Models of Computation
Exploring the Power of Computing

Models of Computation
Exploring the Power of Computing

John E. Savage
Brown University

 **ADDISON-WESLEY**

an imprint of Addison Wesley Longman, Inc.

Reading, Massachusetts • Harlow, England • Menlo Park, California
Berkeley, California • Don Mills, Ontario • Sydney • Bonn • Amsterdam
Tokyo • Mexico City

Executive Editor: Carter Shanklin
Editorial Assistant: Rachel Beavers
Manufacturing Coordinator: Judy Sullivan
Copyeditor: Katrina H. Avery
Proofreader: Cynthia Benn
Cover Designers: Scott Klemmer and Michael Legrand

Access the latest information about Addison-Wesley books at our World Wide Web site:
http://www.awl.com/cseng

Many of the designations used by manufacturers and sellers to distinguish their products are claimed as trademarks. Where those designations appear in this book, and Addison-Wesley was aware of a trademark claim, the designations have been printed in caps or initial caps.

The programs and applications presented in this book have been included for their instructional value. They have been tested with care, but are not guaranteed for any particular purpose. The publisher does not offer any warranties or representations, nor does it accept any liabilities with respect to the programs or applications.

Library of Congress Cataloging-in-Publication Data

Savage, John E., 1939–
    Models of computation : exploring the power of computing / John Savage.
       p. cm.
    Includes bibliographical references and index.
    ISBN 0-201-89539-0
  1. Computer science. 2. System analysis. I. Title.
  QA76.S333 1998   9724307
  004—dc21   CIP

1 2 3 4 5 6 7 8 9 10 MA 0100999897

To Patricia, Christopher, and Timothy

Preface

Theoretical computer science treats any computational subject for which a good model can be created. Research on formal models of computation was initiated in the 1930s and 1940s by Turing, Post, Kleene, Church, and others. In the 1950s and 1960s programming languages, language translators, and operating systems were under development and therefore became both the subject and basis for a great deal of theoretical work. The power of computers of this period was limited by slow processors and small amounts of memory, and thus theories (models, algorithms, and analysis) were developed to explore the efficient use of computers as well as the inherent complexity of problems. The former subject is known today as *algorithms and data structures*, the latter *computational complexity.*

The focus of theoretical computer scientists in the 1960s on languages is reflected in the first textbook on the subject, *Formal Languages and Their Relation to Automata* by John Hopcroft and Jeffrey Ullman. This influential book led to the creation of many language-centered theoretical computer science courses; many introductory theory courses today continue to reflect the content of this book and the interests of theoreticians of the 1960s and early 1970s.

Although the 1970s and 1980s saw the development of models and methods of analysis directed at understanding the limits on the performance of computers, this attractive new material has not been made available at the introductory level. This book is designed to remedy this situation.

This book is distinguished from others on theoretical computer science by its primary focus on real problems, its emphasis on concrete models of machines and programming styles, and the number and variety of models and styles it covers. These include the logic circuit, the finite-state machine, the pushdown automaton, the random-access machine, memory hierarchies, the PRAM (parallel random-access machine), the VLSI (very large-scale integrated) chip, and a variety of parallel machines.

The book covers the traditional topics of formal languages and automata and complexity classes but also gives an introduction to the more modern topics of space-time tradeoffs, memory hierarchies, parallel computation, the VLSI model, and circuit complexity. These modern topics are integrated throughout the text, as illustrated by the early introduction of **P**-complete and **NP**-complete problems. The book provides the first textbook treatment of space-time tradeoffs and memory hierarchies as well as a comprehensive introduction to traditional computational complexity. Its treatment of circuit complexity is modern and substantive, and parallelism is integrated throughout.

Plan of the Book

The book has four parts. Part I (Chapter 1) is an overview. Part II, consisting of Chapters 2–5, provides an introduction to general computational models. Chapter 2 introduces logic circuits and derives upper bounds on the size and depth of circuits for important problems. The finite-state, random-access, and Turing machine models are defined in Chapter 3 and circuits are presented that simulate computations performed by these machines. From such simulations arise results of two kinds. First, computational inequalities of the form $C(f) \leq \kappa ST$ are derived for problems f run on the random-access machine, where $C(f)$ is the size of the smallest circuit for f, κ is a constant, and S and T are storage space and computation time. If ST is too small relative to $C(f)$, the problem f cannot be solved. Second, the same circuit simulations are interpreted to identify **P**-complete and **NP**-complete problems. **P**-complete problems can all be solved in polynomial time but are believed hard to solve fast on parallel machines. The **NP**-complete problems include many important scheduling and optimization problems and are believed not solvable in polynomial time on serial machines.

Part II also contains traditional material on formal languages and automata. Chapter 4 explores the connection between two machine models (the finite-state machine and the pushdown automaton) and language types in the Chomsky hierarchy. Chapter 5 examines Turing machines. It shows that the languages recognized by them are the phrase-structure languages, the most expressive of the language types in the Chomsky hierarchy. This chapter also examines universal Turing machines, reducibility, unsolvable problems, and the functions computed by Turing machines.

Part III, a comprehensive treatment of computational complexity, consists of Chapters 6–12. Chapter 6 introduces algebraic and combinatorial circuits. It contains reference material on the problems used in later chapters to illustrate models and lower-bound arguments. Algebraic and combinatorial circuits are graphs of straight-line programs of the kind typically used for matrix multiplication and inversion, solving linear systems of equations, computing the fast Fourier transform, performing convolutions, and merging and sorting.

Parallel machine models such as the PRAM and networks of computers organized as meshes and hypercubes are studied in Chapter 7. A framework is given for the design of algorithms and derivation of lower bounds on performance.

Chapter 8 provides a comprehensive survey of traditional computational complexity. Using serial and parallel machine models, it examines time- and space-bounded complexity classes, including the **P**-complete, **NP**-complete and **PSPACE**-complete languages as well as the circuit complexity classes **NC** and **P/poly**. This chapter also establishes the connections between deterministic and nondeterministic space complexity classes and shows that the nondeterministic space classes are closed under complements.

Circuit complexity is the topic of Chapter 9. Methods for deriving lower bounds on circuit size and depth are given for general circuits, formulas, monotone circuits, and bounded-depth circuits. This modern treatment of circuit complexity complements Chapter 2, which derives tight upper bounds on circuit size and depth.

Space–time tradeoffs are studied in Chapter 10 using two computational models, the branching program and the pebble game, which capture the notions of space and time for many programs for which branching is and is not allowed, respectively. Methods for deriving lower bounds on the exchange of space for time are presented and applied to a representative set of problems.

Chapter 11 examines models for memory hierarchy systems. It uses the pebble game with pebbles of multiple colors to designate storage locations at different levels of a hierarchy, and also employs block and RAM-based models. Again, lower bounds on performance are derived and compared with the performance of algorithms. This chapter also has a brief treatment of the LRU and FIFO memory-management algorithms that uses competitive analysis to compare their performance to that of the optimal algorithm.

The book closes with Chapter 12 on the VLSI model for integrated circuits. In this model both chip area A and time T are important, and methods are given for deriving lower bounds on measures such as AT^2. Chip layouts and VLSI algorithms are also exhibited whose performance comes close to matching the lower bounds.

Use of the Book

Many different courses can be designed around this book. A core undergraduate computer science course can be taught using Parts I and II and some material from Chapter 8. The first course on theoretical computer science for majors at Brown uses most of Chapters 1–5 except for the advanced material in Chapters 2 and 3. It uses a few elementary sections from Chapters 10 and 11 to emphasize space–time tradeoffs, which play a central role in Chapter 3 and lead into the study of formal languages and automata in Chapter 4. After covering the material of Chapter 5, a few lectures are given on **NP**-complete problems from Chapter 8.

This introductory course has four programming assignments in Scheme that illustrate the ideas embodied in Chapters 2, 3 and 5. The first program solves the circuit-value problem, that is, it executes a straight-line program, thereby producing the outputs defined by this program. The second program writes a straight-line program simulating T steps by a finite-state machine. The third program writes a straight-line program simulating T steps by a one-tape Turing machine (this is the reduction involved in the Cook-Levin theorem) and the fourth one simulates a universal Turing machine.

Several different advanced courses can be assembled from the material of Part III and introductory material of Part II. For example, a course on concrete computational complexity can be assembled around Chapters 10 and 11, which examine tradeoffs between space and time in primary and secondary memory. This course would presume or include introductory material from Chapter 3.

An advanced course emphasizing traditional computational complexity can be based primarily on computability (Chapter 5) and complexity classes (Chapter 8) and some material on circuit complexity from Chapter 9.

An advanced course on circuit complexity can be assembled from Chapter 2 on logic circuits and Chapter 9 on circuit complexity. The former describes efficient circuits for a variety of functions while the latter surveys methods for deriving lower bounds to circuit complexity.

The titles of sections containing advanced material carry an **asterisk**.

Acknowledgments

The raw material for this book is the fruit of the labors of many hundreds of people who have sought to understand computation. It is a great privilege to have the opportunity to convey this exciting body of material to a new audience.

Because the writing of a book involves years of solitary work, it is far too easy for authors to lose sight of their audience. For this reason I am indebted to a number of individuals who have read my book critically. José G. Castaños, currently a Brown Ph.D. candidate and my advisee, has been of immense help to me in this regard. He has read many drafts of the book and has given me the benefit of his keen sense of what is acceptable to my readers. José has also served as a teaching assistant for the undergraduate theory course for which this book was used and contributed importantly to the course and the book in this capacity. Dimitrios Michailidis, also a Brown Ph.D. candidate, has also been a great help; he has read several drafts of the book and has spotted many errors and lacunae. Bill Smart, a third Brown Ph.D. candidate, also carefully read the first nine chapters. I have also benefited greatly from the evaluations done for my publisher by Richard Chang, University of Maryland, Baltimore County; Michael A. Keenan, Columbus State University; Philip Lewis, State University of New York, Stony Brook; George Lukas, University of Massachusetts at Boston; Stephen R. Mahaney, Rutgers University; Friedhelm Meyer auf der Heide, University of Paderborn, Germany; Boleslaw Mikolajczak, University of Massachusetts, Dartmouth; Ramamohan Paturi, University of California, San Diego; Professor Gabriel Robins, and Jeffery Westbrook, AT&T Labs–Research. Others, including Ray Greenlaw of the University of New Hampshire, read an early version of the manuscript for other publishers and offered valuable advice. Gary Rommel of the Eastern Connecticut State College and the Hartford Graduate Center provided feedback on classroom use of the book. Finally, I am indebted to students in my undergraduate and graduate courses at Brown whose feedback has been invaluable.

I very much appreciate advice on the content and organization of the book provided by many individuals including my faculty colleagues the late Paris Kanellakis, Philip Klein, and Franco Preparata as well as Akira Maruoka, a visitor to Brown. Together Franco and I also produced the brief analysis of circuit depth given in Section 2.12.2. Alan Selman offered valuable comments on Chapter 8. Akira Maruoka and Johan Håstad read and commented on the sections of Chapter 9 containing their work. Alan Selman and Ken Regan provided help in identifying references and Allan Borodin commented on many of the chapter notes. I wish to thank Jun Tarui for suggesting that I consider rewriting my 1976 book, *The Complexity of Computing*, which led to my writing this book. I also extend my sincere thanks to Andy Yao for his generous comments on the book for the publisher. Many others contributed to this book in one way or another, including Chuck Fiduccia, Paul Fischer, Bill McColl, Tony Medeiros, Mike Paterson, Eric Rudder, Elizabeth and Kevin Savage, Mark Snir, and many students in my courses.

I express my gratitude to Carter Shanklin, Executive Editor for Corporate & Professional Publishing at Addison Wesley Longman, for his confidence in me and this project. I also thank

Alwyn Velásquez for his attractive design of the book, Patricia Unubun, Production Editor on this project, for her secure guidance of the book in its final stages, and Dimitrios Michailidis, an expert in LaTex, for his preparation of the macros used to typeset the book and his very close reading of the complete, formatted document, for which I am most appreciative. I offer my sincere thanks to Katrina Avery for her high-quality copyediting, Rosemary Simpson for her excellent index which is a great addition to this book, and Cynthia Benn for her careful proofreading of the manuscript. The attractive cover of this book was designed by Michael LeGrand and Scott Klemmer, two very talented juniors at Brown University.

Finally, this book would not have been written without the loving support of my wife Patricia and our young sons, Christopher and Timothy. Their patience and understanding for my long absences during the four and one-half years this project was in process is deeply appreciated.

Contents

II General Computational Models 33

2 Logic Circuits 35

7   Parallel Computation   281

III Computational Complexity   325

8   Complexity Classes   327

Models of Computation
Exploring the Power of Computing

Part I
OVERVIEW OF THE BOOK

1

The Role of Theory in Computer Science

Computer science is the study of computers and programs, the collections of instructions that direct the activity of computers. Although computers are made of simple elements, the tasks they perform are often very complex. The great disparity between the simplicity of computers and the complexity of computational tasks offers intellectual challenges of the highest order. It is the models and methods of analysis developed by computer science to meet these challenges that are the subject of theoretical computer science.

Computer scientists have developed models for machines, such as the random-access and Turing machines; for languages, such as regular and context-free languages; for programs, such as straight-line and branching programs; and for systems of programs, such as compilers and operating systems. Models have also been developed for data structures, such as heaps, and for databases, such as the relational and object-oriented databases.

Methods of analysis have been developed to study the efficiency of algorithms and their data structures, the expressibility of languages and the capacity of computer architectures to recognize them, the classification of problems by the time and space required to solve them, their inherent complexity, and limits that hold simultaneously on computational resources for particular problems. This book examines each of these topics in detail except for the first, analysis of algorithms and data structures, which it covers only briefly.

This chapter provides an overview of the book. Except for the mathematical preliminaries, the topics introduced here are revisited later.

1.1 A Brief History of Theoretical Computer Science

Theoretical computer science uses models and analysis to study computers and computation. It thus encompasses the many areas of computer science sufficiently well developed to have models and methods of analysis. This includes most areas of the field.

1.1.1 Early Years

TURING AND CHURCH: Theoretical computer science emerged primarily from the work of Alan Turing and Alonzo Church in 1936, although many others, such as Russell, Hilbert, and Boole, were important precursors. Turing and Church introduced formal computational models (the Turing machine and lambda calculus), showed that some well-stated computational problems have no solution, and demonstrated the existence of universal computing machines, machines capable of simulating every other machine of their type.

Turing and Church were logicians; their work reflected the concerns of mathematical logic. The origins of computers predate them by centuries, going back at least as far as the abacus, if we call any mechanical aid to computation a computer. A very important contribution to the study of computers was made by Charles Babbage, who in 1836 completed the design of his first programmable Analytical Engine, a mechanical computer capable of arithmetic operations under the control of a sequence of punched cards (an idea borrowed from the Jacquard loom). A notable development in the history of computers, but one of less significance, was the 1938 demonstration by Claude Shannon that Boolean algebra could be used to explain the operation of relay circuits, a form of electromechanical computer. He was later to develop his profound "mathematical theory of communication" in 1948 as well as to lay the foundations for the study of circuit complexity in 1949.

FIRST COMPUTERS: In 1941 Konrad Zuse built the Z3, the first general-purpose program-controlled computer, a machine constructed from electromagnetic relays. The Z3 read programs from a punched paper tape. In the mid-1940s the first programmable electronic computer (using vacuum tubes), the ENIAC, was developed by Eckert and Mauchly. Von Neumann, in a very influential paper, codified the model that now carries his name. With the invention of the transistor in 1947, electronic computers were to become much smaller and more powerful than the 30-ton ENIAC. The microminiaturization of transistors continues today to produce computers of ever-increasing computing power in ever-shrinking packages.

EARLY LANGUAGE DEVELOPMENT: The first computers were very difficult to program (cables were plugged and unplugged on the ENIAC). Later, programmers supplied commands by typing in sequences of 0's and 1's, the machine language of computers. A major contribution of the 1950s was the development of programming languages, such as FORTRAN, COBOL, and LISP. These languages allowed programmers to specify commands in mnemonic code and with high level constructs such as loops, arrays, and procedures.

As languages were developed, it became important to understand their expressiveness as well as the characteristics of the simplest computers that could translate them into machine language. As a consequence, formal languages and the automata that recognize them became an important topic of study in the 1950s. Nondeterministic models – models that may have more than one possible next state for the current state and input – were introduced during this time as a way to classify languages.

1.1.2 1950s

FINITE-STATE MACHINES: Occurring in parallel with the development of languages was the development of models for computers. The 1950s also saw the formalization of the finite-state machine (also called the sequential machine), the sequential circuit (the concrete realization of a sequential machine), and the pushdown automaton. Rabin and Scott pioneered the use of analytical tools to study the capabilities and limitations of these models.

FORMAL LANGUAGES: The late 1950s and 1960s saw an explosion of research on formal languages. By 1964 the Chomsky language hierarchy, consisting of the regular, context-free, context-sensitive, and recursively enumerable languages, was established, as was the correspondence between these languages and the memory organizations of machine types recognizing them, namely the finite-state machine, the pushdown automaton, the linear-bounded automaton, and the Turing machine. Many variants of these standard grammars, languages, and machines were also examined.

1.1.3 1960s

COMPUTATIONAL COMPLEXITY: The 1960s also saw the laying of the foundation for computational complexity with the classification of languages and functions by Hartmanis, Lewis, and Stearns and others of the time and space needed to compute them. Hierarchies of problems were identified and speed-up and gap theorems established. This area was to flower and lead to many important discoveries, including that by Cook (and independently Levin) of **NP**-complete languages, languages associated with many hard combinatorial and optimization problems, including the Traveling Salesperson problem, the problem of determining the shortest tour of cities for which all intercity distances are given. Karp was instrumental in demonstrating the importance of **NP**-complete languages. Because problems whose running time is exponential are considered intractable, it is very important to know whether a string in **NP**-complete languages can be recognized in a time polynomial in their length. This is called the $\mathbf{P} \stackrel{?}{=} \mathbf{NP}$ problem, where **P** is the class of deterministic polynomial-time languages. The **P**-complete languages were also identified in the 1970s; these are the hardest languages in **P** to recognize on parallel machines.

1.1.4 1970s

COMPUTATION TIME AND CIRCUIT COMPLEXITY: In the early 1970s the connection between computation time on Turing machines and circuit complexity was established, thereby giving the study of circuits renewed importance and offering the hope that the $\mathbf{P} \stackrel{?}{=} \mathbf{NP}$ problem could be resolved via circuit complexity.

PROGRAMMING LANGUAGE SEMANTICS: The 1970s were a very productive period for formal methods in the study of programs and languages. The area of programming language semantics was very active; models and denotations were developed to give meaning to the phrase "programming language," thereby putting language development on a solid footing. Formal methods for ensuring the correctness of programs were also developed and applied to program development. The 1970s also saw the emergence of the relational database model and the development of the relational calculus as a means for the efficient reformulation of database queries.

SPACE-TIME TRADEOFFS: An important byproduct of the work on formal languages and semantics in the 1970s is the pebble game. In this game, played on a directed acyclic graph, pebbles are placed on vertices to indicate that the value associated with a vertex is located in the register of a central processing unit. The game allows the study of tradeoffs between the number of pebbles (or registers) and time (the number of pebble placements) and leads to space-time product inequalities for individual problems. These ideas were generalized in the 1980s to branching programs.

VLSI MODEL: When the very large-scale integration (VLSI) of electronic components onto semiconductor chips emerged in the 1970s, VLSI models for them were introduced and analyzed. Ideas from the study of pebble games were applied and led to tradeoff inequalities relating the complexity of a problem to products such as AT^2, where A is the area of a chip and T is the number of steps it takes to solve a problem. In the late 1970s and 1980s the layout of computers on VLSI chips also became an important research topic.

ALGORITHMS AND DATA STRUCTURES: While algorithms (models for programs) and data structures were introduced from the beginning of the field, they experienced a flowering in the 1970s and 1980s. Knuth was most influential in this development, as later were Aho, Hopcroft, and Ullman. New algorithms were invented for sorting, data storage and retrieval, problems on graphs, polynomial evaluation, solving linear systems of equations, computational geometry, and many other topics on both serial and parallel machines.

1.1.5 1980s and 1990s

PARALLEL COMPUTING AND I/O COMPLEXITY: The 1980s also saw the emergence of many other theoretical computer science research topics, including parallel and distributed computing, cryptography, and I/O complexity. A variety of concrete and abstract models of parallel computers were developed, ranging from VLSI-based models to the parallel random-access machine (PRAM), a collection of synchronous processors alternately reading from and writing to a common array of memory cells and computing locally. Parallel algorithms and data structures were developed, as were classifications of problems according to the extent to which they are parallelizable. I/O complexity, the study of data movement among memory units in a memory hierarchy, emerged around 1980. Memory hierarchies take advantage of the temporal and spatial locality of problems to simulate fast, expensive memories with slow and inexpensive ones.

DISTRIBUTED COMPUTING: The emergence of networks of computers brought to light some hard logical problems that led to a theory of distributed computing, that is, computing with multiple and potentially asynchronous processors that may be widely dispersed. The problems addressed in this area include reaching consensus in the presence of malicious adversaries, handling processor failures, and efficiently coordinating the activities of agents when interprocessor latencies are large. Although some of the problems addressed in distributed computing were first introduced in the 1950s, this topic is associated with the 1980s and 1990s.

CRYPTOGRAPHY: While cryptography has been important for ages, it became a serious concern of complexity theorists in the late 1970s and an active research area in the 1980s and 1990s. Some of the important cryptographic issues are a) how to exchange information secretly without having to exchange a private key with each communicating agent, b) how to identify with high assurance the sender of a message, and c) how to convince another agent that you have the solution to a problem without transferring the solution to him or her.

As this brief history illustrates, theoretical computer science speaks to many different computational issues. As the range of issues addressed by computer science grows in sophistication, we can expect a commensurate growth in the richness of theoretical computer science.

1.2 Mathematical Preliminaries

In this section we introduce basic concepts used throughout the book. Since it is presumed that the reader has already met most of this material, this presentation is abbreviated.

1.2.1 Sets

A **set** A is a non-repeating and unordered collection of elements. For example, $A_{50s} = \{\text{Cobol, Fortran, Lisp}\}$ is a set of elements that could be interpreted as the names of languages designed in the 1950s. Because the elements in a set are unordered, $\{\text{Cobol, Fortran, Lisp}\}$ and $\{\text{Lisp, Cobol, Fortran}\}$ denote the same set. It is very convenient to recognize the **empty set** $\emptyset$, a set that does not have any elements. The set $\mathcal{B} = \{0, 1\}$ containing 0 and 1 is used throughout this book.

The notation $a \in A$ means that element a is contained in set A. For example, Cobol $\in A_{50s}$ means that Cobol is a language invented in the 1950s. A set can be finite or infinite. The **cardinality** of a finite set A, denoted $|A|$, is the number of elements in A. We say that a set A is a **subset** of a set B, denoted $A \subseteq B$, if every element of A is an element of B. If $A \subseteq B$ but B contains elements not in A, we say that A is a **proper subset** and write $A \subset B$.

The **union** of two sets A and B, denoted $A \cup B$, is the set containing elements that are in A, B or both. For example, if $A_0 = \{1, 2, 3\}$ and $B_0 = \{4, 3, 5\}$, then $A_0 \cup B_0 = \{5, 4, 3, 1, 2\}$. The **intersection** of sets A and B, denoted $A \cap B$, is the set containing elements that are in both A and B. Hence, $A_0 \cap B_0 = \{3\}$. If A and B have no elements in common, denoted $A \cap B = \emptyset$, they are said to be **disjoint sets**. The **difference** between sets A and B, denoted $A - B$, is the set containing the elements that are in A but not in B. Thus, $A_0 - B_0 = \{1, 2\}$. (See Fig. 1.1.)

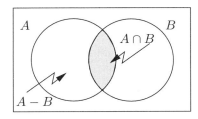

Figure 1.1 A Venn diagram showing the intersection and difference of sets A and B. Their union is the set of elements in both A and B.

The following simple properties hold for arbitrary sets A and B and the operations of set union, intersection, and difference:

$$A \cup B = B \cup A$$
$$A \cap B = B \cap A$$
$$A \cup \emptyset = A$$
$$A \cap \emptyset = \emptyset$$
$$A - \emptyset = A$$

The **power set** of a set A, denoted 2^A, is the set of all subsets of A including the empty set. For example, $2^{\{2,5,9\}} = \{\emptyset, \{2\}, \{5\}, \{9\}, \{2,5\}, \{2,9\}, \{5,9\}, \{2,5,9\}\}$. We use 2^A to denote the power set A as a reminder that it has $2^{|A|}$ elements. To see this, observe that for each subset B of the set A there is a binary n-tuple $(e_1, e_2, \ldots, e_{|A|})$ where e_i is 1 if the ith element of A is in B and 0 otherwise. Since there are $2^{|A|}$ ways to assign 0's and 1's to $(e_1, e_2, \ldots, e_{|A|})$, 2^A has $2^{|A|}$ elements.

The **Cartesian product** of two sets A and B, denoted $A \times B$, is another set, the set of pairs $\{(a, b) \mid a \in A,\ b \in B\}$. For example, when $A_0 = \{1, 2, 3\}$ and $B_0 = \{4, 3, 5\}$, $A_0 \times B_0 = \{(1, 4), (1, 3), (1, 5), (2, 4), (2, 3), (2, 5), (3, 4), (3, 3), (3, 5)\}$. The Cartesian product of k sets $A_1, A_2, \ldots, A_k$, denoted $A_1 \times A_2 \times \cdots \times A_k$, is the set of k-tuples $\{(a_1, a_2, \ldots, a_k) \mid a_1 \in A_1,\ a_2 \in A_2,\ \ldots,\ a_k \in A_k\}$ whose components are drawn from the respective sets. If for each $1 \leq i \leq k$, $A_i = A$, the k-fold Cartesian product $A_1 \times A_2 \times \cdots \times A_k$ is denoted A^k. An element of A^k is a k-tuple $(a_1, a_2, \ldots, a_k)$ where $a_i \in A$. Thus, the binary n-tuple $(e_1, e_2, \ldots, e_{|A|})$ of the preceding paragraph is an element of $\{0, 1\}^n$.

1.2.2 Number Systems

Integers are widely used to describe problems. The infinite set $\mathbb{N}$ consisting of 0 and the positive integers $\{1, 2, 3, \ldots\}$ is called the set of **natural numbers**. The set of positive and negative integers and zero, $\mathbb{Z}$, consists of the integers $\{0, 1, -1, 2, -2, \ldots\}$.

In the **standard decimal representation** of the natural numbers, each integer n is represented as a sum of powers of 10. For example, $867 = 8 \times 10^2 + 6 \times 10^1 + 7 \times 10^0$. Since computers today are binary machines, it is convenient to represent integers over base 2 instead of 10. The **standard binary representation** for the natural numbers represents each integer as a sum of powers of 2. That is, for some $k \geq 0$ each integer n can be represented as a k-tuple $\boldsymbol{x} = (x_{k-1}, x_{k-2}, \ldots, x_1, x_0)$, where each of $x_{k-1}, x_{k-2}, \ldots, x_1, x_0$ has value 0 or 1 and n satisfies the following identity:

$$n = x_{k-1}2^{k-1} + x_{k-2}2^{k-2} + \cdots + x_1 2^1 + x_0 2^0$$

The largest integer that can be represented with k bits is $2^{k-1} + 2^{k-2} + \cdots + 2^1 + 2^0 = 2^k - 1$. (See Problem 1.1.) Also, the k-tuple representation for n is unique; that is, two different integers cannot have the same representation. When leading 0's are suppressed, the standard binary representation for 1, 15, 32, and 97 are (1), $(1, 1, 1, 1)$, $(1, 0, 0, 0, 0, 0)$, and $(1, 1, 0, 0, 0, 0, 1)$, respectively.

We denote with $x + y$, $x - y$, $x * y$, and x/y the results of addition, subtraction, multiplication, and division of integers.

1.2.3 Languages and Strings

A string x is an element $(a_1, a_2, \ldots, a_k)$ of a Cartesian product over a set A (the **alphabet**) in which we drop the commas and parentheses. Thus, we write $x = a_1 a_2 \cdots a_k$, and say that x is a **string over the alphabet** A. A string x in A^k is said to have **length** k, denoted $|x| = k$. Thus, 011 is a string of length three over $\{0, 1\}$.

Consider now the Cartesian product $A^k \times A^l = A^{k+l}$, which is the $(k+l)$-fold Cartesian product of A with itself. Let $x = a_1 a_2 \cdots a_k \in A^k$ and $y = b_1 b_2 \cdots b_l \in A^l$. Then a string $z = c_1 c_2 \cdots c_{k+l} \in A^{k+l}$ can be written as the **concatenation** of strings x and y of length k and l, denoted, $z = x \cdot y$, where

$$x \cdot y = a_1 a_2 \cdots a_k b_1 b_2 \cdots b_l$$

That is, $c_i = a_i$ for $1 \leq i \leq k$ and $c_i = b_{i-k}$ for $k + 1 \leq i \leq k + l$.

The **empty string**, denoted ϵ, is a special string with the property that when concatenated with any other string x it returns x; that is, $x \cdot \epsilon = \epsilon \cdot x = x$. The empty string is said to have zero length. As a special case of A^k, we let A^0 denote the **set containing the empty string**; that is, $A^0 = \{\epsilon\}$.

The **concatenation of sets of strings** A and B, denoted $A \cdot B$, is the set of strings formed by concatenating each string in A with each string in B. For example, $\{00, 1\} \cdot \{a, bb\} = \{00a, 00bb, 1a, 1bb\}$. The concatenation of a set A with the empty set $\emptyset$, denoted $A \cdot \emptyset$, is the empty set because it contains no elements; that is,

$$A \cdot \emptyset = \emptyset \cdot A = \emptyset$$

When no confusion arises, we write AB instead of $A \cdot B$.

A **language** L over an alphabet A is a collection of strings of potentially different lengths over A. For example, $\{00, 010, 1110, 1001\}$ is a **finite language** over the alphabet $\{0, 1\}$. (It is finite because it contains a bounded number of strings.) The set of all strings of all lengths over the alphabet A, including the empty string, is denoted A^* and called the **Kleene closure** of A. For example, $\{0\}^*$ contains ϵ, the empty letter, as well as 0, 00, 000, 0000, ... Also, $\{00 \cup 1\}^* = \{\epsilon, 1, 00, 001, 100, 0000, \ldots\}$. It follows that a language L over the alphabet A is a subset of A^*, denoted $L \subseteq A^*$.

The **positive closure** of a set A, denoted A^+, is the set of all strings over A except for the empty string. For example, $0(0^* 10^*)^+$ is the set of binary strings beginning with 0 and containing at least one 1.

1.2.4 Relations

A subset R of the Cartesian product of sets is called a **relation**. A **binary relation** R is a subset of the Cartesian product of two sets. Three examples of binary relations are $R_0 = \{(0, 0), (1, 1), (2, 4), (3, 9), (4, 16)\}$, $R_1 = \{(\text{red}, 0), (\text{red}, 1), (\text{blue}, 2)\}$, and $R_2 = \{(\text{small}, \text{short}), (\text{medium}, \text{middle}), (\text{medium}, \text{average}), (\text{large}, \text{tall})\}$. The relation R_0 is a **function** because for each first component of a pair there is a unique second component. R_1 is also a function, but R_2 is not a function.

A binary relation R **over a set** A is a subset of $A \times A$; that is, both components of each pair are drawn from the same set. We use two notations to denote membership of a pair (a, b) in a binary relation R over A, namely $(a, b) \in R$ and the new notation aRb. Often it is more convenient to say aRb than to say $(a, b) \in R$.

A binary relation R is **reflexive** if for all $a \in A$, aRa. It is **symmetric** if for all $a, b \in A$, aRb if and only if bRa. It is **transitive** if for all $a, b, c \in A$, if aRb and bRc, then aRc.

A binary relation R is an **equivalence relation** if it is reflexive, symmetric, and transitive. For example, the pairs (a, b), $a, b \in \mathbb{N}$, for which both a and b have the same remainder on division by 3, is an equivalence relation. (See Problem 1.3.)

If R is an equivalence relation and aRb, then a and b are said to be **equivalent elements**. We let $E[a]$ be the set of elements in A that are equivalent to a under the relation R and call it the **equivalence class** of elements equivalent to a. It is not difficult to show that for all $a, b \in A$, $E[a]$ and $E[b]$ are either equal or disjoint. (See Problem 1.4.) Thus, the equivalence classes of an equivalence relation over a set A partition the elements of A into disjoint sets. For example, the partition $\{0^*, 0(0^*10^*)^+, 1(0 + 1)^*\}$ of the set $(0 + 1)^*$ of binary strings defines an equivalence relation R. The equivalence classes consist of strings containing zero or more 0's, strings starting with 0 and containing at least one 1, and strings beginning with 1. It follows that $00R000$ and $1001R11$ hold but not $10R01$.

1.2.5 Graphs

A **graph** $G = (V, E)$ consists of a finite set V of **vertices** and a finite set of pairs of vertices $E = \{(v_1, v_2) \mid v_1, v_2 \in V\}$ called **edges**. That is, $E \subseteq V \times V$. **Edge e is incident on vertex** v if e contains v. A graph is **undirected** if for each edge (v_1, v_2) in E the edge (v_2, v_1) is also in E. A graph that is not undirected is **directed**. Figure 1.2 shows two examples of directed graphs, some of whose vertices are labeled with symbols denoting gates, a topic discussed in Section 1.2.7. In a directed graph the edge (v_1, v_2) is directed from the vertex v_1 to the vertex v_2, shown with an arrow from v_1 to v_2. The **in-degree** of a vertex in a directed graph is the number of edges directed into it; its **out-degree** is the number of edges directed away from it; its **degree** is the sum of its in- and out-degree. In a directed graph an **input vertex** has in-degree zero, whereas an **output vertex** either has out-degree zero or is simply any vertex specially designated as an output vertex. A **path** in a graph (directed or undirected) is a tuple of vertices $(v_1, v_2, \ldots, v_p)$ with the property that (v_i, v_{i+1}) is in E for $1 \le i \le p - 1$. A path $(v_1, v_2, \ldots, v_p)$ is a **cycle** if $v_1 = v_p$ and $p \ge 2$. The **length of a path** is the number of edges on the path. Thus, the path $(v_1, v_2, \ldots, v_p)$ has length $p - 1$. A **directed acyclic graph (DAG)** is a directed graph that has no cycles.

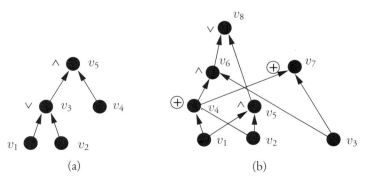

(a)　　　　　　　　　(b)

Figure 1.2 Two directed acyclic graphs representing logic circuits.

Logic circuits are DAGs in which all vertices except input vertices carry the labels of gates. Input vertices carry the labels of **Boolean variables**, variables assuming values over the set $\mathcal{B} = \{0, 1\}$. The graph of Fig. 1.2(a) is the logic circuit of Fig. 1.3(c), whereas the graph of Fig. 1.2(b) is the logic circuit of Fig. 1.4. (The figures are shown in Section 1.4.1, Logic Circuits.) The set of labels of logic gates used in a DAG is called the **basis** Ω for the DAG. The **size** of a circuit is the number of non-input vertices that it contains. Its **depth** is the length of the longest directed path from an input vertex to an output vertex.

1.2.6 Matrices

An $m \times n$ **matrix** is an array of elements containing m rows and n columns. (See Chapter 6.) The **adjacency matrix** of a graph G with n vertices is an $n \times n$ matrix whose entries are 0 or 1. The entry in the ith row and jth column is 1 if there is an edge from vertex i to vertex j and 0 otherwise. The adjacency matrix A for the graph in Fig. 1.2(a) is

$$
A = \begin{bmatrix}
0 & 0 & 1 & 0 & 0 \\
0 & 0 & 1 & 0 & 0 \\
0 & 0 & 0 & 0 & 1 \\
0 & 0 & 0 & 0 & 1 \\
0 & 0 & 0 & 0 & 0
\end{bmatrix}
$$

1.2.7 Functions

The engineering component of computer science is concerned with the design, development, and testing of hardware and software. The theoretical component is concerned with questions of feasibility and optimality. For example, one might ask if there exists a program H that can determine whether an arbitrary program P on an arbitrary input I will halt or not. This is an example of an unsolvable computational problem. While it is a fascinating topic, practice often demands answers to less ethereal questions, such as "Can a particular problem be solved on a general-purpose computer with storage space S in T steps?"

To address feasibility and optimality it is important to have a precise definition of the tasks under examination. Functions serve this purpose. A **function** (or **mapping**) $f : \mathcal{D} \mapsto \mathcal{R}$ is a relation on the Cartesian product $\mathcal{D} \times \mathcal{R}$ subject to the requirement that for each $d \in \mathcal{D}$ there is at most one pair (d, r) in $\mathcal{D} \times \mathcal{R}$. If $(d, r) \in \mathcal{D} \times \mathcal{R}$, we say that the value of f on d is r, denoted $f(d) = r$. Here $\mathcal{D}$ is the **domain** of f and $\mathcal{R}$ is its **range**. The sets $\mathcal{D}$ and $\mathcal{R}$ can be finite or infinite. For example, let $f_{\text{mult}} : \mathbb{N}^2 \mapsto \mathbb{N}$ of domain $\mathcal{D} = \mathbb{N}^2$ and range $\mathcal{R} = \mathbb{N}$ map a pair of natural numbers x and y ($\mathbb{N} = \{0, 1, 2, 3, \ldots\}$) into their product z; that is, $f(x, y) = z = x * y$. A **function** $f : \mathcal{D} \mapsto \mathcal{R}$ **is partial** if for some $d \in \mathcal{D}$ no value in $\mathcal{R}$ is assigned to $f(d)$. Otherwise, a **function is complete**.

If the domain of a function is the Cartesian product of n sets, the function is said to have n **input variables**. If the range of a function is the Cartesian product of m sets, the function is said to have m **output variables**. If the input variables of such a function are all drawn from the set A and the output variables are all drawn from the set B, this information is often captured by the notation $f^{(n,m)} : A^n \mapsto B^m$. However, we frequently do not use exponents or we use only one exponent to parametrize a class of problems.

A **finite function** is one whose domain and range are both finite sets. Finite functions can be completely defined by tables of pairs $\{(d, r)\}$, where d is an element of its domain and r is the corresponding element of its range.

Binary functions are complete finite functions whose domains and ranges are Cartesian products over the binary set $\mathcal{B} = \{0, 1\}$. **Boolean functions** are binary functions whose range is $\mathcal{B}$. The tables below define three Boolean functions on two input variables and one Boolean function on one input variable. They are called **truth tables** because the values 1 and 0 are often associated with the values **True** and **False**, respectively.

x	y	$x \wedge y$	x	y	$x \vee y$	x	y	$x \oplus y$	x	$\overline{x}$
0	0	0	0	0	0	0	0	0	0	1
0	1	0	0	1	1	0	1	1	1	0
1	0	0	1	0	1	1	0	1		
1	1	1	1	1	1	1	1	0		

The above tables define the AND function $x \wedge y$ (its value is **True** when x and y are **True**), the OR function $x \vee y$ (its value is **True** when either x or y or both are **True**), the EXCLUSIVE OR function $x \oplus y$ (its value is **True** only when either x or y is **True**, that is, when x is **True** and y is **False** and vice versa), and the NOT function $\overline{x}$ (its value is **True** when x is **False** and vice versa). The notation $f_{\wedge}^{(2,1)} : \mathcal{B}^2 \mapsto \mathcal{B}$, $f_{\vee}^{(2,1)} : \mathcal{B}^2 \mapsto \mathcal{B}$, $f_{\oplus}^{(2,1)} : \mathcal{B}^2 \mapsto \mathcal{B}$, $f_{\neg}^{(1,1)} : \mathcal{B} \mapsto \mathcal{B}$ for these functions makes explicit their number of input and output variables. We generally suppress the second superscript when functions are Boolean. The physical devices that compute the AND, OR, NOT, and EXCLUSIVE OR functions are called **gates**.

Many computational problems are described by functions $f : \mathcal{A}^* \mapsto \mathcal{C}^*$ from the (unbounded) set of strings over an alphabet $\mathcal{A}$ to the set of strings over a potentially different alphabet $\mathcal{C}$. Since the letters in every finite alphabet $\mathcal{A}$ can be encoded as fixed-length strings over the binary alphabet $\mathcal{B} = \{0, 1\}$, there is no loss of generality in assuming that functions are mappings $f : \mathcal{B}^* \mapsto \mathcal{B}^*$, that is, from strings over $\mathcal{B}$ to strings over $\mathcal{B}$.

Functions with unbounded domains can be used to identify languages. A language L over the alphabet $\mathcal{A}$ is uniquely determined by a **characteristic function** $f : \mathcal{A}^* \mapsto \mathcal{B}$ with the property that $L = \{\boldsymbol{x} \mid \boldsymbol{x} \in A^* \text{ such that } f(\boldsymbol{x}) = 1\}$. This statement means that L is the set of strings $\boldsymbol{x}$ in A^* for which f on them, namely $f(\boldsymbol{x})$, has value 1.

We often restrict a function $f : \mathcal{B}^* \mapsto \mathcal{B}^*$ to input strings of length n, n arbitrary. The domain of such a function is $\mathcal{B}^n$. Its range consists of those strings into which strings of length n map. This set may contain strings of many lengths. It is often convenient to map strings of length n to strings of a fixed length containing the same information. This can be done as follows. Let $h(n)$ be the length of a longest string that is the value of an input string of length n. Encode letters in $\mathcal{B}$ by repeating them (replace 0 by 00 and 1 by 11) and then add as a prefix as many instances of 01 as necessary to insure that each string in the range of f_n has $2h(n)$ characters. For example, if $h(4) = 3$ and $f(0110) = 10$, encode the value 10 as 011100. This encoding provides a function $f_n : \mathcal{B}^n \mapsto \mathcal{B}^{2h(n)}$ containing all the information that is in the original version of f_n.

It is often useful to work with functions $f : \mathbb{R} \mapsto \mathbb{R}$ whose domains and ranges are real numbers $\mathbb{R}$. Functions of this type include linear functions, polynomials, exponentials, and logarithms. A **polynomial** $p(x) : \mathbb{R} \mapsto \mathbb{R}$ of degree $k - 1$ in the variable x is specified by a set of k real coefficients, $c_{k-1}, \ldots, c_1, c_0$, where $p(x) = c_{k-1}x^{k-1} + \cdots + c_1 x^1 + c_0$. A

linear function is a polynomial of degree 1. An **exponential function** is a function of the form $E(x) = a^x$ for some real a – for example, $2^{1.5} = 2.8284271\ldots$. The **logarithm** to the base a of b, denoted $\log_a b$, is the value of x such that $a^x = b$. For example, the logarithm to base 2 of $2.8284271\ldots$ is 1.5 and the logarithm to base 10 of 100 is 2. A function $f(x)$ is **polylogarithmic** if for some polynomial $p(x)$ we can write $f(x)$ as $p(\log_2 x)$; that is, it is a polynomial in the logarithm of x.

Two other functions used often in this book are the floor and ceiling functions. Their domains are the reals, but their ranges are the integers. The **ceiling function**, denoted $\lceil x \rceil$: $\mathbb{R} \mapsto \mathbb{Z}$, maps the real x to the smallest integer greater or equal to it. The **floor function**, denoted $\lfloor x \rfloor$: $\mathbb{R} \mapsto \mathbb{Z}$, maps the real x to the largest integer less than or equal to it. Thus, $\lceil 3.5 \rceil = 4$ and $\lceil 15.0001 \rceil = 16$. Similarly, $\lfloor 3.5 \rfloor = 3$ and $\lfloor 15.0001 \rfloor = 15$. The following bounds apply to the floor and ceiling functions.

$$f(x) - 1 \le \lfloor f(x) \rfloor \le f(x)$$
$$f(x) \le \lceil f(x) \rceil \le f(x) + 1$$

As an example of the application of the ceiling function we note that $\lceil \log_2 n \rceil$ is the number of bits necessary to represent the integer n.

1.2.8 Rate of Growth of Functions

Throughout this book we derive mathematical expressions for quantities such as space, time, and circuit size. Generally these expressions describe functions $f : \mathbb{N} \mapsto \mathbb{R}$ from the non-negative integers to the reals, such as the functions $f_1(n)$ and $f_2(n)$ defined as

$$f_1(n) = 4.5n^2 + 3n$$
$$f_2(n) = 3^n + 4.5n^2$$

When n is large we often wish to simplify expressions such as these to make explicit their dominant or most rapidly growing term. For example, for large values of n the dominant terms in $f_1(n)$ and $f_2(n)$ are $4.5n^2$ and 3^n respectively, as we show. A term dominates when n is large if the value of the function is approximately the value of this term, that is, if the function is within some multiplicative factor of the term.

To highlight dominant terms we introduce the **big Oh**, **big Omega** and **big Theta** notation. They are defined for functions whose domains and ranges are the integers or the reals.

DEFINITION 1.2.1 *Let $f : \mathbb{R} \mapsto \mathbb{R}$ and $g : \mathbb{R} \mapsto \mathbb{R}$ be two functions whose domains and ranges are either the integers or the reals. If there are positive constants x_0 and $K > 0$ such that for all $x \ge x_0$,*

$$f(x) \le K\, g(x)$$

we write

$$f(x) = O(g(x))$$

*and say that "$f(x)$ is **big Oh** of $g(x)$" or it grows no more rapidly in x than $g(x)$. Under the same conditions we also write*

$$g(x) = \Omega(f(x))$$

*and say that "$g(x)$ is **big Omega of** $f(x)$" or that it grows at least as rapidly in x as $f(x)$.*

If $f(x) = O(g(x))$ and $g(x) = O(f(x))$, we write

$$f(x) = \Theta(g(x)) \text{ or } g(x) = \Theta(f(x))$$

*and say that "$f(x)$ is **big Theta of** $g(x)$" and "$g(x)$ is **big Theta of** $f(x)$" or that the two functions have the same rate of growth in x.*

The **big Oh** notation is illustrated by the expressions for $f_1(n)$ and $f_2(n)$ above.

EXAMPLE 1.2.1 *We show that $f_1(n) = 4.5n^2 + 3n$ is $O(n^k)$ for any $k \geq 2$; that is, $f_1(n)$ grows no more rapidly than n^k for $k \geq 2$. We also show that $n^k = O(f_1(n))$ for $k \leq 2$; that is, that n^k grows no more rapidly than $f_1(n)$ for $k \leq 2$. From the above definitions it follows that $f_1(n) = \Theta(n^2)$; that is, $f_1(n)$ and n^2 have the same rate of growth. We say that $f_1(n)$ is a* **quadratic function** *in n.*

To prove the first statement, we need to exhibit a natural number n_0 and a constant $K_0 > 0$ such that for all $n \geq n_0$, $f_1(n) \leq K_0 n^k$. If we can show that $f_1(n) \leq K_0 n^2$, then we have shown $f_1(n) \leq K_0 n^k$ for all $k \geq 2$. To show the former, we must show the following for some $K_0 > 0$ and for all $n \geq n_0$:

$$4.5n^2 + 3n \leq K_0 n^2$$

We try $K_0 = 5.5$ and find that the above inequality is equivalent to $3n \leq n^2$ or $3 \leq n$. Thus, we can choose $n_0 = 3$ and we are done.

To prove the second statement, namely, that $n^k = O(f_1(n))$ for $k \leq 2$, we must exhibit a natural number n_1 and some $K_1 > 0$ such that for all $n \geq n_1$, $n^k \leq K_2 f_1(n)$. If we can show that $n^2 \leq K_1 f_1(n)$, then we have shown $n^k \leq K_2 f_1(n)$. To show the former, we must show the following for some $K_1 > 0$ and for all $n \geq n_1$:

$$n^2 \leq K_1(4.5n^2 + 3n)$$

Clearly, if $K_1 = 1/4.5$ the inequality holds for $n \geq 0$, since $3K_1 n$ is positive. Thus, we choose $n_1 = 0$ and we are done.

EXAMPLE 1.2.2 *We now show that the slightly more complex function $f_2(n) = 3^n + 4.5n^2$ grows as 3^n; that is, $f_2(n) = \Theta(3^n)$, an exponential function in n. Because $3^n \leq f_2(n)$ for all $n \geq 0$, it follows that $3^n = O(f_2(n))$. To show that $f_2(n) = O(3^n)$, we demonstrate that $f_2(n) \leq 2(3^n)$ holds for $n \geq 4$. This is equivalent to the following inequality:*

$$4.5n^2 \leq 3^n$$

To prove this holds, we show that $h(n) = 3^n/n^2$ is an increasing function of n for $n \geq 2$ and that $h(4) \geq 4.5$. To show that $h(n)$ is an increasing function of n, we compute the ratio $r(n) = h(n+1)/h(n)$ and show that $r(n) \geq 1$ for $n \geq 2$. But $r(n) = 3n^2/(n+1)^2$ and $r(n) \geq 1$ when $3n^2 \geq (n+1)^2$ or when $n(n-1) \geq 1/2$, which holds for $n \geq 2$. Since $h(3) = 3$ and $h(4) = 81/16 > 5$, the desired conclusion follows.

1.3 Methods of Proof

In this section we briefly introduce several methods of proof that are used in this book, namely, proof by induction, proof by contradiction, and the pigeonhole principle. In the previous section we saw proof by reduction: in each step the condition to be established was translated into another condition until a condition was found that was shown to be true.

Proofs by induction use **predicates**, that is, functions of the kind $P : \mathbb{N} \mapsto \mathcal{B}$. The truth value of the predicate $P : \mathbb{N} \mapsto \mathcal{B}$ on the natural number n, denoted $P(n)$, is 1 or 0 depending on whether or not the predicate is **True** or **False**.

Proofs by induction are used to prove statements of the kind, "For all natural numbers n, predicate (or property) P is true." Consider the function $S_1 : \mathbb{N} \mapsto \mathbb{N}$ defined by the following sum:

$$S_1(n) = \sum_{j=1}^{n} j \tag{1.1}$$

We use induction to prove that $S_1(n) = n(n+1)/2$ is true for each $n \in \mathbb{N}$.

DEFINITION 1.3.1 *A* **proof by induction** *has a predicate P, a* **basis step**, *an* **induction hypothesis**, *and an* **inductive step**. *The basis establishes that $P(k)$ is true for integer k. The induction hypothesis assumes that for some fixed but arbitrary natural number $n \geq k$, the statements $P(k), P(k+1), \ldots, P(n)$ are true. The inductive step is a proof that $P(n+1)$ is true given the induction hypothesis.*

It follows from this definition that a proof by induction with the predicate P establishes that P is true for all natural numbers larger than or equal to k because the inductive step establishes the truth of $P(n+1)$ for arbitrary integer n greater than or equal to k. Also, induction may be used to show that a predicate holds for a subset of the natural numbers. For example, the hypothesis that every even natural number is divisible by 2 is one that would be defined only on the even numbers.

The following proof by induction shows that $S_1(n) = n(n+1)/2$ for $n \geq 0$.

LEMMA 1.3.1 *For all $n \geq 0$, $S_1(n) = n(n+1)/2$.*

Proof PREDICATE: The value of the predicate P on n, $P(n)$, is **True** if $S_1(n) = n(n+1)/2$ and **False** otherwise.

BASIS STEP: Clearly, $S_1(0) = 0$ from both the sum and the closed form given above.

INDUCTION HYPOTHESIS: $S_1(k) = k(k+1)/2$ for $k = 0, 1, 2, \ldots, n$.

INDUCTIVE STEP: By the definition of the sum for S_1 given in (1.1), $S_1(n+1) = S_1(n) + n + 1$. Thus, it follows that $S_1(n+1) = n(n+1)/2 + n + 1$. Factoring out $n + 1$ and rewriting the expression, we have that $S_1(n+1) = (n+1)((n+1)+1)/2$, exactly the desired form. Thus, the statement of the theorem follows for all values of n. ∎

We now define proof by contradiction.

DEFINITION 1.3.2 *A* **proof by contradiction** *has a predicate P. The complement $\neg P$ of P is shown to be* **False**, *which implies that P is* **True**.

The examples shown earlier of strings in the language $L = \{00 \cup 1\}^*$ suggest that L contains only strings with an odd number of 1's. Let P be the predicate "L contains strings with an even number of 1's." We show that it is true by assuming it is false, namely, by assuming "L contains only strings with an odd number of 1's" and showing that this statement is false. In particular, we show that L contains the string 11. From the definition of the Kleene closure, L contains strings of all lengths in the "letters" 00 and 1. Thus, it contains a string containing two instances of 1 and the predicate P is true.

Induction and proof by contradiction can also be used to establish the pigeonhole principle. The **pigeonhole principle** states that if there are n pigeonholes, $n + 1$ or more pigeons, and every pigeon occupies a hole, then some hole must have at least two pigeons. We reformulate the principle as follows:

LEMMA 1.3.2 *Given two finite sets A and B with $|A| > |B|$, there does not exist a* **naming function** *$\nu : A \mapsto B$ that gives to each element a in A a* **name** *$\nu(a)$ in B such that every element in A has a unique name.*

Proof BASIS: $|B| = 1$. To show that the statement is **True**, assume it is **False** and show that a contradiction occurs. If it is **False**, every element in A can be given a unique name. However, since there is one name (the one element of B) and more than one element in A, we have a contradiction.

INDUCTION HYPOTHESIS: There is no naming function $\nu : A \mapsto B$ when $|B| \leq n$ and $|A| > |B|$.

INDUCTIVE STEP: When $|B| = n+1$ and $|A| > |B|$ we show there is no naming function $\nu : A \mapsto B$. Consider an element $b \in B$. If two elements of A have the name b, the desired conclusion holds. If not, remove b from B, giving the set B', and remove from A the element, if any, whose name is b, giving the set A'. Since $|A'| > |B'|$ and $|B'| \leq n$, by the induction hypothesis, there is no naming function obtained by restricting ν to A'. Thus, the desired conclusion holds. ■

1.4 Computational Models

A variety of computer models are examined in this book. In this section we give the reader a taste of five models, the logic circuit, the finite-state machine, the random-access machine, the pushdown automaton, and the Turing machine. We also briefly survey the problem of language recognition.

1.4.1 Logic Circuits

A **logic gate** is a physical device that realizes a Boolean function. A **logic circuit**, as defined in Section 1.2, is a directed acyclic graph in which all vertices except input and output vertices carry the labels of gates.

Logic gates can be constructed in many different technologies. To make ideas concrete, Fig. 1.3(a) and (b) show electrical circuits for the AND and OR gates constructed with batteries, bulbs, and switches. Shown with each of these circuits is a logic symbol for the gate. These symbols are used to draw circuits, such as the circuit of Fig. 1.3(c) for the function $(x \vee y) \wedge z$. When electrical current flows out of the batteries through a switch or switches in these circuits, the bulbs are lit. In this case we say the value of the circuit is **True**; otherwise it is **False**. Shown below is the truth table for the function mapping the values of the three input variables of the circuit in Fig. 1.3(c) to the value of the one output variable. Here x, y, and z have value 1

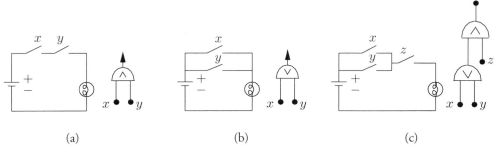

Figure 1.3 Three electrical circuits simulating logic circuits.

when the switch that carries its name is closed; otherwise they have value 0.

x	y	z	$(x \vee y) \wedge z$
0	0	0	0
0	0	1	0
0	1	0	0
0	1	1	1
1	0	0	0
1	0	1	1
1	1	0	0
1	1	1	1

Today's computers use transistor circuits instead of the electrical circuits of Fig. 1.3.

Logic circuits execute **straight-line programs**, programs containing only assignment statements. Thus, they have no loops or branches. (They may have loops if the number of times a loop is executed is fixed.) This point is illustrated by the "full-adder" circuit of Fig. 1.4, a circuit discussed at length in Section 2.7. Each external input and each gate is assigned a unique integer. Each is also assigned a variable whose value is the value of the external input or gate. The ith vertex is assigned the variable x_i. If x_i is associated with a gate that combines the results produced at the jth and kth gates with the operator $\odot$, we write an **assignment operation** of the form $x_i := x_j \odot x_k$. The sequence of assignment operations for a circuit is a straight-line program. Below is a straight-line program for the circuit of Fig. 1.4:

$$x_4 := x_1 \oplus x_2$$
$$x_5 := x_4 \wedge x_3$$
$$x_6 := x_1 \wedge x_2$$
$$x_7 := x_4 \oplus x_3$$
$$x_8 := x_5 \vee x_6$$

The values computed for (x_8, x_7) are the standard binary representation for the number of 1's among x_1, x_2, and x_3. This can be seen by constructing a table of values for x_1, x_2, x_3, x_7,

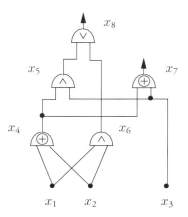

Figure 1.4 A full-adder circuit. Its output pair (x_8, x_7) is the standard binary representation for the number of 1's among its three inputs x_1, x_2, and x_3.

and x_8. Full-adder circuits can be combined to construct an adder for binary numbers. (In Section 2.2 we give another notation for straight-line programs.)

As shown in the truth table for Fig. 1.3(c), each logic circuit has associated with it a binary function that maps the values of its input variables to the values of its output variables. In the case of the full-adder, since x_8 and x_7 are its output variables, we associate with it the function $f_{\text{FA}}^{(3,2)} : \mathcal{B}^3 \mapsto \mathcal{B}^2$, whose value is $f_{\text{FA}}^{(3,2)}(x_1, x_2, x_3) = (x_8, x_7)$.

Algebraic circuits are similar to logic circuits except they may use operations over non-binary sets, such as addition and multiplication over a ring, a concept explained in Section 6.2.1. Algebraic circuits are the subject of Chapter 6. They are also described by DAGs and they execute straight-line programs where the operators are non-binary functions. Algebraic circuits also have associated with them functions that map the values of inputs to the values of outputs.

Logic circuits are the basic building blocks of all digital computers today. When such circuits are combined with binary memory cells, machines with memory can be constructed. The models for these machines are called finite-state machines.

1.4.2   Finite-State Machines

The **finite-state machine** (FSM) is a machine with memory. It executes a series of steps during each of which it takes its current state from the set Q of states and current external input from the set Σ of input letters and combines them in a logic circuit L to produce a successor state in Q and an output letter in Ψ, as suggested in Fig. 1.5. The logic circuit L can be viewed as having two parts, one that computes the **next-state function** $\delta : Q \times \Sigma \mapsto Q$, whose value is the next state of the FSM, and the other that computes the **output function** $\lambda : Q \mapsto \Psi$, whose value is the output of the FSM in the current state. A generic finite-state machine is shown in Fig. 1.5(a) along with a concrete FSM in Fig. 1.5(b) that provides as successor state and output the EXCLUSIVE OR of the current state and the external input. The **state diagram** of the FSM in Fig. 1.5(b) is shown in Fig. 1.8. Two (or more) finite-state machines that operate

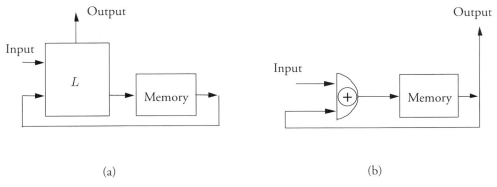

(a)   (b)

Figure 1.5 (a) The finite-state machine (FSM) model; at each unit of time its logic unit, L, operates on its current state (taken from its memory) and its current external input to compute an external output and a new state that it stores in its memory. (b) An FSM that holds in its memory a bit that is the EXCLUSIVE OR of the initial value stored in its memory and the external inputs received to the present time.

in lockstep can be interconnected to form a single FSM. In this case, some outputs of one FSM serve as inputs to the other.

Finite-state machines are ubiquitous today. They are found in microwave ovens, VCRs and automobiles. They can be simple or complex. One of the most useful FSMs is the general-purpose computer modeled by the random-access machine.

1.4.3 Random-Access Machine

The (bounded-memory) **random-access machine** (RAM) is modeled as a pair of intercon-nected finite-state machines, one a **central processing unit** (CPU) and the other a **random-access memory**, as suggested in Fig. 1.6. The random-access memory holds m b-bit words, each identified by an address. It also holds an output word (out_wrd) and a triple of inputs

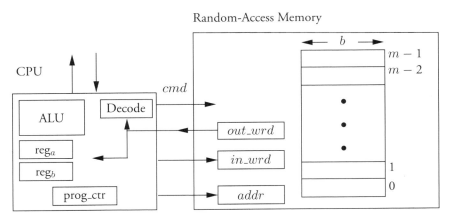

Figure 1.6 The bounded-memory random-access machine.

consisting of a command (cmd), an address ($addr$), and an input data word (in_wrd). cmd is either READ, WRITE, or NO-OP. A NO-OP command does nothing whereas a READ command changes the value of out_wrd to the value of the data word at address $addr$. A WRITE command replaces the data word at address $addr$ with the value of in_wrd.

The random-access memory holds data as well as **programs**, collections of instructions for the CPU. The CPU executes the **fetch-and-execute cycle** in which it repeatedly reads an instruction from the random-access memory and executes it. Its instructions typically include arithmetic, logic, comparison, and jump instructions. Comparisons are used to decide whether the CPU reads the next program instruction in sequence or jumps to an instruction out of sequence.

The general-purpose computer is much more complex than suggested by the above brief sketch of the RAM. It uses a rich variety of methods to achieve high speed at low cost with the available technology. For example, as the number of components that can fit on a semiconductor chip increases, designers have begun to use "super-scalar" CPUs, CPUs that issue multiple instructions in each time step. Also, memory hierarchies are becoming more prevalent as designers assemble collections of slower but larger memories with lower costs per bit to simulate expensive fast memories.

1.4.4   Other Models

There are many other models of computers with memory, some of which have an infinite supply of data words, such as the **Turing machine**, a machine consisting of a **control unit** (an FSM) and a **tape unit** that has a potentially infinite linear array of cells each containing letters from an alphabet that can be read and written by a **tape head** directed by the control unit. It is assumed that in each time step the head may move only from one cell to an adjacent one on the linear array. (See Fig. 1.7.) The Turing machine is a standard model of computation since no other machine model has been discovered that performs tasks it cannot perform.

The **pushdown automaton** is a restricted form of Turing machine in which the tape is used as a pushdown stack. Data is entered, deleted, and accessed only at the top of a stack. A

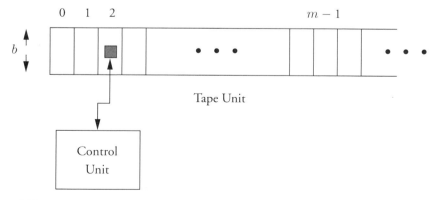

Figure 1.7 The Turing machine has a control unit that is a finite-state machine and a tape unit that controls reading and writing by a tape head and the movement of the tape head one cell at a time to the left or right of the current position.

pushdown stack can be simulated by a tape in which the cell to the right of the tape head is always blank. If the tape moves right from a cell, it writes a non-blank symbol in the cell. If it moves left, it writes a blank in that cell before leaving it.

Some computers are serial: they execute one operation on a fixed amount of data per time step. Others are parallel; that is, they have multiple (usually communicating) subcomputers that operate simultaneously. They may operate synchronously or asynchronously and they may be connected via a simple or a complex network. An example of a simple network is a wire between two computers. An example of a complex network is a crossbar switch consisting of 25 switches at the intersection of five columns and five rows of wires; closing the switch at the intersection of a row and a column connects the two wires and the two computers to which they are attached.

We close this section by emphasizing the importance of models of computers. Good models provide a level of abstraction at which important facts and insights can be developed without losing so much detail that the results are irrelevant to practice.

1.4.5 Formal Languages

In Chapters 4 and 5 the finite-state machine, pushdown automaton, and Turing machine are characterized by their language recognition capability. Formal methods for specifying languages have led to efficient ways to parse and recognize programming languages. This is illustrated by the finite-state machine of Fig. 1.8. Its initial state is q_0, its final state is q_1 and its inputs can assume values 0 or 1. An output of 0 is produced when the machine is in state q_0 and an output of 1 is produced when it is in state q_1. The output before the first input is received is 0.

After the first input the output of the FSM of Fig. 1.8 is equal to the input. After multiple inputs the output is the EXCLUSIVE OR of the 1's and 0's among the inputs, as we show by induction. The inductive hypothesis is clearly true after one input. Suppose it is true after k inputs; we show that it remains true after $k + 1$ inputs, and therefore for all inputs. The output uniquely determines the state. There are two cases to consider: after k inputs either the FSM is in state q_0 or it is in state q_1. For each state, there are two cases to consider based on the value of the $k + 1$st input. In all four cases it is easy to see that after the $k + 1$st input the output is the EXCLUSIVE OR of the first $k + 1$ inputs.

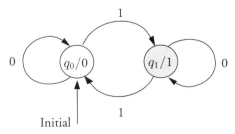

Figure 1.8 A state diagram for a finite-state machine whose circuit model is given in Fig. 1.5(b). q_0 is the initial state of the machine and q_1 is its final state. If the machine is in q_0, it has received an even number of 1 inputs, whereas if it is in q_1, it has received an odd number of 1's.

The **language recognized** by an FSM is defined in two ways. It is the set of input strings that cause the FSM to produce a particular letter as its last output or to enter one of the set of final states on its last input. Thus, the FSM of Fig. 1.8 recognizes the set of binary strings containing an odd number of 1's. It also recognizes the set of binary strings containing an even number of 1's because they result in a last output of 0.

An FSM can also **compute a function**. The most general function that it computes in T steps is the function $f_M^{(T)} : Q \times \Sigma^T \mapsto Q \times \Psi^T$ that maps the initial state s and the T inputs $w_1, w_2, \ldots, w_T$ to the T outputs $y_1, y_2, \ldots, y_T$. It can also compute any other function obtained by ignoring some outputs or fixing either the initial state or some inputs or both.

The class of languages recognized by finite-state machines (the **regular languages**) is not rich enough to describe easily the important programming languages that are in use today. As a consequence, other languages, such as the context-free languages, are employed. **Context-free languages** (which include the regular languages) require computers with potentially unbounded storage for their recognition. The class of computers that recognizes exactly the context-free languages are the nondeterministic pushdown automata, pushdown automata in which the control unit is nondeterministic; that is, some of its states can have multiple potential successor states.

The strings in regular and context-free languages (and other languages as well) can be generated by grammars. A context-free grammar $G = (\mathcal{N}, \mathcal{T}, \mathcal{R}, \mathrm{S})$ consists of sets of **terminal** and **non-terminal symbols**, $\mathcal{T}$ and $\mathcal{N}$ respectively, and rules $\mathcal{R}$ by which each non-terminal is replaced with one or more strings of terminals and non-terminals. All string generations start with the special **start** non-terminal S. The language generated by G, $L(G)$, contains the strings of terminal characters produced by rewriting strings in this fashion. This is illustrated by the context-free grammar G with two rules shown below.

EXAMPLE 1.4.1 $G = (\mathcal{N}, \mathcal{T}, \mathcal{R}, \mathrm{S})$, *where* $\mathcal{N} = \{\mathrm{S}\}$, $\mathcal{T} = \{a, b\}$, *and* $\mathcal{R}$ *consists of the two rules*

$$(a) \quad \mathrm{S} \quad \rightarrow \quad a\mathrm{S}b \qquad (b) \quad \mathrm{S} \quad \rightarrow \quad ab$$

Each application of a rule derives another string, as shown below. This grammar has only two derivations, namely $\mathrm{S} \rightarrow a\mathrm{S}b$ and $\mathrm{S} \rightarrow ab$. The second derivation is always the last to be used. (Recall that the language $L(G)$ contains only terminal strings.)

$$\mathrm{S} \rightarrow a\mathrm{S}b$$
$$\rightarrow aa\mathrm{S}bb$$
$$\rightarrow aaa\mathrm{S}bbb$$
$$\rightarrow aaaabbbb$$

As can be seen by inspection, the only strings in $L(G)$ are of the form $a^k b^k$, where a^k denotes the letter a repeated k times. Thus, $L(G) = \{a^k b^k \mid k \geq 1\}$.

Once a grammar for a regular or context-free language is known, it is possible to **parse** a string in the language. In the above example this amounts to determining the number of times that the first rule is applied.

To develop some intuition for the use of the pushdown automaton as a recognizer for context-free languages, observe that we can determine the number of applications of the first rule in this language by pushing each instance of a onto a stack and then popping a's as b's are encountered. The number of a's can then be matched with the number of b's and if they are not equal, the string is declared not in the language. If equal, the number of instances of the first rule is determined.

Programming languages contain strings of characters and digits representing names and the values of variables. Such strings can typically be scanned with finite-state machines. Once scanned, these strings can be assigned tokens that are then used in a later parsing phase, which today is typically based on a generalization of parsing for context-free languages.

1.5 Computational Complexity

Computational complexity is examined in concrete and abstract terms. The concrete analysis of computational limits is done using models that capture the exchange of space for time. It also is done via the study of circuit complexity, the minimal size and depth of circuits for functions. Computational complexity is studied abstractly via complexity classes, the classification of languages by the time and/or space they need.

1.5.1 A Computational Inequality

Computational inequalities play an important role in this book. We now sketch the derivation of a computational inequality for the finite-state machine and specialize it to the RAM. The idea is very simple: we simulate with a circuit the computation of a function f by an FSM and then compare the size of the circuit produced with the size of the smallest circuit for f. **Simulation**, which we use to derive this result, is a central idea in theoretical computer science. For example, it is used to show that a problem is **NP**-complete. We use it here to relate the resources available to compute a function f with an FSM to the inherent complexity of f.

Shown in Fig. 1.5(a) is the standard model for an FSM. As suggested, a circuit L combines the current state held in the memory M together with an external input to form an external output and a successor state which is held in M. If the input, output, and state are represented as binary tuples, the circuit L can be realized by a logic circuit with Boolean gates. Let the FSM compute the function $f : \mathcal{B}^n \mapsto \mathcal{B}^m$ in T steps; that is, its state and/or T external inputs contain the n Boolean inputs to f and its T outputs contain the m Boolean outputs of f. (The inputs and outputs must appear in the same positions on each computation to prevent the application of hidden computational resources.)

The function f can also be computed by the circuit shown in Fig. 1.9, which is obtained by unwinding the loop of Fig. 1.5(a) using T copies of the logic circuit L for the FSM. This

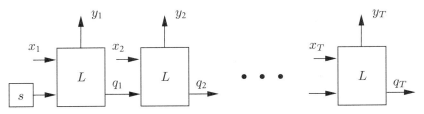

Figure 1.9 A circuit that computes the same function as an FSM (see Fig. 1.5(a)) in T steps. It has the same initial state s, receives the same inputs and produces the same outputs.

follows because the inputs $x_1, x_2, \ldots, x_T$ that would be given to the FSM over time can be given simultaneously to this circuit and it will produce the T outputs that would be produced by the FSM. This circuit has $T \cdot C(L)$ gates, where $C(L)$ is the actual or equivalent number of gates used to realize L. (The circuit L may be realized with a technology that does not formally use gates.) Since this circuit is not necessarily the smallest circuit for the function f, we have the following inequality, where $C(f)$ is the size of the smallest circuit for f:

$$C(f) \leq T \cdot C(L)$$

This result is important because it imposes a constraint on every computation done by a sequential machine. This inequality has two interpretations. First, if the product $T \cdot C(L)$ (the **equivalent number of logic operations employed**) of the number of time steps T and the equivalent number of logic operations $C(L)$ per step is too small, namely, less than $C(f)$, the FSM cannot compute function f because the above inequality would be violated. This is a form of **impossibility theorem for bounded computations.** Second, a complex function, one for which $C(f)$ is large, requires a large value for the product $T \cdot C(L)$. In light of the first interpretation of $T \cdot C(L)$ as the equivalent number of logic operations employed, it makes sense to call $W = T \cdot C(L)$ the **computational work** done by the FSM to compute f.

The above computational inequality can be specialized to the bounded-memory RAM with S bits of memory. When S is large, as it usually is, $C(L)$ for the RAM is proportional to S. As a consequence, for the RAM we have the following computational inequality for some positive constant κ:

$$C(f) \leq \kappa S T$$

This inequality shows the central role of circuit complexity in theoretical computer science. It also demonstrates that the space-time product, ST, is an important measure of the complexity of a problem. Functions with large circuit size can be computed by a RAM only if it either has a large storage capacity or executes many time steps or both. Similar results exist for the Turing machine.

1.5.2   Tradeoffs in Space, Time, and I/O Operations

Computational inequalities of the kind sketched above are important but often difficult to apply because it is hard to show that functions have a large circuit size. For this reason space-time tradeoffs have been studied under the assumption that the type of algorithm or program allowed is restricted. For example, if only straight-line programs are considered, then the *pebble game* sketched below and discussed in detail in Chapter 10 can be used to derive tradeoff inequalities.

The standard **pebble game** is played on a directed acyclic graph (DAG), the graph of a straight-line program. The input vertices of a DAG have no edges directed into them. Output vertices have no edges directed away from them. Internal vertices are non-input vertices. A predecessor of a vertex v is a vertex u that has an edge directed to v. The pebble game is played with pebbles that are placed on vertices according to the following rules:

- Initially no vertices carry pebbles.

- A pebble can be placed on an input vertex at any time.

- A pebble can be placed on an internal vertex only if all of its predecessor vertices carry pebbles.

- The pebble moved to a vertex can be a pebble residing on one of its immediate predecessors.

- A pebble can be removed from a vertex at any time.

- Every output vertex must carry a pebble at some time.

Space S in this game is the maximum number of pebbles used to play the game on a DAG. Time T is the number of times that pebbles are placed on vertices. If enough pebbles are available to play the game, each vertex is pebbled once and T is the number of vertices in the graph. If, however, there are not enough pebbles, some vertices will have to be pebbled more than once. In this case a tradeoff between space and time will be exhibited.

For a particular DAG G we may seek to determine the minimum number of pebbles, $S_{\min}$, needed to place pebbles on all output vertices at some time and for a given number of pebbles S to determine the minimum time T needed when S pebbles are used. Methods for computing $S_{\min}$ and bounding S and T simultaneously have been developed. For example, the four-point (four-input) fast Fourier transform (FFT) graph shown in Fig. 1.10 has $S_{\min} = 3$ and can be pebbled in the minimum number of steps with five pebbles.

Let the FFT graph of Fig. 1.10 be pebbled with the minimum number S of pebbles. Initially no pebbles reside on the graph. Thus, there is a first point in time at which S pebbles reside on the graph. The dark gray vertices identify one possible placement of pebbles at such a point in time. The light gray vertices will have had pebbles placed on them prior to this time and will have to be repebbled again later to pebble output vertices that cannot be reached from the placement of the dark gray vertices. This demonstrates that for this graph if the minimum number of pebbles is used, some vertices will have to be repebbled. Although the n-point FFT graph, n a power of two, has only $n \log n + n$ vertices, we show in Section 10.5.5 that its vertices must be repebbled enough times that S and T satisfy $(S+1)T \geq n^2/24$. Thus, either S is much larger than the minimum space or T is much larger than the number of vertices or both.

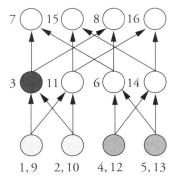

Figure 1.10 A pebbling of a four-input FFT graph at the point at which the maximum number of pebbles (three) is used. Numbers specify the order in which vertices can be pebbled. A maximum of three pebbles is used. Some vertices are pebbled twice.

Space-time tradeoffs can also be studied with the branching program, a type of program that permits data-dependent computations. (See Section 10.9.) While branching programs provide more flexibility than does the pebble game, they are worth considering only for problems in which the algorithms used involve branching and have access to an external random-access memory to permit data-dependent reading of inputs, a strong assumption. For many problems only straight-line programs are used, in which case the pebble game is the model of choice.

A serious problem arises when the storage capacity of a primary memory is too small for a problem, so that a slow secondary memory, such as a disk, must be used for intermediate storage. This results in time-consuming **input/output operations (I/O)** between primary and secondary memory. If too many I/O operations are done, the overall performance of the system can deteriorate markedly. This problem has been exacerbated by the growing disparity between the speed of CPUs and that of memories; the speed of CPUs is increasing over time at a greater rate than that of memories. In fact, the **latency** of a disk, the time between the issuance of a request for data and the time it is answered, can be 100,000 to 1,000,000 times the length of a CPU cycle. As a consequence, the amount of time spent swapping data between primary and secondary memory may dominate the time to perform computations. A second pebble game, the **red-blue pebble game**, has been introduced to study this problem. (See Chapter 11.)

The red-blue pebble game is played with both red and blue pebbles. The (hot) red pebbles correspond to primary memory locations and the (cool) blue pebbles correspond to secondary memory locations. Red pebbles are played according to the rules of the above pebble game. The additional rules that apply to the red and blue pebbles allow a red pebble to be swapped for a blue one and vice versa. In addition, blue pebbles reside only on inputs initially and must reside on inputs finally. The number of red pebbles is limited, but the number of blue pebbles is not.

The goal of the red-blue pebble game is to minimize the number of times that red and blue pebbles are swapped, since each swap corresponds to an expensive input/output (I/O) operation. Let T be the number of I/O operations and S be the number of red pebbles. Upper and lower bounds on the exchange of S for T have been derived for a large number of problems. For example, for the problem of multiplying two $n \times n$ matrices in about $2n^3$ steps with the classical algorithm, it has been shown that a red-blue pebble-game strategy leads to a product ST^2 proportional to n^3 and that this cannot be beaten except by a small multiplicative factor.

1.5.3 Complexity Classes

Complexity classes provide a way to group languages of similar computational complexity. For example, the **nondeterministic polynomial-time languages** (**NP**) are languages that can be solved in time that is polynomial in the size of their input when the machine in question is a nondeterministic Turing machine (TM). nondeterministic Turing machines can have more than one state that is a successor to the current state for the current input. Thus, they can make choices between successor states. A language L is in **NP** if there is a nondeterministic TM such that, given an arbitrary string in L, there is some choice of successor states for the TM control unit that causes the TM to enter an accepting state in a number of steps that is polynomial in the length of the input.

An **NP**-complete language L_0 must satisfy two conditions. First, L_0 must be in **NP** and second, it must be true that for each language L in **NP** a string x in L can be translated into a string y of L_0 using an algorithm whose running time is a polynomial in the length of x such that y is in L_0 if and only if x is in L. As a consequence of this definition, if any **NP**-complete language can be solved in deterministic polynomial time, then every language in **NP** can, including all the other **NP**-complete languages. However, the best algorithms known today for **NP**-complete languages all have exponential running time. Thus, for long strings these algorithms are impractical. If solutions to large **NP**-complete languages are needed, we are limited to approximate solutions.

1.5.4 Circuit Complexity

Circuit complexity is a notoriously difficult subject. Despite decades of research, we have failed to find methods to show that individual functions have super-polynomial circuit size or more than poly-logarithmic depth. Nonetheless, the circuit is such a simple and appealing model that it continues to attract a considerable amount of attention. Some very interesting exponential lower bounds on circuit size have been derived when the circuits are monotone, that is, realized by AND and OR gates but no NOTs.

1.6 Parallel Computation

The VLSI machine and the PRAM are examples of parallel machines. The VLSI machine reflects constraints that exist when finite-state machines are realized through the very large-scale integration of components on semiconductor chips. In the VLSI model the area of a chip is important because large chips have a much higher probability of containing a disabling defect than smaller ones. Consequently, the absolute size of chips is limited. However, the width of lines that can be drawn on chips has been shrinking over time, thereby increasing the number of wires, gates, and binary memory cells that can be placed on them. This has the effect of increasing the effective **chip area**, the real chip area normalized by the cross section of wires.

Figure 1.11(a) is a VLSI diagram representing the types of material that can be deposited on the surface of a pure crystalline semiconductor substrate to form different types of conducting regions. Some of the rectangular regions serve as wires whereas overlaps of other regions create transistors. In turn, collections of transistors form gates. This VLSI diagram describes a NAND gate, a gate whose Boolean function is the NOT of the AND of its two inputs. Shown in Fig. 1.11(b) is the logic symbol for the NAND gate. The small circle at the output of the AND gate denotes the NOT of the gate value.

Given the premium attached to chip real estate, a large number of economical and very regular finite-state machine designs have been made for VLSI chips. One of the most important of these is the **systolic array**, a one- or two-dimensional array of processors (FSMs) that are identical, except possibly for those along the periphery of the array. These processors operate in synchrony; that is, they perform the same operation at the same time. They also communicate only with their nearest neighbors. (The word "systolic" is derived from "systole," a "rhythmically recurrent contraction" such as that of the heart.)

Systolic arrays are typically used to compute specific functions such as the **convolution** $c = a \otimes b$ of the n-tuple $a = (a_0, a_1, \ldots, a_{n-1})$ with the m-tuple $b = (b_0, b_1, \ldots, b_{m-1})$. The jth component, c_j, of the convolution $c = a \otimes b$, $0 \leq j \leq (n + m - 2)$, is defined as

$$c_j = \sum_{r+s=j} a_r * b_s$$

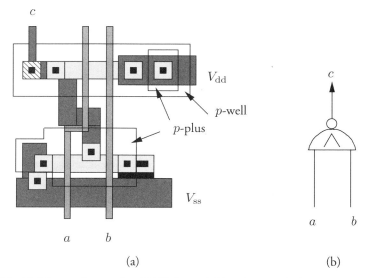

(a)   (b)

Figure 1.11 (a) A layout diagram for a VLSI chip and (b) its logic symbol.

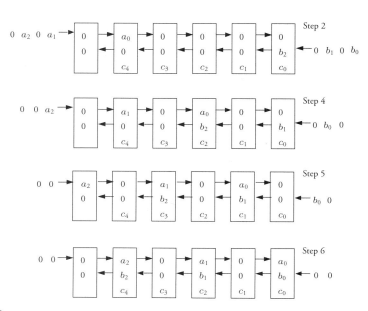

Figure 1.12 A systolic array for the convolution of two binary sequences.

It is assumed that the components of a and b are drawn from a set over which the operations of $*$ (multiplication) and $\sum$ (addition) are defined, such as the integers.

Shown schematically in Fig. 1.12 on page 28 is the one-dimensional systolic array for the convolution $c = a \otimes b$ at the second, fourth, fifth, and sixth steps of execution on input vectors $a = (a_0, a_1, a_2)$ and $b = (b_0, b_1, b_2)$. The components of these vectors are fed from the left and right, respectively, spaced by zero elements. The first component of a enters the array one step ahead of the first component of b. The result of the convolution is the vector $c = (c_0, c_1, c_2, c_3, c_4)$. There is one more cell in the array than there are components in the result. At each step the components of a and b in each cell are multiplied and added to the previous value of the component of c in that cell. After all components of the two input vectors pass through the cell, the convolution is computed.

The processors of a parallel computer generally do not communicate only with nearest neighbors, as in the systolic array. Instead, processors often can communicate with remote neighbors via a network. The type of networks chosen for a parallel computer can have a large impact on their effectiveness.

The processors of the PRAM mentioned in Section 1.1 operate synchronously, alternating between accessing a global memory and computing locally. Since the processors communicate by writing and reading values to and from the global memory, all processors are at the same distance from one another. Although the PRAM model makes two unrealistic assumptions, namely that processors a) can act in synchrony and b) they can communicate directly via global memory, it remains a good model in which to explore problems that are hard to parallelize, even with the flexibility offered by this model.

Problems

MATHEMATICAL PRELIMINARIES

1.1 Show that the sum $S(k)$ below has value $S(k) = 2^k - 1$:

$$S(k) = 2^{k-1} + 2^{k-2} + \cdots + 2^1 + 2^0$$

SETS, LANGUAGES, INTEGERS, AND GRAPHS

1.2 Let $A = \{\text{red, green, blue}\}$, $B = \{\text{green, violet}\}$, and $C = \{\text{red, yellow, blue, green}\}$. Determine the elements in $(A \cap C) \times (B - C)$.

1.3 Let the relation $R \subseteq \mathbb{N} \times \mathbb{N}$ be defined by pairs (a, b) such that a and b have the same remainder on division by 3. Show that R is an equivalence relation.

1.4 Let $R \subset A \times A$ be an equivalence relation. Let the set $E[a]$ be the elements in A equivalent under the relation R to the element a. Show that for all $a, b \in A$ the equivalence classes $E[a]$ and $E[b]$ are either equal or disjoint. Also show that A is the union of all equivalence classes.

1.5 In terms of the Kleene closure and the concatenation of sets, describe the languages containing the following:

a) Strings over $\{0, 1\}$ beginning with 01.

b) Strings beginning with 0 that alternate between 0 and 1.

1.6 Describe an algorithm to convert numbers from decimal to binary notation.

1.7 A graph $G = (V, E)$ can be described by adjacency lists, one list for each vertex in the graph. The **adjacency list** for vertex $v \in V$ is a list of vertices to which there is an edge from v. Generate adjacency lists for the two graphs of Fig. 1.2.

TASKS AS FUNCTIONS

1.8 Let $\mathbb{Z}_5$ be the set $\{0, 1, 2, 3, 4\}$. Let the addition operator $\oplus$ over this set be **modulo** 5; that is, if x and y are two such integers, $x \oplus y$ is obtained by adding x and y as integers and taking the remainder after division by 5. For example, $2 \oplus 2 = 4 \bmod 5$ whereas $3 \oplus 4 = 7 = 2 \bmod 5$. Provide a table describing the function $f_\oplus : \mathbb{Z}_5 \times \mathbb{Z}_5 \mapsto \mathbb{Z}_5$.

1.9 Give a truth table for the Boolean function whose value is **True** exactly when either x or y or both is **True** and z is **False**.

RATE OF GROWTH OF FUNCTIONS

1.10 For each of the fifteen unordered pairs of functions f and g below, determine whether $f(n) = O(g(n))$, $f(n) = \Omega(g(n))$, or $f(n) = \Theta(g(n))$.
   a) n^3;
   c) n^6;
   e) $n^3 \log_2 n$;
   b) $2^{n \log_2 n}$;
   d) $n2^n$;
   f) 2^{2^n}.

1.11 Show that $2.7n^2 + 6\sqrt{n}\lceil \log_2 n \rceil \le 8.7n^2$ for $n \ge 3$.

METHODS OF PROOF

1.12 Let $S_r(n) = \sum_{j=1}^{n} j^r$ denote a sum of powers of integers. Use proof by induction to show that the following identities on arithmetic series hold:
   a) $S_2(n) = \frac{n^3}{3} + \frac{n^2}{2} + \frac{n}{6}$
   b) $S_3(n) = \frac{n^4}{4} + \frac{n^3}{2} + \frac{n^2}{4}$

COMPUTATIONAL MODELS

1.13 Produce a circuit and straight-line program for the Boolean function described in Problem 1.9.

1.14 A **state diagram** for a finite-state machine is a graph containing one vertex (or **state**) for each pattern of data that can be held in its memory and an edge from state p to state q if there is a value for the input data that causes the memory to change from p to q. Such an edge is labeled with the value of the input data that causes the transition. Outputs are generated by a finite-state machine when it is in a state. The vertices of its state diagram are labeled by these outputs.

Provide a state diagram for the finite-state machine described in Fig. 1.5(b).

1.15 Using the straight-line program given for the full-adder circuit in Section 1.4.1, describe how such a program would be placed in the random-access memory of the RAM and how the RAM would run the fetch-and-execute cycle to compute the values produced by the full-adder circuit. This is an example of circuit simulation by a program.

1.16 Describe the actions that could be taken by a Turing machine to simulate a circuit from a straight-line program for it. Illustrate your approach by applying it to the simulation of the full-adder circuit described in Section 1.4.1.

1.17 Suppose you are told that a function is computed in four time steps by a very simple finite-state machine, one whose logic circuit (but not its memory) can be realized with four logic gates. Suppose you are also told that the same function cannot be computed by a logic circuit with fewer than 20 logic gates. What can be said about these two statements? Explain your answer.

1.18 Describe a finite-state machine that recognizes the language consisting of those strings over $\{0, 1\}$ that end in 1.

1.19 Determine the language generated by the context-free grammar $G = (\mathcal{N}, \mathcal{T}, \mathcal{R}, \mathrm{S})$ where $\mathcal{N} = \{\mathrm{S}, \mathrm{M}, \mathrm{N}\}$, $\mathcal{T} = \{0, 1\}$ and $\mathcal{R}$ consists of the rules given below.

a) $\mathrm{S} \rightarrow \mathrm{MN}$ d) $\mathrm{N} \rightarrow c\mathrm{N}d$

b) $\mathrm{M} \rightarrow a\mathrm{M}b$ e) $\mathrm{N} \rightarrow cd$

c) $\mathrm{M} \rightarrow ab$

COMPUTATIONAL COMPLEXITY

1.20 Using the rules for the red pebble game, show how to pebble the FFT graph of Fig. 1.10 with five red pebbles by labeling the vertices with the time step on which it is pebbled. If a vertex has to be repebbled, it will be pebbled on two time steps.

1.21 Suppose that you are told that the n-point FFT graph can be pebbled with $\sqrt{n}$ pebbles in $n/4$ time steps for $n \geq 37$. What can you say about this statement?

1.22 You have been told that the FFT graph of Fig. 1.10 cannot be pebbled with fewer than three red pebbles. Show that it can be pebbled with two red pebbles in the red-blue pebble game by sketching how you would use blue pebbles to achieve this objective.

PARALLEL COMPUTATION

1.23 Using Fig. 1.12 as a guide, design a systolic array to convolve two sequences of length two. Sketch out each step of the convolution process.

1.24 Consider a version of the PRAM consisting of a collection of RAMs (see Fig. 1.13) with small local random-access memories that repeat the following three-step cycle until they halt: a) they simultaneously read one word from a common global memory, b) they execute one local instruction using local memory, and c) they write one word to the common memory. When reading and writing, the individual processors are allowed to read and write from the same location. If two RAMs write to the same location, they must be programmed so that they write a common value. (This is known as the concurrent-read, concurrent-write (CRCW) PRAM.) Each RAM has a unique integer associated with it and can use this number to decide where to read or write in the common memory.

Show that the CRCW PRAM can compute the AND of n Boolean variables in two cycles.

Hint: Reserve one word in common memory and initialize it with 0 and assign RAMs to the appropriate memory cells.

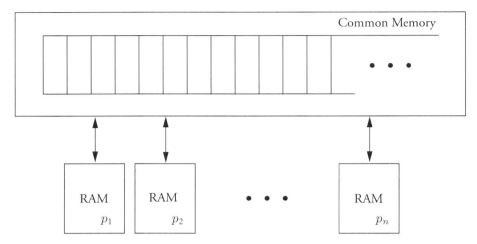

Figure 1.13   The PRAM model is a collection of synchronous RAMs accessing a common memory.

Chapter Notes

Since this chapter introduces concepts used elsewhere in the book, we postpone the bibliographic citations to later chapters. We remark here, however, that the notation for the rate of growth of functions in Section 1.2.8 is due to Knuth [171]. The reader interested in more information on the development of the digital computer, ranging from Babbage's seminal work in the 1830s to the pioneering work of the 1940s, should consult the collection of papers selected and edited by Brian Randell [264].

Part II
GENERAL COMPUTATIONAL MODELS

CHAPTER 2

Logic Circuits

Many important functions are naturally computed with **straight-line programs**, programs without loops or branches. Such computations are conveniently described with **circuits**, directed acyclic graphs of straight-line programs. Circuit vertices are associated with program steps, whereas edges identify dependencies between steps. Circuits are characterized by their **size**, the number of vertices, and their **depth**, the length (in edges) of their longest path. Circuits in which the operations are Boolean are called **logic circuits**, those using algebraic operations are called **algebraic circuits**, and those using comparison operators are called **comparator circuits**. In this chapter we examine logic circuits. Algebraic and comparator circuits are examined in Chapter 6.

Logic circuits are the basic building blocks of real-world computers. As shown in Chapter 3, all machines with bounded memory can be constructed of logic circuits and binary memory units. Furthermore, machines whose computations terminate can be completely simulated by circuits.

In this chapter circuits are designed for a large number of important functions. We begin with a discussion of circuits, straight-line programs, and the functions computed by them. Normal forms, a structured type of circuit, are examined next. They are a starting point for the design of circuits that compute functions. We then develop simple circuits that combine and select data. They include logical circuits, encoders, decoders, multiplexers, and demultiplexers. This is followed by an introduction to prefix circuits that efficiently perform running sums. Circuits are then designed for the arithmetic operations of addition (in which prefix computations are used), subtraction, multiplication, and division. We also construct efficient circuits for symmetric functions. We close with proofs that every Boolean function can be realized with size and depth exponential and linear, respectively, in its number of inputs, and that most Boolean functions require such circuits.

The concept of a reduction from one problem to a previously solved one is introduced in this chapter and applied to many simple functions. This important idea is used later to show that two problems, such as different **NP**-complete problems, have the same computational complexity. (See Chapters 3 and 8.)

35

2.1 Designing Circuits

The logic circuit, as defined in Section 1.4.1, is a directed acyclic graph (DAG) whose vertices are labeled with the names of Boolean functions (logic gates) or variables (inputs). Each logic circuit computes a binary function $f : \mathcal{B}^n \mapsto \mathcal{B}^m$ that is a mapping from the values of its n input variables to the values of its m outputs.

Computer architects often need to design circuits for functions, a task that we explore in this chapter. The goal of the architect is to design efficient circuits, circuits whose size (the number of gates) and/or depth (the length of the longest path from an input to an output vertex) is small. The computer scientist is interested in circuit size and depth because these measures provide lower bounds on the resources needed to complete a task. (See Section 1.5.1 and Chapter 3.) For example, circuit size provides a lower bound on the product of the space and time needed for a problem on both the random-access and Turing machines (see Sections 3.6 and 3.9.2) and circuit depth is a measure of the parallel time needed to compute a function (see Section 8.14.1).

The logic circuit also provides a framework for the classification of problems by their computational complexity. For example, in Section 3.9.4 we use circuits to identify hard computational problems, in particular, the **P**-complete languages that are believed hard to parallelize and the **NP**-complete languages that are believed hard to solve on serial computers. After more than fifty years of research it is still unknown whether **NP**-complete problems have polynomial-time algorithms.

In this chapter not only do we describe circuits for important functions, but we show that most Boolean functions are complex. For example, we show that there are so many Boolean functions on n variables and so few circuits containing C or fewer gates that unless C is large, not all Boolean functions can be realized with C gates or fewer.

Circuit complexity is also explored in Chapter 9. The present chapter develops methods to derive lower bounds on the size and depth of circuits. A lower bound on the circuit size (depth) of a function f is a value for the size (depth) below which there does not exist a circuit for f. Thus, every circuit for f must have a size (depth) greater than or equal to the lower bound. In Chapter 9 we also establish a connection between circuit depth and formula size, the number of Boolean operations needed to realize a Boolean function by a formula. This allows us to derive an upper bound on formula size from an upper bound on depth. Thus, the depth bounds of this chapter are useful in deriving upper bounds on the size of the smallest formulas for problems. Prefix circuits are used in the present chapter to design fast adders. They are also used in Chapter 6 to design fast parallel algorithms.

2.2 Straight-Line Programs and Circuits

As suggested in Section 1.4.1, the mapping between inputs and outputs of a logic circuit can be described by a binary function. In this section we formalize this idea and, in addition, demonstrate that every binary function can be realized by a circuit. Normal-form expansions of Boolean functions play a central role in establishing the latter result. Circuits were defined informally in Section 1.4.1. We now give a formal definition of circuits.

To fix ideas, we start with an example. Figure 2.1 shows a circuit that contains two AND gates, one OR gate, and two NOT gates. (Circles denote NOT gates, AND and OR gates are labeled $\wedge$ and $\vee$, respectively.) Corresponding to this circuit is the following functional de-

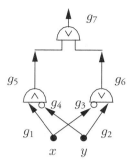

Figure 2.1 A circuit is the graph of a Boolean straight-line program.

scription of the circuit, where g_j is the value computed by the jth input or gate of the circuit:

$$
\begin{array}{llll}
g_1 & := & x; & g_5 & := & g_1 \wedge g_4; \\
g_2 & := & y; & g_6 & := & g_3 \wedge g_2; \\
g_3 & := & \overline{g}_1; & g_7 & := & g_5 \vee g_6; \\
g_4 & := & \overline{g}_2;
\end{array}
\tag{2.1}
$$

The statement $g_1 := x;$ means that the external input x is the value associated with the first vertex of the circuit. The statement $g_3 := \overline{g}_1;$ means that the value computed at the third vertex is the NOT of the value computed at the first vertex. The statement $g_5 := g_1 \wedge g_4;$ means that the value computed at the fifth vertex is the AND of the values computed at the first and fourth vertices. The statement $g_7 := g_5 \vee g_6;$ means that the value computed at the seventh vertex is the OR of the values computed at the fifth and sixth vertices. The above is a description of the functions computed by the circuit. It does not explicitly specify which function(s) are the outputs of the circuit.

Shown below is an alternative description of the above circuit that contains the same information. It is a **straight-line program** whose syntax is closer to that of standard programming languages. Each step is numbered and its associated purpose is given. **Input** and **output steps** are identified by the keywords READ and OUTPUT, respectively. **Computation steps** are identified by the keywords AND, OR, and NOT.

$$
\begin{array}{llll}
(1 & \text{READ} & x) & (6 & \text{AND} & 3 & 2) \\
(2 & \text{READ} & y) & (7 & \text{OR} & 5 & 6) \\
(3 & \text{NOT} & 1) & (8 & \text{OUTPUT} & 5) \\
(4 & \text{NOT} & 2) & (9 & \text{OUTPUT} & 7) \\
(5 & \text{AND} & 1 & 4)
\end{array}
\tag{2.2}
$$

The correspondence between the steps of a straight-line program and the functions computed at them is evident.

Straight-line programs are not limited to describing logic circuits. They can also be used to describe algebraic computations. (See Chapter 6.) In this case, a computation step is identified with a keyword describing the particular algebraic operation to be performed. In the case of logic circuits, the operations can include many functions other than the basic three mentioned above.

As illustrated above, a straight-line program can be constructed for any circuit. Similarly, given a straight-line program, a circuit can be drawn for it as well. We now formally define straight-line programs, circuits, and characteristics of the two.

DEFINITION 2.2.1 *A **straight-line program** is set of steps each of which is an **input step**, denoted* $(s \ \text{READ} \ x)$*, an **output step**, denoted* $(s \ \text{OUTPUT} \ i)$*, or a **computation step**, denoted* $(s \ \text{OP} \ i \ \ldots \ k)$*. Here s is the number of a step, x denotes an input variable, and the keywords* READ, OUTPUT, *and* OP *identify steps in which an input is read, an output produced, and the operation* OP *is performed. In the sth computation step the arguments to* OP *are the results produced at steps $i, \ldots, k$. It is required that these steps precede the sth step; that is, $s \geq i, \ldots, k$.*

*A **circuit** is the graph of a straight-line program. (The requirement that each computation step operate on results produced in preceding steps insures that this graph is a DAG.) The **fan-in** of the circuit is the maximum in-degree of any vertex. The **fan-out** of the circuit is the maximum outdegree of any vertex. A **gate** is the vertex associated with a computation step.*

*The **basis** Ω of a circuit and its corresponding straight-line program is the set of operations that they use. The bases of Boolean straight-line programs and logic circuits contain only Boolean functions. The **standard basis**, Ω_0, for a logic circuit is the set* {AND, OR, NOT}.

2.2.1 Functions Computed by Circuits

As stated above, each step of a straight-line program computes a function. We now define the functions computed by straight-line programs, using the example given in Eq. (2.2).

DEFINITION 2.2.2 *Let g_s be the **function computed by the sth step of a straight-line program**. If the sth step is the input step $(s \ \text{READ} \ x)$, then $g_s = x$. If it is the computation step $(s \ \text{OP} \ i \ \ldots \ k)$, the function is $g_s = \text{OP}(g_i, \ldots, g_k)$, where $g_i, \ldots, g_k$ are the functions computed at steps on which the sth step depends. If a straight-line program has n inputs and m outputs, it computes a function $f : \mathcal{B}^n \mapsto \mathcal{B}^m$. If $s_1, s_2, \ldots, s_m$ are the output steps, then $f = (g_{s_1}, g_{s_2}, \ldots, g_{s_m})$. The function computed by a circuit is the function computed by the corresponding straight-line program.*

The functions computed by the logic circuit of Fig. 2.1 are given below. The expression for g_s is found by substituting for its arguments the expressions derived at the steps on which it depends.

$$
\begin{aligned}
g_1 &:= x; & g_5 &:= x \wedge \overline{y}; \\
g_2 &:= y; & g_6 &:= \overline{x} \wedge y; \\
g_3 &:= \overline{x}; & g_7 &:= (x \wedge \overline{y}) \vee (\overline{x} \wedge y); \\
g_4 &:= \overline{y};
\end{aligned}
$$

The function computed by the above Boolean straight-line program is $f(x, y) = (g_5, g_7)$. The table of values assumed by f as the inputs x and y run through all possible values is shown below. The value of g_7 is the EXCLUSIVE OR function.

x	y	g_5	g_7
0	0	0	0
0	1	0	1
1	0	1	1
1	1	0	0

We now ask the following question: "Given a circuit with values for its inputs, how can the values of its outputs be computed?" One response it to build a circuit of physical gates, supply values for the inputs, and then wait for the signals to propagate through the gates and arrive at the outputs. A second response is to write a program in a high-level programming language to compute the values of the outputs. A simple program for this purpose assigns each step to an entry of an array and then evaluates the steps in order. This program solves the **circuit value problem**; that is, it determines the value of a circuit.

2.2.2 Circuits That Compute Functions

Now that we know how to compute the function defined by a circuit and its corresponding straight-line program, we ask: given a function, how can we construct a circuit (and straight-line program) that will compute it? Since we presume that computational tasks are defined by functions, it is important to know how to build simple machines, circuits, that will solve these tasks. In Chapter 3 we show that circuits play a central role in the design of machines with memory. Thus, whether a function or task is to be solved with a machine without memory (a circuit) or a machine with memory (such as the random-access machine), the circuit and its associated straight-line program play a key role.

To construct a circuit for a function, we begin by describing the function in a table. As seen earlier, the table for a function $f^{(n,m)} : \mathcal{B}^n \mapsto \mathcal{B}^m$ has n columns containing all 2^n possible values for the n input variables of the function. Thus, it has 2^n rows. It also has m columns containing the m outputs associated with each pattern of n inputs. If we let $x_1, x_2, \ldots, x_n$ be the **input variables** of f and let $y_1, y_2, \ldots, y_m$ be its **output variables**,

x_1	x_2	x_3	$f^{(3,2)}_{\text{example}}$ y_1	y_2
0	0	0	1	1
0	0	1	0	1
0	1	0	1	0
0	1	1	0	1
1	0	0	1	1
1	0	1	1	0
1	1	0	0	1
1	1	1	1	1

Figure 2.2 The truth table for the function $f^{(3,2)}_{\text{example}}$.

then we write $f(x_1, x_2, \ldots, x_n) = (y_1, y_2, \ldots, y_m)$. This is illustrated by the function $f_{\text{example}}^{(3,2)}(x_1, x_2, x_3) = (y_1, y_2)$ defined in Fig. 2.2 on page 39.

A **binary function** is one whose domain and range consist of the Cartesian product of $\mathcal{B} = \{0, 1\}$. A **Boolean function** is a binary function whose range consists of the set $\mathcal{B}$. In other words, it has one output.

As we see in Section 2.3, normal forms provide standard ways to construct circuits for Boolean functions. Because a normal-form expansion of a function generally does not yield a circuit of smallest size or depth, methods are needed to simplify the algebraic expressions produced by these normal forms. This topic is discussed in Section 2.2.4.

Before exploring the algebraic properties of simple Boolean functions, we define the basic circuit complexity measures used in this book.

2.2.3   Circuit Complexity Measures

We often ask for the smallest or most shallow circuit for a function. If we need to compute a function with a circuit, as is done in central processing units, then knowing the size of the smallest circuit is important. Also important is the depth of the circuit. It takes time for signals applied to the circuit inputs to propagate to the outputs, and the length of the longest path through the circuit determines this time. When central processing units must be fast, minimizing circuit depth becomes important.

As indicated in Section 1.5, the size of a circuit also provides a lower bound on the space-time product needed to solve a problem on the random-access machine, a model for modern computers. Consequently, if the size of the smallest circuit for a function is large, its space-time product must be large. Thus, a problem can be shown to be hard to compute by a machine with memory if it can be shown that every circuit for it is large.

We now define two important circuit complexity measures.

DEFINITION 2.2.3 *The **size** of a logic circuit is the number of gates it contains. Its **depth** is the number of gates on the longest path through the circuit. The **circuit size**, $C_\Omega(f)$, and **circuit depth**, $D_\Omega(f)$, of a Boolean function $f : \mathcal{B}^n \mapsto \mathcal{B}^m$ are defined as the smallest size and smallest depth of any circuit, respectively, over the basis Ω for f.*

Most Boolean functions on n variables are very complex. As shown in Sections 2.12 and 2.13, their circuit size is proportional to $2^n/n$ and their depth is approximately n. Fortunately, most functions of interest have much smaller size and depth. (It should be noted that the circuit of smallest size for a function may be different from that of smallest depth.)

2.2.4   Algebraic Properties of Boolean Functions

Since the operations AND ($\wedge$), OR ($\vee$), EXCLUSIVE OR ($\oplus$), and NOT ($\neg$ or $^-$) play a vital role in the construction of normal forms, we simplify the subsequent discussion by describing their properties.

If we interchange the two arguments of AND, OR, or EXCLUSIVE OR, it follows from their definition that their values do not change. This property, called **commutativity**, holds for all three operators, as stated next.

COMMUTATIVITY

$$x_1 \vee x_2 = x_2 \vee x_1$$
$$x_1 \wedge x_2 = x_2 \wedge x_1$$
$$x_1 \oplus x_2 = x_2 \oplus x_1$$

When constants are substituted for one of the variables of these three operators, the expression computed is simplified, as shown below.

SUBSTITUTION OF CONSTANTS

$$x_1 \vee 0 = x_1 \qquad x_1 \wedge 1 = x_1$$
$$x_1 \vee 1 = 1 \qquad x_1 \oplus 0 = x_1$$
$$x_1 \wedge 0 = 0 \qquad x_1 \oplus 1 = \overline{x}_1$$

Also, when one of the variables of one of these functions is replaced by itself or its negation, the functions simplify, as shown below.

ABSORPTION RULES

$$x_1 \vee x_1 = x_1 \qquad x_1 \wedge x_1 = x_1$$
$$x_1 \vee \overline{x}_1 = 1 \qquad x_1 \wedge \overline{x}_1 = 0$$
$$x_1 \oplus x_1 = 0 \qquad x_1 \vee (x_1 \wedge x_2) = x_1$$
$$x_1 \oplus \overline{x}_1 = 1 \qquad x_1 \wedge (x_1 \vee x_2) = x_1$$

To prove each of these results, it suffices to test exhaustively each of the values of the arguments of these functions and show that the right- and left-hand sides have the same value.

DeMorgan's rules, shown below, are very important in proving properties about circuits because they allow each AND gate to be replaced by an OR gate and three NOT gates and vice versa. The rules can be shown correct by constructing tables for each of the given functions.

DEMORGAN'S RULES

$$\overline{(x_1 \vee x_2)} = \overline{x}_1 \wedge \overline{x}_2$$
$$\overline{(x_1 \wedge x_2)} = \overline{x}_1 \vee \overline{x}_2$$

The functions AND, OR, and EXCLUSIVE OR are all **associative**; that is, all ways of combining three or more variables with any of these functions give the same result. (An operator $\odot$ is **associative** if for all values of a, b, and c, $a \odot (b \odot c) = (a \odot b) \odot c$.) Again, proof by enumeration suffices to establish the following results.

ASSOCIATIVITY

$$x_1 \vee (x_2 \vee x_3) = (x_1 \vee x_2) \vee x_3$$
$$x_1 \wedge (x_2 \wedge x_3) = (x_1 \wedge x_2) \wedge x_3$$
$$x_1 \oplus (x_2 \oplus x_3) = (x_1 \oplus x_2) \oplus x_3$$

Because of associativity it is not necessary to parenthesize repeated uses of the operators $\vee$, $\wedge$, and $\oplus$.

Finally, the following **distributive laws** are important in simplifying Boolean algebraic expressions. The first two laws are the same as the distributivity of integer multiplication over integer addition when multiplication and addition are replaced by AND and OR.

DISTRIBUTIVITY
$$x_1 \wedge (x_2 \vee x_3) = (x_1 \wedge x_2) \vee (x_1 \wedge x_3)$$
$$x_1 \wedge (x_2 \oplus x_3) = (x_1 \wedge x_2) \oplus (x_1 \wedge x_3)$$
$$x_1 \vee (x_2 \wedge x_3) = (x_1 \vee x_2) \wedge (x_1 \vee x_3)$$

We often write $x \wedge y$ as xy. The operator $\wedge$ has precedence over the operators $\vee$ and $\oplus$, which means that parentheses in $(x \wedge y) \vee z$ and $(x \wedge y) \oplus z$ may be dropped.

The above rules are illustrated by the following formula:

$$\overline{(\overline{x} \wedge (y \oplus z))} \wedge (x \vee y) = (x \vee \overline{(y \oplus z)}) \wedge (x \vee y)$$
$$= (x \vee (\overline{y} \oplus z)) \wedge (x \vee y)$$
$$= x \vee (y \wedge (\overline{y} \oplus z))$$
$$= x \vee ((y \wedge \overline{y}) \oplus (y \wedge z))$$
$$= x \vee (0 \oplus y \wedge z)$$
$$= x \vee (y \wedge z)$$

DeMorgan's second rule is used to simplify the first term in the first equation. The last rule on substitution of constants is used twice to simplify the second equation. The third distributivity rule and commutativity of $\wedge$ are used to simplify the third one. The second distributivity rule is used to expand the fourth equation. The fifth equation is simplified by invoking the third absorption rule. The final equation results from the commutativity of $\oplus$ and application of the rule $x_1 \oplus 0 = x_1$. When there is no loss of clarity, we drop the operator symbol $\wedge$ between two literals.

2.3 Normal-Form Expansions of Boolean Functions

Normal forms are standard ways of constructing circuits from the tables defining Boolean functions. They are easy to apply, although the circuits they produce are generally far from optimal.

In this section we define five normal forms: the disjunctive and conjunctive normal forms, the sum-of-products expansion, the product-of-sums expansion, and the ring-sum expansion.

2.3.1 Disjunctive Normal Form

A **minterm** in the variables $x_1, x_2, \ldots, x_n$ is the AND of each variable or its negation. For example, when $n = 3$, $\overline{x}_1 \wedge \overline{x}_2 \wedge \overline{x}_3$ is a minterm. It has value 1 exactly when each variable has value 0. $x_1 \wedge \overline{x}_2 \wedge x_3$ is another minterm; it has value 1 exactly when $x_1 = 1$, $x_2 = 0$ and $x_3 = 1$. It follows that a minterm on n variables has value 1 for exactly one of the 2^n points in its domain. Using the notation $x^1 = x$ and $x^0 = \overline{x}$, we see that the above minterms can be written as $x_1^0 x_2^0 x_3^0$ and $x_1 x_2^0 x_3$, respectively, when we drop the use of the AND operator $\wedge$. Thus, $x_1^0 x_2^0 x_3^0 = 1$ when $\boldsymbol{x} = (x_1, x_2, x_3) = (0, 0, 0)$ and $x_1^1 x_2^0 x_3^1 = 1$ when $\boldsymbol{x} = (1, 0, 1)$. That is, the minterm $\boldsymbol{x}_{(\boldsymbol{c})} = x_1^{c_1} \wedge x_2^{c_2} \wedge \cdots \wedge x_n^{c_n}$ has value 1 exactly when $\boldsymbol{x} = \boldsymbol{c}$ where $\boldsymbol{c} = (c_1, c_2, \ldots, c_n)$. A **minterm of a Boolean function** f is a minterm $\boldsymbol{x}_{(\boldsymbol{c})}$ that contains all the variables of f and for which $f(\boldsymbol{c}) = 1$.

The word "disjunction" is a synonym for OR, and the **disjunctive normal form (DNF)** of a Boolean function $f : \mathcal{B}^n \mapsto \mathcal{B}$ is the OR of the minterms of f. Thus, f has value 1 when

x_1	x_2	x_3	f
0	0	0	1
0	0	1	0
0	1	0	1
0	1	1	0
1	0	0	1
1	0	1	1
1	1	0	0
1	1	1	1

x_1	x_2	x_3	f
0	0	0	1
0	0	1	0
0	1	0	1
0	1	1	0
1	0	0	1
1	0	1	1
1	1	0	0
1	1	1	1

(a) (b)

Figure 2.3 Truth tables illustrating the disjunctive and conjunctive normal forms.

exactly one of of its minterms has value 1 and has value 0 otherwise. Consider the function whose table is given in Fig. 2.3(a). Its disjunctive normal form (or minterm expansion) is given by the following formula:

$$f(x_1, x_2, x_3) = x_1^0 x_2^0 x_3^0 \vee x_1^0 x_2^1 x_3^0 \vee x_1^1 x_2^0 x_3^0 \vee x_1^1 x_2^0 x_3^1 \vee x_1^1 x_2^1 x_3^1$$

The **parity** function $f_\oplus^{(n)} : \mathcal{B}^n \mapsto \mathcal{B}$ on n inputs has value 1 when an odd number of inputs is 1 and value 0 otherwise. It can be realized by a circuit containing $n - 1$ instances of the EXCLUSIVE OR operator; that is, $f_\oplus^{(n)}(x_1, \ldots, x_n) = x_1 \oplus x_2 \oplus \cdots \oplus x_n$. However, the DNF of $f_\oplus^{(n)}$ contains 2^{n-1} minterms, a number exponential in n. The DNF of $f_\oplus^{(3)}$ is

$$f_\oplus^{(3)}(x, y, z) = \overline{x}\,\overline{y}\,z \vee \overline{x}\,y\,\overline{z} \vee x\,\overline{y}\,\overline{z} \vee xyz$$

Here we use the standard notation for a variable and its complement.

2.3.2 Conjunctive Normal Form

A **maxterm** in the variables $x_1, x_2, \ldots, x_n$ is the OR of each variable or its negation. For example, $x_1 \vee x_2 \vee \overline{x}_3$ is a maxterm. It has value 0 exactly when $x_1 = x_2 = 0$ and $x_3 = 1$. $x_1 \vee \overline{x}_2 \vee \overline{x}_3$ is another maxterm; it has value 0 exactly when $x_1 = 0$ and $x_2 = x_3 = 1$. It follows that a maxterm on n variables has value 0 for exactly one of the 2^n points in its domain. We see that the above maxterms can be written as $x_1^1 \vee x_2^1 \vee x_3^0$ and $x_1^1 \vee x_2^0 \vee x_3^0$, respectively. Thus, $x_1^1 \vee x_2^1 \vee x_3^0 = 0$ when $\boldsymbol{x} = (x_1, x_2, x_3) = (0, 0, 1)$ and $x_1^1 x_2^0 x_3^1 = 1$ when $\boldsymbol{x} = (0, 1, 0)$. That is, the maxterm $\boldsymbol{x}^{(c)} = x_1^{\overline{c}_1} \vee x_2^{\overline{c}_2} \vee \cdots \vee x_n^{\overline{c}_n}$ has value 0 exactly when $\boldsymbol{x} = \boldsymbol{c}$. A **maxterm of a Boolean function** f is a maxterm $\boldsymbol{x}^{(c)}$ that contains all the variables of f and for which $f(\boldsymbol{c}) = 0$.

The word "conjunction" is a synonym for AND, and the **conjunctive normal form (CNF)** of a Boolean function $f : \mathcal{B}^n \mapsto \mathcal{B}$ is the AND of the maxterms of f. Thus, f has value 0 when exactly one of of its maxterms has value 0 and has value 1 otherwise. Consider the function whose table is given in Fig. 2.3(b). Its conjunctive normal form (or maxterm expansion) is given by the following formula:

$$y_1(x_1, x_2, x_3) = (x_1^1 \vee x_2^1 \vee x_3^0) \wedge (x_1^1 \vee x_2^0 \vee x_3^0) \wedge (x_1^0 \vee x_2^0 \vee x_3^1)$$

An important relationship holds between the DNF and CNF representations for Boolean functions. If $\mathrm{DNF}(f)$ and $\mathrm{CNF}(f)$ are the representations of f in the DNF and CNF expansions, then the following identity holds (see Problem 2.6):

$$\mathrm{CNF}(f) = \overline{\mathrm{DNF}(\overline{f})}$$

It follows that the CNF of the parity function $f_{\oplus}^{(n)}$ has 2^{n-1} maxterms.

Since each function $f : \mathcal{B}^n \mapsto \mathcal{B}^m$ can be expanded to its CNF or DNF and each can be realized with circuits, the following result is immediate.

THEOREM 2.3.1 *Every function $f : \mathcal{B}^n \mapsto \mathcal{B}^m$ can be realized by a logic circuit.*

2.3.3 SOPE and POSE Normal Forms

The sum-of-products and product-of-sums normal forms are simplifications of the disjunctive and conjunctive normal forms, respectively. These simplifications are obtained by using the rules stated in Section 2.2.4.

A **product** in the variables $x_{i_1}, x_{i_2}, \ldots, x_{i_k}$ is the AND of each of these variables or their negations. For example, $x_2 \, \overline{x}_5 \, x_6$ is a product. A minterm is a product that contains each of the variables of a function. A **product of a Boolean function** f is a product in some of the variables of f. A **sum-of-products expansion (SOPE)** of a Boolean function is the OR (the sum) of products of f. Thus, the DNF is a special case of the SOPE of a function.

A SOPE of a Boolean function can be obtained by simplifying the DNF of a function using the rules given in Section 2.2.4. For example, the DNF given earlier and shown below can be simplified to produce a SOPE.

$$y_1(x_1, x_2, x_3) = \overline{x}_1 \, \overline{x}_2 \, \overline{x}_3 \vee \overline{x}_1 \, x_2 \, \overline{x}_3 \vee x_1 \, \overline{x}_2 \, \overline{x}_3 \vee x_1 \, \overline{x}_2 \, x_3 \vee x_1 \, x_2 \, x_3$$

It is easy to see that the first and second terms combine to give $\overline{x}_1\overline{x}_3$, the first and third give $\overline{x}_2\overline{x}_3$ (we use the property that $g \vee g = g$), and the last two give x_1x_3. That is, we can write the following SOPE for f:

$$f = x_1 \, x_3 \vee \overline{x}_1 \, \overline{x}_3 \vee \overline{x}_2\overline{x}_3 \tag{2.3}$$

Clearly, we could have stopped before any one of the above simplifications was used and generated another SOPE for f. This illustrates the point that a Boolean function may have many SOPEs but only one DNF.

A **sum** in the variables $x_{i_1}, x_{i_2}, \ldots, x_{i_k}$ is the OR of each of these variables or their negations. For example, $\overline{x}_3 \vee x_4 \vee x_7$ is a sum. A maxterm is a product that contains each of the variables of a function. A **sum of a Boolean function** f is a sum in some of the variables of f. A **product-of-sum expansion (POSE)** of a Boolean function is the AND (the product) of sums of f. Thus, the CNF is a special case of the POSE of a function.

A POSE of a Boolean function can be obtained by simplifying the CNF of a function using the rules given in Section 2.2.4. For example, the conjunction of the two maxterms $x_1 \vee \overline{x}_2 \vee \overline{x}_3$ and $x_1 \vee \overline{x}_2 \vee x_3$, namely $(x_1 \vee \overline{x}_2 \vee \overline{x}_3) \wedge (x_1 \vee \overline{x}_2 \vee x_3)$, can be reduced to $x_1 \vee \overline{x}_2$ by the application of rules of Section 2.2.4, as shown below:

$$(x_1 \vee \overline{x}_2 \vee \overline{x}_3) \wedge (x_1 \vee \overline{x}_2 \vee x_3) =$$

$$= x_1 \vee (\overline{x}_2 \vee \overline{x}_3) \wedge (\overline{x}_2 \vee x_3) \quad \{\text{3rd distributivity rule}\}$$
$$= x_1 \vee \overline{x}_2 \vee (\overline{x}_3 \wedge x_3) \quad \{\text{3rd distributivity rule}\}$$
$$= x_1 \vee \overline{x}_2 \vee 0 \quad \{\text{6th absorption rule}\}$$
$$= x_1 \vee \overline{x}_2 \quad \{\text{1st rule on substitution of constants}\}$$

It is easily shown that the POSE of the parity function is its CNF. (See Problem 2.8.)

2.3.4 Ring-Sum Expansion

The **ring-sum expansion (RSE)** of a function f is the EXCLUSIVE OR ($\oplus$) of a constant and products ($\wedge$) of unnegated variables of f. For example, $1 \oplus x_1 x_3 \oplus x_2 x_4$ is an RSE. The operations $\oplus$ and $\wedge$ over the set $\mathcal{B} = \{0, 1\}$ constitute a ring. (Rings are examined in Section 6.2.1.) Any two instances of the same product in the RSE can be eliminated since they sum to 0.

The RSE of a Boolean function $f : \mathcal{B}^n \mapsto \mathcal{B}$ can be constructed from its DNF, as we show. Since a minterm of f has value 1 on exactly one of the 2^n points in its domain, at most one minterm in the DNF for f has value 1 for any point in its domain. Thus, we can combine minterms with EXCLUSIVE OR instead of OR without changing the value of the function. Now replace $\overline{x}_i$ with $x_i \oplus 1$ in each minterm containing $\overline{x}_i$ and then apply the second distributivity rule. We simplify the resulting formula by using commutativity and the absorption rule $x_i \oplus x_i = 0$. For example, since the minterms of $(\overline{x}_1 \vee x_2)x_3$ are $\overline{x}_1 x_2 x_3$, $\overline{x}_1 \overline{x}_2 x_3$, and $x_1 x_2 x_3$, we construct the RSE of this function as follows:

$$(\overline{x}_1 \vee x_2)x_3 = \overline{x}_1 x_2 x_3 \oplus \overline{x}_1 \overline{x}_2 x_3 \oplus x_1 x_2 x_3$$
$$= (x_1 \oplus 1)x_2 x_3 \oplus (x_1 \oplus 1)(x_2 \oplus 1)x_3 \oplus x_1 x_2 x_3$$
$$= x_2 x_3 \oplus x_1 x_2 x_3 \oplus x_3 \oplus x_1 x_3 \oplus x_2 x_3 \oplus x_1 x_2 x_3 \oplus x_1 x_2 x_3$$
$$= x_3 \oplus x_1 x_3 \oplus x_1 x_2 x_3$$

The third equation follows by applying the second distributivity rule and commutativity. The fourth follows by applying $x_i \oplus x_i = 0$ and commutativity. The two occurrences of $x_2 x_3$ are canceled, as are two of the three instances of $x_1 x_2 x_3$.

As this example illustrates, the RSE of a function $f : \mathcal{B}^n \mapsto \mathcal{B}$ is the EXCLUSIVE OR of a Boolean constant c_0 and one or more products of unnegated variables of f. Since each of the n variables of f can be present or absent from a product, there are 2^n products, including the product that contains no variables; that is, a constant whose value is 0 or 1. For example, $1 \oplus x_3 \oplus x_1 x_3 \oplus x_1 x_2 x_3$ is the RSE of the function $\overline{(\overline{x}_1 \vee x_2)\, x_3}$.

2.3.5 Comparison of Normal Forms

It is easy to show that the RSE of a Boolean function is unique (see Problem 2.7). However, the RSE is not necessarily a compact representation of a function. For example, the RSE of the OR of n variables, $f_\vee^{(n)}$, includes every product term except for the constant 1. (See Problem 2.9.)

It is also true that some functions have large size in some normal forms but small size in others. For example, the parity function has exponential size in the DNF and CNF normal forms but linear size in the RSE. Also, $f_\vee^{(n)}$ has exponential size in the RSE but linear size in the CNF and SOPE representations.

A natural question to ask is whether there is a function that has large size in all five normal forms. The answer is yes. This is true of the Boolean function on n variables whose value is 1 when the sum of its variables is 0 modulo 3 and is 0 otherwise. It has exponential-size DNF, CNF, and RSE normal forms. (See Problem 2.10.) However, its smallest circuit is linear in n. (See Section 2.11.)

2.4 Reductions Between Functions

A common way to solve a new problem is to apply an existing solution to it. For example, an integer multiplication algorithm can be used to square an integer by supplying two copies of the integer to the multiplier. This idea is called a "reduction" in complexity theory because we reduce one problem to a previously solved problem, here squaring to integer multiplication. In this section we briefly discuss several simple forms of reduction, including subfunctions. Note that the definitions given below are not limited to binary functions.

DEFINITION 2.4.1 *A function $f : \mathcal{A}^n \mapsto \mathcal{A}^m$ is a* **reduction** *to the function $g : \mathcal{A}^r \mapsto \mathcal{A}^s$ through application of the functions $p : \mathcal{A}^s \mapsto \mathcal{A}^m$ and $q : \mathcal{A}^n \mapsto \mathcal{A}^r$ if for all $\boldsymbol{x} \in \mathcal{A}^n$:*

$$f(\boldsymbol{x}) = p(g(q(\boldsymbol{x})))$$

As suggested in Fig. 2.4, it follows that circuits for q, g and p can be cascaded (the output of one is the input to the next) to form a circuit for f. Thus, the circuit size and depth of f, $C(f)$ and $D(f)$, satisfy the following inequalities:

$$C(f) \leq C(p) + C(g) + C(q)$$
$$D(f) \leq D(p) + D(g) + D(q)$$

A special case of a reduction is the subfunction, as defined below.

DEFINITION 2.4.2 *Let $g : \mathcal{A}^n \mapsto \mathcal{A}^m$. A* **subfunction** *$f$ of g is a function obtained by assigning values to some of the input variables of g, assigning (not necessarily unique) variable names to the rest, deleting and/or permuting some of its output variables. We say that f is a* **reduction** *to g via the* **subfunction relationship**.

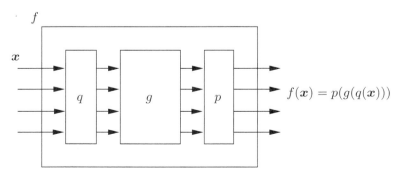

Figure 2.4 The function f is reduced to the function g by applying functions p and q to prepare the input to g and manipulate its output.

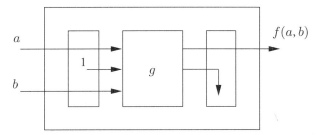

Figure 2.5 The subfunction f of the function g is obtained by fixing some input variables, assigning names to the rest, and deleting and/or permuting outputs.

This definition is illustrated by the function $f_{\text{example}}^{(3,2)}(x_1, x_2, x_3) = (y_1, y_2)$ in Fig. 2.2. We form the subfunction y_1 by deleting y_2 from $f_{\text{example}}^{(3,2)}$ and fixing $x_1 = a$, $x_2 = 1$, and $x_3 = b$, where a and b are new variables. Then, consulting (2.3), we see that y_1 can be written as follows:

$$y_1 = (a\,b) \vee (\overline{a}\,\overline{b}) \vee (\overline{1}\,\overline{b})$$
$$= a\,b \vee \overline{a}\,\overline{b}$$
$$= a \oplus b \oplus 1$$

That is, y_1 contains the complement of the EXCLUSIVE OR function as a subfunction. The definition is also illustrated by the reductions developed in Sections 2.5.2, 2.5.6, 2.9.5, and 2.10.1.

The subfunction definition derives its importance from the following lemma. (See Fig. 2.5.)

LEMMA 2.4.1 *If f is a subfunction of g, a straight-line program for f can be created from one for g without increasing the size or depth of its circuit.*

As shown in Section 2.9.5, the logical shifting function (Section 2.5.1) can be realized by composing the integer multiplication and decoder functions (Section 2.5). This type of reduction is useful in those cases in which one function is reduced to another with the aid of functions whose complexity (size or depth or both) is known to be small relative to that of either function. It follows that the two functions have the same asymptotic complexity even if we cannot determine what that complexity is. The reduction is a powerful idea that is widely used in computer science. Not only is it the essence of the subroutine, but it is also used to classify problems by their time or space complexity. (See Sections 3.9.3 and 8.7.)

2.5 Specialized Circuits

A small number of special functions arise repeatedly in the design of computers. These include logical and shifting operations, encoders, decoders, multiplexers, and demultiplexers. In the following sections we construct efficient circuits for these functions.

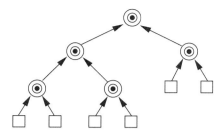

Figure 2.6 A balanced binary tree circuit that combines elements with an associative operator.

2.5.1 Logical Operations

Logical operations are not only building blocks for more complex operations, but they are at the heart of all central processing units. Logical operations include "vector" and "associating" operations. A **vector operation** is the component-wise operation on one or more vectors. For example, the vector NOT on the vector $\boldsymbol{x} = (x_{n-1}, \ldots, x_1, x_0)$ is the vector $\overline{\boldsymbol{x}} = (\overline{x}_{n-1}, \ldots, \overline{x}_1, \overline{x}_0)$. Other vector operations involve the application of a two-input function to corresponding components of two vectors. If $\star$ is a two-input function, such as AND or OR, and $\boldsymbol{x} = (x_{n-1}, \ldots, x_1, x_0)$ and $\boldsymbol{y} = (y_{n-1}, \ldots, y_1, y_0)$ are two n-tuples, the vector operation $\boldsymbol{x} \star \boldsymbol{y}$ is

$$\boldsymbol{x} \star \boldsymbol{y} = (x_{n-1} \star y_{n-1}, \ldots, x_1 \star y_1, x_0 \star y_0)$$

An **associative operator** $\odot$ over a $\mathcal{A}$ satisfies the condition $(a \odot b) \odot c = a \odot (b \odot c)$ for all $a, b, c \in \mathcal{A}$. A **summing operation** on an n-tuple $\boldsymbol{x}$ with an associative two-input operation $\odot$ produces the "sum" y defined below.

$$y = x_{n-1} \odot \cdots \odot x_1 \odot x_0$$

An efficient circuit for computing y is shown in Fig. 2.6. It is a binary tree whose leaves are associated with the variables $x_{n-1}, \ldots, x_1, x_0$. Each level of the tree is full except possibly the last. This circuit has smallest depth of those that form the associative combination of the variables, namely $\lceil \log_2 n \rceil$.

2.5.2 Shifting Functions

Shifting functions can be used to multiply integers and generally manipulate data. A cyclic shifting function rotates the bits in a word. For example, the left cyclic shift of the 4-tuple $(1, 0, 0, 0)$ by three places produces the 4-tuple $(0, 1, 0, 0)$.

The **cyclic shifting function** $f_{\text{cyclic}}^{(n)} : \mathcal{B}^{n+\lceil \log_2 n \rceil} \mapsto \mathcal{B}^n$ takes as input an n-tuple $\boldsymbol{x} = (x_{n-1}, \ldots, x_1, x_0)$ and cyclically shifts it left by $|\boldsymbol{s}|$ places, where $|\boldsymbol{s}|$ is the integer associated with the binary k-tuple $\boldsymbol{s} = (s_{k-1}, \ldots, s_1, s_0)$, $k = \lceil \log_2 n \rceil$, and

$$|\boldsymbol{s}| = \sum_{j=0}^{k-1} s_j 2^j$$

The n-tuple that results from the shift is $\boldsymbol{y} = (y_{n-1}, \ldots, y_1, y_0)$, denoted as follows:

$$\boldsymbol{y} = f_{\text{cyclic}}^{(n)}(\boldsymbol{x}, \boldsymbol{s})$$

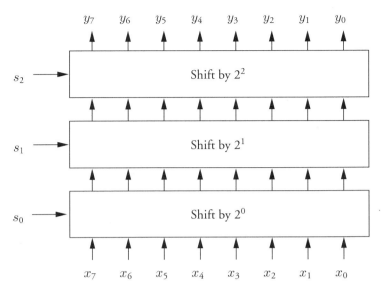

Figure 2.7 Three stages of a cyclic shifting circuit on eight inputs.

A convenient way to perform the cyclic shift of x by $|s|$ places is to represent $|s|$ as a sum of powers of 2, as shown above, and for each $0 \leq j \leq k - 1$, shift x left cyclically by $s_j 2^j$ places, that is, by either 0 or 2^j places depending on whether $s_j = 0$ or 1. For example, consider cyclically shifting the 8-tuple $u = (1, 0, 1, 1, 0, 1, 0, 1)$ by seven places. Since 7 is represented by the binary number $(1, 1, 1)$, that is, $7 = 4 + 2 + 1$, to shift $(1, 0, 1, 1, 0, 1, 0, 1)$ by seven places it suffices to shift it by one place, by two places, and then by four places. (See Fig. 2.7.)

For $0 \leq r \leq n - 1$, the following formula defines the value of the rth output, y_r, of a circuit on n inputs that shifts its input x left cyclically by either 0 or 2^j places depending on whether $s_j = 0$ or 1:

$$y_r = (x_r \wedge \bar{s}_j) \vee (x_{(r - 2^j) \bmod n} \wedge s_j)$$

Thus, y_r is x_r in the first case or $x_{(r - 2^j) \bmod n}$ in the second. The subscript $(r - 2^j) \bmod n$ is the positive remainder of $(r - 2^j)$ after division by n. For example, if $n = 4$, $r = 1$, and $j = 1$, then $(r - 2^j) = -1$, which is 3 modulo 4. That is, in a circuit that shifts by either 0 or 2^1 places, y_1 is either x_1 or x_3 because x_3 moves into the second position when shifted left cyclically by two places.

A circuit based on the above formula that shifts by either 0 or 2^j places depending on whether $s_j = 0$ or 1 is shown in Fig. 2.8 for $n = 4$. The circuit on n inputs has $3n + 1$ gates and depth 3.

It follows that a circuit for cyclic shifting an n-tuple can be realized in $k = \lceil \log_2 n \rceil$ stages each of which has $3n + 1$ gates and depth 3, as suggested by Fig. 2.7. Since this may be neither the smallest nor the shallowest circuit that computes $f_{\text{cyclic}}^{(n)} : \mathcal{B}^{n + \lceil \log_2 n \rceil}$, its minimal circuit size and depth satisfy the following bounds.

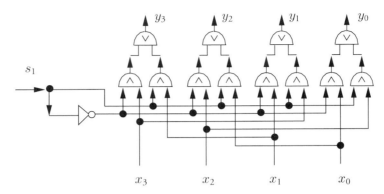

Figure 2.8 One stage of a circuit for cyclic shifting four inputs by 0 or 2 places depending on whether $s_1 = 0$ or 1.

LEMMA 2.5.1 *The cyclic shifting function $f_{\text{cyclic}}^{(n)} : \mathcal{B}^{n+\lceil \log_2 n \rceil} \mapsto \mathcal{B}^n$ can be realized by a circuit of the following size and depth over the basis $\Omega_0 = \{\wedge, \vee, \neg\}$:*

$$C_{\Omega_0}\left(f_{\text{cyclic}}^{(n)}\right) \leq (3n+1)\lceil \log_2 n \rceil$$

$$D_{\Omega_0}\left(f_{\text{cyclic}}^{(n)}\right) \leq 3\lceil \log_2 n \rceil$$

The **logical shifting function** $f_{\text{shift}}^{(n)} : \mathcal{B}^{n+\lceil \log_2 n \rceil} \mapsto \mathcal{B}^n$ shifts left the n-tuple $\boldsymbol{x}$ by a number of places specified by a binary $\lceil \log n \rceil$-tuple $\boldsymbol{s}$, discarding the higher-index components, and filling in the lower-indexed vacated places with 0's to produce the n-tuple $\boldsymbol{y}$, where

$$y_j = \begin{cases} x_{j-|\boldsymbol{s}|} & \text{for } |\boldsymbol{s}| \leq j \leq n-1 \\ 0 & \text{otherwise} \end{cases}$$

REDUCTIONS BETWEEN LOGICAL AND CYCLIC SHIFTING   The logical shifting function $f_{\text{shift}}^{(n)} :$ $\mathcal{B}^{n+\lceil \log_2 n \rceil} \mapsto \mathcal{B}^n$ on the n-tuple $\boldsymbol{x}$ is defined below in terms of $f_{\text{cyclic}}^{(2n)}$ and the "projection" function $\pi_L^{(n)} : \mathcal{B}^{2n} \mapsto \mathcal{B}^n$ that deletes the n high order components from its input $2n$-tuple. Here $\boldsymbol{0}$ denotes the zero binary n-tuple and $\boldsymbol{0} \cdot \boldsymbol{x}$ denotes the concatenation of the two strings. (See Figs. 2.9 and 2.10.)

$$f_{\text{shift}}^{(n)}(\boldsymbol{x}, \boldsymbol{s}) = \pi_L^{(n)}\left(f_{\text{cyclic}}^{(2n)}(\boldsymbol{0} \cdot \boldsymbol{x}, \boldsymbol{s})\right)$$

0	0	0	0	0	x_7	x_6	x_5	x_4	x_3	x_2	x_1	x_0	0	0	0

Figure 2.9 The reduction of $f_{\text{shift}}^{(8)}$ to $f_{\text{cyclic}}^{(8)}$ obtained by cyclically shifting $\boldsymbol{0} \cdot \boldsymbol{x}$ by three places and projecting out the shaded components.

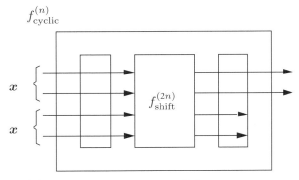

Figure 2.10 The function $f_{\text{cyclic}}^{(n)}$ is obtained by computing $f_{\text{shift}}^{(2n)}$ on $\boldsymbol{xx}$ and truncating the n low-order bits.

LEMMA 2.5.2 *The function $f_{\text{cyclic}}^{(2n)}$ contains $f_{\text{shift}}^{(n)}$ as a subfunction and the function $f_{\text{shift}}^{(2n)}$ contains $f_{\text{cyclic}}^{(n)}$ as a subfunction.*

Proof The first statement follows from the above argument concerning $f_{\text{shift}}^{(n)}$. The second statement follows by noting that

$$f_{\text{cyclic}}^{(n)}(\boldsymbol{x}, \boldsymbol{s}) = \pi_H^{(n)}\left(f_{\text{shift}}^{(2n)}(\boldsymbol{x} \cdot \boldsymbol{x}, \boldsymbol{s})\right)$$

where $\pi_H^{(n)}$ deletes the n low-order components of its input. ∎

This relationship between logical and cyclic shifting functions clearly holds for variants of such functions in which the amount of a shift is specified with some other notation. An example of such a shifting function is integer multiplication in which one of the two arguments is a power of 2.

2.5.3 Encoder

The **encoder function** $f_{\text{encode}}^{(n)} : \mathcal{B}^{2^n} \mapsto \mathcal{B}^n$ has 2^n inputs, exactly one of which is 1. Its output is an n-tuple that is a binary number representing the position of the input that has value 1. That is, it encodes the position of the input bit that has value 1. Encoders are used in CPUs to identify the source of external interrupts.

Let $\boldsymbol{x} = (x_{2^n-1}, \ldots, x_2, x_1, x_0)$ represent the 2^n inputs and let $\boldsymbol{y} = (y_{n-1}, \ldots, y_1, y_0)$ represent the n outputs. Then, we write $f_{\text{encode}}^{(n)}(\boldsymbol{x}) = \boldsymbol{y}$.

When $n = 1$, the encoder function has two inputs, x_1 and x_0, and one output, y_0, whose value is $y_0 = x_1$ because if $x_0 = 1$, then $x_1 = 0$ and $y_0 = 0$ is the binary representation of the input whose value is 1. Similar reasoning applies when $x_0 = 0$.

When $n \geq 2$, we observe that the high-order output bit, y_{n-1}, has value 1 if 1 falls among the variables $x_{2^n-1}, \ldots, x_{2^{n-1}+1}, x_{2^{n-1}}$. Otherwise, $y_{n-1} = 0$. Thus, y_{n-1} can be computed as the OR of these variables, as suggested for the encoder on eight inputs in Fig. 2.11.

The remaining $n - 1$ output bits, $y_{n-2}, \ldots, y_1, y_0$, represent the position of the 1 among variables $x_{2^{n-1}-1}, \ldots, x_2, x_1, x_0$ if $y_{n-1} = 0$ or the 1 among variables $x_{2^n-1}, \ldots, x_{2^{n-1}+1}$, $x_{2^{n-1}}$ if $y_{n-1} = 1$. For example, for $n = 8$ if $\boldsymbol{x} = (0, 0, 0, 0, 0, 0, 1, 0)$, then $y_2 = 0$ and

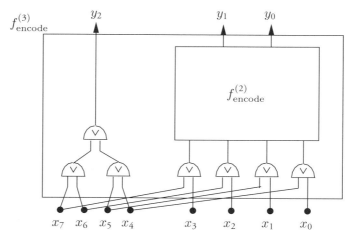

$f_{\text{encode}}^{(3)}$

Figure 2.11 The recursive construction of an encoder circuit on eight inputs.

$(y_1, y_0) = (1, 0)$, whereas if $\boldsymbol{x} = (0, 0, 1, 0, 0, 0, 0, 0)$, then $y_2 = 1$ and $(y_1, y_0) = (1, 0)$. Thus, after computing y_{n-1} as the OR of the 2^{n-1} high-order inputs, the remaining output bits can be obtained by supplying to an encoder on 2^{n-1} inputs the 2^{n-1} low-order bits if $y_{n-1} = 0$ or the 2^{n-1} high-order bits if $y_{n-1} = 1$. It follows that in both cases we can supply the vector $\boldsymbol{\delta} = (x_{2^n-1} \vee x_{2(n-1)-1}, x_{2^n-2} \vee x_{2(n-1)-2}, \ldots, x_{2(n-1)} \vee x_0)$ of $2^{(n-1)}$ components to the encoder on $2^{(n-1)}$ inputs. This is illustrated in Fig. 2.11.

Let's now derive upper bounds on the size and depth of the optimal circuit for $f_{\text{encode}}^{(n)}$. Clearly $C_{\Omega_0}\left(f_{\text{encode}}^{(1)}\right) = 0$ and $D_{\Omega_0}\left(f_{\text{encode}}^{(1)}\right) = 0$, since no gates are needed in this case. From the construction described above and illustrated in Fig. 2.11, we see that we can construct a circuit for $f_{\text{encode}}^{(n)}$ in a two-step process. First, we form y_{n-1} as the OR of the 2^{n-1} high-order variables in a balanced OR tree of depth n using $2^{n-1} - 1$ OR's. Second, we form the vector $\boldsymbol{\delta}$ with a circuit of depth 1 using 2^{n-1} OR's and supply it to a copy of a circuit for $f_{\text{encode}}^{(n-1)}$. This provides the following recurrences for the circuit size and depth of $f_{\text{encode}}^{(n)}$ because the depth of this circuit is no more than the maximum of the depth of the OR tree and 1 more than the depth of a circuit for $f_{\text{encode}}^{(n-1)}$:

$$C_{\Omega_0}\left(f_{\text{encode}}^{(n)}\right) \le 2^n - 1 + C_{\Omega_0}(f_{\text{encode}}^{(n-1)}) \tag{2.4}$$

$$D_{\Omega_0}\left(f_{\text{encode}}^{(n)}\right) \le \max(n - 1, D_{\Omega_0}(f_{\text{encode}}^{(n-1)}) + 1) \tag{2.5}$$

The solutions to these recurrences are stated as the following lemma, as the reader can show. (See Problem 2.14.)

LEMMA 2.5.3 *The encoder function* $f_{\text{encode}}^{(n)}$ *has the following circuit size and depth bounds:*

$$C_{\Omega_0}\left(f_{\text{encode}}^{(n)}\right) \le 2^{n+1} - (n + 3)$$

$$D_{\Omega_0}\left(f_{\text{encode}}^{(n)}\right) \le n - 1$$

2.5.4 Decoder

A decoder is a function that reverses the operation of an encoder: given an n-bit binary address, it generates 2^n bits with a single 1 in the position specified by the binary number. Decoders are used in the design of random-access memory units (see Section 3.5) and of the multiplexer (see Section 2.5.5).

The **decoder function** $f_{\text{decode}}^{(n)} : \mathcal{B}^n \mapsto \mathcal{B}^{2^n}$ has n input variables $\boldsymbol{x} = (x_{n-1}, \ldots, x_1, x_0)$ and 2^n output variables $\boldsymbol{y} = (y_{2^n-1}, \ldots, y_1, y_0)$; that is, $f_{\text{decode}}^{(n)}(\boldsymbol{x}) = \boldsymbol{y}$. Let $\boldsymbol{c}$ be a binary n-tuple corresponding to the integer $|\boldsymbol{c}|$. All components of the binary 2^n-tuple $\boldsymbol{y}$ are zero except for the one whose index is $|\boldsymbol{c}|$, namely $y_{|\boldsymbol{c}|}$. Thus, the minterm functions in the variables $\boldsymbol{x}$ are computed as the output of $f_{\text{decode}}^{(n)}$.

A direct realization of the function $f_{\text{decode}}^{(n)}$ can be obtained by realizing each minterm independently. This circuit uses $(2n-1)2^n$ gates and has depth $\lceil \log_2 n \rceil + 1$. Thus we have the following bounds over the basis $\Omega_0 = \{\wedge, \vee, \neg\}$:

$$C_{\Omega_0}\left(f_{\text{decode}}^{(n)}\right) \leq (2n-1)2^n$$

$$D_{\Omega_0}\left(f_{\text{decode}}^{(n)}\right) \leq \lceil \log_2 n \rceil + 1$$

A smaller upper bound on circuit size and depth can be obtained from the recursive construction of Fig. 2.12, which is based on the observation that a minterm on n variables is the AND of a minterm on the first $n/2$ variables and a minterm on the second $n/2$ variables. For example, when $n = 4$, the minterm $\overline{x}_3 \wedge x_2 \wedge \overline{x}_1 \wedge \overline{x}_0$ is obviously equal to the AND of the minterm $\overline{x}_3 \wedge x_2$ in the variables x_3 and x_2 and the minterm $\overline{x}_1 \wedge \overline{x}_0$ in the variables x_1 and x_0. Thus, when n is even, the minterms that are the outputs of $f_{\text{decode}}^{(n)}$ can be formed by ANDing

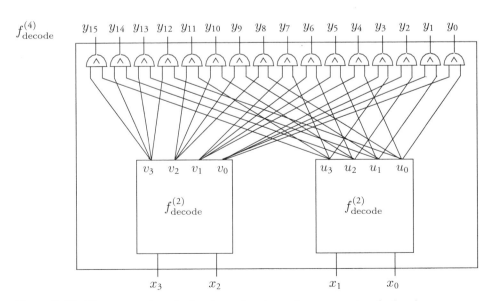

Figure 2.12 The construction of a decoder on four inputs from two copies of a decoder on two inputs.

every minterm generated by a circuit for $f_{\text{decode}}^{(n/2)}$ on the variables $x_{n/2-1}, \ldots, x_0$ with every minterm generated by a circuit for $f_{decode}^{(n/2)}$ on the variables $x_{n-1}, \ldots, x_{n/2}$, as suggested in Fig. 2.12.

The new circuit for $f_{\text{decode}}^{(n)}$ has a size that is at most twice that of a circuit for $f_{\text{decode}}^{(n/2)}$ plus 2^n for the AND gates that combine minterms. It has a depth that is at most 1 more than the depth of a circuit for $f_{\text{decode}}^{(n/2)}$. Thus, when n is even we have the following bounds on the circuit size and depth of $f_{\text{decode}}^{(n)}$:

$$ C_{\Omega_0}\left(f_{\text{decode}}^{(n)}\right) \leq 2C_{\Omega_0}\left(f_{\text{decode}}^{(n/2)}\right) + 2^n $$

$$ D_{\Omega_0}\left(f_{\text{decode}}^{(n)}\right) \leq D_{\Omega_0}\left(f_{decode}^{(n/2)}\right) + 1 $$

Specializing the first bounds given above on the size and depth of a decoder circuit to one on $n/2$ inputs, we have the bound in Lemma 2.5.4. Furthermore, since the output functions are all different, $C_{\Omega_0}\left(f_{\text{decode}}^{(n)}\right)$ is at least 2^n.

LEMMA 2.5.4 *For n even the decoder function $f_{\text{decode}}^{(n)}$ has the following circuit size and depth bounds:*

$$ 2^n \leq C_{\Omega_0}\left(f_{\text{decode}}^{(n)}\right) \leq 2^n + (2n-2)2^{n/2} $$

$$ D_{\Omega_0}\left(f_{\text{decode}}^{(n)}\right) \leq \lceil \log_2 n \rceil + 1 $$

The circuit size bound is linear in the number of outputs. Also, for $n \geq 12$, the exact value of $C_{\Omega_0}\left(f_{\text{decode}}^{(n)}\right)$ is known to within 25%. Since each output depends on n inputs, we will see in Chapter 9 that the upper bound on depth is exactly the depth of the smallest depth circuit for the decoder function.

2.5.5 Multiplexer

The **multiplexer function** $f_{\text{mux}}^{(n)} : \mathcal{B}^{2^n + n} \mapsto \mathcal{B}$ has two vector inputs, $\boldsymbol{z} = (z_{2^n-1}, \ldots, z_1, z_0)$ and $\boldsymbol{x} = (x_{n-1}, \ldots, x_1, x_0)$, where $\boldsymbol{x}$ is treated as an address. The output of $f_{\text{mux}}^{(n)}$ is $v = z_j$, where $j = |\boldsymbol{x}|$ is the integer represented by the binary number $\boldsymbol{x}$. This function is also known as the **storage access function** because it simulates the access to storage made by a random-access memory with one-bit words. (See Section 3.5.)

The similarity between this function and the decoder function should be apparent. The decoder function has n inputs, $\boldsymbol{x} = (x_{n-1}, \ldots, x_1, x_0)$, and 2^n outputs, $\boldsymbol{y} = (y_{2^n-1}, \ldots, y_1, y_0)$, where $y_j = 1$ if $j = |\boldsymbol{x}|$ and $y_j = 0$ otherwise. Thus, we can form $v = z_j$ as

$$ v = \left(z_{2^n-1} \wedge y_{2^n-1}\right) \vee \cdots \vee (z_1 \wedge y_1) \vee (z_0 \wedge y_0) $$

This circuit uses a circuit for the decoder function $f_{\text{decode}}^{(n)}$ plus 2^n AND gates and $2^n - 1$ OR gates. It adds a depth of $n + 1$ to the depth of a decoder circuit. Lemma 2.5.5 follows immediately from these observations.

LEMMA 2.5.5 *The multiplexer function $f_{\text{mux}}^{(n)} : \mathcal{B}^{2^n + n} \mapsto \mathcal{B}$ can be realized with the following circuit size and depth over the basis $\Omega_0 = \{\wedge, \vee, \neg\}$:*

$$C_{\Omega_0}\left(f_{\text{mux}}^{(n)}\right) \leq 3 \cdot 2^n + 2(n-1)2^{n/2} - 1$$

$$D_{\Omega_0}\left(f_{\text{mux}}^{(n)}\right) \leq n + \lceil \log_2 n \rceil + 2$$

Using the lower bound of Theorem 9.3.3, one can show that it is impossible to reduce the upper bound on circuit size to less than $2^{n+1} - 2$. At the cost of increasing the depth by 1, the circuit size bound can be improved to about 2^{n+1}. (See Problem 2.15.) Since $f_{\text{mux}}^{(n)}$ depends on $2^n + n$ variables, we see from Theorem 9.3.1 that it must have depth at least $\log_2(2^n + n) \geq n$. Thus, the above depth bound is very tight.

2.5.6 Demultiplexer

The **demultiplexer function** $f_{\text{demux}}^{(n)} : \mathcal{B}^{n+1} \mapsto \mathcal{B}^{2^n}$ is very similar to a decoder. It has $n + 1$ inputs consisting of n bits, $\boldsymbol{x}$, that serve as an address and a data bit e. It has 2^n outputs $\boldsymbol{y}$ all of which are 0 if $e = 0$ and one output that is 1 if $e = 1$, namely the output specified by the n address bits. Demultiplexers are used to route a data bit (e) to one of 2^n output positions.

A circuit for the demultiplexer function can be constructed as follows. First, form the AND of e with each of the n address bits $x_{n-1}, \ldots, x_1, x_0$ and supply this new n-tuple as input to a decoder circuit. Let $\boldsymbol{z} = (z_{2^n-1}, \ldots, z_1, z_0)$ be the decoder outputs. When $e = 0$, each of the decoder inputs is 0 and each of the decoder outputs except z_0 is 0 and $z_0 = 1$. If we form the AND of z_0 with e, this new output is also 0 when $e = 0$. If $e = 1$, the decoder input is the address $\boldsymbol{x}$ and the output that is 1 is in the position specified by this address. Thus, a circuit for a demultiplexer can be constructed from a circuit for $f_{\text{decode}}^{(n)}$ to which are added n AND gates on its input and one on its output. This circuit has a depth that is at most 2 more than the depth of the decoder circuit. Since a circuit for a decoder can be constructed from one for a demultiplexer by fixing $e = 1$, we have the following bounds on the size and depth of a circuit for $f_{\text{demux}}^{(n)}$.

LEMMA 2.5.6 *The demultiplexer function $f_{\text{demux}}^{(n)} : \mathcal{B}^{n+1} \mapsto \mathcal{B}^{2^n}$ can be realized with the following circuit size and depth over the basis $\Omega_0 = \{\wedge, \vee, \neg\}$:*

$$0 \leq C_{\Omega_0}\left(f_{\text{demux}}^{(n)}\right) - C_{\Omega_0}\left(f_{\text{decoder}}^{(n)}\right) \leq n + 1$$

$$0 \leq D_{\Omega_0}\left(f_{\text{demux}}^{(n)}\right) - D_{\Omega_0}\left(f_{\text{decoder}}^{(n)}\right) \leq 2$$

2.6 Prefix Computations

The prefix computation first appeared in the design of logic circuits, the goal being to parallelize as much as possible circuits for integer addition and multiplication. The carry-lookahead adder is a fast circuit for integer addition that is based on a prefix computation. (See Section 2.7.) Prefix computations are now widely used in parallel computation because they provide a standard, optimizable framework in which to perform computations in parallel.

The **prefix function** $\mathcal{P}_{\odot}^{(n)} : \mathcal{A}^n \mapsto \mathcal{A}^n$ on input $\boldsymbol{x} = (x_1, x_2, \ldots, x_n)$ produces as output $\boldsymbol{y} = (y_1, y_2, \ldots, y_n)$, which is a running sum of its n inputs $\boldsymbol{x}$ using the operator

$\odot$ as the summing operator. That is, $y_j = x_1 \odot x_2 \odot \cdots \odot x_j$ for $1 \le j \le n$. Thus, if the set $\mathcal{A}$ is $\mathbb{N}$, the natural numbers, and $\odot$ is the integer addition operator $+$, then $\mathcal{P}_+^{(n)}$ on the input $\boldsymbol{x} = (x_1, x_2, \ldots, x_n)$ produces the output $\boldsymbol{y}$, where $y_1 = x_1$, $y_2 = x_1 + x_2$, $y_3 = x_1 + x_2 + x_3, \ldots, y_n = x_1 + x_2 + \cdots + x_n$. For example, shown below is the prefix function on a 6-vector of integers under integer addition.

$$\boldsymbol{x} = (2, 1, 3, 7, 5, 1)$$
$$\mathcal{P}_+^{(6)}(\boldsymbol{x}) = (2, 3, 6, 13, 18, 19)$$

A prefix function is defined only for operators $\odot$ that are associative over the set $\mathcal{A}$. An **operator over $\mathcal{A}$ is associative** if a) for all a and b in $\mathcal{A}$, $a \odot b$ is in $\mathcal{A}$, and b) for all a, b, and c in $\mathcal{A}$, $(a \odot b) \odot c = a \odot (b \odot c)$—that is, if all groupings of terms in a sum with the operator $\odot$ have the same value. A pair $(\mathcal{A}, \odot)$ in which $\odot$ is associative is called a **semigroup**. Three semigroups on which a prefix function can be defined are

- $(\mathbb{N}, +)$ where $\mathbb{N}$ are the natural numbers and $+$ is integer addition.

- $(\{0, 1\}^*, \cdot)$ where $\{0, 1\}^*$ is the set of binary strings and $\cdot$ is string concatenation.

- $(\mathcal{A}, \odot_{\text{copy}})$ where $\mathcal{A}$ is a set and $\odot_{\text{copy}}$ is defined by $a \odot_{\text{copy}} b = a$.

It is easy to show that the concatenation operator $\cdot$ on $\{0, 1\}^*$ and $\odot_{\text{copy}}$ on a set $\mathcal{A}$ are associative. (See Problem 2.20.) Another important semigroup is the set of matrices under matrix multiplication (see Theorem 6.2.1).

Summarizing, if $(\mathcal{A}, \odot)$ is a semigroup, the prefix function $\mathcal{P}_\odot^{(n)} : \mathcal{A}^n \mapsto \mathcal{A}^n$ on input $\boldsymbol{x} = (x_1, x_2, \ldots, x_n)$ produces as output $\boldsymbol{y} = (y_1, y_2, \ldots, y_n)$, where $y_j = x_1 \odot x_2 \odot \cdots \odot x_j$ for $1 \le j \le n$.

Load balancing on a parallel machine is an important application of prefix computation. A simple example of load balancing is the following: We assume that p processors, numbered from 0 to $p - 1$, are running processes in parallel. We also assume that processes are born and die, resulting in a possible imbalance in the number of processes active on processors (the work to be done). Finally, we assume that the processes on each processor are ordered. Since it is desirable that all processors be running the same number of processes, processes are periodically redistributed among processors to balance the load. This can be done by a) computing and broadcasting to all processors the number n of processes that are running, b) performing a prefix computation on the number of processes associated with each processor, and c) moving processes between processors. Since the processors are numbered, the prefix computation informs each process of its place in the linear order of processes. Because there are p processors, each processor should have $\lceil n/p \rceil$ processes. This means that the sth process should be located on processor $(s \bmod p)$. The processor owning this process can now send it to the processor on which it should reside to balance the load.

Another important type of prefix computation is the **segmented prefix computation**. In this case two n-vectors are given, a **value vector** $\boldsymbol{x}$ and a **flag vector** $\boldsymbol{\phi}$. The value of the ith entry y_i in the result vector $\boldsymbol{y}$ is x_i if ϕ_i is 1 and otherwise is the associative combination with $\odot$ of x_i and the values between it and the first value x_j to the left of x_i for which the flag $\phi_j = 1$. The first bit of $\boldsymbol{\phi}$ is always 1. An example of a segmented prefix computation is shown below for integer values and integer addition as the associative operation:

$$\boldsymbol{x} = (2, 1, 3, 7, 5, 1)$$

$$\phi = (1, 0, 0, 1, 0, 1)$$
$$y = (2, 3, 6, 7, 12, 1)$$

As shown in Problem 2.21, a segmented prefix computation is a special case of a general prefix computation. This is demonstrated by defining a new associative operation $\otimes$ on value-flag pairs that returns another value-flag pair.

2.6.1 An Efficient Parallel Prefix Circuit

A circuit for the prefix function $\mathcal{P}_\odot^{(n)}$ can be realized with $O(n^2)$ instances of $\odot$ if for each $1 \leq j \leq n$ we naively realize $y_j = x_1 \odot x_2 \odot \cdots \odot x_j$ with a separate circuit containing $j - 1$ instances of $\odot$. If each such circuit is organized as a balanced binary tree, the depth of the circuit for $\mathcal{P}_\odot^{(n)}$ is the depth of the circuit for y_n, which is $\lceil \log_2 n \rceil$. This is a parallel circuit for the prefix problem but uses many more operators than necessary. We now describe a much more efficient circuit for this problem; it uses $O(n)$ instances of $\odot$ and has depth $O(\log n)$.

To describe this improved circuit, we let $x[r, r] = x_r$ and for $r \leq s$ let $x[r, s] = x_r \odot x_{r+1} \odot \cdots \odot x_s$. Then we can write $\mathcal{P}_\odot^{(n)}(x) = y$ where $y_j = x[1, j]$.

Because $\odot$ is associative, we observe that $x[r, s] = x[r, t] \odot x[t + 1, s]$ for $r \leq t < s$. We use this fact to construct the improved circuit. Let $n = 2^k$. Observe that if we form the $(n/2)$-tuple $(x[1, 2], x[3, 4], x[5, 6], \ldots, x[2^k - 1, 2^k])$ using the rule $x[i, i + 1] = x[i, i] \odot x[i + 1, i + 1]$ for i odd and then do a prefix computation on it, we obtain the $(n/2)$-tuple $(x[1, 2], x[1, 4], x[1, 6], \ldots, x[1, 2^k])$. This is almost what is needed. We must only compute $x[1, 1], x[1, 3], x[1, 5], \ldots, x[1, 2^k - 1]$, which is easily done using the rule $x[1, 2i + 1] = x[1, 2i] \odot x_{2i+1}$ for $1 \leq i \leq 2^{k-1} - 1$. (See Fig. 2.13.) The base case for this construction is that of $n = 1$, for which $y_1 = x_1$ and no operations are needed.

If $C(k)$ is the size of this circuit on $n = 2^k$ inputs and $D(k)$ is its depth, then $C(0) = 0$, $D(0) = 0$ and $C(k)$ and $D(k)$ for $k \geq 1$ satisfy the following recurrences:

$$C(k) = C(k - 1) + 2^k - 1$$
$$D(k) = D(k - 1) + 2$$

As a consequence, we have the following result.

THEOREM 2.6.1 *For $n = 2^k$, k an integer, the parallel prefix function $\mathcal{P}_\odot^{(n)} : \mathcal{A}^n \mapsto \mathcal{A}^n$ on an n-vector with associative operator $\odot$ can be implemented by a circuit with the following size and depth bounds over the basis $\Omega = \{\odot\}$:*

$$C_\Omega \left(\mathcal{P}_\odot^{(n)} \right) \leq 2n - \log_2 n - 2$$
$$D_\Omega \left(\mathcal{P}_\odot^{(n)} \right) \leq 2 \log_2 n$$

Proof The solution to the recurrence on $C(k)$ is $C(k) = 2^{k+1} - k - 2$, as the reader can easily show. It satisfies the base case of $k = 0$ and the general case as well. The solution to $D(k)$ is $D(k) = 2k$. ∎

When n is not a power of 2, we can start with a circuit for the next higher power of 2 and then delete operations and edges that are not used to produce the first n outputs.

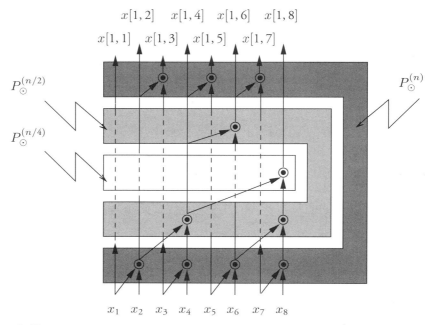

Figure 2.13 A simple recursive construction of a prefix circuit when $n = 2^k = 8$. The gates used at each stage of the construction are grouped into individual shaded regions.

2.7 Addition

Addition is a central operation in all general-purpose digital computers. In this section we describe the standard ripple adder and the fast carry-lookahead addition circuits. The ripple adder mimics the elementary method of addition taught to beginners but for binary instead of decimal numbers. Carry-lookahead addition is a fast addition method based on the fast prefix circuit described in the preceding section.

Consider the binary representation of integers in the set $\{0, 1, 2, \ldots, 2^n - 1\}$. They are represented by binary n-tuples $\boldsymbol{u} = (u_{n-1}, u_{n-2}, \ldots, u_1, u_0)$ and have value

$$|\boldsymbol{u}| = \sum_{j=0}^{n-1} u_j 2^j$$

where $\sum$ denotes integer addition.

The **addition function** $f_{\text{add}}^{(n)} : \mathcal{B}^{2n} \mapsto \mathcal{B}^{n+1}$ computes the sum of two binary n-bit numbers $\boldsymbol{u}$ and $\boldsymbol{v}$, as shown below, where $+$ denotes integer addition:

$$|\boldsymbol{u}| + |\boldsymbol{v}| = \sum_{j=0}^{n-1} (u_j + v_j) 2^j$$

The tuple $((u_{n-1}+v_{n-1}), (u_{n-2}+v_{n-2}), \ldots, (u_0+v_0))$ is not a binary number because the coefficients of the powers of 2 are not Boolean. However, if the integer $u_0 + v_0$ is converted to a binary number (c_1, s_0), where $c_1 2^1 + s_0 2^0 = u_0 + v_0$, then the sum can be replaced by

$$|\boldsymbol{u}| + |\boldsymbol{v}| = \sum_{j=2}^{n-1}(u_j + v_j)2^j + (u_1 + v_1 + c_1)2^1 + s_0 2^0$$

where the least significant bit is now Boolean. In turn, the sum $u_1 + v_1 + c_1$ can be represented in binary by (c_2, s_1), where $c_2 2 + s_1 = u_1 + v_1 + c_1$. The sum $|\boldsymbol{u}| + |\boldsymbol{v}|$ can then be replaced by one in which the two least significant coefficients are Boolean. Repeating this process on all coefficients, we have the **ripple adder** shown in Fig. 2.14.

In the general case, the jth stage of a ripple adder combines the jth coefficients of each binary number, namely u_j and v_j, and the carry from the previous stage, c_j, and represents their integer sum with the binary notation (c_{j+1}, s_j), where

$$c_{j+1}2 + s_j = u_j + v_j + c_j$$

Here c_{j+1}, the number of 2's in the sum $u_j + v_j + c_j$, is the carry into the $(j+1)$st stage and s_j, the number of 1's in the sum modulo 2, is the external output from the jth stage. The circuit performing this mapping is called a **full adder** (see Fig. 2.15). As the reader can easily show by constructing a table, this circuit computes the function $f_{FA} : \mathcal{B}^3 \mapsto \mathcal{B}^2$, where $f_{FA}(u_j, v_j, c_j) = (c_{j+1}, s_j)$ is described by the following formulas:

$$
\begin{aligned}
p_j &= u_j \oplus v_j \\
g_j &= u_j \wedge v_j \\
c_{j+1} &= (p_j \wedge c_j) \vee g_j \\
s_j &= p_j \oplus c_j
\end{aligned}
\tag{2.6}
$$

Here p_j and g_j are intermediate variables with a special significance. If $g_j = 1$, a carry is **generated** at the jth stage. If $p_j = 1$, a carry from the previous stage is **propagated** through the jth stage, that is, a carry-out occurs exactly when a carry-in occurs. Note that p_j and g_j cannot both have value 1.

The full adder can be realized with five gates and depth 3. Since the first full adder has value 0 for its carry input, three gates can be eliminated from its circuit and its depth reduced by 2. It follows that a ripple adder can be realized by a circuit with the following size and depth.

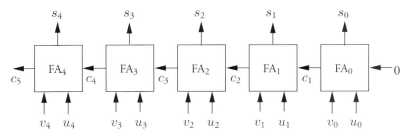

Figure 2.14 A ripple adder for binary numbers.

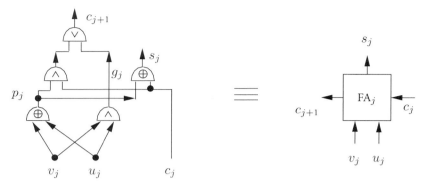

Figure 2.15 A full adder realized with gates.

THEOREM 2.7.1 *The addition function* $f_{add}^{(n)} : \mathcal{B}^{2n} \mapsto \mathcal{B}^{n+1}$ *can be realized with a ripple adder with the following size and depth bounds over the basis* $\Omega = \{\wedge, \vee, \oplus\}$:

$$C_\Omega \left(f_{add}^{(n)} \right) \leq 5n - 3$$

$$D_\Omega \left(f_{add}^{(n)} \right) \leq 3n - 2$$

(Do the ripple adders actually have depth less than $3n - 2$?)

2.7.1 Carry-Lookahead Addition

The ripple adder is economical; it uses a small number of gates. Unfortunately, it is slow. The depth of the circuit, a measure of its speed, is linear in n, the number of bits in each integer. The carry-lookahead adder described below is considerably faster. It uses the parallel prefix circuit described in the preceding section.

The **carry-lookahead adder** circuit is obtained by applying the prefix operation to pairs in $\mathcal{B}^2$ using the associative operator $\diamond : (\mathcal{B}^2)^2 \mapsto \mathcal{B}^2$ defined below. Let (a, b) and (c, d) be arbitrary pairs in $\mathcal{B}^2$. Then $\diamond$ is defined by the following formula:

$$(a, b) \diamond (c, d) = (a \wedge c, (b \wedge c) \vee d)$$

To show that $\diamond$ is associative, it suffices to show by straightforward algebraic manipulation that for all values of a, b, c, d, e, and f the following holds:

$$((a, \ b) \diamond (c, \ d)) \diamond (e, \ f) = (a, \ b) \diamond ((c, \ d) \diamond (e, \ f))$$
$$= (a\,c\,e, \ b\,c\,e \vee d\,e \vee f)$$

Let $\pi[j, j] = (p_j, g_j)$ and, for $j < k$, let $\pi[j, k] = \pi[j, k - 1] \diamond \pi[k, k]$. By induction it is straightforward to show that the first component of $\pi[j, k]$ is 1 if and only if a carry propagates through the full adder stages numbered $j, j + 1, \ldots, k$ and its second component is 1 if and only if a carry is generated at the rth stage, $j \leq r \leq k$, and propagates from that stage through to the kth stage. (See Problem 2.26.)

The prefix computation on the string $(\pi[0, 0], \pi[1, 1], \ldots, \pi[n - 1, n - 1])$ with the operator $\diamond$ produces the string $(\pi[0, 0], \pi[0, 1], \pi[0, 2], \ldots, \pi[0, n - 1])$. The first component of

$\pi[0, j]$ is 1 if and only if a carry generated at the zeroth stage, c_0, is propagated through the jth stage. Since $c_0 = 0$, this component is not used. The second component of $\pi[0, j]$, c_{j+1}, is 1 if and only if a carry is generated at or before the jth stage. From (2.6) we see that the sum bit generated at the jth stage, s_j, satisfies $s_j = p_j \oplus c_j$. Thus the jth output bit, s_j, is obtained from the EXCLUSIVE OR of p_j and the second component of $\pi[0, j - 1]$.

THEOREM 2.7.2 *For $n = 2^k$, k an integer, the addition function $f_{\text{add}}^{(n)} : \mathcal{B}^{2n} \mapsto \mathcal{B}^{n+1}$ can be realized with a carry-lookahead adder with the following size and depth bounds over the basis $\Omega = \{\wedge, \vee, \oplus\}$:*

$$C_\Omega\left(f_{\text{add}}^{(n)}\right) \leq 8n$$

$$D_\Omega\left(f_{\text{add}}^{(n)}\right) \leq 4\log_2 n + 2$$

Proof The prefix circuit uses $2n - \log_2 n - 3$ instances of $\diamond$ and has depth $2\log_2 n$. Since each instance of $\diamond$ can be realized by a circuit of size 3 and depth 2, each of these bounds is multiplied by these factors. Since the first component of $\pi[0, j]$ is not used, the propagate value computed at each output combiner vertex can be eliminated. This saves one gate per result bit, or n gates. However, for each $0 \leq j \leq n - 1$ we need two gates to compute p_j and q_j and one gate to compute s_j, $3n$ additional gates. The computation of these three sets of functions adds depth 2 to that of the prefix circuit. This gives the desired bounds. ∎

The addition function $f_{\text{add}}^{(n)}$ is computed by the carry-lookahead adder circuit with 1.6 times as many gates as the ripple adder but in logarithmic instead of linear depth.

When exact addition is expected and every number is represented by n bits, a carry-out of the last stage of an adder constitutes an **overflow**, an error.

2.8 Subtraction

Subtraction is possible when negative numbers are available. There are several ways to represent negative numbers. To demonstrate that subtraction is not much harder than addition, we consider the **signed two's complement** representation for positive and negative integers in the set $\mathbb{Z}(n) = \{-2^n, \ldots, -2, -1, 0, 1, 2, \ldots, 2^n - 1\}$. Each signed number **u** is represented by an $(n + 1)$-tuple $(\sigma, \boldsymbol{u})$, where σ is its sign and $\boldsymbol{u} = (u_{n-1}, \ldots, u_0)$ is a binary number that is either the magnitude $|\boldsymbol{u}|$ of the number **u**, if positive, or the **two's complement** $2^n - |\boldsymbol{u}|$ of it, if negative. The sign σ is defined below:

$$\sigma = \begin{cases} 0 & \text{the number } \mathbf{u} \text{ is positive or zero} \\ 1 & \text{the number } \mathbf{u} \text{ is negative} \end{cases}$$

The two's complement of an n-bit binary number v is easily formed by adding 1 to $t = 2^n - 1 - |\boldsymbol{v}|$. Since $2^n - 1$ is represented as the n-tuple of 1's, t is obtained by complementing (NOTing) every bit of v. Thus, the two's complement of $\boldsymbol{u}$ is obtained by complementing every bit of $\boldsymbol{u}$ and then adding 1. It follows that the two's complement of the two's complement of a number is the number itself. Thus, the magnitude of a negative number $(1, \boldsymbol{u})$ is the two's complement of $\boldsymbol{u}$.

This is illustrated by the integers in the set $\mathbb{Z}(4) = \{-16, \ldots, -2, -1, 0, 1, 2, \ldots, 15\}$. The two's complement representation of the decimal integers 9 and -11 are

$$9 = (0, 1, 0, 0, 1)$$
$$-11 = (1, 0, 1, 0, 1)$$

Note that the two's complement of 11 is $16 - 11 = 5$, which is represented by the four-tuple $(0, 1, 0, 1)$. The value of the two's complement of 11 can be computed by complementing all bits in its binary representation $(1, 0, 1, 1)$ and adding 1.

We now show that to add two numbers $\mathbf{u}$ and $\mathbf{v}$ in two's complement notation $(\sigma_u, \mathbf{u})$ and $(\sigma_v, \mathbf{v})$, we add them as binary $(n + 1)$-tuples and discard the overflow bit, that is, the coefficient of 2^{n+1}. We now show that this procedure provides a correct answer when no overflow occurs and establish conditions on which overflow does occur.

Let $|\mathbf{u}|$ and $|\mathbf{v}|$ denote the magnitudes of the two numbers. There are four cases for their sum $|\mathbf{u} + \mathbf{v}|$:

Case	$|\mathbf{u}|$	$|\mathbf{v}|$	$|\mathbf{u} + \mathbf{v}|$
I	≥ 0	≥ 0	$|\mathbf{u}| + |\mathbf{v}|$
II	≥ 0	< 0	$2^{n+1} + |\mathbf{u}| - |\mathbf{v}|$
III	< 0	≥ 0	$2^{n+1} - |\mathbf{u}| + |\mathbf{v}|$
IV	< 0	< 0	$2^{n+1} + 2^{n+1} - |\mathbf{u}| - |\mathbf{v}|$

In the first case the sum is positive. If the coefficient of 2^n is 1, an overflow error is detected. In the second case, if $|\mathbf{u}| - |\mathbf{v}|$ is negative, then $2^{n+1} + |\mathbf{u}| - |\mathbf{v}| = 2^n + 2^n - ||\mathbf{u}| - |\mathbf{v}||$ and the result is in two's complement notation with sign 1, as it should be. If $|\mathbf{u}| - |\mathbf{v}|$ is positive, the coefficient of 2^n is 0 (a carry-out of the last stage has occurred) and the result is a positive number with sign bit 0, properly represented. A similar statement applies to the third case. In the fourth case, if $|\mathbf{u}| + |\mathbf{v}|$ is less than 2^n, the sum is $2^{n+1} + 2^n + (2^n - (|\mathbf{u}| + |\mathbf{v}|))$, which is $2^n + (2^n - (|\mathbf{u}| + |\mathbf{v}|))$ when the coefficient of 2^{n+1} is discarded. This is a proper representation for a negative number. However, if $|\mathbf{u}| + |\mathbf{v}| \geq 2^n$, a borrow occurs from the $(n + 1)$st position and the sum $2^{n+1} + 2^n + (2^n - (|\mathbf{u}| + |\mathbf{v}|))$ has a 0 in the $(n + 1)$st position, which is not a proper representation for a negative number (after discarding 2^{n+1}); overflow has occurred.

The following procedure can be used to subtract integer $\mathbf{u}$ from integer $\mathbf{v}$: form the two's complement of $\mathbf{u}$ and add it to the representation for $\mathbf{v}$. The negation of a number is obtained by complementing its sign and taking the two's complement of its binary n-tuple. It follows that subtraction can be done with a circuit of size linear in n and depth logarithmic in n. (See Problem 2.27.)

2.9 Multiplication

In this section we examine several methods of multiplying integers. We begin with the standard elementary integer multiplication method based on the binary representation of numbers. This method requires $O(n^2)$ gates and has depth $O(\log^2 n)$ on n-bit numbers. We then examine a divide-and-conquer method that has the same depth but much smaller circuit size. We also describe fast multiplication methods, that is, methods that have circuits with smaller depths. These include a circuit whose depth is much smaller than $O(\log n)$. It uses a novel representation of numbers, namely, the exponents of numbers in their prime number decomposition.

The integer multiplication function $f_{\text{mult}}^{(n)} : \mathcal{B}^{2n} \mapsto \mathcal{B}^{2n}$ can be realized by the **standard integer multiplication algorithm**, which is based on the following representation for the product of integers represented as binary n-tuples $\boldsymbol{u}$ and $\boldsymbol{v}$:

$$|\boldsymbol{u}||\boldsymbol{v}| = \sum_{i=0}^{n-1} \sum_{j=0}^{n-1} u_i v_j 2^{i+j} \tag{2.7}$$

Here $|\boldsymbol{u}|$ and $|\boldsymbol{v}|$ are the magnitudes of the integers represented by $\boldsymbol{u}$ and $\boldsymbol{v}$. The standard algorithm forms the products $u_i v_j$ individually to create n binary numbers, as suggested below. Here each row corresponds to a different number; the columns correspond to powers of 2 with the rightmost column corresponding to the least significant component, namely the coefficient of 2^0.

2^6	2^5	2^4	2^3	2^2	2^1	2^0		
			$u_0 v_3$	$u_0 v_2$	$u_0 v_1$	$u_0 v_0$	$= z_0$	
		$u_1 v_3$	$u_1 v_2$	$u_1 v_1$	$u_1 v_0$	0	$= z_1$	(2.8)
	$u_2 v_3$	$u_2 v_2$	$u_2 v_1$	$u_2 v_0$	0	0	$= z_2$	
$u_3 v_3$	$u_3 v_2$	$u_3 v_1$	$u_3 v_0$	0	0	0	$= z_3$	

Let the ith binary number produced by this multiplication operation be z_i. Since each of these n binary numbers contains at most $2n - 1$ bits, we treat them as if they were $(2n - 1)$-bit numbers. If these numbers are added in the order shown in Fig. 2.16(a) using a carry-lookahead adder at each step, the time to perform the additions, measured by the depth of a circuit, is $O(n \log n)$. The size of this circuit is $O(n^2)$. A faster circuit containing about the same number of gates can be constructed by adding $z_0, \ldots, z_{n-1}$ in a balanced binary tree with n leaves, as shown in Fig. 2.16(b). This tree has $n - 1$ $(2n - 1)$-bit adders. (A binary tree with n leaves has $n - 1$ internal vertices.) If each of the adders is a carry-lookahead adder, the depth of this circuit is $O(\log^2 n)$ because the tree has $O(\log n)$ adders on every path from the root to a leaf.

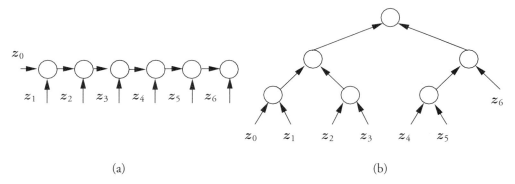

Figure 2.16 Two methods for aggregating the binary numbers $z_0, \ldots, z_{n-1}$.

2.9.1 Carry-Save Multiplication

We now describe a much faster circuit obtained through the use of the carry-save adder. Let u, v, and w be three binary n-bit numbers. Their sum is a binary number t. It follows that $|t|$ can be represented as

$$|t| = |u| + |v| + |w|$$
$$= \sum_{i=0}^{n-1} (u_i + v_i + w_i) 2^i$$

With a full adder the sum $(u_i + v_i + w_i)$ can be converted to the binary representation $c_{i+1} 2 + s_i$. Making this substitution, we have the following expression for the sum:

$$|t| = |u| + |v| + |w|$$
$$= \sum_{i=0}^{n-1} (2c_{i+1} + s_i) 2^i$$
$$= |c| + |s|$$

Here c with $c_0 = 0$ is an $(n + 1)$-tuple and s is an n-tuple. The conversion of (u_i, v_i, w_i) to (c_{i+1}, s_i) can be done with the full adder circuit shown in Fig. 2.15 of size 5 and depth 3 over the basis $\Omega = \{\land, \lor, \oplus\}$.

The function $f_{\text{carry-save}}^{(n)} : \mathcal{B}^{3n} \mapsto \mathcal{B}^{2n+2}$ that maps three binary n-tuples, u, v, and w, to the pair (c, s) described above is the **carry-save adder**. A circuit of full adders that realizes this function is shown in Fig. 2.17.

THEOREM 2.9.1 *The carry-save adder function $f_{\text{carry-save}}^{(n)} : \mathcal{B}^{3n} \mapsto \mathcal{B}^{2n+2}$ can be realized with the following size and depth over the basis $\Omega = \{\land, \lor, \oplus\}$:*

$$C_\Omega \left(f_{\text{carry-save}}^{(n)} \right) \leq 5n$$
$$D_\Omega \left(f_{\text{carry-save}}^{(n)} \right) \leq 3$$

Three binary n-bit numbers u, v, w can be added by combining them in a carry-save adder to produce the pair (c, s), which are then added in an $(n + 1)$-input binary adder. Any adder can be used for this purpose.

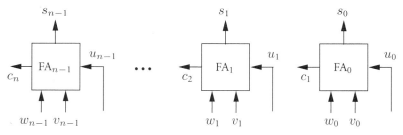

Figure 2.17 A carry-save adder realized by an array of full adders.

A multiplier for two n-bit binary can be formed by first creating the n $(2n-1)$-bit binary numbers shown in Fig. 2.8 and then adding them, as explained above. These n numbers can be added in groups of three, as suggested in Fig. 2.18.

Let's now count the number of levels of carry-save adders in this construction. At the zeroth level there are $m_0 = n$ numbers. At the jth level there are

$$m_j = 2\lfloor m_{j-1}/3 \rfloor + m_{j-1} - 3\lfloor m_{j-1}/3 \rfloor = m_{j-1} - \lfloor m_{j-1}/3 \rfloor$$

binary numbers. This follows because there are $\lfloor m_{j-1}/3 \rfloor$ groups of three binary numbers and each group is mapped to two binary numbers. Not combined into such groups are $m_{j-1} - \lfloor m_{j-1}/3 \rfloor$ binary numbers, giving the total m_j. Since $(x-2)/3 \le \lfloor x/3 \rfloor \le x/3$, we have

$$\left(\frac{2}{3}\right) m_{j-1} \le m_j \le \left(\frac{2}{3}\right) m_{j-1} + \left(\frac{2}{3}\right)$$

from which it is easy to show by induction that the following inequality holds:

$$\left(\frac{2}{3}\right)^j n \le m_j \le \left(\frac{2}{3}\right)^j n + 2\left(1 - \left(\frac{2}{3}\right)^j\right) \le \left(\frac{2}{3}\right)^j n + 2$$

Let s be the number of stages after which $m_s = 2$. Since $m_{s-1} \ge 3$, we have

$$\frac{\log_2(n/2)}{\log_2(3/2)} \le s \le \frac{\log_2 n}{\log_2(3/2)} + 1$$

The number of carry-save adders used in this construction is $n - 2$. This follows from the observation that the number of carry-save adders used in one stage is equal to the decrease in the number of binary numbers from one stage to the next. Since we start with n and finish with 2, the result follows.

After reducing the n binary numbers to two binary numbers through a series of carry-save adder stages, the two remaining binary numbers are added in a traditional binary adder. Since each carry-save adder operates on three $(2n-1)$-bit binary numbers, they use at most $5(2n-1)$ gates and have depth 3. Summarizing, we have the following theorem showing that carry-save addition provides a multiplication circuit of depth $O(\log n)$ but of size quadratic in n.

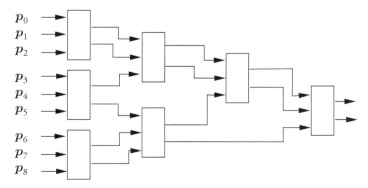

Figure 2.18 Schema for the carry-save combination of nine 18-bit numbers.

THEOREM 2.9.2 *The binary multiplication function* $f_{\text{mult}}^{(n)} : \mathcal{B}^{2n} \mapsto \mathcal{B}^{2n}$ *for* n-*bit binary numbers can be realized by carry-save addition by a circuit of the following size and depth over the basis* $\Omega = \{\wedge, \vee, \oplus\}$:

$$C_\Omega\left(f_{\text{mult}}^{(n)}\right) \leq 5(2n-1)(n-2) + C_\Omega\left(f_{\text{add}}^{(2n)}\right)$$

$$D_\Omega\left(f_{\text{mult}}^{(n)}\right) \leq 3s + D_\Omega\left(f_{\text{add}}^{(2n)}\right)$$

where s, *the number of carry-save adder stages, satisfies*

$$s \leq \frac{\log_2 n}{\log_2(3/2)} + 1$$

It follows from this theorem and the results of Theorem 2.7.2 that two n-bit binary numbers can be multiplied by a circuit of size $O(n^2)$ and depth $O(\log n)$.

2.9.2 Divide-and-Conquer Multiplication

We now examine a multiplier of much smaller circuit size but depth $O(\log^2 n)$. It uses a **divide-and-conquer** technique. We represent two positive integers by their n-bit binary numbers u and v. We assume that n is even and decompose each number into two $(n/2)$-bit numbers:

$$u = (u_h, u_l), \quad v = (v_h, v_l)$$

where u_h, u_l, v_h, v_l are the high and low components of the vectors u and v, respectively. Then we can write

$$|u| = |u_h|2^{n/2} + |u_l|$$
$$|v| = |v_h|2^{n/2} + |v_l|$$

from which we have

$$|u||v| = |u_l||v_l| + (|u_h||v_h| + (|v_h| - |v_l|)(|u_l| - |u_h|) + |u_l||v_l|)2^{n/2} + |u_h||v_h|2^n$$

It follows from this expression that only three integer multiplications are needed, namely $|u_l||u_l|$, $|u_h||u_h|$, and $(|v_h| - |v_l|)(|u_l| - |u_h|)$; multiplication by a power of 2 is done by realigning bits for addition. Each multiplication is of $(n/2)$-bit numbers. Six additions and subtractions of $2n$-bit numbers suffice to complete the computation. Each of the additions and subtractions can be done with a linear number of gates in logarithmic time.

If $C(n)$ and $D(n)$ are the size and depth of a circuit for integer multiplication realized with this divide-and-conquer method, then we have

$$C(n) \leq 3C(n/2) + cn \tag{2.9}$$
$$D(n) \leq D(n/2) + d\log_2 n \tag{2.10}$$

where c and d are constants of the construction. Since $C(1) = 1$ and $D(1) = 1$ (one use of AND suffices), we have the following theorem, the proof of which is left as an exercise (see Problem 2.28).

THEOREM 2.9.3 *If $n = 2^k$, the binary multiplication function $f_{\text{mult}}^{(n)} : \mathcal{B}^{2n} \mapsto \mathcal{B}^{2n}$ for n-bit binary numbers can be realized by a circuit for the divide-and-conquer algorithm of the following size and depth over the basis $\Omega = \{\wedge, \vee, \oplus\}$:*

$$C_\Omega\left(f_{\text{mult}}^{(n)}\right) = O\left(n^{\log_2 3}\right)$$

$$D_\Omega\left(f_{\text{mult}}^{(n)}\right) = O(\log_2^2 n)$$

The size of this divide-and-conquer multiplication circuit is $O(n^{1.585})$, which is much smaller than the $O(n^2)$ bound based on carry-save addition. The depth bound can be reduced to $O(\log n)$ through the use of carry-save addition. (See Problem 2.29.) However, even faster multiplication algorithms are known for large n.

2.9.3 Fast Multiplication

Schönhage and Strassen [299] have described a circuit to multiply integers represented in binary that is asymptotically small and shallow. Their algorithm for the multiplication of n-bit binary numbers uses $O(n \log n \log \log n)$ gates and depth $O(\log n)$. It illustrates the point that a circuit can be devised for this problem that has depth $O(\log n)$ and uses a number of gates considerably less than quadratic in n. Although the coefficients on the size and depth bounds are so large that their circuit is not practical, their result is interesting and motivates the following definition.

DEFINITION 2.9.1 *$M_{\text{int}}(n, c)$ is the size of the smallest circuit for the multiplication of two n-bit binary numbers that has depth at most $c \log_2 n$ for $c > 0$.*

The Schönhage-Strassen circuit demonstrates that $M_{\text{int}}(n, c) = O(n \log n \log \log n)$ for all $n \geq 1$. It is also clear that $M_{\text{int}}(n, c) = \Omega(n)$ because any multiplication circuit must examine each component of each binary number and no more than a constant number of inputs can be combined by one gate. (Chapter 9 provides methods for deriving lower bounds on the size and depth of circuits.)

Because we use integer multiplication in other circuits, it is convenient to make the following reasonable assumption about the dependence of $M_{\text{int}}(n)$ on n. We assume that

$$M_{\text{int}}(dn, c) \leq d M_{\text{int}}(n, c)$$

for all d satisfying $0 \leq d \leq 1$. This condition is satisfied by the Schönhage-Strassen circuit.

2.9.4 Very Fast Multiplication

If integers in the set $\{0, 1, \ldots, N - 1\}$ are represented by the exponents of primes in their prime factorization, they can be multiplied by adding exponents. The largest exponent on a prime in this range is at most $\log_2 N$. Thus, exponents can be represented by $O(\log \log N)$ bits and integers multiplied by circuits with depth $O(\log \log \log N)$. (See Problem 2.32.) This depth is much smaller than $O(\log \log N)$, the depth of circuits to add integers in any fixed radix system. (Note that if $N = 2^n$, $\log_2 \log_2 N = \log_2 n$.) However, addition is very difficult in this number system. Thus, it is a fast number system only if the operations are limited to multiplications.

2.9.5   Reductions to Multiplication

The logical shifting function $f_{\text{shift}}^{(n)}$ can be reduced to integer multiplication function $f_{\text{mult}}^{(n)}$, as can be seen by letting one of the two n-tuple arguments be a power of 2. That is,

$$f_{\text{shift}}^{(n)}(\boldsymbol{x}, \boldsymbol{s}) = f_{\text{mult}}^{(n)}(\boldsymbol{x}, \boldsymbol{y})$$

where $\boldsymbol{y} = f_{\text{decode}}^{(m)}(\boldsymbol{s})$ is the value of the decoder function (see Section 2.5) that maps a binary m-tuple, $m = \lceil \log_2 n \rceil$, into a binary 2^m-tuple containing a single 1 at the output indexed by the integer represented by $\boldsymbol{s}$.

LEMMA 2.9.1 *The logical shifting function $f_{\text{shift}}^{(n)}$ can be reduced to the binary integer multiplication function $f_{\text{mult}}^{(n)}$ through the application of the decoder function $f_{\text{decode}}^{(m)}$ on $m = \lceil \log_2 n \rceil$ inputs.*

As shown in Section 2.5, the decoder function $f_{\text{decode}}^{(m)}$ can be realized with a circuit of size very close to 2^m and depth $\lceil \log_2 m \rceil$. Thus, the shifting function has circuit size and depth no more than constant factors larger than those for integer multiplication.

The **squaring function** $f_{\text{square}}^{(n)} : \mathcal{B}^n \mapsto \mathcal{B}^{2n}$ maps the binary n-tuple $\boldsymbol{x}$ into the binary $2n$-tuple $\boldsymbol{y}$ representing the product of $\boldsymbol{x}$ with itself. Since the squaring and integer multiplication functions contain each other as subfunctions, as shown below, circuits for one can be used for the other.

LEMMA 2.9.2 *The integer multiplication function $f_{\text{mult}}^{(n)}$ contains the squaring function $f_{\text{square}}^{(n)}$ as a subfunction and $f_{\text{square}}^{(3n+1)}$ contains $f_{\text{mult}}^{(n)}$ as a subfunction.*

Proof The first statement follows by setting the two n-tuple inputs of $f_{\text{mult}}^{(n)}$ to be the input to $f_{\text{square}}^{(n)}$. The second statement follows by examining the value of $f_{\text{square}}^{(3n+1)}$ on the $(3n+1)$-tuple input $(\boldsymbol{xzy})$, where $\boldsymbol{x}$ and $\boldsymbol{y}$ are binary n-tuples and $\boldsymbol{z}$ is the zero binary $(n+1)$-tuple. Thus, $(\boldsymbol{xzy})$ denotes the value $a = 2^{2n+1}|\boldsymbol{x}| + |\boldsymbol{y}|$ whose square b is

$$b = 2^{4n+2}|\boldsymbol{x}|^2 + 2^{2n+2}|\boldsymbol{x}||\boldsymbol{y}| + |\boldsymbol{y}|^2$$

The value of the product $|\boldsymbol{x}||\boldsymbol{y}|$ can be read from the output because there is no carry into $2^{2n+2}|\boldsymbol{x}||\boldsymbol{y}|$ from $|\boldsymbol{y}|^2$, nor is there a carry into $2^{4n+2}|\boldsymbol{x}|^2$ from $2^{2n+2}|\boldsymbol{x}||\boldsymbol{y}|$, since $|\boldsymbol{x}|, |\boldsymbol{y}| \leq 2^n - 1$. ∎

2.10 Reciprocal and Division

In this section we examine methods to divide integers represented in binary. Since the division of one integer by another generally cannot be represented with a finite number of bits (consider, for example, the value of $2/3$), we must be prepared to truncate the result of a division. The division method presented in this section is based on Newton's method for finding a zero of a function.

Let $\boldsymbol{u} = (u_{n-1}, \ldots, u_1, u_0)$ and $\boldsymbol{v} = (v_{n-1}, \ldots, v_1, v_0)$ denote integers whose magnitudes are u and v. Then the division of one integer u by another v, u/v, can be obtained as the result of taking the product of u with the reciprocal $1/v$. (See Problem 2.33.) For this reason, we examine only the computation of reciprocals of n-bit binary numbers. For simplicity we assume that n is a power of 2.

The reciprocal of the n-bit binary number $\boldsymbol{u} = (u_{n-1}, \ldots, u_1, u_0)$ representing the integer u is a fractional number r represented by the (possibly infinite) binary number $\boldsymbol{r} = (r_{-1}, r_{-2}, r_{-3}, \ldots)$, where

$$|\boldsymbol{r}| = r_{-1}2^{-1} + r_{-2}2^{-2} + r_{-3}2^{-3} + \cdots$$

Some numbers, such as 3, have a binary reciprocal that has an infinite number of digits, such as $(0, 1, 0, 1, 0, 1, \ldots)$, and cannot be expressed exactly as a binary tuple of finite extent. Others, such as 4, have reciprocals that have finite extent, such as $(0, 1)$.

Our goal is to produce an $(n + 2)$-bit approximation to the reciprocal of n-bit binary numbers. (It simplifies the analysis to obtain an $(n+2)$-bit approximation instead of an n-bit approximation.) We assume that each such binary number $\boldsymbol{u}$ has a 1 in its most significant position; that is, $2^{n-1} \leq u < 2^n$. If this is not true, a simple circuit can be devised to determine the number of places by which to shift $\boldsymbol{u}$ left to meet this condition. (See Problem 2.25.) The result is shifted right by an equal amount to produce the reciprocal.

It follows that an $(n + 2)$-bit approximation to the reciprocal of an n-bit binary number $\boldsymbol{u}$ with $u_{n-1} = 1$ is represented by $\boldsymbol{r} = (r_{-1}, r_{-2}, r_{-3}, \ldots)$, where the first $n - 2$ digits of $\boldsymbol{r}$ are zero. Thus, the value of the approximate reciprocal is represented by the $n + 2$ components $(r_{-(n-1)}, r_{-(n)}, \ldots, r_{-(2n)})$. It follows that these components are produced by shifting $\boldsymbol{r}$ left by $2n$ places and removing the fractional bits. This defines the function $f_{\text{recip}}^{(n)}$:

$$f_{\text{recip}}^{(n)}(\boldsymbol{u}) = \left\lfloor \frac{2^{2n}}{u} \right\rfloor$$

The approximation described below can be used to compute reciprocals.

Newton's approximation algorithm is a method to find the zero x_0 of a continuous function $h : \mathbb{R} \mapsto \mathbb{R}$ on the reals (that is, $h(x_0) = 0$) when h has a non-zero derivative $h'(x)$ in the neighborhood of x_0. As suggested in Fig. 2.19, the tangent to the curve at the point y_i, $h'(y_i)$, is equal to $h(y_i)/(y_i - y_{i+1})$. For the concave increasing function shown in this figure, the value of y_{i+1} is closer to the zero x_0 than is y_i. The same holds for all continuous functions whether increasing, decreasing, convex, or concave in the neighborhood of a zero. It

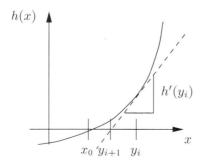

Figure 2.19 Newton's method for finding the zero of a function.

follows that the recurrence

$$y_{i+1} = y_i - \frac{h(y_i)}{h'(y_i)} \tag{2.11}$$

provides values increasingly close to the zero of h as long as it is started with a value sufficiently close to the zero.

The function $h(y) = 1 - 2^{2n}/uy$ has zero $y = 2^{2n}/u$. Since $h'(y) = 2^{2n}/uy^2$, the recurrence (2.11) becomes

$$y_{i+1} = 2y_i - uy_i^2/2^{2n}$$

When this recurrence is modified as follows, it converges to the $(n + 2)$-bit binary reciprocal of the n-bit binary number $\boldsymbol{u}$:

$$y_{i+1} = \left\lfloor \frac{2^{2n+1}y_i - uy_i^2}{2^{2n}} \right\rfloor$$

The size and depth of a circuit resulting from this recurrence are $O(M_{\text{int}}(n) \log n)$ and $O(\log^2 n)$, respectively. However, this recurrence uses more gates than are necessary since it does calculations with full precision at each step even though the early steps use values of y_i that are imprecise. We can reduce the size of the resulting circuit to $O(M_{\text{int}}(n))$ if, instead of computing the reciprocal with $n + 2$ bits of accuracy at every step we let the amount of accuracy vary with the number of stages, as in the algorithm $\texttt{recip}(u, n)$ of Fig. 2.20. The algorithm $\texttt{recip}$ is called $1 + \log_2 n$ times, the last time when $n = 1$.

We now show that the algorithm $\texttt{recip}(u, n)$ computes the function $f_{\text{recip}}^{(n)}(\boldsymbol{u}) = r = \lfloor 2^{2n}/u \rfloor$. In other words, we show that r satisfies $ru = 2^{2n} - s$ for some $0 \le s < u$. The proof is by induction on n.

The inductive hypothesis is that the algorithm $\texttt{recip}(u, m)$ produces an $(m + 2)$-bit approximation to the reciprocal of the m-bit binary number u (whose most significant bit is 1), that is, it computes $r = \lfloor 2^{2m}/u \rfloor$. The assumption applies to the base case of $m = 1$ since $u = 1$ and $r = 4$. We assume it holds for $m = n/2$ and show that it also holds for $m = n$.

Algorithm $\texttt{recip}(u, n)$
    if $n = 1$ **then**
       r := 4;
    else begin
       t := $\texttt{recip}(\lfloor u/2^{n/2} \rfloor, n/2)$;
       r := $\left\lfloor (2^{3n/2+1}t - ut^2)/2^n \right\rfloor$;
       for $j := 3$ **downto** 0 **do**
          if $(u(r + 2^j) \le 2^{2n})$ **then** $r := r + 2^j$;
    end;
    return(r);

Figure 2.20 An algorithm to compute $\mathbf{r}$, the $(n + 2)$-bit approximation to the reciprocal of the n-bit binary number $\mathbf{u}$ representing the integer u, that is, $\mathbf{r} = f_{\text{recip}}^{(n)}(\mathbf{u})$.

Let u_1 and u_0 be the integers corresponding to the most and least significant $n/2$ bits respectively of u, that is, $u = u_1 2^{n/2} + u_0$. Since $2^{n-1} \leq u < 2^n$, $2^{n/2-1} \leq u_1 < 2^{n/2}$. Also, $\lfloor \frac{u}{2^{n/2}} \rfloor = u_1$. By the inductive hypothesis $t = \lfloor 2^n/u_1 \rfloor$ is the value returned by $\mathtt{recip}(u_1, n/2)$; that is, $u_1 t = 2^n - s'$ for some $0 \leq s' < u_1$. Let $w = 2^{3n/2 + 1} t - u t^2$. Then

$$uw = 2^{2n+1} u_1 t + 2^{3n/2 + 1} u_0 t - [t(u_1 2^{n/2} + u_0)]^2$$

Applying $u_1 t = 2^n - s'$, dividing both sides by 2^n, and simplifying yields

$$\frac{uw}{2^n} = 2^{2n} - \left(s' - \frac{t u_0}{2^{n/2}} \right)^2 \tag{2.12}$$

We now show that

$$\frac{uw}{2^n} \geq 2^{2n} - 8u \tag{2.13}$$

by demonstrating that $(s' - t u_0/2^{n/2})^2 \leq 8u$. We note that $s' < u_1 < 2^{n/2}$, which implies $(s')^2 < 2^{n/2} u_1 \leq u$. Also, since $u_1 t = 2^n - s'$ or $t \leq 2^n/u_1$ we have

$$\left(\frac{t u_0}{2^{n/2}} \right)^2 < \left(\frac{2^{n/2} u_0}{u_1} \right)^2 < \left(2^{n/2+1} \right)^2 \leq 8u$$

since $u_1 \geq 2^{n/2-1}$, $u_0 < 2^{n/2}$, and $2^{n-1} \leq u$. The desired result follows from the observation that $(a - b)^2 \leq \max(a^2, b^2)$.

Since $r = \lfloor w/2^n \rfloor$, it follows from (2.13) that

$$ur = u \left\lfloor \frac{w}{2^n} \right\rfloor > u \left(\frac{w}{2^n} - 1 \right) > \frac{uw}{2^n} - u > 2^{2n} - 9u$$

It follows that $r > (2^{2n}/u) - 9$. Also from (2.12), we see that $r \leq 2^{2n}/u$. The three-step adjustment process at the end of $\mathtt{recip}(u, m)$ increases ur by the largest integer multiple of u less than $16u$ that keeps it less than or equal to 2^{2n}. That is, r satisfies $ur = 2^{2n} - s$ for some $0 \leq s < u$, which means that r is the reciprocal of u.

The algorithm for $\mathtt{recip}(u, n)$ translates into a circuit as follows: a) $\mathtt{recip}(u, 1)$ is realized by an assignment, and b) $\mathtt{recip}(u, n)$, $n > 1$, is realized by invoking a circuit for $\mathtt{recip}(\lfloor \frac{u}{2^{n/2}} \rfloor, n/2)$ followed by a circuit for $\lfloor (2^{3n/2 + 1} t - u t^2)/2^n \rfloor$ and one to implement the three-step adjustment. The first of these steps computes $\lfloor \frac{u}{2^{n/2}} \rfloor$, which does not require any gates, merely shifting and discarding bits. The second step requires shifting t left by $3n/2$ places, computing t^2 and multiplying it by u, subtracting the result from the shifted version of t, and shifting the final result right by n places and discarding low-order bits. Circuits for this have size $c M_{\mathrm{int}}(n)$ for some constant $c > 0$ and depth $O(\log n)$. The third step can be done by computing ur, adding $u 2^j$ for $j = 3, 2, 1,$ or 0, and comparing the result with 2^{2n}. The comparisons control whether 2^j is added to r or not. The one multiplication and the additions can be done with circuits of size $c' M_{\mathrm{int}}(n)$ for some constant $c' > 0$ and depth $O(\log n)$. The comparison operations can be done with a constant additional number of gates and constant depth. (See Problem 2.19.)

It follows that $\mathtt{recip}$ can be realized by a circuit whose size $C_{\mathrm{recip}}(n)$ is no more than a multiple of the size of an integer multiplication circuit, $M_{\mathrm{int}}(n, c)$, plus the size of a circuit for the invocation of $\texttt{recip}(\lfloor \frac{u}{2^{n/2}} \rfloor, \texttt{n/2})$. That is,

$$C_{\text{recip}}(n) \leq C_{\text{recip}}(n/2) + cM_{\text{int}}(n)$$
$$C_{\text{recip}}(1) = 1$$

for some constant $c > 0$. This inequality implies the following bound:

$$C_{\text{recip}}(n) \leq c \sum_{j=0}^{\log n} M_{\text{int}}\left(\frac{n}{2^j}, c\right) \leq cM_{\text{int}}(n, c) \sum_{j=0}^{\log n} \frac{1}{2^j}$$
$$= O(M_{\text{int}}(n, c))$$

which follows since $M_{\text{int}}(dn, c) \leq dM_{\text{int}}(n, c)$ when $d \leq 1$.

The depth $D_{\text{recip}}(n)$ of the circuit produced by this algorithm is at most $c \log n$ plus the depth $D_{\text{recip}}(n/2)$. Since the circuit has at most $1 + \log_2 n$ stages with a depth of at most $c \log n$ each, $D_{\text{recip}}(n) \leq 2c \log^2 n$ when $n \geq 2$.

THEOREM 2.10.1 *If $n = 2^k$, the reciprocal function $f_{\text{recip}}^{(n)} : \mathcal{B}^n \mapsto \mathcal{B}^{n+2}$ for n-bit binary numbers can be realized by a circuit with the following size and depth:*

$$C_\Omega\left(f_{\text{recip}}^{(n)}\right) \leq O(M_{\text{int}}(n, c))$$
$$D_\Omega\left(f_{\text{recip}}^{(n)}\right) \leq c \log_2^2 n$$

VERY FAST RECIPROCAL   Beame, Cook, and Hoover [33] have given an $O(\log n)$ circuit for the reciprocal function. It uses a sequence of about $n^2 / \log n$ primes to represent an n-bit binary number $\boldsymbol{x}$, $.5 \leq \boldsymbol{x} < 1$, using arithmetic modulo these primes. The size of the circuit produced is polynomial in n, although much larger than $M_{\text{int}}(n, c)$. Reif and Tate [321] show that the reciprocal function can be computed with a circuit that is defined only in terms of n and has a size proportional to M_{int} (and thus nearly optimal) and depth $O(\log n \log \log n)$. Although the depth bound is not quite as good as that of Beame, Cook, and Hoover, its size bound is very good.

2.10.1   Reductions to the Reciprocal

In this section we show that the reciprocal function contains the squaring function as a sub-function. It follows from Problem 2.33 and the preceding result that integer multiplication and division have comparable circuit size. We use Taylor's theorem [311, p. 345] to establish the desired result.

THEOREM 2.10.2 (Taylor) *Let $f(x) : \mathbb{R} \mapsto \mathbb{R}$ be a continuous real-valued function defined on the interval $[a, b]$ whose kth derivative is also continuous for $k \leq K$ over the same interval. Then for $a \leq x_0 \leq x \leq b$, $f(x)$ can be expanded as*

$$f(x) = f(x_0) + (x - x_0)f^{[1]}(x_0) + \frac{(x - x_0)^2}{2}f^{[2]}(x_0) + \cdots + \frac{(x - x_0)^n}{n!}f^{[n]}(x_0) + r_n$$

where $f^{[n]}$ denotes the nth derivative of f and the remainder r_n satisfies

$$r_n = \int_{x_0}^{x} f^{[n+1]}(t)\frac{(x - t)^n}{n!}\, dt$$

$$= \frac{(x - x_0)^{n+1}}{(n+1)!} f^{[n+1]}(\psi)$$

for some ψ satisfying $x_0 \leq \psi \leq x$.

Taylor's theorem is used to expand $\lfloor 2^{2n-1}/|\mathbf{u}| \rfloor$ by applying it to the function $f(x) = (1 + w)^{-1}$ on the interval $[0, 1]$. The Taylor expansion of this function is

$$(1 + w)^{-1} = 1 - w + w^2 - w^3(1 + \psi)^{-4}$$

for some $0 \leq \psi \leq 1$. The magnitude of the last term is at most w^3.

Let $n \geq 12$, $k = \lfloor n/2 \rfloor$, $l = \lfloor n/12 \rfloor$ and restrict $|\mathbf{u}|$ as follows:

$$|\mathbf{u}| = 2^k + |\mathbf{a}| \text{ where}$$
$$|\mathbf{a}| = 2^l |\mathbf{b}| + 1 \text{ and}$$
$$|\mathbf{b}| \leq 2^{l-1} - 1$$

It follows that $|\mathbf{a}| \leq 2^{2l-1} - 2^l + 1 < 2^{2l-1}$ for $l \geq 1$. Applying the Taylor series expansion to $(1 + |\mathbf{a}|/2^k)^{-1}$, we have

$$\left\lfloor \frac{2^{2n-1}}{(2^k + |\mathbf{a}|)} \right\rfloor = \left\lfloor 2^{2n-1-k} \left(1 - \frac{|\mathbf{a}|}{2^k} + \left(\frac{|\mathbf{a}|}{2^k} \right)^2 - \left(\frac{|\mathbf{a}|}{2^k} \right)^3 (1 + \psi)^{-4} \right) \right\rfloor \quad (2.14)$$

for some $0 \leq \psi \leq 1$. For the given range of values for $|\mathbf{u}|$ both the sum of the first two terms and the third term on the right-hand side have the following bounds:

$$2^{2n-1-k}(1 - |\mathbf{a}|/2^k) > 2^{2n-1-k} \left(1 - 2^{2l-1}/2^k \right)$$
$$2^{2n-1-k}(|\mathbf{a}|/2^k)^2 < 2^{2n-1-k} \left(2^{2l-1}/2^k \right)^2$$

Since $2^{2l-1}/2^k < 1/2$, the value of the third term, $2^{2n-1-k}(|\mathbf{a}|/2^k)^2$, is an integer that does not overlap in any bit positions with the sum of the first two terms.

The fourth term is negative; its magnitude has the following upper bound:

$$2^{2n-1-4k}|\mathbf{a}|^3(1 + \psi)^{-4} < 2^{3(2l-1)+2n-1-4k}$$

Expanding the third term, we have

$$2^{2n-1-3k}(|\mathbf{a}|)^2 = 2^{2n-1-3k}(2^{2l}|\mathbf{b}|^2 + 2^{l+1}|\mathbf{b}| + 1)$$

Because $3(2l - 1) \leq k$, the third term on the right-hand side of this expansion has value $2^{2n-1-3k}$ and is larger than the magnitude of the fourth term in (2.14). Consequently the fourth term does not affect the value of the result in (2.14) in positions occupied by the binary representation of $2^{2n-1-3k}(2^{2l}|\mathbf{b}|^2 + 2^{l+1}|\mathbf{b}|)$. In turn, $2^{l+1}|\mathbf{b}|$ is less than 2^{2l}, which means that the binary representation of $2^{2n-1-3k}(2^{2l}|\mathbf{b}|^2)$ appears in the output shifted but otherwise without modification. This provides the following result.

LEMMA 2.10.1 *The reciprocal function $f_{\text{recip}}^{(n)}$ contains as a subfunction the squaring function $f_{\text{square}}^{(m)}$ for $m = \lfloor n/12 \rfloor - 1$.*

Proof The value of the l-bit binary number denoted by $\mathbf{b}$ appears in the output if $l = \lfloor n/12 \rfloor \geq 1$. ∎

Lower bounds similar to those derived for the reciprocal function can be derived for special fractional powers of binary numbers. (See Problem 2.35.)

2.11 Symmetric Functions

The symmetric functions are encountered in many applications. Among the important symmetric functions is binary sorting, the binary version of the standard sorting function. A surprising fact holds for binary sorting, namely, that it can be realized on n inputs by a circuit whose size is linear in n (see Problem 2.17), whereas non-binary sorting requires on the order of $n \log n$ operations. Binary sorting, and all other symmetric functions, can be realized efficiently through the use of a counting circuit that counts the number of 1's among the n inputs with a circuit of size linear in n. The counting circuit uses AND, OR, and NOT. When negations are disallowed, binary sorting requires on the order of $n \log n$ gates, as shown in Section 9.6.1.

DEFINITION 2.11.1 *A **permutation** $\pi : \mathcal{B}^n \mapsto \mathcal{B}^n$ of an n-tuple $\boldsymbol{x} = (x_1, x_2, \ldots, x_n)$ is a reordering $\pi(\boldsymbol{x}) = (x_{\pi(1)}, x_{\pi(2)}, \ldots, x_{\pi(n)})$ of the components of $\boldsymbol{x}$. That is, $\{\pi(1), \pi(2), \ldots, \pi(n)\} = \{1, 2, 3, \ldots, n\}$. A **symmetric function** $f^{(n)} : \mathcal{B}^n \mapsto \mathcal{B}^m$ is a function for which $f^{(n)}(\boldsymbol{x}) = f^{(n)}(\pi(\boldsymbol{x}))$ for all permutations π. $S_{n,m}$ is the set of all symmetric functions $f^{(n)} : \mathcal{B}^n \mapsto \mathcal{B}^m$ and $S_n = S_{n,1}$ is the set of Boolean symmetric functions on n inputs.*

If $f^{(3)}$ is symmetric, then $f^{(3)}(0, 1, 1) = f^{(3)}(1, 0, 1) = f^{(3)}(1, 1, 0)$.

The following are symmetric functions:

1. **Threshold functions** $\tau_t^{(n)} : \mathcal{B}^n \mapsto \mathcal{B}, 1 \leq t \leq n$:

$$\tau_t^{(n)}(\boldsymbol{x}) = \begin{cases} 1 & \sum_{j=1}^n x_j \geq t \\ 0 & \text{otherwise} \end{cases}$$

2. **Elementary symmetric functions** $e_t^{(n)} : \mathcal{B}^n \mapsto \mathcal{B}, 0 \leq t \leq n$:

$$e_t^{(n)}(\boldsymbol{x}) = \begin{cases} 1 & \sum_{j=1}^n x_j = t \\ 0 & \text{otherwise} \end{cases}$$

3. **Binary sorting function** $f_{\text{sort}}^{(n)} : \mathcal{B}^n \mapsto \mathcal{B}^n$ sorts an n-tuple into descending order:

$$f_{\text{sort}}^{(n)}(\boldsymbol{x}) = (\tau_1^{(n)}, \tau_2^{(n)}, \ldots, \tau_n^{(n)})$$

   Here $\tau_t^{(n)}$ is the tth threshold function.

4. **Modulus functions** $f_{c, \bmod m}^{(n)} : \mathcal{B}^n \mapsto \mathcal{B}, 0 \leq c \leq m - 1$:

$$f_{c, \bmod m}^{(n)}(\boldsymbol{x}) = \begin{cases} 1 & \sum_{j=1}^n x_j = c \bmod m \\ 0 & \text{otherwise} \end{cases}$$

The elementary symmetric functions e_t are building blocks in terms of which other symmetric functions can be realized at small additional cost. Each symmetric function $f^{(n)}$ is determined uniquely by its value $v_t, 0 \leq t \leq n$, when exactly t of the input variables are 1. It follows that we can write $f^{(n)}(\boldsymbol{x})$ as

$$f^{(n)}(\boldsymbol{x}) = \bigvee_{0 \leq t \leq n} v_t \wedge e_t^{(n)}(\boldsymbol{x}) = \bigvee_{t \mid v_t = 1} e_t^{(n)}(\boldsymbol{x}) \qquad (2.15)$$

Thus, efficient circuits for the elementary symmetric functions yield efficient circuits for general symmetric functions.

An efficient circuit for the elementary symmetric functions can be obtained from a circuit for counting the number of 1's among the variables $\boldsymbol{x}$. This **counting function** $f_{\text{count}}^{(n)} : \mathcal{B}^n \mapsto \mathcal{B}^{\lceil \log_2 n \rceil}$ produces a $\lceil \log_2 n \rceil$-bit binary number representing the number of 1's among the n inputs $x_1, x_2, \ldots, x_n$.

A recursive construction for the counting function is shown in Fig. 2.21 (b) when $m = 2^{l+1} - 1$. The m inputs are organized into three groups, the first $2^l - 1$ Boolean variables $\boldsymbol{u}$, the second $2^l - 1$ variables $\boldsymbol{v}$, and the last variable x_m. The sum is represented by l "sum bits" $s_j^{(l+1)}$, $0 \le j \le l - 1$, and the "carry bit" $c_l^{(l+1)}$. This sum is formed by adding in a ripple adder the outputs $s_j^{(l)}$, $0 \le j \le l - 2$, and $c_{l-1}^{(l+1)}$ from the two counting circuits, each on $2^l - 1$ inputs, and the mth input x_m. (We abuse notation and use the same variables for the outputs of the different counting circuits.) The counting circuit on $2^2 - 1 = 3$ inputs is the full adder of Fig. 2.21(a). From this construction we have the following theorem:

LEMMA 2.11.1 *For $n = 2^k - 1$, $k \ge 2$, the counting function $f_{\text{count}}^{(n)} : \mathcal{B}^n \mapsto \mathcal{B}^{\lceil \log_2 n \rceil}$ can be realized with the following circuit size and depth over the basis $\Omega = \{\land, \lor, \oplus\}$:*

$$C_\Omega\left(f_{\text{count}}^{(n)}\right) \le 5(2^k - k - 1)$$

$$D_\Omega\left(f_{\text{count}}^{(n)}\right) \le 4k - 5$$

Proof Let $C(k) = C_\Omega\left(f_{\text{count}}^{(n)}\right)$ and $D(k) = D_\Omega\left(f_{\text{count}}^{(n)}\right)$ when $n = 2^k - 1$. Clearly, $C(2) = 5$ and $D(2) = 3$ since a full adder over $\Omega = \{\land, \lor, \oplus\}$ has five gates and depth 3. The following inequality is immediate from the construction:

$$C(k) \le 2C(k - 1) + 5(k - 1)$$

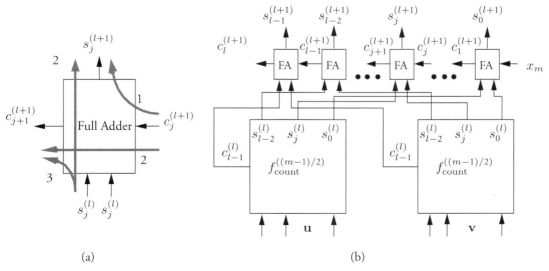

(a)   (b)

Figure 2.21 A recursive construction for the counting function $f_{\text{count}}^{(m)}$, $m = 2^{l+1} - 1$.

The size bound follows immediately. The depth bound requires a more careful analysis.

Shown in Fig. 2.21(a) is a full adder together with notation showing the amount by which the length of a path from one input to another is increased in passing through it when the full-adder circuit used is that shown in Fig. 2.14 and described by Equation 2.6. From this it follows that

$$D_\Omega\left(c_{j+1}^{(l+1)}\right) = \max\left(D_\Omega\left(c_j^{(l+1)}\right) + 2, D_\Omega\left(s_j^{(l)}\right) + 3\right)$$

$$D_\Omega\left(s_j^{(l+1)}\right) = \max\left(D_\Omega\left(c_j^{(l+1)}\right) + 1, D_\Omega\left(s_j^{(l)}\right) + 2\right)$$

for $2 \leq l$ and $0 \leq j \leq l - 1$, where $s_{l-1}^{(l)} = c_{l-1}^{(l)}$. It can be shown by induction that $D_\Omega\left(c_j^{(k)}\right) = 2(k+j)-3, 1 \leq j \leq k-1$, and $D_\Omega\left(s_j^{(k)}\right) = 2(k+j)-2, 0 \leq j \leq k-2$, both for $2 \leq k$. (See Problem 2.16.) Thus, $D_\Omega\left(f_{\text{count}}^{(n)}\right) = D_\Omega\left(c_{k-1}^{(k)}\right) = (4k - 5)$. ∎

We now use this bound to derive upper bounds on the size and depth of symmetric functions in the class $S_{n,m}$.

THEOREM 2.11.1 *Every symmetric function* $f^{(n)} : \mathcal{B}^n \mapsto \mathcal{B}^m$ *can be realized with the following circuit size and depth over the basis* $\Omega = \{\wedge, \vee, \oplus\}$:

$$C_\Omega\left(f^{(n)}\right) \leq m\lceil n/2 \rceil + 5(2^k - k - 1) + 2n + \lceil \log_2 n \rceil \sqrt{2n} + 1$$

$$D_\Omega\left(f^{(n)}\right) \leq 5\lceil \log_2 n \rceil + \lceil \log_2 \lceil \log_2 n \rceil \rceil - 5$$

for $k = \lceil \log_2(n + 1) \rceil$.

Proof Lemma 2.11.1 establishes bounds on the size and depth of the function $f_{\text{count}}^{(n)}$ for $n = 2^k - 1$. For other values of n, let $k = \lceil \log_2(n + 1) \rceil$ and fill out the $2^k - 1 - n$ variables with 0's.

The elementary symmetric functions are obtained by applying the value of $f_{\text{count}}^{(n)}$ as argument to the decoder function. A circuit for this function has been constructed that has size $2n + \lceil \log_2 n \rceil \sqrt{2n}$ and depth $\lceil \log_2 \lceil \log_2 n \rceil \rceil$. (See Lemma 2.5.4. We use the fact that $2^{\lceil \log_2 n \rceil} \leq 2n$.) Thus, all elementary symmetric functions on n variables can be realized with the following circuit size and depth:

$$C_\Omega\left(e_1^{(n)}, e_2^{(n)}, \ldots, e_n^{(n)}\right) \leq 5(2^k - k - 1) + 2n + \lceil \log_2 n \rceil \sqrt{2n}$$

$$D_\Omega\left(e_1^{(n)}, e_2^{(n)}, \ldots, e_n^{(n)}\right) \leq 4k - 5 + \lceil \log_2 \lceil \log_2 n \rceil \rceil$$

The expansion of Equation (2.15) can be used to realize an arbitrary Boolean symmetric function. Clearly, at most n OR gates and depth $\lceil \log_2 n \rceil$ suffice to realize each one of m arbitrary Boolean symmetric functions. (Since the v_t are fixed, no ANDs are needed.) This number of ORs can be reduced to $(n - 1)/2$ as follows: if $\lceil n/2 \rceil$ or more elementary functions are needed, use the complementary set (of at most $\lfloor n/2 \rfloor$ functions) and take the complement of the result. Thus, no more than $\lceil n/2 \rceil - 1$ ORs are needed per symmetric function (plus possibly one NOT), and depth at most $\lceil \log_2 \lfloor (n/2) \rfloor \rceil + 1 \leq \lceil \log_2 n \rceil$. ∎

This theorem establishes that the binary sorting $f_{\text{sort}}^{(n)} : \mathcal{B}^n \mapsto \mathcal{B}^n$ has size $O(n^2)$. In fact, a linear-size circuit can be constructed for it, as stated in Problem 2.17.

2.12 Most Boolean Functions Are Complex

As we show in this section, the circuit size and depth of most Boolean functions $f : \mathcal{B}^n \mapsto \mathcal{B}$ on n variables are at least exponential and linear in n, respectively. Furthermore, we show in Section 2.13 that such functions can be realized with circuits whose size and depth are at most exponential and linear, respectively, in n. Thus, the circuit size and depth of most Boolean functions on n variables are tightly bounded. Unfortunately, this result says nothing about the size and depth of a specific function, the case of most interest.

Each Boolean function on n variables is represented by a table with 2^n rows and one column of values for the function. Since each entry in this one column can be completed in one of two ways, there are 2^{2^n} ways to fill in the column. Thus, there are exactly 2^{2^n} Boolean functions on n variables. Most of these functions cannot be realized by small circuits because there just are not enough small circuits.

THEOREM 2.12.1 *Let* $0 < \epsilon < 1$. *The fraction of the Boolean functions* $f : \mathcal{B}^n \mapsto \mathcal{B}$ *that have size complexity* $C_{\Omega_0}(f)$ *satisfying the following lower bound is at least* $1 - 2^{-(\epsilon/2)2^n}$ *when* $n \geq 2[(1 - \epsilon)/\epsilon] \log_2[(3e)^2(1 - \epsilon/2)]$. *(Here* $e = 2.71828\ldots$ *is Euler's constant.)*

$$C_{\Omega_0}(f) \geq \frac{2^n}{n}(1 - \epsilon) - 2n^2$$

Proof Each circuit contains some number, say g, of gates and each gate can be one of the three types of gate in the standard basis. The circuit with no gates computes the constant functions with value of 1 or 0 on all inputs.

An input to a gate can either be the output of another gate or one of the n input variables. (Since the basis Ω_0 is $\{\text{AND}, \text{OR}, \text{NOT}\}$, no gate need have a constant input.) Since each gate has at most two inputs, there are at most $(g - 1 + n)^2$ ways to connect inputs to one gate and $(g - 1 + n)^{2g}$ ways to interconnect g gates. In addition, since each gate can be one of three types, there are 3^g ways to name the gates. Since there are $g!$ orderings of g items (gates) and the ordering of gates does not change the function they compute, at most $N(g) = 3^g(g + n)^{2g}/g!$ distinct functions can be realized with g gates. Also, since $g! \geq g^g e^{-g}$ (see Problem 2.2) it follows that

$$N(g) \leq (3e)^g[(g^2 + 2gn + n^2)/g]^g \leq (3e)^g(g + 2n^2)^g$$

The last inequality follows because $2gn + n^2 \leq 2gn^2$ for $n \geq 2$. Since the last bound is an increasing function of g, $N(0) = 2$ and $G + 1 \leq (3e)^G$ for $G \geq 1$, the number $M(G)$ of functions realizable with between 0 and G gates satisfies

$$M(G) \leq (G + 1)(3e)^G(G + 2n^2)^G \leq [(3e)^2(G + 2n^2)]^G \leq (x^x)^{1/a}$$

where $x = a(G + 2n^2)$ and $a = (3e)^2$. With base-2 logarithms, it is straightforward to show that $x^x \leq 2^{x_0}$ if $x \leq x_0/\log_2 x_0$ and $x_0 \geq 2$.

If $M(G) \leq 2^{(1-\delta)2^n}$ for $0 < \delta < 1$, at most a fraction $2^{(1-\delta)2^n}/2^{2^n} = 2^{-\delta 2^n}$ of the Boolean functions on n variables have circuits with G or fewer gates.

Let $G < 2^n(1 - \epsilon)/n - 2n^2$. Then $x = a(G + 2n^2) \leq a2^n(1 - \epsilon)/n \leq x_0/\log_2 x_0$ for $x_0 = a2^n(1 - \epsilon/2)$ when $n \geq 2[(1 - \epsilon)/\epsilon] \log_2[(3e)^2(1 - \epsilon/2)]$, as can be shown directly. It follows that $M(G) \leq (x^x)^{1/a} \leq 2^{x_0} = 2^{2^n(1-\epsilon/2)}$. ∎

To show that most Boolean functions $f : \mathcal{B}^n \mapsto \mathcal{B}$ over the basis Ω_0 require circuits with a depth linear in n, we use a similar argument. We first show that for every circuit there is a **tree circuit** (a circuit in which either zero or one edge is directed away from each gate) that computes the same function and has the same depth. Thus when searching for small-depth circuits it suffices to look only at tree circuits. We then obtain an upper bound on the number of tree circuits of depth d or less and show that unless d is linear in n, most Boolean functions on n variables cannot be realized with this depth.

LEMMA 2.12.1 *Given a circuit for a function $f : \mathcal{B}^n \mapsto \mathcal{B}^m$, a tree circuit can be constructed of the same depth that computes f.*

Proof Convert a circuit to a tree circuit without changing its depth as follows: find a vertex v with out-degree 2 or more at maximal distance from an output vertex. Attach a copy of the tree subcircuit with output vertex v to each of the edges directed away from v. This reduces by 1 the number of vertices with out-degree greater than 1 but doesn't change the depth or function computed. Repeat this process on the new circuit until no vertices of outdegree greater than 1 remain. ∎

We count the number of tree circuits of depth d as follows. First, we determine $T(d)$, the number of binary, unlabeled, and unoriented trees of depth d. (Each vertex has fan-in 2, no vertex carries a label, and we count as one tree those trees that differ only by the exchange of the two subtrees at a vertex.) We then multiply $T(d)$ by the number of ways to label the internal vertices with one of at most three gates and the leaves by at most one of n variables or constants to obtain an upper bound on $N(d)$, the number of distinct tree circuits of depth d. Since a tree of depth d has at most $2^d - 1$ internal vertices and 2^d leaves (see Problem 2.3), $N(d) \leq T(d)3^{2^d}(n + 2)^{2^d}$.

LEMMA 2.12.2 *When $d \geq 4$ the number $T(d)$ of depth-d unlabeled, unoriented binary trees satisfies $T(d) \leq (56)^{2^{d-4}}$.*

Proof There is one binary tree of depth 0, a tree containing a single vertex, and one of depth 1. Let $C(d)$ be the number of unlabeled, unoriented binary trees of depth d or less, including depth 0. Thus, $C(0) = 1$, $T(1) = 1$, and $C(1) = 2$. This recurrence for $C(d)$ follows immediately for $d \geq 1$:

$$C(d) = C(d - 1) + T(d) \tag{2.16}$$

We now enumerate the unoriented, unlabeled binary trees of depth $d + 1$. Without loss of generality, let the left subtree of the root have depth d. There are $T(d)$ such subtrees. The right subtree can either be of depth $d - 1$ or less (there are $C(d - 1)$ such trees) or of depth d. In the first case there are $T(d)C(d - 1)$ trees. In the second, there are $T(d)(T(d) - 1)/2$ pairs of different subtrees (orientation is not counted) and $T(d)$ pairs of identical subtrees. It follows that

$$T(d + 1) = T(d)C(d - 1) + T(d)(T(d) - 1)/2 + T(d) \tag{2.17}$$

Thus, $T(2) = 2$, $C(2) = 4$, $T(3) = 7$, $C(3) = 11$, and $T(4) = 56$. From this recurrence we conclude that $T(d+1) \geq T^2(d)/2$. We use this fact and the inequality $y \geq 1/(1-/y)$, which holds for $y \geq 2$, to show that $(T(d+1)/T(d)) + T(d)/2 \leq T(d+1)/2$. Since $T(d) \geq 4$ for $d \geq 3$, it follows that $T(d)/2 \geq 1/(1 - 2/T(d))$. Replacing $T(d)/2$ by this lower bound in the inequality $T(d+1) \geq T^2(d)/2$, we achieve the desired result by simple algebraic manipulation. We use this fact below.

Solving the equation (2.17) for $C(d-1)$, we have

$$C(d-1) = \frac{T(d+1)}{T(d)} - \frac{(T(d)+1)}{2} \tag{2.18}$$

Substituting this expression into (2.16) yields the following recurrence:

$$\frac{T(d+2)}{T(d+1)} = \frac{T(d+1)}{T(d)} + \frac{(T(d+1)+T(d))}{2}$$

Since $(T(d+1)/T(d)) + T(d)/2 \leq T(d+1)/2$, it follows that $T(d+2)$ satisfies the inequality $T(d+2) \leq T^2(d+1)$ when $d \geq 3$ or $T(d) \leq T^2(d-1)$ when $d \geq 5$ and $d-1 \geq 4$. Thus, $T(d) \leq T^{2^j}(d-j)$ for $d - j \geq 4$ or $T(d) \leq (56)^{2^{d-4}}$ for $d \geq 4$. ∎

Combine this with the early upper bound on $N(d)$ for the number of tree circuits over Ω_0 of depth d and we have that $N(d) \leq c^{2^d}$ for $d \geq 4$, where $c = 3((56)^{1/16})(n+2)$. (Note that $3(56)^{1/16} \leq 4$.) The number of such trees of depth 0 through d is at most $(d+1)N(d) \leq c^{2^{d+1}}$. But if $c^{2^{D_0+1}}$ is at most $2^{2^n(1-\delta)}$, then a fraction of at most $2^{-\delta 2^n}$ of the Boolean functions on n variables have depth D_0 or less. But this holds when

$$D_0 = n - 1 - \delta \log_2 e - \log_2 log_2 4(n+2) = n - \log\log n - O(1)$$

since $\ln(1-x) \leq -x$. Note that $d \geq 4$ implies that $n \geq d + 1$.

THEOREM 2.12.2 *For each $0 < \delta < 1$ a fraction of at least $1 - 2^{-\delta 2^n}$ of the Boolean functions $f^{(n)} : \mathcal{B}^n \mapsto \mathcal{B}$ have depth complexity $D_{\Omega_0}(f)$ that satisfies the following bound when $n \geq 5$:*

$$D_{\Omega_0}(f) \geq n - \log\log n - O(1)$$

As the above two theorems demonstrate, most Boolean functions on n variables require circuits whose size and depth are approximately $2^n/n$ and n, respectively. Fortunately, most of the useful Boolean functions are far less complex than these bounds suggest. In fact, we often encounter functions whose size is polynomial in n and whose depth is logarithmic in or a small polynomial in the logarithm of the size of its input. Functions that are polynomial in the logarithm of n are called **poly-logarithmic**.

2.13 Upper Bounds on Circuit Size

In this section we demonstrate that every Boolean function on n variables can be realized with circuit size and depth that are close to the lower bounds derived in the preceding section. We begin by stating the obvious upper bounds on size and depth and then proceed to obtain stronger (that is, smaller) upper bounds on size through the use of refined arguments.

As shown in Section 2.2.2, every Boolean function $f : \mathcal{B}^n \mapsto \mathcal{B}$ can be realized as the OR of its minterms. As shown in Section 2.5.4, the minterms on n variables are produced by the decoder function $f_{\text{decode}}^{(n)} : \mathcal{B}^n \mapsto \mathcal{B}^{2^n}$, which has a circuit with $2^n + (2n - 2)2^{n/2}$ gates and depth $\lceil \log_2 n \rceil$. Consequently, we can realize f from a circuit for $f_{\text{decode}}^{(n)}$ and an OR tree on at most 2^n inputs (which has at most $2^n - 1$ two-input OR's and depth at most n). We have that every function $f : \mathcal{B}^n \mapsto \mathcal{B}$ has circuit size and depth satisfying:

$$C_\Omega(f) \leq C_\Omega\left(f_{\text{decode}}^{(n)}\right) + 2^{n-1} \leq 3 \cdot 2^{n-1} + (2n - 2)2^{n/2}$$

$$D_\Omega(f) \leq D_\Omega\left(f_{\text{decode}}^{(n)}\right) + n + 1 \leq n + \lceil \log_2 n \rceil$$

Thus every Boolean function $f : \mathcal{B}^n \mapsto \mathcal{B}$ can be realized with an exponential number of gates and depth $n + \lceil \log_2 n \rceil$. Since the depth lower bound of $n - O(\log \log n)$ applies to almost all Boolean functions on n variables (see Section 2.12), this is a very good upper bound on depth. We improve upon the circuit size bound after summarizing the depth bound.

THEOREM 2.13.1 *The depth complexity of every Boolean function $f : \mathcal{B}^n \mapsto \mathcal{B}$ satisfies the following bound:*

$$D_{\Omega_0}(f) \leq n + \lceil \log_2 n \rceil$$

We now describe a procedure to construct circuits of small size for arbitrary Boolean functions on n variables. By the results of the preceding section, this size will be exponential in n. The method of approach is to view an arbitrary Boolean function $f : \mathcal{B}^n \mapsto \mathcal{B}$ on n input variables $\boldsymbol{x}$ as a function of two sets of variables, $\boldsymbol{a}$, the first k variables of $\boldsymbol{x}$, and $\boldsymbol{b}$, the remaining $n - k$ variables of $\boldsymbol{x}$. That is, $\boldsymbol{x} = \boldsymbol{ab}$ where $\boldsymbol{a} = (x_1, \ldots, x_k)$ and $\boldsymbol{b} = (x_{k+1}, \ldots, x_n)$.

As suggested by Fig. 2.22, we rearrange the entries in the defining table for f into a rectangular table with 2^k rows indexed by $\boldsymbol{a}$ and 2^{n-k} columns indexed by $\boldsymbol{b}$. The lower right-hand quadrant of the table contains the values of the function f. The value of f on $\boldsymbol{x}$ is the entry at the intersection of the row indexed by the value of $\boldsymbol{a}$ and the column indexed by the value of $\boldsymbol{b}$. We fix s and divide the lower right-hand quadrant of the table into $p - 1$ groups of s consecutive rows and one group of $s' \leq s$ consecutive rows where $p = \lceil 2^k/s \rceil$. (Note that $(p - 1)s + s' = 2^k$.) Call the ith collections of rows A_i. This table serves as the basis for the (k, s)-Lupanov representation of f, from which a smaller circuit for f can be constructed.

Let $f_i : \mathcal{B}^n \mapsto \mathcal{B}$ be f restricted to A_i; that is,

$$f_i(\boldsymbol{x}) = \begin{cases} f(\boldsymbol{x}) & \text{if } \boldsymbol{a} \in A_i \\ 0 & \text{otherwise.} \end{cases}$$

It follows that f can be expanded as the OR of the f_i:

$$f(\boldsymbol{x}) = \bigvee_{i=1}^{p} f_i(\boldsymbol{x})$$

We now expand f_i. When $\boldsymbol{b}$ is fixed, the values for $f_i(\boldsymbol{ab})$ when $\boldsymbol{a} \in A_i$ constitute an s-tuple (s'-tuple) $\boldsymbol{v}$ for $1 \leq i \leq p - 1$ (for $i = p$). Let $B_{i,\boldsymbol{v}}$ be those $(n - k)$-tuples $\boldsymbol{b}$ for

				x_4								
				0	1	0	1	0	1	0	1	x_4
				0	0	1	1	0	0	1	1	x_5
				0	0	0	0	1	1	1	1	x_6
x_1	x_2	x_3										
0	0	0		0	1	0	0	0	1	0	0	
0	0	1		0	1	1	0	0	1	1	1	A_1
0	1	0		1	0	0	1	0	0	0	1	
0	1	1		1	0	1	1	0	0	1	0	
1	0	0		0	0	0	0	1	0	0	1	A_2
1	0	1		1	1	0	1	1	0	0	0	
1	1	0		1	0	1	1	0	1	1	0	
1	1	1		0	1	0	0	0	0	1	0	A_3

Figure 2.22 The rectangular representation of the defining table of a Boolean function used in its (k, s)-Lupanov representation.

which v is the tuple of values of f_i when $a \in A_i$. (Note that the non-empty sets $B_{i,v}$ for different values of v are disjoint.) Let $f_{i,v}^{(c)}(b) : \mathcal{B}^{n-k} \mapsto \mathcal{B}$ be defined as

$$f_{i,v}^{(c)}(b) = \begin{cases} 1 & \text{if } b \in B_{i,v} \\ 0 & \text{otherwise.} \end{cases}$$

Finally, we let $f_{i,v}^{(r)}(a) : \mathcal{B}^k \mapsto \mathcal{B}$ be the function that has value v_j, the jth component of v, when a is the jth k-tuple in A_i:

$$f_{i,v}^{(r)}(a) = \begin{cases} 1 & \text{if } a \text{ is the } j\text{th element of } A_i \text{ and } v_j = 1 \\ 0 & \text{otherwise.} \end{cases}$$

It follows that $f_i(x) = \bigvee_v f_{i,v}^{(r)}(a) f_{i,v}^{(c)}(b)$. Given these definitions, f can be expanded in the following (k, s)-**Lupanov representation**:

$$f(x) = \bigvee_{i=1}^{p} \bigvee_v f_{i,v}^{(r)}(a) \wedge f_{i,v}^{(c)}(b) \tag{2.19}$$

We now bound the number of logic elements needed to realize an arbitrary function $f : \mathcal{B}^n \mapsto \mathcal{B}$ in this representation.

Consider the functions $f_{i,v}^{(r)}(a)$ for a fixed value of v. We construct a decoder circuit for the minterms in a that has size at most $2^k + (k - 2)2^{k/2}$. Each of the functions $f_{i,v}^{(r)}$ can be realized as the OR of s minterms in a for $1 \leq i \leq p - 1$ and s' minterms otherwise. Thus, $(p-1)(s-1) + (s'-1) \leq 2^k$ two-input OR's suffice for all values of i and a fixed value of v. Hence, for each value of v the functions $f_{i,v}^{(r)}$ can be realized by a circuit of size $O(2^k)$. Since there are at most 2^s choices for v, all $f_{i,v}^{(r)}$ can be realized by a circuit of size $O(2^{k+s})$.

Consider next the functions $f_{i,v}^{(c)}(b)$. We construct a decoder circuit for the minterms of b that has size at most $2^{n-k} + (n - k - 2)2^{(n-k)/2}$. Since for each i, $1 \leq i \leq p$, the sets

$B_{i,v}$ for different values of v are disjoint, $f_{i,v}^{(c)}(b)$ can be realized as the OR of at most 2^{n-k} minterms using at most 2^{n-k} two-input OR's. Thus, all $f_{i,v}^{(c)}(b)$, $1 \le i \le p$, can be realized with $p2^{n-k} + 2^{n-k} + (n - k - 2)2^{(n-k)/2}$ gates.

Consulting (2.19), we see that to realize f we must add one AND gate for each i and tuple v. We must also add the number of two-input OR gates needed to combine these products. Since there are at most $p2^s$ products, at least $p2^s$ OR gates are needed for a total of $p2^{s+1}$ gates.

Let $C_{k,s}(f)$ be the total number of gates needed to realize f in the (k, s)-Lupanov representation. $C_{k,s}(f)$ satisfies the following inequality:

$$C_{k,s}(f) \le O(2^{k+s}) + O(2^{(n-k)}) + p(2^{n-k} + 2^{s+1})$$

Since $p = \lceil 2^k/s \rceil$, $p \le 2^k/s + 1$, this expands to

$$C_{k,s}(f) \le O(2^{k+s}) + O(2^{n-k}) + \frac{2^n}{s} + \frac{2^{k+s+1}}{s}$$

Now let $k = \lceil 3 \log_2 n \rceil$ and $s = \lceil n - 5 \log_2 n \rceil$. Then, $k + s \le n - \log_2 n^2 + 2$ and $n - k \le n - \log_2 n^3$. As a consequence, for large n, we have

$$C_{k,s}(f) \le O\left(\frac{2^n}{n^2}\right) + O\left(\frac{2^n}{n^3}\right) + \frac{2^n}{(n - 5 \log_2 n)}$$

We summarize the result in a theorem.

THEOREM 2.13.2 *For each $\epsilon > 0$ there exists some $N_0 > 1$ such that for all $n \ge N_0$ every Boolean function $f : \mathcal{B}^n \mapsto \mathcal{B}$ has a circuit size complexity satisfying the following upper bound:*

$$C_{\Omega_0}(f) \le \frac{2^n}{n}(1 + \epsilon)$$

Since we show in Section 2.12 that for $0 < \epsilon < 1$ almost all Boolean functions $f : \mathcal{B}^n \mapsto \mathcal{B}$ have a circuit size complexity satisfying

$$C_{\Omega_0}(f) \ge \frac{2^n}{n}(1 - \epsilon) - 2n^2$$

for $n \ge 2[(1 - \epsilon)/\epsilon] \log_2[(3e)^2(1 - \epsilon/2)]$, this is a good lower bound.

- -

Problems

MATHEMATICAL PRELIMINARIES

2.1 Show that the following identities on geometric series hold:

$$\sum_{j=0}^{s} a^j = \frac{(a^{s+1} - 1)}{(a - 1)}$$

$$\sum_{j=0}^{s} a^j j = \frac{a}{(a - 1)^2}(sa^{s+1} - (s + 1)a^s + 1)$$

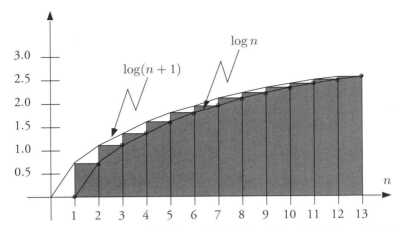

Figure 2.23 The natural logarithm of the factorial $n!$ is $\sum_{k=1}^{n} \ln k$, which is bounded below by $\int_{1}^{n} \ln x \, dx$ and above by $\int_{1}^{n+1} \ln(x+1) \, dx$.

2.2 Derive tight upper and lower bounds on the factorial function $n! = n(n-1) \cdots 3\,2\,1$.

Hint: Derive bounds on $\ln n!$ where $\ln$ is the natural logarithm. Use the information given in Fig. 2.23.

2.3 Let $\mathcal{T}(d)$ be a complete balanced binary tree of depth d. $\mathcal{T}(1)$, shown in Fig. 2.24(a), has a root and two leaves. $\mathcal{T}(d)$ is obtained by attaching to each of the leaves of $\mathcal{T}(1)$ copies of $\mathcal{T}(d-1)$. $\mathcal{T}(3)$ is shown in Fig. 2.24(b).

a) Show by induction that $\mathcal{T}(d)$ has 2^d leaves and $2^d - 1$ non-leaf vertices.

b) Show that any binary tree with n leaves has $n - 1$ non-leaf vertices and depth at least $\lceil \log_2 n \rceil$.

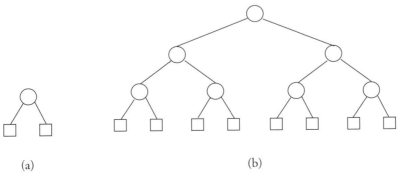

(a)   (b)

Figure 2.24 Complete balanced binary trees a) of depth two and b) depth 4.

BINARY FUNCTIONS AND LOGIC CIRCUITS

2.4 a) Write a procedure EXOR in a language of your choice that **writes** the description of the straight-line program given in equation (2.2).

b) Write a program in a language of your choice that **evaluates** an arbitrary straight-line program given in the format of equation (2.2) in which each input value is specified.

2.5 A set of Boolean functions forms a **complete basis** Ω if a logic circuit can be constructed for every Boolean function $f : \mathcal{B}^n \mapsto \mathcal{B}$ using just functions in Ω.

a) Show that the basis consisting of one function, the NAND gate, a gate on two inputs realizing the NOT of the AND of its inputs, is complete.

b) Determine whether or not the basis {AND, OR} is complete.

2.6 Show that the CNF of a Boolean function f is unique and is the negation of the DNF of $\overline{f}$.

2.7 Show that the RSE of a Boolean function is unique.

2.8 Show that any SOPE (POSE) of the parity function $f_{\oplus}^{(n)}$ has exponentially many terms.

Hint: Show by contradiction that every term in a SOPE (every clause of a POSE) of $f_{\oplus}^{(n)}$ contains every variable. Then use the fact that the DNF (CNF) of $f_{\oplus}^{(n)}$ has exponentially many terms to complete the proof.

2.9 Demonstrate that the RSE of the OR of n variables, $f_{\vee}^{(n)}$, includes every product term except for the constant 1.

2.10 Consider the Boolean function $f_{\mathrm{mod}\ 3}^{(n)}$ on n variables, which has value 1 when the sum of its variables is zero modulo 3 and value 0 otherwise. Show that it has exponential-size DNF, CNF, and RSE normal forms.

Hint: Use the fact that the following sum is even:

$$\sum_{0 \leq j \leq k} \binom{3k}{3j}$$

2.11 Show that every Boolean function $f^{(n)} : \mathcal{B}^n \mapsto \mathcal{B}$ can be expanded as follows:

$$f(x_1, x_2, \ldots, x_n) = x_1 f(1, x_2, \ldots, x_n) \vee \overline{x}_1 f(0, x_2, \ldots, x_n)$$

Apply this expansion to each variable of $f(x_1, x_2, x_3) = x_1 \overline{x}_2 \vee x_2 x_3$ to obtain its DNF.

2.12 In a **dual-rail logic** circuit 0 and 1 are represented by the pairs $(0, 1)$ and $(1, 0)$, respectively. A variable x is represented by the pair $(x, \overline{x})$. A NOT in this representation (called a DRL-NOT) is a pair of twisted wires.

a) How are AND (DRL-AND) and OR (DRL-OR) realized in this representation? Use standard AND and OR gates to construct circuits for gates in the new representation. Show that every function $f : \mathcal{B}^n \mapsto \mathcal{B}^m$ can be realized by a **dual-rail logic** circuit in which the standard NOT gates are used only on input variables (to obtain the pair $(x, \overline{x})$).

b) Show that the size and depth of a dual-rail logic circuit for a function f (measured in terms of standard gates) are at most twice the circuit size and one more than the circuit depth of f, respectively, over the standard basis.

2.13 A function $f : \mathcal{B}^n \mapsto \mathcal{B}$ is **monotone** if for all $1 \leq j \leq n$, $f(x_1, \ldots, x_{j-1}, 0, x_{j+1}, \ldots, x_n) \leq f(x_1, \ldots, x_{j-1}, 1, x_{j+1}, \ldots, x_n)$ for all values of the remaining variables; that is, increasing any variable from 0 to 1 does not cause the function to decrease its value from 1 to 0.

a) Show that every circuit over the basis $\Omega_{\mathrm{mon}} = \{\mathrm{AND}, \mathrm{OR}\}$ computes monotone functions at every gate.

b) Show that every monotone function $f^{(n)} : \mathcal{B}^n \mapsto \mathcal{B}$ can be expanded as follows:

$$f(x_1, x_2, \ldots, x_n) = x_1 f(1, x_2, \ldots, x_n) \vee f(0, x_2, \ldots, x_n)$$

Show that this implies that every monotone function can be realized by a logic circuit over the **monotone basis** $\Omega_{\mathrm{mon}} = \{\mathrm{AND}, \mathrm{OR}\}$.

SPECIALIZED FUNCTIONS

2.14 Complete the proof of Lemma 2.5.3 by solving the recurrences stated in Equation (2.4).

2.15 Design a multiplexer circuit of circuit size 2^{n+1} plus lower-order terms when n is even.

Hint: Construct a smaller circuit by applying the decomposition given in Section 2.5.4 of the minterms of n variables into minterms on the two halves of the n variables.

2.16 Complete the proof of Lemma 2.11.1 by establishing the correctness of the inductive hypothesis stated in its proof.

2.17 The **binary sorting** function is defined in Section 2.11. Show that it can be realized with a circuit whose size is $O(n)$ and depth is $O(\log n)$.

Hint: Consider using a circuit for $f_{\mathrm{count}}^{(m)}$, a decoder circuit and other circuitry. Is there a role for a prefix computation in this problem?

LOGICAL FUNCTIONS

2.18 Let $f_{\mathrm{member}}^{(n)} : \mathcal{B}^{(n+1)b} \mapsto \mathcal{B}$ be defined below.

$$f_{\mathrm{member}}^{(n)}(\boldsymbol{x}_1, \boldsymbol{x}_2, \ldots, \boldsymbol{x}_n, \boldsymbol{y}) = \begin{cases} 1 & \boldsymbol{x}_i = \boldsymbol{y} \quad \text{for some } 1 \leq i \leq n \\ 0 & \text{otherwise} \end{cases}$$

where $\boldsymbol{x}_i, \boldsymbol{y} \in \mathcal{B}^b$ and $\boldsymbol{x}_i = \boldsymbol{y}$ if and only if they agree in each position.

Obtain good upper bounds to $C_\Omega \left(f_{\mathrm{member}}^{(n)} \right)$ and $D_\Omega \left(f_{\mathrm{member}}^{(n)} \right)$ by constructing a circuit over the basis $\Omega = \{\wedge, \vee, \neg, \oplus\}$.

2.19 Design a circuit to compare two n-bit binary numbers and return the value 1 if the first is larger than or equal to the second and 0 otherwise.

Hint: Compare each pair of digits of the same significance and generate three outcomes, **yes**, **maybe**, and **no**, corresponding to whether the first digit is greater than, equal to or less than the second. How can you combine the outputs of such a comparison circuit to design a circuit for the problem? Does a prefix computation appear in your circuit?

PARALLEL PREFIX

2.20 a) Let $\odot_{copy} : S^2 \mapsto S$ be the operation

$$a \odot_{copy} b = a$$

Show that $(S, \odot_{copy})$ is a semigroup for S an arbitrary non-empty set.

b) Let $\cdot$ denote string concatenation over the set $\{0, 1\}^*$ of binary strings. Show that it is associative.

2.21 The segmented prefix computation with the associative operation $\odot$ on a "value" n-vector $\boldsymbol{x}$ over a set S, given a "flag vector" ϕ over $\mathcal{B}$, is defined as follows: the value of the ith entry y_i of the "result vector" $\boldsymbol{y}$ is x_i if its flag is 1 and otherwise is the associative combination with $\odot$ of x_i and the entries to its left up to and including the first occurrence of a 1 in the flag array. The leftmost bit in every flag vector is 1. An example of a segmented prefix computation is given in Section 2.6.

Assuming that $(S, \odot)$ is a semigroup, a segmented prefix computation over the set $S \times \mathcal{B}$ of pairs is a special case of general prefix computation. Consider the operator $\otimes$ on pairs (x_i, ϕ_i) of values and flags defined below:

$$((x_1, \phi_1) \otimes (x_2, \phi_2)) = \begin{cases} (x_2, 1) & \phi_2 = 1 \\ (x_1 \odot x_2, \phi_1) & \phi_2 = 0 \end{cases}$$

Show that $((S, \mathcal{B}), \otimes)$ is a semigroup by proving that $(S, \mathcal{B})$ is closed under the operator $\otimes$ and that the operator $\otimes$ is associative.

2.22 Construct a logic circuit of size $O(n \log n)$ and depth $O(\log^2 n)$ that, given a binary n-tuple $\boldsymbol{x}$, computes the n-tuple $\boldsymbol{y}$ containing the running sum of the number of 1's in $\boldsymbol{x}$.

2.23 Given $2n$ Boolean variables organized as pairs $0a$ or $1a$, design a circuit that moves pairs of the form $1a$ to the left and the others to the right without changing their relative order. Show that the circuit has size $O(n \log n)$.

2.24 Linear recurrences play an important role in many problems including the solution of a tridiagonal linear system of equations. They are defined over "near-rings," which are slightly weaker than rings in not requiring inverses under the addition operation. (Rings are defined in Section 6.2.1.)

A **near-ring** $(\mathcal{R}, \cdot, +)$ is a set $\mathcal{R}$ together with an associative multiplication operator $\cdot$ and an associative and commutative addition operator $+$. (If $+$ is commutative, then for all $a, b \in \mathcal{R}$, $a + b = b + a$.) In addition, $\cdot$ distributes over $+$; that is, for all $a, b, c \in \mathcal{R}$, $a \cdot (b + c) = a \cdot b + a \cdot c$.

A **first-order linear recurrence of length** n is an n-tuple $\boldsymbol{x} = (x_1, x_2, \ldots, x_n)$ of variables over a near-ring $(\mathcal{R}, \cdot, +)$ that satisfies $x_1 = b_1$ and the following set of identities for $2 \le j \le n$ defined in terms of elements $\{a_j, b_j \in \mathcal{R} \mid 2 \le j \le n\}$:

$$x_j = a_j \cdot x_{j-1} + b_j$$

Use the ideas of Section 2.7 on carry-lookahead addition to show that x_j can be written

$$x_j = c_j \cdot x_1 + d_j$$

where the pairs (c_j, d_j) are the result of a prefix computation.

ARITHMETIC OPERATIONS

2.25 Design a circuit that finds the most significant non-zero position in an n-bit binary number and logically shifts the binary number left so that the non-zero bit is in the most significant position. The circuit should produce not only the shifted binary number but also a binary representation of the amount of the shift.

2.26 Consider the function $\pi[j, k] = \pi[j, k-1] \diamond \pi[k, k]$ for $1 \le j < k \le n-1$, where $\diamond$ is defined in Section 2.7.1. Show by induction that the first component of $\pi[j, k]$ is 1 if and only if a carry propagates through the full adder stages numbered $j, j+1, \ldots, k$ and its second component is 1 if and only if a carry is generated at one of these stages, propagates through subsequent stages, and appears as a carry out of the kth stage.

2.27 Give a construction of a circuit for subtracting one n-bit positive binary integer from another using the two's-complement operation. Show that the circuit has size $O(n)$ and depth $O(\log n)$.

2.28 Complete the proof of Theorem 2.9.3 outlined in the text. In particular, solve the recurrence given in equation (2.10).

2.29 Show that the depth bound stated in Theorem 2.9.3 can be improved from $O(\log^2 n)$ to $O(\log n)$ without affecting the size bound by using carry-save addition to form the six additions (or subtractions) that are involved at each stage.

Hint: Observe that each multiplication of $(n/2)$-bit numbers at the top level is expanded at the next level as sums of the product of $(n/4)$-bit numbers and that this type of replacement continues until the product is formed of 1-bit numbers. Observe also that $2n$-bit carry-save adders can be used at the top level but that the smaller carry-save adders can be used at successively lower levels.

2.30 Residue arithmetic can be used to add and subtract integers. Given positive relatively prime integers $p_1, p_2, \ldots, p_k$ (no common factors), an integer n in the set $\{0, 1, 2, \ldots, N-1\}$, $N = p_1 p_2 \cdots p_k$, can be represented by the k-tuple $\boldsymbol{n} = (n_1, n_2, \ldots, n_k)$, where $n_j = n \bmod p_j$. Let n and m be in this set.

a) Show that if $n \ne m$, $\boldsymbol{n} \ne \boldsymbol{m}$.

b) Form $\boldsymbol{n} + \boldsymbol{m}$ by adding corresponding jth components modulo p_j. Show that $\boldsymbol{n} + \boldsymbol{m}$ uniquely represents $(n + m) \bmod N$.

c) Form $n \times m$ by multiplying corresponding jth components of $\boldsymbol{n}$ and $\boldsymbol{m}$ modulo p_j. Show that $n \times m$ is the unique representation for $(nm) \bmod N$.

2.31 Use the circuit designed in Problem 2.19 to build a circuit that adds two n-bit binary numbers modulo an arbitrary third n-bit binary number. You may use known circuits.

2.32 In **prime factorization** an integer n is represented as the product of primes. Let $p(N)$ be the largest prime less than N. Then, $n \in \{2, \ldots, N-1\}$ is represented by the exponents $(e_2, e_3, \ldots, e_{p(N)})$, where $n = 2^{e_2} 3^{e_3} \ldots p(N)^{e_{p(N)}}$. The representation for the product of two integers in this system is the sum of the exponents of their respective prime factors. Show that this leads to a multiplication circuit whose depth is proportional to $\log \log \log N$. Determine the size of the circuit using the fact that there are $O(N/\log N)$ primes in the set $\{2, \ldots, N-1\}$.

2.33 Construct a circuit for the division of two n-bit binary numbers from circuits for the reciprocal function $f_{\text{recip}}^{(n)}$ and the integer multiplication function $f_{\text{mult}}^{(n)}$. Determine the size and depth of this circuit and the accuracy of the result.

2.34 Let $f : \mathcal{B}^n \mapsto \mathcal{B}^n$ be an integer power of $\boldsymbol{x}$; that is, $f(\boldsymbol{x}) = \lceil \boldsymbol{x}^k \rceil$ for some integer k. Show that such functions contain the shifting function $f_{\text{shift}}^{(m)}$ as a subfunction for some integer m. Determine m dependent on n and k.

2.35 Let $f : \mathcal{B}^n \mapsto \mathcal{B}^n$ be a fractional power of $\boldsymbol{x}$ of the form $f(\boldsymbol{x}) = \lceil \boldsymbol{x}^{q/2^k} \rceil$. Show that this function contains the shifting function $f_{\text{shift}}^{(m)}$ as a subfunction. Find the largest value of m for which this holds.

Chapter Notes

Logic circuits have a long history. Early in the nineteenth century Babbage designed mechanical computers capable of logic operations. In the twentieth century logic circuits, called switching circuits, were constructed of electromechanical relays. The earliest formal analysis of logic circuits is attributed to Claude Shannon [302]; he applied Boolean algebra to the analysis of logic circuits, the topic of Section 2.2. Reduction between problems, a technique central to computer science, is encountered whenever one uses an existing program to solve a new problem by pre-processing inputs and post-processing outputs. Reductions also provide a way to identify problems with similar complexity, an idea given great importance by the work of Cook [76], Karp [160], and Levin [199] on **NP**-completeness. (See also [331].) This topic is explored in depth in Chapter 8.

The upper bound on the size of ripple adder described in Section 2.7 cannot be improved, as shown by Red'kin [272] using the gate elimination method of Section 9.3.2. Prefix computations, the subject of Section 2.6, were first used by Ofman [230]. He constructed the adder based on carry-lookahead addition described in Section 2.7. Krapchenko [173] and Brent [59] developed adders with linear size whose depth is $\lceil \log n \rceil + O(\sqrt{\lceil \log n \rceil})$, asymptotically almost as good as the best possible depth bound of $\lceil \log n \rceil$.

Ofman used carry-save addition for fast integer multiplication [230]. Wallace independently discovered carry-save addition and logarithmic depth circuits for addition and multiplication [350]. The divide-and-conquer integer multiplication algorithm of Section 2.9.2 is due to Karatsuba [156]. As mentioned at the end of Section 2.9, Schönhage and Strassen [299] have designed binary integer multipliers of depth $O(\log n)$ whose size is $O(n \log n \log \log n)$.

Sir Isaac Newton around 1665 invented the iterative method bearing his name used in Section 2.10 for binary integer division. Our treatment of this idea follows that given by Tate [321]. Reif and Tate [274] have shown that binary integer division can be done with circuit size $O(n \log n \log \log n)$ and depth $O(\log n \log \log n)$ using circuits whose description is log-space uniform. Beame, Cook, and Hoover [33] have given an $O(\log n)$-depth circuit for the reciprocal function, the best possible depth bound up to a constant multiple, but one whose size is polynomial in n and whose description is not uniform; it requires knowledge of about $n^2 / \log n$ primes.

The key result in Section 2.11 on symmetric functions is due to Muller and Preparata [224]. As indicated, it is the basis for showing that every one-output symmetric function can be realized by a circuit whose size and depth are linear and logarithmic, respectively.

Shannon [303] developed lower bounds for two-terminal switching circuits of the type given in Section 2.12 on circuit size. Muller [222] extended the techniques of Shannon to derive the lower bounds on circuit size given in Theorem 2.12.1. Shannon and Riordan [277] developed a lower bound of $\Omega(2^n/\log n)$ on the size of Boolean formulas, circuits in which the fan-out of each gate is 1. As seen in Chapter 9, such bounds readily translate into lower bounds on depth of the form given Theorem 2.12.2. Gaskov, using the Lupanov representation, has derived a comparable upper bound [111].

The upper bound on circuit size given in Section 2.13 is due to Lupanov [208]. Shannon and Riordan [277] show that a lower bound of $\Omega(2^n/\log n)$ must apply to the formula size (see Definition 9.1.1) of most Boolean functions on n variables. Given the relationship of Theorem 9.2.2 between formula size and depth, a depth lower bound of $n - \log\log n - O(1)$ follows.

Early work on circuits and circuit complexity is surveyed by Paterson [233] and covered in depth by Savage [283]. More recent coverage of this subject is contained in the survey article by Bopanna and Sipser [52] and books by Wegener [354] and Dunne [93].

Machines with Memory

As we saw in Chapter 1, every finite computational task can be realized by a combinational circuit. While this is an important concept, it is not very practical; we cannot afford to design a special circuit for each computational task. Instead we generally perform computational tasks with machines having memory. In a strong sense to be explored in this chapter, the memory of such machines allows them to reuse their equivalent circuits to realize functions of high circuit complexity.

In this chapter we examine the deterministic and nondeterministic finite-state machine (FSM), the random-access machine (RAM), and the Turing machine. The finite-state machine moves from state to state while reading input and producing output. The RAM has a central processing unit (CPU) and a random-access memory with the property that each memory word can be accessed in one unit of time. Its CPU executes instructions, reading and writing data from and to the memory. The Turing machine has a control unit that is a finite-state machine and a tape unit with a head that moves from one tape cell to a neighboring one in each unit of time. The control unit reads from, writes to, and moves the head of the tape unit.

We demonstrate through simulation that the RAM and the Turing machine are universal in the sense that every finite-state machine can be simulated by the RAM and that it and the Turing machine can simulate each other. Since they are equally powerful, either can be used as a reference model of computation.

We also simulate with circuits computations performed by the FSM, RAM, and Turing machine. These circuit simulations establish two important results. First, they show that all computations are constrained by the available resources, such as space and time. For example, if a function f is computed in T steps by the RAM with storage capacity S (in bits), then S and T must satisfy the inequality $C_\Omega(f) = O(ST)$, where $C_\Omega(f)$ is the size of the smallest circuit for f over the complete basis Ω. Any attempt to compute f on the RAM using space S and time T whose product is too small will fail. Second, an $O(\log ST)$-space, $O(ST)$-time program exists to write the descriptions of circuits simulating the above machines. This fact leads to the identification in this chapter of the first examples of **P**-complete and **NP**-complete problems.

3.1 Finite-State Machines

The finite-state machine (FSM) has a set of states, one of which is its initial state. At each unit of time an FSM is given a letter from its input alphabet. This causes the machine to move from its current state to a potentially new state. While in a state, the FSM produces a letter from its output alphabet. Such a machine computes the function defined by the mapping from its initial state and strings of input letters to strings of output letters. FSMs can also be used to accept strings, as discussed in Chapter 4. Some states are called final states. A string is recognized (or accepted) by an FSM if the last state entered by the machine on that input string is a final state. The language recognized (or accepted) by an FSM is the set of strings accepted by it. We now give a formal definition of an FSM.

DEFINITION 3.1.1 *A* **finite-state machine (FSM)** M *is a seven-tuple* $M = (\Sigma, \Psi, Q, \delta, \lambda, s, F)$, *where* Σ *is the* **input alphabet**, Ψ *is the* **output alphabet**, Q *is the* **set of states**, $\delta : Q \times \Sigma \mapsto Q$ *is the* **next-state function**, $\lambda : Q \mapsto \Psi$ *is the* **output function**, s *is the* **initial state** *(which may be fixed or variable), and* F *is the set of* **final states** *($F \subseteq Q$). If the FSM is given input letter a when in state q, it enters state $\delta(q, a)$. While in state q it produces the output letter $\lambda(q)$.*

The FSM M **accepts the string** $w \in \Sigma^*$ *if the last state entered by M on the input string w starting in state s is in the set F. M* **recognizes** *(or* **accepts***)* **the language** L *consisting of the set of such strings.*

When the initial state of the FSM M is not fixed, for each integer T M maps the initial state s and its T external inputs $w_1, w_2, \ldots, w_T$ onto its T external outputs $y_1, y_2, \ldots, y_T$ and the final state $q^{(T)}$. We say that in T steps the FSM M **computes** *the function $f_M^{(T)} : Q \times \Sigma^T \mapsto Q \times \Psi^T$. It is assumed that the sets Σ, Ψ, and Q are encoded in binary so that $f_M^{(T)}$ is a binary function.*

The next-state and output functions of an FSM, δ and λ, can be represented as in Fig. 3.1. We visualize these functions taking a state value from a memory and an input value from an external input and producing next-state and output values. Next-state values are stored in the memory and output values are released to the external world. From this representation an actual machine (a sequential circuit) can be constructed (see Section 3.3). Once circuits are constructed for δ and λ, we need only add memory units and a clock to construct a sequential circuit that emulates an FSM.

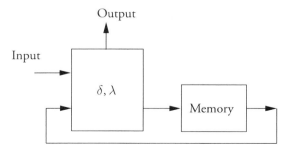

Figure 3.1 The finite-state machine model.

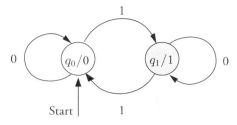

Figure 3.2 A finite-state machine computing the EXCLUSIVE OR of its inputs.

An example of an FSM is shown in Fig. 3.2. Its input and output alphabets and state sets are $\Sigma = \{0, 1\}$, $\Psi = \{0, 1\}$, and $Q = \{q_0, q_1\}$, respectively. Its next-state and output functions, δ and λ, are given below.

q	σ	$\delta(q, \sigma)$		q	$\lambda(q)$
q_0	0	q_0		q_0	0
q_0	1	q_1		q_1	1
q_1	0	q_1			
q_1	1	q_0			

The FSM has initial state q_0 and final state q_1. As a convenience we explicitly identify final states by shading, although in practice they can be associated with states producing a particular output letter.

Each state has a label q_j / v_j, where q_j is the name of the state and v_j is the output produced while in this state. The initial state has an arrow labeled with the word "start" pointing to it. Clearly, the set of strings accepted by this FSM are those containing an odd number of instances of 1. Thus it computes the EXCLUSIVE OR function on an arbitrary number of inputs.

While it is conventional to think of the finite-state machine as a severely restricted computational model, it is actually a very powerful one. The random-access machine (RAM) described in Section 3.4 is an FSM when the number of memory locations that it contains is bounded, as is always so in practice. When a program is first placed in the memory of the RAM, the program sets the initial state of the RAM. The RAM, which may or may not read external inputs or produce external outputs, generally will leave its result in its memory; that is, the result of the computation often determines the final state of the random-access machine.

The FSM defined above is called a **Moore machine** because it was defined by E.F. Moore [221] in 1956. An alternative FSM, the **Mealey machine** (defined by Mealey [214] in 1955), has an output function $\lambda^* : Q \times \Sigma \mapsto \Psi$ that generates an output on each transition from one state to another. This output is determined by both the state in which the machine resides before the state transition and the input letter causing the transition. It can be shown that the two machine models are equivalent (see Problem 3.6): any computation one can do, the other can do also.

3.1.1 Functions Computed by FSMs

We now examine the ways in which an FSM might compute a function. Since our goal is to understand the power and limits of computation, we must be careful not to assume that an FSM can have hidden access to an external computing device. All computing devices must be explicit. It follows that we allow FSMs only to compute functions that receive inputs and produce outputs at data-independent times.

To understand the function computed by an FSM M, observe that in initial state $q^{(0)} = s$ and receiving input letter w_1, M enters state $q^{(1)} = \delta(q^{(0)}, w_1)$ and produces output $y_1 = \delta(q^{(1)})$. If M then receives input w_2, it enters state $q^{(2)} = \delta(q^{(1)}, w_2)$ and produces output $y_2 = \delta(q^{(2)})$. Repeated applications of the functions δ and λ on successive states with successive inputs, as suggested by Fig. 3.3, generate the outputs $y_1, y_2, \ldots, y_T$ and the final state $q^{(T)}$. The function $f_M^{(T)} : Q \times \Sigma^T \mapsto Q \times \Psi^T$ given in Definition 3.1.1 defines this mapping from an initial state and inputs to the final state and outputs:

$$f_M^{(T)}\left(q^{(0)}, w_1, w_2, \ldots, w_T\right) = \left(q^{(T)}, y_1, y_2, \ldots, y_T\right)$$

This simulation of a machine with memory by a circuit illustrates a fundamental point about computation, namely, that the role of memory is to hold intermediate results on which the logical circuitry of the machine can operate in successive cycles.

When an FSM M is used in a T-step computation, it usually does not compute the most general function $f_M^{(T)}$ that it can. Instead, some restrictions are generally placed on the possible initial states, on the values of the external inputs provided to M, and on the components of the final state and output letters used in the computation. Consider three examples of the specialization of an FSM to a particular task. In the first, let the FSM model be that shown in Fig. 3.2 and let it be used to form the EXCLUSIVE OR of n variables. In this case, we supply n bits to the FSM but ignore all but the last output value it produces. In the second example, let the FSM be a programmable machine in which a program is loaded into its memory before the start of a computation, thereby setting its initial state. The program ignores all external inputs and produces no output, leaving the value of the function in memory. In the third example, again let the FSM be programmable, but let the program that resides initially residing in its memory be a "boot program" that treats its inputs as program statements. (Thus, the FSM has a fixed initial state.) The boot program forms a program by loading these statements into successive memory locations. It then jumps to the first location in this program.

In each of these examples, the function f that is actually computed by M in T steps is a subfunction of the function $f_M^{(T)}$ because f is obtained by either restricting the values of

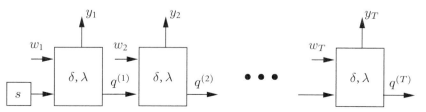

Figure 3.3 A circuit computing the same function, $f_M^{(T)}$, as a finite-state machine M in T steps.

the initial state and inputs to M or deleting outputs or both. We assume that every function computed by M in T steps is a subfunction f of the function $f_M^{(T)}$.

The simple construction of Fig. 3.3 is the first step in deriving a space-time product inequality for the random-access machine in Section 3.5 and in establishing a connection between Turing time and circuit complexity in Section 3.9.2. It is also involved in the definition of the **P**-complete and **NP**-complete problems in Section 3.9.4.

3.1.2   Computational Inequalities for the FSM

In this book we model each computational task by a function that, we assume without loss of generality, is binary. We also assume that the function $f_M^{(T)} : Q \times \Sigma^T \mapsto Q \times \Psi^T$ computed in T steps by an FSM M is binary. In particular, we assume that the next-state and output functions, δ and λ, are also binary; that is, we assume that their input, state, and output alphabets are encoded in binary. We now derive some consequences of the fact that a computation by an FSM can be simulated by a circuit.

The size $C_\Omega \left(f_M^{(T)} \right)$ of the smallest circuit to compute the function $f_M^{(T)}$ is no larger than the size of the circuit shown in Fig. 3.3. But this circuit has size $T \cdot C_\Omega(\delta, \lambda)$, where $C_\Omega(\delta, \lambda)$ is the size of the smallest circuit to compute the functions δ and λ. The depth of the shallowest circuit for $f_M^{(T)}$ is no more than $T \cdot D_\Omega(\delta, \lambda)$ because the longest path through the circuit of Fig. 3.3 has this length.

Let f be the function computed by M in T steps. Since it is a subfunction of $f_M^{(T)}$, it follows from Lemma 2.4.1 that the size of the smallest circuit for f is no smaller than the size of the circuit for $f_M^{(T)}$. Similarly, the depth of f, $D_\Omega(f)$, is no more than that of $f_M^{(T)}$. Combining the observations of this paragraph with those of the preceding paragraph yields the following computational inequalities. A **computational inequality** is an inequality relating parameters of computation, such as time and the circuit size and depth of the next-state and output function, to the size or depth of the smallest circuit for the function being computed.

THEOREM 3.1.1 Let $f_M^{(T)}$ be the function computed by the FSM $M = (\Sigma, \Psi, Q, \delta, \lambda, s, F)$ in T steps, where δ and λ are the binary next-state and output functions of M. The circuit size and depth over the basis Ω of any function f computed by M in T steps satisfy the following inequalities:

$$
\begin{aligned}
C_\Omega(f) &\le C_\Omega \left(f_M^{(T)} \right) &\le TC_\Omega(\delta, \lambda) \\
D_\Omega(f) &\le C_\Omega \left(f_M^{(T)} \right) &\le TD_\Omega(\delta, \lambda)
\end{aligned}
$$

The circuit size $C_\Omega(\delta, \lambda)$ and depth $D_\Omega(\delta, \lambda)$ of the next-state and output functions of an FSM M are measures of its complexity, that is, of how useful they are in computing functions. The above theorem, which says nothing about the actual technologies used to realize M, relates these two measures of the complexity of M to the complexities of the function f being computed. This is a theorem about computational complexity, not technology.

These inequalities stipulate constraints that must hold between the time T and the circuit size and depth of the machine M if it is used to compute the function f in T steps. Let the product $TC_\Omega(\delta, \lambda)$ be defined as the **equivalent number of logic operations performed by** M. The first inequality of the above theorem can be interpreted as saying that the number of equivalent logic operations performed by an FSM to compute a function f must be at least the minimum number of gates necessary to compute f with a circuit. A similar interpretation can be given to the second inequality involving circuit depth.

The first inequality of Theorem 3.1.1 and the interpretation given to $T \cdot C_\Omega(\delta, \lambda)$ justify the following definitions of computational work and power. Here power is interpreted as the time rate at which work is done. These measures correlate nicely with our intuition that machines that contain more equivalent computing elements are more powerful.

DEFINITION 3.1.2 *The **computational work** done by an FSM $M = (\Sigma, \Psi, Q, \delta, \lambda, s, F)$ is $TC_\Omega(\delta, \lambda)$, the number of equivalent logical operations performed by M, which is the product of T, the number of steps executed by M, and $C_\Omega(\delta, \lambda)$, the size complexity of its next-state and output functions. The **power** of an FSM M is $C_\Omega(\delta, \lambda)$, the number of logical operations performed by M per step.*

Theorem 3.1.1 is also a form of **impossibility theorem**: it is impossible to compute functions f for which $TC_\Omega(\delta, \lambda)$ and $TD_\Omega(\delta, \lambda)$ are respectively less than the size and depth complexity of f. It may be possible to compute a function on some points of its domain with smaller values of these parameters, but not on all points. The halting problem, another example of an impossibility theorem, is presented in Section 5.8.2. However, it deals with the computation of functions over infinite domains.

The inequalities of Theorem 3.1.1 also place upper limits on the size and depth complexities of functions that can be computed in a bounded number of steps by an FSM, regardless of how the FSM performs the computation.

Note that there is no guarantee that the upper bounds stated in Theorem 3.1.1 are at all close to the lower bounds. It is always possible to compute a function inefficiently, that is, with resources that are greater than the minimal resources necessary.

3.1.3 Circuits Are Universal for Bounded FSM Computations

We now ask whether the classes of functions computed by circuits and by FSMs executing a bounded number of steps are different. We show that they are the same. Many different functions can be computed from the function $f_M^{(T)}$ by specializing inputs and/or deleting outputs.

THEOREM 3.1.2 *Every subfunction of the function $f_M^{(T)}$ computable by an FSM on n inputs is computable by a Boolean circuit and vice versa.*

Proof A Boolean function on n inputs, f, may be computed by an FSM with $2^{n+1} - 1$ states by branching from the current state to one of two different states on inputs 0 and 1 until all n inputs have been read; it then produces the output that would be produced by f on these n inputs. A fifteen-state version of this machine that computes the EXCLUSIVE OR on three inputs as a subfunction is shown in Fig. 3.4.

The inequalities of Theorem 3.1.1 also place upper limits The proof in the other direction is also straightforward, as described above and represented schematically in Fig. 3.3. Given a binary representation of the input, output, and state symbols of an FSM, their associated next-state and output functions are binary functions. They can be realized by circuits, as can $f_M^{(n)}(s, \boldsymbol{w}) = (q^{(n)}, \boldsymbol{y})$, the function computed by the FSM on n inputs, as suggested by Fig. 3.3. Finally, the subfunction f is obtained by fixing the appropriate inputs, assigning variable names to the remaining inputs, and deleting the appropriate outputs. ■

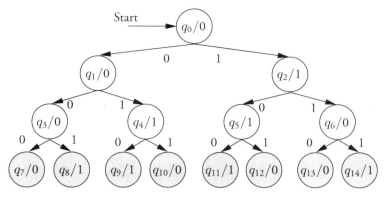

Figure 3.4 A fifteen-state FSM that computes the EXCLUSIVE OR of three inputs as a subfunction of $f_M^{(3)}$ obtained by deleting all outputs except the third.

3.1.4 Interconnections of Finite-State Machines

Later in this chapter we examine a family of FSMs characterized by a computational unit connected to storage devices of increasing size. The random-access machine that has a CPU of small complexity and a random-access memory of large but indeterminate size is of this type. The Turing machine having a fixed control unit that moves a tape head over a potentially infinite tape is another example.

This idea is captured by the **interconnection of synchronous FSMs**. Synchronous FSMs read inputs, advance from state to state, and produce outputs in synchronism. We allow two or more synchronous FSMs to be interconnected so that some outputs from one FSM are supplied as inputs of another, as illustrated in Fig. 3.5. Below we generalize Theorem 3.1.1 to a pair of synchronous FSMs. We model random-access machines and Turing machines in this fashion when each uses a finite amount of storage.

THEOREM 3.1.3 *Let $f_{M_1 \times M_2}^{(T)}$ be a function computed in T steps by a pair of interconnected synchronous FSMs, $M_1 = (\Sigma_1, \Psi_1, Q_1, \delta_1, \lambda_1, s_1, F_1)$ and $M_2 = (\Sigma_2, \Psi_2, Q_2, \delta_2, \lambda_2, s_2, F_2)$.*

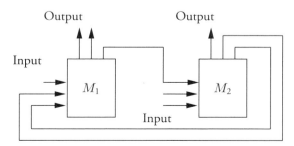

Figure 3.5 The interconnection of two finite-state machines in which one of the three outputs of M_1 is supplied as an input to M_2 and two of the three outputs of M_2 are supplied to M_1 as inputs.

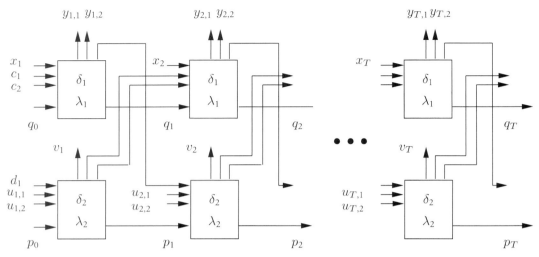

Figure 3.6 A circuit simulating T steps of the two synchronous interconnected FSMs shown in Fig. 3.5. The top row of circuits simulates a T-step computation by M_1 and the bottom row simulates a T-step computation by M_2. One of the three outputs of M_1 is supplied as an input to M_2 and two of the three outputs of M_2 are supplied to M_1 as inputs. The states of M_1 on the initial and T successive steps are $q_0, q_1, \ldots, q_T$. Those of M_2 are $p_0, p_1, \ldots, p_T$.

Let δ_1, λ_1, δ_2, and λ_2 be the size and depth of encodings of the next-state and output functions. Then, the circuit size and depth over the basis Ω of any function f computed by the pair $M_1 \times M_2$ in T steps (that is, a subfunction of $f_{M_1 \times M_2}^{(T)}$) satisfy the following inequalities:

$$C_\Omega(f) \le T[C_\Omega(\delta_1, \lambda_1) + C_\Omega(\delta_2, \lambda_2)]$$
$$D_\Omega(f) \le T[\max(D_\Omega(\delta_1, \lambda_1), D_\Omega(\delta_2, \lambda_2))]$$

Proof The construction that leads to this result is suggested by Fig. 3.6. We unwind both FSMs and connect the appropriate outputs from one to the other to produce a circuit that computes $f_{M_1 \times M_2}^{(T)}$. Observe that the number of gates in the simulated circuit is T times the sum of the number of gates, whereas the depth is T times the depth of the deeper circuit. ∎

3.1.5 Nondeterministic Finite-State Machines

The finite-state machine model described above is called a **deterministic FSM** (DFSM) because, given a current state and an input, the next state of the FSM is uniquely determined. A potentially more general FSM model is the **nondeterministic** FSM (NFSM) characterized by the possibility that several next states can be reached from the current state for some given input letter.

One might ask if such a model has any use, especially since to the untrained eye a non-deterministic machine would appear to be a dysfunctional deterministic one. The value of an NFSM is that it may recognize languages with fewer states and in less time than needed by a DFSM. The concept of nondeterminism will be extended later to the Turing machine, where it is used to classify languages in terms of the time and space they need for recognition. For example, it will be used to identify the class **NP** of languages that are recognized by nondeterministic Turing machines in a number of steps that is polynomial in the length of their inputs. (See Section 3.9.6.) Many important combinatorial problems, such as the traveling salesperson problem, fall into this class.

The formal definition of the NFSM is given in Section 4.1, where the next-state function $\delta : Q \times \Sigma \mapsto Q$ of the FSM is replaced by a next-state function $\delta : Q \times \Sigma \mapsto 2^Q$. Such functions assign to each state q and input letter a a subset $\delta(q, a)$ of the set Q of states of the NFSM (2^Q, the power set, is the set of all subsets of Q. It is introduced in Section 1.2.1.) Since the value of $\delta(q, a)$ can be the empty set, there may be no successor to the state q on input a. Also, since $\delta(q, a)$ when viewed as a set can contain more than one element, a state q can have edges labeled a to several other states. Since a DFSM has a single successor to each state on every input, a DFSM is an NFSM in which $\delta(q, a)$ is a singleton set.

While a DFSM M accepts a string w if w causes M to move from the initial state to a final state in F, an NFSM accepts w if there is some set of next-state choices for w that causes M to move from the initial state to a final state in F.

An NFSM can be viewed as a purely deterministic finite-state machine that has two inputs, as suggested in Fig. 3.7. The first, the **standard input**, accepts the user's data. The second, the **choice input**, is used to choose a successor state when there is more than one. The information provided via the choice input is not under the control of the user supplying data via the standard input. As a consequence, the machine is nondeterministic from the point of view of the user but fully deterministic to an outside observer. It is assumed that the **choice agent** supplies the choice input and, with full knowledge of the input to be provided by the user, chooses state transitions that, if possible, lead to acceptance of the user input. On the other hand, the choice agent cannot force the machine to accept inputs for which it is not designed.

In an NFSM it is not required that a state q have a successor for each value of the standard and choice inputs. This possibility is captured by allowing $\delta(q, a)$ to have no value, denoted $\perp$.

Figure 3.8 shows an NFSM that recognizes strings over $\mathcal{B}^*$ that end in 00101. In this figure parentheses surround the choice input when its value is needed to decide the next state. In this machine the choice input is set to 1 when the choice agent knows that the user is about to supply the suffix 00101.

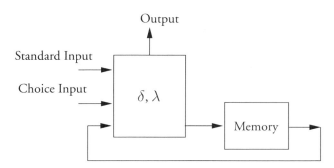

Figure 3.7 A nondeterministic finite-state machine modeled as a deterministic one that has a second choice input whose value disambiguates the value of the next state.

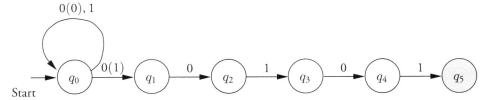

Figure 3.8 A nondeterministic FSM that accepts binary strings ending in 00101. Choice inputs are shown in parentheses for those user inputs for which the value of choice inputs can disambiguate next-state moves.

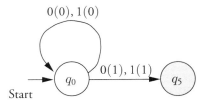

Figure 3.9 An example of an NFSM whose choice agent (its values are in parentheses) accpets not only strings in a language L, but all strings.

Although we use the anthropomorphic phrase "choice agent," it is important to note that this choice agent cannot freely decide which strings to accept and which not. Instead, it must when possible make choices leading to acceptance. Consider, for example, the machine in Fig. 3.9. It would appear that its choice agent can accept strings in an arbitrary language L. In fact, the language that it accepts contains all strings.

Given a string w in the language L accepted by an NFSM, a choice string that leads to its acceptance is said to be a **succinct certificate** for its membership in L.

It is important to note that the nondeterministic finite-state machine is not a model of reality, but is used instead primarily to classify languages. In Section 4.1 we explore the language-recognition capability of the deterministic and nondeterministic finite-state machines and show that they are the same. However, the situation is not so clear with regard to Turing machines that have access to unlimited storage capacity. In this case, we do not know whether or not the set of languages accepted in polynomial time on deterministic Turing machines (the class **P**) is the same set of languages that is accepted in polynomial time by nondeterministic Turing machines (the class **NP**).

3.2 Simulating FSMs with Shallow Circuits*

In Section 3.1 we demonstrated that every T-step FSM computation can be simulated by a circuit whose size and depth are both $O(T)$. In this section we show that every T-step finite-state machine computation can be simulated by a circuit whose size and depth are $O(T)$ and $O(\log T)$, respectively. While this seems a serious improvement in the depth bound, the coefficients hidden in the big-O notation for both bounds depend on the number of states of the FSM and can be very large. Nevertheless, for simple problems, such as binary addition, the

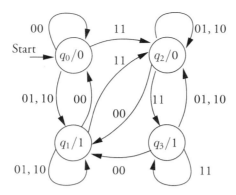

Figure 3.10 A finite-state machine that adds two binary numbers. Their two least significant bits are supplied first followed by those of increasing significance. The output bits represent the sum of the two numbers.

results of this section can be useful. We illustrate this here for binary addition by exhibiting small and shallow circuits for the adder FSM of Fig. 3.10. The circuit simulation for this FSM produces the carry-lookahead adder circuit of Section 2.7. In this section we use matrix multiplication, which is covered in Chapter 6.

The new method is based on the representation of the function $f_M^{(T)} : Q \times \Sigma^T \mapsto Q \times \Psi^T$ computed in T steps by an FSM $M = (\Sigma, \Psi, Q, \delta, \lambda, s, F)$ in terms of the set of **state-to-state mappings** $S = \{\Delta_x : Q \mapsto Q \mid x \in \Sigma\}$, where Δ_x is the following mapping associated with the input letter x for $q \in Q$:

$$\Delta_x(q) = \delta(q, x) \tag{3.1}$$

That is, $\Delta_x(q)$ is the state to which state q is carried by the input letter x.

The FSM shown in Fig. 3.10 adds two binary numbers sequentially by simulating a ripple adder. (See Section 2.7.) Its input alphabet is $\mathcal{B}^2$, that is, the set of pairs of 0's and 1's. Its output alphabet is $\mathcal{B}$ and its state set is $Q = \{q_0, q_1, q_2, q_3\}$. (A sequential circuit for this machine is designed in Section 3.1.) It has the state-to-state mappings shown in Fig. 3.11.

Let $\odot : S^2 \mapsto S$ be the function defined on the set $S = \{\Delta_x : Q \mapsto Q \mid x \in \Sigma\}$ of state-to-state mappings where for arbitrary $x, y \in \Sigma$ and state $q \in Q$ the operator $\odot$ is defined

q	$\Delta_{0,0}(q)$	q	$\Delta_{0,1}(q)$	q	$\Delta_{1,0}(q)$	q	$\Delta_{1,1}(q)$
q_0	q_0	q_0	q_1	q_0	q_1	q_0	q_2
q_1	q_0	q_1	q_1	q_1	q_1	q_1	q_2
q_2	q_1	q_2	q_2	q_2	q_2	q_2	q_3
q_3	q_1	q_3	q_2	q_3	q_2	q_3	q_3

Figure 3.11 The state-to-state mappings associated with the FSM of Fig. 3.10.

as follows:

$$(\Delta_x \odot \Delta_y)(q) = \Delta_x(\Delta_y(q)) \tag{3.2}$$

Below we show that the operator $\odot$ is **associative**, that is, $\odot$ satisfies the property $(\Delta_{w_1} \odot \Delta_{w_2}) \odot \Delta_{w_3} = \Delta_{w_1} \odot (\Delta_{w_2} \odot \Delta_{w_3})$. This means that for each $q \in Q$, $((\Delta_{w_1} \odot \Delta_{w_2}) \odot \Delta_{w_3})(q) = (\Delta_{w_1} \odot (\Delta_{w_2} \odot \Delta_{w_3}))(q)$. Applying the definition of $\odot$ in Equation (3.2), we have the following for each $q \in Q$:

$$
\begin{aligned}
((\Delta_x \odot \Delta_y) \odot \Delta_z)(q) &= \Delta_z((\Delta_x \odot \Delta_y)(q)) \\
&= \Delta_z(\Delta_y(\Delta_x(q))) \\
&= (\Delta_y \odot \Delta_z)(\Delta_x(q)) \\
&= (\Delta_x \odot (\Delta_y \odot \Delta_z))(q)
\end{aligned}
\tag{3.3}
$$

Thus, $\odot$ is associative and $(S, \odot)$ is a semigroup. (See Section 2.6.) It follows that a prefix computation can be done on a sequence of state-to-state mappings.

We now use this observation to construct a shallow circuit for the function $f_M^{(T)}$. Let $\boldsymbol{w} = (w_1, w_2, \ldots, w_T)$ be a sequence of T inputs to M where w_j is supplied on the jth step. Let $q^{(j)}$ be the state of M after receiving the jth input. From the definition of $\odot$ it follows that $q^{(j)}$ has the following value where s is the initial state of M:

$$q^{(j)} = (\Delta_{w_1} \odot \Delta_{w_2} \odot \cdots \odot \Delta_{w_j})(s)$$

The value of $f_M^{(T)}$ on initial state s and T inputs can be represented in terms of $\boldsymbol{q} = (q^{(1)}, \ldots, q^{(T)})$ as follows:

$$f_M^{(T)}(s, \boldsymbol{w}) = \left(q^{(n)}, \lambda(q^{(1)}), \lambda(q^{(2)}), \ldots, \lambda(q^{(T)}) \right)$$

Let $\boldsymbol{\Lambda}^{(T)}$ be the following sequence of state-to-state mappings:

$$\boldsymbol{\Lambda}^{(T)} = (\Delta_{w_1}, \Delta_{w_2}, \ldots, \Delta_{w_T})$$

It follows that $\boldsymbol{q}$ can be obtained by computing the state-to-state mappings $\Delta_{w_1} \odot \Delta_{w_2} \odot \cdots \odot \Delta_{w_j}$, $1 \leq j \leq T$, and applying them to the initial state s. Because $\odot$ is associative, these T state-to-state mappings are produced by the prefix operator $\mathcal{P}_\odot^{(T)}$ on the sequence $\boldsymbol{\Lambda}^{(T)}$ (see Theorem 2.6.1):

$$\mathcal{P}_\odot^{(T)}(\boldsymbol{\Lambda}^{(T)}) = (\Delta_{w_1}, (\Delta_{w_1} \odot \Delta_{w_2}), \ldots, (\Delta_{w_1} \odot \Delta_{w_2} \odot \ldots \odot \Delta_{w_T}))$$

Restating Theorem 2.6.1 for this problem, we have the following result.

THEOREM 3.2.1 *For $T = 2^k$, k an integer, the T state-to-state mappings defined by the T inputs to an FSM M can be computed by a circuit over the basis $\Omega = \{\odot\}$ whose size and depth satisfy the following bounds:*

$$C_\Omega\left(\mathcal{P}_\odot^{(T)}\right) \leq 2T - \log_2 T - 3$$

$$D_\Omega\left(\mathcal{P}_\odot^{(T)}\right) \leq 2\log_2 T - 2$$

The construction of a shallow Boolean circuit for $f_M^{(T)}$ is reduced to a five-step problem: 1) for each input letter x design a circuit whose input and output are representations of states and which defines the state-to-state mapping Δ_x for input letter x; 2) construct a circuit for the associative operator $\odot$ that accepts the representations of two state-to-state mappings Δ_y and Δ_z and produces a representation for the state-to-state mapping $\Delta_y \odot \Delta_z$; 3) use the circuit for $\odot$ in a parallel prefix circuit to produce the T state-to-state mappings; 4) construct a circuit that combines the representation of the initial state s with that of the state-to-state mapping $\Delta_{w_1} \odot \Delta_{w_2} \odot \cdots \odot \Delta_{w_j}$ to obtain a representation for the successor state $\Delta_{w_1} \odot \Delta_{w_2} \odot \cdots \odot \Delta_{w_j}(s)$; and 5) construct a circuit for λ that computes an output from the representation of a state.

We now describe a generic, though not necessarily efficient, implementation of these steps.

Let $Q = \{q_0, q_1, \ldots, q_{|Q|-1}\}$ be the states of M. The state-to-state mapping Δ_x for the FSM M needed for the first step can be represented by a $|Q| \times |Q|$ Boolean matrix $N(x) = \{n_{ij}(x)\}$ in which the entry in row i and column j, $n_{ij}(x)$, satisfies

$$n_{i,j}(x) = \begin{cases} 1 & \text{if } M \text{ moves from state } q_i \text{ to state } q_j \text{ on input } x \\ 0 & \text{otherwise} \end{cases}$$

Consider again the FSM shown in Fig. 3.10. The matrices associated with its four pairs of inputs $x \in \{(0,0), (0,1), (1,0), (1,1)\}$ are shown below, where $N((0,1)) = N((1,0))$:

$$N((0,0)) = \begin{bmatrix} 1 & 0 & 0 & 0 \\ 1 & 0 & 0 & 0 \\ 0 & 1 & 0 & 0 \\ 0 & 1 & 0 & 0 \end{bmatrix} \qquad N((0,1)) = \begin{bmatrix} 0 & 1 & 0 & 0 \\ 0 & 1 & 0 & 0 \\ 0 & 0 & 1 & 0 \\ 0 & 0 & 1 & 0 \end{bmatrix}$$

$$N((1,1)) = \begin{bmatrix} 0 & 0 & 1 & 0 \\ 0 & 0 & 1 & 0 \\ 0 & 0 & 0 & 1 \\ 0 & 0 & 0 & 1 \end{bmatrix}$$

From these matrices the generic matrix $N((u, v))$ parameterized by the values of the inputs (a pair (u, v) in this example) is produced from the following Boolean functions: $t = \overline{u} \wedge \overline{v}$, the **carry-terminate function**, $p = u \oplus v$, the **carry-propagate function**, and $g = u \wedge v$, the **carry-generate function**.

$$N((u, v)) = \begin{bmatrix} t & p & g & 0 \\ t & p & g & 0 \\ 0 & t & p & g \\ 0 & t & p & g \end{bmatrix}$$

Let $\sigma(i) = (0, 0, \ldots, 0, 1, 0, \ldots 0)$ be the unit $|Q|$-vector that has value 1 in the ith position and zeros elsewhere. Let $\sigma(i)N(x)$ denote Boolean vector-matrix multiplication in which addition is OR and multiplication is AND. Then, for each w, $\sigma(i)N(x) = (n_{i,1}, n_{i,2}, \ldots, n_{i,|Q|})$ is the unit vector denoting the state that M enters when it is in state q_i and receives input x.

Let $N(x, y) = N(x) \times N(y)$ be the Boolean matrix-matrix multiplication of matrices $N(x)$ and $N(y)$ in which addition is OR and multiplication is AND. Then, for each x and y the entry in row i and column j of $N(x) \times N(y)$, namely $n_{i,j}^{(2)}(x, y)$, satisfies the following identity:

$$n_{i,j}^{(2)}(x, y) = \bigvee_{q_t \in Q} n_{i,t}(x) \cdot n_{t,j}(y)$$

That is, $n_{i,j}^{(2)}(x, y) = 1$ if there is a state $q_t \in Q$ such that in state q_i, M is given input x, moves to state q_t, and then moves to state q_j on input y. Thus, the composition operator $\odot$ can be realized through the multiplication of Boolean matrices. It is straightforward to show that matrix multiplication is associative. (See Problem 3.10.)

Since matrix multiplication is associative, a prefix computation using matrix multiplication as a composition operator for each prefix $\boldsymbol{x}^{(j)} = (x_1, x_2, \ldots, x_j)$ of the input string $\boldsymbol{x}$ generates a matrix $N(\boldsymbol{x}^{(j)}) = N(x_1) \times N(x_2) \times \cdots \times N(x_j)$ defining the state-to-state mapping associated with $\boldsymbol{x}^{(j)}$ for each value of $1 \leq j \leq n$.

The fourth step, the application of a sequence of state-to-state mappings to the initial state $s = q_r$, represented by the $|Q|$-vector $\sigma(r)$, is obtained through the vector-matrix multiplication $\sigma(r)N(\boldsymbol{x}^{(j)})$ for $1 \leq j \leq n$.

The fifth step involves the computation of the output word from the current state. Let the column $|Q|$-vector $\boldsymbol{\lambda}$ contain in the tth position the output of the FSM M when in state q_t. Then, the output produced by the FSM after the jth input is the product $\sigma(r)N(\boldsymbol{x}^{(j)})\boldsymbol{\lambda}$. This result is summarized below.

THEOREM 3.2.2 *Let the finite-state machine $M = (\Sigma, \Psi, Q, \delta, \lambda, s, F)$ with $|Q|$ states compute a subfunction f of $f_M^{(T)}$ in T steps. Then f has the following size and depth bounds over the standard basis Ω_0 for some $\kappa \geq 1$:*

$$C_{\Omega_0}(f) = O\left(M_{\mathrm{matrix}}(|Q|, \kappa)T\right)$$
$$D_{\Omega_0}(f) = O\left((\kappa \log |Q|)(\log T)\right)$$

Here $M_{\mathrm{matrix}}(n, \kappa)$ is the size of a circuit to multiply two $n \times n$ matrices with a circuit of depth $\kappa \log n$. These bounds can be achieved simultaneously.

Proof The circuits realizing the Boolean functions $\{n_{i,j}(x) \mid 1 \leq i, j \leq |Q|\}$, x an input, each have a size determined by the size of the input alphabet Σ, which is constant. The number of operations required to multiply two Boolean matrices with a circuit of depth $\kappa \log |Q|$, $\kappa \geq 1$, is $M_{\mathrm{matrix}}(|Q|, \kappa)$. (See Section 6.3. Note that $M_{\mathrm{matrix}}(|Q|, \kappa) \leq |Q|^3$.) Finally, the prefix circuit uses $O(T)$ copies of the matrix multiplication circuit and has a depth of $O(\log T)$ copies of the matrix multiplication circuit along the longest path. (See Section 2.6.) ∎

When an FSM has a large number of states but its next-state function is relatively simple, that is, it has a size that is at worst a polynomial in $\log |Q|$, the above size bound will be much larger than the size bound given in Theorem 3.1.1 because $M_{\mathrm{matrix}}(n, \kappa)$ grows exponentially in $\log |Q|$. The depth bound grows linearly with $\log |Q|$ whereas the depth of the next-state function on which the depth bound of Theorem 3.1.1 depends will typically grow either linearly or as a small polynomial in $\log \log |Q|$ for an FSM with a relatively simple next-state function. Thus, the depth bound will be smaller than that of Theorem 3.1.1 for very large values of T, but for smaller values, the latter bound will dominate.

3.2.1 A Shallow Circuit Simulating Addition

Applying the above result to the adder FSM of Fig. 3.10, we produce a circuit that accepts T pairs of binary inputs and computes the sum as T-bit binary numbers. Since this FSM has four states, the theorem states that the circuit has size $O(T)$ and depth $O(\log T)$. The carry-lookahead adder of Section 2.7 has these characteristics.

We can actually produce the carry-lookahead circuit by a more careful design of the state-to-state mappings. We use the following encodings for states, where states are represented by pairs $\{(c, s)\}$.

State Encoding

q	c	s
q_0	0	0
q_1	0	1
q_2	1	0
q_3	1	1

Since the next-state mappings are the same for inputs $0, 1$, and $1, 0$, we encode an input pair (u, v) by (g, p), where $g = u \wedge v$ and $p = u \oplus v$ are the carry-generate and carry-propagate variables introduced in Section 2.7 and used above. With these encodings, the three different next-state mappings $\{\Delta_{0,0}, \Delta_{0,1}, \Delta_{1,1}\}$ defined in Fig. 3.11 can be encoded as shown in the table below. The entry at the intersection of row (c, s) and column (p, g) in this table is the value (c^*, s^*) of the generic next-state function $(c^*, s^*) = \Delta_{p,g}(c, s)$. (Here we abuse notation slightly to let $\Delta_{p,g}$ denote the state-to-state mapping associated with the pair (u, v) and represent the state q of M by the pair (c, s).)

	g		0		0		1	
	p		0		1		0	
c	s		c^*	s^*	c^*	s^*	c^*	s^*
0	0		0	0	0	1	1	0
0	1		0	0	0	1	1	0
1	0		0	1	1	0	1	1
1	1		0	1	1	0	1	1

Inspection of this table shows that we can write the following formulas for c^* and s^*:

$$c^* = (p \wedge c) \vee g, \quad s^* = p \oplus c$$

Consider two successive input pairs (u_1, v_1) and (u_2, v_2) and associated pairs (p_1, g_1) and (p_2, g_2). If the FSM of Fig. 3.10 is in state (c_0, s_0) and receives input (u_1, v_1), it enters the state $(c_1, s_1) = (p_1 \wedge c_0 \vee g_1, p_1 \oplus c_0)$. This new state can be obtained by combining p_1 and g_1 with c_0. Let (c_2, s_2) be the successor state when the mapping Δ_{p_2,g_2} is applied to (c_1, s_1). The effect of the operator $\odot$ on successive state-to-state mappings Δ_{p_1,g_1} and Δ_{p_2,g_2} is shown below, in which (3.2) is used:

$$(\Delta_{p_1,g_1} \odot \Delta_{p_2,g_2})(q) = \Delta_{p_2,g_2}(\Delta_{p_1,g_1}((c_0, s_0)))$$
$$= \Delta_{p_2,g_2}(p_1 \wedge c_0 \vee g_1, p_1 \oplus c_0)$$

$$= (p_2 \wedge (p_1 \wedge c_0 \vee g_1) \vee g_2, p_2 \oplus (p_1 \wedge c_0 \vee g_1))$$
$$= ((p_2 \wedge p_1) \wedge c_0 \vee (g_2 \vee p_2 \wedge g_1)), p_2 \oplus (p_1 \wedge c_0 \vee g_1))$$
$$= (c_2, s_2)$$

It follows that c_2 can be computed from $p^* = p_2 \wedge p_1$ and $g^* = g_2 \vee p_2 \wedge g_1$ and c_0. The value of s_2 is obtained from p_2 and c_1. Thus the mapping $\Delta_{p_1,g_1} \odot \Delta_{p_2,g_2}$ is defined by p^* and g^*, quantities obtained by combining the pairs (p_1, g_1) and (p_2, g_2) using the same associative operator $\diamond$ defined for the carry-lookahead adder in Section 2.7.1.

To summarize, the state-to-state mappings corresponding to subsequences of an input string $((u_0, v_0), (u_1, v_1), \dots, (u_{n-2}, v_{n-2}), (u_{n-1}, v_{n-1}))$ can be computed by representing this string by the carry-propagate, carry-generate string $((p_0, g_0), (p_1, g_1), \dots, (p_{n-2}, g_{n-2}), (p_{n-1}, g_{n-1}))$, computing the prefix operation on this string using the operator $\diamond$, then computing c_i from c_0 and the carry-propagate and carry-generate functions for the ith stage and s_i from this carry-propagate function and c_{i-1}. This leads to the carry-lookahead adder circuit of Section 2.7.1.

3.3 Designing Sequential Circuits

Sequential circuits are concrete machines constructed of gates and binary memory devices. Given an FSM, a sequential machine can be constructed for it, as we show.

A **sequential circuit** is constructed from a logic circuit and a collection of clocked binary memory units, as suggested in Figs. 3.12(a) and 3.15. (Shown in Fig. 3.12(a) is a simple sequential circuit that computes the EXCLUSIVE OR of the initial value in memory and the external input to the sequential circuit.) Inputs to the logic circuit consist of outputs from the binary memory units as well as external inputs. The outputs of the logic circuit serve as inputs to the clocked binary memory units as well as external outputs.

A clocked binary memory unit is driven by a **clock**, a periodic signal that has value 1 (it is **high**) during short, uniformly spaced time intervals and is otherwise 0 (it is **low**), as suggested in Figs. 3.12(b). For correct operation it is assumed that the input to a memory unit does not change when the clock is high. Thus, the outputs of a logic circuit feeding the memory units cannot change during these intervals. This in turn requires that all changes in the inputs to

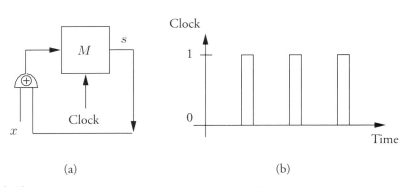

(a)   (b)

Figure 3.12 (a) A sequential circuit with one gate and one clocked memory unit computing the EXCLUSIVE OR of its inputs; (b) a periodic clock pattern.

this circuit be fully propagated to its outputs in the intervals when the clock is low. A circuit that operates this way is considered **safe**. Designers of sequential circuits calculate the time for signals to pass through a logic circuit and set the interval between clock pulses to insure that the operation of the sequential circuit is safe.

Sequential circuits are designed from finite-state machines (FSMs) in a series of steps. Consider an FSM $M = (\Sigma, \Psi, Q, \delta, \lambda, s)$ with input alphabet Σ, output alphabet Ψ, state set Q, next-state function $\delta : Q \times \Sigma \mapsto Q$, output function $\lambda : Q \mapsto \Psi$, and initial state s. (For this discussion we ignore the set of final states; they are important only when discussing language recognition.) We illustrate the design of a sequential machine using the FSM of Fig. 3.10, which is repeated in Fig. 3.13.

The first step in producing a sequential circuit from an FSM is to assign unique binary tuples to each input letter, output letter, and state (the state-assignment problem). This is illustrated for our FSM by the tables of Fig. 3.14 in which the identity encoding is used on inputs and outputs. This step can have a large impact on the size of the logic circuit produced. Second, tables for $\delta : B^4 \mapsto B^2$ and $\lambda : B^2 \mapsto B$, the next-state and output functions of the FSM, respectively, are produced from the description of the FSM, as shown in the same figure. Here c^* and s^* represent the successor to the state (c, s). Third, circuits are designed that realize the binary functions associated with c^* and s^*. Fourth and finally, these circuits are connected to clocked binary memory devices, as shown in Fig. 3.15, to produce a sequential circuit that realizes the FSM. We leave to the reader the task of demonstrating that these circuits compute the functions defined by the tables. (See Problem 3.11.)

Since gates and clocked memory devices can be constructed from semiconductor materials, a sequential circuit can be assembled from physical components by someone skilled in the use of this technology. We design sequential circuits in this book to obtain upper bounds on the size and depth of the next-state and output functions of a sequential machine so that we can derive computational inequalities.

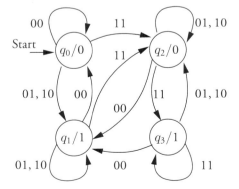

Figure 3.13 A finite-state machine that simulates the ripple adder of Fig. 2.14. It is in state q_r if the carry-and-sum pair (c_{j+1}, s_j) generated by the jth full adder of the ripple adder represents the integer r, $0 \leq r \leq 3$. The output produced is the sum bit.

Input Encoding				Output Encoding		State Encoding		
$\sigma \in \Sigma$		u	v	$\lambda(q) \in \Psi$	$\lambda(q)$	q	c	s
0	0	0	0	0	0	q_0	0	0
0	1	0	1	1	1	q_1	0	1
1	0	1	0			q_2	1	0
1	1	1	1			q_3	1	1

$\delta : B^4 \mapsto B^2$						$\lambda : B^2 \mapsto B$		
c	s	u	v	c^*	s^*	c^*	s^*	s
0	0	0	0	0	0	0	0	0
0	1	0	0	0	0	0	1	1
1	0	0	0	0	1	1	0	0
1	1	0	0	0	1	1	1	1
0	0	0	1	0	1			
0	1	0	1	0	1			
1	0	0	1	1	0			
1	1	0	1	1	0			
0	0	1	0	0	1			
0	1	1	0	0	1			
1	0	1	0	1	0			
1	1	1	0	1	0			
0	0	1	1	1	0			
0	1	1	1	1	0			
1	0	1	1	1	1			
1	1	1	1	1	1			

Figure 3.14 Encodings for inputs, outputs, states, and the next-state and output functions of the FSM adder.

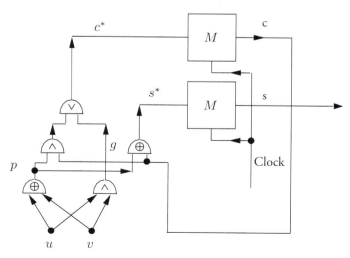

Figure 3.15 A sequential circuit for the FSM that adds binary numbers.

3.3.1 Binary Memory Devices

It is useful to fix ideas about memory units by designing one (a flip-flop) from logic gates. A collection of clocked flip-flops is called a **register**. A clocked **flip-flop** can be constructed from a few AND and NOT gates, as shown in Fig. 3.16(a). The NAND gates (they compute NOT of AND) labeled g_3 and g_4 form the heart of the flip-flop. Consider the inputs to g_3 and g_4, the lines connected to the outputs of NAND gates g_1 and g_2. If one is set to 1 and the other reset to 0, ρ and ρ^* will assume complementary values (one will have value 1 and the other will have value 0), regardless of their previous values. The gate with input 1 will assume output 0 and vice versa.

Now if the outputs of g_1 and g_2 are both set to 1 and the values previously assumed by ρ and ρ^* are complementary, these values will be retained due to the feedback between g_3 and g_4, as the reader can verify. Since the outputs of g_1 and g_2 are both 1 when the clock input (CLK in Fig. 3.16) has value 0, the complementary outputs of g_3 and g_4 remain unchanged when the clock is low. Since the outputs of a flip-flop provide inputs to the logic-circuit portion of a sequential circuit, it is important that the flip-flop outputs remain constant when the clock is low.

When the clock input is 1, the outputs of g_1 and g_2 are $\overline{S}$ and $\overline{R}$, the Boolean complements of S and R. If S and R are complementary, as is true for this flip-flop since $R = \overline{S}$, this device will store the value of S in ρ and its complement in ρ^*. Thus, if $S = 1$, the flip-flop is **set** to 1, whereas if $R = 1$ (and $S = 0$) it is **reset** to 0. This type of device is called a **D-type flip-flop**. For this reason we change the name of the external input to this memory device from S to D.

Because the output of the D-type flip-flop shown in Fig. 3.16(a) changes when the clock pulse is high, it cannot be used as a stable input to a logic circuit that feeds this or another such flip-flop. Adding another stage like the first but having the complementary value for the clock pulse, as shown in Fig. 3.16(b), causes the output of the second stage to change only while the clock pulse is low. The output of the first stage does change when the clock pulse is high to record the new value of the state. This is called a **master-slave flip-flop.** Other types of flip-flop are described in texts on computer architecture.

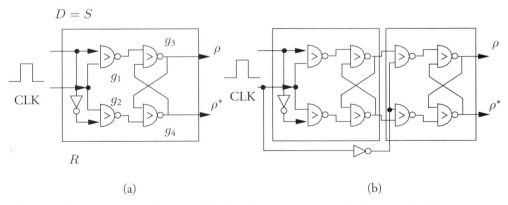

(a)   (b)

Figure 3.16 (a) Design of a D-type flip-flop from NAND gates. (b) A master-slave D-type flip-flop.

3.4 Random-Access Machines

The **random-access machine** (RAM) models the essential features of the traditional serial computer. The RAM is modeled by two synchronous interconnected FSMs, a central processing unit (CPU) and a random-access memory. (See Fig. 3.17.) The CPU has a small number of storage locations called **registers** whereas the random-access memory has a large number. All operations performed by the CPU are performed on data stored in its registers. This is done for efficiency; no increase in functionality is obtained by allowing operations on data stored in memory locations as well.

3.4.1 The RAM Architecture

The CPU implements a **fetch-and-execute cycle** in which it alternately reads an instruction from a program stored in the random-access memory (the **stored-program concept**) and executes it. Instructions are read and executed from consecutive locations in the random-access memory unless a **jump instruction** is executed, in which case an instruction from a non-consecutive location is executed next.

A CPU typically has five basic kinds of instruction: a) arithmetic and logical instructions of the kind described in Sections 2.5.1, 2.7, 2.9, and 2.10, b) memory load and store instructions for moving data between memory locations and registers, c) jump instructions for breaking out of the current program sequence, d) input and output (I/O) instructions, and e) a halt instruction.

The basic random-access memory has an output word (out_wrd) and three input words, an address (addr), a data word (in_wrd), and a command (cmd). The command specifies one of three actions, a) read from a memory location, b) write to a memory location, or c) do nothing. Reading from address addr deposits the value of the word at this location into out_wrd whereas writing to addr replaces the word at this address with the value of in_wrd.

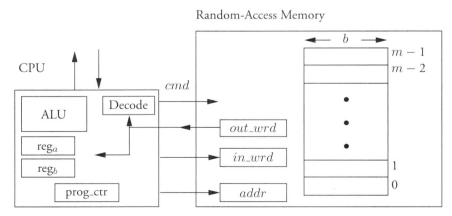

Figure 3.17 The random-access machine has a central processing unit (CPU) and a random-access memory unit.

This memory is called random-access because the time to access a word is the same for all words. The Turing machine introduced in Section 3.7 has a tape memory in which the time to access a word increases with its distance from the tape head.

The random-access memory in the model in Fig. 3.17 has $m = 2^\mu$ storage locations each containing a b-bit word, where μ and b are integers. Each word has a μ-bit address and the addresses are consecutive starting at zero. The combination of this memory and the CPU described above is the **bounded-memory RAM**. When no limit is placed on the number of memory words, this combination defines the **unbounded-memory RAM**. We use the term RAM for these two machines when context unambiguously determines which is intended.

DESIGN OF A SIMPLE CPU   The design of a simple CPU is given in Section 3.10.   (See Fig. 3.31.) This CPU has eight registers, a **program counter** (PC), **accumulator** (AC), **memory address register** (MAR), **memory data register** (MDR), **operation code (opcode) register** (OPC), **input register** (INR), **output register** (OUTR), and **halt register** (HALT). Each operation that requires two operands, such as addition or vector AND, uses AC and MDR as sources for the operands and places the result in AC. Each operation with one operand, such as the NOT of a vector, uses AC as both source and destination for the result. PC contains the address of the next instruction to be executed. Unless a jump instruction is executed, PC is incremented on the execution of each instruction. If a jump instruction is executed, the value of PC is changed. Jumps occur in our simple CPU if AC is zero.

To fetch the next instruction, the CPU copies PC to MAR and then commands the random-access memory to read the word at the address in MAR. This word appears in MDR. The portion of this word containing the identity of the opcode is transferred to OPC. The CPU then inspects the value of OPC and performs the small local operations to execute the instruction represented by it. For example, to perform an addition it commands the arithmetic/logical unit (ALU) to combine the contents of MDR and AC in an adder circuit and deposit the result in AC. If the instruction is a *load accumulator* instruction (LDA), the CPU treats the bits other than opcode bits as address bits and moves them to the MAR. It then commands the random-access memory to deposit the word at this address in MDR, after which it moves the contents of MDR to AC. In Section 3.4.3 we illustrate programming in an assembly language, the language of a machine enhanced by mnemonics and labels. We further illustrate assembly-language programming in Section 3.10.4 for the instruction set of the machine designed in Section 3.10.

3.4.2   The RAM as FSM

As this discussion illustrates, the CPU and the random-access memory are both finite-state machines. The CPU receives input from the random-access memory as well as from external sources. Its output is to the memory and the output port. Its state is determined by the contents of its registers. The random-access memory receives input from and produces output to the CPU. Its state is represented by an m-tuple $(\boldsymbol{w}_0, \boldsymbol{w}_1, \ldots, \boldsymbol{w}_{m-1})$ of b-bit words, one per memory location, as well as by the values of in_wrd, out_word, and addr. We say that the random-access memory has a **storage capacity** of $S = mb$ bits. The RAM has input and output registers (not shown in Fig. 3.17) through which it reads external inputs and produces external outputs.

As the RAM example illustrates, some FSMs are programmable. In fact, a program stored in the RAM memory selects one of very many state sequences that the RAM may execute. The number of states of a RAM can be very large; just the random-access memory alone has more than 2^S states.

The programmability of the unbounded-memory RAM makes it universal for FSMs, as we show in Section 3.4.4. Before taking up this subject, we pause to introduce an assembly-language program for the unbounded-memory RAM. This model will play a role in Chapter 5.

3.4.3   RAM Programs

We now introduce **assembly-language programs** to make concrete the use of the RAM. An assembly language contains one instruction for each machine-level instruction of a CPU. However, instead of bit patterns, it uses mnemonics for opcodes and labels as symbolic addresses. Labels are used in *jump* instructions.

Figure 3.18 shows a simple assembly language. It implements all the instructions of the CPU defined in Section 3.10 and vice versa if the CPU has a sufficiently long word length.

Our new assembly language treats all memory locations as equivalent and calls them registers. Thus, no distinction is made between the memory locations in the CPU and those in the random-access memory. Such a distinction is made on real machines for efficiency: it is much quicker to access registers internal to a CPU than memory locations in an external random-access machine.

Registers are used for data storage and contain integers. Register names are drawn from the set $\{R_0, R_1, R_2, \ldots\}$. The **address of register** R_i is i. Thus, both the number of registers and their size are potentially unlimited. All registers are initialized with the value zero. Registers used as **input registers** to a program are initialized to input values. Results of a computation are placed in **output registers**. Such registers may also serve as input registers. Each instruction may be given a **label** drawn from the set $\{N_0, N_1, N_2, \ldots\}$. Labels are used by jump instructions, as explained below.

Instruction	Meaning
INC R_i	Increment the contents of R_i by 1.
DEC R_i	Decrement the contents of R_i by 1.
CLR R_i	Replace the contents of R_i with 0.
$R_i \leftarrow R_j$	Replace the contents of R_i with those of R_j.
JMP$_+$ N_i	Jump to closest instruction above current one with label N_i.
JMP$_-$ N_i	Jump to closest instruction below current one with label N_i.
R_j JMP$_+$ N_i	If R_j contains 0, jump to closest instruction above current one with label N_i.
R_j JMP$_-$ N_i	If R_j contains 0, jump to closest instruction below current one with label N_i.
CONTINUE	Continue to next instruction; halt if none.

Figure 3.18 The instructions in a simple assembly language.

The meaning of each instruction should be clear except possibly for the CONTINUE and JUMP. If the program reaches a CONTINUE statement other than the last CONTINUE, it executes the following instruction. If it reaches the last CONTINUE statement, the program halts.

The jump instructions R_j JMP$_+$ N_i, R_j JMP$_-$ N_i, JMP$_+$ N_i, and JMP$_-$ N_i cause a break in the program sequence. Instead of executing the next instruction in sequence, they cause jumps to instructions with labels N_i. In the first two cases these jumps occur only when the content of register R_j is zero. In the last two cases, these jumps occur unconditionally. The instructions with JMP$_+$ (JMP$_-$) cause a jump to the closest instruction with label N_i above (below) the current instruction. The use of the suffixes $+$ and $-$ permit the insertion of program fragments into an existing program without relabeling instructions.

A **RAM program** is a finite sequence of assembly language instructions terminated with CONTINUE. A valid program is one for which each jump is to an existing label. A **halting program** is one that halts.

TWO RAM PROGRAMS   We illustrate this assembly language with the two simple programs shown in Fig. 3.19. The first adds two numbers and the second uses the first to square a number. The heading of each program explains its operation. Registers R_0 and R_1 contain the initial values on which the addition program operates. On each step it increments R_0 by 1 and decrements R_1 by 1 until R_1 is 0. Thus, on completion, the value of R_0 is its original value plus the value of R_1 and R_1 contains 0.

The squaring program uses the addition program. It first makes three copies of the initial value x of R_0 and stores them in R_1, R_2, and R_3. R_2 will be used to reset R_1 to x after adding R_1 to R_0. R_3 is used as a counter and decremented $x - 1$ times, after which x is added to itself x times in R_0; that is, x^2 is computed.

	$R_0 \leftarrow R_0 + R_1$	*Comments*			$R_0 \leftarrow R_0^2$	*Comments*
N_0	R_1 JMP$_-$ N_1	End if $R_1 = 0$			$R_2 \leftarrow R_0$	Copy R_0 (x) to R_2
	INC R_0	Increment R_0			$R_3 \leftarrow R_0$	Copy R_0 (x) to R_3
	DEC R_1	Decrement R_1		N_2	$R_1 \leftarrow R_2$	Copy R_2 (x) to R_1
	JMP$_+$ N_0	Repeat		N_0	R_1 JMP$_-$ N_1	$R_0 \leftarrow R_0 + R_1$
N_1	CONTINUE				INC R_0	
					DEC R_1	
					JMP$_+$ N_0	
				N_1	CONTINUE	
					DEC R_3	Decrement R_3
					R_3 JMP$_-$ N_3	End when zero
					JMP$_+$ N_2	Add x to R_0
				N_3	CONTINUE	

Figure 3.19 Two simple RAM programs. The first adds two integers stored initially in registers R_0 and R_1, leaving the result in R_0. The second uses the first to square the contents of R_0, leaving the result in R_0.

As indicated above, with large enough words each of the above assembly-language instructions can be realized with a few instructions from the instruction set of the CPU designed in Section 3.10. It is also true that each of these CPU instructions can be implemented by a fixed number of instructions in the above assembly language. That is, with sufficiently long memory words in the CPU and random-access memory, the two languages allow the same computations with about the same use of time and space.

However, the above assembly-language instructions are richer than is absolutely essential to perform all computations. In fact with just five assembly-language instructions, namely INC, DEC, CONTINUE, R_j JMP$_+$ N_i, and R_j JMP$_-$ N_i, all the other instructions can be realized. (See Problem 3.21.)

3.4.4 Universality of the RAM

The RAM is universal in two senses. First, it can simulate any finite-state machine including another random-access machine, and second, it can execute any RAM program.

DEFINITION 3.4.1 *A machine M is* **universal** *for a class of machines $\mathcal{C}$ if M is in $\mathcal{C}$ and every machine in $\mathcal{C}$ can be simulated by M.*

We now show that the RAM is universal for the class $\mathcal{C}$ of finite-state machines. We show that in $O(T)$ steps and with constant storage capacity S the RAM can simulate T steps of any other FSM. Since any random-access machine that uses a bounded amount of memory can be described by a logic circuit such as the one defined in Section 3.10, it can also be simulated by the RAM.

THEOREM 3.4.1 *Every T-step FSM $M = (\Sigma, \Psi, Q, \delta, \lambda, s, F)$ computation can be simulated by a RAM in $O(T)$ steps with constant space. Thus, the RAM is universal for finite-state machines.*

Proof We sketch a proof. Since an FSM is characterized completely by its next-state and output functions, both of which are assumed to be encoded by binary functions, it suffices to write a fixed-length RAM program to perform a state transition, generate output, and record the FSM state in the RAM memory using the tabular descriptions of the next-state and output functions. This program is then run repeatedly. The amount of memory necessary for this simulation is finite and consists of the memory to store the program plus one state (requiring at least $\log_2 |Q|$ bits). While the amount of storage and time to record and compute these functions is constant, they can be exponential in $\log_2 |Q|$ because the next-state and output functions can be a complex binary function. (See Section 2.12.) Thus, the number of steps taken by the RAM per FSM state transition is constant. ■

The second notion of universality is captured by the idea that the RAM can execute RAM programs. We discuss two execution models for RAM programs. In the first, a RAM program is stored in a private memory of the RAM, say in the CPU. The RAM alternates between reading instructions from its private memory and executing them. In this case the registers described in Section 3.4.3 are locations in the random-access memory. The program counter either advances to the next instruction in its private memory or jumps to a new location as a result of a jump instruction.

In the second model (called by some [10] the **random-access stored program machine** (**RASP**)), a RAM program is stored in the random-access memory itself. A RAM program can be translated to a RASP program by replacing the names of RAM registers by the names of random-access memory locations not used for storing the RAM program. The execution of a RASP program directly parallels that of the RAM program; that is, the RASP alternates between reading instructions and executing them. Since we do not consider the distinction between RASP and RAM significant, we call them both the RAM.

3.5 Random-Access Memory Design

In this section we model the random-access memory described in Section 3.4 as an FSM $M_{\mathrm{RMEM}}(\mu, b)$ that has $m = 2^\mu$ b-bit data words, $\boldsymbol{w}_0, \boldsymbol{w}_1, \ldots, \boldsymbol{w}_{m-1}$, as well as an input data word $\boldsymbol{d}$ (**in_wrd**), an input address $\boldsymbol{a}$ (**addr**), and an output data word $\boldsymbol{z}$ (**out_wrd**). (See Fig. 3.20.) The state of this FSM is the concatenation of the contents of the data, input and output words, and the command word. We construct an efficient logic circuit for its next-state and transition function.

To simplify the design of the FSM M_{RMEM} we use the following encodings of the three input commands:

Name	s_1	s_0
no-op	0	0
read	0	1
write	1	0

An input to M_{RMEM} is a binary $(\mu + b + 2)$-bit binary tuple, two bits to represent a command, μ bits to specify an address, and b bits to specify a data word. The output function of M_{RMEM}, λ_{RMEM}, is a simple projection operator and is realized by a circuit without any gates. Applied to the state vector, it produces the output word.

We now describe a circuit for δ_{RMEM}, the next-state function of M_{RMEM}. Memory words remain unchanged if either **no-op** or **read** commands are executed. In these cases the value of the command bit s_1 is 0. One memory word changes if $s_1 = 1$, namely, the one whose

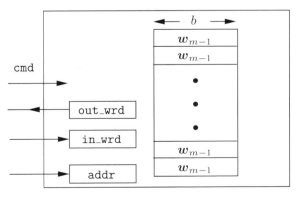

Figure 3.20 A random-access memory unit M_{RMEM} that holds m b-bit words. Its inputs consist of a command (`cmd`), an input word (`in_wrd`), and an address (`addr`). It has one output word (`out_wrd`).

address is $\boldsymbol{a}$. Thus, the memory words $\boldsymbol{w}_0, \boldsymbol{w}_1, \ldots, \boldsymbol{w}_{m-1}$ change only when $s_1 = 1$. The word that changes is determined by the μ-bit address $\boldsymbol{a}$ supplied as part of the input. Let $a_{\mu-1}, \ldots, a_1, a_0$ be the μ bits of $\boldsymbol{a}$. Let these bits be supplied as inputs to an μ-bit decoder function $f_{\text{decode}}^{(\mu)}$ (see Section 2.5.4). Let $y_{m-1}, \ldots, y_1, y_0$ be the m outputs of a decoder circuit. Then, the Boolean function $c_i = s_1 y_i$ (shown in Fig. 3.21(a)) is 1 exactly when the input address $\boldsymbol{a}$ is the binary representation of the integer i and the FSM M_{RMEM} is commanded to **write** the word $\boldsymbol{d}$ at address $\boldsymbol{a}$.

Let $\boldsymbol{w}_0^*, \boldsymbol{w}_1^*, \ldots, \boldsymbol{w}_{m-1}^*$ be the new values for the memory words. Let $w_{i,j}^*$ and $w_{i,j}$ be the jth components of $\boldsymbol{w}_i^*$ and $\boldsymbol{w}_i$, respectively. Then, for $0 \le i \le m - 1$ and $0 \le j \le b - 1$ we write $w_{i,j}^*$ in terms of $w_{i,j}$ and the jth component d_j of $\boldsymbol{d}$ as follows:

$$c_i = s_1 y_i$$
$$w_{i,j}^* = \bar{c}_i w_{i,j} \vee c_i d_j$$

Figures 3.21(a) and (b) show circuits described by these formulas. It follows that changes to memory words can be realized by a circuit containing $C_\Omega \left(f_{\text{decode}}^{(\mu)} \right)$ gates for the decoder, m gates to compute all the terms c_i, $0 \le i \le m - 1$, and $4mb$ gates to compute $w_{i,j}^*$, $0 \le i \le m - 1$, $0 \le j \le b - 1$ (NOTs are counted). Combining this with Lemma 2.5.4, we have that

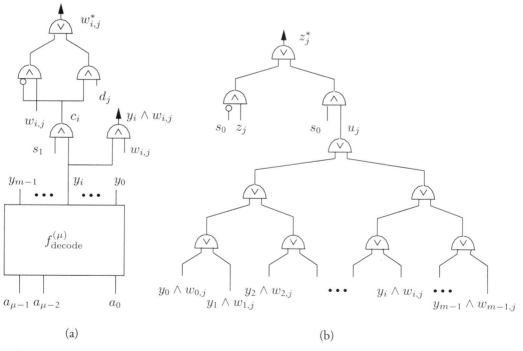

(a)   (b)

Figure 3.21 A circuit that realizes the next-state and output function of the random-access memory. The circuit in (a) computes the next values $\{w_{i,j}^*\}$ for components of memory words, whereas that in (b) computes components $\{z_i^*\}$ of the output word. The output $y_j \wedge w_{i,j}$ of (a) is an input to (b).

a circuit realizing this portion of the next-state function has at most $m(4b + 2) + (\mu - 2)\sqrt{m}$ gates. The depth of this portion of the circuit is the depth of the decoder plus 4 because the longest path between an input and an output $\boldsymbol{w}_0^*, \boldsymbol{w}_1^*, \ldots, \boldsymbol{w}_{m-1}^*$ is through the decoder and then through the gates that form $\overline{c}_i w_{i,j}$. This depth is at most $\lceil \log_2 \mu \rceil + 5$.

The circuit description is complete after we give a circuit to compute the output word $\boldsymbol{z}$. The value of $\boldsymbol{z}$ changes only when $s_0 = 1$, that is, when a **read** command is issued. The jth component of $\boldsymbol{z}$, namely z_j, is replaced by the value of $w_{i,j}$, where i is the address specified by the input $\boldsymbol{a}$. Thus, the new value of z_j, z_j^*, can be represented by the following formula (see the circuit of Fig. 3.21(b)):

$$z_j^* = \overline{s}_0 z_j \vee s_0 \left(\bigvee_{k=0}^{m-1} y_k w_{k,j} \right) \qquad \text{for } 0 \leq j \leq b - 1$$

Here $\bigvee$ denotes the OR of the m terms $y_k w_{k,j}$, $m = 2^\mu$. It follows that for each value of j this portion of the circuit can be realized with m two-input AND gates and $m - 1$ two-input OR gates (to form $\bigvee$) plus four additional operations. Thus, it is realized by an additional $2(m + 3)b$ gates. The depth of this circuit is the depth of the decoder ($\lceil \log \mu \rceil + 1$) plus $\mu = \log_2 m$, the depth of a tree of m inputs to form $\bigvee$, plus three more levels. Thus, the depth of the circuit to produce the output word is $\mu + \lceil \log_2 \mu \rceil + 4$.

The size of the complete circuit for the next-state function is at most $m(6b + 2) + (\mu - 2)\sqrt{m} + 3b$. Its depth is at most $\mu + \lceil \log_2 \mu \rceil + 4$. We state these results as a lemma.

LEMMA 3.5.1 *The next-state and output functions of the FSM $M_{\mathrm{RMEM}}(\mu, b)$, δ_{RMEM} and λ_{RMEM}, can be realized with the following size and depth bounds over the standard basis Ω_0, where $S = mb$ is its storage capacity in bits:*

$$C_{\Omega_0}(\delta_{\mathrm{RMEM}}, \lambda_{\mathrm{RMEM}}) \leq m(6b + 2) + (\mu - 2)\sqrt{m} + 3b = O(S)$$
$$D_{\Omega_0}(\delta_{\mathrm{RMEM}}, \lambda_{\mathrm{RMEM}}) \leq \mu + \lceil \log_2 \mu \rceil + 4 \qquad\quad = O(\log(S/b))$$

Random-access memories can be very large, so large that their equivalent number of logic elements (which we see from the above lemma is proportional to the storage capacity of the memory) is much larger than the tens to hundreds of thousands of logic elements in the CPUs to which they are attached.

3.6 Computational Inequalities for the RAM

We now state computational inequalities that apply for all computations on the bounded-memory RAM. Since this machine consists of two interconnected synchronous FSMs, we invoke the inequalities of Theorem 3.1.3, which require bounds on the size and depth of the next-state and output functions for the CPU and the random-access memory.

From Section 3.10.6 we see that size and depth of these functions for the CPU grow slowly in the word length b and number of memory words m. In Section 3.5 we designed an FSM modeling an S-bit random-access memory and showed that the size and depth of its next-state and output functions are proportional to S and $\log S$, respectively. Combining these results, we obtain the following computational inequalities.

THEOREM 3.6.1 *Let f be a subfunction of $f_{\mathrm{RAM}}^{(T,m,b)}$, the function computed by the m-word, b-bit RAM with storage capacity $S = mb$ in T steps. Then the following bounds hold simultaneously over the standard basis Ω_0 for logic circuits:*

$$C_{\Omega_0}(f) = O(ST)$$
$$D_{\Omega_0}(f) = O(T \log S)$$

The discussion in Section 3.1.2 of computational inequalities for FSMs applies to this theorem. In addition, this theorem demonstrates the importance of the space-time product, ST, as well as the product $T \log S$. While intuition may suggest that ST is a good measure of the resources needed to solve a problem on the RAM, this theorem shows that it is a fundamental quantity because it directly relates to another fundamental complexity measure, namely, the size of the smallest circuit for a function f. Similar statements apply to the second inequality.

It is important to ask how tight the inequalities given above are. Since they are both derived from the inequalities of Theorem 3.1.1, this question can be translated into a question about the tightness of the inequalities of this theorem. The technique given in Section 3.2 can be used to tighten the second inequality of Theorem 3.1.1 so that the bounds on circuit depth can be improved to logarithmic in T without sacrificing the linearity of the bound on circuit size. However, the coefficients on these bounds depend on the number of states and can be very large.

3.7 Turing Machines

The Turing machine model is the classical model introduced by Alan Turing in his famous 1936 paper [334]. No other model of computation has been found that can compute functions that a Turing machine cannot compute. The Turing machine is a canonical model of computation used by theoreticians to understand the limits on serial computation, a topic that is explored in Chapter 5. The Turing machine also serves as the primary vehicle for the classification of problems by their use of space and time. (See Chapter 8.)

The (deterministic) one-tape, bounded-memory **Turing machine (TM)** consists of two interconnected FSMs, a **control unit** and a **tape unit** of potentially unlimited storage capacity.

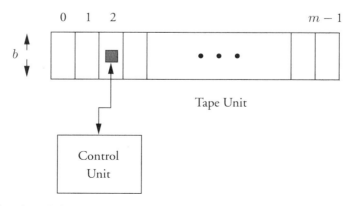

Figure 3.22 A bounded-memory one-tape Turing machine.

(It is shown schematically in Fig. 3.22.) At each unit of time the control unit accepts input from the tape unit and supplies output to it. The tape unit produces the value in the cell under the head, a b-bit word, and accepts and writes a b-bit word to that cell. It also accepts commands to move the head one cell to the left or right or not at all. The bounded-memory tape unit is an array of m b-bit cells and has a **storage capacity** of $S = mb$ bits. A formal definition of the one-tape deterministic Turing machine is given below.

DEFINITION 3.7.1 *A* **standard Turing machine (TM)** *is a six-tuple* $M = (\Gamma, \beta, Q, \delta, s, h)$, *where* Γ *is the* **tape alphabet** *not containing the* **blank symbol** β, Q *is the* **set of states**, $\delta :$ $Q \times (\Gamma \cup \{\beta\}) \mapsto (Q \cup \{h\}) \times (\Gamma \cup \{\beta\}) \times \{\mathbf{L}, \mathbf{N}, \mathbf{R}\}$ *is the* **next-state function**, s *is the* **initial state**, *and* $h \notin Q$ *is the* **accepting halt state**. *A TM cannot exit from h. If M is in state q with letter a under the tape head and* $\delta(q, a) = (q', \mathbf{C})$, *its control unit enters state q' and writes a' in the cell under the head, and moves the head left (if possible), right, or not at all if* $\mathbf{C}$ *is* $\mathbf{L}$, $\mathbf{R}$, *or* $\mathbf{N}$, *respectively.*

The TM M **accepts the input string** $w \in \Gamma^*$ *(it contains no blanks) if, when started in state s with w placed left-adjusted on its otherwise blank tape, the last state entered by M is h. If M has other halting states (states from which it does not exit) these are rejecting states. Also, M may not halt on some inputs.*

M **accepts the language** $L(M)$ *consisting of all strings accepted by M. If a Turing machine halts on all inputs, we say that it* **recognizes the language** *that it accepts. For simplicity, we assume that when M halts during language acceptance it writes the letter 1 in its first tape cell if its input string is accepted and 0 otherwise.*

The **function computed by a Turing machine** *on input string w is the string z written leftmost on the non-blank portion of the tape after halting. The function computed by a TM is* **partial** *if the TM fails to halt on some input strings and* **complete** *otherwise.*

Thus, a TM performs a computation on input string w, which is placed left-adjusted on its tape by placing its head over the leftmost symbol of w and repeatedly reading the symbol under the tape head, making a state change in its control unit, and producing a new symbol for the tape cell and moving the head left or right by one cell or not at all. The head does not move left from the leftmost tape cell. If a TM is used for language acceptance, it accepts w by halting in the accepting state h. If the TM is used for computation, the result of a computation on input w is the string z that remains on the non-blank portion of its tape.

We require that M store the letter 1 or 0 in its first tape cell when halting during language acceptance to simplify the construction of a circuit simulating M in Section 3.9.1. This requirement is not essential because the fact that M has halted in state h can be detected with a simple circuit.

The **multi-tape Turing machine** is a generalization of this model that has multiple tape units. (These models and limits on their ability to solve problems are examined in Chapter 5, where it is shown that the multi-tape TM is no more powerful than the one-tape TM.) Although in practice a TM uses a bounded number of memory locations, the full power of TMs is realized only when they have access to an unbounded number of tape cells.

Although the TM is much more limited than the RAM in the flexibility with which it can access memory, given sufficient time and storage capacity they both compute exactly the same set of functions, as we show in Section 3.8.

A very important class of languages recognized by TMs is the class **P** of polynomial-time languages.

DEFINITION 3.7.2 *A language $L \subseteq \Gamma^*$ is in* **P** *if there is a Turing machine M with tape alphabet Γ and a polynomial $p(n)$ such that, for every $w \in \Gamma^*$, M halts in $p(|w|)$ steps and accepts w if it is in L and rejects it otherwise.*

The class **P** is said to contain all the "feasible" languages because any language requiring more than a polynomial number of steps for its recognition is thought to require so much time for long strings as not to be recognizable in practice.

A second important class of languages is **NP**, the languages accepted in polynomial time by nondeterministic Turing machines. To define this class we introduce the nondeterministic Turing machines.

3.7.1   Nondeterministic Turing Machines

A **nondeterministic Turing machine (NTM)** is identical to the standard TM except that its control unit has an external choice input. (See Fig. 3.23.)

DEFINITION 3.7.3 *A* **non-deterministic Turing machine (NTM)** *is the extension of the TM model by the addition of a choice input to its control unit. Thus an NTM is a seven-tuple $M = (\Sigma, \Gamma, \beta, Q, \delta, s, h)$, where Σ is the* **choice input alphabet**, Γ *is the* **tape alphabet** *not containing the* **blank symbol** β, Q *is the* **set of states**, s *is the* **initial state**, *and $h \notin Q$ is the* **accepting halt state**. *A TM cannot exit from h. When M is in state q with letter a under the tape head, reading choice input c, its* **next-state function** $\delta : Q \times \Sigma \times (\Gamma \cup \{\beta\}) \mapsto (Q \cup \{h\}) \times (\Gamma \cup \{\beta\}) \times \{\mathbf{L}, \mathbf{R}, \mathbf{N}\} \cup \perp$ *has value $\delta(q, c, a)$. If $\delta(q, c, a) = \perp$, there is no successor to the current state with choice input c and tape symbol a. If $\delta(q, c, a) = (q', a', \mathbf{C})$, M's control unit enters state q', writes a' in the cell under the head, and moves the head left (if possible), right, or not at all if $\mathbf{C}$ is $\mathbf{L}$, $\mathbf{R}$, or $\mathbf{N}$, respectively. The choice input selects possible transitions on each time step.*

An NTM M reads one character of its **choice input string** $c \in \Sigma^*$ *on each step. An NTM M* **accepts string** w *if there is some choice string c such that the last state entered by M is h when M is started in state s with w placed left-adjusted on its otherwise blank tape. We assume that when M halts during language acceptance it writes the letter 1 in its first tape cell if its input string is accepted and 0 otherwise.*

An NTM M **accepts the language** $L(M) \subseteq \Gamma^*$ *consisting of those strings w that it accepts. Thus, if $w \notin L(M)$, there is no choice input for which M accepts w.*

Note that the choice input c associated with acceptance of input string w is selected with full knowledge of w. Also, note that an NTM does not accept any string not in $L(M)$; that is, for no choice inputs does it accept such a string.

The NDTM simplifies the characterization of languages. It is used in Section 8.10 to characterize the class **NP** of languages accepted in nondeterministic polynomial time.

DEFINITION 3.7.4 *A language $L \subseteq \Gamma^*$ is in* **NP** *if there is a nondeterministic Turing machine M and a polynomial $p(n)$ such that M accepts L and for each $w \in L$ there is a choice input c such that M on input w with this choice input halts in $p(|w|)$ steps.*

A choice input is said to "verify" membership of a string in a language. The particular string provided by the choice agent is a verifier for the language. The languages in **NP** are thus

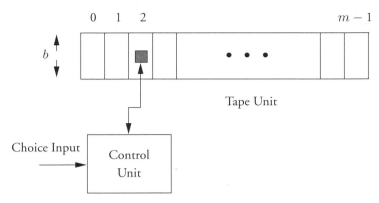

Figure 3.23 A nondeterministic Turing machine modeled as a deterministic one whose control unit has an external choice input that disambiguates the value of its next state.

easy to verify: they can be verified in a polynomial number of steps by a choice input string of polynomial length.

The class **NP** contains many important problems. The **Traveling Salesperson Problem (TSP)** is in this class. TSP is a set of strings of the following kind: each string contains an integer n, the number of vertices (cities) in an undirected graph G, as well as distances between every pair of vertices in G, expressed as integers, and an integer k such that there is a path that visits each city once, returning to its starting point (a **tour**), whose length is at most k. A verifier for TSP is an ordering of the vertices such that the total distance traveled is no more than k. Since there are $n!$ orderings of the n vertices and $n!$ is approximately $\sqrt{2\pi} n^n e^{-n}$, a verifier can be found in a number of steps exponential in n; the actual verification itself can be done in $O(n^2)$ steps. (See Problem 3.24.) **NP** also contains many other important languages, in particular, languages defining important combinatorial problems.

While it is obvious that **P** is a subset of **NP**, it is not known whether they are the same. Since for each language L in **NP** there is a polynomial p such that for each string $\boldsymbol{w}$ in L there is a verifying choice input $\boldsymbol{c}$ of length $p(|\boldsymbol{w}|)$, a polynomial in the length of $\boldsymbol{w}$, the number of possible choice strings $\boldsymbol{c}$ to be considered in search of a verifying string is at most an exponential in $|\boldsymbol{w}|$. Thus, for every language in **NP** there is an exponential-time algorithm to recognize it.

Despite decades of research, the question of whether **P** is equal to **NP**, denoted **P** $\overset{?}{=}$ **NP**, remains open. It is one of the great outstanding questions of computer science today. The approach taken to this question is to identify **NP**-complete problems (see Section 8.10), the hardest problems in **NP**, and then attempt to determine problems whether or not such problems are in **P**. TSP is one of these **NP**-complete problems.

3.8 Universality of the Turing Machine

We show the existence of a universal Turing machine in two senses. On the one hand, we show that there is a Turing machine that can simulate any RAM computation. Since every Turing machine can be simulated by the RAM, the Turing machine simulating a RAM is universal for the set of all Turing machines.

Also, because there is a Turing machine that can simulate any RAM computation, every RAM program can be simulated on this Turing machine. Since it is not hard to see that every Turing machine can be described by a RAM program (see Problem 3.29), it follows that the RAM programs are exactly the programs computed by Turing machines. Consequently, the RAM is also universal.

The following theorem demonstrates that RAM computations can be simulated by Turing-machine computations and vice versa when each operates with bounded memory. Note that all halting computations are bounded-memory computations. A direct proof of the existence of a universal Turing machine is given in Section 5.5.

THEOREM 3.8.1 *Let $S = mb$ and $m \geq b$. Then for every m-word, b-bit Turing machine M_{TM} (with storage capacity S) there is an $O(m)$-word, b-bit RAM that simulates a time T computation of M_{TM} in time $O(T)$ and storage $O(S)$. Similarly, for every m-word, b-bit RAM M_{RAM} there is an $O((m/b) \log m)$-word, $O(b)$-bit Turing machine that simulates a T-time, S-storage computation of M_{RAM} in time $O(ST \log^2 S)$ and storage $O(S \log S)$.*

Proof We begin by describing a RAM that simulates a TM. Consider a b-bit RAM program to simulate an m-word, b-bit TM. As shown in Theorem 3.4.1, a RAM program can be written to simulate one step of an FSM. Since a TM control unit is an FSM, it suffices to exhibit a RAM program to simulate a tape unit (also an FSM); this is straightforward, as is combining the two programs. If the RAM has storage capacity proportional to that of the TM, then the RAM need only record with one additional word the position of the tape head. This word, which can be held in a RAM register, is incremented or decremented as the head moves. The resulting program runs in time proportional to the running time of the TM.

We now describe a b^*-bit TM that simulates a RAM, where $b^* = \lceil \log m \rceil + b + c$ for some constant c, an assumption we examine later. Let RAM words and their corresponding addresses be placed in individual cells on the tape of the TM, as suggested in Fig. 3.24. Let the address **addr** of the RAM CPU program counter be placed on the tape of the TM to the left, as suggested by the shading in the figure. (It is usually assumed that, unlike the RAM, the TM holds words of size no larger than $O(b)$ in its control unit.) The TM simulates a RAM by simulating the RAM fetch-and-execute cycle. This means it fetches a word at

								$\diamond$				♠			
0000	0000	0001	0010	0011	0100	0101	0110	0111	1000	1001	1010	1011	1100	1101	1110	1111
	w_0	w_1	w_2	w_3	w_4	w_5	w_6	w_7	w_8	w_9	w_{10}	w_{11}	w_{12}	w_{13}	w_{14}	w_{15}

Figure 3.24 Organization of a tape unit to simulate a RAM. Each RAM memory word w_j is accompanied by its address j in binary.

address **addr** in the simulated RAM memory unit, interprets it as an instruction, and then executes the instruction (which might require a few additional accesses to the memory unit to read or write data). We return to the simulation of the RAM CPU after we examine the simulation of the RAM memory unit.

The TM can find a word at location **addr** as follows. It reads the most significant bit of **addr** and moves right on its tape until it finds the first word with this most significant bit. It leaves a marker at this location. (The symbol $\diamondsuit$ in Fig. 3.24 identifies the first place a marker is left.) It then returns to the left-hand end of the tape and obtains the next most significant bit of **addr**. It moves back to the marker $\diamondsuit$ and then carries this marker forward to the next address containing the next most significant bit (identified by the marker $\spadesuit$ in Fig. 3.24). This process is repeated until all bits of **addr** have been visited, at which point the word at location **addr** in the simulated RAM is found. Since m tape unit cells are used in this simulation, at most $O(m \log m)$ TM steps are taken for this purpose.

The TM must also simulate internal RAM CPU computations. Each addition, subtraction, and comparison of b-bit words can be done by the TM control unit in a constant number of steps, as can the logical vector operations. (For simplicity, we assume that the RAM does not use its I/O registers. To simulate these operations, either other tapes would be used or space would be reserved on the single tape to hold input and output words.) The jump instructions as well as the incrementing of the program counter require moving and incrementing $\lceil \log m \rceil$-bit addresses. These cannot be simulated by the TM control unit in a constant number of steps since it can only operate on b-bit words. Instead, they are simulated on the tape by moving addresses in b-bit blocks. If two tape cells are separated by $q - 1$ cells, $2q$ steps are necessary to move each block of b bits from the first cell to the second. Thus, a full address can be moved in $2q\lceil \lceil \log m \rceil / b \rceil$ steps. An address can also be incremented using ripple addition in $\lceil \lceil \log m \rceil / b \rceil$ steps using operations on b-bit words, since the blocks of an address are contiguous. (See Section 2.7 for a discussion of ripple addition.) Thus, both of these address-manipulation operations can be done in at most $O(m \lceil \lceil \log m \rceil / b \rceil)$ steps, since no two words are separated by more than $O(m)$ cells.

Now consider the general case of a TM with word size comparable to that of the RAM, that is, a size too small to hold an address as well as a word. In particular, consider a TM with $\hat{b}$-bit tape alphabet where $\hat{b} = cb$, $c > 1$ a constant. In this case, we divide addresses into $\lceil \lceil \log m \rceil / \hat{b} \rceil$ $\hat{b}$-bit words and place these words in locations that precede the value of the RAM word at this address, as suggested in Fig. 3.40. We also place the address **addr** at the beginning of the tape in the same number of tape words. A total of $O((m/b)(\log m))$ $O(b)$-bit words are used to store all this data. Now assume that the TM can carry the contents of a $\hat{b}$-bit word in its control unit. Then, as shown in Problem 3.26, the extra symbols in the TM's tape alphabet can be used as markers to find a word with a given address in at most $O((m/b)(\log^2 m))$ TM steps using storage $O((m/b) \log m)$. Hence each RAM memory access translates into $O((m/b)(\log^2 m))$ TM steps on this machine.

Simulation of the CPU on this machine is straightforward. Again, each addition, subtraction, comparison, and logical vector operation on b-bit words can be done in a constant number of steps. Incrementing of the program counter can also be done in $\lceil \lceil \log m \rceil / b \rceil$ operations since the cells containing this address are contiguous. However, since a jump operation may require moving an address by $O(m)$ cells in the b^*-bit TM, it may now require moving it by $O(m(\log m)/b)$ cells in the $\hat{b}$-bit TM in $O\left(m\left((\log m)/b\right)^2\right)$ steps.

Combining these results, we see that each step of the RAM may require as many as $O((m((\log m)/b)^2)$ steps of the $\hat{b}$-bit TM. This machine uses storage $O((m/b)\log m)$. Since $m = S(n)/b$, the conclusion of the theorem follows. ∎

This simulation of a bounded-memory RAM by a Turing machine assumes that the RAM has a fixed number of memory words. Although this may appear to prevent an unbounded-memory TM from simulating an unbounded-memory RAM, this is not the case. If the Turing machine detects that an address contains more than the number of bits currently assumed as the maximum number, it can increase by 1 the number of bits allocated to each memory location and then resume computation. To make this adjustment, it will have to space out the memory words and addresses to make space for the extra bits. (See Problem 3.28.)

Because a Turing machine with no limit on the length of its tape can be simulated by a RAM, this last observation demonstrates the existence of **universal Turing machines**, Turing machines with unbounded memory (but with fixed-size control units and bounded-size tape alphabets) that can simulate arbitrary Turing machines. This matter is also treated in Section 5.5.

Since the RAM can execute RAM programs, the same is true of the Turing machines. As mentioned above, it is not hard to see that every Turing machine can be simulated by a RAM program. (See Problem 3.29.) As a consequence, the RAM programs are exactly the programs that can be computed by a Turing machine.

While the above remarks apply to the one-tape Turing machine, they also apply to all other Turing machine models, such as double-ended and multi-tape Turing machines, because each of these can also be simulated by the one-tape Turing machine. (See Section 5.2.)

3.9 Turing Machine Circuit Simulations

Just as every T-step finite-state machine computation can be simulated by a circuit, so can every T-step Turing machine computation. We give two circuit simulations, a simple one that demonstrates the concept and another more complex one that yields a smaller circuit. We use these two simulations in Sections 3.9.5 and 3.9.6 to establish computational inequalities that must hold for Turing machines. With a different interpretation they provide examples of **P**-complete and **NP**-complete problems. (See also Sections 8.9 and 8.10.) These results illustrate the central role of circuits in theoretical computer science.

3.9.1   A Simple Circuit Simulation of TM Computations

We now design a circuit simulating a computation of a Turing machine M that uses m memory cells and T steps. Since the only difference between a deterministic and nondeterministic Turing machine is the addition of a choice input to the control unit, we design a circuit for a nondeterministic Turing machine.

For deterministic computations, the circuit simulation provides computational inequalities that must be satisfied by computational resources, such as space and time, if a problem is to be solved by M. Such an inequality is stated at the end of this section.

With the proper interpretation, the circuit simulation of a deterministic computation is an instance of a **P**-complete problem, one of the hardest problems in **P** to parallelize. Here **P** is the class of polynomial-time languages. A first **P**-complete problem is stated in the following section. This topic is studied in detail in Section 8.9.

For nondeterministic computations, the circuit simulation produces an instance of an **NP**-complete problem, a hardest problem to solve in **NP**. Here **NP** is the class of languages accepted in polynomial time by a nondeterministic Turing machine. A first **NP**-complete problem is stated in the following section. This topic is studied in detail in Section 8.10.

THEOREM 3.9.1 *Any computation performed by a one-tape Turing machine M, deterministic or nondeterministic, on an input string $\boldsymbol{w}$ in T steps using m b-bit memory cells can be simulated by a circuit $\mathcal{C}_{M,T}$ over the standard complete basis Ω of size and depth $O(ST)$ and $O(T \log S)$, respectively, where $S = mb$ is the storage capacity in bits of M's tape. For the deterministic TM the inputs to this circuit consist of the values of $\boldsymbol{w}$. For the nondeterministic TM the inputs consist of $\boldsymbol{w}$ and the Boolean choice input variables whose values are not set in advance.*

Proof To construct a circuit $\mathcal{C}_{M,T}$ simulating T steps by M is straightforward because M is a finite-state machine now that its storage capacity is limited. We need only extend the construction given in Section 3.1.1, namely, construct a circuit for the next-state and output functions of M. As shown in Fig. 3.25, it is convenient to view M as a pair of synchronous

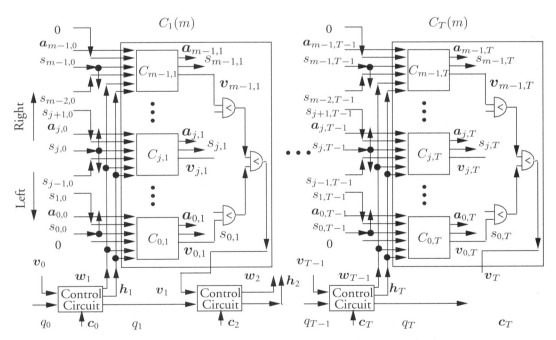

Figure 3.25 The circuit $\mathcal{C}_{M,T}$ simulates an m-cell, T-step computation by a nondeterministic Turing machine M. It contains T copies of M's control unit circuit and T column circuits, $\mathcal{C}_t$, each containing cell circuits $C_{j,t}$, $0 \leq j \leq m-1$, $1 \leq t \leq T$, simulating the jth tape cell on the tth time step. q_t and $\boldsymbol{c}_t$ are M's state on the tth step and its tth set of choice variables. Also, $\boldsymbol{a}_{j,t}$ is the value in the jth cell on the tth step, $s_{j,t}$ is 1 if the head is over cell j at the tth time step, and $\boldsymbol{v}_{j,t}$ is $\boldsymbol{a}_{j,t}$ if $s_{j,t} = 1$ and $\boldsymbol{0}$ otherwise. $\boldsymbol{v}_t$, the vector OR of $\boldsymbol{v}_{j,t}$, $0 \leq j \leq m-1$, supplies the value under the head to the control unit, which computes head movement commands, $\boldsymbol{h}_t$, and a new word, $\boldsymbol{w}_t$, for the current cell in the next simulated time step. The value of the function computed by M resides on its tape after the Tth step.

FSMs, as discussed in Section 3.1.4, and to design separate circuits for M's control and tape units. The design of the circuit for the control unit is straightforward since it is an unspecified NFSM. The **tape circuit**, which realizes the next-state and output functions for the tape unit, contains m **cell circuits**, one for each cell on the tape. We denote by $\mathcal{C}_t(m)$, $1 \le t \le T$, the tth tape circuit. We begin by constructing a tape circuit and determining its size and depth.

For $0 \le j \le m$ and $1 \le t \le T$ let $C_{j,t}$ be the jth cell circuit of the tth tape circuit, $\mathcal{C}_t(m)$. $C_{j,t}$ produces the value $\boldsymbol{a}_{j,t}$ contained in the jth cell after the jth step as well as $s_{j,t}$, whose value is 1 if the head is over the jth tape cell after the tth step and 0 otherwise. The value of $\boldsymbol{a}_{j,t}$ is either $\boldsymbol{a}_{j,t-1}$ if $s_{j,t} = 0$ (the head is not over this cell) or $\boldsymbol{w}$ if $s_{j,t} = 1$ (the head is over the cell). Subcircuit SC_2 of Fig. 3.26 performs this computation.

Subcircuit SC_1 in Fig. 3.26 computes $s_{j,t}$ from $s_{j-1,t-1}$, $s_{j,t-1}$, $s_{j+1,t-1}$ and the triple $\boldsymbol{h}_t = (h_t^{-1}, h_t^0, h_t^{+1})$, where $h_t^{-1} = 1$ if the head moves to the next lower-numbered cell, $h_t^{+1} = 1$ if it moves to the next higher-numbered cell, $(s_{j-1,t-1})$, or $h_t^0 = 1$ if it does not move. Thus, $s_{j,t} = 1$ if $s_{j+1,t-1} = 1$ and $h_t^{-1} = 1$, or if $s_{j-1,t-1}$ and $h_t^{+1} = 1$, or if $s_{j,t-1} = 1$ and $h_t^0 = 1$. Otherwise, $s_{j,t} = 0$.

Subcircuit SC_3 of cell circuit $C_{j,t}$ generates the b-bit word $\boldsymbol{v}_{j,t}$ that is used to provide the value under the head on the tth step. $\boldsymbol{v}_{j,t}$ is $\boldsymbol{a}_{j,t}$ if the head is over the jth cell on the

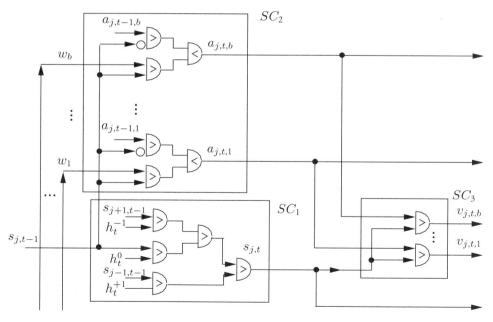

Figure 3.26 The cell circuit $C_{j,t}$ has three components: SC_1, a circuit to compute the new value for the head location bit $s_{j,t}$ from the values of this quantity on the preceding step at neighboring cells and the head movement vector $\boldsymbol{h}_t$, SC_2, a circuit to replace the value in the jth cell on the t step with the input $\boldsymbol{w}$ if the head is over the cell on the $(t-1)$st step ($s_{j,t-1} = 1$), and SC_3, a circuit to produce the new value in the jth cell at the tth step if the head is over this cell ($s_{j,t} = 1$) and the zero vector otherwise. The circuit $C_{j,t}$ has $5(b+1)$ gates and depth 4.

tth step ($s_{j,t} = 1$) and $\mathbf{0}$ otherwise. The vector-OR of $\boldsymbol{v}_{j,t}$, $0 \leq j \leq m-1$, is formed using the tree circuit shown in Fig. 3.25 to compute the value of the b-bit word $\boldsymbol{v}_t$ under the head after the tth step. (This can be done by b balanced binary OR trees, each with size $m-1$ and depth $\lceil \log_2 m \rceil$.) $\boldsymbol{v}_t$ is supplied to the tth copy of the control unit circuit, which also uses the previous state of the control unit, q_t, and the choice input $\boldsymbol{c}_t$ (a tuple of Boolean variables) to compute the next state, q_{t+1}, the new b-bit word $\boldsymbol{w}_{t+1}$ for the current tape cell, and the head movement command $\boldsymbol{h}_{t+1}$.

Summarizing, it follows that the tth tape circuit, $\mathcal{C}_t(m)$, uses $O(S)$ gates (here $S = mb$) and has depth $O(\log S/b)$.

Let C_{control} and D_{control} be the size and depth of the circuit simulating the control unit. It follows that the circuit simulating T computation steps by a Turing machine M has $T\,C_{\text{control}}$ gates in the T copies of the control unit and $O(ST)$ gates in the tape circuits for a total of $O(ST)$ gates. Since the longest path through the circuit of Fig. 3.26 passes through each control and tape circuit, the depth of this circuit is $O(T(D_{\text{control}} + \log S/b)) = O(T \log S)$.

The simulation of M is completed by placing the head over the zeroth cell by letting $s_{0,0} = 1$ and $s_{j,0} = 0$ for $j \neq 0$. The inputs to M are fixed by setting $\boldsymbol{a}_{j,0} = w_j$ for $0 \leq j \leq n-1$ and to the blank symbol for $j \geq n$. Finally, $\boldsymbol{v}_0$ is set equal to $\boldsymbol{a}_{j,0}$, the value under the head at the start of the computation. The choice inputs are sets of Boolean variables under the control of an outside agent and are treated as variables of the circuit simulating the Turing machine M. $\blacksquare$

We now give two interpretations of the above simulation. The first establishes that the circuit complexity for a function provides a lower bound to the time required by a computation on a Turing machine. The second provides instances of problems that are **P**-complete and **NP**-complete.

3.9.2 Computational Inequalities for Turing Machines

When the simulation of Theorem 3.9.1 is specialized to a deterministic Turing machine M, a circuit is constructed that computes the function f computed by M in T steps with S bits of memory. It follows that $C_\Omega(f)$ and $D_\Omega(f)$ cannot be larger than those given in this theorem, since this circuit also computes f. From this observation we have the following computational inequalities.

THEOREM 3.9.2 *The function f computed by an m-word, b-bit one-tape Turing machine in T steps can also be computed by a circuit whose size and depth satisfy the following bounds over any complete basis Ω, where $S = mb$ is the storage capacity used by this machine:*

$$C_\Omega(f) = O(ST)$$
$$D_\Omega(f) = O(T \log S)$$

Since $S = O(T)$ (at most $T + 1$ cells can be visited in T steps), we have the following corollary. It demonstrates that the time T to compute a function f with a Turing machine is at least the square root of its circuit size. As a consequence, circuit size complexity can be used to derive lower bounds on computation time on Turing machines.

COROLLARY 3.9.1 *Let the function f be computed by an m-word, b-bit one-tape Turing machine in T steps, b fixed. Then, over any complete basis Ω the following inequality must hold:*

$$C_\Omega(f) = O\left(T^2\right)$$

There is no loss in assuming that a language L is a set of strings over a binary alphabet; that is, $L \subseteq \mathcal{B}^*$. As explained in Section 1.2.3, a language can be defined by a family $\{f_1, f_2, f_3, \ldots\}$ of characteristic (Boolean) functions, $f_n : \mathcal{B}^n \mapsto \mathcal{B}$, where a string w of length n is in L if and only if $f_n(w) = 1$.

Theorem 3.9.2 not only establishes a clear connection between Turing time complexity and circuit size complexity, but it also provides a potential means to resolve the question $\mathbf{P} \overset{?}{=} \mathbf{NP}$ of whether $\mathbf{P}$ and $\mathbf{NP}$ are equal or not. Circuit complexity is currently believed to be the most promising tool to examine this question. (See Chapter 9.)

3.9.3 Reductions from Turing to Circuit Computations

As shown in Theorem 3.9.1, a circuit $\mathcal{C}_{M,T}$ can be constructed that simulates a time- and space-bounded computation by either a deterministic or a nondeterministic Turing machine M. If M is deterministic and accepts the binary input string w, then $\mathcal{C}_{M,T}$ has value 1 when supplied with the value of w. If M is nondeterministic and accepts the binary input string w, then for some values of the binary choice variables c, $\mathcal{C}_{M,T}$ on inputs w and c has value 1.

The language of strings describing circuits with fixed inputs whose value on these inputs is 1 is called CIRCUIT VALUE. When the circuits also have variable inputs whose values can be chosen so that the circuits have value 1, the language of strings describing such circuits is called CIRCUIT SATISFIABILITY. (See Section 3.9.6.) The languages CIRCUIT VALUE and CIRCUIT SATISFIABILITY are examples of $\mathbf{P}$-complete and $\mathbf{NP}$-complete languages, respectively.

The $\mathbf{P}$-complete and $\mathbf{NP}$-complete languages play an important role in complexity theory: they are prototypical hard languages. The $\mathbf{P}$-complete languages can all be recognized in polynomial time on serial machines, but it is not known how to recognize them on parallel machines in time that is a polynomial in the logarithm of the length of strings (this is called **poly-logarithmic time**), which should be possible if they are parallelizable. The $\mathbf{NP}$-complete languages can be recognized in exponential time on deterministic serial machines, but it is not known how to recognize them in polynomial time on such machines. Many important problems have been shown to be $\mathbf{P}$-complete or $\mathbf{NP}$-complete.

Because so much effort has been expended without success in trying to show that the $\mathbf{NP}$-complete ($\mathbf{P}$-complete) languages can be solved serially (in parallel) in polynomial (poly-logarithmic) time, it is generally believed they cannot. Thus, showing that a problem is $\mathbf{NP}$-complete ($\mathbf{P}$-complete) is considered good evidence that a problem is hard to solve serially (in parallel).

To obtain such results, we exhibit a program that writes the description of the circuit $\mathcal{C}_{M,T}$ from a description of the TM M and the values written initially on its tape. The time and space needed by this program are used to classify languages and, in particular, to identify the $\mathbf{P}$-complete and $\mathbf{NP}$-complete languages.

The simple program $\mathcal{P}$ shown schematically in Fig. 3.27 writes a description of the circuit $\mathcal{C}_{M,T}$ of Fig. 3.25, which is deterministic or nondeterministic depending on the nature of M. (Textual descriptions of circuits are given in Section 2.2. Also see Problem 3.8.) The first loop of this program reads the value of ith input letter w_i of the string w written on

```
for i := 0 to n − 1
    READ_VALUE(w_i)
    WRITE_INPUT(i, w_i)
for j := n to m − 1
    WRITE_INPUT(j, β)
for t := 0 to T
    WRITE_CONTROL_UNIT(t, c_t)
    WRITE_OR(t, m)
    for j := 0 to m − 1
        WRITE_CELL_CIRCUIT(j, t)
```

Figure 3.27 A program $\mathcal{P}$ to write the description of a circuit $\mathcal{C}_{M,T}$ that simulates T steps of a nondeterministic Turing machine M and uses m memory words. It reads the n inputs supplied to M, after which it writes the input steps of a straight-line program that reads these n inputs as well as $m − n$ blanks β into the first copy of a tape unit. It then writes the remaining steps of a straight-line program consisting of descriptions of the T copies of the control unit and the mT cell circuits simulating the T copies of the tape unit.

the input tape of T, after which it writes a fragment of a straight-line program containing the value of w_i. The second loop sets the remaining initial values of cells to the blank symbol β. The third outer loop writes a straight-line program for the control unit using the procedure WRITE_CONTROL_UNIT that has as arguments t, the index of the current time step, and c_t, the tuple of Boolean choice input variables for the tth step. These choice variables are not used if M is deterministic. In addition, this loop uses the procedure WRITE_OR to write a straight-line program for the vector OR circuit that forms the contents v_t of the cell under the head after the tth step. Its inner loop uses the procedure WRITE_CELL_CIRCUIT with parameters j and t to write a straight-line program for the jth cell circuit in the tth tape.

The program $\mathcal{P}$ given in Fig. 3.27 is economical in its use of space and time, as we show. Consider a language L in **P**; that is, for L there is a deterministic Turing machine M_L and a polynomial $p(n)$ such that on an input string w of length n, M_L halts in $T = p(n)$ steps. It accepts w if it is in L and rejects it otherwise. Since $\mathcal{P}$ uses space logarithmic in the values of n and T and $T = p(n)$, $\mathcal{P}$ uses space logarithmic in n. (For example, if $p(n) = n^6$, $\log_2 p(n) = 6 \log_2 n = O(\log n)$.) Such programs are called **log-space programs**.

We show in Theorem 8.8.1 that the composition of two log-space programs is a log-space program, a non-obvious result. However, it is straightforward to show that the composition of two polynomial-time programs is a polynomial-time program. (See Problems 3.2 and 8.19.) Since $\mathcal{P}$'s inner and outer loops each execute a polynomial number of steps, it follows that $\mathcal{P}$ is a polynomial-time program.

If M is nondeterministic, $\mathcal{P}$ continues to be a log-space, polynomial-time program. The only difference is that it writes a circuit description containing references to choice variables whose values are not specified in advance. We state these observations in the form of a theorem.

THEOREM 3.9.3 *Let $L \subseteq \mathbf{P}$ ($L \subseteq \mathbf{NP}$). Then for each string $w \in L$ a deterministic (nondeterministic) circuit $\mathcal{C}_{M,T}$ can be constructed by a program that runs in logarithmic space and polynomial time in $n = |w|$, the length of w, such that the output of $\mathcal{C}_{M,T}$, the value in the first tape cell, is (can be) assigned value 1 (for some values of the choice inputs).*

The program of Fig. 3.27 provides a translation (or **reduction**) from any language in **NP** (or **P**) to a language that we later show is a hardest language in **NP** (or **P**).

We now use Theorem 3.9.3 and the above facts to give a brief introduction to the **P**-complete and **NP**-complete languages, which are discussed in more detail in Chapter 8.

3.9.4   Definitions of P-Complete and NP-Complete Languages

In this section we identify languages that are hardest in the classes **P** and **NP**. A language L_0 is **hardest** in one of these classes if a) L_0 is itself in the class and b) for every language L in the class, a test for the membership of a string w in L can be constructed by translating w with an algorithm to a string v and testing for membership of v in L_0. If the class is **P**, the algorithm must use at most space logarithmic in the length of w, whereas in the case of **NP**, the algorithm must use time at most a polynomial in the length of w. Such a language L_0 is said to be a **complete language** for this complexity class. We begin by defining the **P**-complete languages.

DEFINITION 3.9.1 *A language $L \subseteq \mathcal{B}^*$ is* **P-complete** *if it is in* **P** *and if for every language $L_0 \subseteq \mathcal{B}^*$ in* **P***, there is a log-space deterministic program that translates each $w \in \mathcal{B}^*$ into a string $w' \in \mathcal{B}^*$ such that $w \in L_0$ if and only if $w' \in L$.*

The **NP**-complete languages have a similar definition. However, instead of requiring that the translation be log-space, we ask only that it be polynomial-time. It is not known whether all polynomial-time computations can be done in logarithmic space.

DEFINITION 3.9.2 *A language $L \subseteq \mathcal{B}^*$ is* **NP-complete** *if it is in* **NP** *and if for every language $L_0 \subseteq \mathcal{B}^*$ in* **NP***, there is a polynomial-time deterministic program that translates each $w \in \mathcal{B}^*$ into a string $w' \in \mathcal{B}^*$ such that $w \in L_0$ if and only if $w' \in L$.*

Space precludes our explaining the important role of the **P**-complete languages. We simply report that these languages are the hardest languages to parallelize and refer the reader to Sections 8.9 and 8.14.2. However, we do explain the importance of the **NP**-complete languages.

As the following theorem states, if an **NP**-complete language is in **P**; that is, if membership of a string in an **NP**-complete language can be determined in polynomial time, then the same can be done for every language in **NP**; that is, **P** and **NP** are the same class of languages. Since decades of research have failed to show that **P** = **NP**, a determination that a problem is **NP**-complete is a testimonial to but not a proof of its difficulty.

THEOREM 3.9.4 *If an* **NP***-complete language is in* **P***, then* **P** = **NP***.*

Proof Let L be **NP**-complete and let L_0 be an arbitrary language in **NP**. Because L is **NP**-complete, there is a polynomial-time program that translates an arbitrary string w into a string w' such that $w' \in L$ if and only if $w \in L_0$. If $L \in \mathbf{P}$, then testing of membership of strings in L_0 can be done in polynomial time in the length of the string. It follows that there exists a polynomial-time program to determine membership of a string in L_0. Thus, every language in **NP** is also in **P**. ∎

3.9.5   Reductions to P-Complete Languages

We now formally define CIRCUIT VALUE, our first **P**-complete language.

CIRCUIT VALUE

Instance: A circuit description with fixed values for its input variables and a designated output gate.

Answer: "Yes" if the output of the circuit has value 1.

THEOREM 3.9.5 *The language* CIRCUIT VALUE *is* **P***-complete.*

Proof To show that CIRCUIT VALUE is **P**-complete, we must show that it is in **P** and that every language in **P** can be translated to it by a log-space program. We have already shown the second half of the proof in Theorem 3.9.1. We need only show the first half, which follows from a simple analysis of the obvious program. Since a circuit is a graph of a straight-line program, each step depends on steps that precede it. (Such a program can be produced by a pre-order traversal of the circuit starting with its output vertex.) Now scan the straight-line program and evaluate and store in an array the value of each step. Successive steps access this array to find their arguments. Thus, one pass over the straight-line program suffices to evaluate it; the evaluating program runs in linear time in the length of the circuit description. Hence CIRCUIT VALUE is in **P**. ∎

When we wish to show that a new language L_1 is **P**-complete, we first show that it is in **P**. Then we show that every language $L \in \mathbf{P}$ can be translated to it in logarithmic space; that is, for each string w, there is an algorithm that uses temporary space $O(\log|w|)$ (as does the program in Fig. 3.27) that translates w into a string v such that w is in L if and only if v is in L_1. (This is called a **log-space reduction**. See Section 8.5 for a discussion of temporary space.)

If we have already shown that a language L_0 is **P**-complete, we ask whether we can save work by using this fact to show that another language, L_1, in **P** is **P**-complete. This is possible because the composition of two deterministic log-space algorithms is another log-space algorithm, as shown in Theorem 8.8.1. Thus, if we can translate L_0 into L_1 with a log-space algorithm, then every language in **P** can be translated into L_1 by a log-space reduction. (This idea is suggested in Fig. 3.28.) Hence, the task of showing L_1 to be **P**-complete is reduced to showing that L_1 is in **P** and that L_0, which is **P**-complete, can be translated to L_1 by a log-space algorithm. Many **P**-complete languages are exhibited in Section 8.9.

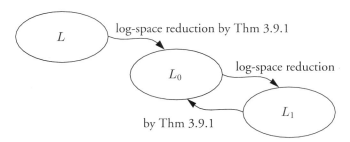

Figure 3.28 A language L_0 is shown **P**-complete by demonstrating that L_0 is in **P** and that every language L in **P** can be translated to it in logarithmic space. A new language L_1 is shown **P**-complete by showing that it is in **P** and that L_0 can be translated to it in log-space. Since L can be L_1, L_1 can also be translated to L_0 in log-space.

3.9.6   Reductions to NP-Complete Languages

Our first **NP**-complete language is CIRCUIT SAT, a language closely related to CIRCUIT VALUE.

CIRCUIT SAT
Instance: A circuit description with n input variables $\{x_1, x_2, \ldots, x_n\}$ for some integer n and a designated output gate.
Answer: "Yes" if there is an assignment of values to the variables such that the output of the circuit has value 1.

THEOREM 3.9.6 *The language* CIRCUIT SAT *is* **NP**-*complete.*

Proof To show that CIRCUIT SAT is **NP**-complete, we must show that it is in **NP** and that every language in **NP** can be translated to it by a polynomial-time program. We have already shown the second half of the proof in Theorem 3.9.1. We need only show the first half. As discussed in the proof of Theorem 3.9.5, each circuit can be organized so that all steps on which a given step depends precede it. We assume that a string in CIRCUIT SAT meets this condition. Design a DTM which on such a string uses choice inputs to assign values to each of the variables in the string. Then invoke the program described in the proof of Theorem 3.9.5 to evaluate the circuit. For some assignment to the variables $x_1, x_2, \ldots, x_n$, this nondeterministic program can accept each string in CIRCUIT SAT but no string not in CIRCUIT SAT. It follows that CIRCUIT SAT is in **NP**. ■

The model used to show that a language is **P**-complete directly parallels the model used to show that a language L_1 is **NP**-complete. We first show that L_1 is in **NP** and then show that every language $L \in \mathbf{NP}$ can be translated to it in polynomial time. That is, we show that there is a polynomial p and algorithm that on inputs of length n runs in time $p(n)$, and that for each string w the algorithm translates w into a string v such that w is in L and only if v is in L_1. (This is called a **polynomial-time reduction**.) Since any algorithm that uses log-space (as does the program in Fig. 3.27) runs in polynomial time (see Theorem 8.5.8), a log-space reduction can be used in lieu of a polynomial-time reduction.

If we have already shown that a language L_0 is **NP**-complete, we can show that another language, L_1, in **NP** is **NP**-complete by translating L_0 into L_1 with a polynomial-time algorithm. Since the composition of two polynomial-time algorithms is another polynomial-time algorithm (see Problem 3.2), every language in **NP** can be translated in polynomial time into L_1 and that L_1 is **NP**-complete. The diagram shown in Fig. 3.28 applies when the reductions are polynomial-time and the languages are members of **NP** instead of **P**. Many **NP**-complete languages are exhibited in Section 8.10.

We apply this idea to show that SATISFIABILITY is **NP**-complete. Strings in this language consist of strings representing the POSE (product-of-sums expansion) of a Boolean function. Thus, they consist of clauses containing literals (a variable or its negation) with the property that for some value of the variables at least one literal in each clause is satisfied.

SATISFIABILITY
Instance: A set of **literals** $X = \{x_1, \overline{x}_1, x_2, \overline{x}_2, \ldots, x_n, \overline{x}_n\}$ and a sequence of **clauses** $C = (c_1, c_2, \ldots, c_m)$ where each clause c_i is a subset of X.
Answer: "Yes" if there is a (satisfying) assignment of values for the variables $\{x_1, x_2, \ldots, x_n\}$ over the set $\mathcal{B}$ such that each clause has at least one literal whose value is 1.

THEOREM 3.9.7 SATISFIABILITY *is* **NP**-*complete.*

Proof SATISFIABILITY is in **NP** because for each string w in this language there is a satisfying assignment for its variables that can be verified by a polynomial-time program. We sketch a nondeterministic RAM program for this purpose. This program reads as many choice variables as there are variables in w and stores them in memory locations. It then evaluates each literal in each clause in w and declares this string satisfied if all clauses evaluate to 1. This program, which runs in time linear in the length of w, can be converted to a Turing-machine program using the construction of Theorem 3.8.1. This program executes in a time quadratic in the time of the original program on the RAM. We now show that every language in **NP** can be reduced to CIRCUIT SAT via a polynomial-time program.

Given an instance of CIRCUIT SAT, as we now show, we can convert the circuit description, a straight-line program (see Section 2.2), into an instance of SATISFIABILITY such that the former is a "yes" instance of CIRCUIT SAT if and only if the latter is a "yes" instance of SATISFIABILITY. Shown below are the different steps of a straight-line program and the clauses used to replace them in constructing an instance of SATISFIABILITY. A DTM can be designed to make these translations in time proportional to the length of the circuit description. Clearly the instance of SATISFIABILITY that it produces is a satisfiable instance if and only if the instance of CIRCUIT SAT is satisfiable.

Step Type				Corresponding Clauses		
(i	READ	x)		$(\overline{g}_i \vee x)$	$(g_i \vee \overline{x})$	
(i	NOT	j)		$(\overline{g}_i \vee \overline{g}_j)$	$(g_i \vee g_j)$	
(i	OR	j	k)	$(g_i \vee \overline{g}_j)$	$(g_i \vee \overline{g}_k)$	$(\overline{g}_i \vee g_j \vee g_k)$
(i	AND	j	k)	$(\overline{g}_i \vee g_j)$	$(\overline{g}_i \vee g_k)$	$(g_i \vee \overline{g}_j \vee \overline{g}_k)$
(i	OUTPUT	j)		(g_j)		

For each gate type it is easy to see that each of the corresponding clauses is satisfiable only for those gate and argument values that are consistent with the type of gate. For example, a NOT gate with input g_j has value $g_i = 1$ when g_j has value 0 and $g_i = 0$ when g_j has value 1. In both cases, both of the clauses $(\overline{g}_i \vee \overline{g}_j)$ and $(g_i \vee g_j)$ are satisfied. However, if g_i is equal to g_j, at least one of the clauses is not satisfied. Similarly, if g_i is the AND of g_j and g_k, then examining all eight values for the triple (g_i, g_j, g_k) shows that only when g_i is the AND of g_j and g_k are all three clauses satisfied. The verification of the above statements is left as a problem for the reader. (See Problem 3.36.) Since the output clause (g_j) is true if and only if the circuit output has value 1, it follows that the set of clauses are all satisfiable if and only if the circuit in question has value 1; that is, it is satisfiable.

Given an instance of CIRCUIT SAT, clearly a DTM can produce the clauses corresponding to each gate using a temporary storage space that is logarithmic in the length of the circuit description because it need deal only with integers that are linear in the length of the input. Thus, each instance of CIRCUIT SAT can be translated into an instance of SATISFIABILITY in a number of steps polynomial in the length of the instance of CIRCUIT SAT. Since it is also in **NP**, it is **NP**-complete. ■

3.9.7   An Efficient Circuit Simulation of TM Computations*

In this section we construct a much more efficient circuit of size $O(Tb \log m)$ that simulates a computation done in T steps by an m-word, b-bit one-tape TM. A similar result on circuit depth is shown.

THEOREM 3.9.8 *Let an m-word, b-bit Turing machine compute in T steps the function f, a projection of $f_{\text{TM}}^{(T,m,b)}$, the function computed by the TM in T steps. Then the following bounds on the size and depth of f over the complete basis Ω must be satisfied:*

$$C_\Omega(f) = O\left(T(\log[\min(bT, S)])\right)$$
$$D_\Omega(f) = O(T)$$

Proof The circuit $\mathcal{C}_{M,T}$ described in Theorem 3.9.1 has size proportional to $O(ST)$, where $S = mb$. We now show that a circuit computing the same function, $N(1, T, m)$, can be constructed whose size is $O\left(T(\log[\min(bT, S)])\right)$. This new circuit is obtained by more efficiently simulating the tape unit portion of a Turing machine. We observe that if the head never reaches a cell, the cell circuit of Fig. 3.26 can be replaced by wires that pass its inputs to its output. It follows that the number of gates can be reduced if we keep the head near the center of a simulated tape by "centering" it periodically. This is the basis for the circuit constructed here.

It simplifies the design of $N(1, T, m)$ to assume that the tape unit has cells indexed from $-m$ to m. Since the head is initially placed over the cell indexed with 0, it is over the middle cell of the tape unit. (The control unit is designed so that the head never enters cells whose index is negative.) We construct $N(1, T, m)$ from a subcircuit $N(c, s, n)$ that simulates s steps of a tape unit containing n b-bit cells under the assumption that the tape head is initially over one of the middle c cells where c and n are odd. Here $n \geq c + 2s$, so that in s steps the head cannot move from one of the middle c cells to positions that are not simulated by this circuit. Let $C(c, s, n)$ and $D(c, s, n)$ be the size and depth of $N(c, s, n)$.

As base cases for our recursive construction of $N(c, s, n)$, consider the circuits $N(1, 1, 3)$ and $N(3, 1, 5)$. They can be constructed from copies of the tape circuit $\mathcal{C}_t(3)$ and $\mathcal{C}_t(5)$ since they simulate one step of tape units containing three and five cells, respectively. In fact, these circuits can be simplified by removing unused gates. Without simplification $\mathcal{C}_t(n)$ contains $5(b + 1)$ gates in each of the n cell circuits (see Fig. 3.26) as well as $(n - 1)b$ gates in the vector OR circuit, for a total of at most $6n(b + 1)$ gates. It has depth $4 + \lceil \log_2 n \rceil$. Thus, $N(1, 1, 3)$ and $N(3, 1, 5)$ each can be realized with $O(b)$ gates and depth $O(1)$.

We now give a recursive construction of a circuit that simulates a tape unit. The $N(1, 2q, 4q + 1)$ circuit simulates $2q$ steps of the tape unit when the head is over the middle cell. It can be decomposed into an $N(1, q, 2q + 1)$ circuit simulating the first q steps and an $N(2q + 1, q, 4q + 1)$ circuit simulating the second q steps, as shown in Fig. 3.29. In the $N(1, q, 2q + 1)$ circuit, the head may move from the middle position to any one of $2q + 1$ positions in q steps, which requires that $2q + 1$ of the inputs be supplied to it. In the $N(2q + 1, q, 4q + 1)$ circuit, the head starts in the middle $2q + 1$ positions and may move to any one of $4q + 1$ middle positions in the next q steps, which requires that $4q + 1$ inputs be supplied to it. The size and depth of our $N(1, 2q, 4q + 1)$ circuit satisfy the following recurrences:

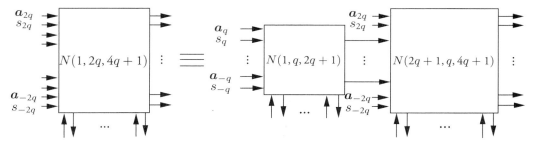

Figure 3.29 A decomposition of an $N(1, 2q, 4q + 1)$ circuit.

$$
\begin{aligned}
C(1, 2q, 4q + 1) &\leq C(1, q, 2q + 1) + C(2q + 1, q, 4q + 1) \\
D(1, 2q, 4q + 1) &\leq D(1, q, 2q + 1) + D(2q + 1, q, 4q + 1)
\end{aligned}
\tag{3.4}
$$

When the number of tape cells is bounded, the above construction and recurrences can be modified. Let $m = 2^p$ be the maximum number of cells used during a T-step computation by the TM. We simulate this computation by placing the head over the middle of a tape with $2m + 1$ cells. It follows that at least m steps are needed to reach each of the reachable cells. Thus, if $T \leq m$, we can simulate the computation with an $N(1, T, 2T + 1)$ circuit. If $T \geq m$, we can simulate the first m steps with an $N(1, m, 2m + 1)$ circuit and the remaining $T - m$ steps with $\lceil (T - m)/m \rceil$ copies of an $N(2m + 1, m, 4m + 1)$ circuit. This follows because at the end of the first m steps the head is over the middle $2m + 1$ of $4m + 1$ cells (of which only $2m + 1$ are used) and remains in this region after m steps due to the limitation on the number of cells used by the TM.

From the above discussion we have the following bounds on the size $C(T, m)$ and depth $D(T, m)$ of a simulating circuit for a T-step, m-word TM computation:

$$
C(T, m) \leq \begin{cases}
C(1, T, 2T + 1) & T \leq m \\
C(1, m, 2m + 1) + \left(\left\lceil \frac{T}{m} \right\rceil - 1 \right) C(2m + 1, m, 4m + 1) & T \geq m
\end{cases}
\tag{3.5}
$$

$$
D(T, m) \leq \begin{cases}
D(1, T, 2T + 1) & T \leq m \\
D(1, m, 2m + 1) + \left(\left\lceil \frac{T}{m} \right\rceil - 1 \right) D(2m + 1, m, 4m + 1) & T \geq m
\end{cases}
$$

We complete the proof of Theorem 3.9.8 by bounding $C(1, 2q, 4q + 1)$, $C(2q + 1, q, 4q + 1)$, $D(1, 2q, 4q + 1)$, and $D(2q + 1, q, 4q + 1)$ appearing in (3.4) and combining them with the bounds of (3.5).

We now give a recursive construction of an $N(2q + 1, q, 4q + 1)$ circuit from which these bounds are derived. Shown in Fig. 3.30 is the recursive decomposition of an $N(4t + 1, 2t, 8t+1)$ circuit in terms of two copies of $N(2t+1, t, 4t+1)$ circuits. The t-centering circuits detect whether the head is in positions $2t, 2t - 1, \ldots, 1, 0$ or in positions $-1, \ldots, -2t$. In the former case, this circuit cyclically shifts the $8t + 1$ inputs inputs down by t positions; in the latter, it cyclically shifts them up by t positions. The result is that the head is centered in the middle $2t + 1$ positions. The OR of $s_{-1}, \ldots, s_{-2t}$ can be used as a signal to determine

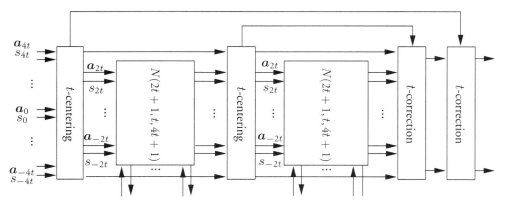

Figure 3.30 A recursive decomposition of $N(4t + 1, 2t, 8t + 1)$.

which shift to take. After centering, t steps are simulated, the head is centered again, and another t steps are again simulated. Two t-correction circuits cyclically shift the results in directions that are the reverse of the first two shifts. This circuit correctly simulates the tape computation over $2t$ steps and produces an $N(4t + 1, 2t, 8t + 1)$ circuit.

A t-centering circuit can be realized as a single stage of the cyclic shift circuit described in Section 2.5.2 and shown in Fig. 2.8. A t-correction circuit is just a t-centering circuit in which the shift is in the reverse direction. The four shifting circuits can be realized with $O(tb)$ gates and constant depth. The two OR trees to determine the direction of the shift can be realized with $O(t)$ gates and depth $O(\log t)$. From this discussion we have the following bounds on the size and depth of $N(4t + 1, 2t, 8t + 1)$:

$$C(4t + 1, 2t, 8t + 1) \le 2C(2t + 1, t, 4t + 1) + O(bt)$$
$$C(3, 1, 5) \le O(b)$$
$$D(4t + 1, 2t, 8t + 1) \le 2D(2t + 1, t, 4t + 1) + 2\lceil \log_2 t \rceil$$
$$D(3, 1, 5) \le O(1)$$

We now solve this set of recurrences. Let $\mathcal{C}(k) = C(2t + 1, t, 4t + 1)$ and $\mathcal{D}(k) = D(2t+1, t, 4t+1)$ when $t = 2^k$. The above bounds translate into the following recurrences:

$$\mathcal{C}(k + 1) \le 2\mathcal{C}(k) + K_1 2^k + K_2$$
$$\mathcal{C}(0) \le K_3$$
$$\mathcal{D}(k + 1) \le 2\mathcal{D}(k) + 2k + K_4$$
$$\mathcal{D}(0) \le K_5$$

for constants K_1, K_2, K_3, K_4, and K_5. It is straightforward to show that $\mathcal{C}(k + 1)$ and $\mathcal{D}(k + 1)$ satisfy the following inequalities:

$$\mathcal{C}(k) \le 2^k(K_1 k/2 + K_2 + K_3) - K_2$$
$$\mathcal{D}(k) \le 2^k(K_5 + K_4 + 2) - 2k - (K_4 + 2)$$

We now derive explicit upper bounds to (3.4). Let $\Lambda(k) = C(1, q, 2q+1)$ and $\Delta(k) = D(1, q, 2q+1)$ when $q = 2^k$. Then, the inequalities of (3.4) become the following:

$$\Lambda(k+1) \leq \Lambda(k) + \mathcal{C}(k)$$
$$\Lambda(0) \leq K_6$$
$$\Delta(k+1) \leq \Delta(k) + \mathcal{D}(k)$$
$$\Delta(0) \leq K_7$$

where $K_6 = C(1, 1, 3) = 7b + 3$ and $K_7 = D(1, 1, 3) = 4$. The solutions to these recurrences are given below.

$$\Lambda(k) \leq \sum_{j=0}^{k-1} \mathcal{C}(j)$$
$$= 2^k (K_1 k/2 + K_2 + K_3 - K_1) - k K_2 + (K_6 - (K_2 + K_3 - K_1))$$
$$= O(k 2^k)$$
$$\Delta(k) \leq \sum_{j=0}^{k-1} \mathcal{D}(j)$$
$$= 2^k (K_5 + K_4 + 2) - k^2 + (1 - (K_4 + 2))k + (K_7 - (K_5 + K_4 + 2))$$
$$= O(2^k)$$

Here we have made use of the identity in Problem 3.1. From (3.5) and (3.6) we establish the result of Theorem 3.9.8. ∎

3.10 Design of a Simple CPU

In this section we design an eleven-instruction CPU for a general-purpose computer that has a random-access memory with 2^{12} 16-bit memory words. We use this design to illustrate how a general-purpose computer can be assembled from gates and binary storage devices (flip-flops). The design is purposely kept simple so that basic concepts are made explicit. In practice, however, CPU design can be very complex. Since the CPU is the heart of every computer, a high premium is attached to making them fast. Many clever ideas have been developed for this purpose, almost all of which we must for simplicity ignore here.

Before beginning, we note that a typical complex instruction set (CISC) CPU, one with a rich set of instructions, contains several tens of thousands of gates, while as shown in the previous section, a random-access memory unit has a number of equivalent gates proportional to its memory capacity in bits. (CPUs are often sold with caches, small random-access memory units that add materially to the number of equivalent gates.) The CPUs of reduced instruction set (RISC) computers have many fewer gates. By contrast, a four-megabyte memory has the equivalent of several tens of millions of gates. As a consequence, the size and depth of the next-state and output functions of the random-access memory, δ_{RMEM} and λ_{RMEM}, typically dominate the size and depth of the next-state and output functions, δ_{CPU} and λ_{CPU}, of the CPU, as shown in Theorem 3.6.1.

3.10.1   The Register Set

A CPU is a sequential circuit that repeatedly reads and executes an instruction from its memory in what is known as the fetch-and-execute cycle. (See Sections 3.4 and 3.10.2.) A machine-language program is a set of instructions drawn from the instruction set of the CPU. In our simple CPU each instruction consists of two parts, an **opcode** and an **address**, as shown schematically below.

1	4	5	16
Opcode		Address	

Since our computer has eleven instructions, we use a 4-bit opcode, a length sufficient to represent all of them. Twelve bits remain in the 16-bit word, providing addresses for 4,096 16-bit words in a random-access memory.

We let our CPU have eight special registers: the 16-bit **accumulator** (AC), the 12-bit **program counter** (PC), the 4-bit **opcode register** (OPC), the 12-bit **memory address register** (MAR), the 16-bit **memory data register** (MDR), the 16-bit **input register** (INR), the 16-bit **output register** (denoted OUTR), and the **halt register** (HLT). These registers are shown schematically together with the random-access memory in Fig. 3.31.

The program counter PC contains the address from which the next instruction will be fetched. Normally this is the address following the address of the current instruction. However, if some condition is true, such as that the contents of the accumulator AC are zero, the program might place a new address in the PC and jump to this new address. The memory address register MAR contains the address used by the random-access memory to fetch a word. The memory data register MDR contains the word fetched from the memory. The halt register HLT contains the value 0 if the CPU is halted and otherwise contains 1.

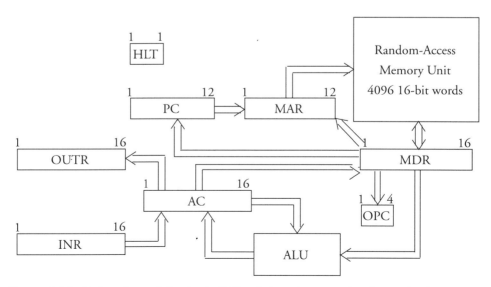

Figure 3.31 Basic registers of the simple CPU and the paths connecting them. Also shown is the arithmetic logic unit (ALU) containing circuits for AND, addition, shifting, and Boolean complement.

3.10.2   The Fetch-and-Execute Cycle

The fetch-and-execute cycle has a fetch portion and an execution portion. The fetch portion is always the same: the instruction whose address is in the PC is fetched into the MDR and the opcode portion of this register is copied into the OPC. At this point the action of the CPU diverges, based on the instruction denoted by the value of the OPC. Suppose, for example, that the OPC denotes a load accumulator instruction. The action required is to copy the word specified by the address part of the instruction into the accumulator. Fig. 3.32 contains a decomposition of the **load accumulator** instruction into eight **microinstructions** executed in six **microcycles**. During each microcycle several microinstructions can be executed concurrently, as shown in the table for the second and fourth microcycles. In Section 3.10.5 we describe implementations of the fetch-and-execute cycle for each of the instructions of our computer.

It is important to note that a realistic CPU must do more than fetch and execute instructions: it must be interruptable by a user or an external device that demands its attention. After fetching and executing an instruction, a CPU typically examines a small set of flip-flops to see if it must break away from the program it is currently executing to handle an **interrupt**, an action equivalent to fetching an instruction associated with the interrupt. This action causes an interrupt routine to be run that responds to the problem associated with the interrupt, after which the CPU returns to the program it was executing when it was interrupted. It can do this by saving the address of the next instruction of this program (the value of the PC) at a special location in memory (such as address 0). After handling the interrupt, it branches to this address by reloading PC with the old value.

3.10.3   The Instruction Set

Figure 3.33 lists the eleven instructions of our simple CPU. The first group consists of arithmetic (see Section 2.7), logic, and shift instructions (see Section 2.5.1). The circulate instruction executes a cyclic shift of the accumulator by one place. The second group consists of instructions to move data between the accumulator and memory. The third set contains a conditional jump instruction: when the accumulator is zero, it causes the CPU to resume fetching instructions at a new address, the address in the memory data register. This address is moved to the program counter before fetching the next instruction. The fourth set contains input/output instructions. The fifth set contains the halt instruction. Many more instruc-

Cycle	Microinstruction	Microinstruction
1	Copy contents of PC to MAR.	
2	Fetch word at address MAR into MDR.	Increment PC.
3	Copy opcode part of MDR to OPC.	
4	Interpret OPC	Copy address part of MDR to MAR.
5	Fetch word at address MAR into MDR.	
6	Copy MDR into AC.	

Figure 3.32 Decomposition of the **load accumulator** instruction into eight microinstructions in six microcycles.

	Opcode	Binary	Description
Arithmetic	ADD	0000	Add memory word to AC
Logic	AND	0001	AND memory word to AC
	CLA	0010	Clear (set to zero) the accumulator
	CMA	0011	Complement AC
	CIL	0100	Circulate AC left
Memory	LDA	0101	Load memory word into AC
	STA	0110	Store AC into memory word
Jump	JZ	0111	Jump to address if AC zero
I/O	IN	1000	Load INR into AC
	OUT	1001	Store AC into OUTR
Halt	HLT	1010	Halt computer

Figure 3.33 Instructions of the simple CPU.

tions could be added, including ones to simplify the execution of subroutines, handle loops, and process interrupts. Each instruction has a mnemonic opcode, such as CLA, and a binary opcode, such as 0010.

Many other operations can be performed using this set, including subtraction, which can be realized through the use of ADD, CMA, and two's-complement arithmetic (see Problem 3.18). Multiplication is also possible through the use of CIL and ADD (see Problem 3.38). Since multiple CILs can be used to rotate right one place, division is also possible. Finally, as observed in Problem 3.39, every two-input Boolean function can be realized through the use of AND and CMA. This implies that every Boolean function can be realized by this machine if it is designed to address enough memory locations.

Each of these instructions is a **direct memory instruction**, by which we mean that all addresses refer directly to memory locations containing the **operands** (data) on which the program operates. Most CPUs also have **indirect memory instructions** (and are said to support **indirection**). These are instructions in which an address is interpreted as the address at which to find the address containing the needed operand. To find such an indirect operand, the CPU does two memory fetches, the first to find the address of the operand and the second to find the operand itself. Often a single bit is added to an opcode to denote that an instruction is an indirect memory instruction.

An instruction stored in the memory of our computer consists of sixteen binary digits, the first four denoting the opcode and the last twelve denoting an address. Because it is hard for humans to interpret such **machine-language** statements, mnemonic opcodes and assembly languages have been devised.

3.10.4 Assembly-Language Programming

An assembly-language program consists of a number of lines each containing either a real or pseudo-instruction. Real instructions correspond exactly to machine-language instructions except that they contain mnemonics and symbolic addresses instead of binary sequences. Pseudo-instructions are directions to the **assembler**, the program that translates an assembly-language program into machine language. A typical pseudo-instruction is ORG 100, which instructs the assembler to place the following lines at locations beginning with location 100. Another example is the DAT pseudo-instruction that identifies a word containing only data. The END pseudo-instruction identifies the end of the assembly-language program.

Each assembly-language instruction fits on one line. A typical instruction has the following fields, some or all of which may be used.

| Symbolic_Address | Mnemonic | Address | Indirect Bit | Comment |

If an instruction has a Symbolic_Address (a string of symbols), the address is converted to the physical address of the instruction by the assembler and substituted for all uses of the symbolic address. The Address field can contain one or more symbolic or real addresses, although the assembly language used here allows only one address. The Indirect Bit specifies whether or not indirection is to be used on the address in question. In our CPU we do not allow indirection, although we do allow it in our assembly language because it simplifies our sample program.

Let's now construct an assembly-language program whose purpose is to boot up a computer that has been reset. The **boot program** reads another program provided through its input port and stores this new program (a sequence of 16-bit words) in the memory locations just above itself. When it has finished reading this new program (determined by reading a zero word), it transfers control to the new program by jumping to the first location above itself. When computers are turned off at night they need to be rebooted, typically by executing a program of this kind.

Figure 3.34 shows a program to boot up our computer. It uses three symbolic addresses, ADDR_1, ADDR_2, ADDR_3, and one real address, 10. We assume this program resides

	ORG	0		Program is stored at location 0.
ADDR_1	IN			Start of program.
	JZ	10		Transfer control if AC zero.
	STA	ADDR_2	I	Indirect store of input.
	LDA	ADDR_2		Start incrementing ADDR_2.
	ADD	ADDR_3		Finish incrementing of ADDR_2.
	STA	ADDR_2		Store new value of ADDR_2.
	CLA			Clear AC.
	JZ	ADDR_1		Jump to start of program.
ADDR_2	DAT	10		Address for indirection.
ADDR_3	DAT END	1		Value for incrementing.

Figure 3.34 A program to reboot a computer.

permanently in locations 0 through 9 of the memory. After being reset, the CPU reads and executes the instruction at location 0 of its memory.

The first instruction of this program after the ORG statement reads the value in the input register into the accumulator. The second instruction jumps to location 10 if the accumulator is zero, indicating that the last word of the second program has been written into the memory. If this happens, the next instruction executed by the CPU is at location 10; that is, control is transferred to the second program. If the accumulator is not zero, its value is stored indirectly at location ADDR_2. (We explain the indirect STA in the next paragraph.) On the first execution of this command, the value of ADDR_2 is 10, so that the contents of the accumulator are stored at location 10. The next three steps increment the value of ADDR_2 by placing its contents in the accumulator, adding the value in location ADDR_3 to it, namely 1, and storing the new value into location ADDR_2. Finally, the accumulator is zeroed and a JZ instruction used to return to location ADDR_1, the first address of the boot program.

The indirect STA instruction in this program is not available in our computer. However, as shown in Problem 3.42, this instruction can be simulated by a self-modifying subprogram. While it is considered bad programming practice to write self-modifying programs, this exercise illustrates the power of self-modification as well as the advantage of having indirection in the instruction set of a computer.

3.10.5   Timing and Control

Now that the principles of a CPU have been described and a programming example given, we complete the description of a sequential circuit realizing the CPU. To do this we need to describe circuits controlling the combining and movement of data. To this end we introduce the assignment notation in Fig. 3.35. Here the expression AC ← MDR means that the contents of MDR are copied into AC, whereas AC ← AC + MDR means that the contents of AC and MDR are added and the result assigned to AC. In all cases the left arrow, ←, signifies that the result or contents on the right are assigned to the register on the left. However, when the register on the left contains information of a particular type, such as an address in the case of PC or an opcode in the case of OPC, and the register on the right contains more information, the assignment notation means that the relevant bits of the register on the right are loaded into the register on the left. For example, the assignment PC ← MDR means that the address portion of MDR is copied to PC.

Register transfer notation uses these assignment operations as well as timing information to break down a machine-level instruction into microinstructions that are executed in succes-

Notation	Explanation
AC ← MDR	Contents of MDR loaded into AC.
AC ← AC + MDR	Contents of MDR added to AC.
MDR ← M	Contents of memory location MAR loaded into MDR.
M ← MDR	Contents of MDR stored at memory location MAR.
PC ← MDR	Address portion of MDR loaded into PC.
MAR ← PC	Contents of PC loaded into MAR.

Figure 3.35 Microinstructions illustrating assignment notation.

Timing	Microinstructions
t_1	MAR ← PC
t_2	MDR ← M, PC ← PC+1
t_3	OPC ← MDR

Figure 3.36 The microcode for the fetch portion of each instruction.

sive microcycles. The jth microcycle is specified by the **timing variable** t_j, $1 \leq j \leq k$. That is, t_j is 1 during the jth microcycle and is zero otherwise. It is straightforward to show that these timing variables can be realized by connecting a decoder to the outputs of a counting circuit, a circuit containing the binary representation of an integer that increments the integer modulo some other integer on each clock cycle. (See Problem 3.40.)

Since the fetch portion of each instruction is the same, we write a few lines of register transfer notation for it, as shown in Fig. 3.36. On the left-hand side of each line is timing variable indicating the cycle during which the microinstruction is executed.

The microinstructions for the execute portion of each instruction of our computer are shown in Fig. 3.37. On the left-hand side of each line is a timing variable that must be ANDed with the indicated **instruction variable**, such as c_{ADD}, which is 1 if that instruction is in

Control		Microcode
ADD		
c_{ADD}	t_4	MAR ← MDR
c_{ADD}	t_5	MDR ← M
c_{ADD}	t_6	AC ← AC + MDR
AND		
c_{AND}	t_4	MAR ← MDR
c_{AND}	t_5	MDR ← M
c_{AND}	t_6	AC ← AC AND MDR
CLA		
c_{CLA}	t_4	AC ← 0
CIL		
c_{CIL}	t_4	AC ← Shift(AC)
LDA		
c_{LDA}	t_4	MAR ← MDR
c_{LDA}	t_5	MDR ← M
c_{LDA}	t_6	AC ← MDR

Control		Microcode
STA		
c_{STA}	t_4	MAR ← MDR
c_{STA}	t_4	MDR ← AC
c_{STA}	t_5	M ← MDR
CMA		
c_{CMA}	t_4	AC ← ¬ AC
JZ		
c_{JZ}	t_4	if (AC = 0) PC ← MDR
IN		
c_{IN}	t_4	AC ← INR
OUT		
c_{OUT}	t_4	OUTR ← AC
HLT		
c_{HLT}	t_4	t_j ← 0 for $1 \leq j \leq k$

Figure 3.37 The execute portions of the microcode of instructions.

the opcode register OPC and 0 otherwise. These instruction variables can be generated by a decoder attached to the output of OPC. Here $\neg A$ denotes the complement of the accumulator.

Now that we understand how to combine microinstructions in microcycles to produce macroinstructions, we use this information to define control variables that control the movement of data between registers or combine the contents of two registers and assign the result to another register. This information will be used to complete the design of the CPU.

We now introduce notation for **control variables**. If a microinstruction results in the movement of data from register B to register A, denoted $A \leftarrow B$ in our assignment notation, we associate the control variable $L(A, B)$ with it. If a microinstruction results in the combination of the contents of registers B and C with the operation $\odot$ and the assignment of the result to register A, denoted $A \leftarrow B \odot C$ in our assignment notation, we associate the control variable $L(A, B \odot C)$ with it. For example, inspection of Figs. 3.36 and 3.37 shows that we can write the following expressions for the control variables $L(\mathrm{OPC}, \mathrm{MDR})$ and $L(\mathrm{AC}, \mathrm{AC+MDR})$:

$$L(\mathrm{OPC}, \mathrm{MDR}) = t_3$$
$$L(\mathrm{AC}, \mathrm{AC+MDR}) = c_{\mathrm{ADD}} \wedge t_6$$

Thus, OPC is loaded with the contents of MDR when $t_3 = 1$, and the contents of AC are added to those of MDR and copied into AC when $c_{\mathrm{ADD}} \wedge t_6 = 1$.

The complete set of control variables can be obtained by first grouping together all the microinstructions that affect a given register, as shown in Fig. 3.38, and then writing expressions for the control variables. Here M denotes the memory unit and HLT is a special register that must be set to 1 for the CPU to run. Inspection of Fig. 3.38 leads to the following expressions for control variables:

$$L(\mathrm{AC}, \mathrm{AC} + \mathrm{MDR}) = c_{\mathrm{ADD}} \wedge t_6$$
$$L(\mathrm{AC}, \mathrm{AC\ AND\ MDR}) = c_{\mathrm{AND}} \wedge t_6$$
$$L(\mathrm{AC}, 0) = c_{\mathrm{CLA}} \wedge t_4$$
$$L(\mathrm{AC}, \mathrm{Shift(AC)}) = c_{\mathrm{CIL}} \wedge t_4$$
$$L(\mathrm{AC}, \mathrm{MDR}) = c_{\mathrm{LDA}} \wedge t_6$$
$$L(\mathrm{AC}, \mathrm{INR}) = c_{\mathrm{IN}} \wedge t_4$$
$$L(\mathrm{AC}, \neg\, \mathrm{AC}) = c_{\mathrm{CMA}} \wedge t_4$$
$$L(\mathrm{MAR}, \mathrm{PC}) = t_1$$
$$L(\mathrm{MAR}, \mathrm{MDR}) = (c_{\mathrm{ADD}} \vee c_{\mathrm{AND}} \vee c_{\mathrm{LDA}} \vee c_{\mathrm{STA}}) \wedge t_4$$
$$L(\mathrm{MDR}, \mathrm{M}) = t_2 \vee (c_{\mathrm{ADD}} \vee c_{\mathrm{AND}} \vee c_{\mathrm{LDA}}) \wedge t_5$$
$$L(\mathrm{MDR}, \mathrm{AC}) = c_{\mathrm{STA}} \wedge t_4$$
$$L(\mathrm{M}, \mathrm{MDR}) = c_{\mathrm{STA}} \wedge t_5$$
$$L(\mathrm{PC}, \mathrm{PC+1}) = t_2$$
$$L(\mathrm{PC}, \mathrm{MDR}) = (AC = 0) \wedge c_{\mathrm{JZ}} \wedge t_4$$
$$L(\mathrm{OPC}, \mathrm{MDR}) = t_3$$
$$L(\mathrm{OUTR}, \mathrm{AC}) = c_{\mathrm{OUT}} \wedge t_4$$
$$L(t_j) = c_{\mathrm{HLT}} \wedge t_4 \text{ for } 1 \leq j \leq 6$$

Control		Microcode	Control		Microcode
AC			**M**		
c_{ADD}	t_6	$\text{AC} \leftarrow \text{AC} + \text{MDR}$	c_{STA}	t_5	$\text{M} \leftarrow \text{MDR}$
c_{AND}	t_6	$\text{AC} \leftarrow \text{AC AND MDR}$			
c_{CLA}	t_4	$\text{AC} \leftarrow 0$	**PC**		
c_{CIL}	t_4	$\text{AC} \leftarrow \text{Shift(AC)}$		t_2	$\text{PC} \leftarrow \text{PC}+1$
c_{LDA}	t_6	$\text{AC} \leftarrow \text{MDR}$	c_{JZ}	t_4	if ($\text{AC} = 0$) $\text{PC} \leftarrow \text{MDR}$
c_{CMA}	t_4	$\text{AC} \leftarrow \neg \text{AC}$			
c_{IN}	t_4	$\text{AC} \leftarrow \text{INR}$	**OPC**		
				t_3	$\text{OPC} \leftarrow \text{MDR}$
MAR					
	t_1	$\text{MAR} \leftarrow \text{PC}$	**OUTR**		
c_{ADD}	t_4	$\text{MAR} \leftarrow \text{MDR}$	c_{OUT}	t_4	$\text{OUTR} \leftarrow \text{AC}$
c_{AND}	t_4	$\text{MAR} \leftarrow \text{MDR}$			
c_{LDA}	t_4	$\text{MAR} \leftarrow \text{MDR}$	**HLT**		
c_{STA}	t_4	$\text{MAR} \leftarrow \text{MDR}$	c_{HLT}	t_4	$t_j \leftarrow 0$ for $1 \leq j \leq k$
MDR					
	t_2	$\text{MDR} \leftarrow \text{M}$			
c_{ADD}	t_5	$\text{MDR} \leftarrow \text{M}$			
c_{AND}	t_5	$\text{MDR} \leftarrow \text{M}$			
c_{LDA}	t_5	$\text{MDR} \leftarrow \text{M}$			
c_{STA}	t_4	$\text{MDR} \leftarrow \text{AC}$			

Figure 3.38 The microinstructions affecting each register.

The expression ($\text{AC} = 0$) denotes a Boolean variable whose value is 1 if all bits in the AC are zero and 0 otherwise. This variable is the AND of the complement of each component of register AC.

To illustrate the remaining steps in the design of the CPU, we show in Fig. 3.39 the circuits used to provide input to the accumulator AC. Shown are registers AC, MDR, and INR as well as circuits for the functions f_{add} (see Section 2.7) and f_{and} that add two binary numbers and take their AND, respectively. Also shown are multiplexer circuits f_{mux} (see Section 2.5.5). They have three control inputs, L_0, L_1, and L_2, and can select one of eight inputs to place on their output lines. However, only seven inputs are needed: the result of adding AC and MDR, the result of ANDing AC and MDR, the zero vector, the result of shifting AC, the contents of MDR or INR, and the complement of AC. The three control inputs encode the seven control variables, $L(\text{AC}, \text{AC} + \text{MDR})$, $L(\text{AC}, \text{AC AND MDR})$, $L(\text{AC}, 0)$, $L(\text{AC}, \text{Shift(AC)})$, $L(\text{AC}, \text{MDR})$, $L(\text{AC}, \text{INR})$, and $L(\text{AC}, \neg\text{AC})$. Since at most one of these control variables has value 1 at any one time, the encoder circuit of Section 2.5.3 can be used to encode these seven control variables into the three bits L_0, L_1, and L_2 shown in Fig. 3.39.

The logic circuit to supply inputs to AC has size proportional to the number of bits in each register. Thus, if the word size of the CPU were scaled up, the size of this circuit would scale linearly with the word size.

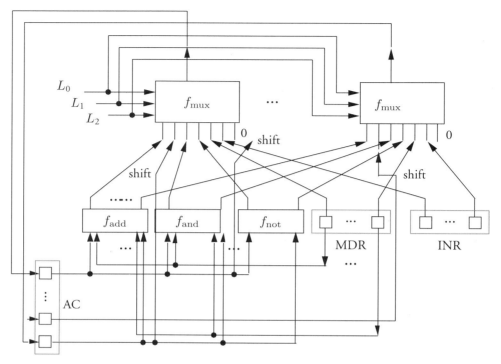

Figure 3.39 Circuits providing input to the accumulator AC.

The circuit for the program counter PC can be designed from an adder, a multiplexer, and a few additional gates. Its size is proportional to $\lceil \log_2 m \rceil$. The circuits to supply inputs to the remaining registers, namely MAR, MDR, OPC, INR, and OUTR, are less complex to design than those for the accumulator. The same observations apply to the control variable to write the contents of the memory. The complete design of the CPU is given as an exercise (see Problem 3.41).

3.10.6 CPU Circuit Size and Depth

Using the design given above for a simple CPU as a basis, we derive upper bounds on the size and depth of the next-state and output functions of the RAM CPU defined in Section 3.4.

All words on which the CPU operates contain b bits except for addresses, which contain $\lceil \log m \rceil$ bits where m is the number of words in the random-access memory. We assume that the CPU not only has an $\lceil \log m \rceil$-bit program counter but can send the contents of the PC to the MAR of the random-access memory in one unit of time. When the CPU fetches an instruction that refers to an address, it may have to retrieve multiple b-bit words to create an $\lceil \log m \rceil$-bit address. We assume the time for such operations is counted in the number T of steps that the RAM takes for the computation.

The arithmetic operations supported by the RAM CPU include addition and subtraction, operations realized by circuits with size and depth linear and logarithmic respectively in b, the length of the accumulator. (See Section 2.7.) The same is true for the logical vector and the shift operations. (See Section 2.5.1.) Thus, circuits affecting the accumulator (see Fig. 3.39) have size $O(b)$ and depth $O(\log b)$. Circuits affecting the opcode and output registers and the memory address and data registers are simple and have size $O(b)$ and depth $O(\log b)$. The circuits affecting the program counter not only support transfer of data from the accumulator to the program counter but also allow the program counter to be incremented. The latter function can be performed by an adder circuit whose size is $O(\lceil \log m \rceil)$ and depth is $O(\log \lceil \log m \rceil)$. It follows that

$$C_\Omega(\delta_{\text{CPU}}) = O(b + \lceil \log m \rceil)$$
$$D_\Omega(\delta_{\text{CPU}}) = O(\log b + \log \lceil \log m \rceil)$$

3.10.7 Emulation

In Section 3.4 we demonstrated that whatever computation can be done by a finite-state machine can be done by a RAM when the latter has sufficient memory. This universal nature of the RAM, which is a model for the CPU we have just designed, is emphasized by the problem of emulation, the simulation of one general-purpose computer by another.

Emulation of a target CPU by a host CPU means reading the instructions in a program for the target CPU and executing host instructions that have the same effect as the target instructions. In Problem 3.44 we ask the reader to sketch a program to emulate one CPU by another. This is another manifestation of universality, this time for unbounded-memory RAMs.

. . . .

Problems

MATHEMATICAL PRELIMINARIES

3.1 Establish the following identity:

$$\sum_{j=0}^{k} j2^j = 2\left((k-1)2^k + 1\right)$$

3.2 Let $p : \mathbb{N} \mapsto \mathbb{N}$ and $q : \mathbb{N} \mapsto \mathbb{N}$ be polynomial functions on the set $\mathbb{N}$ of non-negative integers. Show that $p(q(n))$ is also a polynomial in n.

FINITE-STATE MACHINES

3.3 Describe an FSM that compares two binary numbers supplied as concurrent streams of bits in descending order of importance and enters a rejecting state if the first string is smaller than the second and an accepting state otherwise.

3.4 Describe an FSM that computes the threshold-two function on n Boolean inputs that are supplied sequentially to the machine.

3.5 Consider the full-adder function $f_{FA}(x_i, y_i, z_i) = (c_{i+1}, s_i)$ defined below where $+$ denotes integer addition:

$$2c_{i+1} + s_i = x_i + y_i + c_i$$

Show that the subfunction of f_{FA} obtained by fixing $c_i = 0$ and deleting c_{i+1} is the EXCLUSIVE OR of the variables x_i and y_i.

3.6 It is straightforward to show that every Moore FSM is a Mealey FSM. Given a Mealey FSM, show how to construct a Moore FSM whose outputs for every input sequence are identical to those of the Mealey FSM.

3.7 Find a deterministic FSM that recognizes the same language as that recognized by the nondeterministic FSM of Fig. 3.8.

3.8 Write a program in a language of your choice that writes the straight-line program described in Fig. 3.3 for the FSM of Fig. 3.2 realizing the EXCLUSIVE OR function.

SHALLOW FSM CIRCUITS

3.9 Develop a representation for states in the m-word, b-bit random-access memory so that its next-state mappings form a semigroup.

Hint: Show that the information necessary to update the current state can be succinctly described.

3.10 Show that matrix multiplication is associative.

SEQUENTIAL CIRCUITS

3.11 Show that the circuit of Fig. 3.15 computes the functions defined in the tables of Fig. 3.14.

Hint: Section 2.2 provides a method to produce a circuit from a tabular description of a binary function.

3.12 Design a sequential circuit (an **electronic lock**) that enters an accepting state only when it receives some particular four-bit sequence that you specify.

3.13 Design a sequential circuit (a **modulo-p counter**) that increments a binary number by one on each step until it reaches the integer value p, at which point it resets its value to zero. You should assume that p is not a power of 2.

3.14 Give an efficient design of an **incrementing/decrementing counter**, a sequential circuit that increments or decrements a binary number modulo 2^n. Specify the machine as an FSM and determine the number of gates in the sequential circuit in terms of n.

RANDOM-ACCESS MACHINES

3.15 Given a straight-line program for a Boolean function, describe the steps taken to compute it during fetch-and-execute cycles of a RAM. Determine whether jump instructions are necessary to execute such programs.

3.16 Consulting Theorem 3.4.1, determine whether jump instructions are necessary for all RAM computations. If not, what advantage accrues to using them?

3.17 Sketch a RAM program using time and space $O(n)$ that recognizes strings of the form $\{0^m 1^m \mid 1 \le m \le n\}$.

ASSEMBLY-LANGUAGE PROGRAMMING

3.18 Write an assembly-language program in the language of Fig. 3.18 to subtract two integers.

3.19 The assembly-language instructions of Fig. 3.18 operate on integers. Show that the operations AND, OR, and NOT can be realized on Boolean variables with these instructions. Show also that these operations on vectors can be implemented.

3.20 Write an assembly-language program in the language of Fig. 3.18 to form x^y for integers x and y.

3.21 Show that the assembly-language instructions CLR R_i, $R_i \leftarrow R_j$, JMP$_+$ N_i, and JMP$_-$ N_i can be realized from the assembly-language instructions INC, DEC, CONTINUE, R_j JMP$_+$ N_i, and R_j JMP$_-$ N_i.

TURING MACHINES

3.22 In a standard Turing machine the tape unit has a left end but extends indefinitely to the right. Show that allowing the tape unit to be infinite in both directions does not add power to the Turing machine.

3.23 Describe in detail a Turing machine with unlimited storage capacity that recognizes the language $\{0^m 1^m | 1 \leq m\}$.

3.24 Sketch a proof that in $O(n^2)$ steps a Turing machine can verify that a particular tour of n cities in an instance of the Traveling Salesperson Problem satisfies the requirement that the total distance traveled is less than or equal to the limit k set on this instance of the Traveling Salesperson Problem.

3.25 Design the additional circuitry needed to transform a sequential circuit for a random-access memory into one for a tape memory. Give upper bounds on the size and depth of the next-state and output functions that are simultaneously achievable.

3.26 In the proof of Theorem 3.8.1 it is assumed that the words and their addresses in a RAM memory unit are placed on the tape of a Turing machine in order of increasing addresses, as suggested by Fig. 3.40. The addresses, which are $\lceil \log m \rceil$ bits in length, are organized as a collection of $\lceil \lceil \log m \rceil / b \rceil$ b-bit words. (In the example, $b = 1$.) An address is written on tape cells that immediately precede the value of the corresponding RAM word. A RAM address `addr` is stored on the tape to the left in the shaded region.

Assume that markers can be placed on cells. (This amounts to enlarging the tape alphabet by a constant factor.) Show that markers can be used to move from the first word whose RAM address matches the ib most significant bits of the address $\boldsymbol{a}$ to the next one that matches the $(i + 1)b$ most significant bits. Show that this procedure can

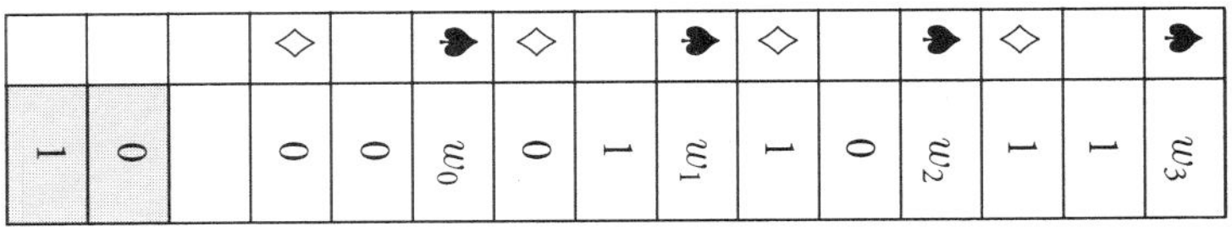

Figure 3.40 A TM tape with markers on words and the first bit of each address.

be used to find the RAM word whose address matches `addr` in $O((m/b)(\log m)^2)$ Turing machine steps by a machine that can store in its control unit only one b-bit subword of `addr`.

3.27 Extend Problem 3.26 by demonstrating that the simulation can be done with a binary tape symbol alphabet.

3.28 Extend Theorem 3.8.1 to show that there exists a Turing machine that can simulate an unbounded-memory RAM.

3.29 Sketch a proof that every Turing machine can be simulated by a RAM program of the kind described in Section 3.4.3.

COMPUTATIONAL INEQUALITIES FOR TURING MACHINES

3.30 Show that a one-tape Turing machine needs time exponential in n to compute most Boolean functions $f : \mathcal{B}^n \mapsto \mathcal{B}$ on n variables, regardless of how much memory is allocated to the computation.

3.31 Apply Theorem 3.2.2 to the one-tape Turing machine that executes T steps. Determine whether the resulting inequalities are weaker or stronger than those given in Theorem 3.9.2.

3.32 Write a program in your favorite language for the procedure WRITE_OR(t, m) introduced in Fig. 3.27.

3.33 Write a program in your favorite language for the procedure WRITE_CELL_CIRCUIT(t, m) introduced in Fig. 3.27.

Hint: See Problem 2.4.

FIRST P-COMPLETE AND NP-COMPLETE PROBLEMS

3.34 Show that the language MONOTONE CIRCUIT VALUE defined below is **P**-complete.

MONOTONE CIRCUIT VALUE
Instance: A description for a monotone circuit with fixed values for its input variables and a designated output gate.
Answer: "Yes" if the output of the circuit has value 1.

Hint: Using dual-rail logic, find a way to translate (reduce) a string in the language CIRCUIT VALUE to a string in MONOTONE CIRCUIT VALUE by converting in logarithmic space (in the length of the string) a circuit over the standard basis to a circuit over the monotone basis. Note that, as stated in the text, the composition of two logarithmic-space reductions is a logarithmic-space reduction. To simplify the conversion from non-monotone circuits to monotone circuits, use even integers to index vertices in the non-monotone circuits so that both even and odd integers can be used in the monotone case.

3.35 Show that the language FAN-OUT 2 CIRCUIT SAT defined below is **NP**-complete.

FAN-OUT 2 CIRCUIT SAT
Instance: A description for a circuit of fan-out 2 with fixed values for its input variables and a designated output gate.
Answer: "Yes" if the output of the circuit has value 1.

Hint: To reduce the fan-out of a vertex, replace the direct connections between a gate and its successors by a binary tree whose vertices are AND gates with their inputs connected together. Show that, for each gate of fan-out more than two, such trees can be generated by a program that runs in polynomial time.

3.36 Show that clauses given in the proof of Theorem 3.9.7 are satisfied only when their variables have values consistent with the definition of the gate type.

3.37 A circuit with n input variables $\{x_1, x_2, \ldots, x_n\}$ is satisfiable if there is an assignment of values to the variables such that the output of the circuit has value 1. Assume that the circuit has only one output and the gates are over the basis $\Omega = \{\text{AND, OR, NOT}\}$.

    a) Describe a nondeterministic procedure that accepts as input the description of a circuit in POSE and returns 1 if the circuit is satisfiable and 0 otherwise.

    b) Describe a deterministic procedure that accepts as input the description of a circuit in POSE and returns 1 if the circuit is satisfiable and 0 otherwise. What is the running time of this procedure when implemented on the RAM?

    c) Describe an efficient (polynomial-time) deterministic procedure that accepts as input the description of a circuit in SOPE and returns 1 if the circuit is satisfiable and 0 otherwise.

    d) By using Boolean algebra, we can convert a circuit from POSE to SOPE. We can then use the result of the previous question to determine if the circuit is satisfiable. What is the drawback of this approach?

CENTRAL PROCESSING UNIT

3.38 Write an assembly-language program to multiply two binary numbers using the simple CPU of Section 3.10. How large are the integers that can be multiplied without producing numbers that are too large to be recorded in registers?

3.39 Assume that the simple CPU of Section 3.10 is modified to address an unlimited number of memory locations. Show that it can realize any Boolean function by demonstrating that it can compute the Boolean operations AND, OR, and NOT.

3.40 Design a circuit to produce the timing variables t_j, $1 \leq j \leq k$, of the simple CPU. They must have the property that exactly one of them has value 1 at a time and they successively become 1.

    Hint: Design a circuit that counts sequentially modulo k, an integer. That is, it increments a binary number until it reaches k, after which it resets the number to zero. See Problem 3.13.

3.41 Complete the design of the CPU of Section 3.10 by describing circuits for PC, MAR, MDR, OPC, INR, and OUTR.

3.42 Show that an indirect store operation can be simulated by the computer of Section 3.10.

Hint: Construct a program that temporarily moves the value of AC aside, fetches the address containing the destination for the store, and uses Boolean operations to modify a STA instruction in the program so that it contains the destination address.

3.43 Write an assembly-language program that repeatedly examines the input register until it is nonzero and then moves its contents to the accumulator.

3.44 Sketch an assembly-language program to emulate a target CPU by a host CPU under the assumption that each CPU's instruction set supports indirection. Provide a skeleton program that reads an instruction from the target instruction set and decides which host instruction to execute. Also sketch the particular host instructions needed to emulate a target add instruction and a target jump-on-zero instruction.

Chapter Notes

Although the concept of the finite-state machine is fully contained in the Turing machine model (Section 3.7) introduced in 1936 [334], the finite-state machine did not become a serious object of study until the 1950s. Mealey [214] and Moore [221] introduced models for finite-state machines that were shown to be equivalent. The Moore model is used in Section 3.1. Rabin and Scott [262] introduced the nondeterministic machine, although not defined in terms of external choice inputs as it is defined here.

The simulation of finite-state machines by logic circuits exhibited in Section 3.1.1 is due to Savage [281], as is its application to random-access (Section 3.6) and deterministic Turing machines (Section 3.9.1) [282]. The design of a simple CPU owes much to the early simple computers but is not tied to any particular architecture. The assembly language of Section 3.4.3 is borrowed from Smith [308].

The shallow circuits simulating finite-state machines described in Section 3.2 are due to Ladner and Fischer [186] and the existence of a universal Turing machine, the topic of Section 3.7, was shown by Turing [334].

Cook [76] identified the first **NP**-complete problem and Karp [160] demonstrated that a large number of other problems are **NP**-complete, including the Traveling Salesperson problem. About this time Levin [199] (see also [331]) was led to similar concepts for combinatorial problems. Our construction in Section 3.9.1 of a satisfiable circuit follows the general outline given by Papadimitriou [231] (who also gives the reduction to SATISFIABILITY) as well as the construction of a circuit simulating a deterministic Turing machine given by Savage [282]. Cook also identified the first **P**-complete problem [77,81]. Ladner [185] observed that the circuit of Theorem 3.9.1 could be written by a program using logarithmic space, thereby showing that CIRCUIT VALUE is **P**-complete. More information on **P**-complete and **NP**-complete problems can be found in Chapter 8.

The more sophisticated simulation of a circuit by a Turing machine given in Section 3.9.7 is due to Pippenger and Fischer [248] with improvements by Schnorr [297] and Savage, as cited by Schnorr.

4

Finite-State Machines and Pushdown Automata

The finite-state machine (FSM) and the pushdown automaton (PDA) enjoy a special place in computer science. The FSM has proven to be a very useful model for many practical tasks and deserves to be among the tools of every practicing computer scientist. Many simple tasks, such as interpreting the commands typed into a keyboard or running a calculator, can be modeled by finite-state machines. The PDA is a model to which one appeals when writing compilers because it captures the essential architectural features needed to parse context-free languages, languages whose structure most closely resembles that of many programming languages.

In this chapter we examine the language recognition capability of FSMs and PDAs. We show that FSMs recognize exactly the regular languages, languages defined by regular expressions and generated by regular grammars. We also provide an algorithm to find a FSM that is equivalent to a given FSM but has the fewest states.

We examine language recognition by PDAs and show that PDAs recognize exactly the context-free languages, languages whose grammars satisfy less stringent requirements than regular grammars. Both regular and context-free grammar types are special cases of the phrase-structure grammars that are shown in Chapter 5 to be the languages accepted by Turing machines.

It is desirable not only to classify languages by the architecture of machines that recognize them but also to have tests to show that a language is not of a particular type. For this reason we establish so-called pumping lemmas whose purpose is to show how strings in one language can be elongated or "pumped up." Pumping up may reveal that a language does not fall into a presumed language category. We also develop other properties of languages that provide mechanisms for distinguishing among language types. Because of the importance of context-free languages, we examine how they are parsed, a key step in programming language translation.

4.1 Finite-State Machine Models

The deterministic finite-state machine (DFSM), introduced in Section 3.1, has a set of states, including an initial state and one or more final states. At each unit of time a DFSM is given a letter from its input alphabet. This causes the machine to move from its current state to a potentially new state. While in a state, the DFSM produces a letter from its output alphabet. Such a machine computes the function defined by the mapping from strings of input letters to strings of output letters. DFSMs can also be used to accept strings. A string is accepted by a DFSM if the last state entered by the machine on that input string is a final state. The language recognized by a DFSM is the set of strings that it accepts.

Although there are languages that cannot be accepted by any machine with a finite number of states, it is important to note that all realistic computational problems are finite in nature and can be solved by FSMs. However, important opportunities to simplify computations may be missed if we do not view them as requiring potentially infinite storage, such as that provided by pushdown automata, machines that store data on a pushdown stack. (Pushdown automata are formally introduced in Section 4.8.)

The nondeterministic finite-state machine (NFSM) was also introduced in Section 3.1. The NFSM has the property that for a given state and input letter there may be several states to which it could move. Also for some state and input letter there may be no possible move. We say that an NFSM accepts a string if there is a sequence of next-state choices (see Section 3.1.5) that can be made, when necessary, so that the string causes the NFSM to enter a final state. The language accepted by such a machine is the set of strings it accepts.

Although nondeterminism is a useful tool in describing languages and computations, non-deterministic computations are very expensive to simulate deterministically: the deterministic simulation time can grow as an exponential function of the nondeterministic computation time. We explore nondeterminism here to gain experience with it. This will be useful in Chapter 8 when we classify languages by the ability of nondeterministic machines of infinite storage capacity to accept them. However, as we shall see, nondeterminism offers no advantage for finite-state machines in that both DFSMs and NFSMs recognize the same set of languages.

We now begin our formal treatment of these machine models. Since this chapter is concerned only with language recognition, we give an abbreviated definition of the deterministic FSM that ignores the output function. We also give a formal definition of the nondeterministic finite-state machine that agrees with that given in Section 3.1.5. We recall that we interpreted such a machine as a deterministic FSM that possesses a choice input through which a choice agent specifies the state transition to take if more than one is possible.

DEFINITION 4.1.1 *A deterministic **finite-state machine (DFSM)** M is a five-tuple $M = (\Sigma, Q, \delta, s, F)$ where Σ is the **input alphabet**, Q is the **set of states**, $\delta : Q \times \Sigma \mapsto Q$ is the **next-state function**, s is the **initial state**, and F is the **set of final states**. The DFSM M **accepts the input string** $w \in \Sigma^*$ if the last state entered by M on application of w starting in state s is a member of the set F. M **recognizes the language** $L(M)$ consisting of all such strings.*

*A **nondeterministic FSM (NFSM)** is similarly defined except that the next-state function δ is replaced by a **next-set function** $\delta : Q \times \Sigma \mapsto 2^Q$ that **associates a set of states with each state-input pair** (q, a). The NFSM M **accepts the string** $w \in \Sigma^*$ if there are next-state choices, whenever more than one exists, such that the last state entered under the input string w is a member of F. M **accepts the language** $L(M)$ consisting of all such strings.*

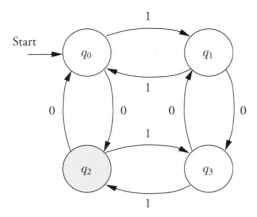

Figure 4.1 The deterministic finite-state machines $M_{\text{odd/even}}$ that accepts strings containing an odd number of 0's and an even number of 1's.

Figure 4.1 shows a DFSM $M_{\text{odd/even}}$ with initial state q_0. The final state is shown as a shaded circle; that is, $F = \{q_2\}$. $M_{\text{odd/even}}$ is in state q_0 or q_2 as long as the number of 1's in its input is even and is in state q_1 or q_3 as long as the number of 1's in its input is odd. Similarly, $M_{\text{odd/even}}$ is in state q_0 or q_1 as long as the number of 0's in its input is even and is in states q_2 or q_3 as long as the number of 0's in its input is odd. Thus, $M_{\text{odd/even}}$ recognizes the language of binary strings containing an odd number of 0's and an even number of 1's.

When the next-set function δ for an NFSM has value $\delta(q, a) = \emptyset$, the empty set, for state-input pair (q, a), no transition is specified from state q on input letter a.

Figure 4.2 shows a simple NFSM ND with initial state q_0 and final state set $F = \{q_0, q_3, q_5\}$. Nondeterministic transitions are possible from states q_0, q_3, and q_5. In addition, no transition is specified on input 0 from states q_1 and q_2 nor on input 1 from states q_0, q_3, q_4, or q_5.

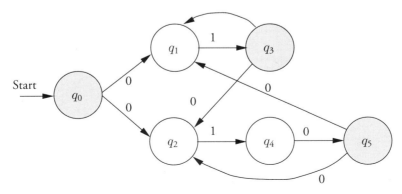

Figure 4.2 The nondeterministic machine ND.

4.2 Equivalence of DFSMs and NFSMs

Finite-state machines recognizing the same language are said to be **equivalent**. We now show that the class of languages accepted by DFSMs and NFSMs is the same. That is, for each NFSM there is an equivalent DFSM and vice versa. The proof has two symmetrical steps: a) given an arbitrary DFSM D_1 recognizing the language $L(D_1)$, we construct an NFSM N_1 that accepts $L(D_1)$, and b) given an arbitrary NFSM N_2 that accepts $L(N_2)$, we construct a DFSM D_2 that recognizes $L(N_2)$. The first half of this proof follows immediately from the fact that a DFSM is itself an NFSM. The second half of the proof is a bit more difficult and is stated below as a theorem. The method of proof is quite simple, however. We construct a DFSM D_2 that has one state for each set of states that the NFSM N_2 can reach on some input string and exhibit a next-state function for D_2. We illustrate this approach with the NFSM $N_2 = ND$ of Fig. 4.2.

Since the initial state of ND is q_0, the initial state of $D_2 = M_{\text{equiv}}$, the DFSM equivalent to ND, is the set $\{q_0\}$. In turn, because q_0 has two successor states on input 0, namely q_1 and q_2, we let $\{q_1, q_2\}$ be the successor to $\{q_0\}$ in M_{equiv} on input 1, as shown in the following table. Since q_0 has no successor on input 1, the successor to $\{q_0\}$ on input 1 is the empty set $\emptyset$. Building in this fashion, we find that the successor to $\{q_1, q_2\}$ on input 1 is $\{q_3, q_4\}$ whereas its successor on input 0 is $\emptyset$. The reader can complete the table shown below. Here q_{equiv} is the name of a state of the DFSM M_{equiv}.

q_{equiv}	a	$\delta_{M_{\text{equiv}}}(q_{\text{equiv}}, a)$	q_{equiv}	q
$\{q_0\}$	0	$\{q_1, q_2\}$	$\{q_0\}$	a
$\{q_0\}$	1	$\emptyset$	$\{q_1, q_2\}$	b
$\{q_1, q_2\}$	0	$\emptyset$	$\{q_3, q_4\}$	c
$\{q_1, q_2\}$	1	$\{q_3, q_4\}$	$\{q_1, q_2, q_5\}$	d
$\{q_3, q_4\}$	0	$\{q_1, q_2, q_5\}$	$\emptyset$	q_R
$\{q_3, q_4\}$	1	$\emptyset$		
$\{q_1, q_2, q_5\}$	0	$\{q_1, q_2\}$		
$\{q_1, q_2, q_5\}$	1	$\{q_3, q_4\}$		

In the second table above, we provide a new label for each state q_{equiv} of M_{equiv}. In Fig. 4.3 we use these new labels to exhibit the DFSM M_{equiv} equivalent to the NFSM ND of Fig. 4.2. A final state of M_{equiv} is any set containing a final state of ND because a string takes M_{equiv} to such a set if and only if it can take ND to one of its final states. We now show that this method of constructing a DFSM from an NFSM always works.

THEOREM 4.2.1 *Let L be a language accepted by a nondeterministic finite-state machine M_1. There exists a deterministic finite-state machine M_2 that recognizes L.*

Proof Let $M_1 = (\Sigma, Q_1, \delta_1, s_1, F_1)$ be an NFSM that accepts the language L. We design a DFSM $M_2 = (\Sigma, Q_2, \delta_2, s_2, F_2)$ that also recognizes L. M_1 and M_2 have identical input alphabets, Σ. The states of M_2 are associated with subsets of the states of Q_1, which is denoted by $Q_2 \subseteq 2^{Q_1}$, where 2^{Q_1} is the power set of Q_1 containing all the subsets of Q_1, including the empty set. We let the initial state s_2 of M_2 be associated with the set $\{s_1\}$ containing the initial state of M_1. A state of M_2 is a set of states that M_1 can reach on a sequence of inputs. A final state of M_2 is a subset of Q_1 that contains a final state of M_1. For example, if $q_5 \in F_1$, then $\{q_2, q_5\} \in F_2$.

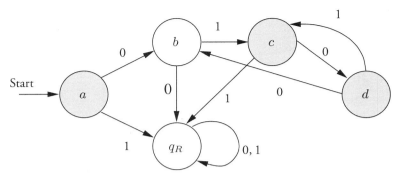

Figure 4.3 The DFSM M_{equiv} equivalent to the NFSM *ND*.

We first give an inductive definition of the states of M_2. Let $Q_2^{(k)}$ denote the sets of states of M_1 that can be reached from s_1 on input strings containing k or fewer letters. In the example given above, $Q_2^{(1)} = \{\{q_0\}, \{q_1, q_2\}, q_R\}$ and $Q_2^{(3)} = \{\{q_0\}, \{q_1, q_2\}, \{q_3, q_4\}, \{q_1, q_2, q_5\}, q_R\}$. To construct $Q_2^{(k+1)}$ from $Q_2^{(k)}$, we form the subset of Q_1 that can be reached on each input letter from a subset in $Q_2^{(k)}$, as illustrated above. If this is a new set, it is added to $Q_2^{(k)}$ to form $Q_2^{(k+1)}$. When $Q_2^{(k)}$ and $Q_2^{(k+1)}$ are the same, we terminate this process since no new subsets of Q_1 can be reached from s_1. This process eventually terminates because Q_2 has at most $2^{|Q_1|}$ elements. It terminates in at most $2^{|Q_1|} - 1$ steps because starting from the initial set $\{q_0\}$ at least one new subset must be added at each step.

The next-state function δ_2 of M_2 is defined as follows: for each state q of M_2 (a subset of Q_1), the value of $\delta_2(q, a)$ for input letter a is the state of M_2 (subset of Q_1) reached from q on input a. As the sets $Q_2^{(1)}, \ldots, Q_2^{(m)}$ are constructed, $m \leq 2^{|Q_1|} - 1$, we construct a table for δ_2.

We now show by induction on the length of an input string z that if z can take M_1 to a state in the set $S \subseteq Q_1$, then it takes M_2 to its state associated with S. It follows that if S contains a final state of M_1, then z is accepted by both M_1 and M_2.

The basis for the inductive hypothesis is the case of the empty input letter. In this case, s_1 is reached by M_1 if and only if $\{s_1\}$ is reached by M_2. The inductive hypothesis is that if w of length n can take M_1 to a state in the set S, then it takes M_2 to its state associated with S. We assume the hypothesis is true on inputs of length n and show that it remains true on inputs of length $n + 1$. Let $z = wa$ be an input string of length $n + 1$. To show that z can take M_1 to a state in S' if and only if it takes M_2 to the state associated with S', observe that by the inductive hypothesis there exists a set $S \subseteq Q_1$ such that w can take M_1 to a state in S if and only if it takes M_2 to the state associated with S. By the definition of δ_2, the input letter a takes the states of M_1 in S into states of M_1 in S' if and only if a takes the state of M_2 associated with S to the state associated with S'. It follows that the inductive hypothesis holds. ∎

Up to this point we have shown equivalence between deterministic and nondeterministic FSMs. Another equivalence question arises in this context: It is, "Given an FSM, is there an equivalent FSM that has a smaller number of states?" The determination of an equivalent FSM with the smallest number of states is called the **state minimization problem** and is explored in Section 4.7.

4.3 Regular Expressions

In this section we introduce regular expressions, algebraic expressions over sets of individual letters that describe the class of languages recognized by finite-state machines, as shown in the next section.

Regular expressions are formed through the concatenation, union, and Kleene closure of sets of strings. Given two sets of strings L_1 and L_2, their **concatenation** $L_1 \cdot L_2$ is the set $\{uv \mid u \in L_1 \text{ and } v \in L_2\}$; that is, the set of strings consisting of an arbitrary string of L_1 followed by an arbitrary string of L_2. (We often omit the concatenation operator $\cdot$, writing variables one after the other instead.) The **union** of L_1 and L_1, denoted $L_1 \cup L_2$, is the set of strings that are in L_1 or L_2 or both. The **Kleene closure** of a set L of strings, denoted L^* (also called the **Kleene star**), is defined in terms of the i-fold concatenation of L with itself, namely, $L^i = L \cdot L^{i-1}$, where $L^0 = \{\epsilon\}$, the set containing the empty string:

$$L^* = \bigcup_{i=0}^{\infty} L^i$$

Thus, L^* is the union of strings formed by concatenating zero or more words of L. Finally, we define the **positive closure** of L to be the union of all i-fold products except for the zeroth, that is,

$$L^+ = \bigcup_{i=1}^{\infty} L^i$$

The positive closure is a useful shorthand in regular expressions.

An example is helpful. Let $L_1 = \{01, 11\}$ and $L_2 = \{0, aba\}$; then $L_1 L_2 = \{010, 01aba, 110, 11aba\}$, $L_1 \cup L_2 = \{0, 01, 11, aba\}$, and

$$L_2^* = \{0, aba\}^* = \{\epsilon, 0, aba, 00, 0aba, aba0, abaaba, \ldots\}$$

Note that the definition given earlier for Σ^*, namely, the set of strings over the finite alphabet Σ, coincides with this new definition of the Kleene closure. We are now prepared to define regular expressions.

DEFINITION 4.3.1 *Regular expressions over the finite alphabet Σ and the languages they describe are defined recursively as follows:*

1. *$\emptyset$ is a regular expression denoting the empty set.*

2. *ϵ is a regular expression denoting the set $\{\epsilon\}$.*

3. *For each letter $a \in \Sigma$, $\boldsymbol{a}$ is a regular expression denoting the set $\{a\}$ containing a.*

4. *If r and s are regular expressions denoting the languages R and S, then (rs), $(r + s)$, and (r^*) are regular expressions denoting the languages $R \cdot S$, $R \cup S$, and R^*, respectively.*

*The languages denoted by regular expressions are called **regular languages**. (They are also often called regular sets.)*

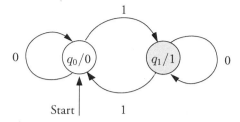

Figure 4.4 A finite-state machine computing the EXCLUSIVE OR of its inputs.

Some examples of regular expressions will clarify the definitions. The regular expression $(\mathbf{0} + \mathbf{1})^*$ denotes the set of all strings over the alphabet $\{0, 1\}$. The expression $(\mathbf{0}^*)(\mathbf{1})$ denotes the strings containing zero or more 0's that end with a single 1. The expression $((\mathbf{1})(\mathbf{0}^*)(\mathbf{1}) + \mathbf{0})^*$ denotes strings containing an even number of 1's. Thus, the expression $((\mathbf{0}^*)(\mathbf{1}))((\mathbf{1})(\mathbf{0}^*)(\mathbf{1}) + \mathbf{0})^*$ denotes strings containing an odd number of 1's. This is exactly the class of strings recognized by the simple DFSM in Fig. 4.4. (So far we have set in boldface all regular expressions denoting sets containing letters. Since context will distinguish between a set containing a letter and the letter itself, we drop the boldface notation at this point.)

Some parentheses in regular expressions can be omitted if we give highest precedence to Kleene closure, next highest precedence to concatenation, and lowest precedence to union. For example, we can write $((0^*)(1))((1)(0^*)(1) + 0)^*$ as $0^*1(10^*1 + 0)^*$.

Because regular expressions denote languages, certain combinations of union, concatenation, and Kleene closure operations on regular expressions can be rewritten as other combinations of operations. A regular expression will be treated as identical to the language it denotes. Two **regular expressions are equivalent** if they denote the same language. We now state properties of regular expressions, leaving their proof to the reader.

THEOREM 4.3.1 *Let $\emptyset$ and ϵ be the regular expressions denoting the empty set and the set containing the empty string and let r, s, and t be arbitrary regular expressions. Then the rules shown in Fig. 4.5 hold.*

We illustrate these rules with the following example. Let $a = 0^*1 \cdot b + 0^*$, where $b = c \cdot 10^+$ and $c = (0 + 10^+1)^*$. Using rule (16) of Fig. 4.5, we rewrite c as follows:

$$c = (0 + 10^+1)^* = (0^*10^+1)^*0^*$$

Then using rule (15) with $r = 0^*10^+$ and $s = 1$, we write b as follows:

$$b = (0^*10^+1)^*0^*10^+ = (rs)^*r = r(sr)^* = 0^*10^+(10^*10^+)^*$$

It follows that a satisfies

$$
\begin{aligned}
a &= 0^*1 \cdot b + 0^* \\
&= 0^*10^*10^+(10^*10^+)^* + 0^* \\
&= 0^*(10^*10^+)^+ + 0^* \\
&= 0^*((10^*10^+)^+ + \epsilon) \\
&= 0^*(10^*10^+)^*
\end{aligned}
$$

$$
\begin{array}{llllll}
(1) & r\emptyset & = & \emptyset r & = & \emptyset \\
(2) & r\epsilon & = & \epsilon r & = & r \\
(3) & r + \emptyset & = & \emptyset + r & = & r \\
(4) & r + r & = & r & & \\
(5) & r + s & = & s + r & & \\
(6) & r(s + t) & = & rs + rt & & \\
(7) & (r + s)t & = & rt + st & & \\
(8) & r(st) & = & (rs)t & & \\
(9) & \emptyset^* & = & \epsilon & & \\
(10) & \epsilon^* & = & \epsilon & & \\
(11) & (\epsilon + r)^+ & = & r^* & & \\
(12) & (\epsilon + r)^* & = & r^* & & \\
(13) & r^*(\epsilon + r) & = & (\epsilon + r)r^* & = & r^* \\
(14) & r^*s + s & = & r^*s & & \\
(15) & r(sr)^* & = & (rs)^*r & & \\
(16) & (r + s)^* & = & (r^*s)^*r^* & = & (s^*r)^*s^*
\end{array}
$$

Figure 4.5 Rules that apply to regular expressions.

where we have simplified the expressions using the definition of the positive closure, namely $r(r^*) = r^+$ in the second equation and rules (6), (5), and (12) in the last three equations. Other examples of the use of the identities can be found in Section 4.4.

4.4 Regular Expressions and FSMs

Regular languages are exactly the languages recognized by finite-state machines, as we now show. Our two-part proof begins by showing (Section 4.4.1) that every regular language can be accepted by a nondeterministic finite-state machine. This is followed in Section 4.4.2 by a proof that the language recognized by an arbitrary deterministic finite-state machine can be described by a regular expression. Since by Theorem 4.2.1 the language recognition power of DFSMs and NFSMs are the same, the desired conclusion follows.

4.4.1 Recognition of Regular Expressions by FSMs

THEOREM 4.4.1 *Given a regular expression r over the set Σ, there is a nondeterministic finite-state machine that accepts the language denoted by r.*

Proof We show by induction on the size of a regular expression r (the number of its operators) that there is an NFSM that accepts the language described by r.

BASIS: If no operators are used, the regular expression is either ϵ, $\emptyset$, or a for some $a \in \Sigma$. The finite-state machines shown in Fig. 4.6 recognize these three languages.

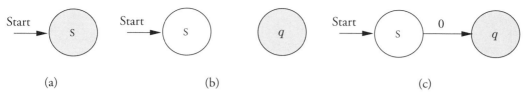

Figure 4.6 Finite-state machines recognizing the regular expressions ϵ, $\emptyset$, and a, respectively. In b) an output state is shown even though it cannot be reached.

INDUCTION: Assume that the hypothesis holds for all regular expressions r with at most k operators. We show that it holds for $k + 1$ operators. Since k is arbitrary, it holds for all k. The outermost operator (the $k + 1$st) is either concatenation, union, or Kleene closure. We argue each case separately.

CASE 1: Let $r = (r_1 \cdot r_2)$. M_1 and M_2 are the NFSMs that accept r_1 and r_2, respectively. By the inductive hypothesis, such machines exist. Without loss of generality, assume that the states of these machines are distinct and let them have initial states s_1 and s_2, respectively. As suggested in Fig. 4.7, create a machine M that accepts r as follows: for each input letter σ, final state f of M_1, and state q of M_2 reached by an edge from s_2 labeled σ, add an edge with the same label σ from f to q. If s_2 is not a final state of M_2, remove the final state designations from states of M_1.

It follows that every string accepted by M either terminates on a final state of M_1 (when M_2 accepts the empty string) or exits a final state of M_1 (never to return to a state of M_1), enters a state of M_2 reachable on one input letter from the initial state of M_2, and terminates on a final state of M_2. Thus, M accepts exactly the strings described by r.

CASE 2: Let $r = (r_1 + r_2)$. Let M_1 and M_2 be NFSMs with distinct sets of states and let initial states s_1 and s_2 accept r_1 and r_2, respectively. By the inductive hypothesis, M_1 and M_2 exist. As suggested in Fig. 4.8, create a machine M that accepts r as follows: a) add a new initial state s_0; b) for each input letter σ and state q of M_1 or M_2 reached by an edge

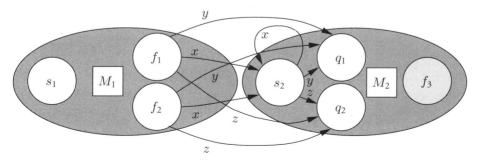

Figure 4.7 A machine M recognizing $r_1 \cdot r_2$. M_1 and M_2 are the NFSMs that accept r_1 and r_2, respectively. An edge with label a is added between each final state of M_1 and each state of M_2 reached on input a from its start state, s_2. The final states of M_2 are final states of M, as are the final states of M_1 if s_2 is a final of M_2. It follows that this machine accepts the strings beginning with a string in r_1 followed by one in r_2.

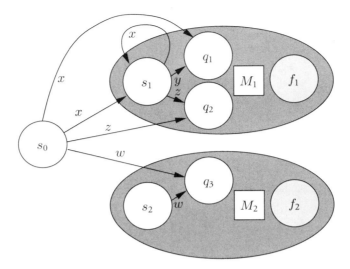

Figure 4.8 A machine M accepting $r_1 + r_2$. M_1 and M_2 are the NFSMs that accept r_1 and r_2, respectively. The new start state s_0 has an edge labeled a for each edge with this label from the initial state of M_1 or M_2. The final states of M are the final states of M_1 and M_2 as well as s_0 if either s_1 or s_2 is a final state. After the first input choice, the new machine acts like either M_1 or M_2. Therefore, it accepts strings denoted by $r_1 + r_2$.

from s_1 or s_2 labeled σ, add an edge with the same label from s_0 to q. If either s_1 or s_2 is a final state, make s_0 a final state.

It follows that if either M_1 or M_2 accepts the empty string, so does M. On the first non-empty input letter M enters and remains in either the states of M_1 or those of M_2. It follows that it accepts either the strings accepted by M_1 or those accepted by M_2 (or both), that is, the union of r_1 and r_2.

CASE 3: Let $r = (r_1)^*$. Let M_1 be an NFSM with initial state s_1 that accepts r_1, which, by the inductive hypothesis, exists. Create a new machine M, as suggested in Fig. 4.9, as follows: a) add a new initial state s_0; b) for each input letter σ and state q reached on σ from s_1, add an edge with label σ between s_0 and state q with label σ, as in Case 2; c) add such edges from each final state to these same states. Make the new initial state a final state and remove the initial-state designation from s_1.

It follows that M accepts the empty string, as it should since $r = (r_1)^*$ contains the empty string. Since the edges leaving each final state are those directed away from the initial state s_0, it follows that M accepts strings that are the concatenation of strings in r_1, as it should. ∎

We now illustrate this construction of an NFSM from a regular expression. Consider the regular expression $r = 10^* + 0$, which we decompose as $r = (r_1 r_2 + r_3)$ where $r_1 = 1$, $r_2 = (r_4)^*$, $r_3 = 0$, and $r_4 = 0$. Shown in Fig. 4.10(a) is a NFSM accepting the languages denoted by the regular expressions r_3 and r_4, and in (b) is an NFSM accepting r_1. Figure 4.11 shows an NFSM accepting the closure of r_4 obtained by adding a new initial state (which is also made a final state) from which is directed a copy of the edge directed away from initial

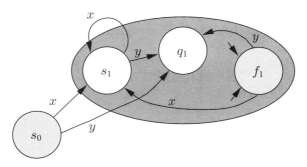

Figure 4.9 A machine M accepts r_1^*. M_1 accepts r_1. Make s_0 the initial state of M. For each input letter a, add an edge labeled a from s_0 and each final of M_1 to each state reached on input a from s_1, the initial state of M_1. The final states of M are s_0 and the final states of M_1. Thus, M accepts ϵ and all states reached by the concatenation of strings accepted by M_1; that is, it realizes the closure r_1^*.

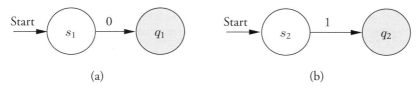

Figure 4.10 Nondeterministic machines accepting 0 and 1.

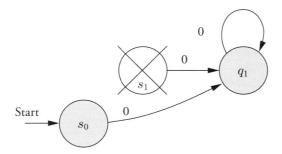

Figure 4.11 An NFSM accepting the Kleene closure of $\{0\}$.

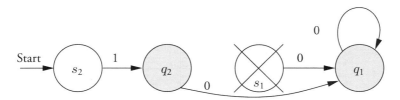

Figure 4.12 A nondeterministic machine accepting 10^*.

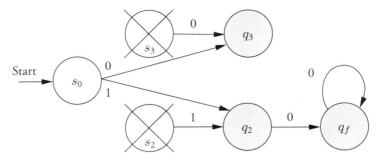

Figure 4.13 A nondeterministic machine accepting $10^* + 0$.

state of M_0, the machine accepting r_4. (The state s_1 is marked as inaccessible.) Figure 4.12 (page 163) shows an NFSM accepting $r_1 r_2$ constructed by **concatenating** the machine M_1 accepting r_1 with M_2 accepting r_2. (s_1 is inaccessible.) Figure 4.13 gives an NFSM accepting the language denoted by $r_1 r_2 + r_3$, designed by forming the **union** of machines for $r_1 r_2$ and r_3. (States s_2 and s_3 are inaccessible.) Figure 4.14 shows a DFSM recognizing the same language as that accepted by the machine in Fig. 4.13. Here we have added a reject state q_R to which all states move on input letters for which no state transition is defined.

4.4.2 Regular Expressions Describing FSM Languages

We now give the second part of the proof of equivalence of FSMs and regular expressions. We show that every language recognized by a DFSM can be described by a regular expression. We illustrate the proof using the DFSM of Fig. 4.3, which is the DFSM given in Fig. 4.15 except for a relabeling of states.

THEOREM 4.4.2 *If the language L is recognized by a DFSM $M = (\Sigma, Q, \delta, s, F)$, then L can be represented by a regular expression.*

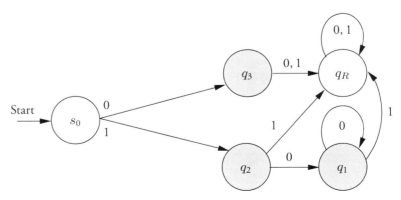

Figure 4.14 A deterministic machine accepting $10^* + 0$.

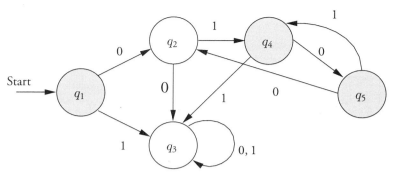

Figure 4.15 The DFSM of Figure 4.2 with a relabeling of states.

Proof Let $Q = \{q_1, q_2, \ldots, q_n\}$ and $F = \{q_{j_1}, q_{j_2}, \ldots, q_{j_p}\}$ be the final states. The proof idea is the following. For every pair of states (q_i, q_j) of M we construct a regular expression $r_{i,j}^{(0)}$ denoting the set $R_{i,j}^{(0)}$ containing input letters that take M from q_i to q_j without passing through any other states. If $i = j$, $R_{i,j}^{(0)}$ contains the empty letter ϵ because M can move from q_i to q_i without reading an input letter. (These definitions are illustrated in the table $T^{(0)}$ of Fig. 4.16.) For $k = 1, 2, \ldots, m$ we proceed to define the set $R_{i,j}^{(k)}$ of strings of length k that take M from q_i to q_j without passing through any state except possibly one in $Q^{(k)} = \{q_1, q_2, \ldots, q_k\}$. We also associate a regular expression $r_{i,j}^{(k)}$ with the set $R_{i,j}^{(k)}$. Since $Q^{(n)} = Q$, the input strings that carry M from s, the initial state, to a final state in F are the strings accepted by M. They can be described by the following regular expression:

$$r_{t,j_1}^{(n)} + r_{t,j_2}^{(n)} + \cdots + r_{t,j_p}^{(n)}$$

This method of proof provides a **dynamic programming** algorithm to construct a regular expression for L.

$$T^{(0)} = \{r_{i,j}^{(0)}\}$$

$i \setminus j$	1	2	3	4	5
1	ϵ	0	1	$\emptyset$	$\emptyset$
2	$\emptyset$	ϵ	0	1	$\emptyset$
3	$\emptyset$	$\emptyset$	$\epsilon + 0 + 1$	$\emptyset$	$\emptyset$
4	$\emptyset$	$\emptyset$	1	ϵ	0
5	$\emptyset$	0	$\emptyset$	1	ϵ

Figure 4.16 The table $T^{(0)}$ containing the regular expressions $\{r_{i,j}^{(0)}\}$ associated with the DFSM in shown in Fig. 4.15.

$R_{i,j}^{(0)}$ is formally defined below.

$$R_{i,j}^{(0)} = \begin{cases} \{a \mid \delta(q_i, a) = q_j\} & \text{if } i \neq j \\ \{a \mid \delta(q_i, a) = q_j\} \cup \{\epsilon\} & \text{if } i = j \end{cases}$$

Since $R_{i,j}^{(k)}$ is defined as the set of strings that take M from q_i to q_j without passing through states outside of $Q^{(k)}$, it can be recursively defined as the strings that take M from q_i to q_j without passing through states outside of $Q^{(k-1)}$ plus those that take M from q_i to q_k without passing through states outside of $Q^{(k-1)}$, followed by strings that take M from q_k to q_k zero or more times without passing through states outside $Q^{(k-1)}$, followed by strings that take M from q_k to q_j without passing through states outside of $Q^{(k-1)}$. This is represented by the formula below and suggested in Fig. 4.17:

$$R_{i,j}^{(k)} = R_{i,j}^{(k-1)} \cup R_{i,k}^{(k-1)} \cdot \left(R_{k,k}^{(k-1)}\right)^* \cdot R_{k,j}^{(k-1)}$$

It follows by induction on k that $R_{i,j}^{(k)}$ correctly describes the strings that take M from q_i to q_j without passing through states of index higher than k.

We now exhibit the set $\{r_{i,j}^{(k)}\}$ of regular expressions that describe the sets $\{R_{i,j}^{(k)} \mid 1 \leq i, j, k \leq m\}$ and establish the correspondence by induction. If the set $R_{i,j}^{(0)}$ contains the letters $x_1, x_2, \ldots, x_l$ (which might include the empty letter ϵ), then we let $r_{i,j}^{(0)} = x_1 + x_2 + \cdots + x_l$. Assume that $r_{i,j}^{(k-1)}$ correctly describes $R_{i,j}^{(k-1)}$. It follows that the regular expression

$$r_{i,j}^{(k)} = r_{i,j}^{(k-1)} + r_{i,k}^{(k-1)} \left(r_{k,k}^{(k-1)}\right)^* r_{k,j}^{(k-1)} \tag{4.1}$$

correctly describes $R_{i,j}^{(k)}$. This concludes the proof. ∎

The dynamic programming algorithm given in the above proof is illustrated by the DFSM in Fig. 4.15. Because this algorithm can produce complex regular expressions even for small DFSMs, we display almost all of its steps, stopping when it is obvious which results are needed for the regular expression that describes the strings recognized by the DFSM. For $1 \leq k \leq 6$,

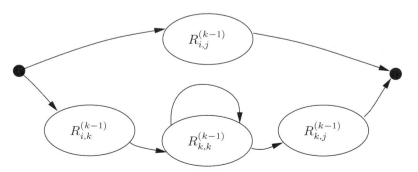

Figure 4.17 A recursive decomposition of the set $R_{i,j}^{(k)}$ of strings that cause an FSM to move from state q_i to q_j without passing through states q_l for $l > k$.

let $T^{(k)}$ denote the table of values of $\{r_{i,j}^{(k)} \mid 1 \le i, j \le 6\}$. Table $T^{(0)}$ in Fig. 4.16 describes the next-state function of this DFSM. The remaining tables are constructed by invoking the definition of $r_{i,j}^{(k)}$ in (4.1). Entries in table $T^{(1)}$ are formed using the following facts:

$$r_{i,j}^{(1)} = r_{i,j}^{(0)} + r_{i,1}^{(0)} \left(r_{1,1}^{(0)}\right)^* r_{1,j}^{(0)}; \quad \left(r_{1,1}^{(0)}\right)^* = \epsilon^* = \epsilon; \quad r_{i,1}^{(0)} = \emptyset \quad \text{for } i \ge 2$$

It follows that $r_{i,j}^{(1)} = r_{i,j}^{(0)}$ or that $T^{(1)}$ is identical to $T^{(0)}$. Invoking the identity $r_{i,j}^{(2)} = r_{i,j}^{(1)} + r_{i,2}^{(1)} \left(r_{2,2}^{(1)}\right)^* r_{2,j}^{(1)}$ and using $\left(r_{2,2}^{(1)}\right)^* = \epsilon$, we construct the table $T^{(2)}$ below:

$$T^{(2)} = \{r_{i,j}^{(2)}\}$$

$i \setminus j$	1	2	3	4	5
1	ϵ	0	$1 + 00$	01	$\emptyset$
2	$\emptyset$	ϵ	0	1	$\emptyset$
3	$\emptyset$	$\emptyset$	$\epsilon + 0 + 1$	$\emptyset$	$\emptyset$
4	$\emptyset$	$\emptyset$	1	ϵ	0
5	$\emptyset$	0	00	$1 + 01$	ϵ

The fourth table $T^{(3)}$ is shown below. It is constructed using the identity $r_{i,j}^{(3)} = r_{i,j}^{(2)} + r_{i,3}^{(2)} \left(r_{3,3}^{(2)}\right)^* r_{3,j}^{(2)}$ and the fact that $\left(r_{3,3}^{(2)}\right)^* = (0+1)^*$.

$$T^{(3)} = \{r_{i,j}^{(3)}\}$$

$i \setminus j$	1	2	3	4	5
1	ϵ	0	$(1 + 00)(0 + 1)^*$	01	$\emptyset$
2	$\emptyset$	ϵ	$0(0 + 1)^*$	1	$\emptyset$
3	$\emptyset$	$\emptyset$	$(0 + 1)^*$	$\emptyset$	$\emptyset$
4	$\emptyset$	$\emptyset$	$1(0 + 1)^*$	ϵ	0
5	$\emptyset$	0	$00(0 + 1)^*$	$1 + 01$	ϵ

The fifth table $T^{(4)}$ is shown below. It is constructed using the identity $r_{i,j}^{(4)} = r_{i,j}^{(3)} + r_{i,4}^{(3)} \left(r_{4,4}^{(3)}\right)^* r_{4,j}^{(3)}$ and the fact that $\left(r_{4,4}^{(3)}\right)^* = \epsilon$.

$$T^{(4)} = \{r_{i,j}^{(4)}\}$$

$i \setminus j$	1	2	3	4	5
1	ϵ	0	$(1 + 00 + 011)(0 + 1)^*$	01	010
2	$\emptyset$	ϵ	$(0 + 11)(0 + 1)^*$	1	10
3	$\emptyset$	$\emptyset$	$(0 + 1)^*$	$\emptyset$	$\emptyset$
4	$\emptyset$	$\emptyset$	$1(0 + 1)^*$	ϵ	0
5	$\emptyset$	0	$(00 + 11 + 011)(0 + 1)^*$	$1 + 01$	$\epsilon + 10 + 010$

Instead of building the sixth table, $T^{(5)}$, we observe that the regular expression that is needed is $r = r_{1,1}^{(5)} + r_{1,4}^{(5)} + r_{1,5}^{(5)}$. Since $r_{i,j}^{(5)} = r_{i,j}^{(4)} + r_{i,5}^{(4)} \left(r_{5,5}^{(4)} \right)^* r_{5,j}^{(4)}$ and $\left(r_{5,5}^{(4)} \right)^* = (10 + 010)^*$, we have the following expressions for $r_{1,1}^{(5)}$, $r_{1,4}^{(5)}$, and $r_{1,5}^{(5)}$:

$$r_{1,1}^{(5)} = \epsilon$$
$$r_{1,4}^{(5)} = 01 + (010)(10 + 010)^*(1 + 01)$$
$$r_{1,5}^{(5)} = 010 + (010)(10 + 010)^* = (010)(10 + 010)^*$$

Thus, the DFSM recognizes the language denoted by the regular expression $r = \epsilon + 01 + (010)(10+010)^*(\epsilon + 1 + 01)$. It can be shown that this expression denotes the same language as does $\epsilon + 01 + (010)(01 + 010)^*$. (See Problem 4.12.)

4.4.3 grep—Searching for Strings in Files

Many operating systems provide a command to find strings in files. For example, the Unix grep command prints all lines of a file containing a string specified by a regular expression. grep is invoked as follows:

            grep regular-expression file_name

Thus, the command grep 'o+' file_name returns each line of the file file_name that contains o^+ somewhere in the line. grep is typically implemented with a nondeterministic algorithm whose behavior can be understood by considering the construction of the preceding section.

In Section 4.4.1 we describe a procedure to construct NFSMs accepting strings denoted by regular expressions. Each such machine starts in its initial state before processing an input string. Since grep finds lines containing a string that starts anywhere in the lines, these NFSMs have to be modified to implement grep. The modifications required for this purpose are straightforward and left as an exercise for the reader. (See Problem 4.19.)

4.5 The Pumping Lemma for FSMs

It is not surprising that some languages are not regular. In this section we provide machinery to show this. It is given in the form of the pumping lemma, which demonstrates that if a regular language contains long strings, it must contain an infinite set of strings of a particular form. We show the existence of languages that do not contain strings of this form, thereby demonstrating that they are not regular.

The **pigeonhole principle** is used to prove the pumping lemma. It states that if there are n pigeonholes and $n + 1$ pigeons, each of which occupies a hole, then at least one hole has two pigeons. This principle, whose proof is obvious (see Section 1.3), enjoys a hallowed place in combinatorial mathematics.

The pigeonhole principle is applied as follows. We first note that if a regular language L is infinite, it contains a string w with at least as many letters as there are states in a DFSM M recognizing L. Including the initial state, it follows that M visits at least one more state while processing w than it has different states. Thus, at least one state is visited at least twice. The substring of w that causes M to move from this state back to itself can be repeated zero or more times to give other strings in the language. We use the notation $\boldsymbol{u}^n$ to mean the string repeated n times and let $\boldsymbol{u}^0 = \epsilon$.

LEMMA 4.5.1 *Let L be a regular language over the alphabet Σ recognized by a DFSM with m states. If $\boldsymbol{w} \in L$ and $|\boldsymbol{w}| \geq m$, then there are strings $\boldsymbol{r}$, $\boldsymbol{s}$, and $\boldsymbol{t}$ with $|\boldsymbol{s}| \geq 1$ and $|\boldsymbol{rs}| \leq m$ such that $\boldsymbol{w} = \boldsymbol{rst}$ and for all integers $n \geq 0$, $\boldsymbol{rs}^n\boldsymbol{t}$ is also in L.*

Proof Let L be recognized by the DFSM M with m states. Let $k = |\boldsymbol{w}| \geq m$ be the length of $\boldsymbol{w}$ in L. Let $q_0, q_1, q_2, \ldots, q_k$ denote the initial and k successive states that M enters after receiving each of the letters in $\boldsymbol{w}$. By the pigeonhole principle, some state q' in the sequence $q_0, \ldots, q_m$ ($m \leq k$) is repeated. Let $q_i = q_j = q'$ for $i < j$. Let $\boldsymbol{r} = w_1 \ldots w_i$ be the string that takes M from q_0 to $q_i = q'$ (this string may be empty) and let $\boldsymbol{s} = w_{i+1} \ldots w_j$ be the string that takes M from $q_i = q'$ to $q_j = q'$ (this string is non-empty). It follows that $|\boldsymbol{rs}| \leq m$. Finally, let $\boldsymbol{t} = w_{j+1} \ldots w_k$ be the string that takes M from q_j to q_k. Since $\boldsymbol{s}$ takes M from state q' to state q', the final state entered by M is the same whether $\boldsymbol{s}$ is deleted or repeated one or more times. (See Fig. 4.18.) It follows that $\boldsymbol{rs}^n\boldsymbol{t}$ is in L for all $n \geq 0$. ∎

As an application of the pumping lemma, consider the language $L = \{0^p1^p \mid p \geq 1\}$. We show that it is not regular. Assume it is regular and is recognized by a DFSM with m states. We show that a contradiction results. Since L is infinite, it contains a string $\boldsymbol{w}$ of length $k = 2p \geq 2m$, that is, with $p \geq m$. By Lemma 4.5.1 L also contains $\boldsymbol{rs}^n\boldsymbol{t}$, $n \geq 1$, where $\boldsymbol{w} = \boldsymbol{rst}$ and $|\boldsymbol{rs}| \leq m \leq p$. That is, $\boldsymbol{rs} = 0^d$ where $d \leq p$. Since $\boldsymbol{rs}^n\boldsymbol{t} = 0^{p+nd}1^p$ for $n \geq 1$ and this is not of the form 0^p1^p, the language is not regular.

The pumping lemma allows us to derive specific conditions under which a language is finite or infinite, as we now show.

LEMMA 4.5.2 *Let L be a regular language recognized by a DFSM with m states. L is non-empty if and only if it contains a string of length less than m. It is infinite if and only if it contains a string of length at least m and at most $2m - 1$.*

Proof If L contains a string of length less than m, it is not empty. If it is not empty, let $\boldsymbol{w}$ be a shortest string in L. This string must have length at most $m - 1$ or we can apply the pumping lemma to it and find another string of smaller length that is also in L. But this would contradict the assumption that $\boldsymbol{w}$ is a shortest string in L. Thus, L contains a string of length at most $m - 1$.

If L contains a string $\boldsymbol{w}$ of length $m \leq |\boldsymbol{w}| \leq 2m - 1$, as shown in the proof of the pumping lemma, $\boldsymbol{w}$ can be "pumped up" to produce an infinite set of strings. Suppose now that L is infinite. Either it contains a string $\boldsymbol{w}$ of length $m \leq |\boldsymbol{w}| \leq 2m - 1$ or it does not.

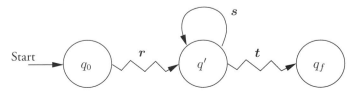

Figure 4.18 Diagram illustrating the pumping lemma.

In the first case, we are done. In the second case, $|w| \geq 2m$ and we apply the pumping lemma to it to find another shorter string that is also in L, contradicting the hypothesis that it was the shortest string of length greater than or equal to $2m$. ∎

4.6 Properties of Regular Languages

Section 4.4 established the equivalence of regular languages (recognized by finite-state machines) and the languages denoted by regular expressions. We now present properties satisfied by regular languages. We say that **a class of languages is closed under an operation** if applying that operation to a language (or languages) in the class produces another language in the class. For example, as shown below, the union of two regular languages is another regular language. Similarly, the Kleene closure applied to a regular language returns another regular language.

Given a language L over an alphabet Σ, **the complement of L** is the set $\overline{L} = \Sigma^* - L$, the strings that are in Σ^* but not in L. (This is also called the **difference** between Σ^* and L.) The **intersection** of two languages L_1 and L_2, denoted $L_1 \cap L_2$, is the set of strings that are in both languages.

THEOREM 4.6.1 *The class of regular languages is closed under the following operations:*
- *concatenation*
- *union*
- *Kleene closure*
- *complementation*
- *intersection*

Proof In Section 4.4 we showed that the languages denoted by regular expressions are exactly the languages recognized by finite-state machines (deterministic or nondeterministic). Since regular expressions are defined in terms of concatenation, union, and Kleene closure, they are closed under each of these operations.

The proof of closure of regular languages under complementation is straightforward. If L is regular and has an associated FSM M that recognizes it, make all final states of M non-final and all non-final states final. This new machine then recognizes exactly the complement of L. Thus, $\overline{L}$ is also regular.

The proof of closure of regular languages under intersection follows by noting that if L_1 and L_2 are regular languages, then

$$L_1 \cap L_2 = \overline{\overline{L_1} \cup \overline{L_2}}$$

that is, the intersection of two sets can be obtained by complementing the union of their complements. Since each of $\overline{L_1}$ and $\overline{L_2}$ is regular, as is their union, it follows that $\overline{L_1} \cup \overline{L_2}$ is regular. (See Fig. 4.19(a).) Finally, the complement of a regular set is regular. ∎

When we come to study Turing machines in Chapter 5, we will show that there are well-defined languages that have no machine to recognize them, even if the machine has an infinite amount of storage available. Thus, it is interesting to ask if there are algorithms that solve certain decision problems about regular languages in a finite number of steps. (Machines that halt on all input are said to **implement algorithms**.) As shown above, there are algorithms

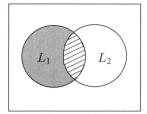 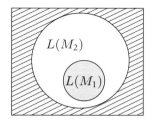

Figure 4.19   (a) The intersection $L_1 \cap L_2$ of two sets L_1 and L_2 can be obtained by taking the complement $\overline{\overline{L_1} \cup \overline{L_2}}$ of the union $\overline{L_1} \cup \overline{L_2}$ of their complements. (b) If $L(M_1) \subseteq L(M_2)$, then $L(M_1) \cap \overline{L(M_2)} = \emptyset$.

that can recognize the concatenation, union and Kleene closure of regular languages. We now show that algorithms exist for a number of decision problems concerning finite-state machines.

THEOREM 4.6.2   *There are algorithms for each of the following decision problems:*
  a)   For a finite-state machine M and a string w, determine if $w \in L(M)$.
  b)   For a finite-state machine M, determine if $L(M) = \emptyset$.
  c)   For a finite-state machine M, determine if $L(M) = \Sigma^*$.
  d)   For finite-state machines M_1 and M_2, determine if $L(M_1) \subseteq L(M_2)$.
  e)   For finite-state machines M_1 and M_2, determine if $L(M_1) = L(M_2)$.

Proof To answer (a) it suffices to supply w to a deterministic finite-state machine equivalent to M and observe the final state after it has processed all letters in w. The number of steps executed by this machine is the length of w. Question (b) is answered in Lemma 4.5.2. We need only determine if the language contains strings of length less than m, where m is the number of states of M. This can be done by trying all inputs of length less than m. The answer to question (c) is the same as the answer to "Is $\overline{L(M)} = \emptyset$?" The answer to question (d) is the same as the answer to "Is $L(M_1) \cap \overline{L(M_2)} = \emptyset$?" (See Fig. 4.19(b).) Since FSMs that recognize the complement and intersection of regular languages can be constructed in a finite number of steps (see the proof of Theorem 4.6.1), we can use the procedure for (b) to answer the question. Finally, the answer to question (e) is "yes" if and only if $L(M_1) \subseteq L(M_2)$ and $L(M_2) \subseteq L(M_1)$. ∎

4.7 State Minimization*

Given a finite-state machine M, it is often useful to have a potentially different DFSM $M_{\min}$ with the smallest number of states (a minimal-state machine) that recognizes the same language $L(M)$. In this section we develop a procedure to find such a machine recognizing a regular language L. As a step in this direction, we define a natural equivalence relation R_L for each language L and show that L is regular if and only if R_L has a finite number of equivalence classes.

4.7.1 Equivalence Relations on Languages and States

The relation R_L is used to define a machine M_L. When L is regular, we show that M_L is a minimal-state DFSM. We also give an explicit procedure to construct a minimal-state DFSM recognizing a regular language L. The approach is the following: a) given a regular expression, an NFSM is constructed (Theorem 4.4.1); b) an equivalent DFSM is then produced (Theorem 4.2.1); c) equivalent states of this DFSM are discovered and coalesced, thereby producing the minimal machine. We begin our treatment with a discussion of equivalence relations.

DEFINITION 4.7.1 *An **equivalence relation** R on a set A is a partition of the elements of A into disjoint subsets called **equivalence classes**. If two elements a and b are in the same equivalence class under relation R, we write aRb. If a is an element of an equivalence class, we represent its equivalence class by $[a]$. An equivalence relation is represented by its equivalence classes.*

An example of equivalence relation on the set $A = \{0, 1, 2, 3\}$ is the set of equivalence classes $\{\{0, 2\}, \{1, 3\}\}$. Then, $[0]$ and $[2]$ denote the same equivalence class, namely $\{0, 2\}$, whereas $[1]$ and $[2]$ denote different equivalence classes.

Equivalence relations can be defined on any set, including the set of strings over a finite alphabet (a language). For example, let the partition $\{0^*, 0(0^*10^*)^+, 1(0 + 1)^*\}$ of the set $(0 + 1)^*$ denote the equivalence relation R. The equivalence classes consist of strings containing zero or more 0's, strings starting with 0 and containing at least one 1, and strings beginning with 1. It follows that $00R000$ and $1001R11$ but not that $10R01$.

Additional conditions can be put on equivalence relations on languages. An important restriction is that an equivalence relation be right-invariant (with respect to concatenation).

DEFINITION 4.7.2 *An equivalence relation R over the alphabet Σ is **right-invariant** (with respect to concatenation) if for all $\boldsymbol{u}$ and $\boldsymbol{v}$ in Σ^*, $\boldsymbol{u}R\boldsymbol{v}$ if for all $\boldsymbol{z} \in \Sigma^*$, $\boldsymbol{uz}R\boldsymbol{vz}$.*

For example, let $R = \{(10^*1 + 0)^*, 0^*1(10^*1 + 0)^*\}$. That is, R consists of two equivalence classes, the set containing strings with an even number of 1's and the set containing strings with an odd number of 1's. R is right-invariant because if $\boldsymbol{u}R\boldsymbol{v}$; that is, if the numbers of 1's in $\boldsymbol{u}$ and $\boldsymbol{v}$ are both even or both odd, then the same is true of $\boldsymbol{uz}$ and $\boldsymbol{vz}$ for each $\boldsymbol{z} \in \Sigma^*$, that is, $\boldsymbol{uz}R\boldsymbol{vz}$.

To each language L, whether regular or not, we associate the natural equivalence relation R_L defined below. Problem 4.30 shows that for some languages R_L has an unbounded number of equivalence classes.

DEFINITION 4.7.3 *Given a language L over Σ, the equivalence relation R_L is defined as follows: strings $\boldsymbol{u}, \boldsymbol{v} \in \Sigma^*$ are equivalent, that is, $\boldsymbol{u}R_L\boldsymbol{v}$, if and only if for each $\boldsymbol{z} \in \Sigma^*$, either both $\boldsymbol{uz}$ and $\boldsymbol{vz}$ are in L or both are not in L.*

The equivalence relation $R = \{(10^*1+0)^*, 0^*1(10^*1+0)^*\}$ given above is the equivalence relation R_L for both the language $L = (10^*1 + 0)^*$ and the language $L = 0^*1(10^*1 + 0)^*$.

A natural right-invariant equivalence relation on strings can also be associated with each DFSM, as shown below. This relation defines two strings as equivalent if they carry the machine from its initial state to the same state. Thus, for each state there is an equivalence class of strings that take the machine to that state.

DEFINITION 4.7.4 *Given a DFSM $M = (\Sigma, Q, \delta, s, F)$, R_M is the equivalence relation defined as follows: for all $\boldsymbol{u}, \boldsymbol{v} \in \Sigma^*$, $\boldsymbol{u}R_M\boldsymbol{v}$ if and only if $\delta(s, \boldsymbol{u}) = \delta(s, \boldsymbol{v})$. (Note that $\delta(q, \epsilon) = q$.)*

It is straightforward to show that the equivalence relations R_L and R_M are right-invariant. (See Problems 4.28 and 4.29.) It is also clear that R_M has as many equivalence classes as there are states of M.

Before we present the major results of this section we define a special machine M_L that will be seen to be a minimal machine recognizing the language L.

DEFINITION 4.7.5 *Given the language L over the alphabet Σ, the DFSM $M_L = (\Sigma, Q_L, \delta_L, s_L, F_L)$ is defined in terms of the right-invariant equivalence relation R_L as follows: a) the states Q_L are the equivalence classes of R_L; b) the initial state s_L is the equivalence class $[\epsilon]$; c) the final states F_L are the equivalence classes containing strings in the language L; d) for an arbitrary equivalence class $[u]$ with representative element $u \in \Sigma^*$ and an arbitrary input letter $a \in \Sigma$, the next-state transition function $\delta_L : Q_L \times \Sigma \mapsto Q_L$ is defined by $\delta_L([u], a) = [ua]$.*

For this definition to make sense we must show that condition c) does not contradict the facts about R_L: that an equivalence class containing a string in L does not also contain a string that is not in L. But by the definition of R_L, if we choose $z = \epsilon$, we have that $u R_L v$ only if both u and v are in L. We must also show that the next-state function definition is consistent: it should not matter which representative of the equivalence class $[u]$ is used. In particular, if we denote the class $[u]$ by $[v]$ for v another member of the class, it should follow that $[ua] = [va]$. But this is a consequence of the definition of R_L.

Figure 4.20 shows the machine M_L associated with $L = (10^*1 + 0)^*$. The initial state is associated with $[\epsilon]$, which is in the language. Thus, the initial state is also a final state. The state associated with $[0]$ is also $[\epsilon]$ because ϵ and 0 are both in L. Thus, the transition from state $[\epsilon]$ on input 0 is back to state $[\epsilon]$. Problem 4.31 asks the reader to complete the description of this machine.

We need the notion of a refinement of an equivalence relation before we establish conditions for a language to be regular.

DEFINITION 4.7.6 *An equivalence relation R over a set A is a **refinement** of an equivalence relation S over the same set if aRb implies that aSb. A refinement R of S is **strict** if there exist $a, b \in A$ such that aSb but it is not true that aRb.*

Over the set $A = \{a, b, c, d\}$, the relation $R = \{\{a\}, \{b\}, \{c, d\}\}$ is a strict refinement of the relation $S = \{\{a, b\}, \{c, d\}\}$. Clearly, if R is a refinement of S, R has no fewer equivalence classes than does S. If the refinement R of S is strict, R has more equivalence classes than does S.

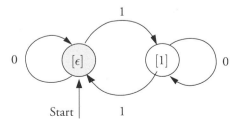

Figure 4.20 The machine M_L associated with $L = (10^*1 + 0)^*$.

4.7.2   The Myhill-Nerode Theorem

The following theorem uses the notion of refinement to give conditions under which a language is regular.

THEOREM 4.7.1 (Myhill-Nerode) *L is a regular language if and only if R_L has a finite number of equivalence classes. Furthermore, if L is regular, it is the union of some of the equivalence classes of R_L.*

> **Proof** We begin by showing that if L is regular, R_L has a finite number of equivalence classes. Let L be recognized by the DFSM $M = (\Sigma, Q, \delta, s, F)$. Then the number of equivalence classes of R_M is finite. Consider two strings $\boldsymbol{u}, \boldsymbol{v} \in \Sigma^*$ that are equivalent under R_M. By definition, $\boldsymbol{u}$ and $\boldsymbol{v}$ carry M from its initial state to the same state, whether final or not. Thus, $\boldsymbol{u}z$ and $\boldsymbol{v}z$ also carry M to the same state. It follows that R_M is right-invariant. Because $\boldsymbol{u}R_M\boldsymbol{v}$, either $\boldsymbol{u}$ and $\boldsymbol{v}$ take M to a final state and are in L or they take M to a non-final state and are not in L. It follows from the definition of R_L that $\boldsymbol{u}R_L\boldsymbol{v}$. Thus, R_M is a refinement of R_L. Consequently, R_L has no more equivalence classes than does R_M and this number is finite.
>
> Now let R_L have a finite number of equivalence classes. We show that the machine M_L recognizes L. Since it has a finite number of states, we are done. The proof that M_L recognizes L is straightforward. If $[\boldsymbol{w}]$ is a final state, it is reached by applying to M_L in its initial state a string in $[\boldsymbol{w}]$. Since the final states are the equivalence classes containing exactly those strings that are in L, M_L recognizes L. It follows that if L is regular, it is the union of some of the equivalence classes of R_L. ∎

We now state an important corollary of this theorem that identifies a minimal machine recognizing a regular language L. Two DFSMs are **isomorphic** if they differ only in the names given to states.

COROLLARY 4.7.1 *If L is regular, the machine M_L is a minimal DFSM recognizing L. All other such minimal machines are isomorphic to M_L.*

> **Proof** From the proof of Theorem 4.7.1, if M is any DFSM recognizing L, it has no fewer states than there are equivalence classes of R_L, which is the number of states of M_L. Thus, M_L has a minimal number of states.
>
> Consider another minimal machine $M_0 = (\Sigma, Q_0, \delta_0, s_0, F_0)$. Each state of M_0 can be identified with some state of M_L. Equate the initial states of M_L and M_0 and let q be an arbitrary state of M_0. There is some string $\boldsymbol{u} \in \Sigma^*$ such that $q = \delta_0(s_0, \boldsymbol{u})$. (If not, M_0 is not minimal.) Equate state q with state $\delta_L(s_L, \boldsymbol{u}) = [\boldsymbol{u}]$ of M_L. Let $\boldsymbol{v} \in [\boldsymbol{u}]$. If $\delta_0(s_0, \boldsymbol{v}) \neq q$, M_0 has more states than does M_L, which is a contradiction. Thus, the identification of states in these two machines is consistent. The final states F_0 of M_0 are identified with those equivalence classes of M_L that contain strings in L.
>
> Consider now the next-state function δ_0 of M_0. Let state q of M_0 be identified with state $[\boldsymbol{u}]$ of M_L and let a be an input letter. Then, if $\delta_0(q, a) = p$, it follows that p is associated with state $[\boldsymbol{u}a]$ of M_L because the input string ua maps q_0 to state p in M_0 and maps s_L to $[\boldsymbol{u}a]$ in M_L. Thus, the next-state functions of the two machines are identical up to a renaming of the states of the two machines. ∎

4.7.3   A State Minimization Algorithm

The above approach does not offer a direct way to find a minimal-state machine. In this section we give a procedure for this purpose. Given a regular language, we construct an NFSM that recognizes it (Theorem 4.4.1) and then convert the NFSM to an equivalent DFSM (Theorem 4.2.1). Once we have such a DFSM M, we give a procedure to minimize the number of states based on combining equivalence classes of the right-invariant equivalence relation R_M that are indistinguishable. (These equivalence classes are sets of states of M.) The resulting machine is isomorphic to M_L, the minimal-state machine.

DEFINITION 4.7.7 *Let $M = (\Sigma, Q, \delta, s, F)$ be a DFSM. The equivalence relation $\equiv_n$ on states in Q is defined as follows: two states p and q of M are **n-indistinguishable** (denoted $p \equiv_n q$) if and only if for all input strings $\boldsymbol{u} \in \Sigma^*$ of length $|\boldsymbol{u}| \leq n$ either both $\delta(p, \boldsymbol{u})$ and $\delta(q, \boldsymbol{u})$ are in F or both are not in F. (We write $p \not\equiv_n q$ if p and q are not n-indistinguishable.) Two states p and q are **equivalent** (denoted $p \equiv q$) if they are n-indistinguishable for all $n \geq 0$.*

For arbitrary states q_1, q_2, and q_3, if q_1 and q_2 are n-indistinguishable and q_2 and q_3 are n-indistinguishable, then q_1 and q_3 are n-indistinguishable. Thus, all three states are in the same set of the partition and $\equiv_n$ is an equivalence relation. By an extension of this type of reasoning to all values of n, it is also clear that $\equiv$ is an equivalence relation.

The following lemma establishes that $\equiv_{j+1}$ refines $\equiv_j$ and that for some k and all $j \geq k$, $\equiv_j$ is identical to $\equiv_k$, which is in turn equal to $\equiv$.

LEMMA 4.7.1 *Let $M = (\Sigma, Q, \delta, s, F)$ be an arbitrary DFSM. Over the set Q the equivalence relation $\equiv_{n+1}$ is a refinement of the relation $\equiv_n$. Furthermore, if for some $k \leq |Q| - 2$, $\equiv_{k+1}$ and $\equiv_k$ are equal, then so are $\equiv_{j+1}$ and $\equiv_j$ for all $j \geq k$. In particular, $\equiv_k$ and $\equiv$ are identical.*

Proof If $p \equiv_{n+1} q$ then $p \equiv_n q$ by definition. Thus, for $n \geq 0$ $\equiv_{n+1}$ refines $\equiv_n$.

We now show that if $\equiv_{k+1}$ and $\equiv_k$ are equal, then $\equiv_{j+1}$ and $\equiv_j$ are equal for all $j \geq$k. Suppose not. Let l be the smallest value of j for which $\equiv_{j+1}$ and $\equiv_j$ are equal but $\equiv_{j+2}$ and $\equiv_{j+1}$ are not equal. It follows that there exist two states p and q that are indistinguishable for input strings of length $l + 1$ or less but are distinguishable for some input string $\boldsymbol{v}$ of length $|\boldsymbol{v}| = l+2$. Let $\boldsymbol{v} = a\boldsymbol{u}$ where $a \in \Sigma$ and $|\boldsymbol{u}| = l+1$. Since $\delta(p, \boldsymbol{v}) = \delta(\delta(p, a), \boldsymbol{u})$ and $\delta(q, \boldsymbol{v}) = \delta(\delta(q, a), \boldsymbol{u})$, it follows that the states $\delta(p, a)$ and $\delta(q, a)$ are distinguishable by some string $\boldsymbol{u}$ of length $l + 1$ but not by any string of length l. But this contradicts the assumption that $\equiv_{l+1}$ and $\equiv_l$ are equal.

The relation $\equiv_0$ has two equivalence classes, the final states and all other states. For each integer $j \leq k$, where k is the smallest integer such that $\equiv_{k+1}$ and $\equiv_k$ are equal, $\equiv_j$ has at least one more equivalence class than does $\equiv_{j-1}$. That is, it has at least $j + 2$ classes. Since $\equiv_k$ can have at most $|Q|$ equivalence classes, it follows that $k + 2 \leq |Q|$.

Clearly, $\equiv_k$ and $\equiv$ are identical because if two states cannot be distinguished by input strings of length k or less, they cannot be distinguished by input strings of any length. ∎

The proof of this lemma provides an algorithm to compute the equivalence relation $\equiv$, namely, compute the relations $\equiv_j$, $0 \leq j \leq |Q| - 2$ in succession until we find two relations that are identical. We find $\equiv_{j+1}$ from $\equiv_j$ as follows: for every pair of states (p, q) in an equivalence class of $\equiv_j$, we find their successor states $\delta(p, a)$ and $\delta(q, a)$ under input letter a for each such letter. If for all letters a, $\delta(p, a) \equiv_j \delta(q, a)$ and $p \equiv_j q$, then $p \equiv_{j+1} q$ because we cannot distinguish between p and q on inputs of length $k + 1$ or less. Thus, the algorithm compares each pair of states in an equivalence class of $\equiv_j$ and forms equivalence classes of $\equiv_{j+1}$ by grouping together states whose successors under input letters are in the same equivalence class of $\equiv_j$.

To illustrate these ideas, consider the DFSM of Fig. 4.14. The equivalence classes of $\equiv_0$ are $\{\{s_0, q_R\}, \{q_1, q_2, q_3\}\}$. Since $\delta(s_0, 0)$ and $\delta(q_R, 0)$ are different, s_0 and q_R are in different equivalence classes of $\equiv_1$. Also, because $\delta(q_3, 0) = q_R$ and $\delta(q_1, 0) = \delta(q_2, 0) = q_1 \in F$, q_R is an different equivalence class of $\equiv_1$ from q_1 and q_2. The latter two states are in the same equivalence class because $\delta(q_1, 1) = \delta(q_2, 1) = q_R \notin F$. Thus, $\equiv_1 = \{\{s_0\}, \{q_R\}, \{q_1\}, \{q_2, q_3\}\}$. The only one of these equivalence classes that could be refined is the last one. However, since we cannot distinguish between the two states in this class under any input, no further refinement is possible and $\equiv \; = \; \equiv_1$.

We now show that if two states are equivalent under $\equiv$, they can be combined, but if they are distinguishable under $\equiv$, they cannot. Applying this procedure provides a minimal-state DFSM.

DEFINITION 4.7.8 *Let $M = (\Sigma, Q, \delta, s, F)$ be a DFSM and let $\equiv$ be the equivalence relation defined above over Q. The DFSM $M_\equiv = (\Sigma, Q_\equiv, \delta_\equiv, s, F_\equiv)$ associated with the relation $\equiv$ is defined as follows: a) the states $Q_\equiv$ are the equivalence classes of $\equiv$; b) the initial state of $M_\equiv$ is $[s]$; c) the final states $F_\equiv$ are the equivalence classes containing states in F; d) for an arbitrary equivalence class $[q]$ with representative element $q \in Q$ and an arbitrary input letter $a \in \Sigma$, the next-state function $\delta_\equiv : Q_\equiv \times \Sigma \mapsto Q_\equiv$ is defined by $\delta_\equiv([q], a) = [\delta(q, a)]$.*

This definition is consistent; no matter which representative of the equivalence class $[q]$ is used, the next state on input a is $[\delta(q, a)]$. It is straightforward to show that $M_\equiv$ recognizes the same language as does M. (See Problem 4.27.) We now show that $M_\equiv$ is a minimal-state machine.

THEOREM 4.7.2 *$M_\equiv$ is a minimal-state machine.*

Proof Let $M = (\Sigma, Q, \delta, s, F)$ be a DFSM recognizing L and let $M_\equiv$ be the DFSM associated with the equivalence relation $\equiv$ on Q. Without loss of generality, we assume that all states of $M_\equiv$ are accessible from the initial state. We now show that $M_\equiv$ has no fewer states than M_L. Suppose it has more states. That is, suppose $M_\equiv$ has more states than there are equivalence classes of R_L. Then, there must be two states p and q of M such that $[p] \neq [q]$ but that uRv, where u and v carry M from its initial state to p and q, respectively. (If this were not the case, any strings equivalent under R_L would carry M from its initial state s to equivalent states, contradicting the assumption that $M_\equiv$ has more states than M_L.) But if uRv, then since R is right-invariant, $uwRvw$ for all $w \in \Sigma^*$. However, because $[p] \neq [q]$, there is some $z \in \Sigma^*$ such that $[p]$ and $[q]$ can be distinguished. This is equivalent to saying that $uzRvz$ does not hold, a contradiction. Thus, $M_\equiv$ and M_L have the same number of states. Since $M_\equiv$ recognizes L, it is a minimal-state machine equivalent to M. ∎

As shown above, the equivalence relation $\equiv$ for the DFSM of Fig. 4.14 is $\equiv$ is $\{\{s_0\}, \{q_R\}, \{q_1\}, \{q_2, q_3\}\}$. The DFSM associated with this relation, $M_\equiv$, is shown in Fig. 4.21. It clearly recognizes the language $10^* + 0$. It follows that the equivalent DFSM of Fig. 4.14 is not minimal.

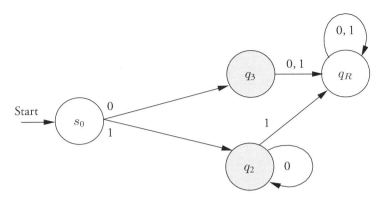

Figure 4.21 *A minimal-state DFSM equivalent to the DFSM in Fig. 4.14.*

4.8 Pushdown Automata

The pushdown automaton (PDA) has a one-way, read-only, potentially infinite input tape on which an input string is written (see Fig. 4.22); its head either advances to the right from the leftmost cell or remains stationary. It also has a stack, a storage medium analogous to the stack of trays in a cafeteria. The **stack** is a potentially infinite ordered collection of initially blank cells with the property that data can be pushed onto it or popped from it. Data is **pushed** onto the top of the stack by moving all existing entries down one cell and inserting the new element in the top location. Data is **popped** by removing the top element and moving all other entries up one cell. The control unit of a pushdown automaton is a finite-state machine. The full power of the PDA is realized only when its control unit is nondeterministic.

DEFINITION 4.8.1 *A **pushdown automaton (PDA)** is a six-tuple $M = (\Sigma, \Gamma, Q, \Delta, s, F)$, where Σ is the **tape alphabet** containing the blank symbol β, Γ is the **stack alphabet** containing the blank symbol γ, Q is the **set of states**, $\Delta \subseteq (Q \times (\Sigma \cup \{\epsilon\}) \times (\Gamma \cup \{\epsilon\}) \times Q \times (\Gamma \cup \{\epsilon\}))$ is the set of **transitions**, s is the **initial state**, and F is the **set of final states**. We now describe transitions.*

If for state p, tape symbol x, and stack symbol y the transition $(p, x, y; q, z) \in \Delta$, then if M is in state p, $x \in \Sigma$ is under its tape head, and $y \in \Gamma$ is at the top of its stack, M may pop y from its stack, enter state $q \in Q$, and push $z \in \Gamma$ onto its stack. However, if $x = \epsilon$, $y = \epsilon$ or $z = \epsilon$, then M does not read its tape, pop its stack or push onto its stack, respectively. The head on the tape either remains stationary if $x = \epsilon$ or advances one cell to the right if $x \neq \epsilon$.

*If at each point in time a unique transition $(p, x, y; q, z)$ may be applied, the PDA is **deterministic**. Otherwise it is **nondeterministic**.*

*The PDA M **accepts the input string** $w \in \Sigma^*$ if when started in state s with an empty stack (its cells contain the **blank stack symbol** γ) and w placed left-adjusted on its otherwise blank tape (its blank cells contain the **blank tape symbol** β), the last state entered by M after reading the components of w and no other tape cells is a member of the set F. M **accepts the language** $L(M)$ consisting of all such strings.*

Some of the special cases for the action of the PDA M on empty tape or stack symbols are the following: if $(p, x, \epsilon; q, z)$, x is read, state q is entered, and z is pushed onto

One-way read-only input tape

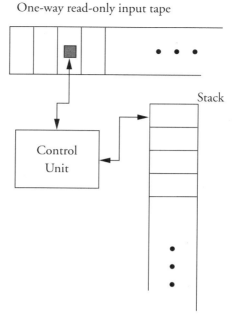

Figure 4.22 The control unit, one-way input tape, and stack of a pushdown automaton.

the stack; if $(p, x, y; q, \epsilon)$, x is read, state q is entered, and y is popped from the stack; if $(p, \epsilon, y; q, z)$, no input is read, y is popped, z is pushed and state q is entered. Also, if $(p, \epsilon, \epsilon; q, \epsilon)$, M moves from state p to q without reading input, or pushing or popping the stack.

Observe that if every transition is of the form $(p, x, \epsilon; q, \epsilon)$, the PDA ignores the stack and simulates an FSM. Thus, the languages accepted by PDAs include the regular languages.

We emphasize that a PDA is nondeterministic if for some state q, tape symbol x, and top stack item y there is more than one transition that M can make. For example, if Δ contains $(s, a, \epsilon; s, a)$ and $(s, a, a; r, \epsilon)$, M has the choice of ignoring or popping the top of the stack and of moving to state s or r. If after reading all symbols of $\boldsymbol{w}$ M enters a state in F, then M accepts $\boldsymbol{w}$.

We now give two examples of PDAs and the languages they accept. The first accepts palindromes of the form $\{\boldsymbol{w}c\boldsymbol{w}^R\}$, where $\boldsymbol{w}^R$ is the reverse of $\boldsymbol{w}$ and $\boldsymbol{w} \in \{a, b\}^*$. The state diagram of its control unit is shown in Fig. 4.23. The second PDA accepts those strings over $\{a, b\}$ of the form $a^n b^m$ for which $n \geq m$.

EXAMPLE 4.8.1 *The PDA $M = (\Sigma, \Gamma, Q, \Delta, s, F)$, where $\Sigma = \{a, b, c, \beta\}$, $\Gamma = \{a, b, \gamma\}$, $Q = \{s, p, r, f\}$, $F = \{f\}$ and Δ contains the transitions shown in Fig. 4.24, accepts the language $L = \{\boldsymbol{w}c\boldsymbol{w}^R\}$.*

The PDA M of Figs. 4.23 and 4.24 remains in the **stacking state** s while encountering a's and b's on the input tape, pushing these letters (the order of these letters on the stack is the reverse of their order on the input tape) onto the stack (Rules (a) and (b)). If it encounters an

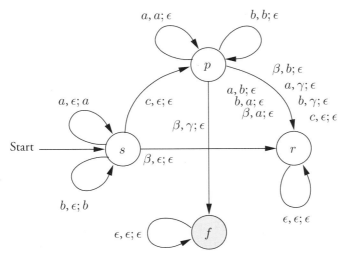

Figure 4.23 State diagram for the pushdown automaton of Fig. 4.24 which accepts $\{wcw^R\}$. An edge label $a, b; c$ between states p and q corresponds to the transition $(p, a, b; q, c)$.

instance of letter c while in state s, it enters the **possible accept state** p (Rule (c)) but enters the **reject state** r if it encounters a blank on the input tape (Rule (d)). While in state p it pops an a or b that matches the same letter on the input tape (Rules (e) and (f)). If the PDA discovers blank tape and stack symbols, it has identified a palindrome and enters the **accept state** f (Rule (g)). On the other hand, if while in state p the tape symbol and the symbol on the top of the stack are different or the letter c is encountered, the PDA enters the reject state r (Rules (h)–(n)). Finally, the PDA does not exit from either the reject or accept states (Rules (o) and (p)).

	Rule	Comment		Rule	Comment
(a)	$(s, a, \epsilon; s, a)$	push a	(i)	$(p, b, a; r, \epsilon)$	reject
(b)	$(s, b, \epsilon; s, b)$	push b	(j)	$(p, \beta, a; r, \epsilon)$	reject
(c)	$(s, c, \epsilon; p, \epsilon)$	accept?	(k)	$(p, \beta, b; r, \epsilon)$	reject
(d)	$(s, \beta, \epsilon; r, \epsilon)$	reject	(l)	$(p, a, \gamma; r, \epsilon)$	reject
(e)	$(p, a, a; p, \epsilon)$	accept?	(m)	$(p, b, \gamma; r, \epsilon)$	reject
(f)	$(p, b, b; p, \epsilon)$	accept?	(n)	$(p, c, \epsilon; r, \epsilon)$	reject
(g)	$(p, \beta, \gamma; f, \epsilon)$	accept	(o)	$(r, \epsilon, \epsilon; r, \epsilon)$	stay in reject state
(h)	$(p, a, b; r, \epsilon)$	reject	(p)	$(f, \epsilon, \epsilon; f, \epsilon)$	stay in accept state

Figure 4.24 Transitions for the PDA described by the state diagram of Fig. 4.23.

	Rule	Comment			Rule	Comment
(a)	$(s, \beta, \gamma; f, \epsilon)$	accept		(g)	$(p, \beta, a; f, \epsilon)$	accept
(b)	$(s, a, \epsilon; s, a)$	push a		(h)	$(p, \beta, \gamma; f, \epsilon)$	accept
(c)	$(s, b, \gamma; r, \epsilon)$	reject		(i)	$(p, a, \epsilon; r, \epsilon)$	reject
(d)	$(s, b, a; p, \epsilon)$	pop a, enter pop state		(j)	$(f, \epsilon, \epsilon; f, \epsilon)$	stay in accept state
(e)	$(p, b, a; p, \epsilon)$	pop a		(k)	$(r, \epsilon, \epsilon; r, \epsilon)$	stay in reject state
(f)	$(p, b, \gamma; r, \epsilon)$	reject				

Figure 4.25 Transitions for a PDA that accepts the language $\{a^n b^m \mid n \geq m \geq 0\}$.

EXAMPLE 4.8.2 *The PDA $M = (\Sigma, \Gamma, Q, \Delta, s, F)$, where $\Sigma = \{a, b, \beta\}$, $\Gamma = \{a, b, \gamma\}$, $Q = \{s, p, r, f\}$, $F = \{f\}$ and Δ contains the transitions shown in Fig. 4.25, accepts the language $L = \{a^n b^m \mid n \geq m \geq 0\}$. The state diagram for this machine is shown in Fig. 4.26.*

The rules of Fig. 4.25 work as follows. An empty input in the **stacking state** s is accepted (Rule (a)). If a string of a's is found, the PDA remains in state s and the a's are pushed onto the stack (Rule (b)). At the first discovery of a b in the input while in state s, if the stack is empty, the input is rejected by entering the **reject state** (Rule (c)). If the stack is not empty, the a at the top is popped and the PDA enters the **pop state** p (Rule (d)). If while in p a b is discovered on the input tape when an a is found at the top of the stack (Rule(e)), the PDA pops the a and stays in this state because it remains possible that the input contains no more b's than a's. On the other hand, if the stack is empty when a b is discovered, the PDA enters the reject state (Rule (f)). If in state p the PDA discovers that it has more a's than b's by reading

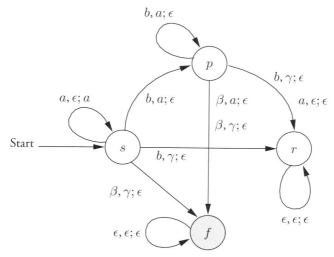

Figure 4.26 The state diagram for the PDA defined by the tables in Fig. 4.25.

the blank tape letter β when the stack is not empty, it enters the **accept state** f (Rule (g)). If the PDA encounters an a on its input tape when in state p, an a has been received after a b and the input is rejected (Rule (i)). After the PDA enters either the accept or reject states, it remains there (Rules (j) and (k)).

In Section 4.12 we show that the languages recognized by pushdown automata are exactly the languages defined by the context-free languages described in the next section.

4.9 Formal Languages

Languages are introduced in Section 1.2.3. A **language** is a set of strings over a finite set Σ called an **alphabet**. Σ^* is the language of all strings over Σ including the **empty string** ϵ, which has zero length. The empty string has the property that for an arbitrary string w, $\epsilon w = w = w\epsilon$. Σ^+ is the set Σ^* without the empty string.

In this section we introduce grammars for languages, rules for **rewriting strings** through the substitution of substrings. A **grammar** consists of alphabets $\mathcal{T}$ and $\mathcal{N}$ of terminal and non-terminal symbols, respectively, plus a set of rules $\mathcal{R}$ for rewriting strings. Below we define four types of language in terms of their grammars: the phrase-structure, context-sensitive, context-free, and regular grammars.

The role of grammars is best illustrated with an example for a small fragment of English. Consider a grammar G whose non-terminals $\mathcal{N}$ contain a start symbol S denoting a generic sentence and NP and VP denoting generic noun and verb phrases, respectively. In turn, assume that $\mathcal{N}$ also contains non-terminals for adjectives and adverbs, namely AJ and AV. Thus, $\mathcal{N} = \{S, NP, VP, AJ, AV, N, V\}$. We allow the grammar to have the following words as terminals: $\mathcal{T} = \{bob, alice, duck, big, smiles, quacks, loudly\}$. Here *bob*, *alice*, and *duck* are nouns, *big* is an adjective, *smiles* and *quacks* are verbs, and *loudly* is an adverb. In our fragment of English a sentence consists of a noun phrase followed by a verb phrase, which we denote by the rule S $\rightarrow$ NP VP. This and the other rules $\mathcal{R}$ of the grammar are shown below. They include rules to map non-terminals to terminals, such as N $\rightarrow$ *bob*

S	$\rightarrow$	NP VP	N	$\rightarrow$	*bob*	V	$\rightarrow$	*smiles*
NP	$\rightarrow$	N	N	$\rightarrow$	*alice*	V	$\rightarrow$	*quacks*
NP	$\rightarrow$	AJ N	N	$\rightarrow$	*duck*	AV	$\rightarrow$	*loudly*
VP	$\rightarrow$	V	AJ	$\rightarrow$	*big*			
VP	$\rightarrow$	V AV						

With these rules the following strings (sentences) can be generated: *bob smiles*; *big duck quacks loudly*; and *alice quacks*. The first two sentences are acceptable English sentences, but the third is not if we interpret *alice* as a person. This example illustrates the need for rules that limit the rewriting of non-terminals to an appropriate context of surrounding symbols.

Grammars for formal languages generalize these ideas. Grammars are used to interpret programming languages. A language is translated and given meaning through a series of steps the first of which is **lexical analysis**. In lexical analysis symbols such as a, l, i, c, e are grouped into tokens such as *alice*, or some other string denoting *alice*. This task is typically done with a finite-state machine. The second step in translation is **parsing**, a process in which a tokenized string is associated with a series of **derivations** or applications of the rules of a grammar. For example, *big duck quacks loudly*, can be produced by the following sequence of derivations: S $\rightarrow$ NP VP; NP $\rightarrow$ AJ N; AJ $\rightarrow$ *big*; N $\rightarrow$ *duck*; VP $\rightarrow$ V AV; V $\rightarrow$ *quacks*; AV $\rightarrow$ *loudly*.

In his exploration of models for natural language, Noam Chomsky introduced four languages types of decreasing expressibility, now called the **Chomsky hierarchy**, in which each language is described by the type of grammar generating it. These languages serve as a basis for the classification of programming languages. The four types are the phrase-structure languages, the context-sensitive languages, the context-free languages, and the regular languages.

There is an exact correspondence between each of these types of languages and particular machine architectures in the sense that for each language type T there is a machine architecture A recognizing languages of type T and for each architecture A there is a type T such that all languages recognized by A are of type T. The correspondence between language and architecture is shown in the following table, which also lists the section or problem where the result is established. Here the **linear bounded automaton** is a Turing machine in which the number of tape cells that are used is linear in the length of the input string.

Level	Language Type	Machine Type	Proof Location
0	phrase-structure	Turing machine	Section 5.4
1	context-sensitive	linear bounded automaton	Problem 4.36
2	context-free	nondet. pushdown automaton	Section 4.12
3	regular	finite-state machine	Section 4.10

We now give formal definitions of each of the grammar types under consideration.

4.9.1   Phrase-Structure Languages

In Section 5.4 we show that the phrase-structure grammars defined below are exactly the languages that can be recognized by Turing machines.

DEFINITION 4.9.1   *A **phrase-structure grammar** G is a four-tuple $G = (\mathcal{N}, \mathcal{T}, \mathcal{R}, \mathrm{S})$ where $\mathcal{N}$ and $\mathcal{T}$ are disjoint alphabets of **non-terminals** and **terminals**, respectively. Let $V = \mathcal{N} \cup \mathcal{T}$. The **rules** $\mathcal{R}$ form a finite subset of $V^+ \times V^*$ (denoted $\mathcal{R} \subseteq V^+ \times V^*$) where for every rule $(\boldsymbol{a}, \boldsymbol{b}) \in \mathcal{R}$, $\boldsymbol{a}$ contains at least one non-terminal symbol. The symbol $\mathrm{S} \in \mathcal{N}$ is the **start symbol**.*

*If $(\boldsymbol{a}, \boldsymbol{b}) \in \mathcal{R}$ we write $\boldsymbol{a} \to \boldsymbol{b}$. If $\boldsymbol{u} \in V^+$ and $\boldsymbol{a}$ is a contiguous substring of $\boldsymbol{u}$, then $\boldsymbol{u}$ can be replaced by the string $\boldsymbol{v}$ by substituting $\boldsymbol{b}$ for $\boldsymbol{a}$. If this holds, we write $\boldsymbol{u} \Rightarrow_G \boldsymbol{v}$ and call it an **immediate derivation**. Extending this notation, if through a sequence of immediate derivations (called a **derivation**) $\boldsymbol{u} \Rightarrow_G \boldsymbol{x}_1, \boldsymbol{x}_1 \Rightarrow_G \boldsymbol{x_2}, \cdots, \boldsymbol{x}_n \Rightarrow_G \boldsymbol{v}$ we can transform $\boldsymbol{u}$ to $\boldsymbol{v}$, we write $\boldsymbol{u} \stackrel{*}{\Rightarrow}_G \boldsymbol{v}$ and say that $\boldsymbol{v}$ **derives** from $\boldsymbol{u}$. If the rules $\mathcal{R}$ contain $(\boldsymbol{a}, \boldsymbol{a})$ for all $\boldsymbol{a} \in V^+$, the relation $\stackrel{*}{\Rightarrow}_G$ is called the **transitive closure** of the relation $\Rightarrow_G$ and $\boldsymbol{u} \stackrel{*}{\Rightarrow}_G \boldsymbol{u}$ for all $\boldsymbol{u} \in V^*$.*

*The **language** $L(G)$ defined by the grammar G is the set of all terminal strings that can be derived from the start symbol S; that is,*

$$L(G) = \{\boldsymbol{u} \in \mathcal{T}^* \mid \mathrm{S} \stackrel{*}{\Rightarrow}_G \boldsymbol{u}\}$$

When the context is clear we drop the subscript G in $\Rightarrow_G$ and $\stackrel{*}{\Rightarrow}_G$. These definitions are best understood from an example. In all our examples we use letters in SMALL CAPS to denote non-terminals and letters in *italics* to denote terminals, except that ϵ, the empty letter, may also be a terminal.

EXAMPLE 4.9.1   *Consider the grammar $G_1 = (\mathcal{N}_1, \mathcal{T}_1, \mathcal{R}_1, \mathrm{S})$, where $\mathcal{N}_1 = \{\mathrm{S}, \mathrm{B}, \mathrm{C}\}$, $\mathcal{T}_1 = \{a, b, c\}$ and $\mathcal{R}_1$ consists of the following rules:*

$$
\begin{array}{llll}
a) & \text{S} & \rightarrow & a\text{SBC} \\
b) & \text{S} & \rightarrow & a\text{BC} \\
c) & \text{CB} & \rightarrow & \text{BC}
\end{array}
\qquad
\begin{array}{llll}
d) & a\text{B} & \rightarrow & ab \\
e) & b\text{B} & \rightarrow & bb \\
f) & b\text{C} & \rightarrow & bc
\end{array}
\qquad
\begin{array}{llll}
g) & c\text{C} & \rightarrow & cc
\end{array}
$$

Clearly the string $aa\text{BCBC}$ can be rewritten as $aa\text{BBCC}$ using rule (c), that is, $aa\text{BCBC} \Rightarrow aa\text{BBCC}$. One application of (d), one of (e), one of (f), and one of (g) reduces it to the string $aabbcc$. Since one application of (a) and one of (b) produces the string $aa\text{BBCC}$, it follows that the language $L(G_1)$ contains $aabbcc$.

Similarly, two applications of (a) and one of (b) produce $aaa\text{BCBCBC}$, after which three applications of (c) produce the string $aaa\text{BBBCCC}$. One application of (d) and two of (e) produce $aaabbb\text{CCC}$, after which one application of (f) and two of (g) produces $aaabbbccc$. In general, one can show that $L(G_1) = \{a^n b^n c^n \mid n \geq 1\}$. (See Problem 4.38.)

4.9.2 Context-Sensitive Languages

The context-sensitive languages are exactly the languages accepted by linear bounded automata, nondeterministic Turing machines whose tape heads visit a number of cells that is a constant multiple of the length of an input string. (See Problem 4.36.)

DEFINITION 4.9.2 *A **context-sensitive grammar** G is a phrase structure grammar $G = (\mathcal{N}, \mathcal{T}, \mathcal{R}, \text{S})$ in which each rule $(\boldsymbol{a}, \boldsymbol{b}) \in \mathcal{R}$ satisfies the condition that $\boldsymbol{b}$ has no fewer characters than does $\boldsymbol{a}$, namely, $|\boldsymbol{a}| \leq |\boldsymbol{b}|$. The languages defined by context-sensitive grammars are called **context-sensitive languages** (CSL).*

Each rule of a context-sensitive grammar maps a string to one that is no shorter. Since the left-hand side of a rule may have more than one character, it may make replacements based on the context in which a non-terminal is found. Examples of context-sensitive languages are given in Problems 4.38 and 4.39.

4.9.3 Context-Free Languages

As shown in Section 4.12, the context-free languages are exactly the languages accepted by pushdown automata.

DEFINITION 4.9.3 *A **context-free grammar** $G = (\mathcal{N}, \mathcal{T}, \mathcal{R}, \text{S})$ is a context-sensitive grammar in which each rule in $\mathcal{R} \subseteq \mathcal{N} \times V^*$ has a single non-terminal on the left-hand side. The languages defined by context-free grammars are called **context-free languages** (CFL).*

Each rule of a context-free grammar maps a non-terminal to a string over V^* without regard to the context in which the non-terminal is found because the left-hand side of each rule consists of a single non-terminal.

EXAMPLE 4.9.2 *Let $\mathcal{N}_2 = \{\text{S}, \text{A}\}$, $\mathcal{T}_2 = \{\epsilon, a, b\}$, and $\mathcal{R}_2 = \{\text{S} \rightarrow a\text{S}b, \text{S} \rightarrow \epsilon\}$. Then the grammar $G_2 = (\mathcal{N}_2, \mathcal{T}_2, \mathcal{R}_2, \text{S})$ is context-free and generates the language $L(G_2) = \{a^n b^n \mid n \geq 1\}$. To see this, let the rule $\text{S} \rightarrow a\text{S}b$ be applied k times to produce the string $a^k \text{S} b^k$. A final application of the last rule establishes the result.*

EXAMPLE 4.9.3 *Consider the grammar G_3 with the following rules and the implied terminal and non-terminal alphabets:*

a)	S	$\to$	cMNc		*d)*	N	$\to$	bNb
b)	M	$\to$	aMa		*e)*	N	$\to$	c
c)	M	$\to$	c					

G_3 *is context-free and generates the language* $L(G_3) = \{ca^n ca^n cb^m cb^m c \,|\, n, m \geq 0\}$, *as is easily shown.*

Context-free languages capture important aspects of many programming languages. As a consequence, the parsing of context-free languages is an important step in the parsing of programming languages. This topic is discussed in Section 4.11.

4.9.4 Regular Languages

DEFINITION 4.9.4 *A **regular grammar** G is a context-free grammar $G = (\mathcal{N}, \mathcal{T}, \mathcal{R}, \mathrm{S})$, where the right-hand side is either a terminal or a terminal followed by a non-terminal. That is, its rules are of the form* A $\to$ a *or* A $\to$ bC. *The languages defined by regular grammars are called **regular languages**.*

Some authors define a regular grammar to be one whose rules are of the form A $\to$ a or A $\to$ $b_1 b_2 \cdots b_k$C. It is straightforward to show that any language generated by such a grammar can be generated by a grammar of the type defined above.

The following grammar is regular.

EXAMPLE 4.9.4 *Consider the grammar $G_4 = (\mathcal{N}_4, \mathcal{T}_4, \mathcal{R}_4, \mathrm{S})$ where $\mathcal{N}_4 = \{\mathrm{S}, \mathrm{A}, \mathrm{B}\}$, $\mathcal{T}_4 = \{0, 1\}$ and $\mathcal{R}_4$ consists of the rules given below.*

a)	S	$\to$	0A		*d)*	B	$\to$	0A
b)	S	$\to$	0		*e)*	B	$\to$	0
c)	A	$\to$	1B					

It is straightforward to see that the rules a) S $\to$ 0, b) S $\to$ 01B, c) B $\to$ 0, and d) B $\to$ 01B generate the same strings as the rules given above. Thus, the language G_4 contains the strings $0, 010, 01010, 0101010, \ldots$, that is, strings of the form $(01)^k 0$ for $k \geq 0$. Consequently $L(G_4) = (01)^* 0$. A formal proof of this result is left to the reader. (See Problem 4.44.)

4.10 Regular Language Recognition

As explained in Section 4.1, a deterministic finite-state machine (DFSM) M is a five-tuple $M = (\Sigma, Q, \delta, s, F)$, where Σ is the input alphabet, Q is the set of states, $\delta : Q \times \Sigma \mapsto Q$ is the next-state function, s is the initial state, and F is the set of final states. A nondeterministic FSM (NFSM) is similarly defined except that δ is a next-set function $\delta : Q \times \Sigma \mapsto 2^Q$. In other words, in an NFSM there may be more than one next state for a given state and input. In Section 4.2 we showed that the languages recognized by these two machine types are the same.

We now show that the languages defined by a regular grammar are exactly those recognized by FSMs.

THEOREM 4.10.1 *The languages generated by regular grammars and recognized by finite-state machines are the same.*

Proof Given a regular grammar G, we construct a corresponding NFSM M that accepts exactly the strings generated by G. Similarly, given a DFSM M we construct a regular grammar G that generates the strings recognized by M.

Let $G = (\mathcal{N}, \mathcal{T}, \mathcal{R}, \text{S})$ be a regular grammar. Then, its rules $\mathcal{R}$ are of the form $\text{A} \rightarrow a$ or $\text{A} \rightarrow b\text{C}$. We first produce a grammar G' that generates the same language by replacing each rule of the form $\text{A} \rightarrow a$ with two rules of the form $\text{A} \rightarrow a\text{B}$ and $\text{B} \rightarrow \epsilon$. Here B is a new non-terminal particular to the rule $\text{A} \rightarrow a\text{B}$.

Every derivation $\text{S} \stackrel{*}{\Rightarrow}_G w$, $w \in \mathcal{T}^*$, corresponds to a derivation $\text{S} \stackrel{*}{\Rightarrow}_{G'} w\text{B}$ in which B is a new non-terminal added to G along with the new rule $\text{B} \rightarrow \epsilon$ to form G'. Hence, the strings generated by G and G' are the same.

Now construct an NFSM $M_{G'}$ whose states correspond to the non-terminals of this new regular grammar and whose input alphabet is its set of terminals. Let the state associated with S be the start state of $M_{G'}$. Let there be a transition from state A to state B on input a if there is a rule $\text{A} \rightarrow a\text{B}$ in G'. Let a state B be a final state if there is a rule of the form $\text{B} \rightarrow \epsilon$ in G'. Clearly, every derivation of a string w in $L(G')$ corresponds to a path in M that begins in the start state and ends on a final state. Hence, w is accepted by $M_{G'}$. On the other hand, if a string w is accepted by $M_{G'}$, given the one-to-one correspondence between edges and rules, there is a derivation of w from S in G'. Thus, the strings generated by G and the strings accepted by $M_{G'}$ are the same.

Now assume we are given a DFSM M that accepts a language L_M. Create a grammar G_M whose non-terminals correspond to the states of M and whose start symbol is the start state of M. G_M has a rule of the form $q_1 \rightarrow aq_2$ if M makes a transition from state q_1 to q_2 on input a. If state q is a final state of M, also add the rule $q \rightarrow \epsilon$. If a string is accepted by M, that is, it causes M to move to a final state, then G_M generates the same string. Since G_M generates only strings of this kind, every language accepted by M is generated by a regular grammar. ∎

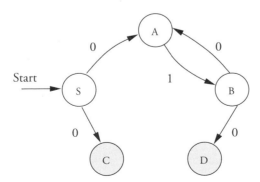

Figure 4.27 A nondeterministic FSM that accepts a language generated by a regular language in which all rules are of the form $\text{A} \rightarrow b\text{C}$ or $\text{A} \rightarrow \epsilon$. A state is associated with each non-terminal, the start symbol S is associated with the start state, and final states are associated with non-terminals A such that $\text{A} \rightarrow \epsilon$. This particular NFSM accepts the language $L(G_4)$ of Example 4.9.4.

A simple example illustrates the construction of an NFSM from a regular grammar. Consider the grammar G_4 of Example 4.9.4. A new grammar G_4' is constructed with the following rules: a) $S \rightarrow 0A$, b) $S \rightarrow 0C$, c) $C \rightarrow \epsilon$, d) $A \rightarrow 1B$, e) $B \rightarrow 0A$, f) $B \rightarrow 0D$, and g) $D \rightarrow \epsilon$. Figure 4.27 (page 185) shows an NFSM that accepts the language generated by this grammar. A DFSM recognizing the same language can be obtained by invoking the construction of Theorem 4.2.1.

4.11 Parsing Context-Free Languages

Parsing is the process of deducing those rules of a grammar G (a **derivation**) that generates a terminal string w. The first rule must have the start symbol S on the left-hand side. In this section we give a brief introduction to the parsing of context-free languages, a topic central to the parsing of programming languages. The reader is referred to a textbook on compilers for more detail on this subject. (See, for example, [11] and [100].) The concepts of Boolean matrix multiplication and transitive closure are used in this section, topics that are covered in Chapter 6.

Generally a string w has many derivations. This is illustrated by the context-free grammar G_3 defined in Example 4.9.3 and described below.

EXAMPLE 4.11.1 $G_3 = (\mathcal{N}_3, \mathcal{T}_3, \mathcal{R}_3, S)$, where $\mathcal{N}_3 = \{S, M, N\}$, $\mathcal{T}_3 = \{A, B, C\}$ and $\mathcal{R}_3$ consists of the rules below:

$$
\begin{array}{llll}
a) & S \rightarrow cMNc & d) & N \rightarrow bNb \\
b) & M \rightarrow aMa & e) & N \rightarrow c \\
c) & M \rightarrow c &
\end{array}
$$

The string $caacaabcbc$ can be derived by applying rules (a), (b) twice, (c), (d) and (e) to produce the following derivation:

$$
\begin{aligned}
S & \Rightarrow cMNc \quad \Rightarrow \quad caMaNc \quad \Rightarrow \quad ca^2Ma^2Nc \\
& \Rightarrow ca^2ca^2Nc \quad \Rightarrow \quad ca^2ca^2bNbc \quad \Rightarrow \quad ca^2ca^2bcbc
\end{aligned}
\tag{4.2}
$$

The same string can be obtained by applying the rules in the following order: (a), (d), (e), (b) twice, and (c). Both derivations are described by the **parse tree** of Fig. 4.28. In this tree each instance of a non-terminal is rewritten using one of the rules of the grammar. The order of the descendants of a non-terminal vertex in the parse tree is the order of the corresponding symbols in the string obtained by replacing this non-terminal. The string ca^2ca^2bcbc, the **yield** of this parse tree, is the terminal string obtained by visiting the leaves of this tree in a left-to-right order. The **height** of the parse tree is the number of edges on the longest path (having the most edges) from the root (associated with the start symbol) to a terminal symbol. A **parser** for a language $L(G)$ is a program or machine that examines a string and produces a derivation of the string if it is in the language and an error message if not.

Because every string generated by a context-free grammar has a derivation, it has a corresponding parse tree. Given a derivation, it is straightforward to convert it to a **leftmost derivation**, a derivation in which the leftmost remaining non-terminal is expanded first. (A **rightmost derivation** is a derivation in which the rightmost remaining non-terminal is expanded first.) Such a derivation can be obtained from the parse tree by deleting all vertices

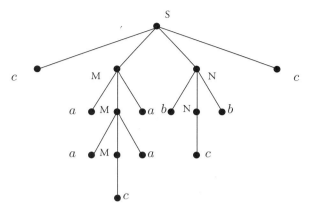

Figure 4.28 A parse tree for the grammar G_3.

associated with terminals and then traversing the remaining vertices in a depth-first manner (visit the first descendant of a vertex before visiting its siblings), assuming that descendants of a vertex are ordered from left to right. When a vertex is visited, apply the rule associated with that vertex in the tree. The derivation given in (4.2) is leftmost.

Not only can some strings in a context-free language have multiple derivations, but in some languages they have multiple parse trees. Languages containing strings with more than one parse tree are said to be **ambiguous languages**. Otherwise languages are **non-ambiguous**.

Given a string that is believed to be generated by a grammar, a **compiler** attempts to parse the string after first scanning the input to identify letters. If the attempt fails, an error message is produced. Given a string generated by a context-free grammar, can we guarantee that we can always find a derivation or parse tree for that string or determine that none exists? The answer is yes, as we now show.

To demonstrate that every CFL can be parsed, it is convenient first to convert the grammar for such a language to Chomsky normal form.

DEFINITION 4.11.1 *A context-free grammar G is in* **Chomsky normal form** *if every rule is of the form* A $\rightarrow$ BC *or* A $\rightarrow$ u, $u \in \mathcal{T}$ *except if* $\epsilon \in L(G)$, *in which case* S $\rightarrow$ ϵ *is also in the grammar.*

We now give a procedure to convert an arbitrary context-free grammar to Chomsky normal form.

THEOREM 4.11.1 *Every context-free language can be generated by a grammar in Chomsky normal form.*

Proof Let $L = L(G)$ where G is a context-free grammar. We construct a context-free grammar G' that is in Chomsky normal form. The process described in this proof is illustrated by the example that follows.

Initially G' is identical with G. We begin by eliminating ϵ-**rules** of the form B $\rightarrow$ ϵ. We keep the rule S $\rightarrow$ ϵ if $\epsilon \in L(G)$ and eliminate the rest as follows. For each rule B $\rightarrow$ ϵ and every rule that has B on the right-hand side, such as A $\rightarrow$ αBβBγ, $\alpha, \beta, \gamma \in (V - \{B\})^*$ $(V = \mathcal{N} \cup \mathcal{T})$, we add a rule for each possible replacement of B by ϵ; for example, we add

A $\rightarrow$ $\alpha\beta B\gamma$, A $\rightarrow$ $\alpha B\beta\gamma$, and A $\rightarrow$ $\alpha\beta\gamma$. Clearly the strings generated by the new rules are the same as are generated by the old rules.

Let A $\rightarrow$ $w_1 \cdots w_i \cdots w_k$ for some $k \geq 1$ be a rule in G' where $w_i \in V$. We replace this rule with the new rules A $\rightarrow$ $Z_1 Z_2 \cdots Z_k$, and $Z_i \rightarrow w_i$ for $1 \leq i \leq k$. Here Z_i is a new non-terminal. Clearly, the new version of G' generates the same language as does G.

With these changes the rules of G' consist of rules either of the form A $\rightarrow$ $u, u \in \mathcal{T}$ (a single terminal) or A $\rightarrow$ $w, w \in \mathcal{N}^+$ (a string of at least one non-terminal). There are two cases of $w \in \mathcal{N}^+$ to consider, a) $|w| = 1$ and b) $|w| \geq 2$. We begin by eliminating all rules of the first kind, that is of the form A $\rightarrow$ B.

Rules of the form A $\rightarrow$ B can be cascaded to form rules of the type C $\stackrel{*}{\Rightarrow}$ D. The number of distinct derivations of this kind is at most $|\mathcal{N}|!$ because if any derivation contains two instances of a non-terminal, the derivation can be shortened. Thus, we need only consider derivations in which each non-terminal occurs at most once. For each such pair C, D with a relation of this kind, add the rule C $\rightarrow$ D to G'. If C $\rightarrow$ D and D $\rightarrow$ w for $|w| \geq 2$ or $w = u \in \mathcal{T}$, add C $\rightarrow$ w to the set of rules. After adding all such rules, delete all rules of the form A $\rightarrow$ B. By construction this new set of rules generates the same language as the original set of rules but eliminates all rules of the first kind.

We now replace rules of the type A $\rightarrow$ $A_1 A_2 \cdots A_k$, $k \geq 3$. Introduce $k - 2$ new non-terminals $N_1, N_2, \cdots, N_{k-2}$ peculiar to this rule and replace the rule with the following rules: A $\rightarrow$ $A_1 N_1$, $N_1 \rightarrow A_2 N_2$, $\cdots$, $N_{k-3} \rightarrow A_{k-2} N_{k-2}$, $N_{k-2} \rightarrow A_{k-1} A_k$. Clearly, the new grammar generates the same language as the original grammar and is in the Chomsky normal form. ∎

EXAMPLE 4.11.2 *Let $G_5 = (\mathcal{N}_5, \mathcal{T}_5, \mathcal{R}_5, E)$ (with start symbol E) be the grammar with $\mathcal{N}_5 = \{E, T, F\}$, $\mathcal{T}_5 = \{a, b, +, *, (,)\}$, and $\mathcal{R}_5$ consisting of the rules given below:*

a)	E $\rightarrow$ E + T	*d)*	T $\rightarrow$ F	*f)*	F $\rightarrow$ a
b)	E $\rightarrow$ T	*e)*	F $\rightarrow$ (E)	*g)*	F $\rightarrow$ b
c)	T $\rightarrow$ T * F				

Here E, T, and F denote expressions, terms, and factors. It is straightforward to show that E $\stackrel{*}{\Rightarrow}$ $(a * b + a) * (a + b)$ and E $\stackrel{*}{\Rightarrow}$ $a * b + a$ are two possible derivations.

We convert this grammar to the Chomsky normal form using the method described in the proof of Theorem 4.11.1. Since $\mathcal{R}$ contains no ϵ-rules, we do not need the rule E $\rightarrow$ ϵ, nor do we need to eliminate ϵ-rules.

First we convert rules of the form A $\rightarrow$ w so that each entry in w is a non-terminal. To do this we introduce the non-terminals (,), +, and * and the rules below. Here we use a boldface font to distinguish between the non-terminal and terminal equivalents of these four mathematical symbols. Since we are adding to the original set of rules, we number them consecutively with the original rules.

h)	**(** $\rightarrow$ (	*j)*	**+** $\rightarrow$ +
i)	**)** $\rightarrow$)	*k)*	***** $\rightarrow$ *

Next we add rules of the form C $\rightarrow$ D for all chains of single non-terminals such that C $\stackrel{*}{\Rightarrow}$ D. Since by inspection E $\stackrel{*}{\Rightarrow}$ F, we add the rule E $\rightarrow$ F. For every rule of the form A $\rightarrow$ B for which B $\rightarrow$ w, we add the rule A $\rightarrow$ w. We then delete all rules of the form A $\rightarrow$ B. These changes cause the rules of G' to become the following. (Below we use a different numbering scheme because all these rules replace rules (a) through (k).)

1)	E	$\rightarrow$	E+T	7)	T	$\rightarrow$	(E)	13)	(	$\rightarrow$	(
2)	E	$\rightarrow$	T*F	8)	T	$\rightarrow$	a	14)	)	$\rightarrow$	)
3)	E	$\rightarrow$	(E)	9)	T	$\rightarrow$	b	15)	+	$\rightarrow$	+
4)	E	$\rightarrow$	a	10)	F	$\rightarrow$	(E)	16)	*	$\rightarrow$	*
5)	E	$\rightarrow$	b	11)	F	$\rightarrow$	a				
6)	T	$\rightarrow$	T*F	12)	F	$\rightarrow$	b				

We now reduce the number of non-terminals on the right-hand side of each rule to two through the addition of new non-terminals. The result is shown in Example 4.11.3 below, where we have added the non-terminals A, B, C, D, G, and H.

EXAMPLE 4.11.3 *Let $G_6 = (\mathcal{N}_6, \mathcal{T}_6, \mathcal{R}_6, E)$ (with start symbol E) be the grammar with $\mathcal{N}_6 = \{A, B, C, D, E, F, G, H, T, +, *, (,)\}$, $\mathcal{T}_6 = \{a, b, +, *, (,)\}$, and $\mathcal{R}_6$ consisting of the rules given below.*

(A)	E	$\rightarrow$	EA	(I)	T	$\rightarrow$	TD	(Q)	H	$\rightarrow$	E)
(B)	A	$\rightarrow$	+T	(J)	D	$\rightarrow$	*F	(R)	F	$\rightarrow$	a
(C)	E	$\rightarrow$	TB	(K)	T	$\rightarrow$	(G	(S)	F	$\rightarrow$	b
(D)	B	$\rightarrow$	*F	(L)	G	$\rightarrow$	E)	(T)	(	$\rightarrow$	(
(E)	E	$\rightarrow$	(C	(M)	T	$\rightarrow$	a	(U)	)	$\rightarrow$	)
(F)	C	$\rightarrow$	E)	(N)	T	$\rightarrow$	b	(V)	+	$\rightarrow$	+
(G)	E	$\rightarrow$	a	(P)	F	$\rightarrow$	(H	(W)	*	$\rightarrow$	*
(H)	E	$\rightarrow$	b								

The new grammar clearly generates the same language as does the original grammar, but it is in Chomsky normal form. It has 22 rules, 13 non-terminals, and six terminals whereas the original grammar had seven rules, three non-terminals, and six terminals.

We now use the Chomsky normal form to show that for every CFL there is a polynomial-time algorithm that tests for membership of a string in the language. This algorithm can be practical for some languages.

THEOREM 4.11.2 *Given a context-free grammar $G = (\mathcal{N}, \mathcal{T}, \mathcal{R}, S)$, an $O(n^3 |\mathcal{N}|^2)$-step algorithm exists to determine whether or not a string $\boldsymbol{w} \in \mathcal{T}^*$ of length n is in $L(G)$ and to construct a parse tree for it if it exists.*

Proof If G is not in Chomsky normal form, convert it to this form. Given a string $\boldsymbol{w} = (w_1, w_2, \ldots, w_n)$, the goal is to determine whether or not $S \stackrel{*}{\Rightarrow} \boldsymbol{w}$. Let $\emptyset$ denote the empty set. The approach taken is to construct an $(n+1) \times (n+1)$ **set matrix** S whose entries are sets of non-terminals of G with the property that the i, j entry, $a_{i,j}$, is the set of non-terminals C such that $C \stackrel{*}{\Rightarrow} (w_i \cdots w_{j-1})$. Thus, the string $\boldsymbol{w}$ is in $L(G)$ if $S \in a_{1,n+1}$, since S generates the entire string $\boldsymbol{w}$. Clearly, $a_{i,j} = \emptyset$ for $j \leq i$. We illustrate this construction with the example following this proof.

We show by induction that set matrix S is the transitive closure (denoted B^+) of the $(n+1) \times (n+1)$ set matrix B whose i, j entry $b_{i,j} = \emptyset$ for $j \neq i+1$ when $1 \leq i \leq n-1$

is defined as follows:

$$b_{i,i+1} = \{ \text{A} \mid (\text{A} \rightarrow w_i) \text{ in } \mathcal{R} \text{ where } w_i \in \mathcal{T} \}$$

$$B = \begin{bmatrix} \emptyset & b_{1,2} & \emptyset & \cdots & \emptyset \\ \emptyset & \emptyset & b_{2,3} & \cdots & \emptyset \\ \vdots & \vdots & \vdots & \ddots & \vdots \\ \emptyset & \emptyset & \emptyset & \cdots & b_{n-1,n} \\ \emptyset & \emptyset & \emptyset & \cdots & \emptyset \end{bmatrix}$$

Thus, the entry $b_{i,i+1}$ is the set of non-terminals that generate the ith terminal symbol w_i of w in one step. The value of each entry in the matrix B is the empty set except for the entries $b_{i,i+1}$ for $1 \leq i \leq n-1$, $n = |w|$.

We extend the concept of matrix multiplication (see Chapter 6) to the product of two set matrices. Doing this requires a new definition for the product of two sets (entries in the matrix) as well as for the addition of two sets. The **product** $S_1 \cdot S_2$ **of sets of terminals** S_1 and S_2 is defined as:

$$S_1 \cdot S_2 = \{ \text{A} \mid \text{there exists B} \in S_1 \text{ and C} \in S_2 \text{ such that } (\text{A} \rightarrow \text{BC}) \in \mathcal{R} \}$$

Thus, $S_1 \cdot S_2$ is the set of non-terminals for which there is a rule in $\mathcal{R}$ of the form $\text{A} \rightarrow \text{BC}$ where $\text{B} \in S_1$ and $\text{C} \in S_2$. The **sum** of two sets is their union.

The i, j entry of the product $C = D \times E$ of two $m \times m$ matrices D and E, each containing sets of non-terminals, is defined below in terms of the product and union of sets:

$$c_{i,j} = \bigcup_{k=1}^{m} d_{i,k} \cdot e_{k,j}$$

We also define the **transitive closure** C^+ of an $m \times m$ matrix C as follows:

$$C^+ = C^{(1)} \cup C^{(2)} \cup C^{(3)} \cup \cdots C^{(m)}$$

where

$$C^{(s)} = \bigcup_{r=1}^{s-1} C^{(r)} \times C^{(s-r)} \text{ and } C^{(1)} = C$$

By the definition of the matrix product, the entry $b_{i,j}^{(2)}$ of the matrix $B^{(2)}$ is $\emptyset$ if $j \neq i+2$ and otherwise is the set of non-terminals A that produce $w_i w_{i+1}$ through a derivation tree of depth 2; that is, there are rules such that $\text{A} \rightarrow \text{BC}$, $\text{B} \rightarrow w_i$, and $\text{C} \rightarrow w_{i+1}$, which implies that $\text{A} \overset{*}{\Rightarrow} w_i w_{i+1}$.

Similarly, it follows that both $B^{(1)} B^{(2)}$ and $B^{(2)} B^{(1)}$ are $\emptyset$ in all positions except $i, i+3$ for $1 \leq i \leq n-2$. The entry in position $i, i+3$ of $B^{(3)} = B^{(1)} B^{(2)} \bigcup B^{(2)} B^{(1)}$ contains the set of non-terminals A that produce $w_i w_{i+1} w_{i+2}$ through a derivation tree of depth 3; that is, $\text{A} \rightarrow \text{BC}$ and either B produces $w_i w_{i+1}$ through a derivation of depth 2 ($\text{B} \overset{*}{\Rightarrow} w_i w_{i+1}$) and C produces w_{i+2} in one step ($\text{C} \rightarrow w_i$) or B produces w_i in one step ($\text{B} \rightarrow w_i$) and C produces $w_{i+1} w_{i+2}$ through a derivation of depth 2 ($\text{C} \overset{*}{\Rightarrow} w_{i+1} w_{i+2}$).

Finally, the only entry in $B^{(n)}$ that is not $\emptyset$ is the $1, n+1$ entry and it contains the set of non-terminals, if any, that generate $\boldsymbol{w}$. If S is in this set, $\boldsymbol{w}$ is in $L(G)$.

The transitive closure $S = B^+$ involves $\sum_{r=1}^{n} r = (n+1)n/2$ products of set matrices. The product of two $(n+1) \times (n+1)$ set matrices of the type considered here involves at most n products of sets. Thus, at most $O(n^3)$ products of sets is needed to form S. In turn, a product of two sets, $S_1 \cdot S_2$, can be formed with $O(q^2)$ operations, where $q = |\mathcal{N}|$ is the number of non-terminals. It suffices to compare each pair of entries, one from S_1 and the other from S_2, through a table to determine if they form the right-hand side of a rule.

As the matrices are being constructed, if a pair of non-terminals is discovered that is the right-hand side of a rule, that is, A $\to$ BC, then a link can be made from the entry A in the product matrix to the entries B and C. From the entry S in $a_{1,n+1}$, if it exists, links can be followed to generate a parse tree for the input string. ∎

The procedure described in this proof can be extended to show that membership in an arbitrary CFL can be determined in time $O(M(n))$, where $M(n)$ is the number of operations to multiply two $n \times n$ matrices [338]. This is the fastest known general algorithm for this problem when the grammar is part of the input. For some CFLs, faster algorithms are known that are based on the use of the deterministic pushdown automaton. For fixed grammars membership algorithms often run in $O(n)$ steps. The reader is referred to books on compilers for such results. The procedure of the proof is illustrated by the following example.

EXAMPLE 4.11.4 *Consider the grammar G_6 of Example 4.11.3. We show how the five-character string $a * b + a$ in $L(G_6)$ can be parsed. We construct the 6×6 matrices $B^{(1)}$, $B^{(2)}$, $B^{(3)}$, $B^{(4)}$, $B^{(5)}$, as shown below. Since $B^{(5)}$ contains E in the $1, n+1$ position, $a * b + a$ is in the language. Furthermore, we can follow links between non-terminals (not shown) to demonstrate that this string has the parse tree shown in Fig. 4.29. The matrix $B^{(4)}$ is not shown because each of its entries is $\emptyset$.*

$$B^{(1)} = \begin{bmatrix} \emptyset & \{E,F,T\} & \emptyset & \emptyset & \emptyset & \emptyset \\ \emptyset & \emptyset & \{*\} & \emptyset & \emptyset & \emptyset \\ \emptyset & \emptyset & \emptyset & \{E,F,T\} & \emptyset & \emptyset \\ \emptyset & \emptyset & \emptyset & \emptyset & \{+\} & \emptyset \\ \emptyset & \emptyset & \emptyset & \emptyset & \emptyset & \{E,F,T\} \\ \emptyset & \emptyset & \emptyset & \emptyset & \emptyset & \emptyset \end{bmatrix}$$

$$B^{(2)} = \begin{bmatrix} \emptyset & \emptyset & \emptyset & \emptyset & \emptyset & \emptyset \\ \emptyset & \emptyset & \emptyset & \{B\} & \emptyset & \emptyset \\ \emptyset & \emptyset & \emptyset & \emptyset & \emptyset & \emptyset \\ \emptyset & \emptyset & \emptyset & \emptyset & \emptyset & \{A\} \\ \emptyset & \emptyset & \emptyset & \emptyset & \emptyset & \emptyset \\ \emptyset & \emptyset & \emptyset & \emptyset & \emptyset & \emptyset \end{bmatrix} \qquad B^{(3)} = \begin{bmatrix} \emptyset & \emptyset & \emptyset & \{E\} & \emptyset & \emptyset \\ \emptyset & \emptyset & \emptyset & \emptyset & \emptyset & \emptyset \\ \emptyset & \emptyset & \emptyset & \emptyset & \emptyset & \{E\} \\ \emptyset & \emptyset & \emptyset & \emptyset & \emptyset & \emptyset \\ \emptyset & \emptyset & \emptyset & \emptyset & \emptyset & \emptyset \\ \emptyset & \emptyset & \emptyset & \emptyset & \emptyset & \emptyset \end{bmatrix}$$

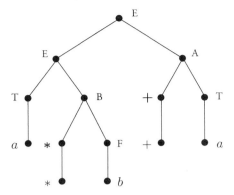

Figure 4.29 The parse tree for the string $a * b + a$ in the language $L(G_6)$.

$$B^{(5)} = \begin{bmatrix} \emptyset & \emptyset & \emptyset & \emptyset & \emptyset & \{E\} \\ \emptyset & \emptyset & \emptyset & \emptyset & \emptyset & \emptyset \\ \emptyset & \emptyset & \emptyset & \emptyset & \emptyset & \emptyset \\ \emptyset & \emptyset & \emptyset & \emptyset & \emptyset & \emptyset \\ \emptyset & \emptyset & \emptyset & \emptyset & \emptyset & \emptyset \\ \emptyset & \emptyset & \emptyset & \emptyset & \emptyset & \emptyset \end{bmatrix}$$

4.12 CFL Acceptance with Pushdown Automata*

While it is now clear that an algorithm exists to parse every context-free language, it is useful to show that there is a class of automata that accepts exactly the context-free languages. These are the nondeterministic pushdown automata (PDA) described in Section 4.8.

We now establish the principal results of this section, namely, that the context-free languages are accepted by PDAs and that the languages accepted by PDAs are context-free. We begin with the first result.

THEOREM 4.12.1 *For each context-free grammar G there is a PDA M that accepts $L(G)$. That is, $L(M) = L(G)$.*

Proof Before beginning this proof, we extend the definition of a PDA to allow it to push strings onto the stack instead of just symbols. That is, we extend the stack alphabet Γ to include a small set of strings. When a string such as $abcd$ is pushed, a is pushed before b, b before c, etc. This does not increase the power of the PDA, because for each string we can add unique states that M enters after pushing each symbol except the last. With the pushing of the last symbol M enters the successor state specified in the transition being executed.

Let $G = (\mathcal{N}, \mathcal{T}, \mathcal{R}, s)$ be a context-free grammar. We construct a PDA $M = (\Sigma, \Gamma, Q, \Delta, s, F)$, where $\Sigma = \mathcal{T}$, $\Gamma = \mathcal{N} \cup \mathcal{T} \cup \{\gamma\}$ (γ is the blank stack symbol), $Q = \{s, p, f\}$, $F = \{f\}$, and Δ consists of transitions of the types shown below. Here $\forall$ denotes "for all" and $\forall(A \mapsto w) \in \mathcal{R}$ means for all transitions in $\mathcal{R}$.

a) $(s, \epsilon, \epsilon; p, \text{S})$

b) $(p, a, a; p, \epsilon)$ $\forall a \in \mathcal{T}$

c) $(p, \epsilon, \text{A}; p, \boldsymbol{v})$ $\forall (\text{A} \mapsto \boldsymbol{v}) \in \mathcal{R}$

d) $(p, \epsilon, \gamma; f, \epsilon)$

Let $\boldsymbol{w}$ be placed left-adjusted on the input tape of M. Since $\boldsymbol{w}$ is generated by G, it has a leftmost derivation. (Consider for example that given in (4.2) on page 186.) The PDA begins by pushing the start symbol S onto the stack and entering state p (Rule (a)). From this point on the PDA simulates a leftmost derivation of the string $\boldsymbol{w}$ placed initially on its tape. (See the example that follows this proof.) M either matches a terminal of G on the top of the stack with one under the tape head (Rule (b)) or it replaces a non-terminal on the top of the stack with a rule of $\mathcal{R}$ by pushing the right-hand side of the rule onto the stack (Rule (c)). Finally, when the stack is empty, M can choose to enter the final state f and accept $\boldsymbol{w}$. It follows that any string that can be generated by G can also be accepted by M and vice versa. ∎

The leftmost derivation of the string $caacaabcbc$ by the grammar G_3 of Example 4.11.1 is shown in (4.2). The PDA M of the above proof can simulate this derivation, as we show. With the notation $T : \ldots$ and $S : \ldots$ (shown below before the computation begins) we denote the contents of the tape and stack at a point in time at which the underlined symbols are those under the tape head and at the top of the stack, respectively. We ignore the blank tape and stack symbols unless they are the ones underlined.

$T : \underline{c}aacaabcbc \qquad S : \underline{\gamma}$

After the first step taken by M, the tape and stack configurations are:

$T : \underline{c}aacaabcbc \qquad S : \underline{\text{S}}$

From this point on M simulates a derivation by G_3. Consulting (4.2), we see that the rule $\text{S} \rightarrow c\text{MN}c$ is the first to be applied. M simulates this with the transition $(p, \epsilon, \text{S}; p, c\text{MN}c)$, which causes S to be popped from the stack and $c\text{MN}c$ to be pushed onto it without advancing the tape head. The resulting configurations are shown below:

$T : \underline{c}aacaabcbc \qquad S : \underline{c}\text{MN}c$

Next the transition $(p, c, c; p, \epsilon)$ is applied to pop one item from the stack, exposing the non-terminal M and advancing the tape head to give the following configurations:

$T : c\underline{a}acaabcbc \qquad S : \underline{\text{M}}\text{N}c$

The subsequent rules, in order, are the following:

1) M $\rightarrow$ $a\text{M}a$ 3) M $\rightarrow$ c 5) N $\rightarrow$ c

2) M $\rightarrow$ $a\text{M}a$ 4) N $\rightarrow$ $b\text{N}b$

The corresponding transitions of the PDA are shown in Fig. 4.30.

We now show that the language accepted by a PDA can be generated by a context-free grammar.

$$
\begin{array}{llll}
T: & c\underline{a}acaabcbc & S: & \underline{a}\text{M}a\text{N}c \\
T: & ca\underline{a}caabcbc & S: & \text{M}a\text{N}c \\
T: & ca\underline{a}caabcbc & S: & \underline{a}\text{M}aa\text{N}c \\
T: & caa\underline{c}aabcbc & S: & \text{M}aa\text{N}c \\
T: & caa\underline{c}aabcbc & S: & \underline{c}aa\text{N}c \\
T: & caac\underline{a}abcbc & S: & \underline{a}a\text{N}c \\
T: & caaca\underline{a}bcbc & S: & \underline{a}\text{N}c \\
T: & caacaa\underline{b}cbc & S: & \text{N}c \\
T: & caacaa\underline{b}cbc & S: & \underline{b}\text{N}bc \\
T: & caacaab\underline{c}bc & S: & \text{N}bc \\
T: & caacaab\underline{c}bc & S: & \underline{c}bc \\
T: & caacaabc\underline{b}c & S: & \underline{b}c \\
T: & caacaabcb\underline{c} & S: & \underline{c} \\
T: & caacaabcbc\underline{\beta} & S: & \underline{\gamma}
\end{array}
$$

Figure 4.30 PDA transitions corresponding to the leftmost derivation of the string $caacaabcbc$ in the grammar G_3 of Example 4.11.1.

THEOREM 4.12.2 *For each PDA M there is a context-free grammar G that generates the language $L(M)$ accepted by M. That is, $L(G) = L(M)$.*

Proof It is convenient to assume that when the PDA M accepts a string it does so with an empty stack. If M is not of this type, we can design a PDA M' accepting the same language that does meet this condition. The states of M' consist of the states of M plus three additional states, a new initial state s', a cleanup state k, and a new final state f'. Its tape symbols are identical to those of M. Its stack symbols consist of those of M plus one new symbol κ. In its initial state M' pushes κ onto the stack without reading a tape symbol and enters state s, which was the initial state of M. It then operates as M (it has the same transitions) until entering a final state of M, upon which it enters the cleanup state k. In this state it pops the stack until it finds the symbol κ, at which time it enters its final state f'. Clearly, M' accepts the same language as M but leaves its stack empty.

We describe a context-free grammar $G = (\mathcal{N}, \mathcal{T}, \mathcal{R}, \text{S})$ with the property that $L(G) = L(M)$. The non-terminals of G consist of S and the triples $< p, y, q >$ defined below denoting goals:

$$ < p, y, q > \in \mathcal{N} \text{ where } \mathcal{N} \subset Q \times (\Gamma \cup \{\epsilon\}) \times Q $$

The meaning of $< p, y, q >$ is that M moves from state p to state q in a series of steps during which its only effect on the stack is to pop y. The triple $< p, \epsilon, q >$ denotes the goal of moving from state p to state q leaving the stack in its original condition. Since M starts with an empty stack in state s with a string w on its tape and ends in a final state f with its stack empty, the non-terminal $< s, \epsilon, f >, f \in F$, denotes the goal of M moving from state s to a final state f on input w, and leaving the stack in its original state.

The rules of G, which represent goal refinement, are described by the following conditions. Each condition specifies a family of rules for a context-free grammar G. Each rule either replaces one non-terminal with another, replaces a non-terminal with the empty string, or rewrites a non-terminal with a terminal or empty string followed by one or two non-terminals. The result of applying a sequence of rules is a string of terminals in the language $L(G)$. Below we show that $L(G) = L(M)$.

1)	S	$\rightarrow$ $< s, \epsilon, f >$	$\forall f \in F$
2)	$< p, \epsilon, p >$	$\rightarrow$ ϵ	$\forall p \in Q$
3)	$< p, y, r >$	$\rightarrow$ $x < q, z, r >$	$\forall r \in Q$ and $\forall (p, x, y; q, z) \in \Delta$, where $y \neq \epsilon$
4)	$< p, u, r >$	$\rightarrow$ $x < q, z, t >< t, u, r >$	$\forall r, t \in Q$, $\forall (p, x, \epsilon; q, z) \in \Delta$, and $\forall u \in \Gamma \cup \{\epsilon\}$

Condition (1) specifies rules that map the start symbol of G onto the goal non-terminal symbol $< s, \epsilon, f >$ for each final state f. These rules insure that the start symbol of G is rewritten as the goal of moving from the initial state of M to a final state, leaving the stack in its original condition.

Condition (2) specifies rules that map non-terminals $< p, \epsilon, p >$ onto the empty string. Thus, all goals of moving from a state to itself leaving the stack in its original condition can be ignored. In other words, no input is needed to take M from state p back to itself leaving the stack unchanged.

Condition (3) specifies rules stating that for all $r \in Q$ and $(p, x, y; q, z)$, $y \neq \epsilon$, that are transitions of M, a goal $< p, y, r >$ to move from state p to state r while removing y from the stack can be accomplished by reading tape symbol x, replacing the top stack symbol y with z, and then realizing the goal $< q, z, r >$ of moving from state q to state r while removing z from the stack.

Condition (4) specifies rules stating that for all $r, t \in Q$ and $(p, x, \epsilon; q, z)$ that are transitions of M, the goal $< p, u, r >$ of moving from state p to state r while popping u for arbitrary stack symbol u can be achieved by reading input x and pushing z on top of u and then realizing the goal $< q, z, t >$ of moving from q to some state t while popping z followed by the goal $< t, u, r >$ of moving from t to r while popping u.

We now show that any string accepted by M can be generated by G and any string generated by G can be accepted by M. It follows that $L(M) = L(G)$. Instead of showing this directly, we establish a more general result.

CLAIM: For all $r, t \in Q$ and $u \in \Gamma \cup \{\epsilon\}$, $< r, u, t > \overset{*}{\Rightarrow}_G \boldsymbol{w}$ if and only if the PDA M can move from state r to state t while reading $\boldsymbol{w}$ and popping u from the stack.

The theorem follows from the claim because $< s, \epsilon, f > \overset{*}{\Rightarrow}_G \boldsymbol{w}$ if and only if the PDA M can move from initial state s to a final state f while reading $\boldsymbol{w}$ and leaving the stack empty, that is, if and only if M accepts $\boldsymbol{w}$.

We first establish the "if" portion of the claim, namely, if for $r, t \in Q$ and $u \in \Gamma \cup \{\epsilon\}$ the PDA M can move from r to t while reading $\boldsymbol{w}$ and popping u from the stack, then $< r, u, t > \overset{*}{\Rightarrow}_G \boldsymbol{w}$. The proof is by induction on the number of steps taken by M. If no step is taken (basis for induction), $r = t$, nothing is popped and the string ϵ is read by M. Since the grammar G contains the rule $< r, \epsilon, r > \rightarrow \epsilon$, the basis is established.

Suppose that the "if" portion of the claim is true for k or fewer steps (inductive hypothesis). We show that it is true for $k + 1$ steps (induction step). If the PDA M can move from r to t in $k + 1$ steps while reading $\boldsymbol{w} = x\boldsymbol{v}$ and removing u from the stack, then on its first step it must execute a transition $(r, x, y; q, z)$, $q \in Q$, $z \in \Gamma \cup \{\epsilon\}$, for $x \in \Sigma$ with either $y = u$ if $u \neq \epsilon$ or $y = \epsilon$. In the first case, M enters state q, pops u, and pushes z. M subsequently pops z as it reads $\boldsymbol{v}$ and moves to state t in k steps. It follows from the inductive hypothesis that $< q, z, t > \overset{*}{\Rightarrow}_G \boldsymbol{v}$. Since $y \neq \epsilon$, a rule of type (3) applies, that is, $< r, y, t > \rightarrow x < q, z, t >$. It follows that $< r, y, t > \overset{*}{\Rightarrow}_G \boldsymbol{w}$, the desired conclusion.

In the second case $y = \epsilon$ and M makes the transition $(r, x, \epsilon; q, z)$ by moving from r to t and pushing z while reading x. To pop u, which must have been at the top of the stack, M must first pop z and then pop u. Let it pop z as it moves from q to some intermediate state t' while reading a first portion $\boldsymbol{v_1}$ of the input word $\boldsymbol{v}$. Let it pop u as it moves from t' to t while reading a second portion $\boldsymbol{v_2}$ of the input word $\boldsymbol{v}$. Here $\boldsymbol{v_1}\boldsymbol{v_2} = \boldsymbol{v}$. Since the move from q to t' and from t' to t each involves at most k steps, it follows that the goals $< q, z, t' >$ and $< t', u, r >$ satisfy $< q, z, t' > \overset{*}{\Rightarrow}_G \boldsymbol{v_1}$ and $< t', u, r > \overset{*}{\Rightarrow}_G \boldsymbol{v_2}$. Because M's first transition meets condition (4), there is a rule $< r, u, t > \rightarrow x < q, z, t' >< t', u, r >$. Combining these derivations yields the desired conclusion.

Now we establish the "only if" part of the claim, namely, if for all $r, t \in Q$ and $u \in \Gamma \cup \{\epsilon\}$, $< r, u, t > \overset{*}{\Rightarrow}_G \boldsymbol{w}$, then the PDA M can move from state r to state t while reading $\boldsymbol{w}$ and removing u from the stack. Again the proof is by induction, this time on the number of derivation steps. If there is a single derivation step (basis for induction), it must be of the type stated in condition (2), namely $< p, \epsilon, p > \rightarrow \epsilon$. Since M can move from state p to p without reading the tape or pushing data onto its stack, the basis is established.

Suppose that the "only if" portion of the claim is true for k or fewer derivation steps (inductive hypothesis). We show that it is true for $k + 1$ steps (induction step). That is, if $< r, u, t > \overset{*}{\Rightarrow}_G \boldsymbol{w}$ in $k + 1$ steps, then we show that M can move from r to t while reading $\boldsymbol{w}$ and popping u from the stack. We can assume that the first derivation step is of type (3) or (4) because if it is of type (2), the derivation can be shortened and the result follows from the inductive hypothesis. If the first derivation is of type (3), namely, of the form $< r, u, t > \rightarrow x < q, z, t >$, then by the inductive hypothesis, M can execute $(r, x, u; q, z)$, $u \neq \epsilon$, that is, read x, pop u, push z, and enter state q. Since $< r, u, t > \overset{*}{\Rightarrow}_G \boldsymbol{w}$, where $\boldsymbol{w} = x\boldsymbol{v}$, it follows that $< q, z, t > \overset{*}{\Rightarrow}_G \boldsymbol{v}$. Again by the inductive hypothesis M can move from q to t while reading $\boldsymbol{v}$ and popping z. Combining these results, we have the desired conclusion.

If the first derivation is of type (4), namely, $< r, u, t > \rightarrow x < q, z, t' >< t', u, t >$, then the two non-terminals $< q, z, t' >$ and $< t', u, t >$ must expand to substrings $\boldsymbol{v_1}$ and $\boldsymbol{v_2}$, respectively, of $\boldsymbol{v}$ where $\boldsymbol{w} = x\boldsymbol{v_1}\boldsymbol{v_2} = x\boldsymbol{v}$. That is, $< q, z, t' > \overset{*}{\Rightarrow}_G \boldsymbol{v_1}$ and $< t', u, t > \overset{*}{\Rightarrow}_G \boldsymbol{v_1}$. By the inductive hypothesis, M can move from q to t' while reading $\boldsymbol{v_1}$ and popping z and it can also move from t' to t while reading $\boldsymbol{v_2}$ and popping u. Thus, M can move from r to t while reading $\boldsymbol{w}$ and popping u, which is the desired conclusion. ∎

4.13 Properties of Context-Free Languages

In this section we derive properties of context-free languages. We begin by establishing a pumping lemma that demonstrates that every CFL has a certain periodicity property. This property, together with other properties concerning the closure of the class of CFLs under the operations of concatenation, union and intersection, is used to show that the class is not closed under complementation and intersection.

4.13.1 CFL Pumping Lemma

The pumping lemma for regular languages established in Section 4.5 showed that if a regular language contains an infinite number of strings, then it must have strings of a particular form. This lemma was used to show that some languages are not regular. We establish a similar result for context-free languages.

LEMMA 4.13.1 *Let $G = (\mathcal{N}, \mathcal{T}, \mathcal{R}, \mathrm{S})$ be a context-free grammar in Chomsky normal form with m non-terminals. Then, if $w \in L(G)$ and $|w| \geq 2^{m-1} + 1$, there are strings r, s, t, u, and v with $w = rstuv$ such that $|su| \geq 1$ and $|stu| \leq 2^m$ and for all integers $n \geq 0$,* $\mathrm{S} \overset{*}{\Rightarrow}_G rs^n tu^n v \in L.$

Proof Since each production is of the form $\mathrm{A} \to \mathrm{BC}$ or $\mathrm{A} \to a$, a subtree of a parse tree of height h has a yield (number of leaves) of at most 2^{h-1}. To see this, observe that each rule that generates a leaf is of the form $\mathrm{A} \to a$. Thus, the yield is the number of leaves in a binary tree of height $h - 1$, which is at most 2^{h-1}.

Let $K = 2^{m-1} + 1$. If there is a string w in L of length K or greater, its parse tree has height greater than m. Thus, a longest path P in such a tree (see Fig. 4.31(a)) has more

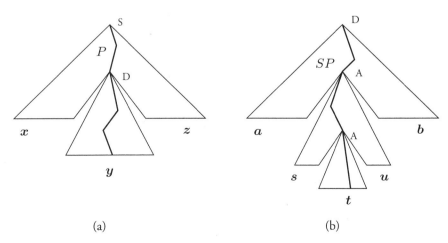

| (a) | (b) |

Figure 4.31 $L(G)$ is generated by a grammar G in Chomsky normal form with m non-terminals. (a) Each $w \in L(G)$ with $|w| \geq 2^{m-1} + 1$ has a parse tree with a longest path P containing at least $m + 1$ non-terminals. (b) SP, the portion of P containing the last $m + 1$ non-terminals on P, has a non-terminal A that is repeated. The derivation $\mathrm{A} \to sA u$ can be deleted or repeated to generate new strings in $L(G)$.

than m non-terminals on it. Consider the subpath SP of P containing the last $m + 1$ non-terminals of P. Let D be the first non-terminal on SP and let the yield of its parse tree be y. It follows that $|y| \leq 2^m$. Thus, the yield of the full parse tree, w, can be written as $w = xyz$ for strings x, y, and z in $\mathcal{T}^*$.

By the pigeonhole principle stated in Section 4.5, some non-terminal is repeated on SP. Let A be such a non-terminal. Consider the first and second time that A appears on SP. (See Fig. 4.31(b).) Repeat all the rules of the grammar G that produced the string y except for the rule corresponding to the first instance of A on SP and all those rules that depend on it. It follows that $D \overset{*}{\Rightarrow} a A b$ where a and b are in $\mathcal{T}^*$. Similarly, apply all the rules to the derivation beginning with the first instance of A on P up to but not including the rules beginning with the second instance of A. It follows that $A \overset{*}{\Rightarrow} s A u$, where s and u are in $\mathcal{T}^*$ and at least one is not ϵ since no rules of the form $A \to B$ are in G. Finally, apply the rules starting with the second instance of A on P. Let $A \overset{*}{\Rightarrow} t$ be the yield of this set of rules. Since $A \overset{*}{\Rightarrow} s A u$ and $A \overset{*}{\Rightarrow} t$, it follows that L also contains $x a t b z$. L also contains $x a s^n t u^n b z$ for $n \geq 1$ because $A \overset{*}{\Rightarrow} s A u$ can be applied n times after $A \overset{*}{\Rightarrow} s A u$ and before $A \overset{*}{\Rightarrow} t$. Now let $r = xa$ and $v = bz$. ■

We use this lemma to show the existence of a language that is not context-free.

LEMMA 4.13.2 *The language $L = \{a^n b^n c^n \mid n \geq 0\}$ over the alphabet $\Sigma = \{a, b, c\}$ is not context-free.*

Proof The proof is by contradiction; that is, we assume that L is context-free and show that L contains strings which are not in the language.

Since L is infinite, the pumping lemma can be applied. Let $r s t u v = a^n b^n c^n$ for $n = n_0$. From the pumping lemma $r s^2 t u^2 v$ is also in L. Clearly if s or u is not empty (and at least one is), then they contain either one, two, or three of the symbols in Σ. If one of them, say s, contains two symbols, then s^2 contains a b before an a or a c before a b, contradicting the definition of the language. The same is true if one of them contains three symbols. Thus, they contain exactly one symbol. But this implies that the number of a's, b's, and c's in $r s^2 t u^2 v$ is not the same, whether or not s and u contain the same or different symbols. ■

4.13.2 CFL Closure Properties

In Section 4.6 we examined the closure properties of regular languages. We demonstrated that they are closed under concatenation, union, Kleene closure, complementation, and intersection. In this section we show that the context-free languages are closed under concatenation, union, and Kleene closure but not complementation or intersection. A class of languages is closed under an operation if the result of performing the operation on one or more languages in the class produces another language in the class.

The concatenation, union, and Kleene closure of languages are defined in Section 4.3. The concatenation of languages L_1 and L_2, denoted $L_1 \cdot L_2$, is the language $\{uv \mid u \in L_1 \text{ and } v \in L_2\}$. The union of languages L_1 and L_2, denoted $L_1 \cup L_2$, is the set of strings that are in L_1 or L_2 or both. The Kleene closure of a language L, denoted L^* and called the Kleene star, is the language $\bigcup_{i=0}^{\infty} L^i$ where $L^0 = \{\epsilon\}$ and $L^i = L \cdot L^{i-1}$.

THEOREM 4.13.1 *The context-free languages are closed under concatenation, union, and Kleene closure.*

Proof Consider two arbitrary CFLs $L(H_1)$ and $L(H_2)$ generated by grammars $H_1 = (\mathcal{N}_1, \mathcal{T}_1, \mathcal{R}_1, S_1)$ and $H_2 = (\mathcal{N}_2, \mathcal{T}_2, \mathcal{R}_2, S_2)$. Without loss of generality assume that their non-terminal alphabets (and rules) are disjoint. (If not, prefix every non-terminal in the second grammar with a symbol not used in the first. This does not change the language generated.)

Since each string in $L(H_1) \cdot L(H_2)$ consists of a string of $L(H_1)$ followed by a string of $L(H_2)$, it is generated by the context-free grammar $H_3 = (\mathcal{N}_3, \mathcal{T}_3, \mathcal{R}_3, S_3)$ in which $\mathcal{N}_3 = \mathcal{N}_1 \cup \mathcal{N}_2 \cup \{S_3\}$, $\mathcal{T}_3 = \mathcal{T}_1 \cup \mathcal{T}_2$, and $\mathcal{R}_3 = \mathcal{R}_1 \cup \mathcal{R}_2 \cup \{S_3 \rightarrow S_1 S_2\}$. The new rule $S_3 \rightarrow S_1 S_2$ generates a string of $L(H_1)$ followed by a string of $L(H_2)$. Thus, $L(H_1) \cdot L(H_2)$ is context-free.

The union of languages $L(H_1)$ and $L(H_2)$ is generated by the context-free grammar $H_4 = (\mathcal{N}_4, \mathcal{T}_4, \mathcal{R}_4, S_4)$ in which $\mathcal{N}_4 = \mathcal{N}_1 \cup \mathcal{N}_2 \cup \{S_4\}$, $\mathcal{T}_4 = \mathcal{T}_1 \cup \mathcal{T}_2$, and $\mathcal{R}_4 = \mathcal{R}_1 \cup \mathcal{R}_2 \cup \{S_4 \rightarrow S_1, S_4 \rightarrow S_2\}$. To see this, observe that after applying $S_4 \rightarrow S_1$ all subsequent rules are drawn from H_1. (The sets of non-terminals are disjoint.) A similar statement applies to the application of $S_4 \rightarrow S_2$. Since H_4 is context-free, $L(H_4) = L(H_1) \cup L(H_2)$ is context-free.

The Kleene closure of $L(H_1)$, namely $L(H_1)^*$, is generated by the context-free grammar $H_5 = (\mathcal{N}_1, \mathcal{T}_1, \mathcal{R}_5, S_1)$ in which $\mathcal{R}_5 = \mathcal{R}_1 \cup \{S_1 \rightarrow \epsilon, S_1 \rightarrow S_1 S_1\}$. To see this, observe that $L(H_5)$ includes ϵ, every string in $L(H_1)$, and, through $i - 1$ applications of $S_1 \rightarrow S_1 S_1$, every string in $L(H_1)^i$. Thus, $L(H_1)^*$ is generated by H_5 and is context-free. ∎

We now use this result and Lemma 4.13.2 to show that the set of context-free languages is not closed under complementation and intersection, operations defined in Section 4.6. The complement of a language L over an alphabet Σ, denoted $\overline{L}$, is the set of strings in Σ^* that are not in L. The intersection of two languages L_1 and L_2, denoted $L_1 \cap L_2$, is the set of strings that are in both languages.

THEOREM 4.13.2 *The set of context-free languages is not closed under complementation or intersection.*

Proof The intersection of two languages L_1 and L_2 can be defined in terms of the complement and union operations as follows:

$$L_1 \cap L_2 = \Sigma^* - (\Sigma^* - L_1) \cup (\Sigma^* - L_2)$$

Thus, since the union of two CFLs is a CFL, if the complement of a CFL is also a CFL, from this identity, the intersection of two CFLs is also a CFL. We now show that the intersection of two CFLs is not always a CFL.

The language $L_1 = \{a^n b^n c^m \mid n, m \geq 0\}$ is generated by the grammar $H_1 = (\mathcal{N}_1, \mathcal{T}_1, \mathcal{R}_1, S_1)$, where $\mathcal{N}_1 = \{S, A, B\}$, $\mathcal{T}_1 = \{a, b, c\}$, and the rules $\mathcal{R}_1$ are:

a)	S	$\rightarrow$	AB	*d)*	B	$\rightarrow$	Bc
b)	A	$\rightarrow$	aAb	*e)*	B	$\rightarrow$	ϵ
c)	A	$\rightarrow$	ϵ				

The language $L_2 = \{a^m b^n c^n \mid n, m \geq 0\}$ is generated by the grammar $H_2 = (\mathcal{N}_2, \mathcal{T}_2, \mathcal{R}_2, S_2)$, where $\mathcal{N}_2 = \{S, A, B\}$, $\mathcal{T}_2 = \{a, b, c\}$ and the rules $\mathcal{R}_2$ are:

$a)$　S　$\rightarrow$　AB　　　　$d)$　B　$\rightarrow$　bBc

$b)$　A　$\rightarrow$　aA　　　　$e)$　B　$\rightarrow$　ϵ

$c)$　A　$\rightarrow$　ϵ

Thus, the languages L_1 and L_2 are context-free. However, their intersection is $L_1 \cap L_2 = \{a^n b^n c^n \mid n \geq 0\}$, which was shown in Lemma 4.13.2 not to be context-free. Thus, the set of CFLs is not closed under intersection, nor is it closed under complementation. ■

Problems

FSM MODELS

4.1 Let $M = (\Sigma, \Psi, Q, \delta, \lambda, s, F)$ be the FSM model described in Definition 3.1.1. It differs from the FSM model of Section 4.1 in that its output alphabet Ψ has been explicitly identified. Let this machine recognize the language $L(M)$ consisting of input strings w that cause the last output produced by M to be the first letter in Ψ. Show that every language recognized under this definition is a language recognized according to the "final-state definition" in Definition 4.1.1 and vice versa.

4.2 The **Mealey machine** is a seven-tuple $M = (\Sigma, \Psi, Q, \delta, \lambda, s, F)$ identical in its definition with the Moore machine of Definition 3.1.1 except that its output function $\lambda : Q \times \Sigma \mapsto \Psi$ depends on both the current state and input letter, whereas the output function $\lambda : Q \mapsto \Psi$ of the Moore FSM depends only on the current state. Show that the two machines recognize the same languages and compute the same functions with the exception of ϵ.

4.3 Suppose that an FSM is allowed to make state ϵ-transitions, that is, state transitions on the empty string. Show that the new machine model is no more powerful than the Moore machine model.

Hint: Show how ϵ-transitions can be removed, perhaps by making the resultant FSM nondeterministic.

EQUIVALENCE OF DFSMS AND NFSMS

4.4 Functions computed by FSMs are described in Definition 3.1.1. Can a consistent definition of function computation by NFSMs be given? If not, why not?

4.5 Construct a deterministic FSM equivalent to the nondeterministic FSM shown in Fig. 4.32.

REGULAR EXPRESSIONS

4.6 Show that the regular expression $0(0^*10^*)^+$ defines strings starting with 0 and containing at least one 1.

4.7 Show that the regular expressions 0^*, $0(0^*10^*)^+$, and $1(0+1)^*$ partition the set of all strings over 0 and 1.

4.8 Give regular expressions generating the following languages over $\Sigma = \{0, 1\}$:

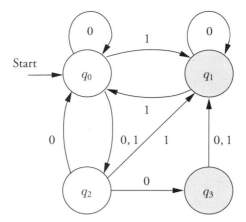

Figure 4.32 A nondeterministic FSM.

    a) $L = \{w \mid w$ has length at least 3 and its third symbol is a 0$\}$
    b) $L = \{w \mid w$ begins with a 1 and ends with a 0$\}$
    c) $L = \{w \mid w$ contains at least three 1s$\}$

4.9 Give regular expressions generating the following languages over $\Sigma = \{0, 1\}$:
    a) $L = \{w \mid w$ is any string except 11 and 111$\}$
    b) $L = \{w \mid$ every odd position of w is a 1$\}$

4.10 Give regular expressions for the languages over the alphabet $\{0, 1, 2, 3, 4, 5, 6, 7, 8, 9\}$ describing positive integers that are:
    a)   even
    b)   odd
    c)   a multiple of 5
    d)   a multiple of 4

4.11 Give proofs for the rules stated in Theorem 4.3.1.

4.12 Show that $\epsilon + 01 + (010)(10 + 010)^*(\epsilon + 1 + 01)$ and $\epsilon + 01 + (010)(01 + 010)^*$ describe the same language.

REGULAR EXPRESSIONS AND FSMS

4.13 a)   Find a simple nondeterministic finite-state machine accepting the language $(01 \cup 001 \cup 010)^*$ over $\Sigma = \{0, 1\}$.
    b)   Convert the nondeterministic finite state machine of part (a) to a deterministic finite-state machine by the method of Section 4.2.

4.14 a)   Let $\Sigma = \{0, 1, 2\}$, and let L be the language over Σ that contains each string w ending with some symbol that does not occur anywhere else in w. For example, 011012, 20021, 11120, 0002, 10, and 1 are all strings in L. Construct a nondeterministic finite-state machine that accepts L.

b) Convert the nondeterministic finite-state machine of part (a) to a deterministic finite-state machine by the method of Section 4.2.

4.15 Describe an algorithm to convert a regular expression to an NFSM using the proof of Theorem 4.4.1.

4.16 Design DFSMs that recognize the following languages:

a) a^*bca^*

b) $(a + c)^*(ab + ca)b^*$

c) $(a^*b^*(b + c)^*)^*$

4.17 Design an FSM that recognizes decimal strings (over the alphabet $\{0, 1, 2, 3, 4, 5, 6, 7, 8, 9\}$ representing the integers whose value is 0 modulo 3.

Hint: Use the fact that $(10)^k = 1 \bmod 3$ (where 10 is "ten") to show that $(a_k(10)^k + a_{k-1}(10)^{k-1} + \cdots + a_1(10)^1 + a_0) \bmod 3 = (a_k + a_{k-1} + \cdots + a_1 + a_0) \bmod 3$.

4.18 Use the above FSM design to generate a regular expression describing those integers whose value is 0 modulo 3.

4.19 Describe an algorithm that constructs an NFSM from a regular expression r and accepts a string w if w contains a string denoted by r that begins anywhere in w.

THE PUMPING LEMMA

4.20 Show that the following languages are not regular:

a) $L = \{a^n b a^n \mid n \geq 0\}$

b) $L = \{0^n 1^{2n} 0^n \mid n \geq 1\}$

c) $L = \{a^n b^n c^n \mid n \geq 0\}$

4.21 Strengthen the pumping lemma for regular languages by demonstrating that if L is a regular language over the alphabet Σ recognized by a DFSM with m states and it contains a string w of length m or more, then any substring z of w ($w = uzv$) of length m can be written as $z = rst$, where $|s| \geq 1$ such that for all integers $n \geq 0$, $urs^n tv \in L$. Explain why this pumping lemma is stronger than the one stated in Lemma 4.5.1.

4.22 Show that the language $L = \{a^i b^j \mid i > j\}$ is not regular.

4.23 Show that the following languages are not regular:

a) $\{w \mid w$ is decimal notation for an integer that is a multiple of 7$\}$

b) $\{u^n z v^m z w^{n+m} \mid n, m \geq 1\}$

PROPERTIES OF REGULAR LANGUAGES

4.24 Use Lemma 4.5.1 and the closure property of regular languages under intersection to show that the following languages are not regular:

a) $\{ww^R \mid w \in \{0, 1\}^*\}$

b) $\{w\overline{w} \mid$ where $\overline{w}$ denotes w in which 0's and 1's are interchanged$\}$

c) $\{w \mid w$ has equal number of 0's and 1's$\}$

4.25 Prove or disprove each of the following statements:

a)   Every subset of a regular language is regular

b)   Every regular language has a proper subset that is also a regular language

c)   If L is regular, then so is $\{xy \mid x \in L \text{ and } y \notin L\}$

d)   If L is a regular language, then so is $\{w : w \in L \text{ and } w^R \in L\}$

e) $\{w \mid w = w^R\}$ is regular

STATE MINIMIZATION

4.26 Find a minimal-state FSM equivalent to that shown in Fig. 4.33.

4.27 Show that the languages recognized by M and $M_\equiv$ are the same, where $\equiv$ is the equivalence relation on M defined by states that are indistinguishable by input strings of any length.

4.28 Show that the equivalence relation R_L is right-invariant.

4.29 Show that the equivalence relation R_M is right-invariant.

4.30 Show that the right-invariance equivalence relation (defined in Definition 4.7.2) for the language $L = \{a^n b^n \mid n \geq 0\}$ has an unbounded number of equivalence classes.

4.31 Show that the DFSM in Fig. 4.20 is the machine M_L associated with the language $L = (10^*1 + 0)^*$.

PUSHDOWN AUTOMATA

4.32 Construct a pushdown automaton that accepts the following language: $L = \{w \mid w$ is a string over the alphabet $\Sigma = \{(,)\}$ of balanced parentheses$\}$.

4.33 Construct a pushdown automaton that accepts the following language: $L = \{w \mid w$ contains more 1's than 0's$\}$.

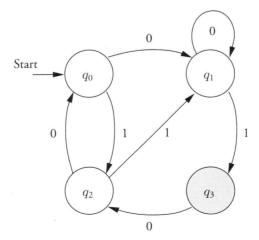

Figure 4.33 A four-state finite-state machine.

PHRASE STRUCTURE LANGUAGES

4.34 Give phrase-structure grammars for the following languages:

  a) $\{ww \mid w \in \{a,b\}^*\}$

  b) $\{0^{2^i} \mid i \geq 1\}$

4.35 Show that the following language can be described by a phrase-structure grammar:

$$\{a^i \mid i \text{ is not prime}\}$$

CONTEXT-SENSITIVE LANGUAGES

4.36 Show that every context-sensitive language can be accepted by a **linear bounded automaton** (LBA), a nondeterministic Turing machine in which the tape head visits a number of cells that is a constant multiple of the number of characters in the input string w.

  Hint: Consider a construction similar to that used in the proof of Theorem 5.4.2. Instead of using a second tape, use a second track on the tape of the TM.

4.37 Show that every language accepted by a linear bounded automaton can be generated by a context-sensitive language.

  Hint: Consider a construction similar to that used in the proof of Theorem 5.4.1 but instead of deleting characters at the end of TM configuration, encode the end markers [and] by enlarging the tape alphabet of the LBA to permit the first and last characters to be either marked or unmarked.

4.38 Show that the grammar G_1 in Example 4.9.1 is context-sensitive and generates the language $L(G_1) = \{a^n b^n c^n \mid n \geq 1\}$.

4.39 Show that the language $\{0^{2^i} \mid i \geq 1\}$ is context-sensitive.

4.40 Show that the context-sensitive languages are closed under union, intersection, and concatenation.

CONTEXT-FREE LANGUAGES

4.41 Show that language generated by the context-free grammar G_3 of Example 4.9.3 is $L(G_3) = \{ca^n ca^n cb^m cb^m c \mid n, m \geq 0\}$.

4.42 Construct context-free grammars for each of the following languages:

  a) $\{ww^R \mid w \in \{a,b\}^*\}$

  b) $\{w \mid w \in \{a,b\}^*,\ w = w^R\}$

  c) $L = \{w \mid w \text{ has twice as many 0's as 1's}\}$

4.43 Give a context-free grammars for each of the following languages:

  a) $\{w \in \{a,b\}^* \mid w \text{ has twice as many } a\text{'s as } b\text{'s}\}$

  b) $\{a^r b^s \mid r \leq s \leq 2r\}$

REGULAR LANGUAGES

4.44 Show that the regular language G_4 described in Example 4.9.4 is $L(G_4) = (01)^*0$.

4.45 Show that grammar $G = (\mathcal{N}, \mathcal{T}, \mathcal{R}, \mathrm{S})$, where $\mathcal{N} = \{\mathrm{A, B, S}\}$, $\mathcal{T} = \{a, b\}$ and the rules $\mathcal{R}$ are given below, is regular.

a) $\mathrm{S} \rightarrow ab\mathrm{A}$ d) $\mathrm{S} \rightarrow \epsilon$ f) $\mathrm{B} \rightarrow a\mathrm{S}$

b) $\mathrm{S} \rightarrow ba\mathrm{B}$ e) $\mathrm{A} \rightarrow b\mathrm{S}$ g) $\mathrm{A} \rightarrow b$

c) $\mathrm{S} \rightarrow \mathrm{B}$

Give a derivation for the string $abbbaa$.

4.46 Provide a regular grammar generating strings over $\{0, 1\}$ not containing 00.

4.47 Give a regular grammar for each of the following languages and show that there is a FSM that accepts it. In all cases $\Sigma = \{0, 1\}$.

a) $L = \{w \mid \text{the length of } w \text{ is odd}\}$

b) $L = \{w \mid w \text{ contains at least three 1s}\}$

REGULAR LANGUAGE RECOGNITION

4.48 Construct a finite-state machine that recognizes the language generated by the grammar $G = (\mathcal{N}, \mathcal{T}, \mathcal{R}, \mathrm{S})$, where $\mathcal{N} = \{\mathrm{S, X, Y}\}$, $\mathcal{T} = \{x, y\}$, and $\mathcal{R}$ contains the following rules: $\mathrm{S} \rightarrow x\mathrm{X}$, $\mathrm{S} \rightarrow y\mathrm{Y}$, $\mathrm{X} \rightarrow y\mathrm{Y}$, $\mathrm{Y} \rightarrow x\mathrm{X}$, $\mathrm{X} \rightarrow \epsilon$, and $\mathrm{Y} \rightarrow \epsilon$.

4.49 Describe finite-state machines that recognize the following languages:

a) $\{w \in \{a, b\}^* \mid w \text{ has an odd number of } a\text{'s}\}$

b) $\{w \in \{a, b\}^* \mid w \text{ has } ab \text{ and } ba \text{ as substrings}\}$

4.50 Show that, if L is a regular language, then the language obtained by reversing the letters in each string in L is also regular.

4.51 Show that, if L is a regular language, then the language consisting of strings in L whose reversals are also in L is regular.

PARSING CONTEXT-FREE LANGUAGES

4.52 Use the algorithm of Theorem 4.11.2 to construct a parse tree for the string $(a * b + a) * (a + b)$ generated by the grammar G_5 of Example 4.11.2, and give a leftmost and a rightmost derivation for the string.

4.53 Let $G = (\mathcal{N}, \mathcal{T}, \mathcal{R}, \mathrm{S})$ be the context-free grammar with $\mathcal{N} = \mathrm{S}$ and $\mathcal{T} = \{(,), 0\}$ with rules $\mathcal{R} = \{\mathrm{S} \rightarrow 0, \mathrm{S} \rightarrow \mathrm{SS}, \mathrm{S} \rightarrow (\mathrm{S})\}$. Use the algorithm of Theorem 4.11.2 to generate a parse tree for the string $(0)((0))$.

CFL ACCEPTANCE WITH PUSHDOWN AUTOMATA

4.54 Construct PDAs that accept each of the following languages:

a) $\{a^n b^n \mid n \geq 0\}$

b) $\{ww^R \mid w \in \{a, b\}^*\}$

c) $\{w \mid w \in \{a, b\}^*, w = w^R\}$

4.55 Construct PDAs that accept each of the following languages:
   a) $\{w \in \{a, b\}^* \mid w \text{ has twice as many } a\text{'s as } b\text{'s}\}$
   b) $\{a^r b^s \mid r \leq s \leq 2r\}$

4.56 Use the algorithm of Theorem 4.12.2 to construct a context-free grammar that accepts the language accepted by the PDA in Example 4.8.2.

4.57 Construct a context-free grammar for the language $\{wcw^R \mid w \in \{a, b\}^*\}$.

   Hint: Use the algorithm of Theorem 4.12.2 to construct a context-free grammar that accepts the language accepted by the PDA in Example 4.8.1.

PROPERTIES OF CONTEXT-FREE LANGUAGES

4.58 Show that the intersection of a context-free language and a regular language is context-free.

   Hint: From machines accepting the two language types, construct a machine accepting their intersection.

4.59 Suppose that L is a context-free language and R is a regular one. Is $L - R$ necessarily context-free? What about $R - L$? Justify your answers.

4.60 Show that, if L is context-free, then so is $L^R = \{w^R \mid w \in L\}$.

4.61 Let $G = (\mathcal{N}, \mathcal{T}, \mathcal{R}, \text{S})$ be context-free. A non-terminal A is **self-embedding** if and only if $\text{A} \overset{*}{\Rightarrow}_G s\text{A}u$ for some $s, u \in \mathcal{T}$.
   a) Give a procedure to determine whether $\text{A} \in \mathcal{N}$ is self-embedding.
   b) Show that, if G does not have a self-embedding non-terminal, then it is regular.

CFL PUMPING LEMMA

4.62 Show that the following languages are not context-free:
   a) $\{0^{2^i} \mid i \geq 1\}$
   b) $\{b^{n^2} \mid n \geq 1\}$
   c) $\{0^n \mid n \text{ is a prime}\}$

4.63 Show that the following languages are not context-free:
   a) $\{0^n 1^n 0^n 1^n \mid n \geq 0\}$
   b) $\{a^i b^j c^k \mid 0 \leq i \leq j \leq k\}$
   c) $\{ww \mid w \in \{0, 1\}^*\}$

4.64 Show that the language $\{ww \mid w \in \{a, b\}^*\}$ is not context-free.

CFL CLOSURE PROPERTIES

4.65 Let M_1 and M_2 be pushdown automata accepting the languages $L(M_1)$ and $L(M_2)$. Describe PDAs accepting their union $L(M_1) \cup L(M_2)$, concatenation $L(M_1) \cdot L(M_2)$, and Kleene closure $L(M_1)^*$, thereby giving an alternate proof of Theorem 4.13.1.

4.66 Use closure under concatenation of context-free languages to show that the language $\{ww^R v^R v \mid w, v \in \{a, b\}^*\}$ is context-free.

Chapter Notes

The concept of the finite-state machine is often attributed to McCulloch and Pitts [209]. The models studied today are due to Moore [220] and Mealey [212]. The equivalence of deterministic and non-deterministic FSMs (Theorem 4.4.1) was established by Rabin and Scott [263].

Kleene established the equivalence of regular expressions and finite-state machines. The proof used in Theorems 4.4.1 and 4.4.2 is due to McNaughton and Yamada [210]. The pumping lemma (Lemma 4.5.1) is due to to Bar-Hillel, Perles, and Shamir [28]. The closure properties of regular expressions are due to McNaughton and Yamada [210].

State minimization was studied by Huffman [143] and Moore [220]. The Myhill-Nerode Theorem was independently obtained by Myhill [224] and Nerode [226]. Hopcroft [138] has given an efficient algorithm for state miminization.

Chomsky [68,69] defined four classes of formal language, the regular, context-free, context-sensitive, and phrase-structure languages. He and Miller [71] demonstrated the equivalence of languages generated by regular grammars and those recognized by finite-state machines. Chomsky introduced the normal form that carries his name [69]. Oettinger [230] introduced the pushdown automaton and Schutzenberger [302], Chomsky [70], and Evey [96] independently demonstrated the equivalence of context-free languages and pushdown automata.

Two efficient algorithms for parsing context-free languages were developed by Earley [93] and Cocke (unpublished) and independently by Kasami [160] and Younger [368]. These are cubic-time algorithms. Our formulation of the parsing algorithm of Section 4.11 is based on Valiant's derivation [339] of the Cocke-Kasami-Younger recognition matrix, where he also presents the fastest known general algorithm to parse context-free languages. The CFL pumping lemma and the closure properties of CFLs are due to Bar-Hillel, Perles, and Shamir [28].

Myhill [225] introduced the deterministic linear-bounded automata and Landweber [187] showed that languages accepted by linear-bounded automata are context-sensitive. Kuroda [182] generalized the linear-bounded automata to be nondeterministic and established the equivalence of such machines and the context-sensitive languages.

5

Computability

The Turing machine (TM) is believed to be the most general computational model that can be devised (the **Church-Turing thesis**). Despite many attempts, no computational model has yet been introduced that can perform computations impossible on a Turing machine. This is not a statement about efficiency; other machines, notably the RAM of Section 3.4, can do the same computations either more quickly or with less memory. Instead, it is a statement about the feasibility of computational tasks. If a task can be done on a Turing machine, it is considered feasible; if it cannot, it is considered infeasible. Thus, the TM is a litmus test for computational feasibility. As we show later, however, there are some well-defined tasks that cannot be done on a TM.

The chapter opens with a formal definition of the standard Turing machine and describes how the Turing machine can be used to compute functions and accept languages. We then examine multi-tape and nondeterministic TMs and show their equivalence to the standard model. The nondeterministic TM plays an important role in Chapter 8 in the classification of languages by their complexity. The equivalence of phrase-structure languages and the languages accepted by TMs is then established. The universal Turing machine is defined and used to explore limits on language acceptance by Turing machines. We show that some languages cannot be accepted by any Turing machine, while others can be accepted but not by Turing machines that halt on all inputs (the languages are unsolvable). This sets the stage for a proof that some problems, such as the Halting Problem, are unsolvable; that is, there is no Turing machine halting on all inputs that can decide for an arbitrary Turing machine M and input string w whether or not M will halt on w. We close by defining the *partial recursive functions*, the most general functions computable by Turing machines.

5.1 The Standard Turing Machine Model

The standard Turing machine consists of a control unit, which is a finite-state machine, and a (single-ended) infinite-capacity tape unit. (See Fig. 5.1.) Each cell of the tape unit initially contains the blank symbol β. A string of symbols from the tape alphabet Γ is written left-adjusted on the tape and the tape head is placed over the first cell. The control unit then reads the symbol under the head and makes a state transition the result of which is either to write a new symbol under the tape head or to move the head left (if possible) or right. (The TM described in Section 3.7 is slightly different; it always replaces the cell contents and always issues a move command, even if the effect in both cases is null. The equivalence between the standard TM and that described in Section 3.7 is easily established. See Problem 5.1.) A move left from the first cell leads to **abnormal termination**, a problem that can be avoided by having the Turing machine write a special **end-of-tape marker** in the first tape cell. This marker is a tape symbol not used elsewhere.

DEFINITION 5.1.1 *A **standard Turing machine (TM)** is a six-tuple $M = (\Gamma, \beta, Q, \delta, s, h)$ where Γ is the **tape alphabet** not containing the **blank symbol** β, Q is the **set of states**, $\delta : Q \times (\Gamma \cup \{\beta\}) \mapsto (Q \cup \{h\}) \times (\Gamma \cup \{\beta\} \cup \{\mathbf{L}, \mathbf{R}\})$ is the **next-state function**, s is the **initial state**, and $h \notin Q$ is the **accepting halt state**. A TM cannot exit from h. If M is in state q with letter a under the tape head and $\delta(q, a) = (q', \mathbf{C})$, its control unit enters state q' and writes a' if $\mathbf{C} = a' \in \Gamma \cup \{\beta\}$ or moves the head left (if possible) or right if $\mathbf{C}$ is $\mathbf{L}$ or $\mathbf{R}$, respectively.*

*The TM M **accepts the input string** $w \in \Gamma^*$ (it contains no blanks) if when started in state s with w placed left-adjusted on its otherwise blank tape, the last state entered by M is h. M **accepts the language** $L(M)$ consisting of all strings accepted by M. Languages accepted by Turing machines are called **recursively enumerable**. A language L is **decidable** or **recursive** if there exists a TM M that halts on every input string, whether in L or not, and accepts strings in L.*

*A function $f : \Gamma^* \mapsto \Gamma^* \cup \perp$, where $\perp$ is a symbol that is not in Γ, is **partial** if for some $w \in \Gamma^*$, $f(w) = \perp$ (f is **not defined** on w). Otherwise, f is **total**.*

*A TM M **computes a function** $f : \Gamma^* \mapsto \Gamma^* \cup \perp$ for those w such that $f(w)$ is defined if when started in state s with w placed left-adjusted on its otherwise blank tape, M enters the accepting halt state h with $f(w)$ written left-adjusted on its otherwise blank tape. If a TM halts on all inputs, it implements an **algorithm**. A task defined by a total function f is **solvable** if f has an algorithm and **unsolvable** otherwise.*

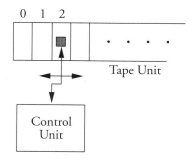

Figure 5.1 The control and tape units of the standard Turing machine.

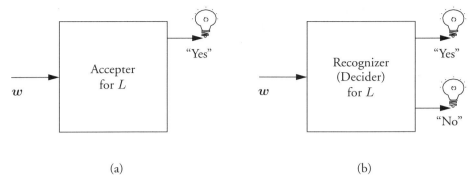

(a)   (b)

Figure 5.2 An accepter (a) for a language L is a Turing machine that can accept strings in a language L but may not halt on all inputs. A decider or recognizer (b) for a language L is a Turing machine that halts on all inputs and accepts strings in L.

The accepting halt state h has been singled out to emphasize language acceptance. However, there is nothing to prevent a TM from having multiple halt states, states from which it does not exit. (A halt state can be realized by a state to which a TM returns on every input without moving the tape head or changing the value under the head.) On the other hand, on some inputs a TM may never halt. For example, it may endlessly move its tape head right one cell and write the symbol a.

Notice that we do not require a TM M to halt on every input string for it to accept a language $L(M)$. It need only halt on those strings in the language. A language L for which there is a TM M accepting $L = L(M)$ that halts on all inputs is decidable. The distinction between accepting and recognizing (or deciding) a language L is illustrated schematically in Fig. 5.2. An accepter is a TM that accepts strings in L but may not halt on strings not in L. When the accepter determines that the string w is in the language L, it turns on the "Yes" light. If this light is not turned on, it may be that the string is not in L or that the TM is just slow. On the other hand, a recognizer or decider is a TM that halts on all inputs and accepts strings in L. The "Yes" or "No" light is guaranteed to be turned on at some time.

The computing power of the TM is extended by allowing **partial computations**, computations on which the TM does not halt on every input. The computation of functions by Turing machines is discussed in Section 5.9.

5.1.1 Programming the Turing Machine

Programming a Turing machine means choosing a tape alphabet and designing its control unit, a finite-state machine. Since the FSM has been extensively studied elsewhere, we limit our discussion of programming of Turing machines to four examples, each of which illustrates a fundamental point about Turing machines. Although TMs are generally designed to perform unbounded computations, their control units have a bounded number of states. Thus, we must insure that as they move across their tapes they do not accumulate an unbounded amount of information.

A simple example of a TM is one that moves right until it encounters a blank, whereupon it halts. The TM of Fig. 5.3(a) performs this task. If the symbol under the head is 0 or 1,

q	a	$\delta(\sigma,q)$		q	a	$\delta(\sigma,q)$
q_1	0	q_1 **R**		q_1	0	q_2 β
q_1	1	q_1 **R**		q_1	1	q_3 β
q_1	β	h β		q_1	β	h β
				q_2	0	q_4 **R**
				q_2	1	q_4 **R**
				q_2	β	q_4 **R**
				q_3	0	q_5 **R**
				q_3	1	q_5 **R**
				q_3	β	q_5 **R**
				q_4	0	q_2 0
				q_4	1	q_3 0
				q_4	β	h 0
				q_5	0	q_2 1
				q_5	1	q_3 1
				q_5	β	h 1

(a)   (b)

Figure 5.3 The transition functions of two Turing machines, one (a) that moves across the non-blank symbols on its tape and halts over the first blank symbol, and a second (b) that moves the input string right one position and inserts a blank to its left.

it moves right. If it is the blank symbol, it halts. This TM can be extended to replace the rightmost character in a string of non-blank characters with a blank. After finding the blank on the right of a non-blank string, it backs up one cell and replaces the character with a blank. Both TMs compute functions that map strings to strings.

A second example is a TM that replaces the first letter in its input string with a blank and shifts the remaining letters right one position. (See Fig. 5.3(b).) In its initial state q_1 this TM, which is assumed to be given a non-blank input string, records the symbol under the tape head by entering q_2 if the letter is 0 or q_4 if the letter is 1 and writing the blank symbol. In its current state it moves right and enters a corresponding state. (It enters q_4 if its current state is q_2 and q_5 if it is q_3.) In the new state it prints the letter originally in the cell to its left and enters either q_2 or q_3 depending on whether the current cell contains 0 or 1. This TM can be used to insert a special end-of-tape marker instead of a blank to the left of a string written initially on a tape. This idea can generalized to insert a symbol anyplace in another string.

A third example of a TM M is one that accepts strings in the language $L = \{a^n b^n c^n \mid n \geq 1\}$. M inserts an end-of-tape marker to the left of a string w placed on its tape and uses a computation denoted $C(x,y)$, in which it moves right across zero or more x's followed by zero or more "pseudo-blanks" (a symbol other than a, b, c, or β) to an instance of y, entering a non-accepting halt state f if some other pattern of letters is found. Starting in the first cell, if M discovers that the next letter is not a, it exits to state f. If it is a, it replaces a by a pseudo-blank. It then executes $C(a,b)$. M then replaces b by a pseudo-blank and executes $C(b,c)$, after which it replaces c by a pseudo-blank and executes $C(c,\beta)$. It then returns to the beginning of the tape. If it arrives at the end-of-tape marker without encountering any instances of a, b, or c, it terminates in the accepting halt state h. If not, then it moves right over pseudo-blanks until it finds an a, entering state f if it finds some other letter. It then resumes the process executed on the first pass by invoking $C(a, b)$. This computation either enters the non-accepting halt state f or on each pass it replaces one instance each of a, b, and c with a pseudo-blank. Thus, M accepts the language $L = \{a^n b^n c^n \,|\, n \geq 1\}$; that is, L is decidable (recursive). Since M makes one pass over the tape for each instance of a, it uses time $O(n^2)$ on a string of length n. Later we give examples of languages that are recursively enumerable but not recursive.

In Section 3.8 we reasoned that any RAM computation can be simulated by a Turing machine. We showed that any program written for the RAM can be executed on a Turing machine at the expense of an increase in the running time from T steps on a RAM with S bits of storage to a time $O(ST \log^2 S)$ on the Turing machine.

5.2 Extensions to the Standard Turing Machine Model

In this section we examine various extensions to the standard Turing machine model and establish their equivalence to the standard model. These extensions include the multi-tape, nondeterministic, and oracle Turing machines.

We first consider the **double-ended tape Turing machine**. Unlike the standard TM that has a tape bounded on one end, this is a TM whose single tape is double-ended. A TM of this kind can be simulated by a two-track one-tape TM by reading and writing data on the top track when working on cells to the right of the midpoint of the tape and reading and writing data on the bottom track when working with cells to its left. (See Problem 5.7.)

5.2.1 Multi-Tape Turing Machines

A k-**tape Turing machine** has a control unit and k single-ended tapes of the kind shown in Fig. 5.1. Each tape has its own head and operates in the fashion indicated for the standard model. The FSM control unit accepts inputs from all tapes simultaneously, makes a state transition based on this data, and then supplies outputs to each tape in the form of either a letter to be written under its head or a head movement command. We assume that the tape alphabet of each tape is Γ. A three-tape TM is shown in Fig. 5.4. A k-tape TM M_k can be simulated by a one-tape TM M_1, as we now show.

THEOREM 5.2.1 *For each k-tape Turing machine M_k there is a one-tape Turing machine M_1 such that a terminating T-step computation by M_k can be simulated in $O(T^2)$ steps by M_1.*

Proof Let Γ and Γ' be the tape alphabets of M_k and M_1, respectively. Let $|\Gamma'| = (2|\Gamma|)^k$ so that Γ' has enough letters to allow the tape of M_1 to be subdivided into k tracks, as suggested in Fig. 5.5. Each cell of a track contains $2|\Gamma|$ letters, a number large enough to allow each cell to contain either a member of Γ or a marked member of Γ. The marked members retain their original identity but also contain the information that they have been marked. As suggested in Fig. 5.5 for a three-tape TM, k heads can be simulated by one head by marking the positions of the k heads on the tracks of M_1.

M_1 simulates M_k in two passes. First it visits marked cells to collect the letters under the original tape heads, after which it makes a state transition akin to that made by M_1. In a second pass it visits the marked cells either to change their entries or to move the simulated

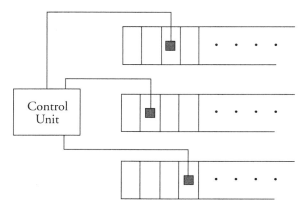

Figure 5.4 A three-tape Turing machine.

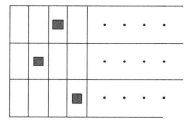

Figure 5.5 A single tape of a TM with a large tape alphabet that simulates a three-tape TM with a smaller tape alphabet.

tape heads. If the k-tape TM executes T steps, it uses at most $T + 1$ tape cells. Thus each pass requires $O(T)$ steps and the complete computation can be done in $O(T^2)$ steps. ∎

Multi-tape machines in which the tapes are double-ended are equivalent to multi-tape single-ended Turing machines, as the reader can show.

5.2.2 Nondeterministic Turing Machines

The **nondeterministic standard Turing machine** (NDTM) is introduced in Section 3.7.1. We use a slightly altered definition that conforms to the definition of the standard Turing machine in Definition 5.1.1.

DEFINITION 5.2.1 *A* **nondeterministic Turing machine (NTM)** *is a seven-tuple* $M = (\Sigma, \Gamma, \beta, Q, \delta, s, h)$ *where* Σ *is the* **choice input alphabet**, Γ *is the* **tape alphabet** *not containing the* **blank symbol** β, Q *is the* **set of states**, $\delta : Q \times \Sigma \times (\Gamma \cup \{\beta\}) \mapsto (Q \cup \{h\}) \times (\Gamma \cup \{\beta\}) \cup \{\mathbf{L}, \mathbf{R}\}) \cup \perp$ *is the* **next-state function**, s *is the* **initial state**, *and* $h \notin Q$ *is the* **accepting halt state**. *A TM cannot exit from* h. *If* M *is in state* q *with letter* a *under the tape head and* $\delta(q, c, a) = (q', \mathbf{C})$, *its control unit enters state* q' *and writes* a' *if* $\mathbf{C} = a' \in \Gamma \cup \{\beta\}$, *or it*

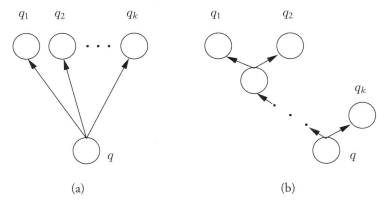

Figure 5.6 The construction used to reduce the fan-out of a nondeterministic state.

moves the head left (if possible) or right if **C** *is* **L** *or* **R**, *respectively. If* $\delta(q, c, a) = \bot$, *there is no successor to the current state with choice input c and tape symbol a.*

An NTM M reads one character of its **choice input string** $c \in \Sigma^*$ *on each step. An NTM M* **accepts string** w *if there is some choice string* c *such that the last state entered by M is h when M is started in state s with* w *placed left-adjusted on its otherwise blank tape.*

An NTM M **accepts the language** $L(M) \subseteq \Gamma^*$ *consisting of those strings* w *that it accepts. Thus, if* $w \notin L(M)$, *there is no choice input for which M accepts* w.

If an NDTM has more than two nondeterministic choices for a particular state and letter under the tape head, we can design another NDTM that has at most two choices. As suggested in Fig. 5.6, for each state q that has k possible next states $q_1, \ldots, q_k$ for some input letter, we can add $k - 2$ intermediate states, each with two outgoing edges such that a) in each state the tape head doesn't move and no change is made in the letter under the head, but b) each state has the same k possible successor states. It follows that the new machine computes the same function or accepts the same language as the original machine. Consequently, from this point on we assume that there are either one or two next states from each state of an NDTM for each tape symbol.

We now show that the range of computations that can be performed by deterministic and nondeterministic Turing machines is the same. However, this does not mean that with the identical resource bounds they compute the same set of functions.

THEOREM 5.2.2 *Any language accepted by a nondeterministic standard TM can be accepted by a standard deterministic one.*

Proof The proof is by simulation. We simulate all possible computations of a nondeterministic standard TM M_{ND} on an input string w by a deterministic three-tape TM M_{D} and halt if we find a sequence of moves by M_{ND} that leads to an accepting halt state. Later this machine can be simulated by a one-tape TM. The three tapes of M_{D} are an input tape, a work tape, and **enumeration tape**. (See Fig. 5.7.) The input tape holds the input and is never modified. The work tape is used to simulate M_{ND}. The enumeration tape contains choice sequences used by M_{D} to decide which move to make when simu-

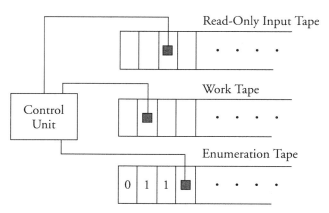

Figure 5.7 A three-tape deterministic Turing machine that simulates a nondeterministic Turing machine.

lating M_{ND}. These sequences are generated in lexicographical order, that is, in the order $0, 1, 00, 01, 10, 11, 000, 001, \ldots$. It is straightforward to design a deterministic TM that generates these sequences. (See Problem 5.2.)

Since a string w is accepted by a nondeterministic TM if there is some choice input on which it is accepted, a deterministic TM M_{D} that accepts the input w accepted by M_{ND} can be constructed by erasing the work tape, copying the input sequence w to the work tape, placing the next choice input sequence in lexicographical order on the enumeration tape (initially this is the sequence 0), and then simulating M_{ND} on the work tape while reading choice inputs from the enumeration tape. If M_{D} runs out of choice inputs before reaching the halt state, the above procedure is repeated; that is, the computation is restarted with the next choice input sequence. This breadth-first searching method deterministically accepts the input string w if and only if there is some choice input to M_{ND} on which it is accepted. ∎

Adding more than one tape to a nondeterministic Turing machine does not increase its computing power. To see this, it suffices to simulate a multi-tape nondeterministic Turing machine with a single-tape one, using a construction parallel to that of Theorem 5.2.1, and then invoke the above result. Applying these observations to language acceptance yields the following corollary.

COROLLARY 5.2.1 *Any language accepted by a nondeterministic (multi-tape) Turing machine can be accepted by a deterministic standard Turing machine.*

We emphasize that this result does not mean that with identical resource bounds the deterministic and nondeterministic Turing machines compute the same set of functions.

5.2.3   Oracle Turing Machines

The **oracle Turing machine** (OTM) is a multi-tape DTM or NDTM with a special **oracle tape** and an associated **oracle** function $h : \mathcal{B}^* \mapsto \mathcal{B}^*$, which need not be computable. (See Fig. 5.8.) After writing a string z on its oracle tape, the OTM signals to the oracle to replace z with the value $h(z)$ of the oracle function. During a computation the OTM may consult

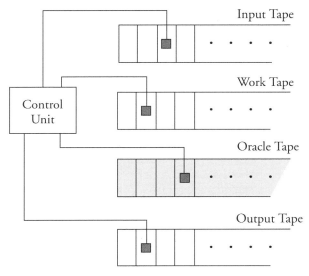

Figure 5.8   The oracle Turing machine has an "oracle tape" on which it writes a string (a problem instance), after which an "oracle" returns an answer in one step.

the oracle as many times as it wishes. **Time** on an OTM is the number of steps taken, where one consultation of the oracle is counted as one step. **Space** is the number of cells used on the work tapes of an OTM not including the oracle tape. The OTM machine can be used to classify problems. (See Problem 8.15.)

5.2.4   Representing Restricted Models of Computation

Now that we have introduced a variety of Turing machine models, we ask how the finite-state machine and pushdown automaton fit into the picture.

The finite-state machine can be viewed as a Turing machine with two tapes, the first a read-only input tape and the second a write-only output tape. This TM reads consecutive symbols on its input tape, moving right after reading each symbol, and writes outputs on its output tape, moving right after writing each symbol. If this TM enters an accepting halt state, the input sequence read from the tape is accepted.

The pushdown automaton can be viewed as a Turing machine with two tapes, a read-only input tape and a pushdown tape. The pushdown tape is a standard tape that pushes a new symbol by moving its head right one cell and writing the new symbol into this previously blank cell. It pops the symbol at the top of the stack by copying the symbol, after which it replaces it with the blank symbol and moves its head left one cell.

The Turing machine can be simulated by two pushdown tapes. The movement of the head in one direction can be simulated by popping the top item of one stack and pushing it onto the other stack. To simulate the movement of the head in the opposite direction, interchange the names of the two stacks.

The nondeterministic equivalents of the finite-state machine and pushdown automaton are obtained by making their Turing machine control units nondeterministic.

5.3 Configuration Graphs

We now introduce configuration graphs, graphs that capture the state of Turing machines with potentially unlimited storage capacity. We begin by describing configuration graphs for one-tape Turing machines.

DEFINITION 5.3.1 *The* **configuration of a standard Turing machine** M *at any point in time is* $[x_1 x_2 \ldots \boldsymbol{p} x_j \ldots x_n]$, *where p is the state of the control unit, the tape head is over the jth tape cell, and $\boldsymbol{x} = (x_1, x_2, \ldots, x_n)$ is the string that contains all the non-blank symbols on the tape as well as the symbol under the head. Here the state p is shown in boldface to the left of the symbol x_j to indicate that the tape head is over the jth cell. x_n and some of the symbols to its left may be blanks.*

To illustrate such configurations, consider a TM M that is in state p reading the third symbol on its tape, which contains xyz. This information is captured by the configuration $[xy\boldsymbol{p}z]$. If M changes to state q and moves its head right, then its new configuration is $[xyz\boldsymbol{q}\beta]$. In this case we add a blank β to the right of the string xyz to insure that the head resides over the string.

Because multi-tape TMs are important in classifying problems by their use of temporary work space, a definition for the configuration of a multi-tape TM is desirable. We now introduce a notation for this purpose that is somewhat more cumbersome than used for the standard TM. This notation uses an explicit binary number for the position of each tape head.

DEFINITION 5.3.2 *The* **configuration of a k-tape Turing machine** M *is $(p, \boldsymbol{h_1}, \boldsymbol{h_2}, \ldots, \boldsymbol{h_k}, \boldsymbol{x_1}, \boldsymbol{x_2}, \ldots, \boldsymbol{x_k})$, where $\boldsymbol{h_r}$ is the position of the head in binary on the rth tape, p is the state of the control unit, and $\boldsymbol{x_r}$ is the string on the rth tape that includes all the non-blank symbols as well as the symbol under the head.*

We now define configuration graphs for DTMs and NDTMs. Because we will apply configuration graphs to machines that halt on all inputs, we view them as acyclic.

DEFINITION 5.3.3 *A* **configuration graph** $G(M_{\mathrm{ND}}, \boldsymbol{w})$ *associated with the NDTM M_{ND} is a graph whose vertices are configurations of M_{ND}. (See Fig. 5.9.) There is a directed edge between two vertices if for some choice input vector $\boldsymbol{c}$ M_{ND} can move from the first configuration to the*

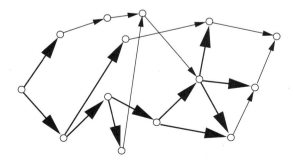

Figure 5.9 The configuration graph $G(M_{\mathrm{ND}}, \boldsymbol{w})$ of a nondeterministic Turing machine M_{ND} on input $\boldsymbol{w}$ has one vertex for each configuration of M_{ND}. The graph is acyclic. Heavy edges identify the nondeterministic choices associated with each configuration.

second in one step. There is one configuration corresponding to the initial state of the machine and one corresponding to the final state. (We assume without loss of generality that, after accepting an input string, M_{ND} enters a cleanup phase during which it places a fixed string on each tape.)

Configuration graphs are used in the next section to associate a phrase-structure language with a Turing machine. They are also used in many places in Chapter 8, especially in Section 8.5.3, where they are used to establish an important relationship between deterministic and nondeterministic space classes.

5.4 Phrase-Structure Languages and Turing Machines

We now demonstrate that the phrase-structure languages and the languages accepted by Turing machines are the same. We begin by showing that every recursively enumerable language is a phrase-structure language. For this purpose we use configurations of one-tape Turing machines. Then, for each phrase-structure language L we describe the construction of a TM accepting L. We conclude that the languages accepted by TMs and described by phrase-structure languages are the same.

With these conventions as background, if a standard TM halts in its accepting halt state, we can require that it halt with $\beta 1 \beta$ on its tape when it accepts the input string $\boldsymbol{w}$. Thus, the TM configuration when a TM halts and accepts its input string is $[\mathbf{h}\beta 1 \beta]$. Its starting configuration is $[\mathbf{s}\beta w_1 w_2 \ldots w_n \beta]$, where $\boldsymbol{w} = w_1 w_2 \ldots w_n$.

THEOREM 5.4.1 *Every recursively enumerable language is a phrase-structure language.*

Proof Let $M = (\Gamma, Q, \delta, s, h)$ be a deterministic TM and let $L(M)$ be the recursively enumerable language over the alphabet Γ that it accepts. The goal is to show the existence of a phrase-structure grammar $G = (\mathcal{N}, \mathcal{T}, \mathcal{R}, \mathsf{s})$ that can generate each string $\boldsymbol{w}$ of L. Since the TM accepting L halts with $\beta 1 \beta$ on its tape when started with $\boldsymbol{w} \in L$, we design a grammar G that produces the configurations of M in reverse order. Starting with the final configuration $[\mathbf{h}\beta 1 \beta]$, G produces the starting configuration $[\mathbf{s}\beta w_1 w_2 \ldots w_n \beta]$, where $\boldsymbol{w} = w_1 w_2 \ldots w_n$, after which it strips off the characters $[\mathbf{s}\beta$ at the beginning and $\beta]$. The grammar G defined below serves this purpose, as we show.

Let $\mathcal{N} = Q \cup \{\mathsf{s}, \beta, [,]\}$ and $\mathcal{T} = \Gamma$. The rules $\mathcal{R}$ of G are defined as follows:

$$
\begin{array}{lllll}
\text{(a)} & \mathsf{s} & \rightarrow & [\mathbf{h}\beta 1 \beta] & \\
\text{(b)} & \beta] & \rightarrow & \beta\beta] & \\
\text{(c)} & [\mathbf{s}\beta & \rightarrow & \epsilon & \\
\text{(d)} & \beta\beta] & \rightarrow & \beta] & \\
\text{(e)} & \beta] & \rightarrow & \epsilon & \\
\text{(f)} & x\mathbf{q} & \rightarrow & \mathbf{p}x & \text{for all } p \in Q \text{ and } x \in (\Gamma \cup \{\beta\}) \\
& & & & \text{such that } \delta(p, x) = (q, \mathbf{R}) \\
\text{(g)} & \mathbf{q}zx & \rightarrow & z\mathbf{p}x & \text{for all } p \in Q \text{ and } x, z \in (\Gamma \cup \{\beta\}) \\
& & & & \text{such that } \delta(p, x) = (q, \mathbf{L}) \\
\text{(h)} & \mathbf{q}y & \rightarrow & \mathbf{p}x & \text{for all } p \in Q \text{ and } x \in (\Gamma \cup \{\beta\}) \\
& & & & \text{such that } \delta(p, x) = (q, y), y \in (\Gamma \cup \{\beta\})
\end{array}
$$

These rules are designed to start with the transition $\mathsf{s} \rightarrow [\mathbf{h}\beta 1 \beta]$ (Rule (a)) and then rewrite $[\mathbf{h}\beta 1 \beta]$ using other rules until the configuration $[\mathbf{s}\beta w_1 w_2 \ldots w_n \beta]$ is reached. At this point Rule (c) is invoked to strip $[\mathbf{s}\beta$ from the beginning of the string, and Rule (d) strips β from the end and (e) removes $]$, thereby producing the string $w_1, w_2, \ldots, w_n$ that was written initially on M's tape.

Rule (b) is used to add blank space at the right-hand end of the tape. Rules (f)–(h) mimic the transitions of M in reverse order. Rule (f) says that if M in state p reading x moves to state q and moves its head right, then M's configuration contained the substring $\mathbf{p}x$ before the move and $x\mathbf{q}$ after it. Thus, we map $x\mathbf{q}$ into $\mathbf{p}x$ with the rule $x\mathbf{q} \to x\mathbf{q}$. Similar reasoning is applied to Rule (g). If the transition $\delta(p, x) = (q, y)$, $y \in \Gamma \cup \{\beta\}$ is executed, M's configuration contained the substring $\mathbf{p}x$ before the step and $\mathbf{q}y$ after it because the head does not move.

Clearly, every computation by a TM M can be described by a sequence of configurations and the transitions between these configurations can be described by this grammar G. Thus, the strings accepted by M can be generated by G. Conversely, if we are given a derivation in G, it produces a series of configurations characterizing computations by the TM M in reverse order. Thus, the strings generated by G are the strings accepted by M. ∎

By showing that every phrase-structure language can be accepted by a Turing machine, we will have demonstrated the equivalence between the phrase-structure and recursively enumerable languages.

THEOREM 5.4.2 *Every phrase-structure language is recursively enumerable.*

Proof Given a phrase-structure grammar G, we construct a nondeterministic two-tape TM M with the property that $L(G) = L(M)$. Because every language accepted by a multi-tape TM is accepted by a one-tape TM and vice versa, we have the desired conclusion.

To decide whether or not to accept an input string placed on its first (input) tape, M nondeterministically generates a terminal string on its second (work) tape using the rules of G. To do so, it puts G's start symbol on its work tape and then nondeterministically expands it into a terminal string using the rules of G. After producing a terminal string, M compares the input string with the string on its work tape. If they agree in every position, M accepts the input string. If not, M enters an infinite loop. To write the derived strings on its work tape, M must either replace, delete, or insert characters in the string on its tape, tasks well suited to Turing machines.

Since it is possible for M to generate every string in $L(G)$ on its work tape, it can accept every string in $L(G)$. On the other hand, every string accepted by M is a string that it can generate using the rules of G. Thus, every string accepted by M is in $L(G)$. It follows that $L(M) = L(G)$. ∎

This last result gives meaning to the phrase "recursively enumerable": the languages accepted by Turing machines (the recursively enumerable languages) are languages whose strings can be enumerated by a Turing machine (a recursive device).

5.5 Universal Turing Machines

A universal Turing machine is a Turing machine that can simulate the behavior of an arbitrary Turing machine, even the universal Turing machine itself. To give an explicit construction for such a machine, we show how to encode Turing machines as strings.

Without loss of generality we consider only deterministic Turing machines $M = (\Gamma, \beta, Q, \delta, s, h)$ that have a binary tape alphabet $\Gamma = \mathcal{B} = \{0, 1\}$. When M is in state p and the value under the head is a, the next-state function $\delta : Q \times (\Gamma \cup \{\beta\}) \mapsto (Q \cup \{h\}) \times (\Gamma \cup \{\beta\} \cup \{\mathbf{L}, \mathbf{R}\})$ takes M to state q and provides output z, where $\delta(p, a) = (q, z)$ and $z \in \Gamma \cup \{\beta\} \cup \{\mathbf{L}, \mathbf{R}\}$.

We now specify a convention for numbering states that simplifies the description of the next-state function δ of M.

DEFINITION 5.5.1 *The **canonical encoding** of a Turing machine M, $\rho(M)$, is a string over the 10-letter alphabet $\Lambda = \{<, >, [,], \#, 0, 1, \beta, \mathbf{R}, \mathbf{L}\}$ formed as follows:*

(a) Let $Q = \{q_1, q_2, \ldots, q_k\}$ where $s = q_1$. Represent state q_i in unary notation by the string 1^i. The halt state h is represented by the empty string.

(b) Let (q, z) be the value of the next-state function when M is in state p reading a under its tape head; that is, $\delta(p, a) = (q, z)$. Represent (q, z) by the string $< z\#q >$ in which q is represented in unary and $z \in \{0, 1, \beta, \mathbf{L}, \mathbf{R}\}$. If $q = h$, the value of the next-state function is $< z\# >$.

(c) For $p \in Q$, the three values $< z'\#q' >$, $< z''\#q'' >$, and $< z''\#q''' >$ of $\delta(p, 0)$, $\delta(p, 1)$, and $\delta(p, \beta)$ are assembled as a triple $[< z'\#q' >< z''\#q'' >< z'''\#q''' >]$. The complete description of the next-state function δ is given as a sequence of such triples, one for each state $p \in Q$.

To illustrate this definition, consider the two TMs whose next-state functions are shown in Fig. 5.3. The first moves across the non-blank initial string on its tape and halts over the first blank symbol. The second moves the input string right one position and inserts a blank to its left. The canonical encoding of the first TM is $[< \mathbf{R}\#1 >< \mathbf{R}\#1 >< \beta\# >]$ whereas that of the second is

$$[< \beta\#11 > \quad < \beta\#111 > \quad < \beta\# >]$$
$$[< \mathbf{R}\#1111 > \quad < \mathbf{R}\#1111 > \quad < \mathbf{R}\#1111 >]$$
$$[< \mathbf{R}\#11111 > < \mathbf{R}\#11111 > < \mathbf{R}\#11111 >]$$
$$[< 0\#11 > \quad < 0\#111 > \quad < 0\# >]$$
$$[< 1\#11 > \quad < 1\#111 > \quad < 1\# >]$$

It follows that the valid encodings of TMs can be described by the regular expression $([[(< \{0, 1, \beta, \mathbf{L}, \mathbf{R}\}\#1^* >)^3])^*$. Consequently, a finite-state machine can determine in one pass over a string drawn from the alphabet Γ whether or not it is a valid encoding.

A **universal Turing machine** (UTM) U is a Turing machine that is capable of simulating an arbitrary Turing machine on an arbitrary input word $\boldsymbol{w}$. The construction of a UTM based on the simulation of the random-access machine is described in Section 3.8. Here we describe a direct construction of a UTM.

Let the UTM U have a 20-letter alphabet $\widehat{\Lambda}$ containing the 10 symbols in Λ plus another 10 symbols that are marked copies of the symbols in Λ. (The marked copies are used to simulate multiple tracks on a one-track TM.) That is, we define $\widehat{\Lambda}$ as follows:

$$\widehat{\Lambda} = \{(,), [,], \#, 0, 1, \beta, \mathbf{R}, \mathbf{L}\} \cup \{\widehat{(}, \widehat{)}, \widehat{[}, \widehat{]}, \widehat{\#}, \widehat{0}, \widehat{1}, \widehat{\beta}, \widehat{\mathbf{R}}, \widehat{\mathbf{L}}\}$$

To simulate the TM M on the input string $\boldsymbol{w}$, we place M's canonical encoding, $\rho(M)$, on the tape of the UTM U followed by $\boldsymbol{w}$, as suggested in Fig. 5.10. The first letter of $\boldsymbol{w}$

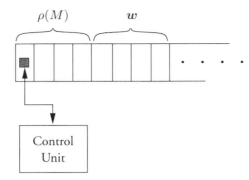

Figure 5.10 The initial configuration of the tape of a universal TM that is prepared to simulate the TM M on input w.

follows the rightmost bracket,], and is marked by replacing it with its marked equivalent, $\widehat{]}$. The current state q of M is identified by replacing the left bracket, [, in q's triple by its marked equivalent, $\widehat{[}$. U simulates M by reading the marked input symbol a, the one that resides under M's simulated head, and advancing its own head to the triple to the right of $\widehat{[}$ that corresponds to a. (Before it moves its head, it replaces $\widehat{[}$ with [.) That is, it advances its head to the first, second, or third triple associated with the current state depending on whether a is 0, 1, or β. It then moves to the symbol following $<$ and takes the required action on the simulated tape. If the action requires writing a symbol, it replaces a with a new marked symbol. If it requires moving M's head, the marking on a is removed and the appropriate adjacent symbol is marked.

The UTM U moves to the next state as follows. It moves its head right two places, at which point it is to the right of $\#$, over the first digit representing the next state. If the symbol in this position is $>$, the next state is h, the halting state, and the UTM halts. If the symbol is 1, U replaces it with $\widehat{1}$ and then moves its head left to the leftmost instance of [. It marks this symbol and then returns to $\widehat{1}$. It replaces $\widehat{1}$ with 1 and moves its head right one place. If U finds the symbol 1, it marks it, moves left to $\widehat{[}$, restores it to [and then moves right to the next instance of [and marks it. It then moves right to $\widehat{1}$ and repeats this operation. However, if the UTM finds the symbol $>$, it has finished updating the current state so it moves right to the marked tape symbol, at which point it reads the symbol under M's head and starts another transition cycle. The details of this construction are left to the reader. (See Problem 5.15.)

5.6 Encodings of Strings and Turing Machines

Given an alphabet $\mathcal{A}$ with an ordering of its letters, strings over this alphabet have an order known as the standard **lexicographical order**, which we now define. In this order, strings of length $n - 1$ precede strings of length n. Thus, if $\mathcal{A} = \{0, 1, 2\}$, $201 < 0001$. Among the strings of length n, if a and b are in $\mathcal{A}$ and $a < b$, then all strings beginning with a precede those beginning with b. For example, if $0 < 1 < 2$ in $\mathcal{A} = \{0, 1, 2\}$, then $022 < 200$. If two strings of length n have the same prefix u, the ordering between them is determined by the order of the next letter. For example, for the alphabet $\mathcal{A}$ and the ordering given on its letters, $201021 < 201200$.

A simple algorithm produces the strings over an alphabet in lexicographical order. Strings of length 1 are produced by enumerating the letters from the alphabet in increasing order. Strings of length n are enumerated by choosing the first letter from the alphabet in increasing order. The remaining $n - 1$ letters are generated in lexicographical order by applying this algorithm recursively on strings of length $n - 1$.

To prepare for later results, we observe that it is straightforward to test an arbitrary string over the alphabet Λ given in Definition 5.5.1 to determine if it is a valid description $\rho(M)$ of a Turing machine M. This follows because the valid forms of $\rho(M)$ can be described by regular expressions and detected by a finite-state machine. If a putative canonical encoding does not correspond to a valid encoding, we associate with it the two-state **null TM** T_{null} with next-state function satisfying $\delta(s, a) = (h, a)$ for all tape letters a. This encoding associates a Turing machine with each string over the alphabet Λ.

We now show how to identify the **jth Turing machine**, M_j. Given an order to the symbols in Λ, strings over this alphabet are generated in lexicographical order. We define the null TM to be the zeroth TM. Each string over Λ that is not a valid encoding is associated with this machine. The first TM is the one described by the lexicographically first string over Λ that is a valid encoding. The second TM is described by the second valid encoding, etc. Not only does a finite-state machine determine which string is a valid encoding, but when combined with an algorithm to generate strings in lexicographical order, this procedure also assigns a Turing machine to each string and allows the jth Turing machine to be found.

Observe that there is no loss in generality in assuming that the encodings of Turing machines are binary strings. We need only create a mapping from the letters in the alphabet Λ to binary strings. Since it may be necessary to use marked letters, we can assume that the 20 strings in $\widehat{\Lambda}$ are available and are encoded into 5-bit binary strings. This allows us to view encodings of Turing machines as binary strings but to speak of the encodings in terms of the letters in the alphabet Λ.

5.7 Limits on Language Acceptance

A language L that is **decidable** (also called **recursive**) has an algorithm, a Turing machine that halts on all inputs and accepts just those strings in L. A language for which there is a Turing machine that accepts just those strings in L, possibly not halting on strings not in L, is **recursively enumerable**. A language that is recursively enumerable but not decidable is **unsolvable**.

We begin by describing some decidable languages and then exhibit a language, $\mathcal{L}_1$, that is not recursively enumerable (no Turing machine exists to accepts strings in it) but whose complement, $\mathcal{L}_2$, is recursively enumerable but not decidable; that is, $\mathcal{L}_2$ is unsolvable. We use the language $\mathcal{L}_2$ to show that other languages, including the halting problem, are unsolvable.

5.7.1 Decidable Languages

Our first decidable problem is the language of pairs of regular expressions and strings such the regular expression describes a language containing the corresponding string:

$$\mathcal{L}_{\text{RX}} = \{R, \boldsymbol{w} \mid \boldsymbol{w} \text{ is in the language described by the regular expression } R\}$$

THEOREM 5.7.1 *The language $\mathcal{L}_{\mathrm{RX}}$ is decidable.*

Proof To decide on a string R, w, use the method of Theorem 4.4.1 to construct a NFSM M_1 that accepts the language described by R. Then invoke the method of Theorem 4.2.1 to construct a DFSM M_2 accepting the same language as M_1. The string w is given to M_2, which accepts it if R can generate it and rejects it otherwise. This procedure decides $\mathcal{L}_{\mathrm{RX}}$ because it halts on all strings R, w, whether in $\mathcal{L}_{\mathrm{RX}}$ or not. ■

As a second example, we show that finite-state machines that recognize empty languages are decidable. Here an FSM encoded as Turing machine reads one input from the tape per step and makes a state transition, halting when it reaches the blank letter.

THEOREM 5.7.2 *The language $L = \{\rho(M) \mid M$ is a DFSM and $L(M) = \emptyset\}$ is decidable.*

Proof $L(M)$ is not empty if there is some string w it can accept. To determine if there is such a string, we use a TM M' that executes a breadth-first search on the graph of the DFSM M that is provided as input to M'. M' first marks the initial state of M and then repeatedly marks any state that has not been marked previously and can be reached from a marked state until no additional states can be marked. This process terminates because M has a finite number of states. Finally, M' checks to see if there is a marked accepting state that can be reached from the initial state, rejecting the input $\rho(M)$ if so and accepting it if not. ■

The third language describes context-free grammars generating languages that are empty. Here we encode the rules of a context-free grammar G as a string $\rho(G)$ over a small alphabet.

THEOREM 5.7.3 *The language $L = \{\rho(G) \mid G$ is a CFG and $L(G) = \emptyset\}$ is decidable.*

Proof We design a TM M' that, when given as input a description $\rho(G)$ of a CFG G, first marks all the terminals of the grammar and then scans all the rules of the grammar, marking non-terminal symbols that can be replaced by some marked symbols. (If there is a non-terminal A that it is not marked and there is a rule $A \rightarrow BCD$ in which B, C, D have already been marked, then the TM also marks A.) We repeat this procedure until no new non-terminals can be marked. This process terminates because the grammar G has a finite number of non-terminals. If S is not marked, we accept $\rho(G)$. Otherwise, we reject $\rho(G)$ because it is not possible to generate a string of terminals from S. ■

5.7.2 A Language That Is Not Recursively Enumerable

Not unexpectedly, there are well-defined languages that are not recursively enumerable, as we show in this section. We also show that the complement of a decidable language is decidable. This allows us to exhibit a language that is recursively enumerable but undecidable.

Consider the language $\mathcal{L}_1$ defined below. It contains the ith binary input string if it is not accepted by the ith Turing machine.

$$\mathcal{L}_1 = \{w_i \mid w_i \text{ is not accepted by } M_i\}$$

THEOREM 5.7.4 *The language $\mathcal{L}_1$ is not recursively enumerable; that is, no Turing machine exists that can accept all the strings in this language.*

	$\rho(M_1)$	$\rho(M_2)$		$\rho(M_k)$	
$\mathbf{w}_1$	reject	accept	$\cdots$	reject	$\cdots$
$\mathbf{w}_2$	accept	accept	$\cdots$	reject	$\cdots$
	$\vdots$	$\vdots$	$\vdots$	$\vdots$	$\vdots$
$\mathbf{w}_k$	accept	reject	$\cdots$	?	$\cdots$
	$\vdots$	$\vdots$	$\vdots$	$\vdots$	$\vdots$

Figure 5.11 A table whose rows and columns are indexed by input strings and Turing machines, respectively. Here $\boldsymbol{w}_i$ is the ith input string and $\rho(M_j)$ is the encoding of the jth Turing machine. The entry in row i, column j indicates whether or not M_j accepts $\boldsymbol{w}_i$. The language $\mathcal{L}_1$ consists of input strings $\boldsymbol{w}_j$ for which the entry in the jth row and jth column is **reject**.

Proof We use proof by contradiction; that is, we assume the existence of a TM M_k that accepts $\mathcal{L}_1$. If $\boldsymbol{w}_k$ is in $\mathcal{L}_1$, then M_k accepts it, contradicting the definition of $\mathcal{L}_1$. This implies that $\boldsymbol{w}_k$ is not in $\mathcal{L}_1$. On the other hand, if $\boldsymbol{w}_k$ is not in $\mathcal{L}_1$, then it is not accepted by M_k. It follows from the definition of $\mathcal{L}_1$ that $\boldsymbol{w}_k$ is in $\mathcal{L}_1$. Thus, $\boldsymbol{w}_k$ is in $\mathcal{L}_1$ if and only if it is not in $\mathcal{L}_1$. We have a contradiction and no Turing machine accepts $\mathcal{L}_1$. ∎

This proof uses **diagonalization**. (See Fig. 5.11.) In effect, we construct an infinite two-dimensional matrix whose rows are indexed by input words and whose columns are indexed by Turing machines. The entry in row i and column j of this matrix specifies whether or not input word $\boldsymbol{w}_j$ is accepted by M_j. The language $\mathcal{L}_1$ contains those words $\boldsymbol{w}_j$ that M_j rejects, that is, it contains row indices (words) for which the word "reject" is found on the diagonal. If we assume that some TM, M_k, accepts $\mathcal{L}_1$, we have a problem because we cannot decide whether or not $\boldsymbol{w}_k$ is in $\mathcal{L}_1$. Diagonalization is effective in ruling out the possibility of solving a computational problem but has limited usefulness on problems of bounded size.

5.7.3 Recursively Enumerable but Not Decidable Languages

We show the existence of a language that is recursively enumerable but not decidable. Our approach is to show that the complement of a recursive language is recursive and then exhibit a recursively enumerable language $\mathcal{L}_2$ whose complement $\mathcal{L}_1$ is not recursively enumerable:

$$\mathcal{L}_2 = \{\boldsymbol{w}_i \mid \boldsymbol{w}_i \text{ is accepted by } M_i\}$$

THEOREM 5.7.5 *The complement of a decidable language is decidable.*

Proof Let L be a recursive language accepted by a Turing machine M_1 that halts on all input strings. Relabel the accepting halt state of M_1 as non-accepting and all non-accepting halt states as accepting. This produces a machine M_2 that enters an accepting halt state only when M_1 enters a non-accepting halt state and vice versa. We convert this non-standard machine to standard form (having one accepting halt state) by adding a new accepting halt state and making a transition to it from all non-accepting halt states. This new machine halts on all inputs and accepts the complement of L. ∎

THEOREM 5.7.6 *The language $\mathcal{L}_2$ is recursively enumerable but not decidable.*

Proof To establish the desired result it suffices to exhibit a Turing machine M that accepts each string in $\mathcal{L}_2$, because the complement $\overline{\mathcal{L}_2} = \mathcal{L}_1$, which is not recursively enumerable, as shown above.

Given a string x in $\mathcal{L}_2$, let M enumerate the input strings over the alphabet of $\mathcal{L}_2$ until it finds x. Let x be the ith string where i is recorded in binary on one of M's tapes. The strings over the alphabet Λ used for canonical encodings of Turing machines are enumerated and tested to determine whether or not they are valid encodings, as described in Section 5.6. When the encoding $\rho(M_i)$ of the ith Turing machine is discovered, M_i is simulated with a universal Turing machine on the input string x. This universal machine will halt and accept the string x if it is in $\mathcal{L}_2$. Thus, $\mathcal{L}_2$ is recursively enumerable. ∎

5.8 Reducibility and Unsolvability

In this section we show that there are many languages that are unsolvable (undecidable). In the previous section we showed that the language $\mathcal{L}_2$ is unsolvable. To show that a new problem is unsolvable we use reducibility: we assume an algorithm A exists for a new language L and then show that we can use A to obtain an algorithm for a language previously shown to be unsolvable, thereby contradicting the assumption that algorithm A exists.

We begin by introducing reducibility and then give examples of unsolvable languages. Many interesting languages are unsolvable.

5.8.1 Reducibility

A new language $\mathcal{L}_{\mathrm{new}}$ can often be shown unsolvable by assuming it is solvable and then showing this implies that an older language $\mathcal{L}_{\mathrm{old}}$ is solvable, where $\mathcal{L}_{\mathrm{old}}$ has been previously shown to be unsolvable. Since this contradicts the facts, the new language cannot be solvable. This is one application of **reducibility**. The formal definition of reducibility is given below and illustrated by Fig. 5.12.

DEFINITION 5.8.1 *The language L_1 is **reducible** to the language L_2 if there is an algorithm computing a total function $f : \mathcal{C}^* \mapsto \mathcal{D}^*$ that translates each string w over the alphabet $\mathcal{C}$ of L_1 into a string $z = f(w)$ over the alphabet $\mathcal{D}$ of L_2 such that $w \in L_1$ if and only if $z \in L_2$.*

In this definition, testing for membership of a string w in L_1 is reduced to testing for membership of a string z in L_2, where the latter problem is presumably a previously solved problem. It is important to note that the latter problem is no easier than the former, even though the use of the word "reduce" suggests that it is. Rather, reducibility establishes a link between two problems with the expectation that the properties of one can be used to deduce properties of the other. For example, reducibility is used to identify **NP**-complete problems. (See Sections 3.9.3 and 8.7.)

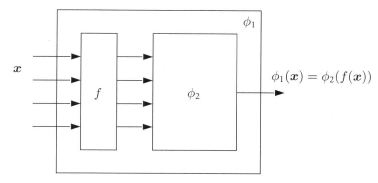

Figure 5.12 The characteristic function ϕ_i of L_i, $i = 1, 2$ has value 1 on strings in L_i and 0 otherwise. Because the language L_1 is reducible to the language L_2, there is a function f such that for all x, $\phi_2(x) = \phi_1(f(x))$.

Reducibility is a fundamental idea that is formally introduced in Section 2.4 and used throughout this book. Reductions of the type defined above are known as **many-to-one reductions**. (See Section 8.7 for more on this subject.)

The following lemma is a tool to show that problems are unsolvable. We use the same mechanism in Chapter 8 to classify languages by their use of time, space and other computational resources.

LEMMA 5.8.1 *Let L_1 be reducible to L_2. If L_2 is decidable, then L_1 is decidable. If L_1 is unsolvable, L_2 is also unsolvable.*

Proof Let T be a Turing machine implementing the algorithm that translates strings over the alphabet of L_1 to strings over the alphabet of L_2. If L_2 is decidable, there is a halting Turing machine M_2 that accepts it. A multi-tape Turing machine M_1 that decides L_1 can be constructed as follows: On input string w, M_1 invokes T to generate the string z, which it then passes to M_2. If M_2 accepts z, M_1 accepts w. If M_2 rejects it, so does M_1. Thus, M_1 decides L_1.

Suppose now that L_1 is unsolvable. Assuming that L_2 is decidable, from the above construction, L_1 is decidable, contradicting this assumption. Thus, L_2 cannot be decidable. ∎

The power of this lemma will be apparent in the next section.

5.8.2 Unsolvable Problems

In this section we examine six representative unsolvable problems. They range from the classical halting problem to Rice's theorem.

We begin by considering the **halting problem** for Turing machines. The problem is to determine for an arbitrary TM M and an arbitrary input string x whether M with input x halts or not. We characterize this problem by the language $\mathcal{L}_H$ shown below. We show it is unsolvable, that is, $\mathcal{L}_H$ is recursively enumerable but not decidable. No Turing machine exists to decide this language.

$$\mathcal{L}_H = \{\rho(M),\, w \mid M \text{ halts on input } w\}$$

THEOREM 5.8.1 *The language $\mathcal{L}_H$ is recursively enumerable but not decidable.*

Proof To show that $\mathcal{L}_H$ is recursively enumerable, pass the encoding $\rho(M)$ of the TM M and the input string w to the universal Turing machine U of Section 5.5. This machine simulates M and halts on the input w if w is in $L(M)$. Thus, $\mathcal{L}_H$ is recursively enumerable.

To show that $\mathcal{L}_H$ is undecidable, we follow the pattern described in Lemma 5.8.1. We assume that $\mathcal{L}_H$ is decidable by a Turing machine M_H and exhibit a TM that translates $\mathcal{L}_1$ to $\mathcal{L}_H$. This implies that $\mathcal{L}_1$ is decidable, which is a contradiction.

We assume that M_H exists and has an encoding $\rho(M_H)$. We use this encoding to construct a Turing machine M_1 that decides $\mathcal{L}_1$ as follows: a) given the input string w, M_1 determines the value of i such that w is the ith string, x_i, in the lexicographical ordering of input strings; b) M_1 generates an encoding for the ith Turing machine M_i using the procedure described in Section 5.6; c) M_1 simulates M_H to determine if M_i halts on $w = x_i$; d) if M_H says that M_i does not halt, M_1 accepts w; e) if M_H says that M_i does halt, M_1 simulates M_i on input string w. M_1 rejects w if M_i accepts it and accepts w if M_i rejects it. Clearly, M_1 recognizes strings in $\mathcal{L}_1$, which contradicts the nature of $\mathcal{L}_1$. Thus, M_H cannot exist. ■

The second unsolvable problem we consider is the **empty tape acceptance problem**: given a Turing machine M, we ask if we can tell whether it accepts the empty string. We reduce the halting problem to it. (See Fig. 5.13.)

$$\mathcal{L}_{ET} = \{\rho(M) \mid L(M) \text{ contains the empty string}\}$$

THEOREM 5.8.2 *The language $\mathcal{L}_{ET}$ is not decidable.*

Proof To show that $\mathcal{L}_{ET}$ is not decidable, we assume that it is and derive a contradiction. The contradiction is produced by assuming the existence of a TM M_{ET} that decides $\mathcal{L}_{ET}$ and then showing that this implies the existence of a TM M_H that decides $\mathcal{L}_H$.

Given an encoding $\rho(M)$ for an arbitrary TM M and an arbitrary input w, the TM M_H constructs a TM $T(M, w)$ that writes w on the tape when it is empty and then simulates M on w, halting if M accepts it. Thus, $T(M, w)$ accepts the empty tape if M halts on w. M_H decides $\mathcal{L}_H$ by constructing $T(M, w)$ and passing it to M_{ET}. (See Fig. 5.13.) The language accepted by $T(M, w)$ includes the empty tape if and only if M halts on w. Thus, M_H decides the halting problem, which as shown earlier cannot be decided. ■

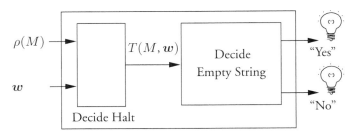

Figure 5.13 Schematic representation of the reduction from $\mathcal{L}_H$ to $\mathcal{L}_{ET}$.

The third unsolvable problem we consider is the **empty set acceptance problem**: Given a Turing machine, we ask if we can tell if the language it accepts is empty. We reduce the halting problem to this language.

$$\mathcal{L}_{\mathrm{EL}} = \{\rho(M) \mid L(M) = \emptyset\}$$

THEOREM 5.8.3 *The language $\mathcal{L}_{\mathrm{EL}}$ is not decidable.*

Proof We reduce $\mathcal{L}_H$ to $\mathcal{L}_{\mathrm{EL}}$, assume that $\mathcal{L}_{\mathrm{EL}}$ is decidable by a TM M_{EL}, and then show that a TM M_H exists that decides $\mathcal{L}_H$, thereby establishing a contradiction.

Given an encoding $\rho(M)$ for an arbitrary TM M and an arbitrary input $\boldsymbol{w}$, the TM M_H constructs a TM $T(M, \boldsymbol{w})$ that accepts the string placed on its tape if it is $\boldsymbol{w}$ and M accepts it; otherwise it enters an infinite loop. M_H can implement $T(M, \boldsymbol{w})$ by entering an infinite loop if its input string is not $\boldsymbol{w}$ and otherwise simulating M on $\boldsymbol{w}$ with a universal Turing machine.

It follows that $T(M, \boldsymbol{w})$ is empty if M does not halt on $\boldsymbol{w}$ and contains $\boldsymbol{w}$ if it does halt. Under the assumption that M_{EL} decides $\mathcal{L}_{\mathrm{EL}}$, M_H can decide $\mathcal{L}_H$ by constructing $T(M, \boldsymbol{w})$ and passing it to M_{EL}, which accepts $T(M, \boldsymbol{w})$ if M does not halt on $\boldsymbol{w}$ and rejects it if it does halt. Thus, M_H decides $\mathcal{L}_H$, a contradiction. ■

The fourth problem we consider is the **regular machine recognition problem**. In this case we ask if a Turing machine exists that can decide from the description of an arbitrary Turing machine M whether the language accepted by M is regular or not:

$$\mathcal{L}_R = \{\rho(M) \mid L(M) \text{ is regular}\}$$

THEOREM 5.8.4 *The language $\mathcal{L}_R$ is not decidable.*

Proof We assume that a TM M_R exists to decide $\mathcal{L}_R$ and show that this implies the existence of a TM M_H that decides $\mathcal{L}_H$, a contradiction. Thus, M_R cannot exist.

Given an encoding $\rho(M)$ for an arbitrary TM M and an arbitrary input $\boldsymbol{w}$, the TM M_H constructs a TM $T(M, \boldsymbol{w})$ that scans its tape. If it finds a string in $\{0^n 1^n \mid n \geq 0\}$, it accepts it; if not, $T(M, \boldsymbol{w})$ erases the tape and simulates M on $\boldsymbol{w}$, halting only if M halts on $\boldsymbol{w}$. (It enters an infinite loop if M halts without accepting $\boldsymbol{w}$.) Thus, $T(M, \boldsymbol{w})$ accepts all strings in $\mathcal{B}^*$ if M halts on $\boldsymbol{w}$ but accepts only strings in $\{0^n 1^n \mid n \geq 0\}$ otherwise. Thus, $T(M, \boldsymbol{w})$ accepts the regular language $\mathcal{B}^*$ if M halts on $\boldsymbol{w}$ and accepts the context-free language $\{0^n 1^n \mid n \geq 0\}$ otherwise. Thus, M_H can be implemented by constructing $T(M, \boldsymbol{w})$ and passing it to M_R, which is presumed to decide $\mathcal{L}_R$. ■

The fifth problem generalizes the above result and is known as **Rice's theorem**. It says that no algorithm exists to determine from the description of a TM whether or not the language it accepts falls into any proper subset of the recursively enumerable languages.

Let **RE** be the set of recursively enumerable languages. For each set $\mathcal{C}$ that is a proper subset of **RE**, define the following language:

$$\mathcal{L}_{\mathcal{C}} = \{\rho(M) \mid L(M) \in \mathcal{C}\}$$

Rice's theorem says that, for all $\mathcal{C}$ such that $\mathcal{C} \neq \emptyset$ and $\mathcal{C} \subset \textbf{RE}$, the language $\mathcal{L}_{\mathcal{C}}$ defined above is undecidable.

THEOREM 5.8.5 (Rice) *Let* $\mathcal{C} \subset \mathbf{RE}$, $\mathcal{C} \neq \emptyset$. *The language* $\mathcal{L}_{\mathcal{C}}$ *is not decidable.*

Proof To prove that $\mathcal{L}_{\mathcal{C}}$ is not decidable, we assume that it is decidable by the TM $M_{\mathcal{C}}$ and show that this implies the existence of a TM M_H that decides $\mathcal{L}_H$, which has been shown previously not to exist. Thus, $M_{\mathcal{C}}$ cannot exist.

We consider two cases, the first in which $\mathcal{B}^*$ is in not $\mathcal{C}$ and the second in which it is in $\mathcal{C}$. In the first case, let L be a language in $\mathcal{C}$. In the second, let L be a language in $\mathbf{RE} - \mathcal{C}$. Since $\mathcal{C}$ is a proper subset of $\mathbf{RE}$ and not empty, there is always a language L such that one of L and $\mathcal{B}^*$ is in $\mathcal{C}$ and the other is in its complement $\mathbf{RE} - \mathcal{C}$.

Given an encoding $\rho(M)$ for an arbitrary TM M and an arbitrary input $\boldsymbol{w}$, the TM M_H constructs a TM $T(M, \boldsymbol{w})$ that scans its tape and if it finds a string in L, it accepts it. If not, $T(M, \boldsymbol{w})$ erases the tape and simulates M on $\boldsymbol{w}$, halting only if M halts on $\boldsymbol{w}$. (It enters an infinite loop if M halts without accepting $\boldsymbol{w}$.) Thus, $T(M, \boldsymbol{w})$ accepts all strings in $\mathcal{B}^*$ if M halts on $\boldsymbol{w}$ but accepts only strings in L otherwise. Thus, $T(M, \boldsymbol{w})$ accepts the regular language $\mathcal{B}^*$ if M halts on $\boldsymbol{w}$ and accepts the language L otherwise. Thus, M_H can be implemented by constructing $T(M, \boldsymbol{w})$ and passing it to $M_{\mathcal{C}}$, which is presumed to decide $\mathcal{L}_{\mathcal{C}}$. ∎

Our last problem is the **self-terminating machine problem**. The question addressed is whether a Turing machine M given a description $\rho(M)$ of itself as input will halt or not. The problem is defined by the following language. We give a direct proof that it is undecidable; that is, we do not reduce some other problem to it.

$$\mathcal{L}_{\mathrm{ST}} = \{\rho(M) \mid M \text{ is self-terminating}\}$$

THEOREM 5.8.6 *The language* $\mathcal{L}_{\mathrm{ST}}$ *is recursively enumerable but not decidable.*

Proof To show that $\mathcal{L}_{\mathrm{ST}}$ is recursively enumerable we exhibit a TM T that accepts strings in $\mathcal{L}_{\mathrm{ST}}$. T makes a copy of its input string $\rho(M)$ and simulates M on $\rho(M)$ by passing $(\rho(M), \rho(M))$ to a universal TM that halts and accepts $\rho(M)$ if it is in $\mathcal{L}_{\mathrm{ST}}$.

To show that $\mathcal{L}_{\mathrm{ST}}$ is not decidable, we assume that it is and arrive at a contradiction. Let M_{ST} decide $\mathcal{L}_{\mathrm{ST}}$. We design a TM M^* that does the following: M^* simulates M_{ST} on the input string $\boldsymbol{w}$. If M_{ST} halts and accepts $\boldsymbol{w}$, M^* enters an infinite loop. If M_{ST} halts and rejects $\boldsymbol{w}$, M^* accepts $\boldsymbol{w}$. (M_{ST} halts on all inputs.)

The new machine M^* is either self-terminating or it is not. If M^* is self-terminating, then on input $\rho(M^*)$, which is an encoding of itself, M^* enters an infinite loop because M_{ST} detects that it is self-terminating. Thus, M^* is not self-terminating. On the other hand, if M^* is not self-terminating, on input $\rho(M^*)$ it halts and accepts $\rho(M^*)$ because M_{ST} detects that it is not self-terminating and enters the accepting halt state. But this contradicts the assumption that M^* is not self-terminating. Since we arrive at a contradiction in both cases, the assumption that $\mathcal{L}_{\mathrm{ST}}$ is decidable must be false. ∎

5.9   Functions Computed by Turing Machines

In this section we introduce the partial recursive functions, a family of functions in which each function is constructed from three basic function types, zero, successor, and projection, and three operations on functions, composition, primitive recursion, and minimalization. Although we do not have the space to show this, the functions computed by Turing machines are exactly the partial recursive functions. In this section, we show one half of this result, namely, that every partial recursive function can be encoded as a RAM program (see Section 3.4.3) that can be executed by Turing machines.

We begin with the primitive recursive functions then describe the partial recursive functions. We then show that partial recursive functions can be realized by RAM programs.

5.9.1 Primitive Recursive Functions

Let $\mathbb{N} = \{0, 1, 2, 3, \ldots\}$ be the set of non-negative integers. The partial recursive functions, $f : \mathbb{N}^n \mapsto \mathbb{N}^m$, map n-tuples of integers over $\mathbb{N}$ to m-tuples of integers in $\mathbb{N}$ for arbitrary n and m. Partial recursive functions may be partial functions. They are constructed from three base function types, the **zero function** $Z : \mathbb{N} \mapsto \mathbb{N}$, where $Z(x) = 0$, the **successor function** $S : \mathbb{N} \mapsto \mathbb{N}$, where $S(x) = x + 1$, and the **projection functions** $U_j^n : \mathbb{N}^n \mapsto \mathbb{N}$, $1 \leq j \leq n$, where $U_j^n(x_1, x_2, \ldots, x_n) = x_j$. These basic functions are combined using a finite number of applications of function composition, primitive recursion, and minimalization.

Function composition is studied in Chapters 2 and 6. A function $f : \mathbb{N}^n \mapsto \mathbb{N}$ of n arguments is defined by the composition of a function $g : \mathbb{N}^m \mapsto \mathbb{N}$ of m arguments with m functions $f_1 : \mathbb{N}^n \mapsto \mathbb{N}$, $f_2 : \mathbb{N}^n \mapsto \mathbb{N}$, $\ldots$, $f_m : \mathbb{N}^n \mapsto \mathbb{N}$, each of n arguments, as follows:

$$f(x_1, x_2, \ldots, x_n) = g(f_1(x_1, x_2, \ldots, x_n), \ldots, f_m(x_1, x_2, \ldots, x_n))$$

A function $f : \mathbb{N}^{n+1} \mapsto \mathbb{N}$ of $n + 1$ arguments is defined by **primitive recursion** from a function $g : \mathbb{N}^n \mapsto \mathbb{N}$ of n arguments and a function $h : \mathbb{N}^{n+2} \mapsto \mathbb{N}$ on $n + 2$ arguments if and only if for all values of $x_1, x_2, \ldots, x_n$ and y in $\mathbb{N}$:

$$f(x_1, x_2, \ldots, x_n, 0) = g(x_1, x_2, \ldots, x_n)$$
$$f(x_1, x_2, \ldots, x_n, y + 1) = h(x_1, x_2, \ldots, x_n, y, f(x_1, x_2, \ldots, x_n, y))$$

In the above definition if $n = 0$, we adopt the convention that the value of f is a constant. Thus, $f(x_1, x_2, \ldots, x_n, k)$ is defined recursively in terms of h and itself with k replaced by $k - 1$ unless $k = 0$.

DEFINITION 5.9.1 *The class of* **primitive recursive functions** *is the smallest class of functions that contains the base functions and is closed under composition and primitive recursion.*

Many functions of interest are primitive recursive. Among these are addition, subtraction, multiplication, and division, as we now show. Let $f_{\text{add}} : \mathbb{N}^2 \mapsto \mathbb{N}$, $f_{\text{sub}} : \mathbb{N}^2 \mapsto \mathbb{N}$, $f_{\text{mult}} : \mathbb{N}^2 \mapsto \mathbb{N}$, and $f_{\text{div}} : \mathbb{N}^2 \mapsto \mathbb{N}$ denote integer addition, subtraction, multiplication, and division.

For the **integer addition function** f_{add} introduce the function $h_1 : \mathbb{N}^3 \mapsto \mathbb{N}$ on three arguments, where h_1 is defined below in terms of the successor and projection functions:

$$h_1(x_1, x_2, x_3) = S(U_3^3(x_1, x_2, x_3))$$

Then, $h_1(x_1, x_2, x_3) = x_3 + 1$. Now define $f_{\text{add}}(x, y)$ using primitive recursion, as follows:

$$f_{\text{add}}(x, 0) = U_1^1(x)$$
$$f_{\text{add}}(x, y + 1) = h_1(x, y, f_{\text{add}}(x, y))$$

The role of h is to carry the values of x and y from one recursive invocation to another. To determine the value of $f_{\mathrm{add}}(x, y)$ from this definition, if $y = 0$, $f_{\mathrm{add}}(x, y) = x$. If $y > 0$, $f_{\mathrm{add}}(x, y) = h_1(x, y - 1, f_{\mathrm{add}}(x, y - 1))$. This in turn causes other recursive invocations of f_{add}. The infix notation $+$ is used for f_{add}; that is, $f_{\mathrm{add}}(x, y) = x + y$.

Because the primitive recursive functions are defined over the non-negative integers, the subtraction function $f_{\mathrm{sub}}(x, y)$ must return the value 0 if y is larger than x, an operation called **proper subtraction**. (Its infix notation is $\dot{-}$ and we write $f_{\mathrm{sub}}(x, y) = x \dot{-} y$.) To define it we introduce the **predecessor function** $P : \mathbb{N} \mapsto \mathbb{N}$; $P(x)$ returns either 0 if $x = 0$ or the integer one less than x:

$$P(0) = 0$$
$$P(x + 1) = U_1^2(x, P(x))$$

We can then define **proper integer subtraction** f_{sub} as follows:

$$f_{\mathrm{sub}}(x, 0) = U_1^1(x)$$
$$f_{\mathrm{sub}}(x, y + 1) = U_3^3(x, y, P(f_{\mathrm{sub}}(x, y)))$$

The value of $f_{\mathrm{sub}}(x, y)$ is x if $y = 0$ and is the predecessor of $f_{\mathrm{sub}}(x, y - 1)$ otherwise. Note that primitive recursion is used in the definition of P and $f_{\mathrm{sub}}(x, y)$.

The **integer multiplication function**, f_{mult}, is defined in terms of the function $h_2 : \mathbb{N}^3 \mapsto \mathbb{N}$:

$$h_2(x_1, x_2, x_3) = f_{\mathrm{add}}(U_1^3(x_1, x_2, x_3),\ U_3^3(x_1, x_2, x_3))$$

Using primitive recursion, we have

$$f_{\mathrm{mult}}(x, 0) = Z(x)$$
$$f_{\mathrm{mult}}(x, y + 1) = h_2(x, y, f_{\mathrm{mult}}(x, y))$$

The value of $f_{\mathrm{mult}}(x, y)$ is zero if $y = 0$ and otherwise is the result of adding x to itself y times. To see this, note that the value of h_2 is the sum of its first and third arguments, x and $f_{\mathrm{mult}}(x, y)$. On each invocation of primitive recursion the value of y is decremented by 1 until the value 0 is reached. The definition of the division function is left as an exercise. (See Problem 5.26.)

Define the function $f_{\mathrm{sign}} : \mathbb{N} \mapsto \mathbb{N}$ so that $f_{\mathrm{sign}}(0) = 0$ and $f_{\mathrm{sign}}(x + 1) = 1$. To show that f_{sign} is primitive recursive it suffices to invoke the projection operator formally. A function with value 0 or 1 is called a **predicate**.

5.9.2 Partial Recursive Functions

The partial recursive functions are obtained by extending the primitive recursive functions to include minimalization. **Minimalization** defines a function $f : \mathbb{N}^n \mapsto \mathbb{N}$ in terms of a second function $g : \mathbb{N}^{n+1} \mapsto \mathbb{N}$ by letting $f(\boldsymbol{x})$ be the smallest integer $y \in \mathbb{N}$ such that $g(\boldsymbol{x}, y) = 0$ and $g(\boldsymbol{x}, z)$ is defined for all $z \leq y$, $z \in \mathbb{N}$. Note that if $g(\boldsymbol{x}, z)$ is not defined for all $z \leq y$, then $f(\boldsymbol{x})$ is not defined. Thus, minimalization can result in partial functions.

DEFINITION 5.9.2 *The set of* **partial recursive functions** *is the smallest set of functions containing the base functions that is closed under composition, primitive recursion, and minimalization.*

A partial recursive function that is defined for all points in its domain is called a **recursive function**.

5.9.3   Partial Recursive Functions are RAM-Computable

It is not difficult to see that every partial recursive function can be described by a program in the RAM assembly language of Section 3.4.3. For example, to compute the zero function, $Z(x)$, it suffices for a RAM program to clear register R_1. To compute the successor function, $S(x)$, it suffices to increment register R_1. Similarly, to compute the projection function U_j^n, one need only load register R_1 with the contents of register R_j. Function composition it is straightforward: one need only insure that the functions f_j, $1 \leq j \leq m$, deposit their values in registers that are accessed by g. Similar constructions are possible for primitive recursion and minimalization. (See Problems 5.29, 5.30, and 5.31.)

- -

Problems

THE STANDARD TURING MACHINE MODEL

5.1   Show that the standard Turing machine model of Section 5.1 and the model of Section 3.7 are equivalent in that one can simulate the other.

PROGRAMMING THE TURING MACHINE

5.2   Describe a Turing machine that generates the binary strings in lexicographical order. The first few strings in this ordering are 0, 1, 00, 01, 10, 11, 000, 001, ...

5.3   Describe a Turing machine recognizing $\{x^i y^j x^k \mid i, j, k \geq 1 \text{ and } k = i \cdot j\}$.

5.4   Describe a Turing machine that computes the function whose value on input $a^i b^j$ is c^k, where $k = i \cdot j$.

5.5   Describe a Turing machine that accepts the string $(\boldsymbol{u}, \boldsymbol{v})$ if $\boldsymbol{u}$ is a substring of $\boldsymbol{v}$.

5.6   The **element distinctness language**, L_{ed}, consists of binary strings no two of which are the same; that is, $L_{\mathrm{ed}} = \{2\boldsymbol{w}_1 2 \ldots 2\boldsymbol{w}_k 2 \mid \boldsymbol{w}_1 \in \mathcal{B}^* \text{ and } \boldsymbol{w}_i \neq \boldsymbol{w}_j, \text{ for } i \neq j\}$. Describe a Turing machine that accepts this language.

EXTENSIONS TO THE STANDARD TURING MACHINE MODEL

5.7   Given a Turing machine with a double-ended tape, show how it can be simulated by one with a single-ended tape.

5.8   Show equivalence between the standard Turing machine and the one-tape **double-headed** Turing machine with two heads that can move independently on its one tape.

5.9   Show that a pushdown automaton with two pushdown tapes is equivalent to a Turing machine.

5.10   Figure 5.14 shows a representation of a Turing machine with a two-dimensional tape whose head can move one step vertically or horizontally. Give a complete definition of a two-dimensional TM and sketch a proof that it can be simulated by a standard TM.

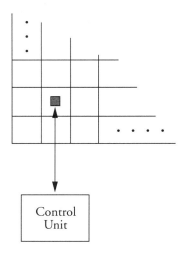

Figure 5.14 A schematic representation of a two-dimensional Turing machine.

5.11 By analogy with the construction given in Section 3.9.7, show that every deterministic T-step multi-tape Turing machine computation can be simulated on a two-tape Turing machine in $O(T \log T)$ steps.

PHRASE-STRUCTURE LANGUAGES AND TURING MACHINES

5.12 Give a detailed design of a Turing machine recognizing $\{a^n b^n c^n \mid n \geq 1\}$.

5.13 Use the method of Theorem 5.4.1 to construct a phrase-structure grammar generating $\{a^n b^n c^n \mid n \geq 1\}$.

5.14 Design a Turing machine recognizing the language $\{0^{2^i} \mid i \geq 1\}$.

UNIVERSAL TURING MACHINES

5.15 Using the description of Section 5.5, give a complete description of a universal Turing machine.

5.16 Construct a universal TM that has only two non-accepting states.

DECIDABLE PROBLEMS

5.17 Show that the following languages are decidable:

    a) $L = \{\rho(M), \boldsymbol{w} \mid M$ is a DFSM that accepts the input string $\boldsymbol{w}\}$

    b) $L = \{\rho(M) \mid M$ is a DFSM and $L(M) = \emptyset\}$

5.18 The **symmetric difference** between sets A and B is defined by $(A - B) \cup (B - A)$, where $A - B = A \cap \overline{B}$. Use the symmetric difference to show that the following language is decidable:

$$\mathcal{L}_{\text{EQ\_FSM}} = \{\rho(M_1), \rho(M_2) \mid M_1 \text{ and } M_2 \text{ are FSMs recognizing the same language}\}$$

5.19 Show that the following language is decidable:

$$L = \{\rho(G), \boldsymbol{w} \mid \rho(G) \text{ encodes a CFG } G \text{ that generates } \boldsymbol{w}\}$$

Hint: How long is a derivation of $\boldsymbol{w}$ if G is in Chomsky normal form?

5.20 Show that the following language is decidable:

$$L = \{\rho(G) \mid \rho(G) \text{ encodes a CFG } G \text{ for which } L(G) = \emptyset\}$$

Hint: Can the derivation of terminal strings be reversed?

5.21 Let $L_1, L_2 \in \mathbf{P}$ where $\mathbf{P}$ is the class of polynomial-time problems (see Definition 3.7.2). Show that the following statements hold:

a) $L_1 \cup L_2 \in \mathbf{P}$
b) $L_1 L_2 \in \mathbf{P}$, where $L_1 L_2$ is the concatenation of L_1 and L_2
c) $\overline{L_1} \in \mathbf{P}$

5.22 Let $L_1 \in \mathbf{P}$. Show that $L_1^* \in \mathbf{P}$.

Hint: Try using dynamic programming, the algorithmic concept illustrated by the parsing algorithm of Theorem 4.11.2.

UNSOLVABLE PROBLEMS

5.23 Show that the problem of determining whether an arbitrary TM starting with a blank tape will ever halt is unsolvable.

5.24 Show that the following language is undecidable:

$$L_{\text{EQ}} = \{\rho(M_1), \rho(M_2) \mid L(M_1) = L(M_2)\}$$

5.25 Determine which of the following problems are solvable and unsolvable. Defend your conclusions.

a) $\{\rho(M), \boldsymbol{w}, p \mid M \text{ reaches state } p \text{ on input } \boldsymbol{w} \text{ from its initial state}\}$
b) $\{\rho(M), p \mid \text{there is a configuration } [u_1 \ldots u_m \boldsymbol{q} v_1 \ldots v_n] \text{ yielding a configuration containing } p\}$
c) $\{\rho(M), a \mid M \text{ writes character } a \text{ when started on the empty tape}\}$
d) $\{\rho(M), a \mid M \text{ writes a non-blank character when started on the empty tape}\}$
e) $\{\rho(M), \boldsymbol{w} \mid \text{on input } \boldsymbol{w} \ M \text{ moves its head to the left}\}$

FUNCTIONS COMPUTED BY TURING MACHINES

5.26 Define the integer division function $f_{\text{div}} : \mathbf{N}^2 \mapsto \mathbf{N}$ using primitive recursion.

5.27 Show that the function $f_{\text{remain}} : \mathbf{N}^2 \mapsto \mathbf{N}$ that provides the remainder of x after division by y is a primitive recursive function.

5.28 Show that the factorial function $x!$ is primitive recursive.

5.29 Write a RAM program (see Section 3.4.3) to realize the composition operation.

5.30 Write a RAM program (see Section 3.4.3) to realize the primitive recursion operation.

5.31 Write a RAM program (see Section 3.4.3) to realize the minimalization operation.

Chapter Notes

Alan Turing introduced the Turing machine, gave an example of a universal machine and demonstrated the unsolvability of the halting problem in [332]. A similar model was independently developed by Post [249]. Chomsky [69] demonstrated the equivalence of phrase-structure languages. Rice's theorem is presented in [274].

Church gave a formal model of computation in [72]. The equivalence between the primitive recursive functions and the Turing computable functions was shown by Kleene [165].

For a more extensive introduction to Turing machines, see the books by Hopcroft and Ullman [140] and Lewis and Papadimitriou [197].

C H A P T E R

6

Algebraic and Combinatorial Circuits

In this chapter we develop algebraic and combinatorial circuits for a variety of generally non-Boolean problems, including multiplication and inversion of matrices, convolution, the discrete Fourier transform, and sorting networks. These problems are used primarily to illustrate concepts developed in later chapters, so that this chapter may be used for reference when studying those chapters.

For each of the problems examined here the natural algorithms are straight-line and the graphs are directed and acyclic; that is, they are circuits. Not only are straight-line algorithms the ones typically used for these problems, but in some cases they are the best possible.

The quality of the circuits developed here is measured by circuit size, the number of circuit operations, and circuit depth, the length of the longest path between input and output vertices. Circuit size is a measure of the work necessary to execute the corresponding straight-line program. Circuit depth is a measure of the minimal time needed for a problem on a parallel machine.

For some problems, such as matrix inversion, we give serial (large-depth) as well as parallel (small-depth) circuits. The parallel circuits generally require considerably more circuit elements than the corresponding serial circuits.

6.1 Straight-Line Programs

Straight-line programs (SLP) are defined in Section 2.2. Each SLP step is an input, computation, or output step. The notation $(s\ \text{READ}\ x)$ indicates that the sth step is an input step on which the value x is read. The notation $(s\ \text{OUTPUT}\ i)$ indicates that the result of the ith step is to be provided as output. Finally, the notation $(s\ \text{OP}\ i\ \ldots\ k)$ indicates that the sth step computes the value of the operator OP on the results generated at steps $i, \ldots, k$. We require that $s > i, \ldots, k$ so that the result produced at step s depends only on the results produced at earlier steps. In this chapter we consider SLPs in which the inputs and operators have values over a set $\mathcal{A}$ that is generally not binary. Thus, the circuits considered here are generally not logic circuits. The basis Ω for an SLP is the set of operators it uses. A **circuit** is the graph of a straight-line program. By its nature this graph is directed and acyclic.

An example of a straight-line program that computes the fast Fourier transform (FFT) on four inputs is given below. (The FFT is introduced in Section 6.7.3.) Here the function $f_{+,\,\alpha}(a, b) = a + b\alpha$ where α is a power of a constant ω that is a principal nth root of unity of a commutative ring $\mathcal{R}$. (See Section 6.7.1.) The arguments a and b are variables with values in $\mathcal{R}$.

$$
\begin{array}{ll}
(1 \quad \text{READ} \quad a_0) & (7 \quad f_{+,\,\omega^0} \quad 3 \quad 4) \\
(2 \quad \text{READ} \quad a_2) & (8 \quad f_{+,\,\omega^2} \quad 3 \quad 4) \\
(3 \quad \text{READ} \quad a_1) & (9 \quad f_{+,\,\omega^0} \quad 5 \quad 7) \\
(4 \quad \text{READ} \quad a_3) & (10 \quad f_{+,\,\omega^1} \quad 6 \quad 8) \\
(5 \quad f_{+,\,\omega^0} \quad 1 \quad 2) & (11 \quad f_{+,\,\omega^2} \quad 5 \quad 7) \\
(6 \quad f_{+,\,\omega^2} \quad 1 \quad 2) & (12 \quad f_{+,\,\omega^3} \quad 6 \quad 8)
\end{array}
$$

The graph of the above SLP is the familiar FFT **butterfly graph** shown in Fig. 6.1. Assignment statements are associated with vertices of in-degree zero and operator statements are associated with other vertices. We attach the name of the operator or variable associated with each step to the corresponding vertex in the graph. We often suppress the unique indices of vertices, although they are retained in Fig. 6.1.

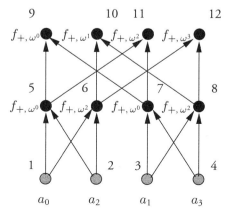

Figure 6.1 The FFT butterfly graph on four inputs.

The function g_s is associated with the sth step. The identity function with value v is associated with the assignment statement $(r \; \text{READ} \; v)$. Associated with the computation step $(s \; \text{OP} \; i \; \ldots \; k)$ is the function $g_s = \text{OP}(g_i, \ldots, g_k)$, where $g_i, \ldots, g_k$ are the functions computed at the steps on which the sth step depends. If a straight-line program has n inputs and m outputs, it computes a function $f : \mathcal{A}^n \mapsto \mathcal{A}^m$. If $s_1, s_2, \ldots, s_m$ are the output steps, then $f = (g_{s_1}, g_{s_2}, \ldots, g_{s_m})$. The function computed by a circuit is the function computed by the corresponding straight-line program.

In the example above, $g_{11} = f_{+, \, \omega^2}(g_5, g_7) = g_5 + g_7\omega^2$, where $g_5 = f_{+, \, \omega^0}(g_1, g_2) = a_0 + a_2\omega^0 = a_0 + a_2$ and $g_7 = f_{+, \, \omega^0}(g_3, g_4) = a_1 + a_3\omega^0 = a_1 + a_3$. Thus,

$$g_{11} = a_0 + a_1\omega^2 + a_2 + a_3\omega^2$$

which is the value of the polynomial $p(x)$ at $x = \omega^2$ when $\omega^4 = 1$:

$$p(x) = a_0 + a_1 x + a_2 x^2 + a_3 x^3$$

The **size** of a circuit is the number of operator statements it contains. Its **depth** is the length of (number of edges on) the longest path from an input to an output vertex. The **basis** Ω is the set of operators used in the circuit. The size and depth of the smallest and shallowest circuits for a function f over the basis Ω are denoted $C_\Omega(f)$ and $D_\Omega(f)$, respectively. In this chapter we derive upper bounds on the size and depth of circuits.

6.2 Mathematical Preliminaries

In this section we introduce rings and matrices, two concepts that are widely used in this chapter.

6.2.1 Rings

A ring is an algebraic system that consists of a set and two operations called addition and multiplication that obey a small set of rules.

DEFINITION 6.2.1 *A* **ring** $\mathcal{R}$ *is a five-tuple* $(R, +, *, \mathbf{0}, \mathbf{1})$, *where* R *is* **closed** *under* **addition** $+$ *and* **multiplication** $*$ *(that is,* $+ : R^2 \mapsto R$ *and* $* : R^2 \mapsto R$*) and* $+$ *and* $*$ *are associative (for all* $a, b, c \in R$, $a + (b + c) = (a + b) + c$ *and* $a * (b * c) = (a * b) * c$*). Also,* $\mathbf{0}, \mathbf{1} \in R$, *where* $\mathbf{0}$ *is the* **identity under addition** *(for all* $a \in R$, $a + \mathbf{0} = \mathbf{0} + a = a$*) and* $\mathbf{1}$ *is the* **identity under multiplication** *(for all* $a \in R$, $a * \mathbf{1} = \mathbf{1} * a = a$*). In addition,* $\mathbf{0}$ *is an* **annihilator under multiplication** *(for all* $a \in R$, $a * \mathbf{0} = \mathbf{0} * a = \mathbf{0}$*). Every element of* R *has an* **additive inverse** *(for all* $a \in R$, *there exists an element* $-a$ *such that* $(-a) + a = a + (-a) = \mathbf{0}$*). Finally, addition is* **commutative** *(for all* $a, b \in R$, $a + b = b + a$*) and multiplication* **distributes over addition** *(for all* $a, b, c \in R$, $a * (b + c) = (a * b) + (a * c)$ *and* $(b + c) * a = (b * a) + (c * a)$*).*

A ring is **commutative** *if multiplication is commutative (for all* $a, b \in R$, $a * b = b * a$*).*

Let $\mathbb{N}$ be the natural numbers (the set of non-negative integers). Then $(\mathbb{N}, +, *, 0, 1)$, where $+$ and $*$ denote integer addition and multiplication and 0 and 1 are the first two integers, is a ring. (See Problem 6.1.) In fact, it is a commutative ring. Similarly, the system $(\{0, 1\}, +, *, 0, 1)$, where $+$ is addition modulo 2 (for all $a, b \in \{0, 1\}$, $a + b$ is the remainder after division by 2 or the EXCLUSIVE OR operation) and $*$ is the AND operation, is a commutative ring, as the reader can show. A third commutative ring is the integers modulo p together with the operations of addition and multiplication modulo p. (See Problem 6.2.) The ring of matrices introduced in the next section is not commutative. Some important commutative rings are introduced in Section 6.7.1.

6.2.2 Matrices

A **matrix over a set** R is a rectangular array of elements drawn from R consisting of some number m of rows and some number n of columns. Rows are indexed by integers from the set $\{1, 2, 3, \ldots, m\}$ and columns are indexed by integers from the set $\{1, 2, 3, \ldots, n\}$. The entry in the ith row and jth column of A is denoted $a_{i,j}$, as suggested in the following example:

$$
A = [a_{i,j}] = \begin{bmatrix} a_{1,1} & a_{1,2} & a_{1,3} & a_{1,4} \\ a_{2,1} & a_{2,2} & a_{2,3} & a_{2,4} \\ a_{3,1} & a_{3,2} & a_{3,3} & a_{3,4} \end{bmatrix} = \begin{bmatrix} 1 & 2 & 3 & 4 \\ 5 & 6 & 7 & 8 \\ 9 & 10 & 11 & 12 \end{bmatrix}
$$

Thus, $a_{2,3} = 7$ and $a_{3,1} = 9$.

The **transpose** of a matrix A, denoted A^T, is the matrix obtained from A by exchanging rows and columns, as shown below for the matrix A above:

$$
A^T = \begin{bmatrix} 1 & 5 & 9 \\ 2 & 6 & 10 \\ 3 & 7 & 11 \\ 4 & 8 & 12 \end{bmatrix}
$$

Clearly, the transpose of the transpose of a matrix A, $(A^T)^T$, is the matrix A.

A **column n-vector** $\boldsymbol{x}$ is a matrix containing one column and n rows, for example:

$$
\boldsymbol{x} = \begin{bmatrix} x_1 \\ x_2 \\ \vdots \\ x_n \end{bmatrix} = \begin{bmatrix} 5 \\ 6 \\ \vdots \\ 8 \end{bmatrix}
$$

A **row m-vector** $\boldsymbol{y}$ is a matrix containing one row and m columns, for example:

$$
\boldsymbol{y} = [y_1, y_2, \ldots, y_m] = [1, 5, \ldots, 9]
$$

The transpose of a row vector is a column vector and vice versa.

A **square matrix** is an $n \times n$ matrix for some integer n. The **main diagonal** of an $n \times n$ square matrix A is the set of elements $\{a_{1,1}, a_{2,2}, \ldots, a_{n-1,n-1}, a_{n,n}\}$. The diagonal below (above) the main diagonal is the elements $\{a_{2,1}, a_{3,2}, \ldots, a_{n,n-1}\}$ ($\{a_{1,2}, a_{2,3}, \ldots, a_{n-1,n}\}$). The $n \times n$ **identity matrix**, I_n, is a square $n \times n$ matrix with value 1 on the main diagonal and 0 elsewhere. The $n \times n$ **zero matrix**, 0_n, has value 0 in each position. A matrix is **upper (lower) triangular** if all elements below (above) the main diagonal are 0. A square matrix A is **symmetric** if $A = A^T$, that is, $a_{i,j} = a_{j,i}$ for all $1 \leq i, j \leq n$.

The **scalar product** of a scalar $c \in R$ and an $n \times m$ matrix A over R, denoted cA, has value $ca_{i,j}$ in row i and column j.

The **matrix-vector product** between an $m \times n$ matrix A and a column n-vector x is the column m-vector b below:

$$b = Ax = \begin{bmatrix} a_{1,1} & a_{1,2} & \cdots & a_{1,n} \\ a_{2,1} & a_{2,2} & \cdots & a_{2,n} \\ \vdots & \vdots & \ddots & \vdots \\ a_{m,1} & a_{n-1,2} & \cdots & a_{m-1,n} \\ a_{m,1} & a_{n,2} & \cdots & a_{m,n} \end{bmatrix} \times \begin{bmatrix} x_1 \\ x_2 \\ \vdots \\ x_{n-1} \\ x_n \end{bmatrix}$$

$$= \begin{bmatrix} a_{1,1} * x_1 & + & a_{1,2} * x_2 & + & \cdots & + & a_{1,n} * x_n \\ a_{2,1} * x_1 & + & a_{2,2} * x_2 & + & \cdots & + & a_{2,n} * x_n \\ \vdots & & \vdots & & \ddots & & \vdots \\ a_{m-1,1} * x_1 & + & a_{m-1,2} * x_2 & + & \cdots & + & a_{m-1,n} * x_n \\ a_{m,1} * x_1 & + & a_{m,2} * x_2 & + & \cdots & + & a_{m,n} * x_n \end{bmatrix}$$

Thus, b_j is defined as follows for $1 \leq j \leq n$:

$$b_j = a_{i,1} * x_1 + a_{i,2} * x_2 + \cdots + a_{i,m} * x_m$$

The matrix-vector product between a row m-vector x and an $m \times n$ matrix A is the row n-vector b below:

$$b = [b_i] = xA$$

where for $1 \leq i \leq n$ b_i satisfies

$$b_i = x_1 * a_{1,i} + x_2 * a_{2,i} + \cdots + x_m * a_{m,i}$$

The special case of a matrix-vector product between a row n-vector, x, and a column n vector, y, denoted $x \cdot y$ and defined below, is called the **inner product** of the two vectors:

$$x \cdot y = \sum_{i=1}^{n} x_i * y_i$$

If the entries of the $n \times n$ matrix A and the column n-vectors x and b shown below are drawn from a ring $\mathcal{R}$ and A and b are given, then the following matrix equation defines a **linear system** of n equations in the n unknowns x:

$$Ax = b$$

An example of a linear system of four equations in four unknowns is

$$\begin{array}{rcrcrcrcr} 1 * x_1 & + & 2 * x_2 & + & 3 * x_3 & + & 4 * x_4 & = & 17 \\ 5 * x_1 & + & 6 * x_2 & + & 7 * x_3 & + & 8 * x_4 & = & 18 \\ 9 * x_1 & + & 10 * x_2 & + & 11 * x_3 & + & 12 * x_4 & = & 19 \\ 13 * x_1 & + & 14 * x_2 & + & 15 * x_3 & + & 16 * x_4 & = & 20 \end{array}$$

It can be expressed as follows:

$$
\begin{bmatrix} 1 & 2 & 3 & 4 \\ 5 & 6 & 7 & 8 \\ 9 & 10 & 11 & 12 \\ 13 & 14 & 15 & 16 \end{bmatrix} \begin{bmatrix} x_1 \\ x_2 \\ x_3 \\ x_4 \end{bmatrix} = \begin{bmatrix} 17 \\ 18 \\ 19 \\ 20 \end{bmatrix}
$$

Solving a linear system, when it is possible, consists of finding values for $\boldsymbol{x}$ given values for A and $\boldsymbol{b}$. (See Section 6.6.)

Consider the set of $m \times n$ matrices whose entries are drawn from a ring $\mathcal{R}$. The **matrix addition function** $f_{A+B}^{(m,n)} : \mathcal{R}^{2mn} \mapsto \mathcal{R}^{mn}$ on two $m \times n$ matrices $A = [a_{i,j}]$ and $B = [b_{i,j}]$ generates a matrix $C = f_{A+B}^{(m,n)}(A, B) = A +_{m,n} B = [c_{i,j}]$, where $+_{m,n}$ is the infix matrix addition operator and $c_{i,j}$ is defined as

$$
c_{i,j} = a_{i,j} + b_{i,j}
$$

The straight-line program based on this equation uses one instance of the ring addition operator $+$ for each entry in C. It follows that over the basis $\{+\}$, $C_+(f_{A+B}^{(m,n)}) = mn$ and $D_+(f_{A+B}^{(m,n)}) = 1$. Two special cases of matrix addition are the addition of square matrices ($m = n$), denoted $+_n$, and the addition of row or column vectors that are either $1 \times n$ or $m \times 1$ matrices.

The **matrix multiplication function** $f_{A\times B}^{(n)} : \mathcal{R}^{(m+p)n} \mapsto \mathcal{R}^{mp}$ multiplies an $m \times n$ matrix $A = [a_{i,j}]$ by an $n \times p$ matrix $B = [b_{i,j}]$ to produce the $m \times p$ matrix $C = f_{A\times B}^{(n)}(A, B) = A \times_n B = [c_{i,j}]$, where

$$
c_{i,j} = \sum_{k=1}^{n} a_{i,k} * b_{k,j} \tag{6.1}
$$

and $\times_n$ is the infix matrix multiplication operator. The subscript on $\times_n$ is usually dropped when the dimensions of the matrices are understood. The **standard matrix multiplication algorithm** for multiplying an $m \times n$ matrix A by an $n \times p$ matrix B forms mp **inner products** of the kind shown in equation (6.1). Thus, it uses mnp instances of the ring multiplication operator and $m(n-1)p$ instances of the ring addition operator.

A fast algorithm for matrix multiplication is given in Section 6.3.1. It is now straightforward to show the following result. (See Problem 6.4.)

THEOREM 6.2.1 *Let $M_{n \times n}$ be the set of $n \times n$ matrices over a ring $\mathcal{R}$. The system $\mathcal{M}_{n \times n} = (M_{n \times n}, +_n, \times_n, 0_n, I_n)$, where $+_n$ and $\times_n$ are the matrix addition and multiplication operators and 0_n and I_n are the $n \times n$ zero and identity matrices, is a ring.*

The ring of matrices $\mathcal{M}_{n \times n}$ is not a commutative ring because matrix multiplication is not commutative. For example, the following two matrices do not commute, that is, $AB \neq BA$:

$$
A = \begin{bmatrix} 0 & 1 \\ 1 & 0 \end{bmatrix} \qquad B = \begin{bmatrix} 1 & 0 \\ 0 & -1 \end{bmatrix}
$$

A **linear combination** of a subset of the rows of an $n \times m$ matrix A is a sum of scalar products of the rows in this subset. A linear combination is **non-zero** if the sum of the scalar product is not the zero vector. A set of rows of a matrix A is **linearly independent** if all linear combinations are non-zero except when each scalar is zero.

The **rank of an** $n \times m$ **matrix** A, $f_{\text{rank}}^{(n)} : \mathcal{R}^{n^2} \mapsto \mathbb{N}$, is the maximum number of linearly independent rows of A. It is also the maximum number of linearly independent columns of A. (See Problem 6.5.) We write $\text{rank}(A) = f_{\text{rank}}^{(n)}(A)$. An $n \times n$ matrix A is **non-singular** if $\text{rank}(A) = n$.

If an $n \times n$ matrix A is non-singular, it has an **inverse** A^{-1} that is an $n \times n$ matrix with the following properties:

$$AA^{-1} = A^{-1}A = I_n$$

where I_n is the $n \times n$ identity matrix. That is, there is a (partial) inverse function $f_{\text{inv}}^{(n)} : \mathcal{R}^{n^2} \mapsto \mathcal{R}^{n^2}$ that is defined for non-singular square matrices A such that $f_{\text{inv}}^{(n)}(A) = A^{-1}$. $f_{\text{inv}}^{(n)}$ is partial because it is not defined for singular matrices. Below we exhibit a matrix and its inverse over the ring of positive and negative integers:

$$\begin{bmatrix} 1 & 1 \\ -1 & 1 \end{bmatrix}^{-1} = \begin{bmatrix} 1 & -1 \\ 1 & 1 \end{bmatrix}$$

Algorithms for matrix inversion are given in Section 6.5.

We now show that the inverse $(AB)^{-1}$ of the product AB of two invertible matrices, A and B, over a ring $\mathcal{R}$ is the product of their inverses in reverse order.

LEMMA 6.2.1 *Let A and B be invertible square matrices over a ring $\mathcal{R}$. Then the following relationship holds:*

$$(AB)^{-1} = B^{-1}A^{-1}$$

Proof To show that $(AB)^{-1} = B^{-1}A^{-1}$, we multiply AB either on the left or right by $B^{-1}A^{-1}$ to produce the identity matrix:

$$\begin{aligned} AB(AB)^{-1} &= ABB^{-1}A^{-1} = A(BB^{-1})A^{-1} = AA^{-1} = I \\ (AB)^{-1}AB &= B^{-1}A^{-1}AB = B^{-1}(A^{-1}A)B = B^{-1}B = I \quad \blacksquare \end{aligned}$$

The transpose of the product of an $m \times n$ matrix A and an $n \times p$ matrix B over a ring $\mathcal{R}$ is the product of their transposes in reverse order:

$$(A\,B)^T = B^T\,A^T$$

(See Problem 6.6.) In particular, the following identity holds for an $m \times n$ matrix A and a column n-vector $\boldsymbol{x}$:

$$\boldsymbol{x}^T A^T = (A\boldsymbol{x})^T$$

A **block matrix** is a matrix in which each entry is a matrix with fixed dimensions. For example, when n is even it may be convenient to view an $n \times n$ matrix as a 2×2 matrix whose four entries are $(n/2) \times (n/2)$ matrices.

Two special types of matrix that are frequently encountered are the Toeplitz and circulant matrices. An $n \times n$ **Toeplitz matrix** T has the property that the entries of its (i, j) entry

$t_{i,j} = a_r$ for $j = i - n + 1 + r$ and $0 \leq r \leq 2n - 2$. A generic Toeplitz matrix T is shown below:

$$T = \begin{bmatrix} a_{n-1} & a_n & a_{n+1} & \cdots & a_{2n-2} \\ a_{n-2} & a_{n-1} & a_n & \cdots & a_{2n-3} \\ a_{n-3} & a_{n-2} & a_{n-1} & \cdots & a_{2n-4} \\ \vdots & \vdots & \vdots & \ddots & \vdots \\ a_0 & a_1 & a_2 & \cdots & a_{n-1} \end{bmatrix}$$

An $n \times n$ **circulant matrix** C has the property that the entries on the kth row are a right cyclic shift by $k - 1$ places of the entries on the first row, as suggested below.

$$C = \begin{bmatrix} a_0 & a_1 & a_2 & \cdots & a_{n-1} \\ a_{n-1} & a_0 & a_1 & \cdots & a_{n-2} \\ a_{n-2} & a_{n-1} & a_0 & \cdots & a_{n-3} \\ \vdots & \vdots & \vdots & \ddots & \vdots \\ a_1 & a_2 & a_3 & \cdots & a_0 \end{bmatrix}$$

The circulant is a type of Toeplitz matrix. Thus the function defined by the product of a Toeplitz matrix and a vector contains as a subfunction the function defined by the product of a circulant matrix and a vector. Consequently, any algorithm to multiply a vector by a Toeplitz matrix can be used to multiply a circulant by a vector.

As stated in Section 2.11, a **permutation** $\pi : \mathcal{R}^n \mapsto \mathcal{R}^n$ of an n-tuple $\boldsymbol{x} = (x_1, x_2, \ldots, x_n)$ over the set $\mathcal{R}$ is a rearrangement $\pi(\boldsymbol{x}) = (x_{\pi(1)}, x_{\pi(2)}, \ldots, x_{\pi(n)})$ of the components of $\boldsymbol{x}$. A $n \times n$ **permutation matrix** P has entries from the set $\{0, 1\}$ (here 0 and 1 are the identities under addition and multiplication for a ring $\mathcal{R}$) with the property that each row and column of P has exactly one instance of 1. (See the example below.) Let A be an $n \times n$ matrix. Then AP contains the columns of A in a permuted order determined by P. A similar statement applies to PA. Shown below is a permutation matrix P and the result of multiplying it on the right by a matrix A on the left. In this case P interchanges the first two columns of A.

$$\begin{bmatrix} 1 & 2 & 3 & 4 \\ 5 & 6 & 7 & 8 \\ 9 & 10 & 11 & 12 \\ 13 & 14 & 15 & 16 \end{bmatrix} \begin{bmatrix} 0 & 1 & 0 & 0 \\ 1 & 0 & 0 & 0 \\ 0 & 0 & 1 & 0 \\ 0 & 0 & 0 & 1 \end{bmatrix} = \begin{bmatrix} 2 & 1 & 3 & 4 \\ 6 & 5 & 7 & 8 \\ 10 & 9 & 11 & 12 \\ 14 & 13 & 15 & 16 \end{bmatrix}$$

6.3 Matrix Multiplication

Matrix multiplication is defined in Section 6.2. The **standard matrix multiplication algorithm** computes the matrix product using the formula for $c_{i,j}$ given in (6.1). It performs nmp multiplications and $n(m - 1)p$ additions. As shown in Section 6.3.1, however, matrices can be multiplied with many fewer operations.

Boolean matrix multiplication is matrix multiplication for matrices over $\mathcal{B}$ when $+$ denotes OR and $*$ denotes AND. Another example is matrix multiplication over the set of integers modulo a prime p, a set that forms a finite field under addition and multiplication modulo p. (See Problem 6.3.)

In the next section we describe Strassen's algorithm, a straight-line program realizable by a logarithmic-depth circuit of size $O(n^{2.807})$. This is not the final word on matrix multiplication, however. Winograd and Coppersmith [81] have improved the bound to $O(n^{2.38})$. Despite this progress, the smallest asymptotic bound on matrix multiplication remains unknown.

Since later in this chapter we design algorithms that make use of matrix multiplication, it behooves us to make the following definition concerning the number of ring operations to multiply two $n \times n$ matrices over a ring $\mathcal{R}$.

DEFINITION 6.3.1 *Let $K \geq 1$. Then $M_{\mathrm{matrix}}(n, K)$ is the size of the smallest circuit of depth $K \log_2 n$ over a ring $\mathcal{R}$ for the multiplication of two $n \times n$ matrices.*

The following assumptions on the rate of growth of $M_{\mathrm{matrix}}(n, K)$ with n make subsequent analysis easier. They are satisfied by Strassen's algorithm.

ASSUMPTION 6.3.1 *We assume that for all c satisfying $0 \leq c \leq 1$ and $n \geq 1$,*

$$M_{\mathrm{matrix}}(cn, K) \leq c^2 M_{\mathrm{matrix}}(n, K)$$

ASSUMPTION 6.3.2 *We assume there exists an integer $n_0 > 0$ such that, for $n \geq n_0$,*

$$2n^2 \leq M_{\mathrm{matrix}}(n, K)$$

6.3.1 Strassen's Algorithm

Strassen [313] has developed a fast algorithm for multiplying two square matrices over a ring $\mathcal{R}$. This algorithm makes use of the additive inverse of ring elements to reduce the total number of operations performed.

Let n be even. Given two $n \times n$ matrices, A and B, we write them and their product C as 2×2 matrices whose components are $(n/2) \times (n/2)$ matrices:

$$C = \begin{bmatrix} u & v \\ w & x \end{bmatrix} = A \times B = \begin{bmatrix} a & b \\ c & d \end{bmatrix} \times \begin{bmatrix} e & f \\ g & h \end{bmatrix}$$

Using the standard algorithm, we can form C with eight multiplications and four additions of $(n/2) \times (n/2)$ matrices. Strassen's algorithm exchanges one of these multiplications for 10 such additions. Since one multiplication of two $(n/2) \times (n/2)$ matrices is much more costly than an addition of two such matrices, a large reduction in the number of operations is obtained. We now derive Strassen's algorithm.

Let D be the the 4×4 matrix shown below whose entries are $(n/2) \times (n/2)$ matrices. (Thus, D is a $2n \times 2n$ matrix.)

$$D = \begin{bmatrix} a & b & 0 & 0 \\ c & d & 0 & 0 \\ 0 & 0 & a & b \\ 0 & 0 & c & d \end{bmatrix}$$

The entries u, v, w, and x of the product $A \times B$ can also be produced by the following matrix-vector product:

$$\begin{bmatrix} u \\ w \\ v \\ x \end{bmatrix} = D \times \begin{bmatrix} e \\ g \\ f \\ h \end{bmatrix}$$

We now write D as a sum of seven matrices as shown in Fig. 6.2; that is,

$$D = A_1 + A_2 + A_3 + A_4 + A_5 + A_6 + A_7$$

Let $P_1, P_2, \ldots, P_7$ be the products of the $(n/2) \times (n/2)$ matrices

$$
\begin{aligned}
P_1 &= (a + d) \times (e + h) & P_5 &= (a + b) \times h \\
P_2 &= (c + d) \times e & P_6 &= (-a + c) \times (e + f) \\
P_3 &= a \times (f - h) & P_7 &= (b - d) \times (g + h) \\
P_4 &= d \times (-e + g)
\end{aligned}
$$

$$A_1 = \begin{bmatrix} a+d & 0 & 0 & a+d \\ 0 & 0 & 0 & 0 \\ 0 & 0 & 0 & 0 \\ a+d & 0 & 0 & a+d \end{bmatrix} \qquad A_2 = \begin{bmatrix} 0 & 0 & 0 & 0 \\ c+d & 0 & 0 & 0 \\ 0 & 0 & 0 & 0 \\ -(c+d) & 0 & 0 & 0 \end{bmatrix}$$

$$A_3 = \begin{bmatrix} 0 & 0 & 0 & 0 \\ 0 & 0 & 0 & 0 \\ 0 & 0 & a & -a \\ 0 & 0 & a & -a \end{bmatrix} \qquad A_4 = \begin{bmatrix} -d & d & 0 & 0 \\ -d & d & 0 & 0 \\ 0 & 0 & 0 & 0 \\ 0 & 0 & 0 & 0 \end{bmatrix}$$

$$A_5 = \begin{bmatrix} 0 & 0 & 0 & -(a+b) \\ 0 & 0 & 0 & 0 \\ 0 & 0 & 0 & a+b \\ 0 & 0 & 0 & 0 \end{bmatrix} \qquad A_6 = \begin{bmatrix} 0 & 0 & 0 & 0 \\ 0 & 0 & 0 & 0 \\ 0 & 0 & 0 & 0 \\ -a+c & 0 & -a+c & 0 \end{bmatrix}$$

$$A_7 = \begin{bmatrix} 0 & b-d & 0 & b-d \\ 0 & 0 & 0 & 0 \\ 0 & 0 & 0 & 0 \\ 0 & 0 & 0 & 0 \end{bmatrix}$$

Figure 6.2 The decomposition of the 4×4 matrix D as the sum of seven 4×4 matrices.

Then the product of the vector $[e, g, f, h]^T$ with D is the following sum of seven column vectors.

$$\begin{bmatrix} u \\ w \\ v \\ x \end{bmatrix} = \begin{bmatrix} P_1 \\ 0 \\ 0 \\ P_1 \end{bmatrix} + \begin{bmatrix} 0 \\ P_2 \\ 0 \\ -P_2 \end{bmatrix} + \begin{bmatrix} 0 \\ 0 \\ P_3 \\ P_3 \end{bmatrix} + \begin{bmatrix} P_4 \\ P_4 \\ 0 \\ 0 \end{bmatrix} + \begin{bmatrix} -P_5 \\ 0 \\ P_5 \\ 0 \end{bmatrix} + \begin{bmatrix} 0 \\ 0 \\ 0 \\ P_6 \end{bmatrix} + \begin{bmatrix} P_7 \\ 0 \\ 0 \\ 0 \end{bmatrix}$$

It follows that u, v, w, and x are given by the following equations:

$$u = P_1 + P_4 - P_5 + P_7 \qquad v = P_3 + P_5$$
$$w = P_2 + P_4 \qquad x = P_1 - P_2 + P_3 + P_6$$

Associativity and commutativity under addition and distributivity of multiplication over addition are used to obtain this result. In particular, commutativity of the ring multiplication operator is not assumed. This is important because it allows this algorithm to be used when the entries in the original 2×2 matrices are themselves matrices, since matrix multiplication is not commutative.

Thus, an algorithm exists to form the product of two $n \times n$ matrices with seven multiplications of $(n/2) \times (n/2)$ matrices and 18 additions or subtractions of such matrices. Let $n = 2^k$ and $M(k)$ be the number of operations over the ring $\mathcal{R}$ used by this algorithm to multiply $n \times n$ matrices. Then, $M(k)$ satisfies

$$M(k) = 7M(k-1) + 18\left(2^{k-1}\right)^2 = 7M(k-1) + (18)4^{k-1}$$

If the standard algorithm is used to multiply 2×2 matrices, $M(1) = 12$ and $M(k)$ satisfies the following recurrence:

$$M(k) = (36/7)7^k - (18/3)4^k$$

The depth (number of operations on the longest path), $D(k)$, of this straight-line algorithm for the product of two $n \times n$ matrices when $n = 2^k$ satisfies the following bound:

$$D(k) = D(k-1) + 3$$

because one level of addition or subtraction is used before products are formed and one or two levels are used after they are formed. Since $D(1) = 2$ if the standard algorithm is used to multiply 2×2 matrices, $D(k) = 3k - 1 = \log n - 1$.

These size and depth bounds can be improved to those in the following theorem by using the standard matrix multiplication algorithm on small matrices. (See Problem 6.8.)

THEOREM 6.3.1 *The matrix multiplication function for $n \times n$ matrices over a ring $\mathcal{R}$, $f^{(n)}_{A+B}$, has circuit size and depth satisfying the following bounds over the basis Ω containing addition, multiplication, and additive inverse over $\mathcal{R}$:*

$$C_\Omega\left(f^{(n)}_{A+B}\right) \leq 4.77 n^{\log_2 7}$$
$$D_\Omega\left(f^{(n)}_{A+B}\right) = O(\log n)$$

We emphasize again that subtraction plays a central role in Strassen's algorithm. Without it we show in Section 10.4 that the standard algorithm is nearly best possible.

Strassen's algorithm is practical for sufficiently large matrices, say with $n \geq 64$. It can also be used to multiply Boolean matrices even though the addition operator (OR) and the multiplication operator (AND) over the set $\mathcal{B}$ do not constitute a ring. (See Problem 6.9.)

6.4 Transitive Closure

The edges of a directed graph $G = (V, E)$, $n = |V|$, specify paths of length 1 between pairs of vertices. (See Fig. 6.3.) This information is captured by the Boolean $n \times n$ **adjacency matrix** $A = [a_{i,j}]$, $1 \leq i, j \leq n$, where $a_{i,j}$ is 1 if there is an edge from vertex i to vertex j in E and 0 otherwise. (The adjacency matrix for the graph in Fig. 6.3 is given after Lemma 6.4.1.) Our goal is to compute a matrix A^* whose i, j entry $a_{i,j}^*$ has value 1 if there is a path of length 0 or more between vertices i and j and value 0 otherwise. A^* is called the **transitive closure** of the matrix A. The transitive closure function $f_{A^*}^{(n)} : \mathcal{B}^{n^2} \mapsto \mathcal{B}^{n^2}$ maps an arbitrary $n \times n$ Boolean matrix A onto its $n \times n$ transitive closure matrix; that is, $f_{A^*}^{(n)}(A) = A^*$. In this section we add and multiply Boolean matrices over the set $\mathcal{B}$ using OR as the element addition operation and AND as the element multiplication operation. (Note that $(\mathcal{B}, \vee, \wedge, 0, 1)$ is not a ring; it satisfies all the rules for a ring except for the condition that each element of $\mathcal{B}$ have an (additive) inverse under $\vee$.)

To compute A^* we use the following facts: a) the entry in the rth row and sth column of the Boolean matrix product $A^2 = A \times A$ is 1 if there is a path containing two edges from vertex r to vertex s and 0 otherwise (which follows from the definition of Boolean matrix multiplication given in Section 6.3), and b) the entry in the rth row and sth column of $A^k = A^{k-1} \times A$ is 1 if there is a path containing k edges from vertex r to vertex s and 0 otherwise, as the reader is asked to show. (See Problem 6.11.)

LEMMA 6.4.1 *Let A be the Boolean adjacency matrix for a directed graph and let A^k be the kth power of A. Then the following identity holds for $k \geq 1$, where $+$ denotes the addition (OR) of Boolean matrices:*

$$(I + A)^k = I + A + \cdots + A^k \tag{6.2}$$

Proof The proof is by induction. The base case is $k = 1$, for which the identity holds. Assume that it holds for $k \leq K - 1$. We show that it holds for $k = K$. Since $(I+A)^{K-1} =$

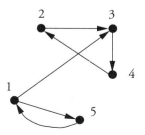

Figure 6.3 A graph that illustrates transitive closure.

$I + A + \cdots + A^{K-1}$, multiply both sides by $I + A$:

$$
\begin{aligned}
(I + A)^K &= (I + A) \times (I + A)^{K-1} \\
&= (I + A) \times (I + A + \cdots + A^{K-1}) \\
&= I + (A + A) + \cdots + (A^{K-1} + A^{K-1}) + A^K
\end{aligned}
$$

However, since A^j is a Boolean matrix, $A^j + A^j = A^j$ for all j and the result follows. ∎

The adjacency matrix A of the graph in Fig. 6.3 is given below along with its powers up to the fifth power. Note that every non-zero entry appearing in A^5 appears in at least one of the other matrices. The reason for this fact is explained in the proof of Lemma 6.4.2.

$$
A = \begin{bmatrix}
0 & 0 & 1 & 0 & 1 \\
0 & 0 & 1 & 0 & 0 \\
0 & 0 & 0 & 1 & 0 \\
0 & 1 & 0 & 0 & 0 \\
1 & 0 & 0 & 0 & 0
\end{bmatrix}
\quad
A^2 = \begin{bmatrix}
1 & 0 & 0 & 1 & 0 \\
0 & 0 & 0 & 1 & 0 \\
0 & 1 & 0 & 0 & 0 \\
0 & 0 & 1 & 0 & 0 \\
0 & 0 & 1 & 0 & 1
\end{bmatrix}
\quad
A^3 = \begin{bmatrix}
0 & 1 & 1 & 0 & 1 \\
0 & 1 & 0 & 0 & 0 \\
0 & 0 & 1 & 0 & 0 \\
0 & 0 & 0 & 1 & 0 \\
1 & 0 & 0 & 1 & 0
\end{bmatrix}
$$

$$
A^4 = \begin{bmatrix}
1 & 0 & 1 & 1 & 0 \\
0 & 0 & 1 & 0 & 0 \\
0 & 0 & 0 & 1 & 0 \\
0 & 1 & 0 & 0 & 0 \\
0 & 1 & 1 & 0 & 1
\end{bmatrix}
\quad
A^5 = \begin{bmatrix}
0 & 1 & 1 & 1 & 1 \\
0 & 0 & 0 & 1 & 0 \\
0 & 1 & 0 & 0 & 0 \\
0 & 0 & 1 & 0 & 0 \\
1 & 0 & 1 & 1 & 0
\end{bmatrix}
$$

LEMMA 6.4.2 *If there is a path between pairs of vertices in the directed graph $G = (V, E)$, $n = |V|$, there is a path of length at most $n - 1$.*

Proof We suppose that the shortest path between vertices i and j in V has length $k \geq n$. Such a path has $k + 1$ vertices. Because $k + 1 \geq n + 1$, some vertex is repeated more than once. (This is an example of the pigeonhole principle.) Consider the subpath defined by the edges between the first and last instance of this repeated vertex. Since it constitutes a loop, it can be removed to produce a shorter path between vertices i and j. This contradicts the hypothesis that the shortest path has length n or more. Thus, the shortest path has length at most $n - 1$. ∎

Because the shortest path has length at most $n - 1$, any non-zero entries in A^k, $k \geq n$, are also found in one of the matrices A^j, $j \leq n - 1$. Since the identity matrix I is the adjacency matrix for the graph that has paths of length zero between two vertices, the transitive closure, which includes such paths, is equal to:

$$
A^* = I + A + A^2 + A^3 + \cdots + A^{n-1} = (I + A)^{n-1}
$$

It also follows that $A^* = (I + A)^k$ for all $k \geq n - 1$, which leads to the following result.

THEOREM 6.4.1 *Over the basis $\Omega = \{\text{AND, OR}\}$ the transitive closure function, $f_{A^*}^{(n)}$, has circuit size and depth satisfying the following bounds (that is, a circuit of this size and depth can be* *constructed with* AND *and* OR *gates for it):*

$$C_\Omega\left(f_{A^*}^{(n)}\right) \leq M_{\text{matrix}}(cn, K)\lceil\log_2 n\rceil$$

$$D_\Omega\left(f_{A^*}^{(n)}\right) \leq K(\log n)\lceil\log_2 n\rceil$$

Proof Let $k = 2^p$ be the smallest power of 2 such that $k \geq n-1$. Then, $p = \lceil\log_2(n-1)\rceil$. Since $A^* = (I + A)^k$, it can be computed with a circuit that squares the matrix $I + A$ p times. Each squaring can be done with a circuit for the standard matrix multiplication algorithm described in (6.1) using $M_{\text{matrix}}(cn, K) = O(n^3)$ operations and depth $\lceil\log_2 2n\rceil$. The desired result follows. ∎

The above statement says that the transitive closure function on $n \times n$ matrices has circuit size and depth at most a factor $O(\log n)$ times that of matrix multiplication. We now show that Boolean matrix multiplication is a subfunction of the transitive closure function, which implies that the former has a circuit size and depth no larger than the latter. We subsequently show that the size bound can be improved to a constant multiple of the size bound for matrix multiplication. Thus the transitive closure and Boolean matrix multiplication functions have comparable size.

THEOREM 6.4.2 *The $n \times n$ matrix multiplication function $f_{A^*}^{(n)} : \mathcal{R}^{2n^2} \mapsto \mathcal{R}^{n^2}$ for Boolean matrices is a subfunction of the transitive closure function $f_{A^*}^{(3n)} : \mathcal{R}^{18n^2} \mapsto \mathcal{R}^{9n^2}$.*

Proof Observe that the following relationship holds for $n \times n$ matrices A and B, since the third and higher powers of the $3n \times 3n$ matrix on the left are 0.

$$\begin{bmatrix} 0 & A & 0 \\ 0 & 0 & B \\ 0 & 0 & 0 \end{bmatrix}^* = \begin{bmatrix} I & A & AB \\ 0 & I & B \\ 0 & A & I \end{bmatrix}$$

It follows that the product AB of $n \times n$ matrices is a subfunction of the transitive closure function on a $3n \times 3n$ matrix. ∎

COROLLARY 6.4.1 *It follows that*

$$C_\Omega\left(f_{A \times B}^{(n)}\right) \leq C_\Omega\left(f_{A^*}^{(3n)}\right)$$

$$D_\Omega\left(f_{A \times B}^{(n)}\right) \leq D_\Omega\left(f_{A^*}^{(3n)}\right)$$

over the basis $\Omega = \{\text{AND, OR}\}$.

Not only can a Boolean matrix multiplication algorithm be devised from one for transitive closure, but the reverse is also true, as we show. Let n be a power of 2 and divide an $n \times n$ matrix A into four $(n/2) \times (n/2)$ matrices:

$$A = \begin{bmatrix} U & V \\ W & X \end{bmatrix} \tag{6.3}$$

Compute X^* recursively and use it to form $Y = U + VX^*W$ by performing two multiplications of $(n/2) \times (n/2)$ matrices and one addition of such matrices. Recursively form Y^* and then assemble the matrix B shown below with four further multiplications and one addition of $(n/2) \times (n/2)$ matrices.

$$B = \begin{bmatrix} Y^* & Y^*VX^* \\ X^*WY^* & X^* + X^*WY^*VX^* \end{bmatrix} \qquad (6.4)$$

We now show that $B = A^*$.

THEOREM 6.4.3 *Under Assumptions 6.3.1 and 6.3.2, a circuit of size $O(M_{\mathrm{matrix}}(n, K))$ and depth $4K(\log_2 n)(\log_2 n + 1)/2$ exists to form the transitive closure of $n \times n$ matrices.*

Proof We assume that n is a power of 2 and use the representation for the matrix A given in (6.3). If n is not a power of 2, we augment the matrix A by embedding it in a larger matrix in which all the new entries, are 0 except for the new diagonal entries, which are 1. Given that $4M(n) \leq M(2n)$, the bound applies.

We begin by showing that $B = A^*$. Let $F \subset V$ and $S \subset V$ be the first and second sets of $n/2$ vertices, respectively, corresponding to the first and second halves of the rows and columns of the matrix A. Then, $F \cup S = V$ and $F \cap S = \emptyset$. Observe that X^* is the adjacency matrix for those paths originating on and terminating with vertices in F and visiting no other vertices. Similarly, $Y = U + VX^*W$ is the adjacency matrix for those paths consisting of an edge from a vertex in F to a vertex in F or paths of length more than 1 consisting of an edge from vertices in F to vertices in S, a path of length 0 or more within vertices in S, and an edge from vertices in S to vertices in F. It follows that Y^* is the adjacency matrix for all paths between vertices in F that may visit any vertices in V. A similar line of reasoning demonstrates that the other entries of A^* are correct.

The size of a circuit realizing this algorithm, $T(n)$, satisfies

$$T(n) = 2T(n/2) + 5M_{\mathrm{matrix}}(n/2, K) + (n/2)^2$$

because the above algorithm (see Fig. 6.4) uses two circuits for transitive closure on $(n/2) \times (n/2)$ matrices, five circuits for multiplying, and one circuit for adding two such matrices.

Because we assume that $n^2 \leq M_{\mathrm{matrix}}(n, K)$, it follows that $T(n) \leq 2T(n/2) + 6M_{\mathrm{matrix}}(n/2, K)$. Let $T(m) \leq cM_{\mathrm{matrix}}(cm, K)$ for $m \leq n/2$ be the inductive hypothesis. Then we have the inequalities

$$T(n) \leq (2c + 6)M_{\mathrm{matrix}}(n/2, K) \leq (c/2 + 1.5)M_{\mathrm{matrix}}(n, K)$$

which follow from $M_{\mathrm{matrix}}(n/2, K) \leq M_{\mathrm{matrix}}(n, K)/4$ (see Assumption 6.3.2). Because $(c/2 + 1.5) \leq c$ for $c \geq 3$, for $c = 3$ we have the desired bound on circuit size.

The depth $D(n)$ of the above circuit satisfies $D(n) = D(n/2) + 4K\log_2 n$, from which we conclude that $D(n) = O(\log^2 n)$. ∎

A **closed semiring** $(S, +, *, 0, 1)$ is a set S, two operations $+$ and $*$ and elements $0, 1 \in S$ with the following properties:

a) S is closed under $+$ and $*$;

b) $+$ and $*$ are associative;

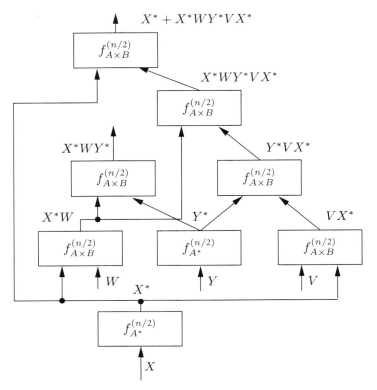

Figure 6.4 A circuit for the transitive closure of a Boolean matrix based on the construction of equation (6.4).

c) for all $a \in S$, $a + 0 = 0 + a = a$;

d) for all $a \in S$, $a * 1 = 1 * a = a$;

e) $+$ is commutative and **idempotent**; i.e. $a + a = a$;

f) $*$ distributes over $+$; i.e. for all $a, b, c \in S$, $a * (b + c) = a * b + a * c$ and $(b + c) * a = b * a + c * a$.

The above definitions and results generalize to matrices over closed semirings. To show this, it suffices to observe that the properties used to derive these results are just these properties. (See Problem 6.12.)

6.5 Matrix Inversion

The inverse of a non-singular $n \times n$ matrix M defined over a ring $\mathcal{R}$ is another matrix M^{-1} whose product with M is the $n \times n$ identity matrix I; that is,

$$MM^{-1} = M^{-1}M = I$$

Given a linear system of n equations in the column vector $\boldsymbol{x}$ of n unknowns defined by the non-singular $n \times n$ coefficient matrix M and the vector $\boldsymbol{b}$, namely,

$$M\boldsymbol{x} = \boldsymbol{b} \tag{6.5}$$

the solution $\boldsymbol{x}$ can be obtained through a matrix-vector multiplication with M^{-1}:

$$\boldsymbol{x} = M^{-1}\boldsymbol{b}$$

In this section we present two algorithms for matrix inversion. Such algorithms compute the (partial) matrix inverse function $f_{A^{-1}}^{(n)} : \mathcal{R}^{n^2} \mapsto \mathcal{R}^{n^2}$ that maps non-singular $n \times n$ matrices over a ring $\mathcal{R}$ onto their inverses. The first result, Theorem 6.5.4, demonstrates that $C_\Omega\left(f_{A^{-1}}^{(n)}\right) = \Theta(M_{\mathrm{matrix}}(n, K))$ with a circuit whose depth is more than linear in n. The second, Theorem 6.5.6, demonstrates that $D_\Omega\left(f_{A^{-1}}^{(n)}\right) = O(\log^2 n)$ with a circuit whose size is $O(nM_{\mathrm{matrix}}(n, K))$.

Before describing the two matrix inversion algorithms, we present a result demonstrating that matrix multiplication of $n \times n$ matrices is no harder than inverting a $3n \times 3n$ matrix; the function defining the former task is a subfunction of the function defining the latter task.

LEMMA 6.5.1 *The matrix inverse function* $f_{A^{-1}}^{(3n)}$ *contains as a subfunction the function* $f_{A \times B}^{(n)} :$ $\mathcal{R}^{2n^2} \mapsto \mathcal{R}^{n^2}$ *that maps two matrices over* $\mathcal{R}$ *to their product.*

Proof The proof follows by writing a $3n \times 3n$ matrix as a 3×3 matrix of $n \times n$ matrices and then specializing the entries to be the identity matrix I, the zero matrix 0, or matrices A and B:

$$\begin{bmatrix} I & A & 0 \\ 0 & I & B \\ 0 & 0 & I \end{bmatrix}^{-1} = \begin{bmatrix} I & -A & AB \\ 0 & I & -B \\ 0 & 0 & I \end{bmatrix}$$

This identity is established by showing that the product of these two matrices is the identity matrix. ∎

6.5.1 Symmetric Positive Definite Matrices

Our first algorithm to invert a non-singular $n \times n$ matrix M has a circuit size linear in $M_{\mathrm{matrix}}(n, K)$, which, in light of Lemma 6.5.1, is optimal to within a constant multiplicative factor. This algorithm makes use of symmetric positive definite matrices, the Schur complement, and LDL$^\mathrm{T}$ factorization, terms defined below. This algorithm has depth $O(n \log^2 n)$.

The second algorithm, Csanky's algorithm, has circuit depth $O(\log^2 n)$, which is smaller, but circuit size $O(nM_{\mathrm{matrix}}(n, K))$, which is larger. Symmetric positive definite matrices are defined below.

DEFINITION 6.5.1 *A matrix M is* **positive definite** *if for all non-zero vectors $\boldsymbol{x}$ the following condition holds:*

$$\boldsymbol{x}^T M \boldsymbol{x} = \sum_{1 \leq i,j \leq n} x_i m_{i,j} x_j > 0 \tag{6.6}$$

A matrix is **symmetric positive definite** *(SPD) if it is both symmetric and positive definite.*

We now show that an algorithm to invert SPD matrices can be used to invert arbitrary non-singular matrices by adding a circuit to multiply matrices.

LEMMA 6.5.2 *If M is a non-singular $n \times n$ matrix, then the matrix $P = M^T M$ is symmetric positive definite. M can be inverted by inverting P and then multiplying P^{-1} by M^T. Let $f_{\text{SPD\_inverse}}^{(n)} : \mathcal{R}^{n^2} \mapsto \mathcal{R}^{n^2}$ be the inverse function for $n \times n$ SPD matrices over the ring $\mathcal{R}$. Then the size and depth of $f_{A^{-1}}^{(n)}$ over $\mathcal{R}$ satisfy the following bounds:*

$$C\left(f_{A^{-1}}^{(n)}\right) \leq C\left(f_{\text{SPD\_inverse}}^{(n)}\right) + M_{\text{matrix}}(n, K)$$

$$D\left(f_{A^{-1}}^{(n)}\right) \leq D\left(f_{\text{SPD\_inverse}}^{(n)}\right) + O(\log n)$$

Proof To show that P is symmetric we note that $\left(M^T M\right)^T = M^T M$. To show that it is positive definite, we observe that

$$\boldsymbol{x}^T P \boldsymbol{x} = \boldsymbol{x}^T M^T M \boldsymbol{x}$$
$$= (M\boldsymbol{x})^T M\boldsymbol{x}$$
$$= \sum_{i=1}^{n} \left(\sum_{j=1}^{n} m_{i,j} x_j \right)^2$$

which is positive unless the product $M\boldsymbol{x}$ is identically zero for the non-zero vector $\boldsymbol{x}$. But this cannot be true if M is non-singular. Thus, P is symmetric and positive definite.

To invert M, invert P to produce $M^{-1}\left(M^T\right)^{-1}$. If we multiply this product on the right by M^T, the result is the inverse M^{-1}. ■

6.5.2 Schur Factorization

We now describe **Schur factorization**. Represent an $n \times n$ matrix M as the 2×2 matrix

$$M = \begin{bmatrix} M_{1,1} & M_{1,2} \\ M_{2,1} & M_{2,2} \end{bmatrix} \tag{6.7}$$

where $M_{1,1}$, $M_{1,2}$, $M_{2,1}$, and $M_{2,2}$ are $k \times k$, $k \times n - k$, $n - k \times k$, and $n - k \times n - k$ matrices, $1 \leq k \leq n - 1$. Let $M_{1,1}$ be invertible. Then by straightforward algebraic manipulation M can be factored as

$$M = \begin{bmatrix} I & 0 \\ M_{2,1}M_{1,1}^{-1} & I \end{bmatrix} \begin{bmatrix} M_{1,1} & 0 \\ 0 & S \end{bmatrix} \begin{bmatrix} I & M_{1,1}^{-1}M_{1,2} \\ 0 & I \end{bmatrix} \tag{6.8}$$

Here I and O denote identity and zero matrices (all entries are zero) of a size that conforms to the size of other submatrices of those matrices in which they are found. This is the Schur factorization. Also,

$$S = M_{2,2} - M_{2,1}M_{1,1}^{-1}M_{1,2}$$

is the **Schur complement** of M. To show that M has this factorization, it suffices to carry out the product of the above three matrices.

The first and last matrix in this product are invertible. If S is also invertible, the middle matrix is invertible, as is the matrix M itself. The inverse of M, M^{-1}, is given by the product

$$M^{-1} = \begin{bmatrix} I & -M_{1,1}^{-1}M_{1,2} \\ 0 & I \end{bmatrix} \begin{bmatrix} M_{1,1}^{-1} & 0 \\ 0 & S^{-1} \end{bmatrix} \begin{bmatrix} I & 0 \\ -M_{2,1}M_{1,1}^{-1} & I \end{bmatrix} \qquad (6.9)$$

This follows from three observations: a) the inverse of a product is the product of the inverses in reverse order (see Lemma 6.2.1), b) the inverse of a 2×2 upper (lower) triangular matrix is the matrix with the off-diagonal term negated, and c) the inverse of a 2×2 diagonal matrix is a diagonal matrix in which the ith diagonal element is the multiplicative inverse of the ith diagonal element of the original matrix. (See Problem 6.13 for the latter two results.)

The following fact is useful in inverting SPD matrices.

LEMMA 6.5.3 *If M is an $n \times n$ SPD matrix, its Schur complement is also SPD.*

Proof Represent M as shown in (6.7). In (6.6) let $x = u \cdot v$; that is, let x be the concatenation of the two column vectors. Then

$$x^T M x = \begin{bmatrix} u^T, v^T \end{bmatrix} \begin{bmatrix} M_{1,1}u + M_{1,2}v \\ M_{2,1}u + M_{2,2}v \end{bmatrix}$$
$$= u^T M_{1,1}u + u^T M_{1,2}v + v^T M_{2,1}u + v^T M_{2,2}v$$

If we say that

$$u = -M_{1,1}^{-1}M_{1,2}\,v$$

and use the fact that $M_{1,2}^T = M_{2,1}$ and $\left(M_{1,1}^{-1}\right)^T = \left(M_{1,1}^T\right)^{-1} = M_{1,1}^{-1}$, it is straightforward to show that S is symmetric and

$$x^T M x = v^T S v$$

where S is the Schur complement of M. Thus, if M is SPD, so is its Schur complement. ∎

6.5.3 Inversion of Triangular Matrices

Let T be $n \times n$ lower triangular and non-singular. Without loss of generality, assume that $n = 2^r$. (T can be extended to a $2^r \times 2^r$ matrix by placing it on the diagonal of a $2^r \times 2^r$ matrix along with a $2^r - n \times 2^r - n$ identity matrix.) Represent T as a 2×2 matrix of $n/2 \times n/2$ matrices:

$$T = \begin{bmatrix} T_{1,1} & 0 \\ T_{2,1} & T_{2,2} \end{bmatrix}$$

The inverse of T, which is lower triangular, is given below, as can be verified directly:

$$T^{-1} = \begin{bmatrix} T_{1,1}^{-1} & 0 \\ -T_{2,2}^{-1}T_{2,1}T_{1,1}^{-1} & T_{2,2}^{-1} \end{bmatrix}$$

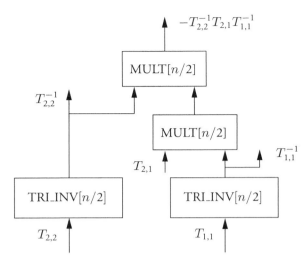

Figure 6.5 A recursive circuit TRI_INV[n] for the inversion of a triangular matrix.

This representation for the inverse of T defines the recursive algorithm TRI_INV[n] in Fig. 6.5. When $n = 1$ this algorithm requires one operation; on an $n \times n$ matrix it requires two calls to TRI_INV[$n/2$] and two matrix multiplications. Let $f_{\text{tri\_inv}}^{(n)} : \mathcal{R}^{(n^2+n)/2} \mapsto \mathcal{R}^{(n^2+n)/2}$ be the function corresponding to the inversion of an $n \times n$ lower triangular matrix. The algorithm TRI_INV[n] provides the following bounds on the size and depth of the smallest circuit to compute $f_{\text{tri\_inv}}^{(n)}$.

THEOREM 6.5.1 _Let n be a power of 2. Then the matrix inversion function $f_{\text{tri\_inv}}^{(n)}$ for $n \times n$ lower triangular matrices satisfies the following bounds:_

$$C\left(f_{\text{tri\_inv}}^{(n)}\right) \leq M_{\text{matrix}}(n, K)$$
$$D\left(f_{\text{tri\_inv}}^{(n)}\right) = O(\log^2 n)$$

Proof From Fig. 6.5 it is clear that the following circuit size and depth bounds hold if the matrix multiplication algorithm has circuit size $M_{\text{matrix}}(n, K)$ and depth $K \log_2 n$:

$$C\left(f_{\text{tri\_inv}}^{(n)}\right) \leq 2C\left(f_{\text{tri\_inv}}^{(n/2)}\right) + 2M_{\text{matrix}}(n/2, K)$$
$$D\left(f_{\text{tri\_inv}}^{(n)}\right) \leq D\left(f_{\text{tri\_inv}}^{(n/2)}\right) + 2K \log n$$

The solution to the first inequality follows by induction from the fact that $M_{\text{matrix}}(1, K) = 1$ and the assumption that $4M_{\text{matrix}}(n/2, K) \leq M_{\text{matrix}}(n, K)$. The second inequality follows from the observation that $d > 0$ can be chosen so that $d \log^2(n/2) + c \log n \leq d \log^2 n$ for any $c > 0$ for n sufficiently large. ∎

6.5.4 LDL^T Factorization of SPD Matrices

Now that we know that the Schur complement S of M is SPD when M is SPD, we can show that every SPD matrix M has a factorization as the product LDL^T of a unit lower triangular matrix L (each of its diagonal entries is the multiplicative unit of the ring $\mathcal{R}$), a diagonal matrix D, and the transpose of L.

THEOREM 6.5.2 *Every $n \times n$ SPD matrix M has a factorization as the product $M = LDL^T$, where L is a unit lower triangular matrix and D is a diagonal matrix.*

Proof The proof is by induction on n. For $n = 1$ the result is obvious because we can write $[m_{1,1}] = [1][m_{1,1}][1]$. Assume that it holds for $n \leq N - 1$. We show that it holds for $n = N$.

Form the Schur factorization of the $N \times N$ matrix M. Since the $k \times k$ submatrix $M_{1,1}$ of M as well as the $n - k \times n - k$ submatrix S of M are SPD, by the inductive hypothesis they can be factored in the same fashion. Let

$$M_{1,1} = L_1 D_1 L_1^T, S = L_2 D_2 L_2^T$$

Then the middle matrix on the right-hand side of equation (6.8) can be represented as

$$\begin{bmatrix} M_{1,1} & 0 \\ 0 & S \end{bmatrix} = \begin{bmatrix} L_1 & 0 \\ 0 & L_2 \end{bmatrix} \begin{bmatrix} D_1 & 0 \\ 0 & D_2 \end{bmatrix} \begin{bmatrix} L_1^T & 0 \\ 0 & L_2^T \end{bmatrix}$$

Substituting the above product for the middle matrix in (6.8) and multiplying the two left and two right matrices gives the following representation for M:

$$M = \begin{bmatrix} L_1 & 0 \\ M_{2,1} M_{1,1}^{-1} L_1 & L_2 \end{bmatrix} \begin{bmatrix} D_1 & 0 \\ 0 & D_2 \end{bmatrix} \begin{bmatrix} L_1^T & L_1^T M_{1,1}^{-1} M_{1,2} \\ 0 & L_2^T \end{bmatrix} \quad (6.10)$$

Since M is symmetric, $M_{1,1}$ is symmetric, $M_{1,2} = M_{2,1}^T$, and

$$L_1^T M_{1,1}^{-1} M_{1,2} = L_1^T (M_{1,1}^{-1})^T M_{2,1}^T = (M_{2,1} M_{1,1}^{-1} L_1)^T$$

Thus, it suffices to compute L_1, D_1, L_2, D_2, and $M_{2,1} M_{1,1}^{-1} L_1$. ∎

When $n = 2^r$ and $k = n/2$, the proof of Theorem 6.5.2 describes a recursive procedure, $LDL^T[n]$, defined on $n \times n$ SPD matrices that produces their LDL^T factorization. Figure 6.6 captures the steps involved. They are also described below.

- The LDL^T factorization of the $n/2 \times n/2$ matrix $M_{1,1}$ is computed using the procedure $LDL^T[n/2]$ to produce the $n/2 \times n/2$ triangular and diagonal matrices L_1 and D_1, respectively.

- The product $M_{2,1} M_{1,1}^{-1} L_1 = M_{2,1} \left(L_1^{-1} \right)^T D_1^{-1}$ which may be computed by inverting the lower triangular matrix L_1 with the operation $TRI\_INV[n/2]$, computing the product $M_{2,1} \left(L_1^{-1} \right)^T$ using $MULT[n/2]$, and multiplying the result with D_1^{-1} using a procedure $SCALE[n/2]$ that inverts D_1 and multiplies it by a square matrix.

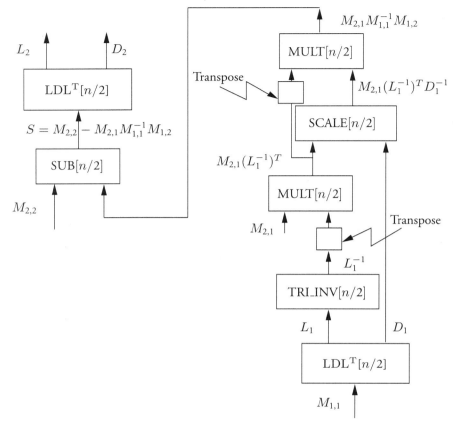

Figure 6.6 An algebraic circuit to produce the LDL^T factorization of an SPD matrix.

- $S = M_{2,2} - M_{2,1} M_{1,1}^{-1} M_{1,2}$ can be formed by multiplying $M_{2,1} \left(L_1^{-1} \right)^T D_1^{-1}$ by the transpose of $M_{2,1} \left(L_1^{-1} \right)^T$ using MULT$[n/2]$ and subtracting the result from $M_{2,2}$ by the subtraction operator SUB$[n/2]$.

- The LDL^T factorization of the $n/2 \times n/2$ matrix S is computed using the procedure LDL$^T[n/2]$ to produce the $n/2 \times n/2$ triangular and diagonal matrices L_2 and D_2, respectively.

Let's now determine the size and depth of circuits to implement the algorithm for LDL$^T[n]$. Let $f_{\text{LDL}^T}^{(n)} : \mathcal{R}^{n^2} \mapsto \mathcal{R}^{(n^2+n)/2}$ be the function defined by the LDL^T factorization of an $n \times n$ SPD matrix, $f_{\text{tri\_inv}}^{(n)} : \mathcal{R}^{(n^2+n)/2} \mapsto \mathcal{R}^{(n^2+n)/2}$ be the inversion of an $n \times n$ lower triangular matrix, $f_{\text{scale}}^{(n)} : \mathcal{R}^{n^2+n} \mapsto \mathcal{R}^{n^2}$ be the computation of $N(D^{-1})$ for an $n \times n$ matrix N and a diagonal matrix D, $f_{\text{mult}}^{(n)} : \mathcal{R}^{2n^2} \mapsto \mathcal{R}^{n^2}$ be the multiplication of two $n \times n$ matrices, and $f_{\text{sub}}^{(n)} : \mathcal{R}^{2n^2} \mapsto \mathcal{R}^{n^2}$ the subtraction of two $n \times n$ matrices. Since a transposition can be done without any operators, the size and depth of the circuit for $\mathrm{LDL^T}[n]$ constructed above satisfy the following inequalities:

$$C\left(f_{\mathrm{LDL^T}}^{(n)}\right) \leq C\left(f_{\mathrm{tri\_inv}}^{(n/2)}\right) + C\left(f_{\mathrm{scale}}^{(n/2)}\right) + 2C\left(f_{\mathrm{mult}}^{(n/2)}\right) + C\left(f_{\mathrm{sub}}^{(n/2)}\right) + 2C\left(f_{\mathrm{LDL^T}}^{(n/2)}\right)$$
$$D\left(f_{\mathrm{LDL^T}}^{(n)}\right) \leq D\left(f_{\mathrm{tri\_inv}}^{(n/2)}\right) + D\left(f_{\mathrm{scale}}^{(n/2)}\right) + 2D\left(f_{\mathrm{mult}}^{(n/2)}\right) + D\left(f_{\mathrm{sub}}^{(n/2)}\right) + 2D\left(f_{\mathrm{LDL^T}}^{(n/2)}\right)$$

The size and depth of a circuit for $f_{\mathrm{tri\_inv}}^{(n)}$ are $M_{\mathrm{matrix}}(n, K)$ and $O(\log^2 n)$, as shown in Theorem 6.5.1. The circuits for $f_{\mathrm{scale}}^{(n)}$ and $f_{\mathrm{sub}}^{(n)}$ have size n^2 and depth 1; the former multiplies the elements of the jth column of N by the multiplicative inverse of jth diagonal element of D_1 for $1 \leq j \leq n$, while the latter subtracts corresponding elements from the two input matrices.

Let $C_{\mathrm{SPD}}(n) = C\left(f_{\mathrm{LDL^T}}^{(n)}\right)$ and $D_{\mathrm{SPD}}(n) = D\left(f_{\mathrm{LDL^T}}^{(n)}\right)$. Since $M_{\mathrm{matrix}}(n/2, K) \leq (1/4)M_{\mathrm{matrix}}(n, K)$ is assumed (see Assumption 6.3.1), and $2m^2 \leq M_{\mathrm{matrix}}(m, K)$ (see Assumption 6.3.2), the above inequalities become

$$\begin{aligned} C_{\mathrm{SPD}}(n) &\leq M_{\mathrm{matrix}}(n/2, K) + (n/2)^2 + 2M_{\mathrm{matrix}}(n/2, K) + (n/2)^2 + 2C_{\mathrm{SPD}}(n/2) \\ &\leq 2C_{\mathrm{SPD}}(n/2) + M_{\mathrm{matrix}}(n, K) \end{aligned} \tag{6.11}$$
$$\begin{aligned} D_{\mathrm{SPD}}(n) &\leq O(\log^2(n/2)) + 1 + 2O(\log(n/2)) + 1 + 2D_{\mathrm{SPD}}(n/2) \\ &\leq 2D_{\mathrm{SPD}}(n/2) + K\log_2^2 n \quad \text{for some } K > 0 \end{aligned} \tag{6.12}$$

As a consequence, we have the following results.

THEOREM 6.5.3 *Let n be a power of two. Then there exists a circuit to compute the $\mathrm{LDL^T}$ factorization of an $n \times n$ matrix whose size and depth satisfy*

$$C\left(f_{\mathrm{LDL^T}}^{(n)}\right) \leq 2M_{\mathrm{matrix}}(n, K)$$
$$D\left(f_{\mathrm{LDL^T}}^{(n)}\right) \leq O\left(n\log^2 n\right)$$

Proof From (6.11) we have that

$$C_{\mathrm{SPD}}(n) \leq \sum_{j=0}^{\log n} 2^j M_{\mathrm{matrix}}(n/2^j, K)$$

By Assumption 6.3.2, $M_{\mathrm{matrix}}(n/2, K) \leq (1/4)M_{\mathrm{matrix}}(n, K)$. It follows by induction that $M_{\mathrm{matrix}}(n/2^j, K) \leq (1/4)^j M_{\mathrm{matrix}}(n, K)$, which bounds the above sum by a geometric series whose sum is at most $2M_{\mathrm{matrix}}(n, K)$. The bound on $D\left(f_{\mathrm{LDL^T}}^{(n)}\right)$ follows from the observation that $(2c)(n/2)\log^2(n/2) + c\log^2 n \leq cn\log^2 n$ for $n \geq 2$ and $c > 0$. ∎

This result combined with earlier observations provides a matrix inversion algorithm for arbitrary non-singular matrices.

THEOREM 6.5.4 *The matrix inverse function $f_{A^{-1}}^{(n)}$ for arbitrary non-singular $n \times n$ matrices over an arbitrary ring $\mathcal{R}$ can be computed by an algebraic circuit whose size and depth satisfy the following bounds:*

$$C\left(f_{A^{-1}}^{(n)}\right) = \Theta(M_{\mathrm{matrix}}(n, K))$$

$$D\left(f_{A^{-1}}^{(n)}\right) = O(n \log^2 n)$$

Proof To invert a non-singular $n \times n$ matrix M that is not SPD, form the product $P = M^T M$ (which is SPD) with one instance of MULT[n] and then invert it. Then multiply P^{-1} by M^T on the right with a second instance of MULT[n]. To invert P, compute its LDL^T factorization and invert it by forming $\left(L^T\right)^{-1} D^{-1} L^{-1}$. Inverting LDL^T requires one application of TRI_INV[n], one application of SCALE[n], and one application of MULT[n], in addition to the steps used to form the factorization. Thus, three applications of MULT[n] are used in addition to the factorization steps. The following bounds hold:

$$C\left(f_{A^{-1}}^{(n)}\right) \leq 4M_{\mathrm{matrix}}(n, K) + n^2 \leq 4.5 M_{\mathrm{matrix}}(n)$$

$$D\left(f_{A^{-1}}^{(n)}\right) = O\left(n \log^2 n\right) + O(\log n) = O\left(n \log^2 n\right)$$

The lower bound on $C\left(f_{A^{-1}}^{(n)}\right)$ follows from Lemma 6.5.1. ∎

6.5.5   Fast Matrix Inversion*

In this section we present a depth-$O(\log^2 n)$ circuit for the inversion of $n \times n$ matrices known as **Csanky's algorithm**, which is based on the method of Leverrier. Since this algorithm uses a number of well-known matrix functions and properties that space precludes explaining in detail, advanced knowledge of matrices and polynomials is required for this section.

The determinant of an $n \times n$ matrix A, $\det(A)$, is defined below in terms of the set of all permutations π of the integers $\{1, 2, \ldots, n\}$. Here the **sign** of π, denoted $\sigma(\pi)$, is the number of swaps of pairs of integers needed to realize π from the identity permutation.

$$\det(A) = \sum_{\pi} (-1)^{\sigma(\pi)} \prod_{i=1}^{n} a_{i,\pi(i)}$$

Here $\prod_{i=1}^{n} a_{i,\pi(i)}$ is the product $a_{1,\pi(1)} \cdots a_{n,\pi(n)}$. The **characteristic polynomial** of a matrix A, namely, $\phi_A(x)$ in the variable x, is the determinant of $xI - A$, where I is the $n \times n$ identity matrix:

$$\phi_A(x) = \det(xI - A)$$
$$= x^n + c_{n-1}x^{n-1} + c_{n-2}x^{n-2} + \cdots + c_0$$

If x is set to zero, this equation implies that $c_0 = \det(-A)$. Also, substituting A for x, we have that $\phi_A(A) = 0$, a fact known as the **Cayley-Hamilton theorem**: A matrix satisfies its own characteristic polynomial. This implies that

$$A\left(A^{n-1} + c_{n-1}A^{n-2} + c_{n-2}A^{n-3} + \cdots + c_1\right) = -c_0 I$$

Thus, when $c_0 \neq 0$ the inverse of A can be computed from

$$A^{-1} = \frac{-1}{c_0}\left(A^{n-1} + c_{n-1}A^{n-2} + c_{n-2}A^{n-3} + \cdots + c_1\right)$$

Once the characteristic polynomial of A has been computed, its inverse can be computed by forming the $n - 1$ successive powers of A, namely, $A, A^2, A^3, \ldots, A^{n-1}$, multiplying them by the coefficients of $\phi_A(x)$, and adding the products together. These powers of A can be computed using a prefix circuit having $O(n)$ instances of the associative matrix multiplication operator and depth $O(\log n)$ measured in the number of instances of this operator. We have defined $M_{\mathrm{matrix}}(n, K)$ to be the size of the smallest $n \times n$ matrix multiplication circuit with depth $K \log n$ (Definition 6.3.1). Thus, the successive powers of A can be computed by a circuit of size $O(nM_{\mathrm{matrix}}(n, K))$ and depth $O(\log^2 n)$. The size bound can be improved to $O(\sqrt{n}M_{\mathrm{matrix}}(n, K))$. (See Problem 6.15.)

To complete the derivation of the Csanky algorithm we must produce the coefficients of the characteristic polynomial of A. For this we invoke **Leverrier's theorem**. This theorem uses the notion of the **trace of a matrix** A, that is, the sum of the elements on its main diagonal, denoted $tr(A)$.

THEOREM 6.5.5 (Leverrier) *The coefficients of the characteristic polynomial of the $n \times n$ matrix A satisfy the following identity, where $s_r = tr(A^r)$ for $1 \leq r \leq n$:*

$$
\begin{bmatrix}
1 & 0 & 0 & \cdots & 0 \\
s_1 & 2 & 0 & \cdots & 0 \\
s_2 & s_1 & 3 & & 0 \\
\vdots & & & \ddots & \vdots \\
s_{n-1} & \cdots & s_2 & s_1 & n
\end{bmatrix}
\begin{bmatrix}
c_{n-1} \\
c_{n-2} \\
c_{n-3} \\
\vdots \\
c_0
\end{bmatrix}
= -
\begin{bmatrix}
s_1 \\
s_2 \\
s_3 \\
\vdots \\
s_n
\end{bmatrix}
\tag{6.13}
$$

Proof The degree-n characteristic polynomial $\phi_A(x)$ of A can be factored over a field of characteristic zero. If $\lambda_1, \lambda_2, \ldots, \lambda_n$ are its roots, we write

$$
\phi_A(x) = \prod_{i=1}^{n} (x - \lambda_i)
$$

From expanding this expression, it is clear that the coefficient c_{n-1} of x^{n-1} is $-\sum_{j=1}^{n} \lambda_j$. Similarly, expanding $\det(xI - A)$, c_{n-1} is the negative sum of the diagonal elements of A, that is, $c_{n-1} = -tr(A)$. It follows that $tr(A) = \sum_{j=1}^{n} \lambda_j$.

The λ_j's are called the **eigenvalues** of A, that is, values such that there exists an n-vector $\boldsymbol{u}$ (an **eigenvector**) such that $A\boldsymbol{u} = \lambda_j \boldsymbol{u}$. It follows that $A^r \boldsymbol{u} = \lambda_j^r \boldsymbol{u}$, which implies that λ_j^r's are eigenvalues of A^r and that $\Pi_{j=1}^{n}(x - \lambda_j^r)$ is the characteristic polynomial of A^r. Since $s_r = tr(A^r)$, $s_r = \sum_{j=1}^{n} \lambda_j^r$.

Let $s_0 = 1$ and $s_k = 0$ for $k < 0$. Then, to complete the proof of (6.13), we must show that the following identity holds for $1 \leq i \leq n$:

$$
s_{i-1}c_{n-1} + s_{i-2}c_{n-2} + \cdots + s_1 c_{n-i+1} + ic_{n-i} = -s_i
$$

Moving s_i to the left-hand side, substituting for the traces, and using the definition of the characteristic polynomial yield

$$
ic_{n-i} + \sum_{j=1}^{n} \frac{\phi_A(\lambda_j) - \left(\lambda_j^{n-i}c_{n-i} + \lambda_j^{n-i-1}c_{n-i-1} + \cdots + \lambda_j c_1 + c_0\right)}{\lambda_j^{n-i}} = 0
$$

Since $\phi_A(\lambda_j) = 0$, when we substitute l for $n - i$ it suffices to show the following for $0 \le l \le n - 1$:

$$(n - l)c_l = \sum_{j=1}^{n} \sum_{k=0}^{l} \frac{c_k}{\lambda_j^l} \tag{6.14}$$

This identity can be shown by induction using as the base case $l = 0$ and the following facts about the derivatives of the characteristic polynomial of A, which are easy to establish:

$$c_0 = (-1)^n \prod_{j=1}^{n} \lambda_j$$

$$c_k = \left. \frac{d^k \phi_A(x)}{dx^k} \right|_{x=0} = (-1)^k c_0 \sum_{j_1} \cdots \sum_{j_k} \prod_{\substack{t=1 \\ j_r \ne j_s}}^{k} \frac{1}{\lambda_{j_t}}$$

The reader is asked to show that (6.14) follows from these identities. (See Problem 6.17.) ∎

Csanky's algorithm computes the traces of powers, namely the s_r's, and then inverts the lower triangular matrix given above, thereby solving for the coefficients of the characteristic polynomial. The coefficients are then used with a prefix computation, as mentioned earlier, to compute the inverse. Each of the n s_r's can be computed in $O(n)$ steps once the powers of A have been formed by the prefix computation described above. The lower triangular matrix is non-singular and can be inverted by a circuit with $M_{\mathrm{matrix}}(n, K)$ operations and depth $O(\log^2 n)$, as shown in Theorem 6.5.1. The following theorem summarizes these results.

THEOREM 6.5.6 *The matrix inverse function for non-singular $n \times n$ matrices over a field of characteristic zero, $f_{A^{-1}}^{(n)}$, has an algebraic circuit whose size and depth satisfy the following bounds:*

$$C\left(f_{A^{-1}}^{(n)} \right) = O(n M_{\mathrm{matrix}}(n, K))$$

$$C\left(f_{A^{-1}}^{(n)} \right) = O(\log^2 n)$$

The size bound can be improved to $O(\sqrt{n} M_{\mathrm{matrix}}(n, K))$, as suggested in Problems 6.15 and 6.16.

6.6 Solving Linear Systems

A general linear system with $n \times n$ coefficient matrix M, n-vector $\boldsymbol{x}$ of unknowns and n-vector $\boldsymbol{b}$ is defined in (6.5) and repeated below:

$$M\boldsymbol{x} = \boldsymbol{b}$$

This system can be solved for $\boldsymbol{x}$ in terms of M and $\boldsymbol{b}$ using the following steps when M is not SPD. If it is SPD, the first step is unnecessary and can be eliminated.

a) Premultiply both sides by the transpose of M to produce the following linear system in which the coefficient matrix $M^T M$ is SPD:

$$M^T M \boldsymbol{x} = M^T \boldsymbol{b} = \boldsymbol{b}^*$$

b) Compute the LDL^T decomposition of $M^T M$.

c) Solve the system (6.15) by solving three subsequent systems:

$$LDL^T \boldsymbol{x} = \boldsymbol{b}^* \tag{6.15}$$

$$L\boldsymbol{u} = \boldsymbol{b}^* \tag{6.16}$$

$$D\boldsymbol{v} = \boldsymbol{u} \tag{6.17}$$

$$L^T \boldsymbol{x} = \boldsymbol{v} \tag{6.18}$$

Clearly, $L\boldsymbol{u} = LD\boldsymbol{v} = LDL^T \boldsymbol{x} = \boldsymbol{b}^*$.

The vector $\boldsymbol{b}^*$ is formed by a matrix-vector multiplication that can be done with n^2 multiplications and $n(n-1)$ additions, for a total of $2n^2 - n$ operations.

Since L is unit lower triangular, the system (6.16) is solved by **forward elimination**. The value of u_1 is b_1^*. The value of u_2 is $b_1^* - l_{2,1}u_1$, obtained by eliminating u_1 from the second equation. Similarly, on the jth step, the values of $u_1, u_2, \ldots, u_{j-1}$ are known and their weighted values can be subtracted from b_j^* to provide the value of u_j; that is,

$$u_j = b_j^* - l_{j,1}u_1 - l_{j,2}u_2 - \cdots - l_{j,j-1}u_{j-1}$$

for $1 \leq j \leq n$. Here $n(n-1)/2$ products are formed and $n(n-1)/2$ subtractions taken for a total of $n(n-1)$ operations.

Since D is diagonal, the system (6.17) is solved for $\boldsymbol{v}$ by multiplying u_j by the multiplicative inverse of $d_{j,j}$; that is,

$$v_j = u_j d_{j,j}^{-1}$$

for $1 \leq j \leq n$. This is called **normalization**. Here n divisions are performed.

Finally, the system (6.18) is solved for $\boldsymbol{x}$ by **backward substitution**, which is forward elimination applied to the elements of $\boldsymbol{x}$ in reverse order.

THEOREM 6.6.1 *Let* $f_{\text{SPD\_solve}}^{(n)} : R^{n^2+n} \mapsto R^n$ *be the (partial) function that computes the solution to a linear system of equations defined by an* $n \times n$ *symmetric positive definite coefficient matrix* M. *Then*

$$C(f_{\text{SPD\_solve}}^{(n)}) \leq C(f_{LDL^T}^{(n)}) + O(n^2)$$

$$D(f_{\text{SPD\_solve}}^{(n)}) \leq C(f_{LDL^T}^{(n)}) + O(n)$$

If M *is not SPD but is non-singular, an additional* $O(M_{\text{matrix}}(n, K))$ *circuit elements and depth* $O(\log n)$ *suffice to compute it.*

6.7 Convolution and the FFT Algorithm

The discrete Fourier transform (DFT) and convolution are widely used techniques with important applications in signal processing and computer science.

In this section we introduce the DFT, describe the fast Fourier transform algorithm, and derive the convolution theorem. The naive DFT algorithm on sequences of length n uses $O(n^2)$ operations; the fast Fourier transform algorithm uses only $O(n \log n)$ operations, a saving of a factor of at least 100 for $n \geq 1,000$. The convolution theorem provides a way to use the DFT to convolve two sequences in $O(n \log n)$ steps, many fewer than the naive algorithm for convolution, which uses $O(n^2)$ steps.

6.7.1   Commutative Rings*

Since the DFT is defined over commutative rings having an nth root of unity, we digress briefly to discuss such rings. (Commutative rings are defined in Section 6.2.)

DEFINITION 6.7.1 *A commutative ring $\mathcal{R} = (R, +, *, 0, 1)$ has a* **principal nth root of unity** *ω if $\omega \in R$ satisfies the following conditions:*

$$\omega^n = 1 \tag{6.19}$$

$$\sum_{k=0}^{n-1} \omega^{lk} = 0 \text{ for each } 1 \leq l \leq n-1 \tag{6.20}$$

The elements $\omega^0, \omega^1, \omega^2, \ldots, \omega^{n-1}$ are the nth **roots of unity** *and the elements $\omega^0, \omega^{-1}, \omega^{-2}, \ldots, \omega^{-(n-1)}$ are the nth* **inverse roots of unity**. *(Note that $\omega^{-j} = \omega^{n-j}$ is the multiplicative inverse of ω^j since $\omega^j \omega^{n-j} = \omega^n = 1$.)*

Two commutative rings that have principal nth roots of unity are the complex numbers and the ring $\mathbb{Z}_m$ of integers modulo $m = 2^{tn/2} + 1$ when $t \geq 2$ and $n = 2^q$, as we show. The reader is asked to show that $\mathbb{Z}_m$ has a principal nth root of unity, as stated below. (See Problem 6.24.)

LEMMA 6.7.1 *Let $\mathbb{Z}_m$ be the ring of integers modulo m when $m = 2^{tn/2} + 1$, $t \geq 2$ and $n = 2^q$. Then $\omega = 2^t$ is a principal nth root of unity.*

An example of the ring $\mathbb{Z}_m$ is given by $t = 2$, $n = 4$, and $m = 2^4 + 1 = 17$. In this ring $\omega = 4$ is a principal fourth root of unity. This is true because $\omega^n = 4^4 = 16 \cdot 16 = (16+1)(16-1) + 1 = 1 \bmod (16+1)$ and $\sum_{j=0}^{n-1} \omega^{pj} = ((4^p)^n - 1)/(4^p - 1) \bmod (17) = ((4^n)^p - 1)/(4^p - 1) \bmod (17) = (1^p - 1)/(4^p - 1) \bmod (17) = 0 \bmod (17)$.

LEMMA 6.7.2 *$e^{2\pi i/n} = \cos(2\pi/n) + i\sin(2\pi/n)$ is a principal nth root of unity over the complex numbers where $i = \sqrt{-1}$ is the "imaginary unit."*

Proof The first condition is satisfied because $(e^{2\pi i/n})^n = e^{2\pi i} = 1$. Also, $\sum_{k=0}^{n-1} \omega^{lk} = (\omega^{ln} - 1)/(\omega^l - 1) = 0$ if $1 \leq l \leq n-1$ for $\omega = e^{2\pi i/n}$. ∎

6.7.2   The Discrete Fourier Transform

The discrete Fourier transform has many applications. In Section 6.7.4 we see that it can be used to compute the convolution of two sequences efficiently, which is the same as computing the coefficients of the product of two polynomials. The discrete Fourier transform can also be used to construct a fast algorithm (circuit) for the multiplication of two binary integers [297]. It is widely used in processing analog data such as speech and music.

The n-point **discrete Fourier transform** $F_n : R^n \mapsto R^n$ maps n-tuples $\boldsymbol{a} = (a_0, a_1, \ldots, a_{n-1})$ over R to n-tuples $\boldsymbol{f} = (f_0, f_1, \ldots, f_{n-1})$ over R; that is, $F_n(\boldsymbol{a}) = \boldsymbol{f}$. The components of $\boldsymbol{f}$ are defined as the values of the following polynomial $p(x)$ at the nth roots of unity:

$$p(x) = a_0 + a_1 x + a_2 x^2 + \cdots + a_{n-1} x^{n-1} \tag{6.21}$$

Then f_r, the rth component of $F_n(\boldsymbol{a})$, is defined as

$$f_r = p(\omega^r) = \sum_{k=0}^{n-1} a_k \omega^{rk} \tag{6.22}$$

This computation is equivalent to the following matrix-vector multiplication:

$$F_n(\boldsymbol{a}) = [w^{ij}] \times \boldsymbol{a} \tag{6.23}$$

where $[w^{ij}]$ is the $n \times n$ **Vandermonde matrix** whose i, j entry is w^{ij}, $0 \le i, j \le n - 1$, and $\boldsymbol{a}$ is treated as a column vector.

The n-point **inverse discrete Fourier transform** $F_n^{-1} : R^n \mapsto R^n$ is defined as the values of the following polynomial $q(x)$ at the inverse nth roots of unity:

$$q(x) = (f_0 + f_1 x + f_2 x^2 + \cdots + f_{n-1} x^{n-1})/n \tag{6.24}$$

That is, the inverse DFT maps an n-tuple $\boldsymbol{f}$ to an n-tuple $\boldsymbol{g}$, namely, $F_n^{-1}(\boldsymbol{f}) = \boldsymbol{g}$, where g_s is defined as follows:

$$g_s = q(\omega^{-s}) = \frac{1}{n} \sum_{l=0}^{n-1} f_l \omega^{-ls} \tag{6.25}$$

This computation is equivalent to the following matrix-vector multiplication:

$$F_n^{-1}(\boldsymbol{f}) = \left[\frac{1}{n} w^{-ij} \right] \times \boldsymbol{f}$$

Because of the following lemma it is legitimate to call F_n^{-1} the **inverse** of F_n.

LEMMA 6.7.3 *For all $\boldsymbol{a} \in R^n$, $\boldsymbol{a} = F_n^{-1}(F_n(\boldsymbol{a}))$.*

Proof Let $\boldsymbol{f} = F_n(\boldsymbol{a})$ and $\boldsymbol{g} = F_n^{-1}(\boldsymbol{f})$. Then g_s satisfies the following:

$$g_s = \frac{1}{n} \sum_{l=0}^{n-1} f_l \omega^{-ls} = \frac{1}{n} \sum_{l=0}^{n-1} \sum_{k=0}^{n-1} a_k \omega^{(k-s)l}$$

$$= \sum_{k=0}^{n-1} a_k \frac{1}{n} \sum_{l=0}^{n-1} \omega^{(k-s)l}$$

$$= a_s$$

The second equation results from a change in the order of summation. The last follows from the definition of nth roots of unity. It follows that the matrix $[w^{-ij}/n]$ is the inverse of $[w^{ij}]$. ∎

The computation of the n-point DFT and its inverse using the naive algorithms suggested by their definitions requires $O(n^2)$ steps. Below we show that a fast DFT algorithm exists for which only $O(n \log n)$ steps suffice.

6.7.3 Fast Fourier Transform

The **fast Fourier transform algorithm** is a consequence of the following observation: when n is even, the polynomial $p(x)$ in equation (6.21) can be decomposed as

$$
\begin{aligned}
p(x) &= a_0 + a_1 x + a_2 x^2 + \cdots + a_{n-1} x^{n-1} \\
&= (a_0 + a_2 x^2 + \cdots + a_{n-2} x^{n-2}) \\
&\quad + x\,(a_1 + a_3 x^2 + \cdots + a_{n-1} x^{n-2}) \\
&= p_e(x^2) + x p_o(x^2)
\end{aligned}
\tag{6.26}
$$

Here $p_e(y)$ and $p_o(y)$ are polynomials of degree $(n/2) - 1$.

Let n be a power of 2, that is, $n = 2^d$. As stated above, the n-point DFT of $\boldsymbol{a}$ is obtained by evaluating $p(x)$ at the nth roots of unity. Because of the decomposition of $p(x)$, it suffices to evaluate $p_e(y)$ and $p_o(y)$ at $y = (\omega^0)^2, (\omega^1)^2, (\omega^2)^2, \ldots, (\omega^{n-1})^2 = (\omega^2)^0, (\omega^2)^1, (\omega^2)^2, \ldots, (\omega^2)^{n-1}$ and combine their values with one multiplication and one addition for each of the n roots of unity. However, because ω^2 is a $(n/2)$th principal root of unity (see Problem 6.25), $(\omega^2)^{(n/2)+r} = (\omega^2)^r$ and the n powers of ω^2 collapse to $n/2$ distinct powers of ω^2, namely, the $(n/2)$th roots of unity. Thus, $p(x)$ at the nth roots of unity can be evaluated by evaluating $p_e(y)$ and $p_o(y)$ at the $(n/2)$th roots of unity and combining their values with one addition and multiplication for each of the nth roots of unity. In other words, the n-point DFT of $\boldsymbol{a}$ can be done by performing the $(n/2)$-point DFT of its even and odd subsequences and combining the results with $O(n)$ additional steps. This is the fast Fourier transform (FFT) algorithm.

We denote by $F^{(d)}$ the directed acyclic graph associated with the straight-line program resulting from this realization of the FFT on $n = 2^d$ inputs. A circuit for the 16-point FFT algorithm inputs, $F^{(4)}$, is shown in Fig. 6.7. It is computed from the eight-point FFT on the even and odd components of $\boldsymbol{a}$, as shown in the boxed regions. These components are permuted because each of these smaller FFTs is computed recursively in turn. (The index of

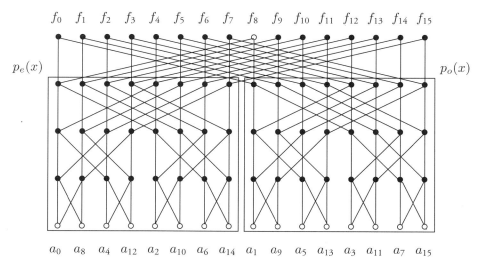

Figure 6.7 A circuit $F^{(4)}$ for the FFT algorithm on 16 inputs.

the ith input vertex from the left is obtained by writing the integer i as a binary number, reversing the bits, and converting the resulting binary number to an integer. This is called the **bit-reverse permutation** of the binary representation of the integer. For example, the third input from the left has index 3, which is (011) in binary. Reversed, the binary number is (110), which represents 12.) Inputs are associated with the open vertices at the bottom of the graph. Each vertex except for input vertices is associated with an addition and a multiplication. For example, the white vertex at the top of the graph computes $f_8 = p_e((\omega^8)^2) + \omega^8 p_o((\omega^8)^2)$, where $(\omega^8)^2 = \omega^{16} = \omega$.

Let $C(F^{(d)})$ and $D(F^{(d)})$ be the size and depth of circuits for the 2^d-point FFT algorithm for integer $d \geq 1$. The construction given above leads to the following recurrences for these two measures:

$$C\left(F^{(d)}\right) \leq 2C\left(F^{(d-1)}\right) + 2^{d+1}$$
$$D\left(F^{(d)}\right) \leq D\left(F^{(d-1)}\right) + 2$$

Also, examination of the base case of $n = 2$ demonstrates that $C\left(F^{(1)}\right) = 3$ and $D\left(F^{(1)}\right) = 2$, from which we have the following theorem.

THEOREM 6.7.1 *Let $n = 2^d$. The circuit for the n-point FFT algorithm over a commutative ring $\mathcal{R}$ has the following circuit size and depth bounds:*

$$C\left(F^{(d)}\right) \leq 2n \log n$$
$$D\left(F^{(d)}\right) \leq 2 \log n$$

The FFT graph is used in later chapters to illustrate tradeoffs between space and time, space and the number of I/O operations, and area and time for computation with VLSI machines. For each of these applications we decompose the FFT graph into sub-FFT graphs. One such decomposition is shown in Fig. 6.7. A more general decomposition is shown in Fig. 6.8 and described below.

LEMMA 6.7.4 *The 2^d-point FFT graph $F^{(d)}$ can be decomposed into 2^e 2^{d-e}-point bottom FFT graphs, $\{F_{b,j}^{(d-e)} \mid 1 \leq j \leq 2^e\}$, and 2^{d-e} 2^e-point top FFT graphs, $\{F_{t,j}^{(e)} \mid 1 \leq j \leq 2^{d-e}\}$. The ith input of $F_{t,j}^{(e)}$ is the jth output of $F_{b,i}^{(d-e)}$.*

In Fig. 6.8 the vertices and edges have been grouped together as recognizable FFT graphs and surrounded by shaded boxes. The edges between boxes are not edges of the FFT graph but instead are used to identify vertices that are simultaneously outputs of bottom FFT subgraphs and inputs to top FFT subgraphs.

COROLLARY 6.7.1 *$F^{(d)}$ can be decomposed into $\lfloor d/e \rfloor$ stages each containing 2^{d-e} copies of $F^{(e)}$ and one stage containing 2^{d-k} copies of $F^{(k)}$, $k = d - \lfloor d/e \rfloor e$. ($F(0)$ is a single vertex.) The output vertices of one stage are the input vertices to the next.*

Proof From Lemma 6.7.4, each of the 2^e bottom FFT subgraphs $F^{(d-e)}$ can be further decomposed into 2^{d-2e} top FFT subgraphs $F^{(e)}$ and 2^e bottom FFT subgraphs $F^{(d-2e)}$. By repeating this process t times, $t \leq d/e$, $F^{(d)}$ can be decomposed into t stages each

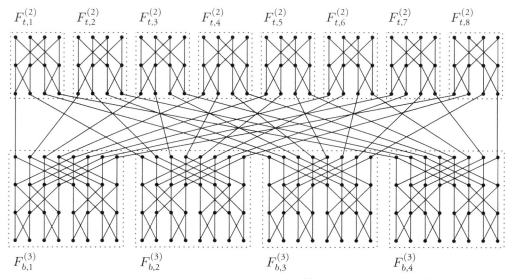

$F_{t,1}^{(2)}$ $F_{t,2}^{(2)}$ $F_{t,3}^{(2)}$ $F_{t,4}^{(2)}$ $F_{t,5}^{(2)}$ $F_{t,6}^{(2)}$ $F_{t,7}^{(2)}$ $F_{t,8}^{(2)}$

$F_{b,1}^{(3)}$ $F_{b,2}^{(3)}$ $F_{b,3}^{(3)}$ $F_{b,4}^{(3)}$

Figure 6.8 Decomposition of the 32-point FFT graph $F^{(5)}$ into four copies of $F^{(3)}$ and 8 copies of $F^{(2)}$. The edges between bottom and top sub-FFT graphs do not exist in the FFT graph. They are used here to identify common vertices and highlight the communication needed among sub-FFT graphs.

containing 2^{d-e} copies of $F^{(e)}$ and one stage containing 2^{d-te} copies of $F^{(d-te)}$. The result follows by setting $t = \lfloor d/e \rfloor$. ∎

6.7.4 Convolution Theorem

The **convolution function** $f_{\mathrm{conv}}^{(n,m)} : R^{n+m} \mapsto R^{n+m-1}$ over a commutative ring $\mathcal{R}$ maps an n-tuple $\boldsymbol{a} = (a_0, a_1, \ldots, a_{n-1})$ and an m-tuple $\boldsymbol{b} = (b_0, b_1, \ldots, b_{m-1})$ onto an $(n+m-1)$-tuple $\boldsymbol{c}$, denoted $\boldsymbol{c} = \boldsymbol{a} \otimes \boldsymbol{b}$, where c_j is defined as follows:

$$c_j = \sum_{r+s=j} a_r * b_s \text{ for } 0 \leq j \leq n + m - 2$$

Here $\sum$ and $*$ are addition and multiplication over the ring $\mathcal{R}$. The direct computation of the convolution function using the above formula takes $O(nm)$ steps. The convolution theorem given below and the fast Fourier transform algorithm described above allow the convolution function to be computed in $O(n \log n)$ steps when $n = m$.

Associate with $\boldsymbol{a}$ and $\boldsymbol{b}$ the following polynomials in the variable x:

$$a(x) = a_0 + a_1 x + a_2 x^2 + \cdots + a_{n-1} x^{n-1}$$
$$b(x) = b_0 + b_1 x + b_2 x^2 + \cdots + b_{n-1} x^{n-1}$$

Then the coefficient of the term x^j in the product polynomial $c(x) = a(x)b(x)$ is clearly the term c_j in the convolution $\boldsymbol{c} = \boldsymbol{a} \otimes \boldsymbol{b}$.

Convolution is used in signal processing and integer multiplication. In signal processing, convolution describes the results of passing a signal through a linear filter. In binary integer multiplication the polynomials $a(2)$ and $b(2)$ represent binary numbers; convolution is related to the computation of their product.

The **convolution theorem** is one of the most important applications of the DFT. It demonstrates that convolution, which appears to require $O(n^2)$ operations when $n = m$, can in fact be computed by a circuit with $O(n)$ operations plus a small multiple of the number needed to compute the DFT and its inverse.

THEOREM 6.7.2 *Let $\mathcal{R} = (R, +, *, \mathbf{0}, \mathbf{1})$ be a commutative ring and let $\boldsymbol{a}, \boldsymbol{b} \in R^n$. Let $F_{2n} : R^{2n} \mapsto R^{2n}$ and $F_{2n}^{-1} : R^{2n} \mapsto R^{2n}$ be the $2n$-point DFT and its inverse over R. Let $F_{2n}(\boldsymbol{a}) \times F_{2n}(\boldsymbol{b})$ denote the $2n$-tuple obtained from the term-by-term product of the components of $F_{2n}(\boldsymbol{a})$ and $F_{2n}(\boldsymbol{b})$. Then, the convolution $\boldsymbol{a} \otimes \boldsymbol{b}$ satisfies the following identity:*

$$\boldsymbol{a} \otimes \boldsymbol{b} = F_{2n}^{-1}(F_{2n}(\boldsymbol{a}) \times F_{2n}(\boldsymbol{b}))$$

Proof The n-point DFT $F_n : R^n \mapsto R^n$ transforms the n-tuple of coefficients $\boldsymbol{a}$ of the polynomial $p(x)$ of degree $n - 1$ into the n-tuple $\boldsymbol{f} = F_n(\boldsymbol{a})$. In fact, the rth component of $\boldsymbol{f}$, f_r, is the value of the polynomial $p(x)$ at the rth of the n roots of unity, namely $f_r = p(w^r)$. The n-point inverse DFT $F_n^{-1} : R^n \mapsto R^n$ inverts the process through a similar computation. If $q(x)$ is the polynomial of degree $n - 1$ whose lth coefficient is f_l/n, then the sth component of the inverse DFT on $\boldsymbol{f}$, namely $F_n^{-1}(\boldsymbol{f})$, is $a_s = q(w^{-s})$.

As stated above, to compute the convolution of n-tuples $\boldsymbol{a}$ and $\boldsymbol{b}$ it suffices to compute the coefficients of the product polynomial $c(x) = a(x)b(x)$. Since the product $c(x)$ is of degree $2n - 2$, we can treat it as a polynomial of degree $2n - 1$ and take the $2n$-point DFT, F_{2n}, of it and its inverse, F_{2n}^{-1}, of the result. This seemingly futile process leads to an efficient algorithm for convolution. Since the DFT is obtained by evaluating a polynomial

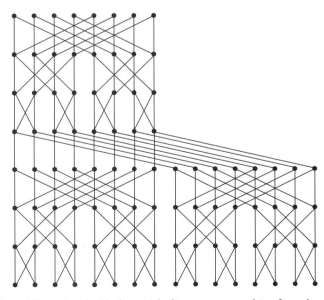

Figure 6.9 The DAG associated with the straight-line program resulting from the application of the FFT to the convolution theorem with sequences of length 8.

at the n roots of unity, the DFT of $c(x)$ can be done at the $2n$ roots of unity by evaluating $a(x)$ and $b(x)$ at the $2n$ roots of unity (that is, computing the DFTs of their coefficients as if they had degree $2n - 1$), multiplying their values together, and taking the $2n$-point inverse DFT, that is, performing the computation stated in the theorem. ∎

The combination of the convolution theorem and the algorithm for the FFT provides a fast straight-line program for convolution, as stated below. The directed acyclic graph for this straight-line program is shown in Fig. 6.9 on page 269.

THEOREM 6.7.3 *Let* $n = 2^d$. *The convolution function* $f_{\text{conv}}^{(n,n)} : R^{2n} \mapsto R^{2(n-1)}$ *over a commutative ring* $\mathcal{R}$ *can be computed by a straight-line program over* $\mathcal{R}$ *with size and depth satisfying the following bounds:*

$$C\left(f_{\text{conv}}^{(n,n)}\right) \leq 12n \log 2n$$
$$D\left(f_{\text{conv}}^{(n,n)}\right) \leq 4 \log 2n$$

6.8 Merging and Sorting Networks

The **sorting problem** is to put into ascending or descending order a collection of items that are drawn from a totally ordered set. A set is **totally ordered** if for every two distinct elements of the set one is larger than the other. The **merging problem** is to merge two sorted lists into one sorted list. Sorting and merging algorithms can be either straight-line or non-straight-line. An example of a non-straight-line merging algorithm is the following:

Create a new sorted list from two sorted lists by removing the smaller item from the two lists and appending it to the new list until one list is empty, at which point append the non-empty list to the end of the new list.

The binary sorting function $f_{\text{sort}}^{(n)} : \mathcal{B}^n \mapsto \mathcal{B}^n$ described in Section 2.11 sorts a Boolean n-tuple into descending order. The combinational circuit given there is an example of a straight-line sorting network, a network realized by a straight-line program. When the set of elements to be sorted is not Boolean, sorting networks can become quite a bit more complicated, as we see below.

In this section we describe **sorting networks**, circuits constructed from comparator operators that take n elements drawn from a finite totally ordered set $\mathcal{A}$ and put them into sorted order. A **comparator function** $\otimes : \mathcal{A}^2 \mapsto \mathcal{A}^2$ with arguments a and b returns their maximum and minimum; that is, $\otimes(a, b) = (\max(a, b), \min(a, b))$.

It is convenient to show a comparator operator as a vertical edge between two lines carrying values, as in Fig. 6.10(a). The values on the two lines to the right of the edge are the values to its left in sorted order, the smaller being on the upper line. A sorting network is an example of a **comparator network**, a circuit in which the only operator is a comparator. Input values appear on the left and output values appear on the right in sorted order.

Shown in Fig. 6.10(b) is an **insertion-sorting network** on five inputs that inserts an element into a previously sorted sublist. Two inputs are sorted at the wavefront labeled A. Between wavefronts A and B a new item is inserted that is compared against the previously sorted sublist and inserted into its proper position. The same occurs between wavefronts B and C and after

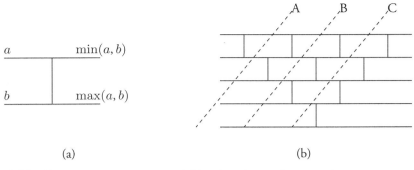

$$a \quad\quad \min(a, b)$$

$$b \quad\quad \max(a, b)$$

(a)   (b)

Figure 6.10   (a) A comparison operator, and (b) an insertion-sorting network.

wavefront C. An insertion-sorting network can be realized with one comparator for the first two inputs and $k - 1$ more for the kth input, $3 \leq k \leq n$. Let $C_{\mathrm{insert}}(n)$ and $D_{\mathrm{insert}}(n)$ denote the size and depth of an insertion-sorting network on n elements. Then $C(2) = 1$ and $D(2) = 1$, and

$$C_{\mathrm{insert}}(n) \leq C_{\mathrm{insert}}(n - 1) + n - 1 = n(n - 1)/2$$
$$D_{\mathrm{insert}}(n) \leq \max(D_{\mathrm{insert}}(n - 1) + 1, n - 1) = n - 1$$

The depth bound follows because there is a path of length $n - 1$ through the chain of comparators added at the last wavefront and every path through the sorting network is extended by one comparator with the addition of the new wavefront. A simple proof by induction establishes these results.

6.8.1   Sorting Via Odd-Even Merging

We now describe **Batcher's odd-even merging network** $BM(m)$, which is the basis for a sorting network. Let $\boldsymbol{x} = (x_1, x_2, \ldots, x_m)$ and $\boldsymbol{y} = (y_1, y_2, \ldots, y_m)$ be ordered sequences of length m. That is, $x_j \leq x_{j+1}$ and $y_j \leq y_{j+1}$. As suggested in Fig. 6.11, the even-indexed components of $\boldsymbol{x}$ are merged with the odd-indexed components of $\boldsymbol{y}$, as are the odd-indexed components of $\boldsymbol{x}$ and the even-indexed components of $\boldsymbol{y}$. Each of the four lists that are merged are themselves sorted. The two lists are interleaved and the kth and $(k + 1)$st elements, k even, are compared and swapped if necessary. To prove correctness of this circuit, we use the zero-one principle which is stated below for sorting networks but applied later to merging networks.

THEOREM 6.8.1 (**Zero-one principle**)   *If a comparator network for inputs over a set $\mathcal{A}$ correctly sorts all binary inputs, it correctly sorts all inputs.*

Proof   The proof is by contradiction. Suppose the network correctly sorts all 0-1 sequences but fails to sort the input sequence $(a_1, a_2, \ldots, a_n)$. Then there are inputs a_i and a_j such that $a_i \leq a_j$ but the network puts a_j before a_i.

Since a sorting network contains only comparators, if we replace each entry a_r in an input sequence $(a_1, a_2, \ldots, a_n)$ with a new entry $h(a_r)$, where $h(a)$ is monotonically non-decreasing in a ($h(a)$ is non-decreasing as a increases), each comparison of entries a_r and a_s is replaced by a comparison of entries $h(a_r)$ and $h(a_s)$. Since $a_r \leq a_s$ if and only

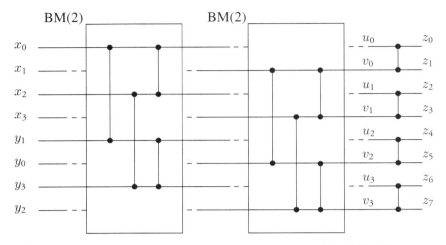

Figure 6.11 A recursive construction of the odd-even merging network $BM(4)$. The even-indexed elements of one sorted sequence are merged with the odd-indexed elements of the other, the resulting sequences interleaved, and the even- and succeeding odd-indexed elements compared. The inputs of one sequence are permuted to demonstrate that $BM(4)$ uses two copies of $BM(2)$.

if $h(a_r) \leq h(a_s)$, the set of comparisons made by the sorting network will be exactly the same on $(a_1, a_2, \ldots, a_n)$ as on $(h(a_1), h(a_2), \ldots, h(a_n))$. Thus, the original output $(b_1, b_2, \ldots, b_n)$ will be replaced by the output sequence $(h(b_1), h(b_2), \ldots, h(b_n))$.

Since it is presumed that the comparator network puts a_i and a_j in the incorrect order, let $h(x)$ be the following monotone function:

$$h(x) = \begin{cases} 0 & \text{if } x \leq a_i \\ 1 & \text{if } x > a_i \end{cases}$$

Then the input and output sequences to the comparator network are binary. However, the output sequence is not sorted (a_j appears before a_i but $h(a_j) = 1$ and $h(a_i) = 0$), contradicting the hypothesis of the theorem. It follows that all sequences over $\mathcal{A}$ must be sorted correctly. ∎

We now show that Batcher's odd-even merging circuit correctly merges two sorted lists. If a correct m-sorter exists, then a correct $2m$-sorter can be constructed by combining two m-sorters with a correct $2m$-input odd-even merging circuit. It follows that a correct $2m$-input odd-even merging circuit exists if and only if the resulting sorting network is correct. This is the core idea in a proof by induction of correctness of the $2m$-input odd-even merging circuit. The basis for induction is the fact that individual comparators correctly sort sequences of two elements.

Suppose that $\boldsymbol{x}$ and $\boldsymbol{y}$ are sorted $0-1$ sequences of length m. Let $\boldsymbol{x}$ have k 0's and $m - k$ 1's, and let $\boldsymbol{y}$ have l 0's and $m - l$ 1's. Then the leftmost merging network of Fig. 6.11 selects exactly $\lceil k/2 \rceil$ 0's from $\boldsymbol{x}$ and $\lfloor l/2 \rfloor$ 0's from $\boldsymbol{y}$ to produce the sequence $\boldsymbol{u}$ consisting of $a = \lceil k/2 \rceil + \lfloor l/2 \rfloor$ 0's followed by 1's. Similarly, the rightmost merging network produces the sequence $\boldsymbol{v}$ consisting of $b = \lfloor k/2 \rfloor + \lceil l/2 \rceil$ 0's followed by 1's. Since $\lceil x \rceil - \lfloor x \rfloor$ is 0 or 1, it follows that either $a = b$, $a = b - 1$, or $a = b + 1$. Thus, when $\boldsymbol{u}$ and $\boldsymbol{v}$ are interleaved to produce the sequence $\boldsymbol{z}$ it contains a sequence of $a + b$ 0's followed by 1's when $a = b$ or $a = b - 1$, or $2a$ 0's followed by 1 0 followed by 1's when $a = b + 1$, as suggested below:

$$\boldsymbol{z} = \overbrace{0, 0, \ldots, 0}^{2a}, 1, 0, 1, \ldots, 1$$

Thus, if for each $0 \le k \le m - 1$ the outputs in positions $2k$ and $2k + 1$ are compared and swapped, if necessary, the output will be properly sorted.

The graph of $BM(4)$ of Fig. 6.11 illustrates that $BM(4)$ is constructed of two copies of $BM(2)$. In addition, it demonstrates that the operations of each of the two $BM(2)$ subnetworks can be performed in parallel. Another important observation is that this graph is isomorphic to an FFT graph when the comparators are replaced by two-input butterfly graphs, as shown in Fig. 6.12.

THEOREM 6.8.2 *Batcher's n-input odd-even merging circuit $BM(n)$ for merging two sorted n-sequences, $n = 2^k$, has the following size and depth bounds over the basis Ω of comparators:*

$$C_\Omega(BM(n)) \le (n/2)(\log n)$$
$$D_\Omega(BM(n)) \le \log n$$

Proof Let $C(k)$ and $D(k)$ be the size and depth of $BM(n)$. Then $C(1) = 1$, $D(1) = 1$, $C(k) = 2C(k - 1) + 2^{k-1}$, and $D(k) = D(k - 1) + 1$. It follows that $C(k) = k2^{k-1}$ and $D(k) = k$. (See Problem 6.29.) ■

This leads us to the recursive construction of a Batcher's odd-even sorting network $BS(n)$ for sequences of length n, $n = 2^k$. It merges the output of two copies of $BS(n/2)$ using a copy of Batcher's n-input odd-even merging circuit $BM(n)$. The proof of the following theorem is left as an exercise. (See Problem 6.28.)

THEOREM 6.8.3 *Batcher's n-input odd-even sorting circuit $BS(n)$ for $n = 2^k$ has the following size and depth bounds over the basis Ω of comparators:*

$$C_\Omega(BS(n)) = \frac{n}{4}[\log^2 n + \log n]$$

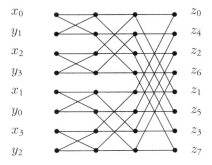

Figure 6.12 The graph resulting from the replacement of comparators in Fig. 6.11 with two-input butterfly graphs and the permutation of inputs. All edges are directed from left to right.

$$D_\Omega(BS(n)) = \frac{1}{2} \log n (\log n - 1)$$

6.8.2   Fast Sorting Networks

Ajtai, Komlós, and Szemerédi [14] have shown the existence of a sorting network (known as the **AKS sorting network**) on n inputs whose circuit size and depth are $O(n \log n)$ and $O(\log n)$, respectively. The question had been open for many years whether such a sorting network existed. Prior to [14] it was thought that sorting networks required $\Omega(\log^2 n)$ depth.

· ·

Problems

MATHEMATICAL PRELIMINARIES

6.1 Show that $(\mathbb{N}, +, *, 0, 1)$ is a commutative ring, where $+$ and $*$ denote integer addition and multiplication and 0 and 1 denote the first two integers.

6.2 Let $\mathbb{Z}_p$ be the **set of integers modulo** p, $p > 0$, under addition and multiplication modulo p with additive identity 0 and multiplicative identity 1. Show that $\mathbb{Z}_p$ is a ring.

6.3 A **field** $\mathcal{F}$ is a commutative ring in which each element other than **0** has a multiplicative inverse. Show that $(\mathbb{Z}_p, +, *, 0, 1)$ is a field when p is a prime.

MATRICES

6.4 Let $M_{n \times n}$ be the set of $n \times n$ matrices over a ring $\mathcal{R}$. Show that $(M_{n \times n}, +_n, \times_n, 0_n, I_n)$ is a ring, where $+_n$ and $\times_n$ are the matrix addition and multiplication operators and 0_n and I_n are the $n \times n$ zero and identity matrices.

6.5 Show that the maximum number of linearly independent rows and of linearly independent columns of an $n \times m$ matrix A are the same.

Hint: Use the fact that permuting the rows and/or columns of A and adding a scalar product of one row (column) of A to any other row (column) does not change its rank. Use row and column permutations as well as additions of scalar products to rows and/or columns of A to transform A into a matrix that contains the largest possible identity matrix in its upper left-hand corner. This is called **Gaussian elimination**.

6.6 Show that $(A B)^T = B^T A^T$ for all $m \times n$ matrices A and $n \times p$ matrices B over a ring $\mathcal{R}$.

MATRIX MULTIPLICATION

6.7 The standard matrix-vector multiplication algorithm for a general $n \times n$ matrix requires $O(n^2)$ operations. Show that at most $O(n^{\log_2 3})$ operations are needed when the matrix is Toeplitz.

Hint: Assume that n is a power of two and treat the matrix as a 2×2 matrix of $n/2 \times n/2$ matrices. Also note that only $2n - 1$ values determine all the entries in a Toeplitz matrix. Thus, the difference between two $n \times n$ Toeplitz matrices does not require n^2 operations.

6.8 Generalize Strassen's matrix multiplication algorithm to matrices that are $m \times m$ for $m = p2^k$, p and k both integers. Derive bounds on the size and depth of a circuit realizing this version of the algorithm.

For arbitrary n, show how $n \times n$ matrices can be embedded into $m \times m$ matrices, $m = p2^k$, so that this new version of the algorithm can be used. Show that upper bounds of $4.77n^{\log_2 7}$ and $O(\log n)$ on the size and depth of this algorithm can be obtained.

6.9 Show that Strassen's matrix multiplication algorithm can be used to multiply square Boolean matrices by replacing OR by addition modulo $n + 1$. Derive a bound on the size and depth of a circuit to realize this algorithm.

6.10 Show that, when one of two $n \times n$ Boolean matrices A and B is fixed and known in advance, A and B can be multiplied by a circuit with $O(n^3/\log n)$ operations and depth $O(\log n)$ to produce the product $C = AB$ using the information provided below.

a) Multiplication of A and B is equivalent to n multiplications of A with an $n \times 1$ vector $\boldsymbol{x}$, a column of B.

b) Since A is a $0 - 1$ matrix, the product $A\boldsymbol{x}$ consists of sums of variables in $\boldsymbol{x}$.

c) The product $A\boldsymbol{x}$ can be further decomposed into the sum $A_1\boldsymbol{x}_1 + A_2\boldsymbol{x}_2 + \cdots + A_k\boldsymbol{x}_k$ where $k = \lceil n/\lceil \log n \rceil \rceil$, A_j is the $n \times \lceil \log n \rceil$ submatrix consisting of columns $(j - 1)\lceil \log n \rceil + 1$ through $j\lceil \log n \rceil$ of A, and $\boldsymbol{x}_j$ is the jth set of $\lceil \log n \rceil$ rows (variables) in $\boldsymbol{x}$.

d) There are at most n distinct sums of $\lceil \log n \rceil$ variables each of which can be formed in at most $2n$ addition steps, thereby saving a factor of $\lceil \log n \rceil$.

TRANSITIVE CLOSURE

6.11 Let $A = [a_{i,j}]$, $1 \leq i,j \leq n$, be a Boolean matrix that is the adjacency matrix of a directed graph $G = (V, E)$ on $n = |V|$ vertices. Give a proof by induction that the entry in the rth row and sth column of $A^k = A^{k-1} \times A$ is 1 if there is a path containing k edges from vertex r to vertex s and 0 otherwise.

6.12 Consider a directed graph $G = (V, E)$ in which each edge carries a label drawn from a semiring. Let the entry in the ith row and jth column of the adjacency matrix of G contain the label of the edge between vertices i and j if there is such an edge and the empty set otherwise. Assume that the labels of edges in G are drawn from a semiring. Show that Theorems 6.4.1, 6.4.2, and 6.4.3 hold for such labeled graphs.

MATRIX INVERSION

6.13 Show that the following properties hold for matrix inversion:

a) The inverse of a 2×2 upper (lower) triangular matrix is the matrix with the off-diagonal term negated.

b) The inverse of a 2×2 diagonal matrix is a diagonal matrix in which the ith diagonal element is the multiplicative inverse of the ith diagonal element of the original matrix.

6.14 Show that a lower triangular Toeplitz matrix T can be inverted by a circuit of size $O(n \log n)$ and depth $O(\log^2 n)$.

Hint: Assume that $n = 2^k$, write T as a 2×2 matrix of $n/2 \times n/2$ matrices, and devise a recursive algorithm to invert T.

6.15 Exhibit a circuit to compute the characteristic polynomial $\phi_A(x)$ of an $n \times n$ matrix A over a ring $\mathcal{R}$ that has $O(\max(n^3, \sqrt{n}M_{\text{matrix}}(n)))$ ring operations and depth $O(\log^2 n)$.

Hint: Consider the case $n = k^2$. Represent the integer i, $0 \le i \le n - 1$, by the unique pair of integers (r, s), $0 \le r, s \le k - 1$, where $i = rk + s$. Represent the coefficient c_{i+1}, $0 \le i \le n - 2$, of $\phi_A(x)$ by $c_{r,s}$. Then we can write $\phi_A(x)$ as follows:

$$\phi_A(x) = \sum_{r=0}^{k-1} A^{rk} \left(\sum_{s=0}^{k-1} c_{r,s} A^s \right)$$

Show that it suffices to perform $k^2 n^2 = n^3$ scalar multiplications and $k(k-1)n^2 \le n^3$ additions to form the inner sums, k multiplications of $n \times n$ matrices, and kn^2 scalar additions to combine these products. In addition, $A^2, A^3, \ldots, A^{k-1}$ and $A^k, A^{2k}, \ldots, A^{(k-1)k}$ must be computed.

6.16 Show that the traces of powers, s_r, $1 \le r \le n$, for an $n \times n$ matrix A can be computed with $O(\sqrt{n}M_{\text{matrix}}(n))$ operations.

Hint: By definition $s_r = \sum_{j=1}^{n} a_{j,j}^{(r)}$, where $a_{j,j}^{(r)}$ is the jth diagonal term of the matrix A^r. Let n be a square. Represent r uniquely by a pair (a, b), where $1 \le a, b \le \sqrt{n} - 1$ and $r = a\sqrt{n} + b$. Then $A^r = A^{a\sqrt{n}}A^b$. Thus, $a_{j,j}^{(r)}$ can be computed as the product of the jth row of $A^{a\sqrt{n}}$ with the jth column of A^b. Then, for each j, $1 \le j \le n$, form the $\sqrt{n} \times n$ matrix R_j whose ath row is the jth row of $A^{a\sqrt{n}}$, $0 \le a \le \sqrt{n} - 1$. Also form the $n \times \sqrt{n}$ matrix C_j whose bth column is the jth column of A^b, $1 \le b \le \sqrt{n} - 1$. Show that the product $R_j C_j$ contains each of the terms $a_{j,j}^{(r)}$ for all values of r, $0 \le r \le n - 1$ and that the products $R_j C_j$, $1 \le j \le n$, can be computed efficiently.

6.17 Show that (6.14) holds by applying the properties of the coefficients of the characteristic polynomial of an $n \times n$ matrix stated in (6.15).

Hint: Use proof by induction on l to establish (6.14).

CONVOLUTION

6.18 Consider the convolution $f_{\text{conv}}^{(n,m)} : R^{n+m} \mapsto R^{n+m-2}$ of an n-tuple $\boldsymbol{a}$ with an m-tuple $\boldsymbol{b}$ when $n \ll m$. Develop a circuit for this problem whose size is $O(m \log n)$ that uses the convolution theorem multiple times.

Hint: Represent the m-tuple $\boldsymbol{b}$ as sequence of $\lceil m/n \rceil$ n-tuples.

6.19 The **wrapped convolution** $f_{\text{wrapped}}^{(n)} : \mathcal{R}^{2n} \mapsto \mathcal{R}^{2n-1}$ maps n-tuples $\boldsymbol{a} = (a_0, a_1, \ldots, a_{n-1})$ and $\boldsymbol{b} = (b_0, b_1, \ldots, b_{n-1})$, denoted $\boldsymbol{a} \star \boldsymbol{b}$, to the $(2n-1)$-tuple $\boldsymbol{c}$ the jth component of which, c_j, is defined as follows:

$$c_j = \sum_{r+s \,=\, j \bmod n} a_r * b_s$$

Show that the wrapped convolution on n-tuples contains the standard convolution on $\lfloor(n+1)/2\rfloor$-tuples as a subfunction and vice versa.

Hint: In both halves of the problem, it helps to characterize the standard and wrapped convolutions as matrix-vector products. It is straightforward to show that the wrapped convolution contains the standard convolution as a subfunction. To show the other result, observe that the matrix characterizing the standard convolution contains a Toeplitz matrix as a submatrix. Consider, for example, the standard convolution of two six-tuples. The matrix associated with the wrapped convolution contains a special type of Toeplitz matrix.

6.20 Show that the standard convolution function $f_{\text{conv}}^{(n,n)} : R^{2n} \mapsto R^{2n-2}$ is a subfunction of the integer multiplication function, $f_{\text{mult}}^{(n)} : \mathcal{B}^{2n\lceil\log n\rceil} \mapsto \mathcal{B}^{2n\lceil\log n\rceil}$ of Section 2.9 when R is the ring of integers modulo 2.

Hint: Represent the two sequences to be convolved as binary numbers that have been padded with zeros so that at most one bit in a sequence appears among $\lceil\log n\rceil$ positions.

DISCRETE FOURIER TRANSFORM

6.21 Let $n = 2^k$. Use proof by induction to show that for all elements a of a commutative ring $\mathcal{R}$ the following identity holds, where $\prod$ is the product operation:

$$\sum_{j=0}^{n-1} a^j = \prod_{j=0}^{n-1} (1 + a^{2^j})$$

6.22 Let $n = 2^k$ and let $\mathcal{R}$ be a commutative ring. For $\omega \in \mathcal{R}$, $\omega \neq 0$, let $m = \omega^{n/2} + 1$. Show that for $1 \leq p < n$

$$\sum_{j=0}^{n-1} \omega^{pj} = 0 \bmod m$$

Hint: Represent p as the product of the largest power of 2 with an odd integer and apply the result of Problem 6.21.

6.23 Let n and ω be positive powers of two. Let $m = \omega^{n/2} + 1$. Show that in the ring $\mathbb{Z}_m$ of integers modulo m the integer n has a multiplicative inverse and that ω is a principal nth root of unity.

6.24 Let n be even. Use the results of Problems 6.21, 6.22, and 6.23 to show that $\mathbb{Z}_m$, the set of integers modulo m, $m = 2^{tn/2} + 1$ for any positive integer $t \geq 2$, is a commutative ring in which $\omega = 2^t$ is a principal nth root of unity.

6.25 Let ω be a principal nth root of unity of the commutative ring $\mathcal{R} = (R, +, *, 0, 1)$. Show that ω^2 is a principal $(n/2)$th root of unit.

6.26 A **circulant** is an $n \times n$ matrix in which the rth row is the rth cyclic shift of the first row, $2 \leq r \leq n$. When n is a prime, show that computing the DFT of a vector of length n is equivalent to multiplying by an $(n-1) \times (n-1)$ circulant.

6.27 Show that the multiplication of circulant matrix with a vector can be done by a circuit of size $O(n \log n)$ and depth $O(\log n)$.

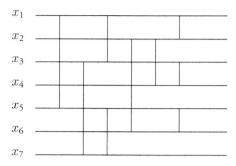

Figure 6.13 A bitonic sorter on seven inputs.

MERGING AND SORTING

6.28 Prove Theorem 6.8.3.

6.29 Show that the recurrences given below and stated in the proof of Theorem 6.8.2 have the solutions shown, where $C(1) = 1$ and $D(1) = 1$:

$$C(k) = 2C(k-1) + 2^k = k2^{k-1}$$
$$D(k) = D(k-1) + 1 = k$$

6.30 A sequence $(x_1, x_2, \ldots, x_n)$ is **bitonic** if there is an integer $0 \le k \le n$ such that $x_1 > \ldots > x_k \le \ldots \le x_n$.

   a) Show that a bitonic sorting network can be constructed as follows: i) sort $(x_1, x_3, x_5, \ldots)$ and $(x_2, x_4, x_6, \ldots)$ in bitonic sorters whose lines are interleaved, ii) compare and interchange the outputs in pairs, beginning with the least significant pairs. (See Fig. 6.13.)

   b) Show that two ordered lists can be merged with a bitonic sorter and that an n-sorter can be constructed from bitonic sorters.

   c) Determine the number of comparators in a 2^k-sorter based on merging with bitonic sorters.

Chapter Notes

The bulk of this chapter concerns matrix computations, a topic with a long history. Many books have been written on this subject to which the interested reader may refer. (See [25], [44], [104], [195], and [356].)

   Among the more important recent results in this area are the matrix multiplication algorithm of Strassen [313]. Many other improvements have been made on this work, among the most significant of which is the demonstration by Coppersmith and Winograd [81] that two $n \times n$ matrices can be multiplied with $O(n^{2.376})$ ring operations.

   The relationships between transitive closure and matrix multiplication embodied in Theorems 6.4.2 and 6.4.3 as well as the generalization of these results to closed semirings are taken from the book by Aho, Hopcroft, and Ullman [10].

Winograd [358] demonstrated that matrix multiplication is no harder than matrix inversion, whereas Aho, Hopcroft, and Ullman [10] demonstrated the converse.

Csanky's algorithm for matrix inversion is reported in [82]. Leverrier's method for computing the characteristic function of a matrix is described in [97].

Although the FFT algorithm became well known through the work of Cooley and Tukey [80], the idea actually begins with Gauss in 1805! (See Heideman, Johnson, and Burrus [129].)

The zero-one principle for the study of comparator networks is due to Knuth [167]. Oddly enough, Batcher's odd-even merging network is due to Batcher [29].

Borodin and Munro [56] is a good early source for arithmetic complexity, the size and depth of arithmetic circuits for problems related to matrices and polynomials. More recent work on the parallel evaluation of arithmetic circuits is surveyed by JáJá [146, Chapter 8] and von zur Gathen [110].

7

Parallel Computation

Parallelism takes many forms and appears in many guises. It is exhibited at the CPU level when microinstructions are executed simultaneously. It is also present when an arithmetic or logic operation is realized by a circuit of small depth, as with carry-save addition. And it is present when multiple computers are connected together in a network. Parallelism can be available but go unused, either because an application was not designed to exploit parallelism or because a problem is inherently serial.

In this chapter we examine a number of explicitly parallel models of computation, including shared and distributed memory models and, in particular, linear and multidimensional arrays, hypercube-based machines, and the PRAM model. We give a broad introduction to a large and representative set of models, describing a handful of good parallel programming techniques and showing through analysis the limits on parallelization. Because of the limited use so far of parallel algorithms and machines, the wide range of hardware and software models developed by the research community has not yet been fully digested by the computer industry.

Parallelism in logic and algebraic circuits is also examined in Chapters 2 and 6. The block I/O model, which characterizes parallelism at the disk level, is presented in Section 11.6 and the classification of problems by their execution time on parallel machines is discussed in Section 8.15.2.

7.1 Parallel Computational Models

A **parallel computer** is any computer that can perform more than one operation at time. By this definition almost every computer is a parallel computer. For example, in the pursuit of speed, computer architects regularly perform multiple operations in each CPU cycle: they execute several microinstructions per cycle and overlap input and output operations (**I/O**) (see Chapter 11) with arithmetic and logical operations. Architects also design parallel computers that are either several CPU and memory units attached to a common bus or a collection of computers connected together via a network. Clearly parallelism is common in computer science today.

However, several decades of research have shown that exploiting large-scale parallelism is very hard. Standard algorithmic techniques and their corresponding data structures do not parallelize well, necessitating the development of new methods. In addition, when parallelism is sought through the undisciplined coordination of a large number of tasks, the sheer number of simultaneous activities to which one human mind must attend can be so large that it is often difficult to insure correctness of a program design. The problems of parallelism are indeed daunting.

Small illustrations of this point are seen in Section 2.7.1, which presents an $O(\log n)$-step, $O(n)$-gate addition circuit that is considerably more complex than the ripple adder given in Section 2.7. Similarly, the fast matrix inversion straight-line algorithm of Section 6.5.5 is more complex than other such algorithms (see Section 6.5).

In this chapter we examine forms of parallelism that are more coarse-grained than is typically found in circuits. We assume that a parallel computer consists of multiple processors and memories but that each processor is primarily serial. That is, although a processor may realize its instructions with parallel circuits, it typically executes only one or a small number of instructions simultaneously. Thus, most of the parallelism exhibited by our parallel computer is due to parallel execution by its processors.

We also describe a few programming styles that encourage a parallel style of programming and offer promise for user acceptance. Finally, we present various methods of analysis that have proven useful in either determining the parallel time needed for a problem or classifying a problem according to its need for parallel time.

Given the doubling of CPU speed every two or three years, one may ask whether we can't just wait until CPU performance catches up with demand. Unfortunately, the appetite for speed grows faster than increases in CPU speed alone can meet. Today many problems, especially those involving simulation of physical systems, require teraflop computers (those performing 10^{12} floating-point operations per second (**FLOPS**)) but it is predicted that pentaflop computers (performing 10^{15} FLOPS) are needed. Achieving such high levels of performance with a handful of CPUs may require CPU performance beyond what is physically possible at reasonable prices.

7.2 Memoryless Parallel Computers

The circuit is the premier parallel memoryless computational model: input data passes through a circuit from inputs to outputs and disappears. A circuit is described by a directed acyclic graph in which vertices are either input or computational vertices. Input values and the results of computations are drawn from a set associated with the circuit. (In the case of logic

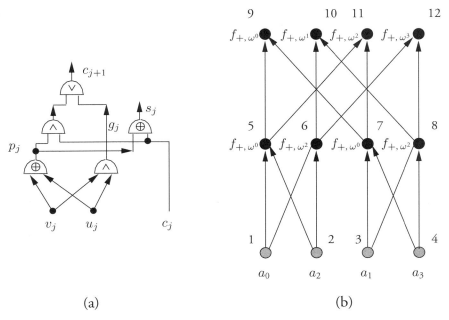

Figure 7.1 Examples of Boolean and algebraic circuits.

circuits, these values are drawn from the set $\mathcal{B} = \{0, 1\}$ and are called Boolean.) The function computed at a vertex is defined through functional composition with values associated with computational and input vertices on which the vertex depends. Boolean logic circuits are discussed at length in Chapters 2 and 9. Algebraic and combinatorial circuits are the subject of Chapter 6. (See Fig. 7.1.)

A circuit is a form of **unstructured parallel computer**. No order or structure is assumed on the operations that are performed. (Of course, this does not prevent structure from being imposed on a circuit.) Generally circuits are a form of **fine-grained parallel computer**; that is, they typically perform low-level operations, such as AND, OR, or NOT in the case of logic circuits, or addition and multiplication in the case of algebraic circuits. However, if the set of values on which circuits operate is rich, the corresponding operations can be complex and coarse-grained.

The **dataflow computer** is a parallel computer designed to simulate a circuit computation. It maintains a list of operations and, when all operands of our operation have been computed, places that operation on a queue of runnable jobs.

We now examine a variety of structured computational models, most of which are coarse-grained and synchronous.

7.3 Parallel Computers with Memory

Many coarse-grained, structured parallel computational models have been developed. In this section we introduce these models as well as a variety of performance measures for parallel computers.

There are many ways to characterize parallel computers. A **fine-grained parallel computer** is one in which the focus is on its constituent components, which themselves consist of low-level entities such as logic gates and binary memory cells. A **coarse-grained parallel computer** is one in which we ignore the low-level components of the computer and focus instead on its functioning at a high level. A complex circuit, such as a carry-lookahead adder, whose details are ignored is a single coarse-grained unit, whereas one whose details are studied explicitly is fine-grained. CPUs and large memory units are generally viewed as coarse-grained.

A parallel computer is a collection of interconnected processors (CPUs or memories). The processors and the media used to connect them constitute a **computer network**. If the processors are in close physical proximity and can communicate quickly, we often say that they are **tightly coupled** and call the machine a **parallel computer** rather than a computer network. However, when the processors are not in close proximity or when their operating systems require a large amount of time to exchange messages, we say that they are **loosely coupled** and call the machine a **computer network**.

Unless a problem is trivially parallel, it must be possible to exchange messages between processors. A variety of low-level mechanisms are generally available for this purpose. The use of software for the exchange of potentially long messages is called **message passing**. In a tightly coupled parallel computer, messages are prepared, sent, and received quickly relative to the clock speed of its processors, but in a loosely coupled parallel computer, the time required for these steps is much larger. The time T_m to transmit a message from one processor to another is generally assumed to be of the form $T_m = \alpha + l\beta$, where l is the length of the message, α (**latency**) is the time to set up a communication channel, and β (**bandwidth**) is the time to send and receive one message. Both α and β are constant multiples of the duration of the CPU clock cycle of the processors. Thus, $\alpha + \beta$ is the time to prepare, send, and receive a single unit-length message. In a tightly coupled machine α and β are small, whereas in a loosely coupled machine α is large.

An important classification of parallel computers with memory is based on the degree to which they share access to memory. A **shared-memory computer** is characterized by a model in which each processor can address locations in a common memory. (See Fig. 7.2(a).) In this model it is generally assumed that the time to make one access to the common mem-

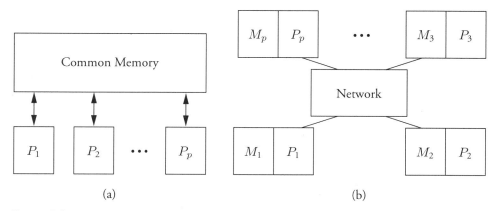

(a)   (b)

Figure 7.2 (a) A shared-memory computer; (b) a distributed-memory computer.

ory is relatively close to the time for a processor to access one of its registers. Processors in a shared-memory computer can communicate with one another via the common memory. The **distributed-memory computer** is characterized by a model in which processors can communicate with other processors only by sending messages. (See Fig. 7.2(b).) In this model it is generally assumed that processors also have local memories and that the time to send a message from one processor to another can be large relative to the time to access a local memory. A third type of computer, a cross between the first two, is the **distributed shared-memory computer**. It is realized on a distributed-memory computer on which the time to process messages is large relative to the time to access a local memory, but a layer of software gives the programmer the illusion of a shared-memory computer. Such a model is useful when programs can be executed primarily from local memories and only occasionally must access remote memories.

Parallel computers are **synchronous** if all processors perform operations in lockstep and **asynchronous** otherwise. A synchronous parallel machine may alternate between executing instructions and reading from local or common memory. (See the PRAM model of Section 7.9, which is a synchronous, shared-memory model.) Although a synchronous parallel computational model is useful in conveying concepts, in many situations, as with loosely coupled distributed computers, it is not a realistic one. In other situations, such as in the design of VLSI chips, it is realistic. (See, for example, the discussion of systolic arrays in Section 7.5.)

7.3.1 Flynn's Taxonomy

Flynn's taxonomy of parallel computers distinguishes between four extreme types of parallel machine on the basis of the degree of simultaneity in their handling of instructions and data. The **single-instruction, single-data (SISD)** model is a serial machine that executes one instruction per unit time on one data item. An SISD machine is the simplest form of serial computer. The **single-instruction, multiple-data (SIMD)** model is a synchronous parallel machine in which all processors that are not idle execute the same instruction on potentially different data. (See Fig. 7.3.) The **multiple-instruction, single-data (MISD)** model describes a synchronous parallel machine that performs different computations on the same data. While not yet practical, the MISD machine could be used to test the primality of an integer (the single datum) by having processors divide it by independent sets of integers. The

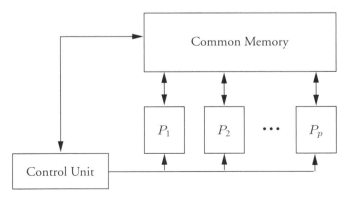

Figure 7.3 In the SIMD model the same instruction is executed on every processor that is not idle.

multiple-instruction, multiple-data (MIMD) model describes a parallel machine that runs a potentially different program on potentially different data on each processor but can send messages among processors.

The SIMD machine is generally designed to have a single instruction decoder unit that controls the action of each processor, as suggested in Fig. 7.3. SIMD machines have not been a commercial success because they require specialized processors rather than today's commodity processors that benefit from economies of scale. As a result, most parallel machines today are MIMD. Nonetheless, the SIMD style of programming remains appealing because programs having a single thread of control are much easier to code and debug. In addition, a MIMD model, the more common parallel model in use today, can be programmed in a SIMD style.

While the MIMD model is often assumed to be much more powerful than the SIMD one, we now show that the former can be converted to the latter with at most a constant factor slowdown in execution time. Let K be the maximum number of different instructions executable by a MIMD machine and index them with integers in the set $\{1, 2, 3, \ldots, K\}$. Slow down the computation of each machine by a factor K as follows: 1) identify time intervals of length K, 2) on the kth step of the jth interval, execute the kth instruction of a processor if this is the instruction that it would have performed on the jth step of the original computation. Otherwise, let the processor by idle by executing its NOOP instruction. This construction executes the instructions of a MIMD computation in a SIMD fashion (all processors either are idle or execute the instruction with the same index) with a slowdown by a factor K in execution time.

Although for most machines this simulation is impractical, it does demonstrate that in the best case a SIMD program is at worst a constant factor slower than the corresponding MIMD program for the same problem. It offers hope that the much simpler SIMD programming style can be made close in performance to the more difficult MIMD style.

7.3.2 The Data-Parallel Model

The **data-parallel model** captures the essential features of the SIMD style. It has a single thread of control in which serial and parallel operations are intermixed. The parallel operations possible typically include vector and shifting operations (see Section 2.5.1), prefix and segmented prefix computations (see Sections 2.6), and data-movement operations such as are realized by a permutation network (see Section 7.8.1). They also include **conditional vector operations**, vector operations that are performed on those vector components for which the corresponding component of an auxiliary flag vector has value is 1 (others have value 0).

Figure 7.4 shows a data-parallel program for **radix sort**. This program sorts n d-bit integers, $\{x[n], \ldots, x[1]\}$, represented in binary. The program makes d passes over the integers. On each pass the program reorders the integers, placing those whose jth least significant bit (**lsb**) is 1 ahead of those for which it is 0. This reordering is **stable**; that is, the previous ordering among integers with the same jth lsb is retained. After the jth pass, the n integers are sorted according to their j least significant bits, so that after d passes the list is fully sorted. The prefix function $\mathcal{P}_+^{(n)}$ computes the running sum of the jth lsb on the jth pass. Thus, for k such that $x[k]_j = 1$, b_k (c_k) is the number of integers with index k or higher whose jth lsb is 1 (0). The value of $a_k = b_k x[k]_j + (c_k + b_1)\overline{x[k]_j}$ is b_k or $c_k + b_1$, depending on whether the lsb of $x[k]$ is 1 or 0, respectively. That is, a_k is the index of the location in which the kth integer is placed after the jth pass.

{ $x[n]_j$ is its jth least significant bit of the nth integer. }
{ After the jth pass, the integers are sorted by their j least significant bits. }
{ Upon completion, the kth location contains the kth largest integer. }

for $j := 0$ **to** $d - 1$
   begin

      $(b_n, \ldots, b_1) := \mathcal{P}_+^{(n)}(x[n]_j, \ldots, x[1]_j);$
           { b_k is the number of 1's among $x[n]_j, \ldots, x[k]_j$. }
           { b_1 is the number of integers whose jth bit is 1. }

      $(c_n, \ldots, c_1) := \mathcal{P}_+^{(n)}(\overline{x[n]_j}, \ldots, \overline{x[1]_j});$
           { c_k is the number of 0's among $x[n]_j, \ldots, x[k]_j$. }

      $(a_n, \ldots, a_1) := \left(b_n x[n]_j + (c_n + b_1)\overline{x[n]_j}, \ldots, b_1 x[1]_j + (c_1 + b_1)\overline{x[1]_j} \right);$
           { $a_k = b_k x[k]_j + (c_k + b_1)\overline{x[k]_j}$ is the rank of the kth key. }

      $(x[a_n], x[a_{n-1}], \ldots, x[a_1]) := (x[n], x[n-1], \ldots, x[1])$
           { This operation permutes the integers. }
   end

Figure 7.4 A data-parallel radix sorting program to sort n d-bit binary integers that makes two uses of the prefix function $\mathcal{P}_+^{(n)}$.

The data-parallel model is often implemented using the **single-program multiple-data (SPMD)** model. This model allows copies of one program to run on multiple processors with potentially different data without requiring that the copies run in synchrony. It also allows the copies to synchronize themselves periodically for the transfer of data. A convenient abstraction often used in the data-parallel model that translates nicely to the SPMD model is the assumption that a collection of virtual processors is available, one per vector component. An operating system then maps these virtual processors to physical ones. This method is effective when there are many more virtual processors than real ones so that the time for interprocessor communication is amortized.

7.3.3 Networked Computers

A **networked computer** consists of a collection of processors with direct connections between them. In this context a processor is a CPU with memory or a sequential machine designed to route messages between processors. The graph of a network has a vertex associated with each processor and an edge between two connected processors. Properties of the graph of a network, such as its **size** (number of vertices), its **diameter** (the largest number of edges on the shortest path between two vertices), and its **bisection width** (the smallest number of edges between a subgraph and its complement, both of which have about the same size) characterize its computational performance. Since a transmission over an edge of a network introduces delay, the diameter of a network graph is a crude measure of the worst-case time to transmit

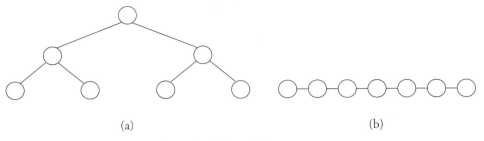

Figure 7.5 Completely balanced (a) and unbalanced (b) trees.

a message between processors. Its bisection width is a measure of the amount of information that must be transmitted in the network for processors to communicate with their neighbors.

A large variety of networks have been investigated. The graph of a **tree network** is a tree. Many simple tasks, such as computing sums and broadcasting (sending a message from one processor to all other processors), can be done on tree networks. Trees are also naturally suited to many recursive computations that are characterized by **divide-and-conquer strategies**, in which a problem is divided into a number of like problems of similar size to yield small results that can be combined to produce a solution to the original problem. Trees can be completely balanced or unbalanced. (See Fig. 7.5.) Balanced trees of fixed degree have a root and bounded number of edges associated with each vertex. The diameter of such trees is logarithmic in the number of vertices. Unbalanced trees can have a diameter that is linear in the number of vertices.

A mesh is a regular graph (see Section 7.5) in which each vertex has the same degree except possibly for vertices on its boundary. Meshes are well suited to matrix operations and can be used for a large variety of other problems as well. If, as some believe, speed-of-light limitations will be an important consideration in constructing fast computers in the future [43], the one-, two-, and three-dimensional mesh may very well become the computer organization of choice. The diameter of a mesh of dimension d with n vertices is proportional to $n^{1/d}$. It is not as small as the diameter of a tree but acceptable for tasks for which the cost of communication can be amortized over the cost of computation.

The hypercube (see Section 7.6) is a graph that has one vertex at each corner of a multidimensional cube. It is an important conceptual model because it has low (logarithmic) diameter, large bisection width, and a connectivity for which it is easy to construct efficient parallel algorithms for a large variety of problems. While the hypercube and the tree have similar diameters, the superior connectivity of the hypercube leads to algorithms whose running time is generally smaller than on trees. Fortunately, many hypercube-based algorithms can be efficiently translated into algorithms for other network graphs, such as meshes.

We demonstrate the utility of each of the above models by providing algorithms that are naturally suited to them. For example, linear arrays are good at performing matrix-vector multiplications and sorting with bubble sort. Two-dimensional meshes are good at matrix-matrix multiplication, and can also be used to sort in much less time than linear arrays. The hypercube network is very good at solving a variety of problems quickly but is much more expensive to realize than linear or two-dimensional meshes because each processor is connected to many more other processors.

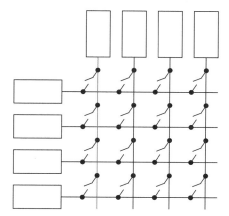

Figure 7.6 A crossbar connection network. Any two processors can be connected.

In designing parallel algorithms it is often helpful to devise an algorithm for a particular parallel machine model, such as a hypercube, and then map the hypercube and the algorithm with it to the model of the machine on which it will be executed. In doing this, the question arises of how efficiently one graph can be embedded into another. This is the **graph-embedding** problem. We provide an introduction to this important question by discussing embeddings of one type of machine into another.

A **connection network** is a network computer in which all vertices except for peripheral vertices are used to route messages. The peripheral vertices are the computers that are connected by the network. One of the simplest such networks is the **crossbar network**, in which a row of processors is connected to a column of processors via a two-dimensional array of switches. (See Fig. 7.6.) The crossbar switch with $2n$ computational processors has n^2 routing vertices. The butterfly network (see Fig. 7.15) provides a connectivity similar to that of the crossbar but with many fewer routing vertices. However, not all permutations of the inputs to a butterfly can be mapped to its outputs. For this purpose the Beneš network (see Fig. 7.20) is better suited. It consists of two butterfly graphs with the outputs of one graph connected to the outputs of the second and the order of edges of the second reversed. Many other permutation networks exist. Designers of connection networks are very concerned with the variety of connections that can be made among computational processors, the time to make these connections, and the number of vertices in the network for the given number of computational processors. (See Section 7.8.)

7.4 The Performance of Parallel Algorithms

We now examine measures of performance of parallel algorithms. Of these, computation time is the most important. Since parallel computation time T_p is a function of p, the number of processors used for a computation, we seek a relationship among p, T_p, and other measures of the complexity of a problem.

Given a p-processor parallel machine that executes T_p steps, in the spirit of Chapter 3, we can construct a circuit to simulate it. Its size is proportional to pT_p, which plays the role of serial time T_s. Similarly, a single-processor RAM of the type used in a p-processor parallel machine but with p times as much memory can simulate an algorithm on the parallel machine in p times as many steps; it simulates each step of each of the p RAM processors in succession. This observation provides the following relationship among p, T_p, and T_s when storage space for the serial and parallel computations is comparable.

THEOREM 7.4.1 *Let T_s be the smallest number of steps needed on a single RAM with storage capacity S, in bits, to compute a function f. If f can be computed in T_p steps on a network of p RAM processors, each with storage S/p, then T_p satisfies the following inequality:*

$$pT_p \geq T_s \tag{7.1}$$

Proof This result follows because, while the serial RAM can simulate the parallel machine in pT_p steps, it may be able to compute the function in question more quickly. ∎

The **speedup** $\mathcal{S}$ of a parallel p-processor algorithm over the best serial algorithm for a problem is defined as $\mathcal{S} = T_s/T_p$. We see that, with p processors, a speedup of at most p is possible; that is, $\mathcal{S} \leq p$. This result can also be stated in terms of the computational work done by serial and parallel machines, defined as the number of equivalent serial operations. (Computational work is defined in terms of the equivalent number of gate operations in Section 3.1.2. The two measures differ only in terms of the units in which work is measured, CPU operations in this section and gate operations in Section 3.1.2.) The **computational work** W_p done by an algorithm on a p-processor RAM machine is $W_p = pT_p$. The above theorem says that the minimal parallel work needed to compute a function is at least the serial work required for it, that is, $W_p \geq W_s = T_s$. (Note that we compare the work on a serial processor to a collection of p identical processors, so that we need not take into account differences among processors.)

A **parallel algorithm is efficient** if the work that it does is close to the work done by the best serial algorithm. A **parallel algorithm is fast** if it achieves a nearly maximal speedup. We leave unspecified just how close to optimal a parallel algorithm must be for it to be classified as efficient or fast. This will often be determined by context. We observe that parallel algorithms may be useful if they complete a task with acceptable losses in efficiency or speed, even if they are not optimal by either measure.

7.4.1 Amdahl's Law

As a warning that it is not always possible with p processors to obtain a speedup of p, we introduce Amdahl's Law, which provides an intuitive justification for the difficulty of parallelizing some tasks. In Sections 3.9 and 8.9 we provide concrete information on the difficulty of parallelizing individual problems by introducing the **P**-complete problems, problems that are the hardest polynomial-time problems to parallelize.

THEOREM 7.4.2 (Amdahl's Law) *Let f be the fraction of a program's execution time on a serial RAM that is parallelizable. Then the speedup S achievable by this program on a p-processor RAM machine must satisfy the following bound:*

$$S \leq \frac{1}{(1-f) + f/p}$$

Proof Given a T_s-step serial computation, fT_s/p is the smallest possible number of steps on a p-processor machine for the parallelizable serial steps. The remaining $(1-f)T_s$ serial steps take at least the same number of steps on the parallel machine. Thus, the parallel time T_p satisfies $T_p \geq T_s[(1-f) + f/p]$ from which the result follows. ∎

This result shows that if a fixed fraction f of a program's serial execution time can be parallelized, the speedup achievable with that program on a parallel machine is bounded above by $1/(1-f)$ as p grows without limit. For example, if 90% of the time of a serial program can be parallelized, the maximal achievable speed is 10, regardless of the number of parallel processors available.

While this statement seems to explain the difficulty of parallelizing certain algorithms, it should be noted that programs for serial and parallel machines are generally very different. Thus, it is not reasonable to expect that analysis of a serial program should lead to bounds on the running time of a parallel program for the same problem.

7.4.2 Brent's Principle

We now describe how to convert the inherent parallelism of a problem into an efficient parallel algorithm. Brent's principle, stated in Theorem 7.4.3, provides a general schema for exploiting parallelism in a problem.

THEOREM 7.4.3 *Consider a computation C that can be done in t parallel steps when the time to communicate between operations can be ignored. Let m_i be the number of primitive operations done on the ith step and let $m = \sum_{i=1}^{t} m_i$. Consider a p-processor machine M capable of the same primitive operations, where $p \leq \max_i m_i$. If the communication time between the operations in C on M can be ignored, the same computation can be performed in T_p steps on M, where T_p satisfies the following bound:*

$$T_p \leq \lceil m/p \rceil + t$$

Proof A parallel step in which m_i operations are performed can be simulated by M in $\lceil m_i/p \rceil \leq (m_i/p) + 1$ steps, from which the result follows. ∎

Brent's principle provides a schema for realizing the inherent parallelism in a problem. However, it is important to note that the time for communication between operations can be a serious impediment to the efficient implementation of a problem on a parallel machine. Often, the time to route messages between operations can be the most important limitation on exploitation of parallelism.

We illustrate Brent's principle with the problem of adding n integers, $x_1, \ldots, x_n$. Under the assumption that at most two integers can be added in one primitive operation, we see that the sum can be formed by performing $n/2$ additions, $n/4$ additions of these results, etc., until the last sum is formed. Thus, $m_i = n/2^i$ for $i \leq \lceil \log_2 n \rceil$. When only p processors are available, we assign either $\lceil n/p \rceil$ or $n - p\lceil n/p \rceil$ integers to each processor. In $\lceil n/p \rceil$ steps, the p processors each compute their local sums, leaving their results in a reserved location. In each subsequent phase, half of the processors active in the preceding phase are active in this one. Each of the active processors fetches the partial sum computed by another processor, adds it to its partial sum, and stores the result in a reserved place. After $O(\log p)$ phases, the sum of the n integers has been computed. This algorithm computes the sum of the n integers in $O(n/p + \log p)$ time steps. Since the maximal speedup possible is n/p, this algorithm is optimal to within a constant multiplicative factor if $\log p \leq (n/p)$ or $p \leq 2n/\log n$ for $n \geq 4$.

It is important to note that the time to communicate between processors is often very large relative to the length of a CPU cycle. Thus, the assumption that it takes one unit of time to communicate between processors, the basis of Brent's principle, holds only for tightly coupled processors.

7.5 Multidimensional Meshes

In this section we examine multidimensional meshes. A **one-dimensional mesh** or **linear array** of processors is a one-dimensional (1D) array of computing elements connected via nearest-neighbor connections. (See Fig. 7.7.) If the vertices of the array are indexed with integers from the set $\{1, 2, 3, \ldots, n\}$, then vertex i, $2 \leq i \leq n - 1$, is connected to vertices $i - 1$ and $i + 1$. If the linear array is a **ring**, vertices 1 and n are also connected. Such an end-to-end connection can be made with short connections by folding the linear array about its midpoint.

The linear array is an important model that finds application in very large-scale integrated (VLSI) circuits. When the processors of a linear array operate in synchrony (which is the usual way in which they are used), it is called a linear **systolic array** (a systole is a recurrent rhythmic contraction, especially of the heart muscle). A systolic array is any mesh (typically 1D or 2D) in which the processors operate in synchrony. The computing elements of a systolic array are called **cells**. A linear systolic array that convolves two binary sequences is described in Section 1.6.

A **multidimensional mesh** (see Fig. 7.8) (or **mesh**) offers better connectivity between processors than a linear array. As a consequence, a multidimensional mesh generally can compute functions more quickly than a 1D one. We illustrate this point by matrix multiplication on 2D meshes in Section 7.5.3.

Figure 7.8 shows 2D and 3D meshes. Each vertex of the 2D mesh is numbered by a pair (r, c), where $0 \leq r \leq n - 1$ and $0 \leq c \leq n - 1$ are its row and column indices. (If the cell

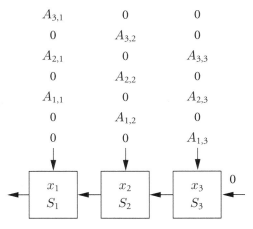

Figure 7.7 A linear array to compute the matrix-vector product $A\boldsymbol{x}$, where $A = [a_{i,j}]$ and $\boldsymbol{x}^T = (x_1, \ldots, x_n)$. On each cycle, the ith processor adds to its current sum S_i the sum to its right, S_{i+1}, and the product of its local value, x_i, with its vertical input.

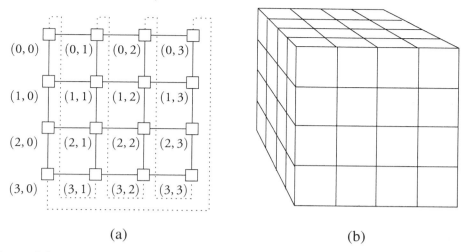

Figure 7.8 (a) A two-dimensional mesh with optional connections between the boundary elements shown by dashed lines. (b) A 3D mesh (a cube) in which elements are shown as subcubes.

(r, c) is associated with the integer $rn + c$, this is the **row-major order** of the cells. Cells are numbered left-to-right from 0 to 3 in the first row, 4 to 7 in the second, 8 to 11 in the third, and 12 to 15 in the fourth.) Vertex (r, c) is adjacent to vertices $(r - 1, c)$ and $(r + 1, c)$ for $1 \leq r \leq n - 2$. Similarly, vertex (r, c) is adjacent to vertices $(r, c - 1)$ and $(r, c + 1)$ for $1 \leq c \leq n - 2$. Vertices on the boundaries may or may not be connected to other boundary vertices, and may be connected in a variety of ways. For example, vertices in the first row (column) can be connected to those in the last row (column) in the same column (row) (this is a **toroidal mesh**) or the next larger column (row). The second type of connection is associated with the dashed lines in Fig. 7.8(a).

Each vertex in a 3D mesh is indexed by a triple (x, y, z), $0 \leq x, y, z \leq n - 1$, as suggested in Fig. 7.8(b). Connections between boundary vertices, if any, can be made in a variety of ways. Meshes with larger dimensionality are defined in a similar fashion.

A d-dimensional mesh consists of processors indexed by a d-tuple $(n_1, n_2, \ldots, n_d)$ in which $0 \leq n_j \leq N_j - 1$ for $1 \leq j \leq d$. If processors $(n_1, n_2, \ldots, n_d)$ and $(m_1, m_2, \ldots, m_d)$ are adjacent, there is some j such that $n_i = m_i$ for $j \neq i$ and $|n_j - m_j| = 1$. There may also be connections between boundary processors, that is, processors for which one component of their index has either its minimum or maximum value.

7.5.1 Matrix-Vector Multiplication on a Linear Array

As suggested in Fig. 7.7, the cells in a systolic array can have external as well as nearest-neighbor connections. This systolic array computes the matrix-vector product $A\boldsymbol{x}$ of an $n \times n$ matrix with an n-vector. (In the figure, $n = 3$.) The cells of the systolic array beat in a rhythmic fashion. The ith processor adds to its current sum, S_i, the product of x_i with its vertical input and the value of S_{i+1} to its right (the value 0 is read by the rightmost cell). Initially, $S_i = 0$ for $1 \leq i \leq n$. Since alternating vertical inputs are 0, the alternating values of S_i are 0. In Fig. 7.7 the successive values of S_3 are $A_{1,3}x_3$, 0, $A_{2,3}x_3$, 0, $A_{3,3}x_3$, 0, 0. The successive values of S_2

are 0, $A_{1,2}x_2 + A_{1,3}x_3$, 0, $A_{2,2}x_2 + A_{2,3}x_3$, 0, $A_{3,2}x_2 + A_{3,3}x_3$, 0. The successive values of S_1 are 0, 0, $A_{1,1}x_1 + A_{1,2}x_2 + A_{1,3}x_3$, 0, $A_{2,1}x_1 + A_{2,2}x_2 + A_{2,3}x_3$, 0, $A_{3,1}x_1 + A_{3,2}x_2 + A_{3,3}x_3$.

The algorithm described above to compute the matrix-vector product for a 3×3 matrix clearly extends to arbitrary $n \times n$ matrices. (See Problem 7.8.) Since the last element of an $n \times n$ matrix arrives at the array after $3n - 2$ time steps, such an array will complete its task in $3n - 1$ time steps. A lower bound on the time for this problem (see Problem 7.9) can be derived by showing that the n^2 entries of the matrix A and the n entries of the matrix x must be read to compute Ax correctly by an algorithm, whether serial or not. By Theorem 7.4.1 it follows that all systolic algorithms using n processors require n steps. Thus, the above algorithm is nearly optimal to within a constant multiplicative factor.

THEOREM 7.5.1 *There exists a linear systolic array with n cells that computes the product of an $n \times n$ matrix with an n-vector in $3n - 1$ steps, and no algorithm on such an array can do this computation in fewer than n steps.*

Since the product of two $n \times n$ matrices can be realized as n matrix-vector products with an $n \times n$ matrix, an n-processor systolic array exists that can multiply two matrices nearly optimally.

7.5.2   Sorting on Linear Arrays

A second application of linear systolic arrays is bubble sorting of integers. A sequential version of the **bubble sort** algorithm passes over the entries in a tuple $(x_1, x_2, \ldots, x_n)$ from left to right multiple times. On the first pass it finds the largest element and moves it to the rightmost position. It applies the same procedure to the first $n - 1$ elements of the resultant list, stopping when it finds a list containing one element. This sequential procedure takes time proportional to $n + (n - 1) + (n - 2) + \cdots + 2 + 1 = n(n + 1)/2$.

A parallel version of bubble sort, sometimes called **odd-even transposition sort**, is naturally realized on a linear systolic array. The n entries of the array are placed in n cells. Let c_i be the word in the ith cell. We assume that in one unit of time two adjacent cells can read words stored in each other's memories (c_i and c_{i+1}), compare them, and swap them if one (c_i) is larger than the other (c_{i+1}). The odd-even transposition sort algorithm executes n stages. In the even-numbered stages, integers in even-numbered cells are compared with integers in the next higher numbered cells and swapped, if larger. In the odd-numbered stages, the same operation is performed on integers in odd-numbered cells. (See Fig. 7.9.) We show that in n steps the sorting is complete.

THEOREM 7.5.2 *Bubble sort of n elements on a linear systolic array can be done in at most n steps. Every algorithm to sort a list of n elements on a linear systolic array requires at least $n - 1$ steps. Thus, bubble sort on a linear systolic array is almost optimal.*

Proof To derive the upper bound we use the zero-one principle (see Theorem 6.8.1), which states that if a comparator network for inputs over an ordered set A correctly sorts all binary inputs, it correctly sorts all inputs. The bubble sort systolic array maps directly to a comparator network because each of its operations is data-independent, that is, **oblivious**. To see that the systolic array correctly sorts binary sequences, consider the position, r, of the rightmost 1 in the array.

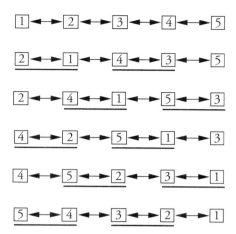

Figure 7.9 A systolic implementation of bubble sort on a sequence of five items. Underlined pairs of items are compared and swapped if out of order. The bottom row shows the first set of comparisons.

If r is even, on the first phase of the algorithm this 1 does not move. However, on all subsequent phases it moves right until it arrives at its final position. If r is odd, it moves right on all phases until it arrives in its final position. Thus by the second step the rightmost 1 moves right on every step until it arrives at its final position. The second rightmost 1 is free to move to the right without being blocked by the first 1 after the second phase. This second 1 will move to the right by the third phase and continue to do so until it arrives at its final position. In general, the kth rightmost 1 starts moving to the right by the $(k + 1)$st phase and continues until it arrives at its final position. It follows that at most n phases are needed to sort the 0-1 sequence. By the zero-one principle, the same applies to all sequences.

To derive the lower bound, assume that the sorted elements are increasing from left to right in the linear array. Let the elements initially be placed in decreasing order from left to right. Thus, the process of sorting moves the largest element from the leftmost location in the array to the rightmost. This requires at least $n - 1$ steps. The same lower bound holds if some other permutation of the n elements is desired. For example, if the kth largest element resides in the rightmost cell at the end of the computation, it can reside initially in the leftmost cell, requiring at least $n - 1$ operations to move to its final position. ■

7.5.3 Matrix Multiplication on a 2D Mesh

2D systolic arrays are natural structures on which to compute the product $C = A \times B$ of matrices A and B. (Matrix multiplication is discussed in Section 6.3.) Since $C = A \times B$ can be realized as n matrix-vector multiplications, C can be computed with n linear arrays. (See Fig. 7.7.) If the columns of B are stored in successive arrays and the entries of A pass from one array to the next in one unit of time, the nth array receives the last entry of B after $4n - 2$ time steps. Thus, this 2D systolic array computes $C = A \times B$ in $4n - 1$ steps. Somewhat more efficient 2D systolic arrays can be designed. We describe one of them below.

Figure 7.10 shows a 2D mesh for matrix multiplication. Each cell of this mesh adds to its stored value the product of the value arriving from above and to its left. These two values pass through the cells to those below and to their right, respectively. When the entries of A are supplied on the left and those of B are supplied from above in the order shown, the cell $C_{i,j}$ computes $c_{i,j}$, the (i, j) entry of the product matrix C. For example, cell $C_{2,3}$ accumulates the value $c_{2,3} = a_{2,1} * b_{1,3} + a_{2,2} * b_{2,3} + a_{2,3} * b_{3,3}$. After the entries of C have been computed, they are produced as outputs by shifting the entries of the mesh to one side of the array. When generalized to $n \times n$ matrices, this systolic array requires $2n - 1$ steps for the last of the matrix components to enter the array. An additional n steps are needed to shift the components of the product matrix out of the array. Thus, this systolic array performs matrix multiplication in $3n - 1$ steps.

We put the following requirements on every systolic array (of any dimension) that computes the matrix multiplication function: a) each component of each matrix enters the array at one location, and b) each component of the product matrix is computed at a unique cell. We now show that the systolic matrix multiplication algorithm is optimal to within a constant multiplicative factor.

THEOREM 7.5.3 *Two $n \times n$ matrices can be multiplied by an $n \times n$ systolic array in $3n - 1$ steps and every two-dimensional systolic array for this problem requires at least $(n/2) - 1$ steps.*

Proof The proof that two $n \times n$ matrices can be multiplied in $3n - 1$ steps by a two-dimensional systolic array was given above. We now show that $\Omega(n)$ steps are required to multiply two $n \times n$ matrices, A and B, to produce the matrix $C = A \times B$. Observe that the number of cells in a two-dimensional array that are within d moves from any particular cell is at most $\sigma(d)$, where $\sigma(d) = 2d^2 + 2d + 1$. The maximum occurs at the center of the array. (See Problem 7.11.)

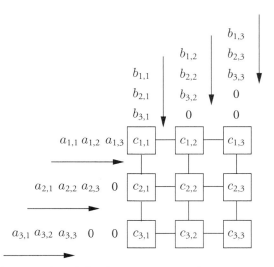

Figure 7.10 A two-dimensional mesh for the multiplication of two matrices. The entries in these matrices are supplied in successive time intervals to processors on the boundary of the mesh.

Given a systolic array with inputs supplied externally over time (see Fig. 7.10), we enlarge the array so that each component of each matrix is initially placed in a unique cell. The enlarged array contains the original $n \times n$ array.

Let $C = [c_{i,j}]$. Because $c_{i,j} = \sum_u a_{i,u} b_{u,j}$, it follows that for each value of i, j, t, and u there is a path from $a_{i,u}$ to the cell at which $c_{i,j}$ is computed as well as a path from $b_{t,j}$ to this same cell. Thus, it follows that there is a path in the array between them arbitrary entries $a_{i,u}$ and $b_{t,j}$ of the matrices $A = [a_{i,u}]$ and $B = [b_{t,j}]$. Let s be the maximum number of array edges between an element of A or B and an element of C on which it depends. It follows that at least s steps are needed to form C and that every element of A and B is within distance $2s$. Furthermore, each of the $2n^2$ elements of A and B is located initially in a unique cell of the expanded systolic array. Since there are at most $\sigma(2s)$ vertices within a distance of $2s$, it follows that $\sigma(2s) = 2(2s)^2 + 2(2s) + 1 \geq 2n^2$, from which we conclude that the number of steps to multiply $n \times n$ matrices is at least $s \geq \frac{1}{2}(n^2 - \frac{1}{4})^{1/2} - \frac{1}{4} \geq \frac{n}{2} - 1$. ∎

7.5.4 Embedding of 1D Arrays in 2D Meshes

Given an algorithm for a linear array, we ask whether that algorithm can be efficiently realized on a 2D mesh. This is easily determined: we need only specify a mapping of the cells of a linear array to cells in the 2D mesh. Assuming that the two arrays have the same number of cells, a natural mapping is obtained by giving the cells of an $n \times n$ mesh the **snake-row ordering**. (See Fig. 7.11.) In this ordering cells of the first row are ordered from left to right and numbered from 0 to $n - 1$; those in the second row are ordered from right to left and numbered from n to $2n - 1$. This process repeats, alternating between ordering cells from left to right and right to left and numbering the cells in succession. Ordering the cells of a linear array from left to right and numbering them from 0 to $n^2 - 1$ allows us to map the linear array directly to the 2D mesh. Any algorithm for the linear array runs in the same time on a 2D mesh if the processors in the two cases are identical.

Now we ask if, given an algorithm for a 2D mesh, we can execute it on a linear array. The answer is affirmative, although the execution time of the algorithm may be much greater on the 1D array than on the 2D mesh. As a first step, we map vertices of the 2D mesh onto vertices of the 1D array. The snake-row ordering of the cells of an $n \times n$ array provides a convenient

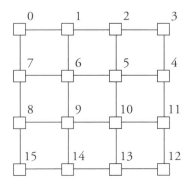

Figure 7.11 Snake-row ordering of the vertices of a two-dimensional mesh.

mapping of the cells of the 2D mesh onto the cells of the linear array with n^2 cells. We assume that each of the cells of the linear array is identical to a cell in the 2D mesh.

We now address the question of communication between cells. When mapped to the 1D array, cells can communicate only with their two immediate neighbors in the array. However, cells on the $n \times n$ mesh can communicate with as many as four neighbors. Unfortunately, cells in one row of the 2D mesh that are neighbors of cells in an adjacent row are mapped to cells that are n cells away in the linear array. We show that with a factor of $4n + 2$ slowdown, the linear array can simulate the 2D mesh. A slowdown by at least a factor of $n/2$ is necessary for those problems and data for which a datum moves from the first to the last entry in the array (in $n^2 - 1$ steps) to simulate a movement that takes $2n - 1$ steps on the array. ($(n^2 - 1)/(2n - 1) \geq n/2$ for $n \geq 2$.)

Given an algorithm for a 2D mesh, slow it down as follows:

a) Subdivide each cycle into six subcycles.

b) In the first of these subcycles let each cell compute using its local data.

c) In the second subcycle let each cell communicate with neighbor(s) in adjacent columns.

d) In the third subcycle let cells in even-numbered rows send messages to cells in the next higher numbered rows.

e) In the fourth subcycle let cells in even-numbered rows receive message from cells in the next higher numbered rows.

f) In the fifth subcycle let cells in odd-numbered rows send messages to cells in next higher numbered rows.

g) In the sixth subcycle let cells in odd-numbered rows receive messages from cells in next higher numbered rows.

When the revised 2D algorithm is executed on the linear array, computation occurs in the first subcycle in unit time. During the second subcycle communication occurs in unit time because cells that are column neighbors in the 2D mesh are adjacent in the 1D array. The remaining four subcycles involve communication between pairs of groups of n cells each. This can be done for all pairs in n time steps: each cell shifts a datum in the direction of the cell for which it is destined. After n steps it arrives and can be processed. We summarize this result below.

THEOREM 7.5.4 *Any T-step systolic algorithm on an $n \times n$ array can be simulated on a linear systolic array with n^2 cells in at most $(4n + 2)T$ steps.*

In the next section we demonstrate that hypercubes can be embedded into meshes. From this result we derive mesh-based algorithms for a variety of problems from hypercube-based algorithms for these problems.

7.6 Hypercube-Based Machines

A d-dimensional **hypercube** has 2^d vertices. When they are indexed by binary d-tuples $(a_d, a_{d-1}, \ldots, a_0)$, adjacent vertices are those whose tuples differ in one position. Thus, the 2D

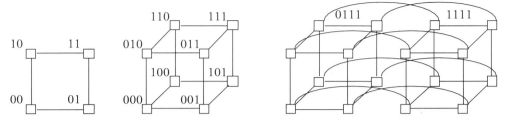

Figure 7.12 Hypercubes in two, three, and four dimensions.

hypercube is a square, the 3D hypercube is the traditional 3-cube, and the four-dimensional hypercube consists of two 3-cubes with edges between corresponding pairs of vertices. (See Fig. 7.12.) The d-dimensional hypercube is composed of two $(d-1)$-dimensional hypercubes in which each vertex in one hypercube has an edge to the corresponding vertex in the other. The degree of each vertex in a d-dimensional hypercube is d and its diameter is d as well.

While the hypercube is a very useful model for algorithm development, the construction of hypercube-based networks can be costly due to the high degree of the vertices. For example, each vertex in a hypercube with 4,096 vertices has degree 12; that is, each vertex is connected to 12 other vertices, and a total of 49,152 connections are necessary among the 4,096 processors. By contrast, a $2^6 \times 2^6$ 2D mesh has the same number of processors but at most 16,384 wires. The ratio between the number of wires in a d-dimensional hypercube and a square mesh with the same number of vertices is $d/4$. This makes it considerably more difficult to realize a hypercube of high dimensionality than a 2D mesh with a comparable number of vertices.

7.6.1   Embedding Arrays in Hypercubes

Given an algorithm designed for an array, we ask whether it can be efficiently realized on a hypercube network. The answer is positive. We show by induction that if d is even, a $2^{d/2} \times 2^{d/2}$ array can be embedded into a d-dimensional, 2^d-vertex hypercube and if d is odd, a $2^{(d+1)/2} \times 2^{(d-1)/2}$ array can be embedded into a d-dimensional hypercube. The base cases are $d = 2$ and $d = 3$.

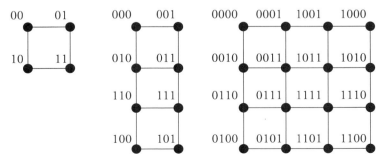

Figure 7.13 Mappings of 2×2, 4×2, and 4×4 arrays to two-, three-, and four-dimensional hypercubes. The binary tuples identify vertices of a hypercube.

When $d = 2$, a $2^{d/2} \times 2^{d/2}$ array is a 2×2 array that is itself a four-vertex hypercube. When $d = 3$, a $2^{(d+1)/2} \times 2^{(d-1)/2}$ array is a 4×2 array. (See Fig. 7.13, page 299.) It can be embedded into a three-dimensional hypercube by mapping the top and bottom 2×2 subarrays to the vertices of the two 2-cubes contained in the 3-cube. The edges between the two subarrays correspond directly to edges between vertices of the 2-cubes.

Applying the same kind of reasoning to the inductive hypothesis, we see that the hypothesis holds for all values of $d \geq 2$. If a 2D array is not of the form indicated, it can be embedded into such an array whose sides are a power of 2 by at most quadrupling the number of vertices.

7.6.2   Cube-Connected Cycles

A reasonable alternative to the hypercube is the **cube-connected cycles (CCC)** network shown in Fig. 7.14. Each of its vertices has degree 3, yet the graph has a diameter only a constant factor larger than that of the hypercube. The (d, r)-CCC is defined in terms of a d-dimensional hypercube when $r \geq d$. Let $(a_{d-1}, a_{d-2}, \ldots, a_0)$ and $(b_{d-1}, b_{d-2}, \ldots, b_0)$ be the indices of two adjacent vertices on the d-dimensional hypercube. Assume that these tuples differ in the jth component, $0 \leq j \leq d - 1$; that is, $a_j = b_j \oplus 1$ and $a_i = b_i$ for $i \neq j$. Associated with vertex $(a_{d-1}, \ldots, a_p, \ldots, a_0)$ of the hypercube are the vertices $(p, a_{d-1}, \ldots, a_p, \ldots, a_0)$, $0 \leq p \leq r - 1$, of the CCC that form a ring; that is, vertex $(p, a_{d-1}, \ldots, a_p, \ldots, a_0)$ is adjacent to vertices $((p + 1) \bmod r, a_{d-1}, \ldots a_p, \ldots, a_0)$ and $((p - 1) \bmod r, a_{d-1}, \ldots, a_p, \ldots, a_0)$. In addition, for $0 \leq p \leq d - 1$, vertex $(p, a_{d-1}, \ldots, a_p, \ldots, a_0)$ is adjacent to vertex $(p, a_{d-1}, \ldots, a_p \oplus 1, \ldots, a_0)$ on the ring associated with vertex $(a_{d-1}, \ldots, a_p \oplus 1, \ldots, a_0)$ of the hypercube.

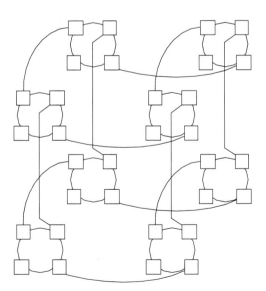

Figure 7.14   The cube-connected cycles network replaces each vertex of a d-dimensional hypercube with a ring of $r \geq d$ vertices in which each vertex is connected to its neighbor on the ring. The jth ring vertex, $0 \leq j \leq d - 1$, is also connected to the jth ring vertex at an adjacent corner of the original hypercube.

The diameter of the CCC is at most $3r/2 + d$, as we now show. Given two vertices $v_1 = (p, a_{d-1}, \ldots, a_0)$ and $v_2 = (q, b_{d-1}, \ldots, b_0)$, let their hypercube addresses $a = (a_{d-1}, \ldots, a_0)$ and $b = (b_{d-1}, \ldots, b_0)$ differ in k positions. To move from v_1 to v_2, move along the ring containing v_1 by decreasing processor numbers until reaching the next lower index at which a and b differ. (Wrap around to the highest index, if necessary.) Move from this ring to the ring whose hypercube index differs in this index. Move around this ring until arriving at the next lower indexed processor at which a and b differ. Continue in this fashion until reaching the ring with hypercube address b. The number of edges traversed in this phase of the movement is at most one for each vertex on the ring plus at most one for each of the $k \leq d$ positions on which the addresses differ. Finally, move around the last ring toward the vertex v_2 along the shorter path. This requires at most $r/2$ edge traversals. Thus, the maximal distance between two vertices, the diameter of the graph, is at most $3r/2 + d$.

7.7 Normal Algorithms

Normal algorithms on hypercubes are systolic algorithms with the property that in each cycle some bit position in an address is chosen and data is exchanged only between vertices whose addresses differ in this position. An operation is then performed on this data in one or both vertices. Thus, if the hypercube has three dimensions and the chosen dimension is the second, the following pairs of vertices exchange data and perform operations on them: $(0, 0, 0)$ and $(0, 1, 0)$, $(0, 0, 1)$ and $(0, 1, 1)$, $(1, 0, 0)$ and $(1, 1, 0)$, and $(1, 0, 1)$ and $(1, 1, 1)$. A **fully normal algorithm** is a normal algorithm that visits each of the dimensions of the hypercube in sequence. There are two kinds of fully normal algorithms, **ascending** and **descending algorithms**; ascending algorithms visit the dimensions of the hypercube in ascending order, whereas descending algorithms visit them in descending order. We show that many important algorithms are fully normal algorithms or combinations of ascending and descending algorithms. These algorithms can be efficiently translated into mesh-based algorithms, as we shall see.

The **fast Fourier transform** (FFT) (see Section 6.7.3) is an ascending algorithm. As suggested in the **butterfly graph** of Fig. 7.15, if each vertex at each level in the FFT graph on $n = 2^d$ inputs is indexed by a pair (l, a), where a is a binary d-tuple and $0 \leq l \leq d$, then at level l pairs of vertices are combined whose indices differ in their lth component. (See Problem 7.14.) It follows that the FFT graph can be computed in levels on the d-dimensional hypercube by retaining the values corresponding to the column indexed by a in the hypercube vertex whose index is a. It follows that the FFT graph has exactly the minimal connectivity required to execute an ascending fully normal algorithm. If the directions of all edges are reversed, the graph is exactly that needed for a descending fully normal algorithm. (The convolution function $f_{\text{conv}}^{(n,m)} : R^{n+m} \mapsto R^{n+m-1}$ over a commutative ring $\mathcal{R}$ can also be implemented as a normal algorithm in time $O(\log n)$ on an n-vertex hypercube, $n = 2^d$. See Problem 7.15.)

Similarly, because the graph of Batcher's odd-even merging algorithm (see Section 6.8.1) is the butterfly graph associated with the FFT, it too is a normal algorithm. Thus, two sorted lists of length $n = 2^d$ can be merged in $d = \log_2 n$ steps. As stated below, because the butterfly graph on 2^d inputs contains butterfly subgraphs on 2^k inputs, $k < d$, a recursive normal **sorting algorithm** can be constructed that sorts on the hypercube in $O(\log^2 n)$ steps. The reader is asked to prove the following theorem. (See Problem 6.29.)

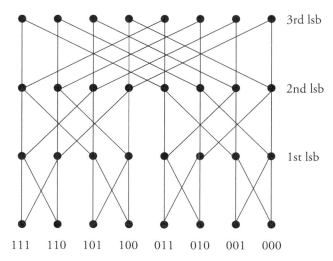

Figure 7.15   The FFT butterfly graph with column numberings. The predecessors of vertices at the kth level differ in their kth least significant bits.

THEOREM 7.7.1   *There exists a normal sorting algorithm on the p-vertex hypercube, $p = 2^d$, that sorts p items in time $O(\log^2 p)$.*

Normal algorithms can also be used to perform a **sum on the hypercube** and **broadcast on the hypercube**, as we show. We give a descending algorithm for the first problem and an ascending algorithm for the second.

7.7.1   Summing on the Hypercube

Let the hypercube be d-dimensional and let $\boldsymbol{a} = (a_{d-1}, a_{d-2}, \ldots, a_0)$ denote an address of a vertex. Associate with $\boldsymbol{a}$ the integer $|\boldsymbol{a}| = a_{d-1}2^{d-1} + a_{d-2}2^{d-2} + \cdots + a_0$. Thus, when $d = 3$, the addresses $\{0, 1, 2, \ldots, 7\}$ are associated with the eight 3-tuples $\{(0, 0, 0), (0, 0, 1), (0, 1, 0), \ldots, (1, 1, 1)\}$, respectively.

Let $V(|\boldsymbol{a}|)$ denote the value stored at the vertex with address $\boldsymbol{a}$. For each $(d - 1)$ tuple $(a_{d-1}, \ldots, a_1)$, send to vertex $(a_{d-1}, \ldots, a_1, 0)$ the value stored at vertex $(a_{d-1}, \ldots, a_1, 1)$. In the summing problem we store at vertex $(a_{d-1}, \ldots, a_1, 0)$ the sum of the original values stored at vertices $(a_{d-1}, \ldots, a_1, 0)$ and $(a_{d-1}, \ldots, a_1, 1)$. Below we show the transmission (e.g. $V(0) \leftarrow V(1)$) and addition (e.g. $V(0) \leftarrow V(0) + V(1)$) that result for $d = 3$:

$$
\begin{aligned}
V(0) &\leftarrow V(1), & V(0) &\leftarrow V(0) + V(1) \\
V(2) &\leftarrow V(3), & V(2) &\leftarrow V(2) + V(3) \\
V(4) &\leftarrow V(5), & V(4) &\leftarrow V(4) + V(5) \\
V(6) &\leftarrow V(7), & V(6) &\leftarrow V(6) + V(7)
\end{aligned}
$$

For each $(d - 1)$ tuple $(a_{d-1}, \ldots, a_1, 0)$ we then send to vertex $(a_{d-1}, \ldots, a_2, 0, 0)$ the value stored at vertex $(a_{d-1}, \ldots, a_2, 1, 0)$. Again for $d = 3$, we have the following data transfers and additions:

$$V(0) \leftarrow V(2), \qquad V(0) \leftarrow V(0) + V(2),$$
$$V(4) \leftarrow V(6), \qquad V(4) \leftarrow V(4) + V(6),$$

We continue in this fashion until reaching the lowest dimension of the d-tuples at which point we have the following actions when $d = 3$:

$$V(0) \leftarrow V(4), \qquad V(0) \leftarrow V(0) + V(4)$$

At the end of this computation, $V(0)$ is the sum of the values stored in all vertices. This algorithm for computing $V(0)$ can be extended to any associative binary operator.

7.7.2 Broadcasting on the Hypercube

The broadcast operation is obtained by reversing the directions of each of the transmissions described above. Thus, in the example, $V(0)$ is sent to $V(4)$ in the first stage, in the second stage $V(0)$ and $V(4)$ are sent to $V(2)$ and $V(6)$, respectively, and in the last stage, $V(0)$, $V(2)$, $V(4)$, and $V(6)$ are sent to $V(1)$, $V(3)$, $V(5)$, and $V(7)$, respectively.

The algorithm given above to broadcast from one vertex to all others in a hypercube can be modified to broadcast to just the vertices in a subhypercube that is defined by those addresses $\boldsymbol{a} = (a_{d-1}, a_{d-2}, \ldots, a_0)$ in which all bits are fixed except for those in some k positions. For example, $\{(0, 0, 0), (0, 1, 0), (1, 0, 0), (1, 1, 0)\}$ are the vertices of a subhypercube of the three-dimensional hypercube (the rightmost bit is fixed). To broadcast to each of these vertices from $(0, 1, 0)$, say, on the first step send the message to its pair along the second dimension, namely, $(0, 0, 0)$. On the second step, let these pairs send messages to their pairs along the third dimension, namely, $(0, 1, 0) \rightarrow (1, 1, 0)$ and $(0, 0, 0) \rightarrow (1, 0, 0)$. This algorithm can be generalized to broadcast from any vertex in a hypercube to all other vertices in a subhypercube. Values at all vertices of a subhypercube can be associatively combined in a similar fashion.

The performance of these normal algorithms is summarized below.

THEOREM 7.7.2 *Broadcasting from one vertex in a d-dimensional hypercube to all other vertices can be done with a normal algorithm in $O(d)$ steps. Similarly, the associative combination of the values stored at the vertices of a d-dimensional hypercube can be done with a normal algorithm in $O(d)$ steps. Broadcasting and associative combining can also be done on the vertices of k-dimensional subcube of the d-dimensional hypercube in $O(k)$ steps with a normal algorithm.*

7.7.3 Shifting on the Hypercube

Cyclic shifting can also be done on a hypercube as a normal algorithm. For $n = 2^d$, consider shifting the n-tuple $\boldsymbol{x} = (x_{n-1}, \ldots, x_0)$ cyclically left by k places on a d-dimensional hypercube. If $k \leq n/2$ (see Fig. 7.16(a)), the largest element in the right half of $\boldsymbol{x}$, namely $x_{n/2-1}$, moves to the left half of $\boldsymbol{x}$. On the other hand, if $k > n/2$ (see Fig. 7.16(b)), $x_{n/2-1}$ moves to the right half of $\boldsymbol{x}$.

Thus, to shift $\boldsymbol{x}$ left cyclically by k places, $k \leq n/2$, divide $\boldsymbol{x}$ into two $(n/2)$-tuples, shift each of these tuples cyclically by k places, and then swap the rightmost k components of the two halves, as suggested in Fig. 7.16(a). The swap is done via edges across the highest

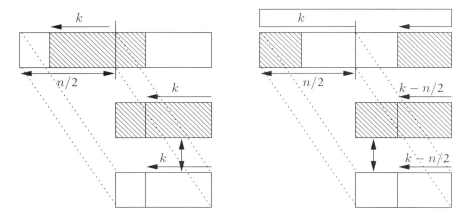

Figure 7.16 The two cases of a normal algorithm for cyclic shifting on a hypercube.

dimension of the hypercube. When $k > n/2$, cyclically shift each $(n/2)$-tuple by $k - n/2$ positions and then swap the high-order $(n/2) - k$ positions from each tuple across the highest dimension of the hypercube. We have the following result.

THEOREM 7.7.3 *Cyclic shifting of an n-tuple, $n = 2^d$, by any amount can be done recursively by a normal algorithm in $\log_2 n$ communication steps.*

7.7.4 Shuffle and Unshuffle Permutations on Linear Arrays

Because many important algorithms are normal and hypercubes are expensive to realize, it is preferable to realize normal algorithms on arrays. In this section we introduce the shuffle and unshuffle permutations, show that they can be used to realize normal algorithms, and then show that they can be realized on linear arrays. We use the unshuffle algorithms to map normal hypercube algorithms onto one- and two-dimensional meshes.

Let $\mathbb{N}(n) = \{0, 1, 2, \ldots, n - 1\}$ and $n = 2^d$. The **shuffle permutation** $\pi_{\text{shuffle}}^{(n)}$: $\mathbb{N}(n) \mapsto \mathbb{N}(n)$ moves the item in position a to position $\pi_{\text{shuffle}}^{(n)}(a)$, where $\pi_{\text{shuffle}}^{(n)}(a)$ is the integer represented by the left cyclic shift of the d-bit binary number representing a. For example, when $n = 8$ the integer 3 is represented by the binary number 011 and its left cyclic shift is 110. Thus, $\pi_{\text{shuffle}}^{(8)}(3) = 6$. The shuffle permutation of the sequence $\{0, 1, 2, 3, 4, 5, 6, 7\}$ is the sequence $\{0, 4, 1, 5, 2, 6, 3, 7\}$. A shuffle operation is analogous to interleaving of the two halves of a sorted deck of cards. Figure 7.17 shows this mapping for $n = 8$.

The **unshuffle permutation** $\pi_{\text{unshuffle}}^{(n)}$: $\mathbb{N}(n) \mapsto \mathbb{N}(n)$ reverses the shuffle operation: it moves the item in position b to position a where $b = \pi_{\text{shuffle}}^{(n)}(a)$; that is, $a = \pi_{\text{unshuffle}}^{(n)}(b) = \pi_{\text{unshuffle}}(\pi_{\text{shuffle}}(a))$. Figure 7.18 shows this mapping for $n = 8$. The shuffle permutation is obtained by reversing the directions of edges in this graph.

An unshuffle operation can be performed on an n-cell linear array, $n = 2^d$, by assuming that the cells contain the integers $\{0, 1, 2, \ldots, n - 1\}$ from left to right represented as d-bit binary integers and then sorting them by their least significant bit using a stable sorting algorithm. (A **stable sorting algorithm** is one that does not change the original order of keys with the same value.) When this is done, the sequence $\{0, 1, 2, 3, 4, 5, 6, 7\}$ is mapped to the

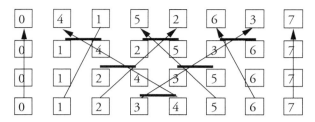

Figure 7.17 The shuffle permutation can be realized by a series of swaps of the contents of cells. The cells between which swaps are done have a heavy bar above them. The result of swapping cells of one row is shown in the next higher row, so that the top row contains the result of shuffling the bottom row.

sequence $\{0, 2, 4, 6, 1, 3, 5, 7\}$, the unshuffled sequence, as shown in Fig. 7.18. The integer b is mapped to the integer a whose binary representation is that of b shifted cyclically right by one position. For example, position 1 (001) is mapped to position 4 (100) and position 6 (110) is mapped to position 3 (011).

Since bubble sort is a stable sorting algorithm, we use it to realize the unshuffle permutation. (See Section 7.5.2.) In each phase keys (binary tuples) are compared based on their least significant bits. In the first phase values in positions i and $i + 1$ are compared for i even. The next comparison is between such pairs for i odd. Comparisons of this form continue, alternating between even and odd values for i, until the sequence is sorted. Since the first phase has no effect on the integers $\{0, 1, 2, \ldots, n - 1\}$, it is not done. Subsequent phases are shown in Fig. 7.18. Pairs that are compared are connected by a light line; a darker line joins pairs whose values are swapped. (See Problem 7.16.)

We now show how to implement efficiently a fully normal ascending algorithm on a linear array. (See Fig. 7.19.) Let the **exchange locations** of the linear array be locations i and $i + 1$ of the array for i even. Only elements in exchange locations are swapped. Swapping between the first dimension of the hypercube is done by swaps across exchange locations. To simulate exchanges across the second dimension, perform a shuffle operation (by reversing the order of the operations of Fig. 7.18) on each group of four elements. This places into exchange locations elements whose original indices differed by two. Performing a shuffle on eight, sixteen, etc.

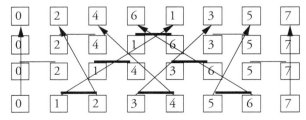

Figure 7.18 An unshuffle operation is obtained by bubble sorting the integers $\{0, 1, 2, \ldots, n - 1\}$ based on the value of their least significant bits. The cells with bars over them are compared. The first set of comparisons is done on elements in the bottom row. Those pairs with light bars contain integers whose values are in order.

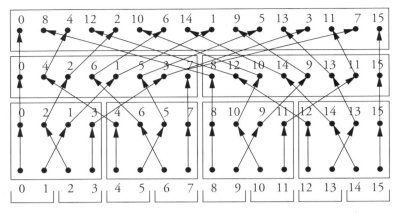

Figure 7.19 A normal ascending algorithm realized by shuffle operations on 2^k elements, $k = 2, 3, 4, \ldots$, places into exchange locations elements whose indices differ by increasing powers of two. Exchange locations are paired together.

positions places into exchange locations elements whose original indices differed by four, eight, etc. The proof of correctness of this result is left to the reader. (See Problem 7.17.)

Since a shuffle on $n = 2^d$ elements can be done in $2^{d-1} - 1$ steps on a linear array with n cells (see Theorem 7.5.2), it follows that this fully normal ascending algorithm uses $T(n) = \phi(d)$ steps, where $T(2) = \phi(1) = 0$ and

$$\phi(d) = \phi(d - 1) + 2^{d-1} - 1 = 2^d - d - 1$$

Summarizing, we have the following theorem.

THEOREM 7.7.4 *A fully normal ascending or descending algorithm that runs in* $d = \log_2 n$ *steps on a d-dimensional hypercube containing* 2^d *vertices can be realized on a linear array of* $n = 2^d$ *elements in* $T(n) = n - \log_2 n - 1$ *parallel steps.*

From the discussion of Section 7.7 it follows that broadcasting, associative combining, and the FFT algorithm can be executed on a linear array in $O(n)$ steps because each can be implemented as a normal algorithm on the n-vertex hypercube. Also, a list of n items can be sorted on a linear array in $O(n)$ steps by translating Batcher's sorting algorithm based on odd-even merging, a normal sorting algorithm, to the linear array. (See Problem 7.20.)

7.7.5 Fully Normal Algorithms on Two-Dimensional Arrays

We now consider the execution of a normal algorithm on a rectangular array. We assume that the $n = 2^{2d}$ vertices of a 2d-dimensional hypercube are mapped onto an $m \times m$ mesh, $m = 2^d$, in row-major order. Since each cell is indexed by a pair consisting of row and column indices, (r, c), and each of these satisfies $0 \leq r \leq m - 1$ and $0 \leq c \leq m - 1$, they can each be represented by a d-bit binary number. Let $\boldsymbol{r}$ and $\boldsymbol{c}$ be these binary numbers. Thus cell (r, c) is indexed by the 2d-bit binary number $\boldsymbol{rc}$.

Cells in positions (r, c) and $(r, c + 1)$ have associated binary numbers that agree in their d most significant positions. Cells in positions (r, c) and $(r + 1, c)$ have associated binary numbers that agree in their d least significant positions. To simulate a normal hypercube algorithm on the 2D mesh, in each row simulate a normal hypercube algorithm on 2^d vertices after which in each column simulate a normal hypercube algorithm on 2^d vertices. The correctness of this procedure follows because every adjacent pair of vertices of the simulated hypercube is at some time located in adjacent cells of the 2D array.

From Theorem 7.7.4 it follows that hypercube exchanges across the lower d dimensions can be simulated in time proportional to the length of a row, that is, in time $O(\sqrt{n})$. Similarly, it also follows that hypercube exchanges across the higher d dimensions can be simulated in time proportional to $O(\sqrt{n})$. We summarize this result below.

THEOREM 7.7.5 *Each step of a fully normal n-dimensional hypercube algorithm (ascending or descending), $n = 2^{2d}$, can be realized in $O(\sqrt{n})$ steps on an $\sqrt{n} \times \sqrt{n}$ array of cells.*

It follows from the discussion of Section 7.7 that broadcasting, associative combining, and the FFT algorithm can be executed on a 2D mesh in $O(\sqrt{n})$ steps because each can be implemented as a normal algorithm on the n-vertex hypercube.

Also, a list of n items can be sorted on a linear array in $O(\sqrt{n})$ steps by translating a normal merging algorithm to the linear array and using it recursively to create a sorting network. (See Problem 7.21.) No sorting algorithm can sort in fewer than $2\sqrt{m} - 1$ steps on an $m \times m$ array because whatever element is positioned in the lower right-hand corner of the array could originate in the upper left-hand corner and have to traverse at least $2\sqrt{m} - 1$ edges to arrive there.

7.7.6 Normal Algorithms on Cube-Connected Cycles

Consider now processors connected as a d-dimensional cube-connected cycle (CCC) network in which each ring has $r = 2^k \geq d$ processors. In particular, let r be the smallest power of 2 greater than or equal to d, so that $d \leq r \leq 2d$. (Thus $k = O(\log d)$.) We call such a CCC network a **canonical CCC network** on n vertices. It has $n = r2^d$ vertices, $d2^d \leq n \leq (2d)2^d$. (Thus $d = O(\log n)$.) We show that a fully normal algorithm can be executed efficiently on such CCC networks.

Let each ring of the CCC network be indexed by a d-tuple corresponding to the corner of the hypercube at which it resides. Let each processor be indexed by a $(d + k)$-tuple in which the d low-order bits are the ring index and the k high-order bits specify the position of a processor on the ring.

A fully normal algorithm on a canonical CCC network is implemented in two phases. In the first phase, the ring is treated as an array and a fully normal algorithm on the k high-order bits is simulated in $O(d)$ steps. In the second phase, exchanges are made across hypercube edges. Rotate the elements on each ring so that ring processors whose k-bit indices are **0** (call these the **lead elements**) are adjacent along the first dimension of the original hypercube. Exchange information between them. Now rotate the rings by one position so that lead elements are adjacent along the second dimension of the original hypercube. The elements immediately behind the lead elements on the rings are now adjacent along the first hypercube dimension and are exchanged in parallel with the lead elements. (This simultaneous execution is called **pipelining**.) Subsequent rotations of the rings place successive ring elements in alignment along increasing bit positions. After $O(d)$ rotations all exchanges are complete. Thus, a total of $O(d)$ time steps suffice to execute a fully normal algorithm. We have the following result.

THEOREM 7.7.6 *A fully normal algorithm (ascending or descending) for an n-vertex hypercube can be realized in $O(\log n)$ steps on a canonical n-vertex cube-connected cycle network.*

Thus, a fully normal algorithm on an n-vertex hypercube can be simulated on a CCC network in time proportional to the time on the hypercube. However, the vertices of the CCC have bounded degree, which makes them much easier to realize in hardware than high-degree networks.

7.7.7 Fast Matrix Multiplication on the Hypercube

Matrix multiplication can be done more quickly on the hypercube than on a two-dimensional array. Instead of $O(n)$ steps, only $O(\log n)$ steps are needed, as we show.

Consider the multiplication of $n \times n$ matrices A and B for $n = 2^r$ to produce the product matrix $C = A \times B$. We describe a normal systolic algorithm to multiply these matrices on a d-dimensional hypercube, $d = 3r$.

Since $d = 3r$, the vertices of the d-dimensional hypercube are addressed by a binary $3r$-tuple, $\boldsymbol{a} = (a_{3r-1}, a_{3r-2}, \ldots, a_0)$. Let the r least significant bits of $\boldsymbol{a}$ denote an integer i, let the next r lsb's denote an integer j, and let the r most significant bits denote an integer k. Then, we have $|\boldsymbol{a}| = kn^2 + jn + i$ since $n = 2^r$. Because of this identity, we represent the address $\boldsymbol{a}$ by the triple (i, j, k). We speak of the processor $P_{i,j,k}$ located at the vertex (i, j, k) of the d-dimensional hypercube, $d = 3r$. We denote by $HC_{i,j,-}$ the subhypercube in which i and j are fixed and by $HC_{i,-,k}$ and $HC_{-,j,k}$ the subhypercubes in which the two other pairs of indices are fixed. There are 2^{2r} subhypercubes of each kind.

We assume that each processor $P_{i,j,k}$ contains three local variables, $A_{i,j,k}$, $B_{i,j,k}$, and $C_{i,j,k}$. We also assume that initially $A_{i,j,0} = a_{i,j}$ and $B_{i,j,0} = b_{i,j}$. The multiplication algorithm has the following five phases:

a) For each subhypercube $HC_{i,j,-}$ and for $1 \leq k \leq n$, broadcast $A_{i,j,0}$ (containing $a_{i,j}$) to $A_{i,j,k}$ and $B_{i,j,0}$ (containing $b_{i,j}$) to $B_{i,j,k}$.

b) For each subhypercube $HC_{i,-,k}$ and for $1 \leq j \leq n$, broadcast $A_{i,k,k}$ (containing $a_{i,k}$) to $A_{i,j,k}$.

c) For each subhypercube $HC_{-,j,k}$ and for $1 \leq i \leq n$, broadcast $B_{k,j,k}$ (containing $b_{k,j}$) to $B_{i,j,k}$.

d) At each processor $P_{i,j,k}$ compute $C_{i,j,k} = A_{i,j,k} \cdot B_{i,j,k} = a_{i,k} b_{k,j}$.

e) At processor $P_{i,j,0}$ compute the sum $C_{i,j,0} = \sum_k C_{i,j,k}$ ($C_{i,j,k}$ now contains $c_{i,j} = \sum_k a_{i,k} b_{k,j}$).

From Theorem 7.7.2 it follows that each of these five steps can be done in $O(r)$ steps, where $r = \log_2 n$. We summarize this result below.

THEOREM 7.7.7 *Two $n \times n$ matrices, $n = 2^r$, can be multiplied by a normal systolic algorithm on a d-dimensional hypercube, $d = 3r$, with n^3 processors in $O(\log n)$ steps. All normal algorithms for $n \times n$ matrix multiplication require $\Omega(\log n)$ steps.*

Proof The upper bound follows from the construction. The lower bound follows from the observation that each processor that is participating in the execution of a normal algorithm combines two values, one that it owns and one owned by one of its neighbors. Thus, if t steps are executed to compute a value, that value cannot depend on more than 2^t other values. Since each entry in an $n \times n$ product matrix is a function of $2n$ other values, t must be at least $\log_2(2n)$. ∎

The lower bound stated above applies only to normal algorithms. If a non-normal algorithm is used, each processor can combine up to d values. Thus, after k steps, up to d^k values can be combined. If $2n$ values must be combined, as in $n \times n$ matrix multiplication, then $k \geq \log_d(2n) = (\log_2 2n)/\log_2 d$. If an n^3-processor hypercube is used for this problem, $d = 3\log_2 n$ and $k = \Omega(\log n/\log\log n)$.

The normal matrix multiplication algorithm described above can be translated to linear arrays and 2D meshes using the mappings based on the shuffle and unshuffle operations. The 2D mesh version has a running time $O(\sqrt{n}\log n)$, which is inferior to the running time of the algorithm given in Section 7.5.3.

7.8 Routing in Networks

A topic of major concern in the design of distributed memory machines is **routing**, the task of transmitting messages among processors via nodes of a network. Routing becomes challenging when many messages must travel simultaneously through a network because they can produce congestion at nodes and cause delays in the receipt of messages.

Some routing networks are designed primarily for the **permutation-routing problem**, the problem of establishing a one-to-one correspondence between n senders and n receivers. (A processor can be both a sender and receiver.) Each sender sends one message to a unique receiver and each receiver receives one message from a unique sender. (We examine in Section 7.9.3 routing methods when the numbers of senders and receivers differ and more than one message can be received by one processor.) If many messages are targeted at one receiver, a long delay will be experienced at this receiver. It should be noted that network congestion can occur at a node even when messages are uniformly distributed throughout the network, because many messages may have to pass through this node to reach their destinations.

7.8.1 Local Routing Networks

In a **local routing network** each message is accompanied by its destination address. At each network node (**switch**) the routing algorithm, using only these addresses and not knowing the global state of the network, finds a path for messages.

A sorting network, suitably modified to transmit messages, is a local permutation-routing network. Batcher's odd-even sorting network described in Section 6.8.1 will serve as such a network. As mentioned in Section 7.7, this network can be realized as a normal algorithm on a hypercube, with running time on an n-vertex hypercube $O(\log^2 n)$. (See Problem 6.28.) On the two-dimensional mesh its running time is $O(\sqrt{n})$ (see Problem 7.21), whereas on the linear array it is $O(n)$ (see Problem 7.20).

Batcher's odd-even sorting network is **data-oblivious**; that is, it performs the same set of operations for all values of the input data. The outcomes of these operations are data-dependent, but the operations themselves are data-independent. Non-oblivious sorting algorithms perform operations that depend on the values of the input data. An example of a local non-oblivious algorithm is one that sends a message from the current network node to the neighboring node that is closest to the destination.

7.8.2 Global Routing Networks

In a **global routing network**, knowledge of the destinations of all messages is used to set the network switches and select paths for the messages to follow. A global permutation-routing network realizes permutations of the destination addresses. We now give an example of such a network, the Beneš permutation network.

A permutation network is constructed of two-input, two-output switches. Such a switch either passes its inputs, labeled A and B, to its outputs, labeled X and Y, or it swaps them. That is, the switch is set so that either X = A and Y = B or X = B and Y = A. A **permutation network** on n inputs and n outputs is a directed acyclic graph of these switches such that for each permutation of the n inputs, switches can be set to create n disjoint paths from the n inputs to the n outputs.

A **Beneš permutation network** is shown in Fig. 7.20. This graph is produced by connecting two copies of an FFT graph on 2^{k-1} inputs back to back and replacing the nodes by switches and edges by pairs of edges. (FFT graphs are described in Section 6.7.3.) It follows that a Beneš permutation network on n inputs can be realized by a normal algorithm

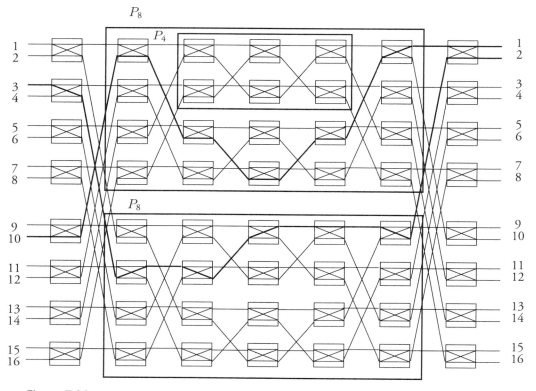

Figure 7.20 A Beneš permutation network.

that executes $O(\log n)$ steps. Thus, a permutation is computed much more quickly (in time $O(\log n)$) with the Beneš offline permutation network than it can be done on Batcher's online odd-even sorting network (in time $O(\log^2 n)$). However, the Beneš network requires time to collect the destinations at some central location, compute the switch settings, and transmit them to the switches themselves.

To understand how the Beneš network works, we provide an alternative characterization of it. Let P_n be the Beneš network on n inputs, $n = 2^k$, defined as back-to-back FFT graphs with nodes replaced by switches. Then P_n may be defined recursively, as suggested in Fig. 7.20. P_n is obtained by making two copies of $P_{n/2}$, placing $n/2$ copies of a two-input, two-output switch at the input and the same number at the output. The first output of the ith new input switch is connected to the ith input of the first copy of $P_{n/2}$, whereas its second output is connected to the ith input of the second copy of $P_{n/2}$. The first input of the jth new output switch is connected to the jth output of the first copy of $P_{n/2}$, whereas its second input is connected to the jth output of the second copy of $P_{n/2}$.

Consider the Beneš network P_2. It consists of a single switch and generates the two possible permutations of the inputs. We show by induction that P_n generates all $n!$ permutations of its n inputs. Assume that this property holds for $n = 2, 4, \ldots, 2^{k-1}$. We show that it holds for $m = 2^k$. Let $\boldsymbol{\pi} = (\pi(1), \pi(2), \ldots, \pi(m))$ be an arbitrary permutation to be realized by P_m. This means that the ith input must be connected to the $\pi(i)$th output. Suppose that $\pi(3)$ is 2, as shown in Fig. 7.20. We can arbitrarily choose to have the third input pass through the first or second copy of $P_{m/2}$. We choose the second. The path taken through the second copy of $P_{m/2}$ must emerge on its first output so that it can then pass to the first switch in the column of output switches. This output switch must pass its inputs without swapping them. The other output of this switch, namely 1, must arrive via a path through the first copy of $P_{m/2}$ and emerge on its first output. To determine the input at which it must arrive, we find the input of P_m associated with the output of 1 and set its switch so that it is directed to the first copy of $P_{m/2}$. Since the other input to this input switch must go to the other copy of $P_{m/2}$, we follow its path through P_m to the output and then reason in the same way about the other output at the output switch at which it arrives. If by tracing paths back and forth this way we do not exhaust all inputs and outputs, we pick another input and repeat the process until all inputs have been routed to outputs.

Now let's determine the number of switches, $S(k)$, in a Beneš network P_n on $n = 2^k$ inputs. It follows that $S(1) = 1$ and

$$S(k) = 2S(k - 1) + 2^k$$

It is straightforward to show that $S(k) = (k - \frac{1}{2})2^k = n(\log_2 n - \frac{1}{2})$.

Although a global permutation network sends messages to their destinations more quickly than a local permutation network, the switch settings must be computed and distributed globally, both of which impose important limitations on the time to realize particular permutations.

7.9 The PRAM Model

The **parallel random-access machine (PRAM)** (see Fig. 7.21), the canonical structured parallel machine, consists of a bounded set of processors and a common memory containing a potentially unlimited number of words. Each processor is similar to the random-access machine (RAM) described in Section 3.4 except that its CPU can access locations in both its local

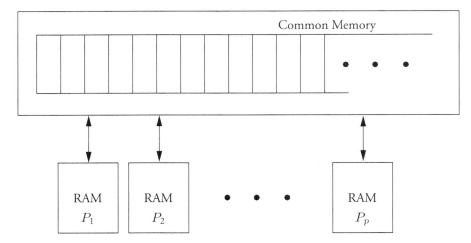

Figure 7.21 The PRAM consists of synchronous RAMs accessing a common memory.

random-access memory and the common memory. During each PRAM step, the RAMs execute the following steps in synchrony: they (a) read from the common memory, (b) perform a local computation, and (c) write to the common memory. Each RAM has its own program and program counter as well as a unique identifying number id_j that it can access to make processor-dependent decisions. The PRAM is primarily an abstract programming model, not a machine designed to be built (unlike mesh-based computers, for example).

The power of the PRAM has been explored by considering a variety of assumptions about the length of local computations and the type of instruction allowed. In designing parallel algorithms it is generally assumed that each local computation consists of a small number of instructions. However, when this restriction is dropped and the PRAM is allowed an unlimited number of computations between successive accesses to the common memory (the **ideal PRAM**), the information transmitted between processors reflects the minimal amount of information that must be exchanged to solve a problem on a parallel computer.

Because the size of memory words is potentially unbounded, very large numbers can be generated very quickly on a PRAM if a RAM can multiply and divide integers and perform vector operations. This allows each RAM to emulate a parallel machine with an unbounded number of processors. Since the goal is to understand the power of parallelism, however, this form of hidden parallelism is usually disallowed, either by not permitting these instructions or by assuming that in t steps a PRAM generates numbers whose size is bounded by a polynomial in t. To simplify the discussion, we limit instructions in a RAM's repertoire to addition, subtraction, vector comparison operations, conditional branching, and shifts by fixed amounts. We also allow load and store instructions for moving words between registers, local memories, and the common memory. These instructions are sufficiently rich to compute all computable functions.

As yet we have not specified the conditions under which access to the common memory occurs in the first and third substeps of each PRAM step. If access by more than one RAM to the same location is disallowed, access is **exclusive**. If this restriction does not apply, access is **concurrent**. Four combinations of these classifications apply to reading and writing. The strongest restriction is placed on the **Exclusive Read/Exclusive Write (EREW) PRAM**, with successively weaker restrictions placed on the **Concurrent Read/Exclusive Write (CREW) PRAM**, the **Exclusive Read/Concurrent Write (ERCW) PRAM**, and the **Concurrent Read/Concurrent Write (CRCW) PRAM**. When concurrent writing is allowed, conflicts are resolved in one of the following ways: a) the **COMMON model** requires that all RAMs writing to a common location write the same value, b) the **ARBITRARY model** allows an arbitrary value to be written, and c) the **PRIORITY model** writes into the common location the value being written by the lowest numbered RAM.

Observe that any algorithm written for the COMMON CRCW PRAM runs without change on the ARBITRARY CRCW PRAM. Similarly, an ARBITRARY CRCW PRAM algorithm runs without change on the PRIORITY CRCW PRAM. Thus, the latter is the most powerful of the PRAM models.

In performing a computation on a PRAM it is typically assumed that the input is written in the lowest numbered locations of the common memory. PRAM computations are characterized by p, the **number of processors** (RAMs) in use, and T (**time**), the number of PRAM steps taken. Both measures are usually stated as a function of the size of a problem instance, namely m, the number of input words, and n, their total length in bits.

After showing that tree, array, and hypercube algorithms translate directly to a PRAM algorithm with no loss in efficiency, we explore the power of concurrency. This is followed by a brief discussion of the simulation of a PRAM on a hypercube and a circuit on a CREW PRAM. We close by referring the reader to connections established between PRAMs and circuits and to the discussion of serial space and parallel time in Chapter 8.

7.9.1 Simulating Trees, Arrays, and Hypercubes on the PRAM

We have shown that 1D arrays can be embedded into 2D meshes and that d-dimensional meshes can be embedded into hypercubes while preserving the neighborhood structure of the first graph in the second. Also, we have demonstrated that any balanced tree algorithm can be simulated as a normal algorithm on a hypercube. As a consequence, in each case, an algorithm designed for the first network carries over to the second without any increase in the number of steps executed. We now show that normal hypercube algorithms are efficiently simulated on an EREW PRAM.

With each d-dimensional hypercube processor, associate an EREW PRAM processor and a reserved location in the common memory. In a normal algorithm each hypercube processor communicates with its neighbor along a specified direction. To simulate this communication, each associated PRAM processor writes the data to be communicated into its reserved location. The processor for which the message is destined knows which hypercube neighbor is providing the data and reads the value stored in its associated memory location.

When a hypercube is not normal, as many as $d - 1$ neighbors can send messages to one processor. Since EREW PRAM processors can access only one cell per unit time, simulation of the hypercube can require a running time that is about d times that of the hypercube.

THEOREM 7.9.1 *Every T-step normal algorithm on the d-dimensional, n-vertex hypercube, $n = 2^d$, can be simulated in $O(T)$ steps on an n-processor EREW PRAM. Every T-step hypercube algorithm, normal or not, can be simulated in $O(Td)$ steps.*

An immediate consequence of Theorems 7.7.1 and 7.9.1 is that a list of n items can be sorted on an n-processor PRAM in $O(\log^2 n)$ steps by a normal oblivious algorithm. Data-dependent sorting algorithms for the hypercube exist with running time $O(\log n)$.

It also follows from Section 7.6.1 that algorithms for trees, linear arrays, and meshes translate directly into PRAM algorithms with the same running time as on these less general models. Of course, the superior connectivity between PRAM processors might be used to produce faster algorithms.

7.9.2   The Power of Concurrency

The CRCW PRAM is a very powerful model. As we show, any Boolean function can be computed with it in a constant number of steps if a sufficient number of processors is available. For this reason, the CRCW PRAM is of limited interest: it represents an extreme that does not reflect reality as we know it. The CREW and EREW PRAMs are more realistic. We first explore the power of the CRCW and then show that an EREW PRAM can simulate a p-processor CRCW PRAM with a slowdown by a factor of $O(\log p)$.

THEOREM 7.9.2   *The CRCW PRAM can compute an arbitrary Boolean function in four steps.*

Proof   Given a Boolean function $f : \mathcal{B}^n \mapsto \mathcal{B}$, represent it by its disjunctive normal form; that is, represent it as the OR of its minterms where a minterm is the AND of each literal of f. (A literal is a variable, x_i, or its complement, $\overline{x}_i$.) Assume that each variable is stored in a separate location in the common memory.

Given a minterm, we show that it can be computed by a CRCW PRAM in two steps. Assign one location in the common memory to the minterm and initialize it to the value 1. Assign one processor to each literal in the minterm. The processor assigned to the jth literal reads the value of the jth variable from the common memory. If the value of the literal is 0, this processor writes the value 0 to the memory location associated with the minterm. Thus, the minterm has value 1 exactly when each literal has value 1. Note that these processors read concurrently with processors associated with other minterms and may write concurrently if more than one of their literals has value 0.

Now assume that a common memory location has been reserved for the function itself and initialized to 0. One processor is assigned to each minterm and if the value of its minterm is 1, it writes the value 1 in the location associated with the function. Thus, in two more steps the function f is computed. ■

Given the power of concurrency, especially as applied to writing, we now explore the cost in performance of not allowing concurrency, whether in reading or writing.

THEOREM 7.9.3   *A p-processor priority CRCW PRAM can be simulated by a p-processor EREW PRAM with a slowdown by a factor equal to the time to sort p elements on this machine. Consequently, this simulation can be done by a normal algorithm in $O(\log^2 p)$ steps.*

Proof   The jth EREW PRAM processor simulates a memory access by the jth CRCW PRAM processor by first writing into a special location, M_j, a pair $(\boldsymbol{a}_j, j)$ indicating that processor j wishes to access (read or write) location $\boldsymbol{a}_j$. If processors are writing to common memory, the value to be written is attached to this pair. If processors are reading from common memory, a return message containing the requested value is provided. If a processor chooses not to access any location, a dummy address larger than all other addresses is used for

a_j. The contents of the locations $M_1, M_2, \ldots, M_p$ are sorted, which creates a subsequence in which pairs with a common address occur together and within which the pairs are sorted by processor numbers. From Theorem 7.7.1 it follows that this step can be performed in time $O(\log^2 p)$ by a normal algorithm. So far no concurrent reads or writes occur.

A processor is now assigned to each pair in the sorted sequence. We consider two cases: a) processors are reading from or b) writing to common memory. Processors now compare the address of its pair to that of the preceding pair. If a processor finds these addresses to be different and case a holds, it reads the item in common memory and sets a flag bit to 1; all other processors except the first set their flag bits to 0; the first sets its bit to 1. (This bit is used later to distribute the value that it read.) However, if case b holds instead, the processor writes its value. Since this processor has the lowest index of all processors and the priority CRCW is the strongest model, the value written is the same value written by either the common or arbitrary CRCW models.

Returning now to case a, the flag bits mark the first pair in each subsequence of pairs that have the same address in the common memory. Associated with the leading pair is the value read at this address. We now perform a segmented prefix computation using as the associative rule the copy-right operation. (See Problem 2.20.) It distributes to each pair (a_j, j) the value the processor wished to read from the common memory. By Problem 2.21 this problem can be solved by a p-processor EREW PRAM in $O(\log p)$ steps. The pairs and their accompanying value are then sorted by the processor number so that the value read from the common memory is in a location reserved for the processor that requested the value. ■

7.9.3   Simulating the PRAM on a Hypercube Network

As stated above, each PRAM cycle involves reading from the global memory, performing a local computation, and writing to the common memory. Of course, a processor need not access common memory when given the chance. Thus, to simulate a PRAM on a network computer, one has to take into account the fact that not all PRAM processors necessarily read from or write to common memory locations on each cycle.

It is important to remember that the latency of network computers can be large. Thus, for the simulation described below to be useful, each PRAM processor must be able to do a lot of work between network accesses.

The EREW PRAM is simulated on a network computer by executing three phases, two of which correspond to reading and writing common memory. (To simulate the CRCW PRAM, we need only add the time given above to simulate a CRCW PRAM by an EREW PRAM.) We simulate an access to common memory by routing a message over the network to the site containing the simulated common memory location. It follows that a message must contain the name of a site as well as the address of a memory location at that site. If the simulated access is a memory read, a return message is generated containing the value of the memory location. If it is a memory write, the transmitted message must also contain the datum to write into the memory location. We assume that the sites are numbered consecutively from 1 to p, the number of processors.

The first problem to be solved is the routing of messages from source to destination processors. This routing problem was partially addressed in Section 7.8. The new wrinkle here is that the mapping from source to destination sites defined by a set of messages is not necessarily a permutation. Not all sources may send a message and not all destinations are guaranteed to receive only one message. In fact, some destination may be sent many messages, which can result in their waiting a long time for receipt.

To develop an appreciation for the various approaches to this problem, we describe an algorithm that distributes messages from sources to destinations, though not as efficiently as possible. Each processor prepares a message to be sent to other processors. Processors not accessing the common memory send messages containing dummy site addresses larger than any other address. All messages are sorted cooperatively by the processors. As seen in Theorem 7.7.1, they can be sorted by a normal algorithm on an p-vertex hypercube, $p = 2^d$, in $O(\log^2 p)$ steps using Batcher's odd-even sorting network described in Section 6.8.1. The $k \leq p$ non-dummy messages are the first k messages in this sorted list. If the sites at which these messages reside after sorting are the sites for which they were destined, the message routing problem is solved. Unfortunately, this is generally not the case.

To route the messages from their positions in the sorted list to their destinations, we first identify duplicates of destination addresses and compute D, the maximum number of duplicates. We then route messages in D stages. In each stage at most one of the D duplicates of each message is routed to its destination. To identify duplicates, we first assign a processor to each message in the sorted list that compares its destination site with that of its predecessor, setting a flag bit to 0 if they are equal and to 1 otherwise. The first processor also sets its flag bit to 1. A segmented prefix operation that segments its messages with these flag bits and uses integer addition on them assigns to each message an integer (a **priority**) between 1 and D that is q if the site address of this message is the qth such address. (Prefix computations can be done on a p-vertex hypercube in $O(\log p)$ steps. See Problem 7.23.) A message with priority q is routed to its destination in the qth stage. An unsegmented prefix operation with max as the operator is then used to determine the value of D.

In the qth stage, $1 \leq q \leq D$, all non-dummy messages with priority q are routed to their destination site on the hypercube as follows:

a) one processor is assigned to each message;

b) each such processor computes the **gap**, the difference between the destination and current sites of its message;

c) each gap $\boldsymbol{g}$ is represented as a binary d-tuple $\boldsymbol{g} = (g_{d-1}, \ldots, g_0)$;

d) For $t = d - 1, d - 2, \ldots, 0$, those messages whose gap contains 2^t are sent to the site reached by crossing the tth dimension of the hypercube.

We show that in at most $O(D \log p)$ steps all messages are routed to their destinations. Let the sorted message sites form an ascending sequence. If there are k non-dummy messages, let gap_i, $1 \leq i \leq k$, be the gap of the ith message. Observe that these gaps must also form a nondecreasing sequence. For example, shown below is a sorted set of destinations and a corresponding sequence of gaps:

gap_i	1	1	2	3	3	6	7	8							
dest_i	1	2	4	5	7	11	13	15							
i	0	1	2	3	4	5	6	7	8	9	10	11	12	13	15

All the messages whose gaps contain 2^{d-1} must be the last messages in the sequence because the gaps would otherwise be out of order. Thus, advancing messages with these gaps by

2^{d-1} positions, which is done by moving them across the largest dimension of the hypercube, advances them to positions in the sequence that cannot be occupied by any other messages, even after these messages have been advanced by their full gaps. For example, shown below are the positions of the messages given above after those whose gaps contain 8 and 4 have been moved by this many positions:

$dest_i$	1	2	4	5	7					11	13				15
i	0	1	2	3	4	5	6	7	8	9	10	11	12	13	15

Repeating this argument on subsequent smaller powers of 2, we find that no two messages that are routed in a given stage occupy the same site. As a consequence, after D stages, each taking d steps, all messages are routed. We summarize this result below.

THEOREM 7.9.4 *Each computation cycle of a p-processor EREW PRAM can be simulated by a fully normal algorithm on a p-vertex hypercube in $O(D \log p + \log^2 p)$ steps, where D is the maximum number of processors accessing memory locations stored at a given vertex of the hypercube.*

This result can be improved to $O(\log p)$ [156] with a probabilistic algorithm that replicates each datum at each hypercube processor a fixed number of times.

Because the simulation described above of a EREW PRAM on a hypercube is fully normal, $O(D\sqrt{p})$- and $O(Dp)$-time simulations of a PRAM on two-dimensional meshes and linear arrays follow. (See Problems 7.32 and 7.33.)

7.9.4 Circuits and the CREW PRAM

Algebraic and logic circuits can also be simulated on PRAMs, in particular the CREW PRAM. For simplicity we assign one processor to each vertex of a circuit (a gate). We also assume that each vertex has bounded fan-in, which for concreteness is assumed to be 2. We also reserve one memory location for each gate and one for each input variable. Each processor now alternates between reading values from its two inputs (concurrently with other processors, if necessary) and exclusively writing values to the location reserved for its value. Two steps are devoted to reading the values of gate inputs. Let $D_\Omega(f)$ be the depth of the circuit for a function f. After $3D_\Omega(f)$ steps the input values have propagated to the output gates, the values computed by them are correct and the computation is complete.

In Section 8.14 we show a stronger result, that CREW PRAMs and circuits are equivalent as language recognizers. We also explore the parallel computation thesis, which states that sequential space and parallel time are polynomially related. It follows that the PRAM and the logic circuit are both excellent models in terms of which to measure the minimal computation time required for a problem on a parallel machine. In Section 8.15 we exhibit complexity classes, that is, classes of languages defined in terms of the depth of circuits recognizing them.

7.10 The BSP and LogP Models

Bulk synchronous parallelism (BSP) extends the MIMD model to potentially different asynchronous programs running on the physical processors of a parallel computer. Its developers believe that the BSP model is both built on realistic assumptions and sufficiently simple to provide an attractive model for programming parallel computers. They expect it will play a role similar to that of the RAM for serial computation, that is, that programs written for the BSP model can be translated into efficient code for a variety of parallel machines.

The BSP model explicitly assumes that a) computations are divided into *supersteps*, b) all processors are synchronized after each superstep, c) processors can send and receive messages to and from all other processors, d) message transmission is non-blocking (computation can resume after sending a message), and e) all messages are delivered by the end of a superstep. The important parameters of this model are p, the number of processors, s, the speed of each processor, l, the latency of the system, which is the number of processor steps to synchronize processors, and g, the additional number of processor steps per word to deliver a message. Here g measures the time per word to transmit a message between processors after the path between them has been set up; l measures the time to set up paths between processors and/or to synchronize all p processors. Each of these parameters must be appraised under "normal" computational and communication loads if the model is to provide useful estimates of the time to complete a task.

For the BSP model to be effective, it must be possible to keep the processors busy while waiting for communications to be completed. If the latency of the network is too high, this will not be possible. It will also not be possible if algorithms are not designed properly. For example, if all processors attempt to send messages to a single processor, network congestion will prevent the messages from being answered quickly. It has been shown that for many important problems data can be distributed and algorithms designed to make good use of the BSP model [342]. It should also be noted that the BSP model is not effective on problems that are not parallelizable, such as may be the case for **P**-complete problems (see Section 8.9).

Although for many problems and machines the BSP model is a good one, it does not take into account network congestion due to the number of messages in transit. The **LogP model** extends the BSP model by explicitly accounting for the overhead time (the o in LogP) to prepare a message for transmission. The model is also characterized by the parameters L, g, and P that have the same meaning as the parameters l, g, and p in the BSP model. The LogP and BSP models are about equally good at predicting algorithm performance.

Many other models have been proposed to capture one aspect or another of practical parallel computation. Chapter 11 discusses some of the parallel I/O issues.

* *

Problems

PARALLEL COMPUTERS WITH MEMORY

7.1 Consider the design of a bus arbitration sequential circuit for a computer containing four CPUs. This circuit has four Boolean inputs and outputs, one per CPU. A CPU requesting bus access sets its input to 1 and waits until its output is set to 1, after which it puts its word and destination address on the bus. CPUs not requesting bus access set their bus arbitration input variable to 0.

At the beginning of each cycle the bus arbitration circuit reads the input variables and, if at least one of them has value 1, sets one output variable to 1. If all input variables are 0, it sets all output variables to 0.

Design two such arbitration circuits, one that grants priority to the lowest indexed input that is 1 and a second that grants priority alternately to the lowest and highest indexed input if more than one input variable is 1.

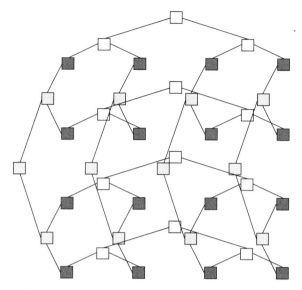

Figure 7.22 A four-by-four mesh-of-trees network.

7.2 Sketch a data-parallel program that operates on a sorted list of keys and finds the largest number of times that a key is repeated.

7.3 Sketch a data-parallel program to find the last record in a linked list where initially each record contains the address of the next item in the list (except for the last item, whose next address is *null*).

Hint: Assign one processor to each list item and assume that accesses to two or more distinct addresses can be done simultaneously.

7.4 The $n \times n$ mesh-of-trees network, $n = 2^r$, is formed from a $n \times n$ mesh by replacing each linear connection forming a row or column by a balanced binary tree. (See Fig. 7.22.) Let the entries of two $n \times n$ matrices be uniformly distributed on the vertices of original mesh. Give an efficient matrix multiplication algorithm on this network and determine its running time.

7.5 Identify problems that arise in a crossbar network when more than one source wishes to connect to the same destination. Describe how to insure that only one source is connected to one destination at the same time.

THE PERFORMANCE OF PARALLEL ALGORITHMS

7.6 Describe how you might apply Amdahl's Law to a data-parallel program to estimate its running time.

7.7 Consider the evaluation of the polynomial $p(x) = a_n x^n + x_{n-1} x^{n-1} + \cdots + a_1 x + a_0$ on a p-processor shared-memory machine. Sketch an algorithm whose running time is $O(\frac{n}{p} + \log n)$ for this problem.

LINEAR ARRAYS

7.8   Generalize the example of Section 7.5.1 to show that the product of an $n \times n$ matrix and an n-vector can be realized in $3n - 1$ steps on a linear systolic array.

7.9   Show that every algorithm on a linear array to compute the product of an $n \times n$ matrix and an n-vector requires at least n steps. Assume that components of the matrix and vector enter cells individually.

7.10 Design an algorithm for a linear array of length $O(n)$ that convolves two sequences each of length n in $O(n)$ steps. Show that no substantially faster algorithm for such a linear array exists.

MULTIDIMENSIONAL ARRAYS

7.11 Show that at most $\sigma(d) = 2d^2 + 2d + 1$ cells are at most d edges away from any cell in a two-dimensional systolic array.

7.12 Derive an expression for the distance between vertices $(n_1, n_2, \ldots, n_d)$ and $(m_1, m_2, \ldots, m_d)$ in a d-dimensional toroidal mesh and determine the maximum distance between two such vertices.

7.13 Design efficient algorithms to multiply two $n \times n$ matrices on a $k \times k$ mesh, $k \leq n$.

HYPERCUBE-BASED MACHINES

7.14 Show that the vertices of the 2^d-input FFT graph can be numbered so that edges between levels correspond to swaps across the dimensions of a d-dimensional hypercube.

7.15 Show that the convolution function $f_{\text{conv}}^{(n,m)} : R^{n+m} \mapsto R^{n+m-1}$ over a commutative ring $\mathcal{R}$ can be implemented by as a fully normal algorithm in time $O(\log n)$.

7.16 Prove that the unshuffle operation on a linear array of $n = 2^d$ cells can be done with $2^d - 1$ comparison/exchange steps.

7.17 Prove that the algorithm described in Section 7.7.4 to simulate a normal hypercube algorithm on a linear array of $n = 2^d$ elements correctly places into exchange locations elements whose indices differ by successive powers of 2.

7.18 Describe an efficient algorithm for a linear array that merges two sorted sequences of the same length.

7.19 Show that Batcher's sorting algorithm based on odd-even merging can be realized on an p-vertex hypercube by a normal algorithm in $O(\log^2 p)$ steps.

7.20 Show that Batcher's sorting algorithm based on odd-even merging can be realized on a linear array of $n = 2^d$ cells in $O(n)$ steps.

7.21 Show that Batcher's sorting algorithm based on odd-even merging can be realized on an $\sqrt{n} \times \sqrt{n}$ array in $O(\sqrt{n})$ steps.

7.22 Design an $O(\sqrt{n})$-step algorithm to implement an arbitrary permutation of n items placed one per cell of an $\sqrt{n} \times \sqrt{n}$ mesh.

7.23 Describe a normal algorithm to realize a prefix computation on a p-vertex hypercube in $O(\log p)$ steps.

7.24 Design an algorithm to perform a prefix computation on an $\sqrt{n} \times \sqrt{n}$ mesh in $\sqrt{n}$ steps. Show that no other algorithm for this problem on this mesh has substantially better performance.

ROUTING IN NETWORKS

7.25 Give a complete description of a procedure to set up the switches in a Beneš network.

7.26 Show how to perform an arbitrary permutation on a linear array.

THE PRAM MODEL

7.27 a) Design an $O(1)$-step CRCW PRAM algorithm to find the maximum element in a list.

 b) Design an $O(\log \log n)$-step CRCW PRAM algorithm to find the maximum element in a list that uses $O(n)$ processors.

 Hint: Construct a tree in which the root and every other vertex has a number of immediate descendants that is about equal to the square root of the number of leaves that are its descendants.

7.28 The goal of the **list-ranking problem** is to assign a rank to each record in a linked list; the rank of a record is its position relative to the last element in the list where the last element has rank zero. Each record has two fields, one for its rank and another for the address of its successor record. The address field of the last record contains its own address.

 Describe an efficient p-processor EREW PRAM algorithm to solve the list-ranking problem for a list of p items stored one per location in the common memory.

 Hint: Use **pointer doubling** in which each address is replaced by the address of its current successor.

7.29 Consider an n-vertex directed graph in which each vertex knows the address of its parent and the roots have themselves as parents. Under the assumption that each vertex is placed in a unique cell in a common PRAM memory, show that the roots can be found in $O(\log n)$ steps.

7.30 Design an efficient PRAM algorithm to find the item in a list that occurs most often.

7.31 Figure 7.23 shows two trees containing one and three copies of a computational element, respectively. This element accepts three inputs and produces three outputs using $\odot$, an associative operator. Tree (a) accepts a, b, and c as input and produces a, $a \odot b$, and $b \odot c$ as output. Tree (b) accepts a, b, c, d, and e as input and produces a, $a \odot b$, $a \odot b \odot c$, $a \odot b \odot c \odot d$, and $b \odot c \odot d \odot e$ as output. If the input and output at the root of the trees are combined with $\odot$, the output of each tree is the prefix computation on its inputs.

 Generalize the constructions of Fig. 7.23 to produce a circuit for the prefix function on n inputs, n arbitrary. Give a convincing argument that your construction is correct and derive good upper bounds on the size and depth of your circuit. Show that to within multiplicative factors your construction has minimal size and depth.

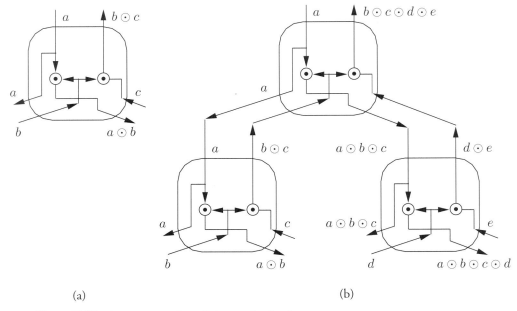

(a)   (b)

Figure 7.23 Components of an efficient prefix circuit.

7.32 Show that each computation cycle of a p-processor EREW PRAM can be simulated on a $\sqrt{p} \times \sqrt{p}$ mesh in $O(D\sqrt{p})$ steps, where D is the maximum number of processors accessing memory locations stored at a given vertex of the mesh.

7.33 Show that each computation cycle of a p-processor EREW PRAM can be simulated on a p-processor linear array in $O(Dp)$ steps, where D is the maximum number of processors accessing memory locations stored at a given vertex of the array.

THE BSP AND LOGP MODELS

7.34 Design an algorithm for the p-processor BSP and/or LogP models to multiply two $n \times n$ matrices when each matrix entry occurs once and entries are uniformly distributed over the p processors. Given the parameters of the models, determine for which values of n your algorithm is efficient.

Hint: The performance of your algorithm will be dependent on the initial placement of data.

7.35 Design an algorithm for the p-processor BSP and/or LogP models for the segmented prefix function. Given the parameters of the models, determine for which values of n your algorithm is efficient.

Chapter Notes

A discussion of parallel algorithms and architectures up to about 1980 can be found in the book by Hockney and Jesshope [134]. A number of recent textbooks provide extensive coverage of parallel algorithms and architectures. They include the books by Akl [16], Bertsekas and Tsitsiklis [38], Gibbons and Spirakis [112], JáJá [147], Leighton [190], Quinn [262], and Reif [274]. In addition, the survey article by Karp and Ramachandran [159] gives an overview of parallel algorithmic methods. References to results on circuit complexity can be found in Chapters 2, 6, and 9.

Flynn introduced the taxonomy of parallel computers that carries his name [101]. The data-parallel style of computing was anticipated in the APL [145] and FP programming languages [26] as well as by Preparata and Vuillemin [259] in their study of parallel algorithms for networked machines. It was developed as the style of choice for programming the Connection Machine [132]. (See also the books by Hatcher and Quinn [128] and Blelloch [45] on data-parallel computing.) The simulation of the MIMD computer by a SIMD one given in Section 7.3.1 is due to Wloka [362].

Amdahl's Law [21] and Brent's principle [58] are widely cited; the latter is used extensively to design efficient parallel algorithms.

Systolic algorithms for convolution, matrix multiplication, and the fast Fourier transform are given by Kung and Leiserson [178] (see also [179]). Odd-even transposition sort is described by Knuth [168]. The lower bound on the time to multiply two matrices given in Theorem 7.5.3 is due to Gentleman [111]. The shuffle network was introduced by Stone [315].

Preparata and Vuillemin [259] give normal algorithms for a variety of problems (including that for shifting in Section 7.7.3) and introduce the cube-connected cycles machine. They also give embeddings of fully normal algorithms into linear arrays and meshes. Dekel, Nassimi, and Sahni [85] developed the fast algorithm for matrix multiplication on the hypercube described in Section 7.7.7.

Batcher [29] introduced odd-even and bitonic sorting methods and noted that they could be used for routing messages in networks. Beneš [36] is the author of the Beneš permutation network.

Variants of the PRAM were introduced by Fortune and Wyllie [102], Goldschlager [117], Savitch and Stimson [295] as generalizations of the idealized RAM model of Cook and Reckhow [77]. The method given in Theorem 7.9.3 to simulate a CRCW PRAM on an EREW PRAM is due to Eckstein [94] and Vishkin [350]. Simulations of PRAMs on networked computers have been developed by Mehlhorn and Vishkin [218], Upfal [337], Upfal and Wigderson [338], Karlin and Upfal [157], Alt, Hagerup, Mehlhorn, and Preparata [19], and Ranade [264]. Cypher and Plaxton [84] have developed a deterministic $O(\log p \log \log p)$-step sorting algorithm for the hypercube. However, it is superior to Batcher's algorithm only for very large and impractical values of p.

The bulk synchronous parallel (BSP) model [345] has been proposed as a bridging model between the needs of programmers and parallel machines. The LogP model [83] is offered as a more realistic variant of the BSP model. Juurlink and Wijshoff [153] and Bilardi, Herley, Pietracaprina, Pucci, and Spirakis [39] report empirical evidence that the BSP and LogP models are about equally good as predictors of performance on real parallel computers.

Part III
COMPUTATIONAL COMPLEXITY

8

Complexity Classes

In an ideal world, each computational problem would be classified at least approximately by its use of computational resources. Unfortunately, our ability to so classify some important problems is limited. We must be content to show that such problems fall into general complexity classes, such as the polynomial-time problems **P**, problems whose running time on a deterministic Turing machine is a polynomial in the length of its input, or **NP**, the polynomial-time problems on nondeterministic Turing machines.

Many complexity classes contain "complete problems," problems that are hardest in the class. If the complexity of one complete problem is known, that of all complete problems is known. Thus, it is very useful to know that a problem is complete for a particular complexity class. For example, the class of **NP**-complete problems, the hardest problems in **NP**, contains many hundreds of important combinatorial problems such as the Traveling Salesperson Problem. It is known that each **NP**-complete problem can be solved in time exponential in the size of the problem, but it is not known whether they can be solved in polynomial time. Whether **P** and **NP** are equal or not is known as the $\mathbf{P} \stackrel{?}{=} \mathbf{NP}$ question. Decades of research have been devoted to this question without success. As a consequence, knowing that a problem is **NP**-complete is good evidence that it is an exponential-time problem. On the other hand, if one such problem were shown to be in **P**, all such problems would be been shown to be in **P**, a result that would be most important.

In this chapter we classify problems by the resources they use on serial and parallel machines. The serial models are the Turing and random-access machines. The parallel models are the circuit and the parallel random-access machine (PRAM). We begin with a discussion of tasks, machine models, and resource measures, after which we examine serial complexity classes and relationships among them. Complete problems are defined and the **P**-complete, **NP**-complete, and **PSPACE**-complete problems are examined. We then turn to the PRAM and circuit models and conclude by identifying important circuit complexity classes such as **NC** and **P/poly**.

8.1 Introduction

The classification of problems requires a precise definition of those problems and the computational models used. Problems are accurately classified only when we are sure that they have been well defined and that the computational models against which they are classified are representative of the computational environment in which these problems will be solved. This requires the computational models to be general. On the other hand, to be useful, problem classifications should not be overly dependent on the characteristics of the machine model used for classification purposes. For example, because of the obviously inefficient use of memory on the Turing machine, the set of problems that runs in time linear in the length of their input on a random-access machine is likely to be different from the set that runs in linear time on the Turing machine. On the other hand, the set of problems that run in polynomial time on both machines is the same.

8.2 Languages and Problems

Before formally defining decision problems, a major topic of this chapter, we give two examples of them, SATISFIABILITY and UNSATISFIABILITY. A set of clauses is **satisfiable** if values can be assigned to Boolean variables in these clauses such that each clause has at least one literal with value 1.

> SATISFIABILITY
> *Instance:* A set of literals $X = \{x_1, \overline{x}_1, x_2, \overline{x}_2, \ldots, x_n, \overline{x}_n\}$, and a sequence of clauses $C = (c_1, c_2, \ldots, c_m)$ where each clause c_i is a subset of X.
> *Answer:* "Yes" if for some assignment of Boolean values to variables in $\{x_1, x_2, \ldots, x_n\}$, at least one literal in each clause has value 1.

The complement of the decision problem SATISFIABILITY, UNSATISFIABILITY, is defined below.

> UNSATISFIABILITY
> *Instance:* A set of literals $X = \{x_1, \overline{x}_1, x_2, \overline{x}_2, \ldots, x_n, \overline{x}_n\}$, and a sequence of clauses $C = (c_1, c_2, \ldots, c_m)$ where each clause c_i is a subset of X.
> *Answer:* "Yes" if for all assignments of Boolean values to variables in $\{x_1, x_2, \ldots, x_n\}$, all literals in at least one clause have value 0.

The clauses $C_1 = (\{x_1, x_2, x_3\}, \{x_1, \overline{x}_2\}, \{x_2, \overline{x}_3\})$ are satisfied with $x_1 = x_2 = x_3 = 1$, whereas the clauses $C_2 = (\{x_1, x_2, x_3\}, \{x_1, \overline{x}_2\}, \{x_2, \overline{x}_3\}, \{x_3, \overline{x}_1\}, \{\overline{x}_1, \overline{x}_2, \overline{x}_3\})$ are not satisfiable. SATISFIABILITY consists of collections of satisfiable clauses. C_1 is in SATISFIABILITY. The complement of SATISFIABILITY, UNSATISFIABILITY, consists of instances of clauses not all of which can be satisfied. C_2 is in UNSATISFIABILITY.

We now introduce terminology used to classify problems. This terminology and the associated concepts are used throughout this chapter.

DEFINITION 8.2.1 *Let Σ be an arbitrary finite alphabet. A* **decision problem** *$\mathcal{P}$ is defined by a set of* **instances** *$I \subseteq \Sigma^*$ of the problem and a condition $\phi_\mathcal{P} : I \mapsto \mathcal{B}$ that has value 1 on "Yes" instances and 0 on "No" instances. Then $I_{\text{yes}} = \{w \in I \mid \phi_\mathcal{P}(w) = 1\}$ are the "Yes" instances. The "No" instances are $I_{\text{no}} = I - I_{\text{yes}}$.*

The **complement of a decision problem** $\mathcal{P}$, *denoted* $\mathbf{co}\mathcal{P}$, *is the decision problem in which the "Yes" instances of* $\mathbf{co}\mathcal{P}$ *are the "No" instances of* $\mathcal{P}$ *and vice versa.*

The "Yes" instances of a decision problem are encoded as binary strings by an **encoding function** $\sigma : \Sigma^* \mapsto \mathcal{B}^*$ *that assigns to each* $w \in I$ *a string* $\sigma(w) \in \mathcal{B}^*$.

With respect to σ, *the* **language** $L(\mathcal{P})$ **associated with a decision problem** $\mathcal{P}$ *is the set* $L(\mathcal{P}) = \{\sigma(w) \mid w \in I_{\text{yes}}\}$. *With respect to* σ, *the language* $L(\mathbf{co}\mathcal{P})$ *associated with* $\mathbf{co}\mathcal{P}$ *is the set* $L(\mathbf{co}\mathcal{P}) = \{\sigma(w) \mid w \in I_{\text{no}}\}$.

The **complement of a language** L, *denoted* $\overline{L}$, *is* $\mathcal{B}^* - L$; *that is,* $\overline{L}$ *consists of the strings that are not in* L.

A decision problem can be generalized to a **problem** $\mathcal{P}$ *characterized by a function* $f : \mathcal{B}^* \mapsto \mathcal{B}^*$ *described by a set of ordered pairs* $(x, f(x))$, *where each string* $x \in \mathcal{B}^*$ *appears once as the left-hand side of a pair. Thus, a* **language** *is defined by problems* $f : \mathcal{B}^* \mapsto \mathcal{B}$ *and consists of the strings on which* f *has value 1.*

SATISFIABILITY and all other decision problems in **NP** have succinct "certificates" for "Yes" instances, that is, choices on a nondeterministic Turing machine that lead to acceptance of a "Yes" instance in a number of steps that is a polynomial in the length of the instance. A certificate for an instance of SATISFIABILITY consists of values for the variables of the instance on which each clause has at least one literal with value 1. The verification of such a certificate can be done on a Turing machine in a number of steps that is quadratic in the length of the input. (See Problem 8.3.)

Similarly, UNSATISFIABILITY and all other decision problems in **coNP** can be disqualified quickly; that is, their "No" instances can be "disqualified" quickly by exhibiting certificates for them (which are certificates for the "Yes" instance of the complementary decision problem). For example, a disqualification for UNSATISFIABILITY is a satisfiable assignment for a "No" instance, that is, a satisfiable set of clauses.

It is not known how to identify a certificate for a "Yes" instance of SATISFIABILITY or any other **NP**-complete problem in time polynomial in length of the instance. If a "Yes" instance has n variables, an exhaustive search of the 2^n values for the n variables is about the best general method known to find an answer.

8.2.1 Complements of Languages and Decision Problems

There are many ways to encode problem instances. For example, for SATISFIABILITY we might represent x_i as i and $\overline{x}_i$ as $\sim i$ and then use the standard seven-bit ASCII encodings for characters. Then we would translate the clause $\{x_4, \overline{x}_7\}$ into $\{4, \sim 7\}$ and then represent it as 123 052 044 126 055 125, where each number is a decimal representing a binary 7-tuple and 4, comma, and $\sim$ are represented by 052, 044, and 126, respectively.

All the instances I of decision problems $\mathcal{P}$ considered in this chapter are characterized by regular expressions. In addition, the encoding function of Definition 8.2.1 can be chosen to map strings in I to binary strings $\sigma(I)$ describable by regular expressions. Thus, a finite-state machine can be used to determine if a binary string is in $\sigma(I)$ or not. We assume that membership of a string in $\sigma(I)$ can be determined efficiently.

As suggested by Fig. 8.1, the strings in $\overline{L}(\mathcal{P})$, the complement of $L(\mathcal{P})$, are either strings in $L(\mathbf{co}\mathcal{P})$ or strings in $\sigma(\Sigma^* - I)$. Since testing of membership in $\sigma(\Sigma^* - I)$ is easy, testing for membership in $\overline{L}(\mathcal{P})$ and $L(\mathbf{co}\mathcal{P})$ requires about the same space and time. For this reason, we often equate the two when discussing the complements of languages.

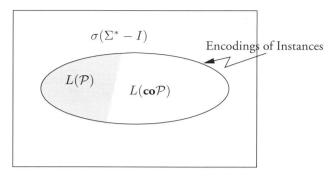

Figure 8.1   The language $L(\mathcal{P})$ of a decision problem $\mathcal{P}$ and the language of its complement $L(\mathbf{co}\mathcal{P})$. The languages $L(\mathcal{P})$ and $L(\mathbf{co}\mathcal{P})$ encode all instances of I. The complement of $L(\mathcal{P})$, $\overline{L}(\mathcal{P})$, is the union of $L(\mathbf{co}\mathcal{P})$ with $\sigma(\Sigma^* - I)$, strings that are in neither $L(\mathcal{P})$ nor $L(\mathbf{co}\mathcal{P})$.

8.3 Resource Bounds

One of the most important problems in computer science is the identification of the computationally feasible problems. Currently a problem is considered feasible if its running time on a DTM (deterministic Turing machine) is polynomial. (Stated by Edmonds [95], this is known as the **serial computation thesis**.) Note, however, that some polynomial running times, such as n^{1000}, where n is the length of a problem instance, can be enormous. In this case doubling n increases the time bound by a factor of 2^{1000}, which is approximately 10^{301}!

Since problems are classified by their use of resources, we need to be precise about **resource bounds**. These are functions $r : \mathbb{N} \mapsto \mathbb{N}$ from the natural numbers $\mathbb{N} = \{0, 1, 2, 3, \ldots\}$ to the natural numbers. The resource functions used in this chapter, where $k \geq 1$, are:

Logarithmic function	$r(n) = O(\log n)$
Poly-logarithmic function	$r(n) = \log^{O(1)} n$
Linear function	$r(n) = O(n)$
Polynomial function	$r(n) = n^{O(1)}$
Exponential function	$r(n) = 2^{n^{O(1)}}$

A resource function that grows faster than any polynomial is called a **superpolynomial function**. For example, the function $f(n) = 2^{\log^2 n}$ grows faster than any polynomial (the ratio $\log f(n)/\log n$ is unbounded) but more slowly than any exponential (for any $k > 0$ the ratio $(\log^2 n)/n^k$ becomes vanishingly small with increasing n).

Another note of caution is appropriate here when comparing resource functions. Even though one function, $r(n)$, may grow more slowly asymptotically than another, $s(n)$, it may still be true that $r(n) > s(n)$ for very large values of n. For example, $r(n) = 10 \log^4 n > s(n) = n$ for $n \leq 1,889,750$ despite the fact that $r(n)$ is much smaller than $s(n)$ for large n.

Some resource functions are so complex that they cannot be computed in the time or space that they define. For this reason we assume throughout this chapter that all resource functions are proper.

DEFINITION 8.3.1 *A function $r : \mathbb{N} \mapsto \mathbb{N}$ is **proper** if it is nondecreasing $(r(n+1) \geq r(n))$ and for some tape symbol a there is a deterministic multi-tape Turing machine M that, on all* *inputs of length n in time $O(n + r(n))$ and temporary space $r(n)$, writes the string $a^{r(n)}$ (**unary notation** for $r(n)$) on one of its tapes and halts.*

Thus, if a resource function $r(n)$ is proper, there is a DTM, M_r, that given an input of length n can write $r(n)$ markers on one of its tapes within time $O(n+r(n))$ and space $r(n)$. Another DTM, M, can use a copy of M_r to mark $r(n)$ squares on a tape that can be used to stop M after exactly $Kr(n)$ steps for some constant K. The resource function can also be used to insure that M uses no more than $Kr(n)$ cells on its work tapes.

8.4 Serial Computational Models

We consider two serial computational models in this chapter, the random-access machine (RAM) introduced in Section 3.4 and the Turing machine defined in Chapter 5.

In this section we show that, up to polynomial differences in running time, the random-access and Turing machines are equivalent. As a consequence, if the running time of a problem on one machine grows at least as fast as a polynomial in the length of a problem instance, then it grows equally fast on the other machine. This justifies using the Turing machine as basis for classifying problems by their serial complexity.

In Sections 8.13 and 8.14 we examine two parallel models of computation, the logic circuit and the parallel random-access machine (PRAM).

Before beginning our discussion of models, we note that any model can be considered either serial or parallel. For example, a finite-state machine operating on inputs and states represented by many bits is a parallel machine. On the other hand, a PRAM that uses one simple RAM processor is serial.

8.4.1 The Random-Access Machine

The random-access machine (RAM) is introduced in Section 3.4. (See Fig. 8.2.) In this section we generalize the simulation results developed in Section 3.7 by considering a RAM in which words are of potentially unbounded length. This RAM is assumed to have instructions for

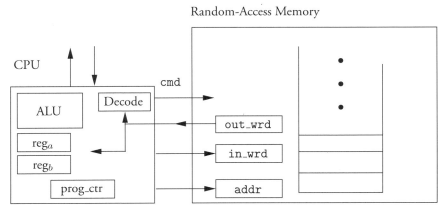

Figure 8.2 A RAM in which the number and length of words are potentially unbounded.

addition, subtraction, shifting left and right by one place, comparison of words, and Boolean operations of AND, OR, and NOT (the operations are performed on corresponding components of the source vectors), as well as conditional and unconditional jump instructions. The RAM also has load (and store) instructions that move words to (from) registers from (to) the random-access memory. Immediate and direct addressing are allowed. An immediate address contains a value, a direct address is the address of a value, and an indirect address is the address of the address of a value. (As explained in Section 3.10 and stated in Problem 3.10, indirect addressing does not add to the computing power of the RAM and is considered only in the problems.)

The **time** on a RAM is the number of steps it executes. The **space** is the maximum number of bits of storage used either in the CPU or the random-access memory during a computation.

We simplify the RAM without changing its nature by eliminating its registers, treating location 0 of the random-access memory as the accumulator, and using memory locations as registers. The RAM retains its program counter, which is incremented on each instruction execution (except for a jump instruction, when its value is set to the address supplied by the jump instruction). The word length of the RAM model is typically allowed to be unlimited, although in Section 3.4 we limited it to b bits. A RAM program is a finite sequence of RAM instructions that is stored in the random-access memory. The RAM implements the stored-program concept described in Section 3.4.

In Theorem 3.8.1 we showed that a b-bit standard Turing machine (its tape alphabet contains 2^b characters) executing T steps and using S bits of storage (S/b words) can be simulated by the RAM described above in $O(T)$ steps with $O(S)$ bits of storage. Similarly, we showed that a b-bit RAM executing T steps and using S bits of memory can be simulated by an $O(b)$-bit standard Turing machine in $O(ST \log^2 S)$ steps and $O(S \log S)$ bits of storage. As seen in Section 5.2, T-step computations on a multi-tape TM can be simulated in $O(T^2)$ steps on a standard Turing machine.

If we could insure that a RAM that executes T steps uses a highest address that is $O(T)$ and generates words of fixed length, then we could use the above-mentioned simulation to establish that a standard Turing machine can simulate an arbitrary T-step RAM computation in time $O(T^2 \log^2 T)$ and space $O(S \log S)$ measured in bits. Unfortunately, words can have length proportional to $O(T)$ (see Problem 8.4) and the highest address can be much larger than T due to the use of jumps. Nonetheless, a reasonably efficient polynomial-time simulation of a RAM computation by a DTM can be produced. Such a DTM places one (`address`, `contents`) pair on its tape for each RAM memory location visited by the RAM. (See Problem 8.5.)

We leave the proof of the following result to the reader. (See Problem 8.6.)

THEOREM 8.4.1 *Every computation on the RAM using time T can be simulated by a deterministic Turing machine in $O(T^3)$ steps.*

In light of the above results and since we are generally interested in problems whose time is polynomial in the length of the input, we use the DTM as our model of serial computation.

8.4.2 Turing Machine Models

The deterministic and nondeterministic Turing machines (DTM and NDTM) are discussed in Sections 3.7, 5.1, and 5.2. (See Fig. 8.3.) In this chapter we use multi-tape Turing machines to define classes of problems characterized by their use of time and space. As shown in The-

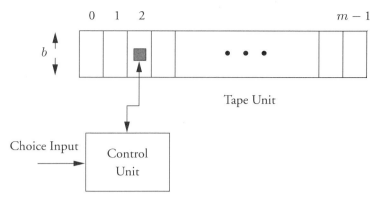

Figure 8.3 A one-tape nondeterministic Turing machine whose control unit has an external choice input that disambiguates the value of its next state.

orem 5.2.2, the general language-recognition capability of DTMs and NDTMs is the same, although, as we shall see, their ability to recognize languages within the same resource bounds is very different.

We recognize two types of Turing machine, the standard one-tape DTM and NDTM and the **multi-tape DTM and NDTM**. The multi-tape versions are defined here to have one read-only input tape, one write-only output tape, and one or more work tapes. The **space** on these machines is defined to be the number of work tape cells used during a computation. This measure allows us to classify problems by a storage that may be less than linear in the size of the input. **Time** is the number of steps they execute. It is interesting to compare these measures with those for the RAM. (See Problem 8.7.) As shown on Section 5.2, we can assume without loss of generality that each NDTM has either one or two choices for next state for any given input letters and state.

As stated in Definitions 3.7.1 and 5.1.1, a DTM M **accepts the language** L if and only if for each string in L placed left-adjusted on the otherwise blank input tape it eventually enters the accepting halt state. A language accepted by a DTM M is **recursive** if M halts on all inputs. Otherwise it is **recursively enumerable**. A DTM M **computes a partial function** f if for each input string w for which f is defined, it prints $f(w)$ left-adjusted on its otherwise blank output tape. A **complete function** is one that is defined on all points of its domain.

As stated in Definition 5.2.1, an NDTM **accepts** the language L if for each string w in L placed left-adjusted on the otherwise blank input tape there is a choice input c for M that leads to an accepting halt state. A NDTM M **computes a partial function** $f : \mathcal{B}^* \mapsto \mathcal{B}^*$ if for each input string w for which f is defined, there is a sequence of moves by M that causes it to print $f(w)$ on its output tape and enter a halt state and there is no choice input for which M prints an incorrect result.

The **oracle Turing machine** (OTM), the multi-tape DTM or NDTM with a special **oracle tape**, defined in Section 5.2.3, is used to classify problems. (See Problem 8.15.) **Time** on an OTM is the number of steps it takes, where one consultation of the oracle is one step, whereas **space** is the number of cells used on its work tapes not including the oracle tape.

A **precise Turing machine** M is a multi-tape DTM or NDTM for which there is a function $r(n)$ such that for every $n \geq 1$, every input w of length n, and every (possibly nondeterministic) computation by M, M halts after precisely $r(n)$ steps.

We now show that if a total function can be computed by a DTM, NDTM, or OTM within a proper time or space bound, it can be computed within approximately the same resource bound by a precise TM of the same type. The following theorem justifies the use of proper resource functions.

THEOREM 8.4.2 *Let $r(n)$ be a proper function with $r(n) \geq n$. Let M be a multi-tape DTM, NDTM, or OTM with k work tapes that computes a total function f in time or space $r(n)$. Then there is a constant $K > 0$ and a precise Turing machine of the same type that computes f in time and space $Kr(n)$.*

> **Proof** Since $r(n)$ is a proper function, there is a DTM M_r that computes its value from an input of length n in time $K_1 r(n)$ for some constant $K_1 > 0$ and in space $r(n)$. We design a precise TM M_p computing the same function.
>
> The TM M_p has an "enumeration tape" that is distinct from its work tapes. M_p initially invokes M_r to write $r(n)$ instances of the letter a on the enumeration tape in $K_1 r(n)$ steps, after which it returns the head on this tape to its initial position.
>
> Suppose that M computes f within a time bound of $r(n)$. M_p then alternates between simulating one step of M on its work tapes and advancing its head on the enumeration tape. When M halts, M_p continues to read and advance the head on its enumeration tape on alternate steps until it encounters a blank. Clearly, M_p halts in precisely $(K_1 + 2)r(n)$ steps.
>
> Suppose now that M computes f in space $r(n)$. M_p invokes M_r to write $r(n)$ special blank symbols on each of its work tapes. It then simulates M, treating the special blank symbols as standard blanks. Thus, M_p uses precisely $kr(n)$ cells on its k work tapes. ∎

Configuration graphs, defined in Section 5.3, are graphs that capture the state of Turing machines with potentially unlimited storage capacity. Since all resource bounds are proper, as we know from Theorem 8.4.2, all DTMs and NDTMs used for decision problems halt on all inputs. Furthermore, NDTMs never give an incorrect answer. Thus, configuration graphs can be assumed to be acyclic.

8.5 Classification of Decision Problems

In this section we classify decision problems by the resources they consume on deterministic and nondeterministic Turing machines. We begin with the definition of complexity classes.

DEFINITION 8.5.1 *Let $r(n) : \mathbb{N} \mapsto \mathbb{N}$ be a proper resource function. Then **TIME$(r(n))$** and **SPACE$(r(n))$** are the **time** and **space Turing complexity classes** containing languages that can be recognized by DTMs that halt on all inputs in time and space $r(n)$, respectively, where n is the length of an input. **NTIME$(r(n))$** and **NSPACE$(r(n))$** are the **nondeterministic time** and **space Turing complexity classes**, respectively, defined for NDTMs instead of DTMs. The union of complexity classes is also a complexity class.*

Let k be a positive integer. Then **TIME**(k^n) and **NSPACE**(n^k) are examples of complexity classes. They are the decision problems solvable in deterministic time k^n and nondeterministic space n^k, respectively, for n the length of the input. Since time and space on a Turing machine are measured by the number of steps and number of tape cells, it is straightforward to show that time and space for a given Turing machine, deterministic or not, can each be reduced by a constant factor by modifying the Turing machine description so that it acts on larger units of information. (See Problem 8.8.) Thus, for a constant $K > 0$ the following classes are the same: a) **TIME**(k^n) and **TIME**(Kk^n), b) **NTIME**(k^n) and **NTIME**(Kk^n), c) **SPACE**(n^k) and **SPACE**(Kn^k), and d) **NSPACE**(n^k) and **NSPACE**(Kn^k).

To emphasize that the union of complexity classes is another complexity class, we define as unions two of the most important Turing complexity classes, **P**, the class of deterministic polynomial-time decision problems, and **NP**, the class of nondeterministic polynomial-time decision problems.

DEFINITION 8.5.2 *The classes* **P** *and* **NP** *are sets of decision problems solvable in polynomial time on DTMs and NDTMs, respectively; that is, they are defined as follows:*

$$\mathbf{P} = \bigcup_{k \geq 0} \mathbf{TIME}(n^k)$$

$$\mathbf{NP} = \bigcup_{k \geq 0} \mathbf{NTIME}(n^k)$$

Thus, for each decision problem $\mathcal{P}$ in **P** there is a DTM M and a polynomial $p(n)$ such that M halts on each input string of length n in $p(n)$ steps, accepting this string if it is an instance w of $\mathcal{P}$ and rejecting it otherwise.

Also, for each decision problem $\mathcal{P}$ in **NP** there is an NDTM M and a polynomial $p(n)$ such that for each instance w of $\mathcal{P}$, $|w| = n$, there is a choice input of length $p(n)$ such that M accepts w in $p(n)$ steps.

Problems in **P** are considered **feasible problems** because they can be decided in time polynomial in the length of their input. Even though some polynomial functions, such as n^{1000}, grow very rapidly in their one parameter, at the present time problems in **P** are considered feasible. Problems that require exponential time are not considered feasible.

The class **NP** includes the decision problems associated with many hundreds of important searching and optimization problems, such as TRAVELING SALESPERSON described below. (See Fig. 8.4.) If **P** is equal to **NP**, then these important problems have feasible solutions. If not, then there are problems in **NP** that require superpolynomial time and are therefore largely infeasible. Thus, it is very important to have the answer to the question $\mathbf{P} \overset{?}{=} \mathbf{NP}$.

TRAVELING SALESPERSON
Instance: An integer k and a set of n^2 symmetric integer distances $\{d_{i,j} \mid 1 \leq i, j \leq n\}$ between n cities where $d_{i,j} = d_{j,i}$.
Answer: "Yes" if there is a **tour** (an ordering) $\{i_1, i_2, \ldots, i_n\}$ of the cities such that the length $l = d_{i_1,i_2} + d_{i_2,i_3} + \cdots + d_{i_n,i_1}$ of the tour satisfies $l \leq k$.

The TRAVELING SALESPERSON problem is in **NP** because a tour satisfying $l \leq k$ can be chosen nondeterministically in n steps and the condition $l \leq k$ then verified in a polynomial number of steps by finding the distances between successive cities on the chosen tour in the description of the problem and adding them together. (See Problem 3.24.) Many other important problems are in **NP**, as we see in Section 8.10. While it is unknown whether a deterministic polynomial-time algorithm exists for this problem, it can clearly be solved deter-

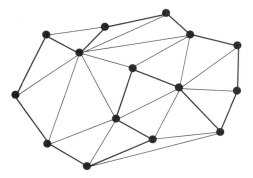

Figure 8.4 A graph on which the TRAVELING SALESPERSON problem is defined. The heavy edges identify a shortest tour.

ministically in exponential time by enumerating all tours and choosing the one with smallest length. (See Problem 8.9.)

The TRAVELING SALESPERSON decision problem is a reduction of the **traveling salesperson optimization problem**, whose goal is to find the shortest tour that visits each city once. The output of the optimization problem is an ordering of the cities that has the shortest tour. By contrast, the TRAVELING SALESPERSON decision problem reports that there is or is not a tour of length k or less. Given an algorithm for the optimization problem, the decision problem can be solved by calculating the length of an optimal tour and comparing it to the parameter k of the decision problem. Since the latter steps can be done in polynomial time, if the optimization algorithm can be done in polynomial time, so can the decision problem. On the other hand, given an algorithm for the decision problem, the optimization problem can be solved through **bisection** as follows: a) Since the length of the shortest tour is in the interval $[n \min_{i,j} d_{i,j}, n \max_{i,j} d_{i,j}]$, invoke the decision algorithm with k equal to the midpoint of this interval. b) If the instance is a "yes" instance, let k be the midpoint of the lower half of the current interval; if not, let it be the midpoint of the upper half. c) Repeat the previous step until the interval is reduced to one integer. The interval is bisected $O(\log n(\max_{i,j} d_{i,j} - \min_{i,j} d_{i,j}))$ times. Thus, if the decision problem can be solved in polynomial time, so can the optimization problem.

Whether $\mathbf{P} \stackrel{?}{=} \mathbf{NP}$ is one of the outstanding problems of computer science. The current consensus of complexity theorists is that nondeterminism is such a powerful specification device that they are not equal. We return to this topic in Section 8.8.

8.5.1 Space and Time Hierarchies

In this section we state without proof the following time and space hierarchy theorems. (See [126,127].) These theorems state that if one space (or time) resource bound grows sufficiently rapidly relative to another, the set of languages recognized within the first bound is strictly larger than the set recognized within the second bound.

THEOREM 8.5.1 (**Time Hierarchy Theorem**) *If $r(n) \geq n$ is a proper complexity function, then* **TIME**$(r(n))$ *is strictly contained in* **TIME**$(r(n) \log r(n))$.

Let $r(n)$ and $s(n)$ be proper functions. If for all $K > 0$ there exists an N_0 such that $s(n) \geq Kr(n)$ for $n \geq N_0$, we say that $\boldsymbol{r(n)}$ **is little oh of** $\boldsymbol{s(n)}$ and write $r(n) = o(s(n))$.

THEOREM 8.5.2 (Space Hierarchy Theorem) *If $r(n)$ and $s(n)$ are proper complexity functions and $r(n) = o(s(n))$, then* **SPACE**$(r(n))$ *is strictly contained in* **SPACE**$(s(n))$.

Theorem 8.5.3 states that there is a recursive but not proper resource function $r(n)$ such that **TIME**$(r(n))$ and **TIME**$(2^{r(n)})$ are the same. That is, for some function $r(n)$ there is a gap of at least $2^{r(n)} - r(n)$ in time over which no new decision problems are encountered. This is a weakened version of a stronger result in [328] and independently reported by [51].

THEOREM 8.5.3 (Gap Theorem) *There is a recursive function $r(n) : \mathcal{B}^* \mapsto \mathcal{B}^*$ such that* **TIME**$(r(n)) = $ **TIME**$(2^{r(n)})$.

8.5.2 Time-Bounded Complexity Classes

As mentioned earlier, decision problems in **P** are considered to be feasible while the class **NP** includes many interesting problems, such as the TRAVELING SALESPERSON problem, whose feasibility is unknown. Two other important complexity classes are the deterministic and nondeterministic exponential-time problems. By the remarks on page 336, TRAVELING SALESPERSON clearly falls into the latter class.

DEFINITION 8.5.3 *The classes* **EXPTIME** *and* **NEXPTIME** *consist of those decision problems solvable in deterministic and nondeterministic exponential time, respectively, on a Turing machine. That is,*

$$\textbf{EXPTIME} = \bigcup_{k \geq 0} \textbf{TIME}(k^n)$$

$$\textbf{NEXPTIME} = \bigcup_{k \geq 0} \textbf{NTIME}(k^n)$$

We make the following observations concerning containment of these complexity classes.

THEOREM 8.5.4 *The following complexity class containments hold:*

$$\textbf{P} \subseteq \textbf{NP} \subseteq \textbf{EXPTIME} \subseteq \textbf{NEXPTIME}$$

However, **P** $\subset$ **EXPTIME**, *that is,* **P** *is strictly contained in* **EXPTIME**.

Proof Since languages in **P** are recognized in polynomial time by a DTM and such machines are included among the NDTMs, it follows immediately that **P** $\subseteq$ **NP**. By similar reasoning, **EXPTIME** $\subseteq$ **NEXPTIME**.

We now show that **P** is strictly contained in **EXPTIME**. **P** $\subseteq$ **TIME**(2^n) follows because **TIME**$(n^k) \subseteq$ **TIME**(2^n) for each $k \geq 0$. By the Time Hierarchy Theorem (Theorem 8.5.1), we have that **TIME**$(2^n) \subset$ **TIME**$(n2^n)$. But **TIME**$(n2^n) \subseteq$ **EXPTIME**. Thus, **P** is strictly contained in **EXPTIME**.

Containment of **NP** in **EXPTIME** is deduced from the proof of Theorem 5.2.2 by analyzing the time taken by the deterministic simulation of an NDTM. If the NDTM executes T steps, the DTM executes $O(k^T)$ steps for some constant k. ∎

The relationships $\mathbf{P} \subseteq \mathbf{NP}$ and $\mathbf{EXPTIME} \subseteq \mathbf{NEXPTIME}$ are examples of a more general result, namely, $\mathbf{TIME}(r(n)) \subseteq \mathbf{NTIME}(r(n))$, where these two classes of decision problems can respectively be solved deterministically and nondeterministically in time $r(n)$, where n is the length of the input. This result holds because every $\mathcal{P} \in \mathbf{TIME}(r(n))$ of length n is accepted in $r(n)$ steps by some DTM $M_{\mathcal{P}}$ and a DTM is also a NDTM. Thus, it is also true that $\mathcal{P} \in \mathbf{NTIME}(r(n))$.

8.5.3 Space-Bounded Complexity Classes

Many other important space complexity classes are defined by the amount of space used to recognize languages and compute functions. We highlight five of them here: the deterministic and nondeterministic logarithmic space classes $\mathbf{L}$ and $\mathbf{NL}$, the square-logarithmic space class $\mathbf{L}^2$, and the deterministic and nondeterministic polynomial-space classes $\mathbf{PSPACE}$ and $\mathbf{NPSPACE}$.

DEFINITION 8.5.4 $\mathbf{L}$ *and* $\mathbf{NL}$ *are the decision problems solvable in logarithmic space on a DTM and NDTM, respectively.* $\mathbf{L}^2$ *are the decision problems solvable in space* $O(\log^2 n)$ *on a DTM.* $\mathbf{PSPACE}$ *and* $\mathbf{NPSPACE}$ *are the decision problems solvable in polynomial space on a DTM and NDTM, respectively.*

Because $\mathbf{L}$ and $\mathbf{PSPACE}$ are deterministic complexity classes, they are contained in $\mathbf{NL}$ and $\mathbf{NPSPACE}$, respectively: that is, $\mathbf{L} \subseteq \mathbf{NL}$ and $\mathbf{PSPACE} \subseteq \mathbf{NPSPACE}$.

We now strengthen the latter result and show that $\mathbf{PSPACE} = \mathbf{NPSPACE}$, which means that nondeterminism does not increase the recognition power of Turing machines if they already have access to a polynomial amount of storage space.

The REACHABILITY problem on directed acyclic graphs defined below is used to show this result. REACHABILITY is applied to configuration graphs of deterministic and nondeterministic Turing machines. Configuration graphs are introduced in Section 5.3.

REACHABILITY
Instance: A directed graph $G = (V, E)$ and a pair of vertices $u, v \in V$.
Answer: "Yes" if there is a directed path in G from u to v.

REACHABILITY can be decided by computing the transitive closure of the adjacency matrix of G in parallel. (See Section 6.4.) However, a simple serial RAM program based on depth-first search can also solve the reachability problem. **Depth-first search** (DFS) on an undirected graph G visits each edge in the forward direction once. Edges at each vertex are ordered. Each time DFS arrives at a vertex it traverses the next unvisited edge. If DFS arrives at a vertex from which there are no unvisited edges, it retreats to the previously visited vertex. Thus, after DFS visits all the descendants of a vertex, it backs up, eventually returning to the vertex from which the search began.

Since every T-step RAM computation can be simulated by an $O(T^3)$-step DTM computation (see Problem 8.5), a cubic-time DTM program based on DFS exists for REACHABILITY. Unfortunately, the space to execute DFS on the RAM and Turing machine both can be linear in the size of the graph. We give an improved result that allows us to strengthen $\mathbf{PSPACE} \subseteq \mathbf{NPSPACE}$ to $\mathbf{PSPACE} = \mathbf{NPSPACE}$.

Below we show that REACHABILITY can be realized in quadratic logarithmic space. This fact is then used to show that $\mathbf{NSPACE}(r(n)) \subseteq \mathbf{SPACE}(r^2(n))$ for $r(n) = \Omega(\log n)$.

THEOREM 8.5.5 (Savitch) REACHABILITY *is in* $\textbf{SPACE}(\log^2 n)$.

Proof As mentioned three paragraphs earlier, the REACHABILITY problem on a graph $G = (V, E)$ can be solved with depth-first search. This requires storing data on each vertex visited during a search. This data can be as large as $O(n)$, $n = |V|$. We exhibit an algorithm that uses much less space.

Given an instance of REACHABILITY defined by $G = (V, E)$ and $u, v \in V$, for each pair of vertices (a, b) and integer $k \leq \lceil \log_2 n \rceil$ we define predicates $\text{PATH}(a, b, 2^k)$ whose value is true if there exists a path from a to b in G whose length is at most 2^k and false otherwise. Since no path has length more than n, the solution to the REACHABILITY problem is the value of $\text{PATH}(u, v, 2^{\lceil \log_2 n \rceil})$. The predicates $\text{PATH}(a, b, 2^0)$ are true if either $a = b$ or there is a path of length 1 (an edge) between the vertices a and b. Thus, $\text{PATH}(a, b, 2^0)$ can be evaluated directly by consulting the problem instance on the input tape.

The algorithm that computes $\text{PATH}(u, v, 2^{\lceil \log_2 n \rceil})$ with space $O(\log^2 n)$ uses the fact that any path of length at most 2^k can be decomposed into two paths of length at most 2^{k-1}. Thus, if $\text{PATH}(a, b, 2^k)$ is true, then there must be some vertex z such that $\text{PATH}(a, z, 2^{k-1})$ and $\text{PATH}(z, b, 2^{k-1})$ are both true. The truth of $\text{PATH}(a, b, 2^k)$ can be established by searching for a z such that $\text{PATH}(a, z, 2^{k-1})$ is true. Upon finding one, we determine the truth of $\text{PATH}(z, b, 2^{k-1})$. Failing to find such a z, $\text{PATH}(a, b, 2^k)$ is declared to be false. Each evaluation of a predicate is done in the same fashion, that is, recursively. Because we need evaluate only one of $\text{PATH}(a, z, 2^{k-1})$ and $\text{PATH}(z, b, 2^{k-1})$ at a time, space can be reused.

We now describe a deterministic Turing machine with an input tape and two work tapes computing $\text{PATH}(u, v, 2^{\lceil \log_2 n \rceil})$. The input tape contains an instance of REACHABILITY, which means it has not only the vertices u and v but also a description of the graph G. The first work tape will contain triples of the form (a, b, k), which are called **activation records**. This tape is initialized with the activation record $(u, v, \lceil \log_2 n \rceil)$. (See Fig. 8.5.)

The DTM evaluates the last activation record, (a, b, k), on the first work tape as described above. There are three kinds of activation records, **complete records** of the form (a, b, k), **initial segments** of the form $(a, z, k - 1)$, and **final segments** of the form $(z, b, k - 1)$. The first work tape is initialized with the complete record $(u, v, \lceil \log_2 n \rceil)$.

An initial segment is created from the current complete record (a, b, k) by selecting a vertex z to form the record $(a, z, k - 1)$, which becomes the current complete record. If it evaluates to true, it can be determined to be an initial or final segment by examining the previous record (a, b, k). If it evaluates to false, $(a, z, k - 1)$ is erased and another value of z, if any, is selected and another initial segment placed on the work tape for evaluation. If no other z exists, $(a, z, k - 1)$ is erased and the expression $\text{PATH}(a, b, 2^k)$ is declared false. If $(a, z, k - 1)$ evaluates to true, the final record $(z, b, k - 1)$ is created, placed on the work tape, and evaluated in the same fashion. As mentioned in the second paragraph of this

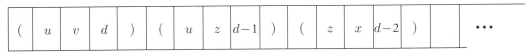

Figure 8.5 A snapshot of the stack used by the REACHABILITY algorithm in which the components of an activation record (a, b, k) are distributed over several cells.

proof, $(a, b, 0)$ is evaluated by consulting the description of the graph on the input tape. The second work tape is used for bookkeeping, that is, to enumerate values of z and determine whether a segment is initial or final.

The second work tape uses space $O(\log n)$. The first work tape contains at most $\lceil \log_2 n \rceil$ activation records. Each activation record (a, b, k) can be recorded in $O(\log n)$ space because each vertex can be specified in $O(\log n)$ space and the depth parameter k can be specified in $O(\log k) = O(\log \log n)$ space. It follows that the first work tape uses at most $O(\log^2 n)$ space. ∎

The following general result, which is a corollary of Savitch's theorem, demonstrates that nondeterminism does not enlarge the space complexity classes if they are defined by space bounds that are at least logarithmic. In particular, it implies that **PSPACE** = **NPSPACE**.

COROLLARY 8.5.1 *Let $r(n)$ be a proper Turing computable function $r : \mathbb{N} \mapsto \mathbb{N}$ satisfying $r(n) = \Omega(\log n)$. Then **NSPACE**$(r(n)) \subseteq$ **SPACE**$(r^2(n))$.*

Proof Let M_{ND} be an NDTM with input and output tapes and s work tapes. Let it recognize a language $L \in$ **NSPACE**$(r(n))$. For each input string $\boldsymbol{w}$, we generate a configuration graph $G(M_{\text{ND}}, \boldsymbol{w})$ of M_{ND}. (See Fig. 8.6.) We use this graph to determine whether or not $\boldsymbol{w} \in L$. M_{ND} has at most $|Q|$ states, each tape cell can have at most c values (there are $c^{(s+2)r(n)}$ configurations for the $s + 2$ tapes), the s work tape heads and the output tape head can assume values in the range $1 \leq h_j \leq r(n)$, and the input head h_{s+1} can assume one of n positions (there are $n r(n)^{s+1}$ configurations for the tape heads). It follows that M_{ND} has at most $|Q| c^{(s+2)r(n)} (n \, r(n)^{s+1}) \leq k^{\log n + r(n)}$ configurations. $G(M_{\text{ND}}, \boldsymbol{w})$ has the same number of vertices as there are configurations and a number of edges at most the square of its number of vertices.

Let $L \in$ **NSPACE**$(r(n))$ be recognized by an NDTM M_{ND}. We describe a deterministic $r^2(n)$-space Turing machine M_{D} recognizing L. For input string $\boldsymbol{w} \in L$ of length n, this machine solves the REACHABILITY problem on the configuration graph $G(M_{\text{ND}}, \boldsymbol{w})$ of M_{ND} described above. However, instead of placing on the input tape the entire configuration graph, we place the input string $\boldsymbol{w}$ and the description of M_{ND}. We keep configurations on the work tape as part of activation records (they describe vertices of $G(M_{\text{ND}}, \boldsymbol{w})$).

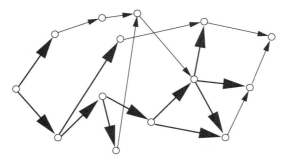

Figure 8.6 The acyclic configuration graph $G(M_{\text{ND}}, \boldsymbol{w})$ of a nondeterministic Turing machine M_{ND} on input $\boldsymbol{w}$ has one vertex for each configuration of M_{ND}. Here heavy edges identify the nondeterministic choices associated with a configuration.

Each of the vertices (configurations) adjacent to a particular vertex can be deduced from the description of M_{ND}.

Since the number of configurations of M_{ND} is $N = O\left(k^{\log n + r(n)}\right)$, each configuration or activation record can be stored as a string of length $O(r(n))$.

From Theorem 8.5.5, the reachability in $G(M_{ND}, \boldsymbol{w})$ of the final configuration from the initial one can be determined in space $O(\log^2 N)$. But $N = O\left(k^{\log n + r(n)}\right)$, from which it follows that **NSPACE**$(r(n)) \subseteq$ **SPACE**$(r^2(n))$. ∎

The classes **NL**, $\mathbf{L}^2$ and **PSPACE** are defined as unions of classes **NSPACE**$(r(n))$. Thus, it follows from this corollary that **NL** $\subseteq$ $\mathbf{L}^2$ $\subseteq$ **PSPACE**. However, because of the space hierarchy theorem (Theorem 8.5.2), it follows that $\mathbf{L}^2$ is contained in but not equal to **PSPACE**, denoted $\mathbf{L}^2 \subset$ **PSPACE**.

We now digress slightly to discuss space-bounded functions.

8.5.4   Relations Between Time- and Space-Bounded Classes

In this section we establish a number of complexity class containment results involving both space- and time-bounded classes. We begin by proving that the nondeterministic $O(r(n))$-space class is contained within the deterministic $O\left(k^{r(n)}\right)$-time class. This implies that **NL** $\subseteq$ **P** and **NPSPACE** $\subseteq$ **EXPTIME**.

THEOREM 8.5.6 *The classes* **NSPACE**$(r(n))$ *and* **TIME**$(r(n))$ *of decision problems solvable in nondeterministic space and deterministic time* $r(n)$, *respectively, satisfy the following relation for some constant* $k > 0$:

$$\mathbf{NSPACE}(r(n)) \subseteq \mathbf{TIME}(k^{\log n + r(n)})$$

Proof Let M_{ND} accept a language $L \in$ **NSPACE**$(r(n))$ and let $G(M_{ND}, \boldsymbol{w})$ be the configuration graph for M_{ND} on input $\boldsymbol{w}$. To determine if $\boldsymbol{w}$ is accepted by M_{ND} and therefore in L, it suffices to determine if there is a path in $G(M_{ND}, \boldsymbol{w})$ from the initial configuration of M_{ND} to the final configuration. This is the REACHABILITY problem, which, as stated in the proof of Theorem 8.5.6, can be solved by a DTM in time polynomial in the length of the input. When this algorithm needs to determine the descendants of a vertex in $G(M_{ND}, \boldsymbol{w})$, it consults the definition of M_{ND} to determine the configurations reachable from the current configuration. It follows that membership of $\boldsymbol{w}$ in L can be determined in time $O\left(k^{\log n + r(n)}\right)$ for some $k > 1$ or that L is in **TIME**$\left(k^{\log n + r(n)}\right)$. ∎

COROLLARY 8.5.2 **NL** $\subseteq$ **P** *and* **NPSPACE** $\subseteq$ **EXPTIME**

Later we explore the polynomial-time problems by exhibiting other important complexity classes that reside inside **P**. (See Section 8.15.) We now show containment of the nondeterministic time complexity classes in deterministic space classes.

THEOREM 8.5.7 *The following containment holds:*

$$\mathbf{NTIME}(r(n)) \subseteq \mathbf{SPACE}(r(n))$$

Proof We use the construction of Theorem 5.2.2. Let L be a language in **NTIME**$(r(n))$. We note that the choice string on the enumeration tape converts the nondeterministic recognition of L into deterministic recognition. Since L is recognized in time $r(n)$ for some

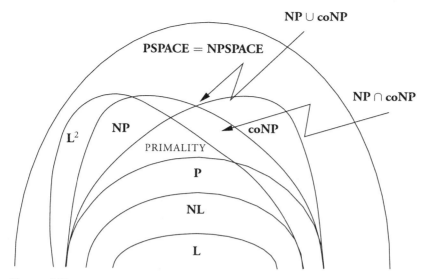

Figure 8.7 The relationships among complexity classes derived in this section. Containment is indicated by arrows.

accepting computation, the deterministic enumeration runs in time $r(n)$ for each choice string. Thus, $O(r(n))$ cells are used on the work and enumeration tapes in this deterministic simulation and L is in **PSPACE**. ∎

An immediate corollary to this theorem is that **NP** $\subseteq$ **PSPACE**. This implies that **P** $\subseteq$ **EXPTIME**. However, as mentioned above, **P** is strictly contained within **EXPTIME**.

Combining these results, we have the following complexity class inclusions:

$$\mathbf{L} \subseteq \mathbf{NL} \subseteq \mathbf{P} \subseteq \mathbf{NP} \subseteq \mathbf{PSPACE} \subseteq \mathbf{EXPTIME} \subseteq \mathbf{NEXPTIME}$$

where **PSPACE** = **NPSPACE**. We also have $\mathbf{L}^2 \subset \mathbf{PSPACE}$, and $\mathbf{P} \subset \mathbf{EXPTIME}$, which follow from the space and time hierarchy theorems. These inclusions and those derived below are shown in Fig. 8.7.

In Section 8.6 we develop refinements of this partial ordering of complexity classes by using the complements of complexity classes.

8.5.5 Space-Bounded Functions

We digress briefly to specialize Theorem 8.5.6 to log-space computations, not just log-space language recognition. As the following demonstrates, log-space computable functions are computable in polynomial time.

THEOREM 8.5.8 *Let M be a DTM that halts on all inputs using space $O(\log n)$ to process inputs of length n. Then M executes a polynomial number of steps.*

Proof In the proof of Corollary 8.5.1 the number of configurations of a Turing machine M with input and output tapes and s work tapes is counted. We repeat this analysis. Let

$r(n)$ be the maximum number of tape cells used and let c be the maximal size of a tape alphabet. Then, M can be in one of at most $\chi \leq c^{(s+2)r(n)}(n\,r(n)^{s+1}) = O(k^{r(n)})$ configurations. Since M always halts, by the pigeonhole principle, it passes through at most χ configurations in at most χ steps. Because $r(n) = O(\log n)$, $\chi = O(n^d)$ for some integer d. Thus, M executes a polynomial number of steps. ∎

8.6 Complements of Complexity Classes

As seen in Section 4.6, the regular languages are closed under complementation. However, we have also seen in Section 4.13 that the context-free languages are not closed under complementation. Thus, complementation is a way to develop an understanding of the properties of a class of languages. In this section we show that the nondeterministic space classes are closed under complements. The complements of languages and decision problems were defined at the beginning of this chapter.

Consider REACHABILITY. Its complement $\overline{\text{REACHABILITY}}$ is the set of directed graphs $G = (V, E)$ and pairs of vertices $u, v \in V$ such that there are no directed paths between u and v. It follows that the union of these two problems is not the entire set of strings over $\mathcal{B}^*$ but the set of all instances consisting of a directed graph $G = (V, E)$ and a pair of vertices $u, v \in V$. This set is easily detected by a DTM. It must only verify that the string describing a putative graph is in the correct format and that the representations for u and v are among the vertices of this graph.

Given a complexity class, it is natural to define the complement of the class.

DEFINITION 8.6.1 *The* **complement of a complexity class of decision problems** $\mathcal{C}$, *denoted* **co**$\mathcal{C}$, *is the set of decision problems that are complements of decision problems in* $\mathcal{C}$.

Our first result follows from the definition of the recognition of languages by DTMs.

THEOREM 8.6.1 *If* $\mathcal{C}$ *is a deterministic time or space complexity class, then* **co**$\mathcal{C} = \mathcal{C}$.

Proof Let $L \in \mathcal{C}$ be a deterministic time or space complexity class. Then it is recognized by a DTM M that halts within its resource bound for every string, whether in L or not. A complementary machine $\overline{M}$ says "Yes" when M says "No" and vice versa. M decides $\mathcal{C}$ and $\overline{M}$ decides **co**$\mathcal{C}$. ∎

In particular, this result says that the class **P** is closed under complements. That is, if the "yes" instances of a decision problem can be answered in deterministic polynomial time, then so can the "No" instances.

We use the above theorem and Theorem 5.7.6 to give another proof that there are problems that are not in **P**.

COROLLARY 8.6.1 *There are languages not in* **P***, that is, languages that cannot be recognized deterministically in polynomial time.*

Proof Since every language in **P** is recursive and $\mathcal{L}_1$ defined in Section 5.7.2 is not recursive, it follows that $\mathcal{L}_1$ is not in **P**. ∎

We now show that all nondeterministic space classes with a sufficiently large space bound are also closed under complements. This leaves open the question whether the nondeterministic time classes are closed under complement. As we shall see, this is intimately related to the question $\mathbf{P} \overset{?}{=} \mathbf{NP}$.

As stated in Definition 5.2.1, for no choices of moves is an NDTM allowed to produce an answer for which it is not designed. In particular, when computing a function it is not allowed to give a false answer for any set of nondeterministic choices.

THEOREM 8.6.2 (Immerman-Szelepscényi) *Given a graph* $G = (V, E)$ *and a vertex* v, *the number of vertices reachable from* v *can be computed by an NDTM in space* $O(\log n)$, $n = |V|$.

Proof Let $V = \{1, 2, \dots, n\}$. Any node reachable from a vertex v must be reachable via a path of length (number of edges) of at most $n - 1$, $n = |V|$. Let $R(k, u)$ be the number of vertices of G reachable from u by paths of length k or less. The goal is to compute $R(n - 1, u)$. A deterministic program for this purpose could be based on the predicate PATH(u, v, k) that has value 1 if there is a path of length k or less from vertex u to vertex v and 0 otherwise and the predicate ADJACENT-OR-IDENTICAL(x, v) that has value 1 if $x = v$ or there is an edge in G from x to v and 0 otherwise. (See Fig. 8.8.) If we let the vertices be associated with the integers in the interval $[1, \dots, n]$, then $R(n - 1, u)$ can be evaluated as follows:

$$R(n - 1, u) = \sum_{1 \le v \le n} \text{PATH}(u, v, n - 1)$$

$$= \sum_{1 \le v \le n} \sum_{1 \le x \le n} \text{PATH}(u, x, n - 2)\text{ADJACENT-OR-EQUAL}(x, v)$$

When this description of $R(n - 1, u)$ is converted to a program, the amount of storage needed grows more rapidly than $O(\log n)$. However, if the inner use of PATH$(u, x, n - 2)$ is replaced by the nonrecursive and nondeterministic test EXISTS-PATH-FROM-u-TO-v-$\le$-LENGTH of Fig. 8.9 for a path from u to x of length $n - 2$, then the space can be kept to $O(\log n)$. This test nondeterministically guesses paths but verifies deterministically that all paths have been explored.

The procedure COUNTING-REACHABILITY of Fig. 8.9 is a nondeterministic program computing $R(n - 1, u)$. It uses the procedure #-VERTICES-AT-$\le$-DISTANCE-FROM-u to compute the number of vertices at distance $dist$ or less from u in order of increasing values of $dist$. (It computes $dist$ correctly or fails.) This procedure has $prev\_num\_dist$ as a parameter, which is the number of vertices at distance $dist - 1$ or less. It passes this

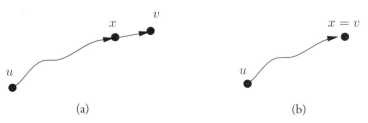

(a)   (b)

Figure 8.8 Paths explored by the REACHABILITY algorithm. Case (a) applies when x and v are different and (b) when they are the same.

COUNTING-REACHABILITY(u)
$\{R(k, u)$ = number of vertices at distance $\leq k$ from u in $G = (V, E)\}$
  $prev\_num\_dist := 1$; $\{num\_dist = R(0, u)\}$
  for $dist := 1$ **to** $n - 1$
    $num\_dist :=$ #-VERTICES-AT-$\leq$-DIST-FROM-$u(dist, u, prev\_num\_dist)$
    $prev\_num\_dist := num\_dist$
      $\{num\_dist = R(dist, u)\}$
  return(num_dist)

#-VERTICES-AT-$\leq$-DISTANCE-FROM-$u(dist, u, prev\_num\_dist)$
$\{$Returns $R(dist, u)$ given $prev\_num\_dist = R(dist - 1, u)$ or fails$\}$
  $num\_nodes := 0$
  for $last\_node := 1$ **to** n
    if IS-NODE-AT-$\leq$-DIST-FROM-$u(dist, u, last\_node, prev\_num\_dist)$ **then**
      $num\_nodes := num\_nodes + 1$
  return (num_nodes)

IS-NODE-AT-$\leq$-DIST-FROM-$u(dist, u, last\_node, prev\_num\_dist)$
  $\{num\_node$ = number of vertices at distance $\leq dist$ from u found so far$\}$
  $num\_node := 0$;
  $reply :=$ **false**
  for $next\_to\_last\_node := 1$ **to** n
    if EXISTS-PATH-FROM-u-TO-v-$\leq$-LENGTH$(u, next\_to\_last\_node, dist - 1)$ **then**
      $num\_node := num\_node + 1$ $\{$count number of next-to-last nodes or fail$\}$
      if ADJACENT-OR-IDENTICAL$(next\_to\_last\_node, last\_node)$ **then**
        $reply :=$ **true**
  if $num\_node < prev\_num\_dist$ **then**
    fail
  else return$(reply)$

EXISTS-PATH-FROM-u-TO-v-$\leq$-LENGTH$(u, v, dist)$
  $\{$nondeterministically choose at most $dist$ vertices, fail if they don't form a path$\}$
  $node\_1 := u$
  for $count := 1$ **to** $dist$
    $node\_2 :=$ NONDETERMINISTIC-GUESS$([1, .., n])$
    if not ADJACENT-OR-IDENTICAL$(node\_1, node\_2)$ **then**
      fail
    else $node\_1 := node\_2$
  if $node\_2 = v$ **then**
    return(**true**)
  else
    return(**false**)

Figure 8.9 A nondeterministic program counting vertices reachable from u. Comments are enclosed in braces $\{, \}$.

value to the procedure IS-NODE-AT-$\leq$-DIST-FROM-u, which examines and counts all possible *next_to_last_node*s reachable from u. #-VERTICES-AT-$\leq$-DISTANCE-FROM-u either fails to find all possible vertices at distance $dist - 1$, in which case it fails, or finds all such vertices. Thus, it nondeterministically verifies that all possible paths from u have been explored. IS-NODE-AT-$\leq$-DIST-FROM-u uses the procedure EXISTS-PATH-FROM-u-TO-v-$\leq$-LENGTH that either correctly verifies that a path of length $dist - 1$ exists from u to *next_to_last_node* or fails. In turn, EXISTS-PATH-FROM-u-TO-v-$\leq$-LENGTH uses the command NONDETERMINISTIC-GUESS($[1, .., n]$) to nondeterministically choose nodes on a path from u to v.

Since this program is not recursive, it uses a fixed number of variables. Because these variables assume values in the range $[1, 2, 3, \ldots, n]$, it follows that space $O(\log n)$ suffices to implement it on an NDTM. ∎

We now extend this result to nondeterministic space computations.

COROLLARY 8.6.2 *If* $r(n) = \Omega(\log n)$ *is proper,* **NSPACE**$(r(n)) = $ **coNSPACE**$(r(n))$.

Proof Let $L \in $ **NSPACE**$(r(n))$ be decided by an $r(n)$-space bounded NDTM M. We show that the complement of L can be decided by a nondeterministic $r(n)$-space bounded Turing machine $\overline{M}$, stopping on all inputs. We modify slightly the program of Fig. 8.9 for this purpose. The graph G is the configuration graph of M. Its initial state is determined by the string w that is initially written on M's input tape. To determine adjacency between two vertices in the configuration graph, computations of M are simulated on one of $\overline{M}$'s work tapes.

$\overline{M}$ computes a slightly modified version of COUNTING-REACHABILITY. First, if the procedure IS-NODE-AT-LENGTH-$\leq$-DIST-FROM-u returns **true** for a vertex u that is a halting accepting configuration of M, then $\overline{M}$ halts and rejects the string. If the procedure COUNTING-REACHABILITY completes successfully without rejecting any string, then $\overline{M}$ halts and accepts the input string because every possible accepting computation for the input string has been examined and none of them is accepting. This computation is nondeterministic.

The space used by $\overline{M}$ is the space needed for COUNTING-REACHABILITY, which means it is $O(\log N)$, where N is the number of vertices in the configuration graph of M plus the space for a simulation of M, which is $O(r(n))$. Since $N = O(k^{\log n + r(n)})$ (see the proof of Theorem 8.5.6), the total space for this computation is $O(\log n + r(n))$, which is $O(r(n))$ if $r(n) = \Omega(\log n)$. Thus, $\overline{L} \in $ **coNSPACE**$(r(n))$ or **NSPACE**$(r(n)) \subseteq $ **coNSPACE**$(r(n))$.

By similar reasoning, if $L \in $ **coNSPACE**$(r(n))$, then $\overline{L} \in $ **NSPACE**$(r(n))$, which implies that **coNSPACE**$(r(n)) \subseteq $ **NSPACE**$(r(n))$; that is, they are equal. ∎

The lowest class in the space hierarchy that is known to be closed under complements is the class **NL**; that is, **NL** = **coNL**. This result is used in Section 8.11 to show that the problem 2-SAT, a specialization of the **NP**-complete problem 3-SAT, is in **P**.

From Theorem 8.6.1 we know that all deterministic time and space complexity classes are closed under complements. From Corollary 8.6.2 we also know that all nondeterministic space complexity classes with space $\Omega(\log n)$ are closed under complements. However, we do not yet know whether the nondeterministic time complexity classes are closed under complements.

This important question is related to the question whether $\mathbf{P} \overset{?}{=} \mathbf{NP}$, because if $\mathbf{NP} \neq \mathbf{coNP}$, then $\mathbf{P} \neq \mathbf{NP}$ because $\mathbf{P}$ is closed under complements but $\mathbf{NP}$ is not.

8.6.1 The Complement of NP

The class **coNP** is the class of decision problems whose complements are in **NP**. That is, **coNP** is the language of "No" instances of problems in **NP**. The decision problem VALIDITY defined below is an example of a problem in **coNP**. In fact, it is log-space complete for **coNP**. (See Problem 8.10.) VALIDITY identifies SOPEs (the sum-of-products expansion, defined in Section 2.3) that can have value 1.

> VALIDITY
> *Instance:* A set of literals $X = \{x_1, \overline{x}_1, x_2, \overline{x}_2, \ldots, x_n, \overline{x}_n\}$, and a sequence of products $P = (p_1, p_2, \ldots, p_m)$, where each product p_i is a subset of X.
> *Answer:* "Yes" if for all assignments of Boolean values to variables in $\{x_1, x_2, \ldots, x_n\}$ every literal in at least one product has value 1.

Given a language L in **NP**, a string in L has a certificate for its membership in L, that is, the set of choices needed to accept it. For example, for VALIDITY a certificate for a string is a set of values for the variables in this string for which all literals in some product are satisfied. For problems in **coNP**, a **disqualification** of a string is a certificate for the string, that is, one that causes it to be a "Yes" instance rather than a "No" instance. For example, a string in the complement $\overline{\text{VALIDITY}}$ is disqualified by an assignment that causes some product to have value 1. (See Problem 8.11.)

As mentioned just before the start of this section, if $\mathbf{NP} \neq \mathbf{coNP}$, then $\mathbf{P} \neq \mathbf{NP}$ because $\mathbf{P}$ is closed under complements. Because we know of no way to establish $\mathbf{NP} \neq \mathbf{coNP}$, we try to identify a problem that is in **NP** but is not known to be in **P**. A problem that is **NP** and **coNP** simultaneously (the class $\mathbf{NP} \cap \mathbf{coNP}$) is a possible candidate for a problem that is in **NP** but not **P**, which would show that $\mathbf{P} \neq \mathbf{NP}$. We show that PRIMALITY is in $\mathbf{NP} \cap \mathbf{coNP}$. (It is straightforward to show that $\mathbf{P} \subseteq \mathbf{NP} \cap \mathbf{coNP}$. See Problem 8.12.)

> PRIMALITY
> *Instance:* An integer n written in binary notation.
> *Answer:* "Yes" if n is a prime.

A disqualification for PRIMALITY is an integer that is a factor of n. Thus, the complement of PRIMALITY is in **NP**, so PRIMALITY is in **coNP**. We now show that PRIMALITY is also in **NP** or that it is in $\mathbf{NP} \cap \mathbf{coNP}$. To prove the desired result we need the following result from number theory, which we do not prove (see [229, p. 222] for a proof).

THEOREM 8.6.3 *An integer $p > 2$ is prime if and only if there is an integer $1 < r < p$ such that $r^{p-1} = 1 \bmod p$ and for all prime divisors q of $p - 1$, $r^{(p-1)/q} \neq 1 \bmod p$.*

As a consequence, to give evidence of primality of an integer $p > 1$, we need only provide an integer r, $1 < r < p$, and the prime divisors $\{q_1, \ldots, q_k\}$ other than 1 of $p - 1$ and then show that $r^{p-1} = 1 \bmod p$ and $r^{(p-1)/q} \neq 1 \bmod p$ for $q \in \{q_1, \ldots, q_k\}$. By the theorem, such integers exist if and only if p is prime. In turn, we must give evidence that the integers $\{q_1, \ldots, q_k\}$ are prime divisors of $p - 1$, which requires showing that they divide $p - 1$ and are prime. We must also show that k is small and that the recursive check of the primes does not grow exponentially. Evidence of the primality of the divisors can be given in the same way, that is, by exhibiting an integer r_j for each prime as well as the prime divisors of $q_j - 1$ for each prime q_j. We must then show that all of this evidence can be given succinctly and verified deterministically in time polynomial in the length n of p.

THEOREM 8.6.4 PRIMALITY *is in* **NP $\cap$ coNP**.

Proof We give an inductive proof that PRIMALITY is in **NP**. For a prime p we give its evidence $E(p)$ as $(p; r, E(q_1), \ldots, E(q_k))$, where $E(q_j)$ is evidence for the prime q_j. We let the evidence for the base case $p = 2$ be $E(2) = (2)$. Then, $E(3) = (3; 2, (2))$ because $r = 2$ works for this case and 2 is the only prime divisor of $3 - 1$, and (2) is the evidence for it. Also, $E(5) = (5; 3, (2))$. The **length $|E(p)|$ of the evidence** $E(p)$ on p is the number of parentheses, commas and bits in integers forming part of the evidence.

We show by induction that $|E(p)|$ is at most $4\log_2^2 p$. The base case satisfies the hypothesis because $|E(2)| = 4$.

Because the prime divisors $\{q_1, \ldots, q_k\}$ satisfy $q_i \geq 2$ and $q_1 q_2 \cdots q_k \leq p-1$, it follows that $k \leq \lfloor \log_2 p \rfloor \leq n$. Also, since p is prime, it is odd and $p - 1$ is divisible by 2. Thus, the first prime divisor of $p - 1$ is 2.

Let $E(p) = (p; r, E(2), E(q_2), \ldots, E(q_k))$. Let the inductive hypothesis be that $|E(p)| \leq 4\log_2^2 p$. Let $n_j = \log_2 q_j$. From the definition of $E(p)$ we have that $|E(p)|$ satisfies the following inequality because at most n bits are needed for p and r, there are $k - 1 \leq n - 1$ commas and three other punctuation marks, and $|E(2)| = 4$.

$$|E(p)| \leq 3n + 6 + 4 \sum_{2 \leq j \leq k} n_j^2$$

Since the q_j are the prime divisors of $p - 1$ and some primes may be repeated in $p - 1$, their product (which includes $q_1 = 2$) is at most $p - 1$. It follows that $\sum_{2 \leq j \leq k} n_j \leq \log_2 \Pi_{2 \leq j \leq k} q_j \leq \log((p-1)/2)$. Since the sum of the squares of n_j is less than or equal to the square of the sum of n_j, it follows that the sum in the above expression is at most $(\log_2 p - 1)^2 \leq (n-1)^2$. But $3n + 6 + 4(n-1)^2 = 4n^2 - 5n + 10 \leq 4n^2$ when $n \geq 2$. Thus, the description of a certificate for the primality of p is polynomial in the length n of p.

We now show by induction that a prime p can be verified in $O(n^4)$ steps on a RAM. Assume that the divisors $q_1, \ldots, q_k$ for $p - 1$ have been verified. To verify p, we compute $r^{p-1} \bmod p$ from r and p as well as $r^{(p-1)/q} \bmod p$ for each of the prime divisors q of $p - 1$ and compare the results with 1. The integers $(p - 1)/q$ can be computed through subtraction of n-bit numbers in $O(n^2)$ steps on a RAM. To raise r to an exponent e, represent e as a binary number. For example, if $e = 7$, write it as $p = 2^2 + 2^1 + 2^0$. If t is the largest such power of 2, $t \leq \log_2(p - 1) \leq n$. Compute $r^{2^j} \bmod p$ by squaring r j times, each time reducing it by p through division. Since each squaring/reduction step takes $O(n^2)$ RAM steps, at most $O(jn^2)$ RAM steps are required to compute r^{2^j}. Since this may be done for $2 \leq j \leq t$ and $\sum_{2 \leq j \leq t} j = O(t^2)$, at most $O(n^3)$ RAM steps suffice to compute one of $r^{p-1} \bmod p$ or $r^{(p-1)/q} \bmod p$ for a prime divisor q. Since there are at most n of these quantities to compute, $O(n^4)$ RAM steps suffice to compute them.

To complete the verification of the prime p, we also need to verify the divisors $q_1, \ldots, q_k$ of $p - 1$. We take as our inductive hypothesis that an arbitrary prime q of n bits can be verified in $O(n^5)$ steps. Since the sum of the number of bits in $q_2, \ldots, q_k$ is $(\log_2(p-1)/2 - 1)$ and the sum of the kth powers is no more than the kth power of the sum, it follows that

$O(n^5)$ RAM steps suffice to verify p. Since a polynomial number of RAM steps can be executed in a polynomial number of Turing machine steps, PRIMALITY is in **NP**. ∎

Since **NP** ∩ **coNP** ⊆ **NP** and **NP** ∩ **coNP** ⊆ **coNP** as well as **NP** ⊆ **NP** ∪ **coNP** and **coNP** ⊆ **NP** ∪ **coNP**, we begin to have the makings of a hierarchy. If we add that **coNP** ⊆ **PSPACE** (see Problem 8.13), we have the relationships between complexity classes shown schematically in Fig. 8.7.

8.7 Reductions

In this section we specialize the reductions introduced in Section 2.4 and use them to classify problems into categories. We show that if problem A is reduced to problem B by a function in the set R and A is hard relative to R, then B cannot be easy relative to R because A can be solved easily by reducing it to B and solving B with an easy algorithm, contradicting the fact that A is hard. On the other hand, if B is easy to solve relative to R, then A must be easy to solve. Thus, reductions can be used to show that some problems are hard or easy. Also, if A can be reduced to B by a function in R and vice versa, then A and B have the same complexity relative to R.

Reductions are widely used in computer science; we use them whenever we specialize one procedure to realize another. Thus, reductions in the form of simulations are used throughout Chapter 3 to exhibit circuits that compute the same functions that are computed by finite-state, random-access, and Turing machines, with and without nondeterminism. Simulations prove to be an important type of reduction. Similarly, in Chapter 10 we use simulation to show that any computation done in the pebble game can be simulated by a branching program.

Not only did we simulate machines with memory by circuits in Chapter 3, but we demonstrated in Sections 3.9.5 and 3.9.6 that the languages CIRCUIT VALUE and CIRCUIT SAT describing circuits are **P**-complete and **NP**-complete, respectively. We demonstrated that each string x in an arbitrary language in **P** (**NP**) could be translated into a string in CIRCUIT VALUE (respectively, CIRCUIT SAT) by a program whose running time is polynomial in the length of x and whose space is logarithmic in its length.

In this chapter we extend these results. We consider primarily transformations (also called **many-one reductions** and just **reductions** in Section 5.8.1), a type of reduction in which an instance of one decision problem is translated to an instance of a second problem such that the former is a "yes" instance if and only if the latter is a "yes" instance. A **Turing reduction** is a second type of reduction that is defined by an oracle Turing machine. (See Section 8.4.2 and Problem 8.15.) In this case the Turing machine may make more than one call to the second problem (the oracle). A transformation is equivalent to an oracle Turing reduction that makes one call to the oracle. Turing reductions subsume all previous reductions used elsewhere in this book. (See Problems 8.15 and 8.16.) However, since the results of this section can be derived with the weaker transformations, we limit our attention to them.

DEFINITION 8.7.1 *If L_1 and L_2 are languages, a* **transformation** *h from L_1 to L_2 is a DTM-computable function $h : \mathcal{B}^* \mapsto \mathcal{B}^*$ such that $x \in L_1$ if and only if $h(x) \in L_2$. A* **resource-bounded transformation** *is a transformation that is computed under a resource bound such as deterministic logarithmic space or polynomial time.*

The classification of problems is simplified by considering classes of transformations. These classes will be determined by bounds on resources such as space and time on a Turing machine or circuit size and depth.

DEFINITION 8.7.2 *For decision problems $\mathcal{P}_1$ and $\mathcal{P}_2$, the notation $\mathcal{P}_1 \leq_R \mathcal{P}_2$ means that $\mathcal{P}_1$ can be transformed to $\mathcal{P}_2$ by a transformation in the class R.*

Compatibility among transformation classes and complexity classes helps determine conditions under which problems are hard.

DEFINITION 8.7.3 *Let C be a complexity class, R a class of resource-bounded transformations, and $\mathcal{P}_1$ and $\mathcal{P}_2$ decision problems. A set of transformations R is **compatible** with C if $\mathcal{P}_1 \leq_R \mathcal{P}_2$ and $\mathcal{P}_2 \in C$, then $\mathcal{P}_1 \in C$.*

It is easy to see that the **polynomial-time transformations** (denoted $\leq_p$) are compatible with **P**. (See Problem 8.17.) Also compatible with **P** are the **log-space transformations** (denoted $\leq_{\text{log-space}}$) associated with transformations that can be computed in logarithmic space. Log-space transformations are also polynomial transformations, as shown in Theorem 8.5.8.

8.8 Hard and Complete Problems

Classes of problems are defined above by their use of space and time. We now set the stage for the identification of problems that are hard relative to members of these classes. A few more definitions are needed before we begin this task.

DEFINITION 8.8.1 *A class R of transformations is **transitive** if the composition of any two transformations in R is also in R and for all problems $\mathcal{P}_1$, $\mathcal{P}_2$, and $\mathcal{P}_3$, $\mathcal{P}_1 \leq_R \mathcal{P}_2$ and $\mathcal{P}_2 \leq_R \mathcal{P}_3$ implies that $\mathcal{P}_1 \leq_R \mathcal{P}_3$.*

If a class R of transformations is transitive, then we can compose any two transformations in the class and obtain another transformation in the class. Transitivity is used to define hard and complete problems.

The transformations $\leq_p$ and $\leq_{\text{log-space}}$ described above are transitive. Below we show that $\leq_{\text{log-space}}$ is transitive and leave to the reader the proof of transitivity of $\leq_p$ and the polynomial-time Turing reductions. (See Problem 8.19.)

THEOREM 8.8.1 *Log-space transformations are transitive.*

Proof A log-space transformation is a DTM that has a read-only input tape, a write-only output tape, and a work tape or tapes on which it uses $O(\log n)$ cells to process an input string w of length n. As shown in Theorem 8.5.8, such DTMs halt within polynomial time. We now design a machine T that composes two log-space transformations in logarithmic space. (See Fig. 8.10.)

Let M_1 and M_2 denote the first and second log-space DTMs. When M_1 and M_2 are composed to form T, the output tape of M_1, which is also the input tape of M_2, becomes a work tape of T. Since M_1 may execute a polynomial number of steps, we cannot store all its output before beginning the computation by M_2. Instead we must be more clever. We keep the contents of the work tapes of both machines as well as (and this is where we are

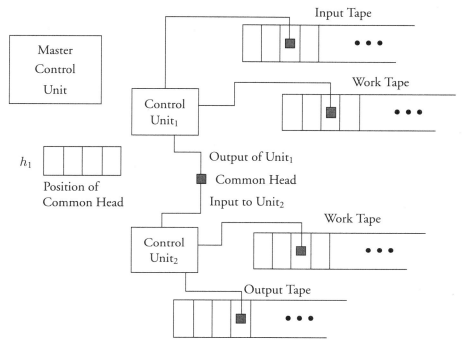

Figure 8.10 The composition of two deterministic log-space Turing machines.

clever) an integer h_1 recording the position of the input head of M_2 on the output tape of M_1. If M_2 moves its input head right by one step, M_1 is simulated until one more output is produced. If its head moves left, we decrement h_1, restart M_1, and simulate it until h_1 outputs are produced and then supply this output as an input to M_2.

The space used by this simulation is the space used by M_1 and M_2 plus the space for h_1, the value under the input head of M_2 and some temporary space. The total space is logarithmic in n since h_1 is at most a polynomial in n. ■

We now apply transitivity of reductions to define hard and complete problems.

DEFINITION 8.8.2 *Let R be a class of reductions, let C be a complexity class, and let R be compatible with C. A problem Q is* **hard for** C **under** R**-reductions** *if for every problem $\mathcal{P} \in C$, $\mathcal{P} \leq_R Q$. A problem Q is* **complete for** C **under** R**-reductions** *if it is hard for C under R-reductions and is a member of C.*

Problems are hard for a class if they are as hard to solve as any other problem in the class. Sometimes problems are shown hard for a class without showing that they are members of that class. Complete problems are members of the class for which they are hard. Thus, complete problems are the hardest problems in the class. We now define three important classes of complete problems.

DEFINITION 8.8.3 *Problems in* **P** *that are hard for* **P** *under log-space reductions are called* **P-complete***. Problems in* **NP** *that are hard for* **NP** *under polynomial-time reductions are called* **NP-complete***. Problems in* **PSPACE** *that are hard for* **PSPACE** *under polynomial-time reductions are called* **PSPACE-complete***.*

We state Theorem 8.8.2, which follows directly from Definition 8.7.3 and transitivity of log-space and polynomial-time reductions, because it incorporates as conditions the goals of the study of **P**-complete, **NP**-complete, and **PSPACE**-complete problems, namely, to show that all problems in **P** can be solved in log-space and all problems in **NP** and **PSPACE** can be solved in polynomial time. It is unlikely that any of these goals can be reached.

THEOREM 8.8.2 *If a* **P***-complete problem can be solved in log-space, then all problems in* **P** *can be solved in log-space. If an* **NP***-complete problem is in* **P***, then* **P** = **NP***. If a* **PSPACE***-complete problem is in* **P***, then* **P** = **PSPACE***.*

In Theorem 8.14.2 we show that if a **P**-complete problem can be solved in poly-logarithmic time with polynomially many processors on a CREW PRAM (they are fully parallelizable), then so can all problems in **P**. It is considered unlikely that all languages in **P** can be fully parallelized. Nonetheless, the question of the parallelizability of **P** is reduced to deciding whether **P**-complete problems are parallelizable.

8.9 P-Complete Problems

To show that a problem $\mathcal{P}$ is **P**-complete we must show that it is in **P** and that all problems in **P** can be reduced to $\mathcal{P}$ via a log-space reduction. (See Section 3.9.5.) The task of showing this is simplified by the knowledge that log-space reductions are transitive: if another problem $\mathcal{Q}$ has already been shown to be **P**-complete, to show that $\mathcal{P}$ is **P**-complete it suffices to show there is a log-space reduction from $\mathcal{Q}$ to $\mathcal{P}$ and that $\mathcal{P} \in$ **P**.

CIRCUIT VALUE
Instance: A circuit description with fixed values for its input variables and a designated output gate.
Answer: "Yes" if the output of the circuit has value 1.

In Section 3.9.5 we show that the CIRCUIT VALUE problem described above is **P**-complete by demonstrating that for every decision problem $\mathcal{P}$ in **P** an instance w of $\mathcal{P}$ and a DTM M that recognizes "Yes" instances of $\mathcal{P}$ can be translated by a log-space DTM into an instance c of CIRCUIT VALUE such that w is a "Yes" instance of $\mathcal{P}$ if and only if c is a "Yes" instance of CIRCUIT VALUE.

Since **P** is closed under complements (see Theorem 8.6.1), it follows that if the "Yes" instances of a decision problem can be determined in polynomial time, so can the "No" instances. Thus, the CIRCUIT VALUE problem is equivalent to determining the value of a circuit from its description. Note that for CIRCUIT VALUE the values of all variables of a circuit are included in its description.

CIRCUIT VALUE is in **P** because, as shown in Theorem 8.13.2, a circuit can be evaluated in a number of steps proportional at worst to the square of the length of its description. Thus, an instance of CIRCUIT VALUE can be evaluated in a polynomial number of steps.

Monotone circuits are constructed of AND and OR gates. The functions computed by monotone circuits form an asymptotically small subset of the set of Boolean functions. Also, many important Boolean functions are not monotone, such as binary addition. But even though monotone circuits are a very restricted class of circuits, the monotone version of CIR-CUIT VALUE, defined below, is also **P**-complete.

> MONOTONE CIRCUIT VALUE
> *Instance:* A description for a monotone circuit with fixed values for its input variables and a designated output gate.
> *Answer:* "Yes" if the output of the circuit has value 1.

CIRCUIT VALUE is a starting point to show that many other problems are **P**-complete. We begin by reducing it to MONOTONE CIRCUIT VALUE.

THEOREM 8.9.1 MONOTONE CIRCUIT VALUE *is* **P**-*complete*.

Proof As shown in Problem 2.12, every Boolean function can be realized with just AND and OR gates (this is known as dual-rail logic) if the values of input variables and their complements are made available. We reduce an instance of CIRCUIT VALUE to an instance of MONOTONE CIRCUIT VALUE by replacing each gate with the pair of monotone gates described in Problem 2.12. Such descriptions can be written out in log-space if the gates in the monotone circuit are numbered properly. (See Problem 8.20.) The reduction must also write out the values of variables of the original circuit and their complements. ∎

The class of **P**-complete problems is very rich. Space limitations require us to limit our treatment of this subject to two more problems. We now show that LINEAR INEQUALITIES described below is **P**-complete. LINEAR INEQUALITIES is important because it is directly related to LINEAR PROGRAMMING, which is widely used to characterize optimization problems. The reader is asked to show that LINEAR PROGRAMMING is **P**-complete. (See Problem 8.21.)

> LINEAR INEQUALITIES
> *Instance:* An integer-valued $m \times n$ matrix A and column m-vector $\boldsymbol{b}$.
> *Answer:* "Yes" if there is a rational column n-vector $\boldsymbol{x} > \boldsymbol{0}$ (all components are non-negative and at least one is non-zero) such that $A\boldsymbol{x} \leq \boldsymbol{b}$.

We show that LINEAR INEQUALITIES is **P**-hard, that is, that every problem in **P** can be reduced to it in log-space. The proof that LINEAR INEQUALITIES is in **P**, an important and difficult result in its own right, is not given here. (See [162].)

THEOREM 8.9.2 LINEAR INEQUALITIES *is* **P**-*hard*.

Proof We give a log-space reduction of CIRCUIT VALUE to LINEAR INEQUALITIES. That is, we show that in log-space an instance of CIRCUIT VALUE can be transformed to an instance of LINEAR INEQUALITIES so that an instance of CIRCUIT VALUE is a "Yes" instance if and only if the corresponding instance of LINEAR INEQUALITIES is a "Yes" instance.

The log-space reduction that we use converts each gate and input in an instance of a circuit into a set of inequalities. The inequalities describing each gate are shown below. (An equality relation $a = b$ is equivalent to two inequality relations, $a \leq b$ and $b \leq a$.) The reduction also writes the equality $z = 1$ for the output gate z. Since each variable must be non-negative, this last condition insures that the resulting vector of variables, $\boldsymbol{x}$, satisfies $\boldsymbol{x} > \boldsymbol{0}$.

	Input		Gates		
Type	TRUE	FALSE	NOT	AND	OR
Function	$x_i = 1$	$x_i = 0$	$w = \neg u$	$w = u \wedge v$	$w = u \vee v$
Inequalities	$x_i = 1$	$x_i = 0$	$0 \leq w \leq 1$ $w = 1 - u$	$0 \leq w \leq 1$ $w \leq u$ $w \leq v$ $u + v - 1 \leq w$	$0 \leq w \leq 1$ $u \leq w$ $v \leq w$ $w \leq u + v$

Given an instance of CIRCUIT VALUE, each assignment to a variable is translated into an equality statement of the form $x_i = 0$ or $x_i = 1$. Similarly, each AND, OR, and NOT gate is translated into a set of inequalities of the form shown above. Logarithmic temporary space suffices to hold gate numbers and to write these inequalities because the number of bits needed to represent each gate number is logarithmic in the length of an instance of CIRCUIT VALUE.

To see that an instance of CIRCUIT VALUE is a "Yes" instance if and only if the instance of LINEAR INEQUALITIES is also a "Yes" instance, observe that inputs of 0 or 1 to a gate result in the correct output if and only if the corresponding set of inequalities forces the output variable to have the same value. By induction on the size of the circuit instance, the values computed by each gate are exactly the same as the values of the corresponding output variables in the set of inequalities. ∎

We give as our last example of a **P**-complete problem DTM ACCEPTANCE, the problem of deciding if a string is accepted by a deterministic Turing machine in a number of steps specified as a unary number. (The integer k is represented as a unary number by a string of k characters.) For this problem it is more convenient to give a direct reduction from all problems in **P** to DTM ACCEPTANCE.

DTM ACCEPTANCE
Instance: A description of a DTM M, a string $\boldsymbol{w}$, and an integer n written in unary.
Answer: "Yes" if and only if M, when started with input $\boldsymbol{w}$, halts with the answer "Yes" in at most n steps.

THEOREM 8.9.3 DTM ACCEPTANCE *is* **P**-complete.

Proof To show that DTM ACCEPTANCE is log-space complete for **P**, consider an arbitrary problem $\mathcal{P}$ in **P** and an arbitrary instance of $\mathcal{P}$, namely $\boldsymbol{x}$. There is some Turing machine, say $M_{\mathcal{P}}$, that accepts instances $\boldsymbol{x}$ of $\mathcal{P}$ of length n in time $p(n)$, p a polynomial. We assume that p is included with the specification of $M_{\mathcal{P}}$. For example, if $p(y) = 2y^4 + 3y^2 + 1$, we can represent it with the string $((2, 4), (3, 2), (1, 0))$. The log-space Turing machine that translates $M_{\mathcal{P}}$ and $\boldsymbol{x}$ into an instance of DTM ACCEPTANCE writes the description of $M_{\mathcal{P}}$ together with the input $\boldsymbol{x}$ and the value of $p(n)$ in unary. Constant temporary space suffices to move the descriptions of $M_{\mathcal{P}}$ and $\boldsymbol{x}$ to the output tape. To complete the proof we need only show that $O(\log n)$ temporary space suffices to write the value in $p(n)$ in unary, where n is the length of $\boldsymbol{x}$.

Since the length of the input x is provided in unary, that is, by the number of characters it contains, its length n can be written in binary on a work tape in space $O(\log n)$ by counting the number of characters in x. Since it is not difficult to show that any power of a k-bit binary number can be computed by a DTM in work space $O(k)$, it follows that any fixed polynomial in n can be computed by a DTM in work space $O(k) = O(\log n)$. (See Problem 8.18.)

To show that DTM ACCEPTANCE is in **P**, we design a Turing machine that accepts the "Yes" instances in polynomial time. This machine copies the unary string of length n to one of its work tapes. Given the description of the DTM M, it simulates M with a universal Turing machine on input w. When it completes a step, it advances the head on the work tape containing n in unary, declaring the instance of DTM ACCEPTANCE accepted if M terminates without using more than n steps. By definition, it will complete its simulation of M in at most n of M's steps each of which uses a constant number of steps on the simulating machine. That is, it accepts a "Yes" instance of DTM ACCEPTANCE in time polynomial in the length of the input. ■

8.10 NP-Complete Problems

As mentioned above, the **NP**-complete problems are the problems in **NP** that are the most difficult to solve. We have shown that **NP** $\subseteq$ **PSPACE** $\subseteq$ **EXPTIME** or that every problem in **NP**, including the **NP**-complete problems, can be solved in exponential time. Since the **NP**-complete problems are the hardest problems in **NP**, each of these is at worst an exponential-time problem. Thus, we know that the **NP**-complete problems require either polynomial or exponential time, but we don't know which.

The CIRCUIT SAT problem is to determine from a description of a circuit whether it can be **satisfied**; that is, whether values can be assigned to its inputs such that the circuit output has value 1. As mentioned above, this is our canonical **NP**-complete problem.

CIRCUIT SAT
Instance: A circuit description with n input variables $\{x_1, x_2, \ldots, x_n\}$ for some integer n and a designated output gate.
Answer: "Yes" if there is an assignment of values to the variables such that the output of the circuit has value 1.

As shown in Section 3.9.6, CIRCUIT SAT is an **NP**-complete problem. The goal of this problem is to recognize the "Yes" instances of CIRCUIT SAT, instances for which there are values for the input variables such that the circuit has value 1.

In Section 3.9.6 we showed that CIRCUIT SAT described above is **NP**-complete by demonstrating that for every decision problem $\mathcal{P}$ in **NP** an instance w of $\mathcal{P}$ and an NDTM M that accepts "Yes" instances of $\mathcal{P}$ can be translated by a polynomial-time (actually, a log-space) DTM into an instance c of CIRCUIT SAT such that w is a "Yes" instance of $\mathcal{P}$ if and only if c is a "Yes" instance of CIRCUIT SAT.

Although it suffices to reduce problems in **NP** via a polynomial-time transformation to an **NP**-complete problem, each of the reductions given in this chapter can be done by a log-space transformation. We now show that a variety of other problems are **NP**-complete.

8.10.1 NP-Complete Satisfiability Problems

In Section 3.9.6 we showed that SATISFIABILITY defined below is **NP**-complete. In this section we demonstrate that two variants of this language are **NP**-complete by simple extensions of the basic proof that CIRCUIT SAT is **NP**-complete.

SATISFIABILITY
Instance: A set of **literals** $X = \{x_1, \overline{x}_1, x_2, \overline{x}_2, \ldots, x_n, \overline{x}_n\}$ and a sequence of **clauses** $C = (c_1, c_2, \ldots, c_m)$, where each clause c_i is a subset of X.
Answer: "Yes" if there is a (satisfying) assignment of values for the variables $\{x_1, x_2, \ldots, x_n\}$ over the set $\mathcal{B}$ such that each clause has at least one literal whose value is 1.

The two variants of SATISFIABILITY are 3-SAT, which has at most three literals in each clause, and NAESAT, in which not all literals in each clause have the same value.

3-SAT
Instance: A set of literals $X = \{x_1, \overline{x}_1, x_2, \overline{x}_2, \ldots, x_n, \overline{x}_n\}$, and a sequence of clauses $C = (c_1, c_2, \ldots, c_m)$, where each clause c_i is a subset of X containing at most three literals.
Answer: "Yes" if there is an assignment of values for variables $\{x_1, x_2, \ldots, x_n\}$ over the set $\mathcal{B}$ such that each clause has at least one literal whose value is 1.

THEOREM 8.10.1 3-SAT *is* **NP**-*complete.*

Proof The proof that SATISFIABILITY is **NP**-complete also applies to 3-SAT because each of the clauses produced in the transformation of instances of CIRCUIT SAT has at most three literals per clause. ∎

NAESAT
Instance: An instance of 3-SAT.
Answer: "Yes" if each clause is satisfiable when not all literals have the same value.

NAESAT contains as its "Yes" instances those instances of 3-SAT in which the literals in each clause are not all equal.

THEOREM 8.10.2 NAESAT *is* **NP**-*complete.*

Proof We reduce CIRCUIT SAT to NAESAT using almost the same reduction as for 3-SAT. Each gate is replaced by a set of clauses. (See Fig. 8.11.) The only difference is that we add the new literal y to each two-literal clause associated with AND and OR gates and to the clause associated with the output gate. Clearly, this reduction can be performed in deterministic log-space. Since a "Yes" instance of NAESAT can be verified in nondeterministic polynomial time, NAESAT is in **NP**. We now show that it is **NP**-hard.

Given a "Yes" instance of CIRCUIT SAT, we show that the instance of 3-SAT is a "Yes" instance. Since every clause is satisfied in a "Yes" instance of CIRCUIT SAT, every clause of the corresponding instance of NAESAT has at least one literal with value 1. The clauses that don't contain the literal y by their nature have not all literals equal. Those containing y can be made to satisfy this condition by setting y to 0, thereby providing a "Yes" instance of NAESAT.

Now consider a "Yes" instance of NAESAT produced by the mapping from CIRCUIT SAT. Replacing every literal by its complement generates another "Yes" instance of NAESAT

Step Type			Corresponding Clauses		
(i	READ	x)	$(\overline{g}_i \vee x)$	$(g_i \vee \overline{x})$	
(i	NOT	j)	$(\overline{g}_i \vee \overline{g}_j)$	$(g_i \vee g_j)$	
(i	OR	j k)	$(g_i \vee \overline{g}_j \vee y)$	$(g_i \vee \overline{g}_k \vee y)$	$(\overline{g}_i \vee g_j \vee g_k)$
(i	AND	j k)	$(\overline{g}_i \vee g_j \vee y)$	$(\overline{g}_i \vee g_k \vee y)$	$(g_i \vee \overline{g}_j \vee \overline{g}_k)$
(i	OUTPUT	j)	$(g_j \vee y)$		

Figure 8.11 A reduction from CIRCUIT SAT to NAESAT is obtained by replacing each gate in a "Yes" instance of CIRCUIT SAT by a set of clauses. The clauses used in the reduction from CIRCUIT SAT to 3-SAT (see Section 3.9.6) are those shown above with the literal y removed. In the reduction to NAESAT the literal y is added to the 2-literal clauses used for AND and OR gates and to the output clause.

since the literals in each clause are not all equal, a property that applies before and after complementation. In one of these "Yes" instances y is assigned the value 0. Because this is a "Yes" instance of NAESAT, at least one literal in each clause has value 1; that is, each clause is satisfiable. This implies that the original CIRCUIT SAT problem is satisfiable. It follows that an instance of CIRCUIT SAT has been translated into an instance of NAESAT so that the former is a "Yes" instance if and only if the latter is a "Yes" instance. ∎

8.10.2   Other NP-Complete Problems

This section gives a sampling of additional **NP**-complete problems. Following the format of the previous section, we present each problem and then give a proof that it is **NP**-complete. Each proof includes a reduction of a problem previously shown **NP**-complete to the current problem. The succession of reductions developed in this book is shown in Fig. 8.12.

INDEPENDENT SET
Instance: A graph $G = (V, E)$ and an integer k.
Answer: "Yes" if there is a set of k vertices of G such that there is no edge in E between them.

THEOREM 8.10.3 INDEPENDENT SET *is* **NP**-*complete.*

Proof INDEPENDENT SET is in **NP** because an NDTM can propose and then verify in polynomial time a set of k independent vertices. We show that INDEPENDENT SET is **NP**-hard by reducing 3-SAT to it. We begin by showing that a restricted version of 3-SAT, one in which each clause contains exactly three literals, is also **NP**-complete. If for some variable x, both x and $\overline{x}$ are in the same clause, we eliminate the clause since it is always satisfied. Second, we replace each 2-literal clause $(a \vee b)$ with the two 3-literal clauses $(a \vee b \vee z)$ and $(a \vee b \vee \overline{z})$, where z is a new variable. Since z is either 0 or 1, if all clauses are satisfied then $(a \vee b)$ has value 1 in both causes. Similarly, a clause with a single literal can be transformed to one containing three literals by introducing two new variables and replacing the clause containing the single literal with four clauses each containing three literals. Since adding

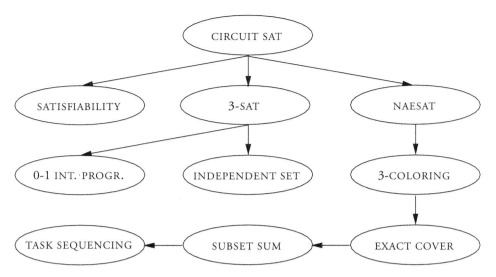

Figure 8.12 The succession of reductions used in this chapter.

distinct new variables to each clause that contains fewer than three literals can be done in log-space, this new problem, which we also call 3-SAT, is also **NP**-complete.

We now construct an instance of INDEPENDENT SET from this new version of 3-SAT in which k is equal to the number of clauses. (See Fig. 8.13.) Its graph G has one triangle for each clause and vertices carry the names of the three literals in a clause. G also has an edge between vertices carrying the labels of complementary literals.

Consider a "Yes" instance of 3-SAT. Pick one literal with value 1 from each clause. This identifies k vertices, one per triangle, and no edge exists between these vertices. Thus, the instance of INDEPENDENT SET is a "Yes" instance. Conversely, a "Yes" instance of INDEPENDENT SET on G has k vertices, one per triangle, and no two vertices carry the label of a variable and its complement because all such vertices have an edge between them. The literals associated with these independent vertices are assigned value 1, causing each clause to be satisfied. Variables not so identified are assigned arbitrary values. ∎

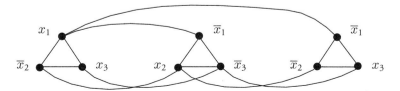

Figure 8.13 A graph for an instance of INDEPENDENT SET constructed from the following instance of 3-SAT: $(x_1 \vee \overline{x}_2 \vee x_3) \wedge (\overline{x}_1 \vee x_2 \vee \overline{x}_3) \wedge (\overline{x}_1 \vee \overline{x}_2 \vee x_3)$.

3-COLORING
Instance: The description of a graph $G = (V, E)$.
Answer: "Yes" if there is an assignment of three colors to vertices such that adjacent vertices have different colors.

THEOREM 8.10.4 3-COLORING *is* **NP**-*complete.*

Proof To show that 3-COLORING is in **NP**, observe that a three-coloring of a graph can be proposed in nondeterministic polynomial time and verified in deterministic polynomial time.

We reduce NAESAT to 3-COLORING. Recall that an instance of NAESAT is an instance of 3-SAT. A "Yes" instance of NAESAT is one for which each clause is satisfiable with not all literals equal. Let an instance of NAESAT consist of m clauses $C = (c_1, c_2, \ldots, c_m)$ containing exactly three literals from the set $X = \{x_1, \overline{x}_1, x_2, \overline{x}_2, \ldots, x_n, \overline{x}_n\}$ of literals in n variables. (Use the technique introduced in the proof of Theorem 8.10.3 to insure that each clause in an instance of 3-SAT has exactly three literals per clause.)

Given an instance of NAESAT, we construct a graph G in log-space and show that this graph is three-colorable if and only if the instance of NAESAT is a "Yes" instance.

The graph G has a set of n **variable triangles**, one per variable. The vertices of the triangle associated with variable x_i are $\{\nu, x_i, \overline{x}_i\}$. (See Fig. 8.14.) Thus, all the variable triangles have one vertex in common. For each clause containing three literals we construct one **clause triangle** per clause. If clause c_j contains literals λ_{j_1}, λ_{j_2}, and λ_{j_3}, its associated clause triangle has vertices labeled (j, λ_{j_1}), (j, λ_{j_2}), and (j, λ_{j_3}). Finally, we add an edge between the vertex (j, λ_{j_k}) and the vertex associated with the literal λ_{j_k}.

We now show that an instance of NAESAT is a "Yes" instance if and only if the graph G is three-colorable. Suppose the graph is three-colorable and the colors are $\{0, 1, 2\}$. Since

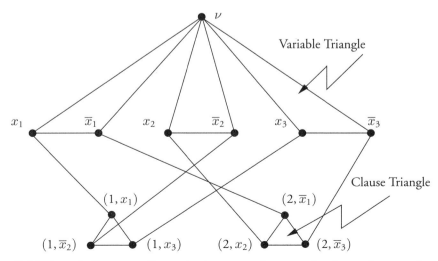

Figure 8.14 A graph G corresponding to the clauses $c_1 = \{x_1, \overline{x}_2, x_3\}$ and $c_2 = \{\overline{x}_1, x_2, \overline{x}_3\}$ in an instance of NAESAT. It has one variable triangle for each variable and one clause triangle for each clause.

three colors are needed to color the vertices of a triangle and the variable triangles have a vertex labeled ν in common, assume without loss of generality that this common vertex has color 2. The other two vertices in each variable triangle are assigned value 0 or 1, values we give to the associated variable and its complement.

Consider now the coloring of clause triangles. Since three colors are needed to color vertices of a clause triangle, consider vertices with colors 0 and 1. The edges between these clause vertices and the corresponding vertices in variable triangles have different colors at each end. Let the literals in the clause triangles be given values that are the Boolean complement of their colors. This provides values for literals that are consistent with the values of variables and insures that not all literals in a clause have the same value. The third vertex in each triangle has color 2. Give its literal a value consistent with the value of its variable. It follows that the clauses are a "Yes" instance of NAESAT.

Suppose, on the other hand, that a set of clauses is a "Yes" instance of NAESAT. We show that the graph G is three-colorable. Assign color 2 to vertex ν and colors 0 and 1 to vertices labeled x_i and $\overline{x}_i$ based on the values of these literals in the "Yes" instance. Consider two literals in clause c_j that are not both satisfied. If x_i $(\overline{x}_i)$ is one of these, give the vertex labeled (j, x_i) $((j, \overline{x}_i))$ the value that is the Boolean complement of the color of x_i $(\overline{x}_i)$ in its variable triangle. Do the same for the other literal. Since the third literal has the same value as one of the other two literals (they have different values), let its vertex have color 2. Then G is three-colorable. Thus, G is a "Yes" instance of 3-COLORING if and only if the corresponding set of clauses is a "Yes" instance of NAESAT. ∎

EXACT COVER
Instance: A set $S = \{u_1, u_2, \ldots, u_p\}$ and a family $\{S_1, S_2, \ldots, S_n\}$ of subsets of S.
Answer: "Yes" if there are disjoint subsets $S_{j_1}, S_{j_2}, \ldots, S_{j_t}$ such that $\cup_{1 \leq i \leq t} S_{j_i} = S$.

THEOREM 8.10.5 EXACT COVER *is* **NP**-*complete.*

Proof It is straightforward to show that EXACT COVER is in **NP**. An NDTM can simply select the subsets and then verify in time polynomial in the length of the input that these subsets are disjoint and that they cover the set S.

We now give a log-space reduction from 3-COLORING to EXACT COVER. Given an instance of 3-COLORING, that is, a graph $G = (V, E)$, we construct an instance of EXACT COVER, namely, a set S and a family of subsets of S such that G is a "Yes" instance of 3-COLORING if and only if the family of sets is a "Yes" instance of EXACT COVER.

As the set S we choose $S = V \cup \{< e, i > \mid e \in E, 0 \leq i \leq 2\}$ and as the family of subsets of S we choose the sets $S_{v,i}$ and $R_{e,i}$ defined below for $v \in V$, $e \in E$ and $0 \leq i \leq 2$:

$$S_{v,i} = \{v\} \cup \{< e, i > \mid e \text{ is incident on } v \in V\}$$
$$R_{e,i} = \{< e, i >\}$$

Let G be three-colorable. Then let c_v, an integer in $\{0, 1, 2\}$, be the color of vertex v. We show that the subsets S_{v,c_v} for $v \in V$ and $R_{e,i}$ for $< e, i > \notin S_{v,c_v}$ for any $v \in V$ are an exact cover. If $e = (v, w) \in E$, then $c_v \neq c_w$ and S_{v,c_v} and S_{w,c_w} are disjoint. By definition the sets $R_{e,i}$ are disjoint from the other sets. Furthermore, every element of S is in one of these sets.

On the other hand, suppose that S has an exact cover. Then, for each $v \in V$, there is a unique c_v, $0 \leq c_v \leq 2$, such that $v \in S_{v,c_v}$. To show that G has a three-coloring, assume that it doesn't and establish a contradiction. Since G doesn't have a three-coloring, there is an edge $e = (v, w)$ such that $c_v = c_w$, which contradicts the assumption that S has an exact cover. It follows that G has a three-coloring if and only if S has an exact cover. ∎

SUBSET SUM
Instance: A set $Q = \{a_1, a_2, \ldots, a_n\}$ of positive integers and a positive integer d.
Answer: "Yes" if there is a subset of Q that adds to d.

THEOREM 8.10.6 SUBSET SUM *is* **NP**-*complete.*

Proof SUBSET SUM is in **NP** because a subset can be nondeterministically chosen in time equal to n and an accepting choice verified in a polynomial number of steps by adding up the chosen elements of the subset and comparing the result to d.

To show that SUBSET SUM is **NP**-hard, we give a log-space reduction of EXACT COVER to it. Given an instance of EXACT COVER, namely, a set $S = \{u_1, u_2, \ldots, u_p\}$ and a family $\{S_1, S_2, \ldots, S_n\}$ of subsets of S, we construct the instance of SUBSET SUM characterized as follows. We let $\beta = n + 1$ and $d = \beta^{n-1} + \beta^{n-2} + \cdots + \beta^0 = (\beta^n - 1)/(\beta - 1)$. We represent the element $u_i \in S$ by the integer β^{i-1}, $1 \le i \le n$, and represent the set S_j by the integer a_j that is the sum of the integers associated with the elements contained in S_j. For example, if $p = n = 3$, $S_1 = \{u_1, u_3\}$, $S_2 = \{u_1, u_2\}$, and $S_3 = \{u_2\}$, we represent S_1 by $a_1 = \beta^2 + \beta^0$, S_2 by $a_2 = \beta + \beta^0$, and S_3 by $a_3 = \beta$. Since S_1 and S_3 forms an exact cover of S, $a_1 + a_3 = \beta^2 + \beta + 1 = d$.

Thus, given an instance of EXACT COVER, this polynomial-time transformation produces an instance of SUBSET SUM. We now show that the instance of the former is a "Yes" instance if and only if the instance of the latter is a "Yes" instance. To see this, observe that in adding the integers corresponding to the sets in an EXACT COVER in base β there is no carry from one power of β to the next. Thus the coefficient of β^k is exactly the number of times that u_{k+1} appears in each of the sets corresponding to a set of subsets of S. The subsets form a "Yes" instance of EXACT COVER exactly when the corresponding integers contain each power of β exactly once, that is, when the integers sum to d. ∎

TASK SEQUENCING
Instance: Positive integers $t_1, t_2, \ldots, t_r$, which are **execution times**, $d_1, d_2, \ldots, d_r$, which are **deadlines**, $p_1, p_2, \ldots, p_r$, which are **penalties**, and integer $k \ge 1$.
Answer: "Yes" if there is a permutation π of $\{1, 2, \ldots, r\}$ such that

$$\left(\sum_{j=1}^{r} [\, \textbf{if } t_{\pi(1)} + t_{\pi(2)} + \cdots + t_{\pi(j)} > d_{\pi(j)} \textbf{ then } p_{\pi(j)} \textbf{ else } 0] \right) \le k$$

THEOREM 8.10.7 TASK SEQUENCING *is* **NP**-*complete.*

Proof TASK SEQUENCING is in **NP** because a permutation π for a "Yes" instance can be verified as a satisfying permutation in polynomial time. We now give a log-space reduction of SUBSET SUM to TASK SEQUENCING.

An instance of SUBSET SUM is a positive integer d and a set $Q = \{a_1, a_2, \ldots, a_n\}$ of positive integers. A "Yes" instance is one such that a subset of Q adds to d. We translate an instance of SUBSET SUM to an instance of TASK SEQUENCING by setting $r = n$, $t_i = p_i = a_i$, $d_i = d$, and $k = (\sum_i a_i) - d$. Consider a "Yes" instance of this TASK

SEQUENCING problem. Then the following inequality holds:

$$\left(\sum_{j=1}^{r} \left[\text{ if } a_{\pi(1)} + a_{\pi(2)} + \cdots + a_{\pi(j)} > d, \text{ then } a_{\pi(j)} \text{ else } 0 \right] \right) \leq k$$

Let q be the expression in parentheses in the above inequality. Then $q = a_{\pi(l+1)} + a_{\pi(l+2)} + \cdots + a_{\pi(n)}$, where l is the integer for which $p = a_{\pi(1)} + a_{\pi(2)} + \cdots + a_{\pi(l)} \leq d$ and $p + a_{\pi(l+1)} > d$. By definition $p + q = \sum_i a_i$. It follows that $q \geq \sum_i a_i - d$. Since $q \leq k = \sum_i a_i - d$, we conclude that $p = d$ or that the instance of TASK SEQUENCING corresponds to a "Yes" instance of SUBSET SUM. Similarly, consider a "Yes" instance of SUBSET SUM. It follows from the above argument that there is a permutation such that the instance of TASK SEQUENCING is a "Yes" instance. ∎

The following **NP**-complete problem is closely related to the **P**-complete problem LINEAR INEQUALITIES. The difference is that the vector $\boldsymbol{x}$ must be a 0-1 vector in the case of 0-1 INTEGER PROGRAMMING, whereas in LINEAR INEQUALITIES it can be a vector of rationals. Thus, changing merely the conditions on the vector $\boldsymbol{x}$ elevates the problem from **P** to **NP** and makes it **NP**-complete.

0-1 INTEGER PROGRAMMING
Instance: An $n \times m$ matrix A and a column n-vector $\boldsymbol{b}$, both over the ring of integers for integers n and m.
Answer: "Yes" if there is a column m-vector $\boldsymbol{x}$ over the set $\{0, 1\}$ such that $A\boldsymbol{x} = \boldsymbol{b}$.

THEOREM 8.10.8 0-1 INTEGER PROGRAMMING *is* **NP**-*complete.*

Proof To show that 0-1 INTEGER PROGRAMMING is in **NP**, we note that a 0-1 vector $\boldsymbol{x}$ can be chosen nondeterministically in n steps, after which verification that it is a solution to the problem can be done in $O(n^2)$ steps on a RAM and $O(n^4)$ steps on a DTM.

To show that 0-1 INTEGER PROGRAMMING is **NP**-hard we give a log-space reduction of 3-SAT to it. Given an instance of 3-SAT, namely, a set of literals $X = (x_1, \overline{x}_1, x_2, \overline{x}_2, \ldots, x_n, \overline{x}_n)$ and a sequence of clauses $C = (c_1, c_2, \ldots, c_m)$, where each clause c_i is a subset of X containing at most three literals, we construct an $m \times p$ matrix $A = [B \mid C]$, where $B = [b_{i,j}]$ for $1 \leq i, j \leq n$ and $C = [c_{r,s}]$ for $1 \leq r \leq n$ and $1 \leq s \leq pm$. We also construct a column p-vector $\boldsymbol{d}$ as shown below, where $p = (m+1)n$. The entries of B and C are defined below.

$$b_{i,j} = \begin{cases} 1 & \text{if } x_j \in c_i \text{ for } 1 \leq j \leq n \\ -1 & \text{if } \overline{x}_j \in c_i \text{ for } 1 \leq j \leq n \end{cases}$$

$$c_{r,s} = \begin{cases} -1 & \text{if } (r-1)n + 1 \leq s \leq rn \\ 0 & \text{otherwise} \end{cases}$$

Since no one clause contains both x_j and $\overline{x}_j$, this definition of $a_{i,j}$ is consistent.

We also let d_i, the ith component of $\boldsymbol{d}$, satisfy $d_i = 1 - q_i$, where q_i is the number of complemented variables in c_i. Thus, the matrix A has the form given below, where B is an $m \times n$ matrix and each row of A contains n instances of -1 outside of B in non-overlapping columns:

$$A = \left[\begin{array}{c|ccccccccc} & -1 & -1 & \ldots & -1 & 0 & \ldots & 0 & 0 & \ldots & 0 \\ & 0 & 0 & & 0 & -1 & \ldots & -1 & \vdots & & 0 \\ B & \vdots & & & \vdots & & & \ddots & 0 & \ldots & 0 \\ & 0 & 0 & \ldots & 0 & 0 & \ldots & 0 & -1 & \ldots & -1 \end{array} \right]$$

We show that the instance of 3-SAT is a "Yes" instance if and only if this instance of 0-1 INTEGER PROGRAMMING is a "Yes" instance, that is, if and only if $A\boldsymbol{x} = \boldsymbol{d}$.

We write the column p-vector $\boldsymbol{x}$ as the concatenation of the column m-vector $\boldsymbol{u}$ and the column mn-vector $\boldsymbol{v}$. It follows that $A\boldsymbol{x} = \boldsymbol{b}$ if and only if $A\boldsymbol{u} \geq \boldsymbol{b}$. Now consider the ith component of $A\boldsymbol{u}$. Let $\boldsymbol{u}$ select k_i uncomplemented and l_i complemented variables of clause c_i. Then, $A\boldsymbol{u} \geq \boldsymbol{b}$ if and only if $k_i - l_i \geq d_i = 1 - q_i$ or $k_i + (q_i - l_i) \geq 1$ for all i. Now let $x_i = u_i$ for $1 \leq i \leq n$. Then k_i and $q_i - l_i$ are the numbers of uncomplemented and complemented variables in c_i that are set to 1 and 0, respectively. Since $k_i + (q_i - l_i) \geq 1$, c_i is satisfied, as are all clauses, giving us the desired result. ■

8.11 The Boundary Between **P** and **NP**

It is important to understand where the boundary lies between problems in **P** and the **NP**-complete problems. While this topic is wide open, we shed a modest amount of light on it by showing that 2-SAT, the version of 3-SAT in which each clause has at most two literals, lies on the **P**-side of this boundary, as shown below. In fact, it is in **NL**, which is in **P**.

THEOREM 8.11.1 *2-SAT is in* **NL**.

Proof Given an instance I of 2-SAT, we construct a directed graph $G = (V, E)$ with vertices V labeled by the literals x and $\overline{x}$ for each variable x appearing in I. There is an edge (α, β) in E directed from vertex α to vertex β if the clause $(\overline{\alpha} \vee \beta)$ is in I. If $(\overline{\alpha} \vee \beta)$ is in I, so is $(\beta \vee \overline{\alpha})$ because of commutativity of $\vee$. Thus, if $(\alpha, \beta) \in E$, then $(\overline{\beta}, \overline{\alpha}) \in E$ also. It follows that if there is a path from α to γ in G, there is a path from $\overline{\gamma}$ to $\overline{\alpha}$. (See the graph in Fig. 8.15.)

To understand why these edges are chosen, note that if all clauses of I are satisfied and $(\overline{\alpha} \vee \beta)$ is in I, then $\alpha = 1$ implies that $\beta = 1$. This implication relation, denoted $\alpha \Rightarrow \beta$, is transitive. If there is a path $(\alpha_1, \alpha_2, \ldots, \alpha_k)$ in G, then there are clauses $(\overline{\alpha}_1 \vee \alpha_2)$, $(\overline{\alpha}_2 \vee \alpha_3), \ldots, (\overline{\alpha}_{k-1} \vee \alpha_k)$ in I. If all clauses are satisfied and if the literal $\alpha_1 = 1$, then each un-negated literal on this path must have value 1.

We now show that an instance I is a "No" instance if and only if there is a variable x such that there is a path in G from x to $\overline{x}$ (which implies that there is a path from $\overline{x}$ to x).

Suppose that there are such paths and that x has value 1. Since $\overline{x}$, the endpoint of this path, has value 0, there is a first edge (α, β) on this path such that $\alpha = 1$ and $\beta = 0$. But this edge corresponds to a clause $(\overline{\alpha} \vee \beta)$ that is not satisfied. Thus I is a "No" instance. If $x = 0$, use the existence of a path from $\overline{x}$ to x to establish the same result.

Conversely, suppose I is a "No" instance. To prove there is a variable x such that there are paths from vertex x to vertex $\overline{x}$ and from $\overline{x}$ to x (by design of the graph, if the first path exists, so does the second), assume that for no variable x does this condition hold and show

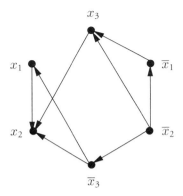

Figure 8.15 A graph capturing the implications associated with the following satisfiable in-
stance of 2-SAT: $(\overline{x}_3 \vee x_2) \wedge (x_3 \vee x_1) \wedge (\overline{x}_3 \vee x_2) \wedge (\overline{x}_1 \vee x_2)$.

that I is a "Yes" instance, that is, every clause is satisfied, which contradicts the assumption
that I is a "No" instance.

Identify a vertex with its associated literal and repeat the following process until done:
pick a vertex α in G that has not been assigned a value and from which there is no directed
path to $\overline{\alpha}$. Assign value 1 to α and each literal λ reachable from it. (This assigns values to
the variables identified by these literals.) If these assignments can be made without assigning
a variable both values 0 and 1, each clause can be satisfied and I is "Yes" instance rather than
a "No" one, as assumed. To show that each variable is assigned a single value, we assume the
converse and show that the conditions under which values are assigned to variables by this
procedure are contradicted. A variable can be assigned contradictory values in two ways: a)
on the current step the literals λ and $\overline{\lambda}$ are both reachable from α and assigned value 1, and
b) a literal λ is reachable from α on the current step that was assigned value 0 on a previous
step. For the first case to happen, there must be a path from α to vertices λ and $\overline{\lambda}$. By design
of the graph, if there is a path from α to $\overline{\lambda}$, there is a path from λ to $\overline{\alpha}$. Since there is a path
from α to λ, there must be a path from α to $\overline{\alpha}$, contradicting the assumption that there are
no such paths. In the second case, let a λ be assigned 1 on the current step that was assigned
0 on a previous step. It follows that $\overline{\lambda}$ was given value 1 on that step. Because there is a path
from α to λ, there is one from $\overline{\lambda}$ to $\overline{\alpha}$ and our procedure, which assigned $\overline{\lambda}$ value 1 on the
earlier step, must have assigned $\overline{\alpha}$ value 1 on that step also. Thus, α had the value 0 before
the current step, contradicting the assumption that it was not assigned a value.

To show that 2-SAT is in **NL**, recall that **NL** is closed under complements. Thus, it suffices to show that "No" instances of 2-SAT can be accepted in nondeterministic logarithmic
space. By the above argument, if I is a "No" instance, there is a variable x such that there is
a path in G from x to $\overline{x}$ and from $\overline{x}$ to x. Since the number of vertices in G is at most linear
in n, the length of I (it may be as small as $O(\sqrt{n})$), an NDTM can propose and then verify
in space $O(\log n)$ a path in G from x to $\overline{x}$ and back by checking that the putative edges are
edges of G, that x is the first and last vertex on the path, and that $\overline{x}$ is encountered before
the end of the path. ∎

8.12 **PSPACE**-Complete Problems

PSPACE is the class of decision problems that are decidable by a Turing machine in space polynomial in the length of the input. Problems in **PSPACE** are potentially much more complex than problems in **P**.

The hardest problems in **PSPACE** are the **PSPACE**-complete problems. (See Section 8.8.) Such problems have two properties: a) they are in **PSPACE** and b) every problem in **PSPACE** can be reduced to them by a polynomial-time Turing machine. The **PSPACE**-complete problems are the hardest problems in **PSPACE** in the sense that if they are in **P**, then so are all problems in **PSPACE**, an unlikely prospect.

We now establish that QUANTIFIED SATISFIABILITY defined below is **PSPACE**-complete. We also show that GENERALIZED GEOGRAPHY, a game played on a graph, is **PSPACE**-complete by reducing QUANTIFIED SATISFIABILITY to it. A characteristic shared by many important **PSPACE**-complete problems and these two problems is that they are equivalent to games on graphs.

8.12.1 A First **PSPACE**-Complete Problem

Quantified Boolean formulas use existential quantification, denoted $\exists$, and universal quantification, denoted $\forall$. **Existential quantification** on variable x_1, denoted $\exists x_1$, means "there exists a value for the Boolean variable x_1," whereas **universal quantification** on variable x_2, denoted $\forall x_2$, means "for all values of the Boolean variable x_2." Given a Boolean formula such as $(x_1 \vee x_2 \vee \overline{x}_3) \wedge (\overline{x}_1 \vee x_2 \vee x_3) \wedge (\overline{x}_1 \vee \overline{x}_2 \vee \overline{x}_3)$, a quantification of it is a collection of universal or existential quantifiers, one per variable in the formula, followed by the formula. For example,

$$\forall x_1 \exists x_2 \forall x_3 [(x_1 \vee x_2 \vee \overline{x}_3) \wedge (\overline{x}_1 \vee x_2 \vee x_3) \wedge (\overline{x}_1 \vee \overline{x}_2 \vee \overline{x}_3)]$$

is a quantified formula. Its meaning is "for all values of x_1, does there exist a value for x_2 such that for all values of x_3 the formula $(x_1 \vee x_2 \vee \overline{x}_3) \wedge (\overline{x}_1 \vee x_2 \vee x_3) \wedge (\overline{x}_1 \vee \overline{x}_2 \vee \overline{x}_3)$ is satisfied?" In this case the answer is "No" because for $x_1 = 1$, the function is not satisfied with $x_3 = 0$ when $x_2 = 0$ and is not satisfied with $x_3 = 1$ when $x_2 = 1$. However, if the third quantifier is changed from universal to existential, then the quantified formula is satisfied. Note that the order of the quantifiers is important. To see this, observe that under the quantification order $\forall x_1 \forall x_3 \exists x_2$ that the quantified formula is satisfied.

QUANTIFIED SATISFIABILITY consists of satisfiable instances of quantified Boolean formulas in which each formula is expressed as a set of clauses.

QUANTIFIED SATISFIABILITY
Instance: A set of literals $X = \{x_1, \overline{x}_1, x_2, \overline{x}_2, \ldots, x_n, \overline{x}_n\}$, a sequence of clauses $C = (c_1, c_2, \ldots, c_m)$, where each clause c_i is a subset of X, and a sequence of quantifiers $(Q_1, Q_2, \ldots, Q_n)$, where $Q_j \in \{\forall, \exists\}$.
Answer: "Yes" if under the quantifiers $Q_1 x_1 Q_2 x_2 \cdots Q_n x_n$, the clauses $c_1, c_2, \ldots, c_m$ are satisfied, denoted

$$Q_1 x_1 Q_2 x_2 \cdots Q_n x_n \, [\phi]$$

where the formula $\phi = c_1 \wedge c_2 \wedge \cdots \wedge c_m$ is in the product-of-sums form. (See Section 2.2.)

In this section we establish the following result, stronger than **PSPACE**-completeness of QUANTIFIED SATISFIABILITY: we show it is complete for **PSPACE** under log-space transformations. Reductions of this type are potentially stronger than polynomial-time reductions because the transformation is executed in logarithmic space, not polynomial time. While it is true that every log-space transformation is a polynomial-time transformation (see Theorem 8.5.8), it is not known if the reverse is true. We prove this result in two stages: we first show that QUANTIFIED SATISFIABILITY is in **PSPACE** and then that it is hard for **PSPACE**.

LEMMA 8.12.1 QUANTIFIED SATISFIABILITY *is in* **PSPACE**.

Proof To show that QUANTIFIED SATISFIABILITY is in **PSPACE** we evaluate in polynomial space a circuit, C_{qsat}, whose value is 1 if and only if the instance of QUANTIFIED SATISFIABILITY is a "Yes" instance. The circuit C_{qsat} is a tree all of whose paths from the inputs to the output (root of the tree) have the same length, each vertex is either an AND gate or an OR gate, and each input has value 0 or 1. (See Fig. 8.16.) The gate at the root of the tree is associated with the variable x_1, the gates at the next level are associated with x_2, etc. The type of gate at the jth level is determined by the jth quantifier Q_j and is AND if $Q_j = \forall$ and OR if $Q_j = \exists$. The leaves correspond to all 2^n the values of the n variables: at each level of the tree the left and right branches correspond to the values 0 and 1 for the corresponding quantified variable. Each leaf of the tree contains the value of the formula ϕ for the values of the variables leading to that leaf. In the example of Fig. 8.16 the leftmost leaf has value 1 because on input $x_1 = x_2 = x_3 = 0$ each of the three clauses $\{x_1, x_2, \overline{x}_3\}$, $\{\overline{x}_1, x_2, x_3\}$ and $\{\overline{x}_1, \overline{x}_2, \overline{x}_3\}$ is satisfied.

It is straightforward to see that the value at the root of the tree is 1 if all clauses are satisfied under the quantifiers $Q_1 x_1 Q_2 x_2 \cdots Q_n x_n$ and 0 otherwise. Thus, the circuit solves the QUANTIFIED SATISFIABILITY problem and its complement. (Note that **PSPACE = coPSPACE**, as shown in Theorem 8.6.1.)

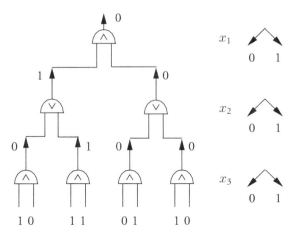

Figure 8.16 A tree circuit constructed from the instance $\forall x_1 \exists x_2 \forall x_3 \phi$ for $\phi = (x_1 \vee x_2 \vee \overline{x}_3) \wedge (\overline{x}_1 \vee x_2 \vee x_3) \wedge (\overline{x}_1 \vee \overline{x}_2 \vee \overline{x}_3)$ of QUANTIFIED SATISFIABILITY. The eight values at the leaves of the tree are the values of ϕ on the eight different assignments to (x_1, x_2, x_3).

```
tree_eval(n, φ, Q, d, w);
  if d = n then
    return(evaluate(φ,  w));
  else
    if first(Q) = ∃ then
      return(tree_eval(n, φ,  rest(Q),  d + 1, w0)
        OR tree_eval(n, φ,  rest(Q),  d + 1, w1));
    else
      return(tree_eval(n, φ,  rest(Q),  d + 1, w0)
        AND tree_eval(n, φ,  rest(Q),  d + 1, w1));
```

Figure 8.17 A program for the recursive procedure `tree_eval`(n, ϕ, Q, d, w). The tuple w keeps track of the path taken into the tree.

The circuit C_{qsat} has size exponential in n because there are 2^n values for the n variables. However, it can be evaluated in polynomial space, as we show. For this purpose consider the recursive procedure `tree_eval`(n, ϕ, Q, d, w) in Fig. 8.17 that evaluates C_{qsat}. Here n is the number of variables in the quantization, d is the depth of recursion, ϕ is the expression over which quantification is done, Q is a sequence of quantifiers, and w holds the values for d variables. Also, `first`(Q) and `rest`(Q) are the first and all but the first components of Q, respectively. When $d = 0$, $Q = (Q_1, Q_2, \ldots, Q_n)$ and $Q_1 x_1 Q_2 x_2 \cdots Q_n x_n \ \phi$ is the expression to evaluate. We show that `tree_eval`$(n, \phi, Q, 0, \epsilon)$ can be computed in space quadratic in the length of an instance of QUANTIFIED SATISFIABILITY.

When $d = n$, the procedure has reached a leaf of the tree and the string w contains values for the variables $x_1, x_2, \ldots, x_n$, in that order. Since all variables of ϕ are known when $d = n$, ϕ can be evaluated. Let `evaluate`(ϕ, w) be the function that evaluates ϕ with values specified by w. Clearly `tree_eval`$(n, \phi, Q, 0, \epsilon)$ is the value of $Q_1 x_1 Q_2 x_2 \cdots Q_n x_n \ \phi$.

We now determine the work space needed to compute `tree_eval`(n, ϕ, Q, d, w) on a DTM. (The discussion in the proof of Theorem 8.5.5 is relevant.) Evaluation of this procedure amounts to a depth-first traversal of the tree. An activation record is created for each call to the procedure and is pushed onto a stack. Since the depth of the tree is n, at most $n + 1$ records will be on the stack. Since each activation record contains a string of length at most $O(n)$, the total space used is $O(n^2)$. And the length of $Q_1 x_1 Q_2 x_2 \cdots Q_n x_n \ \phi$ is at least n, the space is polynomial in the length of this formula. ∎

LEMMA 8.12.2 QUANTIFIED SATISFIABILITY *is log-space hard for* **PSPACE**.

Proof Our goal is to show that every decision problem $\mathcal{P} \in$ **PSPACE** can be reduced in log-space to an instance of QUANTIFIED SATISFIABILITY. Instead, we show that every such $\mathcal{P}$ can be reduced in log-space to a "No" instance of QUANTIFIED SATISFIABILITY (we call this QUANTIFIED UNSATISFIABILITY). But a "No" instance is one for which the formula ϕ, which is in product-of-sums form, is not satisfied under the specified quantification or that its Boolean complement, which is in sum-of-products expansion (SOPE) form, is satisfied under a quantification in which $\forall$ is replaced by $\exists$ and vice versa. Exchanging "Yes" and "No" instances of decision problems (which we can do since **PSPACE** is closed under complements), we have that every problem in **coPSPACE** can be reduced in log-space to QUANTIFIED SATISFIABILITY. However, since **PSPACE = coPSPACE**, we have the desired result.

Our task now is to show that every problem $\mathcal{P} \in$ **PSPACE** can be reduced in log-space to an instance of QUANTIFIED UNSATISFIABILITY. Let $L \in$ **PSPACE** be the language of "Yes" instances of $\mathcal{P}$ and let M be the DTM deciding L. Instances of QUANTIFIED UNSATISFIABILITY will be quantified formulas in SOPE form that describe conditions on the configuration graph $G(M, \boldsymbol{w})$ of M on input $\boldsymbol{w}$. We associate a Boolean vector with each vertex in $G(M, \boldsymbol{w})$ and assume that $G(M, \boldsymbol{w})$ has one initial and final vertex associated with the vectors $\boldsymbol{a}$ and $\boldsymbol{b}$, respectively. (We can make the last assumption because M can be designed to enter a cleanup phase in which it prints blanks in all non-blank tape cells.)

Let $\boldsymbol{c}$ and $\boldsymbol{d}$ be vector encodings of arbitrary configurations c and d of $G(M, \boldsymbol{w})$. We construct formulas $\psi_i(\boldsymbol{c}, \boldsymbol{d})$, $0 \leq i \leq k$, in SOPE form that are satisfied if and only if there exists a path from c to d in $G(M, \boldsymbol{w})$ of length at most 2^i (it computes the predicate PATH$(c, d, 2^i)$ introduced in the proof of Theorem 8.5.5). Then a "Yes" instance of QUANTIFIED UNSATISFIABILITY is the formula $\psi_k(\boldsymbol{a}, \boldsymbol{b})$, where $\boldsymbol{a}$ and $\boldsymbol{b}$ are encodings of the initial and final vertices of $G(M, \boldsymbol{w})$ for k sufficiently large that a polynomial-space computation can be done in time 2^k. Since, as seen in Theorem 8.5.6, a deterministic computation in space S is done in time $O(2^S)$, it suffices for k to be polynomial in the length of the input.

The formula $\psi_0(\boldsymbol{c}, \boldsymbol{d})$ is satisfiable if either $\boldsymbol{c} = \boldsymbol{d}$ or $\boldsymbol{d}$ follows from $\boldsymbol{c}$ in one step. Such formulas are easily computed from the descriptions of M and $\boldsymbol{w}$. $\psi_i(\boldsymbol{c}, \boldsymbol{d})$ can be expressed as shown below, where the existential quantification is over all possible intermediate configurations $\boldsymbol{e}$ of M. (See the proof of Theorem 8.5.5 for the representation of PATH$(c, d, 2^i)$ in terms of PATH$(c, e, 2^{i-1})$ and PATH$(e, d, 2^{i-1})$.)

$$\psi_i(\boldsymbol{c}, \boldsymbol{d}) = \exists \boldsymbol{e} \, [\psi_{i-1}(\boldsymbol{c}, \boldsymbol{e}) \wedge \psi_{i-1}(\boldsymbol{e}, \boldsymbol{d})] \qquad (8.1)$$

Note that $\exists \boldsymbol{e}$ is equivalent to $\exists e_1 \exists e_2 \cdots \exists e_q$, where q is the length of $\boldsymbol{e}$. Universal quantification over a vector is expanded in a similar fashion.

Unfortunately, for $i = k$ this recursively defined formula requires space exponential in the size of the input. Fortunately, we can represent $\psi_i(\boldsymbol{c}, \boldsymbol{d})$ more succinctly using the implication operator $x \Rightarrow y$, as shown below, where $x \Rightarrow y$ is equivalent to $\overline{x} \vee y$. Note that if $x \Rightarrow y$ is TRUE, then either x is FALSE or x and y are both TRUE.

$$\psi_i(\boldsymbol{c}, \boldsymbol{d}) = \exists \boldsymbol{e} \, [\forall \boldsymbol{x} \forall \boldsymbol{y} \, [(\boldsymbol{x} = \boldsymbol{c} \wedge \boldsymbol{y} = \boldsymbol{e}) \vee (\boldsymbol{x} = \boldsymbol{e} \wedge \boldsymbol{y} = \boldsymbol{d})] \Rightarrow \psi_{i-1}(\boldsymbol{x}, \boldsymbol{y})] \quad (8.2)$$

Here $\boldsymbol{x} = \boldsymbol{y}$ denotes $(x_1 = y_1) \wedge (x_2 = y_2) \wedge \cdots \wedge (x_q = y_q)$, where $(x_i = y_i)$ denotes $x_i y_i \vee \overline{x}_i \overline{y}_i$. Then, the formula in the outer square brackets of (8.2) is true when either $(\boldsymbol{x} = \boldsymbol{c} \wedge \boldsymbol{y} = \boldsymbol{e}) \vee (\boldsymbol{x} = \boldsymbol{e} \wedge \boldsymbol{y} = \boldsymbol{d})$ is FALSE or this expression is TRUE and $\psi_{i-1}(\boldsymbol{x}, \boldsymbol{y})$ is also TRUE. Because the contents of the outer square brackets are TRUE, the quantization on $\boldsymbol{x}$ and $\boldsymbol{y}$ requires that $\psi_{i-1}(\boldsymbol{c}, \boldsymbol{e})$ and $\psi_{i-1}(\boldsymbol{e}, \boldsymbol{d})$ both be TRUE or that the formula given in (8.1) be satisfied.

It remains to convert the expression for $\psi_i(\boldsymbol{c}, \boldsymbol{d})$ given above to SOPE form in log-space. But this is straightforward. We replace $g \Rightarrow h$ by $\overline{g} \vee h$, where $g = (r \wedge s) \vee (t \wedge u)$ and $r = (\boldsymbol{x} = \boldsymbol{c})$, $s = (\boldsymbol{y} = \boldsymbol{e})$, $t = (\boldsymbol{x} = \boldsymbol{e})$, and $u = (\boldsymbol{y} = \boldsymbol{d})$. It follows that

$$\overline{g} = (\overline{r} \vee \overline{s}) \wedge (\overline{t} \vee \overline{u})$$
$$= (\overline{r} \wedge \overline{t}) \vee (\overline{r} \wedge \overline{u}) \vee (\overline{s} \wedge \overline{t}) \vee (\overline{s} \wedge \overline{u})$$

Since each of r, s, t, and u can be expressed as a conjunction of q terms of the form $(x_j = y_j)$ and $\overline{(x_j = y_j)} = (\overline{x}_j y_j \vee x_j \overline{y}_j)$, $1 \leq i \leq q$, it follows that $\overline{r}$, $\overline{s}$, $\overline{t}$, and $\overline{u}$ can each be expressed as a disjunction of $2q$ terms. Each of the four terms of the form $(\overline{r} \wedge \overline{t})$ consists of $4q^2$ terms, each of which is a conjunction of four literals. Thus, $\overline{g}$ is the disjunction of $16q^2$ terms of four literals each.

Given the regular structure of this formula for ψ_i, it can be generated from a formula for ψ_{i-1} in space $O(\log q)$. Since $0 \leq i \leq k$ and k is polynomial in the length of the input, all the formulas, including that for ψ_k, can be generated in log-space. By the above reasoning, this formula is a "Yes" instance of QUANTIFIED UNSATISFIABILITY if and only if there is a path in the configuration graph $G(M, \boldsymbol{w})$ between the initial and final states. ∎

Combining the two results, we have the following theorem.

THEOREM 8.12.1 QUANTIFIED SATISFIABILITY *is log-space complete for* **PSPACE**.

8.12.2 Other **PSPACE**-Complete Problems

An important version of QUANTIFIED SATISFIABILITY is ALTERNATING QUANTIFIED SATISFIABILITY.

ALTERNATING QUANTIFIED SATISFIABILITY
Instance: Instances of QUANTIFIED SATISFIABILITY that have an even number of quantifiers that alternate between $\exists$ and $\forall$, with $\exists$ the first quantifier.
Answer: "Yes" if the instance is a "Yes" instance of QUANTIFIED SATISFIABILITY.

THEOREM 8.12.2 ALTERNATING QUANTIFIED SATISFIABILITY *is log-space complete for* **PSPACE**.

Proof ALTERNATING QUANTIFIED SATISFIABILITY is in **PSPACE** because it is a special case of QUANTIFIED SATISFIABILITY. We reduce QUANTIFIED SATISFIABILITY to ALTERNATING QUANTIFIED SATISFIABILITY in log-space as follows. If two universal quantifiers appear in succession, we add an existential quantifier between them in a new variable, say x_l, and add the new clause $\{x_l, \overline{x}_l\}$ at the end of the formula ϕ. If two existential quantifiers appear in succession, add universal quantification over a new variable and a clause containing it and its negation. If the number of quantifiers is not even, repeat one or the other of the above steps. This transformation at most doubles the number of variables and clauses and can be done in log-space. The instance of ALTERNATING QUANTIFIED SATISFIABILITY is a "Yes" instance if and only if the instance of QUANTIFIED SATISFIABILITY is a "Yes" instance. ∎

The new version of QUANTIFIED SATISFIABILITY is akin to a game in which universal and existential players alternate. The universal player attempts to show a fact for all values of its Boolean variable, whereas the existential player attempts to deny that fact by the choice of its existential variable. It is not surprising, therefore, that many games are **PSPACE**-complete. The geography game described below is of this type.

The **geography game** is a game for two players. They alternate choosing names of cities in which the first letter of the next city is the last letter of the previous city until one of the two players (the losing player) cannot find a name that has not already been used. (See Fig. 8.18.) This game is modeled by a graph in which each vertex carries the name of a city and there is an edge from vertex u_1 to vertex u_2 if the last letter in the name associated with u_1 is the first letter in the name associated with u_2. In general this graph is directed because an edge from u_1 to u_2 does not guarantee an edge from u_2 to u_1.

GENERALIZED GEOGRAPHY
Instance: A directed graph $G = (V, E)$ and a vertex v.
Answer: "Yes" if there is a sequence of (at most $|V|$) alternating vertex selections by two players such that vertex v is the first selection by the first player and for each selection of the first player and all selections of the second player of vertices adjacent to the previous selection, the second player arrives at a vertex from which it cannot select a vertex not previously selected.

THEOREM 8.12.3 GENERALIZED GEOGRAPHY *is log-space complete for* **PSPACE**.

Proof To show that GENERALIZED GEOGRAPHY is log-space complete for **PSPACE**, we show that it is in **PSPACE** and that QUANTIFIED SATISFIABILITY can be reduced to it in log-space. To establish the first result, we show that the outcome of GENERALIZED GEOGRAPHY can be determined by evaluating a graph similar to the binary tree used to show that QUANTIFIED SATISFIABILITY is realizable in **PSPACE**.

Given the graph $G = (V, E)$ (see Fig. 8.18(a)), we construct a search graph (see Fig. 8.18(b)) by performing a variant of depth-first search of G from v. At each vertex we visit the next unvisited descendant, continuing until we encounter a vertex on the current path, at which point we backtrack and try the next sibling of the current vertex, if any. In depth-first search if a vertex has been visited previously, it is not visited again. In this variant of the algorithm, however, a vertex is revisited if it is not on the current path. The length of the longest path in this tree is at most $|V| - 1$ because each path can contain no more than $|V|$ vertices. The tree may have a number of vertices exponential in $|V|$.

At a leaf vertex a player has no further moves. The first player wins if it is the second player's turn at a leaf vertex and loses otherwise. Thus, a leaf vertex is labeled 1 (0) if the first player wins (loses). To insure that the value at a vertex u is 1 if the two players reach u and the first player wins, we assign OR operators to vertices at which the first player makes selections and AND operators otherwise. (The output of a one-input AND or OR gate is the

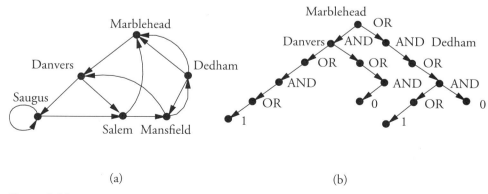

(a)   (b)

Figure 8.18 (a) A graph for the generalized geography game and (b) the search tree associated with the game in which the start vertex is Marblehead.

value of its input.) This provides a circuit that can be evaluated just as was the circuit C_{qsat} used in the proof of Theorem 8.12.1. The "Yes" instances of GENERALIZED GEOGRAPHY are such that the first player can win by choosing a first city. In Fig. 8.18 the value of the root vertex is 0, which means that the first player loses by choosing to start with Marblehead as the first city.

Vertices labeled AND or OR in the tree generated by depth-first search can have arbitrary in-degree because the number of vertices that can be reached from a vertex in the original graph is not restricted. The procedure `tree_eval` described in the proof of Theorem 8.12.1 can be modified to apply to the evaluation of this DAG whose vertex in-degree is potentially unbounded. (See Problem 8.30.) This modified procedure runs in space polynomial in the size of the graph G.

We now show that ALTERNATING QUANTIFIED SATISFIABILITY (abbreviated AQSAT) can be reduced in log-space to GENERALIZED GEOGRAPHY. Given an instance of AQSAT such as that shown below, we construct an instance of GENERALIZED GEOGRAPHY, as shown in Fig. 8.19. We assume without loss of generality that the number of quantifiers is even. If not, add a dummy variable and quantify on it:

$$\exists x_1 \forall x_2 \exists x_3 \forall x_4 [(x_1 \vee x_2 \vee \overline{x}_3) \wedge (\overline{x}_1 \vee x_2 \vee x_3) \wedge (\overline{x}_1 \vee \overline{x}_2 \vee \overline{x}_3) \wedge (x_4 \vee \overline{x}_4)]$$

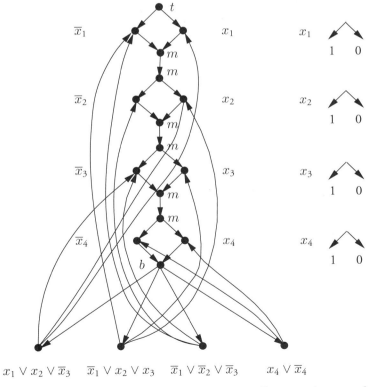

Figure 8.19 An instance of GENERALIZED GEOGRAPHY corresponding to an instance of ALTERNATING QUANTIFIED SATISFIABILITY.

The instance of GENERALIZED GEOGRAPHY corresponding to an instance of AQSAT is formed by cascading a set of diamond-shaped subgraphs, one per variable (see Fig. 8.19), and connecting the bottom vertex b in the last diamond to a set of vertices, one per clause. An edge is drawn from a clause to a vertex associated with a literal (x_i or $\overline{x}_i$) if that literal is in the clause. The literal x_i ($\overline{x}_i$) is associated with the middle vertex on the right-hand (left-hand) side of a diamond. Thus, in the example, there is an edge from the leftmost clause vertex to the left-hand vertex in the diamond for x_3 and to the right-hand vertices in diamonds for x_1 and x_2.

Let the geography game be played on this graph starting with the first player from the topmost vertex labeled t. The first player can choose either the left or right path. The second player has only one choice, taking it to the bottom of the first diamond, and the first player now has only one choice, taking it to the top of the second diamond. The second player now can choose a path to follow. Continuing in this fashion, we see that the first (second) player can exercise a choice on the odd- (even-) numbered diamonds counting from the top. Since the number of quantifiers is even, the choice at the bottom vertex labeled b belongs to the second player. Observe that whatever choices are made within the diamonds, the vertices labeled m and b are visited.

Because the goal of each player is to force the other player into a position from which it has no moves, at vertex b the second player attempts to choose a clause vertex such that the first player has no moves: that is, every vertex reachable from the clause vertex chosen by the second player has already been visited. On the other hand, if all clauses are satisfiable, then for every clause chosen by the second player there should be an edge from its vertex to a diamond vertex that has not been previously visited. To insure that the first player wins if and only if the instance of AQSAT used to construct this graph is a "Yes" instance, the first player always chooses an edge according to the directions in Fig. 8.19. For example, it visits the vertex labeled $\overline{x}_1$ if it wishes to set $x_1 = 1$ because this means that the vertex labeled x_1 is not visited on the path from t to b and can be visited by the first player on the last step of the game. Since each vertex labeled m and b is visited before a clause vertex is visited, the second player does not have a move and loses. ∎

8.13 The Circuit Model of Computation

The complexity classes seen so far in this chapter are defined in terms of the space and time needed to recognize languages with deterministic and nondeterministic Turing machines. These classes generally help us to understand the complexity of serial computation. Circuit complexity classes, studied in this section, help us to understand parallel computation.

Since a circuit is a fixed interconnection of gates, each circuit computes a single Boolean function on a fixed number of inputs. Thus, to compute the unbounded set of functions computed by a Turing machine, a family of circuits is needed. In this section we investigate uniform and non-uniform circuit families. A uniform family of circuits is a potentially unbounded set of circuits for which there is a Turing machine that, given an integer n in unary notation, writes a description of the nth circuit. We show that uniform circuits compute the same functions as Turing machines.

As mentioned below, non-uniform families of circuits are so powerful that they can compute functions not computed by Turing machines. Given the Church-Turing thesis, it doesn't make sense to assume non-uniform circuits as a model of computation. On the other hand, if we can develop large lower bounds on the size or depth of circuits without regard to whether or not they are drawn from a uniform family, then such lower bounds apply to uniform families as well and, in particular, to other models of computation, such as Turing machines. For this reason non-uniform circuits are important.

A circuit is a form of unstructured parallel machine, since its gates can operate in parallel. The parallel random-access machine (PRAM) introduced in Chapter 1 and examined in Chapter 7 is another important parallel model of computation in terms of which the performance of many other parallel computational models can be measured. In Section 8.14 we show that circuit size and depth are related to number of processors and time on the PRAM. These results emphasize the important role of circuits not only in the construction of machines, but also in measuring the serial and parallel complexity of computational problems.

Throughout the following sections we assume that circuits are constructed from gates chosen from the **standard basis** $\Omega_0 = \{\text{AND}, \text{OR}, \text{NOT}\}$.

We now explore uniform and non-uniform circuit families, thereby setting the stage for the next chapter, in which methods for deriving lower bounds on the size of circuits are developed. After introducing uniform circuits we show that uniform families of circuits and Turing machines compute the same functions. We then introduce a number of languages defined in terms of the properties of families of circuits that recognize them.

8.13.1 Uniform Families of Circuits

Families of circuits are useful in characterizing decision problems in which the set of instances is unbounded. One circuit in each family is associated with the "Yes" instances of each length: it has value 1 on the "Yes" instances and value 0 otherwise.

Families of circuits are designed in Chapter 3 to simulate computations by finite-state, random-access, and Turing machines on arbitrary numbers of inputs. For each machine M of one of these types, there is a DTM $S(M)$ such that on an input of length n, $S(M)$ can produce as output the description of a circuit on n inputs that computes exactly the same function as does M on n inputs. (See the program in Fig. 3.27.) These circuits are generated in a uniform fashion.

On the other hand, non-uniform circuit families can be used to define non-computable languages. For example, consider the family in which the nth circuit, C_n, is designed to have value 1 on those strings w of length n in the language $\mathcal{L}_1$ defined in Section 5.7 and value 0 otherwise. Such a circuit realizes the minterm defined by w. As shown in Theorem 5.7.4, $\mathcal{L}_1$ is not recursively enumerable; that is, there is no Turing machine that can recognize it.

This example motivates the need to identify families of circuits that compute functions computable by Turing machines, that is, uniform families of circuits.

DEFINITION 8.13.1 *A **circuit family** $\mathcal{C} = \{C_1, C_2, C_3, \ldots\}$ is a collection of logic circuits in which C_n has n inputs and $m(n)$ outputs for some function $m : \mathbb{N} \mapsto \mathbb{N}$.*

*A time-$r(n)$ (space-$r(n)$) **uniform circuit family** is a circuit family for which there is a deterministic Turing machine M such that for each integer n supplied in unary notation, namely 1^n, on its input tape, M writes the description of C_n on its output tape using time (space) $r(n)$.*

*A **log-space uniform circuit family** is one for which the temporary storage space used by a Turing machine that generates it is $O(\log n)$, where n is the length of the input. The **function** $f : \mathcal{B}^* \mapsto \mathcal{B}^*$ **is computed by** $\mathcal{C}$ if for each $n \geq 1$, f restricted to n inputs is the function computed by C_n.*

8.13.2   Uniform Circuits Are Equivalent to Turing Machines

We now show that the functions computed by log-space uniform families of circuits and by polynomial-time DTMs are the same. Since the family of functions computed by one-tape and multi-tape Turing machines are the same (see Theorem 5.2.1), we prove the result only for the standard one-tape Turing machine and proper resource functions (see Section 8.3).

THEOREM 8.13.1 *Let $p(n)$ be a polynomial and a proper function. Then every total function $f : \mathcal{B}^* \mapsto \mathcal{B}^*$ computed by a DTM in time $p(n)$ on inputs of length n can be computed by a log-space uniform circuit family $\mathcal{C}$.*

Proof Let $f_n : \mathcal{B}^n \mapsto \mathcal{B}^*$ be the restriction to inputs of length n of the function $f : \mathcal{B}^* \mapsto \mathcal{B}^*$ computed by a DTM M in time $p(n)$. It follows that the number of bits in the word $f_n(\boldsymbol{w})$ is at most $p(n)$. Since the function computed by a circuit has a fixed-length output and the length of $f_n(\boldsymbol{w})$ may vary for different inputs $\boldsymbol{w}$ of length n, we show how to create a DTM M^*, a modified version of M, that computes f_n^*, a function that contains all the information in the function f_n. The value of f_n^* has at most $2p(n)$ bits on inputs of length n. We show that M^* produces its output in time $O(p^2(n))$.

Let M^* place a mark in the $2p(n)$th cell on its tape (a cell beyond any reached during a computation). Let it now simulate M, which is assumed to print its output in the first k locations on the tape, $k \leq p(n)$. M^* now recodes and expands this binary string into a longer string. It does so by marking k cells to right of the output string (in at most k^2 steps), after which it writes every letter in the output string twice. That is, 0 appears as 00 and 1 as 11. Finally, the remaining $2(p(n) - k)$ cells are filled with alternating 0s and 1s. Clearly, the value of f_n can be readily deduced from the output, but the length of the value f_n^* is the same on all inputs of length n.

A Turing machine $M_{\mathcal{C}}$ that constructs the nth circuit from n represented in unary and a description of M^* invokes a slightly revised version of the program of Fig. 3.27 to construct the circuit computing f_n. This revised circuit contains placeholders for the values of the n letters representing the input to M. The program uses space $O(\log p^2(n))$, which is logarithmic in n. ∎

We now show that the function computed by a log-space uniform family of circuits can be computed by a polynomial-time Turing machine.

THEOREM 8.13.2 *Let $\mathcal{C}$ be a log-space uniform circuit family. Then there exists a polynomial-time Turing machine M that computes the same set of functions computed by the circuits in $\mathcal{C}$.*

Proof Let $M_{\mathcal{C}}$ be the log-space TM that computes the circuit family $\mathcal{C}$. We design the TM M to compute the same set of functions on an input $\boldsymbol{w}$ of length n. M uses $\boldsymbol{w}$ to obtain a unary representation for the input $M_{\mathcal{C}}$. It uses $M_{\mathcal{C}}$ to write down a description of the nth circuit on its work tape. It then computes the outputs of this circuit in time quadratic in the length of the circuit. Since the length of the circuit is a polynomial in n because the circuit is generated by a log-space TM (see Theorem 8.5.8), the running time of M is polynomial in the length of $\boldsymbol{w}$. ∎

These two results can be generalized to uniform circuit families and Turing machines that use more than logarithmic space and polynomial time, respectively. (See Problem 8.32.)

In the above discussion we examine functions computed by Turing machines. If these functions are **characteristic functions**, $f : \mathcal{B}^* \mapsto \mathcal{B}$; that is, they have value 0 or 1, then those strings for which f has value 1 define a language L_f. Also, associated with each language $L \subseteq \mathcal{B}^*$ is a characteristic function $f_L : \mathcal{B}^* \mapsto \mathcal{B}$ that has value 1 on only those strings in L.

Consider now a language $L \subseteq \mathcal{B}^*$. For each $n \geq 1$ a circuit can be constructed whose value is 1 on binary strings in $L \cap \mathcal{B}^n$ and 0 otherwise. Similarly, given a family $\mathcal{C}$ of circuits such that for each natural number $n \geq 1$ the nth circuit, C_n, computes a Boolean function on n inputs, the language L associated with this circuit family contains only those strings of length n for which C_n has value 1. We say that **L is recognized by $\mathcal{C}$**. At the risk of confusion, we use the same name for a circuit family and the languages they define.

In Theorem 8.5.6 we show that $\mathbf{NSPACE}(r(n)) \subseteq \mathbf{TIME}(k^{\log n + r(n)})$. We now use the ideas of that proof together with the parallel algorithm for transitive closure given in Section 6.4 to show that languages in $\mathbf{NSPACE}(r(n))$, $r(n) \geq \log n$, are recognized by a uniform family of circuits in which the nth circuit has size $O(k^{\log n + r(n)})$ and depth $O(r^2(n))$. When $r(n) = O(\log n)$, the circuit family in question is contained in the class $\mathbf{NC^2}$ introduced in the next section.

THEOREM 8.13.3 *If language $L \subseteq \mathcal{B}^*$ is in $\mathbf{NSPACE}(r(n))$, $r(n) \geq \log n$, there exists a time-$r(n)$ uniform family of circuits recognizing L such that the nth circuit has size $O(k^{\log n + r(n)})$ and depth $O(r^2(n))$ for some constant k.*

Proof We assume without loss of generality that the NDTM accepting L has one accepting configuration. We then construct the adjacency matrix for the configuration graph of M. This matrix has a 1 entry in row i, column j if there is a transition from the ith to the jth configuration. All other entries are 0. From the analysis of Corollary 8.5.1, this graph has $O(k^{\log n + r(n)})$ configurations. The initial configuration is determined by the word $\boldsymbol{w}$ written initially on the tape of the NDTM accepting L. If the transitive closure of this matrix has a 1 in the row and column corresponding to the initial and final configurations, respectively, then the word $\boldsymbol{w}$ is accepted.

From Theorem 6.4.1 the transitive closure of a Boolean $p \times p$ matrix A can be computed by computing $(I + A)^q$ for $q \geq p - 1$. This can be done by squaring A s times for $s \geq \log_2 p$. From this we conclude that the transitive closure can be computed by a circuit of depth $O(\log^2 m)$, where m is the number of configurations. Since $m = O(k^{\log n + r(n)})$, we have the desired circuit size and depth bounds.

A program to compute the dth power of an $p \times p$ matrix A is shown in Fig. 8.20. This program can be converted to one that writes the description of a circuit for this purpose, and both the original and converted programs can be realized in space $O(d \log p)$. (See

```
trans(A, n, d, i, j)
   if d = 0 then
      return(a_{i,j})
   else
      return(∑_{k=1}^{n} trans(A, n, d − 1, i, k) * trans(A, n, d − 1, k, j))
```

Figure 8.20 A recursive program to compute the dth power of an $n \times n$ matrix A.

Problem 8.33.) Invoking this procedure to write a program for the above problem, we see that an $O(r^2(n))$-depth circuit recognizing L can be written by an $O(r^2(n))$-time DTM.∎

8.14 The Parallel Random-Access Machine Model

The PRAM model, introduced in Section 7.9, is an abstraction of realistic parallel models that is sufficiently rich to permit the study of parallel complexity classes. (See Fig. 7.21, repeated as Fig. 8.21.) The PRAM consists of a set of RAM processors with a bounded number of memory locations and a common memory. The words of the common memory are allowed to be of unlimited size, but the instructions that the RAM processors can apply to them are restricted. These processors can perform addition, subtraction, vector comparison operations, conditional branching, and shifts by fixed amounts. We also allow load and store instructions for moving words between registers, local memories, and the common memory. These instructions are sufficiently rich to compute all computable functions.

In the next section we show that the CREW (concurrent read/exclusive write) PRAM that runs in polynomial time and the log-space uniform circuits characterize the same complexity classes. We then go on to explore the parallel complexity thesis, which states that sequential space and parallel time are polynomially related.

8.14.1 Equivalence of the CREW PRAM and Circuits

Because a parallel machine with p processors can provide a speedup of at most a factor of p over a comparable serial machine (see Theorem 7.4.1), problems that are computationally infeasible on serial machines are computationally infeasible on parallel machines with a reasonable number of processors. For this reason the study of parallelism is usually limited to feasible problems, that is, problems that can be solved in serial polynomial time (the class **P**). We limit our attention to such problems here.

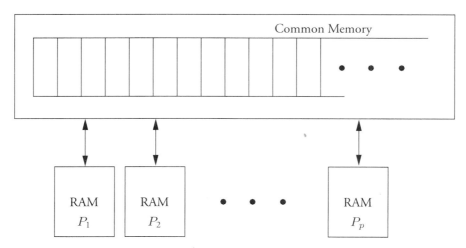

Figure 8.21   The PRAM consists of synchronous RAMs accessing a common memory.

Connections between PRAMs and circuits can be derived that are similar to those stated for Turing machines and circuits in Section 8.13.2. In this section we consider only log-space uniform families of circuits.

Given a PRAM, we now construct a circuit simulating it. This construction is based on that given in Section 3.4. With a suitable definition of **log-space uniform family of PRAMs** the circuits described in the following lemma constitute a log-space uniform family of circuits. (See Problem 8.35.) Also, this theorem can be extended to PRAMs that access memory locations with addresses much larger than $O(p(n)t(n))$, perhaps through indirect addressing. (See Problem 8.37.)

LEMMA 8.14.1 *Consider a function on input words of total length n bits computed by a CREW PRAM P in time $t(n)$ with a polynomial number of processors $p(n)$ in which the largest common memory address is $O(p(n)t(n))$. This function can be computed by a circuit of size $O(p^2(n)t(n) + p(n)t^2(n))$ and depth $O(\log(p(n)t(n)))$.*

Proof Since P executes at most $t(n)$ steps, by a simple extension to Problem 8.4 (only one RAM CPU at a time writes a word), we know that after $t(n)$ steps each word in the common memory of the PRAM has length at most $b = t(n) + n + K$ for some constant $K \geq 0$, because the PRAM can only compare or add numbers or shift them left by one position on each time step. This follows because each RAM CPU uses integers of fixed length and the length of the longest word in the common memory is initially n.

We exhibit a circuit for the computation by P by modifying and extending the circuit sketched in Section 3.4 to simulate one RAM CPU. This circuit uses the next-state/output circuit for the RAM CPU together with the next-state/output circuit for the random-access memory of Fig. 3.21 (repeated in Fig. 8.22). The circuit of Fig. 8.22(a) either writes a new value d_j for $w_{i,j}^*$, the jth component of the ith memory word of the random-access memory, or it writes the old value $w_{i,j}$. The circuit simulating the common memory of the PRAM is obtained by replacing the three gates at the output of the circuit in Fig. 8.22(a) with a subcircuit that assigns to $w_{i,j}^*$ the value of $w_{i,j}$ if $c_i = 0$ for each RAM CPU and the OR of the values of d_j supplied by each RAM CPU if $c_i = 1$ for some CPU. Here we count on the fact that at most one CPU addresses a given location for writing. Thus, if a CPU writes to a location, all other CPUs cannot do so. Concurrent reading is simulated by allowing every component of every memory cell to be used as input by every CPU.

Since the longest word that can be constructed by the CREW PRAM has length $b = t(n)+n+K$, it follows from Lemma 3.5.1 that the next-state/output circuit for the random-access memory designed for one CPU has size $O(p(n)t^2(n))$ and depth $O(\log(p(n)t(n)))$. The modifications described in the previous paragraph add size $O(p^2(n)t(n))$ (each of the $p(n)t(n)$ memory words has $O(p(n))$ new gates) and depth $O(\log p(n))$ (each OR tree has $p(n)$ inputs) to this circuit. As shown at the end of Section 3.10, the size and depth of a circuit for the next-state/output circuit of the CPU are $O(t(n) + \log(p(n)t(n)))$ and $O(\log t(n) + \log \log(p(n)t(n)))$, respectively. Since these sizes and depths add to those for the common memory, the total size and depth for the next-state/output circuit for the PRAM are $O(p^2(n)t(n) + p(n)t^2(n))$ and $O(\log(p(n)t(n)))$, respectively. ∎

We now show that the function computed by a log-space uniform circuit family can be computed in poly-logarithmic time on a PRAM.

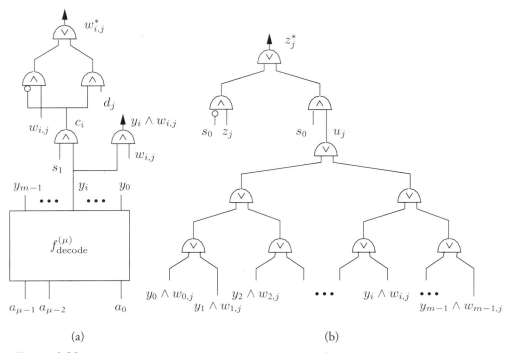

(a)   (b)

Figure 8.22 A circuit for the next-state and output function of the random-access memory. The circuit in (a) computes the next values for components of memory words, whereas that in (b) computes components of the output word. This circuit is modified to generate a circuit for the PRAM.

LEMMA 8.14.2 *Let $\mathcal{C} = (C_1, C_2, \ldots)$ be a log-space uniform family of circuits. There exists a CREW PRAM that computes in poly-logarithmic time and a polynomial number of processors the function $f : \mathcal{B}^* \mapsto \mathcal{B}^*$ computed by $\mathcal{C}$.*

Proof The CREW PRAM is given a string $\boldsymbol{w}$ on which to compute the function f. First it computes the length n of $\boldsymbol{w}$. Second it invokes the CREW PRAM described below to simulate with a polynomial number of processors in poly-logarithmic time the log-space DTM M that writes a description of the nth circuit, $C(M, n)$. Finally we show that the value of $C(M, n)$ can be evaluated from this description by a CREW PRAM in $O(\log^2 n)$ steps with polynomially many processors.

Let M be a three-tape DTM that realizes a log-space transformation. This DTM has a read-only input tape, a work tape, and a write-only output tape. Given a string $\boldsymbol{w}$ on its input tape, it provides on its output tape the result of the transformation. Since M uses $O(\log n)$ cells on its work tape on inputs of length n, it can be modeled by a finite-state machine with $2^{O(\log n)}$ states. The circuit $C(M, n)$ described in Theorem 3.2.2 for the simulation of the FSM M is constructed to simulate M on inputs of length n. We show that $C(M, n)$ has size and depth that are polynomial and poly-logarithmic in n, respectively. We then demonstrate that a CREW PRAM can simulate $C(M, n)$ (and write its output into its common memory) in $O(\log^2 n)$ steps with a polynomial number of processors.

From Theorem 8.5.8 we know that the log-space DTM M generating $C(M, n)$ does not execute more than $p(n)$ steps, $p(n)$ a polynomial in n. Since $p(n)$ is assumed proper, we can assume without loss of generality that M executes $p(n)$ steps on all inputs of length n. Thus, M has exactly $|Q| = O(p(n))$ configurations.

The input string $\boldsymbol{w}$ is placed in the first n locations of the otherwise blank common memory. To determine the length of the input, for each i the ith CREW PRAM processor examines the words in locations i and $i + 1$. If location $i + 1$ is blank but location i is not, $i = n$. The nth processor then computes $p(n)$ in $O(\log^2 n)$ serial steps (see Problem 8.2) and places it in common memory.

The circuit $C(M, n)$ is constructed from representations of next-state mappings, one mapping for every state transition. Since there are no external inputs to M (all inputs are recorded on the input tape before the computation begins), all next-state mappings are the same. As shown in Section 3.2, let this one mapping be defined by a Boolean $|Q| \times |Q|$ matrix M_Δ whose rows and columns are indexed by configurations of M. A configuration of M is a tuple $(q, h_1, h_2, h_3, \boldsymbol{x})$ in which q is the current state, h_1, h_2, and h_3 are the positions of the heads on the input, output, and work tapes, respectively, and $\boldsymbol{x}$ is the current contents of the work tape. Since M computes a log-space transformation, it executes a polynomial number of steps. Thus, each configuration has length $O(\log n)$. Consequently, a single CREW PRAM can determine in $O(\log n)$ time whether an entry in row r and column c, where r and c are associated with configurations, has value 0 or 1. For concreteness, assign PRAM processor i to row r and column c of M_Δ, where $r = \lceil i/p(n) \rceil$ and $c = i - r \times p(n)$, quantities that can be computed in $O(\log^2 n)$ steps.

The circuit $C(M, n)$ simulating M is obtained via a prefix computation on $p(n)$ copies of the matrix M_Δ using matrix multiplication as the associative operator. (See Section 3.2.)

Once $C(M, n)$ has been written into the common memory, it can be evaluated by assigning one processor per gate and then computing its value as many times as the depth of $C(M, n)$. This involves a four-phase operation in which the jth processor reads each of the at most two arguments of the jth gate in the first two phases, computes its value in the third, and then writes it to common memory in the fourth. This process is repeated as many times as the depth of the circuit $C(M, n)$, thereby insuring that correct values for gates propagate throughout the circuit. Again concurrent reads and exclusive writes suffice. ■

These two results (and Problem 8.37) imply the result stated below, namely, that the binary functions computed by circuits with polynomial size and poly-logarithmic depth are the same as those computed by the CREW PRAM with polynomially many processors and poly-logarithmic time.

THEOREM 8.14.1 *The functions $f : \mathcal{B}^* \mapsto \mathcal{B}^*$ computed by circuits of polynomial-size and poly-logarithmic depth are the same as those computed by the CREW PRAM with a polynomial number of processors and poly-logarithmic time.*

8.14.2 The Parallel Computation Thesis

A deep connection exists between serial space and parallel time. The **parallel computation thesis** states that sequential space and parallel time are polynomially related; that is, if there exists a sequential algorithm that uses space S, then there exists a parallel algorithm using time $p(S)$ for some polynomial p and vice versa. There is strong evidence that this hypothesis holds.

In this section we set the stage for discussing the parallel computation thesis in a limited way by showing that every log-space reduction (on a Turing machine) can be realized by a CREW PRAM in time $O\left(\log^2 n\right)$ with polynomially many processors. This implies that if a **P**-complete problem can be solved on a PRAM with polynomially many processors in poly-logarithmic time, then so can every problem in **P**, an unlikely prospect.

LEMMA 8.14.3 *Log-space transformations can be realized by CREW PRAMs with polynomially many processors in time $O(\log^2 n)$.*

> **Proof** We use the CREW PRAM described in the proof of Lemma 8.14.2. The processors in this PRAM are then assigned to perform the matrix operations in the order required for a parallel prefix computation. (See Section 2.6.) If we assign $|Q(n)|^2$ processors per matrix multiplication operation, each operation can be done in $O(\log|Q(n)|^2) = O(\log n)$ steps. Since the prefix computation has depth $O(\log n)$, the PRAM can perform the prefix computation in time $O(\log^2 n)$. The number of processors used is $p(n) \cdot O(|Q(n)|^2)$, which is a polynomial in n. Concurrent reads and exclusive writes suffice for these operations. ∎

Since a log-space transformation can be realized in poly-logarithmic time with polynomially many processors on a CREW PRAM, if a CREW PRAM solves a **P**-complete problem in poly-logarithmic time, we can compose such machines to form a CREW PRAM with poly-logarithmic time and polynomially many processors to solve an arbitrary problem in **P**.

THEOREM 8.14.2 *If a **P**-complete problem can be solved in poly-logarithmic time with polynomially many processors on a CREW PRAM, then so can all problems in **P** and all problems in **P** are fully parallelizable.*

8.15 Circuit Complexity Classes

In this section we introduce several important circuit complexity classes including **NC**, the languages recognized by uniform families of circuits whose size and depth are polynomial and poly-logarithmic in n, respectively, and **P/poly**, the largest set of languages $L \subset \mathcal{B}^*$ with the property that L is recognized by a (non-uniform) circuit family of polynomial size. We also derive relationships among these classes and previously defined classes.

8.15.1 Efficiently Parallelizable Languages

DEFINITION 8.15.1 *The class $\mathbf{NC}^k$ contains those languages L recognized by a uniform family of Boolean circuits of polynomial size and depth $O(\log^k n)$ in n, the length of an input. The class $\mathbf{NC}$ is the union of the classes $\mathbf{NC}^k$, $k \geq 1$; that is,*

$$\mathbf{NC} = \bigcup_{k \geq 1} \mathbf{NC}^k$$

In Section 8.14 we explored the connection between circuit size and depth and PRAM time and number of processors and concluded that circuits having polynomial size and poly-logarithmic depth compute the same languages as do PRAMs with a polynomial number of processors and poly-logarithmic parallel time.

The class **NC** is considered to be the largest feasibly parallelizable class of languages. By **feasible** we mean that the number of gates (equivalently processors) is no more than polynomial in the length n of the input and by **parallelizable** we mean that circuit depth (equivalently computation time) must be no more than poly-logarithmic in n. Feasibly parallelizable languages meet both requirements.

The prefix circuits introduced in Section 2.6 belong to $\mathbf{NC}^1$, as do circuits constructed with prefix operations, such as binary addition and subtraction (see Section 2.7) and the circuits for solutions of linear recurrences (see Problem 2.24). (Strictly speaking, these functions are not predicates and do not define languages. However, comparisons between their values and a threshold converts them to predicates. In this section we liberally mix functions and predicates.) The class $\mathbf{NC}^1$ also contains functions associated with integer multiplication and division.

The fast Fourier transform (see Section 6.7.3) and merging networks (see Section 6.8) can both be realized by algebraic and combinatorial circuits of depth $O(\log n)$, where n is the number of circuit inputs. If the additions and multiplications of the FFT are done over a ring of integers modulo m for some m, the FFT can be realized by a circuit of depth $O(\log^2 n)$. If the items to be merged are represented in binary, a comparison operator can be realized with depth $O(\log n)$ and merging can also be done with a circuit of depth $O(\log^2 n)$. Thus, both problems are in $\mathbf{NC}^2$.

When matrices are defined over a field of characteristic zero, the inverse of invertible matrices (see Section 6.5.5) can be computed by an algebraic circuit of depth $O(\log^2 n)$. If the matrix entries when represented as binary numbers have size n, the ring operations may be realized in terms of binary addition and multiplication, and matrix inversion is in $\mathbf{NC}^3$.

Also, it follows from Theorem 8.13.3 that the nth circuit in the log-space uniform families of circuits has polynomial size and depth $O(\log^2 n)$; that is, it is contained in $\mathbf{NC}^2$. Also contained in this set is the transitive closure of a Boolean matrix (see Section 6.4). Since the circuits constructed in Chapter 3 to simulate finite-state machines as well as polynomial-time Turing machines are log-space uniform (see Theorem 8.13.1), each of these circuit families is in $\mathbf{NC}^2$.

We now relate these complexity classes to one another and to **P**.

THEOREM 8.15.1 *For $k \geq 2$,* $\mathbf{NC}^1 \subseteq \mathbf{L} \subseteq \mathbf{NL} \subseteq \mathbf{NC}^2 \subseteq \mathbf{NC}^k \subseteq \mathbf{NC} \subseteq \mathbf{P}$.

Proof The containment $\mathbf{L} \subseteq \mathbf{NL}$ is obvious. The containment $\mathbf{NL} \subseteq \mathbf{NC}^2$ is a restriction of the result of Theorem 8.13.3 to $r(n) = O(\log n)$. The containments $\mathbf{NC}^2 \subseteq \mathbf{NC}^k \subseteq \mathbf{NC}$ follow from the definitions. The last containment, $\mathbf{NC} \subseteq \mathbf{P}$, is a consequence of the fact that the circuit on n inputs in a log-space uniform family of circuits, call it C_n, can be generated in polynomial time by a Turing machine that can then evaluate C_n in a time quadratic in its length, that is, in polynomial time. (Theorems 8.5.8 and 8.13.2 apply.)

The first containment, namely $\mathbf{NC}^1 \subseteq \mathbf{L}$, is slightly more difficult to establish. Given a language $L \in \mathbf{NC}^1$, consider the problem of recognizing whether or not a string w is in L. This recognition task is done in log-space by invoking two log-space transformations, as is now explained.

The first log-space transformation generates the nth circuit, C_n, in the family recognizing L. C_n has value 1 if w is in L and 0 otherwise. By definition, C_n has size polynomial in n. Also, each gate is described by a straight-line program, as explained in Section 2.2.

The second log-space transformation evaluates the circuit with temporary work space proportional to the maximal length of such strings. If the strings identifying gates have larger length, their transformation would use more space. (Note that it is easy to identify gates with an $O(\log^2 n)$-length string(s) by concatenating the number of each gate on the path to it, including itself.) For this reason we give an efficient encoding of gate locations.

The gates of circuits in $\mathbf{NC}^1$ generally have fan-out exceeding 1. That is, they have more than one parent gate in the circuit. We describe how to identify gates with strings that may associate multiple strings with a gate. We walk the graph, which is the circuit, starting from the output vertex and moving toward input vertices. The output gate is identified with the empty string string ϵ. If we reach a gate g via a parent whose string is $\boldsymbol{p}$, g is identified by $\boldsymbol{p}0$ or $\boldsymbol{p}1$. If the parent has only one descendant, as would be the case for NOT gates and inputs, we represent g by $\boldsymbol{p}0$. If it has two descendants, as would be the case for AND and OR, and g has the smaller gate number, its string is $\boldsymbol{p}0$; otherwise it is $\boldsymbol{p}1$.

The algorithm to produce each of these binary strings can be executed in logarithmic space because one need only walk each path in the circuit from the output to inputs. The tuple defining each gate contains the gate numbers of its predecessors, $O(\log n)$-length numbers, and the algorithm need only carry one such number at a time in its working memory to find the location of a predecessor gate in the input string containing the description of the circuit.

The second log-space transformation evaluates the circuit using the binary strings describing the circuit. It visits the input vertex with the lexicographically smallest string and determines its value. It then evaluates the gate whose string is that of the input vertex minus the last bit. Even though it may have to revisit all gates on the path to this vertex to do this, $O(\log n)$ space is used. If this gate is either a) AND and the input has value 0, b) OR and the input has value 1, or c) NOT, the value of the gate is decided. If the gate has more than one input and its value is not decided, the other input to it is evaluated (the one with suffix 1). Because the second input to the gate is evaluated only if needed, its value determines the value of the gate. This process is repeated at each gate in the circuit until the output gate is reached and its value computed. Since this procedure keeps only one path of length $O(\log n)$ active at a time, the algorithm uses space $O(\log n)$. ∎

An important open question is whether the complexity hierarchy of this theorem collapses and, if so, where. For example, is it true that a problem in $\mathbf{P}$ is also in $\mathbf{NC}$? If so, all serial polynomial-time problems are parallelizable with a number of processing elements polynomial in the length of the input and poly-logarithmic time, an unlikely prospect.

8.15.2 Circuits of Polynomial Size

We now examine the class of languages **P/poly** and show that they are exactly the languages recognized by Boolean circuits of polynomial size. To set the stage we introduce advice and pairing functions.

DEFINITION 8.15.2 *An **advice function** $a : \mathbb{N} \mapsto \mathcal{B}^*$ maps natural numbers to binary strings. A **polynomial advice function** is an advice function for which $|a(n)| \leq p(n)$ for $p(n)$ a polynomial function in n.*

DEFINITION 8.15.3 *A **pairing function** $<,> : \mathcal{B}^* \times \mathcal{B}^* \mapsto \mathcal{B}^*$ encodes pairs of binary strings $\boldsymbol{x}$ and $\boldsymbol{y}$ with two end markers and a separator (a comma) into the binary string $< \boldsymbol{x}, \boldsymbol{y} >$.*

Pairing functions can be very easy to describe and compute. For example, $< x, y >$ can be implemented by representing 0 by 01, 1 by 10, both $<$ and $>$ by 11, and , (comma) by 00. Thus, $< 0010, 110 >$ is encoded as 11010110010010100111. It is clearly trivial to identify, extract, and decode each component of the pair. We are now prepared to define **P/poly**.

DEFINITION 8.15.4 *Let* $a : \mathbb{N} \mapsto \mathcal{B}^*$ *be a polynomial advice function.* **P/poly** *is the set of languages* $L = \{w \mid < w, a(|w|) > \in A\}$ *for which there is a language A in* **P**.

The **advice** $a(|w|)$ given on a string w in a language $L \in$ **P/poly** is the same for all strings of the same length. Furthermore, $< w, a(|w|) >$ must be easy to recognize, namely, recognizable in polynomial time.

The subset of the languages in **P/poly** for which the advice function is the empty string is exactly the languages in **P**, that is, **P** $\subseteq$ **P/poly**.

The following result is the principal result of this section. It gives two different interpretations of the advice given on strings.

THEOREM 8.15.2 *A language L is recognizable by a family of circuits of polynomial size if and only if* $L \in$ **P/poly**.

> **Proof** Let L be recognizable by a family $\mathcal{C}$ of circuits of polynomial size. We show that it is in **P/poly**.
>
> Let $\overline{C}_n$ be an encoding of the circuit C_n in $\mathcal{C}$ that recognizes strings in $L \cap \mathcal{B}^n$. Let the advice function $a(n) = \overline{C}_n$ and let $w \in \mathcal{B}^*$ have length n. Then, $w \in \mathcal{B}^n$ if and only if the value of C_n on w is 1. Since w has length polynomial in n, $w \in \mathcal{B}^n$ if and only if the pairing function $< w, a(|w|) >$ is an instance of CIRCUIT SAT, which has been shown to be in **P**. (See Theorem 8.13.2.)
>
> On the other hand, suppose that $L \in$ **P/poly**. We show that L is recognizable by circuits of polynomial size. By definition there is an advice function $a : \mathbb{N} \mapsto \mathcal{B}^*$ and a language $A \in$ **P** for L such that for all $w \in L$, $< w, a(|w|) > \in A$. Since $A \in$ **P**, there is a polynomial-time DTM that accepts $< w, a(|w|) >$. By Theorem 8.13.1 there is a circuit of polynomial size that recognizes $< w, a(|w|) >$. The string $a(|w|)$ is constant for strings w of length n. Thus, the circuit for $A \cap \mathcal{B}^n$ to which is supplied the constant string $a(|w|)$ is a circuit of length polynomial in n that accepts strings w in L. $\blacksquare$

Problems

MATHEMATICAL PRELIMINARIES

8.1 Show that if strings over an alphabet $\mathcal{A}$ with at least two letters are encoded over a one-letter alphabet (a **unary encoding**), then strings of length n over $\mathcal{A}$ require strings of length exponential in n in the unary encoding.

8.2 Show that the polynomial function $p(n) = K_1 n^k$ can be computed in $O(\log^2 n)$ serial steps from n and for constants $K_1 \geq 1$ and $k \geq 1$ on a RAM when additions require one unit of time.

SERIAL COMPUTATIONAL MODELS

8.3 Given an instance of satisfiability, namely, a set of clauses over a set of literals and values for the variables, show that the clauses can be evaluated in time quadratic in the length of the instance.

8.4 Consider the RAM of Section 8.4.1. Let $l(\mathcal{I})$ be the length, measured in bits, of the contents $\mathcal{I}$ of the RAMs input registers. Similarly, let $l(v)$ be the maximal length of any integer addressed by an instruction in the RAMs program. Show that after k steps the contents of any RAM memory location is at most $k + l(\mathcal{I}) + l(v)$.

Given an example of a computation that produces a word of length k.

Hint: Consider which instructions have the effect of increasing the length of an integer used or produced by the RAM program.

8.5 Consider the RAM of Section 8.4.1. Assume the RAM executes T steps. Describe a Turing-machine simulation of this RAM that uses space proportional to T^2 measured in bits.

Hint: Represent each RAM memory location visited during a computation by an (address, contents) pair. When a RAM location is updated, fill the cells on the second tape containing the old (address, contents) pair with a special "blank" character and add the new (address, contents) pair to the end of the list of such pairs. Use the results of Problem 8.4 to bound the length of individual words.

8.6 Consider the RAM of Section 8.4.1. Using the result of Problem 8.5, describe a multi-tape Turing machine that simulates in $O(T^3)$ steps a T-step computation by the RAM.

Hint: Let your machine have seven tapes: one to hold the input, a second to hold the contents of RAM memory recorded as (address, contents) pairs separated and terminated by appropriate markers, a third to hold the current value of the program counter, a fourth to hold the memory address being sought, and three tapes for operands and results. On the input tape place the program to be executed and the input on which it is to be executed. Handle the second tape as suggested in Problem 8.5. When performing an operation that has two operands, place them on the fifth and sixth tapes and the result on the seventh tape.

8.7 Justify using the number of tape cells as a measure of space for the Turing machine when the more concrete measure of bits is used for the space measure for the RAM.

CLASSIFICATION OF DECISION PROBLEMS

8.8 Given a Turing machine, deterministic or not, show that there exists another Turing machine with a larger tape alphabet that performs the same computation but in a number of steps and number of tape cells that are smaller by constant factors.

8.9 Show that strings in TRAVELING SALESPERSON can be accepted by a deterministic Turing machine in an exponential number of steps.

COMPLEMENTS OF COMPLEXITY CLASSES

8.10 Show that VALIDITY is log-space complete for **coNP**.

8.11 Prove that the complements of **NP**-complete problems are **coNP**-complete.

8.12 Show that the complexity class **P** is contained in the intersection of **NP** and **coNP**.

8.13 Demonstrate that **coNP** $\subseteq$ **PSPACE**.

8.14 Prove that if a **coNP**-complete problem is in **NP**, then **NP** = **coNP**.

REDUCTIONS

8.15 If $\mathcal{P}_1$ and $\mathcal{P}_2$ are decision problems, a **Turing reduction** from $\mathcal{P}_1$ to $\mathcal{P}_2$ is any OTM that solves $\mathcal{P}_1$ given an oracle for $\mathcal{P}_2$. Show that the reductions of Section 2.4 are Turing reductions.

8.16 Prove that the reduction given in Section 10.9.1 of a pebble game to a branching computation is a Turing reduction. (See Problem 8.15.)

8.17 Show that if a problem $\mathcal{P}_1$ can be Turing-reduced to problem $\mathcal{P}_2$ by a polynomial-time OTM and $\mathcal{P}_2$ is in **P**, then $\mathcal{P}_1$ is also in **P**.

Hint: Since each invocation of the oracle can be done deterministically in polynomial time in the length of the string written on the oracle tape, show that it can be done in time polynomial in the length of the input to the OTM.

8.18 a) Show that every fixed power of an integer written as a binary k-tuple can be computed by a DTM in space $O(k)$.

   b) Show that every fixed polynomial in an integer written as a binary k-tuple can be computed by a DTM in space $O(k)$.

Hint: Show that carry-save addition can be used to multiply two k-bit integers with work space $O(k)$.

HARD AND COMPLETE PROBLEMS

8.19 The class of polynomial-time Turing reductions are Turing reductions in which the OTM runs in time polynomial in the length of its input. Show that the class of Turing reductions is transitive.

P-COMPLETE PROBLEMS

8.20 Show that numbers can be assigned to gates in an instance of MONOTONE CIRCUIT VALUE that corresponds to an instance of CIRCUIT VALUE in Theorem 8.9.1 so that the reduction from it to MONOTONE CIRCUIT VALUE can be done in logarithmic space.

8.21 Prove that LINEAR PROGRAMMING described below is **P**-complete.

LINEAR PROGRAMMING
Instance: Integer-valued $m \times n$ matrix A and column m-vectors $\boldsymbol{b}$ and $\boldsymbol{c}$.
Answer: "Yes" if there is a rational column n-vector $\boldsymbol{x} > 0$ such that $A\boldsymbol{x} < \boldsymbol{b}$ and $\boldsymbol{x}$ maximizes $\boldsymbol{b}^T\boldsymbol{x}$.

NP-COMPLETE PROBLEMS

8.22 A **Horn clause** has at most one **positive literal** (an instance of x_i). Every other literal in a Horn clause is a **negative literal** (an instance of $\overline{x}_i$). HORN SATISFIABILITY is an instance of SATISFIABILITY in which each clause is a Horn clause. Show that HORN SATISFIABILITY is in **P**.

Hint: If all literals in a clause are negative, the clause is satisfied only if some associated variables have value 1. If a clause has one positive literal, say y, and negative literals, say $\overline{x}_1, \overline{x}_2, \ldots, \overline{x}_k$, then the clause is satisfied if and only if the implication $x_1 \wedge x_2 \wedge \cdots \wedge x_k \Rightarrow y$ is true. Thus, y has value 1 when each of these variables has value 1. Construct a set $\mathcal{T}$ of variables, if any, that appear alone in positive literals in a clause. Then, cycle through all implications and for each implication all of whose left-hand side variables appear in $\mathcal{T}$ but whose right-hand side variable does not, add this variable to $\mathcal{T}$. Since $\mathcal{T}$ grows until all left-hand sides is satisfied, this procedure terminates.

8.23 Describe a polynomial-time algorithm to determine whether an instance of CIRCUIT SAT is a "yes" instance when the circuit in question consists of a layer of AND gates followed by a layer of OR gates. Inputs are connected to AND gates and the output gate is an OR gate.

8.24 Prove that the CLIQUE problem defined below is **NP**-complete.

CLIQUE
Instance: The description of an undirected graph $G = (V, E)$ and an integer k.
Answer: "Yes" if there is a set of k vertices of G such that all vertices are adjacent.

8.25 Prove that the HALF CLIQUE problem defined below is **NP**-complete.

HALF CLIQUE
Instance: The description of an undirected graph $G = (V, E)$ in which $|V|$ is even and an integer k.
Answer: "Yes" if G contains a clique on $|V|/2$ vertices or has more than k edges.

Hint: Try reducing an instance of CLIQUE on a graph with m vertices and a clique of size k to this problem by expanding the number of vertices and edges to create a graph that has $|V| \geq m$ vertices and a clique of size $|V|/2$. Show that a test for the condition that G contains more than k edges can be done very efficiently by counting the number of bits among the variables describing edges.

8.26 Show that the NODE COVER problem defined below is **NP**-complete.

NODE COVER
Instance: The description of an indirected graph $G = (V, E)$ and an integer k.
Answer: "Yes" if there is a set of k vertices such that every edge contains at least one of these vertices.

8.27 Prove that the HAMILTONIAN PATH decision problem defined below is **NP**-complete.

HAMILTONIAN PATH
Instance: The description of an undirected graph G.
Answer: "Yes" if there is a path visiting each node once.

Hint: 3-SAT can be reduced to HAMILTONIAN PATH, but the construction is challenging. First, add literals to clauses in an instance of 3-SAT so that each clause has

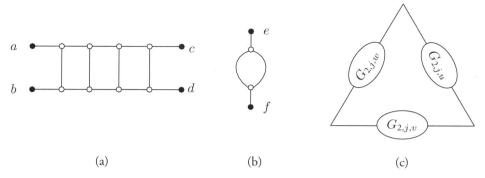

Figure 8.23 Gadgets used to reduce 3-SAT to HAMILTONIAN PATH.

three literals. Second, construct and interconnect three types of subgraphs (gadgets). Figures 8.23(a) and (b) show the first and second of theses gadgets, G_1 and G_2.

There is one first gadget for each variable x_i, $1 \leq i \leq n$, denoted $G_{1,i}$. The left path between the two middle vertices in $G_{1,i}$ is associated with the value $x_i = 1$ and the right path is associated with the complementary value, $x_i = 0$. Vertex f of $G_{1,i}$ is identified with vertex e of $G_{1,i+1}$ for $1 \leq i \leq n-1$, vertex e of $G_{1,1}$ is connected only to a vertex in $G_{1,1}$, and vertex f of $G_{1,n}$ is connected to the clique described below.

There is one second gadget for each literal in each clause. Thus, if x_i ($\overline{x}_i$) is a literal in clause c_j, then we create a gadget $G_{2,j,i,1}$ ($G_{2,j,i,0}$).

Since a HAMILTONIAN PATH touches every vertex, a path through $G_{2,j,i,v}$ for $v \in \{0, 1\}$ passes either from a to c or from b to d.

For each $1 \leq i \leq n$ the two parallel edges of $G_{1,i}$ are broken open and two vertices appear in each of them. For each instance of the literal x_i ($\overline{x}_i$), connect the vertices a and c of $G_{2,j,i,1}$ ($G_{2,j,i,0}$) to the pair of vertices on the left (right) that are created in $G_{1,i}$. Connect the b vertex of one literal in clause c_j to the d vertex of another one, as suggested in Fig. 8.23(c).

The third gadget has vertices g and h and a connecting edge. One of these two vertices, h, is connected in a clique with the b and d vertices of the gadgets $G_{2,j,i,v}$ and the f vertex of $G_{1,n}$.

This graph has a Hamiltonian path between g and the e vertex of $G_{1,1}$ if and only if the instance of 3-SAT is a "yes" instance.

8.28 Show that the TRAVELING SALESPERSON decision problem defined below is **NP-**complete.

TRAVELING SALESPERSON
Instance: An integer k and a set of $n(n-1)/2$ distances $\{d_{1,2}, d_{1,3}, \ldots, d_{1,n}, d_{2,3}, \ldots, d_{2,n}, \ldots, d_{n-1,n}\}$ between n cities.
Answer: "Yes" if there is a **tour** (an ordering) $\{i_1, i_2, \ldots, i_n\}$ of the cities such that the length $l = d_{i_1,i_2} + d_{i_2,i_3} + \cdots + d_{i_n,i_1}$ of the tour satisfies $l \leq k$.

Hint: Try reducing HAMILTONIAN PATH to TRAVELING SALESPERSON.

8.29 Give a proof that the PARTITION problem defined below is **NP**-complete.

PARTITION
Instance: A set $Q = \{a_1, a_2, \ldots, a_n\}$ of positive integers.
Answer: "Yes" if there is a subset of Q that adds to $\frac{1}{2} \sum_{1 \le i \le n} a_i$.

PSPACE-COMPLETE PROBLEMS

8.30 Show that the procedure `tree_eval` described in the proof of Theorem 8.12.1 can be modified slightly to apply to the evaluation of the trees generated in the proof of Theorem 8.12.3.

   Hint: A vertex of in-degree k can be replaced by a binary tree of k leaves and depth $\log_2 k$.

THE CIRCUIT MODEL OF COMPUTATION

8.31 Prove that the class of circuits described in Section 3.1 that simulate a finite-state machine are uniform.

8.32 Generalize Theorems 8.13.1 and 8.13.2 to uniform circuit families and Turing machines that use more than logarithmic space and polynomial time, respectively.

8.33 Write a $O(\log^2 n)$-space program based on the one in Fig. 8.20 to describe a circuit for the transitive closure of an $n \times n$ matrix based on matrix squaring.

THE PARALLEL RANDOM-ACCESS MACHINE MODEL

8.34 Complete the proof of Lemma 8.14.2 by making specific assignments of data to memory locations. Also, provide formulas for the assignment of processors to tasks.

8.35 Give a definition of a **log-space uniform family of PRAMs** for which Lemma 8.14.1 can be extended to show that the function $f : \mathcal{B}^* \mapsto \mathcal{B}^*$ computed by a log-space family of PRAMs can also be computed by a log-space uniform family of circuits satisfying the conditions of Lemma 8.14.1.

8.36 Exhibit a non-uniform family of PRAMs that can solve problems that are not recursively enumerable.

8.37 Lemma 8.14.1 is stated for PRAMs in which the CPU does not access a common memory address larger than $O(p(n)t(n))$. In particular, this model does not permit indirect addressing. Show that this theorem can be extended to RAM CPUs that do allow indirect addressing by using the representation for memory accesses in Problem 8.6.

Chapter Notes

The classification of languages by the resources needed for their recognition is a very large subject capable of book-length study. The reader interested in going beyond the introduction given here is advised to consult one of the readily available references. The *Handbook of Theoretical Computer Science* contains three survey articles on this subject by van Embde Boas [344], Johnson [149], and Karp and Ramachandran [158]

The first examines simulation of one computational model by another for a large range of models. The second provides a large catalog of complexity classes and relationships between them. The third examines parallel algorithms and complexity. Other sources for more information on this topic are the books by Hopcroft and Ullman [140], Lewis and Papadimitriou [198], Balcázar, Díaz, and Gabarrò on structural complexity [27], Garey and Johnson [108] on the theory of **NP**-completeness, Greenlaw, Hoover, and Ruzzo [119] on **P**-completeness, and Papadimitriou [232] on computational complexity.

The Turing machine was defined by Alan Turing in 1936 [335], as was the oracle Turing machine. Random-access machines were introduced by Shepherdson and Sturgis [305] and the performance of RAMs was analyzed by Cook and Reckhow [77].

Hartmanis, Lewis, and Stearns [126,127] gave the study of time and space complexity classes its impetus. Their papers contain many of the basic theorems on complexity classes, including the space and time hierarchy theorems stated in Section 8.5.1. The gap theorem was obtained by Trakhtenbrot [331] and rediscovered by Borodin [51]. Blum [46] developed machine-independent complexity measures and established a speedup theorem showing that for some languages there is no single fastest recognition algorithm [47].

Many individuals identified and recognized the importance of the classes **P** and **NP**. Cook [74] formalized **NP**, emphasized the importance of polynomial-time reducibility, and exhibited the first **NP**-complete problem, SATISFIABILITY. Karp [158] then demonstrated that a number of other combinatorial problems, including TRAVELING SALESPERSON, are **NP**-complete. Cook used Turing reductions in his classification whereas Karp used polynomial-time transformations. Independently and almost simultaneously Levin [197] (see also [332]) was led to concepts similar to the above.

The relationship between nondeterministic and deterministic space (Theorem 8.5.5 and Corollary 8.5.1) was established by Savitch [294]. The proof that nondeterministic space classes are closed under complementation (Theorem 8.6.2 and Corollary 8.6.2) is independently due to Szelepscényi [319] and Immerman [144].

Theorem 8.6.4, showing that PRIMALITY is in **NP** ∩ **coNP**, is due to Pratt [254].

Cook [75] defined the concept of a **P**-complete problem and exhibited the first such problem. He was followed quickly by Jones and Laaser [152] and Galil [107]. Ladner [183] showed that circuits simulating Turing machines (see [283]) could be constructed in logarithmic space, thereby establishing that CIRCUIT VALUE is **P**-complete. Goldschlager [116] demonstrated that MONOTONE CIRCUIT VALUE is **P**-complete. Valiant [342] and Cook established that LINEAR INEQUALITIES is **P**-hard, and Khachian [163] showed that this problem is in **P**. The proof that DTM ACCEPTANCE is **P**-complete is due to Johnson [150].

Cook [74] gave the first proof that SATISFIABILITY is **NP**-complete and also gave the reduction to 3-SAT. Independently, Levin [197] (see also [332]) was led to similar concepts for combinatorial problems. Schäfer [296] showed that NAESAT is **NP**-complete. Karp [158] established that 0-1 INTEGER PROGRAMMING, 3-COLORING, EXACT COVER, SUBSET SUM, TASK SEQUENCING, and INDEPENDENT SET are **NP**-complete.

The proof that 2-SAT is in **NL** (Theorem 8.11.1) is found in Papadimitriou [232].

Karp [158] exhibited a **PSPACE**-complete problem, Meyer and Stockmeyer [313] demonstrated that QUANTIFIED SATISFIABILITY is **PSPACE**-complete and Schäfer established that GENERALIZED GEOGRAPHY is **PSPACE**-complete [296].

The notion of a uniform circuit was introduced by Borodin [52] and has been examined by many others. (See [119].) Borodin [52] established the connection between nondeterministic space and circuit depth stated in Theorem 8.13.3. Stockmeyer and Vishkin [311] show how to simulate efficiently the PRAM with circuits and vice versa. (See also [158].) The class **NC** was defined by Cook [76]. Theorem 8.15.2 is due to Pippenger [243].

A large variety of parallel computational models have been developed. (See van Embde Boas [344] and Greenlaw, Hoover, and Ruzzo [119].) The PRAM was introduced by Fortune and Wyllie [102] and Goldschlager [117,118].

Several problems on the efficient simulation of RAMs are from Papadimitriou [229].

Circuit Complexity

The circuit complexity of a binary function is measured by the size or depth of the smallest or shallowest circuit for it. Circuit complexity derives its importance from the corollary to Theorem 3.9.2; namely, if a function has a large circuit size over a complete basis of fixed fan-in, then the time on a Turing machine required to compute it is large. The importance of this observation is illustrated by the following fact. For $n \geq 1$, let $f_L^{(n)}$ be the characteristic function of an **NP**-complete language L, where $f_L^{(n)}$ has value 1 on strings of length n in L and value 0 otherwise. If $f_L^{(n)}$ has super-polynomial circuit size for all sufficiently large n, then $\mathbf{P} \neq \mathbf{NP}$.

In this chapter we introduce methods for deriving lower bounds on circuit size and depth. Unfortunately, it is generally much more difficult to derive good lower bounds on circuit complexity than good upper bounds; an upper bound measures the size or depth of a particular circuit whereas a lower bound must rule out a smaller size or depth for all circuits. As a consequence, the lower bounds derived for functions realized by circuits over complete bases of bounded fan-in are often weak.

In attempting to understand lower bounds for complete bases, researchers have studied monotone circuits over the monotone basis and bounded-depth circuits over the basis {AND, OR, NOT} in which the first two gates are allowed to have unbounded fan-in. Formula size, which is approximately the size of the smallest circuit with fan-out 1, has also been studied. Lower bounds to formula size also produce lower bounds to circuit depth, a measure of the parallel time needed for a function.

Research on these restricted circuit models has led to some impressive results. Exponential lower bounds on circuit size have been derived for monotone functions over the monotone basis and functions such as parity when realized by bounded-depth circuits. Unfortunately, the methods used to obtain these results may not apply to complete bases of bounded fan-in. Fortunately, it has been shown that the *slice functions* have about the same circuit size over both the monotone and standard (non-monotone) bases. This may help resolve the $\mathbf{P} \overset{?}{=} \mathbf{NP}$ question, since there are **NP**-complete slice problems.

Despite the difficulty of deriving lower bounds, circuit complexity continues to offer one of the methods of highest potential for distinguishing between **P** and **NP**.

9.1 Circuit Models and Measures

In this section we characterize types of logic circuits by their bases and the fan-in and fan-out of basis elements. We consider bases that are complete and incomplete and that have bounded and unbounded fan-in. We also consider circuits in which the fan-out is restricted and unrestricted. Each of these factors can affect the size and depth of a circuit.

9.1.1 Circuit Models

The (general) **logic circuit** is the graph of a straight-line program in which the variables have value 0 or 1 and the operations are Boolean functions $g : \mathcal{B}^p \mapsto \mathcal{B}, p \geq 1$. (Boolean functions have one binary value. Logic circuits are defined in Section 1.2 and discussed at length in Chapter 2.) The vertices in a logic circuit are labeled with Boolean operations and are called **gates**; the set of different gate types used in a circuit is called the **basis** (denoted Ω) for the circuit. The **fan-in of a basis** is the maximal fan-in of any function in the basis. A circuit **computes** the binary function $f : \mathcal{B}^n \mapsto \mathcal{B}^m$, which is the mapping from the n circuit inputs to the m gate outputs designated as circuit outputs.

The **standard basis**, denoted Ω_0, is the set $\{\text{AND}, \text{OR}, \text{NOT}\}$ in which AND and OR have fan-in 2. The **full two-input basis**, denoted B_2, consists of all two-input Boolean functions. The **dyadic unate basis**, denoted U_2, consists of all Boolean functions of the form $(x^a \wedge y^b)^c$ for constants a, b, c in $\mathcal{B}$. Here $x^1 = x$ and $x^0 = \overline{x}$.

A **basis** Ω is **complete** if every binary function can be computed by a circuit over Ω. The bases Ω_0, B_2, and U_2 are complete, as is the basis consisting of the NAND gate computing the function $x \text{ NAND } y = \overline{x \wedge y}$. (See Problem 2.5.)

The bounded fan-out circuit model specifies a bound on the fan-out of a circuit. As we shall see, the **fan-out-1 circuit** plays a special role related to circuit depth. Each circuit of fan-out 1 corresponds to a **formula** in which the operators are the functions associated with vertices of the circuit. Figure 9.1 shows an example of a circuit of fan-out 1 over the standard basis and its associated formula. (See also Problem 9.9.) Although each input variable appears once in this example, Boolean functions generally require multiple instances of variables (have fan-out greater than 1). Formula size is studied at length in Section 9.4.

To define the monotone circuits, we need an ordering of binary n-tuples. Two such tuples, $\boldsymbol{x} = (x_1, x_2, \ldots, x_n)$ and $\boldsymbol{y} = (y_1, y_2, \ldots, y_n)$, are in the relation $\boldsymbol{x} \leq \boldsymbol{y}$ if for all $1 \leq i \leq n$, $x_i \leq y_i$, where $0 \leq 0$, $1 \leq 1$, and $0 \leq 1$, but $1 \not\leq 0$. (Thus, $001011 \leq 101111$, but $011011 \not\leq 101111$.)

A **monotone circuit** is a circuit over the monotone basis $\Omega_{\text{mon}} = \{\text{AND}, \text{OR}\}$ in which the fan-in is 2. There is a direct correspondence between monotone circuits and monotone functions. A **monotone function** is a function $f : \mathcal{B}^n \mapsto \mathcal{B}^m$ that is either **monotone increasing**, that is, for all $\boldsymbol{x}, \boldsymbol{y} \in \mathcal{B}^n$, if $\boldsymbol{x} \leq \boldsymbol{y}$, then $f(\boldsymbol{x}) \leq f(\boldsymbol{y})$, or is **monotone decreasing**, that is, for all $\boldsymbol{x}, \boldsymbol{y} \in \mathcal{B}^n$, if $\boldsymbol{x} \leq \boldsymbol{y}$, then $f(\boldsymbol{x}) \geq f(\boldsymbol{y})$. Unless stated explicitly, a monotone function will be understood to be a monotone increasing function.

A monotone Boolean function has the following expansion on the first variable, as the reader can show. (See Problem 9.10.) A similar expansion is possible on any variable.

$$f(x_1, x_2, \ldots, x_n) = f(0, x_2, \ldots, x_n) \vee (x_1 \wedge f(1, x_2, \ldots, x_n))$$

By applying this expansion to every variable in succession, we see that each monotone function can be realized by a circuit over the monotone basis. Furthermore, the **monotone basis** Ω_{mon}

$$y = ((((x_7 \lor x_6) \land (x_5 \lor x_4)) \lor x_3) \land (x_2 \land x_1))$$

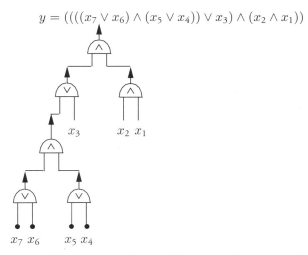

Figure 9.1 A circuit of fan-out 1 over a basis with fan-in 2 and a corresponding formula. The value y at the root is the AND of the value $(((x_7 \lor x_6) \land (x_5 \lor x_4)) \lor x_3)$ of the left subtree with the value $(x_2 \land x_1)$ of the right subtree.

is complete for the monotone functions, that is, every monotone function can be computed by a circuit over the basis Ω_{mon}. (See Problem 2.)

In Section 9.6 we show that some monotone functions on n variables require monotone circuits whose size is exponential in n. In particular, some monotone functions requiring exponential-size monotone circuits can be realized by polynomial-size circuits over the standard basis Ω_0. Thus, the absence of negation can result in a large increase in circuit size.

The **bounded-depth circuit** is a circuit over the standard basis Ω_0 where the fan-in of AND and OR gates is allowed to be unbounded, but the circuit depth is bounded. The conjunctive and disjunctive normal forms and the product-of-sums and sum-of-products normal forms realize arbitrary Boolean functions by circuits of depth 2 over Ω_0. (See Section 2.3.) In these normal forms negations are used only on the input variables. Note that any circuit over the standard basis can be converted to a circuit in which the NOT gates are applied only to the input variables. (See Problem 9.11.)

9.1.2 Complexity Measures

We now define the measures of complexity studied in this chapter. The **depth of a circuit** is the number of gates of fan-in 2 or more on the longest path in the circuit. (Note that NOT gates do not affect the depth measure.)

DEFINITION 9.1.1 *The **circuit size** of a binary function $f : \mathcal{B}^n \mapsto \mathcal{B}^m$ with respect to the basis Ω, denoted $C_\Omega(f)$, is the smallest number of gates in any circuit for f over the basis Ω. The **circuit size with fan-out s**, denoted $C_{s,\Omega}(f)$, is the circuit size of f when the circuit fan-out is limited to at most s.*

The **circuit depth** *of a binary function* $f : \mathcal{B}^n \mapsto \mathcal{B}^m$ *with respect to the basis* Ω, $D_\Omega(f)$, *is the depth of the smallest depth circuit for* f *over the basis* Ω. *The* **circuit depth with fan-out** s, *denoted* $D_{s,\Omega}(f)$, *is the circuit depth of* f *when the circuit fan-out is limited to at most* s.

The **formula size** *of a Boolean function* $f : \mathcal{B}^n \mapsto \mathcal{B}$ *with respect to a basis* Ω, $L_\Omega(f)$, *is the minimal number of input vertices in any circuit of fan-out 1 for* f *over the basis* Ω.

It is important to note the distinction between formula and circuit size: in the former the number of input vertices is counted, whereas in the latter it is the number of gates. A relationship between the two is shown in Lemma 9.2.2.

9.2 Relationships Among Complexity Measures

In this section we explore the effect on circuit complexity measures of a change in either the basis or the fan-out of a circuit. We also establish relationships between circuit depth and formula size.

9.2.1 Effect of Fan-Out on Circuit Size

It is interesting to ask how the circuit size and depth of a function change as the maximal fan-out of a circuit is reduced. This issue is important in understanding these complexity measures and in the use of technologies that limit the fan-out of gates. The following simple facts about trees are useful in comparing complexity measures. (See Problem 9.2.)

LEMMA 9.2.1 *A rooted tree of maximal fan-in* r *containing* k *vertices has at most* $k(r - 1) + 1$ *leaves and a rooted tree with* l *leaves and fan-in* r *has at most* $l - 1$ *vertices with fan-in 2 or more and at most* $2(l - 1)$ *edges.*

From the above result we establish the following connection between circuit size with fan-out 1 and formula size.

LEMMA 9.2.2 *Let* Ω *be a basis of fan-in* r. *For each* $f : \mathcal{B}^n \mapsto \mathcal{B}$ *the following inequalities hold between formula size,* $L_\Omega(f)$, *and fan-out-1 circuit size,* $C_{1,\Omega}(f)$:

$$(L_\Omega(f) - 1)/(r - 1) \leq C_{1,\Omega}(f) \leq 3L_\Omega(f) - 2$$

Proof The first inequality follows from the definition of formula size and the first result stated in Lemma 9.2.1 in which $k = C_{1,\Omega}(f)$. The second inequality also follows from Lemma 9.2.1. A tree with $L_\Omega(f)$ leaves has at most $L_\Omega(f) - 1$ vertices with fan-in of 2 or more and at most $2(L_\Omega(f) - 1)$ edges between vertices (including the leaves). Each of these edges can carry a NOT gate, as can the output gate, for a total of at most $2L_\Omega(f) - 1$ NOT gates. Thus, a circuit of fan-out 1 has at most $3L_\Omega(f) - 2$ gates. ■

As we now show, circuit size increases by at most a constant factor when the fan-out of the circuit is reduced to s for $s \geq 2$. Before developing this result we need a simple fact about a complete basis Ω, namely, that at most two gates are needed to compute the **identity function** $i(x) = x$, as shown in the next paragraph. If a basis contains AND or OR gates, the identity function can be obtained by attaching both of their inputs to the same source.

We are done if Ω contains a function such that by fixing all but one variable, $i(x)$ is computed. If not, then we look for a non-monotone function in Ω. Since some binary functions are non-monotone ($\overline{x}$, for example), some function g in a complete basis Ω is non-monotone. This means there exist tuples x and y for g, $x \leq y$, such that $g(x) = 1 > g(y) = 0$. Let u and v be the largest and smallest tuples, respectively, satisfying $x \leq u \leq v \leq y$ and $g(u) = 1$ and $g(v) = 0$. Then u and v differ in at most one position. Without loss of generality, let that position be the first and let the values in the remaining positions in both tuples be $(c_2, \ldots, c_n)$. It follows that $g(1, c_2, \ldots, c_n) = 0$ and $g(0, c_2, \ldots, c_n) = 1$ or $g(x, c_2, \ldots, c_n) = \overline{x}$. If $l(\Omega)$ is the number of gates from Ω needed to realize the identity function, then $l(\Omega) = 1$ or 2.

THEOREM 9.2.1 *Let Ω be a complete basis of fan-in r and let $f : \mathcal{B}^n \mapsto \mathcal{B}^m$. The following inequalities hold on $C_{s,\Omega}(f)$:*

$$C_{\Omega}(f) \leq C_{s+1,\Omega}(f) \leq C_{s,\Omega}(f) \leq C_{1,\Omega}(f)$$

Furthermore, $C_{s,\Omega}(f)$ has the following relationship to $C_{\Omega}(f)$ for $s \geq 2$:

$$C_{s,\Omega}(f) \leq C_{\Omega}(f)\left(1 + \frac{l(\Omega)(r-1)}{s-1}\right)$$

Proof The first set of inequalities holds because a smallest circuit with fan-out s is no smaller than a smallest circuit with fan-out $s + 1$, a less restrictive type of circuit.

The last inequality follows by constructing a tree of identity functions at each gate whose fan-out exceeds s. (See Fig. 9.2.) If a gate has fan-out $\phi > s$, reduce the fan-out to s and then attach an identity gate to one of these s outputs. This increases the fan-out from s to $s + s - 1$. If ϕ is larger than this number, repeat the process of adding an identity gate k times, where k is the smallest integer such that $s + k(s - 1) \geq \phi$ or is the largest integer such that $s + (k - 1)(s - 1) < \phi$. Thus, $k < (\phi - 1)/(s - 1)$.

Let ϕ_i denote the fan-out of the ith gate in a circuit for f of potentially unbounded fan-out and let k_i be the largest integer satisfying the following bound:

$$k_i < \frac{\phi_i - 1}{s - 1}$$

Then at most $\sum_i (k_i l(\Omega) + 1)$ gates are needed in the circuit of fan-out s to realize f, one for the ith gate in the original circuit and $k_i l(\Omega)$ gates for the k_i copies of the identity

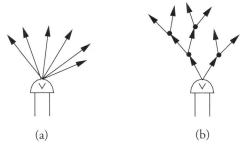

(a) (b)

Figure 9.2 Conversion of a vertex with fan-out more than s to a subtree with fan-out s, illustrated for $s = 2$.

function at the ith gate. Note that $\sum_i \phi_i$ is the number of edges directed away from gates in the original circuit. But since each edge directed away from a gate is an edge directed into a gate, this number is at most $rC_\Omega(f)$ since each gate has fan-in at most r.

It follows that the smallest number of gates in a circuit with fan-out s for f satisfies the following bound:

$$C_{s,\Omega}(f) \le C_\Omega(f) + l(\Omega) \sum_{i=1}^{C_\Omega(f)} \left(\frac{\phi_i - 1}{s - 1}\right) \le C_\Omega(f)\left(1 + \frac{l(\Omega)(r-1)}{s-1}\right)$$

which demonstrates that circuit size with a fan-out $s \ge 2$ differs from the unbounded fan-out circuit size by at most a constant factor. ■

With the construction employed in Theorem 9.2.1, an upper bound can be stated on $D_{s,\Omega}(f)$ that is proportional to the product of $D_\Omega(f)$ and $\log C_\Omega(f)$. (See Problem 9.12.) The upper bound stated above on $C_{s,\Omega}(f)$ can be achieved by a circuit that also achieves an upper bound on $D_{s,\Omega}(f)$ that is proportional to $D_\Omega(f)$ and $\log_r s$ [137].

9.2.2   Effect of Basis Change on Circuit Size and Depth

We now consider the effect of a change in basis on circuit size and depth. In the next section we examine the relationship between formula size and depth, from which we deduce the effect of a basis change on formula size.

LEMMA 9.2.3 *Given two complete bases, Ω_a and Ω_b, and a function $f : \mathcal{B}^n \mapsto \mathcal{B}^m$, the circuit size and depth of f in these two bases differ by at most constant multiplicative factors.*

Proof Because each basis is complete, every function in Ω_a can be computed by a fixed number of gates in Ω_b, and vice versa. Given a circuit with basis Ω_a, a circuit with basis Ω_b can be constructed by replacing each gate from Ω_a by a fixed number of gates from Ω_b. This has the effect of increasing the circuit size by at most a constant factor. It follows that $C_{\Omega_a}(f) = \Theta(C_{\Omega_b}(f))$. Since this construction also increases the depth by at most a constant factor, it follows that $D_{\Omega_a}(f) = \Theta(D_{\Omega_b}(f))$. ■

9.2.3   Formula Size Versus Circuit Depth

A logarithmic relationship exists between the formula size and circuit depth of a function, as we now show. If a formula is represented by a balanced tree, this result follows from the fact that the circuit fan-in is bounded. However, since we cannot guarantee that each formula corresponds to a balanced tree, we must find a way to balance an unbalanced tree.

To balance a formula and provide a bound on the circuit depth of a function in terms of formula size, we make use of the multiplexer function $f_{\text{mux}}^{(n)} : \mathcal{B}^{2^n + n} \mapsto \mathcal{B}$ on three inputs $f_{\text{mux}}^{(1)}(a, y_1, y_0)$. Here the value of a determines which of the two other values is returned.

$$f_{\text{mux}}^{(1)}(a, y_1, y_0) = \begin{cases} y_0 & a = 0 \\ y_1 & a = 1 \end{cases}$$

This function can be realized by

$$f_{\text{mux}}^{(1)}(a, y_1, y_0) = (\overline{a} \wedge y_0) \vee (a \wedge y_1)$$

The measure $d(\Omega)$ of a basis Ω defined below is used to obtain bounds on the circuit depth of a function in terms of its formula size.

DEFINITION 9.2.1 *Given a basis Ω of fan-in r, the constant $d(\Omega)$ is defined as follows:*

$$d(\Omega) = \left(D_\Omega \left(f_{\text{mux}}^{(1)} \right) + 1 \right) / \log_r \left(\frac{r+1}{r} \right)$$

Over the standard basis Ω_0, $d(\Omega_0) = 3.419$.

We now derive a **separator theorem for trees**. This is a theorem stating that a tree can be decomposed into two trees of about the same size by removing one edge. We begin by establishing a property about trees that implies the separator theorem.

LEMMA 9.2.4 *Let T be a tree with n internal (non-leaf) vertices. If the fan-in of every vertex of T is at most r, then for any k, $1 \leq k \leq n$, T has a vertex v such that the subtree T_v rooted at v has at least k leaves but each of its children $T_{v_1}, T_{v_2}, \ldots, T_{v_p}$, $p \leq r$, has fewer than k leaves.*

Proof If the property holds at the root, the result follows. If not, move to some subtree of T that has at least k leaves and apply the test recursively. Because a leaf vertex has one leaf vertex in its subtree, this process terminates on some vertex v at which the property holds. If it terminates on a leaf vertex, each of its children is an empty tree. ∎

COROLLARY 9.2.1 *Let T be a tree of fan-in r with n leaves. Then T has a subtree T_v rooted at a vertex v such that T_v has at least $\lceil n/(r+1) \rceil$ leaves but at most $\lfloor rn/(r+1) \rfloor$.*

Proof Let v be the vertex of Lemma 9.2.4 and let $k = \lceil n/(r+1) \rceil$. Since T_v has at most r subtrees each containing no more than $\lceil n/(r+1) \rceil - 1 \leq n/(r+1)$ leaves, the result follows. ∎

We now apply this decomposition of trees to develop bounds on formula size.

THEOREM 9.2.2 *Let Ω be a complete basis of fan-in r. Any function $f : \mathcal{B}^n \mapsto \mathcal{B}$ with formula size $L_\Omega(f) \geq 2$ has circuit depth $D_\Omega(f)$ satisfying the following bounds:*

$$\log_r L_\Omega(f) \leq D_\Omega(f) \leq d(\Omega) \log_r L_\Omega(f)$$

Proof The lower bound follows because a rooted tree of fan-in r with depth d has at most r^d leaves. Since $L_\Omega(f)$ leaves are needed to compute f with a tree circuit over Ω, the result follows directly.

The derivation of the upper bound is by induction on formula size. We first establish the basis for induction: that $D_\Omega(f) \leq d(\Omega) \log_r L_\Omega(f)$ for $L_\Omega(f) = 2$. To show this, observe that any function f with $L_\Omega(f) = 2$ depends on at most two variables. There are 16 functions on two variables (which includes the functions on one variable), of which 10 have the property that both variables affect the output. Each of these 10 functions can be realized from a circuit for $f_{\text{mux}}^{(1)}$ by adding at most one NOT gate on one input and one NOT on the output. (See Problem 9.13.) But, as seen from the discussion preceding Theorem 9.2.1, every complete basis contains a non-monotone function all but one of whose inputs can be fixed so that the functions computes the NOT of its one remaining input. Thus, a circuit with depth $D_\Omega \left(f_{\text{mux}}^{(1)} \right) + 2$ suffices to realize a function with $L_\Omega(f) = 2$.

The basis for induction is that $D_\Omega\left(f_{\text{mux}}^{(1)}\right) + 2 \leq d(\Omega)\log_r L_\Omega(f)$ for $L_\Omega(f) = 2$, which we now show.

$$d(\Omega)\log_r L_\Omega(f) = \left(D_\Omega\left(f_{\text{mux}}^{(1)}\right) + 1\right)(\log_r 2)/\log_r\left(\frac{r+1}{r}\right)$$

$$= \left(D_\Omega\left(f_{\text{mux}}^{(1)}\right) + 1\right)/\log_2\left(\frac{r+1}{r}\right)$$

$$\geq 1.7\left(D_\Omega\left(f_{\text{mux}}^{(1)}\right) + 1\right) \geq D_\Omega(f_{\text{mux}}^{(1)}) + 2$$

since $(r+1)/r \leq 1.5$ and $D_\Omega\left(f_{\text{mux}}^{(1)}\right) \geq 1$.

The inductive hypothesis is that any function f with a formula size $L_\Omega(f) \leq L_0 - 1$ can be realized by a circuit with depth $d(\Omega)\log_r L_\Omega(f)$.

Let T be the tree associated with a formula for f of size L_0. The value computed by T can be computed from the function $f_{\text{mux}}^{(1)}$ using the values produced by three trees, as suggested in Fig. 9.3. The tree T_v of Corollary 9.2.1 and two copies of T from which T_v has been removed and replaced by 0 in one case (the tree T_0) and 1 in the other (the tree T_1) are formed and the value of T_v is used to determine which of T_0 and T_1 is the value T. Since T_v has at least $\lceil L_0/(r+1)\rceil$ and at most $\lfloor rL_0/(r+1)\rfloor \leq L_0 - 1$ leaves, each of T_0 and T_1 has at most $L_0 - \lceil L_0/(r+1)\rceil = \lfloor rL_0/(r+1)\rfloor$ leaves. (See Problem 9.1.) Thus, all trees have at most $\lfloor rL_0/(r+1)\rfloor \leq L_0 - 1$ leaves and the inductive hypothesis applies. Since the depth of the new circuit is the depth of $f_{\text{mux}}^{(1)}$ plus the maximum of the depths of the three trees, f has the following depth bound:

$$D_\Omega(f) \leq D_\Omega\left(f_{\text{mux}}^{(1)}\right) + d(\Omega)\log_r\frac{rL_\Omega(f)}{(r+1)}$$

The desired result follows from the definition of $d(\Omega)$. ∎

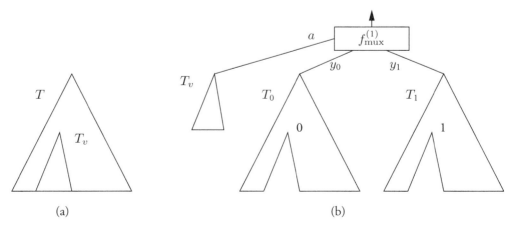

Figure 9.3 Decomposition of a tree circuit T for the purpose of reducing its depth. A large subtree T_v is removed and its value used to select the value computed by two trees formed from the original tree by replacing the value of T_v alternately by 0 and 1.

Combining this result with Lemma 9.2.3, we obtain a relationship between the formula sizes of a function over two different complete bases.

THEOREM 9.2.3 *Let Ω_a and Ω_b be two complete bases with fan-in r_a and r_b, respectively. There is a constant α such that the formula size of a function $f : \mathcal{B}^n \mapsto \mathcal{B}$ with respect to these bases satisfies the following relationship:*

$$L_{\Omega_a}(f) \leq [L_{\Omega_b}(f)]^{\alpha}$$

Proof Let $D_{\Omega_a}(f)$ and $D_{\Omega_b}(f)$ be the depth of f over the bases Ω_a and Ω_b, respectively. From Theorem 9.2.2, $\log_{r_a} L_{\Omega_a}(f) \leq D_{\Omega_a}(f)$ and $D_{\Omega_b}(f) \leq d(\Omega_b) \log_{r_b} L_{\Omega_b}(f)$.

From Lemma 9.2.3 we know there is a constant $d_{a,b}$ such that if a function $f : \mathcal{B}^n \mapsto \mathcal{B}$ has depth $D_{\Omega_b}(f)$ over the basis Ω_b, then it has depth $D_{\Omega_a}(f)$ over the basis Ω_a, where

$$D_{\Omega_a}(f) \leq d_{a,b} D_{\Omega_b}(f)$$

The constant $d_{a,b}$ is the depth of the largest-depth basis element of Ω_b when realized by a circuit over Ω_a.

Combining these facts, we have that

$$
\begin{aligned}
L_{\Omega_a}(f) &\leq (r_a)^{D_{\Omega_a}(f)} \leq (r_a)^{d_{a,b} D_{\Omega_b}(f)} \\
&\leq (r_a)^{d_{a,b} d(\Omega_b) \log_{r_b} L_{\Omega_b}(f)} \\
&\leq L_{\Omega_b}(f)^{d_{a,b} d(\Omega_b)(\log_{r_b} r_a)}
\end{aligned}
$$

Here we have used the identity $x^{\log_y z} = z^{\log_y x}$. ∎

This result can be extended to the monotone basis. (See Problem 9.14.) We now derive a relationship between circuit size and depth.

9.3 Lower-Bound Methods for General Circuits

In Chapter 2 upper bounds were derived for a variety of functions, including logical, arithmetic, shifting, and symmetric functions as well as encoder, decoder, multiplexer, and demultiplexer functions. We also established lower bounds on size and depth of the most complex Boolean functions on n variables. In this section we present techniques for deriving lower bounds on circuit size and depth for particular functions when realized by general logic circuits.

9.3.1 Simple Lower Bounds

A function $f : \mathcal{B}^n \mapsto \mathcal{B}$ on n variables is **dependent on its ith variable**, x_i, if there exist values $c_1, c_2, \ldots, c_{i-1}, c_{i+1}, \ldots, c_n$ such that

$$f(c_1, c_2, \ldots, c_{i-1}, 0, c_{i+1}, \ldots, c_n) \neq f(c_1, c_2, \ldots, c_{i-1}, 1, c_{i+1}, \ldots, c_n)$$

This simple property leads to lower bounds on circuit size and depth that result from the connectivity that a circuit must have to compute a function depending on each of its variables.

THEOREM 9.3.1 *Let* $f : \mathcal{B}^n \mapsto \mathcal{B}$ *be dependent on each of its* n *variables. Then over each basis* Ω *of fan-in* r, *the size and depth of* f *satisfies the following lower bounds:*

$$C_\Omega(f) \geq \left\lceil \frac{n-1}{r-1} \right\rceil$$
$$D_\Omega(f) \geq \lceil \log_r n \rceil$$

Proof Consider a circuit of size $C_\Omega(f)$ for f. Since it has fan-in r, it has at most $rC_\Omega(f)$ edges between gates. After we show that this circuit also has at least $C_\Omega(f) + n - 1$ edges, we observe that $rC_\Omega(f) \geq C_\Omega(f) + n - 1$, from which the conclusion follows.

Since f depends on each of its n variables, there must be at least one edge attached to each of them. Similarly, because the circuit has minimal size there must be at least one edge attached to each of the $C_\Omega(f)$ gates except possibly for the output gate. Thus, the circuit has at least $C_\Omega(f) + n - 1$ edges and the conclusion follows.

The depth lower bound uses the fact that a circuit with depth d and fan-in r with the largest number of inputs is a tree. Such trees have at most r^d leaves (input vertices). Because f depends on each of its variables, a circuit for f of depth d has at least n and at most r^d leaves, from which the depth lower bound follows. ■

This lower bound is the best possible given the information used to derive it. To see this, observe that the function $f(x_1, x_2, \ldots, x_n) = x_1 \wedge x_2 \wedge \cdots \wedge x_n$, which depends on each of its variables, has circuit size $\lceil (n-1)/(r-1) \rceil$ and depth $\lceil \log_r n \rceil$ over the basis containing the r-input AND gate. (See Problem 9.15.)

9.3.2 The Gate-Elimination Method for Circuit Size

The search for methods to derive large lower bounds on circuit size for functions over complete bases has to date been largely unsuccessful. The largest lower bounds on circuit size that have been derived for explicitly defined functions are linear in n, the number of variables on which the functions depend. Since most Boolean functions on n variables have exponential size (see Theorem 2.12.1), functions do exist that have high complexity. Unfortunately, this fact doesn't help us to show that any particular problem has high circuit size. In particular, it does not help us to show that **P** $\neq$ **NP**.

In this section we introduce the gate-elimination method for deriving linear lower bounds. When applied with care, it provides the strongest known lower bounds for complete bases. The **gate-elimination method** uses induction on the properties of a function f on n variables to show two things: a) a few variables of f can be assigned values so that the resulting function is of the same type as f, and b) a few gates in any circuit for f can be eliminated by this assignment of values. After eliminating all variables by assigning values to them, the function is constant. Since the number of gates in the original circuit cannot be smaller than the number removed during this process, the original circuit has at least as many gates as were removed.

We now apply the gate-elimination method to functions in the class $Q_{2,3}^{(n)}$ defined below. Functions in this class have at least three different subfunctions when any pair of variables ranges through all four possible assignments.

DEFINITION 9.3.1 *A Boolean function* $f : \mathcal{B}^n \mapsto \mathcal{B}$ *belongs to the class* $Q_{2,3}^{(n)}$ *if for any two variables* x_i *and* x_j, *f has at least three distinct subfunctions as* x_i *and* x_j *range over all possible* *values. Furthermore, for each variable x_i there is a value c_i such that the subfunction of f obtained by assigning x_i the value c_i is in $Q_{2,3}^{(n-1)}$.*

The class $Q_{2,3}^{(n)}$ contains the function $f_{\text{mod }3,c}^{(n)} : \mathcal{B}^n \mapsto \mathcal{B}$, as we show. Here $z \bmod a$ is the remainder of z after removing all multiples of a.

LEMMA 9.3.1 *For $n \geq 3$ and $c \in \{0, 1, 2\}$, the function $f_{\text{mod }3,c}^{(n)} : \mathcal{B}^n \mapsto \mathcal{B}$ defined below is in $Q_{2,3}^{(n)}$:*

$$f_{\text{mod }3,c}^{(n)}(x_1, x_2, \ldots, x_n) = ((y + c) \bmod 3) \bmod 2$$

where $y = \sum_{i=1}^{n} x_i$ and $\sum$ and $+$ denote integer addition.

Proof We show that the functions $f_{\text{mod }3,c}^{(n)}$, $c \in \{0, 1, 2\}$, are all distinct when $n \geq 1$. When $n = 1$, the functions are different because $f_{\text{mod }3,0}^{(1)}(x_1) = x_1$, $f_{\text{mod }3,1}^{(1)}(x_1) = \overline{x}_1$, and $f_{\text{mod }3,2}^{(1)}(x_1) = 0$. For $n = 2$, y can assume values in $\{0, 1, 2\}$. Because the functions $f_{\text{mod }3,0}^{(2)}(x_1, x_2)$, $f_{\text{mod }3,1}^{(2)}(x_1, x_2)$, and $f_{\text{mod }3,2}^{(2)}(x_1, x_2)$ have value 1 only when $y = x_1 + x_2 = 1, 0, 2$, respectively, the three functions are different.

The proof of membership of $f_{\text{mod }3,c}^{(n)}$ in $Q_{2,3}^{(n)}$ is by induction. The base case is $n = 3$, which holds, as shown in the next paragraph. The inductive hypothesis is that for each $c \in \{0, 1, 2\}$, $f_{\text{mod }3,c}^{(n-1)} \in Q_{2,3}^{(n-1)}$.

To show that for $n \geq 3$, $f_{\text{mod }3,c}^{(n)}$ has at least three distinct subfunctions as any two of its variables range over all values, let y^* be the sum of the $n - 2$ variables that are not fixed and let c^* be the sum of c and the values of the two variables that are fixed. Then the value of the function is $((y^* + c^*) \bmod 3) \bmod 2 = (((y^* \bmod 3) + (c^* \bmod 3)) \bmod 3) \bmod 2$. Since $(y^* \bmod 3)$ and $(c^* \bmod 3)$ range over the values 0, 1, and 2, the three functions are different, as shown in the first paragraph of this proof.

To show that for any variable x_i there is an assignment c_i such that $f_{\text{mod }3,c}^{(n)}$ is in $Q_{2,3}^{(n-1)}$, let $c = 0$. ∎

We now derive a lower bound on the circuit size of functions in the class $Q_{2,3}^{(n)}$.

THEOREM 9.3.2 *Over the basis of all Boolean functions on two inputs, Ω, if $f \in Q_{2,3}^{(n)}$ for $n \geq 3$, then*

$$C_\Omega(f) \geq 2n - 3$$

Proof We show that f depends on each of its variables. Suppose it does not depend on x_i. Then, pick x_i and a second variable x_j and let them range over all four possible values. Since the value of x_i has no effect on f, f has at most two subfunctions as x_i and x_j range over all values, contradicting its definition.

We now show that some input vertex x_i of a circuit for f has fan-out of 2 or more. Consider a gate g in a circuit for f whose longest path to the output gate is longest. (See Fig. 9.4.) Since the circuit does not have loops and no other vertex is farther away from the output, both of g's input edges must be attached to input vertices. Let x_i and x_j be the two inputs to this gate. If the fan-out of both of these input vertices is 1, they influence the value of f only through the one gate to which they are connected. Since this gate has at most two

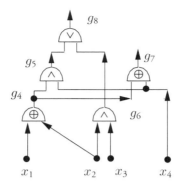

Figure 9.4 A circuit in which gates g_4 has maximal distance from the output gate g_8. The inputs x_1 and x_2 each have fan-out 2.

values for the four assignments to inputs, f has at most two subfunctions, contradicting the definition of f.

If $n = 3$, this fact demonstrates that the fan-out from the three inputs has to be at least 4, that is, the circuit has at least four inputs. From Theorem 9.3.1 it follows that $C_\Omega(f) \geq 2n - 3$ for $n = 3$. This is the base case for a proof by induction.

The inductive hypothesis is that for any $f^* \in Q_{2,3}^{(n-1)}$, $C_\Omega(f^*) \geq 2(n-1) - 3$. From the earlier argument it follows that there is an input vertex x_i in a circuit for $f \in Q_{2,3}^{(n)}$ that has fan-out 2. Let x_i have that value that causes the subfunction f^* of f to be in $Q_{2,3}^{(n-1)}$. Fixing x_i eliminates at least two gates in the circuit for f because each gate connected to x_i either has a constant output, computes the identity, or computes the NOT of its input. The negation, if any, can be absorbed by the gate that precedes or follows it. Thus,

$$C_\Omega(f) \geq C_\Omega(f^*) + 2 \geq 2(n-1) - 3 + 2 = 2n - 3$$

which establishes the result. ∎

As a consequence of this theorem, the function $f_{\text{mod } 3,c}^{(n)}$ requires at least $2n - 3$ gates over the basis B_2. It can also be shown to require at most $2.5n + O(\log^2 n)$ gates. (See Problem 9.17.)

We now derive a second lower-bound result using the gate-elimination method. In this case we demonstrate that the upper bound on the complexity of the multiplexer function $f_{\text{mux}}^{(n)} : \mathcal{B}^{2^n+n} \mapsto \mathcal{B}$ introduced in Section 2.5.5, which is $2^{n+1} + O(n\sqrt{2^n})$, is optimal to within an additive term of size $O(n\sqrt{2^n})$. (The multiplexer function is also called the **storage access function**.) We generalize the storage access function $f_{\text{SA}}^{(n,k)} : \mathcal{B}^{n+k} \mapsto \mathcal{B}$ slightly and write it in terms of a k-bit address $\boldsymbol{a}$ and an n-tuple $\boldsymbol{x}$, as shown below, where $|\boldsymbol{a}|$ denotes the integer represented by the binary number $\boldsymbol{a}$ and $2^k \geq n$.:

$$f_{\text{SA}}^{(n,k)}(a_{k-1}, \ldots, a_1, a_0, x_{n-1}, \ldots, x_0) = x_{|\boldsymbol{a}|}$$

Thus, $f_{\text{mux}}^{(m)} = f_{\text{SA}}^{(2^m, m)}$.

To derive a lower bound on the circuit size of $f_{\text{SA}}^{(n,k)}$ we introduce the class $F_s^{(n,k)}$ of Boolean functions on $n + k$ variables defined below.

DEFINITION 9.3.2 *A Boolean function $f : \mathcal{B}^{n+k} \mapsto \mathcal{B}$ belongs to the class $F_s^{(n,k)}$, $2^k \geq n$, if for some set $S \subseteq \{0, 1, \ldots, n - 1\}$, $|S| = s$,*

$$f(a_{k-1}, \ldots, a_1, a_0, x_{n-1}, \ldots, x_0) = x_{|a|}$$

for $|a| \in S$.

Clearly, $f_{SA}^{(n,k)}$ is a member of $F_n^{(n,k)}$. We now show that every function in $F_s^{(n,k)}$ has circuit size that is at least $2s - 2$.

In the proof of Theorem 9.3.2 the gate-elimination method replaced variables with constants. In the following proof this idea is extended to replacing variables by functions. Applying this result, we have that $C_\Omega(f_{\text{mux}}^{(n)}) \geq 2^{n+1} - 1$.

THEOREM 9.3.3 *Let $f : \mathcal{B}^{n+k} \mapsto \mathcal{B}$ belong to $F_s^{(n,k)}$, $2^k \geq n$. Then over the basis B_2 the circuit size of f satisfies the following bound:*

$$C_\Omega(f) \geq 2s - 2$$

Proof In the proof of Theorem 9.3.2 we used the fact that some input variable has fan-out 2 or more, as deduced from a property of functions in $Q_{2,3}^{(n)}$. This fact does not hold for the storage access function (multiplexer), as can be seen from the construction in Section 2.5.5. Thus, our lower-bound argument must explicitly take into account the fact that the fan-out from some input can be 1.

The following proof uses the fact that the basis B_2 contains functions of two kinds, AND-type and parity-type functions. The former compute expressions of the form $(x^a \wedge y^b)^c$ for Boolean constants a, b, c, where the notation x^c denotes x when $c = 1$ and $\overline{x}$ when $c = 0$. Parity-type functions compute expressions of the form $x \oplus y \oplus c$ for some Boolean constant c. (See Problem 9.19.)

The proof is by induction on the value of s. In the base case $s = 1$ and the lower bound is trivially 0. The inductive hypothesis assumes that for $s = s' - 1$, $C_\Omega(f) \geq 2(s' - 1) - 2$. We let $s = s'$ and consider the following mutually exclusive cases:

a) For some $i \in S$, x_i has fan-out 2. Replacing x_i by a constant allows elimination of at least two gates, replaces S by $S - \{i\}$, which has size $s' - 1$, and reduces f to $f^* \in F_{s'-1}^{(n,k)}$, from which we conclude that

$$C_\Omega(f) \geq 2 + C_\Omega(f^*) \geq 2s' - 2 = 2s - 2$$

b) For some $i \in S$, x_i has fan-out 1, its unique successor is a gate G of AND-type, and G computes the expression $(x_i^a \wedge g^b)^c$ for some function g of the inputs. Setting $x_i = \overline{a}$ sets $x_i^a = \overline{a}^a = 0$, thereby causing the expression to have value 0^c, which is a constant. Since G cannot be the output gate, this substitution allows the elimination of G and at least one successor gate, reduces f to $f^* \in F_{s'-1}^{(n,k)}$, and replaces S by $S - \{i\}$, from which the lower bound follows.

c) For some $i \in S$, x_i has fan-out 1, its unique successor is a gate G of parity-type, and G computes the expression $x_i \oplus g \oplus c$ for some function g of the inputs. Replace S by $S - \{i\}$. Since we ask that the output of the circuit be $x_{|a|}$ for $a \in S - \{i\}$, this output cannot depend on the value of G because a change in x_i would cause the value of G to change. Thus, G is not the output gate and when $\boldsymbol{a} \in S - \{i\}$ we can set its value to any function without affecting the value computed by the circuit. In particular, setting $x_i = g$ causes G to have value c, a constant. This substitution allows the elimination of G and at least one successor gate, and reduces f to $f^* \in F_{s'-1}^{(n,k)}$, from which the lower bound follows.

Thus, in all cases, $C_\Omega(f) \geq 2s' - 2$. ∎

The lower bounds given above are derived for two functions over the basis B_2. The best circuit-size lower bound that has been derived for this basis is $3(n-1)$. When the basis is restricted, larger lower bounds may result, as mentioned in the notes and illustrated by Problems 9.22 and 9.23.

9.4 Lower-Bound Methods for Formula Size

Since formulas correspond to circuits of fan-out 1, the formula size of a function may be much larger than its circuit size. In this section we introduce two techniques for deriving lower bounds on formula size that illustrate this point. Each leads to bounds that are quadratic or nearly quadratic in the number of inputs. The first, due to Nečiporuk [224], applies to any complete basis. The second, due to Krapchenko [171], applies to the standard basis Ω_0.

To fix ideas about formula size, we construct a circuit of fan-out 1 for the **indirect storage access function** $f_{\text{ISA}}^{(k,l)} : \mathcal{B}^{k+lK+L} \mapsto \mathcal{B}$, where $K = 2^k$ and $L = 2^l$:

$$f_{\text{ISA}}^{(k,l)}(\boldsymbol{a}, \boldsymbol{x}_{K-1}, \ldots, \boldsymbol{x}_0, \boldsymbol{y}) = y_{|\boldsymbol{x}_{|\boldsymbol{a}|}|}$$

Here $\boldsymbol{a}$ is a k-tuple, $\boldsymbol{x}_j = (x_{j,l-1}, \ldots, x_{j,0})$ is an l-tuple for $0 \leq j \leq K - 1$, and $\boldsymbol{y} = (y_{L-1}, \ldots, y_0)$ is an L-tuple. The value of $f_{\text{ISA}}^{(k,l)}$ is computed by indirection; that is, the value of $\boldsymbol{a}$ is treated as a binary number with value $|\boldsymbol{a}|$ that is used to select the $|\boldsymbol{a}|$th l-tuple $\boldsymbol{x}_{|\boldsymbol{a}|}$; this, in turn, is treated as a binary number and its value is used to select the $|\boldsymbol{x}_{|\boldsymbol{a}|}|$th variable in $\boldsymbol{y}$.

A circuit realizing $f_{\text{ISA}}^{(k,l)}$ from multiple copies of the multiplexer (direct storage access function) $f_{\text{mux}}^{(n)} : \mathcal{B}^{2^n+n} \mapsto \mathcal{B}$ is shown schematically in Fig. 9.5. This circuit uses l copies of $f_{\text{mux}}^{(k)} : \mathcal{B}^{2^k+k} \mapsto \mathcal{B}$ and one copy of $f_{\text{mux}}^{(l)} : \mathcal{B}^{2^l+l} \mapsto \mathcal{B}$. The copies of $f_{\text{mux}}^{(k)}$ produce the $|\boldsymbol{a}|$th l-tuple, which is supplied to the copy of $f_{\text{mux}}^{(l)}$ to select a variable from $\boldsymbol{y}$. Since, as shown in Lemma 2.5.5, the function $f_{\text{mux}}^{(k)}$ can be realized by a circuit of size linear in 2^k, a circuit for $f_{\text{ISA}}^{(k,l)}$ can be constructed that is also linear in the size of its input.

A formula for $f_{\text{ISA}}^{(k,l)}$ has fan-out of 1 from every gate. The circuit sketched in Fig. 9.5 has fan-out 1 if and only if the fan-out within each multiplexer circuit is also 1. To construct a formula from this circuit, we first construct one for $f_{\text{mux}}^{(l)}$. The total number of times that address bits appear in a formula for $f_{\text{mux}}^{(l)}$ determines the number of copies of the formula for $f_{\text{mux}}^{(k)}$ that are used in the formula for $f_{\text{ISA}}^{(k,l)}$. A proof by induction can be developed to show that a formula for $f_{\text{mux}}^{(p)}$ can be constructed of size $32^p - 2$ in which address bits occur $2(2^p - 1)$ times. (See Problem 9.24.) Since each occurrence of an address bit in $f_{\text{mux}}^{(l)}$ corresponds to a copy of the formula for $f_{\text{mux}}^{(k)}$, by choosing $L = 2^l = n$ and k the smallest integer such that

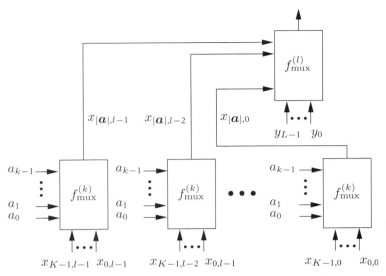

Figure 9.5 The schema used to construct a circuit of fan-out 1 for the indirect storage access function $f_{\text{ISA}}^{(k,l)}$.

$K = 2^k \geq n/l$ we see that $f_{\text{ISA}}^{(k,l)}$ has $2^l + l2^k + k = O(n)$ variables and that its formula size is $2(2^l - 1)L_\Omega\left(f_{\text{mux}}^{(k)}\right) + L_\Omega\left(f_{\text{mux}}^{(l)}\right)$, which is $O(n^2/\log_2 n)$, as summarized in Lemma 9.4.1.

LEMMA 9.4.1 *Let $2^l = n$ and $k = \lceil \log_2 n/l \rceil$. Then the formula size of $f_{\text{ISA}}^{(k,l)} : \mathcal{B}^{k+lK+L} \mapsto \mathcal{B}$ satisfies the following bound:*

$$L_\Omega\left(f_{\text{ISA}}^{(k,l)}\right) = O(n^2/\log_2 n)$$

We now introduce Nečiporuk's method, by which it can be shown that this bound for $f_{\text{ISA}}^{(k,l)}$ is optimal to within a constant multiplicative factor.

9.4.1 The Nečiporuk Lower Bound

The Nečiporuk lower-bound method uses a partition of the variables $X = (x_1, x_2, \ldots, x_n)$ of a Boolean function $f^{(n)} : \mathcal{B}^n \mapsto \mathcal{B}$ into disjoint sets $X_1, X_2, \ldots, X_p$. That is, $X = \bigcup_{i=1}^p X_i$ and $X_i \cap X_j = \emptyset$ for $i \neq j$. The lower bound on the formula size of f is stated in terms of $r_{X_j}(f)$, $0 \leq j \leq p$, the **number of subfunctions of** f when restricted to variables in X_j. That is, $r_{X_j}(f)$ is the number of different subfunctions of f in the variables in X_j obtained by ranging over all values for variables in $X - X_j$.

We now describe Nečiporuk's lower bound on formula size. We emphasize that the strength of the lower bound depends on which partition $X_1, X_2, \ldots, X_p$ of the variables X is chosen. After the proof we apply it to the indirect storage access function. The method cannot provide a lower bound that is larger than $O(n^2/\log n)$ for a function on n variables. (See Problem 9.25.)

THEOREM 9.4.1 *For every complete basis Ω there is a constant c_Ω such that for every function* $f^{(n)} : \mathcal{B}^n \mapsto \mathcal{B}$ *and every partition of its variables X into disjoint sets $X_1, X_2, \ldots, X_p$, the formula size of f with respect to Ω satisfies the following lower bound:*

$$L_\Omega(f) \geq c_\Omega \sum_{j=1}^{p} \log_2 r_{X_j}(f)$$

Proof Consider T, a minimal circuit of fan-out 1 for f. Let n_j be the number of instances of variables in X_j that are labels for leaves in T. Then by definition $L_\Omega(f) = \sum_{i=1}^{p} n_j$. Let d be the fan-in of the basis Ω.

For each j, $1 \leq j \leq p$, we define the subtree T_j of T consisting of paths from vertices with labels in X_j to the output vertex, as suggested by the heavy lines in Fig. 9.6. We observe that some vertices in such a subtree have one input from a vertex in the subtree T_j (called **controllers** — shaded vertices in Fig. 9.6) whereas others have more than one input from a vertex in T_j (**combiners** — black vertices in Fig. 9.6). Each type of vertex typically has inputs from vertices other than those in T_j, that is, from vertices on paths from input vertices in $X - X_j$.

When the variables $X - X_j$ are assigned values, the output of a controller or combiner vertex depends only on the inputs it receives from other vertices in T_j. The function computed by a controller is a function of its one input y in T_j and can be represented as $(a \wedge y) \oplus b$ for some values of the constants a and b. These constants are determined by the values of inputs in $X - X_j$. We assume without loss of generality that each chain of controllers with no intervening combiners is compressed to one controller. The combiner is also some function of its inputs from other vertices in T_j. Since the number of such inputs is as least 2, a combiner (with fan-in at most d) has at most $d - 2$ inputs determined by variables in $X - X_j$.

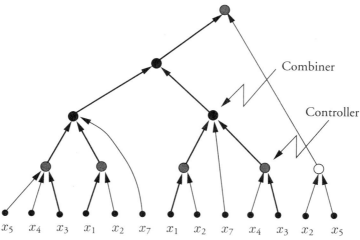

Figure 9.6 The subtree T_j of the tree T is identified by heavy edges on paths from input vertices in the set $X_j = \{x_1, x_3\}$. Vertices in T_j that have one heavy input edge are controller vertices. Other vertices in T_j are combiner vertices.

By Lemma 9.2.1, since T_j has n_j leaves, the number of vertices with fan-in of 2 or more (combiners) is at most $n_j - 1$. Also, by Lemma 9.2.1, T_j has at most $2(n_j - 1)$ edges. Since T_j may have one controller at the output and at most one per edge, T_j has at most $2n_j - 1$ controllers.

The number of functions computed by a combiner is at most one of 2^{d-2} since at most $d - 2$ of its inputs are determined by variables in $X - X_j$. At most four functions are computed by a controller since there are at most four functions on one variable. It follows that the tree T_j associated with the input variables in X_j containing n_j leaves computes r_{X_j} different functions where r_{X_j} satisfies the following upper bound. This bound is the product of the number of ways that each of the controllers and combiners can compute functions.

$$r_{X_j}(f) \leq 2^{(d-2)(n_j-1)} \left(4^{(2n_j-1)} \right) \leq 2^{(d+2)(n_j-1)}$$

Thus, $(d + 2)(n_j - 1) \geq \log_2 r_{X_j}(f)$. Since $L_\Omega(f) = \sum_{i=1}^{p} n_j$, the theorem holds for $c_\Omega = 1/(d + 2)$. ∎

Applying Nečiporuk's lower bound to the indirect storage access function yields the following result, which demonstrates that the upper bound given in Lemma 9.4.1 for the indirect storage access function is tight.

LEMMA 9.4.2 *Let $2^l = n$ and $k = \lceil \log_2(n/l) \rceil$. The formula size of $f_{\text{ISA}}^{(k,l)} : \mathcal{B}^{k+lK+L} \mapsto \mathcal{B}$ satisfies the following bound:*

$$L_\Omega \left(f_{\text{ISA}}^{(k,l)} \right) = \Omega \left(\frac{n^2}{\log_2 n} \right)$$

Proof Let $p = K = 2^k$ and let X_j contain $\boldsymbol{x}_j$. If X_j contains other variables, these are assigned fixed values, which cannot increase $r_{X_j}(f)$. For $0 \leq j \leq K - 1$, set $|\boldsymbol{a}| = j$. f has at least 2^L restrictions since for each of the 2^L assignments to $(y_{L-1}, \ldots, y_0)$ the restriction of f is distinct; that is, if two different such L-tuples are supplied as input, they can be distinguished by some assignment to $\boldsymbol{x}_j$. Thus $r_{X_j}(f) \geq 2^L$. Hence, the formula size of $f_{\text{ISA}}^{(k,l)}$, $L_\Omega \left(f_{\text{ISA}}^{(k,l)} \right) \geq c_\Omega K L$, which is proportional to $n^2/\log n$. ∎

9.4.2 The Krapchenko Lower Bound

Krapchenko's lower bound applies to the standard basis Ω_0 or any complete subset, namely $\{\wedge, \neg\}$ and $\{\vee, \neg\}$. It provides a lower bound on formula size that can be slightly larger than that given by Nečiporuk's method.

We apply Krapchenko's method to the parity function $f_\oplus^{(n)} : \mathcal{B}^n \mapsto \mathcal{B}$, where $f_\oplus^{(n)}(x_1, x_2, \ldots, x_n) = x_1 \oplus x_2 \oplus \cdots \oplus x_n$, to show that its formula size is quadratic in n. Since the parity function on two variables can be expressed by the formula

$$f_\oplus^{(2)}(x_1, x_2) = (x_1 \wedge \overline{x}_2) \vee (\overline{x}_1 \wedge x_2)$$

it is straightforward to show that the formula size of $f_\oplus^{(n)}$ is at most quadratic in n. (See Problem 9.26.)

DEFINITION 9.4.1 *Given two disjoint subsets $A, B \subseteq \{0, 1\}^n$ of the set of the Boolean n-tuples, the* **neighborhood** *of A and B, $\mathcal{N}(A, B)$, is the set of pairs of tuples $(\boldsymbol{x}, \boldsymbol{y})$, $\boldsymbol{x} \in A$ and $\boldsymbol{y} \in B$, such that $\boldsymbol{x}$ and $\boldsymbol{y}$ agree in all but one position.*

The neighborhood of $A = \{0\}$ and $B = \{1\}$ is the pair $\mathcal{N}(A, B) = \{(0, 1)\}$. Also, the neighborhood of $A = \{000, 101\}$ and $B = \{111, 010\}$ is the set of pairs $\mathcal{N}(A, B) = \{(000, 010), (101, 111)\}$.

Given a function $f : \mathcal{B}^n \mapsto \mathcal{B}$, we use the notation $f^{-1}(0)$ and $f^{-1}(1)$ to denote the sets of n-tuples that cause f to assume the values 0 and 1, respectively.

THEOREM 9.4.2 *For any $f : \mathcal{B}^n \mapsto \mathcal{B}$ and any $A \subseteq f^{-1}(0)$ and $B \subseteq f^{-1}(1)$, the following inequality holds over the standard basis Ω_0:*

$$L_{\Omega_0}(f) \geq \frac{|\mathcal{N}(A, B)|^2}{|A||B|}$$

Proof Consider a circuit for f of fan-out 1 over the standard basis that has the minimal number of leaves, namely $L_{\Omega_0}(f)$. Since the fan-in of each gate is either 1 or 2, by Lemma 9.2.1 the number of leaves is one more than the number of gates of fan-in 2. Each fan-in-2 gate is an AND or OR gate with suitable negation on its inputs and outputs.

Consider a minimal formula for f. Assume without loss of generality that the formula is written over the basis $\{\wedge, \neg\}$. We prove the lower bound by induction, the base case being that of a function on one variable. If the function is constant, $|\mathcal{N}(A, B)| = 0$ and its formula size is also 0. If the function is non-constant, it is either x or $\overline{x}$. (If $f(x) = x$, $f^{-1}(1) = \{1\}$ and $f^{-1}(0) = \{0\}$.) In both cases, $|\mathcal{N}(A, B)| = 1$ since the neighborhood has only one pair. (In the first case $\mathcal{N}(A, B) = \{(0, 1)\}$.) Also, $|A| = 1$ and $|B| = 1$, thereby establishing the base case.

The inductive hypothesis is that $L_{\Omega_0}(f^*) \geq |\mathcal{N}(A, B)|/|A||B|$ for any function f^* whose formula size $L_{\Omega_0}(f^*) \leq L_0 - 1$ for some $L_0 \geq 2$. Since the occurrences of NOT do not affect the formula size of a function, apply DeMorgan's theorem as necessary so that the output gate of the optimal (minimal-depth) formula for f is an AND gate. Then we can write $f = g \wedge h$, where g and h are defined on the variables appearing in their formulas. Since the formula for f is optimal, so are the formulas for g and h.

Let $A \subseteq f^{-1}(0)$ and $B \subseteq f^{-1}(1)$. Thus, $f(\boldsymbol{x}) = 0$ for $\boldsymbol{x} \in A$ and $f(\boldsymbol{x}) = 1$ for $\boldsymbol{x} \in B$. Since $f = g \wedge h$, if $f(\boldsymbol{x}) = 1$, then both $g(\boldsymbol{x}) = 1$ and $h(\boldsymbol{x}) = 1$. That is, $f^{-1}(1) \subseteq g^{-1}(1)$ and $f^{-1}(1) \subseteq h^{-1}(1)$. (See Fig. 9.7.) It follows that $B \subseteq g^{-1}(1)$ and $B \subseteq h^{-1}(1)$. Let $B_1 = B_2 = B$. Let $A_1 = A \cap g^{-1}(0)$ (which implies $A_1 \subseteq g^{-1}(0)$) and let $A_2 = A - A_1$. Since $f(\boldsymbol{x}) = 0$ for $\boldsymbol{x} \in A$, but $g(\boldsymbol{x}) = 1$ for $\boldsymbol{x} \in A_2$, as suggested in Fig. 9.7, it follows that $A_2 \subseteq h^{-1}(0)$. (Since $f = g \wedge h$, $f(\boldsymbol{x}) = 0$, and $g(\boldsymbol{x}) = 1$, it follows that $h(\boldsymbol{x}) = 0$.) Finally, observe that $\mathcal{N}(A_1, B_1)$ and $\mathcal{N}(A_2, B_2)$ are disjoint (A_1 and A_2 have no tuples in common) and that $|\mathcal{N}(A, B)| = |\mathcal{N}(A_1, B_1)| + |\mathcal{N}(A_2, B_2)|$.

Given the inductive hypothesis, it follows from the above that

$$L_{\Omega_0}(f) = L_{\Omega_0}(g) + L_{\Omega_0}(h) \geq \frac{|\mathcal{N}(A_1, B_1)|^2}{|A_1||B_1|} + \frac{|\mathcal{N}(A_2, B_2)|^2}{|A_2||B_2|}$$

$$= \frac{1}{|B|} \left(\frac{|\mathcal{N}(A_1, B_1)|^2}{|A_1|} + \frac{|\mathcal{N}(A_2, B_2)|^2}{|A_2|} \right)$$

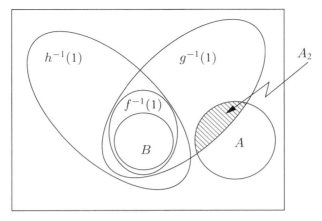

Figure 9.7 The relationships among the sets $f^{-1}(1)$, $g^{-1}(1)$, $h^{-1}(1)$, A_2, and $h^{-1}(0)$.

By the identity $n_1^2/a_1 + n_2^2/a_2 \geq (n_1 + n_2)^2/(a_1 + a_2)$, which holds for positive integers (see Problem 9.3), the desired result follows because $|A| = |A_1| + |A_2|$. ∎

Krapchenko's method is easily applied to the parity function $f_\oplus^{(n)}$. We need only let A (B) contain n-tuples having an even (odd) number of 1's. ($|A| = |B| = 2^{n-1}$.) Then $|\mathcal{N}(A, B)| = n2^{n-1}$ because for any vector in A there are exactly n vectors in B that are neighbors of it. It follows that $L_{\Omega_0}\left(f_\oplus^{(n)}\right) \geq n^2$.

9.5 The Power of Negation

As a prelude to the discussion of monotone circuits for monotone functions in the next section, we consider the minimum number of negations necessary to realize an arbitrary Boolean function $f : \mathcal{B}^n \mapsto \mathcal{B}^m$. From Problem 2.12 on dual-rail logic we know that every such function can be realized by a monotone circuit in which both the variables $x_1, x_2, \ldots, x_n$ and their negations $\overline{x}_1, \overline{x}_2, \ldots, \overline{x}_n$ are provided as inputs. Furthermore, every such circuit need have only at most twice as many AND and OR gates as a minimal circuit over Ω_0, the standard basis. Also, the depth of the dual-rail logic circuit of a function is at most one more than the depth of a minimal-depth circuit, the extra depth being that to form $\overline{x}_1, \overline{x}_2, \ldots, \overline{x}_n$.

Let $f_{\text{NEG}}^{(n)} : \mathcal{B}^n \mapsto \mathcal{B}^n$ be defined by $f_{\text{NEG}}^{(n)}(x_1, x_2, \ldots, x_n) = (\overline{x}_1, \overline{x}_2, \ldots, \overline{x}_n)$. As shown in Lemma 9.5.1, this function can be realized by a circuit of size $O(n^2 \log n)$ and depth $O(\log^2 n)$ over Ω_0 using $\lceil \log_2(n + 1) \rceil$ negations. This implies that most Boolean functions on n variables can be realized by a circuit whose size and depth are within a factor of about 2 of their minimal values when the number of negations is $\lceil \log_2(n + 1) \rceil$.

THEOREM 9.5.1 *Every Boolean function on n variables, $f : \mathcal{B}^n \mapsto \mathcal{B}^m$, can be realized by a circuit containing at most $\lceil \log_2(n + 1) \rceil$ negations. Furthermore, the minimal size and depth of such circuits is at most $2C_{\Omega_0}(f) + O(n^2 \log n)$ and $D_{\Omega_0}(f) + O(\log^2 n)$, respectively, where $C_{\Omega_0}(f)$ and $D_{\Omega_0}(f)$ are the circuit size and depth of f over the standard basis Ω_0.*

Proof The proof follows directly from the dual-rail expansion of Problem 2.12 and the following lemma. ∎

We now show that the function $f_{\text{NEG}}^{(n)} : \mathcal{B}^n \mapsto \mathcal{B}^n$ defined by $f_{\text{NEG}}^{(n)}(x_1, x_2, \ldots, x_n) = (\overline{x}_1, \overline{x}_2, \ldots, \overline{x}_n)$ can be realized by circuit size of $O(n^2 \log n)$ over Ω_0 using $\lceil \log_2(n+1) \rceil$ negations.

LEMMA 9.5.1 $f_{\text{NEG}}^{(n)} : \mathcal{B}^n \mapsto \mathcal{B}^n$ *can be realized with* $\lceil \log_2(n+1) \rceil$ *negations by a circuit over the standard basis that has size* $O(n^2 \log n)$ *and depth* $O(\log n)$.

Proof The **punctured threshold function** $\tau_{t, \neg i}^{(n)} : \mathcal{B}^n \mapsto \mathcal{B}$, $1 \leq t, i \leq n$, is defined below.

$$\tau_{t, \neg i}^{(n)}(\boldsymbol{x}) = \begin{cases} 1 & \sum_{j=1, j \neq i}^n x_j \geq t \\ 0 & \text{otherwise} \end{cases}$$

This function has value 1 if t or more of the variables other than x_i have value 1. The standard threshold function $\tau_t^{(n)} : \mathcal{B}^n \mapsto \mathcal{B}$ has value 1 when t or more of the variables have value 1. Since the function $(\tau_{0, \neg i}^{(n)}, \tau_{1, \neg i}^{(n)}, \ldots, \tau_{n-1, \neg i}^{(n)})$ is the result of sorting all but the ith input, we know from Theorem 6.8.3 that Batcher's odd-even sorting algorithm will produce this output with a circuit of size $O(n \log^2 n)$ and depth $O(\log^2 n)$ because max and min of a comparator unit compute AND and OR on binary inputs. Ajtai, Komlós, and Szemerédi [14] have improved this bound to $O(n \log n)$ but with a very large coefficient, and simultaneously achieve depth $O(\log n)$. Thus, all the functions $\{\tau_{t, \neg i}^{(n)} \mid 1 \leq t, i \leq n\}$ can be realized with $O(n^2 \log n)$ gates and depth $O(\log n)$ over Ω_0.

Observe that for input $\boldsymbol{x}$ there is some largest t, $t = t_0$, such that $\tau_{t_0}^{(n)}(\boldsymbol{x}) = 1$. If $\tau_{t_0, \neg i}^{(n)}(\boldsymbol{x}) = 1$, then $x_i = 0$; otherwise, $x_i = 1$. Let the **implication function** $a \Rightarrow b$ have value 1 when $a = 0$ or when $a = 1$ and $b = 1$ and value 0 otherwise. Then we can express the implication function by the formula $(a \Rightarrow b) = \overline{a} \vee b$. It follows that $\overline{x}_i = (\tau_{t_0}^{(n)}(\boldsymbol{x}) \Rightarrow \tau_{t_0, \neg i}^{(n)}(\boldsymbol{x}))$ because the implication function has value 1 exactly when $x_i = 0$.

We use an indirect method to compute t_0. Since $\tau_t^{(n)}(\boldsymbol{x}) = 0$ for $t > t_0$, $(\tau_t^{(n)}(\boldsymbol{x}) \Rightarrow \tau_{t, \neg i}^{(n)}(\boldsymbol{x})) = 1$ for $t > t_0$. Also, both $\tau_t^{(n)}(\boldsymbol{x})$ and $\tau_{t, \neg i}^{(n)}(\boldsymbol{x})$ have value 1 for $t < t_0$. Using $(x \Rightarrow y) = \overline{x} \vee y$, we can write $\overline{x}_i$ as follows:

$$\overline{x}_i = \left(\overline{\tau_0^{(n)}(\boldsymbol{x})} \vee \tau_{0, \neg i}^{(n)}(\boldsymbol{x}) \right) \wedge \left(\overline{\tau_1^{(n)}(\boldsymbol{x})} \vee \tau_{1, \neg i}^{(n)}(\boldsymbol{x}) \right) \wedge \cdots \wedge \left(\overline{\tau_{n-1}^{(n)}(\boldsymbol{x})} \vee \tau_{n-1, \neg i}^{(n)}(\boldsymbol{x}) \right)$$

The circuit design is complete once a circuit for $\{\overline{\tau_t^{(n)}(\boldsymbol{x})} \mid 1 \leq t \leq n\}$ has been designed. We begin by using a binary sorting circuit that computes $\{\tau_t^{(n)}(\boldsymbol{x}) \mid 1 \leq t \leq n\}$ from $\boldsymbol{x}$, which, as stated above, can be computed with $O(n \log^2 n)$ gates over the standard basis. Let $s_t = \tau_t^{(n)}(\boldsymbol{x})$ for $1 \leq t \leq n$.

For $n = K - 1$, $K = 2^k$ and k an integer, we complete the design by constructing a circuit for the function $\nu^{(k)} : \mathcal{B}^n \mapsto \mathcal{B}^n$, which, given as input the decreasing sequence $s_1, s_2, \ldots, s_n$ ($s_i \geq s_{i+1}$), computes as its jth output $z_j = \overline{s}_j$, $1 \leq j \leq n$. (The case $n \neq 2^k - 1$ is considered below.) That is, $\nu^{(k)}(\boldsymbol{s}) = \boldsymbol{z}$, where $z_t = \overline{\tau_t^{(n)}(\boldsymbol{x})}$. We give a recursive construction of a circuit for $\nu^{(k)}$ whose correctness is established by induction.

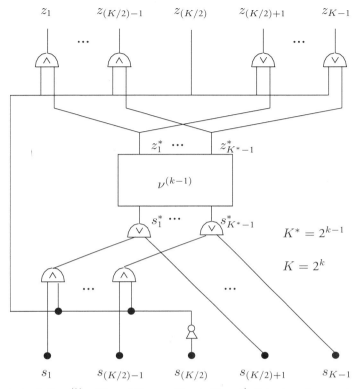

Figure 9.8 A circuit for $\nu^{(k)} : \mathcal{B}^n \mapsto \mathcal{B}^n$, $n = K - 1$, $K = 2^k$. It is given the sorted n-tuple $\boldsymbol{s}$ as input, where $s_j \geq s_{j+1}$ for $1 \leq j \leq n$, and produces as output $\boldsymbol{z}$, where $z_j = \bar{s}_j$.

The base case is a circuit for $\nu^{(1)}$. This circuit has one input, s_1, and one output, $z_1 = \bar{s}_1$, and can be realized by one negation and no other gates.

We construct a circuit for $\nu^{(k)}$ from one for $\nu^{(k-1)}$ using $2n$ additional gates and increasing the depth by three, as shown in Fig. 9.8. Let the inputs and outputs to the circuit for $\nu^{(k-1)}$ be s_i^* and z_i^*, $1 \leq i \leq K^* - 1$, where $K^* = K/2$. It follows that $s_i^* \geq s_{i+1}^*$ for $1 \leq i \leq (K/2) - 1$. By induction $z_i^* = \bar{s}^*_i$ for $1 \leq i \leq n$.

To show that the jth output of the circuit for $\nu^{(k)}$ is $z_j = \bar{s}_j$, we consider cases. If $s_{2^{k-1}} = 0$, then $s_j = 0$ for $j > K/2$. In this case the jth circuit output, $(K/2) < j \leq K - 1$, satisfies $z_j = 1$ (the corresponding output gate is OR), which is the correct value. Also, for $1 \leq j \leq (K/2) - 1$, $z_j = z_j^* = \bar{s}_j$ since the inputs to the circuit for $\nu^{(k-1)}$ are $s_1, s_2, \ldots, s_{(K/2)-1}$ ($s_j = 0$ for $j > K/2$) and its outputs are $\bar{s}_1, \bar{s}_2, \ldots, \bar{s}_{(K/2)-1}$. On the other hand, if $s_{K/2} = 1$, then $s_j = 1$ and $z_j = 0$ for $j \leq (K/2) - 1$ (the corresponding output gate is AND). Also, for $(K/2) + 1 \leq j \leq K - 1$, $z_j = z_j^* = \bar{s}_j$ since the inputs to the circuit for $\nu^{(k-1)}$ are $s_{(K/2)+1}, \ldots, s_{K-1}$ and its outputs are $\bar{s}_{(K/2)+1}, \ldots, \bar{s}_{(K/2)-1}$.

It follows that $k = \log_2(n + 1)$ negations are used. The circuit for $\nu^{(k)}$ uses a total of $C(k) = C(k - 1) + 2^{k+1} - 3$ gates, where $C(1) = 1$. The solution to this recurrence is $C(k) = 4(2^k) - 3k = 4n - 3\log_2 n$. Also, the circuit for $\nu^{(k)}$ has depth $D(k) =$

$D(k-1)+3$, where $D(1)=0$. The solution to this recurrence is $D(k)=3(k-1)$. If n is not of the form 2^k-1, we increase n to the next largest integer of this form, which implies that $k=\lceil\log_2(n+1)\rceil$. Using the upper bounds on the size of circuits to compute $\tau_{t,\neg i}^{(n)}(\boldsymbol{x})$ for $1\le t,i\le n$, we have the desired conclusion. ■

9.6 Lower-Bound Methods for Monotone Circuits

The best lower bounds that have been derived on the circuit size over complete bases of Boolean functions on n variables are linear in n. Similarly, the best lower bounds on formula size that have been derived over complete bases are at best quadratic in n. As a consequence, the search for better lower bounds has led to the study of monotone circuits (their basis is Ω_{mon}) for monotone functions. In one sense, this effort has been surprisingly successful. Techniques have been developed to show that some monotone functions have exponential circuit size. Since most monotone Boolean functions on n variables have circuit size $\Theta(2^n/n^{3/2})$, this is a strong result. On the other hand, the hope that such techniques would lead to strong lower bounds on circuit size for monotone functions over complete bases has not yet been realized.

Some monotone functions are very important. Among these are the **clique function** $f_{\mathrm{clique},k}^{(n)}:\mathcal{B}^{n(n-1)/2}\mapsto\mathcal{B}$. $f_{\mathrm{clique},k}^{(n)}$ is associated with a family of undirected graphs $G=(V,E)$ on $n=|V|$ vertices and $|E|\le n(n-1)/2$ edges, where $V=\{1,2,3,\ldots,n\}$. The variables of $f_{\mathrm{clique},k}^{(n)}$ are denoted $\{x_{i,j}\mid 1\le i<j\le n\}$, where $x_{i,j}=1$ if there is an edge between vertices i and j and $x_{i,j}=0$ otherwise. The value of $f_{\mathrm{clique},k}^{(n)}$ on these variables is 1 if G contains a **k-clique**, a set of k vertices such that there is an edge between every pair of vertices in the set. The value of $f_{\mathrm{clique},k}^{(n)}$ is 0 otherwise. Clearly $f_{\mathrm{clique},k}^{(n)}$ is monotone because increasing the value of a variable from 0 to 1 cannot decrease the value of the function.

As stated in Problem 8.24, the CLIQUE problem is **NP**-complete. Since an instance of CLIQUE on a graph with n vertices can be converted to the input format for $f_{\mathrm{clique},k}^{(n)}$ in time polynomial in n, if the circuit size for $f_{\mathrm{clique},k}^{(n)}$ over a complete basis can be shown to be superpolynomial, then from Corollary 3.9.1, $\mathbf{P}\ne\mathbf{NP}$.

There are important similarities and differences between monotone and non-monotone functions. Every non-monotone function can be realized by a circuit over the standard basis Ω_0 in which negations are used only on inputs. (See Problem 9.11.) On the other hand, since circuits without negation compute only monotone functions (Problem 2), negations on inputs are essential.

The first results showing the existence of monotone functions such that their monotone and non-monotone circuit sizes are different were obtained for multiple-output functions. We illustrate this approach below for the n-input binary sorting function, $f_{\mathrm{sort}}^{(n)}$, whose monotone circuit size is shown to be $\Theta(n\log n)$. As stated in Problem 2.17, this function can be realized by a circuit whose size over Ω_0 is linear in n.

We introduce the path method to show that a gap exists between the monotone and non-monotone circuit size of a family of functions. In Section 9.6.3 the approximation method is introduced and used to show that the clique function $f_{\mathrm{clique},k}^{(n)}$ has exponential monotone circuit size.

9.6.1 The Path-Elimination Method

In this section we illustrate the **path-elimination method** for deriving lower bounds on circuit size for monotone functions. This method demonstrates that a path of gates in a monotone circuit can be eliminated by fixing one input variable. Thus, it is the monotone equivalent of the gate-elimination method for general circuits. We apply the method to two problems, binary sorting and binary merging.

Consider computing the binary sorting function $f_{\text{sort}}^{(n)} : \mathcal{B}^n \mapsto \mathcal{B}^n$ introduced in Section 2.11. This function rearranges the bits in a binary n-input string into descending order. Thus, the first sorted output is 1 if one or more of the inputs is 1, the second is 1 if two or more of them are 1, etc. Consequently, we can write $f_{\text{sort}}^{(n)}(x_1, x_2, \ldots, x_n) = (\tau_1^{(n)}, \tau_2^{(n)}, \ldots, \tau_n^{(n)})$, where $\tau_t^{(n)}$ is the threshold function on n inputs with threshold t whose value is 1 if t or more of its inputs are 1 and 0 otherwise. Ajtai, Komlós, and Szemerédi [14] have shown the existence of a comparator-based sorting network on n inputs of size $O(n \log n)$. (The coefficient on this bound is so large that the bound has only asymptotic value.) Such networks can be converted to a monotone network by replacing the max and min operators in comparators with OR and AND, respectively.

THEOREM 9.6.1 *The monotone circuit size for $f_{\text{sort}}^{(n)}$ satisfies the following bounds:*

$$n\lceil \log_2 n \rceil - 2^{\lceil \log_2 n \rceil} \leq C_{\Omega_{\text{mon}}}\left(f_{\text{sort}}^{(n)}\right) = O(n \log n)$$

Proof To derive the lower bound, we show that in any circuit for $f_{\text{sort}}^{(n)}$ there is an input variable that can be set to 1, thereby allowing at least $\lceil \log_2 n \rceil$ gates along a path from it to the output $\tau_1^{(n)}$ to be removed from the circuit and converting the circuit to one for $f_{\text{sort}}^{(n-1)}$. As a result, we show the following relationship:

$$C_{\Omega_{\text{mon}}}\left(f_{\text{sort}}^{(n)}\right) \geq C_{\Omega_{\text{mon}}}\left(f_{sort}^{(n-1)}\right) + \lceil \log_2 n \rceil$$

A simple proof by induction and a little algebra show that the desired result follows from this bound and the fact that $C_{\Omega}(f_{\text{sort}}^{(2)}) = 2$, which is easy to establish.

Let $x_j = 0$ for $j \neq i$ but let x_i vary. The only functions computed at gates are 0, 1, or x_i. Also, the value of $\tau_1(\boldsymbol{x})$ on such inputs is equal to x_i. Consequently, there must be a path P from the vertex labeled x_i to τ_1 such that at each gate on the path the function x_i is computed. (See Fig. 9.9.) Thus, if we set $x_i = 1$ when $x_j = 0$ for $j \neq i$ the output of each of these gates is 1. Furthermore, since the circuit is monotone, each function computed at a gate is monotone (see Problem 2). Thus, if any other input is subsequently increased from 0 to 1, the value of τ_1 and of all the gates on the path P from x_i remain at 1 and can be removed. This setting of x_i also has the effect of reducing the threshold of all other output functions by 1 and implies that the circuit now computes the binary sorting function on one fewer variable.

Consider a minimal monotone circuit for $f_{\text{sort}}^{(n)}$. The shortest paths from each input to the output $\tau_1^{(n)}$ form a tree of fan-in 2. From Theorem 9.3.1 there is a path in this tree from some input, say x_r, to $\tau_1^{(n)}$ that has length at least $\lceil \log_2 n \rceil$. Consequently the shortest path from x_r to $\tau_1^{(n)}$ has length at least $\lceil \log_2 n \rceil$, implying that at least $\lceil \log_2 n \rceil$ gates can be removed if x_r is set to 1. ∎

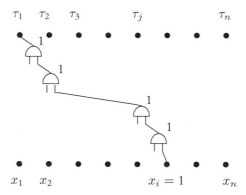

Figure 9.9 When $x_i = 1$ there is a path P to τ_1 such that each gate on P has value 1.

We now derive a stronger result: we show that every monotone circuit for binary merging has a size that is $\Omega(n \log n)$. **Binary merging** is realized by a function $f_{\text{merge}}^{(n)} : \mathcal{B}^n \mapsto \mathcal{B}^n, n = 2k$, defined as follows: given two sorted binary k-tuples $\boldsymbol{x}$ and $\boldsymbol{y}$, the value of $f_{\text{merge}}^{(n)}(\boldsymbol{x}, \boldsymbol{y})$ is the n-tuple that results from sorting the n-tuple formed by concatenating $\boldsymbol{x}$ and $\boldsymbol{y}$. Thus, a binary merging circuit can be obtained from one for sorting simply by restricting the values assumed by inputs to the sorting circuit. (Binary merging is a subfunction of binary sorting.) It follows that a lower bound on $C_{\Omega_{\text{mon}}}\left(f_{\text{merge}}^{(n)}\right)$ is a lower bound on $C_{\Omega_{\text{mon}}}\left(f_{\text{sort}}^{(n)}\right)$.

THEOREM 9.6.2 *Let n be even. Then the monotone circuit size for $f_{\text{merge}}^{(n)} : \mathcal{B}^n \mapsto \mathcal{B}^n$ satisfies the following bounds:*

$$(n/2) \log_2 n - O(n) \leq C_{\Omega_{\text{mon}}}\left(f_{\text{merge}}^{(n)}\right) = O(n \log n)$$

Proof The upper bound on $C_{\Omega_{\text{mon}}}\left(f_{\text{merge}}^{(n)}\right)$ follows from the construction given in Theorem 6.8.2 after max and min comparison operators are replaced by ANDs and ORs, respectively.

Let $k = n/2$. The function $f_{\text{merge}}^{(n)}$ operates on two k-tuples $\boldsymbol{x}$ and $\boldsymbol{y}$ to produce the merged result $f_{\text{merge}}^{(n)}(\boldsymbol{x}, \boldsymbol{y})$, where $\boldsymbol{x}$ and $\boldsymbol{y}$ are in descending order; that is, $x_1 \geq x_2 \geq \cdots \geq x_k$ and $y_1 \geq y_2 \geq \cdots \geq y_k$. As stated above for binary sorting, the output functions are $\tau_1, \tau_2, \ldots, \tau_n$.

Let $x_1 = x_2 = \cdots = x_{r-1} = 1, x_{r+1} = \cdots = x_k = 0, y_1 = y_2 = \cdots = y_s = 1$, and $y_{s+1} = \cdots = y_k = 0$. Let x_r be unspecified. Since the circuit is monotone, the value computed by each gate circuit is 0, 1, or x_r. Also,

$$\tau_t(\boldsymbol{x}, \boldsymbol{y}) = \begin{cases} 1 & t < r + s \\ x_r & t = r + s \\ 0 & t > r + s \end{cases}$$

It follows that there must be a path $P_r^{(r+s)}$ of gates from the input labeled x_r to the output labeled τ_{r+s} such that each gate output is x_r. If $x_r = 0$, since the components of $\boldsymbol{x}$

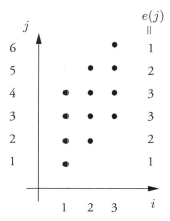

Figure 9.10 Let $f^{(n)}_{\mathrm{merge}}(\boldsymbol{x}, \boldsymbol{y}) = (\tau_1, \ldots, \tau_n)$, where $\boldsymbol{x}$ and $\boldsymbol{y}$ are $(n/2)$-tuples. The dots in the jth row show the inputs on which τ_j depends. $e(j)$ is the number of dots in the jth row.

are sorted, $x_{r+1} = \cdots = x_k = 0$. On the other hand, if $x_r = 1$, by monotonicity the value of τ_{r+s} cannot change under variation of the values $x_{r+1}, \ldots, x_k$. Thus, τ_j is essentially dependent on x_i for i and j satisfying $1 \le i \le k$ and $i \le j \le i + k$. (See Fig. 9.10.) Let $e(j)$ denote the number of variables in $\boldsymbol{x}$ on which τ_j depends; then $e(j) = j$ for $j \le k$ and $e(j) = 2k - j + 1$ for $j > k$.

We show by induction that there exist vertex-disjoint paths between x_1 and τ_{s+1}, x_2 and $\tau_{s+2}, \ldots, x_k$ and τ_{s+k} for $0 \le s \le k$. (See Fig. 9.11.) Thus, there are $k + 1$ sets of vertex-disjoint paths connecting the $k = n/2$ inputs in $\boldsymbol{x}$ and k consecutive outputs.

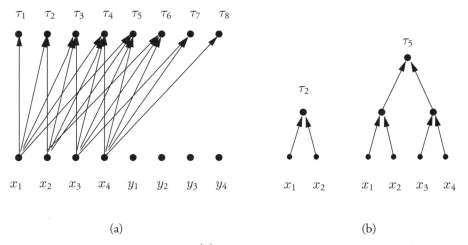

Figure 9.11 (a) In a monotone circuit for $f^{(n)}_{\mathrm{merge}}$, $n = 2k$, $k+1$ sets of k disjoint paths exist between the k inputs $\boldsymbol{x}$ and k consecutive outputs. (b) The paths to an output τ_j form a binary tree.

To show the existence of the vertex-disjoint paths, let $y_1 = y_2 = \cdots = y_s = 1$, $y_{s+1} = \cdots = y_k = 0$ and $x_1 = x_2 = \cdots = x_{r-1} = 1$, but let $x_r, x_{r+1}, \ldots, x_k$ be unspecified. Then $\tau_{r+s} = x_r$ and, as stated above, there is a path $P_r^{(r+s)}$ of gates from an input labeled x_r to the output labeled τ_{r+s} such that each gate has value x_r. Set $x_r = 1$. Reasoning as before, there must be a path $P_{r+1}^{(r+1+s)}$ of gates from an input labeled x_{r+1} to the output labeled τ_{r+1+s} such that each gate has value x_{r+1}. Thus, $P_{r+1}^{(r+1+s)}$ and $P_r^{(r+s)}$ are vertex-disjoint. Extending this idea, we have the desired conclusion about disjoint paths.

We now develop a second fact about these paths that is needed in the lower bound. Let $P_r^{(r+s)}$ be a path from x_r to τ_{r+s}, as suggested in Fig. 9.11(a). Those paths connecting inputs to any one output form a binary tree, as suggested in Fig. 9.11(b). The number of inputs from which there is a path to τ_j is $e(j)$, the number of inputs on which τ_j depends.

To derive the lower bound on $C_{\Omega_{\mathrm{mon}}}(f_{\mathrm{merge}}^{(n)})$, let $d(i,j)$ denote the length (number of edges or non-input vertices (gates)) on the shortest path from an input labeled x_i to the output labeled τ_j. (Clearly, $d(i,j) = 0$ unless $i \leq j \leq i + k$.) Since the path from input x_i to output τ_j described above has a length at least as large as $d(i,j)$, it follows that $C_{\Omega_{\mathrm{mon}}}\left(f_{\mathrm{merge}}^{(n)}\right)$ satisfies the following bound:

$$C_{\Omega_{\mathrm{mon}}}\left(f_{\mathrm{merge}}^{(n)}\right) \geq \max\left\{\sum_{r=1}^{k} d(r, r+s) \mid 0 \leq s \leq k\right\}$$

Since the maximum of a set of integers is at least equal to the average of these integers, we have the following for $k = n/2 \geq 1$:

$$C_{\Omega_{\mathrm{mon}}}\left(f_{\mathrm{merge}}^{(n)}\right) \geq \frac{1}{k+1}\sum_{s=0}^{k}\sum_{r=1}^{k} d(r, r+s) = \frac{1}{k+1}\sum_{j=1}^{2k}\sum_{i=1}^{k} d(i, j)$$

The last identity follows by using the fact that $d(i,j) = 0$ unless $i \leq j \leq i + k$. But $\sum_{i=1}^{k} d(i,j)$ is the sum of the distances of the shortest paths from the relevant inputs of x to output τ_j, $1 \leq j \leq 2k$. Since these paths form a binary tree and τ_j depends on $e(j)$ inputs, this is the external path length of a tree with $e(j)$ leaves. The external path length is at least $e(j)\lceil \log_2 e(j)\rceil - 2^{\lceil \log_2 e(j)\rceil} + e(j)$ (see Problem 9.4). In turn, $x\lceil \log_2 x\rceil - 2^{\lceil \log_2 x\rceil} + x \geq x\log_2 x$, because $\lceil \log_2 x\rceil = (\log_2 x) + \delta$ for $0 \leq \delta < 1$ and $x\lceil \log_2 x\rceil - 2^{\lceil \log_2 x\rceil} + x = x\log_2 x + x(1 - 2^\delta + \delta)$, where $1 - 2^\delta + \delta$ is easily shown to be a concave function whose minimum value occurs at either $\delta = 0$ or $\delta = 1$, both of which are 0. Thus, $1 - 2^\delta + \delta \geq 0$ and the result follows. Thus, the size of smallest monotone circuit satisfies the following lower bound when $n = 2k$:

$$C_{\Omega_{\mathrm{mon}}}\left(f_{\mathrm{merge}}^{(n)}\right) \geq \frac{1}{k+1}\sum_{j=1}^{2k}[e(j)\log_2 e(j)]$$

$$= \frac{2}{k+1}\sum_{j=1}^{k}[j\log_2 j]$$

The last equality uses the definition of $e(j)$ given above. By applying the reasoning in Problem 2.1 and captured in Fig. 2.23, it is easy to show that the above sum is at least as large as $(2/(k+1))(\log_2 e) \int_{j=1}^{k} y \log_e y \; dy$, whose value is $(2/(k+1))[(k^2/2)\log_2 k - (1/4)k^2(\log_2 e) + 1/4]$. From this the desired conclusion follows, since $k = n/2$. ∎

We now present lower bounds on the monotone circuit size of Boolean convolution and Boolean matrix multiplication, problems for which the gap between the monotone and non-monotone circuit size is much larger than for sorting and merging.

9.6.2 The Function Replacement Method

The **function replacement method** simplifies monotone circuits by replacing a function computed at an internal vertex by a new function without changing the function computed by the overall circuit. Since a replacement step eliminates gates and reduces a problem to a subproblem, the method provides a basis for establishing lower bounds on circuit complexity using proof by induction.

We describe two replacement rules and then apply them to Boolean convolution and Boolean matrix multiplication. These two problems are defined in the usual way except that variables assume Boolean values in $\mathcal{B}$ and the multiplication and addition operators are interpreted as AND and OR, respectively.

REPLACEMENT RULES   A **replacement rule** is a rule that allows a function computed at a vertex of a circuit to be replaced by another without changing the function computed by the circuit. Before stating such rules for monotone functions, we introduce some terminology.

DEFINITION 9.6.1 *Let $\boldsymbol{x}$ denote the variables of a Boolean function $f : \mathcal{B}^n \mapsto \mathcal{B}$. An* **implicant** *of f is a product (AND), π, of a subset of the literals of f (the variables and their complements) such that if $\pi(\boldsymbol{x}) = 1$ on input n-tuple $\boldsymbol{x}$, then $f(\boldsymbol{x}) = 1$. (This is denoted $\pi \leq f$.) The* **set of implicants** *of a function f is denoted $I(f)$.*

An implicant π of a Boolean function f is a **prime implicant** *if there is no implicant π_1 different from π such that $\pi \leq \pi_1 \leq f$. The* **set of prime implicants** *of a function f is denoted $PI(f)$.*

A **monotone implicant** *(also called a* **monom***) of a monotone Boolean function $f : \mathcal{B}^n \mapsto \mathcal{B}$ is the product (AND) π of uncomplemented variables of f such that if $\pi(\boldsymbol{x}) = 1$ on input n-tuple $\boldsymbol{x}$, then $f(\boldsymbol{x}) = 1$. The* **empty monom** *has value 1. The* **set of monotone implicants** *of a function f is denoted $I_{\mathrm{mon}}(f)$.*

A monotone implicant π of a Boolean function f is a **monotone prime implicant** *if there is no monotone implicant π_1 different from π such that $\pi \leq \pi_1 \leq f$. The* **set of monotone prime implicants** *of a function f is denoted $PI_{\mathrm{mon}}(f)$.*

The products in the sum-of-products expansion (SOPE) are (non-monotone) implicants of a Boolean function. If a function is monotone, it has monotone implicants (monoms). The prime implicants of a Boolean function f define it completely; the OR of its prime implicants is a formula representing it. In the case of a monotone Boolean function, the prime implicants are monotone prime implicants. (See Problem 9.33.)

When it is understood from context that an implicant or prime implicant is monotone, we may omit the word "monotone" and use the subscript "mon." This will be the case in this section.

The function $c_{j+1} = (p_j \wedge c_j) \vee g_j$ used in the design of a full adder (see Section 2.7) is a monotone function of the variables p_j, c_j, and g_j. Its set of implicants is $I(c_{j+1}) = \{p_j \wedge c_j, g_j, p_j \wedge g_j, c_j \wedge g_j, p_j \wedge c_j \wedge g_j\}$. If any one of these products has value 1 then so does c_{j+1}. Its set of prime implicants is $PI(c_{j+1}) = \{p_j \wedge c_j, g_j\} \subseteq I(c_{j+1})$ because these are the smallest products for which c_{j+1} has value 1. Thus, c_{j+1} is defined by $PI(c_{j+1})$ and represented as $c_{j+1} = (p_j \wedge c_j) \vee g_j$.

We now present a replacement rule for monotone functions that captures the following idea: if a function g computed by a gate of a monotone circuit has a monom π that is not a monom of the function f computed by the complete circuit, then π can be removed from g without affecting the value of f. This idea is valid in monotone circuits because the absence of negation provides only one way to eliminate extra monoms, namely, by ORing them with products containing a subset of their variables. Taking the AND of a monom with another term creates a longer monom. Thus, since monoms that are not monoms of the function f computed by a circuit must be eliminated, there is no loss of generality in assuming that they are not produced in the first place.

DEFINITION 9.6.2 *Let $f : \mathcal{B}^n \mapsto \mathcal{B}$ and $g : \mathcal{B}^n \mapsto \mathcal{B}$ be two monotone functions. Let g be computed within a monotone circuit for f. The following is a replacement rule for g:*

a) *Let $\pi_1 \in PI(g)$ and let h be defined by $PI(h) = PI(g) - \{\pi\}$. Replace the gate computing g by one computing h if for all monoms π' (including the empty monom), $\pi \wedge \pi' \notin PI(f)$.*

We now show that any monom π satisfying Rule (a) can be removed from $PI(g)$ because it contributes nothing to the computation of f.

LEMMA 9.6.1 *Let $f : \mathcal{B}^n \mapsto \mathcal{B}$ and $g : \mathcal{B}^n \mapsto \mathcal{B}$ be two monotone functions and let $\pi \in PI(g)$ be such that for all monoms π' (including the empty monom), $\pi \wedge \pi' \notin PI(f)$. Let h be defined by $PI(h) = PI(g) - \{\pi\}$. If g is computed in some monotone circuit for f, the circuit obtained by replacing g by h also computes f.*

Proof Let $\mathcal{C}$ denote a circuit for f within which the function g is computed. Let $\mathcal{C}^*$ be the circuit obtained by replacing g by h under Rule (a). Since $h \leq g$ and the circuit is monotone, the function f^* computed by $\mathcal{C}^*$ satisfies $f^* \leq f$. We suppose that $f^* \neq f$ and show that a contradiction results.

If $f^* \neq f$, there is some input n-tuple $\boldsymbol{a} \in \mathcal{B}^n$ such that $f^*(\boldsymbol{a}) = 0$ but $f(\boldsymbol{a}) = 1$. Since the only change in the circuit occurred at the gate computing g, by monotonicity, on this tuple $g(\boldsymbol{a}) = 1$ but $h(\boldsymbol{a}) = 0$. It follows that $\pi(\boldsymbol{a}) = 1$. Let π' be a prime implicant of f for which $\pi'(\boldsymbol{a}) = 1$. We show that $\pi' = \pi \wedge \pi_1$ for some monom π_1, in contradiction to the condition of the lemma.

Let x_i be any variable of π. Then $a_i = 1$ since $\pi(\boldsymbol{a}) = 1$. Define the n-tuple $\boldsymbol{b}$ by $b_i = 0$ and $b_j = a_j$ for $j \neq i$. Since $\boldsymbol{b} \leq \boldsymbol{a}$ and $\pi(\boldsymbol{b}) = 0$, h and g both have the same value on $\boldsymbol{b}$. Thus, both circuits compute the same value, which must be 0 by monotonicity and the fact that $f^* = 0$ on $\boldsymbol{a}$. Since $\pi'(\boldsymbol{a}) = 1$ and $\pi'(\boldsymbol{b}) = 0$ but only one variable was changed, namely x_i, π' must contain x_i. Since x_i is an arbitrary variable of π, it follows that π' contains π as a sub-monom. ∎

This last result implies that if a function f has no prime implicants containing more than l variables, then any monoms containing more than l variables can be removed where they are first created. This will be useful later when discussing Boolean convolution and Boolean matrix multiplication, since each of their prime implicants depends on two variables.

BOOLEAN CONVOLUTION   Convolution over commutative rings is defined in Section 6.7. In this section we introduce the Boolean version, which is defined by a monotone multiple-output function, and derive a lower bound of $n^{3/2}$ on its monotone circuit size. We also show that over a complete basis Boolean convolution can be realized by a circuit of nearly linear size.

DEFINITION 9.6.3   *The* **Boolean convolution function** $f_{\text{conv}}^{(n)} : \mathcal{B}^{2n} \mapsto \mathcal{B}^{2n-1}$ *maps Boolean n-tuples* $\boldsymbol{a} = (a_0, a_1, \ldots, a_{n-1})$ *and* $\boldsymbol{b} = (b_0, b_1, \ldots, b_{n-1})$ *onto a* $(2n-1)$*-tuple* $\boldsymbol{c}$*, denoted* $\boldsymbol{c} = \boldsymbol{a} \otimes \boldsymbol{b}$*, where* c_j*,* $0 \le j \le 2n-2$*, is defined as*

$$c_j = \sum_{r+s=j} a_r \wedge b_s$$

Boolean convolution can be realized by a circuit over the standard basis Ω_0 for multiplying binary numbers (see Section 2.9) as follows. Represent $\boldsymbol{a}$ and $\boldsymbol{b}$ by the following integers where $q = \lceil \log_2 n \rceil + 1$:

$$a = \sum_{i=0}^{n-1} a_i 2^{qi}, \qquad b = \sum_{j=0}^{n-1} b_j 2^{qj}$$

That is, each bit in a and b is separated by $\lceil \log_2 n \rceil$ zeros. The formal product of a and b is

$$ab = \sum_{k=0}^{2n-2} \left(\sum_{i+j=k} a_i b_j \right) 2^{qk}$$

Because no inner sum in the above expression is more than $2n-1$, at most q bits suffice to represent it in binary notation. Consequently, there is no carry between any two inner sums. It follows that an inner sum is non-zero if and only if $c_k = 1$. Thus, the value of c_k can be obtained by forming the OR of the bits in positions $kq, kq+1, \ldots, kq+q-1$ of the product. Since two binary m tuples can be multiplied in the standard binary notation by a circuit of size $O\left(m(\log m)(\log\log m)\right)$ (see Section 2.9.3), the function $f_{\text{conv}}^{(n)}$ can be computed by a circuit of size $O\left(n(\log^2 n)(\log\log n)\right)$ since $m = nq = O(n \log n)$.

THEOREM 9.6.3   *The circuit size of* $f_{\text{conv}}^{(n)} : \mathcal{B}^{2n} \mapsto \mathcal{B}^{2n-1}$ *over the standard basis satisfies*

$$C_{\Omega_0}\left(f_{\text{conv}}^{(n)}\right) = O\left(n(\log^2 n)(\log\log n)\right)$$

Our goal is to use the function replacement method to show that every monotone circuit for Boolean convolution has size $\Omega(n^{3/2})$. As explained above, the method is designed to use induction to prove lower bounds on monotone circuit size. Each replacement step removes prime implicants from the function g computed at some gate and changes the function f computed by the circuit. If the new function f^* is in the same family as f, the gate-replacement process can continue and induction can be applied. Since the convolution function does not necessarily change to another instance of itself on fewer variables, we place this function in the class of semi-disjoint bilinear forms.

DEFINITION 9.6.4 *Let $f^{(n,m,p)} = (f_1, f_2, \ldots, f_p)$, where each $f_r : \mathcal{B}^{n+m} \mapsto \mathcal{B}$, $1 \leq r \leq p$, is a monotone function on n-tuple $\boldsymbol{x}$ and m-tuple $\boldsymbol{y}$; that is, $f_r(\boldsymbol{x}, \boldsymbol{y}) \in \mathcal{B}$. $f^{(n,m,p)}$ is a **bilinear form** if each prime implicant of each f_r, $1 \leq r \leq p$, contains one variable of $\boldsymbol{x}$ and one of $\boldsymbol{y}$. A function $f^{(n,m,p)}$ is a **semi-disjoint bilinear form** if in addition $PI(f_r) \cap PI(f_s) = \emptyset$ for $r \neq s$ and each variable is contained in at most one prime implicant of any one function.*

Before deriving a lower bound on the number of gates needed for a semi-disjoint bilinear form, we introduce a new replacement rule peculiar to these forms.

LEMMA 9.6.2 *No gate of a monotone circuit of minimal size for a semi-disjoint bilinear form $f^{(n,m,p)}$ computes a function g whose prime implicants include either two variables of $\boldsymbol{x}$ or of $\boldsymbol{y}$.*

Proof We suppose that a minimal monotone circuit does contain a gate g whose prime implicants contain either two variables of $\boldsymbol{x}$ or two of $\boldsymbol{y}$ and show that a contradiction results. Without loss of generality, assume that $PI(g)$ contains x_i and x_j, $i \neq j$. If there is a gate g satisfying this hypothesis, there is one that is closest to an input variable. This must be an OR gate because AND gates increase the length of prime implicants. Because the gate in question is closest to inputs, at least one of x_i and x_j is either an input to this OR gate or is the input to some OR gate that is on a path of OR gates to this gate. (See Fig. 9.12.)

A simple proof by induction on its circuit size demonstrates that if a circuit for $f^{(n,m,p)} = (f_1, \ldots, f_p)$ contains a gate computing g then f_r, $1 \leq r \leq p$, can be written as follows (see Problem 9.36):

$$f_r(\boldsymbol{x}, \boldsymbol{y}) = (p_r(\boldsymbol{x}, \boldsymbol{y}) \wedge g(\boldsymbol{x}, \boldsymbol{y})) \vee q_r(\boldsymbol{x}, \boldsymbol{y}) \tag{9.1}$$

Here $p_r(\boldsymbol{x}, \boldsymbol{y})$ and $q_r(\boldsymbol{x}, \boldsymbol{y})$ are Boolean functions. Of course, if for no r is f_r a function of g, then we can set $p_r(\boldsymbol{x}, \boldsymbol{y}) = 0$ and the circuit is not minimal.

If f_r depends on g, $p_r(\boldsymbol{x}, \boldsymbol{y}) \neq 0$. However, $p_r(\boldsymbol{x}, \boldsymbol{y}) \neq 1$ because otherwise both x_i and x_j are prime implicants of f_r, contradicting its definition. Also, $PI(p_r(\boldsymbol{x}, \boldsymbol{y}))$ cannot have any monoms containing one or more instances of a variable in $\boldsymbol{x}$ or two or more instances of variables in $\boldsymbol{y}$ because when ANDed with g they produce monoms that could be removed by Rule (a) of Definition 9.6.2 and the circuit would not be minimal. It follows that $PI(p_r(\boldsymbol{x}, \boldsymbol{y}))$ can contain only single variables of $\boldsymbol{y}$. But this implies that for some k, $y_k \wedge g \in I(f_r)$, which together with the fact that $x_i, x_j \in PI(g)$ implies that

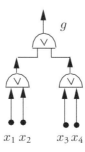

Figure 9.12 If $PI(g)$ for a gate g contains x_i and x_j, then either x_i or x_j is input to an OR gate on a path of OR gates to g.

$y_k \wedge x_i, y_k \wedge x_j \in I(f_r)$. But $y_k \wedge x_i$ and $y_k \wedge x_j$ cannot both be prime implicants of f_r because they violate the requirement that no two prime implicants of f_r contain the same variable. It follows that f_r does not depend on g. ∎

The Boolean convolution function is a semi-disjoint bilinear form. Each implicant of each component of $\boldsymbol{c} = \boldsymbol{a} \otimes \boldsymbol{b}$ contains one variable of $\boldsymbol{a}$ and one of $\boldsymbol{b}$. In addition, the prime implicants of c_i and c_j are disjoint if $i \neq j$. Finally, each variable appears in only one implicant of a component function, although it may appear in more than one such function.

THEOREM 9.6.4 *Let* $f^{(n,m,p)} : \mathcal{B}^{n+m} \mapsto \mathcal{B}^p$, $f^{(n,m,p)} = (f_1, f_2, \ldots, f_p)$, *be a semi-disjoint bilinear form, where* $f_r(\boldsymbol{x}, \boldsymbol{y}) \in \mathcal{B}$. *Let* d_i *be the number of functions in* $\{f_1, f_2, \ldots, f_p\}$ *that are essentially dependent on the input variable* x_i, $1 \leq i \leq n$. *Then the monotone circuit size of* $f^{(n,m,p)}$ *must satisfy the following lower bound:*

$$C_{\Omega_{\mathrm{mon}}} \left(f^{(n,m,p)} \right) \geq \sum_{i=1}^{n} \sqrt{d_i}$$

Proof The proof is by induction. The basis for induction is the semi-disjoint bilinear form on two variables $f^{(1,1,1)}(x, y) = x \wedge y$. In this case $d_1 = 1$ and $C_{\Omega_{\mathrm{mon}}} \left(f^{(1,1,1)} \right) = 1$. We assume that any semi-disjoint bilinear form in $n + m - 1$ or fewer variables satisfies the lower bound. We show that setting $x_i = 0$ produces another function that is a semi-disjoint bilinear form and allows the removal of at least $\sqrt{d_i}$ gates. The lower bound follows by induction. We consider only minimal circuits.

Let u_i denote the number of functions in $\{f_1, f_2, \ldots, f_p\}$ that are essentially dependent on x_i and have a single prime implicant (such as $c_0 = a_0 \wedge b_0$ and $c_{2n-2} = a_{n-1} \wedge b_{n-1}$ for convolution). Setting $x_i = 0$ eliminates the u_i AND gates at which these outputs are computed. We show that at least $\sqrt{d_i - u_i}$ OR gates can also be eliminated. Since $u_i + \sqrt{d_i - u_i} \geq \sqrt{d_i}$ (see Problem 9.8), we have the desired conclusion.

Let V_i denote those outputs that depend on x_i whose associated function has at least two prime implicants. Then $|V_i| = d_i - u_i$. There must be at least one OR gate on each path P from x_i to $f_r \in V_i$ because, if not, each path contains only ANDs and f_r has only one prime implicant that contains x_i, in contradiction to the definition of V_i.

We claim that on each path P from an input labeled x_i to some $f_r \in V_i$ there is an OR gate computing a function g_t such that $x_{i_t} \wedge y_{j_t} \in PI(g_t)$ for some $x_{i_t} \neq x_i$. Let $E_i = \{g_t\}$ be those OR gates closest to an input vertex x_i. Call E_i the **bottleneck for variable** x_i. We shall show that $|E_i| \geq \sqrt{d_i - u_i}$ and that each of the gates in E_i can be eliminated by setting $x_i = 0$.

If the claim is false, then there is a path P from input x_i to output $f_r \in V_i$ such that for each OR gate (let it compute g_t) on P there is no $x_{i_t} \neq x_i$ such that $x_{i_t} \wedge y_{j_t} \in PI(g_t)$. Therefore, either all monoms of $PI(g_t)$ a) contain x_i or b) are monoms that are not implicants of an output (they are not of the form $x_{i_t} \wedge y_{j_t}$). In case a), setting $x_i = 0$ causes the OR gates on P to have value 0, which forces the AND gates on P and f_r to have value 0, contradicting the definition of f_r (it has at least two prime implicants). In the second case under Rule (a) the monoms not containing x_i can be removed without changing the functions computed. Thus, when $x_i = 0$, the output of each OR gate on P has value 0, which contradicts the definition of f_r since it contains at least two prime implicants.

We now show that $|E_i| \geq \sqrt{d_i - u_i}$. Since each of the OR gates in E_i has a prime implicant $x_{i_t} \wedge y_{j_t}$ not containing x_i, their outputs can be set to 1 by setting $x_{i_t} = y_{j_t} = 1$

for $1 \leq t \leq |E_i|$. This eliminates all dependence of $f_r \in V_i$ on x_i. However, since inputs have only been assigned value 1 (and not 0), this dependence on x_i can be eliminated only if all functions in V_i have value 1; that is, at least one prime implicant of each of them is set to 1 by this assignment. Since each variable appears in at most one prime implicant of a function, the number of different variables x_{i_t} (and y_{i_t}) that are set to 1 is at most $|E_i|$. Thus, at most $|E_i|^2$ prime implicants can be assigned value 1 by this assignment. Thus, if $|E_i|^2 < (d_i - u_i)$, we have a contradiction since $|V_i| = (d_i - u_i)$.

We now show that $|E_i|$ OR gates can be eliminated by setting $x_i = 0$. Since each gate is a closest gate to an input labeled x_i with the stated property, there is an OR gate on the path to it with x_i as an input. Thus, setting $x_i = 0$ eliminates one of the two inputs to the OR gate and the need for the gate itself. ∎

Since for each of the n input variables in $\boldsymbol{a}$ there are n output functions in $\boldsymbol{c} = \boldsymbol{a} \otimes \boldsymbol{b}$ that depend on it ($d_i = n$ for $1 \leq i \leq n$), the following corollary is immediate.

COROLLARY 9.6.1 *Let $f_{\text{conv}}^{(n)} : \mathcal{B}^{2n} \mapsto \mathcal{B}^{2n-1}$ be the Boolean convolution function. Then the monotone circuit size of $f_{\text{conv}}^{(n)}$ satisfies the following lower bound:*

$$C_{\Omega_{\text{mon}}} \left(f_{\text{conv}}^{(n)} \right) \geq n^{3/2}$$

Unfortunately, no upper bound on the monotone circuit size of $f_{\text{conv}}^{(n)}$ is known that matches this lower bound. A stronger statement can be made for Boolean matrix multiplication.

BOOLEAN MATRIX MULTIPLICATION   Matrix multiplication over rings is discussed at length in Section 6.3. In this section we introduce the Boolean version. An $I \times J$ matrix $A = [a_{i,j}]$, $1 \leq i \leq I$ and $1 \leq j \leq J$, is a two-dimensional array of elements in which $a_{i,j}$ is the element in the ith row and jth column. We take the entries in a matrix to be Boolean variables.

DEFINITION 9.6.5 *Let $A = [a_{i,k}]$, $1 \leq i \leq n$ and $1 \leq k \leq m$, $B = [b_{k,j}]$, $1 \leq k \leq m$ and $1 \leq j \leq p$, and $C = [c_{i,j}]$, $1 \leq i \leq n$ and $1 \leq j \leq p$, be $n \times m$, $m \times p$, and $n \times p$ matrices, respectively. The* **product** *$C = A \times B$ of A and B is the function $f_{\text{MM}}^{(n,m,p)} : \mathcal{B}^{nm+mp} \mapsto \mathcal{B}^{np}$ whose value on the matrices A and B is the matrix C whose entry in row i and column j, $c_{i,j}$, is defined as*

$$c_{i,j} = \bigvee_{k=1}^{m} a_{i,k} \wedge b_{k,j}$$

In a more general context the AND operator $\wedge$ and the OR operator $\vee$ are replaced by the multiplication and addition operators over rings.

The above definition can be used as an algorithm to compute $c_{i,j}$, $1 \leq i \leq n$ and $1 \leq j \leq p$, from the entries in matrices A and B. We call this the **standard matrix-multiplication algorithm**. It uses nmp ANDs and $n(m-1)p$ ORs. We now show that every monotone circuit for matrix multiplication requires at least this many ANDs and ORs.

Clearly the matrix multiplication function is a bilinear form. We associate the entries in A with the tuple $\boldsymbol{x}$ and those in B with $\boldsymbol{y}$. We strengthen Theorem 9.6.4 to obtain a lower bound on the number of ORs needed to realize it in a monotone circuit.

LEMMA 9.6.3 *Every monotone circuit for Boolean matrix multiplication $f_{\text{MM}}^{(n,m,p)}$ requires at least* $n(m-1)p$ OR *gates.*

Proof In the proof of Theorem 9.6.4 we identified a set E_i of gates called the bottleneck associated with each input variable x_i. We demonstrated that each of these gates can be eliminated by setting $x_i = 0$ and that E_i has at least $\sqrt{d_i - u_i}$ gates, where $d_i - u_i = |V_i|$ is the number of circuit outputs that depend essentially on x_i and have at least two prime implicants. These results were shown by proving that all gates in E_i are OR gates and that the tth of these gates' associated function contains a prime implicant of the form $x_{i_t} \wedge y_{j_t}$ for $x_{i_t} \neq x_i$. We then demonstrated that the dependence of the outputs in V_i on the input x_i can be eliminated by setting $x_{i_t} = y_{j_t} = 1$ for $1 \leq t \leq E_i$ but that this contradicts the definition of a semi-definite bilinear form if $|E_i|^2 < |V_i|$. Finally, we proved that by setting $x_i = 0$ each of the gates in E_i could be eliminated. For this lemma, we need only strengthen the lower bound on E_i for matrix multiplication.

Consider a minimal circuit. The proof is by induction on m, with the base case being $m = 1$. In the base case $c_{i,j} = a_{i,1} \wedge b_{1,j}$ for $1 \leq i \leq n$ and $1 \leq j \leq p$ and no ORs are needed. As inductive hypothesis we assume that $f_{\text{MM}}^{(n,m-1,p)}$ requires at least $n(m-2)p$ OR gates. We show that setting any column of A in $f_{\text{MM}}^{(n,m,p)}$ to 0 eliminates np OR gates and reduces the problem to an instance of $f_{\text{MM}}^{(n,m-1,p)}$. It follows that $f_{\text{MM}}^{(n,m,p)}$ requires $n(m-1)p$ OR gates.

When $m \geq 2$, each output function $c_{i,j}$ has at least two prime implicants. We apply the bottleneck argument to this case. Consider the bottleneck $E_{i,k}$ associated with input variable $a_{i,k}$. We show that $|E_{i,k}| \geq p$, from which it follows that at least p OR gates can be eliminated by setting $x_{i,k} = 0$. This reduces the problem to another set of bilinear forms. Repeating this for $1 \leq i \leq n$, we eliminate np OR gates, one column of A, and one row of B. Let $V_{i,j} = \{c_{i,j} \mid 1 \leq j \leq p\}$ be the outputs that depend on $a_{i,k}$.

To show that $|E_{i,k}| \geq p$, let the tth gate of $E_{i,k}$ compute $x_{i_t} \wedge y_{j_t}$ for $x_{i_t} \neq a_{i,k}$. Here $x_{i_t} = a_{i_t,k_t}$ and $y_{j_t} = b_{l_t,j_t}$ for some i_t, k_t, l_t, and j_t. If we set all entries in $\{a_{i_t,k_t} \mid 1 \leq t \leq |E_{i,k}|\} \cup \{b_{l_t,j_t} \mid 1 \leq t \leq |E_{i,k}|\}$ to 1, we eliminate all dependence of outputs in $V_{i,k}$ on $a_{i,k}$. However, since $|V_{i,j}| = p$, the set $\{b_{l_t,j_t}\}$ must contain at least one variable used in $c_{i,j}$ for each $1 \leq j \leq p$. Thus, $|E_{i,k}| \geq p$. ∎

We now derive a lower bound on the number of AND gates needed for Boolean matrix multiplication.

LEMMA 9.6.4 *Every monotone circuit for Boolean matrix multiplication $f_{\text{MM}}^{(n,m,p)}$ requires at least* nmp AND *gates.*

Proof Consider a minimal circuit. The proof is by induction on m, the base case being $m = 1$. In the base case $c_{i,j} = a_{i,1} \wedge b_{1,j}$ for $1 \leq i \leq n$ and $1 \leq j \leq p$ and np ANDs are needed, since np results must be computed, each requiring one AND, and all functions are different. As inductive hypothesis we assume that $f_{\text{MM}}^{(n,m-1,p)}$ requires at least $n(m-1)p$ AND gates. We show that setting any column of A in $f_{\text{MM}}^{(n,m,p)}$ to 1 and the corresponding row of B to 0 eliminates np AND gates and reduces the problem to an instance of $f_{\text{MM}}^{(n,m-1,p)}$. It follows that $f_{\text{MM}}^{(n,m,p)}$ requires nmp AND gates.

For arbitrary $1 \leq k \leq m$ let $G_{i,j}$ be a gate closest to inputs computing a function g such that $PI(g)$ contains $a_{i,k} \wedge b_{k,j}$. Since the gate associated with $c_{i,j}$ has $a_{i,k} \wedge b_{k,j}$ as a prime implicant, there is such a gate $G_{i,j}$. Furthermore, $G_{i,j}$ must be an AND gate because OR gates cannot generate new prime implicants. Let G_1 and G_2 be gates generating inputs for $G_{i,j}$. Let them compute functions g_1 and g_2. It follows from the definition of $G_{i,j}$ that $a_{i,k} \in PI(g_1)$ and $b_{k,j} \in PI(g_2)$ or vice versa. Let the former hold. If $a_{i,k} = 1$, $g_1 = 1$ and $G_{i,j}$ can be eliminated. We now show that $G_{i,j} \neq G_{i',j'}$ for $(i,j) \neq (i',j')$. Suppose not. Since $i \neq i'$ or $j \neq j'$, there are at least three distinct variables among $a_{i,k}$, $a_{i',k}$, $b_{k,j}$, and $b_{k,j'}$. Therefore either g_1 or g_2 has at least two of these variables as prime implicants. By Lemma 9.6.2 this circuit is not minimal, a contradiction. ■

We summarize the results of this section below.

THEOREM 9.6.5 *The standard algorithm for* $f_{\text{MM}}^{(n,m,p)} : \mathcal{B}^{nm+mp} \mapsto \mathcal{B}^{np}$, *the Boolean matrix multiplication function, is optimal. It uses* nmp *ANDs and* $n(m-1)p$ *ORs.*

We now show that the monotone circuit size of the clique function is exponential.

9.6.3 The Approximation Method

The approximation method is used to derive large lower bounds on the monotone circuit size for certain monotone Boolean functions. In this section we use it to derive an exponential lower bound on the size of the smallest monotone circuit for the clique function $f_{\text{clique},k}^{(n)} : \mathcal{B}^{n(n-1)/2} \mapsto \mathcal{B}$. This method provides an interesting approach to deriving large lower bounds on circuit size. However, as mentioned in the Chapter Notes, it is doubtful that it can be used to obtain large lower bounds on circuit size over complete bases.

The **approximation method** converts a monotone circuit C computing a function f into an approximation circuit $\widehat{C}$ computing a function $\widehat{f}$. This is done by repeatedly replacing a previously unvisited gate farthest away from the output gate by an approximation gate that computes an approximation to the AND or OR gate it replaces. Each replacement operation changes the circuit and increases by a small amount the number of input tuples on which f and the function computed by the new circuit differ. When the entire replacement process is complete, the resulting circuit approximates f poorly; that is, $\widehat{f}$ and f differ on a large number of inputs. For this to happen, the original monotone circuit must have had many gates, each of which contributes a relatively small number of errors to the complete replacement process. This is the essence of the approximation method.

There are a number of ways to approximate AND and OR gates in a monotone circuit. Razborov [264], who introduced the approximation method, used an approximation for gates based on clique indicators, monotone functions associated with a subset of a set of vertices that has value 1 exactly when there is an edge between every pair of vertices in the subset. In this section gates are approximated in terms of the SOPE and POSE forms, a method used by Amano and Maruoka [20] to approximate the clique function.

It is not hard to show that the monotone circuit size of $f_{\text{clique},k}^{(n)}$ is $O(n^n)$. (See Problem 9.37.) We now show that all monotone circuits for $f_{\text{clique},k}^{(n)}$ have size $C_{\Omega_{\text{mon}}}\left(f_{\text{clique},k}^{(n)}\right) \geq \frac{1}{2}(1.8)^{\min(\sqrt{k-1}/2, n/(2k))}$, which is $2^{\Omega(n^{1/3})}$ for k proportional to $n^{2/3}$.

TEST CASES   The quality of an approximation to the clique function $f_{\text{clique},k}^{(n)}$ is determined by providing positive and negative test inputs. A k-**positive test input** is a binary $n(n-1)/2$-tuple that describes a graph containing a single k-clique.

The negative test inputs, defined below, describe graphs that have many edges but not quite enough to contain a k-clique. A special set of negative test inputs is associated with balanced partitions of the vertices of an n-vertex graph $G = (V, E)$. A $(k-1)$-**balanced partition** of $V = \{v_1, \ldots, v_n\}$ is a collection of $k - 1$ disjoint sets, $V_1, V_2, \ldots, V_{k-1}$, such that each set contains either $\lceil n/(k-1) \rceil$ or $\lfloor n/(k-1) \rfloor$ elements. (By Problem 9.5 there are $w = n \bmod (k-1)$ sets of the first kind and $k - 1 - w$ sets of the second kind.) The graph associated with a particular $(k-1)$-balanced partition has an edge between each pair of vertices in different sets and no other edges. For each $(k-1)$-balanced partition, a k-**negative test input** is a binary $n(n-1)/2$-tuple $\boldsymbol{x}$ describing the graph G associated with that partition.

LEMMA 9.6.5   *There are τ_+ k-positive test inputs, where*

$$\tau_+ = \binom{n}{k} = \frac{n!}{k!(n-k)!}$$

and τ_- k-negative test inputs, where for $w = n \bmod (k-1)$

$$\tau_- = \frac{n!}{(\lceil \frac{n}{k-1} \rceil !)^w (\lfloor \frac{n}{k-1} \rfloor !)^{k-1-w} w! (k-1-w)!}$$

Proof   It is well known that $\tau_+ = \binom{n}{k}$. To derive the expression for τ_- we index each element of each set in a $(k-1)$-balanced partition. Such a partition has $w = n \bmod (k-1)$ sets containing $\lceil n/(k-1) \rceil$ elements and $k - 1 - w$ sets containing $\lfloor n/(k-1) \rfloor$ elements. The elements in the first w sets are indexed by the pairs $\{(i,1), (i,2), \ldots, (i, \lceil n/(k-1) \rceil)\}$ for $1 \le i \le w$. Those in the remaining $k - 1 - w$ sets are indexed by the pairs $\{(i,1), (i,2), \ldots, (i, \lfloor n/(k-1) \rfloor)\}$ for $w + 1 \le i \le k - 1$. (See Fig. 9.13.) Let $\mathcal{P}$ be the set of all such pairs. To define a k-negative graph, we assign each vertex in the set $V = \{1, 2, \ldots, n\}$ to a unique pair. This partitions the vertices into $k - 1$ sets. If vertices v_a and v_b are in the same set, the edge variable $x_{a,b} = 0$; otherwise $x_{a,b} = 1$. These assignments define the edges in a graph $G = (V, E)$. There are $n!$ assignments of vertices to pairs. Of these, there are $(\lceil n/(k-1) \rceil !)^w (\lfloor n/(k-1) \rfloor !)^{k-1-w} w! (k-1-w)!$ that

| $(1,1)$ | $(1,2)$ | $(1,3)$ | $(1,4)$ | $(2,1)$ | $(2,2)$ | $(2,3)$ | $(3,1)$ | $(3,2)$ | $(3,3)$ |

| v_3 | v_7 | v_1 | v_2 | v_9 | v_5 | v_{10} | v_6 | v_4 | v_8 |

| v_2 | v_1 | v_3 | v_7 | v_5 | v_{10} | v_9 | v_4 | v_8 | v_6 |

Figure 9.13   A set of pairs $\mathcal{P}$ indexing the elements of sets in a $(k-1)$-balanced partition of a set V of n vertices. In this example $n = 10$ and $k = 4$ and the partition has three sets, V_1, V_2, and V_3 containing four, three, and three elements, respectively. Shown are two assignments of variables to pairs in $\mathcal{P}$ that correspond to the same partition of V.

correspond to each graph. To see this, observe that there are $\lceil n/(k-1) \rceil!$ ways to permute the elements in each of the first w sets and $\lfloor n/(k-1) \rfloor!$ ways to permute the elements in each of the remaining $k-1-w$ sets. Also, each of the first w (the last $k-1-w$) sets have the same size and can be ordered in any of $w!$ $((k-1-w)!)$ ways without changing the graph. ∎

APPROXIMATOR CIRCUITS   It simplifies the development of lower bounds to assume that each AND gate in a circuit is followed by an OR gate and vice versa and that the output gate is an AND gate. This requirement can be met by interposing between successive AND (OR) gates an OR (AND) gate both of whose inputs are connected together. Since this transformation at most triples the number of gates, an exponential lower bound on the size of the transformed circuit yields an exponential lower bound on the size of the original circuit.

A monotone circuit for $f_{\text{clique},k}^{(n)}$ has (edge) variables drawn from the set $\{x_{i,j} \mid 1 \le i < j \le n\}$. The approximation to an input variable $x_{i,j}$ is $x_{i,j}$ itself. Gates in a circuit are successively replaced by approximator circuits starting with a gate that is at greatest distance from the root (output vertex) and continuing with previously unvisited gates at greatest distance from the root. Thus, when an AND or OR gate is replaced, its inputs have previously been replaced by functions f_l and f_r that approximate the functions g_l and g_r computed in the original circuit.

Approximations to AND ($\wedge$) and OR ($\vee$) gates are denoted $\widehat{\wedge}$ and $\widehat{\vee}$, respectively. As seen below, the approximation given to a gate is context dependent. Approximations are defined in terms of endpoint sets. Given a set of edge variables, for example $\{x_{1,2}, x_{1,3}, x_{2,3}, x_{1,4}\}$, its associated **endpoint set** is the set of vertex indices used to define the edge variables, which is $\{1, 2, 3, 4\}$ in this example. Given a term t (a product (AND) or sum (OR) of edge variables), the endpoint set associated with it, $E(t)$, is the endpoint set of the edge variables appearing in the term. For example, if $t = x_{1,2} \wedge x_{1,3} \wedge x_{2,3} \wedge x_{1,4}$ or $t = x_{1,2} \vee x_{1,3} \vee x_{2,3} \vee x_{1,4}$, then $E(t) = \{1, 2, 3, 4\}$. The **endpoint size** of a term t, denoted $|E(t)|$, is the number of indices in $E(t)$.

Consider a gate to be approximated. Let its two inputs be from gates that compute functions f_l and f_r. Like any function, f_r and f_l can be represented in either the monotone SOPE or POSE form. (All SOPEs and POSEs in this section are monotone.) The approximation rules for AND and OR gates are described below and denoted $\widehat{\wedge}$ and $\widehat{\vee}$, respectively. Here we let $p = \lfloor \sqrt{(k-1)}/2 \rfloor$ and $q = \lfloor n/(4k) \rfloor$.

$\widehat{\wedge}$: The approximation $f_l \widehat{\wedge} f_r$ to $f_l \wedge f_r$ is obtained by representing $f_l \wedge f_r$ in the sum-of-products expansion (SOPE) and eliminating all product terms whose endpoint set contains more than p vertices. It follows that $f_l \wedge f_r \ge f_l \widehat{\wedge} f_r$.

$\widehat{\vee}$: The approximation $f_l \widehat{\vee} f_r$ to $f_l \vee f_r$ is obtained by representing $f_l \vee f_r$ in the product-of-sums expansion (POSE) and eliminating all sum terms whose endpoint set contains more than q vertices. It follows that $f_l \vee f_r \le f_l \widehat{\vee} f_r$.

Since $f_l \wedge f_r \ge f_l \widehat{\wedge} f_r$ and $f_l \vee f_r \le f_l \widehat{\vee} f_r$, if a positive test input $\boldsymbol{x}$ causes the output of the approximated circuit to have value 0 when it should have value 1, then there is an approximated AND gate (including the output gate) that has value 0 on $\boldsymbol{x}$ when it should have value 1. Similarly, if there is a negative test input $\boldsymbol{x}$ that causes the approximated output to be 1 when it should be 0, there is an approximated OR gate that has value 1 on $\boldsymbol{x}$ when it should have value 0. We now examine the performance of approximator circuits.

PERFORMANCE OF APPROXIMATOR CIRCUITS   We now show that when the approximation process is complete, the approximation circuit for $f_{\text{clique},k}^{(n)}$ makes a very large number of errors but that each gate approximation introduces a small number of errors. Thus, many gates must have been approximated to produce the large number of errors made by the fully approximated circuit. In fact, we show that the approximating circuit for $f_{\text{clique},k}^{(n)}$ either has output identically 0, thereby making one error on each of the $\tau_+ = \binom{n}{k}$ positive test inputs (it produces 0 when it should produce 1), or makes $\tau_-/2$ errors on the τ_- negative test inputs (it produces 1 when it should produce 0). On the other hand, we also show that approximating one AND or OR gate causes a small number of errors, at most e_{AND} errors per AND gate on positive test inputs and at most e_{OR} errors per OR gate on negative test inputs, quantities for which upper bounds are derived below. It follows that the original circuit for $f_{\text{clique},k}^{(n)}$ either has at least τ_+/e_{AND} AND gates or at least $\tau_-/(2e_{\text{OR}})$ OR gates. The lower bound on the monotone circuit size of $f_{\text{clique},k}^{(n)}$ is the larger of these two lower bounds.

LEMMA 9.6.6 *Let $k \le n + 1$. Then any approximation circuit for $f_{\text{clique},k}^{(n)}$ either computes a function that is identically zero or makes errors on half of the k-negative test inputs.*

Proof   Let the approximation circuit for $f_{\text{clique},k}^{(n)}$ compute the function $\widehat{f_{\text{clique},k}^{(n)}}$. If this function is identically zero, we are done. Suppose not. Since the output gate in the original circuit is an AND gate, the function $\widehat{f_{\text{clique},k}^{(n)}}$ is represented by a SOPE in which each term is the product of variables whose endpoint set (the vertices involved) has size at most p. Because $f_{\text{clique},k}^{(n)}$ is not identically zero, there is a non-zero term t such that $\widehat{f_{\text{clique},k}^{(n)}} \ge t$. An error is made on a negative test input if $t = 1$. But this happens only if each of the endpoints in $E(t)$ is in a different set of the $(k-1)$-balanced partition defining the negative test input.

Let ϕ be the fraction of the negative test inputs on which $t = 1$. We derive a lower bound to ϕ by deriving an upper bound on the fraction χ of the $(k-1)$-balanced partitions with the property that two or more vertices in $E(t)$ fall into the same set. It follows that $\phi \ge 1 - \chi$.

To simplify bounding χ, we use the one-to-one correspondence developed in the proof of Lemma 9.6.5 between the n vertices in $V = \{1, 2, 3, \ldots, n\}$ and the pairs $\mathcal{P}$ associated with a $(k-1)$-balanced partition. Since $E(t)$ has at most p vertices, the number of ways to assign two vertices from $E(t)$ to pairs in $\mathcal{P}$ so that two of them fall into the same set, N_2, is at most the number of ways to choose two vertices from a set of p vertices, $p(p-1)/2$, times the number of ways of assigning these two vertices to pairs in $\mathcal{P}$, m_2, and the number of ways of assigning the remaining $n - 2$ vertices, $(n-2)!$. Here m_2 is at most the product of the number of ways of choosing a pair for the first vertex, $(k-1)\lceil n/(k-1)\rceil$, and the number of ways of choosing a pair for the second from the same set, $\lceil n/(k-1)\rceil - 1$. Thus, N_2 is at most $(p(p-1)/2)(k-1)\lceil n/(k-1)\rceil(\lceil n/(k-1)\rceil - 1)(n-2)!$, which is at most $p^2\lceil n/(k-1)\rceil(n-1)!/2$. Since there are $n!$ assignments of vertices in V to pairs in $\mathcal{P}$, $\chi \le p^2\lceil n/(k-1)\rceil/(2n)$. Because $p = \lfloor\sqrt{(k-1)}/2\rfloor$, χ is at most $1/4$ since $k-1 \le n$. ∎

We now derive upper bounds on the number of errors introduced through the approximation of individual AND and OR gates. Since we have assumed that AND and OR gates alternate on any path between inputs and outputs, it follows that the inputs f_l and f_r to an AND gate are outputs of OR gates (and vice versa). Furthermore, by the approximation rules, if f_l and f_r are inputs to an AND (OR) gate, every sum (product) in their POSE (SOPE) has an endpoint set size of at most q (p). We now show that each replacement of a gate by its approximator introduces a relatively small number of errors. We begin by establishing this fact for OR gates.

LEMMA 9.6.7 *Let an OR gate $\vee$ and its approximation $\widehat{\vee}$ each be given as inputs the functions f_l and f_r whose SOPE contains product terms of endpoint size p or less. Then the number of k-negative test inputs for which $\vee$ and $\widehat{\vee}$ produce different outputs ($\vee$ has value 0 but $\widehat{\vee}$ has value 1) is at most e_{OR} where $w = n \bmod (k-1)$:*

$$e_{OR} = \frac{(n/2)^{q+1}(n-q-1)!}{(\lceil n/(k-1)\rceil!)^w(\lfloor n/(k-1)\rfloor!)^{k-1-w}w!(k-1-w)!}$$

Proof Let $f_{correct} = f_l \vee f_r$ and $f_{approx} = f_l \widehat{\vee} f_r$. Let $t_1, \ldots, t_l$ be the product terms in the SOPE for $f_{correct}$. Since the endpoint size of all terms in the SOPE of $f_{correct}$ is at most p, each term is the product of at most $p(p-1)/2$ variables.

Using the association between $(k-1)$-balanced partitions and pairs of indices given in the proof of Lemma 9.6.5, we count N, the number of one-to-one mappings from V to $\mathcal{P}$ for which $f_{correct}(\boldsymbol{x}) = 0$ but $f_{approx}(\boldsymbol{x}) = 1$, after which we divide by D, the number of mappings corresponding to a single partition of the variables, to compute $e_{OR} = N/D$. From the proof of Lemma 9.6.5 we have that $D = (\lceil n/(k-1)\rceil!)^w(\lfloor n/(k-1)\rfloor!)^{k-1-w}w!(k-1-w)!$.

To derive an upper bound to N, observe that $f_{approx}(\boldsymbol{x})$ is obtained by converting the SOPE of $f_{correct}$ to a POSE and deleting all sums in this POSE whose endpoint set size exceeds q. Thus, N is at most the number of ways to assign vertices to pairs in $\mathcal{P}$ that causes a deleted sum to be 0 because the new POSE may now become 1. But this can happen only if the endpoint set size of the deleted product is at least $q+1$. Thus, only if at least $q+1$ vertices in a sum are assigned values is it possible to have $f_{correct}(\boldsymbol{x}) = 0$ and $f_{approx}(\boldsymbol{x}) = 1$.

Below we show that each vertex can be assigned at most $n/2$ different pairs in $\mathcal{P}$. It follows there are at most $(n/2)^{q+1}(n-q-1)!$ ways to assign pairs to $q+1$ or more vertices because the first $q+1$ can be assigned in at most $(n/2)^{q+1}$ ways and the remaining $(n-q-1)$ vertices can be assigned in at most $(n-q-1)!$ ways. This is the desired upper bound on N.

We now show that every mapping from V to $\mathcal{P}$ that corresponds to a negative test input $\boldsymbol{x}$ assigns each vertex to at most $n/2$ pairs in $\mathcal{P}$.

Let $t_1, \ldots, t_l$ be product terms in the SOPE of $f_{correct}$. We examine these terms in sequence. Consider a partial mapping from V to $\mathcal{P}$ that assigns values to variables so that at least one variable in each of the products $t_1, \ldots, t_{i-1}$ is 0, thereby insuring that each product is 0. Consider now the ith product, t_i. If the partial mapping assigns value 0 to at least one of its variables, we move on to consider t_{i+1}. (It cannot set all variables in t_i to 1 because we are considering mappings causing all terms to be 0.)

Suppose that the partial mapping has not assigned value 0 to any of the variables of t_i. There are two cases to consider. For some variable $x_{a,b}$ of t_i either a) one or b) both of the vertices $v_a, v_b \in V$ has not been assigned a pair in $\mathcal{P}$. In the first case, assign the second vertex to the set containing the first, thereby setting $x_{a,b} = 0$. This can be done in at most $\lceil n/(k-1)\rceil - 1 \leq n/(k-1)$ ways since the set contains at most $\lceil n/(k-1)\rceil$ elements and at least one of them has been chosen previously, namely the first vertex. In the second case the two vertices can be assigned to at most $(k-1)(\lceil n/(k-1)\rceil)(\lceil n/(k-1)\rceil - 1) \leq 2n^2/(k-1)$ pairs because the first can be assigned to $(k-1)$ sets each containing at most $\lceil n/(k-1)\rceil$ elements and the second must be assigned to one of the remaining elements in that set.

The number of ways to choose variables in t_i so that it has value 0 is the number of ways to choose a variable of each kind multiplied by the number of ways to assign values to it. Let α be the number of variables of t_i for which one vertex has previously been assigned a pair and let β be the number of variables for which neither vertex has been assigned a pair. ($\beta \leq p(p-1)/2 - \alpha$ since t_i has at most $p(p-1)/2$ variables.) Thus, a variable of the first kind can be assigned in at most $\alpha n/(k-1)$ ways and the number of ways of assigning the two vertices in variables of the second kind is at most $\beta 2n^2/(k-1)$. Since each vertex associated in such pairs can be assigned in the same number of ways, γ, it follows that $\gamma^2 \leq \beta 2n^2/(k-1)$. Thus, $\gamma \leq \sqrt{\beta 2n^2/(k-1)}$.

Summarizing, the variables in t_i can be assigned in at most the following number of ways so that t_i has value 0:

$$\alpha n/(k-1) + \sqrt{(p(p-1)/2 - \alpha)2n^2/(k-1)}$$

This quantity is largest when $\alpha = 0$ and is at most $n/2$ since $p = \lfloor \sqrt{(k-1)}/2 \rfloor$, which is the desired conclusion. ∎

We now derive an upper bound on the number of errors that can be made by AND gates on k-positive inputs.

LEMMA 9.6.8 *Let an* AND *gate $\wedge$ and its approximation $\widehat{\wedge}$ each be given as inputs the functions f_l and f_r whose POSE contains sum terms of endpoint size q or less. Then the number of k-positive test inputs for which $\wedge$ and $\widehat{\wedge}$ produce different outputs ($\wedge$ has value 1 but $\widehat{\wedge}$ has value 0) is at most e_{AND}:*

$$e_{AND} = \frac{(n/2)^{p+1}(n-p-1)!}{k!(n-k)!}$$

Proof The proof is similar to that of Lemma 9.6.7. Let $f_{correct} = f_l \wedge f_r$ and $f_{approx} = f_l \widehat{\wedge} f_r$. Let $c_1, \ldots, c_l$ be the sum terms in the POSE for $f_{correct}$. Since by induction the endpoint size of all terms in the POSE of f_l and f_r is at most q, each term in $f_{correct}$ is the sum of at most $q(q-1)/2$ variables.

In this case we count the number of k-positive test graphs (they contain one k-clique) that cause $f_{correct}(\boldsymbol{x}) = 1$ but $f_{approx}(\boldsymbol{x}) = 0$. Since a k-positive test graph contains just those edges between a specified set of k vertices, we define each such graph by a one-to-one mapping from the vertices (endpoints) in V to the integers $\mathbb{N}(n) = \{1, 2, \ldots, n\}$, where we adopt the rule that vertices mapped to the first k integers are those in the clique associated with a particular test graph. It follows that each k-positive test graph corresponds to exactly $k!(n-k)!$ of these 1-1 mappings. Then, e_{AND} is the number of such 1-1 mappings for which $f_{correct}(\boldsymbol{x}) = 1$ but $f_{approx}(\boldsymbol{x}) = 0$ divided by $k!(n-k)!$.

We show that any mapping that results in $f_{correct}(\boldsymbol{x}) = 1$ assigns each endpoint to at most $n/2$ values from $\mathbb{N}(n)$. But $f_{approx}(\boldsymbol{x}) = 0$ for positive test inputs only if more than p endpoints are assigned values, because f_{approx} is obtained from $f_{correct}$ by discarding product terms in its SOPE that contain more than p endpoints. It follows that at most $(n/2)^{p+1}(n-p-1)!$ of the positive test inputs result in an error by the approximate AND gate. Dividing by $k!(n-k)!$, we have the desired upper bound on e_{AND}.

To complete the proof we must show that each endpoint is assigned at most $n/2$ values from $\mathbf{N}(n)$. Consider the sum terms $c_1, \ldots, c_l$ in the POSE of f_{correct} in sequence and consider a partial mapping from V to $\mathbf{N}(n)$ that causes at least one variable in each of the sums $c_1, \ldots, c_{i-1}$ to be 1, thereby insuring that the value of each sum is 1. Now consider the ith sum, c_i. If the partial mapping assigns value 1 to at least one variable, we move on to c_{i+1}. (It cannot set all variables in c_i to 0 because we are considering mappings causing all terms to be 1.)

We now extend the mapping by considering the set C_i of variables of c_i that have not been assigned a value. A given variable $x_{a,b}$ in C_i has either one or no endpoints (vertices) previously mapped to an integer in $\mathbf{N}(n)$. If one endpoint, say a, has been assigned an integer, the other endpoint, b, can be assigned to at most one of $k-2$ integers that cause $x_{a,b} = 1$ because endpoint a was previously assigned a value in the range $\{1, 2, \ldots, k\}$ together with at least one other vertex and b must be different from them. Because there are most $q = \lfloor n/(4k) \rfloor$ variables of the first type, there are at most $q(k-2)$ ways to assign the one endpoint of a variable $x_{a,b}$ of the first type so that $x_{a,b} = 1$.

Consider now variables of the second type. There are at most $q(q-1)/2$ such variables and at most $(q(q-1)/2)k(k-1)$ ways to make assignments to both endpoints so that a variable has value 1. This follows because each endpoint is assigned to a distinct integer among the first k integers in $\mathbf{N}(n)$. Since each endpoint can be assigned in the same number of ways, this number is at most $\sqrt{(q(q-1)/2)k(k-1)}$.

It follows that the number of ways to assign an endpoint so that the correct and approximate functions differ is at most $q(k-2) + \sqrt{(q(q-1)/2)k(k-1)} \leq 2qk$, which is no more than $n/2$ since $q = \lfloor n/(4k) \rfloor$. This is the desired conclusion. ∎

The desired result follows from the above lemmas.

THEOREM 9.6.6 *For $n \geq 13$ and $8 \leq k \leq n/2$, every monotone circuit for the clique function $f_{\text{clique},k}^{(n)} : \mathcal{B}^{n(n-1)/2} \mapsto \mathcal{B}$ has a circuit size satisfying the following lower bound:*

$$C_{\Omega_{\text{mon}}}\left(f_{\text{clique},k}^{(n)}\right) \geq \frac{1}{2}(1.8)^{\min(\sqrt{k-1}/2, n/(2k))}$$

The largest value for this lower bound is $C_{\Omega_{\text{mon}}}(f_{\text{clique},k}^{(n)}) = 2^{\Omega(n^{1/3})}$.

Proof From the discussion at the beginning of this section, we see that the monotone circuit size of $f_{\text{clique},k}^{(n)}$ is at least $\min\left(\tau_+/e_{\text{AND}}, \tau_-/(2e_{\text{OR}})\right)$. Thus,

$$C_{\Omega_{\text{mon}}}(f_{\text{clique},k}^{(n)}) \geq \min\left(\frac{n!}{2(n/2)^{p+1}(n-p-1)!}, \frac{n!}{(n/2)^{q+1}(n-q-1)!}\right)$$

$$\geq \min\left(\frac{(n-p)^{p+1}}{2(n/2)^{p+1}}, \frac{(n-q)^{q+1}}{(n/2)^{q+1}}\right)$$

Let $8 \leq k \leq n/2$. It follows that $p = \lfloor \sqrt{(k-1)}/2 \rfloor \leq \sqrt{n}/(2\sqrt{2})$ and $q = \lfloor n/(2k) \rfloor \leq n/16$. Thus, $p, q \leq n/10$ if $n \geq 13$. Hence both $(n-p)$ and $(n-q)$ are at least $9n/10$, and

$$C_{\Omega_{\text{mon}}}\left(f_{\text{clique},k}^{(n)}\right) \geq \min\left(\frac{1}{2}(1.8)^{p+1}, (1.8)^{q+1}\right)$$

The desired conclusion follows from this and the observation that $p + 1 \geq \sqrt{k-1}/2$ and $q + 1 \geq n/(2k)$. That the maximum value of $\min(\sqrt{k-1}/2, n/(2k))$ is $\Omega(n^{1/3})$ under variation of k is left as a problem. (See Problem 9.38.) ■

9.6.4 Slice Functions

Although, as shown above, some monotone functions have exponential circuit size over the monotone basis, it is doubtful that the methods of analysis used to obtain this result can be extended to derive such bounds over the standard basis. (See the Chapter Notes.)

This section introduces a note of optimism by showing that the monotone circuit size of monotone slice functions can provide a strong lower bound on the circuit size of such functions over the standard basis. In addition, there are **NP**-complete languages whose characteristic functions are slice functions. Thus, if such functions can be shown to have super-polynomial monotone circuit size, **P** $\neq$ **NP**.

Let $|\boldsymbol{x}|$ denote the number of 1's in $\boldsymbol{x}$. We now define the slice functions.

DEFINITION 9.6.6 *A function* $s : \mathcal{B}^n \mapsto \mathcal{B}$ *is a* **slice function** *if there is an integer* $0 \leq k \leq n$ *such that* $s(\boldsymbol{x}) = 0$ *if* $|\boldsymbol{x}| < k$ *and* $s(\boldsymbol{x}) = 1$ *if* $|\boldsymbol{x}| > k$. *The* **kth slice of a function** $f : \mathcal{B}^n \mapsto \mathcal{B}$, $0 \leq k \leq n$, *is the function* $f^{[k]} : \mathcal{B}^n \mapsto \mathcal{B}$ *defined below.*

$$
f^{[k]}(\boldsymbol{x}) = \begin{cases} 0 & |\boldsymbol{x}| < k \\ f(\boldsymbol{x}) & |\boldsymbol{x}| = k \\ 1 & |\boldsymbol{x}| > k \end{cases}
$$

It should be clear from this definition that slice functions are monotone. Below we show that if a Boolean function f on n variables has a large circuit size, then one of its slices has a circuit size that differs from the size of f by at most a multiplicative factor that is linear in n. Thus, a function f has a large circuit size if and only if one of its slice functions has a large circuit size.

We set the stage with a lemma that shows that the circuit size of a Boolean function is bounded above by the circuit size of its slices plus an additive term linear in its number of variables.

LEMMA 9.6.9 *Let* Ω_0 *be the standard basis and* $f : \mathcal{B}^n \mapsto \mathcal{B}$. *Then the following holds, where* $C_{\Omega_0}(f^{[0]}, f^{[1]}, \ldots, f^{[n]})$ *is the circuit size of all the slices simultaneously:*

$$
C_{\Omega_0}(f) = C_{\Omega_0}(f^{[0]}, f^{[1]}, \ldots, f^{[n]}) + O(n)
$$

Proof The goal is to construct a circuit for f given the input tuple $\boldsymbol{x}$ and a circuit for all the functions $f^{[0]}, f^{[1]}, \ldots, f^{[n]}$. This is easily done. We construct a circuit to count the number of 1's among the n inputs and represent the result in binary. We then supply this number as an address to a direct storage address function (multiplexer) where the other inputs are the values of the slice functions. If the address is $|\boldsymbol{a}|$, the output of the multiplexer is $f^{[|\boldsymbol{a}|]}$. Since, as shown in Lemma 2.11.1, the counting circuit can be realized with a circuit of size linear in n, and, as shown in Lemma 2.5.5, the multiplexer in question can be realized with a linear-size circuit, the result follows. ■

We now establish the connection between the circuit size of a function and that of one of its slices.

THEOREM 9.6.7 *Let Ω_0 be the standard basis and $f : \mathcal{B}^n \mapsto \mathcal{B}$. Then there exists $0 \leq k \leq n$ such that*

$$\frac{C_{\Omega_0}(f)}{n} - O(1) \leq C_{\Omega_0}\left(f^{[k]}\right) \leq C_{\Omega_0}(f) + O(n)$$

Proof The first inequality follows from Lemma 9.6.9, the following inequality and the observation that at least one term in an average is greater than or equal to the average.

$$C_{\Omega_0}\left(f^{[0]}, f^{[1]}, \ldots, f^{[n]}\right) \leq \sum_i C_{\Omega_0}(f^{[i]})$$

The second inequality uses the fact that the kth slice of a function can be expressed as

$$f^{[k]}(\boldsymbol{x}) = \tau_k^{(n)}(\boldsymbol{x})f(\boldsymbol{x}) + \tau_{k+1}^{(n)}(\boldsymbol{x})$$

Since $\tau_j^{(n)}(\boldsymbol{x})$ can be realized by a circuit of size linear in n (see Theorem 2.11.1), the second inequality follows. ∎

In Theorem 9.6.9 we show that the monotone circuit size of slice functions provides a lower bound on their non-monotone circuit size up to a polynomial additive term. Before establishing this result we introduce the concept of pseudo-negation. A **pseudo-negation** for variable x_i in a monotone Boolean function $f : \mathcal{B}^n \mapsto \mathcal{B}$ is a function h_i such that replacing each instance of $\overline{x}_i$ in a circuit for f by h_i does not change the value computed by the circuit. Thus, the pseudo-negation h_i acts like the real negation $\overline{x}_i$.

In Theorem 9.6.9 we also show that for $1 \leq i \leq n$ the punctured threshold function $\tau_{k,\neg i}^{(n)} : \mathcal{B}^n \mapsto \mathcal{B}$, which depends on all the variables except x_i, is a pseudo-negation for a kth slice of every monotone function. Since for a given k each of these threshold functions can be realized by a monotone circuit of size $O(n \log n)$ (see Theorem 6.8.2), they can all be realized by a monotone circuit of size $O(n^2 \log n)$. Although this result can be used in Theorem 9.6.9, the following stronger result is used instead.

We now describe a circuit that computes all of the above pseudo-negations efficiently. This circuit uses the **complementary number system**, a system that associates with each integer i in the set $\mathbf{N}(n) = \{0, 1, 2, \ldots, n-1\}$ the complementary set $\mathbf{N}(n) - \{i\}$. It makes use of results on sorting networks found in Chapter 6.

THEOREM 9.6.8 *The set $\{\tau_{k,\neg i}^{(n)} \mid 1 \leq i \leq n\}$ of pseudo-negations can be realized by a monotone circuit of size $O(n \log^2 n)$.*

Proof We assume that $n = 2^s$. If not, add variables with value 0 to increase the number to the next power of 2. This does not change the value of the function on the first n variables.

For this proof let the pseudo-negations $\tau_{k,\neg i}^{(n)}$ be defined for $0 \leq i \leq n-1$ and on the variables whose indices are in $\mathbf{N}(n)$. (We subtract 1 from each index.) Let $D_i = \mathbf{N}(n) - \{i\}$ denote the indices of the variables on which $\tau_{k,\neg i}^{(n)}$ depends. An efficient monotone circuit to compute all the pseudo-negations $\{\tau_{k,\neg i}^{(n)} \mid i \in \mathbf{N}(n)\}$ is based on an efficient decomposition of the sets $\{D_i \mid i \in \mathbf{N}(n)\}$.

For $a, b \geq 0$, let $U_{a,b}$ be defined by

$$U_{a,b} = \{a2^b + c \mid 0 \leq c \leq 2^b - 1\}$$

For example, $U_{3,3} = \{24, 25, 26, 27, 29, 30, 31\}$, $U_{1,2} = \{4, 5, 6, 7\}$, and $U_{2,1} = \{4, 5\}$. The set $U_{a,b}$ has size 2^b.

For $n = 2^s$, every set $D_i = \mathbf{N}(n) - \{i\}$ can be represented as the disjoint union of the sets $U_{a,b}$ below, where $0 \le a_{i,j} \le 2^{s-j} - 1$. (This is the complementary number system; see Fig. 9.14.)

$$D_i = U_{a_{i,s-1},s-1} \cup U_{a_{i,s-2},s-2} \cup \cdots \cup U_{a_{i,0},0}$$

To see this, note that if i is in the first (second) half of $\mathbf{N}(n)$, $U_{a_{i,s-1},s-1}$ denotes the second (first) half; that is, $a_{i,s-1} = 1$ ($a_{i,s-1} = 0$). The next set, $U_{a_{i,s-2},s-2}$, is the half of the remaining set $D_i - U_{a_{i,s-1},s-1}$ that does not contain i, etc. Thus, D_i is decomposed as the disjoint union of sets of size $2^{s-1}, 2^{s-2}, \ldots, 2^0$ For example, when $n = 16$, $D_3 = U_{1,3} \cup U_{1,2} \cup U_{0,1} \cup U_{2,0}$. Figure 9.14 shows the values of $a_{i,s-1}, a_{i,s-2}, \ldots, a_{i,0}$ for each $i \in \mathbf{N}(n)$ for $n = 8$.

As suggested in Fig. 9.14, the sets $\{D_i \mid i \in \mathbf{N}(n)\}$ have either $U_{0,s-1}$ or $U_{1,s-1}$ in common. Similarly, they also have either $U_{1,s-1} \cup U_{1,s-2}$, $U_{0,s-1} \cup U_{1,s-2}$, $U_{3,s-1} \cup U_{0,s-2}$, or $U_{2,s-1} \cup U_{0,s-2}$ in common. Continuing in this fashion, we construct the sets $\{D_i \mid i \in \mathbf{N}(n)\}$ by successively forming the disjoint union of 2^j sets, $1 \le j \le s$. Assembling the sets in this fashion is much more economical than assembling them individually.

The value of $\tau_{k,\neg i}^{(n)}$, $i \in \mathbf{N}(n)$, is the kth largest variable whose index is in D_i. From now on we equate the variables with their indices. Sorting the sets into which D_i is decomposed simplifies the computation. But these sets are exactly the sets that are sorted by Batcher's sorting network based on Batcher's merging algorithm. (See Theorem 6.8.3.) Since on Boolean data a comparator consists of one AND for the max operation and one OR for the min operation, a monotone circuit of size $O(n \log^2 n)$ exists to sort the sets $\{U_{i,j} \mid 0 \le i \le 2^{s-j} - 1, 0 \le j \le s - 1\}$.

The functions $\tau_{k,\neg i}^{(n)}$, $0 \le i \le n - 1$, can be obtained by sorting the sets $\{U_{i,j} \mid 0 \le i \le 2^{s-j} - 1, 0 \le j \le s - 1\}$, merging them in groups to form D_i for $i \in \mathbf{N}(n)$, as suggested above, and then taking the kth largest element. A faster way merges the sorted versions of the sets $U_{a_{i,s-1},s-1}$, $U_{a_{i,s-2},s-2}, \ldots, U_{a_{i,0},0}$ in the order in which D_i is assembled above. For each of these sets the sorting network presents its elements in sorted order.

i	$a_{i,0}$	$a_{i,1}$	$a_{i,2}$
0	1	1	1
1	0	1	1
2	3	0	1
3	2	0	1
4	5	3	0
5	4	3	0
6	7	2	0
7	6	2	0

Figure 9.14 The coefficients $a_{i,j}$ of $D_i = \mathbf{N}(n) - \{i\}$ in the expansion $U_{a_{i,s-1},s-1} \cup U_{a_{i,s-2},s-2} \cup \cdots \cup U_{a_{i,0},0}$ for $n = 2^s = 8$ and $s = 3$.

Since only the kth element of D_i is needed, it is not necessary to merge all the elements in each set when two sets are merged. To see which elements need to be merged, let $\Delta_i(j) = U_{a_{i,s-1},s-1} \cup U_{a_{i,s-2},s-2} \cup \cdots \cup U_{a_{i,j},j}$. Then $D_i - \Delta_i(j)$ is a set of size $2^j - 1$. Observe that the kth element of D_i can be obtained by merging elements of rank k and $k-1$ of $\Delta_i(1)$ with the element of $U_{a(i,0),0}$. (They all have value 0 or 1.) The middle element is the kth element in D_i. To obtain elements of rank k and $k-1$ of $\Delta_i(1)$, the elements of rank k, $k-1$, $k-2$ and $k-3$ of $\Delta_i(2)$ are merged with the two elements of $U_{a_{i,1},1}$ and the middle two taken. In general, to obtain the elements of rank $k, \ldots, k-2^j+1$ of $\Delta_i(j)$, the elements of rank $k, \ldots, k-2^{j+1}+1$ of $\Delta_i(j+1)$ are merged with the 2^j elements of $U_{a_{i,j},j}$ and the middle 2^j taken.

We now count the number of extra AND and OR gates needed to perform the merges. There are 2^{s-j} sets $\Delta_i(j)$. The 2^j elements needed from these sets are obtained by merging 2^{j+1} elements of $\Delta_i(j+1)$ with the 2^j elements of $U_{a_{i,j},j}$. Since these sets can be merged in a comparator network with $O(j2^j)$ comparators (see Theorem 6.8.2), it follows that all the sets $\Delta_i(j)$, $0 \leq i \leq n-1$, can be formed with $O(jn)$ gates for $0 \leq j \leq s-1$. Summing over j, $0 \leq j \leq (\log_2 n) - 1$ shows that a total of $O(n \log^2 n)$ extra gates suffice. Since $O(n \log^2 n)$ gates are used to sort the sets $\{U_{i,j} \mid 0 \leq i \leq 2^{s-j} - 1, 0 \leq j \leq s-1\}$, the desired conclusion follows. ∎

We can now show that a large lower bound on the monotone circuit size of a slice function implies a large lower bound on its non-monotone circuit size. The importance of this statement is emphasized by the existence of **NP**-complete slice functions. If such a problem can be shown to have a super-polynomial slice function, then **P** $\neq$ **NP**.

THEOREM 9.6.9 *Let $f : \mathcal{B}^n \mapsto \mathcal{B}$ be a slice function. Then*

$$C_{\Omega_0}(f) \leq C_{\Omega_{\mathrm{mon}}}(f) \leq 2 \cdot C_{\Omega_0}(f) + O(n \log^2 n)$$

Proof The first inequality holds because the standard basis Ω_0 contains the monotone basis. To establish the second inequality, we convert a circuit over Ω_0 by moving all negations to the input variables. This can be done by at most doubling the number of gates. (See Problems 9.11 and 2.12.)

We now show that for slice functions the negation of an input variable x_i can be replaced by the pseudo-negation function $\tau_{k,\neg i}^{(n)}$. To see this, observe that when $|\boldsymbol{x}| > k$, at least $|\boldsymbol{x}| - 1 = k$ of the variables of $\tau_{k,\neg i}^{(n)}$ are 1 and $\tau_{k,\neg i}^{(n)}$ has value 1. On the other hand, when $|\boldsymbol{x}| < k$, then not enough variables can be 1 for $\tau_{k,\neg i}^{(n)}$ to have value 1. Finally, when $|\boldsymbol{x}| = k$, $\tau_{k,\neg i}^{(n)} = 0$ if $x_i = 1$ because not enough of the remaining variables are 1, and $\tau_{k,\neg i}^{(n)} = 1$ when $x_i = 0$ by a similar reasoning. Now replace $\overline{x}_i$ with $\tau_{k,\neg i}^{(n)}$. Since f is a k-slice, $f = 0$ when $|\boldsymbol{x}| < k$, as is $\tau_{k,\neg i}^{(n)}$. If $\overline{x}_i = 1$ when $|\boldsymbol{x}| < k$, replacing $\overline{x}_i$ by its pseudo-negation means replacing $\overline{x}_i$ by 0, which can only decrease the circuit output since it is monotone. Thus, f is computed correctly in this case. The same is true if $|\boldsymbol{x}| > k$, again by monotonicity. Since $\tau_{k,\neg i}^{(n)} = \overline{x}_i$ when $|\boldsymbol{x}| = k$, the circuit correctly computes f for all inputs when $\overline{x}_i$ is replaced by the ith pseudo-negation. ∎

AN NP-COMPLETE SLICE FUNCTION   We now exhibit the language HALF-CLIQUE CENTRAL SLICE and show it is **NP**-complete. The characteristic functions of this language are slice functions. It follows from Theorem 9.6.9 that if these slice functions have exponential circuit size, then $\mathbf{P} \neq \mathbf{NP}$. We show that HALF-CLIQUE CENTRAL SLICE is **NP**-complete by reducing HALF-CLIQUE (see Problem 8.25) to it.

DEFINITION 9.6.7 *A **central slice** of a function* $f : \mathcal{B}^n \mapsto \mathcal{B}$ *on* n *variables,* $f^{[\lceil n/2 \rceil]}$, *is the* $\lceil n/2 \rceil$th *slice.*

A central slice of a function f on n variables is the function that has value 0 if the weight of the input tuple is less than $\lceil n/2 \rceil$, value 1 if the weight exceeds this value, and is equal to the value of f otherwise.

Given the function $f : \mathcal{B}^* \mapsto \mathcal{B}$, $f^{(n)}$ denotes the function restricted to strings of length n. The family of central slice functions $\{(f^{(n)})^{[\lceil n/2 \rceil]} \mid n \geq 2\}$ identifies the language $L_{\text{central}}(f) = \{x \in \mathcal{B}^n \mid (f^{(n)})^{[\lceil n/2 \rceil]}(x) = 1, n \geq 2\}$.

The central clique function $f^{(n)}_{\text{clique}, \lceil n/2 \rceil}$ has value 1 if the input graph contains a clique on $\lceil n/2 \rceil$ vertices. The central slice of the central clique function $f^{(n)}_{\text{clique}, \lceil n/2 \rceil}$ is called the **half-clique central slice function** and denoted $f^{(n)}_{\text{clique slice}}$. It has value 1 if the input graph either contains a clique on $\lceil n/2 \rceil$ vertices or contains more edges than are in a clique of this size.

The language HALF-CLIQUE is defined in Problem 8.25 as strings describing a graph and an integer k such that a graph on n vertices contains an $n/2$-clique or has more than k edges. The language HALF-CLIQUE CENTRAL SLICE associated with the central slice of a central clique function is defined below.

HALF-CLIQUE CENTRAL SLICE
Instance: The description of an undirected graph $G = (V, E)$ in which $|V|$ is even.
Answer: "Yes" if G contains a clique on $|V|/2$ vertices or has more edges than are contained in a $|V|/2$-clique.

It simplifies the following discussion to define $e(k)$ as the number of edges between a set of k vertices. Clearly, $e(k) = \binom{k}{2}$.

THEOREM 9.6.10 *The language* HALF-CLIQUE CENTRAL SLICE *is* **NP**-*complete. Furthermore, for all* $2 \leq k \leq n$

$$C_{\Omega_{\text{mon}}} \left(\left(f^{(n)}_{\text{clique}, \lceil n/2 \rceil} \right)^{[k]} \right) \leq C_{\Omega_{\text{mon}}} \left(f^{(n)}_{\text{clique slice}} \right)$$

For $k < e(n/2)$, $\left(f^{(n)}_{\text{clique}, \lceil n/2 \rceil} \right)^{[k]} = \tau^{e(n)}_{k+1}$.

Proof We show that HALF-CLIQUE CENTRAL SLICE is **NP**-complete by reducing HALF-CLIQUE to it. Given a graph $G = (V, E)$ in HALF-CLIQUE that has n vertices, n even, we construct a graph $G' = (V', E')$ on $5n$ vertices such that G either contains an $n/2$-clique or has more than k edges if and only if G' contains a (central) clique on $5n/2$ vertices or has more than $\lceil e(5n/2) \rceil$ edges. The construction, which can be done in polynomial time, transforms a graph on n vertices to one on $5n$ vertices such that the former is an instance of HALF-CLIQUE if and only if the latter is an instance of HALF-CLIQUE CENTRAL SLICE.

Let $V = \{v_1, v_2, \ldots, v_n\}$. Construct G' from G by adding the $4n$ vertices $R = \{r_1, r_2, \ldots, r_{2n}\}$ and $S = \{s_1, s_2, \ldots, s_{2n}\}$. Represent edges in E' of G' with the edge variables $\{y_{i,j} \mid 1 \leq i < j \leq 5n\}$. Each edge between vertices of G is an edge between vertices V of G'. Let every edge between vertices in R be in G' as well as all edges between vertices in V and R. Set the edge variables so that the edges between r_i and s_i, $1 \le i \le 2n$, are absent. The unassigned variables are between vertices in S, between vertices in R and S, and between vertices in V and S, of which there are $8n^2 - 3n$. Fix these unassigned edges so that the number of edges between vertices in $V \cup R \cup S$ is $\lceil e(5n/2)/2 \rceil - k$, $1 \le k \le n$. There are sufficiently many unassigned edges to do this.

We now show that G contains an $n/2$-clique or has more than k edges if and only if G' contains an $5n/2$-clique or has more than $\lceil e(5n/2)/2 \rceil$ edges. If G has a $n/2$-clique, the edges between V and R combined with the edges between vertices in R and those in G constitute a $5n/2$ clique since $5n/2$ vertices in $V \cup R$ are completely connected. If V has more than k edges, since there are exactly $\lceil e(5n/2)/2 \rceil - k$ edges between vertices in $V \cup R \cup S$, G' has at least $\lceil e(5n/2)/2 \rceil$ edges. On the other hand, if G' has a $(5n/2)$-clique, because there is at least one absent edge between each pair of vertices (r_i, s_i), $1 \le i \le 2n$, the largest clique on vertices in $R \cup S$ has size $2n$. Thus, there must be a $(n/2)$-clique on vertices in V; that is, G contains a $(n/2)$-clique. Similarly, since the number of edges between vertices in V and those in $R \cup S$ is exactly $\lceil e(5n/2)/2 \rceil - k$, if G' contains at least $\lceil e(5n/2)/2 \rceil$ edges, G must contain at least k edges.

The membership of graph G in HALF-CLIQUE is determined by specializing the graph G' by mapping its edge variables to the constants 0 and 1 or to variables of G. Thus, the function testing G's membership is obtained through a subfunction reduction of the function testing G''s membership. (See Definition 2.4.2.) Thus, at no increase in circuit size, for any k a circuit for $\left(f_{\mathrm{clique}, \lceil n/2 \rceil}^{(n)} \right)^{[k]}$ can be obtained from a circuit for $f_{\mathrm{clique\ slice}}^{(n)}$. Thus, the circuit size for the latter is at least as large for the former, which gives the second result of the theorem.

The statement that for $k < e(n/2)$, $\left(f_{\mathrm{clique}, \lceil n/2 \rceil}^{(n)} \right)^{[k]} = \tau_{k+1}^{e(n)}$ follows from the observation that for these values of k the value of the clique function on inputs of weight $e(n/2) - 1$ or less is 0. ∎

As this theorem indicates, the search for a proof that $\mathbf{P} \ne \mathbf{NP}$ can be limited to the study of the monotone circuit size of the central slice of certain monotone functions. Other central slices of $\mathbf{NP}$-complete problems have been shown to be $\mathbf{NP}$-complete also. (See the Chapter Notes.)

9.7 Circuit Depth

Circuit depth and formula size are exponentially related, as shown in Section 9.2.3. In this section we examine the depth of circuits whose operations have either bounded or unbounded fan-in. As seen in Chapter 3, circuits of bounded fan-in are useful in classifying problems by their complexity and in developing relationships between time and space and circuit size and depth.

Circuits of unbounded fan-in are constructed of AND and OR gates with potentially unbounded fan-in whose inputs are the outputs of other such gates or literals, namely, variables and their negations. Every Boolean function can be realized by a circuit of unbounded fan-in and bounded depth, as is seen by considering the DNF of a Boolean function: it corresponds to a depth-2, unbounded fan-in circuit. Knowledge of the complexity of bounded-depth circuits may shed light on the complexity of bounded-fan-in circuits.

In this section we first show that the depth of a function f is equal to the *communication complexity* of a related problem in a two-player game. Communication complexity is a measure of the amount of information that must be exchanged between two players to perform a computation. We establish such a connection for all Boolean functions over the standard basis Ω_0 and monotone functions over the monotone basis Ω_{mon}. These connections are used to derive lower bounds on circuit depth for monotone and non-monotone functions. After establishing these results we examine bounded-depth circuits and demonstrate that some problems require exponential size when realized by such circuits.

9.7.1 Communication Complexity

We define a *communication game* between two players who have unlimited computing power and communicate via an error-free channel. This game has sufficient generality to derive interesting lower bounds on circuit depth.

DEFINITION 9.7.1 *A* **communication game** (U, V) *is defined by sets* $U, V \subseteq B^n$, *where* $U \cap V = \emptyset$. *An instance of the game is defined by* $\boldsymbol{u} \in U$ *and* $\boldsymbol{v} \in V$. $\boldsymbol{u}$ *is assigned to Player I and* $\boldsymbol{v}$ *is assigned to Player II. Players alternate sending binary messages to each other. We assume that the binary messages form a prefix code (no message is a prefix for another) so that one player can determine when the other has finished transmitting a message.*

Although each player has unlimited computing power, each message it sends is a function of just its own n-tuple and the messages it has received previously from the other player. The two functions used by the players to determine the contents of their messages constitute the **protocol** Π *under which the communication game is played. The protocol also determines the first player to send a message and termination of the game. The* **goal** *of the game is to find an index* i, $1 \leq i \leq n$, *such that* $u_i \neq v_i$.

Let $\Pi(\boldsymbol{u}, \boldsymbol{v})$ *denote the number of bits exchanged under* Π *on the instance* $(\boldsymbol{u}, \boldsymbol{v})$ *of the game* (U, V). *The* **communication complexity** $C(U, V)$ *of the communication game* (U, V) *is the minimum over all protocols* Π *of the maximum number of bits exchanged under* Π *on any instance of* (U, V); *that is,*

$$C(U, V) = \min_{\Pi} \max_{\boldsymbol{u} \in U, \boldsymbol{v} \in V} \Pi(\boldsymbol{u}, \boldsymbol{v})$$

Note that there is always a position i, $1 \leq i \leq n$, such that $u_i \neq v_i$ since $U \cap V = \emptyset$.

The communication game models a search problem; given disjoint sets of n-tuples, U and V, the two players search for an input variable on which the two n-tuples differ. A related communication game measures the exchange of information to obtain the value of a function $f : X \times Y \mapsto Z$ on two variables in which one player has a value in X and the other has a value in Y. The players must acquire enough information about each other's variable to compute the function.

Every communication problem (U, V), where $U, V \subseteq B^n$, can be solved with communication complexity $C(U, V) \leq n + \lceil \log_2 n \rceil$ by the following protocol:

- Player I sends $\boldsymbol{u}$ to Player II.

- Player II determines a position in which $\boldsymbol{u} \neq \boldsymbol{v}$ and sends it to Player I using $\lceil \log_2 n \rceil$ bits.

This bound can be improved to $C(U, V) \leq n + \log_2^* n$, where $\log_2^* n$ is the number of times that $\lceil \log_2 \rceil$ must be taken to reduce n to zero. (See Problem 9.39.) The **log-star function** $\log_2^* n$ grows very slowly. For example, $\log_2^* 10^{10^{10}}$ is 8; by contrast, $\left\lceil \log_2 10^{10^{10}} \right\rceil = 33{,}219{,}280{,}949$.

These concepts are illustrated by the **parity communication problem** (U, V), defined below, where $n = 2^k$:

$$U = \{u \mid u \text{ has an even number of 1s}\}$$
$$V = \{v \mid v \text{ has an odd number of 1s}\}$$

The following protocol achieves a communication complexity bound of $C(U, V) \leq 2 \log_2 n$ for this problem. Later we show it is best possible.

1. If $n = 1$, the players know where their tuples differ and no communication is necessary.

2. If $n > 1$, go to the next step.

3. Player I sends the parity of the first $n/2$ bits of u to Player II.

4. Since $u \neq v$, with one bit Player II tells Player I of half of the variables on which u and v are known to differ. Play is resumed at the first step with the half of the variables on which they are known to differ.

Let $\kappa(n)$ denote the number of bits exchanged with this protocol. Then $\kappa(1) = 0$ and $\kappa(n) \leq \kappa(n/2) + 2$, whose solution is $\kappa(n) = 2 \log_2 n$. Thus, $C(U, V) = \kappa(n) \leq 2 \log_2 n$.

9.7.2   General Depth and Communication Complexity

We now establish a relationship between the depth $D_{\Omega_0}(f)$ of a Boolean function $f : \mathcal{B}^n \mapsto \mathcal{B}$ over the standard basis Ω_0 and the communication complexity of a communication game in which $U = f^{-1}(0)$ and $V = f^{-1}(1)$, where $f^{-1}(a)$ is the set of n-tuples for which f has value a. Theorem 9.7.1 asserts that $D_{\Omega_0}(f)$ and $C(f^{-1}(0), f^{-1}(1))$ have exactly the same value. Later we establish a similar result for monotone functions realized over the monotone basis. We divide this result into two lemmas that are proved separately.

THEOREM 9.7.1   *For every Boolean function* $f : \mathcal{B}^n \mapsto \mathcal{B}$,

$$D_{\Omega_0}(f) = C(f^{-1}(0), f^{-1}(1))$$

The communication game allows the two players to have unlimited computing power at their disposal. Thus, the protocol they employ can be an arbitrarily complex function. This power reflects the non-uniformity in the circuit model.

LEMMA 9.7.1   *For all Boolean functions* $f : \mathcal{B}^n \mapsto \mathcal{B}$ *and all* $U, V \subseteq \mathcal{B}^n$ *such that* $U \subseteq f^{-1}(0)$ *and* $V \subseteq f^{-1}(1)$, *the following bound holds:*

$$C(U, V) \leq D_{\Omega_0}(f)$$

Proof   In this lemma we demonstrate that a protocol for the communication game $(f^{-1}(0), f^{-1}(1))$ can be constructed from a circuit of minimal depth for the Boolean function f. We assume that such a circuit has negations only on input variables. By Problem 9.11 there is such a circuit.

Given an instance defined by $u \in f^{-1}(0)$ and $v \in f^{-1}(1)$, the players follow a path from the circuit output to an input at which u and v differ. The invariant that applies at each step is that Player I (which holds u) simulates an AND gate whose value on u is 0 whereas Player II (which holds v) simulates an OR gate whose value on v is 1. The bits transmitted by one player to the other specify which input to the current gate to follow on the way from the output vertex to an input vertex of the circuit for f.

The proof is by induction. The base case applies to those Boolean functions f for which $D_{\Omega_0}(f) = 0$. In this case f is either x_i or $\overline{x}_i$ for some i where x_i is an input variable of f. Thus, for each instance of the problem, both players know in advance a variable (namely, x_i) on which u and v differ. Hence, $C(U, V) = 0$ and the base case is established.

For the induction step, either $f = f_1 \wedge f_2$ or $f = f_1 \vee f_2$. Consider the first case; the second is treated in a similar fashion. Obviously $D_{\Omega_0}(f) = \max(D_{\Omega_0}(f_1), D_{\Omega_0}(f_2)) + 1$. (We are considering circuits of minimal depth.) Let $U_j = U \cap f_j^{-1}(0)$ for $j = 1, 2$. Since (U_j, V) is a communication game associated with f_j (f_j must have value 1 on V) and $D_{\Omega_0}(f_j) < D_{\Omega_0}(f)$, by induction $C(U_j, V) \leq D_{\Omega_0}(f_j)$.

Since the output gate is AND (the other case is treated similarly), both f_1 and f_2 have value 1 on V, but at least one of them has value 0 on U. We use the following protocol for (U, V): Player I sends 0 if $u \in U_1$ (associated with the input f_1 to this AND gate) and 1 if $u \in U_2$ (associated with the input f_2). (If the output gate is OR, we observe that at least one of f_1 and f_2 has value 1 on V and define $V_1 = V \cap f_1^{-1}(1)$ and $V_2 = V \cap f_2^{-1}(1)$. Player II sends a bit to specify the set containing v.) After the first move the players follow the protocol for the f_j defined by the bit sent by Player I. Thus, when the output gate is AND the following bound holds:

$$C(U, V) \leq 1 + \max_{j=1,2}(C(U_j, B)) \leq 1 + \max(D_{\Omega_0}(f_1), D_{\Omega_0}(f_2)) = D_{\Omega_0}(f)$$

The same bound holds when the output gate is OR. ∎

We now prove the second half of Theorem 9.7.1.

LEMMA 9.7.2 *Let $U, V \subseteq \mathcal{B}^n$ be such that $U \cap V = \emptyset$. Then there exists a Boolean function $f : \mathcal{B}^n \mapsto \mathcal{B}$ with $U \subseteq f^{-1}(0)$ and $V \subseteq f^{-1}(1)$ such that the following bound holds:*

$$D_{\Omega_0}(f) \leq C(U, V)$$

Proof In this proof we show how to define a Boolean function and a circuit for it from a protocol for (U, V). From the protocol a tree is constructed. The root is associated with the player who sends the first bit. As in the proof of Lemma 9.7.1, Player I is associated with AND gates and Player II with OR gates. Thus, if the protocol specifies that Player I makes the first move, the root is labeled AND. The two possible descendants are labeled with the player who makes the next transmission or by a variable or its negation (the answer) if this is the last transmission under the protocol. The function associated with the protocol is the function computed by the circuit so constructed.

We establish the result by induction. The base case applies to sets U and V for which $C(U, V) = 0$. In this case, there is an index i known in advance to both players on which $u \in U$ and $v \in V$ differ. Since either $u_i = 1$ or $u_i = 0$ for all $u \in U$ (v_i has the complementary value for all $\boldsymbol{v} \in V$), let $f = \overline{x}_i$ in the first case and $f = x_i$ in the second. Thus, in the first case (the second case is treated similarly) $U \subseteq f^{-1}(0)$, $V \subseteq f^{-1}(1)$ and $D_{\Omega_0}(f) = 0$. This establishes the base case.

For the induction step, without loss of generality, let Player I send the first bit. (The other case is treated similarly.) For some partition of $U = U_0 \cup U_1$, $U_0 \cap U_1 = \emptyset$, Player I sends a 0 if $\boldsymbol{u} \in U_0$ and a 1 if $\boldsymbol{u} \in U_1$, after which the players play with the best protocol for each subcase. It follows that

$$C(U, V) = 1 + \max_{j=1,2}(C(U_j, V))$$

Since $C(U_j, V) < C(U, V)$ for $j = 1, 2$, by induction there exist Boolean functions f_1 and f_2 such that $U_j \subseteq f_j^{-1}(0)$ and $V \subseteq f_j^{-1}(1)$ and $D_{\Omega_0}(f_j) \leq C(U_j, V)$ for $j = 1, 2$. Since the output vertex is assumed to be AND, $f = f_1 \wedge f_2$, f has value 1 only when both f_1 and f_2 have value 1 and has value 0 when either f_1 or f_2 have value 0. Thus, we have

$$V \subseteq f_1^{-1}(1) \cap f_2^{-1}(1) = f^{-1}(1)$$
$$U = U_1 \cup U_2 \subseteq f_1^{-1}(0) \cup f_2^{-1}(0) = f^{-1}(0)$$

from which we conclude that

$$D_{\Omega_0}(f) \leq 1 + \max(D_{\Omega_0}(f_1), D_{\Omega_0}(f_2)) \leq 1 + \max_{j=1,2}(C(U_j, V)) = C(U, V)$$

which is the desired result. ∎

This establishes the connection between the depth of a Boolean function f over the standard basis Ω_0 and the communication complexity associated with the sets $f^{-1}(0)$ and $f^{-1}(1)$.

We now draw some conclusions from Theorem 9.7.1. From the observation made above that $C(U, V) \leq n + \log_2^* n$ for an arbitrary communication problem (U, V) when $U, V \in \mathcal{B}^n$, we have that $D_{\Omega_0}(f) \leq n + \log_2^* n$ for all $f : \mathcal{B}^n \mapsto \mathcal{B}$. A better upper bound of $D_{\Omega_0}(f) \leq n+1$ is given in Theorem 2.13.1. The best upper bound of $n - \log_2 \log_2 n + O(1)$ has been derived by Gaskov [109], matching the lower bound of $n - \Theta(\log \log n)$ derived in Theorem 2.12.2.

The parity communication problem described above is defined in terms of the two sets that are the inverse images of the parity function $f_{\oplus}^{(n)} : \mathcal{B}^n \mapsto \mathcal{B}$. As stated in Problem 9.28, this function has a formula size of at least n^2. Since $D_{\Omega}(f) \geq \log_2 L_{\Omega_0}(f)$ (Theorem 9.2.2), it follows that $D_{\Omega}(f_{\oplus}^{(n)}) \geq 2\log_2 n$, which matches the upper bound on the communication complexity of the parity communication problem. Thus the protocol given earlier for this problem is optimal.

We now introduce the monotone communication game and develop a relationship between its complexity and the depth of monotone functions over a monotone basis.

9.7.3 Monotone Depth and Communication Complexity

We specialize Theorem 9.7.1 to monotone functions by using the fact that if $f : \mathcal{B}^n \mapsto \mathcal{B}$ is monotone and there are two n-tuples $\boldsymbol{u}$ and $\boldsymbol{v}$ such that $f(\boldsymbol{u}) = 0$ and $f(\boldsymbol{v}) = 1$, then there exists an index i, $1 \leq i \leq n$, such that $u_i < v_i$, that is, $u_i = 0$ and $v_i = 1$.

The binary n-tuple $\boldsymbol{x}$ can be defined by the set $\{i \mid x_i = 1\}$ of indices on which variables have value 1. This is a subset of $[n] = \{1, 2, \ldots, n\}$. Let $2^{[n]}$ be the power set of $[n]$, that is, the set of all subsets of $[n]$. A **monotone minterm** (**monotone maxterm**) is a minimal set of indices of variables that if set to 1 (0) cause f to assume value 1 (0). (The variables of a monotone minterm are variables in a monotone prime implicant of f.) Let $min(f)$ and $max(f)$ be the set of monotone minterms and monotone maxterms of f, respectively. Observe that $min(f) \cap max(f) \neq \emptyset$ because if they have no elements in common, f can be made to assume values 0 and 1 simultaneously for some assignment to the variables of f, a contradiction.

DEFINITION 9.7.2 *A **monotone communication game** (A, B) is defined by sets $A, B \subseteq 2^{[n]}$. An instance of the game is a pair (a, b) where $a \in A$ and $b \in B$. a is assigned to Player I and b is assigned to Player II. Players alternate sending messages as in the communication game, using a predetermined protocol. The **goal** of the problem is to find an integer $i \in a \cap b$. The **communication complexity**, $C_{\mathrm{mon}}(A, B)$, is defined as the minimum over all protocols Π of the maximum number of bits exchanged under Π on any instance of (A, B):*

$$C_{\mathrm{mon}}(A, B) = \min_{\Pi} \max_{a \in A, b \in B} \Pi(a, b)$$

We now establish a relationship between this complexity measure and the circuit depth of a Boolean function.

THEOREM 9.7.2 *For every monotone Boolean function $f : \mathcal{B}^n \mapsto \mathcal{B}$,*

$$D_{\Omega_{\mathrm{mon}}}(f) = C(f^{-1}(0), f^{-1}(1)) = C_{\mathrm{mon}}(min(f), max(f))$$

Proof We show that $D_{\Omega_{\mathrm{mon}}}(f) = C(f^{-1}(0), f^{-1}(1))$ by specializing Lemmas 9.7.1 and 9.7.2 to monotone functions. In the base case of Lemma 9.7.1 since the circuit is monotone we always discover a coordinate such that $u_i = 0$ and $v_i = 1$ and negations are not needed. Thus, $C(f^{-1}(0), f^{-1}(1)) \leq D_{\Omega_{\mathrm{mon}}}(f)$. In Lemma 9.7.2, since the protocol provides a coordinate i such that $u_i = 0$ and $v_i = 1$, the circuit defined by it is monotone and $D_{\Omega_{\mathrm{mon}}}(f) \leq C(f^{-1}(0), f^{-1}(1))$.

We show that $C(f^{-1}(0), f^{-1}(1)) = C_{\mathrm{mon}}(min(f), max(f))$ in two stages. First we show that $C_{\mathrm{mon}}(min(f), max(f)) \leq C(f^{-1}(0), f^{-1}(1))$. This follows because, given any $a \in min(f)$ and $b \in max(f)$, we extend a and b to binary n-tuples $\boldsymbol{u}$ and $\boldsymbol{v}$ for which $u_r = 0$ for $r \in a$ and $v_s = 1$ for $s \in b$ and use the protocol for the monotone communication game to find an index i such that $u_i = 0$ and $v_i = 1$, that is, for which $i \in a \cap b$. Thus, the monotone communication game exchanges no more bits than the standard game.

To show that $C(f^{-1}(0), f^{-1}(1)) \leq C_{\mathrm{mon}}(min(f), max(f))$, consider an instance $(\boldsymbol{u}, \boldsymbol{v})$ of (U, V) where $U = f^{-1}(0)$ and $V = f^{-1}(1)$. To solve the communication problem (U, V), let $a(\boldsymbol{u}) \in [n]$ be defined by $r \in a(\boldsymbol{u})$ if and only if $u_r = 0$ and let $b(\boldsymbol{v}) \in [n]$ be defined by $s \in b(\boldsymbol{v})$ if and only if $v_s = 1$. The goal of the standard communication game is to find an index i such that $u_i \neq v_i$. It follows from the definition of minterms and maxterms that there exist $p \in min(f)$ and $q \in max(f)$ such that $p \subseteq a$ and $q \subseteq b$. Since each player has unlimited computing resources available, computation of p and q can be done with no communication cost. Now invoke the protocol on the instance (p, q) of the monotone communication game $(min(f), max(f))$. This protocol returns an index $i \in p \cap q$ that is also an index on which $\boldsymbol{u}$ and $\boldsymbol{v}$ differ. But this is a solution to the instance of $(\boldsymbol{u}, \boldsymbol{v})$ of $(f^{-1}(0), f^{-1}(1))$. Thus, no more bits are communicated to solve the standard communication game than are exchanged with the monotone communication game when the sets U and V are the inverse images of a monotone Boolean function. ∎

In the next section we use the above result to derive a large lower bound on the monotone depth of the clique function.

9.7.4   The Monotone Depth of the Clique Function

In this section we illustrate the use of the monotone communication game by showing that in this game at least $\Omega(\sqrt{k})$ bits must be exchanged between two players to compute the clique function $f_{\text{clique},k}^{(n)} : \mathcal{B}^{n(n-1)/2} \mapsto \mathcal{B}$ defined in Section 9.6 when $k \leq (n/2)^{2/3}$. The inputs to $f_{\text{clique},k}^{(n)}$ are variables associated with the edges of a graph on n vertices. If an edge variable $e_{i,j} = 1$, the edge between vertices i and j is present. Otherwise, it is absent. By Theorem 9.7.2, a lower bound of $\Omega(\sqrt{k})$ on the number of bits that must be exchanged between the two players to compute $f_{\text{clique},k}^{(n)}$ implies that $f_{\text{clique},k}^{(n)}$ has depth $\Omega(\sqrt{k})$.

THE RULES OF THE GAME   Fix n and k. The players in this communication game are each given sets of edges of graphs on n vertices. Player I is given a set of edges that contains a k-clique (an input on which $f_{\text{clique},k}^{(n)}$ has value 1, a **positive instance**) whereas Player II is given a set of edges that does not contain a k-clique (an input on which it has value 0, a **negative instance**). The goal of the game is to exchange the minimum number of bits for the worst-case instances to permit the players to identify an edge variable that is 1 on a positive instance and 0 on a negative one. This number of bits is the communication complexity of the game.

To derive the lower bound on communication complexity, we restrict the graphs under consideration by choosing them so that every protocol must exchange a lot of data (this cannot make the worst cases any worse). In particular, we give Player I only k-cliques, the set of graphs, CLQ, whose only edges are those between an arbitrary set of k vertices. We call Player I the **clique player**. Also, we give Player II a $(k-1)$-coloring drawn from the set COL of all possible assignments of $k-1$ colors to the n vertices of a graph G. The interpretation of a $(k-1)$-coloring is that two vertices can have the same color only if there is no edge between them. Thus, any graph that has a $(k-1)$-coloring cannot contain a k-clique because the k vertices in such a subgraph must have different colors. We call Player II the **color player**. The goal now becomes for the two players to find a monochromatic edge (both endpoints have the same color) owned by the clique player.

In the standard communication game players alternate exchanging binary messages. We simplify our discussion by assuming that each player transmits one bit simultaneously on each round. We then find a lower bound on the number of rounds and use this as a lower bound on the number of bits exchanged between the two players.

AN ADVERSARIAL STRATEGY   We describe an adversarial strategy for the selection of cliques and colorings that insures that many rounds are needed for the two players to arrive at a decision. To present the strategy, we need some notation.

Let CLQ_0 denote the set of graphs $G = (V, E)$ on n vertices that contain only those edges in a k-clique. It follows that CLQ_0 contains $\binom{n}{k}$ graphs. Let COL_0 denote the set of $(k-1)$-colorings of graphs on n vertices, that is, $COL_0 = \{c \mid c : V \mapsto [k-1]\}$, where $[k-1]$ denotes the set $\{1, 2, \ldots, k-1\}$. It follows that COL_0 contains $(k-1)^n$ $(k-1)$-colorings.

We execute a series of rounds. During each round each player provides one bit of information to the other. This information has the effect of reducing the uncertainty of the color player about the possible k-cliques held by the clique player and of reducing the uncertainty of the clique player about the possible $(k-1)$-colorings held by the color player. The adversary makes the uncertainty large after each round so that the number of rounds needed will be large and a structure of the sets of cliques and colorings that can be analyzed will be maintained. The game ends when both players have found a monochromatic edge that is in a clique.

Let $P_t \subseteq V$ and $M_t \subseteq V$ denote the vertices that after the tth round are present in every k-clique and missing from every k-clique, respectively. (Let $p_t = |P_t|$ and $m_t = |M_t|$.) Since vertices in M_t are not in any cliques after the tth round, as we shall see, each such vertex can be assigned the same color as a "friend" after all vertices not in M_t have been colored. Also, after the tth round the vertices in a k-clique consist of vertices in $V - M_t$ of which those in P_t are the same for all such cliques.

Let $\text{CLQ}(V, P_t, M_t)$ denote the set of k-cliques containing P_t but no vertex in M_t. Let $\text{COL}(V, M_t)$ denote the $(k-1)$-colorings of vertices not in M_t after the tth round. Then $|\text{CLQ}(V, P_t, M_t)| = \binom{n-p_t-m_t}{k-p_t-m_t}$ and $|\text{COL}(V, M_t)| = (n-m_t)^{k-1}$ are the maximum numbers of k-cliques and $(k-1)$-colorings that are possible after the tth round. Let CLQ_t and COL_t denote the actual number of cliques and colorings that are consistent with the information exchanged between players after the tth round.

Given two sets A and B, $A \subseteq B$, we introduce a measure $\mu_B(A) = |A|/|B|$ used in deriving our lower bound. For an element $x \in A$, $\mu_B(A)$ is a rough measure of the amount of information that can be deduced about x. The smaller the value of $\mu_B(A)$, the more information we have about x. This measure is specialized to cliques and colorings after the tth round:

$$\mu_{\text{CLQ}(V,P_t,M_t)}(\text{CLQ}_t) = |\text{CLQ}_t|/|\text{CLQ}(V, P_t, M_t)|$$
$$\mu_{\text{COL}(V,M_t)}(\text{COL}_t) = |\text{COL}_t|/|\text{COL}(V, M_t)|$$

Since the color player does not know the identity of vertices in P_t until after the tth round, its information about the clique held by the other player is measured by p_t and $\mu_{\text{CLQ}(V,P_t,M_t)}(\text{CLQ}_t)$. Since the clique player only knows the color of vertices M_t that are missing in all cliques after the tth round, its information about a $(k-1)$-coloring by the color player is measured by m_t and $\mu_{\text{COL}(V,M_t)}(\text{COL}_t)$.

The number of rounds, T, is large if for $t = T$ no edge present in all remaining cliques CLQ_t that is monochromatic in all remaining colorings COL_t. We show that an adversary can choose the sets CLQ_t and COL_t at each round so that many rounds are needed.

SELECTION OF THE SETS CLQ_T AND COL_T BY THE ADVERSARY: Let the value of the bits sent by the clique and color players be b_{CLQ} and b_{COL}, respectively. At the tth round the following algorithm is used to choose CLQ_t and COL_t:

1) Let $P = P_{t-1}$, $p = p_t$, $M = M_{t-1}$ and $m = m_{t-1}$. Let CLQ^1 be the larger of the two subsets of CLQ_{t-1} consistent with the values $b_{\text{CLQ}} = 0$ and $b_{\text{CLQ}} = 1$. Thus, $\mu_{\text{CLQ}(V,P,M)}(\text{CLQ}^1) \geq \mu_{\text{CLQ}(V,P,M)}(\text{CLQ}_{t-1})/2$.

2) Let CLQ be a collection of k-cliques. Then the set of cliques q in CLQ containing the vertex v is denoted $\text{CLQ}(v) = \{q \in \text{CLQ} \mid v \in q\}$.

Let $\mathrm{CLQ} = \mathrm{CLQ}^1$. As long as there exists $v \in V - P - M$ such that the following is true:

$$\mu_{\mathrm{CLQ}(V,P,M)}(\mathrm{CLQ}(v)) \geq \frac{2(k-p-m)}{(n-p-m)}\mu_{\mathrm{CLQ}(V,P,M)}(\mathrm{CLQ}) \tag{9.2}$$

replace P by $P^* = P \cup \{v\}$, p by $p^* = p + 1$, and CLQ by $\mathrm{CLQ}^* = \mathrm{CLQ}(v)$. Here $(k-p-m)\mu_{\mathrm{CLQ}(V,P,M)}(\mathrm{CLQ})/(n-p-m)$ is the average of $\mu_{\mathrm{CLQ}(V,P,M)}(\mathrm{CLQ}(v))$ over all $v \in V - P - M$. Thus, $\mathrm{CLQ}(v)$ has measure at least twice the average.

Since $|\mathrm{CLQ}(V,P^*,M)| = (k-p-m)|\mathrm{CLQ}(V,P,M)|/(n-p-m)$ after each iteration of this loop, the following bound holds:

$$\mu_{\mathrm{CLQ}(V,P^*,M)}(\mathrm{CLQ}^*) \geq 2\mu_{\mathrm{CLQ}(V,P,M)}(\mathrm{CLQ})$$

That is, the renormalized measure of the set of cliques after one iteration of the loop is at least double that of the measure before the iteration.

After exiting from this loop let $\mathrm{CLQ}_t^* = \mathrm{CLQ}^*$ and let $P_t = P$. Since P_t contains $p_t - p_{t-1}$ more items than P_{t-1}, the following inequality holds:

$$\begin{aligned}\mu_{\mathrm{CLQ}(V,P_t,M_t)}(\mathrm{CLQ}_t^*) &\geq 2^{p_t-p_{t-1}}\mu_{\mathrm{CLQ}(V,P_{t-1},M_{t-1})}(\mathrm{CLQ}^1) \\ &\geq 2^{p_t-p_{t-1}}\mu_{\mathrm{CLQ}(V,P_{t-1},M_{t-1})}(\mathrm{CLQ}_{t-1})/2 \end{aligned} \tag{9.3}$$

Furthermore, for any vertex v remaining in $V - P$ the condition expressed in (9.2) is violated, so that the following holds for $v \in V - P$, where $\alpha = 2(k - p_t - m_{t-1})/(n - p_t - m_{t-1})$:

$$\mu_{\mathrm{CLQ}(V,P_t,M_{t-1})}(\{q \in \mathrm{CLQ}_t^* \mid v \in q\}) < \alpha\left(\mu_{\mathrm{CLQ}(V,P_t,M_{t-1})}(\mathrm{CLQ}_t^*)\right) \tag{9.4}$$

3) Let $\mathrm{COL}_t^* = \{c \in \mathrm{COL}_{t-1} \mid c \text{ is } 1\text{-}1 \text{ on } P_t\}$. That is, COL_t^* is the set of $(k-1)$-colorings in COL_t that assigns unique colors to vertices in P_t. By restricting the $(k-1)$-colorings we do not increase the number of rounds. In Lemma 9.7.3 we develop a lower bound on $\mu_{\mathrm{COL}(V,M_{t-1})}(\mathrm{COL}_t^*)$ in terms of $\mu_{\mathrm{COL}(V,M_{t-1})}(\mathrm{COL}_{t-1})$.

4) Let $M = M_{t-1}$ and $m = m_{t-1}$. Let COL^0 and COL^1 denote the subsets of COL_t^* consistent with the values $b_{\mathrm{COL}} = 0$ and $b_{\mathrm{COL}} = 1$, respectively. Let COL be the larger of these two sets. Then $\mu_{\mathrm{COL}(V,M)}(\mathrm{COL}) \geq \mu_{\mathrm{COL}(V,M)}(\mathrm{COL}_t^*)/2$.

5) The set $\mathrm{COL}_t(u,v) = \{c \in \mathrm{COL} \mid c(u) = c(v)\}$ contains those $(k-1)$-colorings in COL for which vertices u and v have the same color.

As long as there exist $u, v \in V - M$ such that the following is true:

$$\mu_{\mathrm{COL}(V,M)}(\mathrm{COL}_t(u,v)) \geq 2\mu_{\mathrm{COL}(V,M)}(\mathrm{COL})/(k-1)$$

let w be one of u and v that is not in P (they cannot both be in P and have the same color because each coloring is 1-1 on P); replace M by $M^* = M \cup \{w\}$, m by $m^* = m + 1$, and COL by $\mathrm{COL}^* = \mathrm{COL}_t(u,v)$.

The term $\mu_{\mathrm{COL}(V,M)}(\mathrm{COL})/(k-1)$ is the average of $\mu_{\mathrm{COL}(V,M)}(\mathrm{COL}_t(u,v))$ over all u and v in $V - M$. Thus, COL^* contains $(k-1)$-colorings whose measure is at least twice the average.

Since $|\mathrm{COL}(V, M^*)| = |\mathrm{COL}(V, M)|/(k-1)$ after each iteration of this loop, the following holds:

$$\mu_{\mathrm{COL}(V,M^*)}(\mathrm{COL}^*) \geq 2\mu_{\mathrm{COL}(V,M)}(\mathrm{COL})$$

That is, the renormalized measure of the set of $(k-1)$-colorings after each loop iteration is at least double that of the measure before the iteration.

After exiting from this loop, let $M_t = M$. Since M_t contains $m_t - m_{t-1}$ more items than M_{t-1}, the following inequality holds:

$$
\begin{aligned}
\mu_{\mathrm{COL}(V,M_{t-1})}(\mathrm{COL}^*) &\geq 2^{m_t - m_{t-1}} \mu_{\mathrm{COL}(V,M_{t-1})}(\mathrm{COL}) \\
&\geq 2^{m_t - m_{t-1}} \mu_{\mathrm{COL}(V,M_{t-1})}(\mathrm{COL}_t^*)/2
\end{aligned}
\tag{9.5}
$$

6) Let $\mathrm{COL}_t = \mathrm{COL}^*$, $M_t = M$, and $\mathrm{CLQ}_t = \{q \in \mathrm{CLQ}_t^* \mid M_t \cap q = \emptyset\}$. Thus, CLQ_t does not contain any cliques with vertices in M_t. In Lemma 9.7.4 we develop a lower bound on $\mu_{\mathrm{CLQ}(V,P_t,M_{t-1})}(\mathrm{CLQ}_t)$ in terms of $\mu_{\mathrm{CLQ}(V,P_t,M_{t-1})}(\mathrm{CLQ}_t^*)$.

PERFORMANCE OF THE ADVERSARIAL STRATEGY   We establish three lemmas and then derive the lower bound on the number of rounds of the communication game.

LEMMA 9.7.3 *After step 3 of the adversarial selection the following inequality holds:*

$$\mu_{\mathrm{COL}(V,M_{t-1})}(\mathrm{COL}_t^*) \geq \left(1 - \frac{(p_t + 1)^2}{k-1}\right) \mu_{\mathrm{COL}(V,M_{t-1})}(\mathrm{COL}_{t-1})$$

Proof Recall the definition of $\mathrm{COL}_t(u,v) = \{c \in \mathrm{COL} \mid c(u) = c(v)\}$. Consider the results of step 3 of the tth round in the adversary selection process. Because of the choices made in step 5 in the $(t-1)$st round and the choice of COL_0, the following inequality holds for all $t > 0$ and $u, v \in V - M_{t-1}$ when $u \neq v$:

$$\mu_{\mathrm{COL}(V,M_{t-1})}(\mathrm{COL}_t(u,v)) < 2\mu_{\mathrm{COL}(V,M_{t-1})}(\mathrm{COL}_{t-1})/(k-1)$$

Because $M_t = M_{t-1}$ at step 3 of the tth round and $P_t \subseteq V - M_t$, the same bound applies for u and v in P_t.

The set COL_{t-1} is reduced to $\mathrm{COL}_t^* = \{c \in \mathrm{COL}_{t-1} \mid c \text{ is 1 to 1 on } P_t\}$ by discarding $(k-1)$-colorings for which u and v are in P_t and have the same color. From the above facts the following inequalities hold (here instances of the measure μ carry the subscript $\mathrm{COL}(V, M_{t-1})$):

$$
\begin{aligned}
\mu(\mathrm{COL}_t^*) &= \mu(\{c \in \mathrm{COL}_{t-1} \mid c \text{ is 1 to 1 on } P_t\}) \\
&= \mu(\mathrm{COL}_{t-1}) - \mu\left(\bigcup_{u,v \in P_t,\ u \neq v} \mathrm{COL}_t(u,v)\right) \\
&\geq \mu(\mathrm{COL}_{t-1}) - \sum_{u,v \in P_t,\ u \neq v} \mathrm{COL}_t(u,v) \\
&> \left(1 - \binom{p_t}{2}\frac{2}{k-1}\right)\mu(\mathrm{COL}_{t-1}) \\
&> \left(1 - \frac{(p_t + 1)^2}{k-1}\right)\mu(\mathrm{COL}_{t-1})
\end{aligned}
$$

From this the conclusion follows. ∎

LEMMA 9.7.4 *After step 6 of the adversarial selection the following inequality holds:*

$$\mu_{\mathrm{CLQ}(V,P_t,M_{t-1})}(\mathrm{CLQ}_t) \geq \left(1 - \frac{2km_t}{n}\right)\mu_{\mathrm{CLQ}(V,P_t,M_{t-1})}(\mathrm{CLQ}_t^*)$$

Proof As stated in (9.4), after step 2 of the tth round of the adversary selection process we have for all $v \in V - P_t - M_{t-1}$ the following inequality:

$$\mu_{\mathrm{CLQ}(V,P_t,M_{t-1})}(\{q \in \mathrm{CLQ}_t^* \mid v \in q\}) < \frac{2(k - p_t - m_{t-1})}{(n - p_t - m_{t-1})}\mu_{\mathrm{CLQ}(V,P_t,M_{t-1})}(\mathrm{CLQ}_t^*)$$

Since $M_t \subseteq V - P_t$, this bound applies to $v \in M_t$. In the rest of this proof all instances of μ carry the subscript $\mathrm{CLQ}(V, P_t, M_{t-1})$.

Since $\mathrm{CLQ}_t = \{q \in \mathrm{CLQ}_t^* \mid M_t \cap q = \emptyset\}$, after step 6 the following inequalities hold:

$$\mu(\mathrm{CLQ}_t) = \mu(\{c \in \mathrm{CLQ}_t \mid M_t \cap q = \emptyset\})$$

$$= \mu(\mathrm{CLQ}_t^*) - \mu\left(\bigcup_{v \in M_t} \{c \in \mathrm{CLQ}_t^* \mid v \in q\}\right)$$

$$\geq \left(1 - \frac{2(k - p_t - m_{t-1})m_t}{(n - p_t - m_{t-1})}\right)\mu(\mathrm{CLQ}_t^*)$$

$$\geq \left(1 - \frac{2km_t}{n}\right)\mu(\mathrm{CLQ}_t^*)$$

From this the conclusion follows. ∎

The third lemma sets the stage for the principal result of this section.

LEMMA 9.7.5 *Let $k \geq 2$ and $t \leq \sqrt{k}/4$ and $t \leq n/(8k)$. Then the following inequalities hold:*

$$\mu_{\mathrm{CLQ}(V,P_t,M_{t-1})}(\mathrm{CLQ}_t) \geq 2^{p_t - 2t}$$

$$\mu_{\mathrm{COL}(V,M_t)}(\mathrm{COL}_t) \geq 2^{m_t - 2t}$$

Proof The inequalities hold for $t = 0$ because $\mu_{\mathrm{CLQ}(V,P_0)}(\mathrm{CLQ}_0) = \mu_{\mathrm{COL}(V,M_0)}(\mathrm{COL}_0) = 1$. We assume as inductive hypothesis that the inequalities hold for the first $t - 1$ rounds and show they hold for the tth round as well.

Using the inductive hypothesis and (9.3), we have

$$\mu_{\mathrm{CLQ}(V,P_t,M_{t-1})}(\mathrm{CLQ}_t^*) \geq 2^{p_t - p_{t-1}}\mu_{\mathrm{CLQ}(V,P_{t-1},M_{t-1})}(\mathrm{CLQ}_{t-1})/2 \geq 2^{p_t - 2t + 1} \quad (9.6)$$

Since $\mu_{\mathrm{CLQ}(V,P_t)}(\mathrm{CLQ}_t^*) \leq 1$, we conclude that $p_t \leq 2t - 1$. Using this result, the assumption that $t \leq \sqrt{k}/4$, Lemma 9.7.3, and the inductive hypothesis, we have

$$\mu_{\mathrm{COL}(V,M_{t-1})}(\mathrm{COL}_t^*) \geq \left(1 - \frac{4t^2}{k-1}\right)\mu_{\mathrm{COL}(V,M_{t-1})}(\mathrm{COL}_{t-1})$$

$$\geq \left(1 - \frac{k}{4(k-1)}\right)\mu_{\mathrm{COL}(V,M_{t-1})}(\mathrm{COL}_{t-1})$$

$$\geq \frac{1}{2}\mu_{\mathrm{COL}(V,M_{t-1})}(\mathrm{COL}_{t-1})$$

$$\geq 2^{m_{t-1} - 2t + 1}$$

Combining this and (9.5) (note that in step 6 we let $\text{COL}_t = \text{COL}^*$), we have the first of the two desired conclusions, namely $\mu_{\text{COL}(V, M_t)}(\text{COL}_t) \geq 2^{m_t - 2t}$. This implies that $m_t \leq 2t$. Applying this to the inequality in Lemma 9.7.4 and using the condition $t \leq n/(8k)$, we get the following inequality:

$$\mu_{\text{CLQ}(V, P_t, M_{t-1})}(\text{CLQ}_t) \geq \mu_{\text{CLQ}(V, P_t, M_{t-1})}(\text{CLQ}_t^*)/2$$

Combining this with the lower bound given in (9.6), we have the second of the two desired conclusions, namely, $\mu_{\text{CLQ}(V, P_t, M_{t-1})}(\text{CLQ}_t) \geq 2^{p_2 - 2t}$. ∎

We now state the principal conclusion of this section.

THEOREM 9.7.3 *Let $2 \leq k \leq (n/2)^{2/3}$. Then the monotone communication complexity of the k-clique function $f_{\text{clique}, k}^{(n)}$ is $\Omega(\sqrt{k})$.*

Proof Run the adversarial selection process for $T = \sqrt{k}/4$ steps to produce sets CLQ_T, COL_T, P_T, and M_T. Below we show that CLQ_T and COL_T are not empty. Give the clique player a k-clique $q \in \text{CLQ}_T$ and the color player a $(k-1)$-coloring $c \in \text{COL}_T$. To show that the two players cannot agree in T or fewer rounds on an edge in a clique in CLQ_T that is monochromatic in all $c \in \text{COL}_T$, assume they can, and let $(u, v) \in q$ be that edge. If follows that both u and v are in M_T. But this cannot happen because, by construction, $q \cap M_T = \emptyset$.

To show that CLQ_T and COL_T are not empty, observe that $k \leq (n/2)^{2/3}$ and $t \leq \sqrt{k}/4$ imply that $t \leq n/(8k)$. Thus, Lemma 9.7.5 can be invoked, which implies that $p_t, m_t \leq 2t \leq \sqrt{k}/2 \leq k/2 < n$. Invoking the definitions, the following inequalities also hold.

$$\text{CLQ}_t \geq 2^{p_t - 2t}\text{CLQ}(V, P_t, M_{t-1}) > 0$$
$$\text{COL}_t \geq 2^{m_t - 2t}\text{COL}(V, M_t) > 0$$

Since the right-hand sides are non-zero, we have the desired conclusion. ∎

9.7.5 Bounded-Depth Circuits

As explained earlier, bounded-depth circuits are studied to help us understand the depth of bounded fan-in circuits. Bounded-depth circuits for arbitrary Boolean functions require that the fan-in of some gates be unbounded because otherwise only a bounded number of inputs can influence the output(s).

In Section 2.3 we encountered the DNF, CNF, SOPE, POSE, and RSE normal forms. Each of these corresponds to a circuit of bounded depth. The DNF and SOPE normal forms represent Boolean functions as the OR of the AND of literals. The OR and each of the ANDs is a function of a potentially unbounded number of literals. The same statement applies to the CNF and POSE normal forms when AND and OR are exchanged. The RSE normal form represents Boolean functions as the EXCLUSIVE OR of the AND of variables, that is, without the use of negation. Again, the fan-in of the two types of operation is potentially unbounded. As stated in Problems 2.8 and 2.9, the SOPE and POSE of the parity function $f_{\oplus}^{(n)}$ have exponential size, as does the RSE of the OR function $f_{\vee}^{(n)}$. In Problem 2.10 it is stated that the function $f_{\text{mod } 3}^{(n)}$ has exponential size in the DNF, CNF, and RSE normal forms.

In this section we show that every bounded-depth circuit for the parity function $f_\oplus^{(n)}$ over the basis containing the NOT gate on one input and the AND and OR gates on an arbitrary number of inputs has exponential size. Thus, the depth-2 result extends to arbitrary depth.

BOUNDED-DEPTH PARITY CIRCUITS HAVE EXPONENTIAL SIZE   We use an approximation method to derive a lower bound on the size of a bounded-depth circuit for $f_\oplus^{(n)}$. This method parallels almost exactly the method of Section 9.6.3. Starting with gates most distant from the output and progressing toward it, replace each gate of a given circuit by an approximating circuit. We show that as each replacement is made, the number of new errors it introduces is small. However, we also show that after all gates are approximated, the number of errors between the approximating circuit and $f_\oplus^{(n)}$ is large. This implies that the number of gates replaced is large.

The approximation method used here replaces each gate in a circuit by a polynomial over $GF(3)$, the three-element field containing $\{-1, 0, 1\}$, with the property that if the variables of such a polynomial assume values in $\mathcal{B} = \{0, 1\}$, the value of the polynomial is in $\mathcal{B}$. For example, the polynomial $x_1(1 - x_2)x_3$ has value 1 over $\mathcal{B}$ only when $x_1 = x_3 = 1$ and $x_2 = 0$ and has value 0 otherwise. Thus, it corresponds exactly to the minterm $x_1\overline{x}_2x_3$. Since every minterm can be represented as a polynomial of this kind, every Boolean function f can realized by a polynomial over $GF(3)$ by forming the sum of one such polynomial for each of its minterms. A **b-approximator** is polynomial of degree b that approximates a Boolean function.

Although we establish the lower bound for the basis containing NOT and the unbounded fan-in AND and OR gates, the result continues to hold if the unbounded fan-in MOD_3 function is added to the basis. (See Problem 9.41.) We begin by showing that the function computed by a circuit C containing $size(C)$ gates cannot differ from its b-approximator on too many input tuples.

LEMMA 9.7.6 *Let $f : \mathcal{B}^n \mapsto \mathcal{B}$ be computed by a circuit C of depth d. There is a $(2k)^d$-approximator circuit $\widehat{C}$ computing $\widehat{f} : \mathcal{B}^n \mapsto \mathcal{B}$ such that f and $\widehat{f}$ differ on at most $size(C)2^{n-k}$ input n-tuples, where n is the number of inputs on which C depends and $size(C)$ is the number of gates that it contains.*

Proof   We construct a b-approximator for C, $b = (2k)^d$, by approximating inputs (x_i and $\overline{x}_i$ are approximated exactly on $\mathcal{B}$ by x_i and $(1 - x_i)$), after which we approximate gates all of whose inputs have been approximated until the output gate has been approximated. We establish the result of the lemma by induction.

We treat the statement of the lemma as our inductive hypothesis and show that if it holds for $d = D - 1$, it holds for $d = D$. The hypothesis holds on inputs, namely, when $d = 0$. Suppose the hypothesis holds for $d = D - 1$. Since C has depth d, each of the inputs to the output gate has depth at most $D - 1$ and satisfies the hypothesis. The output gate is AND, OR, or NOT. Suppose it is NOT. Let g be the function associated with its input. We replace the NOT gate with the function $(1 - g)$, which introduces no new errors. Since g and $1 - g$ have the same degree, the inductive hypothesis holds in this case.

If the output gate is the AND of $g_1, g_2, \ldots, g_m$, it can be represented exactly by the function $g_1 g_2 \cdots g_m$. However, this polynomial has degree $m(2k)^{d-1}$ if each of its inputs has degree at most $(2k)^{d-1}$; this violates the inductive hypothesis if $m > 2k$, which may happen because the fan-in of the gate is potentially unbounded. Thus we must introduce some error in order to reduce the degree of the approximating polynomial. Since the OR of

$g_1, g_2, \ldots, g_m$ can be represented by $1 - (1 - g_1)(1 - g_2) \cdots (1 - g_m)$ using DeMorgan's Rules, both AND and OR of $g_1, g_2, \ldots, g_m$ have the same degree. We find an approximating polynomial for both AND and OR by approximating the OR gate.

We approximate the OR of $g_1, g_2, \ldots, g_m$ by creating subsets $S_1, S_2, \ldots, S_k$ of $\{g_1, g_2, \ldots, g_m\}$, computing $f_i = (\sum_{j \in S_i} g_j)^2$, and combining these results in

$$\text{OR}(f_1, f_2, \ldots, f_k) = 1 - (1 - f_1)(1 - f_2) \cdots (1 - f_k)$$

The degree of this approximation is $2k$ times the maximal degree of any polynomial in the set $\{g_1, g_2, \ldots, g_m\}$ or at most $(2k)^d$, the desired result.

There is no error in this approximation if the original OR has value 0. We now show that there exist subsets $S_1, S_2, \ldots, S_k$ such that the error is at most 2^{n-k} when the original OR has value 1. Let's fix on a particular input n-tuple $\boldsymbol{x}$ to the circuit. Suppose each subset is formed by deciding for each function in $\{g_1, g_2, \ldots, g_m\}$ with probability $1/2$ whether or not to include it in the set. If one or more of $\{g_1, g_2, \ldots, g_m\}$ is 1 on $\boldsymbol{x}$, the probability of choosing a function for set whose value is 1 is at least $1/2$. Thus, the probability that $\text{OR}(f_1, f_2, \ldots, f_k)$ has value 0 when the original OR has value 1 is the probability that each of $f_1, f_2, \ldots, f_k$ has value 0, which is at most 2^{-k}. Since the sets $\{S_1, S_2, \ldots, S_k\}$ result in an error on input $\boldsymbol{x}$ with probability at most 2^{-k}, the average number of errors on input $\boldsymbol{x}$, averaged over all choices for the k sets, is at most 2^{-k} and the average number of errors on the set of 2^n inputs is at most 2^{n-k}. It follows that some set $\{S_1, S_2, \ldots, S_k\}$ (and a corresponding approximating function) has an incorrect value on at most 2^{n-k} inputs. Since by the inductive hypothesis at most $(size(C) - 1)2^{n-k}$ errors occur on all but the output gate, at most $size(C)2^{n-k}$ errors occur on the entire circuit. ∎

The next result demonstrates that a $\sqrt{n}$-approximator (obtained by letting $k = n^{1/2d}/2$) and the parity function must differ on many inputs. This is used to show that the circuit being approximated must have many gates.

LEMMA 9.7.7 *Let $\widehat{f} : \mathcal{B}^n \mapsto \mathcal{B}$ be a $\sqrt{n}$-approximator for $f_\oplus^{(n)}$. Then, $\widehat{f}$ and $f_\oplus^{(n)}$ differ on at least $2^n/50$ input n-tuples.*

Proof Let $U \subseteq \mathcal{B}^n$ be the n-tuples on which the functions agree. We derive an upper bound on $|U|$ of $\beta = (49)2^n/50$ that implies the lower bound of the lemma. We derive this bound indirectly. Since there are $3^{|U|}$ functions $g : U \mapsto \{-1, 0, 1\}$, assign each one a different polynomial and show that the number of such polynomials is at most 3^β, which implies that $|U| \leq \beta$.

Transform the polynomial in the variables $x_1, x_2, \ldots, x_n$ representing $f_\oplus^{(n)}$ by mapping x_i to $y_i = 2x_i - 1$. This mapping sends 1 to 1 and 0 to -1. (Observe that $y_i^2 = 1$.) It does not change the degree of a polynomial. In these new variables $f_\oplus^{(n)}$ can be represented exactly by the polynomial $y_1 y_2 \cdots y_n$.

Given a function $g : U \mapsto \{-1, 0, 1\}$, extend it arbitrarily to a function $\widetilde{g} : \mathcal{B}^n \mapsto \{-1, 0, 1\}$. Let p be a polynomial in $Y = \{y_1, y_2, \ldots, y_n\}$ that represents $\widetilde{g}$ on U exactly. Let $cy_{i_1}y_{i_2} \cdots y_{i_t}$ be a term in p for some constant $c \in \{-1, 1\}$. We show that if t is larger than $n/2$ we can replace this term with a smaller-degree term.

Let $T = \{y_{i_1}, y_{i_2}, \ldots, y_{i_t}\}$ and $\overline{T} = Y - T$. The term $cy_{i_1}y_{i_2} \cdots y_{i_t}$ can be written as $c\Pi T$, where by ΠT we mean the product of all terms in T. With $y_i^2 = 1$, this may be rewritten as $c\Pi Y \Pi \overline{T}$. Since $f_\oplus^{(n)} = \Pi Y$, on the set U this is equivalent to $c\widehat{f}\Pi \overline{T}$, which has degree $\sqrt{n} + n - |\overline{T}|$. Thus, a term $cy_{i_1} y_{i_2} \cdots y_{i_t}$ of degree $t \geq n/2$ can be replaced by a term of degree $\sqrt{n} + n - t$. It follows that the number of polynomials (and functions) representing functions whose values coincide with $f_{\oplus}^{(n)}$ on U is the number of polynomials of degree at most $\sqrt{n} + n/2$. Since there are $\binom{n}{j}$ ways to choose a term containing j variables of Y, there are at most N ways to choose polynomials representing functions $g : U \mapsto \{-1, 0, 1\}$, where N satisfies the following bound:

$$N \leq \sum_{j=0}^{\sqrt{n}+(n/2)} \binom{n}{j}$$

For sufficiently large n, the bound to N is approximately $0.9772 \cdot 2^n < (49/50)2^n$. (See Problem 9.7.) Since each of the N terms can be included in a polynomial with coefficient -1, 0, or 1, there are at most 3^N distinct polynomials and corresponding functions $g : U \mapsto \{-1, 0, 1\}$, which is the desired conclusion. ∎

We summarize these two results in Theorem 9.7.4.

THEOREM 9.7.4 *Every circuit of depth d for the parity function $f_{\oplus}^{(n)}$ has a size exceeding $2^n/50$ for sufficiently large n.*

Proof Let U be the set of n-tuples on which $f_{\oplus}^{(n)}$ and its approximation $\widehat{f}$ differ. From Lemma 9.7.6, $|U|$ is at most size$(C)2^{n-k}$. Now let $k = n^{1/2d}/2$. From Lemma 9.7.7 these two functions must differ on at least $\frac{1}{50}2^n$ input n-tuples. Thus, size$(C)2^{n-k} \geq \frac{1}{50}2^n$ from which the conclusion follows. ∎

Problems

MATHEMATICAL PRELIMINARIES

9.1 Show that the following identity holds for integers r and L:

$$\left\lceil \frac{L}{r+1} \right\rceil + \left\lfloor \frac{rL}{r+1} \right\rfloor = L$$

9.2 Show that a rooted tree of maximal fan-in r containing k internal vertices has at most $k(r-1)+1$ leaves and that a rooted tree with l leaves and fan-in r has at most $l-1$ vertices with fan-in 2 or more and at most $2(l-1)$ edges.

9.3 For positive integers n_1, n_2, a_1, and a_2, show that the following identity holds:

$$\frac{n_1^2}{a_1} + \frac{n_2^2}{a_2} \geq \frac{(n_1 + n_2)^2}{(a_1 + a_2)}$$

9.4 The **external path length** $e(T, L)$ of a binary tree T with L leaves is the sum of the lengths of the paths from the root to the leaves. Show that $e(T, L) \geq L\lceil \log_2 L \rceil - 2^{\lceil \log_2 L \rceil} + L$.

Hint: Argue that the external path length is minimal for a nearly balanced binary tree. Use this fact and a proof by induction to obtain the external path length of a binary tree with $L = 2^k$ for some integer k. Use this result to establish the above statement.

9.5 For positive integers r and s, show that $\lceil s/r \rceil (s \bmod r) + \lfloor s/r \rfloor (r - s \bmod r) = s$.
Hint: Use the fact that for any real number a, $\lceil a \rceil - \lfloor a \rfloor = 1$ if a is not an integer and 0 otherwise. Also use the fact that $s \bmod r = s - \lfloor s/r \rfloor \cdot r$.

9.6 (**Binomial Theorem**) Show that the coefficient of the term $x^i y^{n-i}$ in the expansion of the polynomial $(x + y)^n$ is the binomial coefficient $\binom{n}{i}$. That is,

$$(x + y)^n = \sum_{i=0}^{n} \binom{n}{i} x^i y^{n-i}$$

9.7 Show that the following sum is closely approximated by $0.4772 \cdot 2^n$ for large n:

$$\sum_{i=(n/2)}^{(n/2)+\sqrt{n}} \binom{n}{i}$$

Hint: Use the fact that $n!$ can be very closely approximated by $\sqrt{2\pi n}\, n^n e^{-n}$ to approximate $\binom{n}{i}$. Then approximate a sum by an integral (see Problem 2.23) and consult tables of values for the **error function** $\operatorname{erf}(x) = \int_0^x e^{-t^2} dt$.

9.8 Let $0 \le x \le y$. Show that $x + \sqrt{y - x} \ge \sqrt{y}$.

CIRCUIT MODELS AND MEASURES

9.9 Provide an algorithm that produces a formula for each circuit of fan-out 1 over a basis that has fan-in of at most 2.

9.10 Show that any monotone Boolean function $f^{(n)} : \mathcal{B}^n \mapsto \mathcal{B}$ can be expanded on its first variable as

$$f(x_1, x_2, \ldots, x_n) = f(0, x_2, \ldots, x_n) \vee (x_1 \wedge f(1, x_2, \ldots, x_n))$$

9.11 Show that a circuit for a Boolean function (one output vertex) over the standard basis can be transformed into one that uses negation only on inputs by at most doubling the number of AND, OR, and NOT gates and without changing its depth by more than a constant factor.
Hint: Find the two-input gate closest to the output gate that is connected to a NOT gate. Change the circuit to move the NOT gate closer to the inputs.

RELATIONSHIPS AMONG COMPLEXITY MEASURES

9.12 Using the construction employed in Theorem 9.2.1, show that the depth of a function $f : \mathcal{B}^n \mapsto \mathcal{B}^m$ in a circuit of fan-out s over a complete basis Ω of fan-in r satisfies the inequality

$$D_{s,\Omega}(f) \le D_\Omega(f) \left(1 + l(\Omega) + l(\Omega) \log_s \left(r C_{s,\Omega}(f)/D\right)\right)$$

9.13 Show that there are ten functions f with $L_\Omega(f) = 2$ that are dependent on two variables and that each can be realized from a circuit for $f_{\text{mux}}^{(1)}$ plus at most one instance of NOT on an input to $f_{\text{mux}}^{(1)}$ and on its output.

9.14 Extend the upper bound on depth versus formula size of Theorem 9.2.2 to monotone functions.

LOWER-BOUND METHODS FOR GENERAL CIRCUITS

9.15 Show that the function $f(x_1, x_2, \ldots, x_n) = x_1 \wedge x_2 \wedge \cdots \wedge x_n$ has circuit size $\lceil (n-1)/(r-1) \rceil$ and depth $\lceil \log_r n \rceil$ over the basis containing the r-input AND gate.

9.16 The parity function $f_\oplus^{(n)} : \mathcal{B}^n \mapsto \mathcal{B}$ has value 1 when an odd number of its variables have value 1 and 0 otherwise. Derive matching upper and lower bounds on the size and depth of the smallest and shallowest circuit(s) for $f_\oplus^{(n)}$ over the basis B_2.

9.17 Show that the function $f_{\text{mod } 3,c}^{(n)}$ defined in Section 9.3.2 can be realized by a circuit over the basis B_2 whose size is $2.5n + O(\log^2 n)$.

   Hint: Show that the function is symmetric and devise a circuit to compute the value of a binary number modulo 3.

9.18 Over the basis B_2 derive good upper and lower bounds on the circuit size of the functions $f_4^{(n)} : \mathcal{B}^n \mapsto \mathcal{B}$ and $f_5^{(n)} : \mathcal{B}^n \mapsto \mathcal{B}$ defined as

$$f_4^{(n)} = ((y+2) \bmod 4) \bmod 2$$
$$f_5^{(n)} = ((y+2) \bmod 5) \bmod 2$$

   Here $y = \sum_{i=1}^n x_i$ and $\sum$ and $+$ denote integer addition.

9.19 Show that the set of Boolean functions on two variables that depend on both variables contains only AND-type and parity-type functions. Here an AND-**type function** computes $(x^a \wedge y^b)^c$ for Boolean constants a, b, c whereas a **parity-type function** computes $x \oplus y \oplus c$ for some Boolean constant c.

9.20 The threshold function $\tau_t^{(n)} : \mathcal{B}^n \mapsto \mathcal{B}$ on n inputs has value is 1 if t or more inputs are 1 and 0 otherwise. Show that over the basis B_2 that $C_{B_2}(\tau_2^{(n)}) \geq 2n - 4$.

9.21 A formula for the parity function $f_{\oplus,c}^{(n)} : \mathcal{B}^n \mapsto \mathcal{B}$ on n inputs is given below. Show that it has circuit size exactly $3(n-1)$ over the standard basis when NOT gates are not counted:

$$f_{\oplus,c}^{(n)} = x_1 \oplus x_2 \oplus \cdots \oplus x_n \oplus c$$

9.22 Show that $f_{\oplus,c}^{(n)}$ has circuit size exactly $4(n-1)$ over the standard basis when NOT gates are counted.

9.23 Show that $f_{\oplus,c}^{(n)}$ has circuit size exactly $7(n-1)$ over the basis $\{\wedge, \neg\}$.

LOWER BOUNDS TO FORMULA SIZE

9.24 Show that the multiplexer function $f_{\text{mux}}^{(p)}$ can be realized by a formula of size $32^p - 2$ in which the total number of address variables is $2(2^p - 1)$.

Hint: Expand the function $f_{\text{mux}}^{(p)}$ as suggested below, where $\boldsymbol{a}^{(k)}$ denotes the k components of $\boldsymbol{a}$ with smallest index and $P = 2^p$:

$$f_{\text{mux}}^{(p)}(\boldsymbol{a}^{(p)}, y_{P-1}, \dots, y_0) = f_{\text{mux}}^{(1)}(a_{p-1}, f_{\text{mux}}^{(p-1)}(\boldsymbol{a}^{(p-1)}, y_{P-1}, \dots, y_{P/2}),$$
$$f_{\text{mux}}^{(p-1)}(\boldsymbol{a}^{(p-1)}, y_{P/2-1}, \dots, y_0))$$

Also, represent $f_{\text{mux}}^{(1)}$ as shown below.

$$f_{\text{mux}}^{(1)}(a, y_1, y_0) = (\overline{a} \wedge y_0) \vee (a \wedge y_1)$$

9.25 Show that Nečiporuk's method cannot provide a lower bound larger than $O(n^2/\log n)$ for a function on n variables.

9.26 Derive a quadratic upper bound on the formula size of the parity function $f_{\oplus}^{(n)}$ over the standard basis.

9.27 Nečiporuk's function is defined in terms of an $\lceil n/m \rceil \times m$ matrix of Boolean variables, $\boldsymbol{X} = \{x_{i,j}\}$, $m = \lceil \log_2 n \rceil + 2$, and a matrix $\boldsymbol{\Sigma} = \{\sigma_{i,j}\}$ of the same dimensions in which each entry $\sigma_{i,j}$ is a distinct m-tuple over $\mathcal{B}$ containing at least two 1s. Nečiporuk's function, $N(\boldsymbol{X})$, is defined as

$$N(\boldsymbol{X}) = \bigoplus_{i,j} x_{i,j} \bigwedge \bigoplus_{\substack{k=1 \\ (k \neq i)}} \prod_{\substack{l \text{ such that} \\ \sigma_{i,j}(l)=1}} x_{k,l}$$

Here $\bigoplus$ denotes the **exclusive or** operation. Show that this function has formula size $\Omega(n^2/\log n)$ over the basis B_2.

9.28 Use Krapchenko's method to derive a lower bound of n^2 on the formula size of the parity function $f_{\oplus}^{(n)} : \mathcal{B}^n \mapsto \mathcal{B}$.

9.29 Use Krapchenko's method to derive a lower bound of $\Omega(t(n - t + 1))$ on the formula size over the standard basis of the threshold function $\tau_t^{(n)}$, $1 \le t \le n - 1$.

9.30 Generalize Krapchenko's lower-bound method as follows. Let $f : \mathcal{B}^n \mapsto \mathcal{B}$ and let $A \subseteq f^{-1}(0)$ and $B \subseteq f^{-1}(1)$. Let $Q = [q_{i,j}]$ be defined by $q_{i,j} = 1$ if $\boldsymbol{x}_i \in A$ and $\boldsymbol{x}_j \in B$ are neighbors and $q_{i,j} = 0$ otherwise. Let $P = QQ^T$ and $\overline{P} = Q^T Q$. Then $p_{r,s}$ is the number of common neighbors to $\boldsymbol{x}_r$ and $\boldsymbol{x}_s$ in B. The matrices P and $\overline{P}$ are symmetric and their largest eigenvalues, $\lambda(P)$ and $\lambda(\overline{P})$, are both non-negative and $\lambda(P) = \lambda(\overline{P})$. Show that

$$L_\Omega(f) \ge \lambda(P)$$

9.31 Under the conditions of Problem 9.30, let

$$D(f) = \frac{1}{|B|} \sum_{r,s} p_{r,s}, \quad \overline{D}(f) = \frac{1}{|B|} \sum_{r,s} \overline{p}_{r,s}, \quad K(f) = \frac{|\mathcal{N}(A,B)|^2}{|A||B|}$$

where $K(f)$ is the lower bound given in Theorem 9.4.2. Show that

$$K(f) \leq D(f) \leq \lambda(P)$$
$$K(f) \leq \overline{D}(f) \leq \lambda(\overline{P})$$

Hint: Use the fact that the largest eigenvalue of a matrix P satisfies

$$\lambda(P) = \max_{x \neq 0} \frac{x^T P x}{x^T x}$$

Also, let s_i be the sum of the elements in the ith column of the matrix Q. Show that $\sum_i s_i^2 = \sum_{r,s} p_{r,s}$.

LOWER-BOUND METHODS FOR MONOTONE CIRCUITS

9.32 Consider a monotone circuit on n inputs that computes a monotone Boolean function $f : \mathcal{B}^n \mapsto \mathcal{B}$. Let the circuit have k two-input AND gates, one of them the output gate, and let these gates compute the Boolean functions $g_1, g_2, \ldots, g_k = f$, where the AND gates are inverse-ordered by their distance from the output gate computing f. Since the function g_j is computed using the values of $x_1, x_2, \ldots, x_n, g_1, \ldots, g_{j-1}$, show that g_j can be computed using at most $n + j - 2$ two-input OR gates and one AND gate. Show that this implies the following upper bound on the monotone circuit size of f:

$$C_{\Omega_{\text{mon}}}(f) \leq kn + \binom{k-1}{2} - 1$$

Let $C_\wedge(f)$ denote the minimum number of AND gates used to realize f over the monotone basis. This result implies the following relationship:

$$C_{\Omega_{\text{mon}}}(f) = O\left((C_\wedge(f))^2\right)$$

How does this result change if the gate associated with f is an OR gate?

9.33 Show that the prime implicants of a monotone function are monotone prime implicants.

9.34 Find the monotone implicants of the Boolean threshold function $\tau_t^{(n)} : \mathcal{B}^n \mapsto \mathcal{B}$, $1 \leq t \leq n$.

9.35 Using the gate-elimination method, show that $C_{\Omega_{\text{mon}}}(\tau_2^{(n)}) = 2n - 4$.

9.36 Show that an expansion of the form of equation (9.1) on page 420 holds for every monotone function.

9.37 Show that the $f_{\text{clique},k}^{(n)} : \mathcal{B}^{n(n-1)/2} \mapsto \mathcal{B}$ can be realized by a monotone circuit of size $O(n^n)$.

9.38 Show that the largest value assumed by $\min(\sqrt{k-1}/2, n/(2k))$ under variation of k is $\Omega(n^{1/3})$.

CIRCUIT DEPTH

9.39 Show that the communication complexity of a problem (U, V), $U, V \subseteq B^n$, satisfies $C(U, V) \leq n + \log_2^* n$, where $\log_2^* n$ is the number of times that $\lceil \log_2 \rceil$ must be taken to reduce n to zero.

Hint: Complete the definition of a protocol in which Player I sends Player II $n - \lceil \log_2 n \rceil$ bits on the first round and Player II responds with a message specifying whether or not its n-tuple agrees with that of Player I and if not, where they differ.

9.40 Consider the communication problem defined by the following sets:

$$U = \{\boldsymbol{u} \mid 3 \text{ divides the number of 1s in } \boldsymbol{u}\}$$
$$V = \{\boldsymbol{v} \mid 3 \text{ does not divide the number of 1s in } \boldsymbol{u}\}$$

Show that a protocol exists that solves this problem with communication complexity $3\lceil \log_2 n \rceil$.

9.41 Show that Theorem 9.7.4 continues to hold when the MOD_3 function is added to the basis where MOD_3 is the Boolean function that has value 1 when the number of 1s among its inputs is not divisible by 3.

Chapter Notes

The dependence of circuit size on fan-out stated in Theorem 9.2.1 is due to Johnson et al. [148]. The depth bound implied by this result is proportional to the product of the depth and the logarithm of the size of the original circuit. Hoover et al. [137] have improved the depth bound so that it is proportional to $(\log_r s)D_\Omega(f)$ without sacrificing the size bound of [148].

The relationship between formula size and depth in Theorem 9.2.2 is due to Spira [308], whose depth bound has a coefficient of proportionality of 2.465 over the basis of all Boolean functions on two variables. Over the basis of all Boolean functions except for parity and its complement, Preparata and Muller [253] obtain a coefficient of 1.81. Brent, in a paper on the parallelization of arithmetic formulas [58], has effectively extended the relationship between depth and formula size to monotone functions. (See also [353].)

An interesting relationship between complexity measures that is omitted from Section 9.2, due to Paterson and Valiant [234], shows that circuit size and depth satisfy the inequality

$$D_\Omega(f) \geq \frac{1}{4} C_\Omega(f) \log C_\Omega(f) - O(C_\Omega(f))$$

The lower bounds of Theorem 9.3.2 on functions in $Q_{2,3}^{(n)}$ are due to Schnorr [294], whereas that of Theorem 9.3.3 on the multiplexer function is due to Paul [238]. Blum [48], building on the work of Schnorr [296], has obtained a lower bound of $3(n-1)$ for a particular function of n variables over the basis B_2. This is the best circuit-size lower bound for this basis. Zwick [368] has obtained a lower bound of $4n$ for certain symmetric functions over the basis U_2. Red'kin [268] has obtained lower bounds with coefficients as high as 7 for certain functions over the bases $\{\wedge, \neg\}$ and $\{\vee, \neg\}$. (See Problem 9.23.) Red'kin [270] has used the gate-elimination method to show that the size of the ripple-adder circuit of Section 2.7 cannot be improved.

The coefficient of Nečiporuk's lower-bound method [224] in Theorem 9.4.1 has been improved upon by Paterson (unpublished) and Zwick [367]. Paul [238] has applied Nečiporuk's method to show that the indirect storage access function has formula size $\Omega(n^2/\log n)$ over the basis B_2. Nečiporuk's method has also been applied to many other problems, including the determinant [166], the marriage problem [125], recognition of context-free languages [235], and the clique function [298].

The proof of Krapchenko's lower bound [171] given in Theorem 9.4.2 is due to Paterson, as described by Bopanna and Sipser [50]. Koutsoupias [169] has obtained the results of Problems 9.30 and 9.31, improving upon the Krapchenko lower bounds for the kth threshold function by a factor of at least 2. Andreev [24], building on the work of Subbotovskaya [314], has improved upon Krapchenko's method and exhibits a lower bound of $\Omega(n^{2.5-\epsilon})$ on a function of n variables for every fixed $\epsilon > 0$ when n is sufficiently large. Krichevskii [173] has shown that over the standard basis, $\tau_t^{(n)}$ requires formula size $\Omega(n\log n)$, which beats Krapchenko's lower bound for small and large values of t.

Symmetric functions are examined in Section 2.11 and upper bounds are given on the circuit size of such functions over the basis $\{\wedge, \vee, \oplus\}$. Polynomial-size formulas for symmetric functions are implicit in the work of Ofman [228] and Wallace [350], who also independently demonstrated how to add two binary numbers in logarithmic depth. Krapchenko [172] demonstrated that all symmetric Boolean functions have formula size $O(n^{4.93})$ over the standard basis. Peterson [241], improving upon the results of Pippenger [242] and Paterson [235], showed that all symmetric functions have formula size $O(n^{3.27})$ over the basis B_2. Paterson, Pippenger, and Zwick [236,237] have recently improved these results, showing that over B_2 and U_2 formulas exist of size $O(n^{3.13})$ and $O(n^{3.13})$, respectively, for many symmetric Boolean functions including the majority function, and of size $O(n^{3.30})$ and $O(n^{4.85})$, respectively, for all symmetric Boolean functions.

Markov demonstrated that the minimal number of negations needed to realize an arbitrary binary function on n variables with an arbitrary number of output variables, maximized over all such functions, is at most $\lceil \log_2(n+1) \rceil$. For Boolean functions (they have one output variable) it is at most $\lfloor \log_2(n+1) \rfloor$. Fischer [99] has described a circuit whose size is at most twice that of an optimal circuit plus the size of a circuit that computes $f_{\mathrm{NEG}}(x_1, \ldots, x_n) = (\overline{x}_1, \ldots, \overline{x}_n)$ and whose depth is at most that of the optimal circuit plus the depth of a circuit for f_{NEG}. He exhibits a circuit for f_{NEG} of size $O(n^2 \log n)$ and depth $O(\log n)$. This is the result given in Theorem 9.5.1. Tanaka and Nishino [317] have improved the size bound on f_{NEG} to $O(n \log^2 n)$ at the expense of increasing the depth bound to $O(\log^2 n)$. Beals, Nishino, and Tanaka [32] have further improved these results, deriving simultaneous size and depth bounds of $O(n \log n)$ and $O(\log n)$, respectively.

Using non-constructive methods, a series of upper bounds have been developed on the monotone formula size of the threshold functions $\tau_t^{(n)}$ by Valiant [340] and Bopanna [49], culminating in bounds by Khasin [163] and Friedman [105] of $O(t^{4.3} n \log n)$ over the monotone basis. With constructive methods, Ajtai, Komlós, and Szemerédi [14] obtained polynomial bounds on the formula size $\tau_t^{(n)}$ over the monotone basis. Using their construction, Friedman [105] has obtained a bound on formula size over the monotone basis of $O(t^c n \log n)$ for c a large constant.

Over the basis B_2, Fischer, Meyer, and Paterson [100] have shown that the majority function $\tau_t^{(n)}$, $t = \lceil n/2 \rceil$, and other symmetric functions require formula size $\Omega(n \log n)$. Pudlák [258], building on the work of Hodes and Specker [135], has shown that all but 16 symmetric

Boolean functions on n variables require formula size $\Omega(n \log \log n)$ over the same basis. The 16 exceptional functions have linear formula size.

Using counting arguments such as those given in Section 2.12, Gilbert [113] has shown that most monotone Boolean functions on n variables have a circuit size that is $\Omega(2^n/n^{3/2})$. Red'kin [269] has shown that the lower bound can be achieved to within a constant multiplicative factor by every monotone Boolean function.

Tiekenherinrich [324] gave a $4n$ lower bound to the monotone circuit size of a simple function. Dunne [87] derived a $3.5n$ lower bound on the monotone circuit size for the majority function.

The lower bound on the monotone circuit size of binary sorting (Theorem 9.6.1) is due to Lamagna and Savage [185] using an argument patterned after that of Van Voorhis [345] for comparator-based sorting networks. Muller and Preparata [221,222] demonstrate that binary sorting over the standard basis has circuit size $O(n)$. (See Theorem 2.11.1.) Pippenger and Valiant [247] and Lamagna [184] demonstrate an $\Omega(n \log n)$ lower bound on the monotone circuit size of merging. These results are established in Section 9.6.1. The sorting network designed by Ajtai, Komlós, and Szemerédi [14] when specialized to Boolean data yields a monotone circuit of size $O(n \log n)$ for binary sorting.

The first proof that the monotone circuit size of $n \times n$ Boolean matrix multiplication (see Section 9.6.2) is $\Omega(n^3)$ was obtained by Pratt [250]. Later Paterson [232] and Mehlhorn and Galil [214] demonstrated that it is exactly $n^2(2n - 1)$. Weiss [355] discovered a simple application of the function-replacement method to both Boolean convolution and Boolean matrix multiplication, as summarized in Corollary 9.6.1 and Theorem 9.6.5. (Wegener [354, p. 170] extended Weiss's result to include the number of ORs.) Wegener [351] has exhibited an n-input, n-output Boolean function (Boolean direct product) whose monotone circuit size is $\Omega(n^2)$. Earlier several authors examined the class of multi-output functions known as **Boolean sums** in which each output is the OR of a subset of inputs. Nečiporuk [225] gave an explicit set of Boolean sums and demonstrated that its monotone circuit size is $\Omega(n^{3/2})$. This lower bound for such functions was independently improved to $\Omega(n^{5/3})$ by Mehlhorn [212] and Pippenger [244]. More recently, Andreev [23] has constructed a family of Boolean sums with monotone circuit size that is $\Omega(n^{2-\epsilon})$ for every fixed $\epsilon > 0$.

The first super-polynomial lower bound on the monotone circuit size of the clique function was established by Razborov [264]. Shortly afterward, Andreev [22], using similar methods, gave an exponential lower bound on the monotone circuit size of a problem in **NP**. Because the clique function is complete with respect to monotone projections [304,338], this established an exponential lower bound for the clique function. Alon and Bopanna [17], by strengthening Razborov's method, gave a direct proof of this fact, giving a lower bound exponential in $\Omega\left((n/\log n)^{1/3}\right)$. The stronger lower bound given in Theorem 9.6.6, which is exponential in $\Omega(n^{1/3})$, is due to Amano and Maruoka [20]. They apply *bottleneck counting*, an idea of Haken [124], to establish this result. Amano and Maruoka [20] have also extended the approximation method to circuits that have negations only on their inputs and for which the number of inputs carrying negations is small. They show that, even with a small number of negations, an exponential lower bound on the circuit size of the clique function can be obtained.

Having shown that monotone circuit complexity can lead to exponential lower bounds, Razborov [265] then cast doubt on the likelihood that this approach would lead to exponential non-monotone circuit size bounds by proving that the matching problem on bipartite graphs, a problem in **P**, has a super-polynomial monotone circuit size. Tardos [318] strengthened

Razborov's lower bound, deriving an exponential one. Later Razborov [267] demonstrated that the obvious generalization of the approximation method cannot yield better lower bounds than $\Omega(n^2)$ for Boolean functions on n inputs realized by circuits over complete bases.

Berkowitz [37] introduced the concept of pseudo-inverse and established Theorem 9.6.9. Valiant [341], Wegener [352], and Paterson (unpublished — see [91,354]) independently improved upon the size of the monotone circuit realizing all pseudo-negations from $O(n^2 \log n)$ to $O(n \log^2 n)$ to produce Theorem 9.6.8. Lemma 9.6.9 is due to Dunne [89].

In his Ph.D. thesis Dunne [86] has given the most general definition of pseudo-negation. He shows that a Boolean function h is a pseudo-negation on variable x_i of a Boolean function f on the n variables $x_1, \dots, x_n$ if and only if h satisfies

$$f(\boldsymbol{x})|_{x_i=0} \leq h(x_1, \dots, x_{i-1}, x_{i+1}, \dots, x_n) \leq f(\boldsymbol{x})|_{x_i=1}$$

Here $f(\boldsymbol{x})|_{x_i=a}$ denotes the function obtained from f by fixing x_i at a.

Dunne [88] demonstrated that HALF-CLIQUE CENTRAL SLICE is **NP**-complete (Theorem 9.6.10) and showed that the central slices of the HAMILTONIAN CIRCUIT (there is a closed path containing each vertex once) and SATISFIABILITY are **NP**-complete. As mentioned by Dunne [90], not all **NP**-complete problems have **NP**-complete central slices.

The concept of communication complexity arose in the context of the VLSI model of computation discussed in Chapter 12. In this case it measures the amount of information that must be transmitted from the inputs to the outputs of a function. The communication game described in Section 9.7.1 is different: it characterizes a search problem because its goal is to find an input variable on which two n-tuples in disjoint sets disagree.

Yao [360] developed a method to derive lower bounds on the communication complexity of functions $f : X \times Y \mapsto Z$. He considered the matrix of values of f where the rows and columns are indexed by the values of X and Y. He defined monochromatic rectangles as submatrices in which all entries are the same. He then established that the logarithm of the minimal number of disjoint rectangles in this matrix is a lower bound on the number of bits that must be exchanged to compute f. (This result shows, for example, that the identity function $f : \mathcal{B}^{2n} \mapsto \mathcal{B}$ defined for $f(\boldsymbol{x}, \boldsymbol{y}) = 1$ if and only if $x_i = y_i$ for all $1 \leq i \leq n$ requires the exchange of at least $n + 1$ bits.) Savage [282] adapted the crossing sequence argument from one-tape Turing machines (an application of the pigeonhole principle) to derive lower bounds on predicates. Mehlhorn and Schmidt [216] show that functions $f : X \times Y \mapsto Z$ for which Z is a subset of a field have a communication complexity that is at most the rank of the two-dimensional matrix of values of f.

The development of the relationship between the circuit depth of a function and its communication complexity follows that given by Karchmer and Wigderson [155]. Karchmer [154] cites Yannakakis for independently discovering the connection $D_{\Omega_0}(f) = C(f^{-1}(0), f^{-1}(1))$ of Theorem 9.7.1 for non-monotone functions. Karchmer and Wigderson [155] have examined st-connectivity in this framework. This is the problem of determining from the adjacency matrix of an undirected graph G with n vertices and two distinguished vertices, s and t, whether there is a path from s to t. When characterized as a Boolean function on the edge variables, this is a monotone function. Karchmer and Wigderson [155] have shown that the circuit depth of this function is $\Omega((\log n)^2 / \log \log n)$, a result later improved to $\Omega((\log n)^2)$ independently by Håstad and Boppana in unpublished work. Raz and Wigderson [263] have shown via a complex proof that the clique problem on n-vertex graphs studied in Section 9.7.4 has monotone communication complexity and depth $\Omega(n)$. The simpler but weaker lower bound for this problem developed in Section 9.7.4 is due to Goldmann and Håstad [115].

Furst, Saxe, and Sipser [106] and, independently, Ajtai [13] obtained the first strong lower bounds on the size of bounded-depth circuits. They demonstrated that every bounded-depth circuit for the parity function $f_{\oplus}^{(n)}$ has superpolynomial size. Using a deeper analysis, Yao [362] demonstrated that bounded-depth circuits for $f_{\oplus}^{(n)}$ have exponential size. Håstad [123] strengthened the results and simplified the argument, giving a lower bound on circuit size of $2^{\Omega(n^{1/d}/10)}$ for circuits of depth d.

Razborov [266] examined a more powerful class of bounded-depth circuits, namely, circuits that use unbounded fan-in AND, OR, and parity functions. He demonstrated that the majority function $\tau_{n/2}^{(n)}$ has exponential size over this larger basis. Smolensky [307] simplified and strengthened Razborov's result, obtaining an exponential lower bound on the size of a bounded-depth circuit for the MOD_p function over the basis AND, OR, and MOD_q when p and q are distinct powers of primes. We use a simplified version of his result in Section 9.7.5.

10

Space–Time Tradeoffs

An important question in the study of computation is how best to use the registers of a CPU and/or the random-access memory of a general-purpose computer. In most computations, the number of registers (space) available is insufficient to hold all the data on which a program operates and registers must be reused. If the space is increased, the number of computation steps (time) can generally be reduced. This is an example of a space–versus–time tradeoff. In this chapter we examine tradeoffs between the number of storage locations and computation time using the pebble game and the branching program model.

The pebble game assumes that computations are done with straight-line programs in a data-independent fashion. Each such program is modeled by a directed acyclic graph. A pebble on a vertex indicates that its value is in a register. The goal of the game is to pebble the output vertices of the graph with numbers of pebbles (space) and steps (time) that are minimal, that is, neither can be reduced without increasing the other.

A branching program models data-dependent computation under the assumption that input variables assume a bounded number of values. Such a program is defined by a directed acyclic multigraph (there may be more than one edge between vertices) that specifies the order in which inputs are read. Time is the length of the longest path in a multigraph and space is the logarithm of its number of vertices.

For both models we present techniques to derive lower bounds on the exchange of space S for time T. For most problems examined here these exchanges are of the form $ST = \Omega(n^2)$, where n is the size of the problem input. Upper bounds on ST are obtained by evaluating S and T for particular algorithms.

Because the branching program is more general than the pebble game, it is more difficult to obtain good lower bounds with it, and for this reason we begin with the pebble game. In addition, the pebble game is appropriate for problems such as integer multiplication, convolution, and matrix multiplication on which only straight-line programs are used. For other problems, such as merging and sorting, the algorithms used typically involve branching and for them the branching program is the better model.

We also exhibit extreme results for the pebble game by showing that the time to pebble some graphs goes from minimal to exponential in the size of the graphs when the number of pebbles changes by 1, a warning against trying too hard to minimize the number of CPU registers used in a computation.

10.1 The Pebble Game

The pebble game is a game played on directed acyclic graphs (DAGs), which capture the dependencies of straight-line programs studied in Chapters 2 and 6. Algorithms for many important problems, such as the FFT and matrix multiplication, are naturally computed by straight-line programs. In the pebble game pebbles are placed on vertices of a DAG to indicate that the value associated with a vertex resides in a register. Pebbles are placed on vertices in a data-independent order.

In this game a pebble can be placed on an input vertex at any time and on any non-input vertex whose immediate predecessor vertices carry pebbles. The goal of the game is to place pebbles on each output vertex. A pebble can be removed from a vertex, including an output vertex, at any time after it has been pebbled. These rules are summarized below.

The rules of the **pebble game** are the following:

- (Initialization) A pebble can be placed on an input vertex at any time.

- (Computation Step) A pebble can be placed on (or moved to) any non-input vertex only if all its immediate predecessors carry pebbles.

- (Pebble Deletion) A pebble can be removed at any time.

- (Goal) Each output vertex must be pebbled at least once.

Placement of a pebble on an input vertex models the reading of input data. Placement of a pebble on a non-input vertex corresponds to computing the value associated with the vertex. The removal of a pebble models the erasure or overwriting of the value associated with the vertex on which the pebble resides.

Allowing pebbles to be placed on input vertices at any time reflects the assumption that inputs are readily available. (The multi-level pebble game introduced in the next chapter models the case in which each access to secondary storage is expensive.) The condition that all predecessor vertices carry pebbles when a pebble is placed on a vertex models the natural requirement that an operation can be performed only after all arguments of the operation are located in main memory. Moving (or **sliding**) a pebble to a vertex from an immediate predecessor reflects the design of CPUs that allow the result of a computation to be placed in a memory location holding an operand.

A **pebbling strategy** is the execution of the rules of the pebble game on the vertices of a graph. We assign a step to each placement of a pebble, ignoring steps on which pebbles are removed, and number the steps consecutively from 1 to T, the **time** or number of steps in the strategy. The **space**, S, used by a pebbling strategy is the maximum number of pebbles it uses. The goal of the pebble game is to pebble a graph with values of space and time that are minimal; that is, the space cannot be reduced for the given value of time and vice versa. In general, it is not possible to minimize space and time simultaneously. We derive upper and lower bounds on the possible exchanges of space for time.

10.1.1 The Pebble Game Versus the Branching Program

As stated above, the branching program model introduced in Section 10.9 handles data-dependent computation, and is thus a more general model than the pebble game. However, there are three reasons to study the pebble game. First, the branching program assumes that

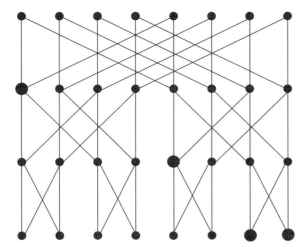

Figure 10.1 An FFT graph $F^{(3)}$ on $n = 2^3$ inputs can be pebbled with four pebbles. A point in time when all four pebbles are needed to pebble the leftmost output.

input variables are held in an auxiliary random-access machine so that it can access them in arbitrary order, a condition not imposed on pebble games. It follows that inputs to a pebble game can be fetched in advance, since the times at which they are needed are data-independent. Second, lower bounds on the exchange of space for time with branching programs are harder to obtain due to their increased flexibility. Third, straight-line programs are used in many problems, such as integer multiplication, convolution, matrix multiplication, and discrete Fourier transform, and the pebble game gives the relevant lower bounds. For other problems, such as sorting and merging, the branching program model is the model of choice since these problems are typically solved with branching programs. We expand upon this topic in Section 10.9.1.

10.1.2 Playing the Pebble Game

The pebble game is illustrated in Fig. 10.1 by pebbling the FFT graph $F^{(3)}$ with eight inputs and 24 non-input vertices. This graph has the property that the set of paths from input vertices to an output vertex forms a complete balanced binary tree. (See Fig. 10.2.) It follows that we can pebble the FFT graph by pebbling each of the trees. Since two of the eight outputs share the same tree at the next lower level, we can pebble two outputs at the same time.

Binary trees form an important class of graphs. A **complete balanced binary tree** of depth 4 is illustrated in Fig. 10.2. (The depth of a directed tree is the number of edges on the longest path from an input vertex to the output (or root) vertex.) This tree has 16 input vertices and one output vertex. A complete balanced binary tree of depth 0, $T(0)$, consists of a single vertex. A complete balanced binary tree of depth $d > 0$, $T(d)$, consists of a root vertex and two copies of $T(d - 1)$ whose root vertices each have one edge directed from them to the root vertex of the full tree. Thus in Fig. 10.2 the complete balanced binary tree of depth four $T(4)$ is constructed of two copies of $T(3)$, which in turn are each constructed of two copies of $T(2)$, and so on. It follows by straightforward induction that a complete balanced binary tree of depth d has 2^d inputs and $2^{d+1} - 1$ vertices. (See Problem 10.8.)

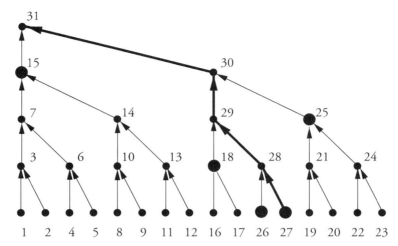

Figure 10.2 A complete balanced binary tree $T(4)$ of depth 4 on 16 inputs. At least five pebbles are needed to pebble it.

The binary tree of Fig. 10.2 can be pebbled with five pebbles by pebbling the vertices in the order shown. Five pebbles are needed at the point in time when the vertex 27 is pebbled. After one pebble is moved to vertex 30, the two outputs of the FFT graph to which vertices 27 and 30 are attached can be pebbled. This tree-pebbling strategy can then be repeated on all remaining outputs. It is a general strategy for pebbling complete balanced binary trees.

This pebbling strategy, explained in detail in the next section, demonstrates that an FFT graph on $n = 2^k$ inputs can be pebbled with no more pebbles than are needed to pebble the trees with n leaves contained within it, namely, $k + 1$. In the next section we show that this is the minimum number of pebbles needed to pebble a complete balanced binary tree on 2^k leaves. This FFT pebbling strategy for the graph in Fig. 10.1 pebbles each vertex on the third and fourth levels once, each vertex on the second level twice, and each vertex on the first level four times. It is clear that inputs must be repebbled if the minimum number of pebbles is used. This is an example of space–time tradeoff. We shall derive a lower bound on the exchange of space for time for this problem.

In the next section we also examine the minimum space required to pebble graphs. In the subsequent section we describe a graph that exhibits an extreme tradeoff. This graph requires a pebbling time exponential in the size of the graph when the minimum number of pebbles is used but can be pebbled with one move per vertex if one more pebble is available.

After studying extreme tradeoffs we define a flow property of functions that, if satisfied, implies a lower bound on the product $(S + 1)T$ (or a related expression) involving the space S and time T needed to compute such functions. This test is used to show that many standard algorithms are optimal with respect to their use of space and time.

10.2 Space Lower Bounds

In this section we derive lower bounds on the **minimum space** $S_{\min}(G)$ needed to pebble a graph G for balanced binary trees, pyramids, and FFT graphs, a representative set of graphs.

Any pebbling strategy will need to use at least as many pebbles as this minimum value of space. It can be shown that no bounded-degree graph on n vertices requires more than $O(n/\log n)$ space (see Theorem 10.7.1) and that some graph requires space proportional to $n/\log n$ (see Theorem 10.8.1).

Complete balanced binary trees were introduced in the previous section. We now derive a lower bound on the space (number of pebbles) needed to pebble them.

LEMMA 10.2.1 *Any pebbling strategy for the complete balanced binary tree of depth k, $T(k)$, requires at least $S_{\min}(T(k)) = k + 1$ pebbles and $2^{k+1} - 1$ steps. There is a pebbling strategy of $T(k)$ that uses exactly this many pebbles and steps.*

Proof Proof of the lemma requires a proof that $k + 1$ pebbles are necessary as well as a strategy that pebbles the tree with $k + 1$ pebbles and makes one pebble placement per vertex. Let's first develop a pebbling strategy.

$T(0)$ obviously can be pebbled with one pebble in one step. Assume that $T(k-1)$ can be pebbled with k pebbles in $2^k - 1$ steps. To pebble $T(k)$, advance a pebble to the root of its left subtree (a copy of $T(k-1)$) using k pebbles and $2^k - 1$ steps. Leave a pebble on its root. Then pebble the right subtree of $T(k)$ using k pebbles and $2^k - 1$ steps. (A snapshot of $T(k)$ when the number of pebbles is maximal under this pebbling strategy is shown in Fig. 10.2.) Thus, $T(k)$ is pebbled in $2 \times (2^k - 1) + 1 = 2^{k+1} - 1$ steps with $k + 1$ pebbles.

The lower bound is derived by showing that no pebbling strategy can use fewer than $k + 1$ pebbles. The argument used is the following: initially no path to the root of the tree (or output) from input vertices carries a pebble because there are no pebbles on the graph. At the end of the computation a pebble resides on the root and all paths to the root carry pebbles. Therefore, there must be a first point in time at which there is a pebble on each path to the root. This must be a time at which a pebble is placed on an input vertex, thereby closing the last path from that input to the root. Such a path is highlighted in Fig. 10.2. Before a pebble is placed on the input vertex of this path, all other paths from input vertices to the root carry pebbles. Each of these paths enters the highlighted path via one edge. Thus, it follows that prior to the placement of this last pebble there is at least one pebble on the tree for each of the k edges on this path except for the input vertex. Consequently, at least $k + 1$ pebbles are on the tree when the last pebble is placed on it. ∎

The FFT graph on 2^k inputs, $F^{(k)}$, is defined recursively in terms of two sub-FFT graphs $F^{(k-1)}$ as shown in Section 6.7.2. It follows that this graph contains many copies of the tree $T(k)$ as a subgraph (see Problem 10.11) and that any pebbling strategy for $F^{(k)}$ requires at least $k + 1$ pebbles. Many other straight-line computations involve tree computations.

A **pyramid graph** on m inputs, $P(m)$ ($P(6)$ is shown in Fig. 10.3), is obtained by slicing an $m \times m$ mesh into two parts along its diagonal, splitting all diagonal nodes (which are now inputs), and then directing edges from the diagonal vertices in one part to the one remaining unsplit corner vertex in this part of the graph. Edges are directed up, a convention we use throughout this chapter. $P(m)$ has $n = m(m + 1)/2$ vertices. (See Problem 10.1.)

We apply to the pyramid graph $P(m)$ the lower bounding argument used in the preceding proof based on closing the last open path to the output vertex.

LEMMA 10.2.2 *Any pebbling strategy for the m-input, n-vertex ($n = m(m + 1)/2$) pyramid graph $P(m)$ requires at least m pebbles; that is, a minimum space $S_{\min}(P(m)) = m \geq \sqrt{2n} -$*

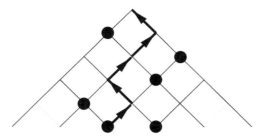

Figure 10.3 The pyramid graph on six inputs.

1. *There exists a pebbling strategy that pebbles $P(m)$ with m pebbles using one pebble placement per vertex.*

> **Proof** The lower-bound proof again uses the fact that there is a first time at which all paths from an input to the output carry pebbles. Highlighted in Fig. 10.3 is a last path to carry a pebble. Prior to the placement of this last pebble, all paths to the output carry pebbles. Thus, with the placement of the last pebble there must be at least as many pebbles on the pyramid graph as there are vertices on a path from an input to the output, namely, m, and $m \geq \sqrt{2n} - 1$. (See Problem 10.1.)
>
> With m pebbles, the vertices can be pebbled in levels by first placing pebbles on each of the m inputs. Pebbles are then advanced to vertices on the second level from left to right, and this process is repeated at all levels to complete the pebbling. Each vertex is pebbled once with this strategy. ∎

In general, it is very hard to determine the minimum number of pebbles needed to pebble a graph. In terms of the complexity classes introduced in Chapter 8, we model this problem as a language consisting of strings each of which contains the description of a graph $G = (V, E)$, a vertex $v \in V$, and an integer S with the property that the vertex can be pebbled with S or fewer pebbles. The language of these strings is **PSPACE**-complete (see Section 8.12).

10.3 Extreme Tradeoffs

We now show that extreme space–time tradeoff behavior is possible. We do this by exhibiting a family of graphs, $H_1, H_2, \ldots, H_k, \ldots$ (Fig. 10.4), that requires a number of steps exponential in the size of the graph when the minimum number of pebbles is used but only one step per vertex when one more pebble is available. This illustrates that excessive minimization of the number of registers used by programs can be harmful!

H_1 has one input and one output vertex and an edge connecting them, as shown in Fig. 10.4. For $k \geq 2$ the kth graph, H_k, has $k + 1$ output vertices and is constructed from one copy of H_{k-1}, a tree (on the left) with k inputs, a two-level bipartite graph (on the top right) with k inputs and $k + 1$ outputs, and a chain of k vertices that connects the tree to the outputs of H_{k-1} and the open vertex. (A **bipartite graph** is a graph in which the vertices are partitioned into two sets and edges join vertices in different sets.)

We summarize our pebbling results for this family of graphs below. Here $n!$ is the factorial function with value $n! = n \cdot (n - 1) \cdot (n - 2) \cdot \ldots \cdot 2 \cdot 1$.

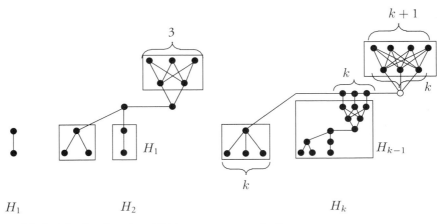

Figure 10.4 A family of graphs exhibiting an extreme tradeoff.

THEOREM 10.3.1 *The graph H_k has $N(k) = 2k^2 + 5k - 6$ vertices for $k \geq 2$. Any pebbling strategy for the graph H_k requires at least $k = \Theta(\sqrt{N(k)})$ pebbles. Any strategy to pebble H_k with k pebbles requires at least $(k + 1)!/2 = 2^{\Omega(\sqrt{N(k)} \log N(k))}$ steps, whereas there exists a pebbling algorithm using $k + 1$ pebbles that pebbles each vertex of H_k once.*

Proof Consider a pebbling strategy that uses $k + 1$ pebbles to pebble H_k. For the case of $k = 1$, H_k can be completely pebbled with one move per vertex. This is also true for H_2 because we can move a pebble to the open vertex connected to the bipartite graph using two pebbles, from which we can advance two of our three pebbles to the bottom layer of the bipartite graph and have one additional pebble with which to pebble the output vertices. Note that this pebbling strategy allows us to pebble output vertices of H_2 from left to right with three pebbles.

Assume that we can pebble the outputs of H_{k-1} from left to right with k pebbles without pebbling any vertex more than once. Then to pebble H_k, advance a pebble to the root of the tree on the left and then pebble the outputs of H_{k-1} from left to right using k pebbles while keeping one additional pebble on the chain. Advance this pebble along the chain until it reaches the open vertex. At this point k pebbles can be advanced to the bottom row of vertices in the bipartite graph and the remaining pebble used to pebble outputs from left to right. This shows that our assumption holds.

The minimum number of pebbles needed to pebble H_k is at least k because at least this many are needed to pebble the tree on the left. To show that this value can be achieved, we give a recursive pebbling strategy. Observe that H_1 can be pebbled with $k = 1$ pebbles. To pebble H_k, assume that we can pebble any one output of H_{k-1} with $k - 1$ pebbles. Advance a pebble to the root of the left tree and then advance it along the chain by pebbling output vertices of H_{k-1} from left to right with $k - 1$ pebbles. Move a pebble to the open vertex and then to all vertices on one side of the bipartite graph. Any one output vertex can now be pebbled. However, doing so requires that one vertex on the bottom side of the bipartite graph lose its pebble. Thus, no other output vertex can be pebbled without repebbling the tree and all vertices of H_{k-1}.

As this pebbling strategy demonstrates, to pebble an output vertex, all k pebbles must move to the bottom of the bipartite graph, thereby removing all pebbles from other vertices of H_k. Let $M(k)$ be the number of pebble placements to pebble H_k with k pebbles. It follows that to pebble each of the $(k+1)$ outputs of H_k with k pebbles, we must pebble each output of H_{k-1} with $k-1$ pebbles. Thus,

$$M(k) \geq (k+1) \times M(k-1)$$
$$\geq (k+1)k(k-1)\cdots 3 \cdot 1 = (k+1)!/2$$

which provides the desired lower bound.

Let the graph H_k have $N(k)$ vertices. Then $N(1) = 2$, $N(2) = 12$ and $N(k) = N(k-1) + 4k + 3$ for $k \geq 3$. A straightforward proof by induction shows that $N(k) = 2k^2 + 5k - 6$ (see Problem 10.13).

To show that $M(k) \geq (k+1)!/2$ is exponential in $N(k) = 2k^2 + 5k - 6$, note that $p! = p \cdot (p-1) \cdot \ldots \cdot 3 \cdot 2 \cdot 1$, which is at least $(p/2)^{(p/2)}$ since each of the first $p/2$ terms is at least $p/2$. Thus, $M(k) \geq .5[(k+1)/2]^{(k+1)/2}$ Also, it is easy to see that $N(k) \leq 3(k+1)^2$ for $k \geq 1$. Since this implies $\sqrt{N(k)/3} \leq (k+1)$, we have that

$$M(k) \geq .5 \left[(\sqrt{N(k)/3})/2 \right]^{(\sqrt{N(k)/3})/2}$$

which is exponential in $N(k)$. ∎

Many vertices in the graph H_k have a fan-in k. A new family $\{G_k\}$ of graphs with fan-in 2 can be obtained by replacing the tree on the left in H_k with the pyramid graph of Fig. 10.3 and replacing the bipartite graph on the top with a new graph (see Problem 10.14). This new graph exhibits an exponential jump in the time to pebble the graph but at a value of space that is the fourth root of the number of vertices in G_k.

10.4 Grigoriev's Lower-Bound Method

In this section we present a method for developing lower bounds on the exchange of space for time in the pebble game. These lower bounds are typically of the form $(S + 1)T = \Omega(n^2)$, where S, T, and n are the space, time, and the size of the input to the problem, and are similar in spirit to those of Theorem 3.6.1. Because they assume a less general model of computation (the pebble game instead of the RAM), lower bounds are easier to derive.

The lower bounds use as a measure the maximum amount of information that can flow from a subset of the inputs to a subset of the outputs, and are much easier to derive than are lower bounds on circuit size for the circuit model. Although the results are stated for straight-line computations, they apply to all "input-output-oblivious" computations by finite-state machines: computations in which inputs are read and outputs produced at times independent of the values of the input variables. (See Problem 10.20.)

10.4.1 Flow Properties of Functions

We start by defining a flow property of functions. (See Fig. 10.5.) A function $f : \mathcal{A}^n \mapsto \mathcal{A}^m$ has a large information flow from input variables in X_1 to output variables in Y_1 if there are values for input variables in $X_0 = X - X_1$ such that many different values can be assumed by

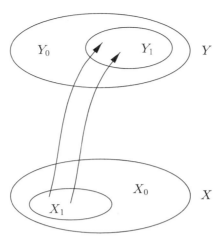

Figure 10.5 A function f that has a large information flow from input variables in X_1 to output variables in Y_1 for some values of input variables in $X_0 = X - X_1$.

outputs in Y_1 as inputs in X_1 range over all their $|\mathcal{A}|^{|X_1|}$ values. This flow property is also used in Section 12.7 to derive lower bounds on the exchange of area for time in the VLSI model of computation.

DEFINITION 10.4.1 *A function* $f : \mathcal{A}^n \mapsto \mathcal{A}^m$ *has a* $\boldsymbol{w(u,v)}$**-flow** *if for all subsets X_1 and Y_1 of its n input and m output variables, with $|X_1| \geq u$ and $|Y_1| \geq v$, there is a subfunction h of f obtained by making some assignment to variables of f not in X_1 (variables in X_0) and discarding output variables not in Y_1 such that h has at least $|\mathcal{A}|^{w(u,v)}$ points in the image of its domain.*

The exponent function $w(u,v)$ is a nondecreasing function of both of its arguments: increasing u, the number of variables that are allowed to vary, can only increase the number of values assumed by f; the same is true if v is increased.

An important class of functions are the (α, n, m, p)-independent functions defined below.

DEFINITION 10.4.2 *A function* $f : \mathcal{A}^n \mapsto \mathcal{A}^m$ *is an* $(\boldsymbol{\alpha, n, m, p})$**-independent function** *for $\alpha \geq 1$ and $p \leq m$ if it has a $w(u,v)$-flow satisfying $w(u,v) > (v/\alpha) - 1$ for $n - u + v \leq p$.*

We illustrate the independence property of a function with matrix multiplication: we show that the function defined by the product of two $n \times n$ matrices is $(1, 2n^2, n^2, n)$-independent. In Section 10.5.4, we show that a stronger property holds for matrix multiplication.

The proof of the independence property of $n \times n$ matrices uses the permutation matrices described in Section 6.2. An $n \times n$ permutation matrix is obtained by permuting either the rows or columns of the $n \times n$ identity matrix. When a permutation matrix B multiplies another matrix A on the right (left) to produce AB (BA), it permutes the columns (rows) of A.

LEMMA 10.4.1 *The matrix multiplication function* $f_{A \times B}^{(n)} : \mathcal{R}^{2n^2} \mapsto \mathcal{R}^{n^2}$ *over the ring $\mathcal{R}$ is $(1, 2n^2, n^2, n)$-independent.*

Proof Let $C = AB$ be the product of $n \times n$ matrices A and B. Consider any set X_0 of input variables (entries of A and B) and any set Y_1 of output variables (entries of C) such that $|X_0| + |Y_1| = n$. The outputs in Y_1 fall into at most $|Y_1|$ columns of C and the inputs in X_0 fall into at most $|X_0|$ columns of A. It follows that at least $n - |X_0|$ columns of A contain only variables in X_1. Fix the entries in B so that it forms a permutation matrix that permutes the columns of A containing only elements in X_1 onto columns of C containing elements of Y_1. (We are free to make the best assignment of variables in B, whether in X_0 or X_1.) It follows that each output variable in Y_1 is assigned to an input variable of A in X_1 by this permutation. Thus these output variables are free to assume $|\mathcal{R}|^{|Y_1|}$ different values. Since this is more than $|\mathcal{R}|^{|Y_1|-1}$, it follows that $f_{A \times B}^{(n)}$ is $(1, 2n^2, n^2, n)$-independent. ∎

As this result illustrates, for any set of y_1 outputs of the matrix multiplication function and any set of x_0 of its inputs satisfying $x_0 + y_1 \leq p$, there is some assignment to these inputs such that there is a large flow of information from the complementary set of inputs, X_1, to any set y_1 of its outputs.

10.4.2 The Lower-Bound Method in the Basic Pebble Game

The following theorem provides a lower bound on the exchange of space for time. Its proof uses a variant of the pigeonhole principle. Since the pebbling of vertices is assumed to occur sequentially, time is divided into intervals in which the number of output vertices pebbled, b, is chosen to be a small multiple of the number of pebbles, S, used in pebbling. The pigeonhole principle is used to show that a large number of inputs must be pebbled in each interval. In particular, we show that if the number of inputs pebbled inside an interval is small, the number of inputs outside the interval is large enough that there is a large flow from the inputs outside the interval to the outputs inside it. However, the flow cannot be any larger than can be supported by the number, S, of vertices carrying pebbles just before the interval. Thus, the number of input variables outside the interval is small, which implies that the number inside is large. That is, many inputs must be pebbled within each interval. Multiplying by the number of intervals in which b outputs are pebbled provides the lower bound.

THEOREM 10.4.1 *Let $f : \mathcal{A}^n \mapsto \mathcal{A}^m$ have an $w(u, v)$-flow and let it be realized by a straight-line program over a basis $\{h : \mathcal{A}^r \mapsto \mathcal{A}^s \mid r, s \geq 1\}$. For arbitrary $b \leq m$, every pebbling of every DAG for f requires space S and time T satisfying the inequality*

$$T \geq \lfloor m/b \rfloor (n - d)$$

where d is the largest integer such that $w(d, b) \leq S$.

Proof Assume that $G = (V, E)$ is pebbled with $S \geq 1$ pebbles in $T \geq 1$ steps. Let $T_I \leq T$ be the number of times that input vertices are pebbled. (This is generally more than the number of input variables.)

Given a pebbling of G with S pebbles, group the consecutive pebbling steps into intervals, the first $\lfloor m/b \rfloor$ of which contain b pebbled outputs and one of which contains $m - b(\lfloor m/b \rfloor)$ pebbled outputs.

Consider an arbitrary interval $\mathcal{I}$ in which b outputs are pebbled. Let Y_1 be these outputs and let x_0 and x_1 be the number of inputs pebbled inside and outside the interval, respectively. By definition, there is an assignment to the x_0 inputs such that that the $b = |Y_1|$

outputs have at least $|\mathcal{A}|^{w(x_1,b)}$ different values. If $w(x_1,b) > S$, the outputs Y_1 assume more values than can be taken by the S pebbles in use just prior to the start of $\mathcal{I}$. Because the values of variables in Y_1 are determined by the inputs pebbled in $\mathcal{I}$, which are fixed, and the values under the S pebbles, this contradicts the definition of f. It follows that x_1 can be no larger than d, where d is the largest value such that $w(d,b) \leq S$. Thus the number of inputs pebbled in $\mathcal{I}$, x_0, satisfies $x_0 \geq (n-d)$.

Since there are $\lfloor m/b \rfloor$ intervals in which b outputs are pebbled, the number of times that inputs are pebbled, T_I, is at least $\lfloor m/b \rfloor (n-d)$. ∎

Grigoriev [120] established the above theorem for $(1,n,m,p)$-independent functions. We restate as a corollary a slightly revised version of his theorem for (α,n,m,p)-independent functions.

COROLLARY 10.4.1 *Let $f : \mathcal{A}^n \mapsto \mathcal{A}^m$ be (α,n,m,p)-independent and let it be realized by a straight-line program over a basis $\{h : \mathcal{A}^r \mapsto \mathcal{A}^s \mid r,s \geq 1\}$. Every pebbling of every DAG for f requires space S and time T satisfying the inequality*

$$\lceil \alpha(S+1) \rceil T \geq mp/4$$

Proof An (α,n,m,p)-independent function on n inputs has a $w(u,v)$-flow satisfying $w(u,v) > (v/\alpha) - 1$ for $n - u + v \leq p$, where $x_0 = n - u \geq 0$. Since b can be freely chosen, let $b = \lceil \alpha(S+1) \rceil$. Thus, $(b/\alpha) - 1 \geq S$ for $(n-d) + b \leq p$, which contradicts the requirement that $w(d,b) \leq S$. It follows that $(n-d) + b > p$ or that $(n-d) \geq p - \lceil \alpha(S+1) \rceil$. With the inequality $\lfloor m/x \rfloor \geq (m - x + 1)/x$ (see Problem 10.2), the following lower bound follows from Theorem 10.4.1:

$$T \geq \frac{(m - \lceil \alpha(S+1) \rceil + 1)(p - \lceil \alpha(S+1) \rceil)}{\lceil \alpha(S+1) \rceil}$$

Since $p \leq m$, if $\lceil \alpha(S+1) \rceil \leq p/2$, the desired lower bound follows. On the other hand, if $\lceil \alpha(S+1) \rceil \geq p/2$, $\lceil \alpha(S+1) \rceil T \geq mp/2$ since $T \geq m$. ∎

It is possible that a function $f : \mathcal{A}^n \mapsto \mathcal{A}^m$ is not (α,n,m,p)-independent but a subfunction $g : \mathcal{A}^r \mapsto \mathcal{A}^s$ is (α,r,s,p)-independent for $r \leq n$ and $s \leq m$. (Subfunctions are defined in Section 2.4.) As shown in Problem 10.18, the lower bound for the subfunction g applies to f.

Lower bounds on space–time exchanges can also be derived using properties of the graphs to be pebbled. For example, if a graph contains a superconcentrator (defined in Problem 10.28), lower bounds on the product can be derived on $(S+1)T$ in terms of the number of inputs of the graph. (See Problem 10.28.)

As mentioned at the beginning of this section, Theorem 10.4.1 is much more general that it appears. In Problem 10.20 the reader is asked to show that the lower bound holds for "input-output-oblivious" finite-state machines, FSMs that compute functions but read their inputs and produce their outputs at data-independent times. Problem 10.21 asks the reader to establish that pebblings of straight-line computations can be translated directly into computations by finite-state machines.

Figure 10.6 Pebbling an inner product graph with three pebbles.

10.4.3   First Matrix Multiplication Bound

The Grigoriev lower-bound method is well illustrated by matrix multiplication. We established its independence property in Section 10.4.1. In this section we apply it to Corollary 10.4.1. The upper bound stated in the following theorem follows from the development of an algorithm for matrix multiplication that uses three pebbles and executes at most $4n^3$ steps. This algorithm, based on the standard matrix multiplication algorithm of Section 6.2.2, forms each of the n^2 inner products defined by the product of two $n \times n$ matrices using three pebbles, as suggested in Fig. 10.6, and $4n - 1$ steps.

THEOREM 10.4.2 *Every pebbling strategy for straight-line programs computing the matrix multiplication function* $f_{A \times B}^{(n)} : \mathcal{B}^{2n^2} \mapsto \mathcal{B}^{n^2}$ *for* $n \times n$ *matrices requires space* S *and time* T *satisfying the following inequality:*

$$(S + 1)T \geq n^3/4$$

The standard algorithm for multiplying $n \times n$ *matrices uses space and time satisfying*

$$(S + 1)T = 16\,n^3$$

Those familiar with fast non-standard matrix multiplication algorithms such as Strassen's fast matrix algorithm (Section 6.3) may find this result surprising. Whereas one learns that the standard matrix multiplication algorithm is not optimal with respect to computation time, the above result states that the standard matrix multiplication algorithm is nearly optimal with respect to the space–time product.

In Section 10.5.4 we specialize Theorem 10.4.1 to the flow properties of matrix multiplication, giving a stronger result: that the space and time for matrix multiplication must satisfy the inequality $ST^2 = \Omega(n^6)$.

10.5   Applications of Grigoriev's Method

Given the above results, to derive a lower bound on $\lceil \alpha(S + 1) \rceil T$ using Corollary 10.4.1 it suffices to establish the independence property of a function. We apply this idea in this section to convolution, cyclic shifting, integer multiplication, matrix-vector multiplication, matrix inversion, and solving linear equations. We apply related arguments to derive lower bounds for the discrete Fourier transform and merging. Finally, we apply Theorem 10.4.1 to derive a lower bound on space–time exchanges for matrix-matrix multiplication that improves upon the bound of Section 10.4.3. Where possible we also derive upper bounds on space–time tradeoffs.

10.5.1   Convolution

The wrapped convolution on strings of length n over the ring $\mathcal{R}$, $f_{\text{wrapped}}^{(n)} : \mathcal{R}^{2n} \mapsto \mathcal{R}^n$, is defined in Problem 6.19. It can be characterized by the following product of a circulant matrix with a vector (see Section 6.2):

$$
\begin{bmatrix} w_0 \\ w_1 \\ w_2 \\ \vdots \\ w_{n-1} \end{bmatrix}
=
\begin{bmatrix}
u_0 & u_{n-1} & u_{n-2} & \cdots & u_1 \\
u_1 & u_0 & u_{n-1} & \cdots & u_2 \\
 & & & \ddots & \\
u_{n-2} & u_{n-3} & u_{n-4} & \cdots & u_{n-1} \\
u_{n-1} & u_{n-2} & u_{n-3} & \cdots & u_0
\end{bmatrix}
\times
\begin{bmatrix} v_0 \\ v_1 \\ v_2 \\ \vdots \\ v_{n-1} \end{bmatrix}
\tag{10.1}
$$

Lemma 10.5.1 demonstrates $(2, 2n, n, n/2)$-independence for the wrapped convolution $f_{\text{wrapped}}^{(n)} : \mathcal{R}^{2n} \mapsto \mathcal{R}^n$ function by showing that for any set X_0 of inputs there is a way to put $|Y_1|/2$ of the inputs in $X - X_0$ into a one-to-one correspondence with $|Y_1|/2$ entries in any set Y_1 of outputs. This is established by setting one component of $\boldsymbol{v}$ to 1 and the rest to 0.

LEMMA 10.5.1 *For n even, the wrapped convolution $f_{\text{wrapped}}^{(n)} : \mathcal{R}^{2n} \mapsto \mathcal{R}^n$ over the ring $\mathcal{R}$ is $(2, 2n, n, n/2)$-independent.*

Proof Consider subsets X_0 and Y_1 of the inputs X and outputs Y of $f_{\text{wrapped}}^{(n)}$ satisfying $|X_0| + |Y_1| = p = n/2$. For $f_{\text{wrapped}}^{(n)}$ to be $(2, 2n, n, n/2)$-independent, there must be an assignment to input variables in X_0 such that the output variables in Y_1 have more than $|\mathcal{R}|^{(|Y_1|/2)-1}$ distinct values as the input variables of $f_{\text{wrapped}}^{(n)}$ in $X_1 = X - X_0$ range over all possible values.

As shown above, $f_{\text{wrapped}}^{(n)}$ is defined by a matrix-vector product $\boldsymbol{w} = M\boldsymbol{v}$, M a circulant matrix, in which each row (column) is a cyclic shift of the first row (column). Let $e = |X_0 \cap \{u_0, u_1, \ldots, u_{n-1}\}|$. Thus, every row of M contains the same number e of entries from X_0. Also, $n - e$ inputs are in $X_1 = X - X_0$. The entries in X_1 are free to vary.

Each output in Y_1 corresponds to a row of M. The number of instances of input variables from X_1 in these rows is $|Y_1|(n - e)$. Since these rows have n columns, there is some column, say the tth, containing at least the average number of instances from X_1. This average is $|Y_1|(1 - e/n) \geq |Y_1|/2$. (The instances of variables from X_1 in a column are distinct.) It follows that by choosing the tth component of $\boldsymbol{v}$, v_t, to be 1 and the others to be 0, at least $|Y_1|/2$ of the inputs in X_1 are mapped onto outputs in Y_1. Since these inputs (and outputs) can assume $|\mathcal{R}|^{|Y_1|/2}$ different values, it follows that $f_{\text{wrapped}}^{(n)}$ is $(2, 2n, n, n/2)$-independent. ■

This implies the lower bound stated below. The upper bound follows from the standard matrix-vector algorithm for the wrapped convolution using the observation that an inner product can be done with three pebbles, as suggested in Fig. 10.6.

THEOREM 10.5.1 *The time T and space S required to pebble any straight-line program for the standard or wrapped convolution must satisfy the following inequality:*

$$(S + 1)T \geq n^2/16$$

This lower bound can be achieved to within a constant multiplicative factor for $S = O(1)$.

10.5.2 Cyclic Shifting

The **cyclic shifting function** $f_{\text{cyclic}}^{(n)} : \mathcal{B}^{n+\lceil \log n \rceil} \mapsto \mathcal{B}^n$ defined in Section 2.5.2 is a subfunction of many functions, including integer multiplication and squaring (see Section 2.9.5), integer reciprocal (see Section 2.10.1), and powers of integers (see Problems 2.34 and 2.35).

Cyclic shifting is another good example of a problem for which a lower bound on the exchange of space and time exists. The method used to establish the independence properties of this function can be generalized to the class of transitive functions. (See Problem 10.22.)

We redefine $f_{\text{cyclic}}^{(n)}$ here. Let $k = \lceil \log n \rceil$. The input variables of $f_{\text{cyclic}}^{(n)}$ are segmented into two groups, an n-tuple $\boldsymbol{x} = (x_{n-1}, \ldots, x_1, x_0)$ of **value variables** and a k-tuple $\boldsymbol{s} = (s_{k-1}, \ldots, s_1, s_0)$ of **control variables**. The control variables specify the integer $|\boldsymbol{s}|$:

$$|\boldsymbol{s}| = s_{k-1} 2^{k-1} + \cdots + s_1 2^1 + s_0$$

$|\boldsymbol{s}|$ is the number of places by which the value inputs must be shifted left cyclically to produce the output n-tuple $\boldsymbol{y} = (y_{n-1}, \ldots, y_1, y_0)$. That is, $f_{\text{cyclic}}^{(n)}(\boldsymbol{x}, \boldsymbol{s}) = (\boldsymbol{y})$, where

$$y_j = x_{(j - |\boldsymbol{s}|) \bmod n} \text{ for } 0 \leq j \leq \lceil \log n \rceil - 1 \qquad (10.2)$$

A circuit to implement $f_{\text{cyclic}}^{(n)}$ is given in Section 2.5.2 that cyclically shifts $\boldsymbol{x}$ left by 2^j places for each of those values of j, $0 \leq j \leq \lceil \log n \rceil - 1$, such that $s_j = 1$.

The independence properties of the cyclic function are shown by demonstrating that some permutation of the input vector $\boldsymbol{x}$ aligns unselected inputs with selected outputs.

LEMMA 10.5.2 $f_{\text{cyclic}}^{(n)} : \mathcal{B}^{n+\lceil \log n \rceil} \mapsto \mathcal{B}^n$ is $(2, n + \lceil \log n \rceil, n, n/2)$-independent.

Proof Consider subsets X_0 and Y_1 of the inputs X and outputs Y of $f_{\text{cyclic}}^{(n)}$ satisfying $|X_0| + |Y_1| = p = n/2$. For $f_{\text{cyclic}}^{(n)}$ to be $(2, n + \lceil \log n \rceil, n, n/2)$-independent, there must be an assignment to input variables in X_0 such that the output variables in Y_1 have more than $|\mathcal{B}|^{(|Y_1|/2)-1}$ distinct values as the input variables of $f_{\text{cyclic}}^{(n)}$ in $X_1 = X - X_0$ range over all possible values.

Let X_0 contain e elements from $\boldsymbol{x}$. Let $y_i \in Y_1$. As $\boldsymbol{s}$ runs through all possible shift values, y_i is made equal to every one of the inputs in $\boldsymbol{x}$. For $n - e$ of these shifts y_i is set equal to an input in $X_1 = X - X_0$. (For example, if $n = 6$ and $e = 2$, say with $X_1 = \{x_0, x_3, x_4, x_5\}$ and $Y_1 = \{y_2, y_3, y_5\}$, then as $\boldsymbol{s}$ ranges over all of its values, each of the three y_i in Y_1 is assigned four different variables in X_1.) Thus, the number of input variables assigned to outputs, summed over all cyclic shifts, is $|Y_1|(n - e)$. Since there are n cyclic shifts, for some shift the number of variables in X_1 that are matched with outputs in Y_1 is at least the average of this quantity; that is, at least $|Y_1|(1 - e/n) \geq |Y_1|/2$. Thus, some shift sets at least $|Y_1|/2$ inputs in X_1 to outputs in Y_1. Since these outputs can assume $|\mathcal{B}|^{|Y_1|/2}$ different values, it follows that $f_{\text{cyclic}}^{(n)}$ is $(2, n + \lceil \log n \rceil, n, n/2)$-independent. ∎

THEOREM 10.5.2 *Every pebbling strategy for straight-line programs computing the cyclic shifting function* $f_{\text{cyclic}}^{(n)} : \mathcal{B}^n \mapsto \mathcal{B}^n$ *requires space S and time T satisfying the inequality*

$$(S + 1)T \geq n^2/16$$

An algorithm exists to compute $f_{\text{cyclic}}^{(n)}$ that uses space $O(n)$ and time $O(n \log n)$, namely, that satisfies the inequality

$$(S + 1)T = O(n^2 \log n)$$

Proof We leave the upper-bound proof to the reader. (See Problem 10.30.) ∎

We now apply this result to integer multiplication.

10.5.3   Integer Multiplication

To apply Grigoriev's method to the binary integer multiplication function $f_{\text{mult}}^{(n)} : \mathcal{B}^{2n} \mapsto \mathcal{B}^{2n}$ of Section 2.9, we assemble a collection of results to show that with the proper encoding of one of its two arguments, $f_{\text{mult}}^{(n)}$ computes the logical shifting function $f_{\text{shift}}^{(n)}$ (see Lemma 2.9.1) and when n is even the logical shifting function $f_{\text{shift}}^{(n)}$ contains the cyclic shift function $f_{\text{cyclic}}^{(n/2)}$ as a subfunction (see Lemma 2.5.2). Thus, $f_{\text{mult}}^{(n)}$ contains $f_{\text{cyclic}}^{(n/2)}$ as a subfunction. We use this fact to obtain a lower bound on the space–time product for integer multiplication.

THEOREM 10.5.3 *Let n be even. Every pebbling strategy for straight-line programs computing the binary integer multiplication function $f_{\text{mult}}^{(n)} : \mathcal{B}^{2n} \mapsto \mathcal{B}^{2n}$ requires space S and time T satisfying the following inequality:*

$$(S + 1)T \geq n^2/64$$

An algorithm exists for multiplying n-bit integers using space $O(\log^2 n)$ and time $O(n^2)$, namely, that satisfies

$$(S + 1)T = O(n^2 \log^2 n)$$

Proof The lower-bound argument is given above. The upper bound follows from a pebbling of an integer multiplication circuit to multiply n-bit binary integers $\boldsymbol{u}$ and $\boldsymbol{v}$. The circuit is based on the following standard expansion of their product:

			$v_3 u_0$	$v_2 u_0$	$v_1 u_0$	$v_0 u_0$
		$v_3 u_1$	$v_2 u_1$	$v_1 u_1$	$v_0 u_1$	0
	$v_3 u_2$	$v_2 u_2$	$v_1 u_2$	$v_0 u_2$	0	0
$v_3 u_3$	$v_2 u_3$	$v_1 u_3$	$v_0 u_3$	0	0	0

To construct a circuit we use the observation that the number of 1s in the jth column is the jth component, w_j, of the convolution $\boldsymbol{w} = \boldsymbol{u} \otimes \boldsymbol{v}$. (See Section 6.7.4.)

To compute w_j we use the counting circuit $f_{\text{count}}^{(n)} : \mathcal{B}^n \mapsto \mathcal{B}^{\lceil \log n \rceil}$ of Section 2.11 on n inputs to count the number of 1s among the products $u_r v_s$ of the Boolean variables u_r and v_s in the sum

$$w_j = \sum_{r+s=j} u_r * v_s \quad \text{for } 0 \leq j \leq 2n - 2$$

To compute the $2n$-bit product we add the binary representations for $w_0, w_1, \ldots, w_{2n-2}$ in a set of $(2n - 1)$ ripple adders, adding w_j to the sum $\sigma(j) = \sum_{0 \leq i \leq j-1} w_i 2^i$, as suggested in Fig. 10.7, where we omit the counting circuits used to compute the values of $w_0, \ldots, w_{2n-2}$.

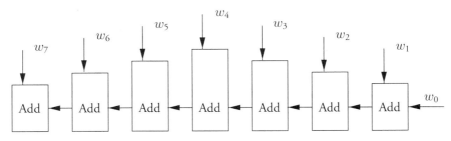

Figure 10.7 A multiplication circuit that can be pebbled in $O(n^2)$ time and $O(\log^2 n)$ space. The counting circuits that generate $w_0, w_1, \ldots, w_{2n-2}$ are not shown.

Each counting function can be pebbled with $O(n)$ steps using $O(\log^2 n)$ pebbles without repebbling vertices. (See Problem 10.10.) After the counting circuit is pebbled, pebbles remain on their outputs until their values have been used elsewhere in the multiplication circuit.

The value of w_j is represented by a k-tuple, $k \leq \lceil \log_2 n \rceil$. The value of $\sigma(j)$ is represented by at most $\lceil \log_2(n(2^j - 1)) \rceil \leq j + \lceil \log_2 n \rceil$ bits since it is the sum of at most n j-bit binary numbers. Because w_j is added after the first j bits, the pebbles on these bits can be discarded. Only $\lceil \log_2 n \rceil$ bits of the running sum and a like number for w_j are needed to hold values on the inputs to the ripple adder. A fixed additional number of pebbles suffices to pebble the internal vertices of the adder. On completion of the sum only $\lceil \log_2 n \rceil$ pebbles are needed. They are used to hold the portion of the running sum that is used in the next stage of addition.

For each value of j, $0 \leq j \leq 2(n - 1)$, $O(\log n)$ steps are executed in the ripple adder and $O(n)$ steps are executed in a counting circuit. Consequently, $O(\log^2 n)$ pebbles and $O(n^2)$ time suffice to compute the product of n-bit binary numbers. ∎

In Section 10.13.2 we show that a lower bound of $\Omega(n^2 / \log^2 n)$ applies under the branching program model. The stronger lower bound of $\Omega(n^2)$ derived here reflects the extra constraints imposed on the pebble game, namely that inputs are read and computations performed at data-independent times.

Similar results apply to the squaring function $f_{\text{square}}^{(n)}$ since, as shown in Lemma 2.9.2, $f_{\text{square}}^{(3n+1)}$ contains $f_{\text{mult}}^{(n)}$ as a subfunction. (See Problem 10.32.)

Similar results also apply to the reciprocal function $f_{\text{recip}}^{(n)} : \mathcal{B}^n \mapsto \mathcal{B}^n$ since, as shown in Lemma 2.10.1, $f_{\text{recip}}^{(n)}$ contains as a subfunction the squaring function $f_{\text{square}}^{(m)}$ for $m = \lfloor n/12 \rfloor - 1$. (See Problem 10.33.)

10.5.4 Matrix Multiplication

In this section we show that the matrix multiplication function is richer than the other functions examined above in that it exhibits a stronger space–time lower bound than given in Theorem 10.4.2. After we derive a lower bound on the function $w(u, v)$ we specialize Theorem 10.4.1 to this case, thereby deriving the stronger lower bound.

LEMMA 10.5.3 *The matrix multiplication function* $f_{A \times B}^{(n)} : \mathcal{R}^{2n^2} \mapsto \mathcal{R}^{n^2}$ *over the ring* $\mathcal{R}$ *has a* $w(u, v)$*-flow, where* $w(u, v)$ *satisfies the following lower bound:*

$$w(u, v) \geq (v - (2n^2 - u)^2/4n^2)/2$$

Proof Let $C = AB$ be the product of $n \times n$ matrices A and B. We establish this result by using characteristic functions to identify the outputs in C in Y_1 and the inputs in A and B in X_1, as indicated below. Here the indices i and j range over $0 \leq i, j \leq n - 1$:

$$\sigma_{i,j} = \begin{cases} 1 & c_{i,j} \in Y_1 \\ 0 & \text{otherwise} \end{cases} \qquad \alpha_{i,j} = \begin{cases} 1 & a_{i,j} \in X_1 \\ 0 & \text{otherwise} \end{cases}$$

$$\beta_{i,j} = \begin{cases} 1 & b_{i,j} \in X_1 \\ 0 & \text{otherwise} \end{cases}$$

Let $\boldsymbol{A}$, $\boldsymbol{B}$, and $\boldsymbol{C}$ denote the matrices $[\alpha_{i,j}]$, $[\beta_{i,j}]$, and $[\sigma_{i,j}]$, respectively. Denote by $|\boldsymbol{A}|$, $|\boldsymbol{B}|$, and $|\boldsymbol{C}|$ the number of 1s in the three corresponding matrices. Note that $|\boldsymbol{A}| + |\boldsymbol{B}| = |X_1|$ and $|\boldsymbol{C}| = |Y_1|$.

The kth $n \times n$ **cyclic permutation matrix** $P(k)$ is the $n \times n$ identity matrix in which the rows are rotated cyclically $k - 1$ times. For example, the following 3×3 matrix is $P(3)$.

$$\begin{bmatrix} 0 & 1 & 0 \\ 0 & 0 & 1 \\ 1 & 0 & 0 \end{bmatrix}$$

Let D be an $n \times n$ matrix. The matrix $P(k)D$ consists of the rows of D shifted cyclically down k places. Similarly, the matrix $DP(k)$ consists of the columns of D shifted cyclically left k places.

Let $\boldsymbol{B}(k)$ be the matrix $\boldsymbol{B}$ obtained by multiplication on the left by $A = P(k)$. Similarly, let $\boldsymbol{A}(k)$ be the matrix $\boldsymbol{A}$ obtained by multiplication on the right by $B = P(k)$. Then, a 1 value for the (i, j) entry in $\boldsymbol{A}(k)$ and $\boldsymbol{B}(k)$ identifies a variable in X_1 that is mapped to an output variable of C through its multiplication by $P(k)$.

Let D and E be $n \times n$ matrices whose entries are drawn from the set $\{0, 1\}$. We denote by $\boldsymbol{D} \cap \boldsymbol{E}$ the $n \times n$ matrix whose (i, j) entry is 1 if $d_{i,j} = e_{i,j} = 1$. Similarly, let $\boldsymbol{D} \cup \boldsymbol{E}$ be the $n \times n$ matrix whose (i, j) entry is 1 if either $d_{i,j} = 1$ or $e_{i,j} = 1$. The following identity applies:

$$|\boldsymbol{D} \cup \boldsymbol{E}| + |\boldsymbol{D} \cap \boldsymbol{E}| = |\boldsymbol{D}| + |\boldsymbol{E}| \tag{10.3}$$

Since $|\boldsymbol{D} \cup \boldsymbol{E}| \leq n^2$ for $n \times n$ matrices, the following inequality holds:

$$|\boldsymbol{D} \cap \boldsymbol{E}| \geq |\boldsymbol{D}| + |\boldsymbol{E}| - n^2 \tag{10.4}$$

Also, since $|\boldsymbol{D} \cap \boldsymbol{E}| \geq 0$ we have

$$|\boldsymbol{D}| + |\boldsymbol{E}| \geq |\boldsymbol{D} \cup \boldsymbol{E}| \tag{10.5}$$

The $w(u, v)$-flow of matrix multiplication is large if for some choice of r or s $|\boldsymbol{C} \cap \boldsymbol{A}(r)|$ or $|\boldsymbol{C} \cap \boldsymbol{B}(s)|$ is large. This follows because choosing A to be the rth cyclic permutation makes many variables of B in X_1 match entries in C in Y_1, and choosing B to be the sth cyclic permutation makes many variables of A in X_1 match entries in C in Y_1. When an input and output variable match, the latter assumes the value of the former. Thus, all the variation in the former is reflected in the latter.

Let $Q = |C \cap A(r)| + |C \cap B(s)|$. Then the $w(u, v)$-flow is at least $Q/2$. Applying (10.5) and then (10.4) to Q, we have the following inequalities:

$$Q \geq |C \cap (|A(r) \cup B(s)|)| \geq |C| + |A(r) \cup B(s)| - n^2$$

Applying (10.3) to $|A(r) \cup B(s)|$ yields the following lower bound on Q:

$$Q \geq |C| + |A(r)| + |B(s)| - |A(r) \cap B(s)| - n^2 \tag{10.6}$$

But $|C| = |Y_1|$, $|A(r)| = |A|$, $|B(s)| = |B|$, and $|A| + |B| = |X_1|$. We now show that there are values for r and s such that $|A(r) \cap B(s)|$ is at most $|A||B|/n^2$.

Consider the following sum:

$$S = \sum_{r=1}^{n} \sum_{s=1}^{n} |A(r) \cap B(s)|$$

Since $A(r)$ and $B(s)$ are formed by the rth and sth cyclic shift of columns and rows of A and B respectively, each 1 in A is aligned once with each 1 in B. It follows that

$$S = |A||B|$$

As a consequence, there are some r and s such that $|A(r) \cap B(s)|$ is at most S/n^2. Applying this result in (10.6), we have the following lower bound on Q:

$$Q \geq |Y_1| + |A| + |B| - |A||B|/n^2 - n^2$$

Since $|X_1| = |A| + |B|$ is fixed, the above lower bound on Q is minimized by maximizing $|A||B|$ under variation of $|A|$. This maximum occurs when $|A| = |X_1|/2$. Consequently we have the following lower bound on Q:

$$Q \geq |Y_1| - n^2 \left(1 - \frac{|X_1|}{2n^2} \right)^2$$

Since $w(u, v) \geq Q/2$ for $u = |X_1|$ and $v = |Y_1|$, we have desired the conclusion. ∎

We now apply this result and Theorem 10.4.1 to derive a stronger result for matrix multiplication than was obtained earlier using its $(1, 2n^2, n^2, n)$-independence property.

THEOREM 10.5.4 *Every pebbling strategy for straight-line programs computing the matrix multiplication function $f_{A \times B}^{(n)} : \mathcal{B}^{2n^2} \mapsto \mathcal{B}^{n^2}$ for $n \times n$ matrices requires space S and time T satisfying the following inequality:*

$$ST^2 \geq 2n^6/9$$

The standard algorithm for multiplying $n \times n$ matrices uses space and time satisfying

$$ST^2 = 48\, n^6$$

Proof From Lemma 10.5.3 we have that the matrix multiplication function has a $w(u, v)$-flow, where

$$w(u, v) \geq (v - (2n^2 - u)^2/4n^2)/2$$

Applying Theorem 10.4.1 to this problem with $b = 3S$, we seek the largest integer d such that $w(d, b) \leq S$, which must satisfy the bound

$$\left(3S - (2n^2 - d)^2/4n^2\right)/2 \leq S$$

This implies that $(2n^2 - d) \geq 2n\sqrt{2S}$. From Theorem 10.4.1, the time to pebble the graph satisfies

$$T \geq 2\sqrt{2S}n\lfloor n^2/3S \rfloor$$
$$\geq 2\sqrt{2S}n(n^2 - 3S + 1)/3S$$

If $S \leq n^2/6$, $T \geq (2\sqrt{2}n^3)/(6\sqrt{S})$ or $ST^2 \geq 2n^6/9$. On the other hand, since $T \geq 3n^2$ just to pebble inputs and outputs, if $S > n^2/6$, then $ST^2 \geq n^6/2$. ∎

10.5.5 Discrete Fourier Transform

The discrete Fourier transform (DFT) is defined in Section 6.7.3. We derive upper and lower bounds on the space–time product needed to compute this function.

LEMMA 10.5.4 *The n-point DFT function $F_n : \mathcal{R}^n \mapsto \mathcal{R}^n$ over a commutative ring $\mathcal{R}$ is $(2, n, n, n/2)$-independent for n even.*

Proof As shown in equation (6.23), the DFT is defined by the matrix-vector product $[w^{ij}]\boldsymbol{a}$, where $[w^{ij}]$ is a Vandermonde matrix. To show that the DFT function is $(2, n, n, n/2)$-independent, consider any set Y_1 of outputs (corresponding to rows of $[w^{ij}]$) and any set X_0 of inputs (corresponding to columns) whose values are to be fixed judiciously, where $p = |X_0| + |Y_1| = n/2$. We show that the outputs in Y_1 have at least $|\mathcal{R}|^{|Y_1|/2}$ values as we vary over the remaining inputs.

It is straightforward to show that the submatrix of $[w^{ij}]$ defined by any $|Y_1|$ rows and any $|Y_1|$ consecutive columns is non-singular. (Its determinant is that of another Vandermonde matrix. Show this by letting the row and column indices be $r_1, r_2, \ldots, r_{|Y_1|}$ and $s, s + 1, \ldots, s + |Y_1| - 1$, respectively, and demonstrating that $w^{r_i s}$ can be factored out of the ith row when computing its determinant.) Our goal is to show that some consecutive group of columns corresponds to at least $|Y_1|/2$ inputs of $\boldsymbol{a}$ in X_1.

Divide the n columns of $[w^{ij}]$ into $\lceil n/|Y_1| \rceil$ groups of consecutive columns with $|Y_1|$ inputs in each group except possibly the last, which may have fewer. There are $n - |X_0|$ inputs that may vary. Since there are $\lceil n/|Y_1| \rceil$ groups, by an averaging argument some group contains at least $(n-|X_0|)/\lceil n/|Y_1| \rceil$ of these inputs. Since $\lceil n/|Y_1| \rceil \leq (n+|Y_1|-1)/|Y_1|$, we show that $(n - |X_0|)/\lceil n/|Y_1| \rceil > |Y_1|/2$ for $p = n/2$. Observe that $(n - |X_0|)/(n + |Y_1| - 1) \geq 1/2$ if $2n - 2|X_0| \geq n + |Y_1| - 1$ or $n \geq |X_0| + p - 1$, which holds because $|X_0| \leq p \leq n/2$.

Since the submatrix defined by k consecutive columns and any k rows where $\lceil |Y_1|/2 \rceil \leq k \leq |Y_1|$ is non-singular, it follows that any subset of $\lceil |Y_1|/2 \rceil$ columns has full rank. Thus, the submatrix contains a non-singular $\lceil |Y_1|/2 \rceil \times \lceil |Y_1|/2 \rceil$ matrix. When all inputs outside of these columns are set to zero, the $\lceil |Y_1|/2 \rceil$ outputs have $|\mathcal{R}|^{\lceil |Y_1|/2 \rceil}$ values, or F_n is $(2, n, n, n/2)$-independent. ∎

The space–time lower bound stated below follows from Corollary 10.4.1.

THEOREM 10.5.5 *To pebble any straight-line program for the n-point DFT over a commutative ring $\mathcal{R}$ requires space S and time T satisfying the following:*

$$(S+1)T \geq n^2/16$$

when n is even. The FFT graph on $n = 2^d$ inputs can be pebbled with space S and time T satisfying the upper bound

$$T \leq 4n^2/(S - \log_2 n) + n \log_2 S$$

Thus, $(S+1)T = O(n^2)$ when $2\log_2 n \leq S \leq (n/\log_2 n) + \log_2 n$.

Proof This lower bound can be achieved up to a constant factor by a pebbling strategy for the FFT algorithm, as we now show. Denote with $F^{(d)}$ the n-point FFT graph (it has n inputs), $n = 2^d$. (Figures. 6.1, 6.7, and 10.8 show 4-point, 16-point, and 32-point FFT graphs.) Inputs are at level 0 and outputs are at level d. We invoke Lemma 6.7.4 to decompose $F^{(d)}$ at level $d - e$ into a set of top 2^{d-e} 2^e-point FFT graphs above the split, $\{F_{t,j}^{(e)} \mid 1 \leq j \leq 2^e\}$, and a set of 2^e 2^{d-e}-point FFT graphs below the split, $\{F_{b,j}^{(d-e)} \mid 1 \leq j \leq 2^e\}$, as suggested in Fig. 10.8. In this figure the vertices and edges have been grouped together as recognizable FFT graphs and surrounded by shaded boxes. The edges between boxes identify vertices that are common to pairs of FFT subgraphs.

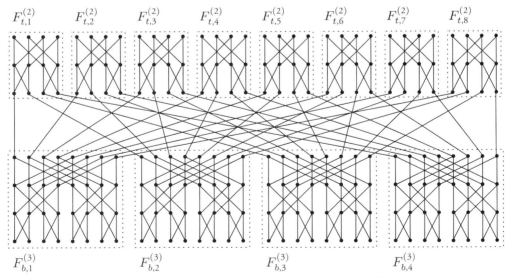

Figure 10.8 Decomposition of the FFT graph $F^{(5)}$ into four copies of $F^{(3)}$ and eight copies of $F^{(2)}$. Edges between bottom and top sub-FFT graphs are fictitious; they identify overlapping vertices between sub-FFT graphs.

A good strategy for pebbling the vertices of an FFT graph is to pebble the top FFT graphs $\{F_{t,j}^{(e)} \mid 1 \le j \le 2^{d-e}\}$ individually. The vertices of a top FFT graph in Fig. 10.8 are highlighted. To pebble its inputs, which are output vertices of FFT graphs below the split, it suffices to pebble the subtrees rooted at these vertices. (They are also highlighted.) Such subtrees are completely balanced binary trees with 2^{d-e} inputs. Thus, $d-e+1$ pebbles and $2^{d-e+1} - 1$ pebble placements suffice to place a pebble on the root of one such subtree. If these subtrees are pebbled in sequence, pebbles can be left on the inputs to a 2^e-point FFT graph $F^{(e)}$ above the split using at most $2^e + d - e$ pebbles and $2^e(2^{d-e+1} - 1)$ pebble placements. Since $2^e + 1$ pebbles and $e2^e$ pebble placements suffice to pebble $F^{(e)}$ level by level without repebbling vertices, it follows that all instances of $F^{(e)}$ above the split can be pebbled using a total of $T = 2^d(2^{d-e+1} + e - 1)$ pebble placements and $S = 2^e + d - e$ pebbles.

We now derive an upper bound on T by deriving upper and lower bounds on the value of e satisfying $S = 2^e + d - e$. Because $S \ge 2^e$, we have $e \le \log_2 S$. Let e_0 be the smallest integer such that $2^{e_0+1} + d \ge S$. Then, $2^{e_0} + d - e_0 \le S$ and $e \ge e_0$. Consequently, $2^e \ge (S - d)/2$, from which we have

$$T = 2^d(2^{d-e+1} + e - 1) \le 4\frac{2^{2d}}{(S - d)} + 2^d \log_2 S$$

Finally, $\log_2 S \le 2^d/(S - d) \le 2\, 2^d/S$ when $2d \le S \le (2^d/d) + d$, from which the desired conclusion follows. ∎

10.5.6 Merging Networks

In this section we consider networks of comparators to merge two sorted lists. Such networks were described in Section 6.8 and an example was given, Batcher's (m, p) odd-even merging network.

A **comparator element** computes the function $\otimes : \mathcal{A}^2 \mapsto \mathcal{A}^2$ that returns the maximum and minimum of its two arguments, that is, $\otimes(a, b) = (\max(a, b), \min(a, b))$.

LEMMA 10.5.5 *Consider a comparator-based merging network that merges two sorted lists of n distinct elements $\boldsymbol{x} = (x_1, x_2, \ldots, x_n)$ $(x_i \le x_{i+1})$ and $\boldsymbol{y} = (y_1, y_2, \ldots, y_n)$ $(y_i \le y_{i+1})$ to produce the sorted list $\boldsymbol{z} = (z_1, z_2, \ldots, z_{2n})$ of $2n$ outputs $(z_i \le z_{i+1})$. There must be r vertex-disjoint paths from any r inputs in $\boldsymbol{x}$ to the outputs in $\boldsymbol{z}$ to which they are mapped by the network.*

Proof Working backwards from the r selected outputs, we see that each output exits from the comparator elements to which it is attached via a disjoint path, as suggested for three outputs in Fig. 10.9. Extending this argument to the remainder of the network establishes the result. ∎

We next show that inputs can be given values to cause a merging network to shift its values in a fashion that permits the derivation of a space–time lower bound.

THEOREM 10.5.6 *Any straight-line comparator-based program that merges two sorted lists of n elements requires space S and time T satisfying*

$$ST = \Omega(n^2)$$

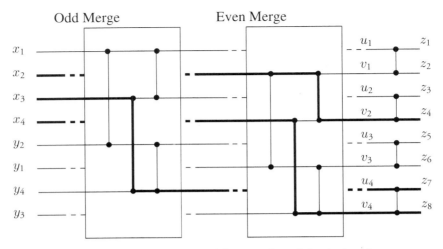

Figure 10.9 Movement of an ordered subset of the items through Batcher's odd-even merge algorithm.

This lower bound can be achieved to within a constant multiplicative factor when $2 \log_2 n \leq S \leq (n/\log_2 n) + \log_2 n$.

Proof Let n be divisible by 2. Any consecutive $n/2$ inputs in $\boldsymbol{x}$ can be shifted to the middle $n/2$ positions in $\boldsymbol{z}$ through a judicious choice of values for $\boldsymbol{y}$. To see this, observe that the first $k = n - n/4 - l$ components of $\boldsymbol{y}$, $l \leq n/2$, can be chosen to be less than the first l components of $\boldsymbol{x}$ with the remaining $n - k$ components of $\boldsymbol{y}$ chosen to be larger than the first $l + n/2$ components of $\boldsymbol{x}$. This will cause elements in positions $l + 1, l + 2, \ldots, l + n/2$ to shift into positions $n - n/4 + 1, \ldots, n + n/4$.

Since coalescing vertices in a graph reduces neither the time nor space needed to pebble it, coalesce input vertices assigned to $\boldsymbol{x}$ whose indices are equivalent modulo $n/2$. By Lemma 10.5.5, the new graph has $n/2$-vertex disjoint paths between the new inputs and the $n/2$ outputs in positions $l + 1, l + 2, \ldots, l + n/2$ for each of the $n/2$ cyclic permutations. It follows that the argument applied to the cyclic shifting function (Lemma 10.5.2) applies to this function. Thus, the merging network computes a function containing a subfunction that is $(2, n/2, n/2, n/4)$-independent. The lower bound follows from Corollary 10.4.1.

As shown in Section 6.8, the graph of Batcher's odd-even merging network is an FFT graph. Thus, the upper bounds given in Theorem 10.5.5 apply. ∎

10.6 Worst-Case Tradeoffs for Pebble Games*

In this section we show that degree-d graphs on n vertices can be pebbled with $O(n/\log n)$ pebbles (Theorem 10.7.1) and that some graphs require this many (Theorem 10.8.1). These results do not answer the question of how bad the space–time tradeoff can be for an arbitrary graph. To address this question we must make it precise. Lengauer and Tarjan [194] state it as follows: is there a value for the space S, say, $S_J(n)$, such that for positive constants $c_1(d)$ and $c_2(d)$ if $S \leq c_1(d)S_J(n)$, some graph on n vertices requires time superpolynomial in

n to pebble it, whereas for $S \geq c_2(d)S_J(n)$ all graphs on n vertices can be pebbled with a polynomial number of steps? They show that there is such a **jump value for space** and that $S_J(n) = \Theta(n/\log\log n)$. Since all graphs on n vertices can be pebbled with $O(n/\log n)$ space, their result shows there exist graphs on n vertices that require time exponential in n when pebbled with this number of pebbles.

10.7 Upper Bounds on Space*

We establish upper bounds on space for the class $\mathcal{G}(n,d)$ of directed acyclic graphs on n vertices that have maximum in-degree d and out-degree 2. We limit the out-degree to 2 because many straight-line programs with fan-out $k > 2$ (and their associated DAGs) can be reorganized so that each computation with fan-out k can be replaced by a binary tree of replicating subcomputations in which edges are directed from the root to the leaves. This at most doubles the number of vertices in the graph. (See Problem 10.12.)

THEOREM 10.7.1 *Let $\mathcal{G}(n,d)$ be graphs with n vertices, in-degree d, and out-degree 2 for d fixed. Then $S_{\min}(n,d)$, the minimum space needed to pebble any DAG in $\mathcal{G}(n,d)$, satisfies $S_{\min}(n,d) = O(n/\log n)$.*

Proof Let $E_{\min}(p,d)$ be the minimum number of edges in any graph in $\mathcal{G}(n,d)$ that requires p pebbles in the pebble game. We show that $E_{\min}(p,d) \geq cp\log_2 p$ for some constant $c > 0$. From this it follows that

$$p \leq 2(E_{\min}(p,d)/c)/\log_2(E_{\min}(p,d)/c)$$

when $p \geq 2$ and $E_{\min}(p,d) \geq 2c$. (See Problem 10.3.)

Consider a graph $G = (V, E)$ in $\mathcal{G}(n,d)$ with $|E|$ edges. The number of edges incident on vertices is $2|E|$. Since each vertex has at most $d+2$ incident edges, $2|E| \leq (d+2)|V| = (d+2)n$. The upper bound on the number of pebbles, p, follows from this fact and the previous discussion.

Let $G = (V, E)$ in $\mathcal{G}(n,d)$ require p pebbles. An edge in E is a pair of vertices (u, v). Let $V_1 \subseteq V$ be vertices that can be pebbled with $p/2$ or fewer pebbles. Let $V_2 = V - V_1$. Thus, every vertex in V_2 requires more than $p/2$ pebbles. Let E_i, $i = 1, 2$, be the set of edges both of whose endpoints are in V_i. Let $G_i = (V_i, E_i)$. Let $A = E - (E_1 \cup E_2)$; that is, A is the set of edges joining vertices in V_1 and V_2.

We now show that there exists a vertex in G_2 that requires more than $p/2 - d$ pebbles if the pebble game is played on G_2 only. Suppose not. Then we show that every vertex in G can be pebbled with fewer than p pebbles. Certainly every vertex in V_1 can be pebbled with fewer than p pebbles. Consider vertices in V_2. We show they can be pebbled with fewer than p pebbles, thereby establishing a contradiction.

Let $\nu \in V_2$ be pebbled with $p/2 - d$ or fewer pebbles when G_2 alone is pebbled. In pebbling ν as part of the complete graph G, we may need to pebble a vertex $\omega \in V_2$ some of whose immediate predecessors are in V_1. As we encounter such vertices ω, advance a pebble to each of ω's predecessors in V_1 one at at time until all predecessors of ω are pebbled. After pebbling a predecessor in V_1, remove pebbles in V_1 not on such predecessors. When all of ω's predecessors in V_1 have been pebbled, pebble ω itself using one of the $p/2 - d$ or fewer pebbles reserved for pebbling on V_2. This strategy uses at most $p/2 + d - 1$ pebbles on vertices in V_1, at most $d - 1$ for all but the last predecessor in V_1 and at most $p/2$

for the last such predecessor, and at most $p/2 - d$ pebbles on vertices in V_2, for a total of at most $p - 1$. This is a contradiction. It follows that G_2 requires at least $p/2 - d + 1$ pebbles when pebbled alone and must have at least $E_{\min}(p/2 - d + 1, d)$ edges. Note that $E_{\min}(p/2 - d + 1, d) \geq E_{\min}(p/2 - d, d)$.

There is also some vertex in G_1 that requires at least $p/2 - d$ vertices, as we show. By assumption every vertex in V_1 must be pebbled. Suppose that each can be pebbled with $p/2 - d - 1$ pebbles. There must be a vertex η in V_2 all of whose predecessors are in V_1. (If not, we can always move backward from a vertex in V_2 to one of its immediate predecessors in V_2, a process that must terminate since the finite acyclic graph does not have a cycle.) Thus, the vertex η can be pebbled with $p/2 - 1$ pebbles using the pebbling strategy described in the preceding paragraph for ω, contradicting the definition of V_2. It follows that G_1 must have at least $E_{\min}(p/2 - d, d)$ edges.

Consider now the set of edges A connecting vertices in V_1 and V_2. If $|A| \geq p/4$, $E_{\min}(p, d) \geq 2E_{\min}(p/2 - d, d) + |A|$ because both G_1 and G_2 have $E_{\min}(p/2 - d, d)$ edges. If $|A| < p/4$, pebbles can be placed on the endpoints of edges of A in V_1 using at most $p/2 + p/4 - 1 \leq 3p/4$ pebbles, with the strategy for ω given above. If we leave at most $p/4$ pebbles on these vertices, $3p/4$ pebbles are available to pebble the vertices in V_2. If V_2 does not require at least $3p/4$ pebbles, we have a contradiction to the assumption that p pebbles are needed. Thus, there must be an output vertex μ that requires at least $3p/4$ pebbles, for if not, none of its predecessors can require more.

We show that a graph requiring at least $3p/4$ pebbles has a subgraph with at least $p/(4d)$ fewer edges that requires at least $p/2$ pebbles. To see this, observe that some predecessor of the output vertex μ requires at least $3p/4 - d$ pebbles. Delete μ and all its incoming edges to produce a subgraph with at least one fewer edge requiring at least $3p/4 - d$ pebbles. Repeat this process $p/(4d)$ times to produce the desired result. It follows that G_2 has at least $E_{\min}(p/2, d) + p/(4d)$ edges.

Thus, when either $|A| \geq p/4$ or $|A| < p/4$, at least $2E_{\min}(p/2 - d, d) + p/(4d)$ edges are required, and

$$E_{\min}(p, d) \geq 2E_{\min}(p/2 - d, d) + \frac{p}{4d}$$

The solution to this recurrence is $E_{\min}(p, d) \geq cp \log p$ for some constant $c \geq 1/8d$ and a sufficiently large value of p. ∎

10.8 Lower Bound on Space for General Graphs*

Now that we have established that every graph in $\mathcal{G}(n, d)$ can be pebbled with $O(n/\log n)$ pebbles, we show that for all n there exists a graph $G(n)$ in $\mathcal{G}(n, d)$ whose minimum space requirement is at least $c_5 n / \log n$ for some constant $c_5 > 0$.

The graph $G(n)$ is obtained from a recursively constructed graph $H(k)$ on 2^k inputs and 2^k outputs, $n/2 < 2^k \leq n$, by adding $n - 2^k$ vertices and no edges. The graph $H(k)$ is composed of two copies of $H(k-1)$ and two copies of an n-superconcentrator, which is defined below.

DEFINITION 10.8.1 *An n-superconcentrator is a directed acyclic graph $G = (V, E)$ with n input vertices and n output vertices and the property that for any r inputs and any r outputs,*

$1 \leq r \leq n$, *there are* r *vertex-disjoint paths in* G *connecting these inputs and outputs. (Paths are* **vertex-disjoint** *if they have no vertices in common.)*

For $n = 2^k$ Valiant [337] has shown the existence of n-superconcentrators $SC(k)$ that have 2^k inputs, 2^k outputs, and $c2^k$ edges. Since his graphs have in-degree greater than 2, replace vertices with in-degree $d > 2$ with binary trees of d leaves, thereby at most doubling the size of the graph. (See Problem 10.12.) This provides the following result.

LEMMA 10.8.1 *For some constant* $c > 0$ *and each integer* k *and* $n = 2^k$ *there exists an* n-*superconcentrator* $SC(k)$ *with* $c2^k$ *vertices.*

We let $H(8) = SC(8)$. For $k \geq 8$ we construct $H(k + 1)$ recursively from two copies of $H(k)$, two copies of $SC(k)$, and extra edges, as suggested in Fig. 10.10. Here edges are directed from left to right. The 2^k output vertices of the first (leftmost) copy of $SC(k)$ (called $SC_1(k)$) are identified with the 2^k input vertices of the first copy of $H(k)$ (called $H_1(k)$), the 2^k output vertices of $H_1(k)$ are identified with the 2^k input vertices of the second copy of $H(k)$ (called $H_2(k)$), and the 2^k output vertices of $H_2(k)$ are identified with the 2^k input vertices of the second copy of $SC(k)$ (called $SC_2(k)$). In addition, we introduce 2^{k+1} new input vertices and 2^{k+1} new output vertices. The first (topmost) half of the new inputs (called I_t) are connected via individual edges to the inputs of $SC_1(k)$. The second (bottommost) half of the new inputs (called I_b) are also connected via individual edges to the inputs of $SC_1(k)$. The new inputs are connected individually to the new outputs. Finally, each output of $SC_2(k)$ is connected via individual edges to two new output vertices, one each in the top (called O_t) and bottom half (called O_b) of the new outputs.

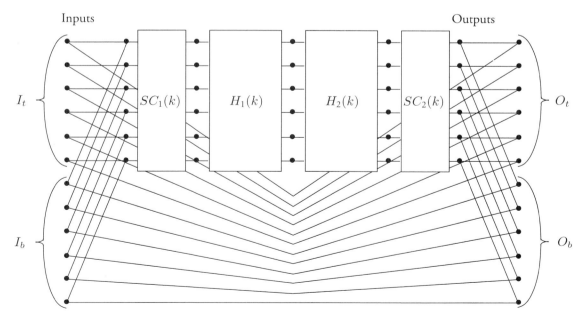

Figure 10.10 A graph $H(k + 1)$ requiring large minimum space.

The graph $H(k)$ has $n(k) = |H(k)|$ vertices, where $n(k)$ satisfies the following:

$$n(8) = c2^8$$
$$n(k + 1) = 2n(k) + (2c + 4)2^k$$

The solution to the recurrence is $n(k) = (k - 7)c2^k + (k - 8)2^{k+1}$, as can be shown directly. The graph $H(k)$ is in $\mathcal{G}(n(k), 2)$.

Important subgraphs of $H(k + 1)$ have the superconcentrator property, as we now show. This result is applied in the subsequent lemma to derive bounds on the amount of space used to pebble outputs of $H(k + 1)$.

LEMMA 10.8.2 *The subgraphs of $H(k+1)$ on 2^k inputs and 2^k outputs defined by vertices and edges on paths from either inputs in I_t or inputs in I_b to the outputs of SC_1 and $H_1(k)$ have the 2^k-superconcentrator property.*

Proof The superconcentrator property applies to the outputs of $SC_1(k)$ by definition. Note that the jth input of $H_1(k)$ is connected to its jth output by an individual edge for $1 \le j \le 2^k$. Thus, any r outputs of $H_1(k)$ have vertex-disjoint paths to the corresponding inputs of $H_1(k)$. By the superconcentrator property of $SC_1(k)$, there are vertex-disjoint paths from these outputs of $SC_1(k)$ to any r of its inputs. These statements obviously apply to inputs in I_t and I_b. ∎

Our goal is to show that pebbling the graph $H(k)$ requires a number of pebbles proportional to $n(k)/\log n(k)$. To do this we establish the following stronger condition, which implies the desired result.

LEMMA 10.8.3 *Let $c_1 = 14/256$, $c_2 = 3/256$, $c_3 = 34/256$, and $c_4 = 1/256$. To pebble at least $c_1 2^k$ outputs of $H(k)$ in any order from an initial placement of at most $c_2 2^k$ pebbles requires there be a time interval $[t_1, t_2]$ during which at least $c_3 2^k$ inputs are pebbled and at least $c_4 2^k$ pebbles remain on the graph.*

Proof The proof is by induction on k with $k = 8$ as the base case. For the base case, consider pebbling $c_1 2^k = 14$ outputs during a time interval $[0, t]$ from an initial placement of no more than $c_2 2^k = 3$ pebbles.

By Problem 10.27 any four outputs of $SC(8)$ are connected via pebble-free paths to $256 - 3 = 253$ inputs. At least one of these four outputs, say v, has pebble-free paths to 64 $= \lceil 253/4 \rceil$ inputs. Let $t_1 - 1$ be the last time at which all 64 of these inputs have pebble-free paths to v. Let t_2 be the last time at which a pebble is placed on these 64 inputs. During the time interval $[t_1, t_2]$ at least $64 \ge c_3 2^k$ inputs are pebbled and at least one pebble remains on the graph; that is, at least $c_4 2^k$ pebbles remain. This establishes the base case.

Now assume the conditions of the lemma (our inductive hypothesis) hold for k. We show they hold for $k + 1$. Assume that at least $c_1 2^{k+1}$ outputs of $H(k + 1)$ are pebbled in any order from an initial placement of at most $c_2 2^{k+1}$ pebbles during a time interval $[t_a, t_b]$.

We consider four cases including the following two cases. There is an interval $[t_1, t_2] \subseteq [t_a, t_b]$ during which at least $c_2 2^k$ pebbles are always on the graph and at least $c_3 2^k$ outputs of either (1) $SC_1(k)$, or (2) $H_1(k)$ are pebbled. By Lemma 10.8.2 the subgraph of $H(k+1)$ consisting of paths from I_t (and I_b) to the outputs of each of these graphs constitutes a 2^k-superconcentrator. This is the only fact about these two cases that we use. Without loss of generality, we show the hypothesis holds for the first of them.

The graph consisting of paths from inputs in I_t to the outputs of $SC_1(k)$ constitutes a 2^k-superconcentrator. Prior to time t_a there are at most $c_2 2^{k+1}$ pebbles on the graph and during the interval $[t_1, t_2]$ there are at least $c_2 2^k$ (but at most $c_2 2^{k+1}$) pebbles on the graph. Thus, there is a latest time t_0 before t_1 when there are at most $c_2 2^{k+1}$ pebbles on the graph. Since $c_3 2^k \geq c_2 2^{k+1} + 1$ outputs of $SC_1(k)$ are pebbled in the interval $[t_1, t_2]$ (and in the interval $[t_0, t_2]$), by Problem 10.27 at time t_0 there are at least $2^k - c_2 2^{k+1} \geq c_3 2^k$ inputs in I_t (and in I_b) that are connected by pebble-free paths to the pebbled outputs of $SC_1(k)$. Thus, at least $c_3 2^{k+1}$ inputs in I_t and I_b are connected via pebble-free paths to the pebbled outputs of $SC_1(k)$. In $[t_0, t_1 - 1]$ there are at least $c_2 2^{k+1}$ pebbles continuously on the graph, whereas there are at least $c_2 2^k$ pebbles during $[t_1, t_2]$. Since $c_2 2^k \geq c_4 2^{k+1}$, the number continuously on the graph in $[t_1, t_2]$ is at least $c_4 2^{k+1}$ and we have the desired conclusion for $H(k + 1)$.

In the third case, there is an interval $[t_1, t_2] \subseteq [t_a, t_b]$ during which at least $c_1 2^k$ outputs of the full graph $H(k+1)$ are pebbled and at least $c_2 2^k$ pebbles are always on the graph. This implies that during $[t_1, t_2]$ either $c_1 2^k/2$ outputs in O_t or in O_b are pebbled, which in turn implies that at least $c_1 2^k/2$ outputs of $SC_2(k)$ are pebbled. Since $c_1 2^k/2 \geq c_2 2^{k+1} + 1$ (at most $c_2 2^{k+1}$ pebbles are on $H(k + 1)$), it follows from Problem 10.27 that at least $2^k - c_2 2^{k+1} \geq c_3 2^k$ inputs in I_t (or I_b) are connected via pebble-free paths to the pebbled outputs of $SC_2(k)$. The total number of such inputs is $c_3 2^{k+1}$. Since $c_2 2^k \geq c_4 2^{k+1}$, there are at least $c_4 2^{k+1}$ pebbles on the graph continuously during $[t_1, t_2]$ and we have the desired conclusion.

In the fourth case none of the previous cases hold. Since $c_1 2^{k+1}$ outputs of $H(k + 1)$ are pebbled during $[t_a, t_b]$, there is an earliest time $t_1 \in [t_a, t_b]$ such that $c_1 2^k$ outputs of $H(k + 1)$ are pebbled in the interval $[t_a, t_1 - 1]$. Since the third case does not hold, there is a time $t_2 \leq t_1$ such that fewer than $c_2 2^k$ pebbles are on the graph at $t_2 - 1$ and at least $c_1 2^k$ outputs of $H(k + 1)$ are pebbled in the interval $[t_2, t_b]$. It follows that at least $c_1 2^k/2$ outputs of $SC_2(k)$ are pebbled during this interval. Since $c_1 2^k/2 \geq c_2 2^k + 1$, it follows from Problem 10.27 that at least $2^k - c_2 2^k \geq c_3 2^k$ inputs to $SC_2(k)$ (which are outputs to $H_2(k)$) are connected via pebble-free paths to the pebbled outputs of $SC_2(k)$ and must be pebbled during $[t_2, t_b]$. Since $c_3 2^k \geq c_1 2^k$, by the inductive hypothesis there is an interval $[t_d, t_e] \subseteq [t_2, t_b]$ during which at least $c_3 2^k$ inputs of $H_2(k)$ (which are outputs of $H_1(k)$) are pebbled and $c_4 2^k$ pebbles reside continuously on $H_2(k)$.

Since the second case does not hold, by an argument paralleling that given in the preceding paragraph there must be a time $t_3 \in [t_d, t_e]$ such that at most $c_3 2^k/2$ outputs of $H_1(k)$ are pebbled during $[t_d, t_3 - 1]$ and fewer than $c_2 2^k$ pebbles reside on $H(k + 1)$ at $t_c - 1$. Thus, during $[t_3, t_e]$ at least $c_3 2^k/2 \geq c_1 2^k$ outputs of $H_1(k)$ are pebbled from an initial configuration of fewer than $c_2 2^k$ pebbles. By the inductive hypothesis there is an interval $[t_f, t_g] \subseteq [t_3, t_e]$ during which at least $c_3 2^k$ inputs of $H_1(k)$ (which are outputs of $SC_1(k)$) are pebbled and $c_4 2^k$ pebbles reside on $H_1(k)$ continuously.

Since the first case does not hold, again paralleling an earlier argument there must be a time $t_4 \in [t_f, t_g]$ such that at most $c_3 2^k/2$ outputs of $SC_1(k)$ are pebbled during $[t_f, t_4 - 1]$ and fewer than $c_2 2^k$ pebbles reside on $H(k + 1)$ at $t_4 - 1$. Thus, during $[t_4, t_g]$ at least $c_3 2^k/2 \geq c_2 2^k + 1$ outputs of $SC_1(k)$ are pebbled from an initial configuration of fewer than $c_2 2^k$ pebbles. By Problem 10.27 at least $2^k - c_2 2^k \geq c_3 2^k$ inputs of $SC_1(k)$ are connected via pebble-free paths to the pebbled outputs. Thus at least $c_3 2^k$ corresponding inputs in both I_t and I_b must be pebbled for a total of at least $c_3 2^{k+1}$ inputs.

Since at least $c_4 2^k$ pebbles reside continuously on both $H_1(k)$ during $[t_d, t_e]$ and on $H_2(k)$ during $[t_f, t_g]$ and $[t_f, t_g] \subseteq [t_d, t_e]$, it follows that $c_4 2^k + c_4 2^k = c_4 2^{k+1}$ reside continuously on $H(k+1)$ during $[t_f, t_g]$. ∎

We are now ready to show the existence of a graph on n vertices that requires $\omega(n/\log n)$ minimal space.

THEOREM 10.8.1 *For integers $n \geq 1$ there exists a graph $G(n)$ in $\mathcal{G}(n, d)$ that requires minimum space $S_{\min}(G(n)) \geq c_5 n/\log n$ for some constant $c_5 > 0$.*

Proof For $n \geq 2^8$, let k be the largest integer such that $n(k) \leq n$; that is, $n(k) \leq n < n(k+1)$. Construct the graph $G(n)$ by adding $n - n(k)$ vertices and no edges to the graph $H(k)$. An optimal pebbling strategy for $G(n)$ pebbles the added vertices one at a time using one pebble, after which $H(k)$ is pebbled. From Lemma 10.8.3 it follows that pebbling $H(k)$ requires at least $c_4 2^k$ pebbles, since at least this many must reside on the graph at one time. Since $n(k+1) \leq 4n(k)$ for $k \geq 8$ and $c \geq 2$, it follows that $n/4 \leq n(k) \leq n$. This implies that $2^k \leq n$ and $k \leq \log_2 n$ and that $n/4 \leq k(c+2)2^k \leq (\log_2 n)(c+2)2^k$. From this we have $2^k \geq c_5 n/\log_2 n$, where $c_5 = 1/(4c + 8)$. The conclusion follows by observing that at least $(c_4 c_5)n/\log_2 n$ pebbles are needed to pebble $G(n)$. ∎

10.9 Branching Programs

The general branching program is a serial computational model that permits data-dependent computation, unlike the pebble game. A branching program is a directed graph consisting of a single starting vertex and in which vertices are labeled with predicates. Each vertex has one outgoing edge for each value of its predicate. (See, for example, Figs. 10.11 and 10.12.) Time in this model is the number of queries performed, and computations other than queries are not counted. The space used by a branching program is the base-2 logarithm of the number of vertices in its graph. Lower bounds on space and input time obtained with the branching program apply to within constant multiplicative factors to the pebble game and the RAM model. (See Section 10.9.1.)

As noted in Section 10.1.1, since the branching program reads inputs in a less constrained manner than the straight-line program, it may be possible to solve some problems with branching programs using less space or time than in the pebble game. As a consequence, space–time lower bounds for branching programs may be smaller than for the pebble game. Thus, if a problem is going to be solved with straight-line programs, such as an algebraic circuit, it is better to use lower bounds derived with the pebble game unless the branching program gives the same lower bounds. In particular, branching programs give smaller space–time lower bounds for integer multiplication and shifting (see Section 10.13.2) than does the pebble game.

We examine two kinds of branching programs in this section, general branching programs and decision branching programs.

DEFINITION 10.9.1 *A **multigraph** is a graph that may have more than one edge between two vertices. A **directed multigraph** is a multigraph in which each edge has a direction. A **directed acyclic multigraph** (DAM) is a multigraph with no directed cycles. A **rooted directed acyclic multigraph** is a multigraph with a **root vertex**, a vertex with no edges directed into it, and is such that every vertex can be reached via some path from the root. A **sink vertex** has no edges directed away from it.*

A **branching program** $\mathcal{P}$ *with input variables* $\boldsymbol{x}$ *over the set* $\mathcal{A}$ *and output variables* $\boldsymbol{y}$ *over the set* $\mathcal{F}$ *is a rooted directed acyclic multigraph that has a query* $q(\boldsymbol{x})$ *associated with each vertex except for sink vertices and has a query outcome associated with every edge directed away from a vertex. Each edge may also carry as a label the values of some output variables, with the proviso that each output variable is assigned exactly one value along any one path from the root to a sink vertex.*

The **decision branching program** is a special kind of branching program in which the queries $q(\boldsymbol{x})$ compare two variables and produce either the two outcomes $\{\leq, >\}$ or the three outcomes $\{<, =, >\}$. Figure 10.11 shows an example of a decision branching program that merges two 2-element sorted lists (u_1, u_2) and (v_1, v_2) $(u_1 \leq u_2$ and $v_1 \leq v_2)$ by using queries that compare the values of two input variables. Each vertex in the example has two out-directed edges corresponding to the results of the query. The outputs appear in sorted order along a path from the root to a leaf.

A **decision tree** is a decision branching program whose DAM (directed acyclic multigraph) is a tree. A decision tree may be constructed for a sequential comparison-based sorting algorithm, such as Batcher's odd-even merging algorithm of Section 6.8, by associating the first comparison with the root, the second comparisons with the roots of the left and right subtrees, etc.

DEFINITION 10.9.2 *A* **computation on a branching program** $\mathcal{P}$ *is a traversal of the unique path in the DAM from the root to a leaf determined by the values of the input variables in* $\boldsymbol{x} = (x_1, x_2, \ldots, x_n)$ *over the set* $\mathcal{A}$. *The* **output of the computation** *is the sequence of output values in* $\boldsymbol{y} = (y_1, y_2, \ldots, y_m)$ *over the set* $\mathcal{F}$ *encountered on the edges of the path traversed.*

A function $f^{(n)} : \mathcal{A}^n \mapsto \mathcal{F}^m$ *with input variables in* $\boldsymbol{x}$ *and output variables in* $\boldsymbol{y}$, *namely*

$$f^{(n)}(x_1, x_2, \ldots, x_n) = (y_1, y_2, \ldots, y_m)$$

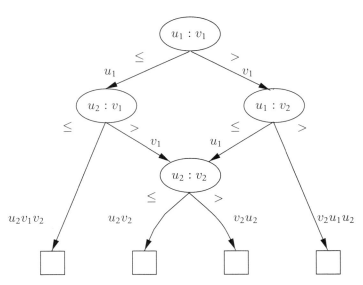

Figure 10.11 A decision branching program that merges the lists (u_1, u_2) and (v_1, v_2) when $u_1 \leq u_2$ and $v_1 \leq v_2$.

is **computed** *by* $\mathcal{P}$ *if for each value of* $\boldsymbol{x}$ *the correct value of each output variable appears exactly once on each path from the root to a leaf.*

The **time associated with a computation** *is the length of the path traversed by the computation. The* **computation time** T **of a branching program** *is the length of its longest path.*

In Fig. 10.11 the computation associated with the input values $(u_1, u_2, v_1, v_2) = (2, 4, 1, 3)$ takes the right branch out of the root and produces the output value $v_1 = 1$, takes the left branch at the next vertex and produces $u_1 = 2$, and takes the right branch at the last vertex and produces $v_2 = 3$ and $u_2 = 4$. The output of this computation is the sorted sequence 1, 2, 3, 4, as expected. This branching program merges the two sorted lists. Each sink vertex corresponds to one of the four ways of merging the two lists. The computation time of this branching program is 3.

Branching programs that compare elements at vertices are well suited to merging and sorting but are not of the most general type.

DEFINITION 10.9.3 *A* **general branching program** $\mathcal{P}$ *with input variables* $\boldsymbol{x}$ *over a finite set* $\mathcal{A}$ *has a query of the form* $x_i = ?$ *associated with a variable* x_i *at each vertex. It also has one edge directed away from the vertex for each value of* x_i. *A general branching program is* **non-redundant** *if along each path from the root to a leaf a query* $x_i = ?$ *appears at most once.*

The general branching program is also known as a **binary decision diagram (BDD)**. BDD's are widely used in the computer-aided design (CAD) of circuits for Boolean functions.

A general branching program that convolves two short binary sequences over the integers is shown in Fig. 10.12. (Convolution is defined in Section 6.7.4.) A computation leaves the left branch of a vertex when the associated variable has value 0 and the right branch when it

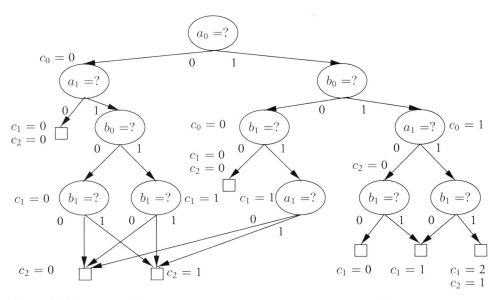

Figure 10.12 A general branching program to compute the convolution of two sequences (a_0, a_1) and (b_0, b_1).

has value 1. This branching program computes the convolution $c = a \otimes b$ of the sequences $a = (a_0, a_1)$ and $b = (b_0, b_1)$; that is,

$$c_0 = a_0 b_0, \quad c_1 = a_0 b_1 + a_1 b_0, \quad c_2 = a_1 b_1$$

The performance of a branching program is also measured by its space complexity.

DEFINITION 10.9.4 *The* **space** *used by branching program $\mathcal{P}$ is the base-2 logarithm of the number of vertices in its directed acyclic multigraph.*

As shown in the next section, this definition permits a lower bound on the space complexity used by any reasonable general-purpose computer model equipped with a random-access read-only memory for its input data.

The following lemma demonstrates that every decision branching program can be simulated by a general branching program, thereby showing the latter to be more general than the former. (See Problem 10.35.)

LEMMA 10.9.1 *Every decision branching program with variables over a finite set $\mathcal{A}$ with computation time T and space S can be simulated by a general branching program with computation time $2T$ and space $S + \log(|\mathcal{A}| + 1)$.*

This result is proved by constructing a general branching program to simulate a comparison operator and substituting it for the comparison operator in a decision branching program. (See Problem 10.35.) The graph that results from this construction is explicitly a multigraph.

While Lemma 10.9.1 establishes that decision branching programs are no more powerful than general branching programs, this does not imply that general branching programs require less space. In fact, the space complexity of a given decision branching program is independent of the size of the set $\mathcal{A}$ over which the variables are defined; this is not true for general branching programs.

If space complexity is not an issue, a **tree program** can be constructed. This is a branching program whose DAM is a tree. The following recursive procedure converts a branching program to a tree program: a) If any immediate descendant of the root has more than one edge directed into it, make as many copies of the submultigraph rooted at that descendant as there are entering edges and direct exactly one edge into each. b) Apply this procedure recursively to each of the submultigraphs until leaf vertices are reached. This procedure does not change the length of any path in the original DAM or the computation time.

The notions of space and time can be generalized to average time and space when a probability distribution is defined on input values. (See Problem 10.37.)

Below we present a key lemma used to derive lower bounds on the space–time product. This lemma is stated for **normal-form branching programs**, general branching programs whose DAMs are **level multigraphs**, that is, multigraphs in which each vertex has a level and adjacent vertices are in adjacent levels. An example of such a graph is shown in Fig. 10.13.

LEMMA 10.9.2 *If there is a general branching program of space S and computation time T for a function f, then there is a normal-form branching program for f that has space $2S$ and computation time T.*

Proof To convert a general branching program to a normal-form branching program, create $T + 1$ copies of the general branching program, one for each time step including the zeroth.

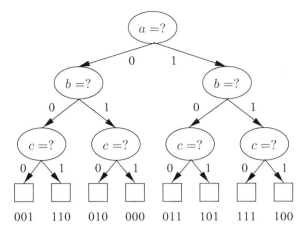

Figure 10.13 A normal-form tree program for table lookup. It has one path for each value of the input.

Delete the original edges and add an edge from vertex u in the ith copy to vertex v in the $(i + 1)$st copy if there was an edge between u and v in the original graph. Now delete all edges and vertices that are not reached from the root of the zeroth branching program. (See Fig. 10.14.)

This procedure increases the number of vertices by at most a factor of T, thereby increasing the space by adding at most $\log T$. However, a branching program with space S has 2^S vertices. Thus, the length of the longest path through the program T cannot exceed 2^S, or $S + \log T \leq 2S$. ∎

Generally the space S used for a branching program computation will be large by comparison with $\log T$, in which case the space bounds for normal-form branching programs and general branching programs will differ by at most a constant factor.

In the rest of this chapter when we speak of a branching program we mean a general branching program.

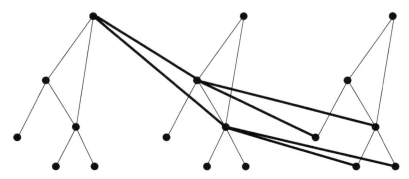

Figure 10.14 Construction of a normal-form general branching program as a level multigraph.

We close this section by describing a normal-form tree program for **table lookup**, an important programming tool that can be used to compute an arbitrary function $f^{(n)} : \mathcal{A}^n \mapsto \mathcal{A}^m$ on n variables whose value is an m-tuple. Each of the n variables is read and the value of the function is found in a table. This is simulated by a tree program with branching factor $|\mathcal{A}|$ in which the variables are read in succession until they are all read, at which point the value of the function is provided. An example of such a tree program for a function $f^{(3)} : \mathcal{B}^3 \mapsto \mathcal{B}^3$ is shown in Fig. 10.13. There is one path through the tree for each of the possible $|\mathcal{A}|^n$ assignments to the n inputs. The sink vertices are labeled by the appropriate m-tuple. Such table-lookup tree programs have computation time n and space proportional to $n \log |\mathcal{A}|$ since they have $(|\mathcal{A}|^{n+1} - 1)/(|\mathcal{A}| - 1)$ vertices with A edges per vertex except for those at the lowest level.

10.9.1 Branching Programs and Other Models

We begin this section with a comparison of branching programs and pebble games and conclude with a brief comparison of branching programs and the RAM model of computation.

The pebble model assumes that computation is serial and straight-line. If all algorithms used for a particular problem are of this type, the pebble game is the appropriate model, especially if the lower bounds on space–time exchanges are larger than those provided by the branching program model. (All algorithms used today for integer multiplication are straight-line and the lower bounds on the space–time product for this problem are larger with the pebble game than with the branching program model.) If the two models give the same lower bounds, then we can invoke Lemma 10.9.3 to derive lower bounds on the space–time exchanges for pebbling from those for branching programs when $\log_2 T_{\mathcal{P}}$ is small by comparison with $S_{\mathcal{P}}$, where $T_{\mathcal{P}}$ and $S_{\mathcal{P}}$ are the time and space used by the pebbling model.

Data-dependent reading of inputs may allow the branching program to perform a computation more quickly than the pebbling model. For example, merging requires a space–time product that is quadratic in the length of the input strings with the pebble game but only linear in the branching program. (See Section 10.10.2.) This demonstrates that the branching program is a much more natural model for this problem.

If the lower bounds derived with the branching program are comparable in strength to those offered by the pebbling model, as is true for most of the problems considered in this chapter, straight-line programs are the better model for these problems. But the extra flexibility offered by branching programs means that when their results are comparable to those provided by the pebble game, one must work harder to obtain them. (See Sections 10.11 and 10.12.)

The branching program measures the time to read inputs but ignores the time for computations and the production of outputs. By contrast, the pebble game measures the time to read inputs, perform computations, and produce outputs. Although the time for computations generally cannot be ignored, the methods available today to derive lower bounds for both models are based on the time spent reading inputs. But while for many problems the time to read inputs dominates computation time for many values of space, when space is large the pebbling model has the potential to give larger lower bounds than the branching program model. For example, no way is known to compute the n-point DFT with fewer than $\Theta(n \log n)$ steps, the number used by the FFT algorithm, although in the limit of large space the branching program gives a lower bound on space proportional to n.

To simulate the pebbling of a DAG by a branching program we must give an **interpretation** to each vertex of the DAG: assign an operation to each non-input vertex and a variable as well as values to each input vertex. Two different interpretations of a DAG may yield different branching programs. Of course, a DAG is pebbled without regard to the interpretation of vertices: the pebble-game lower bounds use only the fact that vertices can hold one of $|\mathcal{A}|$ values and do not depend explicitly on the interpretation given to their operator.

LEMMA 10.9.3 *Given a pebbling $\mathcal{P}$ of an interpreted directed acyclic graph G that uses $S_\mathcal{P}$ pebbles and $T_\mathcal{P}$ input steps to compute a function with operations over a finite set $\mathcal{A}$, there is a branching program with space $S_\mathcal{P} \log |\mathcal{A}| + \log (2T_\mathcal{P})$ and time $T_\mathcal{P}$ that computes the function computed by G. Thus, if $2T_\mathcal{P} \leq |\mathcal{A}|^{S_\mathcal{P}}$, simultaneous lower bounds on the space and time for a branching program for the function imply simultaneous lower bounds on space and time in the pebble game that differ by at most constant multiplicative factors.*

Proof We construct a branching program $\mathcal{Q}$ to simulate the pebbling $\mathcal{P}$ of a directed acyclic graph that uses $S_\mathcal{P}$ pebbles and $T_\mathcal{P}$ steps. (Figure 10.15 illustrates the construction of such a branching program.) Initially the branching program has a single vertex, the root, which is labeled with the first variable to be pebbled according to $\mathcal{P}$. Advance the first pebble as far as possible. Create a vertex in the branching program for each value of the operation or input covered by the first pebble. Label these new vertices with the name of the second input to be pebbled and attach an edge from the root vertex to these new vertices labeled with the corresponding value for the first input. Advance pebbles as far as possible according to $\mathcal{P}$ and create one new vertex in the branching program for each different tuple of values

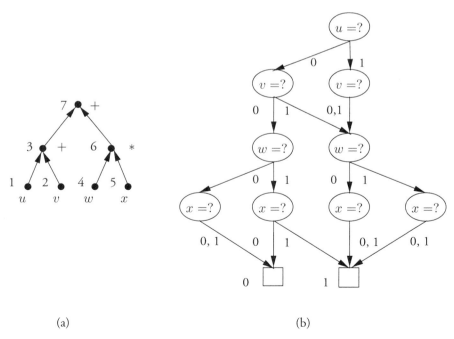

(a)   (b)

Figure 10.15 A general branching program (b) that simulates the pebbling of a DAG (a) in the vertex order 1, 2, 4, 3, 5, 6, 7. The DAG input variables are denoted u, v, w, and x and assume values in $\{0, 1\}$. + denotes OR and $*$ denotes AND.

residing under the pebble(s) currently on the DAG. (In the example of Fig. 10.15, after placing a pebble on the second vertex we advance a pebble to the third vertex and remove all other pebbles. Thus, only two vertices are added to the branching program at this step.) Label the new vertices with the third input to be pebbled. Now repeat the above process by advancing pebbles as far as possible (in the example, pebbles now reside on the third and fourth vertices), add one new vertex for each tuple of pebbles on the DAG (four vertices are added), and connect edges from the previous to the current set of new vertices that conform to the values assumed at the vertices of the DAG. This process is repeated until all inputs have been pebbled.

Since the values of operations are always determined by the values under at most $S_\mathcal{P}$ pebbles, the number of new vertices added in $\mathcal{Q}$ with the pebbling of each new input vertex in G is most $|\mathcal{A}|^{S_\mathcal{P}}$. Since $T_\mathcal{P}$ input vertices of G are pebbled, it follows that $\mathcal{Q}$ has at most $T_\mathcal{P}|\mathcal{A}|^{S_\mathcal{P}} + 1 \le 2T_\mathcal{P}|\mathcal{A}|^{S_\mathcal{P}}$ vertices, from which the conclusion follows. ∎

A branching program can also simulate a computation by a general model of computation, such as the RAM discussed in Section 3.4, as we now show. Let the RAM have M b-bit words of memory and a finite number of b-bit words in its CPU. Consider any program for such a machine. Its **state** is determined by the values in its registers and memory locations. Thus the RAM has at most $O(2^{Mb})$ states. Let the **space used by a RAM** be the base-2 logarithm of the number of its states. Let the RAM execute T_{RAM} steps to read its inputs. We simulate this computation in the same fashion as with the pebble game. After reading an input variable, the branching program enters one of at most $O(2^{Mb})$ vertices corresponding to states of the RAM. Since the RAM reads inputs on T_{RAM} steps, the branching program also takes T_{RAM} steps and has at most $O(T_{\mathrm{RAM}}2^{Mb})$ vertices or uses space of at most $O(Mb + \log T_{\mathrm{RAM}})$. As long as Mb is larger than some multiple of $\log T_{\mathrm{RAM}}$, simultaneous lower bounds on the time to read inputs and space of a branching program for a function computed by the RAM serve as lower bounds on the same quantities on the RAM. The following lemma summarizes this discussion.

LEMMA 10.9.4 *Given a RAM program that uses space S_{RAM} and T_{RAM} input steps to compute $f : \mathcal{A}^n \mapsto \mathcal{A}^m$ there is a branching program with space $O(S_{\mathrm{RAM}} + \log{(2T_{\mathrm{RAM}})})$ and time T_{RAM} that computes f. Thus, if $2T_{\mathrm{RAM}} \le 2^{S_{\mathrm{RAM}}}$, simultaneous lower bounds on the space and time for a branching program for the function imply simultaneous lower bounds on the space and time on the RAM that differ by at most constant multiplicative factors.*

10.10 Straight-Line Versus Branching Programs

In this section we show that some problems can use space and time more efficiently with branching programs than they can with the pebble game. We demonstrate this for the cyclic shifting function $f_{\mathrm{cyclic}}^{(n)} : \mathcal{B}^{n+\lceil \log n \rceil} \mapsto \mathcal{B}^n$ introduced in Section 2.5.2 and the merging problem introduced in Section 6.8. However, for all of the other problems studied in this chapter the lower bounds obtained with these two models are the same up to constant multiplicative factors, except for integer multiplication, where the branching program bound is smaller by a factor of $\log^2 n$.

It is important to note, however, that the superiority of branching programs arises from the assumption that inputs can be read in a data-dependent fashion, an assumption that is not available to straight-line programs. As we know from Problem 10.20, if branching is allowed but inputs must be read in a data-independent fashion by an input-output-oblivious finite-state machine, Theorem 10.4.1 applies. Thus, branching programs that read inputs in a data-independent fashion have no advantage over straight-line programs, at least in terms of lower bounds on space–time exchanges.

10.10.1   Efficient Branching Programs for Cyclic Shift

We present a branching program for $f_{\text{cyclic}}^{(n)}$ that uses space $S = O(\log n)$ and time $T = n + \lceil \log n \rceil$; that is, $ST = O(n \log n)$, a product that is much less than the $\Theta(n^2)$ product required in the pebble game. (See Section 10.5.2.)

The function $f_{\text{cyclic}}^{(n)}$ has $n + \lceil \log n \rceil$ Boolean variables, $\lceil \log n \rceil$ control inputs, and n "value" inputs whose values are shifted by the amount specified by the control inputs. Our efficient branching program is a tree program (see Fig. 10.13) that reads the control inputs and selects one of n paths through the tree. (Note that $n \leq 2^{\lceil \log_2 n \rceil} \leq 2n$.) Each path corresponds to one of the n possible cyclic shifts of the n value inputs. Attached to a leaf of this tree is a chain of vertices, one per value input. These inputs appear in the order specified by the cyclic shift associated with the path. An input value is read and then produced as output at each of these n vertices. Since this branching program has at most $2n + 2n^2$ vertices, it has space $O(\log n)$. It uses time $n + \lceil \log n \rceil$.

If cyclic shifting is to be done by a straight-line program, say in hardware, then it is better to use the pebble game for lower bounds since this model applies to logic circuits and the results it provides are stronger. However, if the problem is to be executed in software, the branching program should be used unless the program is straight-line.

10.10.2   Efficient Branching Programs for Merging

Consider now the merging problem. In Section 10.5.6 we show that it requires an $\Omega(n^2)$ space–time product where n is the size of the input. However, when executed by a branching program it uses space $O(\log n)$ and time $O(n)$, as we show.

Figure 10.11 shows a "pyramid" decision branching program to merge two sequences of length two. It is straightforward to extend this decision branching program to sequences of length n, as suggested in Fig. 10.16. In this figure vertices are labeled by the number of elements that are removed from the two lists being merged before arriving at the vertex carrying the label. For example, prior to arriving at the vertex labeled $(2, 1)$, two elements have been removed from the left list and one from the right list. We assume that the lists to be merged each contain n elements. Thus, all the pyramid vertices below a vertex labeled with (n, k) or (k, n), $1 \leq k \leq n - 1$, are deleted because below such vertices no further comparisons are needed; the outputs produced are those on the list from which k values have been removed. Thus, we attach a chain of $n - k$ vertices, one for each of the input values at the end of the smaller list. If the root is at level 1, vertices labeled (n, k) and (k, n) are at level $n + k + 1 \leq 2n + 1$.

The number of vertices on level l of this decision branching program is at most l. Since $1 \leq l \leq 2n$, it has at most $\sum_{l=1}^{2n+1} l = (n + 1)(2n + 1)$ vertices. The space associated with this program is $O(\log(n + 1)(2n + 1))$. Since the length of the longest path in this program is $2n$, it has time $2n$ associated with it. From Lemma 10.9.2 it follows that merging can be

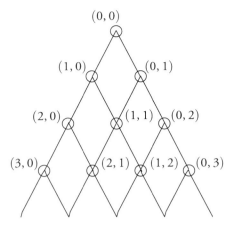

Figure 10.16 The top portion of a decision branching program to merge two sorted lists. The pair of integers at a vertex denotes the number of elements removed from the left and right lists by the program before arriving at the vertex carrying the pair.

realized by a general branching program with space $O(\log n) + \log |\mathcal{A}|$ and time $O(n)$ or a space–time product that is $O(n \log n)$, much smaller than the $O(n^2)$ space–time product that applies to the pebble game.

10.11 The Borodin-Cook Lower-Bound Method

In this section we generalize the method of Borodin and Cook [53] for deriving space-time lower bounds for branching programs. The conditions under which lower bounds can be derived are captured by a property of functions called $(\phi, \lambda, \mu, \nu, \tau)$-distinguishability, which is stronger than the flow property used to derive lower bounds on space-time tradeoffs for the pebble game. In fact, we show that a function that is $(1, \lambda, \mu, \nu, \tau)$-distinguishable has a $(1/\nu, m, \tau)$-flow.

DEFINITION 10.11.1 *Let $\tau : \mathbf{N} \mapsto \mathbf{N}$ be a nondecreasing function. A function $f : \mathcal{A}^n \mapsto \mathcal{F}^m$ is $(\phi, \lambda, \mu, \nu, \tau)$-**distinguishable** for $0 \leq \phi, \lambda, \mu, \nu \leq 1$ if there is a set $\mathcal{D} \subset \mathcal{A}^n$ satisfying $|\mathcal{D}| \geq \phi |\mathcal{A}|^n$ such that for each assignment to a selection of $a \leq \lambda n$ input variables and each assignment to a selection of $b \leq \mu m$ output variables of f, $a \leq \tau(b)$, the number of input n-tuples consistent with the values of the a input variables that cause f to assume the given values for the b output variables is at most $|\mathcal{A}|^{n-a-\nu b}$.*

The meaning of this property for the function f is suggested by Fig. 10.17. For a fraction of ϕ of the input tuples ($\phi = 1$ is the normal case), when any a input variables and any b output variables of f are assigned values, the maximum number of input n-tuples that cause f to produce these output values is no more than $|\mathcal{A}|^{n-a-\nu b}$. This property is used below to derive a lower bound on the space-time product for branching programs. We use $\phi = 1$ for all problems considered below except for the unique elements problem.

This theorem also uses a version of the pigeonhole principle. Time is subdivided into intervals containing equal numbers of input queries. This has the effect of chopping the

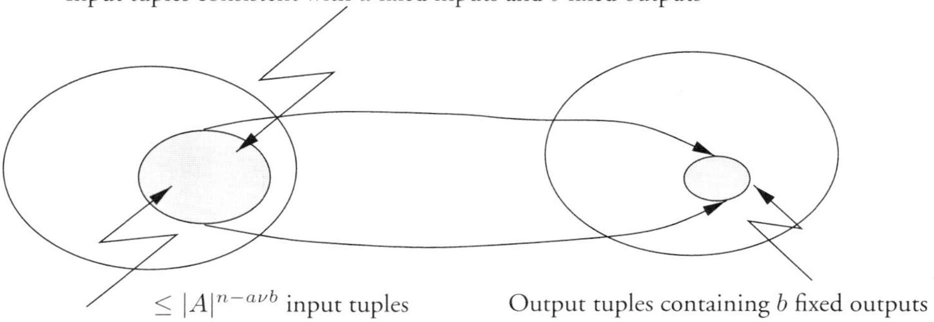

Input tuples consistent with a fixed inputs and b fixed outputs

$\leq |A|^{n-a\nu b}$ input tuples   Output tuples containing b fixed outputs

Figure 10.17 For a fraction of at least ϕ of the input n-tuples, an $(\phi, \lambda, \mu, \nu, \tau)$-distinguishable function f has an upper limit of $|\mathcal{A}|^{n-a-\nu b}$ on the number of input n-tuples consistent with an assignment of values to any a inputs and any b outputs of f when $a \leq \lambda n$, $b \leq \mu m$ and $a \leq \tau(b)$.

branching program up into layers (called stages in the proof). We reason that each input n-tuple follows a rich path through a layer that contains a large number of outputs. Because of the distinguishability property, an upper limit on the number of inputs can be associated with each rich path. It follows that there must be many rich paths or that the branching program must have a large number of vertices (and space).

THEOREM 10.11.1 *Let* $f : \mathcal{A}^n \mapsto \mathcal{F}^m$ *be* $(\phi, \lambda, \mu, \nu, \tau)$-*distinguishable for* $\lambda \leq \mu$. *Then the space S and time $T \geq n$ required by any general branching program $\mathcal{P}$ that computes f must satisfy*

$$S \geq \frac{m\nu a}{4T} \log_2 |\mathcal{A}| + \frac{1}{2} \log_2 \phi$$

where $a \leq \lambda n$ is the largest integer satisfying $a \leq \tau(ma/2T)$ and $n > (\lceil 1/\lambda \rceil - 2)/(1 - \lambda(\lceil 1/\lambda \rceil - 1))$. (Note that $\log_2 \phi$ is a negative constant.)

Proof We show that $S \geq m\nu a/2T \log_2 |\mathcal{A}| + \log_2 \phi$ for normal-form branching programs and then invoke Lemma 10.9.2 to apply it to a general branching program with space $2S$ and time T.

The approach is to break $\mathcal{P}$ into $\sigma = \lceil (T+1)/(a+1) \rceil$ disjoint stages starting with the root at the zeroth level, each stage of which contains $a + 1$ levels, $a \leq \lambda n$, except possibly for the last, which may have fewer levels. ($\sigma \leq 2T/a$ since $T \geq n \geq 1$.) Each stage has depth a. Thus, the last row in one stage is the first row in the next stage. Each stage except for the first typically has multiple roots. (Figure 10.18(a) shows a branching program with $T = 5$ levels. Since $a = 2$, it is divided into $\sigma = \lceil (T+1)/(a+1) \rceil = 2$ layers by the horizontal line. Internal vertices belong to two layers.)

Using a modified version of the technique described on page 491 to create a tree program from a branching program, replace the branching program in each stage by a set of tree programs of depth a, shown in Fig. 10.18(b). Eliminate redundant queries on each path in each tree. Also, pad paths that do not have a queries on them with superfluous but non-redundant queries so that each path through each tree has the same length. A **superfluous**

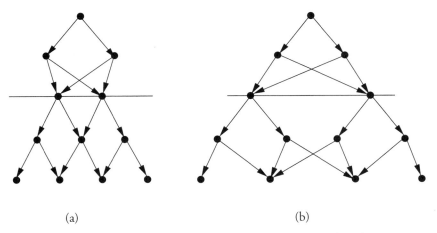

(a)   (b)

Figure 10.18 The transformation of a T-step branching program into a branching program with $\sigma = \lceil (T+1)/(a+1) \rceil$ layers in which each layer consists of a forest of trees.

query has all of its output edges directed to a single successor vertex. Also, move all tree outputs down to the leaves of these trees (which are also roots of trees in the next stage). Let $\mathcal{P}^*$ be the new branching program. Since the roots of trees in each stage are vertices in the original branching program, there are no more than 2^S trees.

Let $\boldsymbol{x}$ be one of the input n-tuples among the fraction ϕ for which $(\phi, \lambda, \mu, \nu, \tau)$-distinguishability is defined. The path through $\mathcal{P}^*$ defined by $\boldsymbol{x}$ passes through σ stages. Therefore, there must be at least one stage containing a tree path that produces at least $b = \lceil m/\sigma \rceil$ outputs (a **rich path**). (As shown in the last paragraph of this proof, $b \leq \lceil \mu m \rceil$ when $\lambda \leq \mu$ for sufficiently large n.) Thus, $\boldsymbol{x}$ defines at least one rich path. Let $a \leq \tau(b)$. Because the function $f : \mathcal{A}^n \mapsto \mathcal{F}^m$ is $(\phi, \lambda, \mu, \nu, \tau)$-distinguishable, each rich path can be associated with at most $|\mathcal{A}|^{n-a-\nu b}$ inputs. (This number is smaller if more than b outputs are produced.) Since there are at most 2^S trees and at most $|\mathcal{A}|^a$ paths through each tree, there are at most $2^S |\mathcal{A}|^a$ rich paths. Furthermore, two distinct rich paths (either the inputs queried or outputs produced are different) are associated with disjoint sets of input n-tuples. Thus, $2^S |\mathcal{A}|^a |\mathcal{A}|^{n-a-\nu b}$ cannot be less than the number of input n-tuples in question, from which the following inequality holds:

$$\phi |\mathcal{A}|^n \leq 2^S |\mathcal{A}|^a |\mathcal{A}|^{n-a-\nu b}$$

We conclude that

$$S \geq \nu b \log_2 |\mathcal{A}| + \frac{1}{2} \log_2 \phi$$

We replace $b = \lceil m/\sigma \rceil$ by its lower bound $ma/2T$. Since $\tau(b)$ is a nondecreasing function, the value of a satisfying $a \leq \tau(b)$ is not increased by replacing b by $ma/2T$. Thus, $S \geq \nu(ma/2T) \log_2 |\mathcal{A}| + \log_2 \phi$, subject to $a \leq \tau(ma/2T)$ and $a \leq \lambda n$.

We show there exists an integer n_α such that for $n > n_\alpha$ the condition $b \leq \lceil \mu m \rceil$ is met by the condition $\lambda \leq \mu$. Note that $b = \lceil m/\sigma \rceil$ is a nondecreasing function of a and a nonincreasing function of T since $\sigma = \lceil (T+1)/(a+1) \rceil$ is a nonincreasing function of a and a nondecreasing function of T. Thus, b is largest when $T = n$ and $a = \lambda n$. It follows that b is largest when $\sigma = \lceil (n+1)/(\lambda n + 1) \rceil \leq \lceil 1/\lambda \rceil$. If $n > (\lceil 1/\lambda \rceil - 2)/(1 - \lambda(\lceil 1/\lambda \rceil - 1))$, then $(n+1)/(\lambda n + 1) > \lceil 1/\lambda \rceil - 1$, which implies that $\lceil (n+1)/(\lambda n + 1) \rceil = \lceil 1/\lambda \rceil$. In other words, when $n > (\lceil 1/\lambda \rceil - 2)/(1 - \lambda(\lceil 1/\lambda \rceil - 1))$, b assumes a value of at most $\lceil m/\lceil 1/\lambda \rceil \rceil \leq \lceil \lambda m \rceil$. ∎

COROLLARY 10.11.1 *Let $f : \mathcal{A}^n \mapsto \mathcal{F}^m$ be $(\phi, \lambda, \mu, \nu, \tau)$-distinguishable for $\lambda \leq \mu$ and $\tau(b) = n$. Then the space S and time T required by any normal-form branching program $\mathcal{P}$ that computes f must satisfy*

$$ST \geq \frac{mn\lambda\nu}{2} \log_2 |\mathcal{A}| + \log_2 \phi$$

when $T \geq n$ and $n > (\lceil 1/\lambda \rceil - 2)/(1 - \lambda(\lceil 1/\lambda \rceil - 1))$.

Proof The result follows from the observation that the maximum value of a in Theorem 10.11.1 is λn. ∎

The connection between the $(1/\nu, m, p)$-flow property and $(1, \lambda, \mu, \nu, \tau)$-distinguishability is given below.

LEMMA 10.11.1 *If $f : \mathcal{A}^n \mapsto \mathcal{F}^m$ is $(1, \lambda, \mu, \nu, \tau)$-distinguishable, it has a $(1/\nu, m, \tau^*)$-flow for $\tau^*(x) = \min(\tau(x), \lambda n, \tau(\mu m))$.*

Proof Consider sets of a input and b output variables to f such that $a \leq \tau(b)$, $a \leq \lambda n$, and $b \leq \mu m$, or equivalently $a \leq \tau^*(b)$, where $\tau^*(x) = \min(\tau(x), \lambda n, \tau(\mu m))$ since $\tau(x)$ is nondecreasing in x. For any particular assignment to the a inputs, the input n-tuples that agree with this assignment but lead to different values for the b outputs must be disjoint, as suggested in Fig. 10.19. We show that for some assignment of values to the a inputs, the number of values assumed by the b outputs is more than $|\mathcal{A}|^{b/\alpha - 1}$ for $\alpha = 1/\nu$. Suppose not. Then there are at most $|\mathcal{A}|^{n-a-\nu b}|\mathcal{A}|^{\nu b - 1}$ input tuples for each assignment to the a inputs, or a total of at most $|\mathcal{A}|^{n-1}$ input tuples. Since f has $|\mathcal{A}|^n$ input tuples, we have a contradiction. Therefore, f has a $(1/\mu, m, \tau^*)$-flow. ∎

The following lemma makes it easier to derive space-time lower bounds for branching programs. It uses the notions of subfunction (see Definition 2.4.2) and reduction (see Definition 2.4.1).

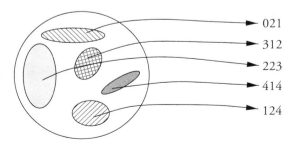

Figure 10.19 On the left are the points in the domain of f that map to individual output b-tuples when the values of a input variables are fixed.

LEMMA 10.11.2 *Let $g : \mathcal{A}^r \mapsto \mathcal{A}^s$ be a reduction of $f : \mathcal{A}^n \mapsto \mathcal{A}^m$ that is either a subfunction or a reduction obtained by restricting f to a subset of its domain. A lower bound to the space-time product ST on branching programs for g is also a lower bound for f.*

Proof Given any branching program for f, we can construct one for g that has no more vertices or longer paths as follows. If g is obtained by deleting outputs, delete these outputs from vertices in the branching program. This may allow the coalescing of vertices. If g is obtained by restricting the set of values that variables of f can assume, this may make some paths and subgraphs inaccessible and therefore removable. If g is obtained by giving two variables of f the same identity, this constrains the branching program and again may make some subgraphs inaccessible. In all cases neither the number of vertices nor the length of any path to a sink vertex is increased by the reduction of f to g. Thus, any lower bound to ST for g must be a lower bound for f. ∎

10.12 Properties of "nice" and "ok" Matrices*

In this section we develop properties of matrices that are γ-nice or γ-ok, concepts we now introduce. (A matrix that is γ-nice is also γ-ok.) These properties are used in Section 10.13 to develop lower bounds on the exchange of space for time using the Borodin-Cook method. This section requires a knowledge of probability theory.

DEFINITION 10.12.1 *An $n \times m$ matrix A, $n \leq m$, is γ-**nice** for $0 < \gamma < 1/2$ if and only if for all $p \leq \lceil \gamma n \rceil$ and $q \geq n - \lceil \gamma n \rceil$ every $p \times q$ submatrix of A has rank p. Such a matrix is γ-**ok** if all such $p \times q$ submatrices have rank at least γp.*

As shown below, most matrices are γ-nice, a fact that is used in several places.

LEMMA 10.12.1 *At least a fraction $(1 - |\mathcal{A}|^{-1}(2/3)^{\gamma n})$ of the $|\mathcal{A}|^{n^2}$ $n \times n$ matrices over a subset $\mathcal{A}$ of a field, $|\mathcal{A}| \geq 2$, are γ-nice for some constant γ, $0 < \gamma < \frac{1}{2}$, independent of n and $\mathcal{A}$. This result also holds for $n \times n$ Toeplitz matrices, matrices $[t_{i,j}]$ with the property that $t_{i,j} = a_{i-j}$; that is, all elements on each diagonal are the same.*

Proof Let $r = \lceil \gamma n \rceil$ and $s = n - r$. The proof is established by deriving upper bounds on the number $N(r,s)$ of $r \times s$ matrices in an $n \times n$ matrix M and the probability $q(r,s)$ that any particular $r \times s$ matrix fails to contain a non-singular $r \times r$ submatrix (it fails to have **rank** r) when each entry in M is equally likely to be an element of $\mathcal{A}$. Since the probability of a union of events is at most the sum of the probabilities of the events, the probability that some $r \times s$ matrix fails to have rank r is at most $q(r,s)N(r,s)$.

It is straightforward to show that

$$N(r, s) = \binom{n}{r}^2$$

since an $r \times s$ submatrix of an $n \times n$ matrix is chosen by selecting a set of r rows and a set of s columns and each can be chosen in $\binom{n}{r}$ ways. (Note that $\binom{n}{s} = \binom{n}{r}$.) We now show that the binomial coefficient $\binom{n}{r}$ is at most $(n/r)^r e^r$. We use the fact that $n!/(n-r)! = n(n-1)\cdots(n-r+1) \leq n^r$ and the observation that $r^r/r!$ is a term in the Taylor-series expansion of e^r, as stated below:

$$\binom{n}{r} = \frac{n!}{r!(n-r)!} \leq \frac{n^r}{r!} = \left(\frac{n}{r}\right)^r \frac{r^r}{r!} \leq \left(\frac{n}{r}\right)^r e^r$$

Later we show that $q(r,s) \leq \rho^{-s} |\mathcal{A}|^{r-1}$, where $\rho = |\mathcal{A}|^2/(2|\mathcal{A}|-1) \leq 2|\mathcal{A}|/3$, from which it follows that

$$q(r,s)N(r,s) \leq |\mathcal{A}|^{-1} \left(\frac{en}{r}\right)^{2r} \rho^{-n} \rho^r |\mathcal{A}|^r$$

$$\leq |\mathcal{A}|^{-1} \left(\frac{2}{3}\right)^r \left[\rho^{-n} \left(\frac{en|\mathcal{A}|}{r}\right)^{2r}\right]$$

since $s = n - r$. Elementary calculus shows that $(e|\mathcal{A}|/r)^{2r}$ is an increasing function of r and that it has value 1 at $r = 0$. Since $r = \lceil \gamma n \rceil$ and $\rho \geq 4/3$, it follows that the quantity in square brackets is less than 1 for some value of $0 < \gamma < 1/2$, which is the desired conclusion.

We now give a proof by induction that $q(r,s)$ satisfies $q(r,s) \leq \rho^{-s}|\mathcal{A}|^{r-1}$. Clearly $q(1,1) \leq 1/|\mathcal{A}|$, since at most one entry in $\mathcal{A}$ is zero. This satisfies the bound. We now assume the inductive hypothesis holds for $q(r-1, s-1)$ and $q(r, s-1)$ and show that it holds for $q(r,s)$.

Consider an $r \times s$ matrix B. It has rank r if the submatrix consisting of the first $s - 1$ columns has rank r. (This occurs with probability $1 - q(r, s-1)$.) If this is not the case, there are many other ways in which it can have rank r. In particular, this is true if the submatrix C consisting of the last $r - 1$ rows and the first $s - 1$ columns of B has rank $r - 1$ (with probability $1 - q(r-1, s-1)$) and the element $b_{1,s}$ has an appropriate value (with probability at least $1 - 1/|\mathcal{A}|$), as we now show.

Consider a submatrix D consisting of some $r - 1$ linearly independent columns of C. Consider the $r \times r$ submatrix of B consisting of these same $r - 1$ columns and its last column. When the determinant of this matrix is expanded on the first row, the multiplier of $b_{1,s}$ is ± 1 times the determinant of D, which is non-zero. Thus, there is at most one value for $b_{1,s}$ that causes the determinant to be zero (the field element causing it to be zero may not be in the set $\mathcal{A}$) or at least $|\mathcal{A}| - 1$ values that cause it to be non-zero. Summarizing this result, we have the following lower bound:

$$1 - q(r,s) \geq 1 - q(r, s-1) + (1 - q(r-1, s-1)) \left(1 - \frac{1}{|\mathcal{A}|}\right)$$

$$\geq (1 - q(r, s-1)) \frac{1}{|\mathcal{A}|} + (1 - q(r-1, s-1)) \left(1 - \frac{1}{|\mathcal{A}|}\right)$$

This implies that

$$q(r,s) \leq q(r, s-1) \frac{1}{|\mathcal{A}|} + q(r-1, s-1) \left(1 - \frac{1}{|\mathcal{A}|}\right)$$

$$\leq \rho^{-s+1} |\mathcal{A}|^{r-1} \frac{1}{|\mathcal{A}|} \left(2 - \frac{1}{|\mathcal{A}|}\right)$$

$$\leq \rho^{-s} |\mathcal{A}|^{r-1}$$

which is the desired conclusion.

The proof also holds for Toeplitz matrices (each element on a diagonal of the matrix is the same) because we reasoned only about the value of elements in the upper right-hand corner of submatrices that are on different diagonals. ∎

The Kronecker product of matrices is used in Section 10.13.5 to derive a lower bound on the space-time product for matrix inversion.

DEFINITION 10.12.2 *The* **Kronecker product** *of two* $n \times n$ *matrices* A *and* B *is the* $n^2 \times n^2$ *matrix* C, *denoted* $C = A \otimes B$, *obtained by replacing the entry* $a_{i,j}$ *of* A *with the matrix* $a_{i,j}B$.

A Kronecker product $C = A \otimes B$ of matrices A and B is shown below:

$$
A = \begin{bmatrix} 1 & 2 \\ 3 & 4 \end{bmatrix}, \qquad
B = \begin{bmatrix} 5 & 6 \\ 7 & 8 \end{bmatrix}, \qquad
C = \begin{bmatrix} 5 & 6 & 10 & 12 \\ 7 & 8 & 14 & 16 \\ 15 & 18 & 20 & 24 \\ 21 & 24 & 28 & 32 \end{bmatrix}
$$

The following property of the Kronecker product of two γ-nice matrices is used to derive the space-time lower bounds stated in Theorem 10.13.5.

LEMMA 10.12.2 *If* A *and* B *are both* $n \times n$ γ-*nice matrices for some* $0 \leq \gamma \leq 1/2$, *then* $C = A \otimes B$ *is an* $n^2 \times n^2$ γ^2-*ok matrix.*

Proof Number the rows and columns of A, B, and C consecutively from 0. For a matrix E, extend the notation $e_{i,j}$ for the entry in the ith row and jth column of E to $e_{I,J}$, by which we denote the submatrix of E consisting of the intersection of the rows in the set I and columns in the set J. Thus, if $I = \{i\}$ and $J = \{j\}$, then $e_{I,J} = e_{i,j}$.

To show that C is γ^2-ok, we must show that every $p \times q$ submatrix S of C satisfying $p \leq \lceil \gamma^2 n^2 \rceil$ and $q \geq n - \lceil \gamma^2 n^2 \rceil$ has rank at least $\gamma^2 p$. Such a matrix S can be represented as $S = c_{I,J}$ for index sets I and J, where $p = |I| \leq \lceil \gamma^2 n^2 \rceil$ and $q = |J| \geq n - \lceil \gamma^2 n^2 \rceil$. We assume that $\gamma n \geq 1$, since otherwise the result holds trivially.

The rth **block row** of C is the submatrix $[a_{r,0}B, a_{r,1}B, \ldots, a_{r,n-1}B]$ containing rows numbered $I_r = \{rn, rn + 1, \ldots, rn + n - 1\}$ and all n^2 columns.

Let $\Delta_r = I \cap \{rn, rn+1, \ldots, rn+n-1\}$ be the indices of the rows of S that fall into the rth block row. Choose a set $\Gamma \subset \{0, 1, 2, \ldots, n-1\}$ of size $|\Gamma| = \lceil \gamma n \rceil$ that maximizes the sum $T = \sum_{r \in \Gamma} |\Delta_r|$. Then, $T \geq \gamma p$ because the lower bound is achieved if the rows of S are uniformly distributed over the rows of C and T is larger if they are not.

Let $\Lambda_r = \Delta_r$ if $|\Delta_r| \leq \lceil \gamma n \rceil$ and let Λ_r consist of the smallest $\lceil \gamma n \rceil$ indices in Δ_r otherwise. Clearly, $|\Lambda_r| \geq |\Delta_r| \gamma$ because Δ_r is chosen from a set of size n. Call rows of C with indices in $\bigcup_{r \in \Gamma} \Lambda_r$ **blue rows**. There must be at least $\gamma^2 p$ blue rows because, if not,

$$
\gamma^2 p > \sum_{r \in \Gamma} |\Lambda_r| \geq \sum_{r \in \Gamma} |\Delta_r| \gamma = \gamma T \geq \gamma^2 p
$$

which is a contradiction.

We now show that the blue rows of S are linearly independent. Suppose not. Then there exist constants $\{\alpha_{r,s} \mid r \in \Gamma, s \in \Delta_r\}$ not all of which are zero such that the linear combination of the blue rows of S is zero:

$$\sum_{r \in \Gamma} \sum_{s \in \Lambda_r} \alpha_{r,s} c_{nr+s,J} = \mathbf{0} \tag{10.7}$$

Here $\mathbf{0}$ is a column vector of zeros, one per blue row. Again, J is the set of columns of C in the submatrix S.

Column j of the $n \times n$ matrix B is *good* if it is associated with at least $(1 - \gamma)n$ columns of S and is *bad* otherwise. Let G be the indices of the good columns in B and let $g = |G|$. Then there are $g \geq (1 - \gamma)n$ good columns and $b \leq \gamma n$ bad columns in B $(g + b = n)$ because, if not, $g \leq (1 - \gamma)n - 1$ and the number of columns altogether in S is at most $gn + b(1 - \gamma)n$, which is an increasing function of g whose value is less than $n^2 - \lceil \gamma^2 n^2 \rceil$ when $g \leq (1 - \gamma)n - 1$, which is less than the number of columns of S.

Since B has at least $g = |G| \geq (1 - \gamma)n$ good columns and B is γ-nice, any set of up to $\lceil \gamma n \rceil$ rows are linearly independent. In particular, the rows of B indexed by Λ_r are linearly independent. This implies that

$$\sum_{s \in \Lambda_r} \alpha_{r,s} b_{s,G} \neq \mathbf{0}$$

where $\mathbf{0}$ is a zero column with $|\Lambda_r|$ rows. Thus, there must be a column index $t \in G$ such that

$$\sum_{s \in \Lambda_r} \alpha_{r,s} b_{s,t} \neq 0 \tag{10.8}$$

Let $K = \{j \mid nj + t \in J\}$ be the columns of S corresponding to the good column of B with index t. It follows that $|K| \geq \lfloor (1 - \gamma)n \rfloor$.

Let $\mathbf{u}_i = c_{i,J \cap K}$, the intersection of the ith row of S with columns whose indices are in K. Similarly, let $\mathbf{v}_i$ be the intersection of the ith row of A with columns in K. It follows from the definition of C that $\mathbf{u}_{ni+j} = b_{j,t}\mathbf{v}_i$. From (10.7) we have that

$$\sum_{r \in \Gamma} \sum_{s \in \Lambda_r} \alpha_{r,s} c_{nr+s,J \cap K} = \mathbf{0}$$

$$\sum_{r \in \Gamma} \left(\sum_{s \in \Lambda_r} \alpha_{r,s} b_{s,t} \right) \mathbf{v}_r = \mathbf{0}$$

However, the rows $|\Gamma|$ rows $\mathbf{v}_r$ constitute a $\lceil \gamma n \rceil \times |K|$ submatrix of the γ-nice matrix A where $|K| \geq \lfloor (1 - \gamma)n \rfloor$. Since its rows are linearly independent, each of the coefficients $\sum_{s \in \Lambda_r} \alpha_{r,s} b_{s,t}$ must be zero, contradicting the statement of (10.8). It follows that $C = A \otimes B$ is γ^2-ok. ∎

10.13 Applications of the Borodin-Cook Method

In this section we illustrate the Borodin-Cook method of Section 10.11 by applying it to a variety of representative problems.

10.13.1 Convolution

The wrapped convolution function $f^{(n)}_{\text{wrapped}} : \mathcal{R}^{2n} \mapsto \mathcal{R}^n$ over the ring $\mathcal{R}$ (see Problem 6.19) of two sequences $\boldsymbol{u}$ and $\boldsymbol{v}$ is described by the matrix-vector product $C\boldsymbol{v}$ of a circulant matrix C in which $c_{i,j} = u_{(i-j) \bmod n}$, as shown in Section 10.5.1.

LEMMA 10.13.1 *For n even, the wrapped convolution $f^{(n)}_{\text{wrapped}} : \mathcal{R}^{2n} \mapsto \mathcal{R}^n$ over the ring $\mathcal{R}$ contains a subfunction $g^{(n)} : \mathcal{R}^{2n} \mapsto \mathcal{R}^{n/2}$ that is $(1, \gamma/2, \gamma/2, 1, 2n)$-distinguishable for some $0 < \gamma < 1/2$.*

Proof Writing C as a 2×2 matrix of $n/2 \times n/2$ matrices, we find that its (1,1) entry is an unrestricted Toeplitz matrix T. That is, each diagonal can contain a different element. Consider the subfunction of $f^{(n)}_{\text{wrapped}}$ defined by this submatrix. By Lemma 10.12.1, a fraction of at least $1 - (2/3)^{(\gamma/2)n}/|\mathcal{R}|$ of such matrices are γ-nice. By Definition 10.12.1, this implies that $\lceil(\gamma/2)n\rceil$ output variables assume $|\mathcal{R}|^{\lceil(\gamma/2)n\rceil}$ different values. If we fix the entries of T to be those of a γ-nice matrix, by Lemma 10.11.2 the lower bound on ST for matrix-vector multiplication with a Toeplitz matrix with n replaced by $n/2$ serves as a lower bound for the original problem. Since for large n most Toeplitz matrices are γ-nice, we have the desired conclusion. ∎

Invoking Theorem 10.11.1, we have the space–time lower bound stated below. The upper bound follows from the design of a branching program to implement the inner product operation, as suggested by Fig. 10.6.

THEOREM 10.13.1 *There is an integer $n_0 > 0$ such that for n even and $n \geq n_0$, the time T and space S used by any general branching program for the wrapped convolution $f^{(n)}_{\text{wrapped}} : \mathcal{R}^{2n} \mapsto \mathcal{R}^n$ over the ring $\mathcal{R}$ must satisfy*

$$ST = \Omega(n^2 \log |\mathcal{R}|) \tag{10.9}$$

Branching programs exist that achieve the following bound for $\log |\mathcal{R}| \leq S \leq n \log |\mathcal{R}|$:

$$ST = O(n^2 \log n \log |\mathcal{R}|)$$

Proof Since the wrapped convolution function depends on $2n$ variables, it can be computed via table lookup with space $O(n \log |\mathcal{R}|)$ and time $O(n)$.

At the limit of small space, namely for $S = \Theta(\log |\mathcal{R}|)$, a branching program can be designed that computes the n inner products defined by the matrix-vector product of (10.1). An example of a branching program to compute the inner product of two 3-vectors is shown in Fig. 10.20. A branching program for the inner product of two n-tuples can be constructed that has $O(n|\mathcal{R}|^2)$ vertices and depth $O(n)$. Hence, a branching program to multiply a general $n \times n$ matrix by a vector can be constructed that has time $O(n^2)$ and space $O(\log n + \log |\mathcal{R}|)$.

To fill in the range between these extremes, let k divide n and note that the product of an $n \times n$ matrix by a column n-vector can be viewed as the product of an $n/k \times n/k$ matrix of $k \times k$ matrices with a column n/k-vector of column k-vectors. Since each product of a $k \times k$ submatrix by a k-vector is a function of $O(k)$ parameters, compute it with table lookup in time $O(k)$ and space $O(k \log |\mathcal{R}|)$. Add two of these matrix-vector products by

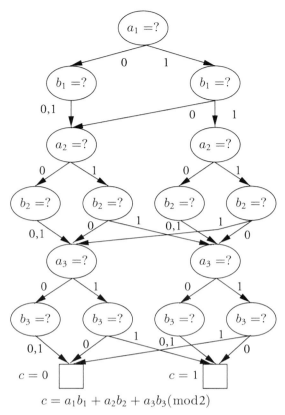

Figure 10.20 A branching program to compute the inner product of two 3-vectors over the set $\mathcal{R}$ of integers modulo 2.

rooting a table-lookup program at each of the $O(|\mathcal{R}|^k)$ final states of a first table-lookup program. Coalesce final states corresponding to the $|\mathcal{R}|^k$ sums of the two column k-vectors. This program has $O(|\mathcal{R}|^{2k})$ vertices or space $O(k \log |\mathcal{R}|)$ and time $O(k)$. n/k such stages increase the number of vertices and time each by a factor of n/k. Since this process is then repeated for each of the n/k rows of the block matrix, the space and time used are $O(k \log |\mathcal{R}| + \log(n/k))$ and $O(n^2/k)$, respectively. ∎

10.13.2   Integer Multiplication

To derive space–time lower bounds for integer multiplication, we could invoke the reductions from this problem to cyclic shifting, as was done in Section 10.5.3. However, as shown in Section 10.10, the space–time product for cyclic shifting is only $O(n \log n)$. Thus, we are forced to use another reduction to obtain a strong space–time product lower bound, namely a reduction from integer multiplication to convolution.

Let $\mathbb{Z}_2$ be the ring of integers modulo 2. As shown in Problem 6.20, the integer multiplication function $f_{\mathrm{mult}}^{(n)} : \mathcal{B}^{2n} \mapsto \mathcal{B}^{2n}$ contains the convolution function over $f_{\mathrm{conv}}^{(n/\log n)} :$ $\mathbb{Z}_2^{2n/\log n} \mapsto \mathbb{Z}_2^{2n/\log n}$. Thus, by Lemmas 10.11.2 and 10.13.1 the following holds:

THEOREM 10.13.2 *There is an integer $n_0 > 0$ such that for $n > n_0$ the time T and space S used by any general branching program for binary integer multiplication $f_{\mathrm{mult}}^{(n)} : \mathcal{B}^{2n} \mapsto \mathcal{B}^{2n}$ must satisfy*

$$ST = \Omega(n^2 / \log^2 n) \tag{10.10}$$

This lower bound can be achieved to within a factor of $O(\log^3 n)$ for space $\Omega(\log n) \leq S \leq O(n)$.

Proof Since the integer multiplication function depends on $2n$ variables, it can be computed via table lookup with space $O(n)$ and time $O(n)$, thereby meeting the lower bound to within a factor of $O(\log^2 n)$.

At the limit of small space, $S = \Theta(\log n)$, the integer multiplication algorithm of Section 10.5.3 provides a branching program. Since at most $\lceil \log_2 n \rceil$ bits suffice for the carry from one power of 2 to the next, a branching program based on this algorithm has at most $O(2^{\lceil \log_2 n \rceil})$ vertices at each of n^2 levels. Thus, this program uses time $O(n^2)$ and space $O(\log n)$, achieving the lower bound to within a factor of $O(\log n)$.

We sketch a procedure to fill in the range of space between these extremes and ask the reader to complete the details. (See Problem 10.39.) Assume that k divides n and represent each n-bit binary number as an (n/k)-component base-2^k number. As in the standard binary integer multiplication algorithm (where $k = 1$), form n/k (n/k)-component numbers through multiplication and shifting of consecutive base-2^k components, as suggested below:

		$v_3 u_0$	$v_2 u_0$	$v_1 u_0$	$v_0 u_0$	
	$v_3 u_1$	$v_2 u_1$	$v_1 u_1$	$v_0 u_1$	0	
$v_3 u_2$	$v_2 u_2$	$v_1 u_2$	$v_0 u_2$	0	0	
$v_3 u_3$	$v_2 u_3$	$v_1 u_3$	$v_0 u_3$	0	0	0

Here u_r and v_s are base-2^k numbers. Multiply two such numbers through table lookup in time and space $O(k)$. Extend the algorithm for the base-2 case by replacing each subprogram that multiplies two binary numbers by the table lookup program to multiply base-2^k numbers. This new program adds products to a running sum of length $O(\log n)$ bits. Thus, it uses space $O(k + \log n)$ and time $O(n^2/k)$, giving a space–time product of $O(n^2 \log n)$ for $k \geq \log n$. ∎

10.13.3 Matrix-Vector Product

The matrix-vector product function $f_{A \times x}^{(n)} : \mathcal{R}^n \mapsto \mathcal{R}^n$ computes the n-tuple $\boldsymbol{y}$ from the n-tuple $\boldsymbol{x}$ for a fixed $n \times n$ matrix A over $\mathcal{R}$ according to the rule

$$\boldsymbol{y} = A\boldsymbol{x}$$

where $y_j = \sum_{k=0}^{n-1} a_{j,k} x_k$ for $0 \leq j \leq n - 1$.

LEMMA 10.13.2 *Let A be a γ-ok $n \times n$ matrix over $\mathcal{R}$ for some $0 < \gamma < 1/2$. Then the matrix-vector product function $f_{A \times \boldsymbol{x}}^{(n)} : \mathcal{R}^n \mapsto \mathcal{R}^n$ is $(1, \gamma, \gamma, \gamma, \tau)$-distinguishable where $\tau(b) = n$.*

Proof To show that $f_{A \times \boldsymbol{x}}^{(n)}$ is $(1, \gamma, \gamma, \gamma, \tau)$-distinguishable, select any $a \leq \lceil \gamma n \rceil$ inputs and any $b \leq \lceil \gamma n \rceil$ outputs. If the ith input is chosen and it has value u_i, introduce the equation $x_i = u_i$. Let B be the $a \times n$ coefficient matrix defining these equations; that is, $B\boldsymbol{x} = \boldsymbol{u}$, where B contains the jth row of the $n \times n$ identity matrix if the jth variable is among the selected inputs.

$$\text{Consider the } (n + a) \times n \text{ matrix } C = \begin{bmatrix} A \\ B \end{bmatrix}. \text{ We show that it has rank } a + \gamma b. \text{ The}$$

submatrix D of A consisting of the intersection of those columns not selected by inputs (of which there are $n - a \geq n - \lceil \gamma n \rceil$) and rows selected by outputs (of which there are b) has rank γb because A is γ-ok. Thus, γb of the $n - a$ columns of A not selected by inputs and the a non-zero columns of B are linearly independent. Thus, the submatrix E of C consisting of the selected rows of B and the rows of D has rank $a + \gamma b$.

The number of n-tuple input vectors $\boldsymbol{x}$ consistent with the linear system $E\boldsymbol{x} = \boldsymbol{d}$ is $|\mathcal{A}|^{n-a-\gamma b}$, as we show. Without loss of generality assume that the first $a + \gamma b$ columns of E (call it F) are linearly independent. (Permute the columns, if necessary, so that this is true.) Fix the values of the b realizable outputs. Then for each assignment to inputs corresponding to the last $n - (a + \gamma b)$ columns there are unique values for the first $a + \gamma b$ inputs, due to the non-singularity of F. Thus the number of assignments to the last $n - (a + \gamma b)$ columns that are consistent with values for the a inputs and b outputs is $|\mathcal{A}|^{n-a-\gamma b}$. ∎

Invoking Corollary 10.11.1 yields the following result.

THEOREM 10.13.3 *Let A be a γ-ok $n \times n$ matrix over $\mathcal{R}$ for some $0 < \gamma < 1/2$. Then there is a constant $0 < \gamma < 1/2$ and an integer n_0 such that for $n \geq n_0$ the space S and time T used by any general branching program for the function $f_{A \times \boldsymbol{x}}^{(n)} : \mathcal{R}^n \mapsto \mathcal{R}^n$ must satisfy the following lower bound when $T \geq n$:*

$$ST = \Omega(n^2 \log |\mathcal{R}|)$$

This lower bound can be met to within a factor of $O(\log n)$ for $\log n \leq S \leq n$.

Proof The lower bound follows from the application of Theorem 10.11.1.

The matrix-vector product $A\boldsymbol{x}$ for an $n \times n$ matrix A can be done with a branching program for the standard algorithm as follows: Compute the inner product of the ith row with the column $\boldsymbol{x}$ for $1 \leq i \leq n$. The inner product of two n-tuples can be computed with a branching program having $O(n|\mathcal{R}|^2)$ vertices, as suggested in Fig. 10.20. (This is true even if A is not fixed.) n branching programs for inner products can be concatenated to form one branching program to multiply an $n \times n$ matrix with an n-vector. This branching program uses space $O(\log n + \log |\mathcal{R}|)$ and time $O(n^2)$, thereby meeting the lower bound to within a factor of $O(\log n)$.

A matrix-vector product for a fixed matrix (this case) can also be computed by table lookup in space $O(n \log |\mathcal{R}|)$ and time $O(n)$ since this function has n variables.

To bridge the gap between these two results, compute the matrix-vector product using a hybrid algorithm similar to that used for convolution in the proof of Theorem 10.13.1. ∎

10.13.4 Matrix Multiplication*

The space–time lower-bound argument for matrix multiplication in the branching program model uses ideas similar to those used for matrix-vector multiplication.

LEMMA 10.13.3 *The matrix multiplication function $f_{A \times B}^{(n)} : \mathcal{R}^{2n^2} \mapsto \mathcal{R}^{n^2}$ over the ring $\mathcal{R}$ is $(1, 1, 1, \gamma/4, \tau)$-distinguishable for some $0 < \gamma < 1/2$, where $\tau(b) = \gamma n \sqrt{b/2}$.*

Proof Consider the subfunction of $f_{A \times B}^{(n)}$ obtained by choosing A and B from the set of $n \times n$ γ-nice matrices. By Lemma 10.11.2, a lower bound on the space–time product for this subfunction provides a lower bound to the matrix multiplication function.

Consider some $a \leq 2n^2$ selected inputs and some $b \leq n^2$ selected outputs such that $a \leq \tau(b)$; that is, $(a/\gamma n)^2 \leq b/2$. The outputs correspond to entries of the product matrix $C = A \times B$. Let row i of C be a **heavy row** if at least γn of the a selected inputs are in row i of A. Similarly, let column j of C be a **heavy column** if at least γn of the a selected inputs are in column j of B. A row or column of C is **light** otherwise. (See Fig. 10.21.)

There are at most $a/\gamma n$ heavy rows and $a/\gamma n$ heavy columns of C. We now show that either a) at least $b/4$ of the selected outputs fall into light rows of C or b) at least $b/4$ of the selected outputs fall into light columns of C. Suppose not. Then both statements are false and less than $b/4$ of the selected outputs fall into light rows and less than $b/4$ of the selected outputs fall into light columns of C. It follows that at least $3b/4$ of the selected outputs fall into heavy rows. Of these at most $(a/\gamma n)^2$ fall into heavy columns, since this is the maximum number of entries of C that could be in both heavy rows and columns. The remaining selected outputs in these rows (of which there are less than $b/4$) fall into light columns. However, because the entries in each row fall into either heavy or light columns, the number of selected outputs that are in heavy rows is less than $(a/\gamma n)^2 + b/4$. But this is less than $3b/4$ since $a \leq \tau(b) = \gamma n \sqrt{b/2}$, contradicting the stated hypothesis.

Without loss of generality, assume that b holds. (If not, a holds and at least $b/4$ selected outputs fall into light rows of C or into light columns of the transpose C^T.) Represent the

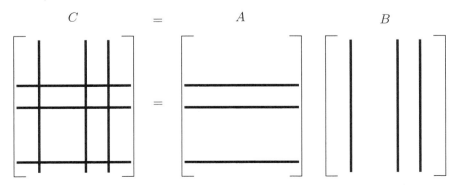

Figure 10.21   Identification of heavy rows and columns of matrices.

product $C = A \times B$ as follows:

$$\begin{bmatrix} A & & \\ & \ddots & \\ & & A \end{bmatrix} \begin{bmatrix} \boldsymbol{B^1} \\ \vdots \\ \boldsymbol{B^n} \end{bmatrix} = \begin{bmatrix} \boldsymbol{C^1} \\ \vdots \\ \boldsymbol{C^n} \end{bmatrix}$$

Here $\boldsymbol{B^i}$ and $\boldsymbol{C^i}$ are the ith columns of the matrices B and C, respectively. Let $\boldsymbol{B}$ and $\boldsymbol{C}$ denote the columns of these columns, respectively, and let $\boldsymbol{D}$ denote the block diagonal matrix on the left.

We show that at most $|\mathcal{R}|^{2n^2 - a - \gamma b/4}$ of the matrix pairs (A, B) are consistent with any assignment to any set of a selected inputs and values of any b selected outputs.

Of the a selected inputs, let a_1 be drawn from A and a_2 be drawn from B, where $a = a_1 + a_2$. The number of γ-nice matrices A consistent with the a_1 selected inputs from A is at most $|\mathcal{R}|^{n^2 - a_1}$. We now bound the number of matrices B that are consistent with the values of selected inputs and outputs.

Let A be fixed and γ-nice. Consider just the (at least $b/4$) selected outputs that fall into light columns of C. Every value for B consistent with the selected inputs and these outputs must satisfy the following linear equation:

$$\begin{bmatrix} E \\ F \end{bmatrix} \boldsymbol{B} = H\boldsymbol{B} = \begin{bmatrix} \boldsymbol{r} \\ \boldsymbol{c} \end{bmatrix}$$

Here E consists of the b rows of $\boldsymbol{D}$ corresponding to selected outputs and F is a submatrix of the $n^2 \times n^2$ identity matrix consisting of the a_2 rows corresponding to selected inputs in B. $\boldsymbol{c}$ is the column of values for the selected inputs in $\boldsymbol{B}$ and $\boldsymbol{r}$ is a column of selected outputs of C that fall into light columns. The number of values for B consistent with a fixed A and the values of the selected inputs and outputs is no more than the number of solutions $\boldsymbol{B}$ to these equations, since we are ignoring outputs in heavy rows.

We now show that H has rank at least $a_2 + \gamma b/4$. A column of H is **queried** if a column of E contains a selected input or the corresponding row of $\boldsymbol{B}$ contains a selected input. a_2 of these columns correspond to selected inputs in B and are linearly independent because the corresponding columns of F are linearly independent. Consider the unqueried columns of H. These columns in F are zero columns. Thus, consider these unqueried columns in E. Consider k rows in E that come from a common copy of A on the diagonal of $\boldsymbol{D}$. The column $\boldsymbol{B^i}$ of B corresponding to this copy of A is light (it has fewer than γn selected entries) because the corresponding column of C is chosen to be light. Thus, this copy of A has at least $n(1 - \gamma)$ unqueried entries, or at least $n(1 - \gamma)$ of its columns are unqueried.

Since A is γ-nice, the unqueried columns of this copy of it have rank at least $\min (k, \gamma n)$. Because there are no dependencies between columns in distinct copies of A in $\boldsymbol{D}$, the number of linearly independent unqueried columns of E is minimal if they all fall in as few common copies of A as possible, because then $\min (k, \gamma n) = \gamma n$. It follows that the unqueried columns of E have rank at least $\gamma b/4$. Since the queried columns have rank at least a_2, the columns of H have rank at least $a_2 + \gamma b/4$. It follows from an argument given in the proof of Lemma 10.13.2 that the number of solutions $\boldsymbol{B}$ to this system is at most $|\mathcal{R}|^{n^2 - a_2 - \gamma b/4}$. Since there are at most $|\mathcal{R}|^{n^2 - a_1}$ matrices A that are γ-nice and consistent with the a_1 selected inputs in A, it follows that the number of pairs consistent with values of the selected inputs and outputs is at most $|\mathcal{R}|^{2n^2 - a - \gamma b/4}$, the desired conclusion. ∎

This result provides a lower bound on the space and time for matrix multiplication. The upper bound cited below is obtained by another hybrid algorithm that mixes a branching program for the standard algorithm with one for table lookup.

THEOREM 10.13.4 *There is an integer $n_0 > 0$ such that for $n > n_0$ the space S and time T needed to compute the matrix multiplication function $f_{A \times B}^{(n)} : \mathcal{R}^{2n^2} \mapsto \mathcal{R}^{n^2}$ over the ring $\mathcal{R}$ using a general branching program satisfies the inequality:*

$$ST^2 \geq \frac{\gamma^3}{16} n^6 \log_2 |\mathcal{R}|$$

for some $0 < \gamma < 1/2$ when $T \geq n^2$. This lower bound can be achieved up to a multiplicative factor of $O(\log n)$ for space in the range $\Omega(\log n + \log |\mathcal{A}|) \leq S \leq O(n \log |\mathcal{A}|)$.

Proof The lower bound follows from Theorem 10.11.1 and Lemma 10.13.3 by letting $a = \lfloor \gamma^2 n^4 / 4T \rfloor$, since this value of a satisfies the two conditions $a \leq \tau(ma/2T) = \gamma n \sqrt{ma/4T}$ and $a \leq 2n^2$ when $T \geq n^2$.

At the extreme of large space, namely $S = O(n^2)$, the upper bound follows from a branching program for table lookup that has one level for each of the $2n^2$ variables in the matrices A and B and the fact that there are $|\mathcal{R}|^{2n^2}$ pairs of such matrices over the ring $\mathcal{R}$. Consequently, the branching program has at most $O(|\mathcal{R}|^{2n^2})$ vertices and space $O(n^2 \log |\mathcal{R}|)$. It uses $O(n^2)$ steps.

At the extreme of small space, namely $S = \Omega(\log n + \log |\mathcal{A}|)$, we use a branching program for the standard matrix multiplication algorithm that forms n^2 inner products of rows and columns of the two matrices. As discussed in the proof of Theorem 10.13.3, a branching program can be constructed to form the inner product of two n-tuples that has $\Theta(n|\mathcal{R}|^2)$ vertices; that is, space $\Omega(\log n + \log |\mathcal{A}|)$ and time $O(n)$. Concatenating n^2 of these programs, one for each of the n^2 entries in the product matrix, we have a branching program with space $\Omega(\log n + \log |\mathcal{A}|)$ and time $O(n^3)$.

To fill in the gap between these extremes, the method applied in Theorem 10.13.3 can be used, as the reader can demonstrate. (See Problem 10.40.) ∎

10.13.5 Matrix Inversion

As an intermediate step to deriving a space–time product lower bound on matrix inversion, we derive a lower bound for the product of three $n \times n$ matrices. This is done by first deriving an alternate representation for this product in terms of the Kronecker product of two matrices. Kronecker products are defined in Section 10.12.

LEMMA 10.13.4 *Let A, B, C, and D be $n \times n$ matrices over a commutative ring. The following two equations define the same set of mappings from entries of A, B, and C to entries in D:*

$$D = ABC$$
$$\boldsymbol{E} = (A \otimes C^T)\boldsymbol{B}$$

where $\boldsymbol{B}$ and $\boldsymbol{E}$ are $n^2 \times 1$ column vectors obtained by concatenating the transposes of the rows of the matrices B and D, respectively.

Proof Let $\boldsymbol{E} = (A \otimes C^T)\boldsymbol{B}$. The goal is to show that the results in the $n^2 \times 1$ column vector $\boldsymbol{E}$ are the same as those in the $n \times n$ matrix D but in a different order. In particular, we show that the $ni + j$ entry in the former, namely $e_{ni+j,1}$, is equal to the (i, j) entry in D, namely $d_{i,j}$.

Given a matrix F, let $f_{i,j}$ denote its entry in the ith row and jth column. Let $f_{i,-}$ and $f_{-,j}$ denote the ith row and jth column of F, respectively. Let rows and columns of matrices be numbered consecutively from zero.

The matrix $A \otimes C^T$ consists of blocks of n consecutive rows with the ith block containing $[a_{i,1}C^T, a_{i,2}C^T, \ldots, a_{i,n}C^T]$. Thus, the $ni + j$th entry of $\boldsymbol{E}$, namely $e_{ni+j,1}$, is the jth entry in the product $[a_{i,1}C^T, a_{i,2}C^T, \ldots, a_{i,n}C^T]\boldsymbol{B}$, as shown below, where $(c_{-,j})^T(b_{k,-})^T$ is the inner product of the row vector $(c_{-,j})^T$ with the column vector $(b_{k,-})^T$.

$$
\begin{aligned}
e_{ni+j,1} &= \sum_{k=0}^{n-1} a_{i,k}(c_{-,j})^T(b_{k,-})^T \\
&= \sum_{k=0}^{n-1}\sum_{l=0}^{n-1} a_{i,k}c_{l,j}b_{k,l} \\
&= \sum_{k=0}^{n-1}\sum_{l=0}^{n-1} a_{i,k}b_{k,l}c_{l,j} \\
&= d_{i,j}
\end{aligned}
$$

This is the desired conclusion. ∎

With this as background, we state the space–time results to compute the product of three matrices.

THEOREM 10.13.5 *There is an integer $n_0 > 0$ such that for $n > n_0$ the time T and space S used by any general branching program to compute the product of three $n \times n$ matrices over a commutative ring $\mathcal{R}$ must satisfy the following inequality:*

$$ST = \Omega(n^4 \log |\mathcal{R}|)$$

Proof Given a general branching program to compute ABC, no more space or time are used when the matrices A and C are given specific values. Let them each be γ-nice for some $0 \le \gamma \le 1/2$. The existence of such matrices is established in Lemma 10.12.1. From Lemma 10.12.2 we know that the matrix $A \otimes C^T$ is γ^2-ok. The result follows from Theorem 10.13.3 since $A \otimes C^T$ is $n^2 \times n^2$. ∎

We are now prepared to state space–time bounds for matrix inversion.

THEOREM 10.13.6 *There is an integer $n_0 > 0$ such that for $n > n_0$ the time T and space S used by any general branching program to compute the inverse of a non-singular $n \times n$ matrix over a commutative ring $\mathcal{R}$ must satisfy the following inequality:*

$$ST = \Omega(n^4 \log |\mathcal{R}|)$$

This lower bound can be achieved to within a multiplicative factor over the range $\Omega(n^2) \le T \le O(n^3)$.

Proof Let n be a multiple of 4. The lower bound follows by reducing matrix inversion to the computation of the product of three arbitrary $n/4 \times n/4$ matrices, as shown below:

$$\begin{bmatrix} I & -A & 0 & 0 \\ 0 & I & -B & 0 \\ 0 & 0 & I & -C \\ 0 & 0 & 0 & I \end{bmatrix}^{-1} = \begin{bmatrix} I & A & AB & ABC \\ 0 & I & B & BC \\ 0 & 0 & I & C \\ 0 & 0 & 0 & I \end{bmatrix}$$

The upper bound for $T = \Theta(n^2)$ is obtained by table lookup using an algorithm of the kind described in the proof of Theorem 10.13.3. For $T = \Theta(n^3)$, the matrix inversion algorithm based on the LDL^T decomposition of a symmetric positive definite matrix of Section 6.5.4 can be used. For intermediate values of time, a hybridized algorithm based on the inversion of block matrices provides the stated upper bound. ■

10.13.6 Discrete Fourier Transform

The discrete Fourier transform (DFT) and the fast Fourier transform algorithm are described in Sections 6.7.2 and 6.7.3. In this section we derive upper and lower bounds on space–time tradeoffs for this problem. The lower bound follows from the result for matrix-vector multiplication and the fact that the coefficient matrix for the DFT is $(1/4)$-ok.

LEMMA 10.13.5 *Consider the n-point DFT over a commutative ring that has a principal nth root of unity. It is defined as a matrix-vector product with $[w^{ij}]$ as its $n \times n$ coefficient matrix. This matrix is $(1/4)$-ok.*

Proof We use the fact, shown in Theorem 10.5.5, that the submatrix of $W = [w^{ij}]$ consisting of any k rows and any k consecutive columns is non-singular. We show that any $p \times q$ submatrix B of W, with $p \le \lceil n/4 \rceil$ and $q \ge n - \lceil n/4 \rceil$, has rank at least $p/4$.

Let I denote the row indices of the submatrix B and let J denote its column indices. Let C be the submatrix of W with row indices in I. Divide the columns of C into $\lceil n/p \rceil$ groups each containing p columns except possibly the last which has at most p columns. We claim that some group has at least $p/2$ columns in common with B. Suppose not. Then every one of the $\lceil n/p \rceil$ groups has at most $(p - 1)/2$ columns in common with B. Thus B has at most $\chi(p) = \lceil n/p \rceil (p - 1)/2$ columns. We show that $\chi(p) < n - (n + 3)/4 \le n - \lceil n/4 \rceil$. But this is a contradiction because B has at least $n - \lceil n/4 \rceil$ columns. Since $\lceil n/p \rceil \le (n + p - 1)/p$, if $(n + p - 1)(p - 1)/2p < n - (n + 3)/4$, the following holds after multiplying both sides by $2p$:

$$(n + p - 1)(p - 1) < \frac{3p(n - 1)}{2} \quad \text{or}$$

$$-n + 1 < p \left(\frac{(n + 1)}{2} - p \right)$$

It suffices to show that the right-hand side of the last equation is positive. But $((n+1)/2) - p$ is positive since $p \le \lceil n/4 \rceil \le (n + 3)/4 \le (n + 1)/2$ for $n \ge 1$. ■

THEOREM 10.13.7 *There is an integer $n_0 > 0$ such that for $n > n_0$ the n-point DFT over a commutative ring $\mathcal{R}$ requires space S and time T with a branching program satisfying the following* *lower bound:*

$$ST = \Omega(n^2 \log |\mathcal{R}|)$$

This lower bound can be achieved to within a constant multiplicative factor.

Proof The upper bound follows by applying Lemma 10.9.3 and Theorem 10.5.5. ∎

10.13.7   Unique Elements

We now derive a lower bound on the space–time product for the sorting problem by reducing sorting to the unique-elements problem. The unique elements problem takes a list of values and returns in any order a list of the non-repeated elements among them.

DEFINITION 10.13.1 *Let $\mathcal{R}$ be a set with at least n distinct elements. The function $f_{\text{unique}}^{(n)}$: $\mathcal{R}^n \mapsto 2^{\mathcal{R}^n}$ defines the* **unique elements** *problem where $2^{\mathcal{R}^n}$ is the power set of $\mathcal{R}^n$ and $f_{\text{unique}}^{(n)}(\boldsymbol{x})$ is the set of non-repeated elements in the input string $\boldsymbol{x}$.*

We emphasize that no order is imposed on the outputs of $f_{\text{unique}}^{(n)}$. Thus, if a set of values appears in the output, their position in the output does not matter.

From Lemma 10.11.2 it follows that a lower bound to ST can be derived by restricting the domain and discarding outputs. We restrict the domain by restricting each input variable to values in a subset $\mathcal{S} \subseteq \mathcal{R}$ containing n elements. We also restrict input tuples to the set $\mathcal{D}$ containing at least $n/(2e)$ unique values (e is the base of the natural logarithm). In the following lemma we show that $|\mathcal{D}| \geq |\mathcal{S}|^n/(2e-1) = \phi n^n$, where $\phi = 1/(2e-1)$. On inputs in $\mathcal{D}$ the function $f_{\text{unique}}^{(n)}$ has at least $n/(2e)$ unique outputs. We define the subfunction $f_{\text{restricted}}^{(n)} : \mathcal{S}^n \mapsto \mathcal{S}^m$, $m = n/(2e)$, of $f_{\text{unique}}^{(n)}$ to be the subfunction obtained by restricting its inputs to $\mathcal{D} \subset \mathcal{S}^n$ and deleting all but the first $n/(2e)$ outputs, which are all unique.

LEMMA 10.13.6 *Let $\mathcal{S}$ be a set of n elements. The fraction ϕ of the input n-tuples over $\mathcal{S}^n$ containing $n/(2e)$ or more unique elements exceeds $1/(2e-1)$.*

Proof We use simple probabilistic arguments. Assign each n-tuple over $\mathcal{S}^n$ probability $1/n^n$. Let $u(\boldsymbol{x})$ be the number of unique elements in $\boldsymbol{x}$. Let $X_i(\boldsymbol{x})$ have value 1 if the ith element of $\mathcal{S}$ occurs uniquely in $\boldsymbol{x}$ and value 0 otherwise. Then

$$u(\boldsymbol{x}) = \sum_{i=1}^{n} X_i(\boldsymbol{x})$$

Let $E[u]$ denote the average value of $u(\boldsymbol{x})$ (the sum of $u(\boldsymbol{x})$ over $\boldsymbol{x}$ weighted by its probability). Because the order of summation can be changed without affecting the sum, we have

$$E[u(\boldsymbol{x})] = \sum_{i=1}^{n} E[X_i(\boldsymbol{x})]$$

$E[X_i(\boldsymbol{x})]$ is also the probability that $X_i = 1$. If $X_i = 1$, then each of the other components of $\boldsymbol{x}$ can assume only one of $n-1$ values. Since the ith value can be in any one of n positions among input variables and since for each position that it occupies there are $(n-1)^{n-1}$ ways to fill the remaining $n-1$ positions so that the ith value is unique, we have that $E[X_i] = f(n)$ where $f(n) = n(n-1)^{n-1}/n^n = (1-1/n)^n/(1-1/n)$. But $f(n)$ is a decreasing function of n, as is shown by calculating its derivative and using the inequality $(1-x) \le e^{-x}$ (see Problem 10.5). The limit of $f(n)$ for large n is e^{-1} because in the limit of small x the function e^{-x} has value $1-x$. It follows that $E[u(\boldsymbol{x})] > n/e$.

Let $\pi = P_r[u(\boldsymbol{x}) \ge n/(2e)]$ be the fraction (or probability) of the input n-tuples for which $u(\boldsymbol{x}) \ge n/(2e))$. Because $u(\boldsymbol{x}) \le n$, it follows that $\pi n + (1-\pi)n/(2e) \ge E[u(\boldsymbol{x})] \ge n/e$, from which we conclude that $\pi > 1/(2e-1)$. (This is known as **Markov's inequality**.) ∎

LEMMA 10.13.7 *Let $|S| = n$. Then $f_{\text{restricted}}^{(n)} : S^n \mapsto S^m$, $m = n/(2e)$, is $(\phi, \lambda, \mu, \nu, \tau)$-distinguishable for $\phi = 1/(2e-1)$, $\lambda = \mu = 1$, $\nu = (1-1/(2e))/\log_2 n$, and $\tau(b) = n$.*

Proof If $f_{\text{restricted}}^{(n)}$ is $(\phi, \lambda, \mu, \nu, \tau)$-distinguishable for $\phi = 1/(2e-1)$, $\lambda = \mu = 1/2$, $\nu = (1-1/(2e))/\log_2 n$, and $\tau(b) = n$, then for at least ϕn^n input tuples and any $a \le \lambda n$ input and $b \le \mu m$ output variables and specified values for them, $f_{\text{restricted}}^{(n)}$ has at most $n^{n-a-\nu b} = n^{n-a}e^{-(1-1/(2e))b}$ input n-tuples that are consistent with these assignments. The order of output values to $f_{\text{restricted}}^{(n)}$ is irrelevant.

Let $\mathcal{B}$ be the values of the b selected and specified unique outputs, $b \le m$, and let $\mathcal{A}$ be the values of the a selected and specified input values. The k values in $\mathcal{B} - \mathcal{A}$ appear in input positions that are not specified. $r = n - k - a$ inputs are in neither $\mathcal{A}$ nor $\mathcal{B}$. We overestimate the number of patterns of inputs consistent with the a inputs and b outputs that are specified if we allow these a inputs to assume any value not in $\mathcal{B}$, since all values in $\mathcal{B}$ are unique. Thus, there are at most $(n-b)^r$ ways to assign values to these r inputs. The k values in $\mathcal{B} - \mathcal{A}$ are fixed, but their positions among the $r + k$ non-selected inputs are not fixed. Since there are $(r+k)!/r!$ ways for these ordered k values to appear among any specific ordering of the remaining r non-selected inputs (see Problem 10.6), the number Q of input patterns consistent with the selected and specified a inputs and b outputs satisfies the following inequality:

$$Q \le \frac{(r+k)!}{r!}(n-b)^r$$

Here $r + k = n - a \le n$ and $k \le b$. Below we bound $(r+k)!/r!$ by $(r+k)^k$ and use the inequality $(1-x) \le e^{-x}$:

$$Q \le (r+k)^k(n-b)^r \le n^{r+k}\left(1-\frac{a}{n}\right)^k\left(1-\frac{b}{n}\right)^r$$
$$\le n^{n-a}e^{-(ka/n+rb/n)} \le n^{n-a}e^{-(ka/n+(n-a-k)b/n)}$$

The exponent $e(a, b, k) = ka/n + (n-a-k)b/n$ is a decreasing function of a whose smallest value is $(1-k/n)b$. In turn, this function is a decreasing function of k whose smallest value is $(1-b/n)b \ge (1-1/(2e))b$. As a consequence, we have

$$Q \le n^{n-a}e^{-(1-1/(2e))b}$$

It follows that $f_{\text{restricted}}^{(n)}$ is $(\phi, \lambda, \mu, \nu, \tau)$-distinguishable for $\phi = 1/(2e-1)$, $\lambda = \mu = 1$, $\nu = (1-1/(2e))/\log_2 n$, and $\tau(b) = n$. ∎

```
b := 0;
for j := 1 to ⌈n/S⌉
{b = (j − 1)S on the jth iteration.}
  begin
    for i := 1 to S
      C[i] := 0;
    for i := 1 to n
      if b ≤ xᵢ ≤ b + S then
        begin
          k := xᵢ − b;
          if C[k] < 2 then C[k] := C[k] + 1;
        end;
    for i := 1 to S
      if C[i] = 1 then print b + i;
    b := b + S;
  end
```

Figure 10.22 A RAM program for the unique-elements problem over the set $\{1, 2, \ldots, n\}$ when $n \geq S \geq O(\log n)$. The input to the program is the n-tuple $\boldsymbol{x}$ in which x_i is the ith entry. The program uses space $O(S)$.

Invoking Theorem 10.11.1, we have a quadratic space–time product lower bound. The RAM program for the unique elements problem given in Fig. 10.22 can be converted to a branching program to obtain an upper bound on the space–time product needed for this problem, as shown in Theorem 10.13.8.

THEOREM 10.13.8 *Let* $|\mathcal{R}| \geq n$. *There is an integer* $n_0 > 0$ *such that for* $n \geq n_0$ *and* $S = \Omega(\log n)$ *the time* T *and space* S *used by any general branching program for the unique elements function* $f_{\text{unique}}^{(n)} : \mathcal{R}^n \mapsto 2^{\mathcal{R}^n}$ *must satisfy*

$$ST = \Omega(n^2)$$

This lower bound can be met to within a constant multiplicative factor for inputs drawn from the set $\{1, 2, 3, \ldots, n\}$.

Proof The lower bound follows directly from Theorem 10.11.1. The upper bound follows from an analysis of the branching program that results from conversion of the RAM program in Fig. 10.22. The RAM program makes $\lceil n/S \rceil$ passes over the input data. On the jth pass the program examines input values in the range $[(j − 1)S, \ldots, jS]$ and determines for each value whether there are zero, one, or more than one instances of it in the input.

The program uses an S-element one-dimensional array $C[1..S]$ that it initializes to zero at the beginning of each pass. If on the jth pass the ith input variable, x_i, is in the interval $[(j − 1)S, \ldots, jS]$, the array element associated with it, namely $C[x_i − (j − 1)S]$, is incremented unless it already has value 2. At the end of the jth pass, if the array element $C[i]$ has value 1, the program prints out the value $jS + i$, namely, the value of an input that appears only once in the input.

The reader is asked to show that the program of Fig. 10.22 can be converted to a branching program of space $O(S)$ and time $O(T)$. (See Problem 10.41.) ■

The program of Fig. 10.22 relies on the fact that input variables are drawn from the set $\{1, 2, 3, \ldots, n\}$. If the set from which they are drawn is much larger, say $\{1, 2, 3, \ldots, n^c\}$, $c > 1$, the outer loop is executed $O(n^c/S)$ times and its total running time is $O(n^c)$. Thus, the program is not optimal in this case.

10.13.8   Sorting

The sorting problem is described in Section 6.8. The general sorting problem is defined by a function $f_{\text{sort}}^{(n)} : \mathcal{R}^n \mapsto \mathcal{R}^n$ that rearranges the values of input variables so they are in descending order. Given a branching program for sorting, we show below that a branching program for the unique-elements problem can be obtained with a small additional amount of space. As a consequence, the space–time product lower bound for unique elements applies to the sorting problem. We also give a nearly matching upper bound.

THEOREM 10.13.9 *Let $|\mathcal{R}| \geq n$. There is an integer $n_0 > 0$ such that for $n \geq n_0$ and $S = \Omega(\log n)$ the time T and space S used by any general branching program for the sorting function $f_{\text{sort}}^{(n)} : \mathcal{R}^n \mapsto \mathcal{R}^n$ must satisfy*

$$ST = \Omega(n^2)$$

This lower bound can be met to within a constant multiplicative factor for inputs drawn from the set $\{1, 2, 3, \ldots, n\}$.

Proof Given a branching program for $f_{\text{sort}}^{(n)}$ that uses space S, we use it to construct a branching program for $f_{\text{unique}}^{(n)}$ that uses space $S + O(\log n) = O(S)$. Since $f_{\text{unique}}^{(n)}$ requires space that is $\Omega(n^2/T)$, the same lower bound applies to sorting.

Let a branching program for $f_{\text{sort}}^{(n)}$ generate the sorted outputs in descending order. By analyzing the outputs the unique elements can be found. Store the last output l along with a bit b that is 1 if l is so far the only occurrence of this value and 0 otherwise. If the next output value is the same as l, set b to 0. If it is different from l and $b = 1$, produce l as an output, replace l with the last output, and set b to 1. Otherwise, do not produce an output.

Given a branching program Π for sorting, we describe a branching program for unique elements that uses modified copies of Π. If more than one output appears on some edge in Π, modify it (yielding Π^*) by replacing edges producing more than one output by a sequence of edges each producing one output separated by vertices testing an arbitrary input. This increases the number of vertices in Π by a factor of at most n and adds at most $\log_2 n$ to its space. Now make $2|\mathcal{R}|$ additional copies of Π^*, two for each value in $\mathcal{R}$, a "one" copy if the value is the first encountered in the sorted output and a "zero" copy if it is not.

Consider an edge in Π^* or one of its copies that produces an output (call it v). There are several cases to examine: the current copy of Π^* is a) the original copy, b) a "one" copy, or c) a "zero" copy. In case a), redirect the edge to the same vertex in the "one" copy of Π^* associated with v. In case b), if v is different from the value c associated with the current copy of Π^*, output c and redirect the edge to the same vertex in the "one" copy of Π^* associated with v. In case c), if v is the same as the value associated with the current copy of Π^*, produce no output; otherwise also produce no output but redirect the edge to the same vertex in the "one" copy of Π^* associated with v. The new branching program has at most $2n + 1$ copies of Π^*, thereby increasing its space by an additive term of size $O(\log n)$. The lower bound on ST for the sorting problem follows.

The upper bound on ST for the sorting problem is obtained by constructing a family of branching programs, one for each value of S. We begin by constructing a "full" branching program for the case $S = \Theta(n)$. Let the variables in the input string be $x_1, x_2, \ldots, x_n$ and let them be tested in sequence. Thus, the root is labeled x_1 and has n successors, each of which tests x_2. There is one successor for each vertex labeled with x_2 for each way two numbers can be chosen with replacement from the set $\{1, 2, \ldots, n\}$. As shown in Problem 10.7, there are $N(n, k)$ ways in which k numbers can be drawn from a set of n elements with replacement where the order among the numbers is unimportant and

$$N(n, k) = \binom{n + k - 1}{k}$$

Thus, $N(n, 1) = n$ and $N(n, 2) = (n + 1)n/2$. The successors to vertices labeled x_2 are labeled x_3. They have $N(n, 3)$ successors, and so on. At the kth level there are $N(n, k)$ successors. Since $N(n, k) < 2^{n+k-1}$, it follows that for $k \leq n$ the above branching program has $O(2^{2n})$ vertices or space $S = \Theta(n)$. It also has time $T = n$ and space–time product $O(n^2)$.

To construct a branching program for space $S = O(n)$, we use $O(n/S)$ pruned copies of the full branching program described above. The idea behind the pruning is the following: we scan the input list looking for variables with values in the set $\{1, 2, \ldots, S\}$. If there are $O(S)$ of them, we record the number of values of each type and produce them in sorted order. However, if there are more than $O(S)$ elements in this range, as we examine additional inputs we reduce the size of the range so that only $O(S)$ space is used to carry the number of values of variables encountered. (This space is represented by $2^{O(S)}$ vertices in the branching program.) On each pass through the input either we reduce the size of the range by $O(S)$ or reduce the number of outputs that must be produced by the same amount. Thus, after $2n/S$ passes the input is sorted. Since each pass tests the value of each variable, the time is $O(n^2/S)$.

It is not difficult to convert the above schema into a branching program. The goal is to have no more than about 2^S vertices on each level of the branching program. The branching program will consist of $O(n/S)$ copies of the full branching program, each having n levels. Thus, the branching program will have $O(n^2 2^S/S)$ vertices or space $O(S)$.

We order vertices at each level in the branching program, placing those with smaller input values to the left. We remove vertices at the jth level that correspond to input values larger than S as well as those to the right of the first 2^S vertices on the jth level. Each edge in the first full branching program that is directed into a removed vertex is redirected to the root of the next copy of the branching program. The second copy of the full branching program is pruned to remove the vertices appearing in the first copy as well as those reached on inputs outside the range $[S + 1, S + 2, \ldots, 2S]$. The edges directed to removed vertices are redirected to the root of the third copy of the full branching program. A similar process is applied to each copy of the full branching program. ∎

Problems

MATHEMATICAL PRELIMINARIES

10.1 Show that the the pyramid graph on m inputs, $P(m)$, has $m(m + 1)/2$ vertices. Let $n = m(m + 1)/2$. Show that $m \geq \sqrt{2n} - 1$.

10.2 Show that the following inequalities hold for integers m and x:

$$m/x \leq \lceil m/x \rceil \leq (m + x - 1)/x$$
$$(m - x + 1)/x \leq \lfloor m/x \rfloor \leq m/x$$

10.3 Suppose that $p \log_2 p \leq q$ for positive integers $p, q \geq 2$. Show that $p \leq 2q/\log_2 q$.

10.4 For n positive integers $x_1, x_2, \ldots, x_n$, show that the following inequality holds between the **geometric mean** on the left and the **arithmetic mean** on the right:

$$(x_1 x_2 \cdots x_n)^{1/n} \leq (x_1 + x_2 + \cdots + x_n)/n$$

10.5 Show that the inequality $(1 - x) \leq e^{-x}$ holds for $x \leq 1$.

10.6 Show that there are $(r + k)!/r!$ ways for k ordered values to appear among r distinct ordered items.

10.7 Show that there are $N(n, k) = \binom{n+k-1}{k} < 2^{n+k-1}$ ways to choose with repetition k numbers from a set $\mathcal{A}$ of size n where the order among the numbers is unimportant. Choosing with repetition means that a number can be chosen more than once.

Hint: Without loss of generality, let $\mathcal{A} = \{1, 2, \ldots, n\}$. Since order is unimportant, assume the chosen numbers are sorted. Let each chosen number be represented by a blue marker. Imagine placing the blue markers on a horizontal line. For $1 \leq i \leq n-1$, place a red marker between the last blue marker associated with the number i and the first blue marker associated with the number $i + 1$, if any. This representation uniquely determines the number of elements of each type chosen. How many ways can the red markers be placed?

10.8 Show that a complete balanced binary tree on 2^{k-1} leaves has $2^k - 1$ vertices including leaves and that each path from a leaf to the root has $k - 1$ edges and k vertices.

THE PEBBLE GAME

10.9 Consider the circuit shown in Fig. 2.15. Treat each gate and each input vertex as a vertex. Give a good pebbling strategy for this graph.

10.10 Give a pebbling strategy for the m-input counting circuit in Fig. 2.21(b) that uses $O(\log^2 m)$ pebbles and $O(m)$ steps. Determine the minimum number of pebbles with which the circuit can be pebbled. Determine the number of steps needed with this minimal pebbling.

SPACE LOWER BOUNDS WITH PEBBLING

10.11 Consider the FFT graph $F^{(k)}$ on $m = 2^k$ inputs. Show that the subgraph connecting inputs to any one output is a complete binary tree on m leaves.

10.12 Consider a directed acyclic graph with n vertices, some of which have out-degree greater than 2. (a) Show that if each vertex of out-degree $k > 2$ is replaced by a binary tree with k leaves and edges directed from the root to the leaves, the number of vertices in the graph is at most doubled. (b) Show that replacing vertices with in-degree greater than 2 with binary trees also at most doubles the number of vertices in the graph.

EXTREME TRADEOFFS WITH PEBBLING

10.13 Let $N(k)$ be the number of vertices in the graph H_k discussed in Section 10.3. Show that the following recurrence holds for $N(k)$:

$$N(k) = N(k - 1) + 4k + 3$$

Show that $N(k) = 2k^2 + 5k - 6$ for $k \geq 2$ since $N(2) = 12$.

10.14 Construct a new family $\{G_k\}$ of graphs with fan-in 2 at each vertex from the graphs $\{H_k\}$ by replacing the tree in Fig. 10.4 by a pyramid graph in k inputs and the bipartite graph with the graph E_k shown in Fig. 10.23. Show that each output of E_k can be pebbled with k pebbles but that after pebbling any one output there is at least one path without pebbles between the input and every other output. Show also that with $k + 1$ pebbles E_k can be pebbled without repebbling any vertex.

Let $T_k(S)$ be the number of steps to pebble G_k with S pebbles. Using the above facts, show the following:

a) $N(k) = |G_k| = O(n^4)$
b) $S_{\min}(G_k) = k$
c) $T_k(k + 1) = N(k)$
d) $T_k(k) = 2^{\Omega(N(k)^{1/4} \log N(k))}$

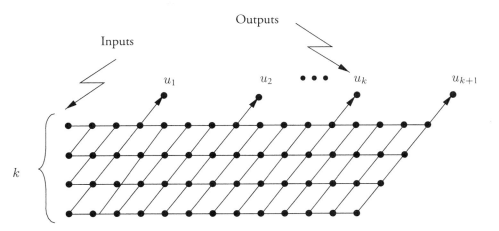

Figure 10.23 The graph E_k used in the construction of the family $\{G_k\}$.

SPACE–TIME LOWER BOUNDS WITH PEBBLING

10.15 Let A be a γ-nice $n \times n$ matrix over a ring $\mathcal{R}$ for some $0 < \gamma < 1/2$. Show that the matrix-vector multiplication function $f^{(n)}_{A \times x} : \mathcal{R}^n \mapsto \mathcal{R}^n$ that maps the input n-tuple x to the output n-tuple Ax is $(1, n^2 + n, n, \gamma n)$-independent.

10.16 Use Lemma 10.12.1 and the result of the previous problem to show that for almost all $n \times n$ matrices A every straight-line program for the matrix-vector multiplication function $f^{(n)}_{A \times x} : \mathcal{R}^n \mapsto \mathcal{R}^n$ over the ring $\mathcal{R}$ requires space S and time T satisfying the inequality

$$(S + 1)T = \Omega(n^2)$$

Furthermore, show that a straight-line program for matrix-vector multiplication can be realized with space $S = 3$ and time $T = n(2n - 1)$, that is, with

$$(S + 1)T = O(n^2)$$

10.17 Linear systems are described in Section 6.2.2. A linear system of n equations in n unknowns x is defined by an $(n \times n)$-coefficient matrix A and an n-vector b, as suggested below:

$$Ax = b \qquad\qquad (10.11)$$

The goal is to solve this equation for x. If A is non-singular, such a solution exists for each vector b. Let $f^{(n)}_{A^{-1} \times b} : \mathcal{R}^{n^2+n} \mapsto \mathcal{R}^n$ denote the **linear system solver function** that maps the matrix A and the vector b onto the solution x when the matrix-vector multiplication is over the ring $\mathcal{R}$ and A is non-singular.

Show that every pebbling strategy for every straight-line program to compute the linear system solver function $f^{(n)}_{A^{-1} \times b} : \mathcal{R}^{n^2} \mapsto \mathcal{R}^{n^2}$ over the ring $\mathcal{R}$ for n even requires space S and time T satisfying the following inequality:

$$(S + 1)T \geq n^3/24$$

Hint: Would it be possible to violate the lower bound on $(S+1)T$ for matrix inversion given in Problem 10.25 if a DAG for the linear system solver function can be pebbled with S pebbles in too few steps?

10.18 Let $f : \mathcal{A}^n \mapsto \mathcal{A}^m$ have $g : \mathcal{A}^r \mapsto \mathcal{A}^s$ as a subfunction. Show that if g is (α, r, s, p)-independent for $r \leq n$ and $s \leq m$, then so is f. Show that, as a consequence, the space S and time T needed to pebble the graph of a straight-line program for f satisfy the following inequality:

$$\lceil \alpha(S + 1) \rceil T \geq sp/4$$

10.19 Show that if a function has an (α, m, p)-flow, it also has an (α, m, q)-flow for $q \leq p$.

Hint: Consider the same set V of outputs in the definition of an (α, m, p)-flow and an (α, m, q)-flow.

10.20 A finite-state machine M computes the function $f_M^{(n)} : Q \times \Sigma^n \mapsto \Psi^n$ that maps the initial state in Q and an input string $\boldsymbol{x}$ of length n over the input alphabet Σ onto an output string $\boldsymbol{y}$ of the same length over the output alphabet Ψ. Such a machine can compute a function $f : \mathcal{A}^n \mapsto \mathcal{A}^n$ by associating inputs and outputs of f with inputs and outputs of $f_M^{(n)}$. A computation of an FSM M of a function f is **input-output oblivious** if the times at which inputs of f are read and its outputs produced are independent of the value of its input variables.

Show that Theorem 10.4.1 can be generalized from straight-line computations to computations by input-output-oblivious FSMs.

Hint: Try to parallel the proof of Theorem 10.4.1 using the FSM M instead of the pebble game. What correspondence can you make between the values under pebbles before the interval $\mathcal{I}$ and the state of M? Let $\log_2 |Q|$, where Q is the set of states of M, be the measure of space associated with it.

10.21 Give a design of an FSM that computes a function f from straight-line programs for it using a number of steps and storage locations proportional to the time and space used by a pebbling strategy for this straight-line program.

Hint: Design the FSM so that it receives the inputs provided to the pebbling strategy as well as instructions to specify which operations are performed on the inputs and temporary storage locations of the FSM.

TRANSITIVE FUNCTIONS

10.22 Many functions for which space–time lower bounds have been derived are transitive. Such functions have the property that for subsets X and Y of their inputs and outputs, respectively, $|X| = |Y| = n$, the (control) inputs not in X can be chosen so as to cause the outputs in Y to be equal to an arbitrary permutation drawn from the set $G(n)$ of the inputs in X. For example, the cyclic shifting function studied in Section 2.5.2 has a set of control inputs that specify the amount by which value inputs are permuted cyclically and assigned to the output variables.

> **DEFINITION 10.13.2** *Let $G(n)$ be a group of permutations of the integers $\mathbf{N}(n) = \{0, 1, 2, \ldots, n-1\}$. That is, if π is in $G(n)$, then $\pi : \mathbf{N}(n) \mapsto \mathbf{N}(n)$. We denote by $\pi(i)$ the integer to which integer i is mapped by π. A function $f_{G(n)} : \mathcal{A}^{n+s} \mapsto \mathcal{A}^n$, where $(y_{n-1}, \ldots, y_1, y_0) = f_{G(n)}(x_{n-1}, \ldots, x_1, x_0, c_{s-1}, \ldots, c_0)$, is said to have* **value inputs** *$x_{n-1}, \ldots, x_1, x_0$,* **control inputs** *$c_{s-1}, \ldots, c_0$, and* **outputs** *$y_{n-1}, \ldots, y_1, y_0$. Such a function is* **transitive of order** *n with respect to the group $G(n)$ if*
>
> a) *For each $0 \le i \le n-1$ and $0 \le j \le n-1$, there exists a permutation $\pi \in G(n)$ such that $\pi(i) = j$, and*
>
> b) *For each $\pi \in G(n)$, there is an assignment to $c_{s-1}, \ldots, c_0$ such that $y_{\pi(i)} = x_i$ for $0 \le i \le n-1$.*

Show that every transitive function of order n with respect to the permutation group $G(n)$, $f_{G(n)} : \mathcal{A}^{n+s} \mapsto \mathcal{A}^n$, is $(2, n+s, n, n/2)$-independent.

10.23 Show that the cyclic shifting function $f_{\text{cyclic}}^{(n)} : \mathcal{B}^{n+\lceil \log n \rceil} \mapsto \mathcal{B}^n$ defined in Section 2.5.2 is transitive of order n.

10.24 Consider the function $f_{PAQ}^{(n)} : \mathcal{R}^{3n^2} \mapsto \mathcal{R}^{n^2}$ whose value is the product PAQ of three $n \times n$ matrices P, A, and Q. Let P and Q be permutation matrices whose entries serve as control inputs. Show that $f_{PAQ}^{(n)}$ is transitive of order n^2.

10.25 The matrix inversion function $f_{M^{-1}}^{(n)} : \mathcal{R}^{n^2} \mapsto \mathcal{R}^{n^2}$ maps a non-singular $n \times n$ matrix over the ring $\mathcal{R}$ to its inverse. (See Section 6.3.) Show that $f_{M^{-1}}^{(n)}$ is $(2, n^2, n, n/2)$-independent.

Hint: Show that $f_{M^{-1}}^{(2n)}$ contains as a subfunction the function $f_{PAQ}^{(n)} : \mathcal{R}^{3n^2} \mapsto \mathcal{R}^{n^2}$ defined in Problem 10.24. In this connection consider the following identity, which holds when the $n \times n$ matrices R and S are non-singular:

$$M = \begin{bmatrix} R & A \\ 0 & S \end{bmatrix}^{-1} = \begin{bmatrix} R^{-1} & -R^{-1}AS^{-1} \\ 0 & S^{-1} \end{bmatrix}$$

PEBBLING SUPERCONCENTRATORS

10.26 Show that the graph consisting of two $n = 2^d$-input FFT graphs connected back to back (as shown in Fig. 10.24 with the second FFT graph reversed) is a superconcentrator. (Valiant [337] has shown the existence of n-superconcentrators with $O(n)$ vertices.)

Hint: Reason that there are unique vertex-disjoint paths from any r input vertices of this graph to any r consecutive vertices that are simultaneously outputs of the first FFT graph and the inputs to the reversed FFT graph. The first and last vertices are consecutive.

10.27 Prove that to pebble any $S + 1$ outputs of an n-superconcentrator, $S + 1 \le n$, from an initial placement of S pebbles requires that at least $n - S$ different inputs be pebbled.

Hint: Suppose that at most $n - (S + 1)$ inputs are pebbled from an initial placement of S pebbles to pebble $S + 1$ outputs. Can you reason from the superconcentration

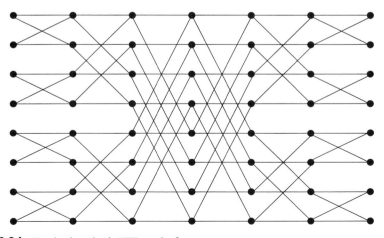

Figure 10.24   Two back-to-back FFT graphs form a superconcentrator.

property that $S + 1$ or more inputs cannot remain unpebbled since $S + 1$ outputs are pebbled?

10.28 Use the result of the previous problem to show that to pebble an n-superconcentrator with S pebbles in time T requires S and T to satisfy the following inequality:

$$(S + 1)T \geq \frac{n^2}{2}$$

Hint: As in the proof of Theorem 10.4.1, divide time up into consecutive intervals. Choose the intervals so that each has the same number of outputs pebbled during it. Apply the results of the previous problem to obtain a lower bound on the sum of the number of input and output vertices that are pebbled during the interval.

10.29 Show that the pebbling of two n-input back-to-back FFT graphs requires space and time that satisfy $S^2 T = \Omega(n^3)$ and that this lower bound can be achieved up to a multiplicative factor.

Hint: From the proof of Lemma 10.5.4 it follows that to pebble any $2S$ outputs with S pebbles at least $n - S + 1$ inputs must be pebbled because if fewer inputs need be pebbled the outputs can have more values than is possible for the FFT.

APPLICATIONS OF THE GRIGORIEV LOWER BOUND

10.30 Show that there is a pebbling for a straight-line program for the cyclic shift function $f_{\text{cyclic}}^{(n)} : \mathcal{B}^{n+\lceil \log n \rceil} \mapsto \mathcal{B}^n$ examined in Section 10.5.2 for which $(S + 1)T = O(n^2 \log n)$.

Hint: Pebble the graph of the circuit described in Section 2.5.1. Construct a circuit for $f_{\text{cyclic}}^{(n)}$ that produces each output with $O(n \log n)$ gates.

10.31 Show that the binary addition function $f_{\text{add}}^{(n)}$ (see Section 2.7) can be realized by a straight-line program using space and time satisfying $ST = O(n)$.

10.32 Derive tight upper and lower bounds on the product $(S + 1)T$ for pebblings of circuits for the squaring function $f_{\text{square}}^{(n)}$.

10.33 Derive tight upper and lower bounds on the product $(S + 1)T$ for pebblings of circuits for the reciprocal function $f_{\text{recip}}^{(n)}$.

10.34 In Section 6.5.3 a straight-line algorithm is given to invert an $n \times n$ triangular matrix. Construct another straight-line algorithm based on it that can be pebbled with $O(n)$ pebbles to produce outputs by columns in $O(n^3)$ steps under the assumption that the standard matrix multiplication algorithm is used for the matrix multiplication steps.

Hint: To produce outputs of a triangular matrix T by columns using the algorithm of Fig. 6.5, it is necessary to read the elements of $T_{2,1}$ by rows and produce the outputs of $T_{2,2}^{-1}$ by rows. Consider modifying this algorithm to generate the elements of the latter matrix first by rows and then by columns.

BRANCHING PROGRAMS

10.35 Give a proof of Lemma 10.9.1 by a) designing a general branching program to simulate a comparison operator and b) using this design in a complete branching program that simulates a decision branching program.

10.36 In Section 10.9 a procedure is given to convert a general branching program to a tree program without increasing the length of any path. Use this fact to show that every decision branching program with queries $\{\leq, =\}$ that sorts a list of n items requires worst-case time of at least $(n/2)\log(n/2)$ when n is even. Show that this lower bound can be achieved up to a constant multiplicative factor.

Hint: Show that every binary tree with m leaves must have a longest path of length at least $\log_2 m$ and determine the number of distinct leaves necessary in every decision branching program for sorting.

THE BORODIN-COOK LOWER-BOUND METHOD

10.37 The computation time of a branching program is the length of the longest path in its directed acyclic multigraph. Assume that a probability is assigned to each input $\boldsymbol{x}$ of length n. The **average computation time**, $\overline{T}$, of a branching program is the sum of the lengths of the paths associated with different inputs weighted by the probabilities of these inputs. To compute the average space of a branching program with k vertices, the integers in the set $\{1, 2, \ldots, k\}$ are assigned to the vertices of the branching program. The space associated with input $\boldsymbol{x}$ is the base-2 logarithm of the largest such integer encountered during the computation associated with $\boldsymbol{x}$. The average space associated with a numbering of vertices is the average of this logarithm. The **average space**, $\overline{S}$, associated with a branching program is the smallest average space over all numberings of vertices.

Given a probability distribution on inputs of length n, let $C_f(a, b)$ denote the maximum over all those tree branching programs of depth a of the probability that b of the m outputs of the function f are computed correctly. Show that Theorem 10.11.1 can be generalized to the above probabilistic setting.

Hint: If $\overline{T}$ is the average time of the branching program P, truncate the branching program at depth $2\overline{T}$, call the new program P^*, and show that P^* solves the problem solved by P with probability at least $1/2$. Also, show that with probability at least $1/2$ there exists a rich path in some stage that produces $b = \lceil m/\sigma \rceil$ outputs. Let p_i be the probability that the subtree with root i in some stage correctly produces b outputs. Now develop an upper bound in terms of the p_i on the probability that some tree in some stage correctly produces b outputs.

APPLICATIONS OF THE BORODIN-COOK LOWER BOUND

10.38 Show that the branching program in Fig. 10.20 computes the inner product of two 3-element sequences over the **set of integers modulo-2**; that is, the integers $\{0, 1\}$ with the EXCLUSIVE-OR function for addition and the AND function for multiplication.

10.39 Complete the proof of Theorem 10.13.2 by filling in the details of the construction of a branching program for integer multiplication for the middle range of space.

10.40 Complete the proof of Theorem 10.13.4 by showing that two $n \times n$ matrices can be multiplied with a hybrid algorithm that combines table lookup with the standard matrix multiplication algorithm on $k \times k$ blocks to achieve space and time satisfying

$$ST^2 = O(n^3 \log |\mathcal{R}|)$$

10.41 Show that the RAM program described in Fig. 10.22 can be converted to a branching program of space $O(S)$ and time $O(T)$.

Chapter Notes

The first formal study of space–time tradeoffs was made by Cobham [73]. He considered computations on one-tape Turing machines using as a space measure the logarithm of the number of configurations, and obtained quadratic lower bounds on the space–time product to recognize strings representing palindromes and perfect squares.

The pebble-game model was implicitly used by Paterson and Hewitt [233] to study program schemas, uninterpreted graphs representing programs. They derived the space lower bound of Lemma 10.2.1, thereby demonstrating that recursive programs are more powerful than nonrecursive ones. Cook [75,79] asked how much space (how many pebbles) was needed to execute a program schema with n vertices and obtained the result for pyramids of Lemma 10.2.2, showing that the minimum space is at least $\Omega(\sqrt{n})$ for some schemas. The minimum-space question was answered by Hopcroft, Paul, and Valiant [139], who proved Theorem 10.7.1, and Paul, Tarjan, and Celoni [240], who obtained Theorem 10.8.1. The pebble model first formally appeared in [139]. Gilbert, Lengauer, and Tarjan [114] and Loui [203] have shown that the languages associated with minimal pebblings of DAGs (described at the end of Section 10.2) are **PSPACE**-complete.

In addition to studying the minimum space needed for a computation, researchers also examined tradeoffs between space and time. Paterson and Hewitt [233] studied the conversion of a linear recursive program schema into a non-recursive one and demonstrated that the time needed satisfies $T = \Omega(n^{1+1/(S-1)})$ for $S \geq 2$. (See Chandra [66] and Swamy and Savage [315]) for more details on this problem.)

A number of other authors have identified graphs exhibiting non-trivial exchanges of space for time. Pippenger [248] gave a graph on n vertices for which $T = \Omega(n \log \log n)$ when $S = O(n/\log n)$, and Savage and Swamy [287] demonstrated that the FFT graph requires S and T satisfying $ST = \Theta(n^2)$. (This is the first tradeoff result for a natural algorithm. Their upper bound is given in Theorem 10.5.5.) Later Tompa [327] and Reischuk [273] exhibited graphs requiring $T = \Omega(n \log n)$ and $T = \Omega(n \log^t n)$ for any integer t, respectively, when $S = \Theta(n/\log n)$.

Paul and Tarjan [239], Lingas [198], and van Emde Boas and van Leeuwen [343] gave graphs with T increasing from $O(n)$ to $T = 2^{\Omega(n^{1/2})}$, $T = 2^{\Omega(n^{1/3})}$, and $T = 2^{\Omega(n^{1/4} \log n)}$, respectively, when S drops by a constant amount from $S = O(n^{1/2})$, $S = O(n^{1/3})$ and $S = O(n^{1/4})$, respectively. Theorem 10.3.1 is from [343], as is Problem 10.14. Carlson and Savage [64] took a different tack and exhibited graphs for which T is superlinear, namely, $T = 2^{\Omega(\log n \log \log n)}$ over a range of values of S, namely, $\Omega(\log n) \leq S \leq O(n^{1/2}/\log n)$. References to the worst-case exchange of space for time are given in Section 10.6.

Grigoriev [120] gave the first space–time lower bounds that apply to all graphs for a problem (see Corollary 10.4.1), the essential idea of which is generalized in Theorem 10.4.1. Savage [286] introduced the $w(u, v)$-flow measure used in this version of a theorem to derive lower bounds on area–time tradeoffs for VLSI algorithms. Grigoriev [120] also established Theorem 10.4.2 and derived a tradeoff lower bound on polynomial multiplication that is equivalent to Theorem 10.5.1 on convolution. The improved version of Theorem 10.4.2, namely Theorem 10.5.4, is original with this book.

Lower bounds using the Grigoriev approach explicitly require that the sets over which functions are defined be finite. Tompa [325,326] eliminated the requirement for finite sets but required instead that functions be linear. Using concentrator properties of matrices deduced by Valiant [337], Tompa derived a lower bound on ST for superconcentrators that he applied to matrix-vector multiplication and polynomial multiplication. He developed a similar lower bound for the DFT. (See Abelson [2] for a generalization of some of these results to continuous functions.) The lower bound of Theorem 10.5.5 uses Tompa's DFT proof but does not require that straight-line programs be linear.

The result on cyclic shift (Theorem 10.5.2) is due to Savage [285]. (This paper also generalizes Grigoriev's model to I/O-oblivious FSMs, extends JáJá's [145] space–time lower bound for matrix inversion, and derives space–time lower bounds for transitive functions and banded matrices.) The result on integer multiplication (Theorem 10.5.3) is due to Savage and Swamy [288]. In [325] Tompa also obtained Theorem 10.5.6 on merging. Transitive functions defined in Problem 10.22 were introduced by Vuillemin [349].

In [327] Tompa examined the graph associated with the algorithm for transitive closure based on successive squarings described in Section 6.4 and demonstrated that it can be pebbled either in a polynomial number of steps or with small space, namely $O(\log^2 n)$, but not both. Carlson [61] demonstrated that algorithms for convolution based on FFT graphs (see Section 6.7.4) require that $T = \Theta(n^3/S^2 + n^2(\log n)/S)$, which doesn't come close to matching the lower bound of Theorem 10.5.1. However, through the judicious replacement of back-to-back FFT subgraphs in the standard convolution algorithm, Carlson [62] was able to achieve the bounds $T = \Theta(n \log S + n^2(\log S)/S)$, which are optimal over all FFT-based convolution algorithms and nearly as good as the $T = \Theta(n^2/S)$ bounds. (See also [63].) Carlson and Savage [65] explored for a number of problems the size of the smallest graphs that can be pebbled with a small number of pebbles and demonstrated a tradeoff between size and space.

Pippenger [245] has surveyed many of the results described above as well as those on the black-white pebble game described below.

Several extensions of the pebble game have been developed. One of these is the red-blue pebble game discussed in Chapter 11 and its generalization, the memory hierarchy game. Another is the black-white pebble game whose rules are the following: a) a black pebble can be placed on an input vertex at any time and on a non-input vertex only if its predecessors carry pebbles, whether white or black; b) a black pebble may be removed at any time; c) a white pebble can be placed on a vertex at any time; d) a white pebble can be removed only if all its predecessors carry pebbles. The placement of white pebbles models a non-deterministic guess. The removal of a white vertex is allowed only when the guess has been verified. Questions this game makes possible are whether the minimum space required for a graph is lower with the black-white pebble game than with the standard game and whether for a given amount of space, the time required is lower. The black-white game was introduced by Cook and Sethi

[78], who showed that the minimum space for the pyramid graph is at least $\sqrt{N/2} - 1$. Meyer auf der Heide [218] proved that this minimum space is at most $\lceil n/2 \rceil + 2$ and established in general that any graph with minimum space n in the black-white game has minimum space at most $(n^2 - n)/2 + 1$ in the standard game. The latter result is the pebbling analog of Savitch's theorem (Theorem 8.5.5).

Loui [202] and Meyer auf der Heide [218] have shown that the minimum space with the black-white game is at least one half that for the standard pebble game for balanced trees, a result extended by Lengauer and Tarjan [193] to all trees and then by Klawe [164]. Wilber [357] has exhibited an infinite family of graphs for which the black-white minimum space is smaller than the minimum space with the standard game by more than a constant factor.

All of the pebble games mentioned above are one-person games; that is, one person plays the game. A two-person game introduced by Venkateswaran and Tompa [346] models parallel complexity classes. Savage and Vitter [290] have also introduced a model of parallel pebbling.

Branching programs have been known as binary decision diagrams for at least 30 years [15], although their importance to CAD was recognized only in the last 10 or 12 years. (See [60]). Branching programs were proposed as a vehicle for studying space–time problems by Pippenger and first studied by Tompa [325], who cites Pippenger for Lemma 10.9.2. Borodin, Fischer, Kirkpatrick, Lynch, and Tompa [55] derived a lower bound of $ST = \Omega(n^2)$ to sort n items with decision branching programs. Borodin and Cook [53] formulated the same problem in terms of the general branching programs of Section 10.9 and developed the general framework used in Theorem 10.11.1.

Yesha [364] developed lower bounds on the space–time product with branching problems for the discrete Fourier transform (see Theorem 10.13.7) and matrix multiplication over restricted domains. Abrahamson [6] (see also [4]) derived the lower bound on ST^2 in Theorem 10.13.4, thereby improving upon the matrix multiplication bound of Yesha. He also extended the Borodin-Cook model to probabilistic branching programs (see Problem 10.37) and derived the lower bound on ST for convolution (Theorem 10.13.1), integer multiplication (Theorem 10.13.2), matrix-vector multiplication (Theorem 10.13.3), and matrix inversion (Theorem 10.13.6). He also developed a lower bound of $\Omega(n^3)$ on ST to compute the product PAQ of three $n \times n$ matrices, where P and Q are permutation matrices. Abrahamson has also studied Boolean matrix multiplication in the general branching program model [5]. Beame [34] has obtained the result of Theorem 10.13.8 showing that the unique elements problem requires that $ST = \Omega(n^2)$ for general branching programs, which implies the lower bound on sorting stated in Theorem 10.13.9.

In the comparison-based branching program model, Borodin, Fich, Meyer auf der Heide, Upfal, and Wigderson [54] derive the lower bound $ST = \Omega(n^{3/2}\sqrt{\log n})$ for the element-distinctness problem on n inputs. For the same computational model, Yao [363] improved this to $ST = \Omega(n^{2-\epsilon(n)})$, where $\epsilon(n)$ is a decreasing function of n.

11

Memory-Hierarchy Tradeoffs

Although serial programming languages assume that programs are written for the RAM model, this model is rarely implemented in practice. Instead, the random-access memory is replaced with a hierarchy of memory units of increasing size, decreasing cost per bit, and increasing access time. In this chapter we study the conditions on the size and speed of these units when a CPU and a memory hierarchy simulate the RAM model. The design of memory hierarchies is a topic in operating systems.

A memory hierarchy typically contains the local registers of the CPU at the lowest level and may contain at succeeding levels a small, very fast, local random-access memory called a cache, a slower but still fast random-access memory, and a large but slow disk. The time to move data between levels in a memory hierarchy is typically a few CPU cycles at the cache level, tens of cycles at the level of a random-access memory, and hundreds of thousands of cycles at the disk level! A CPU that accesses a random-access memory on every CPU cycle may run at about a tenth of its maximum speed, and the situation can be dramatically worse if the CPU must access the disk frequently. Thus it is highly desirable to understand for a given problem how the number of data movements between levels in a hierarchy depends on the storage capacity of each memory unit in that hierarchy.

In this chapter we study tradeoffs between the number of storage locations (space) at each memory-hierarchy level and the number of data movements (I/O time) between levels. Two closely related models of memory hierarchies are used, the memory-hierarchy pebble game and the hierarchical memory model, which are extensions of those introduced in Chapter 10.

In most of this chapter it is assumed not only that the user has control over the I/O algorithm used for a problem but that the operating system does not interfere with the I/O operations requested by the user. However, we also examine I/O performance when the operating system, not the user, controls the sequence of memory accesses (Section 11.10). Competitive analysis is used in this case to evaluate two-level LRU and FIFO memory-management algorithms.

11.1 The Red-Blue Pebble Game

The red-blue pebble game models data movement between adjacent levels of a two-level memory hierarchy. We begin with this model to fix ideas and then introduce the more general memory-hierarchy game. Both games are played on a directed acyclic graph, the graph of a straight-line program. We describe the game and then give its rules.

In the red-blue game, (hot) red pebbles identify values held in a fast primary memory whereas (cold) blue pebbles identify values held in a secondary memory. The values identified with the pebbles can be words or blocks of words, such as the pages used by an operating system. Since the red-blue pebble game is used to study the number of I/O operations necessary for a problem, the number of red pebbles is assumed limited and the number of blue pebbles is assumed unlimited. Before the game starts, blue pebbles reside on all input vertices. The goal is to place a blue pebble on each output vertex, that is, to compute the values associated with these vertices and place them in long-term storage. These assumptions capture the idea that data resides initially in the most remote memory unit and the results must be deposited there.

RED-BLUE PEBBLE GAME

- (Initialization) A blue pebble can be placed on an input vertex at any time.

- (Computation Step) A red pebble can be placed on (or moved to) a vertex if all its immediate predecessors carry red pebbles.

- (Pebble Deletion) A pebble can be deleted from any vertex at any time.

- (Goal) A blue pebble must reside on each output vertex at the end of the game.

- (Input from Blue Level) A red pebble can be placed on any vertex carrying a blue pebble.

- (Output to Blue Level) A blue pebble can be placed on any vertex carrying a red pebble.

The first rule (**initialization**) models the retrieval of input data from the secondary memory. The second rule (a **computation step**) is equivalent to requiring that all the arguments on which a function depends reside in primary memory before the function can be computed. This rule also allows a pebble to move (or **slide**) to a vertex from one of its predecessors, modeling the use of a register as both the source and target of an operation. The third rule allows **pebble deletion**: if a red pebble is removed from a vertex that later needs a red pebble, it must be repebbled.

The fourth rule (the **goal**) models the placement of output data in the secondary memory at the end of a computation. The fifth rule allows data held in the secondary memory to be moved back to the primary memory (an **input operation**). The sixth rule allows a result to be copied to a secondary memory of unlimited capacity (an **output operation**). Note that a result may be in both memories at the same time.

The red-blue pebble game is a direct generalization of the pebble game of Section 10.1 (which we call the **red pebble game**), as can be seen by restricting the sixth rule to allow the placement of blue pebbles only on vertices that are output vertices of the DAG. Under this restriction the blue level cannot be used for intermediate results and the goal of the game becomes to minimize the number of times vertices are pebbled with red pebbles, since the optimal strategy pebbles each output vertex once.

A **pebbling strategy** $\mathcal{P}$ is the execution of the rules of the pebble game on the vertices of a graph. We assign a step to each placement of a pebble, ignoring steps on which pebbles are removed, and number the steps consecutively. The **space** used by a strategy $\mathcal{P}$ is defined as the maximum number of red pebbles it uses. The **I/O time**, T_2, of $\mathcal{P}$ on the graph G is the number of input and output (I/O) steps used by $\mathcal{P}$. The **computation time**, T_1, is the number of computation steps of $\mathcal{P}$ on G. Note that time in the red pebble game is the time to place red pebbles on input and internal vertices; in this chapter the former are called **I/O operations**.

Since accesses to secondary memory are assumed to require much more time than accesses to primary memory, a **minimal pebbling strategy**, $\mathcal{P}_{\min}$, performs the minimal number of I/O operations on a graph G for a given number of red pebbles and uses the smallest number of red pebbles for a given I/O time. Furthermore, such a strategy also uses the smallest number of computation steps among those meeting the other requirements. We denote by $T_1^{(2)}(S, G)$ and $T_2^{(2)}(S, G)$ the number of computation and I/O steps in a minimal pebbling of G in the red-blue pebble game with S red pebbles.

The minimum number of red pebbles needed to play the red-blue pebble game is the maximum number of predecessors of any vertex. This follows because blue pebbles can be used to hold all intermediate results. Thus, in the FFT graph of Fig. 11.1 only two red pebbles are needed, since one of them can be slid to the vertex being pebbled. However, if the minimum number of pebbles is used, many expensive I/O operations are necessary.

In Section 11.2 we generalize the red-blue pebble game to multiple levels and consider two variants of the model, one in which all levels including the highest can be used for intermediate storage, and a second in which the highest level cannot be used for intermediate storage. The second model (the **I/O-limited game**) captures aspects of the red-blue pebble game as well as the red pebble game of Chapter 10.

An important distinction between the pebble game results obtained in this chapter and those in Chapter 10 is that here lower bounds are generally derived for particular graphs, whereas in Chapter 10 they are obtained for all graphs of a problem.

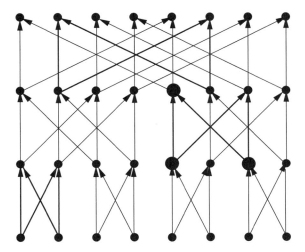

Figure 11.1 An eight-input FFT graph showing three two-input FFT subgraphs.

11.1.1 Playing the Red-Blue Pebble Game

The rules for the red-blue pebble game are illustrated by the eight-input FFT graph shown in Fig. 11.1. If $S = 3$ red pebbles are available to pebble this graph (at least $S = 4$ pebbles are needed in the one-pebble game), a pebbling strategy that keeps the number of I/O operations small is based on the pebbling of sub-FFT graphs on two inputs. Three such sub-FFT subgraphs are shown by heavy lines in Fig. 11.1, one at each level of the FFT graph. This pebbling strategy uses three red pebbles to place blue pebbles on the outputs of each of the four lowest-level sub-FFT graphs on two inputs, those whose outputs are second-level vertices of the full FFT graph. (Thus, eight blue pebbles are used.) Shown on a second-level sub-FFT graph are three red pebbles at the time when a pebble has just been placed on the first of the two outputs of this sub-FFT graph. This strategy performs two I/O operations for each vertex except for input and output vertices. A small savings is possible if, after pebbling the last sub-FFT graph at one level, we immediately pebble the last sub-FFT graph at the next level.

11.1.2 Balanced Computer Systems

A **balanced computer system** is one in which no computational unit or data channel becomes saturated before any other. The results in this chapter can be used to analyze balance. To illustrate this point, we examine a serial computer system consisting of a CPU with a random-access memory and a disk storage unit. Such a system is balanced for a particular problem if the time used for I/O is comparable to the time used for computation.

As shown in Section 11.5.2, multiplying two $n \times n$ matrices with a variant of the classical matrix multiplication algorithm requires a number of computations proportional to n^3 and a number of I/O operations proportional to $n^3/\sqrt{S}$, where S is the number of red pebbles or the capacity of the random-access memory. Let t_0 and t_1 be the times for one computation and I/O operation, respectively. Then the system is balanced when $t_0 n^3 \approx t_1 n^3/\sqrt{S}$. Let the **computational** and **I/O capacities**, C_{comp} and $C_{\text{I/O}}$, be the rates at which the CPU and disk can compute and exchange data, respectively; that is, $C_{\text{comp}} = 1/t_0$ and $C_{\text{I/O}} = 1/t_1$. Thus, balance is achieved when the following condition holds:

$$\frac{C_{\text{comp}}}{C_{\text{I/O}}} \approx \sqrt{S}$$

From this condition we see that if through technological advance the ratio $C_{\text{comp}}/C_{\text{I/O}}$ increases by a factor β, then for the system to be balanced the storage capacity of the system, S, must increase by a factor β^2.

Hennessy and Patterson [131, p. 427] observe that CPU speed is increasing between 50% and 100% per year while that of disks is increasing at a steady 7% per year. Thus, if the ratio $C_{\text{comp}}/C_{\text{I/O}}$ for our simple computer system grows by a factor of $50/7 \approx 7$ per year, then S must grow by about a factor of 49 per year to maintain balance. To the extent that matrix multiplication is typical of the type of computing to be done and that computers have two-level memories, a crisis is looming in the computer industry! Fortunately, multi-level memory hierarchies are being introduced to help avoid this crisis.

As bad as the situation is for matrix multiplication, it is much worse for the Fourier transform and sorting. For each of these problems the number of computation and I/O operations is proportional to $n \log_2 n$ and $n \log_2 n/\log_2 S$, respectively (see Sections 11.5.3). Thus, balance is achieved when

$$\frac{C_{\text{comp}}}{C_{\text{I/O}}} \approx \log_2 S$$

Consequently, if $C_{\text{comp}}/C_{\text{I/O}}$ increases by a factor β, S must increase by a factor of 2^β. Under the conditions given above, a balanced two-level memory-hierarchy system for these problems must have a storage capacity S that grows by a factor of about 128 every year.

11.2 The Memory-Hierarchy Pebble Game

The standard **memory-hierarchy game** (MHG) defined below generalizes the two-level red-blue game to multiple levels. The L-level MHG is played on directed acyclic graphs with p_l pebbles at level l, $1 \le l \le L - 1$, and an unlimited number of pebbles at level L. When $L = 2$, the lower level is the red level and the higher is the blue level. The number of pebbles used at the $L - 1$ lowest levels is recorded in the **resource vector** $\boldsymbol{p} = (p_1, p_2, \ldots, p_{L-1})$, where $p_j \ge 1$ for $1 \le j \le L - 1$. The rules of the game are given below.

STANDARD MEMORY-HIERARCHY GAME

R1. (Initialization) A level-L pebble can be placed on an input vertex at any time.

R2. (Computation Step) A first-level pebble can be placed on (or moved to) a vertex if all its immediate predecessors carry first-level pebbles.

R3. (Pebble Deletion) A pebble of any level can be deleted from any vertex.

R4. (Goal) A level-L pebble must reside on each output vertex at the end of the game.

R5. (Input from Level l) For $2 \le l \le L$, a level-$(l - 1)$ pebble can be placed on any vertex carrying a level-l pebble.

R6. (Output to Level l) For $2 \le l \le L$, a level-l pebble can be placed on any vertex carrying a level-$(l - 1)$ pebble.

The first four rules are exactly as in the red-blue pebble game. The fifth and sixth rules generalize the fifth and sixth rules of the red-blue pebble game by identifying inputs from and outputs to level-l memory. These last two rules allow a level-l memory to serve as temporary storage for lower-level memories.

In the standard MHG, the highest-level memory can be used for storing intermediate results. An important variant of the MHG is the **I/O-limited memory-hierarchy game**, in which the highest level memory cannot be used for intermediate storage. The rules of this game are the same as in the MHG except that rule R6 is replaced by the following two rules:

I/O-LIMITED MEMORY-HIERARCHY GAME

R6. (Output to Level l) For $2 \le l \le L - 1$, a level-l pebble can be placed on any vertex carrying a level-$(l - 1)$ pebble.

R7. (I/O Limitation) Level-L pebbles can only be placed on **output** vertices carrying level-$(L - 1)$ pebbles.

The sixth and seventh rules of the new game allow the placement of level-L pebbles only on output vertices. The two-level version of the I/O-limited MHG is the one-pebble game studied in Chapter 10. As mentioned earlier, we call the two-level I/O-limited MHG the **red pebble game** to distinguish it from the red-blue pebble game and the MHG. Clearly the multi-level I/O-limited MHG is a generalization of both the standard MHG and the one-pebble game.

The I/O-limited MHG models the case in which accesses to the highest level memory take so long that it should be used only for archival storage, not intermediate storage. Today disks are so much slower than the other memories in a hierarchy that the I/O-limited MHG is the appropriate model when disks are used at the highest level.

The **resource vector** $p = (p_1, p_2, \ldots, p_{L-1})$ associated with a pebbling strategy $\mathcal{P}$ specifies the number of l-level pebbles, p_l, used by $\mathcal{P}$. We say that p_l is the **space** used at level l by $\mathcal{P}$. We assume that $p_l \geq 1$ for $1 \leq l \leq L$, so that swapping between levels is possible. The **I/O time** at level l with pebbling strategy $\mathcal{P}$ and resource vector p, $T_l^{(L)}(p, G, \mathcal{P})$, $2 \leq l \leq L$, with both versions of the MHG is the number of inputs from and outputs to level l. The **computation time** with pebbling strategy $\mathcal{P}$ and resource vector p, $T_1^{(L)}(p, G, \mathcal{P})$, in the MHG is the number of times first-level pebbles are placed on vertices by $\mathcal{P}$. Since there is little risk of confusion, we use the same notation, $T_l^{(L)}(p, G, \mathcal{P})$, in the standard and I/O-limited MHG for the number of computation and I/O steps.

The definition of a minimal MHG pebbling is similar to that for a red-blue pebbling. Given a resource vector p, $\mathcal{P}_{\min}$ is a **minimal pebbling** for an L-level MHG if it minimizes the I/O time at level L, after which it minimizes the I/O time at level $L - 1$, continuing in this fashion down to level 2. Among these strategies it must also minimize the computation time. This definition of minimality is used because we assume that the time needed to move data between levels of a memory hierarchy grows rapidly enough with increasing level that it is less costly to repebble vertices at or below a given level than to perform an I/O operation at a higher level.

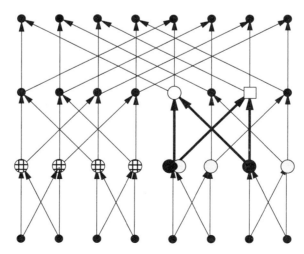

Figure 11.2 Pebbling an eight-input FFT graph in the three-level MHG.

11.2.1 Playing the MHG

Figure 11.2 shows the FFT graph on eight inputs being pebbled in a three-level MHG with resource vector $\boldsymbol{p} = (2, 4)$. Here black circles denote first-level pebbles, shaded circles denote second-level pebbles and striped circles denote third-level pebbles. Four striped, three shaded and two black pebbles reside on vertices in the second row of the FFT. One of these shaded second-level pebbles shares a vertex with a black first-level pebble, so that this black pebble can be moved to the vertex covered by the open circle without deleting all pebbles on the doubly covered vertex.

To pebble the vertex under the open square with a black pebble, we reuse the black pebble on the open circle by swapping it with a fourth shaded pebble, after which we place the black pebble on the vertex that was doubly covered and then slide it to the vertex covered by the open box. This graph can be completely pebbled with the resource vector $\boldsymbol{p} = (2, 4)$ using only four third-level pebbles, as the reader is asked to show. (See Problem 11.3.) Thus, it can also be pebbled in the four-level I/O-limited MHG using resource vector $\boldsymbol{p} = (2, 4, 4)$.

11.3 I/O-Time Relationships

The following simple relationships follow from two observations. First, each input and output vertex must receive a pebble at each level, since every input must be read from level L and every output must be written to level L. Second, at least one computation step is needed for each non-input vertex of the graph. Here we assume that every vertex in V must be pebbled to pebble the output vertices.

LEMMA 11.3.1 *Let α be the maximum in-degree of any vertex in $G = (V, E)$ and let $In(G)$ and $Out(G)$ be the sets of input and output vertices of G, respectively. Then any pebbling $\mathcal{P}$ of G with the MHG, whether standard or I/O-limited, satisfies the following conditions for $2 \leq l \leq L$:*

$$T_l^{(L)}(\boldsymbol{p}, G, \mathcal{P}) \geq |In(G)| + |Out(G)|$$
$$T_1^{(L)}(\boldsymbol{p}, G, \mathcal{P}) \geq |V| - |In(G)|$$

The following theorem relates the number of moves in an L-level game to the number in a two-level game and allows us to use prior results. The lower bound on the level-l I/O time is stated in terms of s_{l-1} because pebbles at levels $1, 2, \ldots, l-1$ are treated collectively as red pebbles to derive a lower bound; pebbles at level l and above are treated as blue pebbles.

THEOREM 11.3.1 *Let $s_l = \sum_{j=1}^{l-1} p_j$. Then the following inequalities hold for every L-level standard MHG pebbling strategy $\mathcal{P}$ for G, where $\boldsymbol{p}$ is the resource vector used by $\mathcal{P}$ and $T_1^{(2)}(S, G)$ and $T_2^{(2)}(S, G)$ are the number of computation and I/O operations used by a minimal pebbling in the red-blue pebble game played on G with S red pebbles:*

$$T_l^{(L)}(\boldsymbol{p}, G, \mathcal{P}) \geq T_2^{(2)}(s_{l-1}, G) \quad \text{for } 2 \leq l \leq L$$

Also, the following lower bound on computation time holds for all pebbling strategies $\mathcal{P}$ in the standard MHG:

$$T_1^{(L)}(\boldsymbol{p}, G, \mathcal{P}) \geq T_1^{(2)}(s_1, G),$$

In the I/O-limited case the following lower bounds apply, where α is the maximum fan-in of any vertex of G:

$$T_l^{(L)}(\boldsymbol{p}, G, \mathcal{P}) \geq T_2^{(2)}(s_{L-1}, G) \quad \text{for } 2 \leq l \leq L$$
$$T_1^{(L)}(\boldsymbol{p}, G, \mathcal{P}) \geq T_2^{(2)}(s_{L-1}, G)/\alpha$$

Proof The first set of inequalities is shown by considering the red-blue game played with $S = s_{l-1}$ red pebbles and an unlimited number of blue pebbles. The S red pebbles and $s_{L-1} - S$ blue pebbles can be classified into $L - 1$ groups with p_j pebbles in the jth group, so that we can simulate the steps of an L-level MHG pebbling strategy $\mathcal{P}$. Because there are constraints on the use of pebbles in $\mathcal{P}$, this strategy uses a number of level-l I/O operations that cannot be larger than the minimum number of such I/O operations when pebbles at level $l - 1$ or less are treated as red pebbles and those at higher levels are treated as blue pebbles. Thus, $T_l^{(L)}(\boldsymbol{p}, G, \mathcal{P}) \geq T_2^{(2)}(s_{l-1}, G)$. By similar reasoning it follows that $T_1^{(L)}(\boldsymbol{p}, G, \mathcal{P}) \geq T_1^{(2)}(s_1, G)$.

In the above simulation, blue pebbles simulating levels l and above cannot be used arbitrarily when the I/O-limitation is imposed. To derive lower bounds under this limitation, we classify $S = s_{L-1}$ pebbles into $L - 1$ groups with p_j pebbles in the jth group and simulate in the red-blue pebble game the steps of an L-level I/O-limited MHG pebbling strategy $\mathcal{P}$. The I/O time at level l is no more than the I/O time in the two-level I/O-limited red-blue pebble game in which all S red pebbles are used at level $l - 1$ or less.

Since the number of blue pebbles is unlimited, in a minimal pebbling all I/O operations consist of placing of red pebbles on blue-pebbled vertices. It follows that if T I/O operations are performed on the input vertices, then at least T placements of red pebbles on blue-pebbled vertices occur. Since at least one internal vertex must be pebbled with a red pebble in a minimal pebbling for every α input vertices that are red-pebbled, the computation time is at least T/α. Specializing this to $T = T_2^{(2)}(s_{L-1}, G)$ for the I/O-limited MHG, we have the last result. ∎

It is important to note that the lower bound to $T_1^{(2)}(S, G, \mathcal{P})$ for the I/O-limited case is not stated in terms of $|V|$, because $|V|$ may not be the same for each values of S. Consider the multiplication of two $n \times n$ matrices. Every graph of the standard algorithm can be pebbled with three red pebbles, but such graphs have about $2n^3$ vertices, a number that cannot be reduced by more than a constant factor when a constant number of red pebbles is used. (See Section 11.5.2.) On the other hand, using the graph of Strassen's algorithm for this problem requires at least $\Omega(n^{.38529})$ pebbles, since it has $O(n^{2.807})$ vertices.

We close this section by giving conditions under which lower bounds for one graph can be used for another. Let a **reduction** of DAG $G_1 = (V_1, E_1)$ be a DAG $G_0 = (V_0, E_0)$, $V_0 \subseteq V_1$ and $E_0 \subseteq E_1$, obtained by deleting edges from E_1 and coalescing the non-terminal vertices on a "chain" of vertices in V_1 into the first vertex on the chain. A **chain** is a sequence $v_1, v_2, \ldots, v_r$ of vertices such that, for $2 \leq i \leq r - 1$, v_i is adjacent to v_{i-1} and v_{i+1} and no other vertices.

LEMMA 11.3.2 *Let G_0 be a reduction of G_1. Then for any minimal pebbling $\mathcal{P}_{\min}$ and $1 \leq l \leq L$, the following inequalities hold:*

$$T_l^{(L)}(\boldsymbol{p}, G_1, \mathcal{P}_{\min}) \geq T_l^{(L)}(\boldsymbol{p}, G_0, \mathcal{P}_{\min})$$

Proof Any minimal pebbling strategy for G_1 can be used to pebble G_0 by simulating moves on a chain with pebble placements on the vertex to which vertices on the chain are coalesced and by honoring the edge restrictions of G_1 that are removed to create G_0. Since this strategy for G_1 may not be minimal for G_0, the inequalities follow. ■

11.4 The Hong-Kung Lower-Bound Method

In this section we derive lower limits on the I/O time at each level of a memory hierarchy needed to pebble a directed acyclic graph with the MHG. These results are obtained by combining the inequalities of Theorem 11.3.1 with a lower bound on the I/O and computation time for the red-blue pebble game.

Theorem 10.4.1 provides a framework that can be used to derive lower bounds on the I/O time in the red-blue pebble game. This follows because the lower bounds of Theorem 10.4.1 are stated in terms of T_I, the number of times inputs are pebbled with S red pebbles, which is also the number of I/O operations on input vertices in the red-blue pebble game. It is important to note that the lower bounds derived using this framework apply to every straight-line program for a problem.

In some cases, for example matrix multiplication, these lower bounds are strong. However, in other cases, notably the discrete Fourier transform, they are weak. For this reason we introduce a way to derive lower bounds that applies to a particular graph of a problem. If that graph is used for the problem, stronger lower bounds can be derived with this method than with the techniques of Chapter 10. We begin by introducing the S-span of a DAG.

DEFINITION 11.4.1 *Given a DAG $G = (V, E)$, the S-**span** of G, $\rho(S, G)$, is the maximum number of vertices of G that can be pebbled with S pebbles in the red pebble game maximized over all initial placements of S red pebbles. (The initialization rule is disallowed.)*

The following is a slightly weaker but simpler version of the Hong-Kung [136] lower bound on I/O time for the two-level MHG. This proof divides computation time into consecutive intervals, just as was done for the space–time lower bounds in the proofs of Theorems 10.4.1 and 10.11.1.

THEOREM 11.4.1 *For every pebbling $\mathcal{P}$ of the DAG $G = (V, E)$ in the red-blue pebble game with S red pebbles, the I/O time used, $T_2^{(2)}(S, G, \mathcal{P})$, satisfies the following lower bound:*

$$\lceil T_2^{(2)}(S, G)/S \rceil \rho(2S, G) \geq |V| - |In(G)|$$

Proof Divide $\mathcal{P}$ into consecutive sequential sub-pebblings $\{\mathcal{P}_1, \mathcal{P}_2, \ldots, \mathcal{P}_h\}$, where each sub-pebbling has S I/O operations except possibly the last, which has no more such operations. Thus, $h = \lceil T_2^{(2)}(S, G, \mathcal{P})/S \rceil$.

We now develop an upper bound Q to the number of vertices of G pebbled with red pebbles in any sub-pebbling $\mathcal{P}_j$. This number multiplied by the number h of sub-pebblings is an upper bound to the number of vertices other than inputs, $|V| - |In(G)|$, that must be pebbled to pebble G. It follows that

$$Qh \geq |V| - |In(G)|$$

The upper bound on Q is developed by adding S new red pebbles and showing that we may use these new pebbles to move all I/O operations in a sub-pebbling $\mathcal{P}_t$ to either the beginning or the end of the sub-pebbling without changing the number of computation steps or I/O operations. Thus, without changing them, we move all computation steps to a middle interval of $\mathcal{P}_t$, between the higher-level I/O operations.

We now show how this may be done. Consider a vertex v carrying a red pebble at some time during $\mathcal{P}_t$ that is pebbled for the first time with a blue pebble during $\mathcal{P}_t$ (vertex 7 at step 11 in Fig. 11.3). Instead of pebbling v with a blue pebble, use a new red pebble to keep a red pebble on v. (This is equivalent to swapping the new and old red pebbles on v.) This frees up the original red pebble to be used later in the sub-pebbling. Because we attach a red pebble to v for the entire pebbling $\mathcal{P}_t$, all later output operations from v in $\mathcal{P}_t$ can be deleted except for the last such operation, if any, which can be moved to the end of the interval. Note that if after v is given a blue pebble in $\mathcal{P}$, it is later given a red pebble, this red pebbling step and all subsequent blue pebbling steps except the last, if any, can be deleted. These changes do not affect any computation step in $\mathcal{P}_t$.

Consider a vertex v carrying a blue pebble at the start of $\mathcal{P}_t$ that later in $\mathcal{P}_t$ is given a red pebble (see vertex 4 at step 12 in Fig. 11.3). Consider the first pebbling of this kind. The red pebble assigned to v may have been in use prior to its placement on v. If a new red pebble is used for v, the first pebbling of v with a red pebble can be moved toward the beginning of $\mathcal{P}_t$ so that, without violating the precedence conditions of G, it precedes all placements of red pebbles on vertices without pebbles. Attach this new red pebble to v during $\mathcal{P}_t$. Subsequent placements of red pebbles on v when it carries a blue pebble during $\mathcal{P}_t$, if any, are thereby eliminated.

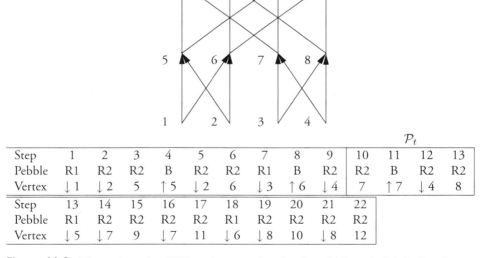

Step	1	2	3	4	5	6	7	8	9	10	11	12	13
Pebble	R1	R2	R2	B	R2	R2	R1	B	R2	R2	B	R2	R2
Vertex	↓ 1	↓ 2	5	↑ 5	↓ 2	6	↓ 3	↑ 6	↓ 4	7	↑ 7	↓ 4	8

Step	13	14	15	16	17	18	19	20	21	22
Pebble	R1	R2	R2	R2	R2	R1	R2	R2	R2	R2
Vertex	↓ 5	↓ 7	9	↓ 7	11	↓ 6	↓ 8	10	↓ 8	12

Figure 11.3 The vertices of an FFT graph are numbered and a pebbling schedule is given in which the two numbered red pebbles are used. Up (down) arrows identify steps in which an output (input) occurs; other steps are computation steps. Steps 10 through 13 of the schedule $\mathcal{P}_t$ contain two I/O operations. With two new red pebbles, the input at step 12 can be moved to the beginning of the interval and the output at step 11 can be moved after step 13.

We now derive an upper bound to Q. At the start of the pebbling of the middle interval of $\mathcal{P}_t$ there are at most $2S$ red pebbles on G, at most S original red pebbles plus S new red pebbles. Clearly, the number of vertices that can be pebbled in the middle interval with first-level pebbles is largest when all $2S$ red pebbles on G are allowed to move freely. It follows that at most $\rho(2S, G)$ vertices can be pebbled with red pebbles in any interval. Since all vertices must be pebbled with red pebbles, this completes the proof. ■

Combining Theorems 11.3.1 and 11.4.1 and a weak lower limit on the size of $T_l^{(L)}(\boldsymbol{p}, G)$, we have the following explicit lower bounds to $T_l^{(L)}(\boldsymbol{p}, G)$.

COROLLARY 11.4.1 *In the standard MHG when $T_l^{(L)}(\boldsymbol{p}, G) \geq \beta(s_{l-1} - 1)$ for $\beta > 1$, the following inequality holds for $2 \leq l \leq L$:*

$$T_l^{(L)}(\boldsymbol{p}, G) \geq \frac{\beta}{\beta + 1} \frac{s_{l-1}}{\rho(2s_{l-1}, G)}(|V| - |In(G)|)$$

In the I/O-limited MHG when $T_l^{(L)}(\boldsymbol{p}, G) \geq \beta(s_{l-1} - 1)$ for $\beta > 1$, the following inequality holds for $2 \leq l \leq L$:

$$T_l^{(L)}(\boldsymbol{p}, G) \geq \frac{\beta}{\beta + 1} \frac{s_{L-1}}{\rho(2s_{L-1}, G)}(|V| - |In(G)|)$$

11.5 Tradeoffs Between Space and I/O Time

We now apply the Hong-Kung method to a variety of important problems including matrix-vector multiplication, matrix-matrix multiplication, the fast Fourier transform, convolution, and merging and permutation networks.

11.5.1 Matrix-Vector Product

We examine here the matrix-vector product function $f_{A\boldsymbol{x}}^{(n)} : R^{n^2+n} \mapsto R^n$ over a commutative ring $\mathcal{R}$ described in Section 6.2.1 primarily to illustrate the development of efficient multi-level pebbling strategies. The lower bounds on I/O and computation time for this problem are trivial to obtain. For the matrix-vector product, we assume that the graphs used are those associated with inner products. The inner product $\boldsymbol{u} \cdot \boldsymbol{v}$ of n-vectors $\boldsymbol{u}$ and $\boldsymbol{v}$ over a ring $\mathcal{R}$ is defined by:

$$\boldsymbol{u} \cdot \boldsymbol{v} = \sum_{i=1}^{n} u_i \cdot v_i$$

The graph of a straight-line program to compute this inner product is given in Fig. 11.4, where the additions of products are formed from left to right.

The matrix-vector product is defined here as the pebbling of a collection of inner product graphs. As suggested in Fig. 11.4, each inner product graph can be pebbled with three red pebbles.

THEOREM 11.5.1 *Let G be the graph of a straight-line program for the product of the matrix A with the vector $\boldsymbol{x}$. Let G be pebbled in the **standard MHG** with the resource vector $\boldsymbol{p}$. There is a*

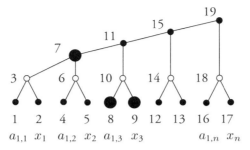

Figure 11.4 The graph of an inner product computation showing the order in which vertices are pebbled. Input vertices are labeled with the entries in the matrix A and vector x that are combined. Open vertices are product vertices; those above them are addition vertices.

pebbling strategy $\mathcal{P}$ of G with $p_l \geq 1$ for $2 \leq l \leq L-1$ and $p_1 \geq 3$ such that $T_1^{(L)}(p, G, \mathcal{P}) \geq 2n^2 - n$, the minimum value, and the following bounds hold simultaneously:

$$n^2 + 2n \leq T_l^{(L)}(p, G, \mathcal{P}) \leq 2n^2 - n$$

Proof The lower bound $T_l^{(L)}(p, G, \mathcal{P}) \geq n^2 + 2n$, $1 \leq l \leq L$, follows from Lemma 11.3.1 because there are $n^2 + n$ inputs and n outputs to the matrix-vector product. The upper bounds derived below represent the number of operations performed by a pebbling strategy that uses three level-1 pebbles and one pebble at each of the other levels.

Each of the n results of the matrix-vector product is computed as an inner product in which successive products $a_{i,j}x_j$ are formed and added to a running sum, as suggested by Fig. 11.4. Each of the n^2 entries of the matrix A (leaves of inner product trees) is used in one inner product and is pebbled once at levels $L, L_1, \ldots, 1$ when needed. The n entries in x are used in every inner product and are pebbled once at each level for each of the n inner products. First-level pebbles are placed on each vertex of each inner product tree in the order suggested in Fig. 11.4. After the root vertex of each tree is pebbled with a first-level pebble, it is pebbled at levels $2, \ldots, L$.

It follows that one I/O operation is performed at each level on each vertex associated with an entry in A and that n I/O operations are performed at each level on each vertex associated with an entry in x, for a total of $3n^2$ I/O operations at each level. This pebbling strategy places a first-level pebble once on each interior vertex of each of the n inner product trees. Such trees have $2n - 1$ internal vertices. Thus, this strategy takes $2n^2 - n$ computation steps. ∎

As the above results demonstrate, the matrix-vector product is an example of an **I/O-bounded problem**, a problem for which the amount of I/O required at each level in the memory hierarchy is comparable to the number of computation steps. Returning to the discussion in Section 11.1.2, we see that as CPU speed increases with technological advances, a balanced computer system can be constructed for this problem only if the I/O speed increases proportionally to CPU speed.

The I/O-limited version of the MHG for the matrix-vector product is the same as the standard version because only first-level pebbles are used on vertices that are neither input or output vertices.

11.5.2   Matrix-Matrix Multiplication

In this section we derive upper and lower bounds on exchanges between I/O time and space for the $n \times n$ matrix multiplication problem in the standard and I/O-limited MHG. We show that the lower bounds on computation and I/O time can be matched by efficient pebbling strategies.

Lower bounds for the standard MHG are derived for the **family $\mathcal{F}_n$ of inner product graphs for $n \times n$ matrix multiplication**, namely, the set of graphs to multiply two $n \times n$ matrices using just inner products to compute entries in the product matrix. (See Section 6.2.2.) We allow the additions in these inner products to be performed in any order.

The lower bounds on I/O time derived below for the I/O-limited MHG apply to all DAGs for matrix multiplication. Since these DAGs include graphs other than the inner product trees in $\mathcal{F}_n$, one might expect the lower bounds for the I/O-limited case to be smaller than those derived for graphs in $\mathcal{F}_n$. However, this is not the case, apparently because efficient pebbling strategies for matrix multiplication perform I/O operations only on input and output vertices, not on internal vertices. The situation is very different for the discrete Fourier transform, as seen in the next section.

We derive results first for the red-blue pebble game, that is, the two-level MHG, and then generalize them to the multi-level MHG. We begin by deriving an upper bound on the S-span for the family of inner product matrix multiplication graphs.

LEMMA 11.5.1 *For every graph $G \in \mathcal{F}_n$ the S-span $\rho(S, G)$ satisfies the bound $\rho(S, G) \leq 2S^{3/2}$ for $S \leq n^2$.*

Proof $\rho(S, G)$ is the maximum number of vertices of $G \in \mathcal{F}_n$ that can be pebbled with S red pebbles from an initial placement of these pebbles, maximized over all such initial placements. Let A, B, and C be $n \times n$ matrices with entries $\{a_{i,j}\}$, $\{b_{i,j}\}$, and $\{c_{i,j}\}$, respectively, where $1 \leq i, j \leq n$. Let $C = A \times B$. The term $c_{i,j} = \sum_k a_{i,k} b_{k,j}$ is associated with the root vertex in of a unique inner product tree. Vertices in this tree are either addition vertices, product vertices associated with terms of the form $a_{i,k} b_{k,j}$, or input vertices associated with entries in the matrices A and B. Each product term $a_{i,k} b_{k,j}$ is associated with a unique term $c_{i,j}$ and tree, as is each addition operator.

Consider an initial placement of $S \leq n^2$ pebbles of which r are in addition trees (they are on addition or product vertices). Let the remaining $S - r$ pebbles reside on input vertices. Let p be the number of product vertices that can be pebbled from these pebbled inputs. We show that at most $p + r - 1$ additional pebble placements are possible from the initial placement, giving a total of at most $\pi = 2p + r - 1$ pebble placements. (Figure 11.5

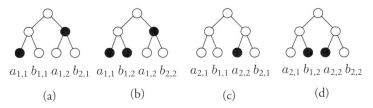

$a_{1,1}\, b_{1,1}\, a_{1,2}\, b_{2,1}$ $a_{1,1}\, b_{1,2}\, a_{1,2}\, b_{2,2}$ $a_{2,1}\, b_{1,1}\, a_{2,2}\, b_{2,1}$ $a_{2,1}\, b_{1,2}\, a_{2,2}\, b_{2,2}$

(a)   (b)   (c)   (d)

Figure 11.5 Graph of the inner products used to form the product of two 2×2 matrices. (Common input vertices are repeated for clarity.)

shows a graph G for a 2×2 matrix multiplication algorithm in which the product vertices are those just below the output vertices. The black vertices carry pebbles. In this example $r = 2$ and $p = 1$. While $p + r - 1 = 2$, only one pebble placement is possible on addition trees in this example.)

Given the dependencies of graphs in $\mathcal{F}_n$, there is no loss in generality in assuming that product vertices are pebbled before pebbles are advanced in addition trees. It follows that at most $p + r$ addition-tree vertices carry pebbles before pebbles are advanced in addition trees. These pebbled vertices define subtrees of vertices that can be pebbled from the $p + r$ initial pebble placements. Since a binary tree with n leaves has $n - 1$ non-leaf nodes, it follows that if there are t such trees, at most $p + r - t$ pebble placements will be made, not counting the original placement of pebbles. This number is maximized at $t = 1$. (See Problem 11.9.)

We now complete the proof by deriving an upper bound on p. Let $\mathcal{A}$ be the $0-1$ $n \times n$ matrix whose (i, j) entry is 1 if the variable in the (i, j) position of the matrix A carries a pebble initially and 0 otherwise. Let $\mathcal{B}$ be similarly defined for B. It follows that the (i, j) entry, $\delta_{i,j}$, of the matrix product $\mathcal{C} = \mathcal{A} \times \mathcal{B}$, where addition and multiplication are over the integers, is equal to the number of products that can be formed that contribute to the (i, j) entry of the result matrix C. Thus $p = \sum_{i,j} \delta_{i,j}$. We now show that $p \leq \sqrt{S}(S - r)$.

Let $\mathcal{A}$ and $\mathcal{B}$ have a and b 1's, respectively, where $a + b = S - r$. There are at most a/α rows of $\mathcal{A}$ containing at least α 1's. The maximum number of products that can be formed from such rows is ab/α because each 1 in $\mathcal{B}$ combine with a 1 in each of these rows. Now consider the product of other rows of $\mathcal{A}$ with columns of $\mathcal{B}$. At most S such row-column inner products are formed since at most S outputs can be pebbled. Since each of them involves a row with at most α 1's, at most αS products of pairs of variables can be formed. Thus, a total of at most $p = ab/\alpha + \alpha S$ products can be formed. We are free to choose α to minimize this sum ($\alpha = ab/S$ does this) but must choose a and b to maximize it ($a = (S - r)/2$ satisfies this requirement). The result is that $p \leq \sqrt{S}(S - r)$. We complete the proof by observing that $\pi = 2p + r - 1 \leq 2\sqrt{S}S$ for $r \geq 0$. ∎

Theorem 11.5.2 states bounds that apply to the computation and I/O time in the red-blue pebble game for matrix multiplication.

THEOREM 11.5.2 *For every graph G in the family $\mathcal{F}_n$ of inner product graphs for multiplying two $n \times n$ matrices and for every pebbling strategy $\mathcal{P}$ for G in the* **red-blue pebble game** *that uses $S \geq 3$ red pebbles, the computation and I/O-time satisfy the following lower bounds:*

$$T_1^{(2)}(S, G, \mathcal{P}) = \Omega(n^3)$$

$$T_2^{(2)}(S, G, \mathcal{P}) = \Omega\left(\frac{n^3}{\sqrt{S}}\right)$$

Furthermore, there is a pebbling strategy $\mathcal{P}$ for G with $S \geq 3$ red pebbles such that the following upper bounds hold simultaneously:

$$T_1^{(2)}(S, G, \mathcal{P}) = O(n^3)$$

$$T_2^{(2)}(S, G, \mathcal{P}) = O\left(\frac{n^3}{\sqrt{S}}\right)$$

The lower bound on I/O time stated above applies for **every graph** *of a straight-line program for matrix multiplication in the* **I/O-limited red-blue pebble game**. *The upper bound on I/O time* *also applies for this game. The computation time in the I/O-limited red-blue pebble game satisfies the following bound:*

$$T_1^{(2)}(S, G, \mathcal{P}) = \Omega\left(\frac{n^3}{\sqrt{S}}\right)$$

Proof For the standard MHG, the lower bound to $T_1^{(2)}(S, G, \mathcal{P})$ follows from the fact that every graph in $\mathcal{F}_n$ has $\Theta(n^3)$ vertices and Lemma 11.3.1. The lower bound to $T_2^{(2)}(S, G)$ follows from Corollary 11.4.1 and Lemma 11.5.1 and the lower bound to $T_1^{(2)}(S, G, \mathcal{P})$ for the I/O-limited MHG follows from Theorem 11.3.1.

We now describe a pebbling strategy that has the I/O time stated above and uses the obvious algorithm suggested by Fig. 11.6. If S red pebbles are available, let $r = \lfloor\sqrt{S/3}\rfloor$ be an integer that divides n. (If r does not divide n, embed A, B and C in larger matrices for which r does divide n. This requires at most doubling n.) Let the $n \times n$ matrices A, B and C be partitioned into $n/r \times n/r$ matrices; that is, $A = [a_{i,j}]$, $B = [b_{i,j}]$, and $C = [c_{i,j}]$, whose entries are $r \times r$ matrices. We form the $r \times r$ submatrix $c_{i,j}$ of C as the inner product of a row of $r \times r$ submatrices of A with a column of such submatrices of B:

$$c_{i,j} = \sum_{q=1}^{r} a_{i,q} \times b_{q,j}$$

We begin by placing blue pebbles on each entry in matrices A and B. Compute $c_{i,j}$ by computing $a_{i,q} \times b_{q,j}$ for $q = 1, 2, \ldots, r$ and adding successive products to the running sum. Keep r^2 red pebbles on the running sum. Compute $a_{i,q} \times b_{q,j}$ by placing and holding r^2 red pebbles on the entries in $a_{i,q}$ and r red pebbles on one column of $b_{q,j}$ at a time. Use two additional red pebbles to compute the r^2 inner products associated with entries of $c_{i,j}$ in the fashion suggested by Fig. 11.4 if $r \geq 2$ and one additional pebble if $r = 1$. The maximum number of red pebbles in use is 3 if $r = 1$ and at most $2r^2 + r + 2$ if $r \geq 2$. Since $2r^2 + r + 2 \leq 3r^2$ for $r \geq 2$, in both cases at most $3r^2$ red pebbles are needed. Thus, there are enough red pebbles to play this game because $r = \lfloor\sqrt{S/3}\rfloor$ implies that $3r^2 \leq S$, the number of red pebbles. Since $r \geq 1$, this requires that $S \geq 3$.

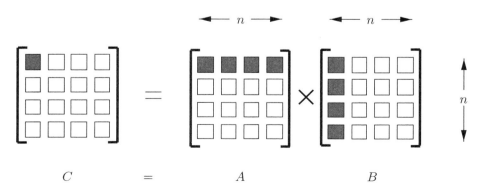

Figure 11.6 A pebbling schema for matrix multiplication based on the representation of a matrix in terms of block submatrices. A submatrix of C is computed as the inner product of a row of blocks of A with a column of blocks of B.

This algorithm performs one input operation on each entry of $a_{i,q}$ and $b_{q,j}$ to compute $c_{i,j}$. It also performs one output operation per entry to compute $c_{i,j}$ itself. Summing over all values of i and j, we find that n^2 output operations are performed on entries in C. Since there are $(n/r)^2$ submatrices $a_{i,q}$ and $b_{q,j}$ and each is used to compute n/r terms $c_{u,v}$, the number of input operations on entries in A and B is $2(n/r)^2 r^2(n/r) = 2n^3/r$. Because $r = \lfloor \sqrt{S/3} \rfloor$, we have $r \geq \sqrt{S/3} - 1$, from which the upper bound on the number of I/O operations follows. Since each product and addition vertex in each inner product graph is pebbled once, $O(n^3)$ computation steps are performed.

The bound on $T_2^{(2)}(S, G, \mathcal{P})$ for the I/O-limited game follows from two observations. First, the computational inequality of Theorem 10.4.1 provides a lower bound to T_I, the number of times that input vertices are pebbled in the red-pebble game when only red pebbles are used on vertices. This is the I/O-limited model. Second, the lower bound of Theorem 10.5.4 on T (actually, T_I) is of the form desired. ∎

These results and the strategy given for the two-level case carry over to the multi-level case, although considerable care is needed to insure that the pebbling strategy does not fragment memory and lead to inefficient upper bounds.

Even though the pebbling strategy given below is an I/O-limited strategy, it provides bounds on time in terms of space that match the lower bounds for the standard MHG.

THEOREM 11.5.3 *For every graph G in the family $\mathcal{F}_n$ of inner product graphs for multiplying two $n \times n$ matrices and for every pebbling strategy $\mathcal{P}$ for G in the* **standard MHG** *with resource vector $\mathbf{p}$ that uses $p_1 \geq 3$ first-level pebbles, the computation and I/O time satisfy the following lower bounds, where $s_l = \sum_{j=1}^{l} p_j$ and k is the largest integer such that $s_k \leq 3n^2$:*

$$T_1^{(L)}(\mathbf{p}, G, \mathcal{P}) = \Omega\left(n^3\right)$$

$$T_l^{(L)}(\mathbf{p}, G, \mathcal{P}) = \begin{cases} \Omega\left(n^3/\sqrt{s_{l-1}}\right) & \text{for } 2 \leq l \leq k \\ \Omega\left(n^2\right) & \text{for } k+1 \leq l \leq L \end{cases}$$

Furthermore, there is a pebbling strategy $\mathcal{P}$ for G with $p_1 \geq 3$ such that the following upper bounds hold simultaneously:

$$T_1^{(L)}(\mathbf{p}, G, \mathcal{P}) = O(n^3)$$

$$T_l^{(L)}(\mathbf{p}, G, \mathcal{P}) = \begin{cases} O\left(n^3/\sqrt{s_{l-1}}\right) & \text{for } 2 \leq l \leq k \\ O\left(n^2\right) & \text{for } k+1 \leq l \leq L \end{cases}$$

In the I/O-limited MHG the upper bounds given above apply. The following lower bound on the I/O time applies to **every graph** *G for $n \times n$ matrix multiplication and every pebbling strategy $\mathcal{P}$, where $S = s_{L-1}$:*

$$T_l^{(L)}(\mathbf{p}, G, \mathcal{P}) = \Omega\left(n^3/\sqrt{S}\right) \quad \text{for } 1 \leq l \leq L$$

Proof The lower bounds on $T_l^{(L)}(\mathbf{p}, G, \mathcal{P})$, $2 \leq l \leq L$, follow from Theorems 11.3.1 and 11.5.2. The lower bound on $T_1^{(L)}(\mathbf{p}, G, \mathcal{P})$ follows from the fact that every graph in $\mathcal{F}_n$ has $\Theta(n^3)$ vertices to be pebbled.

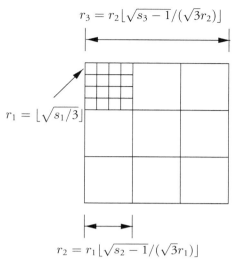

$$r_3 = r_2 \lfloor \sqrt{s_3 - 1}/(\sqrt{3}r_2) \rfloor$$

$$r_1 = \lfloor \sqrt{s_1/3} \rfloor$$

$$r_2 = r_1 \lfloor \sqrt{s_2 - 1}/(\sqrt{3}r_1) \rfloor$$

Figure 11.7 A three-level decomposition of a matrix.

We now describe a multi-level recursive pebbling strategy satisfying the upper bounds given above. It is based on the two-level strategy given in the proof of Theorem 11.5.2. We compute C from A and B using inner products.

Our approach is to successively block A, B, and C into $r_i \times r_i$ submatrices for $i = k, k-1, \ldots, 1$ where the r_i are chosen, as suggested in Fig. 11.7, so they divide on another and avoid memory fragmentation. Also, they are also chosen relative to s_i so that enough pebbles are available to pebble $r_i \times r_i$ submatrices, as explained below.

$$r_i = \begin{cases} \left\lfloor \sqrt{s_1/3} \right\rfloor & i = 1 \\ \\ r_{i-1} \left\lfloor \sqrt{(s_i - i + 1)}/(\sqrt{3}r_{i-1}) \right\rfloor & i \geq 2 \end{cases}$$

Using the fact that $b/2 \leq a\lfloor b/a \rfloor \leq b$ for integers a and b satisfying $1 \leq a \leq b$ (see Problem 11.1), we see that $\sqrt{(s_i - i + 1)/12} \leq r_i \leq \sqrt{(s_i - i + 1)/3}$. Thus, $s_i \geq 3r_i^2 + i - 1$. Also, $r_k^2 \leq n^2$ because $s_k \leq 3n^2$.

By definition, s_l pebbles are available at level l and below. As stated earlier, there is at least one pebble at each level above the first. From the s_l pebbles at level l and below we create a reserve set containing one pebble at each level except the first. This reserve set is used to perform I/O operations as needed.

Without loss of generality, assume that r_k divides n. (If not, n must be at most doubled for this to be true. Embed A, B, and C in such larger matrices.) A, B, and C are then blocked into $r_k \times r_k$ submatrices (call them $a_{i,j}$, $b_{i,j}$, and $c_{i,j}$), and these in turn are blocked into $r_{k-1} \times r_{k-1}$ submatrices, continuing until 1×1 submatrices are reached. The submatrix $c_{i,j}$ is defined as

$$c_{i,j} = \sum_{q=1}^{r_k} a_{i,q} \times b_{q,j}$$

As in Theorem 11.5.2, $c_{i,j}$ is computed as a running sum, as suggested in Fig. 11.4, where each vertex is associated with an $r_k \times r_k$ submatrix. It follows that $3r_k^2$ pebbles at level k or less (not including the reserve pebbles) suffice to hold pebbles on submatrices $a_{i,q}$, $b_{q,j}$ and the running sum. To compute a product $a_{i,q} \times b_{q,j}$, we represent $a_{i,q}$ and $b_{q,j}$ as block matrices with blocks that are $r_{k-1} \times r_{k-1}$ matrices. Again, we form this product as suggested in Fig. 11.4, using $3r_{k-1}^2$ pebbles at levels $k-1$ or lower. This process is repeated until we encounter a product of $r_1 \times r_1$ matrices, which is then pebbled according to the procedure given in the proof of Theorem 11.5.2.

Let's now determine the number of I/O and computation steps at each level. Since all non-input vertices of G are pebbled once, the number of computation steps is $O(n^3)$. I/O operations are done only on input and output vertices. Once an output vertex has been pebbled at the first level, reserve pebbles can be used to place a level-L pebble on it. Thus one output is done on each of the n^2 output vertices at each level.

We now count the I/O operations on input vertices starting with level k. $n \times n$ matrices A, B, and C contain $r_k \times r_k$ matrices, where r_k divides n. Each of the $(n/r_k)^2$ submatrices $a_{i,q}$ and $b_{q,j}$ is used in (n/r_k) inner products and at most r_k^2 I/O operations at level k are performed on them. (If most of the s_k pebbles at level k or less are at lower levels, fewer level-k I/O operations will be performed.) Thus, at most $2(n/r_k)^2(n/r_k)r_k^2 = 2n^2/r_k$ I/O operations are performed at level k. In turn, each of the $r_k \times r_k$ matrices contains $(r_k/r_{k-1})^2$ $r_{k-1} \times r_{k-1}$ matrices; each of these is involved in (r_k/r_{k-1}) inner products each of which requires at most r_{k-1}^2 I/O operations. Since there are at most $(n/r_{k-1})^2$ $r_{k-1} \times r_{k-1}$ submatrices in each of A, B, and C, at most $2n^3/r_{k-1}$ I/O operations are performed at level $k-1$. Continuing in this fashion, at most $2n^3/r_l$ I/O operations are performed at level l for $2 \le l \le k$. Since $r_l \ge \sqrt{(s_i - i + 1)/12}$, we have the desired conclusion.

Since the above pebbling strategy does not place pebbles at level 2 or above on any vertex except input and output vertices, it applies in the I/O-limited case. The lower bound follows from Lemma 11.3.1 and Theorem 11.5.2. ∎

11.5.3 The Fast Fourier Transform

The fast Fourier transform (FFT) algorithm is described in Section 6.7.3 (an FFT graph is given in Fig. 11.1). A lower bound is obtained by the Hong-Kung method for the FFT by deriving an upper bound on the S-span of the FFT graph. In this section all logarithms have base 2.

LEMMA 11.5.2 *The S-span of the FFT graph $F^{(d)}$ on $n = 2^d$ inputs satisfies $\rho(S,G) \le 2S \log S$ when $S \le n$.*

Proof $\rho(S,G)$ is the maximum number of vertices of G that can be pebbled with S red pebbles from an initial placement of these pebbles, maximized over all such initial placements. G contains many two-input FFT (butterfly) graphs, as shown in Fig. 11.8. If v_1 and v_2 are the output vertices in such a two-input FFT and if one of them is pebbled, we

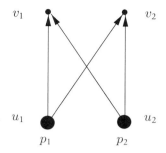

Figure 11.8 A two-input butterfly graph with pebbles p_1 and p_2 resident on inputs.

obtain an upper bound on the number of pebbled vertices if we assume that both of them are pebbled. In this proof we let $\{p_i \mid 1 \leq i \leq S\}$ denote the S pebbles available to pebble G. We assign an integer cost $num(p_i)$ (initialized to zero) to the ith pebble p_i in order to derive an upper bound to the total number of pebble placements made on G.

Consider a matching pair of output vertices v_1 and v_2 of a two-input butterfly graph and their common predecessors u_1 and u_2, as suggested in Fig. 11.8. Suppose that on the next step we can place a pebble on v_1. Then pebbles (call them p_1 and p_2) must reside on u_1 and u_2. Advance p_1 and p_2 to both v_1 and v_2. (Although the rules stipulate that an additional pebble is needed to advance the two pebbles, violating this restriction by allowing their movement to v_1 and v_2 can only increase the number of possible moves, a useful effect since we are deriving an upper bound on the number of pebble placements.)

After advancing p_1 and p_2, if $num(p_1) = num(p_2)$, augment both by 1; otherwise, augment the smaller by 1. Since the predecessors of two vertices in an FFT graph are in disjoint trees, there is no loss in assuming that all S pebbles remain on the graph in a pebbling that maximizes the number of pebbled vertices. Because two pebble placements are possible each time $num(p_i)$ increases by 1 for some i, $\rho(S, G) \leq 2 \sum_{1 \leq i \leq S} num(p_i)$.

We now show that the number of vertices that contained pebbles initially and are connected via paths to the vertex covered by p_i is at least $2^{num(p_i)}$. That is, $2^{num(p_i)} \leq S$ or $num(p_i) \leq \log_2 S$, from which the upper bound on $\rho(S, G)$ follows. Our proof is by induction. For the base case of $num(p_i) = 1$, two pebbles must reside on the two immediate predecessors of a vertex containing the pebble p_i. Assume that the hypothesis holds for $num(p_i) \leq e - 1$. We show that it holds for $num(p_i) = e$. Consider the first point in time that $num(p_i) = e$. At this time p_i and a second pebble p_j reside on a matching pair of vertices, v_1 and v_2. Before these pebbles are advanced to these two vertices from u_1 and u_2, the immediate predecessors of v_1 and v_2, the smaller of $num(p_i)$ and $num(p_j)$ has a value of $e - 1$. This must be p_i because its value has increased. Thus, each of u_1 and u_2 has at least 2^{e-1} predecessors that contained pebbles initially. Because the predecessors of u_1 and u_2 are disjoint, each of v_1 and v_2 has at least $2^e = 2^{num(p_i)}$ predecessors that carried pebbles initially. ∎

This upper bound on the S-span is combined with Theorem 11.4.1 to derive a lower bound on the I/O time at level l to pebble the FFT graph. We derive upper bounds that match to within a multiplicative constant when the FFT graph is pebbled in the standard MHG. We develop bounds for the red-blue pebble game and then generalize them to the MHG.

THEOREM 11.5.4 *Let the FFT graph on* $n = 2^d$ *inputs,* $F^{(d)}$, *be pebbled in the* **red-blue pebble game** *with* S *red pebbles. When* $S \geq 3$ *there is a pebbling of* $F^{(d)}$ *such that the following bounds hold simultaneously, where* $T_1^{(2)}(p_1, F^{(d)})$ *and* $T_2^{(2)}(p_1, F^{(d)})$ *are the computation and I/O time in a minimal pebbling of* $F^{(d)}$:

$$T_1^{(2)}(S, F^{(d)}) = \Theta(n \log n)$$
$$T_2^{(2)}(S, F^{(d)}) = \Theta\left(\frac{n \log n}{\log S}\right)$$

Proof The lower bound on $T_1^{(2)}(S, F^{(d)})$ is obvious; every vertex in $F^{(d)}$ must be pebbled a first time. The lower bound on $T_2^{(2)}(S, F^{(d)})$ follows from Corollary 11.4.1, Theorem 11.3.1, Lemma 11.5.2, and the obvious lower bound on $|V|$. We now exhibit a pebbling strategy giving upper bounds that match the lower bounds up to a multiplicative factor.

As shown in Corollary 6.7.1, $F^{(d)}$ can be decomposed into $\lceil d/e \rceil$ stages, $\lfloor d/e \rfloor$ stages containing 2^{d-e} copies of $F^{(e)}$ and one stage containing 2^{d-k} copies of $F^{(k)}$, $k = d - \lfloor d/e \rfloor e$. (See Fig. 11.9.) The output vertices of one stage are the input vertices to the next. For example, $F^{(12)}$ can be decomposed into three stages with $2^{12-4} = 256$ copies of $F^{(4)}$ on each stage and one stage with 2^{12} copies of $F^{(0)}$, a single vertex. (See Fig. 11.10.) We use this decomposition and the observation that $F^{(e)}$ can be pebbled level by level with $2^e + 1$ level-1 pebbles without repebbling any vertex to develop our pebbling strategy for $F^{(d)}$.

Given S red pebbles, our pebbling strategy is based on this decomposition with $e = d_0 = \lfloor \log_2(S-1) \rfloor$. Since $S \geq 3$, $d_0 \geq 1$. Of the S red pebbles, we actually use only $S_0 = 2^{d_0} + 1$. Since $S_0 \leq S$, the number of I/O operations with S_0 red pebbles is no

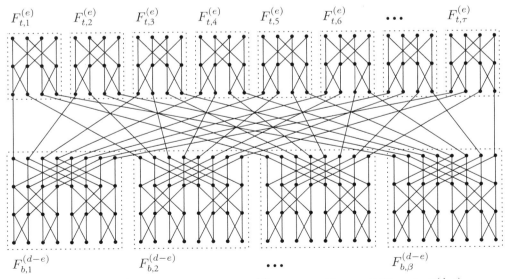

Figure 11.9 Decomposition of the FFT graph $F^{(d)}$ into $\beta = 2^e$ bottom FFT graphs $F^{(d-e)}$ and $\tau = 2^{d-e}$ top $F^{(e)}$. Edges between bottom and top sub-FFT graphs identify common vertices between the two.

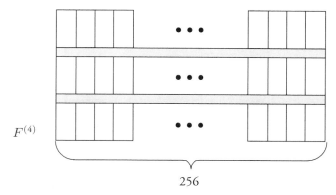

$F^{(4)}$

256

Figure 11.10 The decomposition of an FFT graph $F^{(12)}$ into three stages each containing 256 copies of $F^{(4)}$. The gray areas identify rows of $F^{(12)}$ in which inputs to one copy of $F^{(4)}$ are outputs of copies of $F^{(4)}$ at the preceding level.

less than with S red pebbles. Let $d_1 = \lfloor d/d_0 \rfloor$. Then, $F^{(d)}$ is decomposed into d_1 stages each containing 2^{d-d_0} copies of $F^{(d_0)}$ and one stage containing 2^{d-t} copies of $F^{(t)}$ where $t = d - d_0 d_1$. Since $t \leq d_0$, each vertex in $F^{(t)}$ can be pebbled with S_0 pebbles without re-pebbling vertices. The same applies to $F^{(d_0)}$.

The pebbling strategy for the red-blue pebble game is based on this decomposition. Pebbles are advanced to outputs of each of the bottom FFT subgraphs $F^{(t)}$ using $2^t + 1 \leq S_0$ red pebbles, after which the red pebbles are replaced with blue pebbles. The subgraphs $F^{(d_0)}$ in each of the succeeding stages are then pebbled in the same fashion; that is, their blue-pebbled inputs are replaced with red pebbles and red pebbles are advanced to their outputs after which they are replaced with blue pebbles.

This strategy pebbles each vertex once with red pebbles with the exception of vertices common to two FFT subgraphs which are pebbled twice. It follows that $T_1^{(L)}(S, F^{(d)}) \leq 2^{d+1}(d + 1) = 2n(\log_2 n + 1)$. This strategy also executes one I/O operation for each of the 2^d inputs and outputs to $F^{(d)}$ and two I/O operations for each of the 2^d vertices common to adjacent stages. Since there are $\lceil d/d_0 \rceil$ stages, there are $\lceil d/d_0 \rceil - 1$ such pairs of stages. Thus, the number of I/O operations satisfies $T_2^{(L)}(S, F^{(d)}) \leq 2^{d+1}\lceil d/d_0 \rceil \leq 2n(\log_2 n/(\log_2 S/4) + 1) = O(n \log n / \log S)$. ∎

The bounds for the multi-level case generalize those for the red-blue pebble game. As with matrix multiplication, care must be taken to avoid memory fragmentation.

THEOREM 11.5.5 *Let the FFT graph on $n = 2^d$ inputs, $F^{(d)}$, be pebbled in the **standard MHG** with resource vector $\mathbf{p}$. Let $s_l = \sum_{j=1}^{l} p_j$ and let k be the largest integer such that $s_k \leq n$. When $p_1 \geq 3$, the following lower bounds hold for all pebblings of $F^{(d)}$ and there exists a pebbling $\mathcal{P}$ for* *which the upper bounds are simultaneously satisfied:*

$$T_l^{(L)}(\boldsymbol{p}, F^{(d)}, \mathcal{P}) = \begin{cases} \Theta(n \log n) & l = 1 \\ \Theta\left(\frac{n \log n}{\log s_{l-1}}\right) & 2 \leq l \leq k \\ \Theta(n) & k+1 \leq l \leq L \end{cases}$$

Proof Proofs of the first two lower bounds follow from Lemma 11.3.1 and Theorem 11.5.4. The third follows from the fact that pebbles at every level must be placed on each input and output vertex but no intermediate vertex. We now exhibit a pebbling strategy giving upper bounds that match (up to a multiplicative factor) these lower bounds for all $1 \leq l \leq L$. (See Fig. 11.9.)

We define a non-decreasing sequence $\boldsymbol{d} = (d_0, d_1, d_2, \ldots, d_{L-1})$ of integers used below to describe an efficient multi-level pebbling strategy for $F^{(d)}$. Let $d_0 = 1$ and $d_1 = \lfloor \log(s_1 - 1) \rfloor \geq 1$, where $s_1 = p_1 \geq 3$. Define m_r and d_r for $2 \leq r \leq L-1$ by

$$m_r = \left\lfloor \frac{\lfloor \log \min(s_r - 1, n) \rfloor}{d_{r-1}} \right\rfloor$$
$$d_r = m_r d_{r-1}$$

It follows that $s_r \geq 2^{d_r} + 1$ when $s_r \leq n + 1$ since $a \lfloor b/a \rfloor \leq b$. Because $\lfloor \log a \rfloor \geq (\log a)/2$ when $a \geq 1$ and also $a \lfloor b/a \rfloor \geq b/2$ for integers a and b when $1 \leq a \leq b$ (see Problem 11.1), it follows that $d_r \geq \log(\min(s_r - 1, n))/4$. The values d_l are chosen to avoid memory fragmentation.

Before describing our pebbling strategy, note that because we assume at least one pebble is available at each level in the hierarchy, it is possible to perform an I/O operation at each level. Also, pebbles at levels less than l can be used as though they were at level l.

Our pebbling strategy is based on the decomposition of $F^{(d)}$ into FFT subgraphs $F^{(d_k)}$, each of which is decomposed into FFT subgraphs $F^{(d_{k-1})}$, and so on, until reaching FFT subgraphs $F^{(1)}$ that are two-input, two-output butterfly graphs. To pebble $F^{(d)}$ we apply the strategy described in the proof of Theorem 11.5.4 as follows. We decompose $F^{(2)}$ into d_2/d_1 stages, each containing $2^{d_2-d_1}$ copies of $F^{(1)}$, which we pebble with $s_1 = p_1$ first-level pebbles using this strategy. By the analysis in the proof of Theorem 11.5.4, 2^{d_2+1} level-2 I/O operations are performed on inputs and outputs to $F^{(d_2)}$ as well as another 2^{d_2+1} level-2 I/O operations on the vertices between two stages. Since there are d_2/d_1 stages, a total of $(d_2/d_1)2^{d_2+1}$ level-2 I/O operations are performed. We then decompose $F^{(3)}$ into d_3/d_2 stages each containing $2^{d_3-d_2}$ copies of $F^{(2)}$. We pebble $F^{(3)}$ with s_2 pebbles at level 1 or 2 by pebbling copies of $F^{(2)}$ in stages, using $(d_3/d_2)2^{d_3+1}$ level-3 I/O operations and using $(d_3/d_2)2^{d_3-d_2}$ times as many level-2 I/O operations as used by $F^{(2)}$. Let $n_2^{(3)}$ be the number of level-2 I/O operations used to pebble $F^{(3)}$. Then $n_2^{(3)} = (d_3/d_1)2^{d_3+1}$.

Continuing in this fashion, we pebble $F^{(r)}$, $1 \leq r \leq k$, with s_{r-1} pebbles at levels l or below by pebbling copies of $F^{(r-1)}$ in stages, using $(d_r/d_{r-1})2^{d_r+1}$ level-r I/O operations and using $(d_r/d_{r-1})2^{d_r-d_{r-1}}$ as many level-j I/O operations for $1 \leq j \leq r-1$. Let $n_j^{(r)}$ be the number of level-j I/O operations used to pebble $F^{(r)}$. By induction it follows that $n_j^{(r)} = (d_r/d_j)2^{d_r+1}$.

For $r \geq k$, the number of pebbles available at level r or less is at least $2^d + 1$, which is enough to pebble $F^{(d)}$ by levels without performing I/O operations above level $k+1$; this means that I/O operations at these levels are performed only on inputs, giving the bound $T_l^{(L)}(\boldsymbol{p}, F^{(d)}, \mathcal{P}) = O(n)$, $n = 2^d$, for $k + 1 \leq r \leq L$. When $r \leq k$, we pebble $F^{(d)}$ by decomposing it into $\lceil d/d_k \rceil$ stages such that each stage, except possibly the first, contains 2^{d-d_k} copies of the FFT subgraph $F^{(d_k)}$. The first stage has 2^{d-d^*} copies of $F^{(d^*)}$ of depth $d^* = d - (\lceil d/d_k \rceil - 1)d_k$, which we treat as subgraphs of the subgraph $F^{(d_k)}$ and pebble to completion with a number of operations at each level that is at most the number to pebble $F^{(d_k)}$. Each instance of $F^{(d_k)}$ is pebbled with s_{k-1} pebbles at level $k - 1$ or lower and a pebble at level k or higher is left on its output. Since $s_{k+1} \geq n + 1$, there are enough pebbles to do this.

Thus $T_l^{(L)}(\boldsymbol{p}, F^{(d)}, \mathcal{P})$ satisfies the following bound for $1 \leq l \leq L$:

$$T_l^{(L)}(\boldsymbol{p}, F^{(d)}, \mathcal{P}) \leq \lceil d/d_k \rceil 2^{d-d_k} T_l^{(L)}(\boldsymbol{p}, F^{(d_k)}, \mathcal{P})$$

Combining this with the earlier result, we have the following upper bound on the number of I/O operations for $1 \leq l \leq k$:

$$T_l^{(L)}(\boldsymbol{p}, F^{(d)}, \mathcal{P}) \leq \lceil d/d_k \rceil (d_k/d_l) 2^{d+1}$$

Since, as noted earlier, $d_r \geq \log(\min(s_r - 1, n))/4$, we obtain the desired upper bound on $T_l^{(L)}(\boldsymbol{p}, F^{(d)}, \mathcal{P})$ by combining this result with the bound on $n_l^{(k)}$ given above. ∎

The above results are derived for standard MHG and the family of FFT graphs. We now strengthen these results in two ways when the I/O-limited MHG is used. First, the I/O limitation requires more time for a given amount of storage and, second, the lower bound we derive applies to every graph for the discrete Fourier transform, not just those for the FFT.

It is important to note that the efficient pebbling strategy used in the standard MHG makes extensive use of level-L pebbles on intermediate vertices of the FFT graph. When this is not allowed, the lower bound on the I/O time is much larger. Since the lower bounds for the standard and I/O-limited MHG on matrix multiplication are about the same, this illustrates that the DFT and matrix multiplication make dramatically different use secondary memory. (In the following theorem a **linear straight-line program** is a straight-line program in which the operations are additions and multiplications by constants.)

THEOREM 11.5.6 *Let $FFT(n)$ be **any DAG** associated with the DFT on n inputs when realized by a linear straight-line program. Let $FFT(n)$ be pebbled with strategy $\mathcal{P}$ in the **I/O-limited MHG** with resource vector $\boldsymbol{p}$ and let $s_l = \sum_{j=1}^{l} p_j$. If $S = s_{L-1} \leq n$, then for each pebbling strategy $\mathcal{P}$, the computation and I/O time at level l must satisfy the following bounds:*

$$T_l^{(L)}(\boldsymbol{p}, FFT(n), \mathcal{P}) = \Omega\left(\frac{n^2}{S}\right) \quad \text{for } 1 \leq l \leq L$$

Also, when $n = 2^d$, there is a pebbling $\mathcal{P}$ of the FFT graph $F^{(d)}$ such that the following relations hold simultaneously when $S \geq 2 \log n$:

$$T_l^{(L)}(\boldsymbol{p}, F^{(d)}, \mathcal{P}) = \begin{cases} O\left(\frac{n^2}{S} + n \log S\right) & l = 1 \\ O\left(\frac{n^2}{S} + n \frac{\log S}{\log s_{l-1}}\right) & 2 \leq l \leq L \end{cases}$$

Proof The lower bound follows from Theorem 11.3.1 and Theorem 10.5.5. We show that the upper bounds can be achieved on $F^{(d)}$ under the I/O limitation simultaneously for $1 \leq l \leq L$.

The pebbling strategy meeting the lower bounds is based on that used in the proof of Theorem 10.5.5 to pebble $F^{(d)}$ using $S \leq 2^d + 1$ pebbles in the red pebble game. The number of level-1 pebble placements used in that pebbling is given in the statement of Theorem 10.5.5. A level-2 I/O operation occurs once on each of the 2^d outputs and 2^{d-e} times on each of the 2^d inputs of the bottom FFT subgraphs, for a total of $2^d(2^{d-e} + 1)$ times.

The pebbling for the L-level MHG is patterned after the aforementioned pebbling for the red pebble game, which is based on the decomposition of Lemma 6.7.4. (See Fig. 11.9.) Let e be the largest integer such that $S \geq 2^e + d - e$. Pebble the binary subtrees on 2^{d-e} inputs in the 2^e bottom subgraphs $F_{b,m}^{(d-e)}$ as follows: On an input vertex level-L pebbles are replaced by pebbles at all levels down to and including the first level. Then level-1 pebbles are advanced on the subtrees in the order that minimizes the number of level-1 pebbles in the red pebble game. It may be necessary to use pebbles at all levels to make these advances; however, each vertex in a subtree (of which there are $2^{d-e+1} - 1$) experiences at most two transitions at each level in the hierarchy. In addition, each vertex in a bottom tree is pebbled once with a level-1 pebble in a computation step. Therefore, the number of level-l transitions on vertices in the subtrees is at most $2^{d+1}(2^{d-e+1} - 1)$ for $2 \leq l \leq L$, since this pebbling of 2^e subtrees is repeated 2^{d-e} times.

Once the inputs to a given subgraph $F_{t,p}^{(e)}$ have been pebbled, the subgraph itself is pebbled in the manner indicated in Theorem 11.5.5, using $O(e2^e / \log s_{l-1})$ pebbles at each level l for $2 \leq l \leq L$. Since this is done for each of the 2^{d-e} subgraphs $F_{t,p}^{(e)}$, it follows that on the top FFT subgraphs a total of $O(e2^d / \log s_{l-1})$ level-l transitions occur, $2 \leq l \leq L$. In addition, each vertex in a graph $F_{t,p}^{(e)}$ is pebbled once with a level-1 pebble in a computation step.

It follows that at most

$$T_l^{(L)}(\boldsymbol{p}, F^{(d)}, \mathcal{P}) = O\left(2^d(2^{d-e+1} - 1) + \frac{e2^d}{\log s_{l-1}}\right)$$

level-l I/O operations occur for $2 \leq l \leq L$, as well as

$$T_1^{(L)}(\boldsymbol{p}, F^{(d)}, \mathcal{P}) = O(2^d(2^{d-e+1} - 1) + e2^d)$$

computation steps. It is left to the reader to verify that $2^e < 2^e + d - e \leq S < 2^{e+1} + d - e - 1 \leq 42^e$ when $e + 1 \geq \log d$ (this is implied by $S \geq 2d$), from which the result follows. ∎

11.5.4 Convolution

The convolution function $f_{\text{conv}}^{(n,m)} : R^{n+m} \mapsto R^{n+m-1}$ over a commutative ring $\mathcal{R}$ (see Section 6.7.4) maps an n-tuple $\boldsymbol{a}$ and an m-tuple $\boldsymbol{b}$ onto an $(n + m - 1)$-tuple $\boldsymbol{c}$ and is denoted $\boldsymbol{c} = \boldsymbol{a} \otimes \boldsymbol{b}$. An efficient straight-line program for the convolution is described in Section 6.7.4 that uses the convolution theorem (Theorem 6.7.2) and the FFT algorithm. The convolution theorem in terms of the $2n$-point DFT and its inverse is

$$\boldsymbol{a} \otimes \boldsymbol{b} = F_{2n}^{-1}(F_{2n}(\boldsymbol{a}) \times F_{2n}(\boldsymbol{b}))$$

Obviously, when $n = 2^d$ the $2n$-point DFT can be realized by the $2n$-point FFT. The DAG associated with this algorithm, shown in Fig. 11.11 for $d = 4$, contains three copies of the FFT graph $F^{(2d)}$.

We derive bounds on the computation and I/O time in the standard and I/O-limited memory-hierarchy game needed for the convolution function using this straight-line program. For the standard MHG, we invoke the lower bounds and an efficient algorithm for the FFT. For the I/O-limited MHG, we derive new lower bounds based on those for two back-to-back FFT graphs as well as upper bounds based on the I/O-limited pebbling algorithm given in Theorem 11.5.4 for FFT graphs.

THEOREM 11.5.7 *Let* $G^{(n)}_{\text{convolve}}$ *be the graph of a straight-line program for the convolution of two n-tuples using the convolution theorem, $n = 2^d$. Let* $G^{(n)}_{\text{convolve}}$ *be pebbled in the standard MHG with the resource vector* $\mathbf{p}$. *Let* $s_l = \sum_{j=1}^l p_j$ *and let k be the largest integer such that* $s_k \leq n$. *When $p_1 \geq 3$ there is a pebbling of* $G^{(n)}_{\text{convolve}}$ *for which the following bounds hold simultaneously:*

$$
T_l^{(L)}(\mathbf{p}, F^{(d)}) = \begin{cases} \Theta(n \log n) & l = 1 \\ \Theta\left(\dfrac{n \log n}{\log s_{l-1}}\right) & 2 \leq l \leq k+1 \\ \Theta(n) & k+2 \leq l \leq L \end{cases}
$$

Proof The lower bound follows from Lemma 11.3.2 and Theorem 11.5.5. From the former, it is sufficient to derive lower bounds for a subgraph of a graph. Since $F^{(d)}$ is contained in $G^{(n)}_{\text{convolve}}$, the lower bound follows.

The upper bound follows from Theorem 11.5.5. We advance level-L pebbles to the outputs of each of the two bottom FFT graphs $F^{(2d)}$ in Fig. 11.11 and then pebble the top

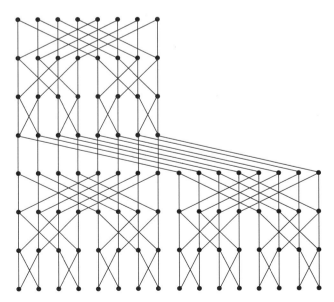

Figure 11.11 A DAG for the graph of the convolution theorem on $n = 8$ inputs.

FFT graph. The number of I/O and computation steps used is triple that used to pebble one such FFT graph. In addition, we perform $O(n)$ I/O and computation steps to combine inputs to the top FFT graph. ∎

The bounds for the I/O-limited version of the MHG for the convolution problem are considerably larger than those for the standard MHG. They have a much stronger dependence on S and n than do those for the FFT graph.

THEOREM 11.5.8 *Let $H_{\text{convolve}}^{(n)}$ be the graph of any DAG for the convolution of two n-tuples using the convolution theorem, $n = 2^d$. Let $H_{\text{convolve}}^{(n)}$ be pebbled in the I/O-limited MHG with the resource vector $\mathbf{p}$ and let $s_l = \sum_{j=1}^{l} p_j$. If $S = s_{L-1} \leq n$, then the time to pebble $H_{\text{convolve}}^{(n)}$ at the lth level, $T_l^{(L)}(\mathbf{p}, H_{\text{convolve}}^{(n)})$, satisfies the following lower bounds simultaneously for $1 \leq l \leq L$:*

$$T_l^{(L)}(\mathbf{p}, H_{\text{convolve}}^{(n)}) = \Omega\left(\frac{n^3}{S^2}\right)$$

when $S \leq n/\log n$.

Proof A lower bound is derived for this problem by considering a generalization of the graph shown in Fig. 11.11 in which the three copies of the FFT graph $F^{(2d)}$ are replaced by an arbitrary DAG for the DFT. This could in principle yield in a smaller lower bound on the time to pebble the graph. We then invoke Lemma 11.3.2 to show that a lower bound can be derived from a reduction of this new graph, namely, that consisting of two back-to-back DFT graphs obtained by deleting one of the bottom FFT graphs. We then derive a lower bound on the time to pebble this graph with the red pebble game and use it together with Theorem 11.3.1 to derive the lower bounds mentioned above.

Consider pebbling two back-to-back DAGs for the DFT on n inputs, n even, in the red pebble game. From Lemma 10.5.4, the n-point DFT function is $(2, n, n, n/2)$-independent. From the definition of the independence property (see Definition 10.4.2), we know that during a time interval in which $2(S + 1)$ of the n outputs of the second DFT DAG on n-inputs are pebbled, at least $n/2 - 2(S + 1)$ of its inputs are pebbled. In a back-to-back DFT graph these inputs are also outputs of the first DFT graph. It follows that for each group of $2(S + 1)$ of these $n/2 - 2(S + 1)$ outputs of the first DFT DAG, at least $n/2 - 2(S + 1)$ of its inputs are pebbled. Thus, to pebble a group of $2(S + 1)$ outputs of the second FFT DAG (of which there are at least $\lfloor n/(2(S + 1)) \rfloor$ groups), at least $\lfloor (n/2 - 2(S + 1))/2(S + 1) \rfloor (n/2 - 2(S + 1))$ inputs of the first DFT must be pebbled. Thus, $T_l^{(L)}(\mathbf{p}, H_{\text{convolve}}^{(n)}) \geq n^3/(64(S + 1)^2)$, since it holds both when $S \leq n/4\sqrt{2}$ and when $S > n/4\sqrt{2}$.

Let's now consider a pebbling strategy that achieves this lower bound up to a multiplicative constant. The pebbling strategy of Theorem 11.5.5 can be used for this problem. It represents the FFT graph $F^{(d)}$ as a set of FFT graphs $F^{(e)}$ on top and a set of FFT graphs $F^{(d-e)}$ on the bottom. Outputs of one copy of $F^{(e)}$ are pebbled from left to right. This requires pebbling inputs of $F^{(d)}$ from left to right once. To pebble all outputs of $F^{(d)}$, 2^{d-e} copies of $F^{(e)}$ are pebbled and the 2^d inputs to $F^{(d)}$ are pebbled 2^{d-e} times.

Consider the graph $G_{\text{convolve}}^{(n/2)}$ consisting of three copies of $F^{(d)}$, two on the bottom and one on top, as shown in Fig. 11.12. Using the above strategy, we pebble the outputs of the

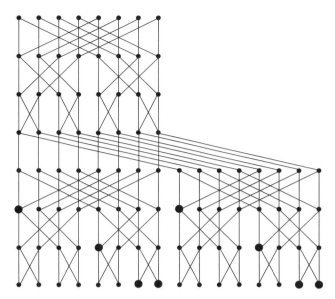

Figure 11.12 An I/O-limited pebbling of a DAG for the convolution theorem showing the placement of eight pebbles.

two bottom copies of $F^{(d)}$ from left to right in parallel a total of 2^{d-e} times. The outputs of these two graphs are pebbled in synchrony with the pebbling of the top copy of $F^{(d)}$. It follows that the number of I/O and computation steps used on the bottom copies of $F^{(d)}$ in $G_{\text{convolve}}^{(n/2)}$ is $2(2^{d-e})$ times the number on one copy, with twice as many pebbles at each level plus the number of such steps on the top copy of $F^{(d)}$. It follows that $G_{\text{convolve}}^{(n/2)}$ can be pebbled with three times the number of pebbles at each level as can $F^{(d)}$, with $O(2^{d-e})$ times as many steps at each level. The conclusion of the theorem follows from manipulation of terms. ∎

The bounds given above also apply to some permutation and merging networks. Since, as shown in Section 6.8, the graph of Batcher's odd-even merging network is an FFT graph, the bounds on I/O and computation time given earlier for the FFT also apply to it. Also, as shown in Section 7.8.2, since a permutation network can be constructed of two FFT graphs connected back-to-back, the lower bounds for convolution apply to this graph. (See the proofs of Theorems 11.5.7 and 11.5.8.) The same order-of-magnitude upper bounds follow from constructions that differ only in details from those given in these theorems.

11.6 Block I/O in the MHG

Many memory units move data in large blocks, not in individual words, as generally assumed in the above sections. (Note, however, that one pebble can carry a block of data.) Data is moved in blocks because the time to fetch one word and a block of words is typically about the same. Figure 11.13 suggests why this is so. A disk spinning at 3,600 rpm that has 40 sectors

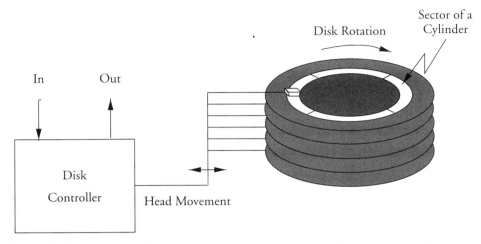

Figure 11.13   A disk unit with three platters and two heads per disk. Each track is divided into four sectors and heads move in and out on a common arm. The memory of the disk controller holds the contents of one track on one disk.

per track and 512 bits per sector (its block size) requires about 10 msec to find data in the track under the head. However, the time to read one sector of 64 bytes (512 bits) is just .42 msec.

To model this phenomenon, we assume that the time to access k disk sectors with consecutive addresses is $\alpha + k\beta$, where α is a large constant and β is a small one. (This topic is also discussed in Section 7.3.) Given the ratio of α to β, it makes sense to move data to and from a disk in blocks of size about equal to the number of bytes on a track. Some operating systems move data in track-sized blocks, whereas others move them in smaller units, relying upon the fact that a disk controller typically keeps the contents of its current track in a fast random-access memory so that successive sector accesses can be done quickly.

The gross characteristics of disks described by the above assumption hold for other storage devices as well, although the relative values of the constants differ. For example, in the case of a tape unit, advancing the tape head to the first word in a consecutive sequence of words usually takes a long time, but successive words can be read relatively quickly.

The situation with **interleaved random-access memory** is similar, although the physical arrangement of memory is radically different. As depicted in Fig. 11.14, an interleaved random-access memory is a collection of 2^r memory modules, $r \geq 1$, each containing 2^k b-bit words. Such a memory can simulate a single 2^{r+k}-word b-bit random-access memory. Words with addresses $0, 2^r, 2\,2^r, 3\,2^r, \ldots, 2^{k-1}2^r$ are stored in the first module, words with addresses $1, 2^r + 1, 2\,2^r + 1, 3\,2^r + 1, \ldots, 2^{k-1}2^r + 1$ in the second module, and words with addresses $2^r - 1, 2\,2^r - 1, 3\,2^r - 1, 4\,2^r - 1, \ldots, 2^{r+k} - 1$ in the last module.

To access a word in this memory, the high order k bits are provided to each module. If a set of words is to be read, the words with these common high-order bits are copied to the registers. If a set of words is to be written, new values are copied from the registers to them.

When an interleaved memory is used to simulate a much faster random-access memory, a CPU writes to or reads from the 2^r registers serially, whereas data is transferred in parallel between the registers and the modules. The use of two sets of registers (**double buffering**) allows the register sets to be alternated so that data can be moved continuously between the

Memory Modules

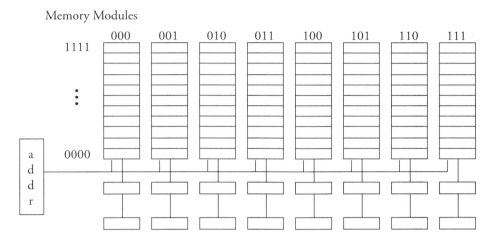

Figure 11.14 Eight interleaved memory modules with double buffering. Addresses are supplied in parallel while data is pipelined into and out of the memory.

CPU and the modules. This allows the interleaved memory to be about 2^r times slower than the CPU and yet, with a small set of fast registers, appear to be as fast as the CPU. This works only if the program accessing memory does not branch to a new set of words. If it does, the startup time to access a new word is about 2^r times the CPU speed. Thus, an interleaved random-access memory also requires time of the form $\alpha + k\beta$ to access k words. For example, for a moderately fast random-access chip technology α might be 80 nanoseconds whereas β might be 10 nanoseconds, a ratio of 8 to 1.

This discussion justifies assuming that the time to move k words with consecutive addresses to and from the lth unit in the memory hierarchy is $\alpha_l + k\beta_l$ for positive constants α_l and β_l, where α_l is typically much larger than β_l. If $k = b_l = \lceil \alpha_l/\beta_l \rceil$, then $\alpha_l + k\beta_l \approx 2\alpha_l$ and the time to retrieve one item and b_l items is about the same. Thus, efficiency dictates that items should be fetched in blocks, especially if all or most of the items in a block can be used if one of them is used. This justifies the block-I/O model described below. Here we let t_l be the time to move a block at level l. We add the requirement that data stored together be retrieved together to reflect physical constraints existing in practice.

DEFINITION 11.6.1 (Block-I/O Model) *At the lth level in a memory hierarchy, I/O operations are performed on blocks. The block size and the time in seconds to access a block at the lth level are b_l and t_l, respectively. For each l, b_l/b_{l-1} is an integer. In addition, any data written as part of a block at level l must be read into level $l - 1$ by reading the entire block in which it was stored.*

The lower bounds on the number of I/O steps given in Section 11.5 can be generalized to the block-I/O case by dividing the number of I/O operations by the size b_l of blocks moving between levels $l - 1$ and l. This lower bound can be achieved for matrix-vector and matrix-matrix multiplication because data is always written to and read from the higher-level memory in the same way for these problems. (See Problems 11.13 and 11.14.)

For the FFT graph in the standard MHG, instead of pebbling FFT subgraphs on 2^{d_r} inputs, we pebble b_l FFT subgraphs on $2^{d_r}/b_l$ inputs (assuming that b_l is a power of 2). Doing so allows all the data moving back and forth in blocks between memories to be used and accommodates the transposition mentioned at the beginning of Section 11.5.3. This provides an upper bound of $O(n \log n/(b_{l-1} \log(s_{l-1}/b_{l-1})))$ on the I/O time at level l. Clearly, when b_{l-1} is much smaller than s_{l-1}, say $b_{l-1} = O(\sqrt{s_{l-1}})$, the upper and lower bounds match to within a multiplicative factor. (This follows because we divide n by b_{l-1} and $\log b_{l-1} = O(\log s_{l-1})$.) These observations apply to the FFT-based problems as well.

11.7 Simulating a Fast Memory in the MHG

In this section we revisit the discussion of Section 11.1.2, taking into account that a memory hierarchy may have many levels and that data is moved in blocks.

We ask the question, "How do we assess the effectiveness of a memory hierarchy on a particular problem?" For several problems we have upper and lower bounds on their number of computation and I/O steps in memory hierarchies parameterized by block sizes and numbers of storage locations. If we add to this mix the time to move a block between levels, we can derive bounds on the time for all computation and I/O steps. We then ask under what conditions this time is the best possible. Since data must typically be stored and retrieved from archival memory, we cannot expect the performance to exceed that of a two-level hierarchy (modeled by the red-blue pebble game) in which all the available storage locations, except for those in the archival memory, are in first-level storage. For this reason we use the two-level memory as our reference model. We now define these terms and state a condition for optimality of a pebbling strategy.

For $1 \leq l \leq L - 1$ we let t_l be the time to move one block of b_l words between levels $l - 1$ and l of a memory hierarchy, measured as a multiple of the time to perform one computation step. Thus, the time for one computation step is $t_1 = 1$.

Let $\mathcal{P}$ be a pebbling strategy for a graph G in the L-level MHG that uses the resource vector $\boldsymbol{p} = (p_1, p_2, \ldots, p_{L-1})$ (p_l pebbles are used at the lth level) and moves data in blocks of size specified by $\boldsymbol{b} = (b_2, b_3, \ldots, b_L)$ (b_l words are moved between levels $(l - 1)$ and l). Let $T_l^{(L)}(\boldsymbol{p}, \boldsymbol{b}, G)$ denote the number of level-l I/O operations with $\mathcal{P}$ on G. We define the **time for the pebbling strategy $\mathcal{P}$**, $T(\mathcal{P}, G)$ on the graph G as

$$T(\mathcal{P}, G) = \sum_{l=1}^{L} t_l \cdot T_l^{(L)}(\boldsymbol{p}, \boldsymbol{b}, G)$$

Thus, $T(\mathcal{P}, G)$ measures the absolute time expended to pebble a graph relative to the time to perform one computation step under the assumption that I/O operations cannot be overlapped.

From the above discussion, a pebbling is efficient if $T(\mathcal{P}, G)$ is at most some small multiple of $T_1^{(2)}(s_{L-1}, G)$, the normalized time to pebble G in the red-blue pebble game when all the pebbles at level $L - 1$ or less in the MHG (there are s_{L-1} such pebbles) are used as if they were red pebbles.

A two-level computation exhibits **locality of reference** if it is likely in the near future to refer to words currently in its primary memory. Such computations perform fewer I/O operations than those that don't meet this condition. This idea extends to multiple levels: a multi-level memory hierarchy exhibits locality of reference if it uses its higher-level memory units much less often that its lower-level units. Formally, we say that a pebbling strategy $\mathcal{P}$ is **c-local** if $T(\mathcal{P}, G)$ satisfies the following inequality:

$$\sum_{l=1}^{L} t_l \cdot T_l^{(L)}(\boldsymbol{p}, \boldsymbol{b}, G, \mathcal{P}) \leq c T_1^{(2)}(s_{L-1}, G)$$

The definition of a c-local pebbling strategy is illustrated by the results for matrix multiplication in the standard MHG when block I/O is not used. Let k be the largest integer such that $s_k \leq 3n^2$. From Theorem 11.5.3 for matrix-matrix multiplication, we see that there exists an optimal pebbling if

$$\sum_{l=2}^{k} \frac{t_l}{b_l \sqrt{s_{l-1}}} + \sum_{l=k+1}^{L} \frac{t_l}{nb_l} \leq c^* \tag{11.1}$$

for some $c^* > 0$ since $T_1^{(2)}(S, G) = \Theta(n^3)$.

We noted in Section 11.1.2 that the imbalance between the computation and I/O times for matrix multiplication is becoming ever more serious with the advance of technology. We re-examine this issue in light of the above condition. Consider the case in which $k + 1 = L$; that is, the highest-level memory is used to store the arguments and results of a computation. In this case the second term on the left-hand side of (11.1) is a relative measure of the time to bring data into lower-level memories from the highest-level memory. It is negligible when nb_L is large. For example, if $t_L = 2,000,000$ and $b_L = 10,000$, say, then n must be at least 200, a modest-sized matrix. The first term on the left-hand side reflects the number of times data moves between the levels of the hierarchy holding the data. It is small when $b_l \sqrt{s_{l-1}}$ is large by comparison with t_l for $2 \leq l \leq k$, a condition that is not hard to meet. For example, if $s_{l-1} = 32 \times 10^6$ (about 4 Mbytes) and $b_l = 1,000$, then t_l must be less than about 45, a condition that certainly applies to low level memories such as today's random-access memories. Problems 11.15 and 11.16 provide opportunities to explore this issue with the FFT and convolution.

11.8 RAM-Based I/O Models

The MHG assumes that computations are done by pebbling the vertices of a directed acyclic graph. That is, it assumes that computations are straight-line. While the best known algorithms for the problems studied earlier in this chapter are straight-line, some problems are not efficiently done in a straight-line fashion. For example, binary search in a tree that holds a set of keys in sorted order (see Section 11.9.1) is much better suited to data-dependent computation of the kind allowed by an unrestricted RAM. Similarly, the merging of two sorted lists can be done more efficiently on a RAM than with a straight-line program. For this reason we consider RAM-based I/O models, specifically the block-transfer model and the hierarchical memory model.

11.8.1 The Block-Transfer Model

The block-transfer model is a two-level I/O model that generalizes the red-blue pebble game to RAM-based computations by allowing programs that are not straight-line.

DEFINITION 11.8.1 *The **block-transfer model** (BTM) is a serial computer in which a CPU is attached to an M-word primary memory and to a secondary memory of unlimited size that stores words in blocks of size B. Words are moved in blocks between the memories and words that leave primary memory in one block must return in that block. An **I/O operation** is the movement of a block to or from secondary memory. The **I/O time** with the BTM is the number of I/O operations.*

The secondary memory in the BTM can be a main memory if the primary memory is a cache, or can be a disk if the primary memory is a random-access memory. In fact, it can model I/O operations between any two devices. Since a block can be viewed as the contents of one track of a disk, the time to retrieve any word on the track is comparable to the time to retrieve the entire track. (See Section 11.6.) Since data is moved in blocks in the BTM, it makes sense to define simple I/O operations.

DEFINITION 11.8.2 *An I/O operation in the BTM is **simple** if, after a block or word is copied from one memory to the other, the copy in the first memory is deleted.*

Simple I/O operations for the pebble game are defined in Problem 11.10. In this problem the reader is asked to show that replacing all I/O operations with simple I/O operations has the effect of at most doubling the number of I/O operations. The proof of this fact applies equally well to the BTM.

We illustrate the use of the block-transfer model by examining the sorting problem. We derive a lower bound on the I/O time for all sorting algorithms and exhibit a sorting algorithm that meets the lower bound, up to a constant multiplicative factor. To derive the lower bound, we limit the range of sorting algorithms to those based on the comparison of keys, as stated below. (Sorting algorithms that are not comparison-based, such as the various forms of **radix sort**, assume that keys consist of individual digits and that digits are used to classify keys.)

ASSUMPTION 11.8.1 *All words to be sorted are located initially in the secondary memory. The **compare-exchange operation** is the only operation available to implement sorting algorithms on the BTM. In addition, an arbitrary permutation of the contents of the primary memory of the BTM can be done during the time required for one I/O operation.*

The assumption that the CPU can perform an arbitrary permutation on the contents of the primary memory during one I/O operation acknowledges that I/O operations take a very long time relative to CPU instructions.

Algorithms consistent with these assumptions are described by the multiway decision trees discussed below. They are a generalization of the **binary decision tree**, a binary tree in which each vertex has associated with it a comparison between two variables. For example, if keys x_1 and x_2 are compared at the root vertex, the comparison has two outcomes, namely $x_1 < x_2$ or $x_1 \geq x_2$, which are associated with the subtrees to the left and right of the root, respectively. Similar comparisons and outcomes are possible at each vertex of these two subtrees. A sequence of comparisons terminates on a leaf node.

Since a binary decision tree captures each of the data-dependent comparisons between keys in comparison-based sorting algorithm, each leaf is associated with the permutation of the original sequence of variables that puts the sequence into sorted order. Thus, a binary decision tree for sorting must have at least $n!$ distinct leaves, one for every permutation of n items. The length of a path through a binary decision tree is the number of comparisons performed on the particular input, and the length of the longest path is a measure of the worst-case number of comparisons. A binary tree with N leaves has a longest path of length at least $\log_2 N$ because if it were smaller, it would have fewer than $2^{\log_2 N} < N$ leaves. Since the length of the longest path is an integer, it must be at least $\lceil \log_2 N \rceil$. We summarize this result as a lemma that uses the lower bound on $n!$ given in Problem 2.23.

LEMMA 11.8.1 *The length of the longest path in a binary decision tree that sorts n inputs is at least $\lceil \log_2 n! \rceil = \Theta(n \log n)$.*

The **multiway decision tree** in Fig. 11.15 extends the above concept by permitting multiple comparisons at each vertex. 2^k outcomes are possible if k comparisons of variable pairs are associated with each vertex.

THEOREM 11.8.1 *Let B divide M and M divide n. Under Assumption 11.8.1 on the BTM, in the worst case the number of block I/O steps to sort a set of n records using M words of primary memory and block size B, $T_{\text{BTMsort}}(n)$, satisfies the following bounds for $B \leq M/2$ and M large:*

$$T_{\text{BTMsort}}(n) = \Theta\left(\max\left[\frac{n}{B}, \frac{(n/B)\log(n/B)}{\log(M/B)}\right]\right)$$

Proof Let's now apply the multiway decision tree to the BTM. Since each path in such a tree corresponds to a sequence of comparisons by the CPU, the tree must have at least $n!$ leaves. To complete the lower-bound derivation we need to determine the number of descendants of vertices in the multiway tree.

Initially the n unsorted words are stored in n/B blocks in the secondary memory. The first time one of these blocks is moved to the primary memory, up to $B!$ permutations can be performed on the words in it. No more permutations are possible between these words no matter how many times they are simultaneously in primary memory, even if they return to the memory as members of different blocks. When a block of B words arrives in the M-word memory, the number of possible permutations between them (given that the order among the $M - B$ words originally in the memory has previously been taken into

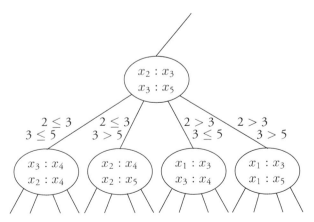

Figure 11.15 A multiway decision tree in which multiple comparisons of keys are made at each vertex.

account, as has the order among the B words in a block) is at most $\rho = \binom{M}{B}$, the binomial coefficient. (To see this, observe that places for the B new (and indistinguishable) words in the primary memory can be any B of the M indistinguishable places.) It follows that the multi-comparison decision tree for every BTM comparison-based sorting algorithm on the BTM has at most n/B vertices with at most $\rho B!$ possible outcomes (vertices corresponding to the first arrival of one of the blocks in primary memory) and that each of the other vertices has at most ρ outcomes.

It follows that if a sorting algorithm executes $T_{\text{BTMsort}}(n)$ block I/O steps, the function $T_{\text{BTMsort}}(n)$ must satisfy the following inequality:

$$(B!)^{n/B} \binom{M}{B}^{T_{\text{BTMsort}}(n)} \geq n!$$

Using the approximation to $n!$ given in Lemma 11.8.1, the upper bound of $(M/B)^B e^B$ on $\binom{M}{B}$ derived in Lemma 10.12.1, and the fact that $T \geq n/B$, we have the desired conclusion.

An upper bound is obtained by extending the standard merging algorithm to blocks of keys. The merging algorithm is divided into phases, an initialization phase and merging phases, each of which takes $(2n/B)$ I/O operations. In the initialization phase, a set of n/M sorted sublists of M keys or M/B blocks is formed by bringing groups of M keys into primary memory, sorting, and then writing them out to secondary memory. In a merging phase, M/B sorted sublists of L blocks ($L = M/B$ in the first merging phase) are merged into one sorted sublist of ML/B blocks, as suggested in Fig. 11.16. The first block of keys (those with the smallest values) in each sublist is brought into memory and the B smallest keys in this set is written out to the new sorted sublist that is being constructed. If any block from an input sublist is depleted, the next block from that list is brought in. There is always sufficient space in primary memory to do this. Thus, after k phases the sorted sublists contain $(M/B)^k$ blocks. When $(M/B)^k \geq n/B$, the merging is done. Thus, $(2n/B)\lceil \log_2(n/B)/\log_2(M/B) \rceil$ I/O operations are performed by this algorithm. ∎

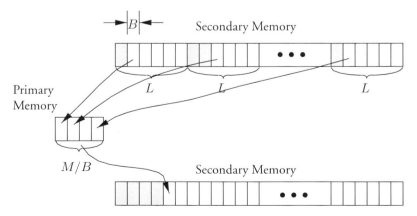

Figure 11.16 The state of the block merging algorithm after merging four blocks. The algorithm merges M/B sublists, each containing L blocks of B keys.

Similar results can be obtained for the permutation networks defined in Section 7.8.2 (see Problem 11.18), the FFT defined in Section 6.7.3 (see Problem 11.19), and matrix transposition defined in Section 6.5.4 (see [9]).

11.9 The Hierarchical Memory Model

In this section we define the hierarchical memory model and derive bounds on the time to do matrix multiplication, the FFT and binary search in this model. These results provide another opportunity to evaluate the performance of memory hierarchies, this time with a single cost function applied to memory accesses at all levels of a hierarchy. We make use of lower bounds derived earlier in this chapter.

DEFINITION 11.9.1 *The **hierarchical memory model** (HMM) is a serial computer in which a CPU without registers is attached to a random-access memory of unlimited size for which the time to access location a for reading or writing is the value of a monotone nondecreasing **cost function** $\nu(a) : \mathbb{N} \mapsto \mathbb{N}$ from the integers $\mathbb{N} = \{0, 1, 2, 3, \ldots\}$ to $\mathbb{N}$. The **cost of computing** $f^{(n)} : \mathcal{A}^n \mapsto \mathcal{A}^m$ **with the HMM** using the cost function $\nu(a)$, $\mathcal{K}_\nu(f)$, is defined as*

$$\mathcal{K}_\nu(f) = \max_{\boldsymbol{x}} \sum_{j=1}^{T(\boldsymbol{x})} \nu(a_j) \tag{11.2}$$

where a_j, $1 \leq j \leq T(\boldsymbol{x})$, is the address accessed by the CPU on the jth computational step and $T(\boldsymbol{x})$ is the number of steps when the input is $\boldsymbol{x}$.

The HMM with cost function $\nu(a) = 1$ is the standard random-access machine described in Section 3.4. While in principle the HMM can model many of the details of the MHG, it is more difficult to make explicit the dependence of $\nu(a)$ on the amount of memory at each level in the hierarchy as well as the time for a memory access in seconds at that level. Even though the HMM can model programs with branching and looping, following [7] we assume straight-line programs when studying the FFT and matrix-matrix multiplication problems with this model.

Let $n(f, \boldsymbol{x}, a)$ be the number of times that address a is accessed in the HMM for f on input $\boldsymbol{x}$. It follows that the cost $\mathcal{K}_\nu(f)$ can be expressed as follows:

$$\mathcal{K}_\nu(f) = \max_{\boldsymbol{x}} \sum_{1 \leq a} n(f, \boldsymbol{x}, a)\nu(a) \tag{11.3}$$

Many cost functions have been studied in the HMM, including $\nu(a) = \lceil \log_2 a \rceil$, $\nu(a) = a^\alpha$, and $\nu(a) = U_m(a)$, where $U_m(a)$ is the following threshold function with threshold m:

$$U_m(a) = \begin{cases} 1 & a \geq m \\ 0 & \text{otherwise} \end{cases}$$

It follows that

$$\mathcal{K}_{U_m}(f) = \max_{\boldsymbol{x}} \sum_{m \leq a} n(f, \boldsymbol{x}, a)$$

For the matrix-matrix multiplication and FFT problems, the cost $\mathcal{K}_{U_m}(f)$ of computing f is directly related to the number of I/O operations with the red-blue pebble game played with $S = m$ red pebbles discussed in Sections 11.5.2 and 11.5.3. For this reason we call this cost **I/O complexity**. The principal difference is that in the HMM no cost is assessed for data stored in the first m memory locations.

Let the differential cost function $\Delta\nu(a)$ be defined as

$$\Delta\nu(a) = \nu(a) - \nu(a-1)$$

As a consequence, we can write $\nu(a)$ as follows if we set $\nu(-1) = 0$:

$$\nu(a) = \sum_{0 \le b \le a} \Delta\nu(b) \tag{11.4}$$

Since $\nu(a)$ is a monotone nondecreasing function, $\Delta\nu(m)$ is nonnegative.

Rewriting (11.3) using (11.4), we have

$$
\begin{aligned}
\mathcal{K}_\nu(f) &= \max_{\boldsymbol{x}} \sum_{1 \le a} n(f, \boldsymbol{x}, a) \sum_{0 \le b \le a} \Delta\nu(b) \\
&= \left[\max_{\boldsymbol{x}} \sum_{c=0}^{\infty} \Delta\nu(c) \sum_{d=c}^{\infty} n(f, \boldsymbol{x}, d) \right] \\
&= \sum_{c=0}^{\infty} \Delta\nu(c) \left[\max_{\boldsymbol{x}} \sum_{d=c}^{\infty} n(f, \boldsymbol{x}, d) \right] \\
&= \sum_{c=0}^{\infty} \Delta\nu(c) \mathcal{K}_{U_c}(f)
\end{aligned}
\tag{11.5}
$$

11.9.1   Lower Bounds for the HMM

Before deriving bounds on the cost to do a variety of tasks in the HMM, we introduce the binary search problem.

A **binary tree** is a tree in which each vertex has either one or two descendants except leaf vertices, which have none. (See Fig. 11.17.) Also, every vertex except the root vertex has one

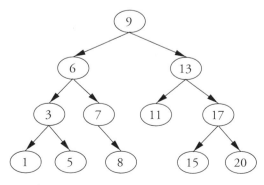

Figure 11.17   A binary search tree.

parent vertex. The **length of a path** in a tree is the number of edges on that path. The **left (right) subtree** of a vertex is the subtree that is detached by removing the left (right) descending edge. A **binary search tree** is a binary tree that has one key at each vertex. (This definition assumes that all the keys in the tree are distinct.) The value of this one key is larger than that of all keys in the left subtree, if any, and smaller than all keys in the right subtree, if any. A **balanced binary search tree** is a binary search tree in which all paths have length k or $k + 1$ for some integer k.

LEMMA 11.9.1 *The length of the longest path in a binary tree with n vertices is at least $\lceil \log_2(n+ 1)/2 \rceil$.*

Proof A longest path in a binary tree with n vertices is smallest when all levels in the tree are full except possibly for the bottom level. If such a tree has a longest path of length l, it has between 2^l and $2^{l+1} - 1$ vertices. It follows that the longest path in a binary search tree containing n keys is at least $\lceil \log_2(n + 1)/2 \rceil$. ∎

The **binary search procedure** searches a binary search tree for a key value v. It compares v against the root value, stopping if they are equal. If they are not equal and v is less than the key at the root, the search resumes at the root vertex of the left subtree. Otherwise, it resumes at the root of the right subtree. The procedure also stops when a leaf vertex is reached.

We can now state bounds on the cost on the HMM for the logarithmic cost function $\nu(a) = \lceil \log_2 a \rceil$. This function applies when the memory hierarchy is organized as a binary tree in which the low-indexed memory locations are located closest to the roots and the time to retrieve an item is proportional to the number of edges between it and the root. We use it to illustrate the techniques developed in the previous section.

Theorem 11.9.1 states lower performance bounds for straight-line algorithms. Thus, the computation time is independent of the particular argument of the function f provided as input. Matching upper bounds are derived in the following section. (The logarithmic cost function is polynomially bounded.)

THEOREM 11.9.1 *The cost function $\nu(a) = \lceil \log_2 a \rceil$ on the HMM for the $n \times n$ matrix multiplication function $f^{(n)}_{A \times B}$ realized by the classical algorithm, the n-point FFT associated with the graph $F^{(d)}$, $n = 2^d$, comparison-based sorting on n keys $f^{(n)}_{\text{sort}}$, and binary search on n keys, $f^{(n)}_{\text{BS}}$, satisfies the following lower bounds:*

Matrix multiplication: $\qquad \mathcal{K}_\nu(f^{(n)}_{A \times B}) = \Omega(n^3)$

Fast Fourier transform: $\qquad \mathcal{K}_\nu(F^{(d)}) = \Omega(n \log n \log \log n)$

Comparison-based sorting: $\quad \mathcal{K}_\nu(f^{(n)}_{\text{sort}}) = \Omega(n \log n \log \log n)$

Binary search: $\qquad \mathcal{K}_\nu(f^{(n)}_{\text{BS}}) = \Omega(\log^2 n)$

Proof The lower bounds for the logarithmic cost function $\nu(a) = \lceil \log_2 a \rceil$ use the fact that $\Delta\nu(a) = 1$ when $a = 2^k$ for some integer k but is otherwise 0. It follows from (11.5) that

$$\mathcal{K}_\nu(f) = \sum_{k=1}^{t} \mathcal{K}_{U_{2^k}}(f) \tag{11.6}$$

for the task characterized by f, where t satisfies $2^t \leq N$ and N is the space used by task. $N = 2n^2$ for $n \times n$ matrix multiplication, $N = n$ for the FFT graph $F^{(d)}$, and $N = n$ for binary search.

In Theorem 11.5.3 it was shown that the number of I/O operations to perform $n \times n$ matrix multiplication with the classical algorithm is $\Omega(n^3/\sqrt{m})$. The model of this theorem assumes that none of the inputs are in the primary memory, the equivalent of the first m memory locations in the HMM.

Since no charge is assessed by the $U_m(a)$ cost function for data in the first m memory locations, a lower bound on cost with this measure can be obtained from the lower bound obtained with the red-blue pebble game by subtracting m to take into account the first m I/O operations that need not be performed.

Thus for matrix multiplication, $\mathcal{K}_{U_m}(f_{A \times B}^{(n)}) = \Omega\left((n^3/\sqrt{m}) - m\right)$. Since

$$(n^3/\sqrt{m}) - m \geq (\sqrt{8} - 1)n^3/\sqrt{8m}$$

when $m \leq n^2/2$, it follows from (11.6) that $\mathcal{K}_\nu(f_{A \times B}^{(n)}) = \Omega(n^3)$ because $\sum_{k=0}^{t} n^3/2^k = \Omega(n^3)$.

For the same reason, $\mathcal{K}_{U_m}(F^{(d)}) = \Omega\left((n \log n)/\log m - m\right)$ (see Theorem 11.5.5) and $(n \log n/\log m) - m \geq n \log n/(2 \log m)$ for $m \leq n/2$. It follows that $\mathcal{K}_\nu(F^{(d)})$ satisfies

$$\mathcal{K}_\nu(F^{(d)}) = \Omega\left(\sum_k \frac{n \log n}{\log(2^k)}\right)$$

$$= \Omega\left(\sum_{k=1}^{\log n} \frac{n \log n}{k}\right) = \Omega\left(n \log n \log \log n\right)$$

The last equation follows from the observation that $\sum_{k=1}^{p} 1/k$ is closely approximated by $\int_1^p \frac{1}{x}\, dx$, which is $\ln p$. (See Problem 11.2.)

The lower bound for comparison-based sorting uses the $\Omega(n \log n/\log m)$ sorting lower bound for the BTM with a block size $B = 1$. Since the BTM assumes that no data are resident in the primary memory before a computation begins, the lower bound for the HMM cost under the U_m cost function is $\Omega\left((n \log n/\log m) - m\right)$. Thus, the FFT lower bound applies in this case as well.

Finally, we show that the lower bound for binary search is $\mathcal{K}_{U_m}(f_{BS}^{(n)}) = \Omega(\log n - \log m)$. Each path in the balanced binary search tree has length $d = \lceil \log(n + 1)/2 \rceil$ or $d - 1$. Choose a query path that visits the minimum number of variables located in the first m memory locations. To make this minimum number as large as possible, place the items in the first m memory locations as close to the root as possible. They will form a balanced binary subtree of path length $l = \lceil \log_2(m + 1)/2 \rceil$ or $l - 1$. Thus no full path will have more than l edges and $l - 1$ variables from the first m memory locations. It follows that there is a path containing at least $d - 1 - (l - 1) = d - l = \lceil \log(n + 1) \rceil - \lceil \log(m + 1) \rceil$

variables that are not in the first m memory locations. At least one I/O operation is needed per variable to operate on them. It thus follows that

$$
\begin{aligned}
\mathcal{K}_\nu(f_{\mathrm{BS}}^{(n)}) &= \sum_{d=0}^{\log n} \Omega(\log n - \log(2^d)) \\
&= \sum_{d=0}^{\log n} \Omega(\log n - d) \\
&= \Omega(\log^2 n)
\end{aligned}
$$

The last inequality is a consequence of the fact that $\log n - d$ is greater than $(\log n)/2$ for $d \le (\log n)/2$. ■

Lower bounds on the I/O complexity for these problems can be derived for a large variety of cost functions. The reader is asked in Problem 11.20 to derive such bounds for the cost function $\nu(a) = a^\alpha$.

11.9.2 Upper Bounds for the HMM

A natural question in this context is whether these lower bounds can be achieved. We already know from Theorems 11.5.3 and 11.5.5 that for each allocation of memory to each memory-hierarchy level, it is possible to match upper and lower bounds on the number of I/O operations and computation time. As a consequence, for each of these problems near-optimal solutions exist for any cost function on memory accesses for these problems.

11.10 Competitive Memory Management

The results stated above for the hierarchical memory model assume that the user has explicit control over the location of data, an assumption that does not apply if storage is allocated by an operating system. In this section we examine **memory management** by an operating system for the HMM model, that is, algorithms that respond to memory requests from programs to move stored items (instructions and data) up and down the memory hierarchy. We examine offline and online memory management algorithms. An **offline algorithm** is one that has complete knowledge of the future. **Online algorithms** cannot predict the future and must act only on the data received up to the present time.

We use **competitive analysis**, a type of analysis not appearing elsewhere in this book, to show that the two widely used online page-replacement algorithms, least recently used (LRU) and first-in, first-out (FIFO), use about twice as many I/O operations as does MIN, the optimal offline page-replacement algorithm, when these two algorithms are allowed to use about twice as much memory as MIN. Competitive analysis bounds the performance of an online algorithm in terms of that of the optimum offline algorithm for the problem without knowing the performance of the optimum algorithm.

Virtual memory-management systems allow the programmer to program for one large virtual random-access memory, such as that assumed by the HMM, although in reality the memory contains multiple physical memory units one of which is a fast random-access unit accessed by the CPU. In such systems the hardware and operating system cooperate to move data from secondary storage units to the primary storage unit in **pages** (a collection of items). Each reference to a virtual memory location is checked to determine whether or not the referenced item is in primary memory. If so, the virtual address is converted to a physical one and the item fetched by the CPU. If not (if a **page fault** occurs), the page containing the virtual address is moved into primary memory and the tables used to translate virtual addresses are updated. The item at the virtual address is then fetched. To make room for the newly fetched page, one page in the fast memory is moved up the memory hierarchy.

A **page-replacement algorithm** is an algorithm that decides which page to remove from a full primary memory to make space for a new page. We describe and analyze page-replacement algorithms for two-level memory hierarchies both because they are important in their own right and because they are used as building blocks for multi-level page-replacement algorithms. A two-level hierarchy has primary and secondary memories. Let the primary memory contain n pages and let the secondary memory be of unlimited size.

The **FIFO** (first-in, first-out) page-replacement algorithm is widely used because it is simple to implement. Under this replacement policy, the page replaced is the first page to have arrived in primary memory. The **LRU** (least recently used) replacement algorithm requires keeping for each page the time it was last accessed and then choosing for replacement the page with the earliest time, an operation that is more expensive to implement than the FIFO shift register.

Under the **optimal two-level page-replacement algorithm**, called **MIN**, primary memory is initialized with the first n pages to be accessed. **MIN** replaces the page p_i in primary memory whose time t_i of next access is largest. If some other page, p_j, were replaced instead of p_i, p_j would have to return to the primary memory before p_i is next accessed, and one more page replacement would occur than is required by MIN.

Implementing MIN requires knowledge of the future, a completely unreasonable assumption on the part of the operating system designer. Nonetheless, MIN is very useful as a standard against which to compare the performance of other page-replacement algorithms such as FIFO and LRU.

11.10.1   Two-Level Memory-Management Algorithms

To compare the performance of FIFO, LRU, and MIN, we characterize memory use by a **memory-address sequence** $s = \{s_1, s_2, \ldots\}$ of HMM addresses accessed by a computation. We assume that no memory entries are created or destroyed. We let $F_{\mathrm{FIFO}}(n, s)$, $F_{\mathrm{LRU}}(n, s)$, and $F_{\mathrm{MIN}}(n, s)$ be the number of page faults with each page-replacement algorithm on the memory address sequence s when the primary memory holds n pages.

We now bound the performance of the FIFO and LRU page-replacement algorithms in terms of that of MIN. We show that if the number of pages available to FIFO and LRU is double the number available to MIN, the number of page faults with FIFO and LRU is at most about double the number with MIN. It follows that FIFO and LRU are very good page-replacement algorithms, a result seen in practice.

THEOREM 11.10.1 *Let n_{FIFO}, n_{LRU}, and n_{MIN} be the number of primary memory pages used by the FIFO, LRU, and MIN algorithms. Let $n_{\mathrm{FIFO}} \geq n_{\mathrm{MIN}}$ and $n_{\mathrm{LRU}} \geq n_{\mathrm{MIN}}$. Then, for any memory-address sequence s the following inequalities hold:*

$$F_{\mathrm{FIFO}}(n_{\mathrm{FIFO}}, s) \leq \frac{n_{\mathrm{FIFO}}}{n_{\mathrm{FIFO}} - n_{\mathrm{MIN}} + 1} F_{\mathrm{MIN}}(n_{\mathrm{MIN}}, s) + n_{\mathrm{MIN}}$$

$$F_{\mathrm{LRU}}(n_{\mathrm{LRU}}, s) \leq \frac{n_{\mathrm{LRU}}}{n_{\mathrm{LRU}} - n_{\mathrm{MIN}} + 1} F_{\mathrm{MIN}}(n_{\mathrm{MIN}}, s) + n_{\mathrm{MIN}}$$

Proof We establish the result for FIFO, leaving it to the reader to show it for LRU. (See Problem 11.23.) Consider a contiguous subsequence t of s that immediately follows a page fault under FIFO and during which FIFO makes $\phi^{\mathrm{FIFO}} = f \leq n_{\mathrm{FIFO}}$ page faults. In the next paragraph we show that at least f different pages are accessed by FIFO during t. Let MIN make ϕ^{MIN} faults during t. Because MIN has n_{MIN} pages, $\phi^{\mathrm{MIN}} \geq f - n_{\mathrm{MIN}} + 1 \geq 0$. Thus, the ratio of page faults by FIFO and MIN is $f/\phi^{\mathrm{MIN}} \leq f/(f - n_{\mathrm{MIN}} + 1)$.

Let p_i be the page on which the fault occurs just before the start of t. To show that at least f different pages are accessed by FIFO during t, consider the following cases: a) FIFO faults on p_i in t; b) FIFO faults on some other page at least twice in t; and c) neither case applies. In the first case, FIFO accesses at least n_{FIFO} different pages because if it accessed fewer, then p_i would still be in its primary memory the second time it is accessed. In the second case, the same statement applies to the page accessed multiple times. In the third case, FIFO can have only f faults if it accesses at least f different pages during t.

Now subdivide the memory access sequence s into subsequences $t_0, t_1, \ldots, t_k$ such that t_i, $i \geq 1$, starts immediately after a page fault under FIFO and contains n_{FIFO} faults and t_0 contains at most n_{FIFO} page faults. This set of subsequences can be found by scanning s backwards. Since MIN makes $\phi_j^{\mathrm{MIN}} \geq n_{\mathrm{FIFO}} - n_{\mathrm{MIN}} + 1$ faults on the jth interval, $j \geq 1$, and $\phi_0^{\mathrm{MIN}} \geq \phi_0^{\mathrm{FIFO}} - n_{\mathrm{MIN}}$ faults on the zeroth interval (that is, $\phi_0^{\mathrm{FIFO}} \leq \phi_0^{\mathrm{MIN}} + n_{\mathrm{MIN}}$), the number of faults by FIFO, $F_{\mathrm{FIFO}}(n_{\mathrm{FIFO}}, s) = \phi_0^{\mathrm{FIFO}} + \phi_1^{\mathrm{FIFO}} + \cdots + \phi_k^{\mathrm{FIFO}}$ satisfies the condition of the theorem because $\phi_j^{\mathrm{FIFO}} \leq n_{\mathrm{FIFO}} \phi_j^{\mathrm{MIN}}/(n_{\mathrm{FIFO}} - n_{\mathrm{MIN}} + 1)$ for $j \geq 1$. ∎

The upper bounds are almost best possible because, as stated in Problem 11.24, for any online algorithm A there is a memory-access sequence such that the number of page faults $F_A(s)$ satisfies the following lower bound:

$$F_A(n_A, s) \geq \frac{n_A}{n_A - n_{\mathrm{MIN}} + 1} F_{\mathrm{MIN}}(n_{\mathrm{MIN}}, s)$$

The difference between this lower bound and the upper bounds given for FIFO and LRU is n_{MIN}, which takes into account for the possibility that the initial entries in the primary memory of MIN and FIFO can be completely different.

It follows that the FIFO and LRU page-replacement strategies are very effective strategies for two-level memory hierarchies.

Problems

MATHEMATICAL PRELIMINARIES

11.1 Let a and b be integers satisfying $1 \leq a \leq b$. Show that $b/2 \leq a\lfloor b/a \rfloor \leq b$.

    Hint: Consider values of b in the range $ka \leq b \leq (k + 1)a$ for k an integer.

11.2 Derive a good lower bound on $\sum_{k=1}^{m}(1/k)$ of the form $\Omega(\log m)$ using an approach similar to that of Problem 2.2.

PEBBLING MODELS

11.3 Show that the graph of Fig. 11.2 can be completely pebbled in the three-level MHG with resource vector $\boldsymbol{p} = (2, 4)$ using only four third-level pebbles.

11.4 Consider pebbling a graph with the red-blue game. Suppose that each I/O operation uses twice as much time as a computation step. Show by example that a red-blue pebbling minimizing the total time to pebble a graph does not always minimize the number of I/O operations.

I/O TIME RELATIONSHIPS

11.5 Let $S_{\min}$ be the minimum number of pebbles needed to pebble the graph $G = (V, E)$ in the red pebble game. Show that if in the MHG a pebbling strategy $\mathcal{P}$ uses s_k pebbles at level l or less and $s_k \geq S_{\min} + k - 1$, then no I/O operations at level $k + 1$ or higher are necessary except on input and output vertices of G.

11.6 The rules of the red-blue pebble game suggest that inputs should be prefetched from high-level memory units early enough that they arrive when needed. Devise a schedule for delivering inputs so that the number of I/O operations for matrix multiplication is minimized in the red-blue pebble game.

THE HONG-KUNG LOWER-BOUND METHOD

11.7 Derive an expression for the S-span $\rho(S, G)$ of the binary tree G shown in Fig. 11.4.

11.8 Consider the pyramid graph G on n inputs shown in Fig. 11.18. Determine its S-span $\rho(S, G)$ as a function of S.

11.9 In Problem 2.3 it is shown that every binary tree with k leaves has $k - 1$ internal vertices. Show that if t binary trees have a total of p pebbles, at most $p - 1$ pebbling steps are possible on these trees from an arbitrary initial placement without re-pebbling inputs.

Hint: The vertices that can be pebbled from an initial placement of pebbles form a set of binary trees.

11.10 An I/O operation is **simple** if after a pebble is placed on a vertex the pebble currently residing on that vertex is removed. Show that at most twice as many I/O operations are used at each level by the MHG when every I/O operation is simple.

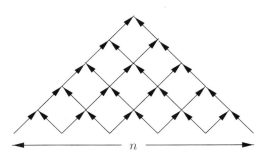

Figure 11.18 The pyramid graph.

Hint: Compare pebble placement with and without the requirement that placements be simple, arguing that if a pebble removed by a simple I/O operation is needed later it can be obtained by one simple I/O operation for each of the original I/O operations.

TRADEOFFS IN THE MEMORY HIERARCHIES

11.11 Using the results of Problem 11.8, derive good upper and lower bounds on the I/O time to pebble the pyramid graph of Fig. 11.18 in terms of n.

11.12 Under the conditions of Problem 11.4, show that any pebbling of a DAG for convolution of n-sequences with the minimal pebbling strategy when $S \geq S_{\min}$ and n is large has much larger total cost than a strategy that treats blue pebbles as red pebbles.

BLOCK I/O IN THE MHG

11.13 Determine how efficiently matrix-vector multiplication can be done in the block-I/O model described in Section 11.6.

11.14 Show that matrix-matrix multiplication can be done efficiently in the block-I/O model described in Section 11.6.

SIMULATING FAST MEMORIES

11.15 Determine conditions on a memory hierarchy under which the FFT can be executed efficiently in the standard MHG. Discuss the extent to which these conditions are likely to be met in practice.

11.16 Repeat the previous problem for convolution realized by the algorithm stated in the convolution theorem.

11.17 The definition of a minimal pebbling stated in Section 11.2 assumes that it is much more expensive to perform a high-level I/O operation than a low-level one. Determine the extent to which the lower bound of Theorem 11.4.1 depends on this assumption. Apply your insight to the problem of matrix multiplication of $n \times n$ matrices in the three-level MHG in which $s_1 < 3n^2$ and $s_2 \geq 3n^2$. (See Theorem 11.5.3.) Determine whether increasing the number of level-3 I/O operations affects the number of level-2 I/O operations.

THE BLOCK-TRANSFER MODEL

11.18 Derive a lower bound on the time to realize a permutation network on n inputs in the block-transfer model.

Hint: Count the number of orderings possible between the n inputs. Base your argument on the number of orderings within blocks and between elements in the primary memory, and the number of ways of choosing which block from the secondary memory to move into the primary memory.

11.19 Derive a lower bound on the time to realize the FFT graph on n inputs in the block-transfer model.

Hint: Use the result of Section 7.8.2 to argue that an n-point FFT graph cannot have many fewer vertices than there are switches in a permutation network.

THE HIERARCHICAL MEMORY MODEL

11.20 Derive the following lower bounds on the cost of computing the following functions when the cost function is $\nu(a) = a^\alpha$:

$$\text{Matrix multiplication:} \quad \mathcal{K}_\nu(f_{A \times B}^{(n)}) = \begin{cases} \Omega(n^{2\alpha+2}) & \text{if } \alpha > 1/2 \\ \Omega(n^3 \log n) & \text{if } \alpha = 1/2 \\ \Omega(n^3) & \text{if } \alpha < 1/2 \end{cases}$$

$$\text{Fast Fourier transform:} \quad \mathcal{K}_c^{(n)}(F^{(d)}) = \Omega(n^{\alpha+1})$$

$$\text{Binary search:} \quad \mathcal{K}_\nu(f_{\text{BS}}^{(n)}) = \Omega(n^\alpha)$$

Hint: Use the following identity to recast expressions for the computation time:

$$\sum_{k=1}^n \Delta g(k)h(k) = -\sum_{k=1}^{n-1} \Delta h(k)g(k+1) + g(n+1)h(n) - g(1)h(1)$$

11.21 A cost function $\nu(a)$ is **polynomially bounded** if for some $K > 1$ and all $a \geq 1$, $\nu(2a) \leq K\nu(a)$. Let the cost function $\nu(a)$ be polynomially bounded. Show that there are positive constants c and d such that $\nu(a) \leq ca^d$.

11.22 Derive a good upper bound on the cost to sort in the HMM with the logarithmic cost function $\lceil \log a \rceil$.

COMPETITIVE MEMORY MANAGEMENT

11.23 By analogy with the proof for FIFO in the proof of Theorem 11.10.1, consider any memory-address sequence s and a contiguous subsequence t of s that immediately follows a page fault under LRU and during which LRU makes $\phi^{\text{LRU}} = f \leq n_{\text{LRU}}$ page faults. Show that at least f different pages are accessed by LRU during t.

11.24 Let A be any online page-replacement algorithm that uses n_A pages of primary memory. Show that there are arbitrarily long memory-address sequences s such that the number of page faults with A, $F_A(s)$, satisfies the following lower bound, where n_{MIN} is the number of pages used by the optimal algorithm MIN:

$$F_A(s) \geq \frac{n_A}{n_A - n_{\text{MIN}} + 1} F_{\text{MIN}}(s)$$

Hint: Design a memory-address sequence s of length n_A with the property that the first $n_A - n_{\text{MIN}} + 1$ accesses by A are to pages that are neither in A's or MIN's primary memory. Let $\mathcal{S}$ be the $n_A + 1$ pages that are either in MIN's primary memory initially or those accessed by A during the first $n_A - n_{\text{MIN}} + 1$ accesses. Let the next $n_{\text{MIN}} - 1$ page accesses by A be to pages not in $\mathcal{S}$.

Chapter Notes

Hong and Kung [136] introduced the first formal model for the I/O complexity of problems, the red-blue pebble game, an extension of the pebble game introduced by Paterson and Hewitt [233]. The analysis of Section 11.1.2 is due to Kung [175]. Hong and Kung derived lower bounds on the number of I/O operations needed for specific graphs for matrix multiplication (Theorem 11.5.2), the FFT (Theorem 11.5.4), odd-even transposition sort and a number of other problems. Savage [289] generalized the red-blue pebble game to the memory-hierarchy game, simplified the proof of Theorem 11.4.1, and obtained Theorems 11.5.3 and 11.5.5 and the results of Section 11.3. Lemma 11.5.2 is implicit in the work of Hong and Kung [136]; the simplified proof given here is due to Agrawal and Vitter [9]. The results of Section 11.5.4 are due to Savage [289].

The two-level contiguous block-transfer model of Section 11.8.1 was introduced by Savage and Vitter [290] in the context of parallel space–time tradeoffs. The analysis of sorting of Section 11.8.1 is due to Agrawal and Vitter [9]. In this paper they also derive similar bounds on the I/O time to realize the FFT, permutation networks and matrix transposition.

The hierarchical memory model of Section 11.9 was introduced by Aggarwal, Alpern, Chandra, and Snir [7]. They studied a number of problems including matrix multiplication, the FFT, sorting and circuit simulation, and examined logarithmic, linear, and polynomial cost functions. The two-level bounds of Section 11.10 are due to Sleator and Tarjan [305]. Aggarwal, Alpern, Chandra, and Snir [7] extended this model to multiple levels. The MIN page-replacement algorithm described in Section 11.10 is due to Belady [35].

Two other I/O models of interest are the BT model and the uniform memory hierarchy. Aggarwal, Chandra, and Snir [8] introduced the **BT model**, an extension of the HMM model supporting block transfers in which a block of size b ending at location x is allowed to move in time $f(x) + b$. They establish tight bounds on computation time for problems including matrix transpose, FFT, and sorting using the cost functions $\lceil \log x \rceil$, x, and x^α for $1 \leq \alpha \leq 1$.

Alpern, Carter, and Feig [18] introduced the **uniform memory hierarchy** in which the uth memory has capacity $\alpha\rho^{2u}$, block size ρ^u, and time $\rho^u/\beta(u)$ to move a block between levels; $\beta(u)$ is a bandwidth function. They allow I/O overlap between levels and determine conditions under which matrix transposition, matrix multiplication, and Fourier transforms can and cannot be done efficiently.

Vitter and Shriver [348] have examined three parallel memory systems in which the memories are disks with block transfer, of the HMM type, or of the BT type. They present a randomized version of distribution sort that meets the lower bounds for these models of computation. Nodine and Vitter [226] give an optimal deterministic sorting algorithm for these memory models.

12

VLSI Models of Computation

The electronics revolution initiated by the invention of the transistor by Schockley, Brattain, and Bardeen in 1947 accelerated with the invention of the integrated circuit in 1958 and 1959 by Jack Kilby and Robert Noyce. An **integrated circuit** contains wires, transistors, resistors, and other components all integrated on the surface of a **chip**, a piece of semiconductor material about the size of a thumbnail. And the revolution continues. The number of components that can be placed on a semiconductor chip has doubled almost every 18 months for about 40 years. Today more than 10 million of them can fit on a single chip. Integrated circuits with very large numbers of components exhibit what is known as very large-scale integration (VLSI). This chapter explores the new models that arise as a result of VLSI.

As the size of the electronic components decreased in size, the area occupied by wires consumed an increasing fraction of chip area. In fact, today some applications devote more than half of their area to wires. In this chapter we examine VLSI models of computation that take this fact into account. Using simulation techniques analogous to those employed in Chapter 3, we show that the performance of algorithms on VLSI chips can be characterized by the product AT^2, where A is the chip area and T is the number of steps used by a chip to compute a function. We relate AT^2 to the planar circuit size $C_{p,\Omega}(f)$ of a function f, a measure that plays the role for VLSI chips that circuit size plays for FSMs. The AT^2 measure is the direct analog of the measure $C_\Omega(\delta, \lambda)T$ for the finite-state machine that was introduced in Chapter 3, where $C_\Omega(\delta, \lambda)$ is the size of a circuit to simulate the next-state and output functions of the FSM. We also relate the measure A^2T to $C_{p,\Omega}(f)$.

12.1 The VSLI Challenge

The design of VLSI chips represents an enormous intellectual challenge akin to that of constructing very large programs. They each involve the assembly of millions of elements, instructions in the case of software, and electronic components in the case of chips. The design and implementation of VLSI chips is also challenging because it involves many steps and many technologies. In this section we provide a brief introduction to this process as preparation for the introduction of the VLSI models and algorithms that are the principal topics of this chapter.

12.1.1 Chip Fabrication

A VLSI chip consists of a number of conducting, insulating, and doped layers that are placed on a semiconductor substrate. (A **doped layer** is created on the surface of the substrate by infusing small concentrations of impurities into the semiconductor. This is called **doping**.) The layers are created using **masks**, templates with open regions through which ionizing radiation is projected onto the surface of the semiconductor. The radiation changes the chemical properties of a previously deposited photosensitive material so that the exposed regions can be washed away with a solvent. The material that is now exposed can be doped or removed. Doping is used to create transistors and wires. A removal step is used when a metallic layer has been previously deposited from which sections are to be removed, leaving wires. A chip may have several layers of wires separated by layers of insulating material in addition to the doped layers that form transistors and wires. The layout of a NAND gate is shown schematically in Fig. 12.1, in which the shadings of rectangles and annotations identify to a chip designer the types of materials used to realize the gate.

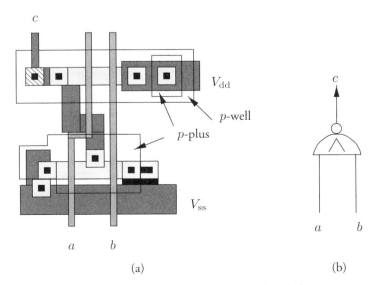

Figure 12.1   The schematic layout of a NAND gate and its logical symbol.

Geometric design rules specify the amounts of overlap of and separation between metal and dopant rectangles that are needed to guarantee the desired electrical and electronic properties of a VLSI circuit. If wires are too thin, electrons, which move through them at very high speeds, can cause excess heating as well as dislodge atoms and create an open circuit (this is called **metal migration**), especially at points at which a wire bends to descend into a well created during chip fabrication. Similarly, if wires are too close, an error in registration of masks may cause short circuits between wires. Also, since transistors are constructed through the doping and overlaying of insulating and conducting materials, if the regions defining a transistor are too small, it will not behave as expected.

The geometric design rules for a particular chip technology can be quite complex. For the purpose of analysis they are simplified into a few rules concerning the width and separation of rectangles, the amount of area required for contacts between wires on layers separated by insulation, and the size of the various rectangular regions that form gates and transistors. As suggested by this discussion, a VLSI chip is **quasiplanar**; that is, its components lie on a few layers, which are separated by insulation except where contacts are made between layers.

12.1.2 Design and Layout

Many tools and techniques have been developed to address the complexity of chip layout. Typically these tools and techniques use abstraction; that is, they decompose a problem into successively lower level units of increasing complexity. At each level the number of units involved in a design is kept small so that the design is comprehensible.

The design of a VLSI chip begins with the specification of its functionality at the **functional** or **algorithmic level**. Either a function or an algorithm is given as the starting point. An algorithm is then produced and translated into a specification at the **architectural level**. At this level a chip is specified in terms of large units such as a CPU, random-access memory, bus, floating-point unit, and I/O devices. (The material of Chapters 3 and 4 is relevant at this level.) After an architectural specification is produced, design commences at the **logical level**. Here particular methods for realizing architectural units are chosen. For example, an adder could be realized either as a ripple or a carry-lookahead adder depending on the stated speed and cost objectives. (The material of Chapter 2 applies at this level.)

At the **gate level**, the next level in the design process, a technology, such as NMOS and CMOS, is chosen in which to realize the transistors and wires. This involves specifications of widths for wires, the number of layers of metal, and other things. If new transistor layouts are used, their physics is often simulated to determine their electrical properties.

At the next level, the **layout level**, a gate-level design is translated into physical positions for modules, gates, and wires. Often at this level a rough layout is produced manually, after which automatic routing and compaction algorithms are invoked to route wires between modules and squeeze out the unnecessary area. Space must be reserved on each layout for **I/O pads**, rectangular regions large enough to connect external wires. They serve as **ports** through which data is read and written. Because these wires and pads are very large by comparison with the wires on the chip, there is a practical limit on the number of I/O ports on a chip. A port can be both an input and an output port.

Once a layout is complete it is usually simulated logically, that is, at the level of Boolean gates. Parts of it may also be simulated electrically, a much more time-consuming process given the much lower level of detail that it entails.

After a chip has been fabricated it is then tested. Because the testing process for a complete chip cannot be exhaustive, due to the number of configurations that are possible, subunits are often isolated and tested. Testing circuitry is often built into a chip to simplify the testing process.

Because the design, layout, simulation, and testing of VLSI chips is complex and error prone, **computer-aided design (CAD)** tools have been developed. CAD is very large subject beyond the scope of this book. Instead, we limit our attention in this chapter to the performance of VLSI chips.

12.2 VLSI Physical Models

Of all the parameters that affect the performance of a VLSI chip, its **area** is one of the most important. Equally important are the **width of** and **separation between wires**, both of which are directly related to area. Area is important for two reasons. First, a larger area means a chip can have more computing elements and do more work. Also, more area means a chip can have more I/O ports to facilitate data movement on and off the chip.

Unfortunately, the area of a chip has a practical limit due to imperfections that occur in the chip manufacturing process. A single very small piece of dust or a dislocation in the crystalline semiconductor substrate, each of which can be large by comparison with the dimensions of components, can destroy a chip. As a consequence, only a small fraction (the **yield**) of the chips resulting from a fabrication process work. The rest must be discarded.

The yield of a chip is very sensitive to its size. If the number of faults per unit area is F, with very high probability a fault occurs if the area A of a chip exceeds $1/F$. As F is reduced by improvements in the manufacturing process, the area of any one chip can increase. However, if F is fixed, so is the value of A at which an economical yield is possible. (F has not decreased much over time.) To make chip manufacture economical, dozens of chips are manufactured together on a circular wafer of 4 to 8 inches in diameter. The wafer is then sliced into individual chips. If the die size is chosen correctly, a fixed fraction of the chips on a wafer will work. The importance of testing becomes evident in light of these observations.

Because the area of a chip has a practical upper limit, the width and separation of wires determine the number of components that can be placed on a chip. As mentioned above, the technology for chip manufacture places a lower limit on these parameters as well as the area of chip components.

To simplify our modeling and analysis, we assume that the minimal width and separation of wires is λ (the **minimum feature size**) and that each gate, memory cell, port, and pair of crossing wires has area λ^2. There is no great loss in assuming a single number for wire width and separation and one number for the minimal area of components because in practice the width and separation of wires of different kinds and the area of components are all small multiples of common values. The only component for which these assumptions are weak is the pads for I/O ports, which are generally very much larger than λ^2. It is important to be cognizant of this fact in drawing conclusions.

Since chips are quasiplanar, we assume that **each chip has at most** $\nu \geq 1$ **layers** on which wires can reside but that there is only one layer of gates. Also, since wires are rectangular, it is impractical for them to meet at angles that are not close to 0 or 45 degrees. In fact, wires are usually rectilinear, that is, run horizontally and vertically. Thus, we assume that **wires are rectilinear**.

To complete the physical modeling of chips we recognize three types of **transmission model**, the synchronous, transmission-line, and diffusion models. The **synchronous model** assumes that one unit of time is needed to transmit a bit across a wire, independent of its length. This is a good model when the switching time of gates is large by comparison with the time to transmit data through a wire or when wires are short, a situation that prevails for most designs. When it does not prevail, the unit of transmission time can be increased so that it does apply. The **transmission-line model** assumes that the time to transmit a bit across a wire is proportional to its length (see Problems 12.1 and 12.2), whereas the **diffusion model** assumes it is quadratic in its length. The models apply to VLSI chip technologies at different wire lengths. The synchronous, transmission-line, and diffusion models apply to wires that are short, medium-length, and long, respectively.

Although we do not examine **energy consumption** in this chapter, the type of gate used can have a large impact on the amount of energy consumed during a computation. NMOS transistors consume energy all the time, whereas CMOS transistors consume energy only when they change their state.

When the area of I/O pads and gates are comparable, the placement of the pads on a VLSI chip can have a big impact on the area occupied by a chip. For example, if the chip realizes a tree and its n leaves (and their pads) are placed on the boundary of a convex region, as noted in Problem 12.3, the chip must have area proportional to $n \log n$. However, as shown in Section 12.5.1, when its leaves can be placed anywhere, there is a layout for a tree (known as the H-tree) that has area proportional to n. If the I/O pads are much larger than the gates, the impact of their placement is diminished.

12.3 VLSI Computational Models

We assume that a VLSI chip implements a finite-state machine instantiated as a clocked sequential machine. (A chip could also model an analog computer rather than a digital one, a topic not discussed in this book.) Although every FSM is eventually realized from two-input gates, binary memory cells, and wires carrying binary values (see Section 3.1), chips are generally designed around an aggregate model for data. That is, if operations are done on integers, the wires associated with an integer travel together on the chip surface. Although the time required for an operation on data depends on the size of alphabet from which the data is drawn and on the complexity of the operation itself, we simplify the analysis by assuming that one unit of time is taken. A more sophisticated analysis takes these factors into account.

To be concrete we let the states of an FSM be represented as tuples over a set X of binary b-tuples. We also assume that gates realize functions $\{h : X^2 \mapsto X\}$ and that memory cells hold one value of X. We recognize a **logic circuit over the set** X as the graph of a straight-line in which the operations are drawn from a basis $\{h : X^2 \mapsto X\}$. This model is used to study problems defined over non-binary alphabets, such as matrix multiplication and the discrete Fourier transform over rings.

We continue to use the notation λ for the minimum feature size of a VLSI chip even though we now allow data to be treated as values in the set X. When the set X is big, it will be important to make use of its size in accounting for the area occupied by wires and gates, an issue that we ignore in this chapter.

Computation **time** in the synchronous model is the number of steps executed by a chip. This is the same measure of time used for finite-state machines. Computation **time** in the other models is the elapsed time in seconds, which is approximated by the number of steps multiplied by the length of the longest step. This time is generally a function of the area of the chip and the problem for which the chip is designed.

Another measure of time, but one that is given only a cursory examination, is the **period** P of a VLSI chip. This is the time between successive inputs to a pipelined chip, one designed to receive a new set of inputs while the previous inputs are propagating through it. Pipelining is illustrated in Section 12.5.1 on H-trees and Section 11.6 on block I/O.

In this chapter **we assume that VLSI chips compute a single function** $f : X^n \mapsto X^m$, a perfectly general assumption that allows any FSM computation to be performed. While this allows the VLSI chip to be a CPU or a RAM, to convey ideas we limit our attention to functions that are simply defined, such as matrix multiplication and the discrete Fourier transform.

The variables of the function computed by a VLSI chip are supplied via its I/O ports. A single port can receive the values of multiple variables but at different time instances. Also, the value of a variable can be supplied at multiple ports, either in the same time step or in multiple time steps. However, the outputs of a function computed by a chip are supplied once to an output port. As noted above, a port can be either an input or output port or serve both purposes, but not in the same time step.

As with the FSM, we cannot allow either the time or the I/O port at which data is received as input or is supplied as output to be data-dependent. To do otherwise is to assume that an external agent not included in the model is performing computations on behalf of the user. We can expect misleading results if this is allowed. Thus, we assume that each I/O operation is **where-** and **when-oblivious**; that is, where an input or output occurs is data-independent, as are the times at which the I/O operations occur.

For many VLSI computations it is important that the input data be read once by the chip even if it may be convenient to read it multiple times. (These are called **semellective** or **read-once** computations.) For example, if a chip is connected to a common bus it may be desirable to supply the data on which the chip operates once rather than add hardware to the chip to allow it to request external data. However, in other situations it may be desirable to provide data to a chip multiple times. Such computations are called **multilective**. Multilective computations must be where- and when-oblivious.

If a multilective VLSI algorithm reads its n input variables $\beta\mu n$ times but only μn times when multiple inputs of a variable (at multiple time steps) at one I/O port are treated as a single input, then the algorithm is (β, μ)**-multilective**.

12.4 VLSI Performance Criteria

As stated in Theorem 7.4.1, the product pT_p of the time, T_p, and the number of processors, p, in a parallel network of RAM processors to solve a problem cannot be less than the serial time, T_s, on a serial RAM with the same total storage capacity for that problem. Applying this result to the VLSI model, since the number of processors of any given size that can be placed on a chip of area A is proportional to A, it follows that the product AT of area with the time T for a chip to complete a task cannot be less than the serial time to compute the same function using a single processor; that is, $AT = \Omega(T_s)$.

In the next section we show that the matrix-vector multiplication and prefix functions can be realized optimally with respect to the AT measure. This holds because these problems have low complexity. For problems of higher complexity, such as $n \times n$ matrix-matrix multiplication, we cannot achieve AT-optimality because stronger lower bounds apply. In particular, both AT^2 and A^2T must grow as n^4 for this problem, as we show. AT, AT^2 and A^2T are the only measures of VLSI performance considered in this chapter.

12.5 Chip Layout

In this section we describe and discuss layouts for a number of important graphs and problems. These include balanced binary trees, multi-dimensional meshes, and the cube-connected cycle.

12.5.1 The H-Tree Layout

H-trees are embeddings of binary trees that use area efficiently. Let H_k be an H-tree with 4^k leaves. Figure 12.2 shows the H-tree H_2 with 16 darkly shaded squares that can be viewed either as subtrees or leaves. The lightly shaded regions are internal vertices of the binary tree. Leaves often perform special functions that are not performed by internal vertices whereas internal vertices of a tree often perform the same function. Each quadrant of the tree shown in Fig. 12.2 can be viewed as the H-tree H_1 on four subtrees or leaves.

The layout of H_k is recursively defined as follows: replace each of the four subtrees (leaves) of a copy of H_1 with copies of H_{k-1}. Thus, H_2 in Fig. 12.2 is obtained by replacing each leaf in H_1 with a copy of itself.

We now derive an upper bound on the area of an H-tree under the assumption that each vertex is square, leaf vertices occupy area b^2, and the separation between leaf vertices is c. If $S(k)$ is the length of a side of H_k, then $S(1) = 2b + c$. Also, from the recursive construction of H_k the following recurrence holds:

$$S(k) = 2S(k-1) + c$$

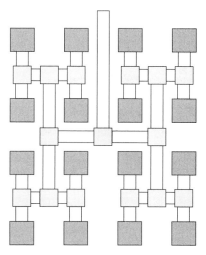

Figure 12.2 The H-tree H_2 containing 16 subtrees (or leaves).

The solution to this recurrence is $S(k) = (b + c)2^k - c$ as the reader can verify. Since H_k has $n = 4^k$ leaves and area $A_n = (S(k))^2$, it follows that an n-vertex H-tree has area $A_n \leq n(b + c)^2$.

To appreciate the importance of the H-tree construction, observe that its leaves are interior to the layout. Given the usual drawing of a binary tree one is tempted to place its leaves along the boundary of a chip. If this boundary is convex, the area of a binary tree on n leaves must be at least proportional to $n \log n$. (See Problem 12.3.)

MATRIX-VECTOR MULTIPLICATION ON AN H-TREE   We now describe an algorithm based on an H-tree that multiplies an $n \times n$ matrix A with an n-vector $\boldsymbol{x}$, $n = 2^k$, by forming the n inner products of the n rows of A with $\boldsymbol{x}$. (Matrix-vector multiplication is defined in Section 6.2.2.) This algorithm assumes that one unit of time is taken to store one piece of data and to perform an addition or multiplication on data.

On the first time step of our algorithm the components of the vector $\boldsymbol{x}$ are supplied in parallel to the n leaves of the tree and stored there. On the second time step components of the first row of A are also provided in parallel to the leaves. In the third time step the product of corresponding components of $\boldsymbol{x}$ and the first row of A are multiplied. In $k = \log_2 n$ additional time steps these products are added in the H-tree and the result supplied as output. In the next two steps the second row of A is supplied as input and its components multiplied by those of $\boldsymbol{x}$. After k additional steps these products are summed and the result generated as output. This process is repeated for each of the remaining rows of A. This algorithm is semellective.

Since we treat the time to add and multiply as the basis for measuring the time required by this H-tree, each inner product requires $O(\log n)$ time and the n inner products require $O(n \log n)$ time. However, if each addition vertex in this tree can also store its result (thereby causing a slight increase in area), a new row of A can be supplied to the H-tree in each unit of time (we say the **period** of the computation is $P = 1$) because a series of partial results can move through the tree in parallel. This is an example of pipelining. In this case the time to perform the n inner products is $O(n + \log n) = O(n)$. If pipelining is not used, this matrix-vector multiplication algorithm does not make the best use of area and time, as we now show.

Even without pipelining there exists an AT optimal algorithm for matrix-vector multiplication. Let n be such that $n/\log_2 n$ is a power of 4. Decompose each row of A as well as $\boldsymbol{x}$ into $(\log_2 n)$-tuples. This is equivalent to representing the $n \times n$ matrix A by a $n \times (n/\log_2 n)$ matrix B whose entries are $1 \times \log_2 n$ matrices (equivalently, $(\log_2 n)$-vectors) and to representing $\boldsymbol{x}$ by an $(n/\log_2 n)$-vector $\boldsymbol{y}$ whose components are $(\log_2 n)$-vectors.

We implement this computation on an H-tree with $O(n/\log n)$ area. To compute the inner product of A's jth row with $\boldsymbol{x}$, sequentially supply to each H-tree leaf the components of one $(\log_2 n)$-vector of $\boldsymbol{y}$ and the corresponding vector in the jth row of B. Supply the individual components of these $(\log_2 n)$-vectors in alternate cycles. After a leaf vertex receives the corresponding components of A and $\boldsymbol{x}$, it multiplies them and adds the result to its running sum. Upon completion of an inner product of two $(\log_2 n)$-vectors, the leaf vertices make their values available to be added in the H-tree in $O(\log n)$ steps. After n of these operations, all n inner products of $A\boldsymbol{x}$ are computed.

This algorithm uses $T = O(n \log n)$ time but only has area $A = O(n/\log n)$. Thus, its area–time product satisfies $AT = O(n^2)$, which is optimal since each of the $n^2 + n$

components of A and x must be read. This algorithm is multilective because it supplies each component of x n times.

PREFIX COMPUTATION ON AN H-TREE   The H-tree is also an effective way to do a prefix computation. Prefix computations (let $\odot$ be the associative operator) are naturally executed on trees. A tree-based prefix computation is described in Problem 7.31. One datum enters the root of the tree; the rest travel up from the leaves. When implemented on an H-tree, this algorithm uses area $O(n)$ on n inputs and time $O(\log n)$, giving an AT product of $O(n \log n)$. This algorithm is semellective.

This algorithm can be converted into an AT-optimal algorithm using a technique similar to that used above. We subdivide the input n-tuple x into $(\log_2 n)$-tuples, of which there are $(n/\log_2 n)$, and serially form the associative combination of the $(\log_2 n)$ components of each tuple using $\odot$ in $(\log_2 n)$ steps. We then perform the prefix computation on these $(n/\log_2 n)$ results. To complete the computation, for $1 \leq j \leq (n/\log_2 n) - 1$ we reread each of the original $(\log_2 n)$-tuples in parallel and add the $(j - 1)$st result (the zeroth result is 0) to the first component of the jth $(\log_2 n)$-tuple, and then serially perform a prefix computation on these new $(\log_2 n)$-tuples.

We increase $(n/\log_2 n)$ to the next power of 4 (adding inputs whose corresponding outputs are ignored) and embed the tree of Fig. 7.23 directly into an H-tree. The initial associative combination of $(\log_2 n)$-tuples and the final prefix computation on $(\log_2 n)$-tuples are done at vertices of the H-tree that are I/O vertices of the prefix tree. This algorithm takes time $O(\log n)$ on the initial and final phases as well as on the prefix computation. Since the area of the layout is $O(n/\log_2 n)$ and every one of the n inputs must be read, its area–time product, AT, is $O(n)$ which is optimal. This algorithm is multilective since each input is supplied twice.

12.5.2 Multi-dimensional Mesh Layouts

As explained in Section 7.5, many important problems can be solved with systolic arrays. If the cells of one- and two-dimensional systolic arrays are of fixed size and quasiplanar, they can be embedded directly onto a chip with area proportional to the number of cells. Applying the results of Theorems 7.5.1, 7.5.2, and 7.5.3 we have the following facts concerning the area and time for three important problems when realized by such arrays.

Problem	Dimensions	Area	Time
$n \times n$ Matrix-Vector Multiplication	1D	$O(n)$	$O(n)$
Bubble Sort of n items	1D	$O(n)$	$O(n)$
Batcher's Odd-Even Sorting of n items	1D	$O(n)$	$O(n)$
$\sqrt{n} \times \sqrt{n}$ Matrix-Matrix Multiplication	2D	$O(n)$	$O(\sqrt{n})$

Fully normal algorithms for problems such as shifting, summing, broadcasting, and fast Fourier transform on $n = 2^{2d}$ inputs can each be done in $O(\log n)$ steps on the n-vertex hypercube or the canonical cube-connected cycles network on n vertices. From Theorems 7.7.4 and 7.7.5 these problems can also be solved in $O(n)$ and $O(\sqrt{n})$ steps, respectively, on n-vertex one- and two-dimensional systolic arrays. We summarize these facts in Figure 12.3.

Problem	Dimensions	Area	Time
Shifting of n-vector	1D	$O(n)$	$O(n)$
	2D	$O(n)$	$O(\sqrt{n})$
Summing n items	1D	$O(n)$	$O(n)$
	2D	$O(n)$	$O(\sqrt{n})$
Broadcasting to n locations	1D	$O(n)$	$O(n)$
	2D	$O(n)$	$O(\sqrt{n})$
n-point FFT	1D	$O(n)$	$O(n)$
	2D	$O(n)$	$O(\sqrt{n})$

Figure 12.3 Area vs. time performance of VLSI algorithms for four problems.

In Section 12.6 we show that shifting of an n-vector, the n-point FFT, and $n \times n$ matrix-matrix multiplication each require area A and time T satisfying $AT^2 = \Omega(n^2)$. Consequently, the 2D algorithms cited above for these problems are optimal to within a constant factor.

In the next section we now show that every normal algorithm can be implemented on the cube-connected cycles (CCC) network in time T satisfying $\Omega(\log n) \leq T \leq O(\sqrt{n})$ and that the CCC network can be embedded in the plane using area $A = O(n^2/T^2)$. In Theorems 12.7.2 and 12.7.3 we show that these implementations are optimal up to constant multiplicative factors with respect to area and time for the three problems mentioned above.

12.5.3 Layout of the CCC Network

In Section 7.7.6 we describe the realization of a fully normal algorithm on the canonical CCC network. The realization extends directly from the canonical CCC network to a general (k, d)-CCC network in which there are 2^d cycles and 2^k vertices on each cycle. (See Fig. 12.4.)

A fully normal algorithm is simulated on the CCC network by giving the processors on the jth cycle, $0 \leq j \leq 2^d - 1$, the addresses $i + j2^k$ where $0 \leq i \leq 2^k - 1$. The cycles are treated as 1D arrays and used to simulate a normal algorithm on the first k dimensions exactly as is done in Section 7.7.6. These simulations are done in parallel after which the swaps across the higher-order d dimensions are simulated by first rotating the leading element on each cycle to the first of the inter-cycle edges. After executing one swap, each cycle is advanced one step so that the second elements on each cycle are aligned with the first of the high-order dimensions. At this point the first elements on each cycle are aligned with the edge associated with the second of the high-order dimensions. Thus, while swaps are done between the second elements on each cycle across the first of the high-order dimensions, swaps occur between leading elements along the second of the high-order dimensions. This rotating and swapping is done until all cycle elements have been swapped across all high-order dimensions.

This algorithm performs $O(2^k)$ steps on the cycles to perform swaps across low-order dimensions and align the cycles for swaps at higher dimensions. An additional $O(d)$ steps are used to perform swaps on the d high-order dimensions. Thus, the number of steps used by this algorithm, T, satisfies $T = O(2^k + d)$. The number of processors used in (k, d)-CCC network, n, satisfies $n = 2^{d+k}$.

Figure 12.4 shows a layout of a $(3, 4)$-CCC network. A layout for a general (k, d)-CCC network, $2^k \geq d$, can be developed following this pattern. Place each cycle of length 2^k in

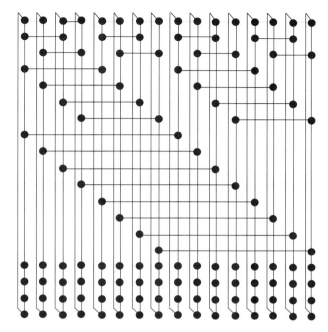

Figure 12.4 An embedding of a (k, d)-CCC network in the plane for $k = 3$ and $d = 4$. The 2^d columns represent cycles of length $2^k \geq d$. For $1 \leq j \leq d$, the jth vertex on each cycle is connected to the jth vertex on another cycle.

a column. Use $2^d - 1$ rows to make connections between columns. These rows are divided into d sets. The first set, consisting of one row, connects adjacent columns. The second set, containing two rows, connects every other column. The jth set, containing 2^{j-1} rows, connects every 2^jth column. The number of rows used for these connections is $1 + 2 + 4 + \cdots + 2^{d-1} = 2^d - 1$. Since d processors are used in each column to make these connections, each column contains $2^k - d \geq 0$ processors not connected to other columns. (These are suggested by the lightly shaded vertices.) It follows that this layout has $2^d + 2^k - (d+1)$ rows and 2^{d+1} columns. If a wire is assumed to have the same width as a processor, the layout has area $A = 2^{d+1}(2^d + 2^k - (d + 1))$.

Recall that $n = 2^{d+k}$ and $2^k \geq d$ or $k \geq \log_2 d$. It follows that $T = \Theta(2^k + d) = \Theta(2^k)$. Since $k \geq \log_2 d$, $T = \Omega(d) = \Omega(\log n)$. Also, when $k \leq d$, $2^{2k} \leq n$ and $T \leq O(\sqrt{n})$. We summarize this result below.

THEOREM 12.5.1 *Every fully normal algorithm for a d-dimensional hypercube can be implemented on a CCC network whose VLSI layout has area A and uses time T satisfying the following bound for $\Omega(\log n) \leq T = O(\sqrt{n})$.*

$$AT^2 = O(n^2)$$

This result can be applied to any of the fully normal algorithms described in Section 7.6 and the Beneš permutation network discussed in Section 7.8.2.

12.6 Area–Time Tradeoffs

The AT^2 measure encountered in the last section is fundamental to VLSI computation. This is established by deriving a lower bound on AT^2 in terms of the planar circuit complexity, $C_{p,\Omega}(f)$, of the function f computed by a VLSI chip of area A in T steps. A similar result is derived for the product A^2T. The planar circuit size of f is the size of the smallest memoryless planar circuit for f. The measures AT^2 and A^2T are the sizes of two different memoryless planar circuits that compute the same mapping from inputs to outputs as a VLSI chip of area A that executes T steps.

12.6.1 Planar Circuit Size

We now formally define planar circuit size and show how it relates to the standard circuit size measure.

DEFINITION 12.6.1 *A **planar circuit** over the set X is a logic circuit over the set X that has been embedded in the plane in such a way that gates do not overlap but edges may cross. A planar circuit is **semellective** if there is a unique vertex at which each input variable is supplied. Otherwise, the planar circuit is **multilective**.*

*The **size of a planar circuit** is the number of inputs, edge crossings, and gates drawn from a basis $\Omega = \{h : X^2 \mapsto X\}$ that the circuit contains. The **planar circuit size** of a function $f : X^n \mapsto X^m$ over Ω, $C_{p,\Omega}(f)$, is the size of the smallest planar circuit for f over the basis Ω.*

A multilective circuit of order μ, $\mu \geq 1$, for a function $f : \mathcal{B}^n \mapsto \mathcal{B}^m$ has μn input vertices. The size of the smallest multilective planar circuit of order μ for f is denoted $C_{p,\Omega}^{(\mu)}(f)$. If the planar circuit is semellective, the planar circuit size of f is denoted $C_{p,\Omega}^{(1)}(f)$ or $C_{p,\Omega}(f)$ when confusion is not likely.

Every binary function has a planar circuit. To see this, observe that every function has a circuit, which is a graph, and that every graph has a planar embedding with edge crossings. The planar circuit size of a function is at worst quadratic in its standard circuit size, as we now show.

LEMMA 12.6.1 *The (multilective) planar circuit and standard size of $f : \mathcal{B}^n \mapsto \mathcal{B}^m$ relative to the basis Ω are in the following relationship where r is the fan-in of Ω.*

$$C_\Omega(f) + n \leq C_{p,\Omega}(f) \leq r^2 C_\Omega^2(f)/2 + C_\Omega(f) + n$$

Proof The first inequality follows because the planar circuit size measure includes inputs, crossings, and gates, whereas the circuit size measure includes only gates.

Consider an embedding of a standard circuit for f containing $C_\Omega(f)$ gates. In such an embedding it is not necessary for any two edges to intersect more than once because if they violate this condition the edge segments between any two successive crossings can be swapped so that these two crossings can be eliminated. Since every gate has at most r inputs, a minimal standard circuit for f has at most $rC_\Omega(f)$ edges connecting gates. It follows that the number of crossings does not exceed $r^2 C_\Omega(f)^2/2$ because there are at most $\binom{q}{2}$ ways of forming pairs drawn from a set of size q and $q = rC_\Omega(f)$. Combining this with the number of inputs and gates, we have the desired upper bound. ■

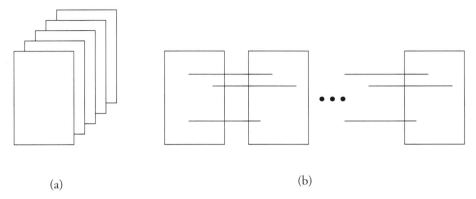

(a)   (b)

Figure 12.5 Two simulations of a T-step VLSI chip computation by a planar circuit.

In Section 12.7 we show that $f_{\text{cyclic}}^{(n)}$ nearly meets the upper bound of Lemma 12.6.1. That is, the planar circuit size of this function is nearly quadratic in its standard circuit size.

12.6.2 Computational Inequalities

We now show that every VLSI chip computation can be simulated by planar circuits of size $O(AT^2)$ and $O(A^2T)$. The simulation is patterned on the simulations of Chapter 3; that is, the loop that constitutes the computation by the chip with memory is unwound to create a planar circuit. Instead of passing the outputs of the next-state/output circuit to binary memory cells they are passed to another copy of the circuit.

Figure 12.5 shows two simulations of a T-step VLSI chip computation by a planar circuit. The first is obtained by placing T copies of the chip one above the other and supplying the state output of one copy to the state input of the next copy. The second is simulated by placing T copies of the chip side by side and running wires from the state output of one chip to the state input of the next. We convert each of these memoryless circuits to planar circuits and bound the number of inputs, crossings and gates they contain. Recall that we assume that wires are rectilinear; that is, they run only horizontally and vertically.

Since the number of wire layers on a single chip is bounded, it does not hurt to assume that the centerlines of parallel wires on different planes are displaced slightly. (It is bad practice to overlap wires because one wire can induce currents in the other.) Now make the width of wires and the area of gates infinitesimal. (Wires are shrunk to their centerline.) As shown in Fig. 12.6(a), each two-input gate is replaced by an infinitesimal vertex connected by a straight-line to its output and the two connections from its inputs are made by wires that contain bends (two wires touch). This converts a single chip to a planar graph with wires that touch or cross. (See Fig. 12.6(b) and (c)).

We now bound n_{w}, the number of wires, and n_{g}, the number of gates on a chip of area A. Since each wire has width λ and length at least λ and each gate occupies area λ^2, n_{w} and n_{g} satisfy the following bounds.

$$n_{\text{w}} \leq A/\lambda^2$$
$$n_{\text{g}} \leq A/\lambda^2$$

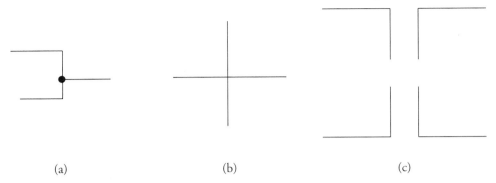

(a)   (b)   (c)

Figure 12.6   (a) The result of shrinking a physical gate to a point. (b) A crossing of two wires, and (c) four types of connection between two wires.

Because each point of crossing or touching of wires occupies area at least λ^2, the number of points at which wires cross and touch on each of the ν layers of a chip that has area A is at most A/λ^2. As shown in Fig. 12.6(a), when gates are made infinitesimal two additional bends are created at the point at which the output wire touches the gate. This can be viewed as adding four wire bends per gate. Since the number of gates is at most A/λ^2, we have the following bound on n_{cr}, the number of wire crossings and touchings.

$$n_{\mathrm{cr}} \leq (\nu + 4)A/\lambda^2$$

Consider the first of the two simulations. T layers of one chip are placed one above the other. To expose overlapping wires, displace all layers to the northeast by an infinitesimal amount. Every pair of wires that cross or meet has the potential to introduce crossings, as suggested in Fig. 12.7(a) and (b). The maximum number of crossings that can be introduced per touching or crossing of wires is T^2. Since the number of input vertices is $O(AT)$, this provides an upper bound of $O(AT^2)$ on the number of inputs, gates, and crossings of the resultant planar circuit.

Now consider the second simulation. T copies of one chip are laid side-by-side and the layout of each chip opened and at most n_{w} parallel wires inserted to make connections to adjacent chips. Since there are n_{w} wire segments on a single chip, at most n_{w}^2 new wire crossings are introduced on one chip. Thus, the number of inputs, gates, and crossings in this layout is $O(AT + n_{\mathrm{w}}^2 T) = O(A^2 T)$.

The following theorem, which is an application of Theorem 3.1.1 to the VLSI model, summarizes the above results. It makes use of the fact the planar circuit size of a function f computed by a VLSI chip of the kind described above is no larger than that of the planar circuits just constructed. This theorem demonstrates the importance of the measures AT^2 and A^2T as characterizations of the complexity of VLSI computations. It also shows that lower bounds on the performance of VLSI chips can be obtained in terms of the planar circuit size of the functions computed by them.

THEOREM 12.6.1   *Let $f_M^{(T)}$ be the function computed by a VLSI chip that realizes the FSM M in T steps. The planar circuit size over a basis $\Omega = \{h : X^2 \mapsto X\}$ of any function f computed*

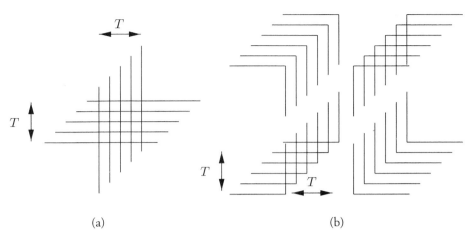

(a)   (b)

Figure 12.7 Crossings obtained by translating infinitesimally to the northeast T copies of (a) one crossing and (b) the four possible connections between two wires.

by M in T steps satisfies the following inequalities:

$$C_{p,\Omega_0}(f) = O(AT^2)$$
$$C_{p,\Omega_0}(f) = O(A^2T)$$

If M is multilective of order μ, then $C_{p,\Omega}(f)$ is replaced by $C_{p,\Omega}^{(\mu)}(f)$.

It is important to note that these relationships between planar circuit size and the measures AT^2 and A^2T hold for all functions computed by VLSI algorithms, both multi-output functions and predicates.

In the next section we develop the planar separator theorem that is used in the next section to derive lower bounds on the planar circuit size of important problems.

12.6.3 The Planar Separator Theorem

The **planar separator theorem** applies to graphs $G = (V, E)$ for which a non-negative cost function c is defined on V. The cost of V, denoted, $c(V)$, is the sum of the costs of every vertex in V. The theorem states that the vertices of every planar graph G on N vertices can be partitioned into three sets, A, B, and C such that no edge connects a vertex in A with one in B, the cost of vertices in A, $c(A)$, and those in B, $c(B)$, satisfy $c(A), c(B) \leq 2c(V)/3$ and C contains at most $4\sqrt{N}$ vertices.

The following lemma uses the concept of the **spanning tree** of a graph, a tree that contains every vertex of a connected graph G. It shows the existence of a cycle that divides a planar graph into an "inside" and an "outside" containing about the same number of vertices. The **radius** of a rooted spanning tree is the number of edges on the longest path from the root to a vertex. (See Problem 12.8 for an illustration of the following lemma.)

LEMMA 12.6.2 *Let $G = (V, E)$ be a finite connected planar graph. Let c be a non-negative cost function defined on V and let $c(V)$ be the total cost of all vertices in V. If G has a rooted*

spanning tree of radius r, then V can be partitioned into sets A, B, and C such that $c(A), c(B) \le$
$2c(V)/3$, no edge joins a vertex of A with one of B, and C contains at most $2r + 1$ vertices.

Proof   Let $G = (V, E)$ be embedded in the plane. A **face of a planar graph** is a region
bounded by vertices and edges that does not contain any other vertices and edges. The
external face of a finite planar graph consists of the region outside all edges and vertices.
Since G is finite, it has an external face. A **triangular planar graph** is a planar graph in
which each face is a **triangle**; that is, the face has three vertices and three edges. If a planar
graph is not triangular, it can be made triangular by choosing one vertex on the boundary of
each face and adding an edge between it and every other vertex on this face to which it does
not already have an edge. Without loss of generality we assume that G is triangular.

Let T be the spanning tree of radius r postulated in the lemma. Each edge e in E not
on T defines a unique cycle $\xi(e)$ of length at most $2r + 1$. The cycle divides V into three
sets, vertices on $\xi(e)$, and vertices on each side of $\xi(e)$. Let $c_1(e)$ and $c_2(e)$ be the cost of
vertices on either side. (The side with the larger cost is called the **inside of the cycle**.) We
claim that for some e not on T the larger of $c_1(e)$ and $c_2(e)$ is no more than $2c(V)/3$. We
suppose the larger is no more than $2c(V)/3$ and establish a contradiction.

Let $e = (x, y)$ be an edge not on T such that $\mu(e) = \max(c_1(e), c_2(e))$ is smallest and
for all other e^* such that $\mu(e^*) = \mu(e)$, and the inside of $\xi(e)$ has the fewest faces. In case
of ties, let e be chosen arbitrarily. We show the assumption that $\mu(e) > 2c(V)/3$ is false.

Consider the triangle containing the edge $e = (x, y)$ on the side of the cycle $\xi(e)$ that
has largest cost. Let z be the third vertex in this triangle. z is on the spanning tree because
every vertex is on the tree. We consider two cases for z: (a) either edge (x, z) or (y, z) is in
T and (b) neither edge is in T.

In case (a) without loss of generality, let (y, z) be in T. There are two subcases to
consider: (a1) z is on $\xi(e)$ (see Fig. 12.8(a)) and (a2) it is not on $\xi(e)$ (see Fig. 12.8(b)). In
(a1) the edge $e' = (x, z)$ cannot be a tree edge since T contains no cycles unless the cycle
consists of just the vertices x, y, and z, which is impossible since the inside of $\xi(e)$ contains
at least one vertex. But $\xi(e')$ includes the same set of vertices of V inside it (and has the
same cost) as does $\xi(e)$, although it has fewer faces, contradicting the choice for $e = (x, y)$.

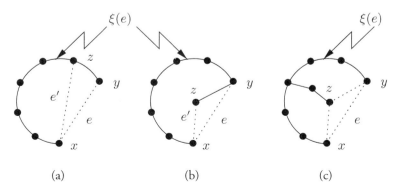

(a)   (b)   (c)

Figure 12.8   A non-tree edge $e = (x, y)$ in a triangular planar graph with spanning tree T
defines a cycle $\xi(e)$. The triangle containing e on the larger side of $\xi(e)$ contains a third vertex
z. In (a) and (b) (y, z) is on T, whereas in (c) neither (x, z) nor (y, z) is on T. In (a) (y, z) is
on $\xi(e)$, whereas in (b) it is not.

In case (a2) the edge $e' = (x, z)$ is a non-tree edge since T contains no cycles. The inside of $\xi(e')$ contains no more cost and one less face than $\xi(e)$. If the cost inside $\xi(e')$ is greater than the cost outside, e' would have been chosen instead of e. On the other hand, if the cost inside $\xi(e')$ is at most the cost outside, since the latter is equal to the cost outside $\xi(e)$, which is at most $c(V)/3$, the cost inside $\xi(e')$ is at most $c(V)/3$. However, this contradicts the assumption that $\mu(e^*) > 2c(V)/3$ for all edges e^*.

Consider the case (b) in which neither edge (x, z) nor (y, z) is in T. (See Fig. 12.8(c).) The edges (x, z) and (y, z) each define a cycle contained within the inside of the cycle defined by e. Without loss of generality assume that the cycle defined by (x, z) has more cost on the inside of the original cycle than does the cycle defined by (y, z). Because the cost of vertices on the inside of the original cycle is more than $2c(V)/3$, the cost inside and on the cycle defined by (x, z) is more than $c(V)/3$. Thus, the cost outside this cycle is less than or equal to $2c(V)/3$, contradicting the assumption that $\mu(e^*) > 2c(V)/3$ for all edges e^*. ∎

The following theorem uses Lemma 12.6.2 together with a spanning tree constructed through a breadth-first traversal of a connected planar graph to show the existence of a small separator that divides the vertices into approximately two equal cost parts.

THEOREM 12.6.2 *Let $G = (V, E)$ be an N-vertex planar graph having non-negative vertex costs summing to $c(V)$. Then, V can be partitioned into three sets, A, B, and C, such that no edge joins vertices in A with those in B, neither A nor B has cost exceeding $2c(V)/3$, and C contains no more than $4\sqrt{N}$ vertices.*

Proof We assume that G is connected. If not, embed it in the plane and add edges as appropriate to make it connected. Assume that it has been triangulated, that is, every face except for the outermost is a triangle.

Pick any vertex (call it the root) and perform a breadth-first traversal of G. This traversal defines a **BFS spanning tree T of G**. A vertex v has level d in this tree if the length of the path from the root to v has d edges. There are no vertices at level q where q is the level one larger than that of all vertices. Let R_d be the vertices at level d and let $r_d = |R_d|$.

The reader is asked to show that there is some level m such that the cost of vertices at levels below and above m each is at most $c(V)/2$. (See Problem 12.9.) Let l and h, $l \leq m \leq h$, be levels closest to m that contain at most $\sqrt{N}$ vertices. That is, $r_l \leq \sqrt{N}$ and $r_h \leq \sqrt{N}$. There are such levels because level 0 contains a single vertex and there are none at level q.

The vertices in G are partitioned into the following five sets: a) $L = \bigcup_{d<l} R_d$, b) R_l, c) $M = \bigcup_{l<d<h} R_d$, d) R_h, and e) $L = \bigcup_{h<d} R_d$. Since L and H are subsets of the sets of vertices with levels less than and more than m, $c(L), c(H) \leq c(V)/2$. Also, by construction, $r_l, r_h \leq \sqrt{N}$. If $R_l = R_h = R_m$ (which implies that M is empty), let $A = L$, $B = H$, and $C = R_l = R_h$. Then, C is a separator of size at most $\sqrt{N}$ and the theorem holds. If $r_l \neq r_h$, then $r_h - r_l - 1 \geq 1$. Since each of the $r_h - r_l - 1$ levels between r_l and r_h has at least $\sqrt{N} + 1$ vertices, it follows that $r_h - r_l - 1 \leq \sqrt{N}$ because these levels cannot have more than $N - 1$ vertices altogether.

Consider the subgraph of G consisting of the vertices in M and the edges between them. Add a new vertex v_0 to replace the vertices in $L \cup R_l$ and add an edge from v_0 to each of the vertices at level r_{l+1}. This operation retains planarity and the resulting graph remains triangulated because adjacent vertices on R_{l+1} have an edge between them. Also, it defines a spanning tree T^* consisting of v_0, the new edges, and the projection of the original spanning tree to the vertices in M. T^* has radius at most $\sqrt{N}$.

Apply Lemma 12.6.2 to T^* giving v_0 zero cost. This lemma identifies three sets of vertices, A_0, B_0 and C_0, from which we delete v_0. Since $c(M) \leq c(V)$, it follows that there are no edges between vertices in A_0 and B_0, $c(A_0), c(B_0) \leq 2c(V)/3$, and $|C_0| \leq 2\sqrt{N}$. Let $C = C_0 \cup R_l \cup R_h$. It follows that $|C| \leq 4\sqrt{N}$.

Each of the four sets A_0, B_0, L, and H has cost at most $2c(V)/3$. If any one of them has cost more than $c(V)/3$, let it be A and let B be the union of the remaining sets. If none of them has cost more than $c(V)/3$ vertices, order the sets by size and let A be the union of the fewest of these sets whose cost is at least $c(V)/3$ vertices. This procedure insures that A has cost between $c(V)/3$ and $2c(V)/3$ which implies that B satisfies the same condition as A and the theorem is established. ∎

The preceding version of the planar separator theorem only guarantees that the vertices of a planar graph are divided into two sets whose costs are nearly balanced and a small separator. It does not insure that the number of vertices in the two sets are balanced. The following lemma remedies this situation. We leave its proof to the reader. (See Problem 12.10.)

LEMMA 12.6.3 *Let $G = (V, E)$ be an N-vertex planar graph having non-negative vertex costs summing to $c(V)$. Then V can be partitioned into three sets, A, B, and C, such that no edge joins vertices in A with those in B, neither A nor B has cost exceeding $2c(V)/3$, $|A|, |B| \leq 5N/6$, and C contains no more than $K_1 \sqrt{N}$ vertices, where $K_1 = 4(\sqrt{2/3} + 1)$.*

This new result can be applied to show that the vertices of a planar graph can be partitioned into many sets each having about the same cost and such that a small set of vertices can be removed to separate each set from all other sets. This result is also left to the reader. (See Problem 12.11.)

LEMMA 12.6.4 *Let $G = (V, E)$ be an N-vertex planar graph and let c be a non-negative cost function on V with total cost of $c(V)$. Let $P \geq 2$. There are constants $2P/3 \leq q \leq 3P$ and $K_2 = 4(\sqrt{2/3} + 1)/(1 - \sqrt{5/6})$ such that V can be partitioned into q sets, $A_1, A_2, \ldots, A_q$ such that for $1 \leq i \leq q$*

$$c(V)/(3P) \leq c(A_i) \leq 3c(V)/(2P)$$

and there are sets C_i, $|C_i| \leq K_2 \sqrt{N}$, and $B_i = V - A_i - C_i$ such that no edges join vertices in A_i with vertices in B_i.

12.7 The Performance of VLSI Algorithms

Using Theorem 12.6.1 and Lemma 12.6.4, we now derive lower bounds on AT^2 and A^2T for individual functions by deriving lower bounds on their planar circuit size. In the following section we derive lower bounds to the planar circuit size for multi-output functions using the $w(u, v)$-flow property of these functions. In Section 12.7.2 we set the stage for deriving lower bounds on the planar circuit size of predicates.

12.7.1 The Performance VLSI Algorithms on Functions

The $w(u, v)$-flow property of functions is introduced in Section 10.4.1 and applied to the study of space–time tradeoffs in the pebble game. In this section we use this property to derive lower bounds on the semellective planar circuit size of multi-output functions.

DEFINITION 12.7.1 *A function $f : X^n \mapsto X^m$ has a $\boldsymbol{w(u, v)}$-flow if for all subsets U_1 and V_1 of its n input and m output variables with $|U_1| \geq u$ and $|V_1| \geq v$ there is some assignment to variables not in U_1 (variables in U_0) such that the resulting subfunction h of f that maps input variables in U_1 to output variables in V_1 (the other outputs are discarded) has at least $|X|^{w(u,v)}$ points in the image of its domain. (Note that $w(u, v) \geq 0$.)*

A lower bound on planar circuit size of a function f is now derived from its $w(u, v)$-flow property. For some functions the parameter P will need to be large for $w(u, v) > 0$, as is seen Lemma 12.7.1.

THEOREM 12.7.1 *Let $f : X^n \mapsto X^m$ have a $w(u, v)$-flow. Then its semellective planar circuit size must satisfy the following lower bound for $u \geq n(1 - 3/2P)$, $v \geq m/(3P)$, and $P \geq 2$, where $K_2 = 4(\sqrt{2/3} + 1)/(1 - \sqrt{5/6})$.*

$$C_{\mathrm{p},\Omega}(f) \geq \frac{w^2(u, v)}{4K_2^2}$$

Proof Consider a minimal semellective planar circuit for $f : X^n \mapsto X^m$ on n inputs containing $N = C_{\mathrm{p},\Omega}(f)$ inputs, gates, and crossings. We apply the version of the planar separator theorem given in Lemma 12.6.4 to this circuit by assigning unit weight to each input vertex and zero weight to all other vertices. For any integer $P \leq |V|$ we conclude that the inputs, gates, and crossings of this circuit can be partitioned into q sets $\{A_1, A_2, \ldots, A_q\}$, for $2P/3 \leq q \leq 3P$, such that each set has at least $n/(3P)$ and at most $3n/(2P)$ input vertices. Since the average number of output vertices in these sets is m/q, at least one set, call it A_1, has at least the average of output vertices or at least $m/3P$ vertices. Let U_0 and V_1 be the sets of inputs and outputs in A_1, respectively. Then, $n/(3P) \leq |U_0| \leq 3n/(2P)$ and $|V_1| \geq m/3P$.

For some assignment of values to variables in U_0, there are at least $|X|^{w(u,v)}$ values for the outputs in V_1 when $u = n - |U_0| \geq n(1 - 3/2P)$ and $v = |V_1| \geq m/(3P)$. But all of the values assumed by the outputs in V_1 must be assumed by the inputs, gates, and crossing wires of the separator. Since at most two wires cross, a separator C of size $|C|$ has at most $2|C|$ inputs, gates, and wires each of which can have at most $|X|$ values. Thus, if C_1, the separator for A_1, has a size satisfying $2|C_1| < w(u, v)$, a contradiction results and the output variables in V_1 cannot assume $|X|^{w(u,v)}$ values. It follows that $|C_1| \geq w(u, v)/2$. Since $C_1 \leq K_2\sqrt{N}$, this implies that $N \geq w^2(u, v)/(2K_2)^2$, the desired conclusion. ∎

We apply this general result to (α, n, m, p)-independent functions and matrix multiplication. A function is (α, n, m, p)-independent (see Definition 10.4.2) if it has a $w(u, v)$-flow satisfying $w(u, v) > (v/\alpha) - 1$ for $n - u + v \leq p$, where $n - u \geq 0$.

LEMMA 12.7.1 *Let* $f : X^n \mapsto X^m$ *be* (α, n, m, p)*-independent. Then for* $P \geq (m/3 + 3n/2)/p$ *and* $m \geq 2\alpha$, f *has semellective planar circuit size satisfying the following lower bound:*

$$C_{p,\Omega}(f) \geq \frac{m^2}{144(\alpha P)^2 K_2^2}$$

Proof f has a $w(u,v)$-flow satisfying $w(u,v) > (v/\alpha) - 1$ for $n - u + v \leq p$. When $u \geq n(1 - 3/2P)$, $n - u + v \leq p$ is satisfied if $v \leq p - 3n/(2P)$. Since we also require that $v \geq m/(3P)$, this implies that $P \geq (m/3 + 3n/2)/p$. Also, $v/\alpha - 1 \geq v/2\alpha$ if $v \geq 2\alpha$. Substituting $m/3P$ for v, we have the desired conclusion. ∎

In Section 10.5 we have shown that many functions are (α, n, m, p)-independent. We summarize these results below.

Name	Function	Independence Property
Wrapped convolution	$f^{(n)}_{\mathrm{wrapped}} : \mathcal{R}^{2n} \mapsto \mathcal{R}^n$	$(2, 2n, n, n/2)$
Cyclic shift	$f^{(n)}_{\mathrm{cyclic}} : \mathcal{B}^{n + \lceil \log n \rceil} \mapsto \mathcal{B}^n$	$(2, n + \lceil \log n \rceil, n, n/2)$
Integer multiplication	$f^{(n)}_{\mathrm{mult}} : \mathcal{B}^{2n} \mapsto \mathcal{B}^{2n}$	$(2, 2n, n, n/2)$
n-point DFT	$F_n : \mathcal{R}^n \mapsto \mathcal{R}^n$	$(2, n, n, n/2)$

It follows that for each case Lemma 12.7.1 holds when $P = 4$. Thus, each of the (α, n, m, p)-independent function has a planar circuit size that is quadratic in n, its number of inputs. The following theorem results from this observation and Theorem 12.6.1.

THEOREM 12.7.2 *The area* A *and time* T *required to compute* $f^{(n)}_{\mathrm{wrapped}} : \mathcal{R}^{2n} \mapsto \mathcal{R}^n$, $f^{(n)}_{\mathrm{cyclic}} : \mathcal{B}^{n + \lceil \log n \rceil} \mapsto \mathcal{B}^n$, $f^{(n)}_{\mathrm{mult}} : \mathcal{B}^{2n} \mapsto \mathcal{B}^{2n}$, *and* $F_n : \mathcal{R}^n \mapsto \mathcal{R}^n$ *on a semellective VLSI chip satisfy the following bounds:*

$$AT^2, A^2 T = \Omega(n^2)$$

The AT^2 *lower bound can be achieved up to a constant multiplicative factor for each of these functions for* $\Omega(\log n) \leq T \leq \sqrt{n}$.

Proof From Theorem 12.5.1 we know that any fully normal algorithm can achieve the $AT^2 = O(n^2)$ for $\Omega(\log n) = T = O(\sqrt{n})$ on an embedded CCC network. Since cyclic shift and FFT are shown to be fully normal (see Section 7.7), we have matching upper and lower bounds for them. From Problem 12.13 we have that the wrapped convolution can be realized with matching bounds on AT^2 over the same range of values for T. The same statement applies to integer multiplication (see Problem 12.16). ∎

In Section 12.6.1 we said that we would exhibit a function whose planar circuit size is nearly quadratic in its standard circuit size. This property holds for the cyclic shifting function because, as shown in Section 2.5.2, $f^{(n)}_{\mathrm{cyclic}} : \mathcal{B}^{n + \lceil \log n \rceil} \mapsto \mathcal{B}^n$ has circuit size no larger than $O(n \log n)$, whereas from the above its planar circuit size is $\Theta(n^2)$.

The cyclic shift function is also an example of a function for which most of the chip area is occupied by wires when $T = O(\sqrt{n/\log n})$, because in this case the area is $\Omega(n \log n)$ but the number of gates needed to realize it is $O(n \log n)$.

Lower bounds on AT^2 and A^2T also exist for matrix multiplication. From Lemma 10.5.3 we know that the matrix multiplication function $f_{A \times B}^{(n)} : \mathcal{R}^{2n^2} \mapsto \mathcal{R}^{n^2}$ has a $w(u, v)$-flow, where $w(u, v) \geq (v - (2n^2 - u)^2/4n^2)/2$. Using this we have the following lower bound on the planar circuit size of this function.

THEOREM 12.7.3 *The area A and time T required to compute the matrix multiplication function $f_{A \times B}^{(n)} : \mathcal{R}^{2n^2} \mapsto \mathcal{R}^{n^2}$ with a semellective VLSI algorithm satisfies the following lower bound:*

$$AT^2, A^2T = \Omega(n^4)$$

The AT^2 lower bound can be met to within a constant multiplicative factor.

Proof Apply Theorem 12.7.1 to matrix multiplication by replacing the number of input variables n by $2n^2$ and the number of output variables m by n^2. The $w(u, v)$-flow function has value

$$w(u, v) = (v - (2n^2 - u)^2/4n^2)/2 \geq \frac{n^2}{2} \left(\frac{1}{3P} - \left(\frac{3}{2P} \right)^2 \right)$$

The right-hand side is maximized when $P = 14$ and has value greater than $n^2/163$, from which the conclusion follows.

As shown in Section 7.5.3, two $n \times n$ matrix can be multiplied with area $A = O(n^2)$ and time $T = n$, which meets the lower bound up to a multiplicative factor. Other near-optimal solutions also exist. (See Problem 12.15.) ∎

12.7.2 The Performance of VLSI Algorithms on Predicates

The approach taken above can be extended to predicates, functions whose range is $\mathcal{B}$. Again we derive lower bounds on the size of the smallest planar circuit for a function. However, since the flow of information from inputs to outputs is at most one bit, we must find some other way to measure the amount of information that must be exchanged between the two halves of a planar circuit. An extension of the communication complexity measure introduced in Section 9.7.1 serves this purpose.

The communication complexity measure of Section 9.7.1 assumes that two players exchange bits to compute the value of a Boolean function $f : \mathcal{B}^n \mapsto \mathcal{B}$. The input variables of f are partitioned into two sets U and V and assigned to two players. Given this partition, the players choose a protocol (a scheme for alternating the transmission of bits from one to the other) by which to decide the value of f for every input n-tuple of f. The bits of each n-tuple are partitioned between the two players according to the division of the n input variables between the sets U and V. The players then use their protocol to determine the value of f. The **communication complexity** $C(U, V)$ of this game is the minimum over protocols of the maximum over input n-tuples of the number of bits exchanged by the players to compute f given the partition of the input variables into sets U and V. This measure and its associated game are naturally extended to predicates $f : X^n \mapsto \mathcal{B}$, whose variables assume values over the set X. Players now exchange values drawn from the set X.

We can derive a lower bound on planar circuit size by applying the planar separator theorem. Since this theorem partitions the input variables into three sets, A, B, and a separator C, where A and B contain at most two-thirds of the total number of input vertices, it is natural to extend the standard communication complexity measure to the following VLSI communication complexity measure for functions $f : X^n \mapsto \mathcal{B}$.

DEFINITION 12.7.2 *The* **VLSI communication complexity** *of a predicate* $f : X^n \mapsto \mathcal{B}$, $CC_{\text{vlsi}}(f)$, *is the minimum of the communication complexity* $C(U, V)$ *over all partitions* (U, V) *of the variables of* f *into two sets of size at most* $2n/3$.

The following theorem, which is left as an exercise (see Problem 12.17), summarizes the result of applying the VLSI communication complexity measure $CC_{\text{vlsi}}(f)$ together with the planar separator theorem to derive a lower bound on the semellective planar circuit size of predicates.

THEOREM 12.7.4 *Let* $f : X^n \mapsto \mathcal{B}$ *have VLSI communication complexity* $CC_{\text{vlsi}}(f)$. *Then, the following bounds hold for the computation of* f *by a semellective VLSI chip with area* A *in* T *steps.*

$$(CC_{\text{vlsi}}(f))^2 = O(AT^2), O(A^2T)$$

Note that in a planar circuit all the information passed from each side of the separator to the other is sent simultaneously, whereas in the communication game players alternate in sending values drawn from the set X. Because more freedom is granted to players in the communication game (each player can choose data to send based on responses previously received from the other player), a lower bound on communication complexity is a lower bound on the amount of information that must be exchange in a planar circuit.

A number of techniques have been developed to derive lower bounds on the planar circuit size of predicates. One of these uses the pigeonhole principle (also known as a **crossing-sequence argument**) to derive lower bounds for predicates that are $w(u, v)$-separated. This new property is similar to the $w(u, v)$-flow property of multi-output functions. It is defined below.

DEFINITION 12.7.3 *A function* $f : X^n \mapsto \mathcal{B}$ *is* $w(u, v)$-separated *if its variables can be permuted and partitioned into three sets* U, V, *and* Z, $|U| \geq u$ *and* $|V| \geq v$, *such that there is some value* $\boldsymbol{z}$ *for variables in* Z *and values* $\boldsymbol{u}_i$ *and* $\boldsymbol{v}_i$, $1 \leq i \leq |X|^{w(u,v)}$, *for variables in* U *and* V, *respectively, such that the following holds:*

$$f(\boldsymbol{u}_i, \boldsymbol{v}_j, \boldsymbol{z}) = \begin{cases} 1 & \text{if } i = j \\ 0 & \text{otherwise} \end{cases}$$

This definition can be applied to predicates that are associated with multi-output functions. These functions are defined below.

DEFINITION 12.7.4 *The characteristic predicate* $p_f : X^{(n+m)} \mapsto \mathcal{B}$ *of* $f : X^{(n)} \mapsto X^{(m)}$ *is defined below.*

$$p_f(\boldsymbol{x}, \boldsymbol{y}) = \begin{cases} 1 & \text{if } \boldsymbol{y} = f(\boldsymbol{x}) \\ 0 & \text{otherwise} \end{cases}$$

It is straightforward to show that the characteristic predicate of a function that has a $w(u, v)$-flow is $w(u, v)$-separated. (See Problem 12.18.) As a consequence, quadratic lower bounds exist on the semellective planar circuit size of the characteristic predicates of the convolution, cyclic shift, integer multiplication, discrete Fourier transform, matrix multiplication functions, and many others.

12.8 Area Bounds

We now derive lower bounds on the area used by semellective VLSI chip algorithms for a variety of functions. For the functions considered here, these bounds are linear in their number of variables. As explained in the Chapter Notes, not all functions are amenable to the type of analysis presented in this section.

The technique used to derive area lower bounds is similar to that used in Section 10.4.2 to derive lower bounds on the exchange of space for time in the pebble game. If a chip has many I/O ports, it has large area. On the other hand, if it has a small number of ports, the inputs to the function computed are received over many cycles. If the function has a large $w(u, v)$-flow, by direct analogy with the pebble game, the area must be large to insure that enough information be stored between cycles.

THEOREM 12.8.1 *Let $\beta \geq 1$. If $f : X^n \mapsto X^m$ has a $w(u, v)$-flow, every chip computing f requires area $A = \Omega(\min((m/2\beta), w(u, v)))$, where $u = n(1 - 1/\beta)$ and $v = (m/4\beta)$.*

Proof If the chip has π I/O pads or can store S values over the alphabet X, it has area $A \geq \lambda^2 \min(\pi, S)$. Fix $\beta \geq 1$. Its value is chosen later to provide a strong lower bound. If $\pi \geq m/2\beta$, we are done. Thus, we show that $S \geq w(u, v)$ when $\pi < m/2\beta$.

Let the VLSI algorithm have T time steps and let $h_i \leq \pi$ outputs be generated on the ith time step, $1 \leq i \leq T$. Create q intervals of consecutive time steps as follows: The first interval contains the first k_1 time steps, where k_1 is such that the total number of outputs produced during the first k_1 steps is as large as possible without exceeding m/β. Successive intervals are created in the same way, namely by grouping consecutive later time steps to satisfy the same requirement on the number of outputs produced. For all intervals except possibly the last, the number of outputs produced is at least $(m/\beta) - \pi + 1 > (m/2\beta)$. If the last interval contains fewer than $(m/2\beta)$ outputs, redistribute the elements in the last two intervals, of which there are at least $(m/\beta) - \pi + 2 \geq (m/2\beta) + 2$, so that each has at least $(m/4\beta) + 1$ outputs. It follows that the number of intervals, q, satisfies $\beta \leq q \leq 4\beta$.

We now examine the inputs read during intervals. Since there are n inputs to be read and each is read once, the average number read per interval is n/q which is at most n/β. It follows that there is some interval I in which at least $(m/4\beta) + 1$ outputs are pebbled and at most n/β inputs are read.

Fix the inputs that are read during I. The remaining inputs, of which there are at least $u = n(1 - 1/\beta)$, are free to vary. The number of outputs produced during I is at least $v = (m/4\beta)$. Since f has a $w(u, v)$-flow, if $S < w(u, v)$, the v outputs, whose values are determined by the values stored on the chip at the beginning of I, cannot assume all their values. It follows that $S \geq w(u, v)$, which is the desired conclusion. ∎

We now apply this bound to (α, n, m, p)-independent functions. Later we apply it to the matrix multiplication function.

THEOREM 12.8.2 *Let $f : X^n \mapsto X^m$ be (α, n, m, p)-independent. It requires area $A = \lambda^2((mp/(n + m/4)\alpha) - 1)$ when realized by a semellective VLSI algorithm.*

Proof We apply Theorem 12.8.1 with $u = n(1 - 1/\beta)$ and $v = (m/4\beta)$. Because f is (α, n, m, p) independent, $w(u, v) > v/\alpha - 1$ for $n - u + v \le p$. Since $n - u = n/\beta$ and $v = (m/4\beta)$, this implies that $\beta \ge (n + m/4)/p$. The lower bound of Theorem 12.8.1 then is the smaller of $(m/2\beta)$ and $(m/4\alpha\beta) - 1$. Since we are free to choose β, we choose it to make the smaller of the two as large as possible. In particular, we set $\beta = (n + m/4)/p$, which provides the desired result. ∎

Because all of the (α, n, m, p)-independent functions listed in Theorem 12.7.2 have n, m, and p proportional to one another, each requires area $A = \Omega(n)$, as stated below. It follows that the lower bound $AT^2 = \Omega(n^2)$ for these problems cannot be achieved to within a constant multiplicative factor if T grows more rapidly with n than $\sqrt{n}$.

COROLLARY 12.8.1 *The functions $f_{\text{wrapped}}^{(n)} : \mathcal{R}^{2n} \mapsto \mathcal{R}^n$, $f_{\text{cyclic}}^{(n)} : \mathcal{B}^{n + \lceil \log n \rceil} \mapsto \mathcal{B}^n$, $f_{\text{mult}}^{(n)} : \mathcal{B}^{2n} \mapsto \mathcal{B}^{2n}$, and $F_n : \mathcal{R}^n \mapsto \mathcal{R}^n$ each require area $A = \Omega(n)$ when realized by a semellective VLSI algorithm.*

A similar result applies to matrix multiplication.

THEOREM 12.8.3 *The area A required to compute the matrix multiplication function $f_{A \times B}^{(n)} : \mathcal{R}^{2n^2} \mapsto \mathcal{R}^{n^2}$ with a semellective VLSI algorithm satisfies $A = \Omega(n^2)$*

Proof We apply Theorem 12.8.1 with n and m replaced by $2n^2$ and n^2, respectively. Since $u = 2n^2(1 - 1/\beta)$ and $v = (n^2/4\beta)$, the lower bound on $w(u, v)$-flow for matrix multiplication function satisfies the following

$$w(u, v) = (v - (2n^2 - u)^2/4n^2)/2 \ge \frac{n^2}{2}\left(\frac{1}{4\beta} - \frac{1}{\beta^2}\right)$$

The lower bound is a positive multiple of n^2 if $\beta > 4$ and largest for $\beta = 8$, from which the desired conclusion follows. ∎

. . . .

Problems

VLSI COMPUTATIONAL MODELS

12.1 Assume the I/O ports are on the periphery of a convex chip. In the speed-of-light model show that if p such ports all have paths to some point on the chip, then the time for data supplied to each port to reach that point is $\Theta(p)$.

12.2 Under the assumptions of Problem 12.1, derive a lower bound on the time to compute a function f on n inputs under the additional assumption that there is a path on the chip from the port at which each variable arrives to the port at which f is produced.

Hint: Show that the time required is at least the sum of the number of cycles needed to read all n inputs and the time for data to travel across the chip. State these times in terms of p and choose p to maximize the smaller of these two lower bounds.

CHIP LAYOUT

12.3 Show that every layout of a binary tree on n leaves in which the leaves are placed on the boundary of a convex region and every vertex of the tree has the same area is proportional to $n \log n$.

12.4 The $n \times n$ mesh-of-trees network, $n = 2^r$, is described in Problem 7.4. Give an area-efficient layout for an arbitrary graph in this family of graphs and derive an expression for its area.

12.5 Let $n = 2^k$. As suggested in Fig. 12.9, the $n \times n$ **tree of meshes** T_n is a binary tree in which each vertex is a mesh and the meshes are decreasing in size with distance from the root. The edges between vertices are bundles of parallel wires. The root vertex is an $n \times n$ mesh, its immediate descendants are $n/2 \times n$ meshes, and their immediate descendants are $n/2 \times n/2$ descendants, and so on.

The depth-d, $n \times n$ mesh of trees, $T_{n,d}$, is T_n that has been truncated to vertices at distance d or less from the root.

Determine the area of an area-efficient layout of the tree $T_{n,d}$.

COMPUTATIONAL INEQUALITIES

12.6 Use the results of Problem 12.11 to extend Theorem 12.7.1 to multilective planar circuits of order μ.

12.7 Further extend the results of Problem 12.6 to (β, μ)-multilective VLSI algorithms by showing that, at the expense of a small increase in AT^2 and A^2T, multiple inputs of a variable at the same I/O port can be treated as a single input, thereby possibly reducing the multilective order of the corresponding planar circuit. This implies that if multiple copies of each variable are read at a single port, then the semellective planar circuit size is a lower bound to both AT^2 and A^2T.

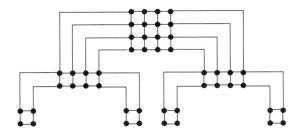

Figure 12.9 The 4×4 tree of meshes, T_4.

THE PLANAR SEPARATOR THEOREM

12.8 The **pizza pie graph** $G = (V, E)$ has $n = |V| - 1$ vertices that are uniformly spaced points on a circle as well as a vertex at the center of the circle. E consists of the arcs between vertices on the circle and edges between the central vertex and vertices on the circle.

When $n = 12$, triangulate G by adding edges between vertices on its external face. Illustrate Lemma 12.6.2 by choosing a cost function c and constructing two sets whose cost at most $2\,c(V)/3$ and a separator containing at most three vertices.

12.9 In a spanning tree for a graph $G = (V, E)$ the level of a vertex is the length of the path to it. Given a non-negative cost function on the vertices of G totaling $c(V)$, show there is some level m such that the cost of vertices at levels less than and more than m each is at most $c(V)/2$.

12.10 (**Two-Cost Planar Separator Theorem**) Let $G = (V, E)$ be an N-vertex planar graph having non-negative vertex costs summing to $c(V)$. Show that V can be partitioned into three sets, A, B, and C, such that no edge joins vertices in A with those in B, neither A nor B has cost exceeding $2c(V)/3$, $|A|$ and $|B|$ contain at most $5N/6$ vertices, and C contains no more than $K_1\sqrt{N}$ vertices, where $K_1 = 4(\sqrt{2/3} + 1)$.

Hint: Apply the planar separator theorem twice. The first time use it to partition V into two sets of about the same size and a separator. If each of the two sets has cost at most $2c(V)/3$, the result holds. If not, make a second application of the planar separator theorem to the set with larger cost. Show that it is possible to combine sets to simultaneously meet both the size and cost requirements.

12.11 Let $G = (V, E)$ be an N-vertex planar graph and let c be a non-negative cost function on V with total cost $c(V)$. Let $P \geq 2$. Show there are constants $2P/3 \leq q \leq 3P$ and $K_2 = 4(\sqrt{2/3} + 1)/(1 - \sqrt{5/6})$ such that V can be partitioned into q sets, $A_1, A_2, \ldots, A_q$ such that for $1 \leq i \leq q$

$$c(V)/(3P) \leq c(A_i) \leq 3c(V)/(2P)$$

and there are sets C_i, $|C_i| \leq K_2\sqrt{N}$, and $B_i = V - A_i - C_i$ such that no edges join vertices in A_i with vertices in B_i.

Hint: When $P = 2$, use the result of Problem 12.10 and combine the vertices of the separator with the other two sets to satisfy the necessary conditions. When $P > 2$, subdivide any set with cost exceeding $c(V)/P$ into two sets and a separator using the two-cost planar separator theorem. Assign vertices of the separator to these two sets to keep the cost in balance.

THE PERFORMANCE OF VLSI ALGORITHMS

12.12 Show that the function defined by the product of three square matrices has a semellective planar circuit size that is quadratic in its number of variables and that it can be realized by a VLSI chip with AT^2 that meets the semellective planar circuit size lower bound.

12.13 Show that the wrapped convolution function $f_{\text{wrapped}}^{(n)} : \mathcal{R}^{2n} \mapsto \mathcal{R}^n$, can be realized as an embedded CCC network on a VLSI circuit with area A and time T satisfying $AT^2 = \Theta(n^2)$ for $\Omega(\log n) \leq T \leq \sqrt{n}$.

12.14 Design a VLSI chip for $n \times n$ matrix multiplication that achieves $AT^2 = n^4 \log^2 n$ for $T = O(\log n)$.

Hint: Represent each matrix as a 2×2 matrix of $(n/2) \times (n/2)$ matrices and use the standard algorithm that performs eight multiplications of $(n/2) \times (n/2)$ matrices. A multiplier has one side longer than the other. Place the long side of the $(n/2) \times (n/2)$ matrix multiplier at right angles to the long side of the $n \times n$ matrix multiplier. Apply this rule to the recursive construction of the multiplier.

12.15 Show that an algorithm of the kind described in Problem 12.14 can be combined with a mesh-based matrix multiplication algorithm of the kind described in Section 7.5.3 to produce a family of algorithms that achieve the lower bound on $n \times n$ matrix multiplication for $\Omega(\log n) \leq T \leq n$.

12.16 Devise a VLSI chip for n-bit integer multiplication function chip that uses area A and time T efficiently.

Hint: Let $\boldsymbol{x}$ and $\boldsymbol{y}$ denote binary numbers. Recursively form the product of these integers as the sum of two products, that of $\boldsymbol{x}$ with the high-order $(n/2)$ bits of $\boldsymbol{y}$ and that of $\boldsymbol{x}$ with the low-order $(n/2)$ bits of $\boldsymbol{y}$. Use carry-save addition where possible.

12.17 Give a proof of Theorem 12.7.4.

12.18 Show that the characteristic predicate of a function that has a $w(u, v)$-flow is $w(u, v)$-separated.

AREA BOUNDS

12.19 Show that any VLSI algorithm that realizes a superconcentrator on n inputs requires area $\Theta(n)$.

Chapter Notes

Mead and Conway wrote an influential book [178] that greatly simplified the design rules for VLSI chips and made VLSI design accessible to a large audience. Ullman [333] summarized the status of the field around 1984 and Lengauer [190] addressed the VLSI layout problem. Lengauer has also written a survey paper [191] that provides an overview of the theory of VLSI algorithms as of about 1990. The three transmission models described in Section 12.2 reflect the analysis of Zhou, Preparata, and Khang [366].

Thompson [320] obtained the first important tradeoff results for the VLSI model of computation. He demonstrated that under a suitable model a lower bound of $AT^2 = \Omega(n^2)$ could be derived for the discrete Fourier transform, a result he subsequently extended to sorting [321]. Generalizations of this model were made to convex chips [59], compact plane regions [192], and other closely related models [199]. Vuillemin [349] extended the models to include pipelining. Chazelle and Monier [67] introduced the transmission-line model described in Problems 12.1 and 12.2. For a discussion of other models that take into account the effects of distributed resistance, capacitance and inductance, see [40] and [366].

Systolic algorithms, which make good use of area and time, were popularized by Kung [174] and others (see, for example, [103,121,176,177,178,187]). The H-tree featured in Section 12.5.1 is due to Mead and Rem [210]. Prefix computations are discussed in Chapter 2. The cube-connected cycles network (its layout is given in Section 12.5.3) and the efficient realization of normal algorithms are due to Preparata and Vuillemin [256], as explained in Chapter 7. Lengauer [190] provides an in-depth treatment of algorithms for VLSI chip layout.

Most authors prefer to derive lower bounds on AT^2 by partitioning the planar region occupied by chips [59,192,320]. In effect, they employ a physical version of the planar separator theorem. The characterization of VLSI lower bounds in terms of planar circuit complexity introduced by Savage [282] reinforces the connection between memoryless and memory-based computation explored in Chapter 3 but for planar computations by VLSI chips. It also provides an opportunity to introduce the elegant planar separator theorem of Lipton and Tarjan [200]. Lipton and Tarjan [201] developed quadratic lower bounds on the planar circuit size of shifting and matrix multiplication before the connection was established between VLSI complexity and planar circuit size. Improving upon results of [282], McColl [206] and McColl and Paterson [207] show that almost all Boolean functions on n variables require a planar circuit size of $\Omega(2^n)$ and that this lower bound can be achieved for all functions to within a constant multiplicative factor close to 1. Turán [330] has shown that the upper bound of Lemma 12.6.1 is tight by exhibiting a family of functions of linear standard circuit size whose planar circuit size is quadratic.

Abelson [1] and Yao [360] studied communication complexity with fixed partitions. Yao [361] and Lipton and Sedgewick [199] made explicit the implicit connection between VLSI communication complexity and the derivation of the AT^2 lower bounds. (See also [230], [12], and [191] for a discussion of the conditions under which lower bounds can be derived on the VLSI communication complexity measure.)

Many authors have contributed to the derivation of semellective lower bounds for particular functions. Among these are Thompson [320,321,322,323], who obtained bounds of the form $AT^2 = \Omega(n^2)$ for the DFT and sorting, as did Abelson and Andreae [3] and Brent and Kung [59] for integer multiplication, JáJá and Kumar [147] for a variety of problems, Bilardi and Preparata [41] for sorting, Savage for matrix multiplication, inversion, and transitive closure [283] and binary integer powers and reciprocals [282], and Vuillemin for transitive functions [349] (see Problem 10.22). These authors generally show that the lower bounds for functions can be met either to within a small multiplicative constant factor.

Good VLSI designs have been given by Baudet, Preparata, and Vuillemin [31] for convolution, Guibas and Liang [122] for systolic stacks, queues, and counters, and Kung and Song [180] and Kung, Ruane, and Yen [179] on 2D convolution. Also, Luk and Vuillemin [204] give an optimal VLSI integer multiplier and Mehlhorn has provided optimal algorithms for integer division and square rooting [213] whose range of optimality has been extended by Mehlhorn and Preparata [215]. Preparata [252] has given a mesh-based optimal VLSI multiplier for large integers and Preparata and Vuillemin have given optimal algorithms for multiplying square [255] and triangular matrices [254]. C. Savage [278] has given a systolic algorithm for graph connectivity.

Lower bounds for the semellective computation of predicates by VLSI algorithms have been derived by Yao [361] for graph isomorphism, by Lipton and Sedgewick [199] for the recognition of context-free languages, pattern matching, and binary integer factorization testing, and by Savage [282] for the characteristic predicates of multi-output functions.

Hochschild [133], Kedem and Zorat [160,161], Savage [284,286], and Turán [331] have developed lower bounds on performance of multilective VLSI algorithms. Savage has explored multilective planar circuit size [286], giving a multi-output function with a $\Omega(n^{4/3})$ lower bound. Turán [331] exhibits a function and a predicate with $\Omega(n^{3/2} \log n)$ and $\Omega(n \log n)$ lower bounds to their multilective planar circuit size, respectively. The $w(u, v)$-flow and $w(u, v)$-separated properties used in Section 12.7 were introduced in [286].

Lower bounds on the area of chips have been explored by a number of authors. Yao [361] examined addition; Baudet [30] studied functions that do not have a large information flow; Heintz [130] derived bounds for matrix-matrix multiplication; Leighton [188] introduced and used the crossing number of a graph to derive area bounds; Siegel [303] derived bounds for sorting; and Savage [282] examined functions with many subfunctions. Bilardi and Preparata [42] have generalized arguments of [30] and [150] to derive stronger area–time lower bounds for functions, such as prefix, for which the information flow arguments give weak results. Lower bounds on the area of multilective chips were obtained by Savage [286], Hromkovič [141,142], and Ďuriš and Galil [92].

Models for 3D VLSI chips, which are not yet a reality, have been introduced by Rosenberg [276,277] and studied by Preparata [257].

Bibliography

[1] H. Abelson, "Lower Bounds on Information Transfer in Distributed Computations," *19th Ann. IEEE Symp. Foundations of Computer Science* (1978), 151–158.

[2] H. Abelson, "A Note on Time-Space Tradeoffs for Computing Continuous Functions," *Inf. Proc. Letters* 8 (1979), 215–217.

[3] H. Abelson and P. Andreae, "Information Transfer and Area-Time Tradeoffs for VLSI Multiplication," *Comm. ACM* 23 (1980), 20–23.

[4] K. Abrahamson, "Time-Space Tradeoffs for Branching Programs Contrasted with Those for Straight-Line Programs," *Proc. 27th Ann. IEEE Symp. Foundations of Computer Science* (1986), 402–409.

[5] K. Abrahamson, "A Time-Space Tradeoff for Boolean Matrix Multiplication," *Proc. 31st Ann. IEEE Symp. Foundations of Computer Science* (1990), 412–419.

[6] K. Abrahamson, "Time-Space Tradeoffs for Algebraic Problems on General Sequential Machines," *J. Comp. Systems Sci.* 43 (1991), 269–289.

[7] A. Aggarwal, B. Alpern, A. Chandra, and M. Snir, "A Model for Hierarchical Memory," *Proc. 19th Ann. ACM Symp. Theory of Computing* (1987), 305–314.

[8] A. Aggarwal, A. Chandra, and M. Snir, "Hierarchical Memory with Block Transfer," *Proc. 28th Ann. IEEE Symp. Foundations of Computer Science* (1987), 204–216.

[9] A. Aggarwal and J. S. Vitter, "The Input/Output Complexity of Sorting and Related Problems," *Comm. ACM* 31 (1988), 1116–1127.

[10] A. V. Aho, J. E. Hopcroft, and J. D. Ullman, *The Design and Analysis of Computer Algorithms*, Addison-Wesley, Reading, MA, 1974.

[11] A. V. Aho, R. Sethi, and J. D. Ullman, *Compilers: Principles, Techniques and Tools*, Addison-Wesley, Reading, MA, 1986.

[12] A. V. Aho, J. D. Ullman, and M. Yannakakis, "On Notions of Information Transfer in VLSI Circuits," *15th Ann. ACM Symp. Theory of Computing* (1983), 133–139.

[13] M. Ajtai, "Σ_1^1-Formulae on Finite Structures," *Ann. Pure and Applied Logic* 24 (1983), 1–48.

[14] M. Ajtai, J. Komlós, and E. Szemerédi, "Sorting in $c \log n$ Parallel Steps," *Combinatorica* 3 (1983), 1–19.

[15] S. B. Akers, "Binary Decision Diagrams," *IEEE Trans. Computers* C-27 (1978), 509–516.

[16] S. G. Akl, *Parallel Computation: Models and Methods*, Prentice-Hall, Inc., Upper Saddle River, NJ, 1997.

[17] N. Alon and R. B. Bopanna, "The Monotone Circuit Complexity of Boolean Functions," *Combinatorica* 7 (1987), 1–22.

[18] B. Alpern, L. Carter, and E. Feig, "Uniform Memory Hierarchies," *Proc. 31st Ann. IEEE Symp. Foundations of Computer Science* (1990), 600–608.

[19] H. Alt, T. Hagerup, K. Mehlhorn, and F. P. Preparata, "Deterministic Simulation of Idealized Parallel Computers on More Realistic Ones ," *SIAM J. Computing* 16 (1987).

[20] K. Amano and A. Maruoka, "Potential of the Approximation Method," *Proc. 37th Ann. IEEE Symp. Foundations of Computer Science* (1996), 431–440.

[21] G. M. Amdahl, "Validity of the Single Processor Approach to Achieving Large Scale Computing Capabilities," *AFIPS JCC* 30 (1967), 483–485.

[22] A. E. Andreev, "On a Method for Obtaining Lower Bounds for the Complexity of Individual Monotone Functions," *Dokl. Akad. Nauk SSSR (Soviet Math. Dokl.)* 282 (1985), 1033–1037.

[23] A. E. Andreev, "A Family of Boolean Matrices," *Vestnik Moskov. Univ. Mat.* 41 (1986), 97–100, (in Russian); English translation in *Moscow University Math. Bull.* 41 (2) (1986), 79–82.

[24] A. E. Andreev, "On a Method for Obtaining More Than Quadratic Effective Lower Bounds for the Complexity of π-Schemes," *Vestnik Moskov Univ. Math.* 42 (1987), 63–66.

[25] S. Axler, *Linear Algebra Done Right*, Springer, Berlin, Heidelberg, and New York, 1996.

[26] J. Backus, "Can Programming Be Liberated from the von Neumann Style? A Function Style and Its Algebra of Programs," *Comm. ACM* 21 (1978), 613–641.

[27] J. L. Balcázar, J. Díaz, and J. Gabarrò, *Structural Complexity I*, Springer-Verlag, Berlin, Heidelberg, and New York, 1995.

[28] V. Bar-Hillel, M. Perles, and E. Shamir, "On Formal Properties of Simple Phrase-Structure Grammars," *Zeitschr. Phonetik, Sprachwissenschaft und Kommunikationsforschung* 14 (1961), 143–172.

[29] K. E. Batcher, "Sorting Networks and Their Applications," *Proc. AFIPS SJCC* 32 (1968), 307–314.

[30] G. M. Baudet, "On the Area Required by VLSI Circuits," in *VLSI Systems and Computations*, H. T. Kung, B. Sproull, and G. Steele, eds., Computer Science Press, Rockville, MD, 1981, 100–107.

[31] G. M. Baudet, F. P. Preparata, and J. E. Vuillemin, "Area-Time Optimal VLSI Circuits for Convolution," *IEEE Trans. on Computers* C-32 (July 1983), 684–688.

[32] R. Beals, T. Nishino, and K. Tanaka, "More on the Complexity of Negation-Limited Circuits," *Proc. 27th Ann. ACM Symp. Theory of Computing* (1995), 585–595.

[33] P. W. Beame, S. A. Cook, and H. J. Hoover, "Log Depth Circuits for Division and Related Problems," *SIAM J. Comput.* 15 (1986), 994–1003.

[34] P. Beame, "A General Sequential Time-Space Tradeoff for Finding Unique Elements," *Proc. 21st Ann. ACM Symp. Theory of Computing* (1989), 197–203.

[35] L. Belady, "A Study of Replacement Algorithms for a Virtual-Store Computer," *IBM Systems J.* 5 (1966), 78–101.

[36] V. E. Beneš, "Permutation Groups, Complexes, and Rearrangeable Multistage Connecting Networks," *Bell Syst. Techn. J.* 43 (1964), 1619–1640.

[37] S. Berkowitz, "On Some Relationships Between Monotone and Non-monotone Circuit Complexity," University of Toronto, Technical Report, 1982.

[38] D. P. Bertsekas and J. N. Tsitsiklis, *Parallel and Distributed Computation: Numerical Methods*, Prentice-Hall, Inc., Englewood Cliffs, NJ, 1989.

[39] G. Bilardi, K. T. Herley, A. Pietracaprina, G. Pucci, and P. Spirakis, "BSP vs. LogP," *Proc. 8th Ann. ACM Symp. Parallel Algorithms and Architectures* (1996), 25–32.

[40] G. Bilardi, M. Pracchi, and F. P. Preparata, "A Critique of Network Speed in VLSI Models of Computation," *IEEE J. Solid-State Circuits* SC-17 (1982), 696–702.

[41] G. Bilardi and F. P. Preparata, "Area-Time Lower-Bound Techniques with Applications to Sorting," *Algorithmica* 1 (1986), 65–91.

[42] G. Bilardi and F. P. Preparata, "Size-Time Complexity of Boolean Networks for Prefix Computations," *JACM* 36 (1989), 362–382.

[43] G. Bilardi and F. P. Preparata, "Horizons of Parallel Computation," *J. Parallel and Distributed Computing* 27 (1995), 172–182.

[44] D. Bini and V. Y. Pan, *Polynomial and Matrix Computations*, Birkhauser, Boston, 1994.

[45] G. E. Blelloch, *Vector Models for Data-Parallel Computing*, MIT Press, Cambridge, MA, 1990.

[46] M. Blum, "A Machine-Independent Theory of the Complexity of Recursive Functions," *JACM* 14 (1967), 322–336.

[47] M. Blum, "On Effective Procedures for Speeding Up Algorithms," *JACM* 18 (1971), 290–305.

[48] N. Blum, "A Boolean Function Requiring $3n$ Network Size," *Theoret. Comp. Sci.* 28 (1984), 337–345.

[49] R. B. Bopanna, "Amplification of Probabilistic Boolean Functions," in *Advances in Computer Research, Vol. 5: Randomness and Computation*, S. Micali, ed., JAI Press, Greenwich, CT, 1989, 27–45.

[50] R. B. Bopanna and M. Sipser, "The Complexity of Finite Functions," in *Handbook of Theoretical Computer Science, Vol. A*, J. van Leeuwen, ed., Elsevier, Amsterdam, NY, Oxford, Tokyo; MIT Press, Cambridge, MA, 1990, 757–804.

[51] A. Borodin, "Computational Complexity and the Existence of Complexity Gaps," *JACM* 19 (1972), 158–174.

[52] A. Borodin, "On Relating Time and Space to Size and Depth," *SIAM J. Comput.* 6 (1977), 733–744.

[53] A. Borodin and S. Cook, "A Time-Space Tradeoff for Sorting on a General Sequential Model of Computation," *SIAM J. Comput.* 11 (1982), 287–297.

[54] A. Borodin, F. Fich, F. Meyer auf der Heide, E. Upfal, and A. Wigderson, "A Time-Space Tradeoff for Element Distinctness," *SIAM J. Comput.* 16 (1987), 97–99.

[55] A. Borodin, M. J. Fischer, D. G. Kirkpatrick, N. A. Lynch, and M. Tompa, "A Time-Space Tradeoff for Sorting and Related Non-Oblivious Computations," *J. Comp. Systems Sci.* 22 (1981), 351–364.

[56] A. Borodin and I. Munro, *The Computational Complexity of Algebraic and Numeric Problems*, American Elsevier, New York, 1975.

[57] R. P. Brent, "On the Addition of Binary Numbers," *IEEE Trans. Computers* 19 (1970), 758–759.

[58] R. P. Brent, "The Parallel Evaluation of General Arithmetic Expressions," *JACM* 21 (1974), 201–206.

[59] R. P. Brent and H. T. Kung, "The Area-Time Complexity of Binary Multiplication," *JACM* 28 (July 1981), 521–534.

[60] R. E. Bryant, "Symbolic Boolean Manipulation with Ordered Binary Decision Diagrams," *ACM Comput. Surveys* 24 (1992), 293–318.

[61] D. A. Carlson, "Time-Space Tradeoffs for Back-to-Back FFT Algorithms," *IEEE Trans. Computers* C-32 (1983), 585–589.

[62] D. A. Carlson, "Time-Space Efficient Algorithms for Computing Convolutions and Related Problems," *Info. and Computation* 75 (1987), 1–14.

[63] D. A. Carlson, "Upper and Lower Bounds on Time-Space Tradeoffs for Computations with Embedded Fast Fourier Transforms," *SIAM J. Discr. Math.* 1 (1988), 22–37.

[64] D. A. Carlson and J. E. Savage, "Extreme Time-Space Tradeoffs for Graphs with Small Space Requirements," *Inf. Proc. Letters* 14 (1982), 223–227.

[65] D. A. Carlson and J. E. Savage, "Size-Space Tradeoffs for Oblivious Computations," *J. Comp. Systems Sci.* 2 (1983), 65–81.

[66] A. K. Chandra, "Efficient Compilation of Linear Recursive Programs," *Proc. 14th Ann. IEEE Symp. Switching and Automata Theory* (1973), 16–25.

[67] B. Chazelle and L. Monier, "A Model of Computation for VLSI with Related Complexity Results," *JACM* 32 (1985), 573–588.

[68] N. Chomsky, "Three Models for the Description of Languages," *PGIT* 2 (1956), 113–124.

[69] N. Chomsky, "On Certain Formal Properties of Grammars," *Info. and Control* 2 (1959), 137–167.

[70] N. Chomsky, "Context-Free Grammar and Pushdown Storage," MIT Research Laboratory in Electronics, Quarterly Progress Report, Cambridge, MA, 1965.

[71] N. Chomsky and G. A. Miller, "Finite-State Languages," *Info. and Control* 1 (1958), 91–112.

[72] A. Church, "An Unsolvable Problem of Elementary Number Systems," *Amer. J. Math.* 58 (1936), 345–363.

[73] A. Cobham, "The Recognition Problem for the Set of Perfect Squares," *IEEE 7th Ann. IEEE Symp. Switching Automata Theory* (1966), 78–87.

[74] S. A. Cook, "The Complexity of Theorem-Proving Procedures," *Proc. 3rd Ann. ACM Symp. Theory of Computing* (1971), 151–158.

[75] S. A. Cook, "An Observation on Time-Storage Trade Off," *Proc. 5th Ann. Symp. Theory of Computing* (1973), 29–33.

[76] S. A. Cook, "Deterministic CFL's Are Accepted Simultaneously in Polynomial Time and Log Squared Space," *Proc. 11th Ann. ACM Symp. Theory of Computing* (1979), 338–345.

[77] S. A. Cook and R. A. Reckhow, "Time-Bounded Random Access Machines," *J. Comp. Systems Sci.* 7 (1973), 354–475.

[78] S. A. Cook and R. Sethi, "Storage Requirements for Deterministic Polynomial Finite Recognizable Languages," *J. Comp. Systems Sci.* 13 (1976), 25–37.

[79] S. A. Cook, "An Observation on Time-Storage Trade Off," *J. Comp. Systems Sci.* 9 (1974), 308–316.

[80] J. W. Cooley and J. W. Tukey, "An Algorithm for the Machine Calculation of Complex Fourier Series," *Math. Computation* 19 (1965), 297–301.

[81] D. Coppersmith and S. Winograd, "Matrix Multiplication via Arithmetic Progressions," *J. Symbolic Computing* 9 (1990), 251–280.

[82]   L. Csanky, "Fast Parallel Matrix Inversion," *SIAM J. Comput.* 5 (1976), 618–623.

[83]   D. E. Culler, R. M. Karp, D. Patterson, A. Sahay, E. E. Santos, K. E. Schauser, R. Subramonian, and T. von Eicken, "LogP: A Practical Model of Parallel Computation," *Comm. ACM* 39 (1996), 78–85.

[84]   R. Cypher and G. Plaxton, "Deterministic Sorting in Nearly Logarithmic Time on the Hypercube and Related Computers," *Proc. 22nd Ann. ACM Symp. Theory of Computing* (1990), 193–203.

[85]   E. Dekel, D. Nassimi, and S. Sahni, "Parallel Matrix and Graph Algorithms," *SIAM J. Comput.* 10 (1981), 657–675.

[86]   P. E. Dunne, "Techniques for the Analysis of Monotone Boolean Networks," University of Warwick, Ph.D. Dissertation, Theory of Computation Report No. 69, Coventry, England, 1984.

[87]   P. E. Dunne, "Lower Bounds on the Monotone Network Complexity of Threshold Functions," *Proc. 22nd Ann. Allerton Conf. Communication, Control and Computing* (1984), 911–920.

[88]   P. E. Dunne, "The Complexity of Central Slice Functions," *Theoret. Comp. Sci.* 44 (1986), 247–257.

[89]   P. E. Dunne, "On Monotone Simulations of Non-monotone Networks," *Theoret. Comp. Sci.* 66 (1989), 15–25.

[90]   P. E. Dunne, "Relationships Between Monotone and Non-monotone Network Complexity," in *Boolean Function Complexity*, M. S. Paterson, ed., London Math. Soc., Lecture Note Series 169, Cambridge University Press, Cambridge, 1992, 1–24.

[91]   P. E. Dunne, *The Complexity of Boolean Networks*, Academic Press, London, 1988.

[92]   P. Ďuriš and Z. Galil, "On the Power of Multiple Reads in a Chip," *Info. and Control* 104 (1993), 277–287.

[93]   J. Earley, "An Efficient Context-Free Parsing Algorithm," *Comm. ACM* 13 (1970), 94–102.

[94]   D. M. Eckstein, "Simultaneous Memory Access," Computer Science Dept., Iowa State University, TR-79-6, Ames, IA, 1979.

[95]   J. Edmonds, "Paths, Trees, Flowers," *Canad. J. Math.* 17 (1965), 449–467.

[96]   J. Evey, "Application of Pushdown Store Machines," *Proc. AFIPS FJCC* (1963), 215–217.

[97]   D. K. Faddeev and V. N. Faddeeva, *Computional Methods in Linear Algebra*, W. H. Freeman, San Francisco, 1963.

[98]   C. N. Fischer and R. J. Le Blanc, Jr., *Crafting a Compiler*, Benjamin/Cummings, Menlo Park, CA, 1988.

[99]   M. J. Fischer, "The Complexity of Negation-Limited Networks – A Brief Survey," in *Automata Theory and Formal Languages*, H. Brakhage, ed., Springer-Verlag, Lecture Notes in Computer Science, 33, Berlin, Heidelberg, and New York, 1975, 71–82.

[100] M. J. Fischer, A. R. Meyer, and M. S. Paterson, "$\Omega(n \log n)$ Lower Bounds on Length of Boolean Formulas," *SIAM J. Comput.* 11 (1982), 416–427.

[101] M. J. Flynn, "Very High-Speed Computing Systems," *Proc. IEEE* 54 (1966), 1901–1909.

[102] S. Fortune and J. Wyllie, "Parallelism in Random Access Machines," *Proc. 10th Ann. ACM Symp. Theory of Computing* (1978), 114–118.

[103] M. J. Foster, "The Design of Special-Purpose VLSI Chips and H. T. Kung," *Computer* 13 (1980), 26–40.

[104] J. B. Fraleigh and R. A. Beauregard, *Linear Algebra, Third Edition*, Addison-Wesley, Reading, MA, 1995.

[105] J. Friedman, "Constructing $O(n \log n)$ Size Monotone Formulae for the kth Elementary Symmetric Polynomial of n Boolean Variables," *SIAM J. Comput.* 15 (1986), 641–654.

[106] M. Furst, J. Saxe, and M. Sipser, "Parity Circuits and the Polynomial Time Hierarchy," *Math. Systems Theory* 17 (1984), 13–27.

[107] Z. Galil, "Some Open Problems in the Theory of Computation as Questions About Two-Way Deterministic Pushdown Automaton Languages," *Math. Systems Theory* 10 (1974), 211–218.

[108] M. R. Garey and D. S. Johnson, *Computers and Intractability: A Guide to the Theory of NP-Completeness*, W. H. Freeman, San Francisco, 1979.

[109] S. B. Gaskov, "The Depth of Boolean Functions," *Probl. Kibern.* 34 (1978 (in Russian)), 265–268.

[110] J. vonzur Gathen, "Parallel Linear Algebra," in *Synthesis of Parallel Algorithms*, John H. Reif, ed., Morgan Kaufmann, San Mateo, CA, 1993.

[111] A. M. Gentleman, "Complexity Results for Matrix Computations on Parallel Processors," *JACM* 25 (1978), 112–115.

[112] A. Gibbons and P. Spirakis, *Lectures on Parallel Computation*, Cambridge University Press, Cambridge, 1993.

[113] E. N. Gilbert, "Lattice-Theoretic Properties of Frontal Switching Functions," *J. Math. and Phys.* 33 (1954), 57–97.

[114] J. R. Gilbert, T. Lengauer, and R. E. Tarjan, "The Pebbling Problem Is Complete in Polynomial Space," *SIAM J. Comput.* 9 (1980), 513–524.

[115] M. Goldmann and J. Håstad, "A Simple Lower Bound for Monotone Cliques Using a Communication Game," *Inf. Proc. Letters* 41 (1992), 221–226.

[116] L. M. Goldschlager, "The Monotone and Planar Circuit Value Problems," *ACM SIGACT News* 9 (1977), 25–29.

[117] L. M. Goldschlager, "A Unified Approach to Models of Synchronous Parallel Machines," *JACM* 29 (1982), 1073–1086.

[118] L. M. Goldschlager, "A Universal Interconnection Pattern for Parallel Computers," *JACM* 30 (1983), 1073–1086.

[119] R. Greenlaw, H. J. Hoover, and W. L. Ruzzo, *Limits to Parallel Computation*, Oxford University Press, Oxford, 1995.

[120] D. Y. Grigoriev, "An Application of Separability and Independence Notions for Proving Lower Bounds of Circuit Complexity," *Notes of Scientific Seminars, Steklov Math. Inst.* 60 (1976), 35–48.

[121] L. J. Guibas, H. T. Kung, and C. D. Thompson, "Direct VLSI Implementation of Combinatorial Algorithms," *Proc. Conf. Very Large Scale Integration: Architecture, Design, Fabrication* (1979).

[122] L. J. Guibas and F. M. Liang, "Systolic Stacks, Queues, and Counters," *Proc. Conf. on Advanced Research in VLSI* (1982), 155–164.

[123] J. Håstad, "Almost Optimal Lower Bounds for Small Depth Circuits," in *Advances in Computer Research, Vol. 5: Randomness and Computation*, S. Micali, ed., JAI Press, Greenwich, CT, 1989, 143–170.

[124] A. Haken, "Counting Bottlenecks to Show Monotone $\mathbf{P} \neq \mathbf{NP}$," *Proc. 36th Ann. IEEE Symp. Foundations of Computer Science* (1995), 36–40.

[125] L. H. Harper and J. E. Savage, "On the Complexity of the Marriage Problem," *Adv. Math* 9 (1972), 299–312.

[126] J. Hartmanis, P. M. Lewis II, and R. E. Stearns, "Hierarchies of Memory-Limited Computations," *Proc. 6th Ann. Symp. Switching Circuit Theory and Logic Design* (1965), 179–190.

[127] J. Hartmanis and R. E. Stearns, "On the Computational Complexity of Algorithms," *Trans. AMS* 117 (1965), 285–306.

[128] P. J. Hatcher and M. J. Quinn, *Data-Parallel Programming on MIMD Computers*, MIT Press, Cambridge, MA, 1991.

[129] M. T. Heideman, D. H. Johnson, and C. S. Burrus, "Gauss and the History of the Fast Fourier Transform," *Arch. Hist. Exact Sci.* 34 (1985), 265–277.

[130] C. A. Heintz, LRI, Univ. Paris-Sud, On the Area Required for Matrix Multiplication with VLSI Algorithms, Orsay, France, 1981.

[131] J. Hennessy and D. Patterson, *Computer Architecture — A Quantitative Approach*, Morgan Kaufmann, San Mateo, CA, 1990.

[132] W. D. Hillis and G. L. Steele, Jr., "Data-Parallel Algorithms," *Comm. ACM* 29 (1986), 1170–1183.

[133] P. Hochschild, "Multiple Cuts, Input Repetition, and VLSI Complexity," *Info. Processing Letters* 24 (1987), 19–24.

[134] R. W. Hockney and C. R. Jesshope, *Parallel Computers*, Adam Hilger, Bristol, 1981.

[135] L. Hodes and E. Specker, "Length of Formulas and Elimination of Quantifiers I," in *Contributions to Mathematical Logic*, H. A. Schmidt, K. Schutte, and J.-J. Thiele, eds., North-Holland, Amsterdam, 1968, 175–188.

[136] J. -W. Hong and H. T. Kung, "I/O Complexity: The Red-Blue Pebble Game," *Proc. 13th Ann. ACM Symp. Theory of Computing* (1981), 326–333.

[137] H. J. Hoover, M. M. Klawe, and N. J. Pippenger, "Bounding Fan-Out in Logical Networks," *JACM* 31 (1984), 13–18.

[138] J. E. Hopcroft, "An $n \log n$ Algorithm for Minimizing States in a Finite Automaton," in *Theory of Machines and Computations*, Z. Kohavi and A. Paz, eds., Academic Press, New York, 1971, 189–196.

[139] J. E. Hopcroft, W. J. Paul, and L. G. Valiant, "On Time Versus Space," *JACM* 24 (1977), 332–337.

[140] J. E. Hopcroft and J. D. Ullman, *Introduction to Automata Theory, Languages, and Computation*, Addison-Wesley, Reading, MA, 1979.

[141] J. Hromkovič, "Nonlinear Lower Bounds on the Number of Processors of Circuits with Sublinear Separators," *Info. and Computation* 95 (1991), 117–128.

[142] J. Hromkovič, "Branching Programs Provide Lower Bounds on the Areas of Multilective Deterministic and Nondeterministic VLSI-Circuits," *Info. Processing Letters* 95 (1992), 168–178.

[143] D. A. Huffman, "The Synthesis of Sequential Switching Circuits," *J. Franklin Inst.* 257 (1954), 161–190, 275–303.

[144] N. Immerman, "Nondeterministic Space is Closed under Complementation," *SIAM J. Comput.* 17 (1988), 935–938.

[145] K. Iverson, *A Programming Language*, John Wiley & Sons, New York, 1962.

[146] J. JáJá, "Time-Space Tradeoffs for Some Algebraic Problems," *JACM* 30 (1983), 657–667.

[147] J. JáJá, *An Introduction to Parallel Algorithms*, Addison-Wesley, Reading, MA, 1992.

[148] J. JáJá and V. K. P. Kumar, "Information Transfer in Distributed Computing with Applications to VLSI," *JACM* 31 (January 1984), 150–162.

[149] D. Johnson, J. E. Savage, and L. R. Welch, "Combinational Complexity Measures as a Function of Fan-Out," Jet Propulsion Laboratory, Technical Report No. 32-1526, 1972.

[150] D. S. Johnson, "A Catalog of Complexity Classes," in *Handbook of Theoretical Computer Science, Vol. A*, J. van Leeuwen, ed., Elsevier, Amsterdam, NY, Oxford, Tokyo; MIT Press, Cambridge, MA, 1990, 68–161.

[151] R. B. Johnson, "The Complexity of a VLSI Adder," *Info. Processing Letters* 11 (1980), 92–93.

[152] N. D. Jones and W. T. Laaser, "Complete Problems for Deterministic Polynomial Time," *Theoret. Comp. Sci.* 3 (1976), 105–117.

[153] B. H. H. Juurlink and H. A. G. Wijshoff, "A Quantitative Comparison of Parallel Computational Models," *Proc. 8th Ann. ACM Symp. Parallel Algorithms and Architectures* (1996), 13–24.

[154] A. Karatsuba and Y. Ofman, "Multiplication of Multidigit Numbers on Automata," *Dokl. Akad. Nauk SSSR (Soviet Math. Dokl.)* 145 (1962), 293–294, (in Russian); English translation in *Sov. Phys.–Dokl.* 19 (1963), 595–596.

[155] M. Karchmer, *Communication Complexity: A New Approach to Circuit Depth*, MIT Press, Cambridge, MA and London, England, 1989.

[156] M. Karchmer and A. Wigderson, "Monotone Circuits for Connectivity Require Superlogarithmic Depth," *Proc. 20th Ann. ACM Symp. Theory of Computing* (1988), 539–550.

[157] A. R. Karlin and E. Upfal, "Parallel Hashing – An Efficient Implementation of Shared Memory," *Proc. 18th Ann. ACM Symp. Theory of Computing* (1986), 160–168.

[158] R. Karp, "Reducibility Among Combinatorial Problems," in *Complexity of Computer Computations*, R. E. Miller and J. Thatcher, eds., Plenum, New York, 1972, 85–104.

[159] R. M. Karp and V. Ramachandran, "A Survey of Parallel Algorithms for Shared-Memory Machines," in *Handbook of Theoretical Computer Science, Vol. A*, J. van Leeuwen, ed., Elsevier, Amsterdam, NY, Oxford, Tokyo; MIT Press, Cambridge, MA, 1990, 870–941.

[160] T. Kasami, "An Efficient Recognition and Syntax Algorithm for Context-Free Languages," Air Force Cambridge Research Laboratory, Report AFCRL-65-758, Cambridge, MA, 1965.

[161] Z. M. Kedem and A. Zorat, "Replication of Inputs May Save Computational Resources in VLSI," in *VLSI Systems and Computations*, H. T. Kung, B. Sproull, and G. Steele, eds., Computer Science Press, Rockville, MD, 1981, 52–60.

[162] Z. M. Kedem and A. Zorat, "On Relations Between Input and Communication/Computation," *Proc. 22nd Ann. IEEE Symp. Foundations of Computer Science* (1981), 37–44.

[163] L. G. Khachian, "A Polynomial Time Algorithm for Linear Programming," *Dokl. Akad. Nauk SSSR (Soviet Math. Dokl.)* 244 (1979), 1093–1096.

[164] L. S. Khasin, "Complexity Bounds for the Realization of Monotone Symmetrical Functions by Means of Formulas in the Basis +, ·, −," *Dokl. Akad. Nauk SSSR (Soviet Math. Dokl.)* 189 (1970), 752–755, (in Russian); English translation in *Soviet Phys. Dokl.* 14(12) (1970), 1149–1151.

[165] M. M. Klawe, "A Tight Bound for Black and White Pebbles on the Pyramid," *Proc. 24th Ann. IEEE Symp. Foundations of Computer Science* (1983), 410–419.

[166] S. C. Kleene, "General Recursive Functions of Natural Numbers," *Math. Annalen* 112 (1936), 727–742.

[167] M. Kloss, "Estimates of the Complexity of Solutions of Systems of Linear Equations," *Dokl. Akad. Nauk SSSR (Soviet Math. Dokl.)* 171 (1966), 781–783, (in Russian); English translation in *Soviet Math. Dokl.* 7 (6) (1966), 1537–1540.

[168] D. E. Knuth, *The Art of Computer Programming – Sorting and Searching, Vol. 3*, Addison-Wesley, Reading, MA, 1973.

[169] D. E. Knuth, "Big Omicron and Big Omega and Big Theta," *ACM SIGACT News* 8 (1976), 18–24.

[170] E. Koutsoupias, "Improvements on Khrapchenko's Theorem," *Theoret. Comp. Sci.* 116 (1993), 399–403.

[171] V. M. Krapchenko, "Asymptotic Estimation of Addition Time of a Parallel Adder," *Probl. Kibern.* 19 (1967), 107–122, (in Russian); English translation in *Syst. Theory Res.* 19 (1970), 105–122.

[172] V. M. Krapchenko, "A Method of Determining Lower Bounds for the Complexity of Π-Schemes," *Aametki* 10 (1971), 83–92, (in Russian); English translation in *Math. Notes.* 10(1) (1971), 474–479.

[173] V. M. Krapchenko, "The Complexity of Symmetrical Functions by Formulae," *Mat. Zametki* 11 (1972), 109–120, (in Russian); English translation in *Math. Notes* 11(1) (1972), 70–76.

[174] R. E. Krichevskii, "Complexity of Contact Circuits Realizing a Function of Logical Algebra," *Dokl. Akad. Nauk SSSR (Soviet Math. Dokl.)* 151 (1963), 803–806, (in Russian); English translation in *Soviet Phys. Dokl.* 8(8) (1964), 770–772.

[175] H. T. Kung, "Let's Design Algorithms for VLSI Systems," *Proc. Caltech Conf. VLSI: Architecture, Design, Fabrication* (1979), 65–90.

[176] H. T. Kung, "Memory Requirements for Balanced Computer Architectures," *J. Complexity* 1 (1985), 147–157.

[177] H. T. Kung and P. L. Lehman, "Systolic (VLSI) Arrays for Relational Database Operations," *Proc. ACM SIGMOD Int. Symp. Management of Data* (1980), 105–116.

[178] H. T. Kung and C. E. Leiserson, "Systolic Arrays (for VLSI)," in *Sparse Matrix Proceedings 1978*, I. S. Duff and G. W. Stewart, eds., SIAM, 1979, 256–282.

[179] H. T. Kung and C. E. Leiserson, "Algorithms for VLSI Processor Arrays," in *Introduction to VLSI Systems*, C. Mead and L. Conway, eds., Addison-Wesley, Reading, MA, 1980, 271–292.

[180] H. T. Kung, L. M. Ruane, and D. W. L. Yen, "A Two-Level Pipelined Systolic Array for Convolutions," in *VLSI Systems and Computations*, H. T. Kung, B. Sproull, and G. Steele, eds., Computer Science Press, Rockville, MD, 1981, 255–264.

[181] H. T. Kung and S. W. Song, "A Systolic 2-D Convolution Chip," in *Multicomputers and Image Processing: Algorithms and Programs*, K. Preston, Jr. and L. Uhr, eds., Academic Press, New York, 1982, 373–384.

[182] S. Y. Kuroda, "Classes of Languages and Linear-Bounded Automata," *Info. and Control* 7 (1964), 207–223.

[183] R. E. Ladner, "The Circuit Value Problem Is Log-Space Complete for **P**," *ACM SIGACT News* 7 (1975), 18–20.

[184] R. E. Ladner and M. J. Fischer, "Parallel Prefix Computation," *JACM* 27 (1980), 831–838.

[185] E. A. Lamagna, "The Complexity of Monotone Networks for Certain Bilinear Forms," *IEEE Trans. Computers* 28 (1979), 773–782.

[186] E. A. Lamagna and J. E. Savage, "Combinational Complexity of Some Monotone Functions," *Proc. 15th Ann. IEEE Symp. Switching and Automata Theory* (1974), 140–144.

[187] P. S. Landweber, "Three Theorems on Phrase-Structure Grammars of Type 1," *Info. and Control* 6 (1963), 131–136.

[188] P. L. Lehman, "A Systolic (VLSI) Array for Processing Simple Relational Queries," in *VLSI Systems and Computations*, H. T. Kung, B. Sproull, and G. Steele, eds., Computer Science Press, Rockville, MD, 1981, 285–295.

[189] F. T. Leighton, "New Lower Bound Techniques for VLSI," *Math. Systems Theory* 17 (1984), 47–70.

[190] F. T. Leighton, *Introduction to Parallel Algorithms and Architectures: Arrays, Trees, Hypercubes,* Morgan Kaufman, San Mateo, CA, 1992.

[191] T. Lengauer, "VLSI Theory," in *Handbook of Theoretical Computer Science, Vol. A,* J. van Leeuwen, ed., Elsevier, Amsterdam, NY, Oxford, Tokyo; MIT Press, Cambridge, MA, 1990, 836–868.

[192] T. Lengauer, *Combinatorial Algorithms for Integrated Circuit Layout,* John Wiley & Sons, Chichester, England, 1990.

[193] T. Lengauer and K. Mehlhorn, "Four Results on the Complexity of VLSI Computations," in *Advances in Computing Research,* F. P. Preparata, ed. #2, JAI Press, Greenwich, CT, 1984, 1–22.

[194] T. Lengauer and R. E. Tarjan, "The Space Complexity of Pebble Games on Trees," *Inf. Proc. Letters* 10 (1980), 184–188.

[195] T. Lengauer and R. E. Tarjan, "Asymptotically Tight Bounds on Time-Space Tradeoffs in a Pebble Game," *JACM* 29 (1982), 1087–1130.

[196] S. J. Leon, *Linear Algebra with Applications,* Prentice-Hall, Englewood Cliffs, NJ, 1997 .

[197] L. A. Levin, "Universal Sorting Problems," *Probl. Peredaci Informacii* 9 (1973), 115–116, (in Russian); English translation in *Problems of Information Transmission* 9 (1973) 265–266.

[198] H. R. Lewis and C. H. Papadimitriou, *Elements of the Theory of Computation,* Prentice-Hall, Englewood Cliffs, NJ, 1981.

[199] A. Lingas, "A PSPACE-Complete Problem Related to a Pebble Game," in *Automata Languages and Programming,* G. Aussiello and C. Boehm, eds., Springer-Verlag, Lecture Notes in Computer Science, 62 , Berlin, Heidelberg, and New York, 1978, 300–321.

[200] R. J. Lipton and R. Sedgewick, "Lower Bounds for VLSI," *Proc. 13th Ann. ACM Symp. Theory of Computing* (1981), 300–307.

[201] R. J. Lipton and R. E. Tarjan, "A Separator Theorem for Planar Graphs," *SIAM J. Appl. Math.* 36 (1979), 177–189.

[202] R. J. Lipton and R. E. Tarjan, "Applications of a Planar Separator Theorem," *SIAM J. Comput.* 9 (1980), 615–627.

[203] M. C. Loui, "Minimum Register Allocation Is Complete in Polynomial Space," Lab. Comp. Sci., MIT, Technical Memorandum TM-128, Cambridge, MA, 1979.

[204] M. C. Loui, "The Space Complexity of Two Pebble Games on Trees," Lab. Comp. Sci., MIT, Technical Memorandum TM-133, Cambridge, MA, 1979.

[205] W. K. Luk and J. E. Vuillemin, "Recursive Implementation of Optimal-Time VLSI Integer Multiplier," in *Advances in Computing Research, 2,* F. P. Preparata, ed., JAI Press, Greenwich, CT, 1984, 67–93.

[206] O. B. Lupanov, "A Method of Circuit Synthesis," *Ivz. V.U.Z. Radiofiz.* 1 (1958), 120–140.

[207] W. F. McColl, "Planar Circuits Have Short Specifications," in *Proc. Symp. Theoretical Aspects of Computer Science,* K. Mehlhorn, ed. #2, Springer-Verlag, Lecture Notes in Computer Science, 182, 1985, 231–242.

[208] W. F. McColl and M. S. Paterson, "The Planar Realization of Boolean Functions," *Info. Processing Letters* 24 (1987), 165–170.

[209] W. S. McCulloch and E. Pitts, "A Logical Calculus of the Ideas Immanent in Nervous Activity," *Bull. Math. Biophysics* 5 (1943), 115–133.

[210] R. McNaughton and H. Yamada, "Regular Expressions and State Graphs for Automata," *IEEE Trans. Electronic Computers* EC-9 (1960), 39–47.

[211] C. A. Mead and M. Rem, "Cost and Performance of VLSI Computing Structures," *IEEE J. Solid State Circuits* SC-14 (1979), 455–462.

[212] G. H. Mealey, "A Method for Synthesizing Sequential Circuits," *Bell Syst. Techn. J.* 34 (1955), 1045–1079.

[213] K. Mehlhorn, "Some Remarks on Boolean Sums," *Acta Informatica* 12 (1979), 371–375.

[214] K. Mehlhorn, "AT^2 Optimal VLSI Integer Division and Integer Square Rooting," *Integration* 2 (1984), 163–167.

[215] K. Mehlhorn and Z. Galil, "Monotone Switching Circuits and Boolean Matrix Product," *Computing* 16 (1976), 99–111.

[216] K. Mehlhorn and F. P. Preparata, "Area-Time Optimal Division for $T = O((\log n)^{1+\epsilon})$," *Info. and Computation* 72 (1987), 270–282.

[217] K. Mehlhorn and E. M. Schmidt, "Las Vegas Is Better than Determinism in VLSI and Distributive Computing," *Proc. 14th Ann. ACM Symp. Theory of Computing* (1982), 330–337.

[218] K. Mehlhorn and U. Vishkin, "Randomized and Deterministic Simulations of PRAMs by Parallel Machines with Restricted Granularity of Parallel Memories," *Acta Informatica* 21 (1984), 339–374.

[219] F. Meyer auf der Heide, "A Comparison Between Two Variations of a Pebble Game on Graphs," *Theoret. Comp. Sci.* 13 (1981), 315–322.

[220] E. F. Moore, "Gedanken-Experiments on Sequential Machines," in *Automata Studies (Annals of Mathematics Studies, No. 34)*, Princeton University Press, Princeton, NJ, 1956, 129–153.

[221] D. E. Muller, "Complexity in Electronic Switching Circuits," *IRE Trans. Comput.* EC-5 (1956), 15–19.

[222] D. E. Muller and F. P. Preparata, "Minimal Delay Networks for Sorting and Switching," *Proc. 6th Ann. Princeton Conf. Information Sciences and Systems* (1972), 138–139.

[223] D. E. Muller and F. P. Preparata, "Bounds to Complexities of Networks for Sorting and Switching," *JACM* 22 (1975), 195–201.

[224] J. Myhill, "Finite Automata and the Representation of Events," Wright Patterson AFB, Technical Note WADD 57-624, Dayton, OH, 1957.

[225] J. Myhill, "Linear Bounded Automata," Wright-Patterson Air Force Base, Ohio, WADD Tech. Note, 1960.

[226] A. Nerode, "Linear Automaton Transformations ," *Proc. Amer. Math. Soc.* 9 (1958), 541–544.

[227] E. I. Nečiporuk, "A Boolean Function," *Dokl. Akad. Nauk SSSR (Soviet Math. Dokl.)* 169 (1966), 765–766, (in Russian); English translation in *Soviet Math. Dokl.* 7 (4) (1966), 999–1000.

[228] E. I. Nečiporuk, "A Boolean Matrix," *Probl. Kibern.* 21 (1969), 237–240, (in Russian); English translation in *Systems Theory Research* 21(4) (1971), 236–239.

[229] M. H. Nodine and J. S. Vitter, "Large-Scale Sorting in Parallel Memories (Extended Abstract)," *Proc. 3rd Ann. Symp. Parallel Algorithms and Architectures* (1991), 29–39.

[230] A. G. Oettinger, "Automatic Syntactic Analysis and the Pushdown Store," *Proc. Symp. Applied Math.* 12 (1961).

[231] Y. Ofman, "On the Algorithmic Complexity of Discrete Functions," *Dokl. Akad. Nauk SSSR (Soviet Math. Dokl.)* 145 (1962), 48–51, (in Russian); English translation in *Soviet Math. Dokl.* 7 (7) (1963), 589–591.

[232] C. H. Papadimitriou, *Computational Complexity*, Addison-Wesley, Reading, MA, 1994.

[233] C. H. Papadimitriou and M. Sipser, "Communication Complexity," *J. Comp. System Sciences* 28 (1984), 260–269.

[234] M. S. Paterson, "An Introduction to Boolean Function Complexity," *Astérique* 38-39 (1976), 183–201.

[235] M. S. Paterson, "Complexity of Monotone Networks for Boolean Matrix Product," *Theoret. Comp. Sci.* 1 (1979), 13–20.

[236] M. S. Paterson and C. E. Hewitt, "Comparative Schematology," in *Proc. Project MAC Conf. Concurrent Systems and Parallel Computation*, Woods Hole, MA, 1970, 119–127.

[237] M. S. Paterson and L. G. Valiant, "Circuit Size Is Nonlinear in Depth," *Theoret. Comp. Sci.* 2 (1976), 397–400.

[238] M. S. Paterson, "New Bounds on Formula Size," in *Proc. 3rd GI Conf. Theoret. Computer Science*, Springer-Verlag, Lecture Notes in Computer Science, 48 , Berlin, Heidelberg, and New York, 1977, 17–26.

[239] M. S. Paterson, N. Pippenger, and U. Zwick, "Faster Circuits and Shorter Formulae for Multiple Addition, Multiplication and Symmetric Boolean Functions," *Proc. 31st Ann. IEEE Symp. Foundations of Computer Science* (1990), 642–650.

[240] M. S. Paterson, N. Pippenger, and U. Zwick, "Optimal Carry-Save Networks," in *Boolean Function Complexity*, M. S. Paterson, ed., Cambridge University Press, London Mathematical Society Lecture Note Series, 169, Cambridge, 1992, 174–201.

[241] W. Paul, "A $2.5N$ Lower Bound for the Combinational Complexity of Boolean Functions," *SIAM J. Comput.* 6 (1977), 427–443.

[242] W. J. Paul and R. E. Tarjan, "Time-Space Trade-Offs in a Pebble Game," *Acta Informatica* 10 (1978), 111–115.

[243] W. J. Paul, R. E. Tarjan, and J. R. Celoni, "Space Bounds for a Game on Graphs," *Math. Systems Theory* 10 (1977), 239–251.

[244] G. L. Peterson, "An Upper Bound on the Size of Formulae for Symmetric Boolean Functions," Dept. Computer Science, Univ. Washington, Tech. Report 78-03-01, 1978.

[245] N. Pippenger, "Short Formulae for Symmetric Functions," IBM T. J. Watson Research Center, Research Report RC-5143, Yorktown Heights, NY, 1974.

[246] N. Pippenger, "On Simultaneous Resource Bounds," *JACM* 26 (1979), 361–381.

[247] N. Pippenger, "On Another Boolean Matrix," *Theoret. Comp. Scii.* 11 (1980), 49–56.

[248] N. Pippenger, "Pebbling," *Proc. 5th Ann. IBM Symp. Math. Foundations of Computer Science* (1980).

[249] N. Pippenger and M. J. Fischer, "Relations Among Complexity Measures," *JACM* 26 (1979), 361–381.

[250] N. Pippenger and L. G. Valiant, "Shifting Graphs and Their Properties," *JACM* 23 (1976), 423–432.

[251] N. Pippenger, "A Time-Space Trade-off," *JACM* 25 (1978), 509–512.

[252] E. L. Post, "Finite Combinatory Processes," *J. Symbolic Logic* 1 (1936), 103–105.

[253] V. R. Pratt, "The Power of Negative Thinking in Multiplying Boolean Matrices," *SIAM J. Comput.* 4 (1974), 326–330.

[254] V. R. Pratt, "Every Prime Has a Succinct Certificate," *SIAM J. Comput.* 4 (1975), 214–220.

[255] F. P. Preparata, "A Mesh-Connected Area-Time Optimal VLSI Multiplier of Large Integers," *IEEE Trans. Computers* C-32 (1983), 194–198.

[256] F. P. Preparata and D. E. Muller, "Efficient Parallel Evaluation of Boolean Expressions," *IEEE Trans. Computers* C-25 (1976), 548–549.

[257] F. P. Preparata and J. E. Vuillemin, "Area-Time Optimal VLSI Networks for Multiplying Matrices," *Info Processing Letters* 11 (1980), 77–80.

[258] F. P. Preparata and J. E. Vuillemin, "Optimal Integrated-Circuit Implementation of Triangular Matrix Inversion," *Parallel Processing* (1980), 211–216.

[259] F. P. Preparata and J. E. Vuillemin, "The Cube-Connected Cycles: A Versatile Network for Parallel Computation," *Comm. ACM* 24 (1981), 300–309.

[260] F. P. Preparata, "Optimal Three-Dimensional VLSI Layouts," *Math. Systems Theory* 16 (1983), 1–8.

[261] P. Pudlák, "Bounds for Hodes-Specker Theorem," in *Logic and Machines: Decision Problems and Complexity*, Springer-Verlag, Lecture Notes in Computer Science, 171 , Berlin, Heidelberg, and New York, 1984, 421–445.

[262] M. J. Quinn, *Parallel Computing: Theory and Practice*, McGraw-Hill, New York, 1994.

[263] M. O. Rabin and D. Scott, "Finite Automata and Their Decision Problems," *IBM J. Res. Devel.* 3 (1959), 114–125.

[264] A. Ranade, "How to Emulate Shared Memory," *Proc. 28th Ann. IEEE Symp. Foundations of Computer Science* (1987), 185–194.

[265] B. Randell, ed., *The Origins of Digital Computers: Selected Papers*, Springer-Verlag, Berlin, Heidelberg, and New York, 1982.

[266] R. Raz and A. Wigderson, "Monotone Circuits for Matching Require Linear Depth," *Proc. 22nd Ann. ACM Symp. Theory of Computing* (1990), 287–292.

[267] A. A. Razborov, "A Lower Bound on the Monotone Network Complexity of the Logical Permanent," *Mat. Zametki* 37 (1985), 887–900, (in Russian); English translation in *Math. Notes* 37 (6) (1985), 485–493.

[268] A. A. Razborov, "Lower Bounds on the Monotone Complexity of Some Boolean Functions," *Dokl. Akad. Nauk SSSR (Soviet Math. Dokl.)* 281 (1985), 798–801, (in Russian); English translation in *Soviet Math. Dokl.* 31 (1985), 354–357.

[269] A. A. Razborov, "Lower Bounds on the Size of Bounded Depth Networks over a Complete Basis with Logical Addition," *Mat. Zametki* 41 (1987), 598–607, (in Russian); English translation in *Math. Notes* 41 (4) (1987), 333–338.

[270] A. A. Razborov, "On the Method of Approximations," *Proc. 21st Ann. ACM Symp. Theory of Computing* (1989), 167–176.

[271] N. P. Red'kin, "Proof of Minimality of Circuits Consisting of Functional Elements," *Probl. Kibern.* 23 (1973), 83–102, (in Russian); English translation in: *Syst. Theory Research* 23 (1973) 102–107.

[272] N. P. Red'kin, "On the Realization of Monotone Boolean Functions by Contact Circuits," *Probl. Kibern.* 35 (1979), 87–110.

[273] N. P. Red'kin, "Minimal Realization of a Binary Adder," *Probl. Kibern.* 38 (1981), 181–216, 272.

[274] J. H. Reif, ed., *Synthesis of Parallel Algorithms*, Morgan Kaufmann, San Mateo, CA, 1993.

[275] J. H. Reif and S. R. Tate, "Optimal Size Integer Division Circuits," *Proc. 21st Ann. ACM Symp. Theory of Computation* (1989), 264–273.

[276] R. Reischuk, "Improved Bounds on the Problem of Time-Space Trade-off in the Pebble Game," *JACM* 27 (1980), 839–849.

[277] H. G. Rice, "Classes of Recursively Enumerable Sets and Their Decision Problems," *Trans. AMS* 74 (1953), 358–366.

[278] J. Riordan and C. E. Shannon, "The Number of Two-Terminal Series-Parallel Networks," *J. Math. Phys.* 21 (1942), 83–93.

[279] A. L. Rosenberg, "Three-Dimensional Integrated Circuitry," in *VLSI Systems and Computations*, H. T. Kung, B. Sproull, and G. Steele, eds., Computer Science Press, Rockville, MD, 1981, 69–80.

[280] A. L. Rosenberg, "Three-Dimensional VLSI: A Case Study," *JACM* 30 (1983), 397–416.

[281] C. Savage, "A Systolic Design for Connectivity Problems," *IEEE Trans. Computers* C-33 (1984), 99–104.

[282] J. E. Savage, "The Complexity of Decoders – Part II: Computational Work and Decoding Time," *IEEE Trans. Inf. Theory* IT-17 (1971), 77–84.

[283] J. E. Savage, "Computational Work and Time on Finite Machines," *JACM* 19 (1972), 660–674.

[284] J. E. Savage, *The Complexity of Computing*, John Wiley & Sons, New York, 1976.

[285] J. E. Savage, "Planar Circuit Complexity and the Performance of VLSI Algorithms," in *VLSI Systems and Computations*, H. T. Kung, B. Sproull, and G. Steele, eds., Computer Science Press, Rockville, MD, 1981, 61–68.

[286] J. E. Savage, "Area-Time Tradeoffs for Matrix Multiplication and Related Problems in VLSI Models," *J. Comp. Systems Sci.* (1981), 230–242.

[287] J. E. Savage, "Multilective Planar Circuit Size," *Proc. 20th Ann. Allerton Conf. on Communication, Control, and Computing* (1982), 665–671.

[288] J. E. Savage, "Space-Time Tradeoffs for Banded Matrix Problems," *JACM* 31 (1984), 422–437.

[289] J. E. Savage, "The Performance of Multilective VLSI Algorithms," *J. Comp. Systems Sci.* 29 (1984), 243–273.

[290] J. E. Savage and S. Swamy, "Space-Time Tradeoffs on the FFT Algorithm," *IEEE Trans. Info. Th.* IT-24 (1978), 563–568.

[291] J. E. Savage and S. Swamy, "Space-Time Tradeoffs for Oblivious Integer Multiplication," in *Automata, Languages and Programming*, H. A. Maurer, ed., Springer-Verlag, Lecture Notes in Computer Science, 71, Berlin, Heidelberg, and New York, 1979, 498–504.

[292] J. E. Savage, "Extending the Hong-Kung Model to Memory Hierarchies," in *Computing and Combinatorics*, Ding-Zhu Du and Ming Li, eds., Springer-Verlag, Lecture Notes in Computer Science, 959 , 1995, 270–281.

[293] J. E. Savage and J. S. Vitter, "Parallelism in Space-Time Tradeoffs," in *VLSI: Algorithms and Architectures*, P. Bertolazzi and F. Luccio, eds., Elsevier Science Publishers (North Holland), 1985, 49–58.

[294] W. J. Savitch, "Relationships Between Nondeterministic and Deterministic Tape Complexities," *J. Comp. Systems Sci.* 4 (1970), 177–192.

[295] W. J. Savitch and M. J. Stimson, "Time-Bounded Random Access Machines with Parallel Processing," *JACM* 26 (1979), 103–118.

[296] T. J. Schaefer, "The Complexity of Satisfiability Problems," *Proc. 10th Ann. ACM Symp. Theory of Computing* (1978), 216–226.

[297] C. P. Schnorr, "Zwei Lineare untere Schranken fur die Komplexitat Boolescher Funktionen," *Computing* 13 (1974), 155–171.

[298] C. P. Schnorr, "The Network Complexity and the Turing Machine Complexity of Finite Functions," *Acta Informatica* 7 (1976), 95–107.

[299] C. P. Schnorr, "A $3n$-Lower Bound on the Network Complexity of Boolean Functions," *Theoret. Comp. Sci.* 10 (1980), 83–92.

[300] A. Schönhage and V. Strassen, "Schnelle Multiplikation grosser Zahlen," *Computing* 7 (1971), 281–292.

[301] U. Schürfeld, "New Lower Bounds on the Formula Size of Boolean Functions," *Acta Informatica* 19 (1983), 183–194.

[302] M. P. Schutzenberger, "On Context-Free Languages and Pushdown Automata," *Info. and Control* 6 (1963), 246–264.

[303] C. E. Shannon, "A Symbolic Analysis of Relay and Switching Circuits," *Trans. AIEE* 57 (1938), 713–723.

[304] C. E. Shannon, "The Synthesis of Two-Terminal Switching Circuits," *Bell Syst. Techn. J.* 28 (1949), 59–98.

[305] J. C. Shepherdson and H. E. Sturgis, "Computability of Recursive Functions," *JACM* 10 (1963), 217–255.

[306] A. Siegel, "Tight Area Bounds and Provably Good AT^2 Bounds for Sorting Circuits," New York University, Report No. 122, New York, 1985.

[307] S. Skyum and L. G. Valiant, "A Complexity Theory Based on Boolean Algebra," *JACM* 32 (1985), 484–502.

[308] D. D. Sleator and R. E. Tarjan, "Amortized Efficiency of List Update and Paging Rules," *Comm. ACM* 28 (1985), 202–208.

[309] C. H. Smith, *A Recursive Introduction to the Theory of Computation*, Springer-Verlag, New York, 1994.

[310] R. Smolensky, "Algebraic Methods in the Theory of Lower Bounds for Boolean Circuit Complexity," *Proc. 19th Ann. ACM Symp. Theory of Computing* (1987), 77–82.

[311] P. M. Spira, "On Time-Hardware Complexity Tradeoffs for Boolean Functions," *Proc. 4th Hawaii Int. Symp. System Science* (1971), 525–527.

[312] M. Spivak, *Calculus*, W. A. Benjamin, San Francisco, 1976.

[313] L. J. Stockmeyer and A. R. Meyer, "Word Problems Requiring Exponential Time," *Proc. 5th Ann. ACM Symp. Theory of Computing* (1973), 1–9.

[314] L. Stockmeyer and U. Vishkin, "Simulation of Parallel Random Access Machines by Circuits," *SIAM J. Comput.* 13 (1984), 409–422.

[315] H. S. Stone, "Parallel Processing with the Perfect Shuffle," *IEEE Trans. Computers* C-20 (1971), 153–161.

[316] V. Strassen, "Gaussian Elimination Is Not Optimal," *Numer. Math* 13 (1969), 354–356.

[317] B. A. Subbotovskaya, "Realizations of Linear Functions by Formulas Using +, ·, −," *Dokl. Akad. Nauk SSSR (Soviet Math. Dokl.)* 136 (1961), 553–555, (in Russian); English translation in *Soviet Math. Dokl.* 2 (1961), 110–112.

[318] S. Swamy and J. E. Savage, "Space-Time Tradeoffs for Linear Recursion," *Math. Systems Theory* 16 (1983), 9–27.

[319] R. Szelepscényi, "The Method of Forcing for Nondeterministic Automata," *Bull. EATCS* 33 (1987), 96–100.

[320] K. Tanaka and T. Nishino, "On the Complexity of Negation-Limited Boolean Networks (Preliminary Version)," *Proc. 26th Ann. ACM Symp. Theory of Computing* (1994), 38–47.

[321] É. Tardos, "The Gap Between Monotone and Non-Monotone Circuit Complexity is Exponential," *Combinatorica* 8 (1988), 141–142.

[322] S. R. Tate, "Newton Iteration and Integer Division," in *Synthesis of Parallel Algorithms*, John H. Reif, ed., Morgan Kaufmann, San Mateo, CA, 1993.

[323] C. D. Thompson, "Area-Time Complexity for VLSI," *Proc. 11th Ann. ACM Symp. Theory of Computing* (1979), 81–88.

[324] C. D. Thompson, "A Complexity Theory for VLSI," Dept. Computer Science, Carnegie-Mellon University, Ph.D. Thesis, 1980.

[325] C. D. Thompson, "The VLSI Complexity of Sorting," *IEEE Trans. Computers* C-32 (1983), 1171–1184.

[326] C. D. Thompson, "Fourier Transforms in VLSI," *IEEE Trans. Computers* C-32 (1983), 1047–1057.

[327] J. Tiekenherinrich, "A $4n$ Lower Bound on the Monotone Network Complexity of a One-Output Boolean Function," *Inf. Proc. Letters* 18 (1984), 201–202.

[328] M. Tompa, "Time-Space Tradeoffs for Computing Functions, Using Connectivity Properties of Their Circuits," *J. Comp. Systems Sci.* 20 (1980), 118–132.

[329] M. Tompa, "Corrigendum: Time-Space Tradeoffs for Computing Functions, Using Connectivity Properties of Their Circuits," *J. Comput. System Sci.* 23 (1981), 106.

[330] M. Tompa, "Two Familiar Transitive Closure Algorithms Which Admit No Polynomial Time, Sublinear Space Implementations," *SIAM J. Comput.* 11 (1982), 130–137.

[331] B. A. Trakhtenbrot, "Turing Computations with Logarithmic Delays," *Algebra i Logika* 3 (1964), 33–48.

[332] B. A. Trakhtenbrot, "A Survey of Russian Approaches to Perebor (Brute-Force Search) Algorithms," *Ann. Hist. of Comput.* 6 (1984), 384–400.

[333] G. Turán, "Lower Bounds for Synchronous Circuits and Planar Circuits," *Info. Processing Letters* 30 (1989), 37–40.

[334] G. Turán, "On restricted Boolean circuits," in *Proceedings of the International Conference on Fundamentals of Computation Theory*, J. Csirik, J. Demetrovics and F. Gécseg, eds., Springer, Lecture Notes in Computer Science, 380, New York, 1989, 460–469.

[335] A. M. Turing, "On Computable Numbers with an Application to the Entscheidungsproblem," *Proc. London Math. Soc.* 42 (1936), 230–265, Correction in Vol. 43, pp. 544–546.

[336] J. D. Ullman, *Computational Aspects of VLSI*, Computer Science Press, Rockville, MD, 1984.

[337] E. Upfal, "A Probabilistic Relation Between Desirable and Feasible Models of Parallel Computation," *Proc. 16th Ann. ACM Symp. Theory of Computing* (1984), 258–265.

[338] E. Upfal and A. Wigderson, "How to Share Memory in a Distributed System," *JACM* 34 (1987), 116–127.

[339] L. G. Valiant, "General Context-Free Recognition in Less Than Cubic Time," *J. Comp. Systems Sci.* 10 (1975), 308–315.

[340] L. G. Valiant, "Graph-Theoretic Properties in Computational Complexity," *J. Comp. Systems Sci.* 13 (1976), 278–285.

[341] L. G. Valiant, "Completeness Classes in Algebra," *Proc. 11th Ann. ACM Symp. Theory of Computing* (1979), 249–261.

[342] L. G. Valiant, "Reducibility by Algebraic Projections," *L'Enseignement Math.* XXVIII (1982), 253–268.

[343] L. G. Valiant, "Short Monotone Formulae for the Majority Function," *J. Algorithms* 5 (1984), 363–366.

[344] L. G. Valiant, "Negation is Powerless for Slice Functions," *SIAM J. Comput.* 15 (1986), 531–535.

[345] L. G. Valiant, "A Bridging Model for Parallel Computation," *Comm. ACM* 33 (1990), 103–111.

[346] P. van Emde Boas and J. van Leeuwen, "Move Rules and Trade-Offs in the Pebble Game," Vakgroep Informatica, Univ. Utrecht, Report RUU-CS-78-4, Utrecht, Netherlands, 1978.

[347] P. van Emde Boas, "Machine Models and Simulations," in *Handbook of Theoretical Computer Science, Vol. A*, J. van Leeuwen, ed., Elsevier, Amsterdam, NY, Oxford, Tokyo; MIT Press, Cambridge, MA, 1990, 2–66.

[348] C. C. Van Voorhis, "An Improved Lower Bound for Sorting Networks," *IEEE Trans. Computers* C-21 (1972), 612–613.

[349] H. Venkateswaran and M. Tompa, "A New Pebble Game That Characterizes Parallel Complexity Classes," *SIAM J. Comput.* 18 (1989), 53–549.

[350] U. Vishkin, "Implementation of Simultaneous Memory Address Access in Models That Forbid It," *J. Algorithms* 4 (1983), 45–50.

[351] J. S. Vitter and E. A. M. Shriver, "Optimal Disk I/O with Parallel Block Transfer," *Proc. 22nd Ann. ACM Symp. Theory of Computing* (1990), 159–169.

[352] J. Vuillemin, "A Combinatorial Limit to the Computing Power of VLSI Circuits," *Proc. 21st Ann. IEEE Symp. Foundations of Computer Science* (Oct. 13-15, 1980), 294–300.

[353] C. S. Wallace, "A Suggestion for a Fast Multiplier," *IEEE Trans. Computers* EC-13 (1964), 14–17.

[354] I. Wegener, "Boolean Functions Whose Monotone Complexity Is of Size $n^2 / \log n$," *Theoret. Comp. Sci.* 21 (1982), 213–224.

[355] I. Wegener, "On the Complexity of Slice Functions," *Theoret. Comp. Sci.* 38 (1985), 55–68.

[356] I. Wegener, "Relating Monotone Formula Size and Monotone Depth of Boolean Functions," *Inf. Proc. Letters* 16 (1983), 41–42.

[357] I. Wegener, *The Complexity of Boolean Functions*, Wiley-Teubner, Stuttgart and New York, 1987.

[358] J. Weiss, "An $n^{3/2}$ Lower Bound on the Monotone Network Complexity of the Boolean Convolution," *Info. and Control* 59 (1983), 184–188.

[359] J. R. Wicks, *Linear Algebra: An Interactive Laboratory Approach with Mathematica*, Addison Wesley Longman, Reading, MA, 1996.

[360] R. Wilber, "White Pebbles Help," *J. Comp. Systems Sci.* 36 (1988), 108–124.

[361] S. Winograd, "On the Algebraic Complexity of Functions," *Actes Congrès Int. Math.* 3 (1970), 283–288.

[362] M. Wloka, "Parallel VLSI Synthesis," Dept. of Computer Science, Brown University, CS-91-35, 1991.

[363] A. C-C. Yao, "Some Complexity Questions Related to Distributive Computing," *Proc. 11th Ann. ACM Symp. Theory of Computing* (1979), 209–213.

[364] A. C-C. Yao, "The Entropic Limitations on VLSI Computations," *Proc. 13th Ann. ACM Symp. Theory of Computing* (1981), 308–311.

[365] A. C-C. Yao, "Separating the Polynomial-Time Hierarchy by Oracles," *Proc. 26th Ann. IEEE Symp. Foundations of Computer Science* (1985), 1–10.

[366] A. C-C. Yao, "Near-Optimal Time-Space Tradeoff for Element Distinctness," *Proc. 29st Ann. IEEE Symp. Foundations of Computer Science* (1988), 91–97.

[367] Y. Yesha, "Time-Space Tradeoffs for Matrix Multiplication and the Discrete Fourier Transform on Any General Sequential Random-Access Computer," *J. Comp. Systems Sci.* 29 (1984), 183–197.

[368] D. H. Younger, "Recognition and Parsing of Context-Free Languages in Time n^3," *Info. and Control* 10 (1967), 189–208.

[369] D. Zhou, F. P. Preparata, and S. M. Khang, "Interconnection Delay in Very High-Speed VLSI," *IEEE Trans. Circuits and Systems* 38 (1991), 779–790.

[370] U. Zwick, "Optimizing Nečiporuk's Theorem," Dept. Computer Science, Tel Aviv Univ., Tech. Report 86/1987, 1987.

[371] U. Zwick, "A $4n$ Lower Bound on the Combinational Complexity of Certain Symmetric Boolean Functions over the Basis of Unated Dyadic Boolean Functions," *SIAM J. Comput.* 20 (1991), 499–505.

Index

Note to the Reader: (*) identifies a reference to a section.